India
a travel survival kit

India – a travel survival kit

Published by
Lonely Planet Publications
PO Box 88, South Yarra, Victoria 3141, Australia
Also at: PO Box 2001A, Berkeley, California, USA 94702

Printed by
Colorcraft, Hong Kong

Photographs by
Tony Wheeler – 160A, 192AB, 193ABC, 257AB, 288ABC, 289AB, 352BC, 353B, 384ABC, 385AB, 481AB
Peter Campbell – 161ABC, 256AB, 289C, 352A, 353A
Geoff Crowther – 257C, 385C, 448ABC, 449AB, 480ABC, 481C
Mark Carter – 160B

Cartoons by
Tony Jenkins

Cover miniature & other illustrations by
Peter Campbell

Design by
Graham Imeson

First published
October 1981

This edition
August 1984

National Library of Australia
Cataloguing-in-publication entry

Crowther, Geoff.
India, a travel survival kit.

2nd ed.
Previous ed.: South Yarra, Vic.: Lonely
Planet, 1981.
Includes index.
ISBN 0 908086 54 7.

1. India – Description and travel – 1981– –
Guide-books. I. Raj, Prakash A., 1943– .
II. Wheeler, Tony, 1946– . III. Title.

915.4'0452

Copyright © Geoff Crowther, Prakash A Raj, Tony Wheeler 1981, 1984

The Authors

Geoff Crowther was born in Yorkshire, England and started his travelling days as a teenage hitch-hiker. Later, after many short trips around Europe, two years in Asia and Africa and short spells in the overgrown fishing village of Hull and on the bleak and beautiful Cumberland fells, Geoff got involved with the London underground information centre BIT. He helped put together their first, tatty, duplicated overland guides and was with them from their late '60s heyday right through to the end. With Lonely Planet Geoff has written or collaborated on guides to Africa, South America, Malaysia, Korea and Taiwan as well as this book for which he also drew the majority of the maps. Geoff now lives with Hyung Pun, whom he met in Korea, on an old banana plantation in the rainforests near the New South Wales/Queensland border. In between travel he spends his time pursuing noxious weeds, cultivating tropical fruits and brewing mango wine.

Prakash A Raj was born in Nepal and later spent five years at university in Michigan, Nevada and Massachusetts in the USA. Following that he studied for a year in the Netherlands, travelled extensively in Europe and then returned to Nepal where he worked on the Kathmandu Enlgish language daily as a journalist and also for the Nepalese government's planning agency. Prakash currently works for the UN in New York. For Lonely Planet he wrote *Kathmandu & the Kingdom of Nepal* and he has also written several other books about Nepal and his life there in both English and Nepali.

Tony Wheeler was born in England but spent most of his younger years overseas due to his father's occupation with British Airways. Those years included a lengthy spell in Pakistan, a shorter period in the West Indies and all his high school years in the USA. He returned to England and did a university degree in engineering, worked for a short time as an automotive design engineer, returned to university again and did an MBA then dropped out on the Asian trail with his wife Maureen. They've been travelling, writing and publishing travel guidebooks ever since. Tony has written a number of the Lonely Planet books including the popular *South-East Asia on a Shoestring*. Travel for Tony and Maureen is considerably enlivened by their children Tashi (born soon after their return from researching the first edition of India) and Kieran. All four Wheelers were in India while researching this edition.

Lonely Planet

Lonely Planet Publications started in the early '70s when Tony and Maureen Wheeler made a lengthy overland trip and turned their experiences and the information they had gathered into the first edition of *Across Asia on the Cheap* (now titled *West Asia on a Shoestring*). Since then Lonely Planet has grown to a list of 30 travel titles, many of them unique; a permanent office in Melbourne, Australia, and (since 1984) a second office in Berkeley, California; and, most important of all, thousands of 'our' travellers out there on the road.

This Book

This book, in terms of people involved, research undertaken and expense was the biggest project yet tackled at Lonely Planet. The preliminary steps were taken when Tony and Maureen made an exploratory trip in south India to see what information would be needed, how long gathering it would take and how big the resulting book would be. It took longer and it turned out bigger!

The following year Geoff, Prakash and Tony – all of whom had visited India on numerous occasions in the past – all returned to India and spent a combined total of a year's more-or-less non-stop travel. Back in Australia much additional work went into desk research and producing maps and other illustrations. The end result exceeded all our hopes and expectations – it instantly became our best selling guide and went on to have 60,000 copies in print on its first edition. In Britain it won the Thomas Cook 'Guidebook of the Year Award' and in India it became the most popular guide to the country; a book used even by Indians to explore their own country.

This Edition

To prepare this second edition all three original writers returned to India. Tony's visit – accompanied this time by his two children, Tashi and Kieran, as well as

Maureen – was a brief one and Geoff Crowther covered not only all the areas he had researched for the first edition but also many of those originally covered by Tony. As well as the three main writers thanks must go to a long list of other contributors.

This edition contains two new features on travelling in India. Motorcycle enthusiasts who visit India are always delighted with the Enfield Indias – splendid recreations of a British single-cylinder motorcycle of 30 years ago. Australian Roman Wowk took that one step further by making a marvellous trip across India on an old Enfield he bought in Amritsar and sold, at a break even price, in Calcutta. His tale is told in 'India on an Enfield'. American Ann Sorrel explored India by bicycle and her advice on making a similar trip – with your own bike brought from abroad or with an 'Indian clunker' bought in India – follows in 'India by Bicycle'.

Carryovers from the first edition include English traveller Mark Carter's description of 'gricing' – tracking down the old steam engines which still ply India's railway lines. Australian Peter Campbell painted the delightful cover picture and provided some of the illustrations and colour pictures. Davindra Garbyal, an experienced trek leader in the Garwhal Himal region, provided us with the information for trekking in that area. In India special thanks go to Ashok Khanna, a longtime friend of Tony and Maureen's, who came with them to Kashmir for the first edition. During the research for the second edition they stayed with Ashok and his wife Lalita; and Ashok lent them the most valuable thing anybody could lend in Calcutta – a car and chauffeur!

Canadian Tony Jenkins, cartoonist for the *Toronto Globe & Mail* drew the controversial cartoons. Controversial because although most India travellers love them we've also had a few complaints from people who find them 'offensive' and 'insulting to Indians'. We're told they've even been discussed in Indian parliament! Well we don't agree that they're offensive, they show India as it is and even some Indian papers and magazines have commented on them favourably – and used them without asking! Perhaps some people are unduly sensitive or perhaps lampooning the people of India has simply not been done before? Whatever, we've pulled out one or two which seemed most likely to upset people and put two or three others in instead. If you like Tony's work you can find much more of it (including the ones most likely to upset people!) in our forthcoming 'Travellers' Tales' cartoon book. And you should see what he does with South Africans!

Back here at Lonely Planet thanks must go to the whole gang who pushed this book through to completion but particularly to Mary Covernton for editing and proofreading, Ann Logan for typesetting and Graham Imeson for design and paste up.

Finally very special thanks to those most important people – 'our travellers'. For two years you've swamped us with letters and cards from India. They've amused and informed us and contributed much new information to this book. Very special thanks must go to Alan Samagalski who wrote us so many letters he ended up working for us and was one of the two researchers on our forthcoming China guide. Australians Tim Willing and Alison Spencer provided us with much information on the western part of Gujarat. Several of the new maps in that section are based on their work for which we are very thankful. Numerous other travellers also helped to fill in missing gaps in the first edition and we're particularly grateful to 'regular' writers who correspond over and over again.

A list of people who have written to us is included at the back of the book.

And the Next Edition

Travel guides are only kept up to date by travelling. Corrections, suggestions, improvements and additions are all greatly appreciated and the best letters score a free copy of the next edition, or any other Lonely Planet guide if you prefer.

Contents

Introduction

India, it is often said, is not a country but a continent. From north to south and east to west the people are different, the languages are different, the customs are different, the country is different. There are few countries on earth with the enormous variety that India has to offer and it's a place which somehow gets into your blood. Love it or hate it you can never ignore India. It's not an easy country to handle and more than a few visitors are only too happy to finally be getting on that aircraft and flying away. Yet a year later they'll be hankering to get back.

It all comes back to that amazing variety – it's as vast as it is crowded, as luxurious as it is squalid, the plains are as flat and featureless as the Himalaya are high and spectacular, the food is as terrible as it can be magnificent, the transport as ex-hilarating as it can be boring and uncomfortable. Nothing is ever quite the way you expect it to be.

India is far from the easiest country in the world to travel around. It can be hard going, the poverty will get you down, Indian bureaucracy would try the patience of even a Hindu saint and the most experienced travellers find themselves at the end of their tempers at some point in India. Yet it's all worth it.

Very briefly India is a triangle with the top formed by the mighty Himalayan mountain chain. Here you will find the intriguing Tibetan region of Ladakh and the astonishingly beautiful Himalayan areas of Kashmir, Himachal Pradesh, the Garwhal of Uttar Pradesh and the Darjeeling and Sikkim regions. South of this is the flat Ganges basin with the colourful and comparatively affluent Punjab to the north-west, the capital city New Delhi and important tourist attractions like Agra (with the Taj Mahal), Khajuraho, Varanasi and the holy Ganges itself. This plain reaches the sea at the

CALCUTTA COPS
A diverse lot in smoggy white. I found them courteous and helpful. They speak softly and DO carry a very big stick.

northern end of the Bay of Bengal where you find teeming Calcutta, a city which seems to sum up all of India's enormous problems.

South of this northern plain the Deccan plateau rises. Here you will find cities that tell of the rise and fall of the Hindu and Moslem kingdoms and the modern metropolis that their successors, the British, built at Bombay. India's story is one of many different kingdoms competing with each other and this is never more clear than in places like Bijapur, Mandu, Golconda and other centres of central India. Finally there is the steamy south where Moslem influence only reached fleetingly. Here Hinduism was least altered by outside influences and is at its most exuberant. The temple towns of the south are quite unlike those of the north and superbly colourful.

Basically India is what you make of it and what you want it to be. If you want temples there are temples in profusion and with enough styles and types to confuse anybody. If it's history you want India has plenty of it and the forts, abandoned cities, ruins, battlefields and monuments all have their tales to tell. If you want to simply lie on the beach there are enough of those to satisfy the most avid sun worshipper. If walking and the open air is your thing then head for the

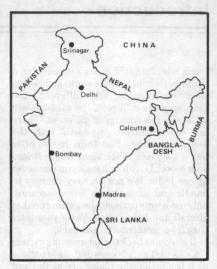

trekking routes of the Himalayas, some of them are as wild and deserted as you could ask for. If you simply want to meet the real India you'll come face to face with it all the time – on Indian trains and buses getting there may not always be half the fun but it certainly is half the experience. A visit to India is just that, it's not a place you simply and clinically 'see'. India is a total experience, an assault on all the senses, a place you'll never forget.

Facts about the Country

HISTORY
India is the home for one of the world's 'great' civilisations – its social structure as it exists today can be traced back thousands of years and empires of great size and complexity existed here far earlier than anything comparable in Europe. Yet India as an entity is a comparatively recent invention put together by the British. Even the mightiest of India's ancient civilisations did not encompass all of modern India and today India is still as much a country of diversities as unities. Few people in the Tamil speaking south speak Hindi, the national language, for example. Beyond India's own history and development its role as the birth place for two of the world's great religions is enough to ensure its historical importance.

Indus Valley Civilisation
India's first major civilisation flourished for a thousand years from around 2500 BC along the Indus River valley in what is now Pakistan. Its great cities were Mocnjodaro and Harappa and here a civilisation of great complexity developed. The major city sites were only discovered during this century but subsequently other, lesser, cities have been unearthed at sites like Lothal, near Ahmedabad in India.

The Indus Valley cities were ruled by a religious group rather than by kings but the most interesting things about these cities was their highly developed city engineering. Four thousand years ago they already had a sophisticated drainage system and even organised garbage collection! Despite the extensive excavations conducted at the sites comparatively little is known about the development and eventual demise of this civilisation. Their script has still not been deciphered nor is it known why such an advanced civilisation collapsed so quickly with the invasion of the Aryans.

Early Invasions
The early Aryan invasions were vague and disjointed although the people of north India today are defined as Aryans while those of the south as Dravidians. The Aryans came from the north from around 1500 BC and gradually spread across India from the Punjab and Sind (now in Pakistan) and down the Ganges towards Bengal. Under Darius (521-486 BC) the Punjab and Sind became part of the Persian empire but this was still peripheral to India itself.

Alexander the Great reached India, in his epic march from Greece, in 326 BC but his troops refused to march further than the Beas River, the easternmost extent of the Persian empire he had conquered, and he turned back without extending his power into India itself. The most lasting reminder of his appearance in the east was the development of Gandharan art, that strange mixture of Grecian artistic ideals with the new religious beliefs of Buddhism.

The Rise of Religions
Two great religions have had their birth on the sub continent – Buddhism and Hinduism. The Hindu religion is one of the oldest in the world. Even the priest dominated Indus Valley civilisation bears many similarities to Hinduism. The great Hindu books are all thought to refer to actual historical events. The Vedas, written around 1500 to 1200 BC, tell of the victory of Brahma over Indra, the god of thunder and battle. This probably refers to the revival of Brahmanism (the predecessor of Hinduism from which Hinduism evolved) following the Aryan invasions.

Hinduism has had a series of declines and revivals, most recently during the past

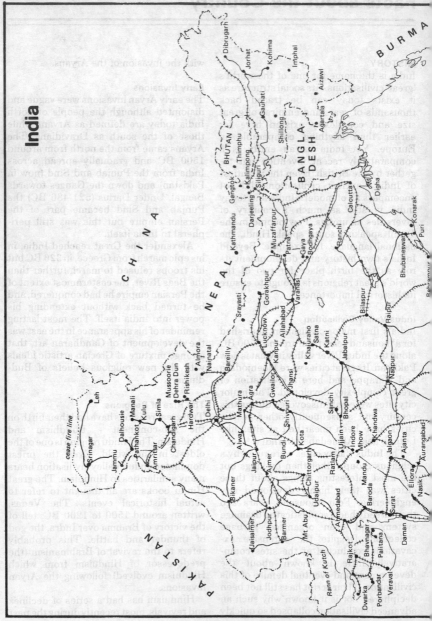

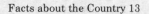

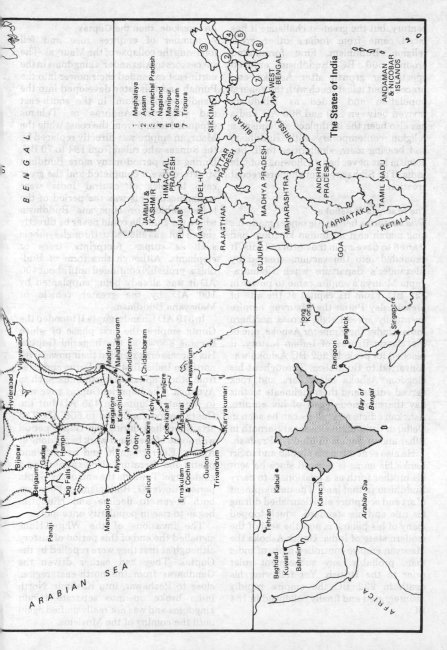

The States of India

century, but the greatest challenge it has faced came from India's other great religion, Buddhism. First formulated around 500 BC Buddhism enjoyed spectacular growth after Ashoka embraced it but it lost touch with the general population and faded as Hinduism revived between 200 and 800 AD. India has also been the birthplace of Jainism, a religion contemporary with Buddhism and bearing many similarities to it, but Jainism has never had a following outside India. The Sikhs are a much more recent creation.

The Mauryas & Ashoka

Two centuries before Alexander made his long march east an Indian kingdom had started to develop in the north of India. It expanded into the vacuum created by Alexander's departure when Chandragupta Maurya's empire came to power in 321 BC. From its capital at the site of present day Patna the Mauryan empire eventually spread right across northern India. Under the Emperor Ashoka, one of the classic figures of Indian history, it reached its peak. In 262 BC Ashoka was converted to Buddhism. Throughout his kingdom Ashoka left pillars and rock carved edicts and these delineate to this day the enormous span of his empire. Ashokan edicts and pillars can be seen in Delhi, in Gujarat, in Orissa, at Sarnath in Bihar and at Sanchi in Madhya Pradesh.

He also sent missions abroad and in Sri Lanka his name is revered since he sent his brother forth as a missionary to carry Buddhism to that land. The development of art and sculpture also flourished during his rule and his standard, which topped many of his pillars, is now the seal of the modern state of India. Under Ashoka the Mauryan empire controlled more of India than, probably, any subsequent ruler prior to the British. Yet following his death in 232 BC the empire rapidly disintegrated and finally collapsed in 184 BC.

An Interlude, then the Guptas

A number of empires rose and fell following the collapse of the Mauryas. The successors to Alexander's kingdoms in the north-east expanded their power into the Punjab and this later developed into the Gandharan kingdom. In the south-east and east the Andhras or Telugus expanded inland from the coast while the Mauryan empire was directly replaced by the Sungas who ruled from 184 to 70 BC. During this period many more Buddhist structures were completed and the great cave temples of central India were commenced. This was the period of the lesser vehicle or Hinayana Buddhism where the Buddha could never be directly shown but was alluded to through symbols such as stupas, footprints, trees or elephants. Although this form of Buddhism probably continued until about 400 AD it was already being supplanted by 100 AD by the greater vehicle or Mahayana Buddhism.

In 319 AD Chandragupta II founded the Gupta empire, the first phase of which became known as the Imperial Guptas. His successors extended their power over northern India, first from Patna and later from other capitals in north India, such as Ayodhya. The Imperial Guptas gave way to the later Guptas in 455 AD but the Gupta period continued to 606 AD. The arts flourished during the Gupta period with some of the finest work being done at Ajanta, Ellora, Sanchi and Sarnath and poetry and literature also experiencing a golden age. Towards the end of the Gupta period, however, Buddhism and Jainism both began to decline and Hinduism began to rise in popularity once more.

The invasions of the White Huns signalled the end of this period of history although at first they were repelled by the Guptas. They had earlier driven the Gandharas from the north-east region, close to Peshawar, into Kashmir. North India broke up into separate Hindu kingdoms and was not really unified again until the coming of the Moslems.

Meanwhile in the South

A continuing theme of Indian history has been that events in one part of the country do not necessarily effect those in another. The kingdoms that rose and fell in the north of the country generally had no influence or connection with those in the south. While Buddhism, and to a lesser extent Jainism, was displacing Hinduism in the centre and north of India, Hinduism continued to flourish in the south.

The south's prosperity was based upon its long established trading links with other civilisations. The Egyptians and later the Romans both traded by sea with the south of India and later strong links were formed with South-East Asia. For a time Buddhism and later Hindulsm flourished in the Indonesian islands and the people of the region looked towards India as their cultural mentor. The Ramayana, that most famous of Hindu epics, is even today told and retold in various forms in many South-East Asian countries. Yet outside influences also came to the south of India. In 52 AD St Thomas the Apostle is said to have arrived in Kerala and to this day there is a strong Christian influence in this region.

Great empires that rose in the south included the Cholas, the Pandyas, the Cheras, the Chalukyas and the Pallavas. The Chalukyas ruled mainly over the Deccan region of central India although at times their power extended further north. With a capital at Badami in Karnataka they ruled from 550 to 753 AD before falling to the Rashtrakutas only to rise again in 972 and continued their rule through to 1190. Further south the Pallavas pioneered the form of Dravidian architecture with its exuberant, almost baroque style. They also carried Indian culture to Java in Indonesia, to Thailand and Cambodia.

In 850 AD the Cholas rose to power and gradually superseded the Pallavas. They too were great builders as their temple at Tanjore indicates. They also carried their power overseas with raids into Ceylon and a long-running war with the Sumatran-based Srivijaya empire. At times they actually controlled part of Sumatra and the Malay peninsula.

The First Moslem Invasions

While the Hindu kingdoms ruled in the south and Buddhism was rising and falling in the north, Moslem power was creeping towards India from the Middle East. It was in 622 AD that Mohammed fled from Mecca and 630 AD when he marched back in and started Islam's period of rapid expansion. Less than a century later there were raids to the Sind and even Gujarat by Arabs carrying, as Mohammed had recommended, the Koran and the sword.

Moslem power first made itself strongly felt on the sub-continent with the raids of Mahmud of Ghazni. Today Ghazni is just a grubby little town between Kabul and Kandahar in Afghanistan but from 1001 Mahmud conducted raids on a virtually annual basis. His army would descend upon India destroying infidel temples and carrying off everything of value that could be moved. In 1033, after his death, one of his successors actually took Varanasi but in 1038 the Seljuk Turks, also expanding eastwards, took Ghazni and the raids into India soon ceased.

These early visits were no more than banditry and it was not until 1192 that Moslem power arrived on a permanent basis. In that year Mohammed of Ghori, who had been expanding his powers across the Punjab, broke into India and took Ajmer. The following year his general Qutb-ud-din took Varanasi and then Delhi and, after Mohammed of Ghori was killed in 1206, he became the first of the Sultans of Delhi. Within 20 years they had brought the whole of the Ganges basin under their control but the Sultans of Delhi were never consistent in their powers. With each new ruler the kingdom grew or shrunk depending on his personal abilities.

In 1297 Ala-ud-din Khilji pushed the

borders south into Gujarat and his general subsequently moved much further south but did not maintain the extension. In 1338 Mohammed Tughlaq decided to move his capital south from Delhi to Daulatabad, near Aurangabad in Maharashtra, but having marched most of Delhi's population south eventually had to return north. Soon after the Bahmani kingdom arose here and the Delhi Sultanate began to retreat north only to be further weakened when Timur made a devastating raid from Samarkand into India in 1398. From then on the power of this Moslem kingdom steadily contracted, until it was supplanted by another Moslem kingdom, the mighty Moghuls.

Meanwhile in the South (again)

Once again events in the south of India took a different path than the north. Just as the Aryan invasions never reached the south so the Moslem invasions also failed to permanently effect events in the south. Between 1000 and 1300 AD the Hoysala empire, with centres at Belur, Halebid and Somnathpur, was at its peak but fell to a predatory raid by Mohammed Tughlaq in 1328 and then the combined opposition of other Hindu kingdoms.

Two other great kingdoms developed in the north of modern day Karnataka – one Moslem and one Hindu. With its beautiful capital at Hampi the Hindu kingdom of Vijayanagar was founded in 1336 and was probably the strongest Hindu kingdom in India, during the time the Moslem Sultans of Delhi were dominating the north of the country. Meanwhile the Bahmani Moslem kingdom also developed but in 1489 it split into five separate kingdoms at Berar, Ahmednagar, Bijapur, Golconda and Ahmedabad. In 1520 Vijayanagar took Bijapur but in 1565 the kingdom's Moslem opponents combined to destroy Vijayanagar in the epic battle of Talikota. Later the Bahmani kingdoms were to fall to the Moghuls.

The Moghuls

Only Ashoka is as giant a figure in Indian history as the Moghul Emperors. These larger than life individuals ushered in another Indian golden age and spread their control over India to an extent rivalled only by Ashoka and the British. Their rise to power was rapid but the decline was equally quick; there were only six great Moghuls; after Aurangzeb they were emperors in name only.

The Moghuls did more than simply rule, however, they also had a passion for building which resulted in some of the great buildings in India – indeed Shah Jahan's magnificent Taj Mahal ranks as one of the greatest buildings in the world. Art and literature also flourished under the Moghuls and the magnificence of their court stunned early European visitors.

The six great Moghuls were:

Babur	1527-1530
Humayan	1530-1556
Akbar	1556-1605
Jehangir	1605-1627
Shah Jahan	1627-1658
Aurangzeb	1658-1707

Babur, a descendant of both Timur and Genghis Khan, marched into the Punjab from his capital at Kabul in Afghanistan and defeated the Sultan of Delhi at Panipat. This initial success did not totally destroy opposition to the Moghuls and in 1540 the Moghul empire came to an abrupt end when Sher Shah defeated Humayun, the second great Moghul. For 15 years he lived in exile until he was able to return and regain his throne. By 1560 Akbar, his son and successor, who had come to the throne aged only 14, was able to claim effective and complete control of his empire.

Akbar was probably the greatest of the Moghuls for he not only had the military ability required of a ruler in that time but he was also a man of culture, wisdom and with a sense of fairness. He saw, as previous Moslem rulers had not, that the number of Hindus in India was too great to simply subjugate them. Instead he integrated them into his empire and made use of many Hindu advisers, generals and administrators. Akbar also had a deep interest in religions and spent many hours in discussion with religious experts of all persuasions including Christians, and eventually formulated a religion of his own devising which combined the best points of all those he had studied.

Jehangir followed Akbar but devoted much of his reign to expressing his love for Kashmir and eventually died while en route there. His tomb is at Lahore in Pakistan. Shah Jahan, however, stuck much more to Agra and Delhi and during his reign some of the most vivid and permanent reminders of the Moghul's glory were constructed. Best known, of course, is the Taj Mahal but that was only one of many magnificent buildings Shah Jahan constructed. Indeed some say that it was his passion for building that led to his downfall and that his son, Aurangzeb, deposed his father in part to put a halt to his architectural extravagances.

Aurangzeb was the last of the great Moghuls and although he extended the empire's boundaries to their furthest extent he also ensured its downfall by failing to follow the ground rules Akbar had so successfully established. Akbar had combined his flair for magnificence and grandeur with a sense of fairness. He had kept his Hindu subjects 'on side' by including them in the governing process and respecting their beliefs.

In contrast Aurangzeb was a penny pincher and a religious zealot. His belief in Islam was deep, austere and puritanical and the result was that he soon lost the trust and respect of his subjects and had to cope with revolts on all sides. In many parts of India there are mosques which Aurangzeb had built on the foundations of temples which had been destroyed due to his fanatical beliefs. With his death in 1707 the Moghul empire rapidly disintegrated. Although there were 'Moghul

Emperors' right up to the time of the mutiny, when the British exiled the last emperor and executed his sons, they were emperors in name only. In sharp contrast to the magnificent tombs of his Moghul predecessors, Aurangzeb's tomb is a simple affair at Rauza, near Aurangabad.

The smaller states which followed on from the Moghul empire did in some case continue for some time. In the south the viceroyalty in Hyderabad became one of the British-tolerated princely states and survived right through to independence. The Nawabs of Oudh in north India ruled eccentrically, flamboyantly and badly until 1854 when the British 'retired' the last Nawab. In Bengal the Moghuls unwisely clashed with the British far earlier and their rule was terminated by the Battle of Plassey in 1757.

The Marathas

Moghul power was not simply supplanted by another, greater power. It fell through a series of factors and to a number of other rulers. Not least of these were the Marathas. Throughout the Moslem period in the north of India there were still strong Hindu powers, most notably Rajputs. Centred in Rajasthan the Rajputs were a sort of warrior caste, a race of chivalrous princes whose place in Indian history is much like that of the gallant knights of England. The Rajputs opposed every foreign foot that tried to walk into India but they were never united or organised in any fashion, and when the Rajputs were not battling foreign oppression they were usually fighting with each other. During the Moghul era they were brought into the emperor's army and some of their best military men were Rajputs.

The Marathas first rose to prominence with Shivaji, who took over his father's kingdom and between 1646 and 1680 performed feats of arms and heroism all over central India. Retelling the tales of his larger-than-life exploits is still a popular activity by wandering storytellers in small villages. He is a particular hero in Maharashtra, where many of his wildest exploits took place, but Shivaji is revered as much as for the fact that he was a lower caste Sudra, who showed that you did not have to be a Brahmin to be a great leader, as for his abilities in confronting the Moghuls. At one time Shivaji was even captured by the Moghuls and taken back to Agra but, naturally, he managed to escape and continue his adventures.

Shivaji's son was captured, blinded and executed by Aurangzeb and his grandson was not made of the same sturdy stuff but the Maratha empire continued under the Peshwas, hereditary government ministers who became the real rulers. They gradually took over more and more of the weakening Moghul empire's powers, first by supplying troops and then by actually taking control of Moghul land.

When Nadir Shah from Persia sacked Delhi in 1739 the declining Moghuls were even further weakened but the expansion of Maratha power came to an abrupt halt in 1761 at Panipat. There, where Babur had won the battle that established the Moghul empire over 200 years earlier, the Marathas were defeated by Ahmad Shah Durani from Afghanistan. Their expansion to the west halted, they nevertheless consolidated their control over central India and their region known as Malwa. Soon, however, they were to fall to India's final great imperial power, the British.

The Expansion of British Power

The British were not the first European power to arrive in India nor were they the last to leave – both those honours go to the Portuguese. In 1498 Vasco da Gama arrived on the coast of modern day Kerala having sailed around the African Cape of Good Hope. Pioneering this route gave the Portuguese a century of uninterrupted monopoly control of Indian trade with Europe and in 1510 they captured Goa, the enclave in India which they controlled

right through to 1961, 14 years after the British had left.

It was in 1612 that the British made their first permanent inroad into India when they established a trading post at Surat in Gujarat. In 1600 Queen Elizabeth I had granted a charter to a London trading company giving them a monopoly on British trade with India. For 250 years British power was exercised in India not by the government but by the East India Company which developed from this initial charter. British trading posts were established on the other coast at Madras in 1640, at Bombay in 1668 and at Calcutta in 1690. The British and Portuguese were not the only Europeans in India. The Dutch also had trading posts and in 1672 the French established themselves at Pondicherry, an enclave they, like the Portuguese in Goa, would hold even after the British had finally departed.

Naturally Anglo-French enmity spread to India and in 1746 the French took Madras only to hand it back in 1749. In subsequent years there was to be much intrigue between the imperial powers. If the British were involved in a struggle with one local ruler they could be certain the French would be backing him with arms, men or expertise. In 1756 Suraj-ud-daula, the Nawab of Bengal, attacked Calcutta and outraged Britain with the 'black hole of Calcutta' incident. A year later Robert Clive retook Calcutta and in the Battle of Plassey defeated Suraj-ud-daula and his French supporters thus not only extending British power but also curtailing French influence.

India at this time was in a state of flux due to the power vacuum created by the disintegration of the Moghul Empire. The Marathas were the only real Indian power to step into this gap and they were more a group of local kingdoms who sometimes co-operated, sometimes did not, than a power in their own right. In the south, where Moghul influence had never been so great, the picture was confused by the strong British-French rivalries with one ruler consistently played off against another.

This was never clearer than in the series of Mysore Wars with that nemesis of British power, Tipu Sultan. In the Fourth Mysore War in 1789-99, Tipu was killed at Srirangapatnam and British power took another step forward, French influence another step back. The long running British struggle with the Marathas was finally concluded in 1803 which left only the Punjab outside British control and that too came under British control in 1849 after the two Sikh Wars. Britain also took on the Nepalese whom they defeated but did not annexe and the Burmese whom they did.

The Rise & Fall of British India

By the early 19th century India was effectively under British control. In part this take over had come about because of the vacuum left by the demise of the Moghuls but the British also followed the rules Akbar had laid down so successfully. To them India was principally a place to make money and the Indians' culture, beliefs and religions were left strictly alone. Indeed it was said the British didn't give a damn what religion a person held so long as he made a good cup of tea. Furthermore the British had a disciplined, efficient army and astute political advisers. They followed the policy of divide and rule with great success and negotiated distinctly one-sided treaties giving them the right to intervene in local states if they were inefficiently run; 'inefficient' could be and was defined as the British saw fit.

Even under the British, India remained a patchwork of states, many of them nominally independent but actually under strong British influence. This policy of maintaining 'princely states' governed by Maharajas, Nawabs or whatever continued right through to independence and was to cause a number of problems at that time. The British interest in trade and

profit resulted in expansion of iron and coal mining; the development of tea, coffee and cotton growing; the construction of the vast Indian railways network; massive irrigation projects which revolutionised agriculture and other important and worthwhile developments.

In the sphere of government and law Britain gave India a well developed and smoothly functioning government and civil service structure. The fearsome love of bureaucracy which India also inherited from Britain may be a downside of that, but overall the country reached independence with a better organised, more efficient and less corrupt administrative system than most ex-colonial countries.

Britain also made some much less helpful moves in India. Cheap textiles from the new manufacturing industry of Britain flooded in to India, virtually crippling the local cottage industries. On one hand the British outlawed sati, the practise of adding the wife to a husband's funeral pyre, but on the other hand they encouraged the system of zamindars. These absentee landlords eased the burden of administrative and tax collection for the British but also contributed to an impoverished and landless peasantry in parts of India; a problem which in Bihar and West Bengal is still chronic today. The British also instituted English as the local language of administration; in a country with so many different languages it still partially fulfils that function of nationwide communication today. On the other hand many British also kept themselves to some extent at 'arms length' from the Indians.

In 1857, less than a half century after Britain had taken firm control of India, they had their first serious setback. Even today the causes of the 'Indian Mutiny' are hard to unravel – it's even hard to define if it really was the 'War of Independence' by which it is referred to in India or merely a mutiny. The causes were a combination of an administration which had been run down and other more specific cases. The dismissal of local rulers, inefficient and unpopular as they might have been, proved to be a flashpoint in certain areas but the main single cause was, believe it or not, bullets. A rumour, quite possibly true, leaked out that a new type of bullet issued to the troops, many of whom were Moslem, was greased with pig fat. A similar rumour developed that the bullets were actually greased with cow fat. Pigs, of course, are unclean to Moslems and cows are holy to Hindus.

The British were slow to deny these rumours and even slower to prove that either they were incorrect or that changes had been made. The result was a loosely co-ordinated mutiny of the Indian battalions of the Bengal Army. Of the 74 battalions seven (one of them Gurkhas) remained loyal, 20 were disarmed and the other 47 mutinied. The mutiny first broke out at Meerut, close to Delhi, and soon spread right across north India. There were massacres and acts of senseless cruelty on both sides, long sieges, decisive victories and protracted struggles, but in the end the mutiny died out rather than conclusively finished. It never spread beyond the north of India, and although there were brilliant self-made leaders on the Indian side, there was never any real co-ordination or common aim.

The British made two moves with the conclusion of the mutiny. First, they wisely decided not to look for scapegoats or to exact official revenge, although revenge and looting had certainly taken place on an unofficial level. Second, the East India Company was wound up and administration of the country was belatedly handed over to the British government. The remainder of the century was the peak period for the empire on which 'the sun never set' and in which India was one of its brightest stars. Two parallel developments during the latter part of the 19th century gradually paved the way for the independent India of today. First, the British slowly began to

hand over power and bring more people into the decision-making processes. Democratic systems began to be implemented in India although the British government retained overall control. In the civil service higher and higher posts were opened up for Indians and not simply retained for colonial administrators.

At the same time Hinduism began to go through another wholesale resurgence and adjustment. The Hindu religion is one of the world's oldest religions but once before, when it shrank before the growth of Buddhism, it had failed to keep in touch with its mass support. Once again it was realised that it had lost touch with the masses and required a complete shake-up to turn it away from its role as a religion for the priests and high caste Brahmins. Reformers like Ram Mohan Roy, Ramakrishna and Swami Vivekananda pushed through sweeping changes in Hindu society and paved the way for the Hindu beliefs of today, beliefs which have proved to have an enormous appeal to modern western society.

With the turn of the century opposition to British rule began to take on a new light. The 'Congress' which had been established to give India a degree of self-rule now began to push for the real thing. Outside of the Congress more hot-blooded individuals pressed for independence by more violent means. Eventually the British mapped out a path towards independence similar to that pursued in Canada or Australia. However, WW I not only shelved these plans; the events in Turkey, a Moslem country, alienated many Indian Moslems. After the war the struggle was on in earnest and its leader was Mahatma Gandhi.

Gandhi & Passive Resistance

In 1915 Mohandas Gandhi returned from South Africa, where he had practised as a lawyer and devoted himself to righting the wrongs the country's many Indian settlers had to face. In India he soon turned his abilities to the question of independence, particularly after the massacre at Amritsar in 1919 when a British army contingent opened fire on an unarmed crowd of protestors. Gandhi, who subsequently became known as Mahatma, the 'great soul', adopted a policy of passive resistance or 'satyagraha' to British rule. His central achievement was to change the independence struggle from a middle class one to a village level one. He led movements to refuse to pay the iniquitous salt tax and boycotts of British textiles, and for his efforts made a number of visits to British prisons.

Others involved in the struggle did not follow Gandhi's policy of non-cooperation and non-violence and at times the battle was bitter and bloody. Nevertheless the Congress Party and Mahatma Gandhi were in the forefront, although it was not until after WW II that a conclusion was finally reached. By then independence was inevitable as the war had dealt a death blow to colonialism and the myth of European superiority. Britain no longer had the power or the desire to maintain a vast empire, but within India a major problem had developed. The large Moslem minority had realised that an independent India would also be a Hindu-dominated India, and that despite Gandhi's fair-minded and even-handed approach others in the Congress Party would not be so willing to share power.

Independence

With the close of WW II it was clear that the European colonial era was over and that independence for India would have to come soon, but how? Congress' refusal to deal with the Moslem League had rebounded on them with the Moslem demand for an independent Pakistan, to be carved out of India and separate from it. The abrupt end of the war with the atomic bombing of Japan and the July 1945 Labour party victory in the British election made the search for a solution to the Indian problem imperative.

Elections within India revealed the obvious – the country was split on purely religious grounds with the Moslem League, led by Muhammad Ali Jinnah, speaking for the overwhelming majority of Moslems and the Congress Party, led by Jawaharlal Nehru, commanding the Hindu population. Mahatma Gandhi remained the father figure for Congress but without an official role and, as events were to prove, his political influence was slipping.

'I will have India divided, or India destroyed', were Jinnah's words. This direct conflict with the Congress desire for an independent greater-India was the greatest stumbling block to the British granting independence but with each passing day the prospects for inter-communal strife and bloodshed increased. In early 1946 a British mission failed to bring the two sides together and the country slid increasingly towards civil war. A 'Direct Action Day', called by the Moslem League in August 1946, led to a slaughter of Hindus in Calcutta followed by reprisals against Moslems. Attempts to make the two sides see reason had no effect and in February 1947 the British government made a momentous decision. The current viceroy, Lord Wavell, would be replaced by Lord Louis Mountbatten and independence would come by June 1948.

Already the Punjab region of northern India was in a state of chaos and the Bengal region in the east was close to it. The new viceroy made a last ditch attempt to convince the rival factions that a united India was a more sensible proposition but they, Jinnah in particular, remained intransigent and the reluctant decision was made to divide the country. Only Gandhi stood firmly against the division, preferring the possibility of a civil war to the chaos he so rightly expected.

As in so many other parts of the world neatly slicing the country in two proved to be an impossible task. Although there were areas which were clearly Hindu or Moslem there were also parts which had very evenly mixed populations and still others where, however the country was divided, isolated 'islands' of Moslems would remain surrounded by Hindu regions. The complete impossibility of dividing all the Moslems from all the Hindus is illustrated by the fact that after partition India was still the third largest Moslem country in the world – only Indonesia and Pakistan had greater populations of Moslems. Even today India has a greater Moslem population than any of the Arab countries or Turkey or Iran.

Worse, the two overwhelmingly Moslem regions were on the exact opposite sides of the country – Pakistan would inevitably have an eastern and western half divided by a hostile India. The instability of this arrangement was self-evident, but it took 25 years before the predestined split came and East Pakistan became Bangladesh.

Other problems showed up only after the actual independence. Pakistan was painfully short of the administrators and clerical workers with which India is so well endowed. It was an occupation simply not followed by many Moslems. Many other occupations, such as money lenders, were purely Hindu callings and the unfortunate untouchables did the dirty work not only for their higher caste Hindu brothers but also for the Moslems.

Mountbatten decided to follow a breakneck pace to independence and announced that it would come on 14 August 1947. Historians have wondered ever since if much bloodshed might not have been averted if the impetuous and egotistical Mountbatten had not decided on such a hasty process.

Once the decision had been made to divide the country there were countless administrative decisions to be made, the most important being the actual location of the dividing line. Since a locally adjudicated dividing line was certain to bring recriminations from either side, an independent British referee was given the odious task of drawing the line, knowing that its effects would be disastrous for countless people. The most difficult decisions had to be made in Bengal and the Punjab. In the former, Calcutta, with its Hindu majority, its port facilities and its jute mills was divided from East Bengal, with a Moslem majority and jute production as its major industry but without a single jute mill for its processing or a suitable port for its export.

The problem was far worse in the Punjab where inter-communal antagonisms were already running at a fever pitch. Here one of the most fertile and affluent regions of the country had large percentages of Moslems (55%) and Hindus (30%) but also a substantial number of India's militant Sikhs. The Punjab contained all the ingredients for an epic disaster and with the announcement of the division line, only days after independence, the resulting bloodshed was even worse than expected. All over India huge exchanges of population took place as Moslems moved to Pakistan and Hindus to India, but in the Punjab the exchange was complete. The dividing line cut neatly between the Punjab's two major cities – Lahore and Amritsar. Prior to independence Lahore's population of 1.2 million included approximately 500,000 Hindus and 100,000 Sikhs. When the dust had finally settled Lahore had a Hindu & Sikh population of only a thousand.

For months the greatest exodus in human history took place east and west across the Punjab. Trainloads of Moslems, fleeing westward, would be held up and slaughtered by Hindu and Sikh mobs. Hindus and Sikhs fleeing to the east would suffer the same fate. The army force sent to maintain order proved totally inadequate and at times all too ready to join the partisan carnage. By the time the Punjab chaos had run its course, over 10 million people had changed sides and even the most conservative estimates calculate that a quarter of a million people had lost their lives. The figure may well have been over a half million. An additional million people changed sides in Bengal.

Nor was the outright division of the Punjab to be the only excuse for carnage. Throughout the British era India had retained many 'princely states' and

Nor was the outright division of the Punjab to be the only excuse for carnage. Throughout the British era India had retained many 'princely states' and incorporating these into independent India and Pakistan proved to be a considerable headache. Guarantees of a substantial measure of independence convinced most of them to opt for inclusion into the new countries but at the time of Independence there were still three holdouts.

One was Kashmir, predominantly Moslem but with a Hindu Maharaja. In October the Maharaja had still not opted for India or Pakistan and a ragtag Pathan army crossed the border from Pakistan, intent on racing to Srinagar and annexing Kashmir without provoking a real India-Pakistan conflict. Unfortunately for the Pakistanis the Pathans had been inspired to this little invasion by the promise of plunder and they did so much plundering on the way that India had time to rush troops to Srinagar and prevent the town's capture. The indecisive Maharaja finally opted for India, a brief India-Pakistan war took place, the UN eventually stepped in and Kashmir has remained a central cause for disagreement between the two countries ever since. With its overwhelming Moslem majority and its geographic links to Pakistan many people are inclined to support Pakistan's claims to the region. But Kashmir is Kashmir and India has consistently evaded a promised plebiscite. India and Pakistan are divided in this region by a demarcation line and neither side agrees to this day on an official border.

The final stages of independence had one final tragedy to be played out. On 30 January, 1948 Gandhi, deeply disheartened by partition and the subsequent bloodshed, was assasinated by a Hindu fanatic.

Independent India

Since independence, India has made enormous strides but faced enormous problems. The mere fact that India has not, like so many third world countries, bowed to dictatorships, military rule or foreign invasion is a testament to the basic strength of the country's government and institutions. Economically it has made major steps forward in improving agricultural output and its industries have expanded to the stage where India is one of the world's top 10 industrial powers.

Jawaharlal Nehru, India's first Prime Minister, tried to follow a strict policy of non-alignment although India has maintained generally excellent relations with its former coloniser – a fact which has caused some little annoyance to the critics of imperialism. Despite this non-aligned policy India has moved towards the USSR – partially because of conflicts with China and partially because of US support for arch-enemy Pakistan. Since independence, Gandhi's belief in peaceful neutrality has on a number of occasions had to be thrown out of the window. Three times India has clashed with Pakistan (1948, 1965, 1971) over bitter disputes concerning Kashmir or the Bangladesh issue. Border wars have been fought with China and India still disputes the area of Aksai Chin in Ladakh which China seized in 1962.

These outside events have taken the attention from India's often serious internal problems. Like any third world country population growth continues to hold the potential for ultimate disaster. India weathered the first energy crisis of the early 70s remarkably well and no better advertisement could be found for the green revolution, but whether this will continue to be enough is an open question.

Indira's India

Politically India's major problem since independence has been the personality cult that has developed with its leaders. There have only been two real Prime Ministers – Nehru and his daughter, Indira Gandhi (no relation to the Mahatma). Having won election in 1966 Indira Gandhi faced serious opposition and unrest in 1975 and countered it by declaring a state of emergency, a situation which in many other countries might quickly have become a dictatorship.

During the 'Emergency' a mixed bag of good and bad policies were followed. Freed of much of the usual parliamentary constraints she was able to control inflation remarkably well, boost the economy and decisively increase efficiency. On the negative side political opponents often found themselves behind bars, India's judicial system was turned into a puppet theatre, the press was fettered and there was more than a hint of personal aggrandisement, as in the disastrous Sanjay Gandhi 'people's car' plan. An equally disastrous programme of virtually forced sterilisations, also masterminded by her son Sanjay, caused much anger. Despite murmurings of discontent Indira decided that the people were behind her and in 1977 called a general election to give credence to her emergency powers. Sanjay had counselled against holding the election and his opinion proved to be a wise one, because Indira and her Congress Party were bundled out of power in favour of the hastily assembled Janata, Peoples' Party.

Janata, however, was a device with only one function, defeating Indira. Once it had won, it had no other cohesive function and its leader, Moraji Desai, seemed more interested in protecting cows, banning alcohol and getting his daily glass of urine than coming to grips with the country's problems. With inflation soaring, unrest rising and the economy stumbling nobody was surprised when Janata fell apart in late 1979 and the 1980 election brought Indira back to power with a larger majority than ever.

Unhappily for Mrs Gandhi, her political touch seems to have faded since the emergency days and she has failed to grapple with the problems that grew so rapidly in the Janata era. The accidental death of her son and potential heir, the none too popular Sanjay, seemed to further sap her vitality. India has been further plagued by communal unrest, violent actions against untouchables, upheaval in the north-west and the Punjab, and numerous cases of police brutality and corruption – all of which you'll read about in the papers while in India.

Despite all these problems it's worth remembering two important points about this vast country. Of all the people in the world who live in what we know as democratic societies nearly 50% of them are Indians; as 1977 indicated it's a democratic society with teeth. Furthermore India, despite its population problems and vast poverty, manages to do something neither the USSR or China can manage, feed its own people without importing food. The average Indian may not eat all that well but those old tales of famine and starvation are, hopefully, a thing of the past – at least at the present population levels.

GOVERNMENT

India has a parliamentary system of government with, however, certain similarities to the US government. Basically there are two houses – a lower house known as the Lok Sabha (House of the People) and the upper house known as the Rajya Sabha (Council of States). The lower house has up to 500 members elected on a population basis while the upper has up to 250 members. As in the British House of Commons or the Australian House of Representatives, the lower house can be dissolved but the upper house, unlike Britain or Australia,

Guardsman
HOUSE OF PARLAIMENT,
NEW DELHI

the constitution provides for special facilities and assistance for India's Harijans and for the tribal groups still found in various parts of the country.

POPULATION & PEOPLE

India had a population in 1981 of 687 million. Despite extensive birth control programmes it is still growing far too rapidly for comfort. In the last 20 years it has gone from 439 million at the 1961 census to 547 million at the 1971 census to the present figure. Despite India's many large cities the country is still overwhelmingly rural. It is estimated that only about 100 million of the total population live in cities or towns but with increasing industrialisation the shift from village to city will continue to grow.

The Indian people are not a homogeneous group. It is quite easy to tell the difference visually between the shorter Bengalis of the east, the taller and lighter skinned people of the centre and north, the Kashmiris with their distinctly central Asian appearance, the Tibetan people of Ladakh and the north of Himachal Pradesh, or the dark skinned Tamils of the south. Despite these regional variations the government has managed to successfully establish an 'Indian' ethos and nationalistic feeling.

Although India is overwhelmingly Hindu there are large minorities of other religions. These include 76 million Moslems, making India one of the largest Moslem countries in the world, much larger than any of the Arab Middle East nations. Christians number about 19 million, Sikhs 13 million, Buddhists five million and Jains three million. About 7% of the population is classified as 'tribal'. They are found scattered throughout the country although there are concentrations of them in the north-east corner of the country as well as in Orissa and a number of other states.

Birth Control

India's attempts at birth control have

cannot. There are also state governments with legislative assemblies known as Vidhan Sabha. The two national houses and the various state houses elect the Indian President but he or she is really a figurehead while the Prime Minister wields the real power.

There is a strict division between the activities handled by the states and by the national government. The police force, education, agriculture and industry are all reserved for the state governments. Certain other areas are jointly administered by the two levels of government. All adult Indians have the vote and

MATRIMONIALS

MATRIMONIALS FOR BRIDES	MATRIMONIALS FOR BRIDES	MATRIMONIALS FOR BRIDES	MATRIMONIALS FOR GROOMS

OFFER OF A LIFE TIME!

REPEAT YOUR MATRIMONIAL ADVERTISEMENT

been varied but although there has been success to some extent at slowing the rate of increase the picture is far from a happy one. Today many international experts feel that the solution to the population increase problem in the third world is not to slow the birth rate, which will then bring prosperity in its wake, but to establish a degree of prosperity which will then bring a desire for fewer children. So long as children are a source of security in old age and so long as male heirs are so avidly desired it will be difficult to successfully bring population pressures under control.

In the early '70s India had a birth control blitz with slogans and posters appearing all over the country and the famous 'transistor radio in exchange for sterilisation' campaign. Many of those wall paintings showing the happy two child family are still visible around the country. More sinister was the brief campaign of the emergency era when squads of sterilisers terrorised half the country and people were afraid to go out after dark. That over-kill campaign probably put the birth control programme in India back by years and it currently enjoys a very low priority in the government's platform.

Castes

The caste system is one of India's more confusing mysteries — how it came about, how it has managed to survive for so long, how much harm it causes, are all topics of discussion for visitors to India. Its origins are lost in the mists of history but basically it seems to have been developed at first by the Brahmins or priest class in order to make their own superior position more permanent. Later it was probably extended by the invading Aryans who felt themselves superior to the indigenous pre-Aryan Indians. Eventually the caste system became formalised into four distinct classes, each with rules of conduct and behaviour.

At the top of the heap is the Brahmin class who are priests and the arbiters of what is right and wrong in matters of religion and caste. Beneath them come the Kshatriyas who are soldiers and administrators, then the Vaisyas who are the artisan and commercial class, finally the Sudras are the farmers and the peasant class. These four castes are said to have come from Brahma's mouth (the Brahmins), his arms (the Kshatriyas), his thighs (the Vaisyas) and his feet (the Sudras). Beneath these four castes is a fifth group, the untouchables, who literally have no caste. They perform the most menial and degrading jobs and at one time to a high caste Hindu to have an untouchable use the same temple, touch you, even have his shadow cast across you, was to be polluted and involve a rigorous series of rituals to be cleansed.

Today the caste system has been much weakened but it still has considerable power, particularly amongst the less educated people. Gandhi put great effort into bringing the untouchables into society including renaming them the 'Harijans' or 'children of god'. But an untouchable by any other name .... It must be remembered that being born into a certain caste does not really limit you strictly to one occupation or position in life just as being black in the USA does not mean you are poverty-stricken and live in Harlem. Many Brahmins are poor peasants for example, and hundreds of years ago the great Maratha leader Shivaji was a Sudra. None of the later Marathas who controlled much of India after the demise of the Moghuls was a Brahmin. Nevertheless you can generalise that the better-off Indians will generally be higher caste and that the 'sweeper' who you see cleaning the toilet in your hotel in a desultory fashion will certainly be a Harijan. In fact when Indian Airlines appointed their first untouchable airline stewardess it was certainly front page news on Indian newspapers.

How do you tell what caste a Hindu is? Well, apart from knowing that if his job is a

BUREAUCRACY India is an innovator and world leader in the field of red tape, buck passing and lunacy in quadruplicate.

The glass globe paperweight is the orb of real power. The more you have the more bureaucratic clout.

Some desks look like rock gardens...

menial one such as cleaning streets or in some way defiling such as working in leather he is a Harijan, there is not really any way you can tell. If you see a man with his shirt off and he has the sacred thread looped round one shoulder he is a Brahmin but then Pharsis also wear a sacred thread. Of course if an Indian is a Sikh or a Moslem he will have no caste.

In many ways the caste system today also functions as an enormous unofficial trade union with strict rules to avoid demarcation disputes. Each caste can have many subdivisions so that the servant who polishes the brass cannot, due to his caste, also polish silver. Many of the old caste rules have been considerably relaxed although less educated or more

isolated Hindus may still be worried about pollution from having a lower caste person prepare their food. Better educated people probably are not too worried about shaking hands with a caste-less westerner though! Nor does the thought of going abroad, and thus losing caste completely, carry too much weight these days.

The caste system still produces enormous burdens for India, however. During the last couple of years there have been frequent and violent outbreaks of violence towards lower caste Hindus. In isolated rural communities higher caste Hindus have lynched Harijans whom they felt were getting 'uppity' and there are often latent tensions between the castes which can easily spill over into violence. In

1980 in one village a number of Harijans were killed after a riot broke out over a bridegroom not dismounting from his wedding horse when passing a group of higher caste men! In 1981 there were a whole series of violent riots in Ahmedabad in Gujarat due to the practice of reserving university places for Harijans, whether or not there were sufficient Harijan applicants for the places. Higher caste Hindus who could not obtain university places despite having good qualifications prompted these outbreaks.

It's interesting to compare these problems with the situation in the US where, during the desegregation era, many blacks experienced great difficulties in being allowed into 'all white' schools and restaurants. Similarly in the US today there is a degree of protest about the reservation of college positions for disadvantaged minorities. Going far back into western history it's interesting that the medieval ideal of heaven was developed in part to keep the peasants in their place – behave yourself, work hard, put up with your lot and you'll go to heaven. Probably caste developed in a similar fashion – your life may be pretty miserable but that's your caste, behave yourself and you may be born into a better one next time around.

ECONOMY

India is still a predominantly agricultural country but it is also one of the world's major industrial powers with important iron and steel works and a growing manufacturing industry. Textiles are still the backbone of India's industrial exports, however. Recently major efforts have been made to launch Indian industry into modern 'high tech' areas, away from the traditional heavy engineering areas. Nevertheless a recent Japanese study indicated that India's policy of protection of local industry from imports rather than a conscious effort to promote exports, even when it meant importing foreign technology, has been far less successful

than the opposite policy followed in countries like Japan or South Korea.

The central planning policies and mountains of red tape and paperwork to be surmounted have also held economic development back. It's interesting that China, which followed similar protectionist and isolationist policies under Mao, has made an abrupt about turn and India also seems to have become intent upon updating key industries, even if that necessitates importing modern technology.

Despite these industrial and manufacturing activities 70% of India's population is engaged in work on the land – much of it inefficient and unproductive. Small landholdings, poor methods and lack of investment all contribute to this record although since independence the agricultural production levels have actually increased at a faster rate than the population. The green revolution, involving new strains and improved use of fertilisers, has had dramatic results in India which has managed to produce a food surplus for several years now. The 1983 monsoon was the best for a number of years producing a particularly good harvest. India also has nearly 200 million cattle but although some of them serve as work animals and there is some dairy production, most of them, due to their religious protection, are totally useless.

GEOGRAPHY

India has a total area of 3,287,782 square km. The north of the country is decisively bordered by the long sweep of the Himalaya, the highest mountains on earth. They run in a south-east to north-west direction right across the north of India and separate it from China. Bhutan in the east and Nepal in the centre actually lie along the Himalaya as does Darjeeling, the northern part of Uttar Pradesh, Himachal Pradesh and Jammu & Kashmir.

The Himalaya are not a single mountain range but a series of ranges with beautiful

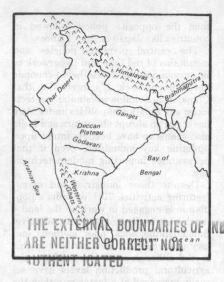

THE EXTERNAL BOUNDARIES OF INDIA
ARE NEITHER CORRECT NOR
AUTHENTICATED

South of the northern plains the land rises up into the high plateau known as the Deccan. The Deccan Plateau is bordered on both sides by ranges of hills which parallel the coast to the east and west. The Western Ghats are higher and have a wider coastal strip than the Eastern Ghats. The two ranges meet in the extreme south in the Nilgiri Hills. The southern hill stations are in these hills – Matheran and Mahabaleshwar near Bombay in the Western Ghats, Ooty in the extreme south in the Nilgiri Hills. The major rivers of the south are the Godavari and the Krishna. Both rise on the eastern slope of the Western Ghats, flow right across the Deccan and into the sea on the east coast.

The eastern boundary of India is also made by ranges of hills, foothills of the Himalaya, which separate the country from Burma. In this north-eastern region India bends right around Bangladesh, a low-lying country at the delta of the Ganges, and almost meets the sea to totally surround it.

On the western side India is separated from Pakistan by three distinct regions. In the north, in the disputed area of Kashmir, the Himalaya forms the boundary between the two countries. The Himalaya drops down to the plains of the Punjab and then merges into the Great Indian Thar Desert. In the eastern part of Rajasthan this is an area of great natural beauty and extreme barrenness. Finally the Indian state of Gujarat is separated from the Sind in Pakistan by the unusual marshland known as the Rann of Kutch. In the dry season the Rann dries right out leaving isolated salt islands on an expansive plain while in the wet it floods over to become a vast inland sea.

valleys wedged between them. The Kulu Valley in Himachal Pradesh and the Vale of Kashmir in J&K are both Himalayan valleys, as is the Kathmandu Valley in Nepal. Nanda Devi (7819 metres) is the highest mountain in India. Beyond the Himalaya stretches the high, dry and barren Tibetan plateau and in Ladakh a small part of this plateau actually lies within India's boundaries.

The final range of the Himalaya, the Siwalik Hills, ends abruptly in the great northern plains of India. In complete contrast to the soaring mountain peaks, the northern plain is oppressively flat and slopes so gradually that all the way from Delhi to the Bay of Bengal it drops only 200 metres. The mighty Ganges River, which has its source in the Himalaya, drains a large part of the northern plain and is the major river of India. The Brahmaputra, flowing down from the north-east of the country, is the other major river of the north. In the north-west the Indus River starts out flowing through Ladakh in India but soon dives off into Pakistani territory and is the most important river of that nation.

CLIMATE

India is so vast that the climatic conditions in the far north have little relation to that of the extreme south. While the heat is building up to breaking point on the plains, the people of Ladakh will still be waiting for the snow to melt on the high passes. Basically India has a three-season year – the hot, the wet, the cool.

The Hot The heat starts to build up on the plains of India from around February and by April or May it has become unbearable. In central India temperatures of 45°C and above are commonplace. It's dry and dusty and everything is seen through a haze. From the air the country looks parched and barren but usually all you can see below is a blanket of hazy brown from all the dust in the air. Later in May the first signs of the monsoon are seen, short sharp rainstorms, violent electric storms, duststorms that turn day into night and cover everything with a film of dust. The heat towards the end of the hot season is like a hammer blow, you feel listless and tired and tempers are short. It's said to be the time of year when murders and suicides take place!

The hot season is the time to leave the plains, which are at their worst, and retreat to the hills. Kashmir comes into its own and all the Himalayan hill stations are at their best. The hill stations further south – Mt Abu in Rajasthan, Matheran in Maharashtra, Ooty in Tamil Nadu – are generally not high enough to be really cool but they are better than being down at sea level. By early June the snow on the passes into Ladakh should be all melted and the road will be open. You can also get into Keylong from Manali in Himachal Pradesh. This is the best trekking season in Kashmir and Ladakh.

The Wet When the monsoon finally arrives it's a great relief. It doesn't arrive in one day as the chart on the next page indicates. After a period of advance warning the rain comes in steadily, starting around 1 June in the extreme south and sweeping north to have covered the whole country by early July. The monsoon doesn't really cool things off, at first you simply trade the hot, dry, dusty weather for hot, humid, muddy con-

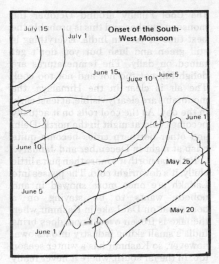

Onset of the South-West Monsoon
July 15
July 1
June 15
June 10 June 5
June 1
June 10
May 25
June 5
May 20
June 1

ditions. Even so it's a great relief, not least for farmers who now have the busiest time of year ahead of them as they prepare their fields for the rice planting. During the monsoon it doesn't simply rain solidly, all day, every day. It certainly rains every day but it tends to come down in buckets for a while then the sun comes out and it's quite pleasant.

Some places are at their best during the monsoon – like Rajasthan with its many palaces in lakes. While in Nepal the monsoon is a very bad time to trek, in the north-west Indian Himalayan regions this is a good trekking time. In Nepal the trekking season commences when the monsoon finishes but the regions of Himachal Pradesh, Kashmir and Ladakh in India are further north and the winter is too cold for trekking. Although the monsoon brings life to India it also brings its share of death. Every year there are many destructive floods and thousands of people are made homeless. Rivers rise and sweep away road and railway lines and many flight schedules are disrupted. Travel can definitely be more difficult during the monsoon.

The Cool Finally around October the monsoon finishes and this is probably the best time of year in India. Everything is still green and lush but you don't get rained on daily. The temperatures are delightful, not too hot and not too cool. The air is clear in the Himalaya, the mountains are clearly visible, at least early in the day. As the cool rolls on it actually becomes cold at night in the north. Delhi and other northern cities become quite crisp at night in December and January.

In the far north it's more than just a little chilly, it's downright cold. The passes into Ladakh are once more snowed in and nobody wants to be staying on a houseboat on Dal Lake in Kashmir when the lake is frozen over. Snow does bring India's small skiing industry into its own, however, so Kashmir has a winter season too. In the far south, where it never really gets less than hot, the temperatures do become comfortably warm rather than hot. Then around February the temperatures start to climb again and before you know it you're back in the hot weather.

Some Regional Variations As in Sri Lanka the south-east coast is also affected by the north-east monsoon and brings rain from mid-October to the end of December. The usual monsoon is the south-west since it comes from that direction. It can get surprisingly wet during the north-east monsoon.

It's easy to forget just how cold it can get in the far north. Even along the Ganges you'll need a sweater or jacket at night and in Kashmir the snow will be up to your neck. Basically the best time to visit India is November through February, except for the northern Himalayan region where April through July is the best time.

RELIGION

India has a positive kaleidoscope of religions. There is probably more diversity of religions and sects in India than anywhere else on earth. Apart from having

nearly all the world's great religions represented here, India was also the birthplace of two of the world's greatest (Hinduism and Buddhism), an important home for one of the world's oldest (Zoroastrianism) and also home for an ancient religion which is unique to India (Jainism).

Hindus

India's major religion, Hinduism, is followed by approximately 80% of the population, over 500 million people. Only in Nepal and on the Indonesian island of Bali do Hindus also predominate, but it is the largest religion in Asia in terms of number of adherents. Despite its colourful, comic book, almost Disneyland appearance it is actually one of the oldest extant religions with firm roots extending back to beyond 1000 BC.

The Indus Valley civilisation developed a religion which shows a close relationship to Hinduism in many ways and later it further developed through the combined religious practices of the southern Dravidians and the Aryan invaders who arrived in the north of India around 1500 BC. Around 1000 BC the Vedic scriptures were introduced and gave the first loose framework to the religion. Hinduism today has a number of holy books including the *Bhagavad Gita* which is credited to Krishna, the *Mahabharata*, the *Ramayana*, the story of Rama; the *Vedas*, the *Upanishads* and the *Puranas*.

Basically it postulates that we will all go through a series of rebirths or reincarnations that eventually lead to *moksha*, the spiritual salvation which frees one from the cycle of rebirths. With each rebirth you can move closer or further from eventual moksha, the deciding factor on this is your *karma* which is literally a law of cause and effect. Bad actions during your life result in bad karma which ends in a lower reincarnation. Conversely if your deeds and actions have been good you will reincarnate on a higher level and be a step closer to eventual freedom from rebirth.

Dharma or the natural law defines the total social, ethical and spiritual harmony of your life. There are three categories of dharma, the first being the eternal harmony which involves the whole universe. The second category is the dharma that controls castes and the relations between castes. The third dharma is the moral code which an individual should follow.

The Hindu religion has three basic practices. They are *puja* or worship, the cremation of the dead and the rules and regulations of the caste system. There are four main castes defined as the *Brahmin* or priest caste, the *Kshatriyas* – soldiers and governors, the *Vaisyas* are tradespeople and farmers while the *Sudras* are menial workers and craftspeople. These basic castes are then sub-divided into a great number of lesser divisions. Beneath all the castes are the *Harijans* or untouchables, the lowest caste-less class for whom all the most menial and degrading tasks are reserved.

Westerners have trouble understanding Hinduism principally because of the vast pantheon of gods involved. In fact you can look upon all these different gods simply as pictorial representations of the many attributes of a god. The one omnipresent god usually has three physical representations. *Brahma* is the creator, *Vishnu* is the preserver while *Shiva* is the destroyer and reproducer. All three gods are usually shown with four arms, but Brahma has the added advantage of four heads to represent his all-seeing presence. The four *Vedas* are supposed to have emanated from his mouths.

The gods also have an associated animal known as the god's vehicle on which he or she rides. Each god has a consort who also has certain attributes and abilities. The gods generally have symbols which they hold in their hands. You can often pick out which god is being represented by their vehicles or their symbols. Brahma's consort is *Sarasvati*, the goddess of learning. She rides upon a white swan and holds the stringed musical instrument known as a *veena*.

Vishnu, the preserver, is usually shown in one of the physical forms in which he has visited earth. In all Vishnu has paid nine visits and on his tenth he is expected as a *Kalki*, riding a horse. On his earlier visits he appeared in animal form as in his boar incarnation or his man-lion (*Narsingh*) incarnation but on visit seven he appeared as *Rama*, regarded as the personification of the ideal man and the hero of the Ramayana. Rama also managed to provide a number of secondary gods including his helpful ally *Hanuman*, the Monkey God. Hanuman's faithful nature is illustrated by the representation of Hanuman which is often found guarding fort or palace entrances. Naturally incarnations can also have consorts and Rama's lady was *Sita*.

On visit eight Vishnu came as *Krishna* who was brought up with peasants and thus became a great favourite of the working classes. Krishna is renowned for his exploits with the *gopis* or shepherdesses and his consorts are *Radha*, the head of the gopis, *Rukmani* and *Satyabhama*. Krishna is often blue in colour and plays a flute. Vishnu's final recent incarnation was on visit nine when he came as the Buddha. This was probably a ploy to bring the Buddhist splinter group back into the Hindu fold.

When Vishnu appears as Vishnu, rather than one of his incarnations, he sits on a couch made from the coils of a serpent and in his hands he holds two symbols, the conch shell and the discus. Vishnu's vehicle is the half man-half eagle known as the *Garuda*. The Garuda is a firm dogooder and has a deep dislike of snakes – Indonesia's national airline is named after the Garuda. His consort is the beautiful *Lakshmi* (Laxmi) who came from the sea and is the goddess of wealth and prosperity.

Shiva's creative role is phallically

symbolised by his representation as the frequently worshipped lingam. Shiva rides on the bull *Nandi* and his matted hair is said to have *Ganga*, the goddess of the river Ganges in it. Shiva is supposed to live in the Himalayas and devote much time to smoking dope. He also has the third eye in the middle of his forehead and carries a trident. Shiva is also known as *Nataraja*, the cosmic dancer whose dance shook the cosmos and created the world. Shiva's consort is *Parvati*, the beautiful. She, however, has a dark side when she appears as *Durga* the terrible. In this role she holds weapons in her 10 hands and rides a tiger. As *Kali*, the fiercest of the gods, she demands sacrifices and wears a garland of skulls. Kali usually handles the destructive side of Shiva's personality.

Shiva and Parvati have two children. *Ganesh* is the elephant headed god of prosperity and wisdom and is probably the most popular of all the gods. Ganesh obtained his elephant head due to his father's notorious temper. Coming back

from a long trip Shiva discovered Parvati in in her room with a young man, not pausing to think that their son might have grown up a little during his absence Shiva lopped his head off! He was then forced by Parvati to bring his son back to life but could only do so by giving him the head of the first living thing he saw – which happened to be an elephant. Ganesh's vehicle is a rat! Shiva and Parvati's other son is *Kartikkaya*, the god of war.

A variety of lesser gods and goddesses also crowd the scene. Most temples are dedicated to one or other of the gods but curiously there are very few Brahma temples – perhaps just two or three in all of India. Most Hindus profess to be either *Vaishnavites* (followers of Vishnu) or *Shaivites* (followers of Shiva). The cow is, of course, the holy animal of Hinduism. Hinduism is not a proselytising religion since you cannot be converted to Hinduism. You're either born a Hindu or you are not, you can never become one. Similarly once you are a Hindu you cannot change your caste – you're born into it and are stuck with it for the rest of that lifetime. Nevertheless Hinduism has a great attraction to many westerners and India's 'export gurus' are many and successful.

A *guru* is not so much a teacher as a spiritual guide, somebody who by his example or simply by his presence indicates what path you should follow. In a spiritual search one always needs a guru. A *sadhu* is an individual on a spiritual search. They're an easily recognised group, usually wandering around half-naked, smeared in dust with their hair and beard matted. Sadhus following Shiva will often carry his symbol, the trident. A sadhu is often someone who has decided that his business and family life has reached its natural conclusion and it is time to throw everything aside and go out on a spiritual search. He may previously have been the village postman, or a businessman. Sadhus perform various feats of self-mortification and wander all over India, occasionally coming together in great pilgrimages and other religious gatherings. Many sadhus are, of course, simply beggars following a more sophisticated approach to gathering in the paise but many of them are completely genuine in their search.

Buddhists

Although there are only about five million Buddhists in India the religion is of great importance because it had its birth here and there are many reminders of its historic role. Strictly speaking Buddhism is not a religion, since it is not centred on a god, but is a system of philosophy and a code of morality. Buddhism was founded in northern India about 500 BC when Siddhartha Gautama, born a prince, achieved enlightenment. Gautama Buddha was not the first Buddha but the fourth and is not expected to be the last 'enlightened one'. Buddhists believe that the achievement of enlightenment is the goal of every being so eventually we will all reach Buddhahood.

The Buddha never wrote down his *dharma* or teachings and a schism later developed so that today there are two major Buddhist schools. The *Theravada, Hinayana*, 'doctrine of the elders' or 'small vehicle' holds that the path to *nirvana*, the eventual aim of all Buddhists, is an individual pursuit. In contrast the *Mahayana* or 'large vehicle' school holds that the combined belief of all followers will eventually be great enough to encompass all mankind and bear it all to salvation. To some the less austere and ascetic Mahayana school is a 'soft option'. Today it is chiefly practised in Viet Nam, Japan and amongst Chinese Buddhists while the Hinayana school is followed in Sri Lanka, Burma and Thailand. There are other, sometimes more esoteric, divisions of Buddhisms such as the *Hindu-Tantric* Buddhism of Tibet which you can see in Ladakh and other parts of north India.

The Buddha renounced his material life to search for enlightenment but, unlike other prophets, found that starvation did not lead to discovery. Therefore he developed his rule of the 'middle way', moderation in everything. The Buddha taught that all life is suffering but that suffering comes from our sensual desires and the illusion that they are important. By following the 'eight-fold path' these desires will be extinguished and a state of nirvana, where they are extinct and we are free from their delusions, will be reached. Following this process required going through a series of rebirths until the goal is eventually reached and no more rebirths into the world of suffering are necessary. The path that takes you through this cycle of births is *karma* but this is not simply fate. Karma is a law of cause and effect, your actions in one life determine the role you will play and what you will have to go through in your next life.

In India Buddhism developed rapidly when it was embraced by the great Emperor Ashoka. As his empire extended over much of India so was Buddhism carried forth. He also sent out missions to other lands to preach the Buddha's word and his own son is said to have carried Buddhism to Sri Lanka. Later, however, Buddhism began to contract in India because it had never really taken a hold on the great mass of people. As Hinduism revived Buddhism in India was gradually reabsorbed into the older religion.

Today Buddha, to Hindus, is simply another incarnation of Vishnu. At its peak, however, Buddhism was responsible for magnificent structures erected wherever it held sway. The earlier Theravada form of Buddhism did not believe in the representation of the Buddha in human form, his presence was always alluded to in Buddhist art or architecture through symbols such as the Bo tree (under which he was sitting when he attained enlightenment), the elephant which his mother dreamed of before he was born or the wheel of life. Today, however, even Theravada Buddhists produce Buddha images.

Moslems

Moslems, the followers of the Islamic religion, are India's largest religious minority. They number about 75 million in all, over 10% of India's population. This makes India one of the largest Islamic nations in the world. India has had two Moslem presidents, several cabinet ministers and State Chief Ministers since independence. It is the most recent and most widespread of the Asian religions and predominates from the Mediterranean right across to India and is the major religion east of India in Bangladesh, Malaysia and Indonesia.

The religion's founder, the prophet Mohammed, was born in 570 AD in Mecca, now in Saudi Arabia. He had his first revelation from God, Allah, in 610 and this and later visions were compiled into the Moslem holy book, the *Koran*. As his purpose in life was revealed to him Mohammed began to preach against the

idolatry that Mecca was then the centre for. Moslems are strictly monotheistic and believe that to search for God through images is a sin. Moslem teachings correspond closely with the Old Testament of the Bible, and Moses and Jesus are both accepted as Moslem prophets although Jesus is not the son of God.

Eventually Mohammed's attacks on local business led to him and his followers being run out of town in 622. They fled to Medina, the 'city of the prophet' and by 630 were strong enough to march back into Mecca and take over. Although Mohammed died in 632 most of Arabia had been converted to Islam within two decades. The Moslem faith was more than just a religion. It also called on its followers to spread the word – if necessary by the sword. In succeeding centuries Islam was to expand over three continents. The Arabs, who first propagated the faith, developed a reputation as being ruthless opponents but reasonable masters so people often found it advisable to surrender to them. In this way the Moslems swept aside the crumbling Byzantine empire, whose people felt no desire to support their distant Christian emperor.

Islam only travelled west for a hundred years before being pushed back at Poitiers, in France, in 732, but it continued east for centuries. It regenerated the Persian Empire, which was then declining from its protracted struggles with Byzantium, and in 711, the same year the Arabs landed in Spain, they sent dhows up the Indus River into India. This was more a casual raid than a full scale invasion but in the 11th centuries all of north India fell into Moslem hands. Eventually the Moghul empire controlled most of the sub-continent. From here it was spread by Indian traders on into South-East Asia.

At an early stage Islam suffered a fundamental split that remains to this day. The third Caliph, successor to Mohammed, was murdered and followed by

Ali, the prophet's son-in-law, in 656. Ali was assassinated in 661 by the Governor of Syria who set himself up as Caliph in preference to the descendants of Ali. Most Moslems today are *Sunnites*, followers of the succession from the Caliph, while the others are *Shias* or *Shi'ites* who follow the descendants of Ali.

Strangely today Islam, which spread out from its initial foundation with such vigour, has become inertial and unchanging. Women in Islamic society may not exactly be second class citizens but they are certainly a second type of citizen. Despite its long period of control over India Islam never managed to make great inroads into Hindu society and the Hindu religion. Converts to Islam were principally made from the lowest castes with the result, at partition, that Pakistan found itself with a shortage of the educated clerical workers and government officials with which India is so liberally endowed. Although it did not make great numbers of converts the visible effects of Moslem influence in India are strong in architecture, art and in food.

Converts to Islam have only to announce that 'There is no God but Allah and Mohammed is his prophet' and they become Moslems. Friday is the Moslem holy day and the main mosque in each town is known as the Jami Masjid or Friday Mosque. The eventual aim of every Moslem is to make the pilgrimage to Mecca and become a *haji*.

Sikhs

The Sikhs number 13 million and are chiefly found in the Punjab although they are also all over India. They are probably the most visible of the Indian religious groups because of the five symbols introduced by Guru Gobind Singh so that Sikh men could easily recognise each other. They are known as the five *kakkars* and are: *kesha* or uncut hair; *kangha* the wooden or ivory comb; *kachha* or shorts;

kara which is a steel bracelet and *kirtipan* or the sword. Because of their kesha Sikh men wear their hair tied up in a bun and hidden by a long turban. The wearing of kachha (shorts) and carrying a (kirtipan) sword, came about because of the Sikh's military tradition – they didn't want to be tripping over a long *dhoti* or caught without a weapon. Normally the sword is simply represented by a tiny image set in the comb. The steel bracelet has the useful secondary function of making a good bottle opener. With their beards and turbans and their upright, military bearing the 'noble' Sikh is hard to miss!

The Sikh religion was founded by Guru Nanak who was born in 1469. It was originally intended to bring together the best of the Hindu and Islamic religions. Its basic tenets are similar to that of Hinduism with the important modification that the Sikhs are opposed to caste distinctions and pilgrimages to rivers. They are not, however, opposed to pilgrimages to holy sites. They worship at temples known as *gurdwaras*, baptise their children when they are old enough to understand the religion in a ceremony known as *pahul* and they cremate their dead. The holy book of the Sikhs is the *Granth Sahib* which contains the works of the ten Sikh gurus together with Hindu and Moslem writings.

In the 16th century Guru Gobind Singh introduced the military overtones into the religion in an attempt to halt the persecution the Sikhs were then suffering. From that time all Sikhs have borne the surname Singh or 'Lion'. In all there were 10 gurus, the last one dying in 1708. Sikhs believe in one god and are opposed to idol worship. They practise tolerance and love of others and their belief in hospitality extends to offering shelter to anyone who comes to their gurdwaras. Because of their get-on-with-it attitude to life they are one of the better-off groups in Indian society. They have a well known reputation for mechanical aptitude and specialise in handling machinery of every type from auto-rickshaws to jumbo jets.

By 1982 the Akalis, the political wing of the Sikh's main party, had been demanding more autonomy for the Punjab. Some Sikh leaders, mainly those settled outside India, were actually demanding an independent state to be called Khalistan. There is little real support for this idea among the Sikhs in India but the demands for greater autonomy have increased and caused much strife in the Punjab.

Jains

The Jain religion is contemporaneous with Buddhism and bears many similarities to it. It was founded around 500 BC by Mahavira who was the 24th and last of the Jain prophets known as *Tirthankars* or 'finders of the path'. The Jains now number only about 3½ million and are found all over India but predominantly to the west and south-west. The Jains believe that the universe is infinite and was not created by a deity. They believe in reincarnaation and eventual spiritual salvation or *moksha* through following the path of the Tirthankars. One factor in the search for salvation is *ahimsa* or reverence for all life and the avoidance of injury to all living things. Due to this belief Jains are strict vegetarians and some monks actually cover their mouths with a piece of cloth in order to avoid the risk of accidentally swallowing an insect.

The Jains are divided into two sects, the *Shvetambara* and the *Digambara*. The Digambaras are the more austere sect and their name literally means 'sky clad' since as a sign of their contempt for material possessions, they do not even wear clothes. Not surprisingly Digambaras are chiefly monks who confine their nudity to the monasteries! Jain temples are noted for the large number of similar buildings which are often erected at one place. Their temples also often have many columns, no two of which are ever identical. The Jains tend to be clever and commercially successful and have an influence disproportionate to their actual numbers.

Their temples are often extremely well kept. There are many Jains in Rajasthan, Gujarat and Bombay.

Parsis

This is one of the oldest religions on earth and was founded in Persia by the prophet Zarathustra in the 6th or 7th century BC. He was born in Mazar-i-Sharif in what is now Afghanistan. At one time Zoroastrinism stretched all the way from India to the Mediterranean but today is found only around Shiraz in Iran, Karachi in Pakistan and Bombay in India. The followers of Zoroastrinism are known as Parsis since they originally fled to India to escape persecution in Persia.

Zoroastrinism was one of the first religions to postulate an omnipotent and invisible god. Their scripture is the *Zend-Avesta* which describes the continual conflict between the forces of good and evil. Their god is *Ahura Mazda*, the god of light who is symbolised by fire. Man ensures the victory of good over evil by following the principles of *humata* or good thoughts, *hukta* or good words and *huvarshta* or good deeds.

Parsis worship in fire temples and wear a *sadra* or sacred shirt and a *kasti* or sacred thread. When children first wear these sacred items it is done in a ceremony known as *Navjote*. They keep eternally burning flames in their fire temples but they worship the fire as a symbol of God, not the fire itself. Because Parsis believe in the purity of elements they will not cremate or bury their dead since it would pollute the fire, earth, air or water. Instead they leave the bodies in 'Towers of Silence' where they are soon cleaned off by vultures.

Although there are only about 85,000 Parsis, concentrated in Bombay, they are very successful in commerce and industry and have become notable philanthropists. Parsis have influence far greater than their numbers would indicate and often acted as a channel of communication between India and Pakistan when the two countries were at loggerheads. Because of the strict requirements that a Parsi must only marry another Parsi and children must have two Parsi parents to be Parsis, their numbers are gradually declining.

Christians & Jews

India also has around 18 million Christians. There have been Christian communities in Kerala as long as Christianity has been in Europe for St Thomas the Apostle is supposed to have arrived here in 54 AD. The Portuguese, who unlike the English were as enthusiastic about spreading their brand of Christianity as making money from trade, left a large Christian community in Goa. Generally though, Christianity has not had great success in India, if success is counted in number of converts. Indians who have become Christians have generally been from the lowest castes.

There are, however, two small states (Mizoram and Nagaland) where Christians form a majority of the population. A quarter of the population of Kerala and a third of Goa are also Christian. There are small Jewish communities in a number of cities but the Jews of Cochin in Kerala are of interest because a group claims to have arrived here in 587 BC.

CULTURE

Painting, Sculpture & Architecture

Indian art and sculpture is basically religious in its themes and developments and appreciation requires at least some knowledge of its religious background. The earliest Indian artifacts are found in the Indus Valley cities in modern day Pakistan. Pieces are mainly small items of sculpture and it is not until the Mauryan period that India's first major artistic period flowered. This classical school of Buddhist art reached its peak during the reign of Ashoka. The superb sculpture of this period can be seen at its best at Sanchi. The Sungas, who followed the Mauryas, continued their artistic traditions.

When this empire ended the Gandharan period came into its own in the north-west. Close to Peshawar in Pakistan today the Gandharan period combined Buddhism with a strong Greek influence from the descendants of Alexander the Great's invading army. During this period the Buddha began to be represented directly in human form rather than by symbols such as the footprint or the stupa. Meanwhile in India proper another school began to develop at Mathura, between Agra and Delhi. Here the religious influence was also Buddhist but began to be altered by the revival of Brahmanism, the forerunner of Hinduism. It was in this school that the tradition of sculpturing *yakshinis*, those well endowed heavenly damsels, began to appear.

During the Gupta period from 320 to 600 AD Indian art went through a golden age, and it was during this period that the Buddha images developed to their present day form – even today in Buddhist countries the attitudes, clothing and hand positions have scarcely altered. This was, however, also the end of Buddhist art in India for Hinduism now began to reassert itself. At the same time as the Guptas were bringing Buddhist art to its final zenith in the north a strongly Hindu tradition was developing in the south. Both schools of art produced metal cast sculptures by the lost wax method as well as larger sculptures in stone.

The following thousand years saw a slow but steady development through to the exuberant mediaeval period of Indian Hindu art. This development can be studied at the caves of Ajanta and Ellora where there are some of the oldest wall paintings in India and the sculpture can be traced from the older, stiff and unmoving Buddhist sculptures through to the dynamic and dramatic Hindu figures.

These reached their culmination in the period when sculpture became an integral part of architecture and it is impossible to tell where building ends and sculpture begins. Some of the finest examples of this era can be seen in the Hoysala temples of Karnataka, the elaborate sun temple at Konarak and the Chandelas' temples at Khajuraho. In all of these the architecture competes valiantly to match the art work which manages to combine high quality with quite awesome quantity. An interesting common element is the highly detailed erotic scenes. The heavenly maidens of an earlier period have blossomed into scenes, positions and possibilities that leave little to the imagination. Art of this period was not purely a representation of gods and goddesses. Every aspect of human life appeared in the sculptures and obviously in India sex was considered a fairly important aspect!

The arrival of the Moslems with their hatred of other religions and 'idols' caused enormous damage to India's artistic relics. The early invaders' art was chiefly confined to paintings but Indian art went through yet another golden period with the Moghuls. Best known of the art forms they encouraged is the miniature painting tradition. These delightfully detailed and brightly coloured paintings showed the events and activities of the Moghuls in their magnificent palaces. Other paintings included portraits, or studies of wildlife and plants.

At the same time there had been a massive revival of folk art and some of these developments also embraced the Moghul miniature concepts but combined them with Indian religious arts. The popular Rajasthan or Mewar schools often included scenes from Krishna's life and escapades – he's always blue. Interestingly this school followed the Persian-influenced Moghul school in its miniaturised and highly detailed approach but made no use of the Persian developed sense of perspective, and are generally almost two dimensional.

In the north of India – at Jammu, Basohli and Kangra – the Pahari miniatures followed the Moghul school in having a definite sense of perspective but in their often religious themes were closer to the Rajasthan school. The Basohli paintings are very dark and use much gold colouring while the other Pahari paintings are often pale and delicate looking.

The Moghuls' greatest achievements were, however, in the architectural field and it is chiefly for their magnificent buildings that they are remembered. After the Moghuls there has not been another major artistic period of purely Indian background. During the British period art became imitative of western trends and ideals. Although there is much British painting in India it is interesting chiefly as an historical record rather than as art itself.

Music

Indian music is in so many ways so unlike the concept of music in the west that it is very difficult for a westerner to appreciate it without a lengthy introduction and much time spent in listening. The basic difficulty is that harmony, so important to western music, has no place in Indian music. Indian music has two basic elements, the *tala* and the *raga*. Tala is the rhythm and is characterised by the number of beats. *Teental* is a tala of 16 beats. The audience follows the tala by clapping at the appropriate beat which on teental is at 1, 5 and 13. There is no clap at the beat of 9 since that is the *khali* or 'empty section' and indicated by a wave of the hand.

Just as tala is the rhythm so is raga the melody and just as there are a number of basic talas so there are many set ragas. The classical Indian music groups consists of three players who provide the drone, the melody and the rhythm – in other words a background drone, a tala and a raga. The musicians are basically soloists – the concept of an orchestra of Indian musicians is impossible since there is not that harmony that a western orchestra provides – each musician selects his own tala and raga. The players then zoom off in their chosen directions, as dictated by the tala and the raga selected, and, to the audience's delight, meet every once in a while before once again diverging.

Yehudi Menuhin, who has devoted much time and energy to understanding Indian music, suggests that Indian music is much like Indian society. A group of individuals not working together but every once in a while meeting at some common point and western music is analogous to western democratic societies, a group of individuals (the orchestra) who each surrender part of their freedom to the harmony of the whole. Although Indian classical music has one of the longest continuous histories of any music form the music has not, until quite recently, ever been recorded in any written notation. Furthermore within the basic framework set by the tala and the raga the musicians improvise – providing variations on the basic melody and rhythm.

Best known of the Indian instruments are the *sitar* and the *tabla*. The sitar is the large stringed instrument popularised by Ravi Shankar in the west – and which more than a few westerners have discovered is more than just slightly difficult to tune. This is the instrument with which the soloist plays the raga. Other less popular stringed instruments are the *sarod* (which is plucked) or the *sarangi* (which is played with a bow). The *tabla*, a twin drum rather like a western bongo drum, provides the tala. The drone, which runs on two basic notes, is provided by the oboe-like *shehnai* or the *tampura*.

Dance

Indian dancing all relates back to *Shiva's* role as *Nataraj*, the King of Dancers. Lord Shiva's first wife was *Sati* and when her father, who disliked Shiva, insulted him Sati committed suicide in a sacrifice by fire that later took her name – Sati. Outraged Shiva killed his father-in-law and danced the *Tandava* – the Dance of Destruction. Later Sati reincarnated as

Parvati, married Shiva again and danced the *Lasya*. Thus the Tandava became the male form of dance, the Lasya the female form. Dancing at first was a part of the religious temple rituals and the dancers were known as *devadasis*. Their dances retold stories from the *Ramayana* or the *Mahabharata*.

Temple dancing is no longer practised but classical Indian dancing is still based on its religious background. Indian dance is divided into *nritta* – the rhythmic elements, *nritya* – the combination of rhythm with expression, and *natya* – the dramatic element. Nritya is usually expressed through eye, hand and facial movements and with nritta makes up the usual dance programmes. To appreciate natya, dance drama, you have to understand and appreciate Indian legends and mythology.

Dance is divided into four basic forms known as *Bharat Natya, Kathakali, Kathak* and *Manipuri*. Bharat Natya is further sub-divided into three other classical forms. It is one of the most popular forms of classical dance, originated in the great temples of the south and usually tells of events in *Krishna's* life. Bharat Natya dancers are always women and, like the sculptures they take their positions from, always dance bent-kneed, never standing upright, and use a huge repertoire of hand movements. *Orissi, Mohini Attam* and *Kuchipudi* are variations of Bharat Natya which take their names from the places where they originated.

Kathakali, the second major dance form, originated in Kerala and is exclusively danced by men. It tells of epic battles of gods and demons and is as dynamic and dramatic as Bharat Natya is austere and expressive. Kathakali dancing is noted for the elaborate make up and painted masks which the dancers wear. Eyedrops even turn their eyes a bloodshot red!

Manipuri dances come, as the name indicates, from the Manipur region in the north-east. These are a folk dance and the message is made through body and arm movements. The women dancers wear hooped skirts and conical caps which are extremely picturesque.

The final classical dance type is Kathak which originated in the north and at first was very similar to the Bharat Natya school. Persian and Moslem influences later altered the dance from a temple ritual to a courtly entertainment. The dances are performed straight legged and there are intricately choreographed foot movements to be followed. The ankle bells which dancers wear must be adeptly controlled and the costumes and themes are often similar to those in Moghul miniature paintings.

There are many opportunities to see classical Indian dancing while you are in India. The major hotels often put on performances to which outsiders as well as hotel guests are welcome.

FESTIVALS & HOLIDAYS

Due to its religious and regional variations India has a great number of holidays and festivals. Most of them follow the lunar calendar which differs from the western calendar, thus they fall on a different date each year. Apart from the holidays and festivals celebrated nationally there are many local and regional occasions. PH – public holiday.

January

Sankranti/Pongal Celebrated predominantly in Andhra Pradesh and amongst the Tamil people of the south, this is a harvest festival marking the change of season when the sun is supposed to move to its northern home and the days get longer, the nights shorter.

January 26

Republic Day Celebrating the anniversary of India's establishment as a republic in 1950 there are activities in all the state capitals but most spectacularly in New Delhi where there is an enormously colourful military parade. (PH)

February-March

Shivaratri This day of fasting is dedicated to Lord Shiva. Processions to the temples are followed by the chanting of mantras and annointing of lingams.

Holi This is one of the most exuberant Hindu festivals with people marking the advent of spring by throwing coloured water or powder at one another – don't wear good clothes on this day! On the night before Holi bonfires are built to symbolise the destruction of the evil demon Holika. (PH)

March-April

Mahavir Jayanti This major Jain festival marks the birth of Mahavira, the 24th and last Jain Tirthankar. (PH)

Ramanavami In temples all over India the birth of Rama, an incarnation of Vishnu, is celebrated on this day. (PH)

Good Friday This Christian holiday is also celebrated in India. (PH)

May-June

Buddha Purnima The Buddha's birth, enlightenment and his reaching of nirvana are all celebrated on this day. The Buddha is supposed to have gone through each of these experiences on the same day but of different years. (PH)

June-July

Festival of the Cars Lord Jagannath's great temple chariot makes its stately journey from his temple in Puri, Orissa. Similar, but far less grandiose, festivals take place in other locations.

July-August

Naga Panchami This festival is dedicated to Ananta, the serpent upon whose coils Vishnu rested between universes. Offerings are made to snake images and snake charmers do a roaring trade. Snakes are supposed to have power over the monsoon rainfall and keep evil from homes.

Janai Purnima After a day long fast high caste Hindus replace the sacred thread which they always wear looped over their left shoulder.

August 15
Independence Day The anniversary of India's independence from Britain in 1947. The Prime Minister delivers an address from the ramaparts of Delhi's Red Fort. (PH)

August
Nariel Purnima A celebration of the official end of the monsoon, observed by sailors and fishermen.

Raksha Bandhan On the same day girls fix amulets known as rakhis to their brothers' wrists to protect them in the coming year. The brothers give their sisters gifts.

Pateti Parsis celebrate their migration from Persia on this day but one sect of Parsis sets the date a month earlier. A week later *Khordad Sal* celebrates the birth of Zarathustra.

August-September
Janmastami The anniversary of Krishna's birth is celebrated with happy abandon – in tune with Krishna's own mischievious moods. Although it is a national holiday Agra, Bombay and Mathura (his birthplace) are the main centres (PH)

Ganesh Chaturthi This festival is dedicated to the popular elephant-headed god Ganesh. Pune, Madras and Bombay are important centres for its celebration. In Bombay images of the god are carried down into the sea.

Onam Harvest Festival During this Kerala festival the famous snake boat races are held.

September-October
Dussehra (Dassehra in the south) This is the most popular of all the Indian festivals and takes place over 10 days. It celebrates Rama's victory over the demon king Ravana and in many places it culminates with the burning of huge images of Ravana and his accomplices in effigy. In Delhi it is known as Ram Lila and there are re-enactments of the Ramayana and fireworks. In Mysore and Ahmedabad there are great processions. In West Bengal the festival is known as Durga Puja since Durga aided Rama in his defeat of Ravana. In Kulu in the north the festival takes place a little later than elsewhere and is a delightful festival when the Kulu Valley shows why it is known as the 'Valley of the Gods'. (PH – two days)

October 2
Gandhi Jayanti A solemn celebration of Gandhi's birth-date with prayer meetings at the Raj Ghat in Delhi where he was cremated. (PH)

October-November
Diwali This is the happiest festival of the Hindu calendar and at night countless oil lamps are lit to show Rama the way home from his period of exile. Today the festival is also dedicated to Lakshmi (particularly in Bombay) and to Kali in Calcutta. In all the festival lasts five days with day one the start of the new business year, day two dedicated to Krishna, the third to Shiva, the fourth to the friendly (but uppity) demon Bali whom Vishnu put in his place. On the fifth day men visit their sisters to have a tika put on their forehead. (PH)

November
Govardhana Puja A Hindu festival dedicated to that holiest of animals, the cow. (PH)

Pushkar Cattle Fair This incredibly colourful cattle fair in Rajasthan includes camel races amongst other events.

Nanak Jayanti The birthday of Guru Nanak, the founder of the Sikh religion, is celebrated with prayer readings and processions, particularly in Amritsar and Patna. (PH)

December

Feast of St Francis Xavier On December 3 this festival and the feast of Our Lady of the Immaculate Conception are two of the most important festivals in Goa.

December 25

Christmas Day Also a holiday in India. (PH)

The dates of Moslem festivals vary very widely from year to year so it is not easy to list what month they will fall in.

Ramadan The most important Moslem festival is a 30-day dawn to dusk fast. In Moslem countries this can be a difficult time for travellers since restaurants are closed and tempers tend to run short. Fortunately, despite India's large Moslem minority, it causes no difficulties for visitors.

Id-ul-Fitr This day celebrates the end of Ramadan. (PH)

Id-ul-Zuhara A Moslem festival commemorating Abraham's attempt to sacrifice his son Ishmael, celebrated with prayers and feasts. (PH)

Muharram A 10-day festival commemorating the martyrdom of Mohammed's grandson, Imam Hussain. (PH)

Festival Calendar

Festival (Place)	1984	1985
Basant Pancahmi	7 Feb	26 Jan
Republic Day (New Delhi)	26 Jan	26 Jan
Shivaratri	29 Feb	17 Feb
Holi	17 Mar	7 Mar
Ramanavami	10 Apr	30 Mar
Buddha's Birthday	15 May	4 May
Festival of Cars (Orissa)	30 June	20 June

Naga Panchami	18 July	22 July
Janmastami	20 Aug	7 Aug
Teej (Rajasthan)	29 Aug	16 Sept
Bijya Dasami	4 Oct	22 Oct
Diwali	24 Oct	12 Nov
Kartik Purnima (Rajasthan)	8 Nov	27 Nov

Seasons/Months of the Year

		Hindi	English
Spring	Vasanta	Chait	Mar-Apr
		Baisakh	Apr-May
Hot season	Grishma	Jeth	May-June
		Asarh	June-July
Rains	Varsha	Sawan	July-Aug
		Bhadon	Aug-Sep
Autumn	Sharada	Asvin	Sep-Oct
		Kartik	Oct-Nov
Winter	Hemanta	Aghan	Nov-Dec
		Pus	Dec-Jan
Cold season	Shishira	Magh	Jan-Feb
		Phagun	Feb-Mar

WILDLIFE IN INDIA

The following description of India's flora and fauna and its national parks and wildlife sanctuaries was written by Murray D Bruce and Constance S Leap Bruce.

The concept of forest and wildlife conservation is not new to India. Here, since time immemorial, wildlife has enjoyed a privileged position of protection through religious ideals and sentiment. Early Indian literature, including the Hindu epics, the Buddhist Jatakas, the Panchatantra and the Jain strictures, teach non-violence and respect for even lowly animal forms. Many of the gods are associated with certain animals: Brahma with the deer, Vishnu the lion, and Ganesh, the eternal symbol of wisdom, is half man and half elephant. The earliest known conservation laws come from India in the third century BC when King Asoka wrote the Fifth Pillar Edict, forbidding the slaughter of certain wildlife and the burning of forests.

Unfortunately, during the recent turbulent history of India, much of this tradition has been lost. Extensive hunting by the British and Indian Rajas, the large-scale clearing of forests for agriculture, the availability of guns and strong pesticides and the ever-increasing population has had disastrous effects on India's environment. However, in the past few decades, the Government has taken serious steps toward environmental management and has since established over 100 parks, santuaries and reserves.

A visit to one or more of these wildlife refuges is a must on any traveller's itinerary. Protected areas have been established throughout India and many are readily accessible, eg Bharatpur Bird Sanctuary near Agra. Parks such as Corbett and Manas offer the best opportunity to experience India's outstanding natural scenic beauty and, for abundance and visibility of a variety of wildlife, parks such as Kaziranga compare with the best in East Africa.

Many of the wildlife sanctuaries, and some national parks, are established in the former private hunting reserves of the British and Indian aristocracy. Often the parks offer a speciality, such as the Asian lion in Gir, Indian rhinoceros in Kaziranga, elephant in Periyar, and tiger in Kanha and Corbett; other areas are established to preserve unique habitat such as lowland tropical rain-forest or the mangrove forest of the Sunderbans.

Some parks offer modern-style guest houses with electricity, while in others only Dak-style bungalows are available. Facilities usually include van and jeep rides, and at some you can take an elephant ride or boat trip to approach wildlife more discreetly. In addition, watch-towers and hides are often available and provide good opportunities to observe and photograph wildlife at close range.

National parks and other protected areas in India are administered at the state level and are often promoted as part of each state's tourist attractions. To encourage more visitors, road systems, transport, accommodation and other facilities continue to be developed and upgraded. Whenever possible, book in advance for transport and accommodation through the local tourist offices or state departments, and check if a permit is required, particularly in border areas. Various fees are charged for your visit (entrance, photography, etc) and these are usually included with advance arrangements. Meals may also be arranged when you book, but in some cases you must take in your food and have it prepared for you.

The diversity of India's climate and topography, varying from arid desert and tropical rain-forest, to some of the world's highest mountains, is reflected in its rich flora and fauna, with many species found only in India. Among more than 500 species of mammals, the tiger, elephant and rhinoceros still exist in India and many conservation projects have been established to preserve them. For some species the protection came too late; the Indian cheetah was last recorded in 1948.

A variety of deer and antelope species can be seen, but these are now virtually confined to the protected areas, most recently as a result of competition with domestic animals and the effects of their diseases. They include the graceful Indian gazelle (chinkara); the Indian antelope (blackbuck); the diminutive four-horned antelope (chowsingha); the large and ungainly-looking blue bull (nilgai), capable of great speed; the rare swamp deer (barasingha); the sambar, India's largest deer; the beautiful spotted deer (chital), usually seen in herds; the larger barking deer (muntjac); and the tiny mouse deer (chevrotain).

Also seen are the wild buffalo; the massive Indian bison (gaur); the shaggy sloth bear; striped hyena; wild pig; jackal; Indian fox; wolf, although much more local in range now; the Indian wild dog (dhole), resembling a giant fox but found in packs in forest; and amongst the smaller mammals are the mongooses, renowned as snake killers, and giant squirrels.

Cats include leopard, or panther; the short-tailed jungle cat; and the beautiful leopard cat. Various monkeys can be seen, with rhesus macaque, bonnet macaque (south only), and the long-tailed common langur as the most likely.

With over 2000 species and varieties of birds, few countries outside of tropical America can compete with India. The diverse bird life of the forests includes the large hornbills, serpent eagles and fishing owls, as well as the elegant national bird, the peacock. Waterbirds, such as herons, ibises, storks, cranes, pelicans and others, are seen not only in parks, but also at numerous special waterbird sanctuaries. These sanctuaries contain large breeding colonies, and are also of great importance for the countless numbers of migrating birds which visit India annually.

Among the other wildlife are over 500 species of reptiles and amphibians, including the infamous cobra, other large snakes such as pythons, crocodiles, large freshwater tortoises and monitor lizards (goannas). Then there are the 30,000 insect species, including large and colourful butterflies.

The vegetation types, from dry desert scrub to alpine meadow, comprise some 15,000 species of plant to date.

Geographically, India is divided into three main regions, each with many subregions, with distinctive altitudinaal climatic variations. From these regions, 24 national parks, wildlife sanctuaries and reserves are listed below.

Northern India

This is a region of extremes ranging from the snow-bound peaks and deep valleys of the Himalaya to flat plains and tropical lowlands.

Dachigam Wildlife Sanctuary (Kashmir) A very

scenic valley with a large meandering river. The surrounding mountainsides contain the rare Kashmir stag (hangul), also black and brown bears. A trek to the upper reaches, where you can camp, offers spectacular vistas. There you may also see the musk deer, a small species widely hunted for the male's musk gland, considered valuable in treating impotence and a major export to Europe's perfumeries. The sanctuary is 22 km by road from Srinagar and certainly worth a visit. Best time: June–July.

Flower Valley National Park (Uttar Pradesh) This

'garden on top of the world' is in the north of Uttar Pradesh near Badrinath, at an elevation of 3500 metres. The famous Valley of Flowers is now a national park and when in bloom, an unforgettable experience. Best time: June–July. See also page 291.

The Gangetic Plain

Some of the most famous parks in Asia are located in this region. It contains the flat, alluvial plains of the Indus, Ganges and Brahmaputra Rivers – an immense tract of level land stretching from sea to sea and separating the Himalayan region from the southern peninsula proper. Climate varies greatly, from the arid, sandy deserts of Rajasthan and Gujarat, with temperatures up to 50°C, to the cool highlands of Assam, where rainfall can exceed 15 *metres*, perhaps the wettest place on earth.

Corbett National Park (Uttar Pradesh) The most

famous park for the tiger, now rare throughout India, but saved from extinction by India's successful Project Tiger. Other wildlife includes chital and hog deer, also elephant, leopard, sloth bear and muntjac. There are numerous watchtowers, but only daylight photography is allowed. The park has magnificent scenery, from sal forest (giant, teak-like hardwood trees) to extensve river plains. The Ramganga River offers tranquil settings and good fishing. A bit touristy, but worth a visit. Best time: November–May. See also page 284.

Hazaribagh Wildlife Sanctuary (Bihar) An area of

rolling, forested hills with large herds of deer, notably sambar, also nilgai and chital, as well as tiger and leopard. Best time: February–March. See also page 304.

Palamau Game Preserve (Bihar) Smaller than

Hazaribagh, but with good concentrations on wildlife, including tiger, leopard, elephant, gaur, sambar, chital, nilgai, and muntjac; also rhesus macaque, common langur and (rarely) wolf. It is 150 km south of Ranchi, with bungalows at Betla. Best time: February–March.

Sunderbans Tiger Reserve (West Bengal) These

extensive mangrove forests of the Ganges Delta are an important haven for tiger. The reserve is south-east of Calcutta, bordering Bangladesh. The area protects the largest area of mangroves in India and offers an exceptional chance to see tiger and other wildlife, such as the fishing cat, looking for fish at the water's edge. The only access is by chartered boat (Sunderbans Launch Association, Calcutta). Best time: February–March. See also page 325.

Jaldapara Wildlife Sanctuary (West Bengal) The

tropical forests extending from South-East Asia end around here, and if you don't go further east, this is your chance to see the Indian rhinoceros, elephant and other wildlife. The area protects 100 square km of lush forest and grasslands, cut by the wide Torsa River. It is 224 km from Darjeeling, via Siliguri and Jalpaiguri (nearest railhead, Hashimara). There is a rest house at Jaldapara. Best time: March–May.

Manas Wildlife Sanctuary (Assam) This lovely

area is formed from the watershed of the Manas, Hakua and Beki Rivers and borders with Bhutan. The bungalows at Mothanguri, on the banks of the Manas, offer views of jungle-clad hills. Established trails enter nearby forests and follow the river banks. Try to arrange a cruise around by boat. Besides tiger, the grassland is home to wild buffalo, elephant, sambar, swamp deer and other wildlife; the rare and beautiful golden langur may be seen on the Bhutan side of the Manas. Best time: January–March. See also page 365.

Kaziranga National Park (Assam) The most famous place to see the one-horned Indian rhinoceros, hunted almost to extinction for its prize as big game and for the Chinese apothecary trade. The park is dominated by tall (up to six metres) grasslands and swampy areas (jheels). Travelling is best done by elephant, which can be arranged at the park. The first sighting of a rhinoceros is always impressive and awesome as they can reach a height of over two metres and weight more than two tonnes. Despite the prehistoric appearance, rhinos are incredibly agile and fast. Spotting them in the tall grass may be difficult. Watch for egrets and other birds who use the rhino's armoured back as a perch, and also listen for the 'churring' sound of a large animal moving through the grass. Best viewing may be by the jheels, where they bathe. Best time: February–March. See also page 365.

Sariska Wildlife Sanctuary; Sawai Madhopur Wildlife Sanctuary (Rajasthan) Both areas provide good opportunities to see the wildlife of the Indian plains. Sariska is notable for night viewing and its nilgai herds. Sawai Madhopur (or Ranthambore) is smaller, which can make seeing animals easier, and has a lake with crocodiles. It is on the Delhi-Bombay railway line, and 160 km south of Jaipur by road. You can stay at the Sawai Madhopur railway retiring rooms. Best time: February–June (Sariska), November–May (Sawai Madhopur). See also page 380.

Keoladeo Ghana Bird Sanctuary (Rajasthan) The best known and most touristy bird sanctuary (usually just called Bharatpur), this features large numbers of breeding waterbirds and thousands of migrating birds from Siberia and China, including herons, storks, cranes and geese. The network of cross-roads and tracks through the sanctuary can increase the opportunities to see the birds, deer and other wildlife there. It is also on the Delhi–Bombay railway line. Best time: September–February. See also page 379.

Gir National Park (Gujarat) Famous for the last surviving Asian lions (under 200), Gir also supports a large variety of other wildlife,

notably the chowsingha. This forested oasis in the desert contains Lake Kamaleshwar, complete with crocodiles. The lake and other watering holes are good places to spot animals. Best time: January–May. See also page 447.

Velavadar National Park (Gujarat) A new park, 65 km north of Bhavnagar, it protects the rich grasslands in the delta region on the west side of the Gulf of Cambay. The main attraction is a large concentration of the beautiful blackbuck. There is a park lodge available for visitors. Best time: October–June.

Little Rann of Kutch Wildlife Sanctuary (Gujarat) A new sanctuary designated for the protection of the desert region of north-west Gujarat, especially the outer rim and a narrow belt of adjacent land. A variety of desert life can be found here, notably the surviving herds of the Indian wild ass (khur); also wolf and caracal (a large, pale cat with tufted ears). Access can be arranged at Bhuj. Best time: October–June.

Shivpuri National Park (Madhya Pradesh) Picturesque, open forests surrounding a lake, and good for photographing various deer, including chinkara, chowsingha and nilgai, also tiger and leopard. It is close to Gwalior. Best time: February–May. See also page 453.

Kanha National Park (Madhya Pradesh) One of India's most spectacular and exciting parks for both variety and numbers of wildlife and well worth a visit. Originally proposed to protect a unique type of swamp deer (barasingha), it is also important for tiger (about 60). There are large herds of chital, plus blackbuck, gaur, leopard and hyena. Best time: November–March. See also page 490.

Similipal Tiger Reserve (Orissa) A vast and beautiful area protecting India's largest region of sal forest, with magnificent scenery and a variety of wildlife, including tiger, elephant, leopard, sambar, chital, muntjac and chevrotain. Best time: November–June. See also page 507.

Southern India

Here is the Deccan Peninsula, which takes the form of a triangular plateau, ranging in altitude from 300 to 900 metres, intersected with rivers, scattered peaks and hill ranges, including the Western and Eastern Ghats. The Ghats form a natural barrier to the monsoons and have created areas of great humidity and rainfall as on the Malabar Coast, where lush lowland tropical rain-forest still occurs, and drier regions on the mountains' leeward sides.

Krishnagiri Upavan National Park (Maharashtra)

This park, formerly known as Borivilli, protects an important and scenic area close to Bombay and other attractions. Amongst the smaller types of wildlife to be seen is a variety of waterbirds. Best time: October–June. See also page 529.

Taroba National Park (Maharashtra)

A large park featuring mixed teak forests and a lake, with night viewing available to see its large wildlife populations. These include tiger, leopard, gaur, nilgai, sambar and chital. It is 45 km from Chandrapur, south-west from Kaanha National Park. You can arrange to stay in the park. Best time: March–May.

Periyar Wildlife Sanctuary (Kerala)

A large and scenic park formed by the watershed of a reservoir developed around a large, man-made lake. It is famous for the large elephant population which can easily be seen as you travel by boat along the watercourses leading to the lake. Other wildlife to be seen from the boat are the gaur, Indian wild dog and nilgiri langur, as well as otters, large tortoises, and a rich bird life, including flights of hornbills. Along the

Know Your Monkey

Rats apart, the monkey is the most commonly seen wild mammal in India. The common or sacred langur is probably seen most often. This is a large monkey of slender build with pale grey fur and black face, hands and feet. It is often seen in large troops in woods, ruins and even in towns (like Pushkar). Because of its association with the monkey-god, Hanuman, it is venerated by Hindus.

The rhesus macaque is the other common monkey of northern India. A stocky monkey with a pink face, short tail and grey-brown fur tending to reddish on the rump. Again it is found in woods and sometimes towns (as at the Durga Temple in Varanasi). The related bonnet macaque is similar with a longer tail and takes the place of the rhesus in southern India.

Another commonly seen animal is the striped palm squirrel – that cute little fellow with the white back stripes open seen scampering on and about trees.

Lloyd Jones

Common Langur

Rhesus Macaque

water's edge you may see the flashing, brilliant hues of several kinds of kingfisher, perhaps even a fishing owl. Best time: February–May. See also page 674.

Jawahar National Park This is a recent proposal to cover Bandipur National Park (Karnataka), Nagarhole National Park (Karnataka), Mudumulai Wildlife Sanctuary (Tamil Nadu), and Wynaad Wildlife Sanctuary (Kerala).

Situated at the junction of the Western Ghats, the Nilgiri Hills and the Deccan Plateau, the merging of these contiguous areas protects the largest elephant population in India, as well as one of the most extensive forested areas in the south. The mixed, diverse forests and their

terrain also protect a large variety of other wildlife, including many rare species such as leopard, gaur, sambar, chital, muntjac, chevrotain, bonnet macaque, and giant squirrels. The very rich bird life includes many spectacular species such as hornbills, barbets, trogons, parakeets, racquet-tailed drongos, and streamertailed Asian paradise flycatchers. The two most popular areas are Bandipur and Mudumulai. Not to be missed if you visit the south. Best time: January–June. See also pages 605,614.

Murray D Bruce &
Constance S Leap Bruce

Facts for the Visitor

VISAS

If you're from a Commonwealth country (Australia, New Zealand, Great Britain, Canada, etc) including Ireland but not including Pakistan you do not need a visa. If you're from the Scandinavian countries, West Germany or a couple of other places you do not need a visa for a stay of up to 90 days. Otherwise you're going to need a visa which will normally be valid for a 90 day stay. They're available from Indian consular offices and generally take 24 hours to issue and cost about US$2.50. Some places can be worse than others when it comes to speed in issuing visas. Athens is one place which has had the thumbs down. If there is no diplomatic representation in the country the British embassy will be able to advise you.

If your stay in India is going to be more than 90 days a few little hassles pop up. First of all if you are in India on a '90 days without visa' basis you now have to obtain one. If you already have a 90 day visa then you have to extend it. Either activity can be a bit of a hassle – not due to any Indian reluctance to permit people to stay longer but simply due to the usual Indian red tape and bureaucracy. Set aside at least a day for coping with this problem. Whatever your visa situation at 90 days you have to register with the 'Foreigner's Registration Office'. Furthermore if you've been in India more than 90 days you have to get an income tax clearance before you leave. This is relatively simple in that you just have to show a handful of currency exchange forms to indicate that you did spend your own money and weren't working while in India. But as usual it involves a fair bit of form filling and rubber stamping and takes a little time.

All in all it's worth avoiding the 90 day hassles if at all possible. A simple way to do just that is to leave India then come back and start the 90 days again. If you are planning to combine a visit to India with, say, Sri Lanka or Nepal then just make sure you arrive there by day 89. Since the first edition, however, we've had a letter saying that after a brief visit to Pakistan only a 30-day stay was permitted on returning to India. The writer thought that the same situation applied to Nepal.

Prohibition has disappeared in India in the last few years so you no longer need a 'liquor permit' to buy a beer in the 'dry' states. Curiously, however, the price of a beer has increased dramatically in states, like Tamil Nadu, where prohibition has recently been repealed. In Gujarat, however, prohibition or not finding a beer will still not be easy.

Foreigners' Registration Offices

The main foreigners' registration offices include:

Bombay	Special Branch II, Annexe 2, Office of the Commissioner of Police (Greater Bombay), Dadabhoy Naroji Rd (tel 268111)
Calcutta	237 Acharya Jagdish Bose Rd (tel 443301)
New Delhi	lst floor, Hans Bhavan, Tilak Bridge (tel 272790)
Madras	13 Victoria Crescent Rd, Egmore (tel 88864)

Special Permits

Even with a visa you are not allowed everywhere in India. Certain places require special additional permits. These are covered in the appropriate sections in the main text but briefly they are:

Darjeeling Permits can be obtained from consular offices abroad or from the main Foreigner's Registration Offices in Bombay, Calcutta, Delhi or Madras. They cannot be obtained while en route to Darjeeling from Calcutta or at the border if you are coming through Nepal from Kathmandu. The permits are generally valid for an initial stay of 15 days and are quite easy to obtain. The only exception from the permit system is if you fly to and from Bagdogra, the airport for Darjeeling.

Assam & Meghalaya You require a permit for these remote north-east states and you are also restricted where you may go. The permits can be obtained at the offices in Calcutta.

Andaman & Nicobar Islands For these islands you need a permit from an embassy or consulate abroad or from the Ministry of Home Affairs in New Delhi. The application to these places must be made at least six weeks in advance although they recommend you allow 12 weeks. In Madras, however, you can get a permit in just three days.

Sikkim Similar ground rules apply as for the Andaman and Nicobar Islands. Your initial permit allows a stay of only four days but this is easily extended once in Sikkim. You are restricted as to where you may go in Sikkim.

Bhutan Officially this remote Himalayan region beside Sikkim is still an independent entity although actually India has firm control over foreign policy and most other things in Bhutan. Applications to visit Bhutan must be made through the Director of Tourism, Ministry of Finance, Tachichho Dzong, Thimpu, Bhutan or from the Bhutan Foreign Mission, Chandragupta Marg, New Delhi 110021, India (tel 74075) or from the Bhutanese mission in New York. Before applying you must have the relevant permits for the restricted areas of India you must pass through in order to get to Bhutan. And don't hold your breath – unless you have high up Indian connections or a personal friend in the Bhutanese aristocracy you needn't expect to get a permit. At present permits appear to be issued only to groups and then generally only for tours costing over US$100 per day.

Other Visas
If you're heading to other places around India the visa stories are as follows:

Afghanistan Probably not at the moment if you value your life but there is an embassy in Delhi although it may be easier and cheaper in Pakistan.

Burma The embassy in New Delhi is fast and efficient – 24 hours, Rs 40 – but the usual 'seven days, no longer' rule applies. Note there is no longer a Burmese consulate in Calcutta. There is one in Kathmandu.

Nepal The Nepalese embassy in New Delhi is on Barakhamba Rd, quite close to Connaught Place, not out at Chanakyapuri like most other embassies. There is also a consulate in Calcutta. Visas take 24 hours and cost Rs 45. A seven day visa is available on arrival in Nepal and this can be extended but doing so involves rather a lot of form filling and queueing – better to have a visa in advance if possible.

Sri Lanka Most western nationalities do not require a visa to visit Sri Lanka but there are diplomatic offices in New Delhi, Bombay and Madras.

Thailand There are Thai embassies in New Delhi and Calcutta. The visa costs Rs 25 and is issued in 24 hours. Note that if you are flying in and flying out of Thailand within 15 days a visa is not required.

Tax Clearance Certificates
You need one of these if you have stayed in India for more than 90 days and are about to leave. Applies to anyone.

Many travel agencies will offer to do this for you and although this saves time you will be charged Rs 50-100 for the service. You can do it yourself for Rs 10 but you need to set the wheels in motion three days in advance of when you wish to collect. The procedure is as follows:

(1) Locate a Notary Public solicitor and tell him you need an affidavit for tax clearance. He will type this out on special

legal paper which costs Rs 2, attach an excise stamp (Rs 3), get you to sign it and charge you a Rs 5 fee.

(2) Take the affidavit to the local Income Tax Office and ask for the Enforcement Directorate. Here you will be asked to produce all the bank receipts you have been given for encashment of travellers' cheques or cash plus all the remaining travellers' cheques and cash you hold. These will be added up and ought to tally with the amount you declared you were carrying on entry (a declaration of this sort is only required if you are carrying US$1000 or more on entry). No need to worry if they don't, you lost them or forgot to ask the bank to endorse your Currency Declaration Form at the time. The Enforcement Directorate will issue you with a 'No Objection Certificate'.

(3) Take the affidavit and the 'No Objection Certificate' to the main income tax office and ask for Form No 31. This form is an application for a Clearance Certificate under Section 230 (1) of the Income Tax Act 1961. Fill in the form and attach the affidavit and 'No Objection Certificate'. Hand in the form and return three days later to collect it.

It is possible to get the Clearance Certificate in less than three days if you have a very good excuse but it will cost you. One of the perks of office for tax officers is *baksheesh* (bribery). This is why getting the tax certificate through a travel agent is expensive (they take their cut too). One traveller wrote, however, that 'an exemption certificate can be obtained from a crowded Delhi Income Tax Office inside an hour. No money, no basksheesh'. Another wrote that you only need it if you leave by air? Still another visitor said the first time it took only five minutes, the second time half a day including visits to two offices but on that second occasion the document was not even asked for when he left.

CUSTOMS

The usual bottle of whisky and 200 cigarettes type of duty free regulations apply in India. If you bring in more than US$1000 in cash and/or travellers' cheques you are supposed to fill in a currency declaration form. You're allowed to bring in all sorts of western technological wonders but big ticket items are likely to be entered on a 'Tourist Baggage Re-Export' form to ensure you take them out with you when you go. If you wonder why your battered Instamatic has been singled out to be honoured with a TBRE form perhaps it's because section 3 of customs regulation number 499/15/74 applies to you (our italics):

There is also likelihood of abuse by tourists holding Indian passports and *hippies*. In the case of such tourists therefore, even a camera or transistor radio should be entered on Tourist Baggage Re-Export form before allowing clearance.

MONEY

A$1 = Rs 9.4	Rs 1 = A$0.10
US$1 = Rs 10.4	Rs 1 = US$0.10
£1 = Rs 15.0	Rs 1 = £0.07

The rupee (Rs) is divided into 100 paise (p). There are coins of 1, 2, 3, 5, 10, 20, 25 and 50 paise and notes of Rs 1, 2, 5, 10, 20, 50, 100 and 500. Once upon a time the rupee was divided into 16 annas and you may still hear prices referred to in annas – particularly in markets. Eight annas is half a rupee or 50 paise, four annas is a quarter rupee or 25 paise.

Currency Exchange Forms

You are not allowed to bring Indian currency into the country or take it out of the country. You are allowed to bring in unlimited amounts of foreign currency or travellers cheques but you are supposed to declare it all on arrival. All money is supposed to be changed at official banks or money changers and you are supposed to be given a currency exchange form for each transaction. In actual practice you can surreptitiously bring rupees into the country with you – they can be bought at a useful discount price in places like Singapore or Bangkok. Indian rupees can be brought in fairly openly from Nepal and again you can get a slightly better rate there.

Banks will usually not give you a currency exchange form unless you specifically ask for one. It is worth getting them for several reasons. First of all you will need one for any re-exchange when you depart India. Secondly certain official purchases, such as airline tickets, must be paid for either with foreign currency or your rupees must be accompanied by sufficient exchange forms to account for the ticket price. This is actually a complete waste of time since some little note will be scrawled on the form to the effect that it was sighted when you bought a ticket from A to B. When you buy a ticket from B to C somebody else can quite easily scrawl a similar little note on another corner of the same form! The third reason for saving exchange forms is that if you stay in India longer than 90 days

then you have to get an income tax clearance and this requires production of a handful of exchange forms to prove you've been changing money all along and not earning money locally.

Which Currency or TC?

In major cities you can change most foreign currencies or travellers' cheques – Australian dollars, Deutschmarks, yen or whatever – but out of town it's best to stick to US dollars or pounds sterling. The pound still has a sentimental appeal in India. Thomas Cook and American Express are both popular travellers' cheques and have a number of branches in India.

Many people make the mistake of bringing too many small denomination cheques. Unless you are moving rapidly from country to country you only need a handful of small denominations for end of stay conversions. In between change as much as you feel happy carrying. This applies particularly in India where

Bank Guards
State Bank of India
Chowk, Varanasi

changing money can be such a time consuming bore. Even in major cities it sometimes takes a long time. In smaller towns – and that means even quite large places if they have little tourist appeal – changing money can take forever. To change a single travellers' cheque can easily take several hours in some towns. You can also spend a lot of time finding which bank will change money. The answer is to change money as infrequently as possible and try to change it only in big banks in big cities.

In some major cities there are now special foreign exchange counters which are more efficient and stay open longer hours. Big hotels also often offer exchange facilities but generally at a poorer rate than the banks.

Money Problems

There is still a small black market in India but it is so small that it is not worth the effort of searching it out and the risks involved. A particular catch with Indian currency and declaration forms may arise if you are buying an airline ticket out of India. You can often get tickets at very useful discounts but these sorts of large purchases must be made with a specific bank exchange form. If you are buying a ticket overseas which costs, say, Rs 8000 officially an agent may be able to offer it to you at Rs 5000. But you must exchange officially Rs 8000 so you get the balance as a Rs 3000 refund from the agent. Since you cannot use your Rs 8000 document to reconvert it (the form specifies it was used to purchase an airline ticket) you're stuck. Two answers – either buy the ticket far enough ahead of your departure that you will use up the money or else have plenty of exchange forms saved up to permit you to re-exchange it on departure.

Credit Cards

Credit cards are now widely accepted in India, particularly Diners Club. With American Express you can use your card to obtain more funds locally from an Amex office. With their love of forms and carbon paper Indians delight in credit cards. You'll be delighted when you get back and all those bills eventually turn up and you find that superb splash out meal at the Ritz actually cost $8 or something equally ridiculous. Note that the warning above on airline tickets also applies to credit card purchases. You can buy an overseas ticket on your card and end up with several thousand rupees in your pocket too.

Cash Problems

When changing money take two precautions in the rupees you are given. First don't take it all in larger denominations. Breaking big notes down is always a problem in India and there is a permanent shortage of small change. So always break big notes (Rs 100 in particular) down as much as possible. Secondly don't accept torn, damaged or dirty notes – when so many are just that it is hard not to but disposing of a damaged note is always difficult. This particularly applies in small towns where money has to be in better condition than in the big cities to be acceptable.

Transferring Money

Finally don't run out of money in India. Getting money transferred to India is a time consuming, boring, tricky and unpleasant operation. Even transferred by cable it can take weeks and weeks and by mail it can take forever. Banks have a reputation for not telling people that money has arrived when it actually has – better in their balance than your pocket seems to be the mood. If you must have money sent to you in India specify the bank, the branch and the address you want it sent to and keep your fingers crossed. Preferably send it to a foreign bank since they are much more efficient when it comes to overseas transactions than Indian banks. Overseas banks with branches in India include American Express, Bank of America, Chartered Bank and, particularly, National &

Grindlays which has many branches in smaller cities as well as in the major cities where Amex also operate. With a European Cheque Card it's possible to cash British Lloyds Bank cheques. Thomas Cook has also been recommended as a good organisation to transfer money through.

Special Note We got a little (very little) amount of flak over the above paragraph in the first edition of this guide. If you have money transferred to you in India and have any big (or amusing) problems please write and tell us about them. Best letters will win the Lonely Planet 'Forward Exchange Rate International Transfer Balance of Payments Gold Card Bankoro M1 Award'.

Indian money has its own special angles and curiosities. For a start there is never any change. The restaurant may have been crowded all day but when you give them five rupees for a two rupee drink they won't have any change. Actually the shortage of change is not quite as bad as they'd like to make out. Often they do have change but are trying to bluff you into parting with yours rather than vice versa. The solution is to always insist that you haven't got any change, then with luck when you meet up with someone who really doesn't have any you will.

Bus conductors never start trips with change. You pay for a Rs 6.60 fare with a Rs 10 note and your ticket is marked to indicate you're owed Rs 3.40. Don't lose it and don't forget to demand your change at the end of the trip.

Giving you change is also open to game playing. Change is never counted out as it is in the west, you're simply handed a handful. Very often if you stand there looking blank you'll be handed some more. Then some more. Post offices are particularly good at this. You ask for a couple of aerograms, a couple of stamps to America, one for a card to England. Total amount, who knows. Everybody behind you in the queue is jostling to get to the front. You can be certain that first handful of change isn't the total due. Wait. This isn't, so I have subsequently been told, necessarily a way of doing you, it's just the way change is given!

The quality of change is also important.

Notes circulate for far longer than they do in the west and the small notes in particular become very tatty. A note can have holes right through it and be quite acceptable but if it's torn at the top or bottom on the crease line then it's no good and you'll have trouble spending it. The answer to this is to simply accept it philosophically or think of clever uses. Use it for tips, or for official purposes. I'd love to pay the Rs 100 departure tax with 100 totally disreputable Rs 1 notes although someone who did just that wrote to say he had some trouble getting them to accept it! Of course you could just take it to a bank but who wants to visit Indian banks more than necessary?

COSTS

Of course it is virtually impossible to say what travelling around India will cost you. It depends on where you stay, what you eat, how you travel and how fast you travel. Two people travelling at exactly the same standard can spend vastly different amounts on a daily basis if one travels twice as fast as the other. A week lying on the beach at Goa watching the waves roll in brings daily costs down very rapidly.

From top to bottom: If you stay in luxury hotels, fly everywhere, see a lot of India in a very short trip you can spend a lot of money. India has plenty of hotels at US$50 or more a day. At the other extreme if you scrimp and save, stay in dormitories or the cheapest hotels, always travel second class on trains, learn to exist on dhal and rice, you can see Indian on less than US$5 a day for everything.

Most travellers will probably be looking for something between those extremes. If you stay in reasonable hotels – the sort of standard the tourist bungalows provide in many states where you have a clean but straightforward room with fan cooling and an attached bathroom. If you eat in regular restaurants but occasionally splash out on a fancy meal when you're in a big town. If you mix your travel, try second class sometimes for short trips, opt for 1st class if you're travelling on a long overnight trip. If you take taxis occasionally rather than always looking for a bus or rickshaw. In that case India could cost you something like US$10 to 20 a day on average. It totally depends on what you're looking for.

As everywhere in Asia remember that you get pretty much what you pay for and many times it's worth paying a little more for the experience it offers. That old fashioned Raj-style luxury is part of India's charm and sometimes it's foolish not to lay out the money and enjoy it.

DOCUMENTS

You have to have a passport, it's the most basic travel document. A health certificate while not necessary in India will probably be required for onward travel. Student cards are not the wonder workers they once were – many student concessions have either been eliminated or replaced by 'youth fares' or similar age concessions. Nevertheless a student card still can have many uses so if you can get one then do. Similarly a youth hostel card is not generally required for India's many hostels but you do pay slightly less with one.

There is not much opportunity to get behind the wheel in India but if you do intend to drive then get an International Driving Permit from your local national motoring organisation. It's worth having a batch of 'photo booth' photos for visa applications and other uses. If you run out Indian photo studios will do excellent portraits at pleasantly low prices.

TIPPING

In most Asian countries tipping is virtually unknown but India is an exception to that rule although tipping has a rather different role in India than in the west. The term *baksheesh*, which encompasses tipping and a lot more besides, aptly describes the concept in India. You 'tip' not so much for good services but to get things done. A 'tip' to a station porter will ensure you a seat when the train is packed out to the very limit.

Judicious baksheesh will open closed doors, find missing letters, perform other small miracles. Tipping is not necessary for taxis nor for cheaper restaurants but if you're going to be using something repeatedly an initial tip will ensure the standards are kept up – if you wonder why the service is slower every time in your hotel restaurant for example. Keep things in perspective though. Demands for baksheesh can quickly become never ending. Ask yourself if it's really necessary or desirable before shelling it out.

In tourist restaurants or hotels, where service will usually be tacked on in any case, the normal 10% figure normally applies. In smaller places, where tipping will be optional, you need only tip a few rupees, not a percentage of the bill.

CONSULATES & EMBASSIES

Countries with diplomatic relations with India will generally have their consular offices in New Delhi, the capital, although many also have offices in Bombay and/or Calcutta. See the relevant sections for addresses. Some of the major Indian consular offices overseas include:

Australia	92 Mugga Way, Red Hill, ACT 2603 (tel 062 95 0045)
Burma	545-547 Merchant St, Rangoon (tel 15933, 16381)
Malaysia	Asian Bank Berhad Building, 19 Malacca St, Kuala Lumpur (tel 21728)
Nepal	Lainchaur, Kathmandu (tel 11300)
Singapore	31 Grange Rd (tel 737 6809)
Sri Lanka	3rd floor, State Bank of India Building, 18-3/1 Sir Baron Jayatilaka Mawatha, Colombo 1 (tel 21604, 22788)
Thailand	139 Pan Lane, Bangkok (tel 35065)
UK	India House, Aldwych, London WC2B 4NA (tel 01 836 8484)
UN	3 East 64th St, New York, NY 10021
USA	2107 Massachusetts Ave NW, Washington DC 2008 (tel 265 5050)

INFORMATION

The Government of India Tourist Office maintains a string of tourist offices overseas where you can get brochures, leaflets and some information about India. The tourist office leaflets and brochures are often very high in their informational quality and worth getting hold of. On the other hand some of the overseas offices are not always as useful for obtaining information as those within the country. The overseas offices are listed below, there are also smaller 'promotion offices' in Osaka (Japan) and Dallas, Miami, San Francisco and Washington DC (all USA).

Australia	Carlton Centre, 55 Elizabeth St, Sydney, NSW 2000 (tel 02 232 1600)
	8 Parliament Court, 1076 Hay St, West Perth, WA 6005 (tel 06 321 6932)
Austria	Opernring 1/E/II, 1010 Vienna (tel 571402)
Belgium	60 Rue Ravenstein, Boite 15, 1000 Brussels (tel 02 5111796)
Canada	Suite 1016, Royal Trust Tower (PO Box 342), Toronto Dominion Centre, Toronto, Ontario M5K 1K7 (tel 416 362 3188)
France	8 Boulevard de la Madeleine, 75009 Paris 9 265 83 86)
Italy	Via Albricci 9, 20122 Milan (tel 804952)
Japan	Pearl Building, 9-18 Ginza, 7 Chome, Chuo ku, Tokyo 104 (tel 571 5062/3)
Kuwait	Saadoun Al-Jassim Building, Fahad Al-Salem St (PO Box 4769), Safat (tel 426088)
Singapore	Podium Block, 4th floor, Ming Court Hotel, Tanglin Rd, Singapore 1024 (tel 235 5737)
Sweden	Sveavagen 9-11 (Box 40016), S-III-57 Stockholm (tel 08 215081)
Switzerland	1-3 Rue de Chantepoulet, 1201 Geneva (tel 022 321813)
Thailand	Singapore Airlines Building, 3rd floor, 62/5 Thaniya Rd, Bangkok (tel 235 2585)
UK	7 Cork St, London WIX QAB (tel 01 437 3677-8) 3678)

USA	30 Rockefeller Plaza, 15 North Mezzanine, New York, NY 10020 (tel 212 586 4901)
	201 North Michigan Ave, Chicago, Illinois 60601 (tel 312 236 6899)
	3550 Wilshire Blvd, Suite 204, Los Angeles, California 90010 (tel 213 380 8855)
West Germany	Kaiserstrasse 77-III, 6 Frankfurt Main (tel 232380)

Within India the tourist office story is somewhat blurred by the overlap between the national and state tourist offices. As well as the national tourist office each state maintains its own tourist office and this can lead to some confusion. In some cities there will be a state and a national tourist office but sometimes the national office will be much larger than the state one or the state one will be virtually non-existent. Government of India Tourist Offices are:

Agra	191 The Mall (tel 72377)
Aurangabad	Krishna Vilas, Station Rd (tel 4817)
Bombay	123 M Karve Rd (tel 293144)
Calcutta	4 Shakespeare Sarani (tel 441402)
Cochin	Willingdon Island (tel 6045)
New Delhi	88 Janpath (tel 320005)
Gauhati	B K Kakati Rd, Ulubari
Jaipur	State Hotel (tel 72200)
Khajuraho	Near Western Group Temples (tel 47)
Madras	154 Anna Salai (tel 86240)
Shillong	Directorate of Tourism, Police Bazaar
Varanasi	15B The Mall (tel 64189)

The state offices vary widely in their efficiency and usefulness. Some of them are very good, some completely hopeless. In many states the tourist offices also run a chain of Tourist Bungalows which generally offer good accommodation at very reasonable prices. State tourist offices will usually be located in the Tourist Bungalows.

The confusion and overlap between the

national and state tourist offices often causes wasteful duplication. Both offices produce a brochure on place A, neither produces anything on place B. More confusion comes in with the division between the Government of India Tourist Office and the Indian Tourism Development Corporation (ITDC). The latter is more an actual 'doing' organisation than a 'telling' one. The ITDC will actually operate the tour bus on the tour for which the tourist office sells tickets. The ITDC also runs a series of hotels and Travellers' Lodges around the country under the Ashoka name.

GENERAL INFORMATION
Postal Services

The Indian postal services and poste restantes are generally excellent. Expected letters almost always are there and letters you send almost invariably get there. American Express, in its major city locaations, is an alternative to the poste restante system but the latter is quite OK. Have letters addressed to you with your surname in capitals and underlined, the poste restante, GPO, the city in question. Many 'lost' letters are simply misfiled under Christian names so always check under both your names.

You can often buy stamps at good hotels, saving a lot of queueing in crowded post offices.

Posting a parcel from India

Most people discover how to do this the hard way in which case it demands all morning or all afternoon. If you're not that keen to reach a peak of hitherto unknown frustration then go about it this way:

(1) Take the parcel to a tailor and tell him you'd like it stitched up in cheap linen and the seams sealed with sealing wax. The wax has to be pressed with a seal which cannot be duplicated (if all else fails a non-Indian coin will serve). At some larger post offices this stitching up service is offered outside. For a small parcel it should cost

between Rs 4-7.

(2) Go to the post office with your parcel and ask for two customs declaration forms. Fill them in and glue one to the parcel. Write your passport number (or any likely looking number) somewhere on the forms together with 'bona fide tourist'. To avoid excise duty at the delivery end it's best to specify that the contents are a 'gift'. The value of the parcel can be up to Rs 1000. (This concession is for tourists only. Internal parcels cannot exceed Rs 500 in value.)

(3) Get the parcel weighed and ask how much it's going to cost.

(4) Buy the stamps (usually not sold at the parcel counter) and stick them on.

(5) Hand the parcel in at the parcel counter and get a receipt for it.

Even if you do it this way it can still take up to two hours. Any other way and you say goodbye to the whole day. That is if you don't take the easy way out and pay somebody else to do the whole thing! Be cautious with places which offer to mail things home for you after you buy them. Government emporiums are usually OK but although most people who buy things from other places get them eventually some items never turn up (were they ever sent?) or what turns up isn't what they bought.

Time

India is 5½ hours ahead of GMT, 4½ hours behind Australian Eastern Standard Time, 10½ hours ahead of American Eastern Standard Time.

Business Hours

Indian shops, offices and post offices are not early starters. Generally shops are open from 10 am to 5 pm daily and on Saturdays. Some government offices open on alternate Saturdays and some commercial offices are open for Saturday mornings. Post offices are open 10 am to 5 pm on weekdays and on Saturday mornings. Main city offices may be open longer hours, such as 8 am to 6 pm in Delhi.

Banks are open for business between 10 am and 2 pm on weekdays and 10 am and 12 noon on Saturdays. The Ashoka Hotel in New Delhi has a bank branch open 24 hours a day for money changing. Sunday is the general closing day.

From *The Statesman*, Calcutta:

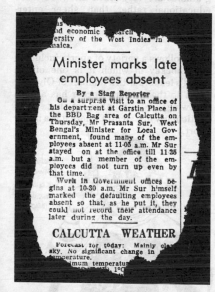

Minister marks late employees absent

By a Staff Reporter

On a surprise visit to an office of his department at Garstin Place in the BBD Bag area of Calcutta on Thursday, Mr Prasanta Sur, West Bengal's Minister for Local Government, found many of the employees absent at 11-05 a.m. Mr Sur stayed on at the office till 11-35 a.m. but a member of the employees did not turn up even by that time.

Work in Government offices begins at 10-30 a.m. Mr Sur himself marked the defaulting employees absent so that, as he put it, they could not record their attendance later during the day.

CALCUTTA WEATHER

Forecast for today: Mainly clear sky. No significant change in temperature.
imum temperature 1°C

Telephones

The telephone system in India is hit and miss. Local calls sometimes work, sometimes don't. Trunk calls are even more a matter of chance. Many calls can be dialled direct but if you get through it feels like a pure fluke. It's probably even more flukey if you can actually hear anything. It's more time-consuming but more positive putting trunk calls through the operator but again there's no guarantee you'll have a clear line.

For long distance calls within India you can make it through the operator or direct dial by STD (Standard Trunk Dialling) or you can make a Demand Call or Lightning

Call. A Demand Call is made faster than a regular call and costs more too. A Lightning Call is supposed to go through, more or less, immediately and costs eight times the regular rate. It's often possible to make phone calls from big hotels far more quickly than from the crowded phone centres.

As for international calls – well, sometimes you can get through in 20 minutes, sometimes you won't be able to get through in 24 hours. If you're intending to make an overseas call from

AGRA - DECEMBER 25th
A call home for Christmas and a telephone clerk who looked much like Santa

the GPO you should come prepared for a long, long wait – bring something to read, something to sit on, food and drink. In some places you can direct dial overseas calls and get through very quickly and reliably.

Telex

Domestic and international telex services in India are good and reasonably priced and not heavily used, like the telephone services. It is a good way to reconfirm flights as you have evidence of having done so. The bigger hotels will sometimes let you use their telex.

Electricity

230-240 volts, 50 cycles, alternating current. Electricity is widely available in India but breakdowns and blackouts are not uncommon. You can buy small immersion elements, perfect for boiling water for tea or coffee, for Rs 20.

MEDIA

There are a number of daily newspapers in English in India – all of the heavy news variety, there are no tabloids on the subcontinent. The *Times of India* and *The Statesman* are probably the best papers. The former is headquartered in Bombay and the latter in Calcutta but there are many regional editions in both cases. The *Indian Express* is also good, and is 'much more readable than the *Times* or *The Statesman*'.

The *Illustrated Weekly of India* makes good reading on long train rides and is readily available at train and bus station news-stands. The same applies to the fortnightly *India Today*, a news magazine very Time-like in its size, format, approach and layout. The problem with all these Indian publications is that they are so inward looking that you soon become starved for outside news. *India Today*, in particular, is stuffed full of dull stories about state government politics. One traveller recommended *Gentleman*, despite its misleading title, as a good Indian news magazine.

Time and *Newsweek* are readily available throughout India although once you've become used to Indian prices they seem very expensive! There are all sorts of other Indian magazines in English although many are of very limited interest

to western visitors – it takes a long time to build up an interest in Indian movie stars and their film-fan magazines! Indian women's magazines, so alike yet so unlike their western counterparts, are definitely worth looking at.

India also has a wide network of radio stations and TV stations are becoming increasingly widespread. The TV programmes are very much intended to be educational rather than sheer entertainment, however.

Sports

India follows a variety of sports including field hockey in which it is one of the world's leaders with a number of Olympic golds to their credit. Soccer has a keen following in a number of big cities particularly in Calcutta where it is a major sport.

A national pastime. Test cricket by transistor radio...

India's national sport has to be cricket. There's something about a game with as many idiosyncrasies and peculiarities as cricket which simply has to appeal to the Indian temperament. During the cricket season, if Australia or England are touring India and there is a test match on, you'll see crowds at every street corner in the big cities clamouring to hear what the latest score is from some transistor listener. Test matches with Pakistan, one sign of the thaw in relations between the countries, always have a particularly strong following.

HEALTH
Immunisations
Apart from yellow fever and smallpox vaccinations for people coming from infected areas, there are no vaccination requirements for visitors to India. You may consider that some protection is worthwhile, nevertheless, and should consult your doctor as to what he thinks is necessary. Smallpox vaccinations provide protection for three years but smallpox, it is believed, has now been totally eradicated worldwide.

Cholera is a disease of insanitation and usually occurs in epidemics. Protection against cholera is recommended for India and the vaccination is good for six months. A very useful vaccination, although not required by health authorities, is TABT. This provides protection against typhoid, paratyphoid A and B and tetanus. Typhoid and paratyphoid are both diseases of insanitation, spread by contaminated food. Tetanus is usually caused by a cut or skin puncture. All three are prevalent in hot climates. There are a number of medical centres in India where it is possible to get free or low cost cholera and other vaccinations.

Polio is also a disease spread by insanitation and found more frequently in hot climates. A booster every five years is recommended by many doctors. The other vaccination you may wish to consider taking is against infectious hepatitis. This disease is, once again, spread by infected water or food but the degree of protection provided by the gamma globulin injection prescribed against it is still a subject of controversy. Improved procedures are now believed to provide good protection for up to six months.

Malaria
It is not (yet) possible to be vaccinated against malaria but it is absolutely necessary to take precautions against it while you are in India. Malaria is spread by mosquitoes and the disease has a nasty habit of coming back in later years even if you are cured at the time – and it can be fatal. Protection is simple – a daily or weekly tablet depending on which your doctor recommends.

Pregnant women should not take Chloroquine (daily) tablets. Some doctors recommend Proguanil as the best anti-malarial for pregnancy – while researching the first edition of this book Maureen was pregnant and used Proguanil without ill effects. When travelling with very small children try to avoid using daily tablets – getting a tablet into a small child every day of the week is not a pleasant task.

Rabies
Rabies is also widespread in India – don't be friendly to India's numerous stray dogs and beware of those picturesque monkeys. If you are bitten by a possibly rabid animal you should wash the wound thoroughly and then embark on a 14 day series of injections which will prevent the disease developing. Rabies, once developed, is almost always fatal. New rabies vaccines have been developed which have fewer side effects than the older animal-derived serums and vaccines.

Stomach Problems
The usual health problem afflicting visitors to India is far more mundane than rabies, hepatitis or malaria. It's simply

Delhi belly, the old upset stomach. Often this can be due simply to a change of diet or a system unused to spicy food. Many times, however, contaminated food or water is the problem.

There are two answers to the upset stomach problem. First avoid getting it in the first place by taking care in what you eat and drink. Uncooked foods are always more likely to harbour germs but so are cooked foods once they have been allowed to cool. Try to eat only freshly cooked foods and beware of places where food is left sitting around for long periods, particularly if exposed to flies.

The main cause of upset stomachs is probably drinking water – the answer is to either drink hot tea or bottled soft drinks from reputable bottlers. This doesn't always work in the thirsty hot season so if you must drink water try to either have it boiled or carry water purification tablets. These are available from pharmacies in the west or, with more difficulty, in India. Water is more effectively sterilised by iodine solution than by tablets – it kills amoebic cysts as well but does require practice drinking swimming pool water! Even in good hotels 'drinking water' may be just filtered, not boiled.

If avoidance fails and you do get a stomach bug the first thing to do is nothing. If you can simply get back to health by yourself you'll probably build up some immunity against it recurring. Stick to hot tea and try not to eat too much. People who take antibiotics at the first sign of an upset stomach are only asking for trouble. Not only does it make another assault more difficult to repel, it also kills off the useful organisms in your digestive tract just as efficiently as it kills off the harmful ones. People whose travels in India are one long series of stomach problems are often the people who overdid the modern medicines. India is also a good place to catch the stomach upset known as giardiasis.

Some advice from two doctors in Nepal on diarrhoea and dysentery:

Diarrhoea is very different from dysentery, and it might be a good idea to define dysentery which will require good drugs. Dysentery is diarrhoea with blood, pus or fever. Diarrhoea with blood or pus but without fever is usually amoebic dysentery and requires an anti-amoebic drug like metronidazole or flagyl. Diarrhoea with blood or pus and fever is usually bacillary dysentery and requires antibiotics like tetracycline, or a sulfa drug. None of these drugs need to be given under the supervision of a doctor if a traveller has dysentery, and they can all be obtained in India or from a family doctor before leaving home. Most over the counter proprietary stomach upset cures in India are worthless or dangerous and if travellers save the drugs suggested above for true dysentery they will avoid one long series of stomach problems.

Most of the diarrhoea that travellers pick up is named appropriately 'travellers diarrhoea' and is without pus, blood or fever. Here the most important advice is to keep drinking to avoid dehydration. Lomotil is neither a heavy gun nor a general cure; it doesn't cure anything but just slows down the guts so that the cramps go away and you don't have to run to the toilet all the time. Lomotil is available over the counter in India but plain codeine is cheaper and works as well.

Hot Season Health
During the hot season there are some additional precautions to take to ensure good health. First of all protect yourself from the sun as much as possible – it doesn't burn, due to all the dust haze, so you won't get sunburnt but it certainly does you no good. Secondly keep your liquid intake up. If you find you are urinating very infrequently or your urine turns a deep yellow or orange you're becoming dehydrated. It's very easy to do just that in the hot season. At times like this you have to balance the dangers of drinking water against the dangers of

dehydration. The first is possible, the second is definite so if necessary throw caution to the winds and drink more water. In good restaurants and hotels drinking water is generally OK anyway. During the dry season water is much less likely to be polluted. It's during the monsoon that you must be especially careful about drinking water.

Hospitals

Although India does have a few excellent hospitals such as the Mission Hospital in Vellore in Tamil Nadu, the Jaslok Hospital in Bombay and the All India Medical Institute in Delhi, most Indian cities do not have the quality of medical care available in the west. Usually hospitals run by western missionaries have better facilities than government hospitals where long waiting lines are common. India does have, however, many qualified doctors with their own private clinics. These can be quite good. The usual fee for a clinic visit is about Rs 25 or Rs 40 for a specialist. Home calls usually cost Rs 50.

Other better known hospitals in India are the Holy Family Hospital near Okhla in Delhi, the Benares Hindu University Hospital in Varanasi and the Kurji Hospital in Patna.

General Thoughts

Finally some miscellaneous thoughts: make sure your teeth are in good shape before departing – dentists' equipment is not always what we've got used to in the west. It's wise to clean your teeth with 'safe' water as well. Always carry a spare pair of glasses or your prescription in case of loss or breakage. It's relatively easy to get glasses made up in an emergency. Don't walk around in bare feet, that is how you get hookworms or worse. Thongs are useful protectors in hotel showers against athletes' foot or other fungal infections. Treat any simple scratch or cut with care – clean it thoroughly with antiseptic and keep it clean. In India's tropical climate

it's very easy for the most straightforward scratch to get infected.

A straightforward medical kit is a wise thing to carry. Apart from medicines, band-aids, antiseptic and so on a small clinical thermometer can be very useful. Take extra care in this department if you're travelling with children. You rarely need a prescription to buy medicines in India – if it's available at all it will be available over the counter. Be aware of possible differences in names, however. If you're after a specific drug it's worthwhile knowing the scientific as well as the trade name. Remember that drugs may not be of the same strength as in other countries or may have deteriorated due to age or poor storage conditions. They most probably will, however, be far cheaper than in the west. Prices for common drugs in Europe or the USA are often 10 or more times the retail price in India.

If a simple stomach upset turns out to be real down-to-earth dysentery the most important thing is not to become dehydrated. Get plenty of liquids. If you get the dreaded hep, rest, good food, no alcohol and generally taking it easy is the cure. Make sure you have a good medical insurance policy, one that covers flying you home in emergencies. If you do need a doctor or other medical help your embassy or consulate or a five star hotel should be able to recommend someone.

It's probably wise to carry your health certificate with you just like your passport. One traveller wrote of having his bus stopped at a 'Cholera Inoculation Checkpoint'. All those who couldn't produce proof of immunisation got a jab on the spot, without benefit of sterilising the needle between goes! *The Traveller's Health Guide* by Dr Anthony Turner (Roger Lascelles, London) has some good basic advice on staying healthy while travelling. A traveller recommended *In Search of the Masters*, a book about ashrams in India, for its resume on health problems in India.

It hardly needs saying but street corner

acupuncturists or ear cleaners (!) are not to be trusted in India. Amazingly some people do let these folk have a go at them and regret it afterwards!

Most important of all don't get overly concerned about your health. Most people survive India with very few problems. During the course of researching the first edition of this book Tony and Maureen spent three months in India in one stretch, during the hot season, and while Maureen was pregnant, with nothing more than a couple of mild stomach upsets between them.

WOMEN TRAVELLERS

India doesn't present the problems for solo women travellers that some Asian countries can—Pakistan in particular—but some care can help. Since the first edition several women travellers have written with their thoughts and suggestions.

One women suggested that: 'you should keep your upper arms, chest and back covered because these areas are, for some reason, considered erotic. A big shawl of light cloth will provide some privacy. Don't return male stares', she continued, 'it is considered a come-on. Turning away haughtily and draping your shawl over your head will have the desired effect. Getting involved in inane conversations with men is also considered a turn-on. Keep discussions down to a necessary minimum unless you're interested in getting hassled. If you get the uncomfortable feeling 'is he encroaching on my space' the chances are that he is. A firm request to keep away, use your best memsahib tone, may help. Firmly return any errant limbs, put some item of luggage in between you and if all else fails find a new spot, with offended dignity. You're also within your rights to tell him to push off!'

A couple of women wrote in some anger over the way they were treated in India. It came down, they decided, to a belief that if you're not married there's something wrong with you and if you are married then what are you doing here all alone!

Being a women also has some advantages. There is often a special ladies' queue for train tickets or even a ladies' quota and ladies' carriages! One women wrote that these ladies' carriages were often nearly empty – another said that they were full of screaming children. Special ladies' facilities are also sometimes found in cinemas and other places.

WHAT TO TAKE & HOW TO TAKE IT

The usual travellers' rule applies – bring as little as possible. It's much better to have to get something you've left behind than find you have too much and need to get rid of it. In the south of India you can count on shirtsleeve weather year round but in the north it can get cool enough to require a sweater or light jacket in the evenings during the winter. In the far north it will get down to freezing and you will need all the warm weather gear you can muster.

Remember that clothes are easily and cheaply purchased in India. You can buy things off the peg or have clothes made to measure in the small tailor shops that are found everywhere in India. In the big cities there are plenty of the Indian fashions that are so popular in the west and the prices often approximate in rupees to what they cost in dollars in the west! One item of clothing to have made as soon as possible is a pair of lightweight pyjama style trousers. You'll find them far cooler and more comfortable than jeans and they'll only cost a few rupees.

Modesty rates highly in India, as in most Asian countries. Although men wearing shorts is accepted as a western eccentricity women should dress more discreetly. A reasonable clothes list would include:

underwear & swimming gear
one pair of jeans, one pair of shorts
a few T-shirts or short sleeved shirts
sweater for cold nights

one pair of sneakers or shoes
sandals and/or thongs
lightweight jacket or raincoat
a 'dress up' set of clothes

On the non-clothing side take along:

washing gear
medical & sewing kit
sunglasses
padlock

Other non-clothing items to consider include an umbrella, invaluable in the monsoon.

Sleeping Bag A sleeping bag can be a hassle to carry but can serve as something to sleep in (and avoid unsavoury-looking hotel bedding), a cushion on hard train seats, a seat for long waits on railway platforms, a bed top-cover (since cheaper hotels rarely give you one) and, of course, as a sleeping bag. If you're going trekking in the north then a sleeping bag will be absolutely necessary. Note that trekking gear cannot be easily hired in India the way it can be in Nepal. A sheet sleeping bag, like those required by youth hostels in the west, can be very useful, particularly if you don't trust a hotel's sheets. Mosquito nets are also rare so your own sheet or sheet sleeping bag will also help to keep mosquitoes at bay and/or keep you warm at night.

Some travellers find that a plastic sheet is useful for a number of reasons including bed-bug proofing unhealthy looking beds. Others have recommended an inflatable pillow as a useful accessory.

Toilet Paper
Toilet paper is a necessity if you can't adapt to the Indian method of a jug of water and your left hand. Since not many trees end up as toilet paper in India the stuff can be very hard to find outside of the big cities and tourist centres. And when you do find it Indian toilet paper is often lousy (either the British masochist-style

waxed paper stuff or a tube of cardboard cms thick with about a metre and a half of paper wrapped around it) and horrendously expensive. One solution is to come to India with an absurd quantity of this western luxury. That makes more sense than it sounds – toilet paper is extremely light and also extremely bulky. Having your pack half full of paper is one way of ensuring that when it's used up you'll have plenty of space for all those interesting things you'll be buying.

Toiletries Soap, toothpaste and other toiletries are readily available but toilet paper can sometimes be difficult to find outside of major centres. A sink plug is worth having since few cheaper hotels have plugs. A nail brush can be very useful. Women will find tampons are virtually unobtainable in India. Except in 'strange, varied, toxic shock inducing forms,' wrote one women.

How to Carry It Where to put all this gear – well for budget travellers the backpack is still the best carrying container. Adding a little thief proofing protection by sewing on tabs so you can padlock it shut is worthwhile. An alternative is a large, soft, zip bag with a wide shoulder strap. It's not so easy to carry for distances but it is rather more thief proof and less prone to damage. Some airlines will no longer accept responsibility for damage or theft from backpacks. Suitcases are only for jet-setters! Lots of plastic bags will keep your gear in some sort of order and will also be invaluable for keeping things dry during the wet season.

Miscellaneous Useful Things
It's amazing how many things you wish you had with you when you're in India. One of the most useful for budget travellers is a padlock. In fact a padlock is a virtual necessity. Many cheaper hotels, in fact most of them, have doors locked by a hasp and padlock. You'll find having your own sturdy lock on the door instead

of the flimsy thing the hotel supplies does wonders for your peace of mind. Other uses are legion. You can lock a pack onto a railway luggage rack at night for example. It may not make it thief proof but it helps. You can buy a good lock in India for Rs 12 to 15. 'Combination locks are relatively unknown so they are very effective', was one reader suggestion.

A universal sink plug is useful since sinks never have them. Ever tried to wash your underwear in a sink without a plug? A knife (Swiss Army for preference) finds a whole field of uses, in particular for peeling fruit. Some travellers rhapsodise about how useful a miniature electric element to boil water in a cup is.

Insect repellant can also be extremely useful. You may find a clothesline and clothes pegs worthwhile. Power cuts are common in India ('load shedding' as it is euphemistically known) and there's little street lighting at night so a torch (flashlight) and candles can be handy. Clear cellophane tape was one suggestion, enables you to flawlessly repair torn banknotes! Bring along your spectacle prescription if you're short sighted. Should you lose or damage your glasses a new pair can be made up very cheaply and in good quality.

Hot weather survival requires another book of rules in India. First of all a sun hat is essential. Stepping out into the sun in India in the hot season is like using your head as a blacksmith's anvil. You don't just feel the sun, it reaches out and hits you. Secondly a water bottle should always be by your side and thirdly have water purification tablets. In the heat you need water – cups of tea, fruit and soft drinks are just not going to do the job. Purification tabs are not 100% effective but when it gets really hot you're not going to care how effective they are! In hot weather you'll really need something with long sleeves, particularly if you're going to ride a bicycle very far.

INDIAN CLOTHING

Many travellers start wearing Indian clothes while in India – after all much of it is a lot more appropriate to India's climate than jeans and T-shirts. Best known Indian clothing style, and one the wearing of which few western women can carry off properly, is the *sari*. This supremely graceful attire is simply one length of material, a bit over a metre in width and five to nine metres long (usually around six metres long). It's worn without any pins, buttons or fastenings to hold it in place so in part its graceful appearance is a necessity. The tightly fitted, short blouse worn under a sari is a *choli*. The final length of the sari, which is draped over the wearer's shoulder, is known as the *pallav* or *palloo*.

There are a number of variations in types of saris and styles of wearing them but there are also other styles of women's costume in India. Sikh women wear pyjama like trousers drawn tightly in at the waist and the ankles. Over these trousers, known as *salwars*, they wear a long, loose tunic known as a *kameez*. This attire is comfortable and 'respectable'. A *churidhar* is similar to salwars but tighter fitting at the hips. Over this goes a collarless or mandarin collar *kurta* – an item of clothing just as popular in the west, where it is worn by men as much as women, as in India.

Although the overwhelming majority of Indian women wear traditional costume many Indian men wear quite conventional western clothing. Indeed a large proportion of India's consumer advertising appears to be devoted to 'suitings & shirtings' – the material made for tailor made western-style business suits and shirts. The traditional *lungi* originated in the south and today is worn by women as well as men. It's simply a short length of material worn around the thighs rather like a sarong. A *dhoti* is like a longer lungi but with a length of material pulled up between the legs, effective but a long way from elegant! Pyjama-like trousers, worn by countryfolk, are known as *lenga*.

There are many religious and regional variations such as the brightly mirrored Rajasthani skirts and their equally colourful tie-dye materials. In Ladakh the women wear superbly picturesque Tibetan costumes with high 'top hats'. Their men wear long dressing gown-like coats. Moslem women, of course, wear much more staid and all-covering attire than their Hindu sisters. More traditional Moslems even wear the all-enveloping tent-like *burkha*.

Dhobi Wallahs

Your clothes will undoubtedly become involved at some point in your travels with the Indian ability to make systems of amazing ocmplexity function smoothly. Travelling in India there's hardly any need for more than one change of clothes. Everyday there will be a knock on your door and the laundry boy will collect all those dusty, sweaty clothes you wore yesterday and every evening those same clothes will re-appear — washed and ironed with more loving care than any washing powder ad-mum every lavished upon anything. And all for a rupee or two per item. But what happened to your clothes between their departure and their like-new return?

INDIANS TRYING TO BREAK
STONES WITH WET WASHING...
RANA GHAT – VARANASI

Well, they certainly did not get anywhere near a washing machine. First of all they're collected and taken to the *dhobi ghat*. A ghat is a place with water, a dhobi is a washerman so the dhobi ghat is where the dhobi plys his trade and washes clothes. In big cities dhobi ghats will be huge places with hundreds of dhobis doing their thing with thousands of articles of clothing.

First of all the clothes are separated – all the white shirts are washed together, all the grey trousers, all the red skirts, all the blue jeans. By now, if this was the west, your clothes would either be hopelessly lost or you'd need a computer to keep track of them all. Your clothes are soaked in soapy water for a few hours, following which the dirt is literally beaten out of them. No multi-programmed, miracle of technology can wash as clean as a determined dhobi although admittedly after a few visits to the Indian laundry your clothes do begin to look distinctly thinner. Buttons also tend to get shattered so bring some spares.

Once clean the clothes are strung out on miles of clothes line to quickly dry in the Indian sun then taken to the ironing sheds where hundreds of ironers wielding primitive irons press your jeans like they've never been pressed before. Not just your jeans – your socks, your T-shirts, even your underwear will come back with knife edge creases. Then the Indian miracle takes place. Out of the thousands upon thousands of items washed that day somehow your very own brown socks, blue jeans, yellow T-shirt and red underwear all find their way back together and head back for your hotel room. There's a system of marking clothes, known only to the dhobis, which is the real reason behind this feat. They say criminals have been tracked down simply by those tell-tale 'dhobi marks'.

FILM & CAMERA

Film is available in India but mainly black and white or colour print film and the colour film is not cheap. Count on Rs 120 to 150 for a reel of 36 exposure 35 mm slide film – *without* developing and mounting. If you're taking slides then bring it with you, and bring plenty, India is a photogenic country. Black and white film and colour prints can be developed and printed quickly and cheaply in India as can regular colour transparencies but you will need to send Kodachrome or other 'includes developing film' overseas. It's up to you whether you send them straight back or carry them back with you at the end of your trip. Film manufacturers warn that once exposed films should be developed as quickly as possible but in practice they seem to last, even in India's summer heat, without deterioration for months.

There are plenty of camera shops who should be able to make minor repairs should you have any camera problems in India. Photography in India presents some special problems. In the dry season the hazy atmosphere makes it difficult to get sharp shots or to get much contrast between what you are photographing and the background. Everything looks washed out and flat even using a polarising filter. In the mountains you should allow for the extreme clarity of the air and light intensity and take care not to over-expose your shots.

Be careful what you photograph. India is touchy about places of military importance – this can include train stations, bridges, airports and any military installations. If in doubt ask. In general most people are happy to be photographed but care should be taken in pointing cameras at Moslem women. Again, if in doubt, ask.

THEFT

Having things stolen is a problem in India, not so much because it's a theft prone country – it isn't – but because you can become involved in a lot of hassles getting it replaced. If your passport is stolen you may have a long trip back to an embassy to replace it. Travellers' cheques may be replaceable if stolen but first of all avoid theft. Always lock your room, preferably with your own padlock in cheaper hotels.

Never leave those most important valuables (passport, tickets, health certificates, money, travellers' cheques) in your room, they should be with you at all times. Either have a stout leather passport wallet on your belt, or a passport pouch under your shirt, or simply extra internal pockets in your clothing. On trains at night keep your gear near to you, padlocking a bag to a luggage rack can be useful. Never walk around with valuables casually slung over your shoulder. Take extra care in crowded public transport. In Bombay, for example, pickpockets are adept at the razor on the back pocket or shoulder bag technique.

Thieves are particularly prevalent on train routes where there are lots of tourists. The Delhi-Agra express service is notorious and Delhi-Jammu Tawi, Delhi-Calcutta and Delhi-Bombay are other routes to take care on. Train departure time, when the confusion and crowds are at their worst, is the time to be most careful. Just as the train is about to leave your bags suddenly fly out the window to a waiting accomplice. On the Delhi-Jammu service the 'instant crowd' technique is the usual method. Young guys work in teams, you suddenly find yourself surrounded and jostled by people and your bags disappear in an instant. Airports are another place to be careful especially for international arrivals which often take place in the middle of the night, when you are unlikely to be at your most wakeful and alert.

Beware also of your fellow travellers. Unhappily there are more than a few backpackers who make the money go further by helping themselves to other peoples'. At places like Goa be very careful with things on the beach – while you're in the water your camera or money can walk away very fast.

Remember that backpacks are very easy to be rifled through. Don't leave valuables in them, especially for flights. Remember also that something may be of little or no value to a thief but to lose it would be a real heartbreak to you – like film. Finally a good travel insurance policy helps.

Travellers' Cheques If you're unlucky enough to have things stolen some precautions can ease the pain. All travellers cheques are replaceable but it does you little immediate good if you have to go home and apply to your bank to do that. What you want is instant replacement. Furthermore what do you do if you lose your cheques and money and have a day or more to travel to the replacement office? The answer to that is to keep an emergency cash stash in some totally separate place. In that same place you should keep a record of the cheque serial numbers and your passport number.

American Express make considerable noise about 'instant replacement' of their cheques but a lot of people find out, to their cost, that without a number of precautions it ain't necessarily so. For a start 'no bank', reported one unhappy traveller, 'will give an instant refund if the amount stolen is over US$1000'. A good reason for carrying more than one brand of cheque. The same person said that it is necessary to get a receipt to prove that you phoned the nearest American Express office after the theft. The receipt should indicate the number you called and the date. 'Keep the original receipt from when you bought the cheques separate from the cheques themselves', he continued. 'Without that, you won't even get a single dollar for weeks and weeks'.

Another traveller wrote that he had travellers' cheques stolen and didn't discover the loss for a month. They had been left in his hotel room and the thief (presumably from the hotel) had neatly removed a few cheques from the centre of the book of cheques. Explaining that sort of theft is really difficult and, of course, the thief has had plenty of time to dispose of them.

We've had a number of letters concerning theft in India since the first edition of this book, including one woman who was so upset by having her camera stolen soon after arrival that she left on the next available flight. Other writers were ripped off from a beach hut at Goa, on various trains, from the top of the bus to Darjeeling, on internal flights and from their hotel rooms. One guy had his camera stolen at knife point by a rickshaw rider who was supposedly about to buy it – down a quiet, deserted street. Geoff even had stuff stolen while researching this second edition. What can we say – be careful. But, of course, there's a reserve side. In many years travel I (Tony speaking here) have had various things stolen in France, Italy, Thailand (more than once), Malaysia, Indonesia and even Australia. On all my visits to India I've never once lost anything. India has no world exclusive on thieves, it's just a matter of luck.

I'll leave the final word to an elderly visitor (he and two friends who visited India and told us about it had a combined age of 200 years!): 'I have never had anything stolen while in transit or in hotels. I am not a particularly careful person and can only conclude that the risk is exaggerated. We found it only too easy to be suspicious and were frequently humbled by realising that people we thought were trying to con us were only trying to be helpful. Every time we misplaced some item of luggage our first thought was that it had been stolen; but we lost absolutely nothing in that way. On the other hand we were several times followed with things we had inadvertantly left in teashops or buses'.

PLACES TO STAY

India has a very wide range of accommodation possibilities apart from straightforward hotels. Some of them include:

Cheap Hotels

There are hotels all over India with conditions ranging from extremely drab and dismal (but prices at rock bottom levels) up to quite reasonable standards

and at quite reasonable prices. Lazily swishing ceiling fans, mosquito nets on the beds, private toilets and bathrooms are all possibilities even in rooms costing Rs 35 or less a night for a double.

A standard term you'll find throughout India is the definition of hotels as 'western' or 'Indian'. It's basically a pretty meaningless differentiation although expensive hotels are always western, cheap ones always Indian. 'Indian' hotels will be more simply and economically furnished but the acid test is likely to be the toilet. 'Western' hotels have to have a sit up style toilet, 'Indian' ones are usually (but not always) the traditional Asian squat style. You can find modern, well equipped, clean places with Indian toilets and dirty, dismal dumps with western toilets so don't be put off them.

Although prices are generally quoted in this book for singles and doubles most hotels will put an extra bed in a room to make a triple for about an extra 25%. This is a considerable economy if there are more than two of you. In some smaller hotels it's often possible to bargain a little if you really want to. on the other hand these places will often put their prices up if there's an accommodation shortage.

Expensive Hotels

You won't find 'International Standard' hotels throughout India. The big, air-con, swimming pool places are generally confined to the major tourist centres and the big cities. There are a number of big hotel chains in India. They include the government operated ITDC chain who usually append the name 'Ashoka' to their hotels. There's an Ashoka hotel in virtually every town in India so that test isn't foolproof but the ITDC places include a number of smaller, but higher standard, units in places like Sanchi or Konarak where accommodation possibilities are limited.

The Taj Group has some of India's flashiest hotels including the luxurious Taj Mahal Inter-Continental in Bombay, the romantic Rambagh Palace in Jaipur and Lake Palace in Udaipur and other interesting hotels such as the Taj Coromandel in Madras and the Fort Aguada Resort in Goa. The Oberoi chain is, of course, well known outside India as well as within. Clarks are a small chain with popular hotels in Varanasi and Agra amongst other places. The Welcom Group and the Air India associated Centaur hotels are other chains.

The more expensive hotels in India are not the great bargain they might seem at first. Although labour costs in India are low it takes a lot of people to get anything done. Combine that with high costs for imported equipment and fittings plus the high cost of electricity and power in India and room costs are certainly not low in India compared to other countries' more expensive hotels.

Beware of extra taxes and charges in the more expensive hotels. There will almost always be a 10% service charge but in addition there will often be a 'luxury tax'. This tax, which is usually either 5% or 10%, seems to depend on the room cost or other factors like whether the room has air-conditioning or not. In some places, where there are different off season and high-season rates, you may find the luxury tax is higher in the high season – presumably because the higher room rate in season moves it from one bracket to another. Sometimes a room rate will be broken down into individual charges thereby keeping the basic room rate low enough to avoid luxury tax. Thus you might find the total price is Rs x for the room plus Rs y for the phone (which you never used). On x alone there is no tax but on x plus y there would be. Anyway rates quoted in this book are generally the basic rate only – taxes and charges are additional.

Government Accommodation

Back in the days of the Raj a whole string of government run accommodation units were set up with labels like Rest Houses, Dak Bungalows, Circuit Houses, PWD (Public Works Department) Bungalows, Forest Rest Houses and so on. Today most of these are reserved for government officials although in some places they may still be available for tourists, if there is room. In an approximate pecking order the Dak Bungalows are the most basic, they often have no electricity and only basic equipment in out of the way places. Rest Houses are next up and then comes the Circuit Houses which are strictly for travelling VIPs.

Tourist Bungalows

These often serve as replacements for the older government-run accommodation units. Tourist Bungalows are generally well kept and are often excellent value. They often have dorm beds but rooms are usually doubles only so they're often not much good for solo travellers who want a room rather than a dormitory. The typical tourist bungalow will have rooms at Rs 30 to 60 for a double. The rooms will be well kept, have a fan, double bed, attached bathroom and there may also be more expensive air-conditioned rooms. There will generally be a restaurant or 'dining hall'. There are particularly good Tourist Bungalows in Rajasthan and Orissa although almost every state has some towns where the Tourist Bungalow is definitely the best place to stay.

In tourist bungalows, as in many other government run places in India, you will find a curiously Indian institution, the 'complaints book'. In this you can write your complaints and periodically someone higher up the chain of command comes along, reads the terrible tales and the tourist bungalow manager gets his knuckles rapped. In disputes or other arguments calling for the complaints book is the angry customer's final weapon. In many places the complaints book can provide interesting and amusing reading. Try the Madurai Tourist Bungalow's complaints book suggested one traveller.

Railway Retiring Rooms

These are just like regular hotels or dormitories except they are at the railway stations. To stay there you are generally supposed to have a railway ticket or Indrail Pass although a Tourist Introduction Card will often do the trick. The rooms are, of course, excellent if you want to be handy for a train departure although they can be noisy if it is a busy station. They are often very cheap and in some places they are also excellent value. Some stations have retiring rooms of definite Raj pretensions with huge rooms and enough furniture to do up a flat or apartment back home.

Railway Waiting Rooms

Emergency accommodation when all else fails or when you just need a few hours shut-eye before your train departs at 2 am. These are a free place to rest your weary head. The trick is to rest it in the comfortable lst class waiting room and not the depressing and crowded lower class one. Officially you need a lst class ticket to be allowed to use the lst class room and its superior facilities. In practice, luck and your Tourist Introduction Card or 2nd class Indrail Pass may work.

Youth Hostels

Indian youth hostels are generally very cheap and sometimes in excellent condition with superb facilities. They are, however, often rather inconveniently situated, some distance from the town centres. You are not usually required to be a YHA member, as in other countries, to use the hostels although your YHA card will generally get you a lower rate. Nor do the usual rules about arrival and departure times, lights out times or not using the hostel during the day apply. A list of Government of India hostels includes:

Andhra Pradesh	Youth Hostel, near Secunderabad Sailing Club, Secunderabad
Goa	Youth Hostel, Panaji (tel 2433)
Gujarat	Youth Hostel, Sector 16, Gandhinagar (tel 2364)
Haryana	Panchkula Youth Hostel, Haryana Tourist Complex, Panchkula, Ambala
Himachal Pradesh	Youth Hostel, bus stand, Dalhousie (tel 89)
Jammu & Kashmir	Patni Top Youth Hostel, c/o Tourist Office, Kud (tel 7)
Kerala	Youth Hostel, Veli, Trivandrum
Madhya Pradesh	Youth Hostel, North TT Nagar, Bhopal (tel 63671)
Maharashtra	Youth Hostel, Padampura, Station Rd, Aurangabad (tel 3801)
Orissa	Youth Hostel, Sea Beach, Puri (tel 424)
Punjab	Youth Hostel, Mal Mandi, GT Rd, Amritsar (tel 48165)
Rajasthan	Youth Hostel, SMS Stadium, Bhagwandas Rd, Jaipur (tel 69084)
Tamil Nadu	Youth Hostel, Indira Nagar, Madras (tel 412882)
	Youth Hostel, Solaithandam Kuppam, Pondicherry
Uttar Pradesh	Youth Hostel, Malli Tal near Ardwell Camp, The Mall, Nainital (tel 513)
West Bengal	Darjeeling Youth Hostel, 16 Dr Zakir Hussain Rd, Darjeeling (tel 2290)

Other

There are YMCAs and YWCAs in many big cities – some of these are modern, well equipped, more expensive (but still good value) places. There are also a few Salvation Army Hostels – in particular in Bombay and Calcutta. There are a few camping places around India but travellers with their own vehicles can almost always find hotels with gardens where they can park and camp.

Free accommodation is available at some Sikh Temples where there is a tradition of hospitality to visitors. It can be an interesting insight to try it but please don't abuse this hospitality and spoil it for other travellers. At many pilgrimage sites there are dharamsalas offering accommodation to pilgrims and travellers are often welcome to use these. This particularly applies at isolated sites like Ranakpur in Rajasthan.

Staying with an Indian family can be real education. It's a change from dealing strictly with tourist-oriented people and the differences and curiousities of everyday Indian life can be very interesting. 'I was shown great hospitality by Indian friends of friends', wrote one visitor.

Touts

Hordes of accommodation touts operate in many towns in India, Jaipur and Varanasi are two particular places. Very often they are the rickshaw-wallahs who meet you at the bus or train station. The technique is simple – they take you to hotel A and rake off a commission for bringing you there rather than to hotel B. The problem with this procedure is that you may well end up not at the place you want to go to but at the place that pays the best commission. Some very good cheap hotels simply refuse to pay the touts and you'll then hear lots of stories about the hotel you want being 'full up', 'closed for repairs' or 'no good anymore'. Nine chances out of 10 they will be just that – stories.

Touts do have use though – if you arrive in a town where some big festival is on (or a cricket test match against England or Australia!) finding a place to stay can be very difficult. Hop in a rickshaw, tell him what price range you want a hotel in and off you go. He'll know which places have rooms available and unless the search is a long one you shouldn't have to pay him more than Rs 5; Rs 10 at the most. Remember he'll be getting a commission from the hotel too!

FOOD

Despite the very fine food that can be prepared in India you'll often find food a great disappointment. In many smaller centres there is simply not a great choice of food and you'll get bored with rice and *dhal*. When you're in larger cities where the food can be excellent take advantage of it.

Contrary to popular belief not all Hindus are officially vegetarians. Strict vegetarianism is confined more to the south which has not had the meat eating influence of the Aryan and later Moslem invasions. On the other hand eating meat is not always a great pleasure in India – the quality tends to be low (most chickens give the impression that they died from starvation) and the hygiene is not all that it might be. Beef, from the holy cow, is strictly taboo of course – and leads to interesting Indian dishes like the mutton-burger. Pork is equally taboo to the Moslems. All in all whether you're vegetarian or not you'll end up eating a lot more vegetarian food in India.

Railway station restaurants are always a good bet in India. Their food is generally safe and if one more curry will kill you they also have a western menu – at higher prices. Of course no culinary achievement awards are ever going to be made to station restaurants but in general they're not bad. Indian interpretations of western cuisine can be pretty horrific, it's usually best to let them stick to preparing Indian food. Meals served on trains are usually palatable too, and reasonably cheap. At every stop you will be besieged by food and drink sellers. Even in the middle of the night that raucous cry of 'chai, chai' breaks into your sleep. The sheer bedlaam of an Indian station when a train is in is a part of India you never forget.

If, after some time in India, you do find the food is getting you down physically or psychologically, there are a couple of escapes. It is very easy for budget travellers to lose weight in India and feel lethargic and drained of energy. The answer is to up your protein intake – eat more eggs which are readily available; buy bananas, mandarin oranges or peanuts, all readily available at stations or in the markets. Many travellers carry multi-vitamins with them. Another answer, if you're travelling on a budget, is to occasionally splash out on a meal in a fancy hotel or restaurant – compared to what you have been paying it may seem amazingly expensive but try translating the price into what it would be at home.

There are considerable regional variations from north to south, partly because of climatic conditions and partly because of historical influences. In the north, as already mentioned, much more meat is eaten and the cooking is often 'Moghul style' which bears a closer relationship to food of the Middle East and central Asia. The emphasis is more on spices and less on curry heat. In the north there are also much more grains and breads eaten and less rice. In the south the food is more strictly vegetarian, more rice is eaten and the curries tend to be hotter. Sometimes very hot. Another peculiarity of southern vegetarian food is you do not need eating utensils, it is always eaten with fingers (of the right hand only). Scooping up food that way takes a little practice but you soon become quite adept at it. It is said that eating this way allows you to get the 'feel' of the food, as important to south Indian cuisine as the aroma or the arrangement is for other cooking styles, but it also offers the added protection that you never need worry if the eating utensils have been properly washed.

In the most basic Indian restaurants and eating places the cooking is usually done right out front so you can actually see exactly what is going on and how it is done. Vegetables will be on the simmer all day and tend to be cooked out and mushy to western tastes. In these basic places dhal is usually free but you pay for *chappatis, parathas, puris* or rice. *Sabzi* (vegetable stew), dhal and a few chappatis makes a passable meal for less than Rs 5. If you order half plates of the various dishes brewing out front you get half the quantity at half the price and get a little more variety. With chutneys and a small plate of onions, which come free, you can put together a reasonable vegetarian meal for, say, Rs 5, or non-vegetarian for Rs 7 to 10. In railway station restaurants and other cheaper restaurants always check the prices and add up your bill. If it's incorrect query it.

At the other end of the price scale there are many restaurants in India's five star hotels that border on the luxurious and by western standards are really absurdly cheap. Paying US$8 to 12 for a meal in India seems exorbitant after you've been there for a while but check what a meal in your friendly local Hilton would cost you. As one traveller put it:

If not on a starvation budget the occasional splurge on a really good meal is very worthwhile in India. Best value are the unlimited 'buffet lunches' which are available at a number of the larger hotels. The *Taj Mahal Inter-Continental* in Bombay is one of the best. A large, opulent dining room complete with orchestra and an astonishing array of every kind of food imaginable. Rs 60, including service, covers all you can eat.

The *Oberoi Grand* in Calcutta comes a close second – a much smaller dining room here and perhaps not quite so much variety but the quality is even higher. Where else can you find a tray of steaks to help yourself from? It's slightly more expensive than the Taj but in Madras the *Connemara* is rather cheaper. The food here is not in quite such abundant variety but you can still eat yourself silly. Extras like soft drinks are very expensive in these hotels – drink water or make yourself a milk shake from the ice cream!

Many other international standard hotels, like the *Oberoi Palace* in Srinagar, offer similar deals. For budget travellers it makes a very pleasant change from dhal and rice.

Finally a couple of hints on how to cope with curry. After a while in India you'll get used to even the fiercest curries and you find western food surprisingly bland. If, however, you do find your mouth is on fire don't reach for water. In emergencies that hardly helps at all. Curd (yoghurt) or fruit do the job much more efficiently.

Curry & Spice

Believe it or not there is no such thing as 'curry' in India. It's an English invention, an all purpose term to cover the whole range of Indian food spicing. *Carhi*, incidentally, is a Gujarati dish but never ask for it in Kumaon where it's a very rude word!

Although all Indian food is certainly not curry this is still the basis of Indian cuisine. Curry doesn't have to be hot enough to blow your head off although it certainly can do that if it's made that way. Curry most definitely is not something found in a packet of curry powder. The Indian cook has about 25 spices on his or her regular list and it is from these that they produce the curry flavour. Usually the spices are freshly ground in a mortar and pestle known as a *sil-vatta*. Spices are usually blended in certain combinations to produce *masalas*. *Garam masala*, for example, is often a red hot combination of cloves and cinnamon with peppercorns.

Popular spices include *saffron*, an expensive spice produced from flowers. This is used to give rice that yellow biriyani colouring and delicate fragrance. *Turmeric* also has a colouring property, acts as a preservative and has a distinctive smell and taste. *Chillies* are ground, dried or added whole to supply that curry heat. They come in red and green varieties but it's the green ones which are hottest. *Ginger* is supposed to be good for the digestion while many masalas contain *coriander* because it is said to cool the body. Strong and sweet *cardamom* is used in many desserts and in rich meat dishes. Other popular spices include *nutmeg, cinnamon, poppy seeds, caraway seeds, cummin, fenugreek, mace, garlic* and *cloves*.

Breads & Grains

Rice is, of course, the basic Indian staple but although it is eaten throughout the country it's only in the south where it is all-important. In the north (where wheat is the staple) rice is supplemented by a whole range of breads known as *rotis* or in the Punjab by *phulka* (blown up). You can also find western style sliced bread (*double roti*) in India but it is almost always horrible, sickly sweet and nearly inedible. The best Indian rice, it is generally agreed, is found in the north where *Basmati* rice grows in the Dehra Dun Valley. It has long grains, is yellowish and has a slightly sweetish or 'bas' smell.

Indian breads are varied but always delicious. Simplest is the *chappati* which is just flour and water fried up like a thin pancake – it's really an English invention. Rotis are flour and water cooked on a hot *tawa* griddle. Direct heat blows it up but it depends on the glutin content of the wheat how well that works. Bast your roti in butter or ghee and it becomes a *paratha*. If you deep fried it you would have a *pouri* in the north or a *loochi* in the east. Made of lentil flour it would be a *dosa* in the south; dosas are actually found all over India and wrapped around curried vegetables you have *masala dosa*, a terrific snack meal. Another type of deep fried bread with a stuffing is the *kachori*. Bake the bread in an oven and you have *nan*. Whatever you do with it Indian rotis taste great.

Use your chappati or paratha to mop up or scoop up your curry. An *idli* is a kind of rice dumpling, often served with a spicy curd sauce or with spiced lentils and chutney. *Papadums* are crispy deep fried wafers often served with thalis or other meals.

Outside the Delhi Jami Masjid you may see 'big' chappatis known as *rumali* (handkerchiefs). Note that Hindus use their tawa concavely, Moslems convexly! In some hill stations (like Nainital or Mussoorie) you can get quite good western-style bread.

Basic Dishes

Curries can be vegetable, meat (usually chicken or lamb) or fish but they are always fried in *ghee*, clarified butter, or vegetable oil. North or south they will be accompanied by rice but in the north the various excellent breads will also come with them. There are a number of dishes which aren't really curries but are close enough to them for western tastes. *Vindaloos* have a vinegar marinade and tend to be hotter than most curries. *Pork vindaloo* is a favourite dish in Goa. *Kormas*, on the other hand, are rich, substantial dishes prepared by braising. *Doopiaza* literally means 'two onions' and is a type of korma which uses onions at two stages in its preparation.

Probably the most basic of Indian dishes is *dhal*, rather like a thick lentil soup. Lentils are *malka*. Dhal is almost always there whether as an accompaniment to a curry or as a very basic meal in itself with chappatis or rice. In many places dhal and rice is just about all there is on the menu so you'll get heartily sick of it before you leave! The favourite dhal of Bengal and Gujarat is yellow *arhar*, in Bengal *channa* is also yellow, *mung* is green, *rajma* is the Heinz 57 varieties of dhal!

Other basic dishes include *mattar panir* – cheese and peas in gravy; *saag gosht* – meat and spinach; *alu dum* – potato curry; *alu chhole* – spicy-sour chick peas and diced potatoes.

Tandoori & Biriyani

Tandoori food is a northern speciality and refers to the clay oven in which the food is cooked after first being marinaded in a complex mix of herbs and yoghurt. Tandoori food – tandoori chicken is a special favourite – is not as hot as curry dishes and usually tastes terrific.

Biriyani, and again chicken is a popular biriyani dish, is another northern Moghul dish. Here the chicken or other meat is mixed with a deliciously flavoured, orange-coloured rice which is sometimes spiced with nuts or dried fruit. A *pulao* is a simpler version of a biriyani and you will also find it in other Asian countries further west. Those who have the idea that Indian food is always curry and always fiery hot will be surprised by tandoori and biriyani dishes.

Regional Specialities

Rogan Josh is a straightforward curried lamb which is always popular in the north and in Kashmir where it originated. *Gushtaba*, pounded and spiced meat balls cooked in a yoghurt sauce, is another Kashmiri speciality. Still in the north *chicken makhanwala* is a rich dish cooked in a butter sauce.

Many coastal areas have excellent seafood including Bombay where the *pomfret*, a flounder like, fish is popular; as is Bombay duck which is not a duck at all but another fish dish. *Dhansak* is a Pharsi speciality found in Bombay – lamb or chicken cooked with curried lentils and steamed rice. Further south Goa also has excellent fish and prawns and in Kerala State, Cochin is famous for its prawns.

Another indication of the influence of central Asian cooking styles on north Indian food is the popularity of *kababs*. You'll find them all across north India with a number of local variations and specialities. The two basic forms are *sikka* (skewered) or *shami* (wrapped). In Calcutta *kati kababs* are a local favourite. Another Bengali dish is *dahi maach* – curried fish in yoghurt sauce, flavoured with ginger and turmeric. Further south in Hyderabad you could try *haleen*, pounded wheat with a lightly spiced mutton gravy. 'In Tamil Nadu', wrote a visitor, 'I particularly enjoyed *pongal* at breakfast, I think it's made of semolina with whole peppercorns'.

Side Dishes

Indian food generally has a number of side dishes to go alongside the main meal. Probably the most popular is *dahi* – curd or yoghurt. It has the useful ability of instantly cooling an over-heated curry – either blend it into the curry or, if it's too late, you can administer it straight to your mouth. Curd is often used in the cooking or as a dessert as well as appearing in the popular drink *lassi*. *Raita* is another popular side dish consisting of curd mixed with cooked or raw vegetables, particularly cucumber (just like Greek zatziki) or tomato.

Sabzi are curried vegetables, *bhartha* is pureed or minced vegetables (particularly in the north), *bhujias* are fresh vegetables. *Mulligatawny* is a soup like dish which is really just a milder, more liquid curry. It's a dish adopted into the English menu by the Raj. *Chutney* is pickled fruit or vegetables and is the standard relish for a curry

Thali

A *thali* is the all purpose Indian vegetarian dish. Although it is basically a product of south India you will find restaurants serving thalis or 'vegetarian plate meals' all over India. Often the sign will simply announce 'Meals'. In addition there are some regional variations like the particularly sumptuous Gujarati thalis.

It takes its name from the 'thali' dish in which it is served. This consists of a metal plate with a number of small metal bowls known as *katoris* on it. Sometimes the small bowls will be replaced by simple indentations right in the plate and in more basic places the 'plate' will be a big, fresh banana leaf. A thali consists of a variety of curry vegetable dishes, relishes, a couple of papadums, puris or dosas and a mountain of rice. A fancy thali may have a *palu*, a rolled leaf stuffed with fruit and nuts. There'll probably be a bowl of curd and possibly even a small dessert.

Thalis are consistently tasty and good food value but they have two other unbeatable plus points for the budget traveller – they're cheap and they're usually 100% filling. Thalis can be as little as Rs 4 and will rarely cost much more than Rs 10 at the very most – big hotel

apart. A thali is usually 100% filling because they're almost always 'all you can eat'. When your plate starts to get empty they come round, add another mountain of rice and refill the katoris. Thalis are always eaten with fingers although you may get a spoon for the dahi or dhal. Always wash your hands before you eat a thali – a sink or other place to wash your hands is always provided in a thali restaurant.

Street vendor setting up...

Snacks

Samosa, tasty little curried vegetable snacks, fried up in a pastry triangle, are found all over India. *Bhelpuri* is a popular Bombay snack peddled all over the city. *Chana* is spiced chick peas *(gram)* served with puris. *Sambhar* is a soup like lentil and vegetable dish with a sour tamarind flavour.

Western Food

Sometimes Indian food simply becomes too much and you want to escape to something familiar and reassuring. It's not always easy but railway station restaurants often have something palatable and close to 'back home'. The Indian food blues are particularly prone to hit you at breakfast time – somehow idlis never really feel like a breakfast. Fortunately that's the meal where you'll find an approximation to the west most easily obtained. All those wonderful Indian varieties of eggs can be obtained – half-fried, omelettes, you name it.

Toast and jam can almost always be found and very often you can get cornflakes and hot milk, although Indian cornflakes would definitely be rejects from Mr Kellogg's production line. The Scots must have visited India too, because porridge is often available on the breakfast menu. If you ask for toast and marmalade say it slowly because you may end up with 'toast and aamlet' – omlette.

That peculiar Raj-era term for a mid-morning snack still lives – tiffin. Today tiffin means any sort of light meal or snack. One western dish which Indians seem to have come 100% to terms with is chips (French fries). It's quite amazing how, if they are available, they will almost always be excellent. To be safe ask for 'finger chips' or you may end up with what the English know as 'potato crisps' although to Americans they'll be 'potato chips'! Some Indian cooks call French fries 'Chinese potatoes'.

Other Asian foods, apart from Indian, are also often available. There's still a small Chinese population, particularly in Calcutta and Bombay, so you can find Chinese food in the larger cities. In the north where many Tibetans have settled, following the Chinese invasion of Tibet, you'll find some Tibetan restaurants in places like Dharamsala, Manali or Srinagar.

Desserts & Sweets

Indians have quite a sweet tooth and an amazing selection of desserts and sweets to satisfy it. Kulfi is a widely available dessert, a sort of Indian interpretation of ice cream. You can, of course, also get normal ice cream all over India. The major brands are healthy and very good. Rasgullas are another very popular Indian dessert, sweet little balls of rose water flavoured cream cheese.

The desserts are basically rice or milk puddings, various interesting things in sweet syrup or else sweet pastries. Gulub jamuns are a typical example of the small 'things' in syrup – they're made of flour, yoghurt and ground almonds. Jalebi are pancakes in syrup. Milk dishes are usually boiled until the liquid has been removed and then have various ingredients added to make a dessert like barfi which has coconut with almond or pistachio flavouring. Sandesh is another variety of milk dish, a particular favourite in Calcutta. Payasam is a southern sweet made from milk simmered with crushed cashews, cereals and sugar, topped with raisins. Firnee is a rice-pudding dessert with almonds, raisins and pistachios.

Many of the Indian sweets come covered in a thin layer of silver, as do some of the desserts. It's just that, silver beaten paper thin. Don't peel it off, it's quite edible. There are countless sweet shops with their goodies all lined up in glass showcases. Prices vary from Rs 5 to 10 for a kg but you can order 50 or 100 gm at a time or simply ask for a rupee's worth. These shops also often sell dahi (curd) which makes a very pleasant dessert as well as being a good curry cooler. Sweets include all sorts of unidentifiable goodies, try them and see. Halwa is a translucent, vividly coloured sweet rather like Turkish delight.

Fruit

If your sweet tooth simply isn't sweet enough to cope with too many Indian desserts you'll be able to fall back on

India's wide variety of fruit. It varies all the way from tropical delights in the south to apples, apricots and other temperate region fruits in the north. Some local specialities include cherries and strawberries in Kashmir. Apricots are found in Ladakh and in Himachal Pradesh. Apples are found all over this north-western region but particularly in the Kulu Valley of Himachal Pradesh.

Melons are widespread all over India, particularly watermelons which are a fine thirst quencher when you're unhappy about the water and fed up with soft drinks. Try to get the first slice before the flies discover it. Coconuts are even better and in the hot season there'll be coconut stalls on many city street corners. When you've drunk the milk the stall holder will split the coconut open and cut you a slice from the outer covering to scoop the flesh out with.

Mangoes and bananas are also found in many parts of India and also pineapples in Assam and elsewhere. You don't see oranges all over the place (lots in Kerala though) but tangerines are widespread in central India, particularly during the hot season. You can go through an awful lot of them in a day.

Pan

An Indian meal should properly be finished with *pan* – the name given to the collection of spices and condiments chewed with *betel*. Found throughout eastern Asia betel is a mildly intoxicating and addictive nut but by itself it is quite inedible. After a meal you chew a pan as a mild digestive.

Pan sellers have a whole collection of little trays, boxes and containers in which they mix up either *sadha* (plain or *mitha* (sweet) pans. The ingredient may include, apart from the betel nut itself, lime paste (the chemical not the fruit), the powder known as *catachu*, various spices and even a dash of opium in a pricey pan. The whole concoction is folded up in a piece of edible leaf which you pop in your mouth and chew. When finished you simply spit the left-overs out and add another red blotch to the sidewalk. Over a long period of time indulgence in pan will turn your teeth red-black and even addict you to the betel nut. But trying one occasionally won't do you any harm.

Cooking Back Home

There are all sorts of books about Indian cooking should you want to continue the experiment after you leave India. *Indian Cookery* by Dharamjit Singh (Penguin, London, 1970) is a useful paperback introduction to the art.

Drinks – Non-Alcoholic

Surprisingly tea is not the all purpose and all important drink it is in Iran and Afghanistan. Worse the Indians, for all the tea they grow, make some of the most hideously over-sweetened, murkily-milky excuse for that fine beverage you ever saw. It may go by the name of *chai*, just like the rest of Asia, but what a let down. Still some people like it and it is cheap. Don't think of bazaar tea as tea in the western sense was the advice one traveller gave!

Better tea can be obtained if you ask for 'tray tea' which gives you the tea, the milk and the sugar separately and allows you to combine them as you see fit. Usually tea is 'mixed tea' which means it has been made by putting cold water, milk, sugar and tea all into one pot and bringing the whole concoction to the boil then letting it stew for a long time. The result can be imagined.

Tea is more popular in the north while in the south coffee, which is generally good, is the number one drink. There are Indian Coffee Houses all over the country. You should not drink water unless you know it has been boiled but frankly that is often a difficult thing to do. In the hot season it is simply too dry not to drink water – if you quenched your thirst all the time on Indian soft drinks you'd drop dead from a sugar overdose.

Water is generally safer in the dry

season than the monsoon (when it really can be dangerous) and adding your own purifying tablets can further improve it. Some travellers report that in the major cities it is 'certainly chlorinated' and can be drunk without ill effect. You can probably count on the water being reasonably safe in big hotels and the better restaurants. Although it is no safer than the water it's made with, lemon squash, *nimbu pani*, is almost always excellent in India. Bottled mineral water can be bought in many centres.

Soft drinks are a safe substitute for water although they tend to have a high sugar content. Coca Cola got the boot from India a few years back for not co-operating with the government but there are many substitutes with names like Campa Cola, Thums Up, Limca, Fanta, Gold Spot or Double Seven. By Asian standards they are pretty expensive at around Rs 1.50 to 2.50 for a 190 ml bottle. They're also very sickly sweet if you drink too many of them, as you're virtually forced to do in the hot season. One very pleasant escape is the Kashmiri apple juice drink Apco but unfortunately it's only really available in Kashmir. Apple juice drinks are also available in Himachal Pradesh and from Bhutan.

Coconut milk, straight from the young coconut, is a popular street side drink. Another escape from soft drinks is soda water – Bisleri Soda is particularly widely available and has the further advantage over soft drinks of coming in a larger bottle. With soda water you can get excellent, and safe, lemon squash sodas. Finally there's *lassi*, that oh so cool, refreshing and delicious iced curd (yoghurt) drink.

Drinks – Alcoholic

Alcohol is expensive – a bottle of Indian beer can cost anything from Rs 8 up to Rs 30 or more in a flashy hotel; Rs 8 to 20 is the usual price range. Some states (like Goa) are very cheap, some (like Tamil Nadu) very expensive. Indian beers have

delightful names like Golden Eagle, Rosy Pelican, Cannon Extra Strong, Kingfisher, Guru or Punjab. They're not too bad if you can find them cold but all tend to be rather gassy.

Beer and other Indian interpretations of western alcoholic drinks are known as IMFL – Indian Made Foreign Liquor. Local drinks are known as Country Liquor and include *toddy*, a mildly alcoholic extract from the coconut palm flower, and *feni*, a distilled liquor produced from fermented cashew nuts or from coconuts. The two varieties taste quite different.

Indian Menus

One of the delights of Indian menus is the amazing way writers can have with English. Start the morning, for example, with corn flaks, also useful for shooting down enemy aircraft. Or perhaps corn flex, Indian corn flakes are often so soggy they'll do just that.

Even before your corn-whatever you should have some tea and what a variety of types of tea India can offer. You can try bed tea, milk tea, light tea, mixed tea, tray tea, plain tea, half set tea and even (of course) full set tea. Eggs also offer unlimited possibilities. Like half fried eggs, or pouch eggs or (alternatively) egg pooch, or bolid eggs, sliced omelettes, or skerem boil eggs (interesting combination there) or simply aggs. Finally you could finish off breakfast with that popular Scottish dish – pordge.

Soup before a meal – how about French onion soap? Or Scotch brath, mughutoni or perhaps start with a parn coactale. Follow that up with some amazing interpretations of western dishes, like the restaurant that not only had Napoleon spaghetti but also Stalin spaghetti! Perhaps a seezling plator sounds more like it? Or simply bum chicken? A light meal – well why not have a sandwitch? And if you want a drink how about orange squish or that popular Indian soft drink Thumps Up.

Chinese dishes offer a whole new range of

possibilities including mashrooms and bamboo sooghts, spring rolos, plane fried rice and park fried rice. Finally for dessert you could try apple pai or treat yourself to leeches & cream!

Travellers sent in lots more menu suggestions since the first edition of this book. Like 'tired fruit juice' (tinned you know), 'plane tost' (the stuff they serve on Indian Airlines?), 'omlet & began', 'scram bled eggs', 'banana frilters' and 'chocolet padding'.

BOOKS

India is a great place for reading – there's plenty to read about, on those never ending bus or train trips there is plenty of time to read, and when you get to the big cities you'll find plenty of bookshops to get the reading matter from. The suggested books that follow are only a few ideas of interesting books that should be readily available. Of course there are far more books of great interest but now long out of print. In addition there are many beautiful coffee table books on India – ideal for whetting the appetite or for conjuring up the magic of India after your return. India has equally spawned a large number of cookery books – if you want to get into curry and all those spices you'll have no trouble finding plenty of instructions. Indian art has also generated a great number of interesting books of all types.

India is also one of the world's largest publishers of books in English. After the USA and the UK it's up there with Canada or Australia as a major English language publisher. You'll find a great number of interesting books on India by Indian publilshers, books which are generally not available in the west. At the other extreme Indian publishers also do cheap reprints of western bestsellers at prices far below western levels. A meaty Leon Uris or Arthur Hailey novel, ideal for an interminable train ride, will often cost less than $2. Compare that with your local bookshop prices. Recently published

British and American books also reach Indian bookshops remarkably fast and with very low markups.

Novels

Plenty of authors have taken the opportunity of setting their novels in a continent as colourful as India. Rudyard Kipling with books like *Kim* and *Plain Tales from the Hills* is the Victorian English interpreter of India par excellence. In *A Passage to India* E M Forster perfectly captures that collision of incomprehension between the English in India and the Indians. A very readable book.

Much more recent but again following that curious question of why the English and Indians, so dissimilar in many ways were also so similar in others, is Ruth Prawer Jhabwala *The Heat and The Dust*. The contemporary narrator of the tale also describes the backpacker's India in a flawless fashion.

Probably the most widely acclaimed Indian novel since the war was Salman Rushdie's *Midnight's Children* which won the Booker Prize. It tells of the children who were born, like modern India itself, at the stroke of midnight on that August night in 1947 and how one particular 'midnight's child' has his life inextricably intertwined with events in India itself. His follow up, *Shame*, is set in modern Pakistan.

Paul Scott's *The Raj Quartet* and *Staying On* are other important novels set in India. The big 'bestseller' Indian novel of recent years was the monster tome *Far Pavilions* by M M Kaye. Women's magazine romance in some ways but also some interesting angles on India.

General Books

John Keay's *Into India* (John Murray, London, 1973) is a fine general introduction to travelling in India. One traveller's observations and perceptions of life in India today provide an illuminating idea of what it's really like.

Paul Theroux's best selling railway odyssey *The Great Railway Bazaar* takes you up and down India by train (and across most of the rest of Asia) and turns the whole world into a railway carriage. Engrossing, like most such books, as much for insights into the author as into the people he meets. *Slow Boats to China* by Gavin Powell follows much the same path but this time by boat and has interesting accounts of a number of boat trips around India. *Slowly Down the Ganges* by Eric Newby is another boat trip tale, this one borders, at times, on sheer masochism!

Karma Kola by Gita Mehta is accurately subtitled 'the marketing of the mystic east'. It amusingly and cynically describes the unavoidable and hilarious collision between India looking to the west for technology and modern methods while the west was descending upon India in search of ancient wisdom.

Ved Mehta has written a number of interesting personal views of India. *Walking the Indian Streets* (Penguin paperback) is a slim and highly readable account of the culture shock he went through on returning to India after a long period abroad. *Portrait of India* is by the same author. Ronald Segal's *The Crisis of India* (Penguin, London, 1965) is written by a South African Indian on the theme that spirituality is not always more important than a full stomach – a counter argument to all the praise of Hinduism and its spirituality. Readers have recommended *Eating the Indian Air* by John Morris; *The Gorgeous East* by Rupert Croft-Cooke; *Delhi is Far Away* and *The Grand Trunk Road* by John Wiles and books by Jan and Rumer Godden.

Finally no survey of personal insights into India can ignore V S Naipaul's two controversial books *An Area of Darkness* and *India – A Wounded Civilisation*. Born in Trinidad but of Indian descent Naipaul tells in the first book of how India, unseen and unvisited, had haunted him and the impact upon him when he finally did make

the pilgrimage to the motherland. You may well find that much of this book rings very true with your own experiences while in India. In the second book he writes of India's unsuccessful search for a new purpose and meaning for its civilisation.

History

If you want a thorough introduction to Indian history then look for the Pelican two volume *A History of India*. In volume 1 Romila Thapar follows Indian history from about 1000 BC to the coming of the Moghuls in the 16th century AD. Volume 2 by Percival Spear follows the rise and fall of the Moghuls through to India since independence. At times both volumes are a little dry but if you want a reasonably detailed history in a handy paperback format they're worth having.

The Wonder that was India by A L Basham gives detailed descriptions of the Indian civilisations, origins of the caste system and social customs, detailed information on Hinduism, Buddhism and other religions in India and is very informative about art and architecture. It has a wealth of background material on ancient India without being overly academic.

Christopher Hibbert's *The Great Mutiny – India 1857* (Penguin, London, 1980) is a recently published single volume description of the often lurid events of the Mutiny. This readable paperback is illustrated with contemporary photographs.

Plain Tales from the Raj edited by Charles Allen (Futura paperback, London, 1976) is the delightful book derived from the delightful series of radio programmes of the same name. It consists of a series of interviews with people who took part in British India on both sides of the table. Extremely readable and full of fascinating little insights into life during the Raj era.

Freedom at Midnight is India's best selling book of the past decade. Its authors Larry Collins and Dominique

Lapierre have written other equally popular modern histories but you could hardly ask for a more enthralling series of events than those that led to India's independence in 1947. In India you can find *Freedom at Midnight* in a cheap Bell Books paperback (Vikas Publishing, Delhi, 1976).

Religion

If you want to understand India's religions a little better there are plenty of books about them available in India. The English series of Penguin paperbacks are amongst the best and are generally available in India. In particular *Hinduism* by K M Sen (Penguin, London, 1961) is brief and to the point. If you want to read the Hindu holy books those are also available in translations: *The Upanishads* (Penguin, London, 1965) and *The Bhagavad Gita* (Penguin, London, 1962).

Penguin also have a translation of the Koran and if you want to know more about Buddhism *Buddhism* by Christmas Humphreys (Penguin, London, 1949) is an excellent introduction.

Guides

First published in 1859 the 22nd edition of *A Handbook for Travellers in India, Pakistan, Nepal, Bangladesh & Sri Lanka* (John Murray, London, 1975) is that rarest of animals, a Victorian travel guide. If you've got a deep interest in Indian architecture and can afford the somewhat hefty price then take along a copy of this immensely detailed guidebook. Unfortunately its system of following 'routes', in the manner of all good Victorian guidebooks, makes it somewhat difficult to locate things but the effort is worth it. Along the way you'll find a lot of places where the British army made gallant stands and find more than a few statues of Queen Victoria – most of which have been replaced by statues of Mahatma Gandhi.

There are a great number of regional and local guidebooks published in India. Many of them are excellent value and describe certain sites (the Ajanta and Ellora Caves or Sanchi for example) in much greater detail than is possible in this book. The guides produced by the Archaeological Survey of India are particularly good. Many of the other guides have a most amusing way with English.

Other Lonely Planet Regional Guides

It's pleasant to be able to claim that for more information on India's neighbours and for travel beyond India most of the best guides come from Lonely Planet! If you're heading north to Nepal then look for *Kathmandu & the Kingdom of Nepal* with complete information on the mountain nation. If you're planning on trekking in Nepal or simply want more information on trekking in general then look for *Trekking in the Nepal Himalaya* and the forthcoming *Trekking in the Indian Himalaya*.

For other Indian neighbours there is also, generally, a Lonely Planet guide. *Pakistan – a travel survival kit* was published at the same time as this India guide and is the first guide to the 'unknown land of the Indus'. *Burma – a travel survival kit* covers that thoroughly delightful and totally eccentric country. If your travels take you south to Sri Lanka then you need *Sri Lanka – a travel survival kit* whether you're planning to explore the ancient cities or simply laze on the beaches. A Lonely Planet guide to Bangladesh is on its way. Finally if you simply want more information on the north-west of India then look for our comprehensive guide to *Kashmir, Ladakh & Zanskar*.

If you're travelling further than India across Asia to Europe (Iran permitting) then our book is *West Asia on a Shoestring*. If it's further east you want then look for *South-East Asia on a Shoestring*.

FILMS

Once you've read all you can about India keep your eyes open for a showing of Louis

Malle's two-part film *Phantom India*. Running about seven hours in all this is a fascinating in-depth look at India today. At times it's very self-indulgent but as an overall view it can't be beaten – and it has been banned in India. The Australian ABC TV channel has produced two excellent documentary series on India, one titled *Journey into India*, the other *Journey into the Himalayas*. Both of them, but particularly the former, are worth seeing if you get a chance.

Of course the epic film *Gandhi* has been the major recent India film and it's also spawned a host of new and reprinted books on the Mahatma. *Heat and Dust* has also been made into an excellent film and the success of *Gandhi* will, no doubt, inspire other films on Indian themes in the next few years.

MAPS

Bartholomew's map of *India, Pakistan, Nepal, Bangladesh & Sri Lanka* is probably the most useful general map for India. It gives you plenty of detail of small towns and villages to help speed along those long bus or train trips. If it has any fault for the traveller it is that it does not always include places of great interest but small population. The map is widely available in India as well as overseas.

Locally the Government Map Office produces a series of maps covering all of India. In Delhi their office is opposite the tourist office on Janpath. It's upstairs, above the cafeteria beside the Central Cottage Industries Emporium. The maps are not really all that useful since they will not allow production of anything at a reasonable scale which shows India's sea or land borders. It is illegal to take any Survey of India map of larger than 1:250,000 scale out of the country.

The Government of India Tourist Office has a number of excellent give-away city maps and also a reasonable all India map. State tourist offices do not have much by the way of maps but the Himachal Pradesh office has three excellent trekking maps which cover the trekking routes in that state.

THINGS TO BUY (AND SELL)

India is packed with beautiful things to buy – you could easily load yourself up to the eyeballs with goodies you pick up around the country. The cardinal rule with purchasing handicrafts is to bargain and bargain hard. You can get a good idea of what is reasonable in quality and in price by visiting the various state emporiums, particularly in New Delhi, and the Central Cottage Industries Emporiums. Here you can inspect items from all over the country at fixed prices which indicate fairly well what you can knock the regular dealers down below.

As with handicrafts in any country don't buy until you have developed a little understanding and appreciation. Rushing in and buying the first thing you see will inevitably lead to later disappointment. In touristy places, particularly places like Varanasi, take extreme care with the commission merchants – these guys hang around waiting to pick you up and cart you off to their favourite dealers where whatever you pay will have a hefty margin built in to it to pay their commission. Stories about 'my family's place', 'special deal at my friend's place', are just stories and nothing more.

Carpets

It may not surprise you that India produces and exports more hand crafted carpets than Iran but it probably is more of a surprise that some of them are of virtually equal quality. In Kashmir, where India's best carpets are produced, the carpet making techniques and styles were brought in from Persia even before the Moghul era. The art flourished under the Moghuls and today Kashmir is packed with small carpet producers. There are many carpet dealers in Delhi as well as in Kashmir. Persian motifs have been much embellished on Kashmiri carpets which come in a variety of sizes – three by five foot, four by six foot and so on. They are either made of pure wool, wool with a small percentage of silk to give a sheen (known as silk touch) or pure silk. The latter are more for decoration than hard wear. Expect to pay from Rs 5000 for a good quality four by six carpet and don't be surprised if the price is more than twice as high.

Other carpet making areas include Badhoi and Mirzapur in Uttar Pradesh or Warangal and Eluru in Andhra Pradesh. In Kashmir and Rajasthan the coarsely woven woollen *numdas* are made. These are more primitive and folksy than the fine carpets. Around the Himalayas and Uttar Pradesh *daris*, flat weave cotton warp and weft rugs are woven. In Kashmir *gabbas* are applique-like rugs. The many Tibetan refugees in India have brought their craft of making superbly colourful Tibetan rugs with them. A three by five foot Tibetan rug will be less than Rs 1000.

Unless you're an expert it is best to have expert advice or buy from a reputable dealer if you're spending large amounts of money on carpets. Check prices back home too, many western carpet dealers sell at prices you would have difficulty matching even at source.

Papier Mache

This is probably the most characteristic Kashmiri craft work. The basic papier mache article is made in a mould then painted and polished in successive layers until the final intricate design is produced. Prices depend upon the complexity and quality of the painted design and the amount of gold leaf used. Items made include bowls, cups, containers, jewel boxes, letter holders, tables, lamps, coasters, trays and so on. A cheap bowl might cost only Rs 10, a large, well made item might approach Rs 1000.

Pottery

In Rajasthan interesting white glazed pottery is made with hand-painted blue flower designs. They're attractively

simple in their design. Terracotta images of the gods and children's toys are made in Bihar.

Metal Work

Copper and brass items are popular throughout India. Candle holders, trays, bowls, tankards, ashtrays are all made in Bombay and other centres. In Rajasthan and Uttar Pradesh the brass is inlaid with exquisite designs in red, green and blue enamel. *Bidhri* is a craft of Andhra Pradesh and particularly Hyderabad where silver is inlaid into gunmetal. Hookah pipes, lamp bases and jewellery boxes are all made in this manner.

Jewellery

Many Indian women put most of their wealth into jewellery so it is no wonder that there is so much of it available. For western tastes the heavy folk-art jewellery of Rajasthan has particular appeal. You'll find it all over the country but in Rajasthan in the greatest profusion of all. In the north you'll also find Tibetan jewellery, even chunkier and more folk-like than the Rajasthan variety.

Leatherwork

Of course Indian leatherwork is not made from cow-hide but from buffalo-hide or some other substitute. Chappals, those basic sandals found all over India are the most popular purchase. In craft shops in Delhi you can find well made leather bags, handbags and other items. In Kashmir leather shoes and boots, often of quite good quality, are made, along with coats and jackets of often abysmally low quality.

Textiles

This is still India's major industry and 40% of the total production is made at the village level where it is known as *khadi*. Bedspreads, table cloths, cushion covers or material for clothes are all popular purchases. There are an amazing variety of styles, types and techniques around the country. In Gujarat and Rajasthan heavy material is embroidered with tiny mirrors and beads to produce the mirror-work used in everything from dresses to stuffed toys to wall hangings. Tie-dye work is also popular in Rajasthan.

In Kashmir embroidered materials are made into shirts and dresses. Fine shawls of *pashmina* goats' wool also come from Kashmir. *Phulkari* bedspreads or wall hangings come from the Punjab. *Batik* is a recent introduction from Indonesia but already widespread, *Kalamkari* cloth from Andhra Pradesh and Gujurat is an associated but far older craft.

Bronze Figures

In the south delightful small images of the gods are made by the age old lost wax process. In this a wax figure is made then a mould formed around it and the wax melted and poured out. The molten metal is poured in and when solidified the mould is broken open. Figures of Shiva as dancing Nataraj are amongst the most popular.

Wood Carving

In the south images of the gods are also carved out of sandalwood. Rosewood is used to carve animals, elephants in particular. Carved wooden furniture and other household items, either in natural finish or lacquered, are also made in various locations. In Kashmir intricately carved wooden screens, tables, jewellery boxes, trays and the like are carved from Indian walnut. They follow a similar pattern to that seen on the decorative trim of houseboats. Old temple carvings can be delightful.

Clothes & Saris

In Bombay and Delhi in particular you can find many readymades exactly like those you'll find from India in western boutiques. Indeed they're most probably the rejects from some export order or other. The prices are so low you need hardly worry but as usual it's wise to check

the quality. Saris, the most Indian of women's outfits, are made in various styles and types of material around the country. In Varanasi they're made of silk, often with gold edging.

Paintings

Reproductions of the beautiful old miniatures are painted in many places but beware of paintings claimed to be antique – they're highly unlikely to be so. Also note that quality can vary very widely, low prices often mean low quality and if you buy before you've had a chance to look at a lot of miniatures and develop some appreciation you'll inevitably find you bought unwisely.

Other

Marble inlay pieces from Agra are pleasant reminders of the beauty of the Taj, they either come as simple little pieces or larger items like jewellery boxes. Applique work is popular in many places such as Orissa but in the Kutch region of Gujarat interesting stuffed toys are made. Indian musical instruments always have an attraction to travellers although you don't see nearly as many backpackers lugging sitars around as you did 10 years ago. A more sensible Indian music buy might be records or tapes. You can always take back Indian tea, food products like mango pickles or papadums, packs of beedies. At the many Bata shoe shops in India western style shoes are cheap and reasonably well made. Their best quality men's shoes are about US$20 to 25, fgar less than shoes of similar quality in London or New York.

Antiques

Articles over 100 years are not allowed to be exported out of India. If you have doubts about some item and consider that it could be defined as an antique you can check with:

Bombay – Superintending Archaeologist,

Antiquities, Archaeological Survey of India, Sion Fort.

Calcutta – Superintending Archaeologist, Eastern Circle, Archaeological Survey of India, Narayani Building, Brabourne Rd.

New Delhi – Director, Antiquities, Archaeological Survey of India, Janpath.

Madras – Superintending Archaeologist, Southern Circle, Archaeological Survey of India, Fort St George.

Srinagar – Superintending Archaeologist, Frontier Circle, Archaeological Survey of India, Minto Bridge.

Things to Sell

All sorts of western technological items are good things to sell in India but note that cameras, tape recorders, typewriters and the like will most probably be entered into your passport to ensure they leave the country with you. Particularly in Calcutta, Delhi and Madras there is a good market for your bottle of duty free whisky (say Rs 250). The same applies in Patna if you fly down from Nepal. It has been suggested that prices are even better in smaller towns.

Pocket calculators and watches are popular things to sell and are less likely to be recorded in your passport. The best market is for high quality watches, not cheap digital things. Don't try and bring several of the same items through customs – it's a bit obvious. Make sure they have 'made in.....' prominently marked on them. Japan or West Germany are preferable to Taiwan, Korea, etc. Your selling price will be much better if you can supply original boxes, instruction manuals and the lot. It's necessary to bargain hard. In Delhi the underground market is a good place to sell, in Bombay along D Naoragi Rd between Victoria Terminus and Flora Fountain.

Be very wary of the buying to sell later game – most people buying things in India to sell elsewhere know what they are about and have spent a lot of time testing the market and establishing good relations with suppliers. Buying precious stones in Agra and Jaipur to sell in Nepal is a favourite game which is unlikely to return the average traveller any profit.

LANGUAGE

There is no 'Indian' language which is part of the reason why English is still so widely spoken, over 30 years after the British left. The country is divided up into a great number of local languages and in many cases the state boundaries have been drawn on linguistic lines. In all there are 14 major languages in India and probably over two hundred minor languages and dialects. The scope for misunderstanding can be easily appreciated!

The most important Indian language is Hindi, spoken by about 50% of the population. In recent years major efforts have been made to promote Hindi as the national language of India and to gradually phase out English. A stumbling block to this plan is that while Hindi is the predominant language in the north and also related to other northern languages such as Punjabi, Gujarati, Oriya and Bengali it bears little relation to the Dravidian languages of the south and in the south very few people speak Hindi. Tamil is the most important Dravidian language while others include Telugu, Kanada and Malayalam. It is from the south where the most vocal opposition to the adoption of Hindi comes and the strongest support for the retention of English.

For many educated Indians, English is virtually their first language and for a great number of Indians who speak more than one language it will be their second language rather than another Indian language. Thus it is very easy to get around India with English – after all many Indians have to speak English to each other if they wish to communicate. Nevertheless it's always nice to know at least a little of the local language so the following words and phrases are in Hindi:

where is a hotel (tourist office)?	hotal (turist afis) kahan hai?
how far is....?	....kitni dur hai?
how do I get to....?	....kojane ke liye kaise jana parega?
hello, goodbye	namaste
yes/no	han/nahin
please	meharbani se
thank you	shukriya, dhanyawad
how much?	kitne paise?
this is expensive	yeh bahut mehnga hai
what is your name?	apka shubh nam?
what is the time?	kya baja hai?
come here	yahan ao
show me the menu	mujha minu dikhao
the bill please	bill lao
big	bara
small	chota
today	aaj
day	din
night	rat
week	saptah
month	mahina
year	sal
medicine	dawa
ice	baraf
egg	anda
fruit	phal
vegetables	sabzi
water	pani
rice	chawal
tea	chai
coffee	kafi
milk	dudh
sugar	chini
butter	makkhan

Beware of *acha*, that all purpose word for 'OK'. It can also mean 'OK, I understand what you mean, but it isn't OK'. As in 'have you got a room available?' to which the answer 'acha' means 'I understand you want a room but I haven't got one'.

Tamil

Although Hindi is being promoted as the 'official' language of India it won't get you very far in the south where Tamil reigns supreme. The following words and phrases are in Tamil:

I want to go to.....	naan .... kku poka-vendum
how do I get there?	naan anke eppadi povathu
where is ....?	yenge irukkirathu
good morning /good night	vanakkam
good bye	poi varukiren
good bye (to you)	poi varungal
how do you do	nalama
yes/no	aam/illai
thank you	nandri
how much?	vilai enna
too expensive	athika vilai
big	perithu
small	siriyathu
good	nallathu
bad	kettathu
today	indru
day	naal
day	pahal neram
night	iravu neram
week	vaaram
month	maatham
year	varudam
eat	sappidu
drink	kudi

There are many phrase books and teach yourself books available in India for Hindi and the other major languages, if you want to learn more of the language. Some of them are typically and amusingly Indian. A section on a visit to the doctor in one phrase book included the following useful series of phrases, the first of which is quite unlikely in India:

I suffer from severe constipation
I am feeling a bit out of sorts today
The patient is sinking fast
He has much run down

The patient is in a precarious condition

Cholera has broken out in the city

He is dying by inches

Numbers

A peculiarity of Indian numbers is that whereas we count in tens, hundreds, thousands, millions, billions the Indian numbering system goes tens, hundreds, thousands, hundred thousands, ten millions. A hundred thousand is a *lakh* and ten million is a *crore*.

These two words are almost always used in place of their English equivalent. Thus you will see ten lakh rather than one million and one crore rather than ten million. Furthermore the numerals are generally written that way too – thus 3,00,000 (three lakh) not 300,000 (three hundred thousand) or 1,05,00,000 (one crore, five lakh) not 10,500,000 (ten million, five hundred thousand). If you say something costs five crore or someone is worth ten lakh it always means 'worth of rupees'.

	Hindi	*Tamil*
1	ek	onru
2	do	irandu
3	tin	moonru
4	char	naangu
5	panch	ainthu
6	chhe	aaru
7	sat	ezhu
8	ath	ettu
9	nau	onpathu
10	das	paththu
100	sau	nooru
1000	hazar	aayiram
100,000	lakh	
10,000,000	crore	

WHERE TO FIND WHAT

India can offer almost anything you want whether it's beaches, forts, amazing travel experiences, fantastic spectacles or simply a search for yourself. Below are just a few of those possibilities and where to start looking.

Beaches

People don't generally come all the way to India simply to laze on a beach – but there are some superb beaches here if you're in that mood. On the west coast, at the southern end of Kerala there's Kovalam while further north Goa has a whole collection of beautiful beaches complete with the soft white sand, the gentle lapping waves, the swaying palms, just like on the postcards. Over on the east coast you could try the beach at Mahabalipuram in Tamil Nadu. From the Shore Temple the beaches stretch north towards Madras and there are some fine places to stay. In Orissa the great temple of Konarak is only a couple of km away from another superb, and virtually deserted, beach.

Faded Touches of the Raj

Although the British have been gone from India for over 30 years there are still many places where you'd hardly know it. Of course much of India's government system, bureaucracy, communications, sport (the Indians are crazy over cricket) and media are British to the core but you'll also find the British touch in more unusual, enjoyable and amusing ways. For example the Fairlawn Hotel in Calcutta where the Raj definitely lives in totally unfaded glory. The imposing Victoria Memorial, also in Calcutta, where they tried to build an imitation British Taj Mahal. The Maharajah's Palace in Mysore, rebuilt after it burnt down earlier this century.

Could anything be more British than the Dal Lake houseboats, all chintz, overstuffed armchairs and understatement? Or the Residency at Lucknow where with stiff upper lip the British held out against those pesky mutineers in 1857. Or relax in true British style for afternoon tea at Gleneary's Tea Rooms in Darjeeling, come to think of it all of Darjeeling is a touch of the Raj.

Freak Centres

India has been the ultimate goal of the on-the-road-hippy-dream for years and somehow the '60s still continues in India's kind climate. From the clothes, the attitude and the music, Woodstock lives and the Beatles haven't even broken up yet. Goa has always been a great freak centre, the beaches are an attraction at any time of the year and every full moon is the occasion for a great gathering of the clans – but Christmas is Goa's peak period when half the freaks in India seem to flock to its beaches.

In Rajasthan the holy lake of Pushkar has a smaller, but semi-permanent, freak population. Or south at Kovalam the fine beaches attract a steady clientele. The technicolour Tibetan outlook on life (they've got a way with hotels and restaurants too) works well in Kathmandu so why not in India – you'll find Dharamsala and Manali, both in Himachal Pradesh, also have longer-term populations of visitors. Varanasi and the holy Ganges also has a freak centre reputation as does Mysore in the south. Hampi, capital of the Vijayanagar kingdom, is very small in terms of number of visitors but definitely on the circuit. Finally Mahabalipuram, south of Madras on the east coast, has temples and beaches too, a sure-fire combination.

Great Places to Stay

India has some superb hotels – it's also got a large number of bug-infested filthy dumps and a fair number of 'internattional class' hotels which are mediocre in standards and service but decidedly first class in price. But it's hard to think of a more enchanting hotel than the Lake Palace in Udaipur – it's far more than merely a palace; elegant, whimsical and romantic are all labels that can be applied to it. Or in Kashmir staying on a housebout is half the fun of going there, they come in all price ranges from the rock bottom 'doonga boats' to 'five star' luxury complete with television.

The Fairlawn Hotel in Calcutta is Raj style elegance totally untarnished by time, a shame if this one ever fades. In Bombay the elegant Taj Mahal Inter-Continental Hotel is probably the best in India – even if you don't stay there its air-conditioned lounge and strategic location is a magnet for everyone from back-packers on up. There are some very fine Tourist Bungalows, run by the state government tourist offices, scattered around India. They're often in fine locations and they're cheap. At the Ajanta Caves the Fardapur Holiday Camp (a tourist bungalow in all but name) is absurdly cheap, very comfortable and has a great verandah to sit around on and sip a lukewarm beer. Pushkar has the delightful fortress-like Sarovar Tourist Bungalow overlooking the lake. Tanjore also has an excellent tourist bungalow.

In Cochin the Bolghatty Palace Hotel is

an old Dutch Palace built in 1744 and later a British residency – now a cheap hotel. The *Kovalam Beach Hotel* is also superb as are the more expensive hotels on the beaches north of Mahabalipuram. Finally the *Naggar Castle*, high up on the valley side between Kulu and Manali, is a fairytale eagle's nest and so romantic it's ridiculous!

Getting There is Half the Fun

A lot of travel in India can be indescribably dull, boring and uncomfortable. Trains take forever, buses fall apart and shake your fillings loose, even Indian Airlines contrives to make your delay time far longer than your flying time. Despite the hassles there are a fair number of trips where getting there is definitely half the fun. Trains of course are the key to Indian travel and elsewhere in this book you'll find a section on India's unique and wonderful old steam trains. The Darjeeling Toy Train, which winds back and forth on its long climb up to the hill station, is half the fun of visiting Darjeeling. Other 'toy trains' include the run up to Matheran, just a couple of hours outside of Bombay, and the 'rack train' which makes the climb to Ooty from Mettupalayam in Tamil Nadu.

Then there is the delightful backwater trip through the waterways between Allepey and Qulon – not only is it a fascinating trip it's also quite absurdly cheap. Indian buses are generally a refined form of torture but the two day trip

between Srinagar in Kashmir and Leh in Ladakh is simply too good to miss. Just to show there are comfortable buses in India you could take the super de-luxe bus between Delhi and Chandigarh which actually shows a movie en route. Finally there could hardly be a more spectacular flight in the world than the Srinagar-Leh route which crosses the full width (and height) of the Himalaya.

Places to be/When to be there

India is a country of festivals and there are a number of places and times simply not to be missed. Starting with the Independence Day festival in New Delhi each January – elephants, procession and military might with Indian princely splendour. In June-July the great Festival of the Cars at Puri is another superb spectacle as the gigantic temple car of Lord Jagannath makes its annual journey, pulled by thousands of eager devotees.

September-October is the time to head for the hills to see the delightful Festival of the Gods in Kulu. That is part of the Dussehra festivall which in the south is known as Dassehra and is at its most spectacular in Mysore. November is the time for the huge and colourful Cattle Festival at Pushkar in Rajasthan. Finally at Christmas where else is there to be in India than Goa?

Deserted Cities

There are a number of places in crowded India where great cities of the past have been deserted and left. Fatehpur Sikri, near Agra, is the most famous since Akbar founded, built and left this impressive centre in less than 20 years. Hampi, the centre of the Vijayanagar Empire is equally impressive. Not too far from there are the ancient centres of Aihole and Badami. Some of the great forts that follow are also really deserted cities.

Great Forts

India has more than its share of great forts, many of them now deserted, to tell of its tumultuous history. The Red Fort in Delhi is one of the most impressive but Agra Fort is an equally massive reminder of Moghul power at its height. A short distance south is the huge, impregnable looking Gwalior Fort. The Rajputs in Rajasthan could build forts like nobody else and they've got them in all shapes and

sizes and with every imaginable tale to tell. Chittorgarh Fort is tragic, Bundi and Kota Forts are whimsical, Jodhpur Fort huge and high, Amber Fort simply beautiful.

Further south there's Mandu, another fort impressive in its size and architecture but with a tragic tale to tell. Further south again at Daulatabad it's a tale of power, ambition and not all that much sense with another immense fort (they went in for large size) which was built and soon deserted. Important forts in the south include Bijapur and Golconda.

Naturally the European invaders had their forts too. You can see Portuguese forts in Goa and at Daman. The British too built their share – Fort William in Calcutta is, unfortunately, not open to the public but Fort St George in Madras certainly is and has a fascinating museum.

Where Gandhi Went

Following the success of the film *Gandhi* you might be interested in making a Gandhi trek round India. Starting at Porbandar where he was born and Rajkot where he spent the early years of his life. From his period in South Africa he returned to India at Bombay and visited that city on numerous occasions. The massacre of two thousand peaceful protesters, one of the seminal events in the march to Independence, took place in Amritsar. For many years Gandhi had his ashram at Sabarmati, across the river from Ahmedabad. The British interned him in the Aga Khan's Palace in Pune. Finally he was assassinated in the garden of the wealthy Birla family in New Delhi and his cremation took place at Rajghat.

Gurus & Religion

With India's great importance as a religious centre it's no wonder that so many people embark on some sort of spiritual quest while they're there. There are all sorts of places and all sorts of gurus. One of the best known would have to be Bhagwan Rajneesh and his orange folk but he has deserted Pune for greener pastures in Oregon, USA. The Pune ashram continues but on a much diminished scale.

Rishikesh has been a guru centre ever since the Beatles went there with the Maharishi Mahesh Yogi, it's still popular today. Vrindaban near Mathura, which is between Delhi and Agra, is the centre for the Hare Krishna movement. Muktananda, who has died since the first edition,

has his ashram at Ganeshpuri while the Theosophical Society is headquartered in Madras. The Ramakrishna Mission has centres all over India although Calcutta is its headquarters. There are plenty of other centres but one guru you won't find in India is the Divine Light Mission's Muharaj ji; when he's there he stays in a hotel, his followers report.

Holy Cities

Yes, in amongst all India's holy cities there are seven of them of particular holiness. Some of them, like Varanasi, are obvious while some, like Dwarka, are not so straightforward. Three of them are dedicated to Shiva, three to Vishnu, Kanchipuram covers both gods. India's richest temple, however, is the Tirupathi and Tirumula complex in Andhra Pradesh.

Getting There

FROM THE UK

The official fare from London to Bombay or New Delhi is £522 economy one-way or £927 in 1st class. Return fares are double. There are two different roundtrip excursion fares available but only to UK residents. The 28/90 (28 day minimum stay, 90 day maximum stay) ticket is £662 and permits one stopover on the round trip. The 14/120 day excursion costs £570 but no stopovers are permitted.

If economy is important then you can do considerably better than that through London's many cheap ticket specialists or 'bucket shops'. Check the travel page ads in *The Times, Business Traveller*, weekly what's on magazine *Time Out*, or in giveaway papers like the *Australasian Express* or *LAM*. Two reliable London bucket shops are Trailfinders at 46 Earls Court Rd, London W8 and STA Travel at 74 Old Brompton Rd, London SW7 or 117 Euston Rd, London NW1.

Typical fares being quoted range from around £200 one-way or £300 return. Fares depend very much on the carrier. The very cheapest fares are likely to be on something like Ariana Afghan Airlines or Iraqi Airways which (surprise, surprise) nobody wants to fly on these days. You'll also find very competitive fares to the sub-continent with Bangladesh Biman or with Air Lanka.

If you want to stop in India en route to Australia you're looking at about £500. You'll probably find fares via Karachi (Pakistan) or Colombo (Sri Lanka) are slightly cheaper than fares via India.

FROM THE USA

Air India has the lowest fare for roundtrip regularly scheduled flights – US$1323 from New York to Delhi. There's a minimum 14 day, maximum 120 day stay requirement. Out of San Francisco the same ticket is US$1413. Some travel agencies will discount these tickets about US$150. AM-Jet Travels (tel 212 697 53320 has daily charters from New York to Delhi for US$1150 roundtrip. Their address is 501 Fifth Ave, Room 2008, New York, NY 10017.

FROM CANADA

The regular one-way economy fare from Toronto to New Delhi is C$1479. The roundtrip excursion fare from Toronto, with a 14 day minimum, 120 days maximum stay, is C$1800. One-way apex fares, with the usual advance booking and cancellation penalties, are C$1132 in the low season, C$1240 in the high. Round the world fares which take in India are available through Canada for around C$2000.

FROM AUSTRALIA

The regular one-way fare to Bombay or Delhi from the Australian east coast is A$1081 in economy, A$1513 in 1st class. Return fares are double. There are also 10/270 (10 day minimum stay, 270 day maximum stay) round trip excursion fares available. From the Australian east coast (Melbourne, Sydney, Adelaide, Brisbane) to Bombay or Delhi the fare is A$1451. From Darwin or Perth it's A$1233. Fares are slightly cheaper to Calcutta, slightly cheaper again to Madras but the largest difference is only A$23. You are allowed one stopover in each direction – which usually means Singapore.

Alternatively there are advance purchase tickets available one-way or return. These must be booked and paid for 21 days in advance and after that time the usual cancellation penalties apply. There's a minimum five day and maximum one year stay requirement. One stopover is permitted on the one-way or the roundtrip tickets. The year is divided into two periods – basic March to

September, peak October to February.

The one-way fare from the Australian east coast to Bombay or Delhi is A$725 basic or A$824 peak. From Darwin or Perth it's A$616 or 701. Calcutta and Madras are somewhat cheaper. The round trip fare from the east coast to Bombay or Delhi is A$980 basic or A$1218 peak. From Darwin or Perth it's A$834 and A$1036. Again Calcutta and Madras are somewhat cheaper.

FROM NEW ZEALAND
Round trip excursion fares are also available from Auckland. To Bombay or Delhi it's NZ$2059, slightly cheaper to Calcutta or Madras.

ROUND THE WORLD FARES
Round the world (RTW) fares have become all the rage in the past few years. Basically they're of two types – airline tickets and agent tickets. An airline RTW ticket usually means two airlines have joined together to market a ticket which takes you right round the world on their combined routes. Within certain limitations of time and number of stopovers you can fly pretty well anywhere you choose using their combined routes so long as you keep moving in the same direction. Compared to the full fare tickets which permit you to go absolutely anywhere you choose on any IATA airline you choose so long as you do not exceed the 'maximum permitted mileage' these tickets are much less flexible. But they are also much cheaper.

Quite a few of these combined airline RTW tickets go through India including the Air India-Continental Airlines one which will also allow you to make several stopovers within India. RTW tickets typically cost from around £1000 (US$1500) for northern hemisphere routes. If you want to include the southern hemisphere (ie Australia) then you're probably looking at around US$2000. The other type of RTW ticket, the agent ticket, is simply a combination of cheap

fares strung together by an enterprising agent. This will probably use a wider variety of airlines and may provide routes which the 'off the shelf' tickets cannot manage.

OVERLAND – FROM EUROPE
The classic way of getting to India has always been overland but sadly the events in Iran and Afghanistan have turned the cross-Asian flow into a trickle. In the old days you travelled through Europe to Greece, crossed from Europe into Asia at Istanbul in Turkey, crossed Turkey by a number of routes to Iran. You then continued to Tehran, possibly made a loop down to see Isfahan and Shiraz, then it was on to Mashed and finally Afghanistan. In that magical country you followed the well beaten track through Herat, Kandahar and Kabul with possibly an excursion further north to the Bamiyan Valley and then Mazar-i-Sharif. From Kabul you crossed the Khyber Pass into Pakistan then followed the Grand Trunk Road through Peshawar to Lahore and eventually into India near Amritsar in the Punjab.

Today Afghanistan is virtually completely off limits and Iran is certainly difficult, although it's only really impossible for Americans. Despite the tensions and uncertainties many overlanders did continue to go through Iran right through the year of the US hostage drama and even Iraq has not stopped intrepid travellers. The Iraq situation has also made the alternative route of going down through the Middle East to the Arabian Gulf and then flying or shipping from there to either Pakistan or India more difficult but again travellers are still managing it. In all the Asia overland trip is certainly not the breeze it once was although people continue to do it. Many travellers combine the sub-continent with the Middle East by flying between India or Pakistan and Amman in Jordan or one of the Gulf cities. A number of the London based overland companies still operate their bus or truck trips across Asia on a regular basis. Check with Exodus, Encounter Overland, Top Deck or Hann Overland for more information.

For more detail on Asia overlanding see the Lonely Planet guide *West Asia on a Shoestring*.

OVERLAND – THROUGH SOUTH-EAST ASIA

In contrast to the difficulties in central Asia the South-East Asian overland trip is still wide open and as popular as ever. From Australia the first step is to Indonesia, either Bali or Jakarta. Although most people fly from an east coast city or from Perth to Bali there are also flights from Darwin and from Port Hedland in the north of Western Australia. From Bali you head north through Java to Jakarta from where you either ship or fly to Singapore or continue north through Sumatra and then cross across to Penang in Malaysia. After travelling around Malaysia you can ship or fly from Penang to Madras in India or, more popularly, continue north to Thailand and eventually fly out from Bangkok to India, preferably via Burma.

An interesting variation on the straight-forward route is to start out from Australia to Papua New Guinea and from there cross to Irian Jaya, then Sulawesi in Indonesia. There are all sorts of travel variations possible in South-East Asia, the region is a delight to travel through, good value for money, the food is generally excellent and healthy and all in all it's an area of the world not to be missed. For full details see the Lonely Planet guide *South-East Asia on a Shoestring*.

TO/FROM MIDDLE EAST & AFRICA

There are many flights between Bombay and the Gulf states. There may still be ships operating between Bombay and Kuwait – the route would probably be Bombay-Karachi-Port Qaboos-Dubai-Doha-Bahrain. The trip takes about six days Bombay-Kuwait but about 13 in the

opposite direction. Fares from Bombay to Kuwait are approximately US$175 in bunk class, US$222 in cabin class. Check with the shipping agents in Bombay. Boats between Karachi and the gulf are probably more frequent.

There are also plenty of flights between East Africa and Bombay due to the large Indian population there. The shipping services between Africa and India will now only carry freight, including cars, not passengers.

TO/FROM PAKISTAN

Relations between India and Pakistan have certainly improved if travel connections between the two countries are anything to go by. After the Bangladesh war they were limited to one road crossing point which was open for one morning each week. Connections are still very limited but you now have a choice of road or rail crossing (every day of the week) as well as a variety of direct flights.

Air

Pakistan International Airlines and Indian Airlines operate flights Karachi-Bombay (seven times weekly) for Pakistan Rs 1130 (approximately US$85), Karachi-Delhi (four times weekly) for Rs 1403 (US$105) and Lahore-Delhi (four times weekly) for Rs 921 (US$70).

Land

There is a daily direct train between Lahore in Pakistan and Amritsar in India, and vice versa. You have to buy one ticket from Lahore to Attari, the border town, for Rs 4.10 and another from Attari to Amritsar (Rs 6). The train departs Lahore at 2 pm and you get to Amritsar around 6 pm after a couple of hours at the border passing through immigration and customs. Going the other way you leave Amritsar at 9.30 am and get to Lahore at 2 pm. Pakistan immigration and customs are handled at Lahore station. Sometimes, however, border delays can make the trip much longer.

From Amritsar you cannot buy a ticket until the morning of departure and there are no seat reservations. So arrive early and push. Money changers offer good rates for Pakistan rupees on the platform but you cannot get Indian rupees coming the opposite way. Travellers have reported that whichever direction you're travelling the exchange rate between Indian and Pakistan rupees is more advantageous to you on the Pakistan side of the border but you can change Indian rupees to Pakistani, or vice versa at Wagah and in Amritsar – no matter what the Pakistanis may tell you! Overall the crossing is trouble free with no hassles from officials on either side.

The old road crossing is still open but fewer travellers use this since the rail route has opened. This entails taking a bus to the border at Wagah, again between Lahore and Amritsar, walking across the actual border then taking another bus into Amrisar. Border formalities here are quite fast so going this way can be rather less time consuming than by rail where the train takes a long time at the border.

From Lahore buses depart from near the General Bus Station on Badami Bagh. The fare is Rs 2.50 by bus or Rs 3 by minibus. The border opens at 9.15 am and closes at 3.30 pm, if you're stuck there (on the Pakistan side) you can stay at the *PTDC Motel* where dorm beds are Rs 30 and doubles Rs 86. From the border into Amritsar costs Rs 2.50.

Prior to partition there were, of course, many more routes but the roads have been cut, the railway lines have been torn up. There used to be a railway across the desert from Jodhpur in Rajasthan to Hyderabad in the Sind. Similarly there used to be road connections from Rawalpindi to Srinagar in Kashmir, in fact this used to be the main route to Kashmir and was much more heavily used than the Jammu-Srinagar route. There was also a route into Kashmir and Ladakh from Skardu to Kargil on the Srinagar-Leh road.

TO/FROM BANGLADESH

You can enter or exit Bangladesh from several points although the Calcutta-Dhaka route is the most used. Note that if you are departing Bangladesh by land you must make absolutely certain you have the current correct border checkpoint listed on your exit permit. They often don't know what is going on at the Immigration Office in Dhaka and you can have a lot of hassles if your exit permit lists an exit point which is not in use. People have taken days to cross the border. A typical tale from one traveller:

I left Bangladesh by land through the north to Siliguri and Darjeeling. I crossed the border north of Titalya or, on other maps, Tetulia. The army camp on the Bangladesh side near the frontier is called Banglabanda. The border is closed – by this I mean there is no frontier checkpost, no customs or immigration. The road is blocked off and has grass growing over it, however the Department of Immigration and passports in Dhaka are not aware of this so they issued me with a Road Permit authorising me to leave Bangladesh by this route. At first the army near the frontier (at Tetulla) would not let me proceed but eventually the Road Permit impressed them enough to let me walk across the border. No stamps on the passport!

From Calcutta

It takes several steps but the cost is low and it can be quite interesting. Calcutta to Bangaon takes two to three hours by rail and costs about Rs 5 in 2nd class. It is then about six km and something either side of Rs 5 by rickshaw to the border, followed by a shorter ride on the other side to Benapol. Two bus rides follow from there to Khulna and then Jessore, total time about four hours at a cost of about T12. It is also possible to do it by share taxi. From here you can fly, bus or train to Dhaka. The train costs T45 and departs early (very) in the morning. Ditto for the all-day bus ride.

Of course you could always fly direct from Calcutta for about US$40, there are a couple of flights daily. With the current tense situation in north-east India, particularly along the border with Bangladesh, it's probable that the Calcutta route will be the only easily available route into or out of Bangladesh. There are, however, Calcutta-Chittagong flights for US$52.

From Darjeeling

Travelling from India to Bangladesh head south to Siliguri first of all then bus via Jalpaiguri to Haldibari (total about 2½ hours) or train direct. The Indian border checkpoint is here but you have got a little travelling yet before you reach Bangladesh. First an hour by bus to Hemkumari, then a two km walk to Chilhat. You are in Bangladesh then but Dhaka is still a long way away. The train trip is long and crowded so train first to Saidpur then bus to Bogra and again to Dhaka. A couple of days travel.

From Shillong

This trip is likely to be difficult while the crisis in the north-east continues. From Shillong you bus to Dawki where you leave India after a km walk. Tamabil is the first village in Bangladesh, from where you bus to Sylhet and train to Dhaka. The train takes 11 hours and costs from T25 depending on the class. You can also fly Sylhet-Dhaka.

TO/FROM SRI LANKA

The transport situation between Sri Lanka and India has improved dramatically since the revived Sri Lankan airline Air Lanka took the air. After its predecessor, Ceylon Air, went bankrupt in spectacular fashion Indian Airlines were the only airline flying the India-Sri Lanka routes and, as a result, were even more hopelessly overbooked than usual. This flowed on to the heavily booked Rameswaram-Talaimannar ferry service which also became hopelessly overbooked.

In the last couple of years connections between the two countries have been affected by several factors. First of all more flights have taken the pressure off the air and sea connections. Secondly when imports of consumer products into Sri Lanka became much easier the country became a pipeline for these desirable goods into India. The ferry service then became much more heavily used as many Indians made shopping trips to Sri Lanka, often bringing entourages of friends and servants with them in order to bring more goods through customs! Finally the riots and upheavals in Sri Lanka in '83 soured relations with India and considerably reduced the flow of visitors between the two countries. Nevertheless the flights can still be heavily booked and you should book as far ahead as possible.

Air

The Colombo-Madras services are the most frequent and most popular and cost US$83 one-way but there are also connections to Colombo from Bombay (US$178), Trivandrum (US$56) and Tiruchirapalli (US$58).

Sea

The ferry service from Rameswaram at the southern end of India to Talaimannar in Sri Lanka is usually suspended in November and December due to the monsoon. At other times it operates three times weekly. Fares from Rameswaram are about Rs 60 in upper deck. From Talaimannar, in Sri Lankan rupees, it's about Rs 120. It's said that at present tourists are not allowed to travel lower deck although there's very little difference between upper and lower deck.

Going to Sri Lanka if you are not pausing at Rameswaram, you should take the night train from Madurai which gets you to the port just before dawn. It's only a few minutes walk from the station to the port, say Rs 3 in a horse cart. The doors to the ferry terminal open at 8 am and it's a bit of a stampede to get in and get your tickets. The slightly more expensive upper deck tickets are a wise investment – not for the extra comfort but because you get precedence for getting off and therefore have more chance of a berth on the train from Talaimannar.

The Indian bureaucracy takes several hours to get through so it will probably be after 11 am when they start loading passengers on the *Ramanujam*. She was built in 1929 but is in good shape, reasonably cleaan and has good food. Loading also takes a long time since there are no deep water docking facilities and you have to get out to the ship by lighter. With the inevitable delays it will probably be after dark by the time you've completed the 3½ hour crossing to Sri Lanka. Make sure you have some Sri Lankan currency on you to pay the Rs 10 port charges on arrival. If you're fast off the boat rush to the booking office at Talaimannar station (which is right at the dock) and try to book a berth on the train. The train is supposed to depart around 10.30 am but usually doesn't leave until the ferry is totally cleared, which may mean after midnight. If you don't get a berth be prepared for a fairly sleepless night and keep a close eye on your gear.

Much the same story applies from Sri Lanka, there is an overnight train from Colombo which gets you to Talaimannar at dawn for the departure to Rameswaram. Try to book ahead, the ferry can get very crowded at certain peak times. Note that Rameswaram is virtually an island connected by a causeway to the mainland. The only way there is by rail but cars can be taken on the train. Cars can also be transported on the ferry but the loading process, involving two lighters tied together, is guaranteed to put grey hairs on any car owner's head.

TO/FROM NEPAL

There are a number of road crossings into Nepal and also a variety of air links with India.

Air

You can fly to Kathmandu, the capital of Nepal, from Delhi (US$142), Calcutta (US$96), Varanasi (US$71) or Patna (US$41). Note that flying Delhi-Patna and Patna-Kathmandu is much cheaper than flying Delhi-Kathmandu direct.

Land

For full details on the land routes into Nepal see the appropriate sections in the book. Most popular is the route where you cross the border from Raxaul to Birgunj and take the daily all day bus up to Kathmandu. See the Patna section in Bihar for details on this trip. Second is the Bhairawa crossing near Lumbini from where buses run to Pokhara. This crossing point is reached via Gorakhpur in Uttar Pradesh. Finally there is the crossing from Darjeeling which then involves a lengthy bus trip along the southern lowlands known as the Terai before you intersect the Birgunj-Kathmandu road. See Darjeeling in West Bengal for details. There are other roads into Nepal from northern Bihar to the east of Birgunj but they are rarely used by travellers.

TO/FROM THE MALDIVES

Although most people fly to Male in the Maldive Islands via Colombo in Sri Lanka there are also direct flights from Trivandrum to Male for US$63. This is, incidentally, cheaper than the Colombo-Male flight which costs US$88.

TO/FROM MALAYSIA

Not many travellers connect between Malaysia and India because it is so much cheaper from Thailand but there are sea and air connections between Penang and Madras. Malaysian Airlines Systems fly Penang-Madras for M$847 although you can generally pick up that ticket from travel agents for less than M$500.

The *Chidambaram*, which crosses between Penang and Madras every two weeks is the most reliable shipping service between South-East Asia and Asia proper. It's used by many travellers who take cars or motorcycles across Asia. A VW Kombi would cost you about US$500 to transport across, a motorcycle about US$150. Plus port charges at both ends. Fares on the *Chidambaram* vary widely depending on the berth and class you travel. A two berth cabin with 'English diet' would be about US$200, a four berth cabin with 'Indian diet' about US$140. More expensive fares also allow you to use the swimming pool and other de-luxe facilities during the four day crossing. In Madras the agent is the Shipping Corporation of India, c/o KPV Shaikh Mohamed Rowther, 41 Linghi Chetty St. In Penang it's R Jumabhoy & Sons, 39 Green Hall.

TO/FROM SINGAPORE

Singapore is a great cheap ticket centre and you can pick up Singapore-Bombay tickets for about S$600, Singapore-Madras for about S$500. The ship *Chidambaram* also operates from Singapore but there is nothing to be gained by taking it from there rather than Penang in Malaysia.

TO/FROM THAILAND

Bangkok is the most popular jumping off point from South-East Asia into Asia proper because of the flights from there to Calcutta or to Rangoon in Burma, Dhaka in Bangladesh or Kathmandu in Nepal. The popular Bangkok-Kathmandu flight is about US$220. You can stopover on this route in Burma and make the seven day circuit of that fascinating country. Bangkok-Calcutta is about US$170, Bangkok-Delhi about US$230.

TO/FROM BURMA

There are no land crossing points between Burma and India, or any other country for that matter. If you want to visit Burma your only choice is to fly there. Burma Airways Corporation flies Calcutta-Rangoon, Bangladesh Biman flies Dhaka-Rangoon.

CHEAP TICKETS IN INDIA

Although you can also get cheap tickets in Bombay and Calcutta it is in Delhi where the real wheeling and dealing goes on. There are countless 'bucket shops' around Connaught Place but enquire with fellow travellers about their current trustworthiness! If you purchase any cheap ticket you have to pay the full official fare through a bank – the agent gets you a bank form stating what the official fare is, you pay the bank, the bank then pays the agent. You then receive a refund from the agent but in rupees. So it is wise either to buy your ticket far enough ahead that you can use those rupees up or have plenty of bank exchange certificates in hand in order to change the rupees back. This also applies to credit card purchases.

Some typical fares from India would be Delhi-Australia for about Rs 6000, Delhi to various European capitals for around Rs 4000 or a bit less from Bombay. The cheapest flights to Europe will be with airlines like Aeroflot, LOT, Kuwait Airways, Syrian Arab Airways or Iraqi Airways.

AIRPORT TAX

India now has one of the highest airport taxes in the world for international flights. For flights to neighbouring countries (Pakistan, Sri Lanka, Bangladesh, Nepal) it's Rs 50 but to more distant countries it's a hefty Rs 100. India's neighbours are also getting into rip-off airport taxes, it's Rs 100 in Nepal and Sri Lanka although, fortunately, that's a fair bit less than Indian Rs 100 in both cases. Note that this airport tax applies to everybody, even to babies who do not occupy a seat – in most countries airport tax applies only to seat occupants or only to adults. It's also important to ensure the tax is for the specific carrier you're flying with. An Air India departure tax is no good on a British Airways flight!

Communications

Communication in India has special rules, not altogether unlike other places in Asia but totally unlike those that prevail in the west. Any answer rather than a negative one for example –will the bus stop here? 'Yes'. Which could equally mean 'No, but I'd hate to disappoint you by telling you so'. Or 'I've got no idea' or 'I simply can't raise the energy to think about that question'. Similarly 'am I heading in the right direction for the Grand Hotel?' 'Yes', which might mean 'Good grief, you've come so far in the wrong direction already I'd hate to be the one to tell you'.

The answer is to always word questions so that a commitment must be made. Not 'is this the way' but 'which is the way?'. But then you can fall for the any answer rather than no answer syndrome – 'down that way and round the corner then straight for a km' just might mean 'I've got no idea at all'. Never ask directions just once.

More annoying than fouled up com-munications are no communications at all. Many Indians, and away from the main tourist centres taxi or auto-rickshaw drivers are particularly prone to this, simply feel that communicating with a foreigner is completely impossible. Hop in an auto-rickshaw and ask for the 'Grand Hotel'. Complete incomprehension. Pronounce 'Grand Hotel' 20 different ways but, despite the fact that the Grand Hotel is the town's number one landmark, it's not getting through. Eventually an English-speaking passer-by is found, 'where do you want to go?', 'Grand Hotel' you tell him, 'Grand Hotel' he says to the auto-rickshaw driver and you're saved.

Even more annoying than that is the pre-cognated communication. He knows better than you do what you want. The fact that you're saying airport quietly, loudly or even screaming it has no bearing on the conviction that what you really want is a hotel and if I can get you into the Hotel Super I'll get a commission on it!

Is Madras airport really this bad or have I just forgotten what flying is like in India? I've finished my short stint of updating and I'm at Madras airport about to fly to Sri Lanka. It's chaotic. Madras airport is small and cramped, everybody falling over everybody and their luggage and this is only a half-full 737, God knows what happens with a full 747 or DC-10, both of which fly out of Madras.

This is my first departure from India since they brought in the departure tax and true to form they've managed to make a real meal of it. Anywhere else you pay your money and they rubber stamp or stick a stamp on your ticket or boarding card and it takes seconds. In India they form a separate queue, tick your name off on a passenger list, write it down somewhere else and copy down your ticket number! To add insult to injury they even charge the departure tax to Kieran, my eight-month old son. All this takes ages, of course, so a full half hour passes before I'm even in the queue to check in.

It's already evident that the flight is going to be late as it's due to depart in 15 minutes and I've now been standing in the queue, totally unmoving, for over 15 minutes. The reason it's not moving is the usual one that people are continually joining the queue at the front. And, of course, there's only one check-in counter although there are half a dozen people milling around behind it. Finally I get close to the front but since it's impossible to hand my bags over across the mountainous heaps of bags piled there by would-be queue jumpers I have to throw them over.

Finally we're all through immigration to find our bags waiting on the other side. We hand them on again, go through security and then find the reason our bags were waiting there was for an outgoing customs check which should have ended with a stamp on our boarding passes. Never mind, Maureen goes back and tells a customs official at one end of the room that the official at the other end (the one heavily involved in form filling at the moment) forgot to stamp the cards. He stamps them and we're away. Finally board and depart only half an hour late so it's really almost early for Indian Airlines. But why is it always this way?

Tony Wheeler

Getting Around

TRAINS

The Indian Railways system is the fourth largest in the world with a route length of over 60,000 km and nine million passengers carried every day. The first step in Indian Railways is to get a timetable. The *Indian Bradshaw* is the complete timetable for every service in India. It's more than most people need so unless you have a real passion for train timetables it can be safely ignored – although if you do intend to head off down the narrow gauge lines on the local passenger trains and would like to know the name of every station you'll be stopping at it can be an interesting investment.

Trains at a Glance is a handier volume but it can be difficult to find. For Rs 3 and in less than 100 pages it covers all the faster trains on all the main routes and for most travellers will provide more than sufficient detail. There will often be useful through carriages not shown in the timetable. Simplest of all is just to get any regional timetable; which should be available at any reasonable size station newstand for Rs 2. This will have all the local train services but, more important, a pink section will give you the timetables for the major mail and express trains (the fast ones) throughout the country.

There are a number of factors to be considered when coming to grips with Indian railways. First of all getting there may not be always be half the fun but it is certainly 90% of the experience. Indian rail travel is quite unlike any other sort of travel in any other place on earth. At times it can be incredibly frustrating, since the trains are not exactly fast, and at times it can be quite uncomfortable. But an experience it certainly is. Money aside if you simply want to get from A to B then fly, if getting from A to B is as much a part of India as what you see at both ends then take the train.

Note that during and shortly after the monsoon rail services in India can be drastically affected by floods and high rivers. This particularly applies in low-lying areas along the Ganges basin or where major rivers run to the sea such as on the north coast region of Andhra Pradesh. The timetables indicate the km distance between major stations and a table in front shows the equivalent fares for distances from 1 km to 5000 km for the various train types. With this information it is very easy to calculate the fare between any two stations. The fares quoted in this guide are simply approximations of the fares on the faster trains. Travel times vary widely between trains and the times indicated are usually for the faster mail or express services. In any case Indian trains often suffer delays.

Classes There are generally two classes – first and second – but there are a number of subtle variations on this basic distinction. For a start there is 1st class and 1st class air-conditioned. The air-con carriages only operate on certain trains and on certain routes. Then there is second class reserved and second class unreserved. In second class reserved you have a seat assigned to you and you alone. In unreserved the train carries as many people as can be crammed on board. Which usually means there is not a square cm of sitting, standing, squatting or hanging space left. Train travel in India is always more comfortable if you can travel reserved.

Trains What you want is a mail or express train. What you do not want is a passenger train. No Indian train travels very fast but at least the mail and express trains do keep travelling for more of the time. Passenger trains spend a lot of time at a lot of stations which quickly becomes very boring unless you have a keen interest in small town stations. Passenger trains are usually 2nd class only; 2nd class fares on passenger trains are less than on a mail or express train over the same route. Recently 'superfast express' services have been introduced on certain main routes. They are often all 2nd class but the trains are comparatively modern and luxurious and they really are much faster.

Gauge What you want nearly as much as a mail or express train is broad gauge. There are three gauges in India, well three types of gauges. In broad gauge the rails are 1.676 metres apart. Metre gauge is, as it says, one metre apart. Narrow gauge is either 0.762 metres (2 foot 6 inches) or 0.610 metres (2 foot). Broad gauge has two advantages – first it is much faster and second the carriages are much wider so they're more comfortable. On the narrow gauges you'll spend longer getting there and do it in carriages which are more crowded and uncomfortable. In areas where there are no broad gauge lines it is always worth considering taking a bus which will usually be faster. These areas include Rajasthan and the northern Bihar and Uttar Pradesh areas towards the Nepalese border.

Life on Board It's India for real on board the trains. In 2nd class, unreserved travel can really be a nightmare since they are always hopelessly crowded and not only with people; Indians seem unable to travel without the kitchen sink and everything that goes with it. There's an ongoing campaign to educate people not to carry so much junk but it doesn't seem to have much effect.

Combined with the crowds, the noise and the confusion there's the discomfort. Fans and lights always seem to have a habit of failing when trains are stationary for prolonged stops and there's no air moving through the carriage. Toilets are often so dirty as to be unusable and in any

case there'll be somebody asleep in it. And worst of all there are the stops. Trains seem to stop often, interminably and for no apparent reason. Often it's because somebody has pulled the emergency stop cable because he's close to home – well so it's said, some people deny it. Still, it's all part of life on the rails.

Costs Fares all operate on a distance basis. The timetables indicates the distance in km between all the stations and from this it is quite simple to calculate the cost between any two stations. If you have a ticket for at least 400 km you can break your journey at the rate of one day per 200 km so long as you travel at least 200 km to the place you leave the train. This can save a lot of hassling around buying tickets and also, of course, results in a small cost saving. Rail fares were increased considerably during 1983 but it is said that the 2nd class fares are still set at an uneconomic level and 1st class fares subsidise them to some extent. Listed below are costs (Rs) and distances for mail and express trains; passenger trains are cheaper.

km	air-con	1st class	air-con chair	2nd class
50	51	24	14	5.00
100	84	39	22	9.00
200	132	66	36	17.00
300	187	94	51	24.00
400	242	121	66	31.00
500	286	143	78	36.50
1000	495	248	135	63.00
2000	836	418	228	106.50

Reservations The cost of reservations is nominal – it's only the time it takes which hurts! Reservations can be made up to six months in advance and the longer in advance you make them the better. Your reservation ticket will indicate which carriage and berth you have and when the train comes into the station you will find a sheet of paper affixed to each carriage listing the names of the various passengers beside their appropriate berth number. Sometimes this information is posted on noticeboards on the platform. It's Indian rail efficiency at its best. Reservation costs are Rs 10 in air-con class, Rs 4 in 1st class, Rs 2 in air-con chair class, Rs 2 in 2nd class sleeper class and Rs 1 in 2nd class sitting. There are also now some 'Superfast Express Trains' for which there is an additional supplementary charge.

If you've not had time to get a reservation or been unable to get one it's worth just getting on the train in the reserved carriage. If there are seats spare the ticket inspector will come round and charge you an extra reservation fee. If they are taken, or will be taken at a station down the line, you'll simply be banished back to the crush and confusion in the unreserved carriages. This trick only really works for day travel. At night sleepers are booked out well in advance.

If you can plan your trip well ahead you can avoid all the hassles by booking in advance from abroad. A good Indian travel agent, Cox & Kings has been recommended, will book and obtain tickets in advance for you and have them ready at your hotel when you arrive.

Sleepers There are second class and first class sleepers. First class sleepers are generally private compartments with two or four sleepers in them, often with a toilet as well. Usually the sleeping berths fold up to make a sitting compartment during the daytime. First class air-con sleepers are more luxurious, and more expensive, than

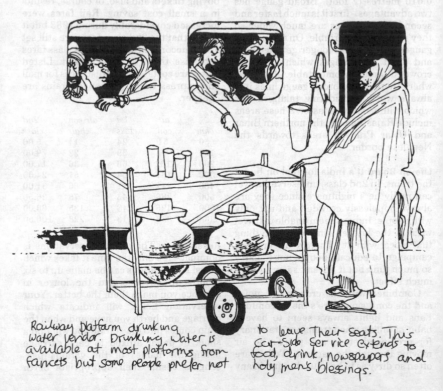

Railway platform drinking water vendor. Drinking water is available at most platforms from faucets but some people prefer not to leave their seats. This car-side service extends to food, drink, newspapers and holy men's blessings.

regular 1st class sleepers. Sleeping berths are only available between 9 pm and 6 am.

There is no additional sleeper charge in 1st class but there is an additional charge in 2nd. Sleeper charges are on top of the sleeper reservation charge. The 2nd class charge is Rs 10 for the first night, Rs 5 for the 2nd night, no charge for subsequent night. For any sleeper reservation you must book at least several days ahead. At busy times, such as on the Delhi-Jammu route for Kashmir during the hot season, you need to plan weeks ahead. There is usually a board up in the station indicating what is available or how long before the next free sleeper comes up on the various routes. You have to fill in a sleeper reservation form so save time by doing this before you get to the front of the queue. They're usually found in boxes around the reservation hall.

Two-Tier v Three-Tier On second class sleepers there are two sorts of sleepers, two-tier and three-tier. Superficially the padded two-tier sleepers seem more comfortable than the hard wooden three-tier ones although on many broad gauge routes three-tier sleepers are padded now. During the day the three-tier sleepers are folded up to make seats for six or eight. At night they are folded down, everybody has to bed down at the same time and a guard ensures nobody unreserved gets into the carriage.

In the two-tier compartments there are still regular seats down below the padded bunks so people get on and off and it's noisier and more difficult to sleep. In any case the racket and noise from the chai-wallahs and other merchants operating at every station makes sleeping on Indian trains a pretty hit and miss affair.

Getting a Space Despite Everything If you've got to travel on a certain date and it's a long trip you will want a sleeper. If there are none left then it's time to try and break into the quotas. Ask at the tourist office if there is a tourist quota on that train. Ask the stationmaster, usually helpful men who speak English, if he has a station quota or if there is a VIP quota. The latter is often a good last bet because VIPs rarely turn up to use their quotas.

If all that fails then you're going to be travelling unreserved and that can be no fun at all. To ease the pain get yourself some expert help. For a few rupees baksheesh you can get a porter, or the tourist officer may find one for you, who will absolutely ensure you get a seat. If it's a train starting from your station the key to success is to be on the train before it arrives in at the station. Your porter will do just that so when it rolls in you simply dawdle on board and take the seat he has warmed for you. If it's a through train then it's every man for himself and you can be certain he'll be better at it than you are – he'll also not be encumbered with baggage or backpacks.

Left Luggage Most stations have a left luggage facility where backpacks can be left for Rs 1 per day. This is a very useful facility if you're visiting, but not staying in, a town. Or if you want to find a place to stay, unencumbered by your gear.

Special Trains There's a special 'palace on wheels' which makes a regular circuit around Rajasthan – you not only travel by train you also stay in the 'fit for a Maharaja' carriages. See the Rajasthan section for more details. The English travel agent Trailfinders operates a regular train tour of India using a special carriage in which you travel, eat and sleep. It's known as the 'Indian Rail Rover'. The carriage is hooked on to regular trains from town to town, then disconnected and left on a siding while you visit the town. The accommodation facilities are basic, this is no palace on wheels, but you cover a lot of India. Tours from 18 to 32 days are available and prices ex-Delhi are around £380.

Indrail Passes

The very popular Indrail Passes permitting unlimited travel on Indian trains for the period of their validity are available overseas or from the main railways offices in New Delhi, Bombay, Calcutta or Madras. In India they are available only if paid for in US dollars or pounds sterling. The costs and period of validity, in US dollars, are as follows:

days	air-con	lst class	2nd class
7 days	160	80	35
15 days	200	100	45
21 days	240	120	55
30 days	300	150	65
60 days	450	225	100
90 days	600	300	130

Children aged five to 12 years pay half the above fares. Indrail tickets can be bought overseas through travel agents or in India at certain major railway offices. Payment in India must be made in either US dollars or pounds sterling, cash or travellers' cheques. Indrail passes cover all reservation and berth costs at night. They can be extended if you wish to keep on travelling. The main offices in India which handle Indrail passes are:

New Delhi	Railway Tourist Guide, Northern Railway Baroda House
New Delhi	Central Reservation Office, Northern Railway, Connaught Place
Bombay	Railway Tourist Guide, Western Railway, Churchgate
Bombay	Railway Tourist Guide, Central Railway, Victoria Terminal
Calcutta	Railway Tourist Guide, Eastern Railway, Fairlie Place
Calcutta	Central Reservation Office, South-Eastern Railway, Esplanade Mansion
Madras	Central Reservation Office, Southern Railway, Madras Central

They are also available from Central Reservation Offices at Secunderabad-Hyderabad, Rameswaram, Bangalore, Vasco-da-Gama, Jaipur, Trivandrum and at certain 'recognised Tourist Agencies'.

Is the Indrail Pass worth having? – well yes and no. In purely financial terms they're probably not. While researching the first edition of this book Tony made 16 rail trips during one fairly intensive 38 day period of travel. He generally made short trips by 2nd class and longer trips by lst class, overnight trips included a sleeper. The 11 2nd class trips and five 1st class trips cost a total of US$42 (fares have increased since then). Travelling only by 2nd class it would have cost only US$18, by lst class it would have cost US$66. By comparison a 30 day Indrail Pass then cost US$40 in 2nd class, US$95 in lst. So even the 2nd class pass would have been more expensive than a pay-as-you-go mixture of 2nd and lst. Even if bus trips taken during the period were made, if possible, by rail there would still not have been a financial saving.

At 90 days, however, the pass comes closer to breaking even. Travelling at the same intensity the 2nd class pass would still be much more expensive than paying as you go but the lst class is virtually on a par. The reason the lst class pass makes more sense is because it only costs about 2.5 times the cost of a 2nd class pass whereas the actual cost of lst class is about four times as high. This comparison involves a pretty heavy schedule and if you start travelling less and pausing more your pass will quickly begin to look like bad value. This particularly applies to the very short passes. A seven day 2nd class pass breaks even when you travel 300 km a day for the whole period. At the usual speed of Indian trains that virtually means being on a train all the time. Or two 1600 km trips, say a 36 hour trip Bombay-Calcutta and then back again, all in the same week.

That's the downside of Indrail passes but pure cost isn't all there is to it. First of all you never need to join the interminable queues to buy tickets. You already have your ticket so if you're travelling unreserved you simply hop aboard. If you are travelling reserved then you still have to get a reservation and that's where the second advantage comes in. Train reservations aren't just issued from A to Z and then they're all used up. There is always a tourist quota, a VIP quota, a station-master's quota and so on. Breaking into that quota is never easy but Indrail pass users report that when the train is 'full' production of their pass often results in another quota making a miraculous appearance.

One traveller reported that 'I always went round the back to the Chief Reservations Office instead of queueing up, he usually shook my hand and came back in five minutes with the reservations. Only in Bombay did this method not succeed'. Another traveller reported this series of steps for breaking into the tourist quota:

If the train is fully booked go directly to the area officer or station superintendent and ask for 'special permission' to get a berth on the train. You will have to fill out a form and then be given a note to take to the reservation counter where your berth is allocated. Sometimes you're told that your berth is booked and there is nothing further to do. Always insist that they write their berth number on your ticket (especially if you have a tourist quota berth) because your name may not appear on the train listings. If you do not have proof of your bookings you have no recourse with the conductor.

Your Indrail pass also allows you use of the station waiting rooms, often a peaceful haven in the 1st class variety, and makes it easier to get into the retiring rooms. The retiring room dormitories are often used by Indian travelling salesmen who speak English and know all the best local places to eat. The main virtue of the Indrail Pass, however, is its ability to produce a seat or a sleeper when there isn't one. That can be worth far more than mere money so overall, yes an Indrail Pass can be a good

buy but it's convenience and simplicity (both very important features in India) which are the plus points, not just cost saving. In particular, short term passes are not so worthwhile, especially the 2nd class ones. If you're going to travel by Indrail then go the whole hog and get a 1st class pass. Since the first edition of this book rail fares have increased considerably and Indrail passes by an equal or even larger margin.

Gricing

For some travellers, India's rail system is more than just public transport. This description of gricing is by Mark Carter.

Just what gricing is will become apparent over the next couple of pages. Gricing is usually carried out by a gricer, a term that defies description, but is used loosely to identify one of that strange breed, the railway enthusiast. Somewhere in amongst the temples, villages, gurus and instant karma of India is to be found the largest treasure trove of steam locomotives in the world. Eight and a half thousand of them still at work at chores long given over to the infernal combustion engine in the western world. As steam crumbles to the forces of progress elsewhere in the world, in India where nothing moves too fast, steam remains supreme.

Three gricers, all crazy Englishmen, of whom I was one, spent five months travelling the length and breadth of India chasing these steam engines. The stations and locomotive sheds became our temples, the locomotives the gods we worshipped and our tributes were not measured in gold or silver, but more in the profits of Kodak and Agfa. I don't expect you to become madly enthused over steam locomotives but it's worth checking a few out while in India, some are real museum pieces and some of you have probably never seen a steam locomotive. It will also give you a feel for what held India together for so long and still does to a certain extent.

The locomotives come in all shapes, sizes and colours and from a variety of countries around the world. Although British built engines predominated at one time, over a third of those now in use were built in India between 1950 and 1972. The railways of India are now formed of nine railway zones but these were derived from a much greater number of former independent and state operations. Names such as the Great Indian Peninsular Railway and the Oudh and Rohilkhand have long since passed into obscurity.

This patchwork of companies led to a rather haphazard development of steam locomotives so in 1903 the BESA (British Engineering Standards Association) designs were introduced in an attempt to achieve some sort of standardisation. A further attempt was made during the 1920s with the IRS design (Indian Railway Standard). Nearly all the BESA and IRS designs were of British construction and when locomotives had to be ordered from foreign manufacturers, because of full order books in Britain, angry questions were asked in Parliament. During WW II large numbers of American locomotives were brought in to cope with increased traffic and these paved the way for the standard post-war designs. Although Britain contributed to these, a large number

were home grown and builders from America, Germany, Japan and Eastern Europe competed. Unfortunately the attractive BESA and classic British IRS designs are now rather old and rapidly heading for the scrapyards.

A good place to get to grips with the Indian steam locomotive is the Rail Transport Museum at Shantipath, New Delhi, near the Chanakyapuri diplomatic enclave. Locomotives from all gauges –broad (5 foot 6 inches), metre and narrow (2 foot and 2 foot 6 inches) – are on show in beautiful external condition. The oldest surviving engine in India, built in 1855, is on show along with a diminutive 2 foot gauge loco from Darjeeling, placed strategically next to a 234 ton Beyer Garratt locomotive. The museum is closed on Mondays.

One train to watch out for while in Delhi is the Taj Express which leaves for Agra just after 7 am and is usually worked by an immaculate WP-type locomotive painted blue and white. These bullet nosed passenger engines never seem to attain the speeds they look capable of,

'Tweed' is probably the oldest regularly working engine in the world, built in Glasgow in 1873 and seen at the Saraya Sugar Mills, Sardarnagar, Gorakhpur.

100 kph being about top whack. Over seven hundred were built between 1947 and 1967 and all require a crew of four – driver, two firemen and a coolie to break up the large lumps of coal.

Other broad gauge engines to watch out for, if you are on your way to Pakistan, are the HPS class at Amritsar and Jullunder. They can also be seen at Lucknow and Ranaghat (north of Calcutta) and although built in 1950 they look very similar to the 1906 BESA designs which they are based on (look for the classification on the cabside numberplate). At Howrah (Calcutta) and along the east coast route HSM locomotives built between 1913 and 1924 can still be seen shunting and the similar HGS class are scattered throughout the Bengal coalfields. The international train from Amritsar to Lahore is worked by a Pakistan Railways HGS loco.

The BESA SGS class look real antiques but are now more numerous in Pakistan, only a few remaining in India at Sealdah (Calcutta). The IRS designs (XB, XC, XD, XE) are scattered all over the country and are starting to be retired. Burdwan and Asansol both have about a dozen or so engines used on shunting and a few are scattered around Kerala for similar duties. The standard design WP and WG are found just about everywhere. If you want a ride on a steam locomotive there's plenty of room on the footplate of these and many crews are quite willing to have you on board for some of the journey.

The metre gauge system has been built up since 1973 and while not quite as extensive as broad gauge it is possible to travel from the eastern extremities of Assam to within 80 km of Cape Comorin on the metre gauge. The engines are generally cleaner and more colourful than their broad gauge counterparts.

One of the main attractions is the rack railway running from Mettupallaiyum to the hill resort of Ootacamund in the Nilgiri Hills, about 100 km south of Mysore. Smart blue engines built in Switzerland push their trains of blue and white coaches through quite spectacular scenery. When the gradient gets too steep a second pair of cylinders on the locomotive activate a mechanism underneath the locomotive which engages the toothed rail in the middle of the track, giving the engine extra 'push'. Wellington is a good place to watch the train climb one side of the valley, cross it by a bridge, then double back and climb the opposite side.

The old BESA engines have mainly disappeared now, most of the remnants of these designs being on the Western Railway. However the short branch from Mathura to Vrindaban (birthplace of Lord Krishna) is still worked by P class engines, originally designed for the passenger trains of the 1920s. The rather attractive IRS engines of classes YB and YD can be seen at their best between Goa and Hubli, resplendent in their livery of orange and green.

The standard post-war types YP (passenger) and YG (goods) are found everywhere, a large number having been built in India. A couple of interesting metre gauge lines run from Jodhpur to the Thar Desert towns of Barmer and Jaisalmer, worked by ten specially built locomotives from America, one of which is kept in its original Jodhpur Railways condition for visiting enthusiasts. One metre gauge line even runs through the Gir Forest Lion Reserve in Gujurat, but the chances of seeing a lion from it are nil.

For a real adventure you can't beat the narrow gauge lines, built to serve more remote areas and connect them with the main lines. Years ago my Mum told me of the little toy train that used to take her to school and I've wanted to see it ever since. Let's hear it for the Darjeeling Himalayan Railway. The diary reads....

> The little tank engine barks its way up steep grades, around tight bends, all at quite a speed. There are loops and reverses, places where you can look down and see where you

A standard broad guage WP passenger locomotive at Jhansi— specially rolled out for visiting railway enthusiasts to photograph.

were half an hour ago. Soon out of Tindhana we stall on a curve, so a following freight train comes and gives us a push, but no go. Then it backs down and takes another run at our train. Wham! and we're on our way again!

Opened in 1880 the railway has been going strong ever since and is arguably the most famous steam railway in the world. The oldest engine, 779 'Mountaineer', was built in 1892 and others of the same design followed until 1927. The bus from Siliguri to Darjeeling takes 3½ hours, the train can take all day but you'd never know what you're missing. If you stand at Batasia loop you may be lucky enough to get a picture of the morning school train from Kurseong with the snow capped Kanchenjunga in the background.

The two other spectacular hill railways from Kalka to Simla and from Neral (near Bombay) to Matheran are plagued by diesels although the Matheran line does see one or two trains a day and is good for panoramic views of the Western Ghats. The first narrow gauge railways in India were built by the Gaekwar of Baroda in 1873 and these lines still exist south of Baroda, based on the town of Dhaboi, which sees 44 steam trains a day.

While of no great significance, two lines on the east coast appealed to me. The line from Naupada to Ginupur is worked by eight delightful little engines built at Stoke-on-Trent, the first in 1903 and now painted up to look like something out of Mickey Mouse, have you ever seen a pink steam engine? Further north runs the line from Rupsa to Bangriposi into the land of the Sontal people. Immaculate red and black engines, decorated with paintings of peacocks, operate this line. They were all built by the North British Company of Glasgow between 1906 and 1908.

Finally India boasts perhaps the greatest steam gem of all – 'Tweed', a metre gauge relic built by Dubs of Glasgow in 1873. It is still at work at the Saraya Sugar Mills near Gorakhpur and is probably the oldest steam engine in the world, still in regular use.

A word of warning if you decide to take a few snaps of steam locomotives for the folks back home, the Indians can go a bit overboard when it comes to security on the railways, so either make sure there are no police or other officials, or get a permit from the Indian consular office before you leave home. If it sounds silly the

joke's on you when you are facing the guy at New Jalpaiguri station who is threatening to burn your film and smash your camera. Luckily I talked my way out of it – Happy Gricing!

Mark Carter

Unhappily for gricing enthusiasts since Mark wrote the above there has been more modernisation and a number of types have disappeared. In brief the HPS and HSM classes are now all finished. The SGS, SPS, HPS and SGC class locomotives are now only found in Pakistan. XB and XC are now finished while the XD and XE classes are barely hanging on. The YB and YD are still hanging on, the YD on the Goa line. The P class metre gauge engines are also finished but there is still plenty of British steam to be seen in the narrow two foot and two foot six inch gauges.

BUS

Travelling around India by train has such an overpowering image – those up and down mail trains, the sights, sounds and smells of the stations, the romantic names and exotic old steam engines – that people forget there is also an extensive and well developed bus system. In many cases this simply extends from the railway system, fanning out from railhead stations, or goes where the railways do not or cannot go, up to Kashmir for example. There are, however, many places where buses offer a parallel service to the railways and in some cases a better or faster one. In places where the only railways are on the narrower gauges it will often be much faster to take a bus – this includes the routes in northern Bihar and Uttar Pradesh up to the Nepal border. Agra-Jaipur, Delhi-Jaipur and Bombay-Goa are other examples of routes where buses are faster and more convenient than the trains.

Buses vary widely from state to state although you can make the general observation that travel by bus is crowded, cramped, slow and none too comfortable.

In some states there is a choice of buses on the main routes – thus in Jammu & Kashmir there are A and B class buses, even de-luxe and air-conditioned buses on the popular Jammu-Srinagar run. There are also a variety of buses in Haryana, particularly on the Delhi-Chandigar route where there is even a bus which shows movies en route!

There is generally a state operated bus company in each state but in some states (Orissa, J&K for example) this is backed up by privately operated buses although they may only operate on certain routes. Despite the extra speed buses often offer (and lesser safety) they generally become very uncomfortable rather sooner than trains. If it's a long trip, and particularly one involving overnight travel, you're generally best opting for a train. A constant barrage of loud and discordant Hindi pop music is another disadvantage of bus travel – 'as if the roads aren't rough enough'.

As long as there's two of you it's worth working out a bus-boarding plan where one of you can guard the gear while the other storms the bus in search of a seat. The big advantage of buses over trains is that they go so frequently (in comparison with trains) and getting a bus involves so little pre-departure hassle (again in comparison to trains). You can, however, often make advance reservations for a small additional fee – usually Rs 0.50 or Rs 1. Waving that magic ticket in front of you can sometimes get you on board when space is at a premium or can get you a better seat – not at the back, not over a wheel, on the scenic side.

Baggage is generally carried on the roof of buses so it's an idea to take a few precautions. Make sure it's tied on properly and that nobody dumps a tin trunk on top of your fragile backpack. Sometimes a tarpaulin will be tied across the baggage – make sure it covers your gear adequately. Theft is sometimes a problem so keep an eye on your bags at chai stops. Having a large, heavy duty bag into which your pack will fit can be a very good idea; not only for bus travel but also for air travel. On long distance bus trips chai stops can be far too frequent or, conversely, agonisingly infrequent. They can be a real hassle for women travellers – toilet facilities will generally be inadequate to say the least.

There are extensive bus routes in all the major cities. These vary from city to city – in Bombay they're surprisingly good, in Delhi they're surprisingly crowded, in Calcutta they are also very crowded but backed up by a more expensive and marginally less crowded minibus service.

AIR

The Indian domestic airline, Indian Airlines, operates an extensive service throughout the nation and also operates connections to neighbouring countries. Air India also operates a number of domestic services, principally on the Bombay-Delhi, Bombay-Calcutta and Bombay-Madras routes. Indian Airlines is the largest regional carrier in South Asia with a fleet of 10 A300 Airbuses, 25 Boeing 737s and also a number of turboprop HS-748s. The recent expansion of the Airbus and 737 fleet, together with some heavy fare increases has to some extent taken the strain off the heavily booked Indian Airlines flights.

Booking Flights

Much of the problem with flying Indian Airlines relates not to aircraft shortages but to the lack of an efficient booking system. To say that Indian Airlines is Indian Railways airborne is probably being unfair to Indian Railways – at least the railways equipment and booking system are appropriate to each other. Indian Airlines have multi-million dollar wide-body jet aircraft backed up by a Victorian booking system. Until they finally get their computer system worked out it means, for the traveller, endless wasted hours and continual uncertainty.

Without a computer it is virtually

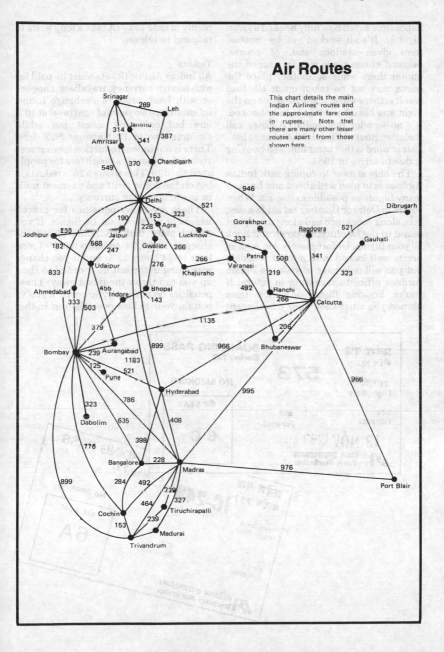

Air Routes

This chart details the main Indian Airlines' routes and the approximate fare cost in rupees. Note that there are many other lesser routes apart from those shown here.

impossible to tell how fully booked a given flight is. It's all worked out by 'quotas' from given stations and, of course, demand at one place may far exceed the quotas there while at another place the quota may not be taken up at all. End result is there will actually be space on the flight you have been told is fully booked. It's no wonder that Indian Airlines call their (lengthy) waiting list the 'chance list'. Latest word is that computerised booking is due to arrive in 1984.

The only answer to coping with Indian Airlines is to plan well ahead and book as many flights as possible in one hit. When you're in Delhi or Bombay set aside a day, take along your lunch and a long novel, trot round to the IA office, sit down and book all your flights. Unfortunately you're then pretty well locked in to a fixed schedule but you will only have to visit the Indian Airlines office to reconfirm in future. If you're booking flights in India from abroad you must allow your travel agent

plenty of time too – IA take a long while to respond to telexes.

Tickets

All Indian Airline tickets must be paid for with foreign currency, travellers' cheques or with bank proof of exchange forms. Infants up to two years of age travel at 10% fare but only one infant per adult. Children two to 12 travel at 50% fare. There is no student reduction for overseas visitors but there is a youth fare for people aged 12 to 30. This allows a 25% reduction but on the dollar tariff and payment must be made in foreign currency.

There are heavy penalties for cancellations or no shows on IA flights. If you cancel more than 48 hours ahead the charge is Rs 20, 24-48 hours it is 10%, one hour to 24 hours 25%, and if you change your mind in the last hour or fail to show up you can throw the ticket away. These penalties do not apply, however, if you've bought your tickets overseas but in that

case you pay a more expensive 'dollar tariff. Unlike almost every other airline in the world IA accepts no responsibility if you lose your tickets. They absolutely will not replace lost tickets so treat them like cash, not travellers' cheques.

Fares

The accompanying chart details the main IA domestic routes and fares. Indian Airlines also has a 21 day 'Discover India' fare which costs US$375. This allows unlimited travel on their domestic routes and is OK if you really plan to rush around India. Strictly for the short term visitor although it's much better value than at the time of the first edition of this book when the price was the same but the validity only 15 days. This ticket must be paid for in foreign currency. 'It took us nearly two hours pay for the ticket at the Indian Airlines office in Bombay', reported a traveller, 'and another four hours were spent looking the flights and they were only on request after all that'.

Indian Airlines have a number of excursion fare circuit trips which give you a 20% discount on the normal fare. An example is Bombay-Colombo (Sri Lanka)-Madras-Calcutta-Dhaka (Bangladesh)-Kathmandu (Nepal)-Delhi-Rawalpindi (Pakistan)-Peshawar (Pakistan)-Karachi (Pakistan)-Bombay. There is also a 21 day South India excursion fare which allows a 30% discount if you combine an India-Sri Lanka or India-Maldives ticket with domestic tickets in the south.

In Flight

All IA flights have vegetarian and non-vegetarian (veg & non-veg) meals but unless you request otherwise westerners will always be assumed to be non-veg. The food is not very good in either case and IA's stewardesses make even Aeroflot's mighty ladies look smiling and happy. Two other IA irritations are the complete lack of effort to keep you informed of the whys and wherefores of the almost inevitable delays and the snails pace at which luggage is unloaded at the end of most flights.

Offices

The Indian Airlines office addresses are listed below together with the distance from the office to the airport:

Agartala	Khosh Mahal Building, Central Rd (tel 60)	12 km
Agra	Hotel Clarks-Shiraz, 54 Taj Rd (tel 73434, 72421)	7 km
Ahmedabad	Airlines House, Lal Darwaja (tel 391736, 391797, 391619)	10 km
Allahabad	18 Tashkant Marg, Tata Auto Sales Building (tel 42607, 61633)	12 km
Amritsar	48 The Mall (tel 42607)	11 km
Aurangabad	Anvikar Building, Adalat Rd (tel 4864)	10 km
Bagdogra	Hotel Sinclairs, Mallaguri PO Pradhanagar, Siliguri (tel 20692)	14 km
Bangalore	Karnataka Housing Board Building, District Office Rd (tel 75911, 29769, 76851)	13 km
Belgaum	Hotel Sanman Deluxe, College Rd (tel 20801, 25898)	14 km
Bhavnagar	Diwanpara Rd (tel 27144, 23214)	8 km
Bhopal	Bhadbhada Rd, TT Nagar (tel 61633, 61155)	11 km
Bhubaneswar	V11-C/8 Raj Path, Bapuji Nagar (tel 50533, 50544)	4 km
Bhuj	Outside Waniawad Gate, Station Rd (tel 34)	6 km
Bombay	Air-India Building, 1st Floor, Madam Cama Rd, Nariman Point (tel 233 031, 233521, 233154)	26 km
Calcutta	Airlines House, 39 Chittaranjan Ave (tel 263135, 260730, 260731, 263390, 262954)	16 km
Chandigarh	SCO-186-187-188 Sector 17C (tel 28721, 26443)	11 km
Chittagong	Hotel Agrabad (tel 838542)	
Cochin	Durbar Hall Rd, Ernakulam (tel 32065, 33826)	6 km

Coimba-tore	503 Trichy Rd (tel 22743, 22208)	11 km
Colombo	95 Sir Baron Jayatilaka Mawatha (tel 23136)	18 km
Dabolim	Dempo House, Campal, Panaji (tel 3826, 4190)	37 km
Delhi	Kanchanjunga, Barak-hamba Rd (tel 40052, 40071)	13 km
Dhaka	Hotel International (tel 231687)	7 km
Dibru-garh	CIWTC Bungalow, Assam Medical College Rd, (tel 114)	26 km
Dimapur	Dimapur-Imphal Rd (tel 2375)	5 km
Gauhati	Paltan Bazar (tel 23128, 26655, 23734)	22 km
Gorakh-pur	Park Rd (tel 3940)	7 km
Gwalior	Tansen Marg, Barrar (tel 21773)	12 km
Hydera-bad	Saifabad, opposite Ravindra Bharati (tel 36902, 77531)	9 km
Imphal	Mahatma Gandhi Rd (tel 28/1377)	7 km
Indore	164/1 Rabindranath Tagore Marg (tel 7069)	9 km
Jabalpur	Chadha Travels, Jackson Hotel, Civil Lines (tel 21324, 22178, 21320)	15 km
Jaipur	Mundhara Bhawan, Ajmer Rd (tel 72940, 74500)	15 km
Jammu	Tourist Reception Centre, Veer Marg (tel 42735, 47577)	7 km
Jamnagar	Indra Mahal, near Bhind Bhanjan Temple (tel 4285)	10 km
Jodhpur	Rupali Tourist Bungalow, High Court Rd (tel 20909)	5 km
Jorhat	Garhali (tel 11)	6 km
Kabul	Chanrahi Malick, Asghar Desh (tel 31469, 32920)	7 km
Kanpur	15/69 Civil Lines (tel 63356, 65042)	13 km
Karachi	Hotel Inter-continental (c/o PIA) (tel 511577, 515021, 522034)	15 km
Kath-mandu	Durbar Marg (tel 11198, 13053)	8 km
Keshod	Rajmahal Plot, New Railway Station (tel 344)	3 km
Khaj-uraho	Khajuraho Hotel (tel 35)	5 km
Lahore	33 Falletis Hotel, Eager-ton Rd (tel 305712)	10 km
Leh	Ibex Guest House (tel 76)	8 km
Lucknow	Clarks Avadh, 5 Mahatma Gandhi Marg (tel 48081)	15 km
Madras	19 Marshalls Rd, Egmore (tel 848711, 848712 847 098, 847522)	16 km
Madurai	Pandyan House, 7A West Veli St (tel 26795, 415 987, 26707)	12 km
Male	Beach Hotel (tel 2106, 3003, 3004)	3 km
Manga-lore	Moti Mahal, Falnir Rd (tel 23504, 27207, 21300, 24669)	20 km
Nagpur	242A Manohar Niwar, Rabindranath Tagore Rd, Civil Lines (tel 23186, 25057)	10 km
Patna	South Gandhi Maidan (tel 54984, 25936)	8 km
Porban-dar	Harish Mansion, opposite Indian Oil petrol pump (tel 18)	5 km
Port Blair	Middle Point G-55 (tel 208)	4 km
Pune	15 Sadhu Vaswani (tel 28179, 24940)	8 km
Raipur	Natraj Hotel, GE Rd (tel 26460)	19 km
Rajkot	Angel Chamber, Jhabar Rd (tel 23306, 24857, 34122)	4 km
Ranchi	Nataya Flat 4, Kedru, B/258 Sector 3 (tel 23350, 21841)	7 km
Silchar	Red Cross Rd (tel 72)	25 km
Srinagar	Tourist Reception Centre (tel 73538, 73270) 73271)	13 km
Tezpur	Jankin Rd (tel 83, 162)	18 km
Tiruchi-rapalli	Southern Railway Employees Co-op Credit Society Building, Dindigul Rd (tel 23116)	8 km
Tirupati	Room 9 & 10, TT Devasthanam Guest House (tel 2818, 2884, 2732)	15 km
Trivan-drum	Air Centre, Muscat Junction (tel 60181, 62288, 66923, 60070, 62110, 61776, 63965, 66370)	7 km

Udaipur LIC Building, outside
Delhi Gate (tel 3952) 25 km
Vadodara University Rd, Fateh Ganj
(Baroda) (tel 63868,
65677) 6 km
Varanasi Mint House Motel, opp
Nadesar Palace, Canton-
ment (tel 64146, 66116) 22 km
Vijaya- Shriniketan 27-1-26,
wada Eluru Rd, Covernorpet
(tel 72218) 22 km
Visak- Jeevan Prakash, LIC
hapatnam Building Complex (tel
64665, 62673) 14 km

DRIVING

There are no car rental systems along the lines of those in the west in India but it is possible to hire chauffeur-driven cars quite easily. This tends to be a little expensive, not because of the chauffeur but because of the cost of the cars, fuel and upkeep. All are very expensive in India by western standards. Basically a chauffeur driven car is just a long distance taxi. In some places they run fairly regular services, such as Chandigarh-Manali or Jammu-Srinagar in the north-west. It is also possible to hire jeeps for the two day run from Srinagar to Leh in Ladakh.

Fewer people bring their own vehicles to India since the overland trip became so curtailed because of the Russians in Afghanistan and the current situation in Iraq and Iran. If you do decide to bring a car or motorcycle to India it has to be brought in under a carnet, a customs document guaranteeing you will remove the car at the end of your stay. Failing to do so will be very expensive.

Driving in India is a matter of low speeds and great caution. Indian roads are narrow and crowded. At night there are unlit cars and ox carts and in daytime there are fearless bicycle riders. Day and night there are the crazy truck drivers to contend with. A loud horn definitely helps in India since the normal driving technique is to put your hand firmly on the horn, close your eyes and plough through regardless. Vehicles always have the right

of way over pedestrians and bigger vehicles always have the right of way over smaller ones. On the Indian roads might is right.

Because of the extreme congestion in the cities and the narrow bumpy roads in the country driving is often a slow, stop-start process, hard on you, on the car, on your fuel economy. Service is so-so in India, parts and tyres are hard to obtain. All in all driving is no great pleasure.

People driving across India on the overland trip will most likely be starting out either from Calcutta, Madras or Bombay. Madras is the usual shipping point since there is a regular shipping service between there and Penang in Malaysia. The route from Madras crosses the country to Bombay then heads north to Delhi and on out to Pakistan.

From Madras & Bombay

	Sector	Total
Route A47	km	km
Madras-Chittoor	157	157
Chittoor-Bangalore	174	331
Bangalore Chitradurga	202	533
Chitradurga-Hubli	206	739
Hubli-Belgaum	94	833
Belgaum-Kolhapur	103	936
Kolhapur Pune	234	1170
Pune-Bombay	185	1355
Bombay-Nasik	197	1552
Nasik-Malegan	106	1658
Malegan-Indore	310	1968
Indore-Shivpuri	376	2344
Shivpuri-Gwalior	113	2457
Gwalior-Agra	117	2574

Route A1		
Agra-Delhi	204	2778
Delhi-Ambala	294	3072
Ambala-Jullundur	174	3246
Jullundur-Amritsar	77	3323
Amritsar-Wagah (border)	26	3349

From Madras the road crosses a plain then climbs up to Bangalore. Karnataka between Bangalore and Belgaum is heavily cultivated and part of the Deccan plateau. From Belgaum the road leaves the hilly Deccan area and runs down to the coast at Bombay. Leaving Bombay it climbs up over the hill range known as the Western Ghats then traverses a number of hill ranges through Dhulia, Indore and Shivpuri, at times the road is very winding. At Shivpuri you can diverge east and visit Khajuraho, then rejoin the route at Gwalior, adding 422 km to the trip. At Agra the route meets the busy Grand Trunk Road and continues to Delhi then across the flat Punjab region to Amritsar and the border with Pakistan.

From Calcutta

Route A1	Sector km	Total km
Calcutta-Asansol	222	222
Asansol-Varanasi	454	676
Varanasi-Allahabad	128	804
Allahabad-Kanpur	192	996
Kanpur-Agra	288	1284
Agra-Wagah (border)	775	2059

From Calcutta the road crosses the heavily populated and fertile West Bengal plain. Traffic all the way is heavy and slow as this route traverses the most densely populated part of India. From Agra the route is the same as from Madras or Bombay.

Road Safety

India suffers about 60 road deaths a day, 20,000 or so a year, an astonishing total in relation to the number of vehicles on the road. The reasons are numerous and many of them fairly obvious – starting with the congestion on the roads and the equal congestion in vehicles. When a bus runs off the road there are plenty of people stuffed inside to get injured and it's unlikely too many of them will be able to escape in a hurry if need be.

Many of the deaths are pedestrians involved in hit and run accidents. The propensity to disappear after the incident is not wholly surprising – lynch mobs can assemble remarkably quickly, even when the driver is not at fault! Most accidents are caused by trucks for on Indian roads might is right and trucks are the biggest, heaviest and mightiest. You either get out of their way or get run down. As with so many Indian vehicles they're likely to be grossly overloaded and not in the best of condition. Trucks are actually licensed and taxed to carry a load 25% more than the maximum recommended by the manufacturer!

The karma theory of driving also helps to push up the statistics – it's not so much the vehicle which collides with you as the events of your previous life which caused the accident.

Indian Vehicles

There is a small, but active, vehicle manufacturing industry in India. Basically it makes two cars, the Fiat 1100 and the Hindustan Ambassador. The Fiat is a licence-made copy of the 1100 cc Fiat of the early '60s. It's India's most popular car, particularly since the demise of the licence built Triumph Herald, and is manufactured in Bombay. The Calcutta-made Ambassador is nothing less than an early-50s British Morris Oxford. By modern standards it is big, heavy, slow and thirsty for the amount of space it offers so it is hardly surprising that sales have been steadily declining. Also the manufacturing equipment – the jigs, presses and so on – is now so old and worn that making doors and other body parts fit accurately is very difficult.

There has been a lot of talk about producing new Indian cars but private car ownership has a very low priority in India. Sanjay Gandhi was involved in a plan to produce an Indian 'peoples' car' and the techniques used to raise finance for this project and to obtain cheap land for the factory were major questions raised in the post-emergency period. Only a handful of the Sanjay mini-cars were ever built. Now, however, it appears that the factory constructed for his doomed project may finally be completed and a new mini-car manufactured with Japanese technical assistance. Since a modern small car would be the final nail in the coffin for the current antiquated cars, new technology may also be allowed to be imported to update the present vehicles.

India's truck and bus industry is a much larger and more thriving business with companies like Tata and Ashok Leyland turning out sturdy trucks which you see all over India. There is also an active motorcycle and motor-scooter industry. The motorcycles include the splendid Enfield India – a replica of the old single cylinder 350 cc British Royal Enfield Bullet. Enthusiasts for the old British

singles will be delighted to see these modern-day vintage bikes still being made. Motor-scooters include Indian versions of both the Italian Lambretta and the Vespa. When production ceased in Italy, India bought the manufacturing plant from them lock, stock and barrel. Finally there are also a variety of different model mopeds.

TWO-WHEELED EXPERIENCES

The following descriptions of two different ways of travelling independently in India were contributed by Roman Wowk and Ann Sorrel

INDIA ON AN ENFIELD

The possibility of touring India on an Indian motorcycle started as a wild brainstorm with three friends. We jetted into India from Europe via Karachi and first made our way, by bus, train and taxi, to the snow-covered slopes of

A single cylinder, 350cc Enfield India

Gulmarg in Kashmir. There we met our long-lost Scottish companion who had spent six months getting there from Europe via Turkey, Iran and Pakistan on a custom-built touring bicycle. From Kashmir we headed back across the mountain passes to Amritsar on the plains. For a change I relieved my friend of the bicycle and chased the others back south.

We had decided that the Enfield Bullet (350 cc, single-cylinder, four-stroke, vintage British design) was the only feasible machine for our trip and started looking for suitable machines to purchase at the army depots in Jammu and Pathankot. New ones, at around Rs 15,000, were out of the question as this would have left us with no money to pay for the petrol and running costs. So for three weeks we resided at the Golden Temple in Amritsar, courtesy of the ever-hospitable Mr Singh, while we surveyed the used motorcycle scene.

Having tried and tested what felt like every Enfield Bullet for sale in the city and having even stretched the patience of many an Indian we finally purchased two 1971 models and took them on a trial run over the plains and up the mountains to Dharamsala and back. After some incredibly cheap major repairs and adjustments to the machines by a befriended mechanic we were finally ready to go. We grabbed our packed lunch and compass, adjusted our goggles, pointed the bikes in the general direction of east (bearing north-east to south!), kicked them over and took off.

Some 8000 km and 16 weeks later, after innumerable adventures, misadventures, pleasures, trials, punctures, repairs, rip-offs and arguments we had traversed India, visited Nepal and ended up in Calcutta, the end of the road and of our money. Here our patience and the Indians' was tested once again as we bartered the Enfields for a healthy bundle of rupees and departed in different directions.

Perhaps the only better and less obtrusive way to enjoy the kaleidoscopic activity of India would have been by bicycle. But for this you must be willing to expend a much greater amount of physical energy and have much more time although you would also need much less money in the pocket. We found that the feeling of participation offered by this method of travel was much preferable to crowded buses.

Costs

It's possible to fully recover your initial expenditure on a motorcycle if you have the time, patience and some knowledge of prices. We purchased two 1971 models for Rs 6000 and 6500 and managed to sell them for the same price, having spent around Rs 6500 in running and repair costs over four months and 8000 km. Divided by four people this came to a cost of around Rs 1600 each over the period, much less than a rupee a km. Of course the costs are double if you ride solo. As another example another couple we met in Calcutta paid Rs 14,000 for their almost new Bullet, sold it three months later for Rs 10,500 but spent almost nothing on repairs.

Which Motorcycle?

The Indian market is very limited so your choice of motorised two-wheelers is fairly simple. At the bottom of the range are various 50 cc mopeds which cost new around Rs 4000 on the road. Next up are a number of single cylinder two-stroke scooters. The new price of a Lamby 150 cc is Rs 8900, the Lamby 175 cc is Rs 9300 and the Alwyn 150 cc is Rs 9200.

Motorcycles start with three single cylinder two-strokes. The 175 cc Rajdoot is Rs 9400, the 250 cc Yezdi is Rs 10,300 and the 200 cc Enfield Mini Bullet is Rs 10,200. Then there's the 350 cc, single cylinder, four-stroke Enfield Bullet costing Rs 15,500 new. Finally there's the 350 cc, twin cylinder, two-stroke Yamaha Rajdoot which costs Rs 22,600. Also available are old imported originals of these now locally manufactured machines (Jawa, Lambretta, Vijay, Vespa) and the occasional, but rare, old British Ariel, Matchless or BSA.

If you intend to cover any reasonable distance there is only one choice – the Bullet. The other machines are really more suitable for the crowded city streets and short distance runs, they are not so practical over longer distances. The recently released Yamaha licensed 350 is the hottest thing on the market but the price, the four month delivery time and the limited availability of spare parts puts it out of contention.

Price New Bullets cost Rs 15,500. One under three years old and in as-new condition should cost around Rs 14,000. Older bikes up to around six years old in original condition will be in the Rs 12,000 to 13,000 range. The price of older models depends more on condition than age. If it's very good expect to pay Rs 8000 to 10,000; if it's just good Rs 7000 to 8000. A reasonably well kept bike should cost Rs 6000 to 7000 while a very scrappy example will be Rs 5000 to 6000.

For the smaller two-stroke motorcycles and scooters you can expect to pay Rs 2000 or 3000 less for older models. The price will also depend on availability. For example in Amritsar, where the majority of the traffic is two-wheeled due to the narrowness of the streets, the prices may be lower than in other cities.

Where & How to Purchase

India does not have used vehicle dealers, motorcycle magazines or weekend newspapers with pages of motorcycle classified advertisements. To purchase a second hand machine one simply needs to enquire. A good place to start is at mechanics. They are likely to know somebody who is selling a bike. Also there are a number of commission agents who merely act as middlemen to bring buyers and sellers together. They will usually be able to show you a number of machines to suit your price bracket. These agents can also be found by enquiring or may sometimes advertise on their shop fronts.

The commission to these agents is usually Rs 100 each from the buyer and the seller. For an additional fee, which usually covers a bribe to officials, they will assist you in transferring the ownership papers through the bureaucratic system. Without their help this could take a couple of weeks. I can highly recommend the assistance of Mr Ved Rattan Sharma, Punjab Tyre Retreading Works, Outside Gandhi Gate, Near Footbridge, Amritsar. Please don't give him a hard time like we did – and trust him, he will do his best to help you!

Alternatively, if you intend to purchase a new machine this can be done directly through your Enfield (or other motorcycle) dealer in the capital city of any state.

Ownership Papers A needless hint perhaps but do not part with your money until you have the ownership papers, receipt and affidavit signed by a magistrate authorising the owner (as recorded in the ownership papers) to sell the machine. Not to mention the keys to the bike and the bike itself!

Each state has a different set of formalities regarding transfer of ownership. Assistance may be obtained from the agent through whom you are purchasing the machine or from one of the many 'attorneys' hanging around under tin

roofs by the Motor Vehicles Office. They will charge you a fee of up to Rs 100 which will consist largely of a bribe to expedite matters.

Alternatively you could approach one of the many typing clerk services and request them to type out the necessary forms and handle the matter yourself at a much cheaper rate – but with no guarantee of a quick result. Remember to dress very neatly to transact this business as Indian officials have a great contempt for dirty foreigners, and inversely great respect for a well dressed, well spoken one. If you are female or there is a female in your party send her to do it, especially if she is blonde!

Check that your name has been recorded in the ownership book and stamped and signed by the head of the department. If you intend to sell your motorcycle in a different state then you will need a 'No Objections Certificate'. This confirms your ownership and is issued by the Motor Vehicles Department in the state where you bought it so get it immediately when transferring ownership papers to your name. The standard form can be typed up for about Rs 10 or more speedily and expensively through one of the many attorneys. We were unaware of the necessity of obtaining this certificate and discovered that nobody was willing to risk purchasing our machines without it. I had the pleasure of the return train trip from Calcutta to Amritsar (2000 km each way) to collect these pieces of paper!

Other Formalities You can obtain an Indian licence on application but it is more convenient if you have an international driving permit or a licence from your country of residence, even if it is out of date or does not cover riding a motorcycle. It is sufficient if it has 'driver's licence' written on it, and your name. In some state, for example the Punjab, it is forbidden for females to ride a motorcycle (chauvinists!), they can travel only as the pillion passenger. Also in the Punjab it is against the law for two males to ride together on one motorcycle. This is to reduce the number of armed holdups as motorcycles, being the fastest thing on the road, are used as getaway vehicles. Being a foreigner, however, this law will not necessarily apply to you.

As in most countries it is compulsory to have third party insurance. The New India Assurance Company or the National Insurance Company are just two of a number of companies who can provide it. The cost will be approximately Rs 60 for a year or Rs 45 for six months. Road tax must also be paid and costs around Rs 16 per quarter. Delhi is the only place in India where the wearing of crash helmets is enforced. At a pinch you can get away with not wearing one there either.

Repairs & Maintenance

Anyone that can handle a screwdriver and spanner in India can be called a mechanic or 'mistri' so be careful. If you have any mechanical knowledge it may be better to buy your own set of tools and to learn how to do your own repairs. This will save a lot of arguments over the price of repairs. If, however, you are in need of a mechanic try to find a Mr Singh (look for the tell tale turban, beard and steel bangle!). He may charge a little more but you can be assured of proud work at a non rip-off price.

Original Enfield parts purchased from an 'Authorised Enfield Dealer' can be rather expensive in comparison to the copy parts available from your spare parts wallah. Again a Mr Singh can be trusted and is not impartial to a little bargaining. Some costs of typical spare parts or labour costs include an air filter element for around Rs 5. A battery will be Rs 50 on exchange or Rs 100 new, a battery recharge will cost Rs 2. Cables are Rs 7, clutch plates RS 30 (and Rs 10 to fit them), chains Rs 75 front and rear. A new carburettor is Rs 100 but a Japanese one will cost Rs 350. Front fork oil seals are Rs 6 and Rs 4 to fit. You can have a complete engine overhaul for Rs 350 to 400. Points are Rs 20, piston rings Rs 25 (Rs 40 for genuine Enfield), a head gasket Rs 8. Wheelbearings cost Rs 40, a rear wheel sprocket Rs 25.

These prices are only approximate and as a foreigner you're an obvious target for a quick rupee for a not-so-honest mechanic. Beware of 15 minute jobs, which should cost about Rs 10 for labour, taking three hours and costing nearly Rs 100. As a guide a good mechanic makes about Rs 50 per day, so calculate your labour costs on this.

If you purchase an older machine you would do well to check and tighten all nuts and bolts every few days. Indian roads and engine vibration tend to work things loose and constant checking could save you rupees and trouble. Check the engine and gearbox oil level regularly and with the quality of oil it is advisable to change it and clean the oil filter every couple of thousand km.

Punctures Either you're lucky or you're not. One of our bikes did not have a single puncture the whole trip. The other had innumerable punctures including three in one day! In some places I even suspected (paranoia?) nails being scattered on the road to boost business. Pushing a loaded motorcycle is hard enough with a flat tyre it's like pushing a tractor. Puncture wallahs are quite frequent (you'll be surprised where you find them) but it's advisable to at least have sufficient tools to be able to remove your own wheel and take *it* to the puncture wallah (*punkucha wallah* in Hindi).

To remove the rear wheel a pair of adjustable multigrips is the only tool necessary although spanners may be easier to work with. First remove the brake adjusting nut, then the brake cover plate anchor nut. Loosen but do not remove the hub spindle nuts on either side, disconnect the chain at the spring link and disconnect the speedo cable (in the unlikely event that it's currently connected!). Finally loosen the exhaust and silencer nuts if necessary and off comes the wheel.

A puncture repair will cost Rs 5 for one hole while a new tube will cost Rs 15. Tyres are Rs 100 to 150 retread or Rs 250 to 350 new. When replacing the rear wheel ensure that the chain connecting link fastener has its split end pointing in the opposite direction to that in which the chain travels. Adjust the chain with the cam-shaped adjusters so that the chain tension allows about three cm of up and down movement. Check that each cam plate is set on the same number of notches. Finally adjust the footbrake.

Fuel

Petrol is about Rs 6 per litre although it varies slightly from state to state. It's relatively expensive compared to the west and compared to the cost of living in India. A tank of petrol, good for 300 to 400 km, will cost about Rs 80. Note that the Enfield Bullet petrol tank holds 14.5 litres so when the pump reading shows 18 litres you can safely assume the meter has been fixed!

Petrol is usually readily available in all larger towns and along the main roads so there is no need to carry spare fuel. Should you run out try flagging down a passing car (not a truck or bus since they use diesel) and beg for some. Most Indians are willing to let you have some if you have a hose or syphon and a container in which to pour it. Alternatively you could hitch a ride on a truck to the nearest petrol station.

Maps

Bartholomew's Indian Subcontinent is probable the best road map although it's not really detailed enough and not readily available outside the larger cities. Alternatively tourist maps of each state, available from tourist offices, are quite good. If you have no maps then ask the locals. Tell them which direction you're heading and they will probably give you a list of every town, together with distances between each one from here to there. Then again you can work out your general dirion from the sun and head off that way. We found this the most adventurous.

Truck or Train Transport

If you break down well away from a mechanic and spare parts wallah it is possible to catch a ride with a truck for around Rs 5 per 10 km. For the price the driver will drop you off at the doorstep of the nearest mechanic. It's also possible to transport a motorcycle by train over longer distances. As an example a trip of nearly 2000 km costs about Rs 100 for a passenger in 2nd class, Rs 45 for a bicycle or Rs 180 for a motorcycle.

Going Abroad

No special permission is needed to take your motorcycle into Nepal so long as you have your normal visa and you are the registered owner. The motorcycle is declared at customs at the border on entry and is free for the first 15 days. Thereafter it costs Nepalese Rs 15 per day. Before you can take a motorcycle on to the ferry to Sri Lanka you have to obtain special permission in Madras.

Selling It

Selling is really a matter of waiting. The better your patience and the more time you have available the better price you will get, or rather the closer you will get to the market value. You will undoubtedly be offered ridiculous prices, your first counter offer is likely to be half what you ask so when questioned for the selling price ask the prospective purchaser whether he wants the 'Indian price' or the 'English price'. The Indian price being twice the English!

If you have time it is well worth dressing the machine up, particularly if it looks scrappy. A paint job for Rs 120 to 500 (depending on the number of coats of paint) will more than likely

recover its cost. You can get new mudguards for Rs 45, mirrors for Rs 20, a seat cover for Rs 25. Word spreads quickly that you have a machine to sell and if the bike 'looks nice' you'll soon get offers.

Roman Wowk

AND INDIA ON A BICYCLE

Every day millions of Indians pedal along the country's roads. If they can do it so can you. India offers an immense array of challenges for a long distance biker tourer/traveller – there are high altitude passes and rocky dirt tracks; smooth surfaced well-graded highways with roadside restaurants and lodges; coastal routes through coconut palms and winding country roads through coffee plantations. Not to mention city streets with all manner of animal and human powered carts and vehicles as well as the spectacle of the Asian bazaar. Hills, plains, plateaus, deserts – you name it, India's got it!

As elsewhere in the world long distance cycling is not for the faint of heart or weak of knee. You'll need physical endurance to cope with the roads and the climate plus you'll face cultural challenges which I called 'the people factor'.

Books to Read

Before you set out read some books on bicycle touring like *Bike Touring* by Raymond Bridge (Sierra Club, 1979), *Bike Tripping* by Tom Cuthbertson (10 Speed Press, 1972) or *The Bicycle Touring Book* by Tom and Glenda Wilhelm (Rodale Press, 1980). Cycling magazines in your own country will also provide useful information, addresses of spare parts suppliers which may be vital if you have to send for a part, and they're good places to look for a riding companion. For a real feel of the adventure of bike touring in strange places there's Dervla Murphy's classic *Full Tilt – From Ireland to India on a Bike* now available in paperback or Lloyd Summer's *The Long Ride*.

Bring Your Own Bike

Bringing your own lightweight touring bicycle will give you lots of mechanical advantages and make mountainous areas much more approachable but it does have disadvantages. Your machine is likely to be a real curiosity and subject to much pushing, pulling and probing. If you can't tolerate people touching your quality bicycle don't bring it to India!

There are also technical problems so have a working knowledge of your machine and bring any special tools with you. Bring a compact bike manual with lots of diagrams and pictures in case the worst happens and you need to get your rear derailleur or another strategic part remade – the right Indian mechanic/tinkerer can do wonders and illustrations help break down language barriers.

Either bring a good quality bicycle equipped with top line touring components or a no-name 10-speed that you won't regret parting with due to damage, theft or sale. Make sure it's a machine that you're comfortable with.

Spare Parts If you bring a bicycle to India apart from all the normal tools and spares (plenty of spokes) bring a good wire cutter to cleanly cut brake and gear cables. Finding a suitable tool or chisel always seems to be difficult. Long, thin cables for derailleurs aren't available outside major cities so bring enough spares. Bike or moped brake cables bought in India (Rs 30) have to modified to fit brake levers correctly – I found a spoke nipple threaded through the cable is perfect. Be ready to make do and improvise. Roads don't have paved shoulders and hence are very dusty so take care to keep your chain lubricated.

Although India is theoretically metricated, you will find that tools and bike parts are 'standard' or 'English' measurement. So don't expect to find tyres for 700c rims although 27 x 1¼ tyres are produced in India by Dunlop and Sawney. Indian cycle pumps cater to a tube valve different from the Presta and Schraeder valves common on bikes in the west. If you're travelling with Presta valves (most high pressure 27 x 1¼ tubes) bring a Schraeder (car type) adapter. In India you can then obtain another adapter to Indian pumps, which means you'll have an adapter on your adapter! But bring your own pump as well, most Indian pumps require two or three men to get air down the leaky cable.

In big cities Japanese tyres and components (derailleurs, freewheels, chains) can be obtained but they're pricey but then so are postage costs and transit time can be considerable. If you receive bike parts from abroad beware of exorbitant customs charges. Say you want the goods as 'in transit' to avoid these charges. They may list the parts in your passport!

There are a number of shops where you may locate parts. Try Metre Cycle, Kalba Devi Rd,

Bombay or their branch in Trivandrum; the cycle bazaar in the old city around Esplanade Rd, Delhi; Popular Cycle Importing Company on Broadway, Madras; Nundy & Company, Bentinck St, Calcutta. Or locate the cycle market and ask around, bring your bike and there'll be someone who'll know which shop would be most likely to have things for your 'special' cycle. Beware of Taiwanese imitations and do watch out for old rubber on tyres which may have been sitting collecting dust for years.

Luggage Your cycle luggage should be as strong, durable and waterproof as possible. I don't recommend a set with lots of zippers as it makes it easier for the contents to be pilfered. As you'll frequently need to remove luggage to bring cycles into lodge rooms (*never* leave your cycle in the lobby or outside – take it to bed with you!) a set designed to easily remove from racks is a must and the less the number of items the better. Thing about a large capacity handlebar bag and a rear pannier set. Front bags mean two more items to haul about. Richard Jones, PO Box 919, Fort Collins, Colorado 80522, USA makes a set of bike luggage that can be easily reassembled into a backpack. Just the thing when you want to park your bike and go by train or go on a trek.

Theft If you're on an imported bike try to avoid the loss of your pump (and the water bottle from your frame) – they're popular items for theft because of their novelty and their loss is of great inconvenience. Don't leave anything on your bike that can be easily removed when it's unattended. Don't be paranoid about theft – outside of the four big cities it would be well nigh impossible for a thief to resell your bike as it'll stick out too much. And not many folk have the wherewithal to figure out quick-release levers on wheels. In that sense your bike is safer in India than in cities in the west.

Buying a Bike in India
Finding an Indian bike is no problem, every Indian town will have at least a couple of cycle shops. Shop around to find the prices and remember to bargain. Try to get a few extras – bell, stand, spare tube – thrown in. There are many different brands of Indian clunkers – *Hero, Atlas, BSA, Raleigh, Bajaj, Avon* – but they all follow the same basic, sturdy design. *Raleigh* is considered to be the finest quality,

followed by *BSA* which has a big line of models including some sporty jobs. *Hero* and *Atlas* both claim to be the biggest seller but basically you can look for the cheapest or the one with the snazziest plate label.

One you've decided on the bike you have a choice of luggage carriers – most of the rat trap type but varying in size, price and sturdiness. There's a wide range of saddles available but all are equally bum-breaking. A stand is certainly a useful addition and a bell or airhorn can be considered an absolute necessity in India. An advantage of buying a new bike is that the brakes actually work when they're brand new. Centre-pull and side-pull brakes are also available but at extra cost and may actually make the bike more difficult to sell at the end. The average Indian will prefer the standard model.

Spare Parts As there are so many repair 'shops' (some consist of a pump, box of tools, tube of rubber solution and water pan under a tree) there is no need to carry spare parts, especially as you'll only own the bike for a few weeks or months. Just take a roll of tube patch rubber, a tube of Dunlop patch glue, two tyre irons and a wonderful 'universal' bike spanner for Indian bikes (Rs 1) which will fit all the nuts. There are plenty of puncture wallahs in all towns and villages who will patch tubes for Rs 1 so chances are you won't have to fix a puncture yourself anyway. Besides Indian tyres are pretty heavy duty so with luck you won't have a flat during the time you own the bike.

Luggage Easiest is to simply get a rack modified to suit your pack or travel bags. You may want to have special canvas bags for your rear pannier or adopt the popular green canvas school bags for the job.

Selling It Reselling the bike is no problem. Ask the proprietor of your lodge if they know anyone who is interested in buying a bike. Negotiate a price and do the deal personally or through the hotel. Most people will be only too willing to help you. Count on losing Rs 50 to 100 depending on local prices. Retail bike stores are not usually interested in buying or selling second-hand bikes. A better bet would be a bike hire shop which may be interested in expanding their fleet at less cost than for a new bike.

On the Road
The 'people factor' makes a bike ride in India both rewarding and frustrating. It is greatly reduced for those with Indian bikes and can be a decisive element in opting not to bring a 10-speed sports bike. Mob scenes are likely to occur. A halt for tea can bring a crowd of 50 men and boys to encircle you and your machine, offer comments to one another about its operation – one points to the water-bottle saying 'petrol', another twists shifter lever saying 'clutch', another squeezes tyres saying 'tubeless' or 'airless', yet others nod knowingly as 'gear system', 'automatic' and 'racing bike' are mouthed. in some areas you'll even get 'disco bike'!

Worst is on a city street when you stop for a banana, look up as you are about to push off and find rickshaws, cyclists, pedestrians all blocking your way! At times the crowd may be unruly –schoolboys especially. If the mob is just too big just request a lathi-wielding policeman to come. The boys scatter pronto! Sometimes hostile boys may throw rocks. Best advice is to keep pedalling, don't turn around or stop, don't leave your bike and chase them as this will only incite them further. Appeal to adults to discipline them. Children, especially boys seven to 13 years old, aren't disciplined and are dangerous in crowds. Avoid riding by a boys' school at recess.

Routes You can go anywhere on a bike that you would using trains and buses with the added pleasure of seeing all the places in between. Those in great shape and with good cycles may want to ride the Jammu-Srinagar-Leh road which appears to have become the ride 'to do' if you're a long-distance cyclist in India.

Try to avoid the major highways up north like NH1 through Haryana and NH2 – the Grand Trunk (GT) between Delhi and Calcutta. They're plagued by speeding buses and trucks. Other national highways can be pleasant, often lonely country roads and are very well marked with a stone every km. Learn the Hindi script to read signs although at least one marker in five will be in English.

Distances If you've never cycled distances before start with 20 to 40 km per day and build up as you gain stamina and confidence. Cycling long distances is 80% determination and 20% perspiration. Don't be ashamed to push up steep hills either. For an eight-hour pedal a serious cyclist and interested tourist will average 125-150 km a day on undulating plains or 80-100 km in mountainous areas.

Accommodation There's no need to bring a tent as cheap lodges are available almost everywhere and a tent pitched by the road would draw crowds. There's also no need to bring a stove and cooking kit unless you cannot tolerate Indian food as there are plenty of tea stalls and restaurants (called 'hotels'). When you want to eat ask for a 'hotel', when you want a room ask for a 'lodge'. On big highways stop at 'dhabhas', the Indian version of a truck stop. The one with the most trucks parked in front has the best food (or serves alcohol). Dhabhas have charpois (string beds) to serve as tables and seats or as a bed for weary cyclists. They're not recommended for single women riders and you should keep your cycle next to you throughout the night. There will be no bathroom or toilet facilities and plenty of road noise.

This is the best part of travelling on a bike – finding places to stay between the cities or touristically important places. You get to meet Indians in places like Iglas, Hunsur, Santoli, Ramdeora, Cuddalore or Nandyal – places that may only be whistle stops or small hamlets which the buses speed straight through. First, to make it understood that you're seeking a place to stay, use the expression 'night halt'. Then go down the following list: dak bungalow, PWD resthouse, inspection bungalow, travellers bungalow, municipal or panchayat guest house. These are dirt cheap (Rs 4 to 10) government accommodation.

Circuit houses are more expensive while dharmsalas (lodges for pilgrims) offer primitive conditions (furniture-less rooms) but some can be pleasant and for free or just Rs 3 to 5 they can't be beat. Ashrams and meditation centres are good bets for lodging and a meal for wandering cyclists. In a village off the road you may end up with a teacher or bank clerk (the most likely people to speak English). They may put you in the school building or simply invite you home to stay with their families. Accommodation will always turn up in some manner or form.

Towns will have lodges and real hotels – start looking near the bus and train stations.

Directions Asking directions can be a real frustration. Approach people who look like they can speak English and aren't in a hurry. Always ask three or four different people just to be certain, use traffic police only as a last resort. Try to be patient but be careful about 'left' and 'right' and be prepared for instructions like 'go straight and turn here and there'!

Maps The most detailed maps are the *Travel & Tourism* plates of the National Atlas prepared by the National Atlas Organisation, 1 Acharya Jagadish Bose Rd, Calcutta 20 and available at most major Automobile Assocation offices. The AA has other road maps too. The plates mark places of historic and architectural interest, indicate types of roads, temples, mosques and dak bungalows. India is covered in 15 plates costing approximately Rs 4 to 5 each, their weight and bulk is the major disadvantage.

A small, light book entitled *The Maps Road Atlas of India* costs Rs 12 and is highly recommended. It's published by Tamilnad Printers & Traders, Chrompet, Madras 600044. It includes street maps of major cities, distance charts and an excellent concise guide to the states. The Government of India Tourist Information booklets not only have fairly good road maps of each state but also road distances to places of tourist interest and break-up distances. They also issue certain road route maps specially meant for tourists with vehicles. Bartholomew's Indian Subcontinent map includes roads and can be useful in some areas because it includes small town maps and gives an idea of geographic features. It's best to have two or three different maps of the same region.

Transporting Your Bike Sometimes you may want to quit pedalling – for sports bikes air travel is easy. With luck airline staff may not be familiar with procedures so use it to your advantage. Tell them it doesn't need to be dismantled and you've never had to pay for it. Remove all luggage and accessories and let the tyres down a bit.

Bus travel with a bike varies from state to state. Generally it goes free on the roof. If it's a sports bike stress that it's lightweight. Secure it well to the roof rack, check it's in a place where it won't get damaged and take all your luggage inside.

Train travel is more complex – pedal up to the railway station, buy a ticket, explain you want to book a cycle for the journey. You'll be directed to the luggage offices or officer where a triplicate form is prepared. Fill out and note down your bike's serial number and a good description of it. Again only the bike, not luggage or accessories. Your bike gets decorated with one copy of the form, usually pasted on the seat, and you get another. God only knows what happens to the other. The minimum rate is Rs 8 but overall it's not too expensive. Produce your copy of the form to claim the bicycle from the luggage van at your destination. If you change trains en route *personally* ensure the cycle changes too!

Final Words Just how unique is a cycle tourist in India? I'd venture to guess about 500 foreign cyclists each year go on a month or more ride somewhere on the sub-continent. And the number's rapidly growing. Perhaps 5000 Indians do tours too – mostly young men and college students. Kashmir to Kanyakumari or a pilgrimage to holy places are their most common goals. For your ego newspaper attention is there for the asking.

If you're a serious cyclist or amateur racer and want to contact counterparts while in India there's the Cycle Federation of India; contact the Secretary, Yamun Velodrome, New Delhi. Last words of advice – make sure your rubber solution is gooey, all your winds are tailwinds and remember to go straight and turn here and there.

Ann Sorrel

BOATS

Apart from ferries across rivers – of which there are a great number – there are not many boat trips to be made in India although a couple are really good. One is the popular trip between Bombay and Goa, since rail connections between the two places are not particularly good this shipping service is very popular. It is suspended during the monsoon, however. Further south the backwater trip in Kerala is an excellent way of not only getting from A to B but also experiencing Kerala as you travel – a not to be missed trip. There is also a three times weekly ferry service between India and Sri Lanka.

HITCH-HIKING

Possible but not always easy. There are not that many private cars streaking across India so you are likely to be on

board trucks. You are then stuck with the old 'do they understand what I am doing, should I be paying for this, will the driver expect to be paid/unhappy if I don't offer to pay/unhappy if I do or simply want too much' quandary. But it is possible.

LOCAL TRANSPORT

Although there are comprehensive local bus networks in most major towns unless you have time to familiarise yourself with the routes you're better sticking to taxis, auto-rickshaws and rickshaws. In the big cities the buses are usually so hopelessly overcrowded that you can only really use them if you get on at the starting point – and get off at the terminus!

A basic ground rule applies to any form of transport where the fare is not ticketed or fixed (like a bus or train), or metered – agree the fare beforehand. If you fail to do that you can expect enormous arguments and hassles when you get to your destination. And agree the fare clearly – if there is more than one of you make sure it covers both of you. One writer suggested an alternative plan of attack with drivers who will not use the meter – jump aboard without agreeing any fare and at the end of the trip pay what you think it should be. If he doesn't agree then suggest he calls the police to settle the matter. In that traveller's experience agreement usually quickly resulted! If you have baggage make sure there is no extra charge for baggage. If you don't you can be certain there will be more extra charges than you could dream of.

In almost all forms of powered transport in India from taxis and auto-rickshaws through to jet aircraft note how a disproportionate number of the operators are Sikhs. In India's chaotic traffic conditions a martial background helps.

Airport Transport

There are official buses, either government operated, Indian Airlines or some local co-operative, to most airports in India. Where there isn't one there will be taxis or auto-rickshaws. There are even some airports close enough to town to get to by cycle-rickshaw! The bus services keep other operators reasonably honest so it is not difficult getting to or from any of India's airports.

Taxis

There are taxis in most towns in India and in most of them, certainly in all the major cities, the taxis will be metered. Getting a metered fare is rather a different situation. First of alll the meter may be 'broken'. Threatening to get another taxi will usually fix the meter immediately, except during rush hours.

Secondly the meter will certainly be out of date. Fares are adjusted upwards so much faster and more frequently than meters are recalibrated that drivers almost always have 'fare adjustment cards' indicating what you should pay compared to what the meter indicates. This is, of course, wide open to abuse. You have no idea if you're being shown the right card or even if the taxi's meter has

actually been recalibrated and you're being shown the card anyway. The only answer is to try and get an idea of what the fare should be before departure (ask information desks at the airport or your hotel). You'll soon begin to develop a feel for what the meter says, what the cards say and what the two together should indicate.

Auto-Rickshaw

An auto-rickshaw is a noisy three wheel device with a driver up front, a two-stroke motorcycle engine and seats for two passengers behind. They're generally about half the price of a taxi, are usually metered and the same ground rules apply as for taxis. Because of their size they are often faster than taxis for short distance trips and their drivers are often decidedly nuttier – glancing blow collisions are not infrequent. Also known as scooters or motor trishaws.

Tempos

Somewhat like a large auto-rickshaw

A TEMPO

these ungainly looking devices operate rather like mini-buses or share taxis along fixed routes. In Delhi there are three-wheeler vehicles pulled by old Harley Davidson motorcycles which perform the same function.

Cycle-Rickshaw

Also known as a trishaw this is effectively a three-wheeler bicycle with a seat for two passengers behind the rider. Although they no longer operate in the big cities you will still find them in all the smaller towns and they're the basic means of transport there. Fares must always be agreed in advance with a trishaw rider, about a rupee a km is a good rule of thumb rate. In places like Agra, where there are a lot of them, the riders are as talkative and opinionated as any New York cabbie. Once upon a time there also used to be the old man-powered rickshaws but today these only exist in Calcutta.

It's quite feasible to hire a rickshaw-wallah by time, not just for a straight trip. Hiring one for a day or even several days can make quite good sense. One traveller commented how, when taking on a rickshaw for several days, the rider would insist that he should 'pay as you like, I just want to please' but, he continued, 'no matter where we went, no matter how generous we were, we were always told at leaving that we had not given them enough'. Settle a price beforehand, no matter how much they insist they don't want to.

Hassling over the fares is the biggest difficulty of cycle-rickshaw travel. They'll often go all out for a fare higher than it would cost you by taxi or auto-rickshaw. Nor does actually agreeing a fare always make a difference, there is always a greater possibility of a post-travel fare disagreement when you travel by cycle-rickshaw than by taxi or auto-rickshaw – metered or not.

Other

In some places tongas (horse drawn two-wheelers) and victorias (horse drawn carriages) still operate. Calcutta has an extensive tramway network and will soon have India's first underground railway. Bombay has suburban trains.

Bicycles

India is a country of bicycles and they're an ideal way of getting around the sights in a city or even making longer trips – see the section on touring India by bicycle. Bicycle shops in most commercial centres will have bicycles for hire and you can often find them even in quite small villages. They charge from around 0.50 an hour or Rs 4 or 6 per day. In some places they may be unwilling to hire to you since you are a stranger but you can generally get around this by offering some sort of ID card as security. Check the time they put in the log book before you pedal off. If you should be so unfortunate as to get a puncture you'll soon spot men sitting under trees with puncture repair outfits at the ready less than a rupee to fix it. If you're asking distances you'll often be told in furlongs – eight to a mile, five to a km.

If you're travelling with small children and would like to use bikes a lot consider getting a bicycle seat made up. If you find a shop making cane furniture they'll quickly make up a child's bicycle seat from a sketch. Get it made to fit on a standard size rear carrier and it can be securely attached with a few lengths of cord. Tony Wheeler's two children, Tashi and Kieran, have both done a bit of travelling on the back of Indian bicycles.

TOURS

At almost any place of tourist interest in India, and a good few places where there's not much tourist interest, there will be tours operated either by the Government of India Tourist office, the state tourist office or the local transport company – sometimes by all three. These tours are usually excellent value particularly in cities or places where the tourist sights are widespread. You probably could not even get around the sights in New Delhi on public transport as cheaply as you could on a half day or day tour of that city.

These tours are not strictly for western tourists, you will almost always find yourself far outnumbered by local tourists and in many places just a little off the beaten track you will often be the only westerner on the bus. Despite this the tours are usually conducted in English – which is possibly the only common language for the middle class Indian tourists in any case. These tours are an excellent place for meeting Indians.

If they have a drawback it is simply that many of them try to cram far too much into too short a period of time. A one day tour which whisks you from Madras to Kanchipuram, Tirukalikundram, Mahabalipuram and back to Madras is not going to give you time for more than the most fleeting glimpse. If a tour looks simply too hectic you're better doing it yourself at a more appropriate pace or taking the tour simply to find out what places you really want to devote more time to.

Coping with India – Getting Things Done

You soon realise why better off Indians have lots of servants. It's nothing to do with being lazy, it's simply that everything takes so long in India that if you did it all yourself you'd never have had the time to become better off in the first place. Travellers too find that a lot of their time is tied up in interminable queues or trying to find out when things depart or where a room is available. The answer is don't do it – get somebody to do it for you. In India labour is cheap, there'll always be some boy at the hotel who will happily stand in the line for hours to pick up your train ticket – all for a few rupees baksheesh.

Similarly those hotel touts who swoop out to meet new arrivals in any reasonable size town really do fill a need if every place in town is full. They'll know exactly where the last free room is and save you a lot of futile marching around. If you want something in India and you don't know where to get it don't waste your time looking – announce loudly 'I want to take a taxi to X tomorrow'. Nine chances out of 10 somebody at your hotel will have heard about the empty taxi going back to X and willing to take a passenger for half price. Get somebody else to do the leg work!

Ganja

Yes there's an awful lot of that well known weed in India. Shiva, the most worshipped of gods, is supposed to devote a fair amount of time to smoking dope in his remote Himalayan home so it would be pretty difficult to ignore it. In fact there are government hashish shops in places like Varanasi, Puri and Jaipur but effectively it's illegal unless you happen to be a Hindu sadhu or someone similar who clearly needs it!

If you want to find it you'll have little problem anywhere in India. Goa with its large resident travellers' population, Kashmir and the Kulu Valley, where it grows in profusion, and Varanasi, with its religious connections, are all good places. Discretion is the key word wherever you are. Don't smoke in public and don't leave it lying around in hotel rooms.

The places to avoid it include the airports and a number of railway stations. Often dope searches are simply ways of extracting a little backsheesh but it's still wise not to get involved. Along the popular Delhi-Bombay railway route, at Allahabad, from Patna up to the Nepalese border, are all places where dope searches have been known to take place. In Delhi there are occasional dope raids on the cheaper hotels, particularly around Pahar Ganj, and in Agra in the cheap hotels just south of the Taj.

New Delhi

Population: 4.5 million
Area: 1485 square km
Main Languages: Hindi, Urdu & Punjabi

New Delhi is the capital of India and also the third largest city. The city actually consists of two parts. Delhi or 'Old' Delhi was the capital of Moslem India between the 12th and 19th centuries. In Old Delhi you will find many mosques, monuments and forts relating to India's Moslem history. The other Delhi is New Delhi, the imperial city created as a capital of India by the British. It is a spacious open city and contains many embassies and government buildings. New Delhi has a third important factor apart from its historic interest and role as the government centre – it is also a major travel gateway. New Delhi is one of India's busiest entrance points for overseas airlines, is on the overland route across Asia and is also the hub of the north Indian travel network.

History

Delhi has not always been the capital of India but it has played an important role in Indian history ever since the epic Mahabharata, 5000 years ago. Under the emperor Ashoka, over 2000 years ago, Pataliputra, near modern day Patna, was the capital of his kingdom. More recently the Moghul emperors made Agra the capital through the 16th and 17th centuries. Under the British, Calcutta was the capital until the construction of New Delhi in 1911. Of course, it is only comparatively recently that India as we know it has been unified as one country. Even at the height of their powers the Moghuls did not control the south of India for example. But Delhi has always been an important city or a capital of the northern region of the sub-continent.

There have been at least eight cities

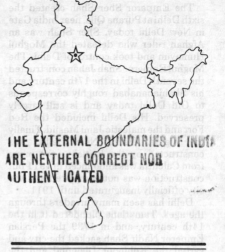

THE EXTERNAL BOUNDARIES OF INDIA
ARE NEITHER CORRECT NOR
AUTHENTICATED

around modern Delhi. The first four were south of modern New Delhi around the area where the Qutab Minar stands. The earliest known Delhi was called Indraprastha and was centred near the present day Purana Qila. At the beginning of the 12th century AD the last Hindu kingdom of Delhi was ruled by the Tomar and Chauthan dynasties and was also near the Qutab Minar and Suran Kund, now in Haryana.

This city was followed by Siri which was constructed by Allah-ud-Din near the present day Hauz Khas in the 12th century. The third Delhi was Tughlaqabad, now entirely in ruins, which stood 10 km south-east of the Qutab Minar. The fourth Delhi dates from the 14th century and was also a creation of the Tughlaqs. Known as Jahanpanah, it also stood near the Qutab Minar.

The fifth Delhi, Ferozabad, was sited at Ferozshah Kotla in present day Old Delhi. Its ruins contain an Ashoka pillar, moved here from elsewhere, and traces of a mosque in which Tamerlane prayed during his attack on India.

The Emperor Sher Shah created the sixth Delhi at Purana Qila, near India Gate in New Delhi today. Sher Shah was an Afghan ruler who defeated the Moghul Humayun and took control of Delhi. The Moghul Emperor Shah Jahan constructed the seventh Delhi in the 17th century and his Shahjahanabad roughly corresponds to Old Delhi today and is still largely preserved. His Delhi included the Red Fort and the majestic Jami Masjid. Finally the eighth Delhi, New Delhi, was constructed by the British – the move from Calcutta was announced in 1911 but construction was not completed and the city officially inaugurated until 1911.

Delhi has seen many invaders through the ages. Tamarlane plundered it in the 14th century, and in 1739 the Persian Emperor Nadir Shah sacked the city and carted the Kohinoor Diamond and the famous Peacock Throne off to Iran. The British captured it in 1803, but during the Indian mutiny in 1857 Delhi was a centre of resistance against the British. Prior to partition Delhi had a very large Moslem population and Urdu was the main language. Now Punjabis have replaced many of the Moslems and Hindi predominates.

Orientation

Delhi is a relatively easy city to find your way around although it is very spread out. All of Delhi of interest to visitors is on the west bank of the Yamuna River and is divided basically into two parts – old Delhi and New Delhi. Desh Bandhu Gupta Rd and Asaf Ali Rd mark the boundary between the tightly packed streets of the old city and the spaciously planned areas of the new capital.

Old Delhi is the 17th century walled city with city gates, narrow alleys, the enormous Red Fort and Jami Masjid of Shah Jahan, temples, mosques, bazaars and the famous street known as Chandni Chowk. Here you will also find the Old Delhi Railway Station and, a little further north, the Interstate Bus Terminal near Kashmiri Gate. Near New Delhi Railway Station, and acting as a sort of 'buffer zone' between the old and new cities, is Pharganj. There are a number of popular cheap hotels and restaurants in this area.

The 'hub' of New Delhi is the great circle of Connaught Place and the streets that radiate out from it. Here you will find most of the airline offices, banks, travel agents, the various state tourist offices and the national one, more budget accommodation and several of the big hotels. The Regal Cinema, at the south side of the circle, and the Plaza Cinema, at the north, are two important Connaught Place landmarks and are very useful for telling taxi or auto-rickshaw drivers where you want to go.

Janpath, running off Connaught Place to the south, is one of the most important streets with the Government of India Tourist Office, the Student Travel Information Centre in the Imperial Hotel and a number of other useful addresses. New Delhi is a planned city of wide, tree-lined streets, parks and fountains. It can be further sub-divided into the business and living areas around Connaught Place and the government areas around Raj Path to the south. At one end of Raj Path is the India Gate memorial and at the other end is the Indian Parliament building.

South of the New Delhi government areas are Delhi's more expensive residential areas with names like Defence Colony, Lodi Colony or Friend's Colony. Delhi airport is to the south-west of the city and about half-way between the airport and Connaught Place is Chanakyapuri, the diplomatic enclave. Most of Delhi's embassies are concentrated in this modern area and there are also a number of the major hotels here.

Information

The Government of India Tourist Office (tel 43005-8) is at 88 Janpath and is open from 8 am to 7 pm in summer, 9 am to 7 pm in winter. The office has a lot of

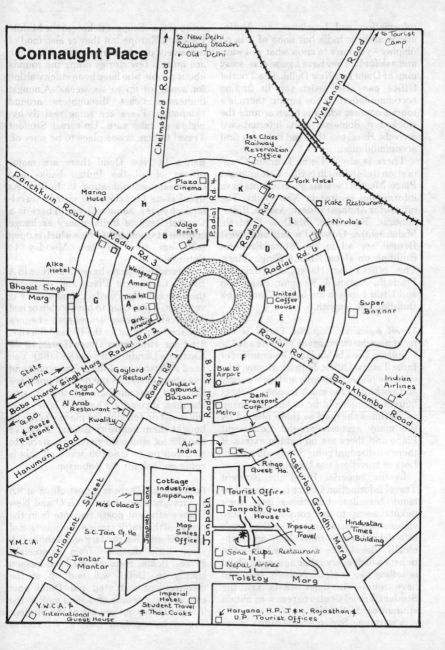

Connaught Place

to New Delhi Railway Station + Old Delhi

to Tourist Camp

Chelmsford Road

Vivekanand Road

1st Class Railway Reservation Office

Plaza Cinema

York Hotel

Marina Hotel

Kake Restaurant

Panchkuin Road

Volga Rest.

Nirula's

Radial Rd. 3

Radial Rd.

Wengers
Amex
Thai Int
P.O.
Brit. Airways

United Coffee House

Radial Rd. 6

Super Bazaar

Alka Hotel

Bhagat Singh Marg

Radial Rd. 2

Radial Rd. 7

State Emporia

Radial Rd. 1

Bus to Airport

Indian Airlines

Baba Kharak Singh Marg

Gaylord Restaurant

Underground Bazaar

Radial Rd. 8

Delhi Transport Corp.

Barakhamba Road

Kegal Cinema

Metro

Al Arab Restaurant

Kwality

G.P.O. + Poste Restante

Hanuman Road

Air India

Ringo Guest Ho.

Tourist Office

Janpath Guest House

Hindustan Times Building

Parliament Street

Mrs Colaca's

Cottage Industries Emporium

Janpath Lane

Tripsout Travel

S.C. Jain G. Ho.

Map Sales Office

Janpath

Kasturba Gandhi Marg

Sona Rupa Restaurant

Nepal Airlines

Jantar Mantar

Y.M.C.A.

Y.W.C.A.
International Guest House

Imperial Hotel, Student Travel + Thos. Cooks

Tolstoy Marg

Haryana, H.P., J+K, Rajasthan + U.P. Tourist Offices

information and brochures on destinations all over India but none of it is on display – you have to know what you want and ask for it. They have a good give-away map of Delhi and New Delhi. The Tourist Office can also assist you in finding accommodation. At the airport there is a tourist counter which is open around the clock for domestic and international arrivals. Here, too, they can help you find accommodation.

There is also a Delhi Tourism Corporation (tel 46356) in N Block, Connaught Place. Most of the state governments have information centres in New Delhi. The offices for Andhra Pradesh, Assam, Bihar, Gujurat, Karnataka, Madhya Pradesh, Maharashtra, Orissa, Punjab and West Bengal are all in the State Emporia Building on Baba Kharak Singh Marg. The offices for Harayana, Himachal Pradesh, Jammu & Kashmir, Rajasthan and Uttar Pradesh are in the Chandralok Building, 36 Janpath.

Travel Agencies Tripsout Travel is the most popular travel agent by far, it's at 72/7 Tolstoy Lane behind the Government of India Tourist Office, Janpath. Sonny, who runs the place, is friendly and trustworthy and nothing is too much trouble. Tickets bought here should be at least as cheap (sometimes cheaper) as those offered by the many agencies around Connaught Place and there are no hidden extras. If there's a discount going Sonny will have it. Lots of travellers use the place.

In the Imperial Hotel the Student Travel Information Centre is also used by many travellers but these days their tickets seem to be consistently more expensive than elsewhere. Also they won't sell tickets which they claim are technically illegal, like discounted Aeroflot tickets which every other agency in Delhi is selling like confetti. Nobody seems to have trouble with these tickets. Visit the Student Travel Centre to renew or obtain student cards, though.

A warning – Syrian Arab Airlines offers some of the cheapest tickets to the Middle East and Europe but they're also fond of massively overbooking flights and there are quite a few stories doing the rounds about people who have been stuck waiting for seats for up to six weeks! Amongst numerous ticket discounters around Connaught Place are some real fly-by-nights so take care. Universal Student Travel Centre is one place to be wary of.

Banks In New Delhi there are major offices of all the Indian banks and overseas ones operating in Indian. As usual some branches will change travellers' cheques, some will not. There is a Central Bank of India money exchange counter at Connaught Place which is open 8.30 am to 7.30 pm, Monday to Saturday.

American Express have their office in A Block, Connaught Place and, although they are usually crowded, their service is very fast. If you need to have stolen or lost American Express travellers' cheques replaced you must go the Refund Service, 8th floor, Hindustan Times House, 18-20 Kasturba Gandhi Marg (tel 385362). You need a photocopy of the police report and one photo as well as the proof of purchase slip and the numbers of the missing cheques. If you don't have the latter they will insist on telexing the place where you bought them before re-issuing. If you've had the lot stolen they are empowered to give you up to US$200 while all this is going on. Ask for Mr Robinson.

Post Offices There is a post office at 9A Connaught Place but the GPO and New Delhi's efficient poste restante is in the centre of the traffic circle at the junction of Baba Kharak Singh Marg and Ashoka Rd, some little distance from Connaught Place. Poste restante mail addressed simply to 'Delhi' will end up at the inconveniently-situated old Delhi post office. Some people also send mail to the Tourist Office on Janpath or the Student Travel Information Centre. Of course

American Express have their clients' mail service.

Bookshops There are a number of excellent bookshops around Connaught Place – a good place to stock up with hefty paperbacks to while away those long train rides or to look for interesting Indian books. Some of the better shops include the New Book Depot at 18 B Block, Connaught Place; the English Book Depot; the Piccadilly Book Store; the Oxford Book Shop in N Block, Connaught Place and the Bookworm in B Block, Connaught Place. There are lots of books for sale near the Regal Cinema.

Libraries and Organisations The US Information Service is at 24 Kasturba Gandhi Marg and is open from 10 am to 6 pm. The British Council's Library is open from 10 am to 7 pm and is in the AIFACS Building, Rafi Marg. There are also cultural centres from France, Bulgaria, Italy, Japan and the USSR.

Sapru House on Barakhamba Rd is an institution devoted to the study of people of the world and has a good library. The India International Centre, beside the Lodi Tombs, has lectures each week on art, economics and other contemporary issues by Indian and foreign experts.

Airlines Addresses of airlines that fly to Delhi include:

Aeroflot	Kanchenjunga Building, Barakhamba Rd (tel 42843)
Air France	6 Scindia House, Connaught Place (tel 374775)
Air India	Scindia House, Connaught Place (tel 344225)
Alitalia	19 Kasturba Gandhi Marg (tel 351019)
British Airways	1A Connaught Place (tel 343428)
Indian Airlines	Kanchenjunga Building, Barakhamba Rd (tel 40052)
KLM	9A Connaught Place (tel 343998)
Lufthansa	56 Janpath (tel 321142)

Pan Am	Chandralok Building, 36 Janpath (tel 322322)
Nepal Airlines	44 Janpath (tel 321572)
Thai International	12A Connaught Place (tel 343608)
SAS	12A Connaught Place (tel 343638)

Embassies Addresses of some of the embassies in Delhi include:

Australia	1/50G Shantipath, Chanakyapuri (tel 690336)
Bangladesh	56 Mahatma Gandhi Marg (tel 515668)
Bhutan	Chandra Gupta Marg (tel 699227)
Burma	3/50F Nyaya Marg, Chanakyapuri (tel 690251)
Canada	7/8 Shantipath, Chanakyapuri (tel 619461)
China	50D Shantipath, Chanakyapuri (tel 690448)
Denmark	2 Golf Links (tel 618354)
Finland	42 Golf Links (tel 611547)
Germany (West)	6/60G Shantipath, Chanakyapuri (tel 694301)
Indonesia	50A Chanakyapuri (tel 692392)
Iran	65 Golf Links (tel 609521)
Ireland	13 Jor Bagh (tel 617435)
Japan	4/50G Chanakyapuri (tel 694271)
Malaysia	50M Satya Marga, Chanakyapuri (tel 690314)
Nepal	Barakhamba Rd (tel 381484)
Netherlands	6/50F Shantipath, Chanakyapuri (tel 699271)
Norway	Kautilya Marg, Chanakyapuri (tel 615982)
Pakistan	Shantipath, Chanakyapuri (tel 699271)
Singapore	48 Golf Links (tel 618139)
Sri Lanka	27 Kautilya Marg, Chanakyapuri (tel 370201)
Sweden	Nyaya Marg, Chanakyapuri (tel 694225)
Thailand	56N Nyaya Marg, Chanakyapuri (tel 615985)
UK	Shantipath, Chanakyapuri (tel 690371)
USA	Shantipath, Chanakyapuri (tel 690351)
USSR	Shantipath, Chanakyapuri (tel 615708)
UN	56 Lodi Estate (tel 690410)

New Delhi is a good place for getting visas. In particular Thai visas are issued with less fuss here than in Kathmandu.

Other Information If Delhi's summer heat (night temperatures in June average 37°C after days in the 41 to 45°C bracket) gets too much hotel pools are a good retreat. You can use the Ashoka Hotel pool for Rs 20 a day or the pool at the Imperial Hotel for Rs 23.

At the Town Hall opposite the Jantar Mantar you can get cholera injections for Rs 5.

Delhi Architecture

The various periods of Delhi's history can be traced in the many historic buildings around the city. These can be roughly divided into early, middle and late Pathan periods followed by early, middle and late Moghul periods.

Early Pathan (1193-1320) The Qutab Minar complex dates from this period, which was characterised by a combination of Hindu designs with those of the Moslem invaders. Domes and arches were the chief imported elements.

Middle Pathan (1320-1414) The Tughlaqabad buildings date from the beginning of this period. Later buildings include the Feroz Shah Kotla mosque, the Hauz Khas tomb, the Nizam-ud-din mosque and the Khirki mosque. At first local stone and red sandstone was used, later giving way to stone and mortar walls with plaster facing. Characteristic design elements include sloping walls and high platforms for the mosques.

Late Pathan (1414-1556) The Saiyad and Lodi tombs and the Purana Qila date from this period. The impressive domes and coloured marble or tile decorations are characteristic of this period.

Moghul (1556-1754) During the early Moghul period buildings were of red sandstone with marble details, Humayun's and Azam Khan's tombs are typical examples. During the middle period much more use of marble was made, and buildings had bulbous domes and towering minarets. The Red Fort, the Jami Masjid and the Fatehpur mosque are all good examples, but the supreme building from this period is, of course, the Taj Mahal in Agra. In the later Moghul period the style became over-elaborate, good examples of this decadent period are the Sonehri mosque on Chandni Chowk in old Delhi and the Safdar Jang tomb, probably the last notable Moghul building.

Old Delhi

The old walled city of Shahjahanabad stands to the west of the Red Fort and was at one time surrounded by a sturdy defensive wall, only fragments of which now exist. The Kashmiri Gate, at the northern end of the walled city, was the scene for desperate fighting when the British retook Delhi during the Mutiny. West of here, near Sabzi Mandi, is the British-erected Mutiny Memorial to the soldiers who lost their lives in the events of the uprising. Near the monument is another Ashoka pillar. Like the one in Feroz Kotla, it was brought here by Feroz Shah Tughlaq.

The main street of old Delhi is the colourful shopping bazaar known as Chandni Chowk. It's hopelessly congested day and night, a very sharp contrast to the open, spacious streets of New Delhi. At the east (Red Fort) end of Chandni Chowk, and north of the Jami Masjid, there is a Jain temple with a small marble courtyard surrounded by a colonnade. Next to the Kotwali (police station) is the Sunehri Masjid. In 1739 Nadir Shah, the Persian invader who carried off the Peacock Throne when he sacked Delhi, stood on the roof of the mosque and watched while his soldiers conducted a bloody massacre of the Delhi inhabitants.

The west end of Chandni Chowk is marked by the Fatehpuri Mosque which one of Shah Jahan's wives erected in 1650.

Red Fort

The red sandstone walls of Lal Qila, the Red Fort, extend for two km and vary in height from 18 metres on the river side to 33 metres on the city side. Shah Jahan commenced construction of the massive fort in 1638 and it was completed in 1648. He never completely moved his capital from Agra to his new city of Shahjahanabad in Delhi because his son Aurangzeb deposed him and imprisoned him in Agra Fort.

The Red Fort dates from the very peak of Moghul power. When the emperor rode out on elephant back into the streets of old Delhi it was a display of pomp and power at its most magnificent. The Moghul period at the top was a short one, however. Aurangzeb was the first and last great Moghul emperor to rule from here. Today the fort is typically Indian with would-be guides leaping forth to offer their services as soon as you enter. It's still a calm haven of peace if you've just left the frantic streets of old Delhi. The city noise and confusion is light years away from the fort gardens and pavilions. If you look out over the fort wall towards the Yamuna River there will probably be assorted musicians, contortionists, rope climbers, magicians, dancing bears and rope climbers down below. Entry to the fort is Rs 0.50.

Lahore Gate The main gate to the fort takes its name from the fact that it faces towards Lahore, now in Pakistan. You enter the fort here and immediately find yourself in a vaulted arcade, now given over to small shops. This was once the Meena Bazaar – the shopping centre for ladies of the court. The arcade of shops leads into the Naubat Khana, which used to be a gallery for musicians, but is now just an open courtyard.

Diwan-i-Am The 'Hall of Public Audiences' was where the emperor would sit to hear complaints or disputes from his subjects. His alcove in the wall was marble panelled and set with precious stones –

many of which were looted following the Mutiny. This elegant hall was restored by Lord Curzon.

Diwan-i-Khas The 'Hall of Private Audiences' was the luxurious chamber where the emperor would hold private meetings. Centrepiece of the hall, until Nadir Shah carted it off to Iran in 1739, was the magnificent Peacock Throne. The solid gold throne had figures of peacocks standing behind it, their beautiful colours coming from countless inlaid precious stones. Between them was the figure of a parrot carved out of a single emerald. This masterpiece in precious metals, sapphires, rubies, emeralds and pearls was broken up, and the so-called Peacock Throne displayed in Tehran simply utilises various bits of the original.

In 1760 the Marathas also removed the silver ceiling from the hall so today it is a pale shadow of its former glory. Inscribed on the walls of the Diwan-i-Khas is that famous Persian couplet:

If there is a paradise on earth
it is this, it is this, it is this

Royal Baths Next to the Diwan-i-Khas are the hamams or baths – three large rooms surmounted by domes, with a fountain in the centre. One of the baths was set up as a sauna!

Moti Masjid Built in 1659 by Aurangzeb the Pearl Mosque is next to the baths. It is made of marble and there is an additional Rs 0.50 charge to the mosque (free on Fridays).

Other The Rang Mahal pavilion or 'Painted Palace' took its name from the painted interior which has now gone. The Khas Mahal was the private palace of the emperor and was divided into rooms for worship, sleeping and living. There is a small Museum of Archaeology in the Mumtaz Mahal. The Delhi Gate to the south of the fort led to the Jami Masjid.

Sound & Light Show Each evening a son et lumiere show recreates events of India's history, particularly those connected with the Red Fort. There are shows in English and Hindi and tickets are available from the ITDC in L Block, Connaught Place (tel 42336, 40982), or at the fort. They cost Rs 3 and Rs 5. Timings vary with the season so check at the Tourist Office. One of the slogans in the fight for independence was that the tri-coloured Indian flag would replace the Union Jack over the Red Fort.

Jami Masjid
The great mosque of old Delhi is both the largest mosque in India and the final architectural extravagance of Shah Jahan. Commenced in 1644, the mosque was not completed until 1658. The mosque has three great gateways, four angle towers and two minarets which stand 40 metres high and are constructed of alternating vertical strips of red sandstone and white marble. Broad flights of steps lead up to the imposing gateway and for Rs 2 (plus Rs 2 for a camera if you have one) you can ascend the minarets. Women are only allowed up if they are accompanied by 'the responsible male relatives'. There's also a fine view of the Red Fort from the east side of the mosque. The Jami Masjid has a capacity of 25,000 people.

Raj Ghat
North-east of Feroz Shah Kotla, on the banks of the Yamuna, a simple square platform of black marble marks the spot where Mahatma Gandhi was cremated following his assasination in 1948. A ceremony takes place each Friday, the day he was killed. Jawaharlal Nehru, the first Indian Prime Minister, was also cremated here in 1964. The Raj Ghat is now a beautiful park, complete with labelled trees planted by a mixed bag of notables including QE2, Gough Whitlam, Dwight Eisenhower and Ho Chi Minh!

Feroz Shah Kotla
Erected by Feroz Shah Tughlaq in 1354 the ruins of Ferozabad, the fifth city of Delhi, are between the old and new Delhis. In the fortress-palace is an Ashoka pillar with Ashoka's edicts (and a later inscription) on the 13 metre high column. The ruins of an old mosque and a fine well can also be seen in the area, but the ruins were used for the construction of later cities.

Connaught Place
At the northern end of New Delhi, Connaught Place is the business and tourist centre of New Delhi. It's a vast traffic circle with an architecturally uniform series of buildings around the edge – mainly devoted to shops, airline offices and the like. It's spacious but busy, and you're continually approached by people willing to provide you with every imaginable necessity from an airline ticket to Timbuktu to having your fortune read.

Jantar Mantar
Only a short stroll down Parliament St from Connaught Place, this strange collection of salmon-coloured structures is another of Maharaja Jai Singh II's observatories. The ruler from Jaipur constructed this observatory in 1725 and it is dominated by a huge sundial known as the 'Prince of Dials'. Other instruments plot the course of heavenly bodies, the paths of stars and predict eclipses.

Laxmi Narayan Temple
Due west of Connaught Place, this garishly coloured modern temple was erected by the industrialist Birla in 1938. It's dedicated to Vishnu and his consort Laxmi, the goddess of wealth.

India Gate
The 42-metre high stone arch of triumph stands at the eastern end of the Raj Path. It bears the name of 90,000 Indian Army soldiers who died in the campaigns of WW

I, the North-West Frontier operations of the same time and the 1919 Afghan fiasco.

Rashtrapati Bhavan

The official residence of the President of India stands on Raisini Hill, at the opposite end of the Raj Path to India Gate. Completed in 1929, the palace-like building has an elegant Moghul garden and occupies 130 hectares. Prior to independence this was the Viceroy's House, the residence of the Viceroy of India. At the time of Mountbatten, India's last Viceroy, the number of servants needed to maintain the 340 rooms of the building and its extensive gardens was enormous. There were 418 gardeners alone, 50 of them boys whose sole job was to chase away birds!

Parliament House

Sansad Bhavan, the Indian Parliament Building, stands at the end of Sansad Marg, Parliament St, just north of the Raj Path. This is one of the key elements in the design of New Delhi. A straight line drawn from the parliament building, down Parliament St, passes through the centre of Connaught Place and extended beyond it intersects the Jami Masjid. The building is a circular colonnaded structure 171 metres in diameter.

Museums

Delhi has a wide range of museums and galleries. Some of the most interesting include:

National Museum On Janpath just south of Rajpath, the National Museum has a good collection of Indian bronzes, terra cotta and wood sculptures dating back to the Mauryan period (2nd-3rd century BC), exhibits from the Vijayanagar period in south India, miniature and mural paintings and costumes of the various tribal peoples. The museum is definitely worth visiting and is open from 10 am to 5 pm daily, but closed on Mondays. Entry

fee is Rs 0.25 on Tuesday-Wednesday-Thursday, Rs 1 on Friday, free on Saturday-Sunday. There are film shows most days of the week.

Nehru Museum On Teen Murti Rd near Chanakyapuri, the diplomatic enclave, the residence of the first Indian prime minister has been converted into a museum and has items and documents related to his life. During the tourist season there is a sound and light show about his life and the independence movement. The museum is open from 10 am to 5 pm daily, closed on Mondays, admission is free.

Rail Transport Museum Located at Chanakyapuri the railway museum will be of great interest to anyone who becomes fascinated by India's exotic collection of railway engines. The collection includes an 1855 steam engine, still in working order, and a large number of oddities such as the skull of an elephant that charged a mail train in 1894, and lost.

The museum is open from 9.30 am to 7.30 pm from 1 May to 15 July and 10.30 am to 5.30 pm for the rest of the year. It is closed on Mondays and admission is Rs 1 and an additional Rs 5 for taking photographs.

Tibet House This small museum has a fascinating collection of ceremonial items brought out of Tibet when the Dalai Lama fled before the Chinese. Downstairs there is a shop selling a wide range of Tibetan handicrafts. It's at 16 Jorbagh, near the Oberoi Inter-Continental Hotel. It's open 9.30 am to 1 pm and 2.30 to 6 pm, April-September and 9 am to 1 pm and 2 to 5 pm the rest of the year. It's closed Sundays and admission is free.

International Dolls Museum Located in Nehru House on Bahadur Shah Zafar Marg the museum displays 6000 dolls from 85 different countries. Over a third of them are from India and an exhibit is

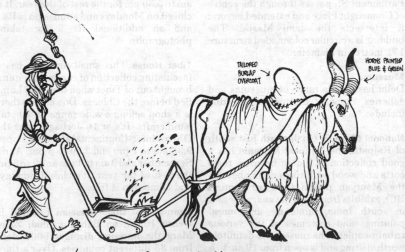

being prepared that will show 500 dolls in the costumes worn all over India. The museum is open from 10 am to 6 pm daily, closed Mondays. Admission is Rs 0.50, half price for children.

Crafts Museum Recently relocated to the Aditi Pavilion at the Exhibition Grounds, Mathura Rd, this museum contains a collection of traditional Indian crafts in textiles, metal, wood and ceramics. The museum is now part of a village life complex where you can visit rural India without ever leaving Delhi. Opening hours are 9.30 am to 4.30 pm, closed Sundays. Admission is free.

Other The Museum of Natural History is opposite the Nepalese Embassy on Barakhamba Rd. It has a modest collection of fossils and a few stuffed animals and birds. Nothing special. There is a National Philatelic Museum at Dak Tar Bhavan, Sardar Patel Square on Parliament St. It's closed on Sunays. At Palam Airport there is an Air Force

Museum open from 10 am to 1.30 pm daily except Tuesdays, admission is free.

Purana Qila
Just south-east of Indian Gate and north of Humayan's Tomb and the Nizam-ud-in Railway Station is the old fort, Purana Qila. This is the supposed site of Indraprastha, the original city of Delhi. The fort has massive walls and three large gateways. Sher Shah, who briefly interrupted the Moghul empire by defeating Humayun, built the fort during his period of rule from 1538 to 1545 before Humayun wrested control of India back.

Entering from the south gate the small octagonal red sandstone tower, the Sher Manzil, was later used by Humayun as a library. It was in this tower that he slipped, fell and recieved injuries from which he died. Just beyond this is the Qila-i-Kuhran Mosque of Sher Shah.

Humayun's Tomb
Built in the mid-16th century by Haji Begum, wife of Humayuan, the second Moghul emperor, this is an early example

lawn mower, Parlaiment Buildings, NEW DELHI.

of Moghul architecture. The elements in its design - a squat building, lighted by high arched entrances, topped by a bulbous dome and surrounded by formal gardens - were to be refined over the years to the magnigficence of the Taj Mahal in Agra. This earlier is thus of great interest for its relation to the later Taj. Humayun's wife is also buried in the red and white sandstone, black and yellow marble tomb.

Other tombs in the garden include that of Humayun's barber, while to the right is the tomb of Isa Khan, a good example of Pathan (Afghan) architecture from the time of the Lodi dynasty. Entry to Humayun's tomb is Rs 0.50, except on Fridays when it is tree. There's a fine view over the surrounding country from the terraces of Humayun's Tomb. One traveller noted that just up the main stairs of the tomb building, to the left, are the graves of the five engineers who built it - 'Old Haji Begum had a strange way of saying thank you for a job well done'.

Zoo

The Delhi Zoo is on the south side of the fort and is open from 8 am to 6 pm in summer, 9 am to 5 pm in winter. Entry fee is Rs 0.50.

Hazrat Nizam-ud-din Aulia

Across the road from Humayun's Tomb is the shrine of the Moslem saint Nizam-ud-din Chisti. He died in 1325, aged 92 and his shrine, with its large tank, is only one of a number of interesting tombs here. They include the later grave of Jahanara, the daughter of Shah Jahan who stayed with him during his imprisonment by Aurangzeb.

Mirza Ghalib, a renowned Urdu poet, also has his tomb here as does Azam Khan, a favourite of Humayun and Akbar, who was murdered by Adham Khan in Agra. In turn Akbar and Adham Khan terminated and his grave is near the Qutab Minar. The construction of Nizan-ud-din's tank caused a dispute between the saint and the constructor of Tughlaqabad further to the south of Delhi - see Tughlaqabad for details. The tomb of a modern Sufi saint, the Hazrat Inayat Khan, is also near hear and every Friday evening about 7 pm Kawali singers perform ar the tomb.

Lodi Tombs

About three km to the west and adjoining the Indian International Centre are the Lodi Gardens. In these well - kept gardens there are the tombs of the Sayyik and Lodi rulers. Muhammad Shah's tomb (1450) is a protype for the later Moghul-style tomb of Humayun, a design which would eventually develop into the Taj Mahal. Other tombs include those of his predecessor Mubarak Shah (1433), Ibrahim Lodi (1526) and Silkander Lodi (1517). The Bara Gambad Mosque is a fine example of its type of plaster decoration.

Safdarjang Tomb

Beside the smaller Safdarjang airport, where Indira Gandhi's son was killed in a light plane accident in 1980, is the Safdarjang Tomb. It was built in 1753-54 by the Nawab of Oudh for his father Safdarjang and is one of the last examples of Moghul architecture before the final remnants of the great empire completely collapsed. The tomb stands on a high terrace in an extensive garden. There are good views from the roof of the tomb which costs Rs 0.50 to enter, free on Fridays.

Moth ki Masjid

South again from the Safdarjang Tomb, this mosque is said to be the finest mosque in the Lodi style. It was around this area that Timur defeated the forces of Muhammad Shah Tughlaq in 1398.

Hauz Khas

About midway between Safdarjang and the Qutab Minar this area was once the reservoir for the second city of Delhi, Siri,

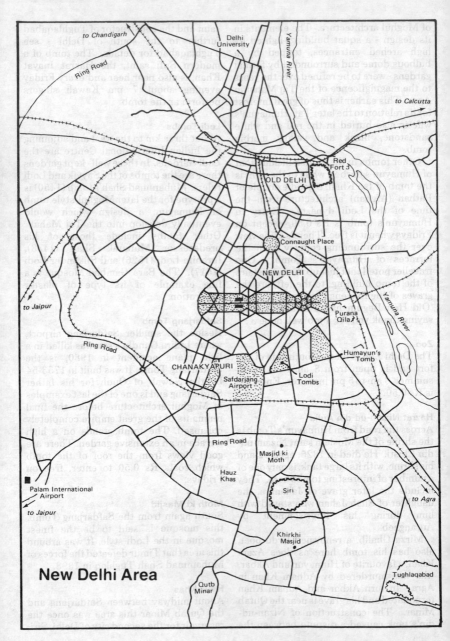

New Delhi Area

which lies slightly to the east. Interesting sights here include Feroz Shah's Tomb (1398) and the remains of an ancient college.

Khirki Masjid & Jahanpath

This interesting mosque with its four open courts dates from 1380. The nearby village of Khirki also takes its name from the mosque. Close to the mosque are remains of the fourth city of Delhi, Jahanpanah, including the high Bijai Mandal platform and the Begumpur Mosque with its multiplicity of domes.

Tughlaqabad

The massively strong walls of Tughlaqabad, the third city of Delhi, are east of the Qutab Minar. The walled city and fort with its 13 gateways was built by Ghiyas-ud-din Tughlaq and its construction involved a legendary quarrel with the saint Nizam-ud-din. When the Tughlaq ruler took the workers whom Nizam-ud-din wanted for work on his shrine the saint cursed the king with the warning that his city would be inhabited only by Gujars (shepherds). Today that is indeed the situation.

The dispute between king and saint did not end with curse and counter-curse. When the king prepared to take vengeance on the saint, Nizam-ud-din calmly told his followers, in a saying that is still current in India today, 'Delhi is a long way off'. Indeed it was, for the king was murdered on his way from Delhi in 1325.

The fort walls are constructed of massive blocks and outside the south wall of the city is an artificial lake with the king's tomb in its centre. A long causeway connects the tomb to the fort, both of which have walls that slope inward.

Qutab Minar Complex

Situated 15 km south of New Delhi, the buildings in this complex date from the onset of Moslem rule in India, and are fine examples of early Afghan architecture.

The Qutab Minar itself is a soaring tower of victory which was commenced in 1193, immediately after the defeat of the last Hindu kingdom in Delhi. It reaches 73 metres high and tapers from a 15-metre diameter base to just 2.5 metres at the top.

The tower has five distinct storeys, each marked by a projecting balcony. The first three storeys are made of red sandstone, the fourth and fifth of marble and sandstone. Although Qutb-ud-din commenced construction of the tower, he only got to the first storey. His successors completed it, and in 1368 Feroz Shah Tughlaq rebuilt the top storeys and added a cupola. An earthquake brought the cupola down in 1803 and it was replaced, and other modifications made at the same time, in 1829.

Today this impressively ornate tower has a slight tilt, but otherwise has worn the centuries remarkably well. At present the tower is closed for renovations and repairs but at other times visitors in groups of four can go up the tower to the first storey, from where there is a fine view. It's said that people are only allowed up in groups in order to discourage suicides.

Quwwat-ul-Islam Mosque At the foot of the Qutab Minar stands the first mosque to be built in India, the 'Might of Islam' mosque. Qutb-ud-din commenced construction of the mosque in 1193, but it has had a number of additions and extensions over the centuries. The original mosque was built on the foundations of a Hindu temple, and an inscription over the east gate states that it was built with materials obtained from demolishing '27 idolatrous temples'. Many of the elements in the mosque's construction indicate their Hindu or Jain origins. The original small mosque was surrounded by a cloistered court by Altamish in 1210-20. Ala-ud-din added a court to the east and the magnificent Alai Darwaza gateway in 1300. Points of interest in and around the mosque include:

The Iron Pillar This seven-metre high pillar stands in the courtyard of the mosque, and has been there since long before the mosque's construction. It was originally erected there in the 5th century AD by the Hindu king Chandra Varman, but a six-line Sanskrit inscription indicates that is was probably brought here from elsewhere. It is thought to date from the Gupta period and may once have been crowned by a Garuda figure, indicating that it may have been in a temple to Vishnu. What those lines of poetry do not tell is how it was made, for the iron in the pillar is of quite exceptional purity. Scientists have never discovered how iron of such purity that it has not rusted after 2000 years could be cast with the technology of the time. It is said that if you can encircle the pillar with your hands your wish will be fulfilled.

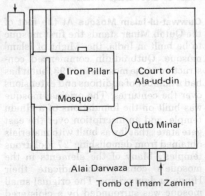

Qutab Minar Complex

Alai Minar At the same time as Ala-ud-din made his additions to the mosque he also conceived a far more ambitious construction programme. He would build a second tower of victory, exactly like the Qutab Minar except it would be twice as high! When he died the tower had reached 27 metres and no-one was willing to continue his over-ambitious project. The uncompleted tower stands to the north of the Qutab Minar and the mosque.

Other Ala-ud-din's Alai Darwaza gateway is the main entrance to the whole complex. It was built in 1310 of red sandstone and stands just south-east of the Qutab Minar. The tomb of Imam Zamin stands beside the gateway while the tomb of Altamish, who died in 1235, is by the north-west corner of the mosque.

Getting There You can get out to the Qutab Minar by bus or minibus. The 505 bus departs from in front of the Delhi Transport Corporation office in Connaught Place and costs Rs 0.90. The minibus goes from in front of the Super Bazaar and costs Rs 1.

Around the Qutab
There are a number of other points of interest around this complex. West of the enclosure is the tomb of Adham Khan who, amongst oher things, drove Rupmati to suicide following the capture of Mandu (see Mandu). When Akbar became displeased with him he ended up being heaved off a terrace in the Agra Fort.

There some summer palaces in the area and also the tombs of the final kings of Delhi, who succeeded the final Moghuls. An empty space between two of the tombs was intended for the last king of Delhi, who died in exile in Rangoon, Burma, in 1862, following his implication in the 1857 Indian Mutiny.

Tours
Delhi is very spread out, so taking a city tour makes a lot of sense. Even by public

transport getting from, say, the Red Fort to the Qutab Minar would be comparatively expensive.

There three major organisations which arrange Delhi tours – beware of agents offering cut-price (and inferior) tours. The ITDC (Indian Tourism Development Corporation) have tours which include guides and a luxury coach – they tend to be overbooked. Their office is in L Block, Connaught Place but their tours also start from the major hotels. Delhi Tourism, a branch of the city government, also arrange similar tours and their office is in Block. Finally, the Delhi Transport Corporation tours which are cheaper than the others. They do not always include guides but are exceptionally good value.

A four-hour morning tour costs Rs 8 (Rs 20 with an air-con coach) with the ITDC or Delhi Tourism, Rs 6 with Delhi Transport. Starting at 9 am the morning tour includes the Qutab Minar, Humayun's Tomb, India Gate, the Jantar Mantar and the Laxmi Narayan Temple. The similarly priced afternoon tour covers the Red Fort, Jami Masjid, Raj Ghat, Shantiban and Feroz Shah Kotla. If you take both tours on the same day it costs Rs 16 (Rs 35 for an air-con coach) with the ITDC, Rs 15 with Delhi Tourism and Rs 10 with Delhi Transport.

There are various cultural performances on in Delhi at night. 'Dances of India' takes place from 7 to 8 pm every night at Bhiwandiwall Hall. It's 'well worth the Rs 25 entry charge'.

Places to Stay – Bottom End

Delhi is certainly no bargain when it comes to cheap hotels. You can easily pay Rs 30 for the most basic single – a price that elsewhere in India will generally get you a quite reasonable double with attached bathroom. There are basically three areas for cheap accommodation in Delhi. First there are a number of places on or around Janpath near Connaught Place in New Delhi. Near New Delhi Railway Station in Paharganj there are

also some places – this is about midway between old and New Delhi. Finally there are a number of rock bottom hotels in old Delhi itself. The last is too far away from the agents, offices, airlines and so on of New Delhi for most travellers – given Delhi's difficult public transport situation – but it is certainly colourful.

Janpath Area There are a number of cheaper 'lodges' or 'guest houses' near the Indian Government Tourist Office but single rooms can cost Rs 50 or more. For shoestring travellers there are often dormitories, however. The ITDC *Yatri Niwas*, see the medium price places below, is such excellent value that it's always worth trying there ahead of any of these bottom end places. In fact it offers better facilities than the cheap places and at lower cost. Usually, however, it's full.

Since many of these places are so popular you may find that your specific choice is full. If that's the case simply stay at one of the others until a room becomes available – it's unlikely you'll have to wait more than a day. High on most people's list is the well known *Ringo Guest House* (tel 40605) at number 17, round Scindia House behind Air India. It has air-cooled dormitories for Rs 14, singles/doubles with common bath for Rs 30-35/50 and doubles with attached bath for Rs 60-80. The management are very friendly, it's clean and the showers and toilets are well maintained. Meals are available in the rooftop courtyard, although at a higher price than in the nearby restaurants, and there's always an interesting collection of people to talk to in the afternoons and evenings.

Other places with very similar prices include the nearby *Sunny Guest House* (tel 46033) at 152 Scindia House or the *Laguna Guest House* (tel 42600), which has air-cooled singles/doubles for Rs 50/85. The somewhat spartan *Asian Guest House* (tel 43393), 14 Scindia House, has regular singles/doubles for Rs 55/80 as well as a number of more expensive air-

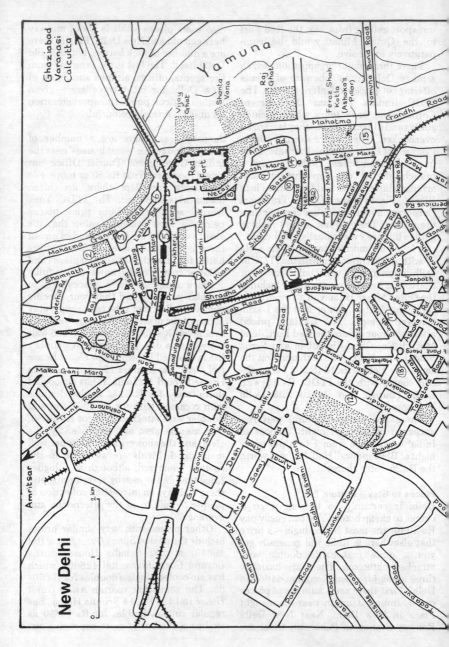

New Delhi

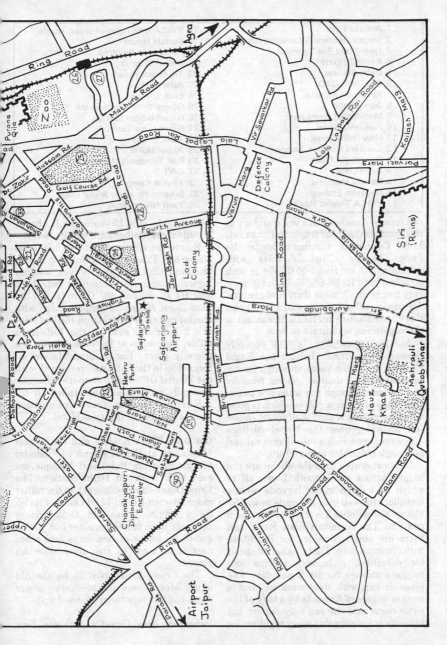

1 Ashoka Pillar	18 YWCA International Guest House
2 Qudsia Gardens & Camping Ground	19 Baroda House
3 Inter-State Bus Terminal	20 Parliament Building
4 Kashmiri Gate	21 Indian Museum
5 Delhi Station	22 Taj Mahal Hotel
6 Old Delhi GPO	23 Ashoka Hotel
7 Fatehpuri Mosque	24 Lodi Tombs
8 Jami Masjid	25 Oberoi Inter-Continental
9 Moti Mahal Restaurant	26 Nizam-ud-din Station
10 President Hotel	27 Humayun's Tomb
11 New Delhi Station	28 Tibet House
12 Lakshmi Narayan Temple	29 Akbar Hotel
13 Connaught Place	30 Rail Transport Museum
14 Delhi Gate	31 GPO
15 Gandhi Memorial	32 Tourist Camp
16 Nepalese Embassy	33 Bikaner House — Jaipur buses
17 YMCA Tourist Hostel	34 Yatri Niwas Hotel

con rooms. Another place you could try in this group is the *Hotel Bright* (tel 350414), M-85 Connaught Circus, opposite the Super Bazaar. Singles/doubles with common bath are Rs 52-55/55-68 or with attached bath Rs 55-66/55-77 but it's not very bright at all, more dirty and grubby. Air-con is available for an extra Rs 30 and there's a dormitory for Rs 25. Breakfast in the vegetarian restaurant is Rs 8.

Another possibility is the recently opened *Tara Homes* behind the Regal Cinema, excellent value although pretty basic at Rs 35 a double – 'clean, friendly and secure although the walls are paper thin'. One of the new places which is good value for money is the *Royal Guest House* (tel 353485), near the Nepal Airlines office on Janpath. It's four flights up and has singles/doubles at Rs 60/90.

Less expensive than the above are the lodges across on Janpath Lane, all of which have been minor legends among travellers for well over a decade now. *Mrs Colaco's* at number 3 is the first one you'll come to. The dormitory costs Rs 15 and there are singles/doubles for Rs 30/40 with common bath. There's a safe deposit for valuables, a laundry service and baggage storage for Rs 2 per day. The place is run with determination and a certain degree of firmness by a lady of the same name and one can only admire her tenacity at keeping this place together for

what must be all of 15 years now. It's basic, crowded, and rather hard on the nerves.

Round the corner, *Mr S C Jain's Guest House* at 7 Pratap Singh Building is also on Janpath Lane and is yet another legend. Rooms with common bath here cost Rs 40, 50 and 60. There is also the *Soni Guest House* on Janpath Lane with similar prices. *R C Mehta* on the 3rd floor at 52 Janpath, next to the Lufthansa office, has rooms at Rs 35 to 45 and is a friendly place. For accommodation information in the Janpath area check with the Tourist Office at 88 Janpath – they can generally recommend something. Or try the helpful Student Travel Information Centre in room 6, Imperial Hotel.

Old Delhi The *Khushdil* and the *Crown Hotels* are at the west end of Chandni Chowk near the Fatehpuri Mosque, an easy walk from old Delhi Station. The Crown has better facilities than the rather more spartan Khusdil and charges Rs 35 for a single. These old Delhi places certainly have more character but you've got to be aware of bed bugs and other nasties in some of the more dive-like places.

The *Crown Hotel* used to be the old hippy Mecca back in the flower power days, but has now been 'cleaned up'.

Paharganj Area Directly opposite New

Delhi Railway Station is the start of Main Bazaar which stretches due west for about a km. There are any number of cheap hotels along this road, offering varying degrees of quality. Many are very popular with budget travellers. Other than the general air of decay and neglect the problem with the ultra-cheap places here is that they are subject to police raids. Don't let this put you off – there are plenty of places offering excellent value for money without the indignity of being searched for narcotics. It can always provide some amusement too as one traveller reported: 'while being raided by the drug squad no amount of warnings would stop them all from tasting the dessicating crystals (silica?) I used to keep my films dry which had poison written all over them. They took them away and we promptly checked out in case any of them croaked'.

Walking up Main Bazaar from the station some of the better places include the *Hotel Kiran* (tel 526104) at 4473 Main Bazaar. It's friendly and clean with singles/doubles at Rs 40/50 or Rs 50/60 with attached bathroom. The *Hotel Vivek* (tel 521948), 1541-50 Main Bazaar, is another friendly place with 24-hour room service and a range of rooms from Rs 30 to 80. The higher-priced rooms have their own bath. *Hotel Vishal* (tel 527629) is similar to the Vivek but with its own attached restaurant. A dorm bed costs Rs 15 on night one, Rs 12 on subsequent nights. Singles/doubles are Rs 30/35 with common bath, a double with attached bathroom is Rs 65.

Hotel Sapna (tel 528273), 5153 Main Bazaar, has small but clean rooms for Rs 30-35 for a double with attached bathroom. Other slightly pricier places you can try in this area are the *Hotel Natraj*, next to the well known Metropolis Restaurant on Chitragupta Rd. Rooms cost from around Rs 45 but make certain of the agreed price when you check in. The rooms have attached baths and fans. The *Hotel Chanakya* charges Rs 40/55 for

singles/doubles and there is also a dormitory. It's clean, has iced water dispensers on each floor and is run by pleasant people. Find it on the road that leads off Main Bazaar Rd before you get to the Metropolis Restaurant, towards and past the Imperial Theatres on the left.

It's suggested you avoid the dark, dingy, noisy and cramped *Venus Hotel* and the similar *Hotel Bright* unless you're flat broke. They're definitely at the grim and desperate end of the budget bracket.

The *White House Tourist Lodge* at 8177 Arakashan Rd, off Desh Bandhu Gupta Rd in Paharganj has 'really good, clean and comfortable rooms' for Rs 60 and 70. The *Apsara Tourist Lodge* next door at 8501/1 Arakashan Rd is similar in standards and price but the people are not so friendly. Rooms there range from Rs 40 for a single to Rs 100 for a double with air-con. At 8126 Arakashan Rd there's also the slightly more expensive *Hotel Crystal* run by the same people. The *Farid Guest House*, look for the sign opposite the Sheila Cinema on Desh Bandhu Gupta Rd, has doubles at Rs 25 and 30.

Other Places Out at Chanakyapuri (where most of the embassies are situated) is the *Vishwa Yuvak Kendra* (tel 373631) on Circular Rd. Dorm beds here are Rs 12, singles cost Rs 25-40-45, doubles Rs 25-50-55. The rooms are excellent and there's also a cafeteria with good food at low prices. It's a good place to stay if you don't mind the 20-minute bus trip or shorter auto-rickshaw ride from Connaught Place. To get there take a 620 bus from the Plaza in Connaught Place and get off near the Indonesian Embassy. Or take a 662 from Old Delhi Station and get off at the Ashok Hotel. It's right behind the Chinese Embassy and near the Chanakyapuri Police Station and is also known as the International Youth Centre.

There is a *Youth Hostel* (tel 376285) at 5 Nyaya Marg, Chanakyapuri where there are dorm beds for Rs 15 for members, Rs 18 for non-members. Bring your own padlock. There's a bank and a travel agency which will arrange trips to Agra, Jaipur, Delhi sightseeing and so on. Good for the embassies too.

Even further out is the *Ashoka Youth Hostel* at Mehrauli, near the Qutab Minar on the southern outskirts of New Delhi. It's very pleasant and somewhat cheaper if you don't mind the long bus ride (easy coming into Delhi but a real hassle getting back out again). Also near the Qutab Minar is the *Sri Aurobindo Ashram* (tel 669225) on Aurobindo Marg. Take a bus to the Indian Institute of Technology gate and ask for 'Mother's School'. It's clean and well organised with rooms with bath for Rs 25, including meals. There's also a dorm.

If you want to camp there are several possibilities in Delhi. The *Tourist Camp* (tel 278929) is one of the cheapest places to stay in Delhi. It's actually situated in old Delhi, near Delhi Gate on Jawaharlal Nehru Marg, across from the J P Narayan Hospital (Irwin Hospital), only two km from Connaught Place. It is very popular with overland tours and campers and is run by retired Indian Army officers. You can camp with your own tent for Rs 14 (two people) or use a hired tent for Rs 22. Or there are dorm beds for Rs 10 or basic rooms with share bathrooms cost Rs 20/30 for singles/doubles. They're spartan but OK, this is a place which generally gets good recommendations from travellers who stay there. The restaurant offers western-style meals which are served in decent-sized proportions – well cooked too. Or at least it is according to some people – 'expensive and not that good', according to others. They have a left luggage room where you can leave your accumulated junk for up to four months. It's quite an interesting place with lots of different nationalities including Afghanis and Iranians. You can reach the camp by taking a six-seater from the Regal Cinema at Connaught Place. There is also a camping site near the *Qudsia Gardens* (which is near the Kashmir Gate Bus Terminal) with similar prices.

If all else fails there are *Railway Retiring Rooms* at both railway stations. Doubles cost Rs 35-40 or dormitory beds are Rs 7.50 in a small dorm, Rs 5 in a larger one. There are also *Airport Retiring Rooms* at the airport so long as you have a confirmed ticket. They're booked through the duty manager at the airport manager's office and cost Rs 75 for a bed in a four-bed dorm, there are also smaller rooms available.

Places to Stay – Middle

There are a number of hotels around Janpath and Connaught Place which fall into the lower and upper part of the middle bracket. In 1983 the ITDC opened a new hotel with such excellent facilities at such a low cost that it's really difficult to believe it's there. It's close to the centre, has good facilities and reasonable prices – everything the budget traveller could ask. The *Ashok Yatri Niwas* (tel 344511) is just 10 minutes from the Tourist Office and singles/doubles cost Rs 50/60 or a four-bed room is Rs 72. Air-con singles/doubles are Rs 140/180. There are no less than 556 rooms. It also has a cheap cafeteria and a lounge with TV. If you can get a room, this new hotel is recommended. It's on Panchkuin Marg, a road running north-west from Connaught Place. The whole story of this hotel has been highly political and it's probable that the ITDC are losing money hand over fist at current price levels. Expect them to rise.

The *Puri Yatri Paying Guest House* (tel 525463) is at Yatri House, 3/4 Rani Jhansi Rd (at the junction of Panchkuin Rd and Mandir Marg, near Connaught Place). It's calm, secure and moderately priced at Rs 140 for a double. The *Ekant Boarding House* (tel 527783) is also at this junction.

A small but very popular place is the *Roshan Villa Guest House* (tel 324770, 324240) at 7 Babar Lane, close to the Bengali Market. Although it's a good 10 minutes' walk from Connaught Place it's one of the cleanest places you're likely to come across in India and the owners, Mr & Mrs Roshan Lal, are very friendly and hospitable. If there's anything you need they'll either get it for you or make sure you know where to find it. It's quiet, meals are available on request and you can store excess gear there for a small charge. A double costs Rs 100 with own bathroom (hot and cold water) or Rs 80 sharing a bathroom with one other room. There's also a room for three or four which costs Rs 80.

Back in the centre, *Nirula's Hotel* (tel 352419) is on L Block, Connaught Place, right beside the Nirula restaurants and snack bars. Singles/doubles range from Rs 200/300 in this small but good standard hotel. *Hotel Fifty Five* (tel 321244) at H-55 Connaught Circus is a beautifully designed and spotlessly clean place with air-con throughout. Rooms with balcony and attached bathroom are Rs 155/195. The *Alka Hotel* (tel 344328) is also centrally located at 16/90 Connaught Place and has air-con singles/doubles from around Rs 222/290 but recent reports indicate that its standards have fallen.

Hotel Palace Heights (tel 351361) in D Block, Connaught Place is a moderately-priced place close to Nirula's. Situated on the third floor of an office building it has a huge verandah overlooking Connaught Place – great for breakfast or afternoon tea. Rooms cost Rs 65 a singles or Rs 82 for a double with own bathroom, Rs 98 with air-con. It has been recommended as good value although it's somewhat scruffy and indifferently kept.

Other centrally located hotels include the *Janpath Guest House* (tel 321935-7) a few doors down from the Tourist Office at 82-84 Janpath. It's popular with travellers, reasonably well kept, clean and the staff re freindly but the rooms are claustrophobically small and most don't have a window to talk of. Singles/doubles cost Rs 85/120, more if you want air-con.

The *Hotel Marina* on the outer circle of Connaught Place and the *Hotel Metro* (tel 48905) on the inner circle are both pretty drab looking places. The Metro is, however, better than initial impressions might indicate with air-con rooms for Rs 110-150/160-200 as well as cheaper rooms without air-con. The old fashioned *Hotel Airlines* (tel 517571-73), directly opposite the New Delhi Railway Station, is rather drab, although located in an interesting area.

The *YMCA Tourist Hotel* (tel 311915) is very central, near the Regal Cinema on Jai Singh Rd and opposite the Jantar Mantar. It's excellent value with rooms with hot and cold water, showers, plus gardens, lounges and a restaurant with western, Indian and Muglai cuisine. Including breakfast rooms with common bath are Rs 70/125 or with attached bath and air-con they're Rs 130/220. There's also a transient membership fee of Rs 5 which is valid for 30 days.

The *YWCA International Guest House* (tel 311561, 383080) at 10 Parliament St (Sansad Marg) has singles/doubles at Rs 100/150 and all rooms have bath and air-con. It's also convenient for Connaught Place. There's a second, lesser known YWCA, the *YWCA Blue Triangle Family Hostel* (tel 310133, 310875) on Ashoka Rd just off Parliament Rd (Sansand Marg). It's clean and well run and has a restaurant. Rates, including breakfast, range from Rs 95 to 135 for singles, Rs 170 to 260 for doubles, all with attached bathroom. There are rooms with and without air-con and there's also a dormitory. The newer Blue Triangle Y is run by the Delhi YWCA, the International Y is run by the national organisation.

The *Lodhi Hotel* (tel 619422) is in south Delhi on Lala Rajput Rai Marg, a long way from Connaught Place, and has air-con rooms at Rs 225/290. A good place for a longer stay in Delhi is the *India International Centre* (tel 619431) beside the Lodi tombs in the south of New Delhi.

It is a good place to meet people involved with international aid agencies and each week there are lectures on art, economics and other contemporary issues by Indian and foreign experts. The centre, which is near the UN offices in Delhi, has rooms with air-con for Rs 125/200.

Places to Stay – Top End

Many of the 'tourist class' hotels are at Chanakyapuri, where the foreign embassies are chiefly located. This is about midway between the airport and the New Delhi city centre. A number of new hotels have opened in this category recently, spurred on in part by New Delhi hosting the Asian Games. New hotels include the Centaur at the airport and the Hyatt Regency. Prices quoted below are before a 10-15% 'luxury tax' and 5-10% 'service charge'. Some of the more important hotels include:

Hotel Akbar (tel 370251) is at Chanakyapuri and is an ITDC hotel but rather smaller than the Ashok. Singles/doubles cost from Rs 500/600.

Ashok Hotel (tel 370101) is at 50B Chanakyapuri and is the 589-room flagship of the ITDC hotel fleet. It offers everything from restaurants, coffee shops, bars, discos, conference rooms and swimming pool to full air-conditioning. Singles/doubles cost Rs 600/700 and up.

The Centaur Hotel is on Gurgaon Rd at the airport. It's a big new hotel with rooms from Rs 450/525.

Claridges Hotel (tel 370211) is at 12 Aurangzeb Rd, south of the Raj Path in New Delhi. Singles/doubles cost from Rs 450/550.

Hyatt Regency (tel 699516, 699521) is another big new hotel with 550 rooms. It's on Bhikaji Cama Place and costs from Rs 650-750/750-850 for singles/doubles.

Hotel Imperial (tel 311511) is conveniently situated on Janpath near the centre. It's a rather more old-fashioned looking hotel with a very pleasant shopping arcade. Singles/doubles cost Rs 400/500-550.

Hotel Janpath (tel 350070) is beside the Imperial and is run by the ITDC. Rooms cost from Rs 250/300-350.

Hotel Kanishka (tel 343400), situated next to the Hotel Janpath, is a new ITDC hotel with rooms at Rs 400/475.

Hotel Maurya Sheraton (tel 370271) is on Sardar Patel Marg at Chanakyapuri and has 300 plus rooms with usual 'international class' features. Singles/doubles cost Rs 725/850.

Hotel Oberoi Inter-Continental (tel 699571) is on Dr Zakir Hussain Rd in the south of New Delhi, near the Purana Qila. There are 350 rooms with the usual luxuries and services and singles/doubles cost Rs 875/975.

The Taj Mahal Hotel (tel 386162) is at 1 Man Singh Rd. It's part of the Taj group of hotels and is fairly central, yet fairly quiet. Singles/doubles cost from Rs 700/800.

Places to Eat

Like places to stay Delhi's many restaurants and snack bars can be divided by price range and location.

Janpath & Connaught Place There has been been a real spate of Indian-style fast food places opening up around here. Their plus point is that they have quite good food at quite reasonable prices and they're clean and healthy. Their minus is that very few of them have any place to sit – it's stand, eat and run. They serve Indian (from samosas to dosas) and western (burgers to sandwiches) food.

Nirula's is probably the most popular and long running of these places and does a wide variety of excellent light snacks, both Indian and western. They've also got good cold drinks, milkshakes and ice cream or they will pack you a box lunch for around Rs 10, ideal to take on train trips. Next door to the snack bar place on one side is an ice cream parlour and on the other it's pizzas. Above the ice cream bar there's the fourth part of Nirula's, a sit down restaurant called *Pot Pourri* with appetising food including a Rs 25 eat-all-you-like salad smorgasbord. They've also got pizzas for Rs 15 (Rs 5 for extras), chili con carne with rice for Rs 15 and a good range of soups and sweets. It's a very pleasant place to eat, the service is good, all in all it's probably the number one place for a minor splurge.

Opposite Nirula's is the *National*

Restaurant which is clean and has excellent non-vegetarian food and somewhat lower prices than Nirula's. Most dishes are in the Rs 4 to 6 range but they also have tandoori dishes for Rs 10 to 15. Also near Nirula's is *The Embassy* with a kitsch 'airport lounge' decor but good food – excellent korma and biriyani for around Rs 35 per person.

Other places around Connaught Place include *Sona Rupa* on Janpath with very good south Indian vegetarian food plus a Rs 15 all-you-can-eat lunch buffet including dessert and coffee. The *United Coffee House* on Connaught Place is also pleasantly relaxed but their prices have gone up although it is still popular. Just round the corner from American Express on Radial Rd there's a place that does great milkshakes.

Kalpana is more-or-less behind the Tourist Office at 84A Tolstoy Lane. It's a popular place for breakfast and prices are low. As well as the stand-up snack bars, 21-flavour ice cream parlours have also hit Delhi with a vengeance. Nice ice cream though.

There's a good collection of cheap restaurants and food markets in Mohan Singh Place, in the same block as the Regal Cinema in Connaught Place. Look for fresh and dried fruits, curd, sweets and so on. Upstairs in the market *Ding Dong* serves good Chinese food for prices which are quite reasonable for Delhi. The fresh milk is excellent at *Keventers*, the small milk bar at the corner of Connaught Place and Radial Road Number 3; banana splits cost Rs 7 and ice cream Rs 4. If you just want a cheap soft drink and somewhere cool to drink it descend into the air-conditioned underground market between Janpath and Parliament St at Connaught Place. Opposite the underground bazaar and close to where the airport buses start from is the increasingly popular *Delhicacy*. The food is good although the helpings are rather small. There is a choice of 'dish of the day' or an a la carte menu.

Moving up a price category there are several higher price restaurants worth considering on Parliament St and by the Regal Cinema. The *Kwality Restaurant* on Parliament St is probably the flagship of the chain. It's spotlessly clean and very efficient and the food is excellent. The prices may be higher by Indian standards (ie a really good meal could cost you more than Rs 50 for two), but you'll probably decide it's worth it. This is also a good place for non-Indian food if you want a break and a good place for breakfast.

Al Arab, right on the corner, is more expensive again but has an interesting Middle Eastern menu with most dishes in the Rs 15 to 30 bracket and a Rs 30 buffet lunch or dinner. Round the corner is *Gaylords* with big mirrors and chandeliers and excellent Indian food but count on around Rs 60 per person. *The Cellar*, also on Connaught Place, has pizzas that, for India, are not bad. Good vegetarian food at the *Volga*, it's a little expensive but it's air-conditioned.

A typical 'dawa'-like Indian place, popular with Delhi residents from all walks of life, is the famous *Kaka's Hotel*, across the street from Nirula's on Connaught Place. Curiously it does not yet seem to have been discovered by westerners at all. Despite having no atmosphere whatsoever it is quite crowded most of the time. Try the excellent butter chicken for just Rs 20.

Finally there's one Delhi food place that should not be forgotten. *Wenger's* on Connaught Place is a cake shop with an awesome range of little cakes which they'll put in a cardboard box, tie up with a bow and you can self-consciously carry them back to your hotel room for private consumption. Take care though – 'in great anticipation as about to devour a famous Wenger's cake this bloody hawk deftly lifted my cake out of my hands and near gave me a heart attack in the process'.

Old Delhi & Paharganj The *Inderpuri Restaurant*, just around the corner from the west end of Chandni Chowk, has a good selection of vegetarian dishs. Good cheap Moghul food at the *Karim Hotel* in a small alley just off the south side of the Jami Masjid – Rs 12 to 15 for a good meal. The stalls in front of the Jami Masjid are very cheap at about Rs 2 to 4 for a meal. Go for the ones with the big chappatis outside.

In the Paharganj area near New Delhi Station is the long running and ever popular *Metropolis Restaurant*. Food is Chinese and western and a little expensive, but it has been a travellers' hangout for years and the food is not bad. Underneath the Hotel Sapna is the considerably cheaper *Restaurant Light* where you can get very good vegetarian food for just Rs 2 to 3 per dish. It's very popular with budget travellers in the evenings. The *Khalsa Punjabi Hotel*, on the left side of Main Bazaar Rd, towards the station, beyond the Vishal and Venus Hotels, has good food.

Gobind is a narrow-fronted place on the opposite side towards the Metropolis and is good for lassi or expresso coffee. There are good breakfast places down towards the Chankya Hotel where you can get fried eggs, chips and tomatoes for Rs 5. Puris and bean and pea curry is a tasty snack from stalls around here. A good cheap breakfast, including fantastic porridge, is available at the *Lakshmi Restaurant* at the end of the main bazaar furthest from New Delhi Station, it's very popular with overlanders. *Cafe Gaylord*, half-way down the main bazaar, is also good. *Neelkamal*, in Chitragupta Rd in Paharganj, is a 'dawa' like place serving good cheap vegetarian food. In the interstate bus station the *ISBT Workers' Canteen* has good food at low prices.

At the other end of the price scale there are two well known tandoori restaurants to consider. The *Tandoor* at the *Hotel President* on Asaf Ali Rd is an excellent place with the usual two waiters per diner service and sitarist playing in the background. A meal for two might come to Rs 100 or more, but the food is really excellent and the tandoori kitchen can be seen through a glass panel. *Moti Mahal's* on Netaji Subhash Marg in Darayaganj in old Delhi is famous for its tandoori dishes including murga musalam, but it seems to live more on reputation than actual ability these days.

Other Places The *YWCA International Guest House's* restaurant has good food, or if you are out at Chanakyapuri (waiting for a visa perhaps), good and inexpensive Indian food can be had in the *International Youth Centre* near the Indonesian Embassy. The numerous 'international class' hotels have 'international standard' restaurants if you want to splash out.

The *Casa de Medici* in the Taj Mahal Hotel has excellent and authentic Italian cuisine. In the same hotel the *House of Ming* has some of the best Chinese food in India, cooked in both Sichuan and Cantonese styles. The *Cafe Chinoise* in the *Oberoi Inter-Continental* also has excellent Chinese food as does the lower priced *Shanghai* in the *Hotel Diplomat*. *Fujiya* on Malcha Marg in Chanakyapuri has good Japanese and Chinese food.

Bukhara in the Maurya Sheraton has many central Asian specialities including tandoori dishes. In the *Ashok* the *Bar-e-Kabab* is famous (and expensive) for its tandoori and Moghul dishes. Also in the Ashoka the *Samovar Coffee Shop* 'has cheaper hamburgers than Nirula's and they're just as good' reported one traveller. *Gulnar* in the *Hotel Janpath* is cheaper for tandoori food.

Getting There

Delhi is a major international gateway to India and for details on arriving from overseas see the introduction. At certain times of year international flights out of Delhi can be heavily booked so it's wise to make reservations as early as possible. This particularly applies to some of the airlines heavily discounted out of Europe – double check your reservations and make sure you reconfirm.

Delhi is also a major centre for domestic travel with extensive bus, rail and air connections.

Air Indian Airlines flights depart from Delhi to all the major Indian centres. Some important connections include Bombay (Rs 938, around 10 flights daily), Madras (Rs 1183), Calcutta (Rs 946, three daily), Srinagar (Rs 549), Jaipur (Rs 190), Agra (Rs 153) and Varanasi (Rs 521).

India is not a great place for airfare bargains on domestic flights – Indian Airlines fly too close to 100% capacity to need to worry about the hard sell. The Indian Airlines Office in Delhi (tel 40052, 40071) is in the Kanchenjunga Building on Barakhamba Rd. The office occupies a large open area upstairs around the back of the building – you wouldn't know it was there, if you didn't know it was there! Reservations can be made for flights all over India but, as usual with Indian Airlines, it usually takes rather a long time.

Rail Delhi is an important rail centre and an excellent place to make rail bookings. Baroda House (tel 387889) is just north of India Gate on Kasturba Gandhi Marg (entrance on Copernicus Rd). They don't actually make bookings for you here but they do give you a *foreigner's permission form* which you then take to the appropriate station to make the actual booking. This form will often ensure you a berth on an otherwise 'full' train because it draws on a separate quota – the tourist quota. They can also advise on rail travel in general.

First and air-con class reservations are made at the Northern Railway Reservation Office, State Entry Rd, Connaught Place. If Baroda House is closed 'for yet another public holiday' then 'go to counter 43 on the first floor of the New Delhi Station, the woman in charge there has the tourist quota' was a suggestion

from one traveller. At the old Delhi Station there are separate reservation counters for *advance* travel (inside) and *current* travel (outside). Current means today! You can waste a lot of time getting in the wrong queue.

Remember that there are two main stations in Delhi – Delhi Station in old Delhi and New Delhi Station. The latter is much closer to Connaught Place and if you're departing from Delhi Station you should allow adequate time to wind your way through the traffic snarls of old Delhi. Between the Delhi and New Delhi Stations you can take the number 6 bus for just Rs 1. There's also the Nizam-ud-din Station south of the New Delhi area.

There are several tourist special trains operating from Delhi. The Taj Express is ideal for day-tripping to Agra. The train departs from and returns to the New Delhi Station and takes three hours each way. The fare is Rs 72 in 1st class, Rs 18 in 2nd. The tourist quota on this service is very limited, but it's generally possible to get a seat. If you want to be certain then check at Baroda House before you go to the Central Reservation Office. Air-con class to Agra costs about Rs 120.

The Pink City Express is a direct train from Delhi Station to Jaipur, departing at 5.55 am and arriving five hours later. Fare is about Rs 110 in 1st class, Rs 25 in 2nd.

Some other important connections by mail or express train include:

	Minimum time	1st class Rs	2nd class Rs
Amritsar	8 hours	120	30
Bombay	17 hours	345	90
Calcutta	17 hours	160	40
Jammu Tawi	13 hours	320	80
Madras	40 hours	435	105
Varanasi	12 hours	200	50

Bus The large Inter-State Bus Terminal is at Kashmiri Gate, north of the Delhi Railway Station in old Delhi. Buses depart from here for locations all around Delhi –

ring 229083 for details. State government bus companies operating from here are:

Haryana Government Roadways (tel 221292), bookings 6 am to 12 noon & 1.30 to 9 pm.

Jammu & Kashmir Government Roadways (tel 224559), bookings 10 am to 5 pm but only on air-con buses.

Rajasthan Roadways (tel 222276), bookings 6 am to 8 pm.

Uttar Pradesh Roadways (tel 226175, 273379), bookings 8 am to 4 pm.

Popular buses include the approximately hourly service to Agra which costs Rs 18. There is also a frequent and fast service to Jaipur for Rs 28. For Chandigarh, from where you can bus or take the narrow gauge train up to Simla, the buses cost Rs 24, but there are also de-luxe buses for Rs 50 and even an air-con bus for Rs 65. You can also get buses direct to Simla (10 hours) or Amritsar (nine hours) for Rs 40 or to Bharatpur for Rs 20.

Getting Around

Distances in Delhi are large and the buses are generally hopelessly crowded, which in the past meant that taxis or auto-rickshaws were the only alternative. Recently, however, a de-luxe service has been introduced which runs the same routes as the regular buses and charges Rs 1 instead of Rs 0.50.

Airport Fortunately airport to city and vice-versa transport is relatively simple. EATS, Ex-Servicemen's Air Link Transport Service, have a regular bus service between the airport and their office in Connaught Place. The fare is Rs 8 and they will drop off or pick up at most of the major hotels en route. Departures, from opposite the underground bazaar, are at 4.40, 5.15, 5.45, 7, 7.45, 10 and 11.30 am, 2.30, 3.30, 5, 6.45, 8.30, 9.30, 10.30 and 11.30 pm. Departures from the airport to the centre are timed according to aircraft arrivals.

A taxi runs about Rs 35 to 40 from the airport to Connaught Place although they frequently ask for considerably more. Auto-rickshaws will also run out to the airport although your teeth will be shaking by the time you get there! If you can find a driver willing to use the meter it should cost about Rs 17, otherwise expect to pay Rs 20 to 25. There is a public bus service to the airport (780) from the Super Bazaar at Connaught Place but it can get very crowded.

If you're arriving at New Delhi airport from overseas, the State Bank foreign exchange counter is within the arrivals hall, after you've gone through customs and immigration. Once you've left the arrivals hall you won't be allowed back in. The service is quite fast and efficient. Many international flights to Delhi arrive and depart at terrible hours in the early morning. Take especial care if this is your first foray into India and you arrive exhausted and jet-lagged. If you're leaving Delhi in the early hours of the morning book a taxi the afternoon before. They'll be hard to find in the night. See the accommodation section for information about the retiring rooms at the airport.

Bus Avoid buses during the rush hours when the situation is hopeless and whenever possible try to board (and leave too) at a starting or finishing point – more chance of a seat, less chance of being trampled. The Regal and Plaza Cinemas in Connaught Place are such places. There are some seats reserved for women on the left side of the bus. The Delhi Transport Corporation (DTC) run the buses and you can get a route guide from their office in Scindia House for Rs 2.

Some buses include the 504 to the Qutab Minar from the Super Bazaar; the 502 from the Red Fort; 504 will also take you to the Youth Hostel there. The 101 runs between the Interstate Bus Terminal and Connaught Place. A 620 or 630 will take you between Connaught Place and Chanakyapuri. Several buses run between the Regal Cinema bus stand the Red Fort. A short bus ride (like Connaught Place-Red Fort) will only be about Rs 0.50. Buses to New Delhi Railway Station from Connaught Place (Regal Cinema) include the 157 and the R40.

Taxis & Auto-Rickshaws All taxis and auto-rickshaws are metered but the meters are invariably out of date, allegedly 'not working' or the drivers will simply refuse to use them. It matters not a jot that they are legally required to do so. A threat to report them to the police results in little more than considerable mirth so you will often have to negotiate a price before you set out. Naturally, this will always be more than it should be. Of course there are exceptions, occasionally a driver will re-set the meter without even a word from you. At places like New Delhi Station or the airport, where there are always plenty of police hanging around, you can generally rely on the meter being used because it's too easy to report a driver. Trips during the rush hour or middle of the night journeys to the airport are the times when meters are least likely to be used.

At the end of a journey you will have to pay according to a scale of revised charges. Some drivers have these cards displayed in the cab; others consign them to the oily rag compartment; still others simply feed them to the cows. So if you do come across a legible copy it's worth noting a few of the conversions down, paying what you think is the right price and leaving it at that. You may rest assured that no-one is going to be out of pocket, except yourself, despite hurt or angry protestations to the contrary.

Connaught Place to the Red Fort could be, depending on traffic, around Rs 12 by taxi, Rs 6 by auto-rickshaw. There are also old Harley-Davidson 'four-seater' or 'six-seater' auto-rickshaws running fixed routes at fixed prices. From Connaught Place their starting point is by the Regal Cinema and your Sikh driver will chop his

way through the traffic as far as the fountain in Chandni Chowk via the Red Fort in old Delhi. They only cost between Rs 1 and Rs 1.50 each and are good value especially during rush hours.

Things to Buy
Good buys in Delhi include silk products, precious stones, leather and woodwork, but the most important thing about Delhi is that here you can find almost anything from almost anywhere in India. If this is your first stop in India, and you intend to buy something while you are here, then it's a chance to compare what is available from all over India. If this is your last stop and there was something you missed elsewhere in the country it's a last chance to find it.

Two good places to start are in New Delhi near Connaught Place. The Central Cottage Industries Emporium is on Janpath, right across from the Tourist Office. In this large building you will find items from all over India. Generally they are of good quality and generally they are reasonably priced. Whether it's wood-carvings, brasswork, paintings, clothes, textiles or furniture you'll find it all here. Along Baba Kharak Singh Marg, two streets round from Janpath, are the various State Emporiums run by the state governments. Each displays and sells handicrafts from their state. There are many other shops around Connaught Place and Janpath. By the nearby Imperial Hotel there are a number of stalls and small shops run by Tibetan refugees where they sell carpets, jewellery and many (often instant) antiques.

In old Delhi Chandni Chowk is the famous shopping street. Here you will find carpets and jewellery, and in the narrow street called Cariba Kalan perfumes are made as well. You can find an interesting variety of perfumes, oils and soaps at Chhabra Perfumery at 1573 Main Bazaar, Paharganj, near the Vivek Hotel. More than a hundred oils are available in small bottles at Rs 3 or 4 each.

Punjab & Haryana

Haryana
Population: 10 million
Area: 44,222 square km
Capital: Chandigarh
Main language: Hindi

Punjab
Population: 15 million
Area: 50,362 square km
Capital: Chandigarh
Main language: Punjabi

THE EXTERNAL BOUNDARIES OF INDIA ARE NEITHER CORRECT NOR AUTHENTICATED

The Punjab was probably the part of India which suffered the most destruction and damage at the time of partition, yet today it is far and away the most affluent state in India. There's no natural resource or natural advantage that has given the Punjabis this enviable position, it was simply sheer hard work. Prior to partition the Punjab extended across both sides of what is now the Pakistan-India border. Its capital was Lahore, which today is the capital of the Pakistan state of the Punjab. But the population of the Punjab was split between Moslems and Sikhs and by the grim logic of partition that meant slicing the region in two. As millions of Sikhs and Hindus fled eastward and equal numbers of Moslems fled west, there were innumerable atrocities and killings on both sides. More recently Sikh political demands have wracked the state, and particularly Amritsar, with violence throughout 1983. The demands are somewhat vague and difficult for out-siders to understand but the escalating violence between Sikh and Hindu factions has made the Punjab a somewhat uncomfortable place of late.

The major city in the Punjab is Amritsar, the holy city of the Sikhs, but it is so close to the Pakistan border that it was thought wise to build a safer capital further within the borders of India. At first Simla, the old imperial summer capital, served as capital but Chandigarh, a new planned city, was conceived and built to serve as the capital of the new Punjab. In 1966, however, the Punjab was to undergo another split. This time it was divided into the predominantly Sikh and Punjabi speaking state of Punjab and the state of Haryana. At the same time some of the northern parts of the Punjab were hived off to Himachal Pradesh. Chandigarh, which now stands on the border of the Punjab and Haryana, remains the capital of both states.

At the time of partition the Punjab was devastated but the Sikh's no-nonsense approach to life has won for the Punjab a position that statistics sum up admirably. The Punjab's per capita income is 50% higher than the all– India average (in second place is Haryana). Although Punjabis comprise less than 2½% of the population of India they provide 60% of India's wheat surplus and 50% of its rice surplus. The Punjab provides a third of all the milk produced in India. Punjabis have 5% of India's total bank deposits, they own 1% of India's television sets, their life

158

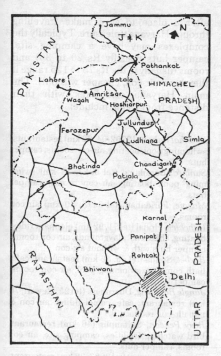

Kashmir a lot of people do pass through them.

The Sikhs

The Sikhs are the reason for the Punjab's success story and they're amongst the most interesting people in India. See the introductory section on religions for a description of their religion and customs. Apart from anything else the Sikhs are the most instantly recognisable people in India. The requirement that they do not cut their hair (*kesh*) ensures that all Sikh men are bearded and turbaned. For some reason they all look big, bulky men too –

Sikhs, always very dapper...

expectancy is 65 years against the all-India average of 47 years. Although the Punjab is predominantly an agricultural state, it also has thriving industries including, at Ludhiana, Hero Bicycles which are India's biggest bicycle manufacturer. The Punjabis also have the highest consumption of alcohol in India – the iron bangle (*kara*), which all Sikh men must wear, is an ideal instrument for taking the caps off beer bottles!

From the traveller's point of view, neither the Punjab nor Haryana has an enormous amount to offer though. In Haryana the chief attraction is the planned city of Chandigarh, while in the Punjab it is the Sikh's golden city of Amritsar. Those cities apart the two states are mainly places of transit. Since they're on the way to the hill stations of Himachal Pradesh and the delights of you never see a weedy looking Sikh. Sikh women also have a unique costume – the *salvar-kamiz*: wide pyjama-style trousers which are fastened at the ankles, topped by a long shirt which almost reaches the knees. All Sikh's have the surname Singh, 'lion'.

Curiously, despite their undoubted success, the Sikhs have a reputation in India, rather like the Irish in the west. The Indians have as many Sikh jokes as the west has Irish jokes. Not many translate very well but they basically follow the same line, which is strange since the stereotyped Sikh is quite unlike the stereotyped Irishman. The Irish joke Irishman is supposed to be all thumbs, the Sikhs have a reputation for great dexterity and mechanical ability – Sikhs have always been at home with machines and in India any activity with machines, from driving an auto-rickshaw to piloting a 747, will employ a disproportionate number of Sikhs. Despite this other Indians mock Sikhs as being blunt and straightforward to the point of stupidity!

HARYANA

The state of Haryana has one of the most successful tourist departments in India, which is very interesting when you consider how few tourist attractions the state has. What the clever Haryanans have done is take advantage of their position – if you're going from Delhi to almost any major attraction in the north – Jaipur, Agra, Kashmir, Amritsar – you go through Haryana. So they've built a series of 'service centres' along the main roads. The sort of motel-restaurant-service station complexes which, in the west are quite common, but in India are all too rare. They're clean and well kept and, if you're after a place to stay, make travelling through Haryana a pleasure. Typically the complexes may have a camping site, camper huts (usually Rs 20 to 30) and rooms (usually in the Rs 75 to 125 range if they have air-con, cheaper without). The main Haryana complexes with their distance from Delhi, include:

Badkhal Lake (tel 2202-04, 32 km) restaurants, swimming pool, boating, air-con rooms, camper huts.

Sunbird, Surajkund (tel 5357, 18 km) swimming pool, boating, air-con rooms, camper huts.

Magpie, Faridabad (tel 3473, 30 km) air-con rooms.

Dabchick, Hodal (tel 91, 92 km) elephant rides, boating, childrens' playgrounds, air-con rooms, camper huts with & without air-con.

Barbet, Sohna (tel 56, 56 km) restaurant, cafe, bath complex, swimming pool, air-con rooms, camper huts.

Jangle Babbleng, Dharuhera (tel 25, Rewari, 70 km) restaurant, cafe, camel riding, air-con & non air-con rooms.

Rosy Pelican, Sultanpur (46 km) restaurant, bird watching facilities, camping site, air-con rooms, camper huts.

Shama Restaurant (tel 2683, 32 km) restaurant, non air-con rooms.

Mor Pankh (70 km) restaurant, non air-con rooms.

Ulchana, Karnal (tel 2179, 124 km) restaurant, cafe, kebab corner, boating, air-con rooms, camper huts.

Parakeet, Pipli (tel 250, 152 km) restaurant, cafe, camping facilities, air-con rooms, camper huts.

Blue Jay, Samalkha (tel 10, 60 km) restaurant, air-con & non air-con rooms, camper huts.

Yadavindra Gardens, Pinjore (tel 155, 281 km) at the Moghul gardens, restaurant, open air cafe, dosa shop, mini-zoo, children's games, air-con rooms, camper huts.

Panchkula Youth Hostel (270 km) dorm beds.

A   Film hoardings in Calcutta (WB)
B   Toy train to Darjeeling (WB)

Skylark, Panipat (tel 3579, 90 km) restaurant, air-con rooms.

Tilyar, Rohtak (tel 3966, 70 km) restaurant, boating, air-con & non air-con rooms.

Myna, Rohtak (tel 2394, 72 km) restaurant, camper huts.

Flamingo, Hissar (tel 2602, 160 km) restaurant, air-con rooms.

Bulbul, Jind (127 km) restaurant, camper huts.

Kala Teetar, Abubshehr (325 km) restaurant, boating, air-con rooms.

DELHI TO CHANDIGARH

There are a number of sites of interest along the 260-km route from Delhi to Chandigarh. The road, part of the Grand Trunk Road, is one of the busiest in India with a lot of traffic of all types.

Panipat

Panipat, 92 km north of Delhi, is reputed to be one of the most fly-infested places in India – due, it is said, to a Moslem saint who is buried here. He is supposed to have totally rid Panipat of flies, but when the people complained that he had done too good a job he gave them all the flies back, times a thousand.

It is also the site of three great battles, although there is nothing much to be seen of these today. In 1526 Babur defeated Ibrahim Lodi, King of Delhi, at Panipat and thus founded the Moghul empire in India. In 1556 Akbar defeated the Pathans at this same site. Finally in 1761 the Mahrattas, who had succeeded the Moghuls, were defeated here by the Afghan forces of Ahmad Shah Durani.

Gharaunda

The gateways of an old Moghul *sarai* (rest house) stand to the west of this village, 102 km north of Delhi. Shah Jahan built

kos minars, 'milestones', along the road from Delhi to Lahore and *sarais* at longer intervals. Most of the *kos minars* still stand but there is little left of the various *sarais*.

Karnal & Kurukshetra

Events in the *Mahabharata* are supposed to have occurred here, 118 km from Delhi, and also at the tank of Kurukshetra, a little further north. It was at Karnal that Nadir Shah, the Persian who took the Peacock Throne from Delhi, defeated the Moghul Emperor Muhammed Shah in 1739. The Kurukshetra tank has attracted as many as half a million pilgrims at times of eclipses – for at these times the water in the tank is also said to contain water from every other sacred tank in India. Thus its ability to wash away sins is unsurpassed – during the eclipse. Kurukshetra also has an interesting small mosque, the Lal Masjid, and a finely designed tomb.

CHANDIGARH (population 250,000)

When the Punjab was partitioned its capital, Lahore, went to Pakistan. Initially Amritsar became the capital of the Indian Punjab, but since it was uncomfortably close to the Pakistan border the decision was made to construct a totally new capital and the French architect, Le Corbusier, produced the plan. Later the Punjab was split into the two states of the Punjab and Haryana so today Chandigarh serves as the capital of both states. It is directly administered from New Delhi as a union territory. Construction of Chandigarh commenced in the '50s and although to many westerners it appears rather sterile and hopelessly sprawling, Indians are proud of it and the residents feel it is a good place to live.

A Jantar Mantar in New Delhi (ND)
B Golden Temple in Amristar (P)
C Sikh guard at the Golden Temple (P)

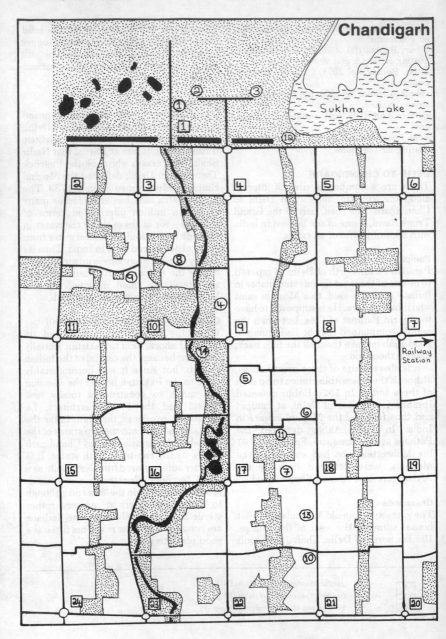

Chandigarh

Sukhna Lake

Railway
Station

1 Secretariat	8 Hotel Mount View
2 Vidhan Sabha	9 YMCA
3 High Court	10 Aroma Hotel
4 Museum & Art Gallery	11 Kwality Restaurant
5 GPO	12 Rock Garden
6 Indian Airliens & Air India	13 Piccadily Hotel
7 Tourist Office & Bus Station	14 Rose Garden

Chandigarh is a great disappointment – dismal and dull. Like so many examples of mid-20th century urban planning (read 'pre oil-crisis') it was very much designed with wheeled transport in mind. Plus, between buildings there are long, ugly, barren stretches of wasteland. In Le Corbusier's home environment they might be parks or gardens, but in India empty ground is obviously doomed. Still the 'rock garden' is an eccentric little amusement.

Information & Orientation

Chandigarh is on the edge of the Siwalik Hills, the outermost edge of the Himalaya. It is divided into 47 numbered sectors, separated by broad avenues. The bus station and modern shopping centre are in Sector 17. The railway station is inconveniently far out of Chandigarh so buses are much more convenient than trains but you can now make rail bookings from the office above the central bus terminus.

The Secretariat and other important government buildings are in Sector 1, to the north. The museum is in Sector 10 and the Rose Garden in Sector 16, next to the bus station. The shopping centre has restaurants, ice cream parlours, books shops and a wide variety of other retail outlets. The Tourist Office is upstairs in the bus station.

Government Buildings

The Secretariat and the Legislative Assembly Buildings are in Sector 1. Between 10 am and 12 noon you can go to the top of the Secretariat from where there is an excellent view over Chandigarh. Eventually, it is intended to build a huge revolving hand to be the centrepiece of the government sector and the symbol of Chandigarh.

Close to the government buildings is a not-to-be-missed attraction, the bizarre Rock Garden (25p admission) – a sort of concrete maze with a lot of rocks and very little garden. A very strange and whimsical fantasy. Close to this is the artificial Sukhna Lake which covers about three square km. You can rent row boats on the lake or just stroll round its two km perimeter.

Museum & Art Gallery

In Sector 10 and open daily except Mondays, the art gallery contains a modest collection of Indian stone sculptures dating back to the Gandhara period, together with some miniature paintings and modern art. The adjacent museum has fossils and implements of pre-historic man, which have been found in India.

Rose Garden

The Sector 16 Rose Garden is claimed to be the biggest in Asia and contains more than a thousand varieties of roses.

Places to Stay – Bottom End

The new *Youth Hostel* is at Panchkula, between Chandigarh and the Pinjore Gardens – a little way out of town, but there are many buses and the hostel is good value. It is also possible to get cheaper dormitory-style accommodation in the *Panchayat Bhawan* (tel 23698) in Sector 18. This is a government accommodation unit but rather far from the city centre and bus station.

Maharajah Tourist Lodge, just a Rs 2 trishaw ride from the bus stand, has clean rooms for Rs 30 or less and even has hot water, but the guys who run it are 'a real hassle'. There is a *YMCA* (tel 26532) in Sector 11 and three less expensive hotels opposite the bus station – *Jullundur, Amar* and *Alankar*.

Places to Stay – Top End
The *Mount View* in Sector 10 (tel 24729, 26021) is Chandigarh's top hotel. Rooms cost from Rs 300 and the hotel has all modern facilities. Two new recently opened hotels are the *Hotel Dhillon* and the *Hotel Piccadilly*. The Piccadilly (tel 32223-7) is in Sector 22 and has singles/doubles, all air-con, at Rs 240/320.

Hotel Aroma in Sector 22 (tel 23359) is somewhat cheaper, but often rather crowded – as are many of Chandigarh's hotels. Rooms cost from Rs 40. It's about 10 minutes' walk from the bus station. There are some rooms with air-con.

Places to Eat
There are many restaurants in the modern shopping centre. *Sai Sweets* at 1102 in Sector 22 (about midway between the bus halt and the Aroma Hotel) has good chat. *Hotel Dibyadwip* in the same area has relatively expensive, but very good thalis. The *Indian Coffee House*, in the shopping centre, is also a good, economic place to eat.

Getting There
Air There are air connections between Chandigarh and Delhi (daily) for Rs 219, Jammu Rs 341 and Srinagar Rs 464. Recently air connections have also been started between Chandigarh and Leh in Ladakh (twice weekly) for Rs 387 and to Kulu in the Kulu Valley for Rs 239.

Bus & Rail Buses depart from the Interstate Bus Terminal in Delhi (near Kashmir Gate) every hour for the five hour trip to Chandigarh. There is a much wider choice of buses than usual on this route. Apart from the regular buses (Rs 24), there are about six de-luxe buses daily (Rs 50) and three or four air-con buses (Rs

65), which actually show Indian movies en route. Although the de-luxe buses cost twice as much as the regular ones they're no faster and do not appear to be much better, especially in the winter.

Buses are equally frequent from Chandigarh to other centres – to Simla costs Rs 16 (Rs 32 de-luxe), Dharamsala Rs 32 or Manali Rs 42. It takes about 14 hours to Manali by bus, only nine by taxi. It's five hours to Simla, 12 hours to Kulu, six hours to Amritsar, 10 hours to Dharamsala and seven hours to Pathankot.

Buses are more convenient than trains to or from Chandigarh, but reservations can be made at the booking agency in Sector 22 (tel 29117) or at the office above the central bus station. Enquiries can be made by phoning 27605.

Getting Around
Chandigarh is much too spread out to get around on foot, but a day is certainly sufficient to see all it has to offer. There is an extensive bus network and this is the cheapest way of getting around – Bus 1 runs by the Aroma Hotel as far as the government buildings in Sector 1. Buses 6, 6A and 6B all run to the railway station.

Cycle rickshaws operate on the normal bargaining basis but Chandigarh is a bit big even for them – if you're planning a longer trip across the city consider an auto-rickshaw, they're metered. If you do want to try walking start off at Sector 1 and stroll back through Sector 10 (Museum & Art Gallery) and 16 (Rose Garden) to the bus station and shopping centre in Sector 17.

Things to Buy
Woollen sweaters and shawls from the Punjab are good buys, especially in the Government Emporium. The Chandigarh shopping centre is probably the most extensive in India.

NEAR CHANDIGARH
Pinjore

The Moghul gardens at Pinjore were designed by Fidai Khan, Aurangzeb's foster brother, who also designed the Badshahi Mosque in Lahore, Pakistan. Situated 20 km from Chandigarh the gardens include the Rajasthani-Moghul style Shish Mahal palace. Below it is the Rang Mahal and the cubical Jal Mahal. An otter house and other animals can be seen in the mini-zoo near the gardens. The fountains only operate on weekends.

Places to Stay The rest house here has air-con rooms for around Rs 100 and one camper hut at Rs 15.

DELHI TO AMRITSAR
Patiala (population 160,000)

A little south of the road and rail lines from Delhi to Amritsar, Patiala was once the capital of an independent Sikh state. There is a museum in the Moti Bagh and the palace of the Maharaja in the Baradari Gardens.

Sirhind

This was once a very important town and the capital of the Pathan Sur dynasty. In 1555 Humayun defeated Sikander Shah here and a year later his son, Akbar, completed the destruction of the Sur dynasty at Panipat. From then until 1709 Sirhind was a rich Moghul city, but clashes between the declining Moghul and rising Sikh powers led to the city's sacking in 1709 and complete destruction in 1763.

The Pathan-style Tomb of Mir Miran and the later Moghul Tomb of Pirbandi Nakshwala, both ornamented with blue tiles, are worth seeing. The mansion or *haveli* of Salabat Beg is probably the largest private home remaining from the Moghul period. South-east of the city is an important Moghul *sarai*.

Ludhiana (population 450,000)

An important textile centre, a great battle of the First Sikh War was fought in Ludhiana. Hero bicycles are manufactured here.

Jullundur (population 325,000)

Only 80 km from Amritsar, this was once the capital of an ancient Hindu kingdom. It survived being sacked by Mahmud of Ghazni nearly a thousand years ago and later became an important Moghul city. The town has a large *sarai* built in 1857 and this is a good place to get out and see some Sikh farming villages.

Places to Stay Not far from the bus stand the *Skylark Hotel* has excellent doubles at Rs 50 and very good food.

Getting There Trains take about six hours from Delhi and there's also a bus stand from where frequent services run to other northern centres.

AMRITSAR (population 500,000)

Travellers heading overland always pass through Amritsar, it's close to the only land crossing open to Pakistan and every traveller crossing Asia inevitably passes through the city. Founded in 1577 by Ram Das, the fourth Guru of the Sikhs, Amritsar is both the centre of the Sikh religion and the major city of the Punjab state – where the majority of Sikhs live. The name Amritsar translates as 'pool of nectar', the name of the sacred pool by which the Sikh's golden temple is built.

The original site for the city was granted by the Moghul emperor Akbar, but in 1761 Ahmad Shah Durani sacked the town and destroyed the temple. The temple was rebuilt in 1764 and in 1802 it was roofed over with copper gilded plates by Ranjit Singh and became known as the golden temple. During the turmoil of the partition of India in 1948, Amritsar was a flashpoint for the terrible events that shook the Punjab. The region's recovery has been remarkable and today Amritsar even looks better off than other parts of India. You see few beggars in the streets. Although the Punjab is currently wracked

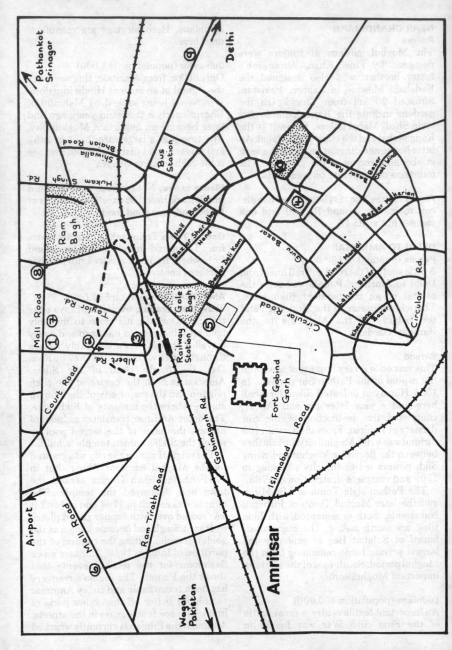

Amritsar

1 Indian Airlines	7 Hotel Ritz
2 G.P.O.	8 Kwality Restaurant
3 Punjab Government Tourist Office	9 Youth Hostel
4 Golden Temple	10 Jallianwala Bagh
5 Durgiana Temple	
6 Mrs. Bhandari's Guest House	Main Hotel & Restaurant Area

by political violence travellers have commented on the friendliness and helpfulness of the Sikhs.

Information & Orientation

The old city is south of the main railway station and is surrounded by a circular road which used to contain the massive city walls. There are 18 gates still in existence but only the gate to the north, facing the Ram Bagh gardens, is original. The Golden Temple and the narrow alleys of the bazaar area are in the interior of the old city. The more modern part of Amritsar is north-east of the railway station where you will also find the beautiful gardens known as Ram Bagh, the Mall and the 'posh' Lawrence St. The bus station is a km east of the railway station on the road to Delhi. The Tourist Office is opposite the railway station.

The Golden Temple

The holiest shrine of the Sikh religion is in the centre of the old part of town. The temple itself is surrounded by the lake which gave the town its name. A causeway connects the temple in the middle of the pool and a loudspeaker broadcasts a continuous reading of the *Granth Sahib* in Punjabi. The high priest who reads from the Sikh's holy book sits on the east side of the temple. The original copy of the *Granth Sahib* is kept in the Golden Temple and is occasionally taken out on procession. There is also a temple garden to the south side of the temple enclosure and the Baba Atal Tower stands in this garden. The tall Ramgarhia Minars stand outside the temple enclosure.

Pilgrims and visitors to the Golden Temple must remove their shoes and cover their heads before entering the temple precincts. An English-speaking guide is available at the clock tower which marks the temple entrance. The Central Sikh Museun is upstairs in the clock tower.

The Old City

A 15-minute walk from the Golden Temple, through the narrow alleys of the old city, brings you to the Hindu temple known as Durgiana. This small temple, dedicated to the goddess Durga, dates back to the 16th century. A larger temple, built like the Golden Temple in the centre of a lake, is dedicated to the Hindu deities Laxmi and Narayan. There are a number of mosques in the old city including the mosque of Muhammad Jan with three white domes and slender minarets. To the south-west of the city stands the Fort of Govindgarh which was built in 1805-09 by Ranjit Singh, who was also responsible for the city walls.

Jalianwala Bagh

This park is just five minutes' walk from the Golden Temple and commemorates the death of 2000 Indians at this site, who were shot indiscriminately by the British in 1919. This was one of the major events in India's struggles for independence and was movingly recreated in the film *Gandhi*. Bullet marks and the well into which some people jumped to escape can still be seen.

Ram Bagh

This beautiful garden is in the new part of town and also has a museum in the small palace built there by the Sikh Maharajah Ranjit Singh. The museum contains weapons dating back to the Moghul times and some portraits of the ruling houses of the Punjab. It's closed on Wednesdays.

Other

The Govindgarh Fort, built by Rajit Singh in 1809, is a little south-west of the city centre. Tarn Taran is an important Sikh tank, about 25 km south of Amritsar. There's a temple and tower on the east side of the tank which was also constructed by Ranjit Singh. The temple predates Amritsar. It's said that any leper who can swim across the tank will be miraculously cured.

Places to Stay – Bottom End

The *Tourist Guest House*, across from the railway station and near Hotel Airlines, has rooms from Rs 25 and is popular with shoestring travellers. The *Hotel Temple View* has rooms at Rs 20 a double – 'clean, real Sikh friendliness and one of the best views of the Golden Temple in town'.

If you're on a really tight budget the state government operated *Youth Hostel* is three km out of town on the Delhi road. There are dorm beds (cheaper for YHA members) and also cheap (but doorless!) doubles. The hotel has hot showers and good, albeit expensive, food. It's one of the better youth hostels in India and also has camping facilities.

The Golden Temple at Amritsar

If you'd really like to come to grips with the Sikh religion you can stay for a few days for free at the guest house of the Golden Temple. Be considerate, don't smoke and don't complain if the standards are not what you expect. Mattresses can be loaned for a returnable Rs 10 deposit. Accommodation is dormitory style. There are many cheap hotels around the temple such as the *Vikas Guest House* (rooms for Rs 30) or the slightly cheaper *Amritsar Majestic Hotel*.

Places to Stay – Middle

Station Links Rd, opposite the railway station, has three moderately priced hotels. *Hotel Skylark* (tel 46738) and *Hotel China* (tel 99455) cost from Rs 50. *Hotel Palace*, which also houses the state tourist information office, has some cheaper rooms. Close by is the similarly priced *Grand Hotel*.

Near the Mall, in the new area of the city and about a km from the railway station, you'll find the pleasant *Hotel Blue Moon* with rooms at Rs 60/90 or at Rs 90/120 with air con. In the same area the *Hotel Odeon* (tel 43474) has rooms with attached bath from only Rs 40. This is also the area for a number of restaurants including a Kwality branch, opposite the Ram Bagh.

Places to Stay – Top End

Built by the Punjab state government the *Amritsar International Hotel* (tel 31991) is a new building near the bus station. Equipped with all modern facilities, such as air-conditioning, rooms range from Rs 160. Other more expensive hotels include the *Airlines Hotel* (tel 44545) on Cooper Rd near the railway station; rooms from Rs 75, air-con from Rs 125.

The *Ritz Hotel* (tel 44199, 43135) is at 45 The Mall and singles/doubles, all air-con, are Rs 180/250. Or there's the *Astoria* (tel 48979) on Queens Rd with rooms at a wide variety of prices from Rs 45 to 95 without air-con, from Rs 90 to 135 with air-con.

Places to Eat

There are a number of more expensive restaurants in the new part of town such as *Napoli*, *Kwality* and *Crystal*. Near the Kwality restaurant there is an ice cream parlour with 20 flavours of ice cream.

Amritsar also has a number of cheaper and locally popular places such as *Kasar de Dhawa* near the Durgiana Temple and the telephone exchange in the old town. Parathas and other vegetarian dishes are the speciality here and you can eat well for less than Rs 10. *Kundan di Dhawa* near the railway station and *Mangal de Dhawa* are other popular cheapies. *Sharma Vaishna Dhaba*, near the temple, also has good vegetarian food. Also near the temple entrance the *Losy Restaurant* has 'superb, real Punjabi food'. The railway restaurant is good.

Getting There

Air Amritsar is on the popular daily Delhi-Amritsar-Srinagar route. Flights to or from Delhi cost Rs 370, to or from Srinagar is Rs 314.

Rail & Bus Amritsar is 447 km from Delhi and takes seven hours by mail or express train (Rs 34 in second class, Rs 132 in first). It's rather less comfortable by the bus which takes 10 hours. Amritsar is a jumping off point to other places in north-west India – Pathankot (on the way to Kashmir) is three hours away by bus and Chandigarh is four. Jammu takes five hours (215 km) for Rs 18. Dharamsala takes 6½ hours (250 km) for Rs 23.

It is only 30 km from Amritsar to Wagah, the road crossing point into Pakistan. There are two buses an hour to the border and formalities on both sides are pretty quick. You just walk across the border and then take another bus into Lahore. The border doesn't open until 9.15 am and closes at 3.30 pm. You can get from Amritsar to Lahore in around three hours. A train service now operates between Amritsar and Lahore as well but because of long delays at the border this can take much longer. See the 'Entry & Exits' section for more details.

Things to Buy

Woollen blankets and sweaters are supposed to be cheaper in Amritsar than in other places in India as they are locally manufactured. Katra Jaimal Singh, near the telephone exchange in the old city, is a good shopping area.

PATHANKOT

In the extreme north of the Punjab, 107 km from Amritsar, the town of Pathankot is important to travellers purely for its crossroads function. It's the gateway to Jammu in the state of Jammu and Kashmir, which in turn is the jumping off point for the bus trip up to Srinagar. Pathankot is also the bus centre for departures to the Himachal Pradesh hill stations – particularly Dalhousie and Dharamsala. Otherwise it's a dull little place, although there's the picturesque Shahpur Kandi Fort, about 13 km north of the town on the River Ravi.

Getting There

The dusty bus station and the railway station are only a hundred or so metres apart. Buses to Jammu take about three hours and cost Rs 8. To Dalhousie it's Rs 11 and about four hours, to Dharamsala

Rs 13 and five hours. You can also get taxis for these longer trips from beside the railway station.

Places to Stay

Pathankot has a rest house and cheap hotels like the *Green Hotel* and the *Imperial Hotel*. Reasonable food in the railway station restaurant.

DELHI TO FEROZEPORE

This route takes you through Haryana and the Punjab, further south than the Delhi-Chandigarh and Delhi-Amritsar routes. From Delhi the railway line runs through Rohtak, 70 km out, which was once a border town between the Sikhs and Marathas and the subject of frequent clashes.

Bhatinda, 296 km from Delhi, was an important town of the Pathan Sur dynasty. Sirsa, to the south of Bhatinda, was an ancient city but little remains apart from the city walls. Hansi, south-east of Sirsa, towards Rohtak, was where Colonel Skinner, of the legendary regiment 'Skinner's Horse', died. Faridkot, 350 km from Delhi, was once the capital of a Sikh state of the same name. It has a 700-year-old fort. Ferozepore is 382 km from Delhi and the railway line continued to Lahore from here, until partition.

Keeping Your Cool

Sometimes India can simply be too much for anyone to take. It has been called culture shock enough times and in a way that is what it is. Remember that habits and practices which annoy or even revolt you – the continuous hawking and spitting that sometimes seems to go on, the practice of making every wall a public urinal – are probably matched by some western habits that an Asian would find just as incomprehensible. Westerners blithely walk into houses without pausing to take their shoes off, they sit on toilet seats, they carry dirty handkerchiefs in their pockets.

The habit of fixedly staring at you is one you just have to get used to. It's simply un-embarrassed interest and there is nothing you can do about it. Staring right back is not going to change anything.

Summon up as much understanding as you can, but sometimes pushing and shoving, cutting into queues, continuously trying to get you to do something you don't want to, the inevitable rip-offs all become too much and even the most easy going travellers lose their temper. Treat it as part of life, practise staying more relaxed next time, but if it starts to happen too often perhaps it's time you took a break from India. After all that's what Nepal and Sri Lanka are there for, isn't it?

Himachal Pradesh

Population: 3.5 million
Area: 55,673 square km
Capital: Simla
Main languages: Hindi, Pahari

The state of Himachal Pradesh came into being in its present form with the partition of the Punjab into Punjab and Haryana in 1966. Himachal Pradesh is essentially a mountain state – it takes in the transition zone from the plains to the high Himalaya and in the trans-Himalayan region of Lahaul and Spiti actually crosses that mighty barrier to the Tibetan plateau. It's a delightful state for visitors, particularly during the hot season when people flock to its hill stations to escape the searing heat of the plains.

High points for the visitor include Simla, the 'summer capital' of British India and still one of India's most important hill stations. The Kulu Valley is simply one of the most beautiful areas on earth – a lush, green valley with the sparkling Beas River running through it and the snow-capped Himalayan peaks forming the background. Then there's Dharamsala, home-in-exile for the Dalai Lama; and a host of other hill stations, lakes, walks and mountains. In the far north of the state the winter snow melts to permit visitors for a few brief summer months to explore the Tibetan culture of Keylong in Lahaul and Spiti.

Trekking & Mountaineering
There is a wide variety of trekking possibilities which, as yet, have been barely exploited. The forthcoming Lonely Planet guidebook *Trekking in the Indian Himalaya* will have much more information on trekking in this region. The Himachal Pradesh Tourist Office can supply a booklet titled *Trekkers Guide to Himachal Pradesh* which concentrates on treks in the Kulu and Manali area. They

also have three excellent large scale maps of Himachal Pradesh which are invaluable for intending trekkers. The trekking season in Himachal Pradesh runs from mid-may to mid-October. In Manali there is a Department of Mountaineering & Allied Sports (tel 42) which can advise you on trekking possibilities in the state and also on the numerous unscaled peaks. Unlike in Nepal no trekking permits are necessary in Himachal Pradesh and this helps to make trekking here relatively cheap.

Equipment and provisions will depend very much on where you trek. In the lower country in the Kulu or Kangra Valleys, or around Simla, there are many rest houses and villages. On the other hand in Lahaul and Spiti the population is much less dense and conditions much more severe. You will need to be much better equipped in terms of cold weather gear and also food and provisions. Some of the better known treks are detailed in the appropriate sections. There are a great number of Forest Rest Houses, PWD Rest Houses and other semi-official accommodation possibilities along the Himachal Pradesh trekking routes. Enquire at local tourist offices about using these places before setting off.

The HPTD's *Trekking Guide* lists 136 mountains over 5000 metres high. The majority of them are unclimbed, most not even named. It's virgin territory for mountaineers.

Wildlife

There are fishing possibilities in many places in Himachal Pradesh and a number of trout hatcheries have been established. The various local tourist offices can advise you on where to fish and how to obtain fishing licences. These are much cheaper than in Kashmir.

There is a variety of deer, antelope, mountain goats and sheep which may be seen in the state, some of which are now rather rare. Himalayan black bears and brown bears are found in many parts of the state; the black bear is fairly common but the brown bear is usually only found at higher elevations. Wild boar are found at lower elevations in certain districts. Snow leopards are now very rare and only found at high elevations in the most remote parts of the state. Panther and leopards are, however, still found in many forested regions. Himachal Pradesh has a numerous kinds of pheasants and partridges and many mountain birds.

Temples

Although Himachal Pradesh does not have any particularly renowned temples, at least so far as being touristically well known goes, it does have many quite interesting and architecturally very diverse ones. In the Kangra and Chamba valleys there are several 8th to 10th century temples in the Indo-Aryan shikhara style. Pagoda-style temples with multi-tiered roofs are found in the Kulu Valley. There are many temples of purely local design, often with interesting wood carvings, particularly in the Chamba region.

In the south of the state there are numerous temples with elements of Moghul and Sikh design while in several locations there are cave temples. Finally the Tibetans, who came to the state following the Chinese invasion of their country, have built colourful gompas (monasteries) and temples. The people of Lahaul and Spiti in the north of the state are also of Tibetan extraction and have many interesting gompas.

Things to Buy

The Kulu Valley is full of spinners and weavers, mostly men, and the fine shawls made in Kulu are very popular. These are made from the fleece shed in the summer by mountain goats. The shawls made from pashmina hair from the pashmina goat are the finest. Chamba is well known for its leather chappals (sandals). In the high Himalayas fleecy soft blankets known as gudmas are woven, and traditional rugs and namdas. In the bazaars you can find locally made jewellery and metalwork. Tibetan handicrafts include coral jewellery, Tibetan carpets and religious paraphernalia.

Transport

Apart from two railway lines which are both narrow gauge and hence rather more 'fun' than 'transport', getting around Himachal Pradesh means taking a bus – unless you can afford a taxi. The two trains run from Kalka – just north of Chandigarh – to Simla, and from Pathankot along the Kangra Valley to Jogindarnargar. Himachal Pradesh buses are generally the Indian norm – slow, crowded, uncomfortable and tiring. Things are made a little worse by the mountainous terrain. If you can manage to average 20 kph on a bus trip you're doing well. Taxis are readily available but rather expensive. One way you can make a saving is to find a taxi on a return trip – in that case you can often knock the price down a bit. Ask the people running your hotel, they often know who's going where and when.

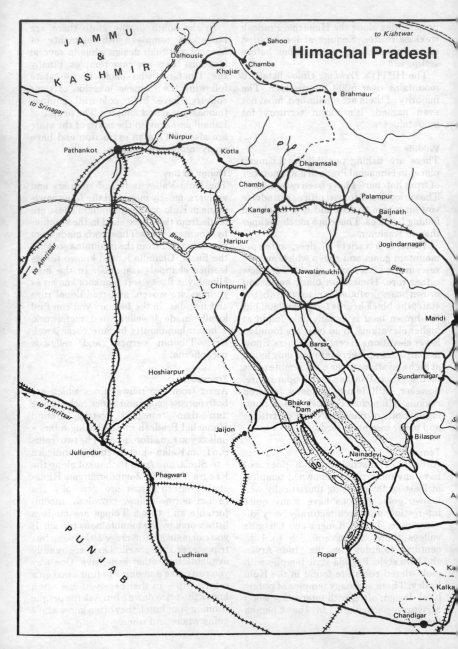

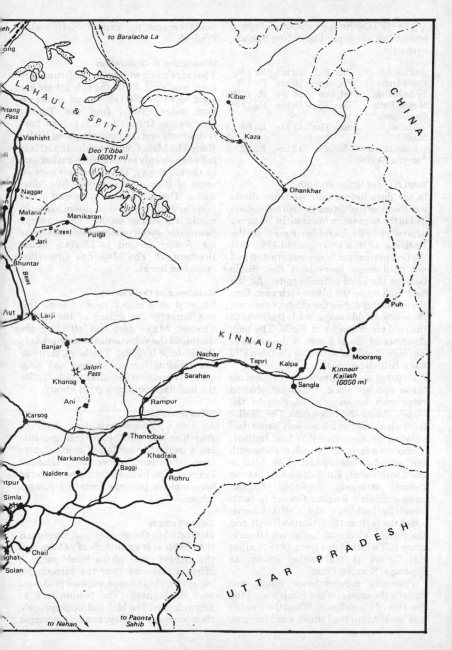

The HPTDC have a number of de-luxe tourist bus services. They often operate overnight.

Delhi-Simla	Thu, Sat	10 hrs	Rs 125
Simla-Delhi	Fri, Sun	10 hrs	Rs 125
Delhi-Manali	Fri, Sun	16 hrs	Rs 130*
Manali-Delhi	Tue, Thu	16 hrs	Rs 130*
Chandigarh-Manali	Sun, Thu	11 hrs	Rs 80
Manali-Chandigarh	Mon, Fri	11 hrs	Rs 80

*air-con Rs 200

SIMLA (population 60,000)

In the days before independence Simla was the most important British hill station and in the hot season became the 'summer capital' of India. First 'discovered' by the British in 1819 it was not until 1822 that the first permanent house was erected and not until many years later that Simla became the semi-official capital. As the heat built up on the plains each year, first the memsahibs, then the sahibs, or at least those who could escape, made their way to the cool mountain air of Simla. The high flown social life of Simla in the summer was legendary and somehow the town still has a British air about it.

Situated at an altitude of 2130 metres Simla sprawls along a crescent shaped ridge with its suburbs clinging to the slopes. Along the ridge runs The Mall – from which the British not only banned all vehicles but also, until WW I, all Indians. Today it's a busy scene each evening with throngs of holidaymakers. The Mall is lined with stately English-looking houses bearing strangely displaced English names. Simla's English flavour is continued by buildings like Christ Church which dates from 1857, Gorton Castle and the former Viceroyal Lodge on Observatory Hill which dates from 1888. Lajpat Rai Chowk is still better known as Kipling's 'Scandal Point'.

Following independence Simla was initially the capital of the Punjab until the creation of Chandigarh. When the Punjab was broken into the Punjab and Haryana, Simla became the capital of Himachal Pradesh.

Information & Orientation

The ridge along which The Mall runs dips away westward. From the ridge there are good views of the valleys and peaks on both sides. You'll find the Tourist Information Office (tel 3311), the best restaurants and the main shopping centre along The Mall. From the ridge the streets fall away steeply to colourful local bazaars on the hill slopes. The streets are narrow, some of them with verandah-like 'sidewalks'. The bus station is located in the middle of the crowded southern slope. In winter it is warmer on the southern slope than on the cooler northern side where the ice skating ground is located. Maria Brothers, 78 The Mall, has interesting maps and books.

Residence of the Viceroy

Situated on a hillock west of Simla this was formerly the palace of the British Viceroy. Many decisions affecting the destiny of the sub-continent were made in this historic building. The huge, fortress-like building has six storeys and magnificent reception and dining halls. Today the building contains a good library.

State Museum

An hour's pleasant walk down from the church on The Mall the nice little museum has a modest collection of stone statues from different places in Himachal Pradesh. The Indian miniatures exhibited here include pictures from the Kangra school.

Jakhu Temple

Dedicated to the monkey god, Hunuman, the temple is at an altitude of 2455 m near the highest point of the Simla ridge. It offers a fine view over the surrounding valleys, out to the snow-capped peaks and over Simla itself. The temple is a 45 min walk from The Mall and, appropriately, there are many monkeys around the temple.

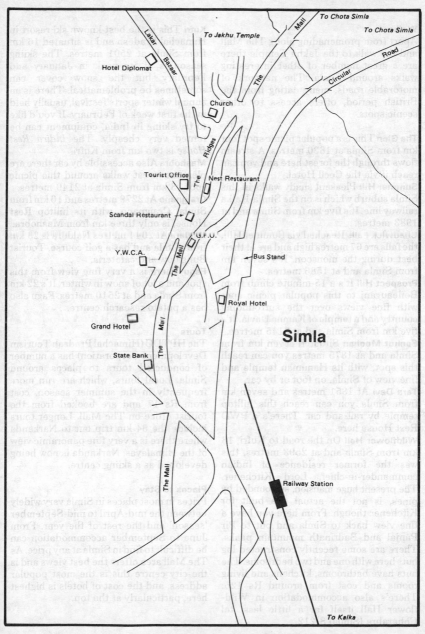

To Chota Simla

To Jakhu Temple

Hotel Diplomat

Church

The Ridges

Tourist Office

Nest Restaurant

Scandal Restaurant

G.P.O.

Y.W.C.A.

Bus Stand

Royal Hotel

Grand Hotel

State Bank

Simla

Railway Station

To Kalka

Walks

Apart from promenading along The Mall and the walk to the Jakhu Temple there are a great number of other interesting walks around Simla. The network of motorable roads, many dating from the British period, offers access to other scenic spots.

The Glen This is a popular picnic spot four km from Simla at 1830 metres. A stream flows through the forest here and you can reach it via the Cecil Hotel.

Summer Hill Pleasant shady walks in this Simla suburb which is on the Simla-Kalka railway line. It's five km from Simla and at 1983 metres.

Chadwick Falls Reached via Summer Hill, the falls are 67 metres high and are at their best during the monsoon. It's seven km from Simla and at 1586 metres.

Prospect Hill It's a 15-minute climb from Boileauganj to this popular picnic spot with fine views over the surrounding country and a temple of Kamna Devia. It's five km from Simla and at 2145 metres.

Sankat Mochan Situated seven km from Simla and at 1875 metres you can reach this spot, with its Hanuman temple and fine view of Simla, on foot or by car.

Tara Devi At 1851 metres and seven km from Simla you can reach this hilltop temple by rail and car. There's a PWD Rest House here.

Wildflower Hall On the road to Kufri, 13 km from Simla and at 2593 metres, this was the former residence of Indian commander-in-chief, Lord Kitchener. The present huge mansion, surrounded by pines, is not the actual one built for Kitchener though. From here you have a fine view back to Simla and out to Pir Panjal and Badrinath mountain peaks. There are some recently constructed log huts here with one and two bedrooms. The huts have bathrooms, kitchens and living rooms and cost from around Rs 125. There's also accommodation in Wildflower Hall itself for a little less; tel Chharabra (Simla) 8/212.

Kufri This is the best known ski resort in Himachal Pradesh and is situated 16 km from Simla at 2501 metres. The skiing season is at its peak in January and February but the snow cover can sometimes be problematical. There is an annual winter sports festival, usually held in the first week of February. If you'd like to try skiing in India, equipment can be rented very cheaply. The *Indira Rest House* is two km from Kufri.

Mashobra Also accessible by car there are pleasant forest walks around this picnic spot 13 km from Simla at 2149 metres.

Craignano At 2279 metres and 16 km from Simla, Craignano, with its hilltop Rest House, is only three km from Mashobra.

Naldera At 2044 metres Naldera is 23 km from Simla and has a golf course, Tourist Bungalow and cafeteria.

Fagu There is a very fine view from this spot and a lot of snow in winter. It's 22 km from Simla and at 2510 metres. Fagu also has a potato research centre.

Tours

The HPTDC (Himachal Pradesh Tourism Development Corporation) has a number of conducted tours to places around Simla. Local tours, which are run more frequently in the summer season, cost from Rs 17 and are booked from the tourist office on The Mall. Longer tours include the 64-km trip out to Narkanda where there is a very fine panoramic view of the Himalayas. Narkanda is now being developed as a skiing centre.

Places to Stay

Prices in most places in Simla vary widely between the mid-April to mid-September 'season' and the rest of the year. From June to September accommodation can be difficult to find in Simla at any price. As The Mall area offers the best views and is the city centre this is the most popular address, and the cost of hotels is highest here, particularly at the top.

Places to Stay – Bottom End

Hotel Shingar (tel 2881) and *Hotel Samrat* are both situated near the 'lift' at the eastern end of the mall. They're OK although the Samrat, at Rs 60 for a double, is cheaper. The *Grand Hotel* (tel 2121) is also on The Mall and prices range from Rs 16. This is possibly the best value in Simla, but it's reserved for Government of India officials between April and mid-July.

The very clean and quiet *YMCA* is good value at Rs 30 a double and it has good food. You get a fireplace, carpets, blankets and there's a gymnasium!

The *Tashkent Hotel*, near the bus stand, has rooms from around Rs 20. There are many other cheap hotels around the bus station, including the *Hotel Vikrant*, where singles/doubles cost Rs 20/70 and there is also a dorm. *Hotel Ashoka* has doubles with bathroom for Rs 30. Not to mention monkeys clattering around on the corrugated iron roof at 6 am! Simla has plenty of other hotels and dharamsalas.

Places to Stay – Top End

Simla's two top end hotels are the *Oberoi Clarkes* (tel 6091-95) and the *Oberoi Cecil* (tel 2073), both on the Mall. Both have singles/doubles at Rs 365/495, including all meals. The Cecil is one of the older and better known hotels in Simla, but it is only open in May and June. Simla's other western-style hotel is the *Himland Hotel* (tel 3595) on Circular Rd. It's most convenient for people with cars and has singles at Rs 65, doubles at Rs 90 to 100.

The state government Tourist Corporation's *Holiday Home* (tel 3971) is on Cart Rd in the eastern part of the city on the southern slope of the ridge. This is probably the best hotel in Simla with pleasant rooms and good service. Singles range from Rs 100 to 200 and there are also more expensive suites. If you want to stay on The Mall the *Hotel Diplomat* (tel 3033) is situated on the north-east corner and has doubles from Rs 100. There's

running hot water in this completely new hotel and it seems good value for money.

Lord's Grey Hotel (tel 5146) on Circular Rd has fine views of the mountains and rooms with attached bathroom and hot water for Rs 110 to 165. It's conveniently near to the centre and good value.

Places to Eat

All the better known restaurants are along The Mall – the best known is probably *Balaji's*. Often crowded, it has pleasant decor and a meal will cost from Rs 15. Upstairs there is another restaurant known as *Fascination*.

The *Alfa Restaurant* is also on The Mall. The various *Indian Coffee Houses* along The Mall offer south Indian food and snacks at reasonable prices and they're also a good place to sit, watch the world pass by, and talk. The State Tourism Department has recently opened two restaurants on the ridge, opposite the Tourist Office. The more expensive *Asiana* also has a live band. *Gufa* is for the budget travellers but both are quite good.

Getting There

Rail By rail to Simla involves a change from broad gauge to narrow gauge at Kalka, a little north of Chandigarh. The narrow gauge trip to Simla takes nearly six hours. Add on two or more hours to change train at Kalka plus the trip from Delhi and you'll find it much faster by bus. On the other hand the rail trip is great fun! It costs Rs 59 in 1st class or Rs 15 in 2nd. It takes less than an hour between Chandigarh and Kalka by bus and costs about Rs 2.50.

Bus A bus from Chandigarh is the easiest way to get to Simla. The 117-km trip takes four hours and costs Rs 16 in an ordinary bus or Rs 31 in a de-luxe bus. You can reach Chandigarh from Delhi by a variety of buses and by air. A bus straight from Delhi takes 10+ hours and costs Rs 40.

There are buses north from Simla to other hill stations in Himachal Pradesh such as Dharamsala or the Kulu Valley. From Simla to Manali or Dharamsala costs about Rs 40 and takes 10 to 12 hours. To Mandi it's about six hours for Rs 20.

Getting Around

Local bus services operate from the Cart Rd bus stand. A bus runs from the bus station to Boileauganj in the west. Apart from that the best way around Simla is to walk. A recently constructed 'tourist lift' takes you to The Mall from the lower part of town, saving a long and tedious climb.

AROUND SIMLA

Kalka

The narrow gauge railway line from Kalka to Simla was built in 1903-04. Although it is cheaper and quicker to go by road, the rail trip is fun. Pinjor, 21 km south-east of Kalka, has a Moghul summerhouse and garden, built by Fidai Khan, who also built the Badshahi Mosque in Lahore, Pakistan.

Chail

This was once the summer capital of the princely state of Patalia – today the old palace is a luxurious hotel. Chail is 45 km from Simla via Kufri or you can reach it via Kandaghat on the Simla-Kalka road or narrow gauge rail line. Chail, at an altitude of 2250 metres, is built on three hills, one of which is topped by the Chail Palace, and one by the ancient Sidh temple. Chail also boasts a temple of quite another religion – cricket, here you will find the highest cricket pitch in the world!

Places to Stay In the *Chail Palace Hotel* (tel Chail 43 & 47) some rooms go down to Rs 125 but the Maharaja and Maharani suites are Rs 300 and Rs 450. Chail also has a number of HPTDC cottages and log huts and the *Himneel Hotel* with rooms from around Rs 40. There are also a number of local hotels.

Getting There There are direct buses to Chail from Kalka and Simla.

Kasauli

A pleasant little hill station at 1927 metres only a little north of Kalka. It's an interesting 15-km trek from Kalka to Kasauli or you can get there from Dharampur, which is on the Kalka-Simla railway line. Only four km from Kasauli is Monkey Point, a picnic spot and lookout with a very fine view over the plains of the south and to the mountains in the north. Sabathu, 38 km from Kasauli, has a 19th century Gurkha built fortress.

Places to Stay There is a *PWD Rest House* and a number of private guest houses such as the *Alasia, Morris* and *Kalyan*. In Dharampur the simple *Mazdoor Dhaba* restaurant near the station has good (and cheap) vegetarian meals and a dormitory upstairs.

Solan

Betweek Kalka and Simla, on both the railway line and the road, this town is named after the Soloni Devi temple at the southern side of the town. There are pleasant picnic spots and streams around this 1350-metre hill station.

Places to Stay The *HPTDC Tourist Bungalow* has rooms from Rs 50 and also dorm beds. Plus the *Talk o' Town Cafeteria* – they certainly think up some names!

Narkanda

At 2700 metres, 64 km from Simla, this is a popular spot for viewing the Himalayas, particularly from the 3300-metre Hattu peak. Narkanda has recently been developed as a skiing centre. The season lasts from late-December to early March. A beginner's skiing course costs Rs 550 for 10 days including room and board!

From Narkanda you can make trips to Baggi and Khadrala which are on the Hindustan-Tibet road leading to the

Tibetan border. Or you can visit the apple growing area around Kotgarh or continue to the Kulu Valley via Luhri.

Places to Stay Narkanda has an old *Rest House* and a *Tourist Bungalow* with rooms from Rs 50 plus a dormitory. Or there's the *PWD Rest House*. Reservations are made through the Tourist Office in Simla.

Tattapani

There's a direct bus to these popular sulphur hot springs, 51 km from Simla and at only 655 metres. Accommodation is available here in the *PWD Rest House*.

Chabba

Five km from Basantpur, which is on the road to Tattapani, it's a pleasant walk to this *Rest House*, 35 km from Simla.

Thanedhar

A centre for apple growing, 82 km from Simla on the route past Narkanda.

Baggi & Khadrala

Also past Narkanda there are *Rest Houses* in both these places. Baggi is 82 km from Simla and at 2648 metres, Khadrala is 11 km further on and at 2987 metres.

Rohru

Situated 129 km from Simla this is the site for the Rohru Fair which takes place for two days each April. The temple of Devta Shikri is the centre for this colourful fair. The Pabar River, which runs through Rohru, is noted for its trout; there's a trout hatchery 13 km upstream at Chirgaon. Haktoti, a little before Rohru, has an interesting ancient Hindu temple dedicated to the goddess Durga. The temple contains a metre high image of the eight-armed goddess made of copper and bronze.

Places to Stay There's a *Rest House* in Rohru, a small *Forest Rest House* (booked in Rohru) at Chirgaon and log cabins at Seema, eight km upstream towards Chirgaon.

OTHER PLACES IN THE SOUTH

There are a number of other places of interest in the south of the state, where Himachal Pradesh borders with Uttar Pradesh and Haryana. This district is known as Sirmur.

Paonta Sahib

Situated on the Yamuna River, on the border with Uttar Pradesh, Paonta Sahib is a transit point for travellers from the hill stations of northern Uttar Pradesh to Simla and other hill stations in Himachal Pradesh. It is linked with Gobind Sigh, 10th of the Sikh's gurus who lived here and at Bhangani, 23 km away, achieved a great military victory when his forces defeated the combined might of 22 hill country kingdoms. His weapons are displayed in the town and his gurdwara still overlooks the river.

Places to Stay There's an *HPTDC Tourist Bungalow*, *Rest Houses* and local hotels.

Renuka

North-west of Paonta Sahib there is a major festival held each November at this lake. The lake also has a small zoo and a wildlife sanctuary with deer and many water birds. There is a *Tourist Inn* at the lake.

Nahan

Situated at 932 metres, Nahan is in the Shivalik hills, where the climb to the Himalayan heights commences. There are a number of interesting walks around the town including the trek to Choordhar (3647 metres) from where there are fine views of the plains to the south and the Sutlej River. Saketi, 14 km south of Nahan, has a fossil park with life size fibreglass models of prehistoric animals whose fossilised skeletons were unearthed here.

Places to Stay There are a number of *Rest Houses* and local hotels.

IN THE SOUTH-WEST
Bhakra-Nangal
The giant Bhakra Dam, one of the largest in the world, provides irrigation water for a vast area of the Punjab and also produces hydro-electric power. The public relations office at the dam arranges permits to inspect this major project.

Bilaspur & Naina Devi
On the shore of the Gobindsagar Lake the interesting Vyas Gufa, Lakshmi Narayan and Radhashyam temples are at this town on the Chandigarh-Mandi route. There are fine views over the lake from Naina Devi.

MANDI
The town of Mandi, on the Beas River, is the gateway to the Kulu Valley. From here you climb up the narrow, spectacular gorge of the river and emerge from this grey and barren stretch into the green and inviting Kulu Valley. At an altitude of only 760 metres it is still quite hot and mainly serves as a travel crossroads as its name, which means 'market', might suggest. Mandi is 202 km north of Chandigarh and 110 km south of Manali. The road from Pathankot and Dharamsala (150 km away) also meets here whether you are going south to Chandigarh or north to the Kulu Valley.

The town is famous for its beautiful stone-carved temples – Bhutnath, Triloknath, Panchavaktra, Ardhanari and Shyamakli.

Rewabar Lake
The Rewabar Lake, a pilgrimage centre for Hindus, Buddhists and Sikhs, is 24 km south-east. There is also a mountain cave-refuge for many foreign Buddhists near here. You can stay in the Tibetan Buddhist monastery for Rs 2 and there's also a hotel.

Places to Stay
Mandi has a *Tourist Lodge* with a variety of rooms from around Rs 30 to 75. For real Maharaja standards try the *Raj Mahal* with rooms at Rs 70/90. It's next to the palace which is a crazy Moghul-Chinese mix and well worth a quick look.

There are also a number of cheap hotels in the town. The *Adarsh Hotel*, second hotel on the right over the bridge, has big clean doubles with bathrooms for Rs 25 and a good restaurant. The *Cafe Shiraz* is run by the state tourist office.

KANGRA VALLEY
The beautiful Kangra Valley starts near Mandi, runs north then bends east and extends to Shahpur near Pathankot. To the north the valley is flanked by the Dhauladhar mountain range to the side of which Dharamsala clings. There are a number of places of interest along the valley, including the popular hill station Dharamsala. The main Pathankot-Mandi road runs through the Kangra Valley and there is a narrow gauge railway line from Pathankot as far as Jogindarnagar. The Kangra school of painting developed in this valley.

Baijnath
Only 16 km from Palampur the small town of Baijnath is an important pilgrimage place due to its very old Shiva temple. The temple is said to date originally from 804 AD. There is a *PWD Rest House* in Baijnath.

Palampur
A pleasant little town surrounded by tea plantations, Palampur is 35 km from Dharamsala and stands at 1260 metres. The main road runs right through Palampur and there are some pleasant walks around the town.

Places to Stay There is an *HPTDC Tourist Bungalow* here. Situated about a km from the bus station it has rooms from Rs 50.

Kangra

There is little to see in this ancient town, 18 km almost directly south of Dharamsala, but at one time it was a place of considerable importance. The famous temple of Bajreshwari Devi was of such legendary wealth that every invader worth his salt took time to sack it. Mahmud of Ghazni carted off a fabulous fortune in gold, silver and jewels in 1009. In 1360 it was plundered once again by Tughlaq but it was still able to recover and, in Jehangir's reign, was paved in plates of pure silver.

The disastrous earthquake which shook the valley in 1905 destroyed the temple which has since been rebuilt. Kangra also has a much ruined fort on a ridge overlooking the Baner and Manjhi Rivers. It too was sacked by Mahmud and severely damaged in the 1905 quake. Kangra has a *PWD Rest House*.

Jawalamukhi

In the Beas Valley, 34 km south of Kangra, the temple of Jawalamukhi is famous for its eternally burning flame. It's the most popular pilgrimage site in Himachal Pradesh. Jawalamukhi has a *PWD Rest House* and there is another pleasant rest house at Nadaun, south of Jawalamukhi on the Beas River.

Chintpurni

Near Bharwain, 80 km south of Dharamsala and across the Beas, this town also has an important temple.

Masrur

Situated three km from Haripur, about 15 km south of Kangra, there are 15 rock-cut temples here. In the Indo-Aryan style and richly carved they are now partly ruined but still show their relationship to the better known, and much larger, temples at Ellora in Maharashtra.

Nurpur

Only 24 km frm Pathankot on the Mandi-Pathankot road, the town acquired its name in 1622 when Jehangir named it after his wife, Nurjahan. Nurpur fort is now in ruins but still has some finely carved reliefs. A ruined Krishna temple, also finely carved, stands within the fort. Nurpur has a *PWD Rest House*.

TREKS FROM KANGRA VALLEY

From Baijnath you can make an interesting trek to Dharamsala, Chamba or Manali. The first day's trek to Bir Khas can be done by bus. At Bara Bhangal, reached on Day 6, you can choose to go east to Manali or west to Dharamsala or Chamba.

Day 1	Baijnath-Bir Khas	1600 m	26 km
Day 2	Bir Khas–		
	Rajgaunda	2500 m	13 km
Day 3	Rajgaunda–		
	Palachak Deota	2750 m	8 km
Day 4	Palachak Deota–		
	Panardu Got	3700 m	8 km
Day 5	Panardu Got–		
	Thamsar Jot	4750 m	6 km
Day 6	Thamsar Jot–Bara		
	Bhangal	2541 m	14 km

From here you can turn west and in four days reach Chanota which is on the Chamba-Dharamsala trek – see Treks from Chamba for details. The days' walk are:

Day 7	Bara Bhangal-Dhardi	21 km
Day 8	Dhardi-Naya Graun	24 km
Day 9	Naya Graun-Holi	16 km
Day 10	Holi-Chanota	13 km

Alternatively you can turn east and a day's trek will bring you to the Manali Pass treks described under Treks from Manali. There are a number of possible routes down to Manali.

DHARAMSALA (population 12,000)

The hill station of Dharamsala is actually split into two totally separate parts. Close to the snowline the town is built along a spur of the Dhauladhar range and varies in height from 1250 metres at the Civil and

Depot Bazaar up through Kotwali Bazaar and Forsyth Ganj to McLeod Ganj at close to 2000 metres. There's quite a temperature variation between the top and bottom.

As in other hill stations there is a wide variety of short and long walks around the station, but Dharamsala also has the additional attraction of its strong Tibetan influence. It was here that the Dalai Lama and his followers fled after the Chinese invasion of Tibet. For the serious student of Tibetan culture there's the monastery up at McLeod Ganj and the school of Tibetan studies and its library, one of the best in the world for studying Tibet and its culture, about midway between McLeod Ganj and the lower town.

For the not so serious, McLeod Ganj is a real little freak centre with lots of Tibetan-run hotels and restaurants, all the menu favourites, low prices, crowds of western travellers – another Kathmandu in fact. McLeod Ganj is full of colour and energy; those little Tibetan terriers (yappy but spry) scoot around everywhere; right in the middle of the main street there's a small temple with a giant prayer wheel and you may even catch a glimpse of the Dalai Lama cruising by in his Mercedes.

Of course Dharamsala was originally a British hill resort and one of the most poignant memorials of that era is the pretty little Church of St John in the Wilderness, only a short distance below McLeod Ganj. It has beautiful stained glass windows and here Lord Elgin, Viceroy of India, was buried after his death in 1863. There are many fine walks and even finer views around Dharamsala. The sheer rock wall of Dhauladhar rises up right behind McLeod Ganj. From the road up from the lower town it seems just an arm's length away.

From McLeod Ganj interesting walks include the two km stroll to Bhagsu where there is an old temple, a spring, slate quarries and a small waterfall. It's a popular picnic spot and you can continue on beyond here on the ascent to the

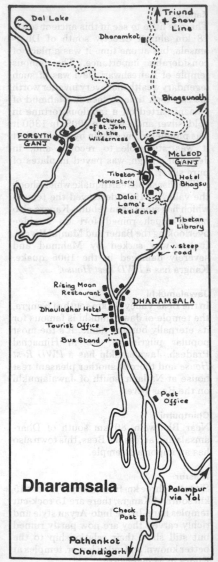

snowline. Dal Lake is a bit brown and dull, about three km from McLeod Ganj, just beyond the Tibetan Children's Village

School. A similar distance from McLeod Ganj takes you to the popular picnic spot at Dharamkot where you'll also enjoy a very fine view.

An eight km trek from McLeod Ganj will bring you to Triund at 2827 metres. Situated at the foot of Dhauladhar it's another five km to the snowline at Ilaqa. There is a *Forest Rest House* for overnight accommodation.

Information & Orientation
The Tourist Office is in the lower town close to the bus stand and the Dhauladhar Hotel. It's about 10 km from the lower part to McLeod Ganj – a 45-minute ride for Rs 1.50. Walking down, take the steep short cut round to the left of the monastery, by the Dalai Lama's home and down to the Cantonment by the library. It takes about 30 to 40 minutes to walk. There are lots of Tibetan handicrafts up in McLeod Ganj, small square Tibetan carpets for around Rs 100, bigger five foot by three foot carpets for Rs 750.

The Tibetan Medical Centre, just across from the Koko Nor Hotel, will be of interest to followers of alternative medicine.

Places to Stay & Eat – Dharamsala
Dharamsala has two accommodation areas – the lower part of town and the upper part known as McLeod Ganj. In the lower part Dharamsala's de-luxe hotel is the *Dhauladhar* with a Rs 12 dorm or doubles at Rs 60, 100 and 150. There's a restaurant and a pleasant garden patio – ideal for sipping a sunset beer while you look out over the plains below.

As in McLeod Ganj the pick of the cheapies are all Tibetan. There's the very popular and extremely laid back *Rising Moon Hotel & Restaurant*. A friendly place with a long menu, good food, good music and quite amazingly slow service. The hotel side has dorm beds at Rs 8, doubles at around Rs 20, some with bathroom. Almost directly behind it there's the slightly cheaper *Tibetan Rest House*. The *Free Tibet Restaurant* has a limited menu but excellent food.

Just left from the fountain you'll find the *Dekyi Palber Hotel & Restaurant* and the *Rose Hotel* – the restaurant for the latter is close to the junction while the hotel is a little further up, then down off the street to the right. The *Tibet United Association Hotel* has doubles at Rs 15 and

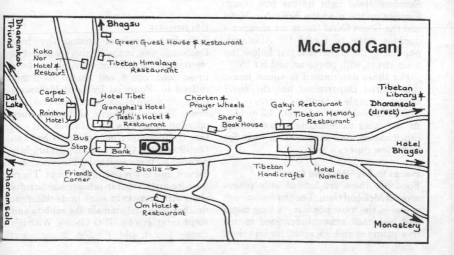

good food. Rooms at the Rose range from around Rs 10 to 25. Finally there's the *Hotel Simla*, opposite the tourist office, with doubles at Rs 20, and the not-so-special *B Mehra* and *Sun & Snow*.

Places to Stay – McLeod Ganj

Most western visitors to Dharamsala stay not in the main part of town but 500 metres (and 10 km by road) higher up the hill at McLeod Ganj. Here the Tibetan community who followed the Dalai Lama into exile have set up a whole series of hotels and restaurants. The accent is very much on cheapness but the hotels are clean and the restaurants are surprisingly good. For those heartily sick of dahl and rice they offer a whole range of Tibetan-Chinese dishes plus those western-travellers' menu favourites such as banana pancakes.

McLeod Ganj is very popular and, due to its popularity, many places are permanently full, but a quick wander will soon turn something up. The Bhagsu road from the bus station is the best bet – doubles at Rs 30 (own bathroom) and Rs 20 at the *Hotel Tibet*. There's a pleasant roof terrace where you can have breakfast. Similar style accommodation at the *Rainbow Hotel* right by the bus stand. Further up the road the *Koko Nor Hotel* and the *Green Guest House* are cheaper – doubles down to Rs 12-15. Also very popular is the *Om Hotel*, just below the main street, with prices around Rs 15.

For those determined to spend more, the Tourist Department has the *Hotel rhagsu*, a couple of hundred metres out of town, with doubles for Rs 60, 100 or 150. At the other extreme, long-stay visitors can find accommodation out of town for just a few rupees a day.

Places to Eat – McLeod Ganj

Foodwise there are lots of little places around McLeod Ganj. The *Om Restaurant* is one of the most popular – a long menu and laid back atmosphere, good music, free plain tea and it's noted for its cakes.

The *Tibetan Himalaya Restaurant*, about midway between the Hotel Tibet and the Green Guest House, has good pancakes amongst other things.

Pema House has good home-made noodles but you have to order in advance, it's in an alley off the same street as the popular *Tibetan Memory Restaurant*. There are a number of cheaper and rather more basic places such as the *Gakyi Restaurant. Friend's Corner* is good for a drink either downstairs or up on the roof. Food in McLeod Ganj is more expensive than the India average, but then it's also a lot better.

Getting There

If you're taking an early morning bus it's probably an idea to spend the night down in the lower town – all the buses start from there. Approximate distances, times and fares from Dharamsala are:

	distance	time	fare
Manali	253 km	12½ hrs	Rs 40
Kulu	214 km	10	Rs 34
Simla	317 km	10	Rs 40
Chandigarh	248 km	9	Rs 30
Pathankot	90 km	3½	Rs 13
Delhi	526 km	14	Rs 56
Jullundur	197 km	8	Rs 25

DALHOUSIE

Sprawling over and around five hills Dalhousie was, in the British era, a sort of 'second string' hill station. A place where those who could not aspire to Simla retired to. Founded by Lord Dalhousie there are some pleasant walks around the town. Today Dalhousie also has a busy population of Tibetan refugees – if you take the footpath from Subhash Chowk to Gandhi (GPO) Chowk you'll pass brightly painted pictures which the Tibetans have carved into low relief on the rocks. There is a nice little Tibetan refugee handicrafts shop with carpets in some quite different designs (unusual animals like rabbits and elephants). It's by GPO Chowk. With it's dense forest, old English houses and

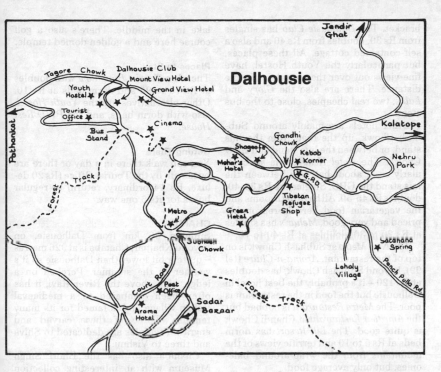

Dalhousie

colourful Tibetans, Dalhousie can be a good place to spend a little time.

About two km from GPO Chowk along Ajit Singh Rd, Panchpulla (five bridges) could be quite a pleasant spot but it's disfigured by the series of horrible concrete steps and seats built over the stream. Along the way there's a small, and easily missed, fresh water spring known as Satdhara. Kalatop is 8.5 km from the GPO and offers a fine view over the surrounding country. There's a *Forest Rest House* here. Lakhi Mandi, 15 km out and at around 3000 metres, has stupendous mountain views.

Information & Orientation

The Tourist Office (tel 36) is by the bus stand but Dalhousie is very scattered. Most shops are clustered around GPO Chowk while the 'town', if Dalhousie can

be spoken of as such a thing, is crowded down the hillside close to Subhash Chowk. The houses almost stand on top of one another.

Places to Stay & Eat

Dalhousie has plenty of hotels although a fair number of them have a run-down, left-by-the-Raj aspect to them. Close to the bus stand the *Mount View Hotel* is an old fashioned place with big doubles from Rs 50 but even a pillow costs extra! And the food in the restaurant is lousy. A little up the hill there's the *Tourist Bungalow*, doubles at Rs 45 but they're often full.

Just below the bus stand there's the *Youth Hostel* (a sign points the way) with dorm beds at Rs 8 while up above the Mount View there's the *Grand View Hotel* with rooms all the way from Rs 50 to 150, although most are in the Rs 60 to 100 bracket. The *Dalhousie Club* has singles from Rs 30, doubles from Rs 40 and also a self-contained cottage. All these places, but particularly the Youth Hostel, have fine views out over the mountains in the distance. There are also the *Glory* and *Lall's*, two real cheapies, close to the bus stand.

Other hotels are mainly around Subhash Chowk, up the road from the bus stand, or between the bus stand and GPO Chowk. The *Hotel Hemkunt* is spectacularly sited about half-way between the bus stand the GPO. Singles are Rs 35-40, doubles Rs 45-50. All have bathrooms and the vegetarian food here is reasonably priced and very good. *Mehar's* has singles at Rs 20 to 30, doubles at Rs 40 to 75.

The *New Metro* at Subhash Chowk is on top of the restaurant. *Aroma-n-Claire* (tel 99), beyond Subhash Chowk, has doubles at Rs 120 – it's probably the best hotel in Dalhousie but the food in the restaurant is poor. The *Metro Restaurant* is not bad but the *Amritsar Restaurant* at Chandi Chowk is quite good. The *Lill Resort* has dorm beds at Rs 5 to 10 and terrific views of the mountains from the wrap-around balconies, but only average food.

Getting There

Pathankot, 80 km away, is the usual departure point for buses to Dalhousie. The trip takes about four hours and costs Rs 12 to 15 depending on the bus company. Jammu-Pathankot buses cost Rs 8 and take three hours.

From Pathankot on to Dharamsala costs Rs 12, there are some straight-through buses from Dalhousie to Dharamsala but although the 'short route' is much more direct on the map it is a bad road and the trip very time-consuming. The 8.30 am bus arrives around 5 pm! Only 30 km is unsurfaced.

KHAJJIAR

This grassy 'marg' is 22 km from Dalhousie. Over a km long and nearly a km wide it is ringed by pine trees and with a

lake in the middle. There's also a golf course here and a golden domed temple.

Places to Stay

There's a *Tourist Bungalow* with doubles at Rs 75 to 95 and dorm beds at Rs 10. Other alternatives are the *Youth Hostel*, also with dorm beds, and the *PWD Rest House*.

Getting There

You can walk there in a day or there are buses run by the Tourist Office (Rs 20 deluxe, Rs 14 ordinary, return) or regular buses for Rs 5 one way.

CHAMBA

Situated 56 km from Dalhousie, on beyond Khajjiar, Chamba is at 926 metres – quite a bit lower than Dalhousie so it's warmer in the summer. Perched on a ledge, high above the River Ravi, it has often been compared to a mediaeval Italian village and is famed for its many temples. Three of these carved and engraved temples are dedicated to Shiva and three to Vishnu.

Chamba also has the Bhuri Singh Museum with an interesting collection relating to the art and culture of this region – particularly the miniature paintings of the Basoli and Kangra schools. The Rang Mahal palace in the upper part of town had been badly fire damaged. Some of its murals are now in the museum.

Chamba has a grassy promenade known as the 'chaugan' – it's only 75 metres wide and less than a km long. The village is a busy local trading centre for villagers from the surrounding hills and each year is the site for the Minjar festival in August with a colourful procession and busy crowds of Gaddi Churachi, Bhatti and Gujjar people. An image of Lord Raghuvira leads the procession and other gods and goddesses follow in palanquins.

Chamba is the centre of the Gaddis, traditional shepherds who move their flocks up to the high alpine pastures during the summer and descend to Kangra, Mandi and Bilaspur in the winter. The Gaddis are found only on the high range which divides Chamba from Kangra.

Places to Stay

The *Akhand Chanoi* is the better hotel – rooms from Rs 50 and there's also a restaurant. The *Tourist Bungalow* (tel 94) has rooms from Rs 20 and also a dorm. Behind the police station there's a *Youth Hostel* with rooms at Rs 25 and dorm beds at Rs 6. The *Janta Hotel* is similarly economical. Meals are available in the *Ravi View Cafe*.

Getting There

Taxis and jeeps can be hired in Dalhousie but they're expensive. The local bus is Rs 8 and takes two hours or you can walk there in two days, resting overnight in Khajjiar. From Chamba trekkers can make an interesting, but hard going, trek through Bharmour and Triund to Dharamsala. Or via Tisa you can trek all the way into Lahaul or into Kashmir.

TREKS FROM CHAMBA

There are a number of interesting treks from Chamba, both short out-and-back treks and longer treks to places like Dharamsala. Shorter treks include the eight-km walk to Sarol, 24 km to Bandal or the 40-km trek to Chhatrari. The temple of Devi Adi Shakti here is dedicated to the goddess of primaeval energy. Chhatrari is on the route to Brahmaur.

Brahmaur (Brahmpura)

Vehicles can cover the whole 65 km from Chamba to Brahmaur although the last 16 km from Kharamukh is either four-wheel drive or foot. Buses run the first distance. Also known as Shivbhumi this is the heart of the Gaddi's land. There are some very old temples grouped in a compound known as the *chaurasi* in Brahmaur and accommodation is available in a *Forest Rest House*.

From Brahmaur it is about 80 km to Dharamsala and takes about six days to walk:

Day 1	Brahmaur-Chanota	22 km
Day 2	Chanota-Kuarsi	13 km
Day 3	Kuarsi-Chatta	13 km
Day 4	Chatta-Lakagot	10 km
Day 5	Lakagot-Triund	6 km
Day 6	Triund-Dharamsala	13 km

The Chatta to Lakagot sector crosses the 4300 metre Indrahas Pass with fine views over the Kangra Valley.

From Brahmaur you can make the 35 km trek to Manimahesh Lake at 3950 metres. This important pilgrimage spot is at the base of the 5575-metre Manimahesh Kailash. Thousands flock here on the 15th day after Janamashtami which falls in August or September each year.

Pangi Valley

Kilar, 167 km north-east of Chamba, is situated in the deep and narrow gorge of the Chenab River. Here you are in the high Himalaya, in the scenic but lightly populated Pangi Valley, between the Pangi and Zanskar Ranges. From Kilar you can trek north-west to Kishtwar in Jammu and Kashmir, or turn east about half-way to Kishtwar and cross the Umasi La Pass into the Zanskar Valley, or trek south-east to Keylong and Manali.

THE KULU VALLEY

The fertile Kulu Valley tilts northward from Mandi, at 760 metres, to the Rohtang Pass, at 3915 metres, the gateway to Lahaul and Spiti. In the south the valley is little wider than a precipitous gorge, with the Beas River (pronounced Bee-Ahs) sometimes a sheer 300 metres below the narrow road. Further up the valley widens and the main part of it is 80 km long, though rarely more than a couple of km wide. Here there are stone fruit and apple orchards, rice paddies and wheat fields along the valley floor and lower slopes and deodar forests higher up the

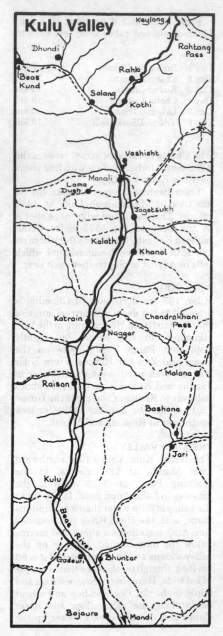

Kulu Valley

slopes with snow-crowned rocky peaks towering behind. The main towns, Kulu and Manali, are in this fertile section of the valley.

The light-complexioned people are friendly, devout, hard working and relatively prosperous. The men wear the distinctive Kulu cap, a pillbox with a flap around the back in which they may stick flowers, while the women wear long garments of homespun wool secured with great silver pins, lots of silver jewellery, and they are rarely without a large conical-shaped basket on their backs, filled with fodder, firewood or even a goat kid.

Other people of the valley are the nomads (Gaddis) who take their flocks of black sheep and white goats up to the mountain pastures in the early summer and retreat before the winter snows. You don't really know what wool smells like until you've travelled in an over-crowded bus of rain-soaked villagers. The valley also has many Tibetan refugees, some running restaurants and hotels in Manali, but many others in camps near the rivers, prayer flags fluttering. The Tibetans are great traders, you'll find them in all the bazaars but many work in road gangs, whole families toiling together.

KULU (population 10,000)

At an altitude of 1200 metres Kulu is the district headquarters but it is not the main tourist centre, that honour goes to Manali. Nevertheless there are a number of interesting things to see around Kulu and some fine walks to be made. The town, which sprawls on the western bank of the Beas, is dominated by the grassy maidans at the southern side of town. They're the site for Kulu's fairs and festivals, in particular the colourful Dussehra festival, from which the Kulu Valley has gained the name 'valley of the gods'.

Dussehra Festival

The Dussehra Festival, in October after the monsoons, is celebrated all over India but most particularly in Kulu. The festival starts on the 10th day of the rising moon, known as 'Vijay Dashmi' and continues for seven days. Dussehra celebrates Rama's victory over the demon king Ravana but in Kulu the festival does not include the burning of Ravana and his brothers, as in other places around India.

Kulu's festival is a great gathering of the gods from temples all around the valley. Approximately 200 gods are brought from their temples down to Kulu to pay homage to Raghunathji from the temple in Raghunathpura in Kulu. The festival cannot commence until the powerful goddess Hadimba, patron deity of the Kulu rajas, arrives from Manali. Like the other gods she is pulled in her own temple car or 'rath' and Hadimba likes speed and has to be pulled as fast as possible. She not only arrives before all the other gods but also leaves before them. Another curiosity is that the Jamlu god from Manali comes to the festival but does not take part – this god stays on the opposite side of the river from the Dhalpur maidan.

The Raghunathji chariot is brought down, decked with garlands and surrounded by the other important gods. Priests and the descendants of Kulu's rajas circle the 'rath' before the car is pulled to the other side of the maidan. There is great competition to aid in pulling the car since this is a very auspicious thing to do. The procession with the cars and bands takes place on the evening of the first day of the festival. During the following days and nights of the festival there are dances, music, a market and festivities far into the night. On the penultimate day the gods assemble for the 'Devta darbar' with Raghunathji and on the final day the temple car is taken to the riverbank where a small heap of grass is burnt to symbolise Ravana's destruction. Raghunathji is carried back to his main temple in a wooden palanquin.

Information & Orientation

The Tourist Information Office (tel 7) is

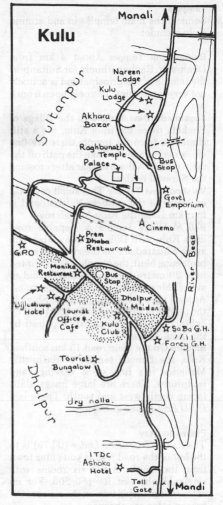

by the maidan at the southern side of town. There's a bus halt area here and all the HPTDC accommodation units and several of the hotels are around the maidan but the main bus station is in the northern area of the town.

Temples

Some of the main temples in and around Kulu include:

Raghunathji Temple About a km from Dhalpur in Raghunathpura (or Sultanpur) the temple of the principal god is actually not very interesting. It is only open from 5 pm.

Jagannathi Devi Temple In the village of Bhekhli, three km from Kulu, it's a stiff climb but from the temple there are fine views over the town. Take the path off the main road to Akhara bazaar after crossing the Sarawai bridge.

Vaishno Devi Temple This small cave has an image of the goddess Vaishno and is four km along the Kulu-Manali road.

Bijli Mahadev Temple A jeepable road links Kulu with Bijli Mahadev, eight km away. Situated across the river, high on a projecting bluff, the temple is surmounted by a 20-metre high rod which is said to attract blessings in the form of lightning. At least once a year the image of Shiva in the temple is supposed to be shattered by lightning, then miraculously repaired by the temple *pujari.*

Bajaura On the main road 15 km south of Kulu, the famous temple of Basheshar Mahadev has fine stone carvings and sculptures. There are large image slabs facing north, west and south. There is a *PWD Rest House* in Bajaura.

Places to Stay

The *Ashok Traveller's Lodge* (tel 79) is to the left of the road just as you enter town from the south. It has six rooms with singles/doubles at Rs 150/200. For an extra charge they'll turn on the air-con. Off season rates are cheaper.

Only a little south of the maidan, but a short walk off the main road, is the *HPTDC Tourist Bungalow* (tel 33) – a well run place with doubles at Rs 75 and also dorm beds at Rs 12. The Tourist Office is right beside the maidan, opposite the bus halt. Beside it is the generally full *Rest House* and between the two are *'Aluminium Huts'* – comfortable enough double rooms at Rs 35, but you can do better elsewhere.

Right behind the Tourist Office is the excellent *Bijleshwar Hotel.* It's a new place, very friendly and well run and has doubles with own bathroom for Rs 40. Across the other side of the maidan, towards the river, are the *Sa Ba Guest House* with rooms from Rs 35 and the *Fancy Guest House* with rooms from Rs 25 – OK.

At the other side of town, by the main bus stand, is the newish *Kulu Lodge* with rooms from Rs 35, more expensive with bath. There are other places around here like the *Kailash Lodge* and the *Newman Hotel* which has rooms for Rs 20.

Places to Eat

The *Tourist Bungalow* has the usual sort of dining hall. By the Tourist Office there's the *Tourist Department Cafe* with good light meals and snacks, but painfully slow service. Fine if you have plenty of time. In the main street close to the bus halt there's the *Monika Restaurant* and just downhill from the main street is the *Prem Dhaba.*

Getting There

Air There is an airport at Bhuntar, 10 km south of Kulu, and there is now a twice-weekly flight from Delhi via Chandigarh. Fares are from Delhi Rs 426, from Chandigarh Rs 239.

A   Kashmiri children on the Pahalgam-Aru walk (J&K)
B   A 'supermarket' shikara on Dal Lake in Kashmir (J&K)

Bus & Taxi There are direct buses to Kulu from Dharamsala, Simla (235 km), Chandigarh (270 km) or Delhi (512 km). Note that Kulu-Chandigarh buses do not go via Simla. All these direct buses will be continuing to Manali, 42 km further north.

A direct bus from Delhi is supposed to take 15 hours but probably takes a good bit more. It costs about Rs 75. Chandigarh-Kulu takes about 12 hours and costs Rs 35. Plenty of taxis make the trip up from the plains but count on around Rs 750 or more for Simla or Chandigarh to Kulu or Manali. A Kulu-Manali taxi would cost about Rs 150, it's Rs 6 by bus.

AROUND KULU

You can make some interesting excursions from Kulu to the adjoining valleys which run in to the Kulu Valley. See also the Treks from Manali section.

Parvati Valley

The Parvati Valley runs off north-east from Bhuntar, which is south of Kulu. You can travel up the valley by bus. Manikaran is built near sulphur hot springs and it's interesting to watch the locals cook their food in the pools of hot water at the Sikh temple. There are also hot baths, separate for men and women, at the temple and, of course, free accommodation too. Hot water is nice to have in Manikaran because the valley is so steep-sided not much sun gets through.

There are a lot of French and Italian freaks in the area, they've been in Manikaran so long 'it's hard to tell them from the locals. Unfortunately there is much friction between freaks and locals although the locals are friendly and

helpful'. There's great trekking and wonderful scenery here.

Places to Stay Rooms in shops or houses are easily available if you ask around. The *Phoda Family House*, near the bridge, is an excellent place where quite a few travellers stay. There are big, clean rooms with rope beds for Rs 15 and less. And there's a private sulphur rock bath indoors. You can also get food and expensive, though beautiful, wild bee honey.

In the local chai shops try *kihr*, a delicious rice dessert made with milk, sugar, fresh coconut and sultanas. It's said that Shiva sat and meditated for two thousand years at Kilu Ganga, a 30-km walk from Manikaran.

Getting There Buses from Kulu to Bhuntar take 1½ hours and cost Rs 3.50. Bhuntar to Manikaran is another 1½ hours for Rs 3.

Sainj Valley

From Aut to Sainj is not as beautiful as the other valleys but it still has a charm of its own. Plus it's very untouristed so the locals love visitors. There is no accommodation as such but rooms are easily available if you ask around.

Getting There A bus from Bhuntar to Aut takes an hour and costs Rs 3.

KULU TO MANALI

There are a number of interesting things to see along the 42 km between Kulu and Manali. There are actually two Kulu-Manali roads, the direct road runs along the west bank of the Beas while the much rougher and more winding east bank road

A   Flying Srinagar-Leh (J&K)
B   Tikse monastery in Ladakh (J&K)
C   Kulu Valley from Nagar Castle (NP)

is not so regularly used, but does take you via Naggar with its delightful *Rest House*.

Raison

Only eight km from Kulu there's a camping place on the grassy meadow beside the river. It's a good base for treks in the vicinity. There are huts at the site, which cost Rs 12 and can be booked through the Kulu Tourist Office.

Katrain

At about the mid-point on the Kulu-Manali road this is the widest point in the Kulu Valley and is overlooked by the 3325-metre Baragarh peak. Two km up the road on the left side there is a trout hatchery.

Places to Stay There's a small *Rest House* and a pleasant *HPTDC Tourist Bungalow* with doubles at Rs 40. It's an interesting alternative to staying in Kulu or Manali.

Naggar

High above Katrain, on the east bank of the river, is Naggar with its superb castle *Rest House*. Transport to the castle is a little problematical but the effort is worthwhile for it is a stunning place to look around or stay at. At one time Naggar was the capital of the Kulu Valley and the castle was the Raja's headquarters. Around 1660 Sultanpur, now known as Kulu, became the new capital. The quaint old fort is built around a courtyard with verandahs right round the outside and absolutely stupendous views over the valley. It feels an eon away from any of the hassles India can dish up! Inside the courtyard is a small temple containing a slab of stone with an intriguing legend about how it was carried there by wild bees.

There are a number of interesting temples around the castle. The grey sandstone Shiva temple of Gauri Shankar is at the foot of the small bazaar below the castle and dates from the 11th or 12th century. Almost opposite the front of the castle is the curious little Chatar Bhuj temple to Vishnu. Higher up the hill is the pagoda-like Tripura Sundri Devi Temple and higher still, on the ridge above Naggar, the Murlidhar Krishna temple. Also up the hill above the castle is the Roerich Gallery, a fine old house displaying the art works of both Professor Nicholas Roerich, who died in 1947, and his son. Its location is delightful and the views over the valley are very fine.

Places to Stay The *Castle Rest House* has just five double rooms which cost Rs 45. It's deservedly popular and often booked out, the Kulu Tourist Office can make reservations but plan ahead. There's also a *Forest Rest House* in Naggar.

Kulu-Manali Transport

Buses run regularly along the main road for Rs 6, the trip takes under two hours. There are only one or two buses daily on the east side of the river and the trip can take a long time, up to two hours from Manali to Naggar alone. Another 1½ hours Naggar to Kulu. The combined fare is not much different than the direct one, though.

There is a daily tour bus from Manali which costs about Rs 20. Cars can get to Naggar by crossing the river at Patlikuhl near Katrain – the bridge is very narrow. Or you can get off the Kulu-Manali bus there and walk up. It's six km up to the castle by road but much less on foot although the path is very steep.

MANALI (population 2500)

Manali, at the top end of the Kulu Valley, is the main resort in the valley. It's beautifully situated, there are many pleasant walks around the town and a large number of hotels and restaurants. It's also very much a 'scene' – at the height of the tourist season it's packed out with Indian and western tourists. Smaller villages around Manali have semi-permanent 'hippy' populations.

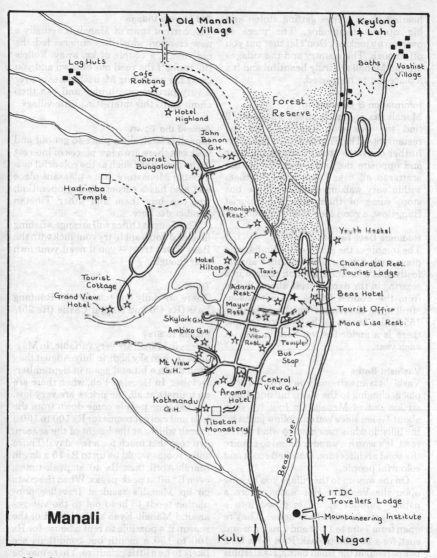

Manali

↑ Old Manali Village

↑ Keylong & Leh

Log Huts

Cafe Rohtang

Baths

Vashist Village

Forest Reserve

Hotel Highland

John Banon G.H.

Tourist Bungalow

Hadrimba Temple

Moonlight Rest.

Youth Hostel

Hotel Hiltop

P.O.

Taxis

Chandratal Rest.
Tourist Lodge

Tourist Cottage

Adarsh Rest.

Beas Hotel

Grand View Hotel

Mayur Rest.

Tourist Office

Skylark G.H.

Mt. View Rest.

Mona Lisa Rest.

Ambika G.H.

Temple

Mt. View G.H.

Bus Stop

Aroma Hotel

Central View G.H.

Kathmandu G.H.

Tibetan Monastery

Beas River

ITDC Travellers Lodge

Mountaineering Institute

Kulu ↓

Nagar ↓

Manali is famous for its marijuana, which is not only esteemed by connoisseurs, but also grows wild all around. However, there have been a number of police busts on the more popular freak hotels so smokers should beware. One recent letter complained that the place 'has really gone sour. There is much friction between the freaks and locals, and freaks and tourists. We were forever hearing about things getting stolen and big rip-offs happening. The place is overrun by junkies'. Don't let that put you off, though. The country and the villages around Manali are truly beautiful and it's a place not to be missed.

Information & Orientation

Manali has one main street where you'll find the bus stop and most of the restaurants. The Tourist Office (tel 25) is further down the street towards the river and opposite the taxi stand. Hotels are scattered all over town, some of them within easy walking distance of the bus stop, some of them, like the Tourist Bungalow, a good long stretch uphill.

Hadimba Devi Temple

The temple of the goddess Hadimba, who plays such a major part in Kulu's annual festival, is a sombre, wooden temple in a clearing in the dense forest about 2½ km from the Tourist Office. It's a pleasant stroll up to the temple which was built in 1553. Also known as the Dhungri Temple there is a major festival here in May of each year.

Vashisht Baths

Vashisht is an extremely picturesque little place, clinging to the steep hillside about six km out of Manali. On foot it's only about 4½ km since you can follow paths up the hillside while cars have to wind up the road. It's worth a wander round to admire the solid architecture, thatched roofs and colourful people.

On the way up to the village you'll come upon the Vashisht Hot Baths where a natural sulphur spring is piped into a recently constructed bath-house. They're open from 7 am to 1 pm and 2 to 7 pm and cost, for a 20 minute soak, Rs 6 (plus Rs 2 per person) in the small baths, Rs 10 (plus Rs 3 per person) in the large de-luxe ones. If you've suffered a long, rough bus trip up to Manali there's no better way to soak away the strain.

Old Manali Village

The current town of Manali is actually a new creation which has superseded the old village, a couple of km away. Follow the trail off the road out of town and you cross the cascading Manaslu stream over a very picturesque bridge and can then climb up to this interesting little village.

Around the Town

Manali is basically a place to get out and walk but there are a few places of interest in the town itself such as the colourful new Tibetan Monastery. It's a pleasant place and also has a carpet making operation; you can buy them and other Tibetan handicrafts here.

The Tourist Office will arrange a fishing licence if you want to try your luck with the Beas River trout – you'll need your own gear though.

Tours

There are daily bus tours to the Rohtang Pass (Rs 45) and Naggar Castle (Rs 25).

Places to Stay

Prices in Manali are very variable. In May-June they go sky high, in July-August they drop down a bit and again in September-October. In Dec-Jan-Feb, when there are no tourists at all, the prices are very low. At that time people come down from the hills and can get rooms for Rs 100 to 150 a month which, at the height of the season, can cost that much for a few days! Those same rooms would be up to Rs 15 a day in March-April then Rs 40 at peak times, even Rs 60 at peak-peaks. When the costs go up Manali's resident traveller population tends to head out to the villages around Manali. Even at the height of the season it's possible to rent a house for Rs 100 to 150 a month but conditions are likely to be a little primitive. There may be a stove but you'll need your own cooking utensils and you may have a long walk to get water.

Back in town there are a number of places run by the HPTDC. They can all be reserved through the tourism development officer, tel 25. The *Tourist Bungalow* is up the hill a little from the town, it's totally covered in ivy and quite a picture. Doubles cost from Rs 80 and there's a Rs 15 dorm. There are also *Tourist Cottages* and *Log Huts* – these are self-contained, with their own kitchens and living rooms and modern facilities. Nightly costs range from Rs 60 to 300 right up to Rs 500 for the flashier Log Huts.

The *Janata Lodge* is much simpler, with rooms from Rs 40. There's also the *Beas Hotel*, right beside the Beas River, with singles at Rs 40, doubles at Rs 50 to 90 and even dorm beds. All this HPTDC accommodation tends to be fairly heavily booked so plan ahead. The ITDC have an *Ashok Travellers' Lodge* (tel 31) in Manali, a little out of town on the Naggar road. There are just 10 rooms with singles/doubles at Rs 150/200, lower in the off-season. The doubles are really suites with a sitting room and fine views of the snow-capped peaks around Manali.

In the private hotel sector your best bet is simply to wander around and have a look at a few, bearing in mind that prices are likely to be quite variable, depending on when you're there and how many rooms they happen to have vacant. Some names to start with include the *Skylark Guest House* (rooms Rs 50 to 75), *Kathmandu Guest House* (close to the gompa, Rs 40 to 60), *Sunflower Hotel* (also near the gompa, around Rs 40, not really clean), *Mount View Guest House* (Rs 50 to 75 again, a pleasant place), *John Banon Guest House* (tel 35, a bit more expensive) and so on. The Tourist Office can supply a more-or-less complete list of Manali's 40 or so hotels and guest houses, together with their official prices.

Places to Eat

Right beside the bus station is the *Monalisa Restaurant*, a popular little place with excellent food, great music, a varied menu and attentive (uniformed no less) service. It's probably a little expensive for some pockets but if you'd like to eat well in Manali it's highly recommended.

There are quite a few other places around Manali – like the *Mount View Restaurant*, just down from the bus stop, for excellent Chinese-Tibetan food and good music to eat it by. Or the *Adarsh Restaurant* and the *Mayur Restaurant*. The *Chandratal Restaurant* is run by the HPTDC with the standard tourist department menu – not so special. Between the Tourist Office and the bus stop there's a little place with delicious, and cold, bottled apple juice.

Following the road out of town you'll come to the *Moonlight Restaurant* – a spartan little place with good bread and cakes, the local freak centre. The HPTDC's *Cafe Rohtang*, up the hill overlooking the river, has fine views but is rather unfriendly.

Places to Stay around Manali

Vashisht, the picturesque little village just above the hot baths, is probably the main centre for Manali's longer term western residents. There's the *Mount Hotel* and the *Brine Ram Restaurant* by the baths. Further up the hill, at the start of the village, is *Demroh's Restaurant*, the freak food centre for Vashisht. Very laid back. Other little snack places can be found in the village.

There are other villages around Manali with summer populations of westerners – you just have to ask around, talk to people, don't expect to find something on the first day.

Getting There

Chandigarh is the usual departure point for buses to Manali if you're coming up from Delhi. Chandigarh-Manali is 312 km, takes about 14 hours by bus (nine by car) and costs Rs 42. Mandi-Manali is 5½ hours for Rs 14. There are also direct buses from Simla (247 km) for Rs 40 and from Dharamsala (253 km) also for Rs 40. It's a long trip to Manali from wherever you start! From Kulu there are frequent buses for Rs 6. Note the introductory details on HPTDC buses in Himachal Pradesh. There are daily buses between Manali and Delhi at 11.30 am and 5.30 pm. The latter is superfast, taking 15 hours.

You can fly to Kulu from Delhi or Chandigarh, see the Kulu section for details.

AROUND MANALI
Jagatsukh

About 12 km north of Naggar and six km south of Manali on the east bank road, Jagatsukh was another former capital of Kulu State until it was supplanted by Naggar. There are some very old temples in the village, particularly the Shiva temple in the shikhara style. Shooru village, nearby, has the old and historically interesting Devi Sharvali temple.

Other Places

Arjun Gufa, with a legendary cave, is near the village of Prini, five km from Manali. A cold water spring named the Nehru Kund after Prime Minister Nehru, is six km from Manali on the Keylong road. The Solang Valley is a little north-west of Manali, but before Kothi. Then nearest glacier to Manali is here, only 13 km from Manali. You can get there by bus to Palchan village, then follow the jeep track.

Kothi is a pretty little village, 12 km from Manali on the Keylong road. Its *Rest House* is a popular resting place for trekkers heading for the Rohtang Pass. It's surrounded by glaciers and mountains, two old tea stalls and nothing else. Doubles with attached bathroom are just Rs 18 – two big beds, carpets, a balcony, goodfood and it's quiet. There are very fine views from Kothi and the Beas River flows through a very deep and narrow gorge at this point. The Rahla Falls, 16 km away, are another popular excursion.

The Rohtang Pass to Lahaul is 51 km from Manali and is a favourite day excursion or trekking trip quite apart from its role as the gateway into Lahaul. The view of mountains from the pass crest is very spectacular. In early summer and late autumn the pass can be subject to strong winds and snow blizzards in the afternoon – so try to cross it early.

TREKS FROM MANALI

There are many treks from Manali, either round trip or further afield.

Malana Valley

It is less than 30 km from Katrain, on the Kulu-Manali road, across the Chandrakhani Pass to the interesting Malana Valley. The pass is at less than 3600 metres and is open from March to December. Malana can also be reached from the Parvati Valley – either from Manikaran over the 3150-metre Rashoi Pass or from Jari. Jari is connected with the Kulu Valley by a jeepable road and it is only 12 km from Jari to Malana.

There are only about 500 people in Malana and they speak a peculiar dialect with strong Tibetan elements. The 6001-metre peak of Deo Tibba overlooks Malana and from the top of the Chandrakhani Pass you can see snow-capped peaks on the border of Spiti to the east. Starting from Naggar it is possible to climb up to the pass summit and return to Naggar on the same day – but it is fairly hard going.

Local legends relate that when Jamlu, the main deity of Malana, first came to Malana he bore a casket containing all the other Kulu gods. At the top of the pass he opened the casket and the breeze carried the gods to their present homes, all over the valley.

At the time of the Dussehra festival in Kulu, Jamlu plays a special part. He is a very powerful god with something of the demon in him. He does not have a temple image so, unlike the other Kulu gods, has no temple car to be carried in. Nor does he openly show his allegiance to Ragbhunathji, the paramount Kulu god, like the other Kulu gods. At the time of the festival Jamlu goes down to Kulu but stays on the east side of the river from where he watches the proceedings. Every few years a major festival is held for Jamlu in the month of Bhadon. In the temple there is a silver elephant with a gold figure on its back which is said to have been a gift from the Emperor Akbar.

It takes three days to trek from Naggar to Malana, spend a day there, then return to Naggar or continue to Jari. A seven-day trek Manali to Malana could be:

Day 1	Manali-Rumsu	2060 m	24 km
Day 2	Rumsu-Chandrakhani	3650 m	8 km
Day 3	Chandrakhani Malana	2100 m	7 km
Day 4	Malana-Kasol	1580 m	8 km
Day 5	Kasol-Jari	1560 m	15 km
Day 6	Jari-Bhuntar	900 m	12 km
Day 7	Bhuntar-Manali	by bus	

The trek can be extended by continuing from Jari along the east bank of the Beas via Bijli Mahadev, with its famous temple, and Naggar to Manali.

Deo Tibba Trek

This is an easy trek east of Manali to the base of 6000-metre Deo Tibba. The trek offers fine views and pleasant walking through forests and alpine meadows. From Manali you start via Jagatsukh to Khanol and Chhika (not the Chhika north-east of Manali on the way to the Hamta Pass). Seri is at the base of Deo Tibba and from here you can make an excursion to Lake Chandratal.

Day 1	Manali-Khanol	8 km
Day 2	Khanol-Chhika	6 km
Day 3	Chhika-Seri	5 km
Day 4	Seri-Bhanara	14 km
Day 5	Bhanara-Manali	

Chandratal

This circular trek from Manali over the Hamta, Chandratal and Baralacha 1a passes is one of the finest in Himachal Pradesh and takes 11 days to complete. From Manali you start at Jagatsukh, on the east bank road to Kulu. At the village of Prini you turn north-east and climb up to Chhika – a steep climb at first but later it becomes easier over grassy downs and pleasant meadows.

The next day involves a long and wearisome climb over the 4270-metre Hamta Pass, then a quick descent to Chhatru on the Chandra River. The pass is generally open from June to September although it may be open longer. There are fine views of Deo Tibba (6001 metres) and Indrasan (6221 metres) from the pass. Two days' walk takes you through Chhota Dara to Batal where the route branches off north-east to Spiti through the Kunzam Pass. There are magnificent views of the Bara Shigri glacier from here.

Succeeding days take you north over the Chandratal (lake of the moon) Pass, the Likhim Gongma (upper) and Likhim Yongma (lower) and the Tokpo Yongma before reaching the Keylong-Leh road at the Baralacha 1a Pass. Three more days walking brings you to Keylong from where you can bus back to Manali. It may be possible to get a bus earlier and shorten the time to Keylong.

Day 1	Manali – Chhika	2960 m	21 km
Day 2	Chhika – Chhatru	3360 m	16 km
Day 3	Chhatru – Chhota Dara	3740 m	16 km
Day 4	Chhota Dara – Batal	3960 m	16 km
Day 5	Batal – Chandratal	4270 m	18 km
Day 6	Chandratal – Likhim Yongma	4320 m	12 km
Day 7	Likhim Yongma – Topko Gongma	4640 m	11 km
Day 8	Topko Gongma – Baralacha 1a	4885 m	10 km
Day 9	Baralacha 1a – Patsio	3820 m	19 km
Day 10	Patsio – Jispa	3320 m	14 km
Day 11	Jispa – Keylong	3340 m	21 km

Parbati Valley

The Parbati Valley is now accessible by bus from Kulu or Bhuntar (Rs 7 from

Kulu). The last part of the Malana Valley trek descends the Parbati Valley to its junction with the Kulu Valley. An interesting alternative is to ascend the Parbati Valley to its upper reaches. The Parbati Valley is much wilder and more rugged than the Kulu Valley. From Bhuntar, near the junction of the Beas and Parbati, you can visit the Adibrahma temple in Khokhan, about a km from Nhuntar, or the pagoda-shaped temple of Triyugi Narain in Diar village. The first day's walk takes you to Jari, on a hillside high above the Parbati and near where the Malana joins the Parbati.

It's a short trek to Kasol with its pleasantly sited *Tourist Hut* and *Forest Rest House*. Good trout fishing here. Manikaran is a very short walk but the river is wild at this point and Manikaran is also famed for its hot springs. The spring, close to the river as you enter the village, is boiling hot. There are several guest houses in Manikaran and be sure not to miss the evening worship accompanied by harmonium, tablas and singing.

It's a long walk, rough and stony at first, to Pulga where again there is a very pleasant *Forest Rest House*. The pretty little village is 300 metres above the river. This is the usual end point of this trek, although hardy and well-equipped trekkers could continue further up the Parbati and cross the Pin Parbati Pass into Spiti. Khirganga, just 10 km upstream from Pulga, has more hot springs. Or you could explore the Tos Nullah which joins the Parbati from the north-east, just upstream from Pulga.

Day 1	Bhuntar-Jari	15 km
Day 2	Jari-Kasol	8 km
Day 3	Kasol-Manikaran	3 km
Day 4	Manikaran-Pulga	16 km

Seraj Valley to Narkanda

The Seraj Valley branches off south-east from the southern end of the Kulu Valley and makes an interesting alternative route between the Kulu Valley and Simla. Aut, on the main road between Kulu and Manali, is the starting point and Larji, at the junction of the Sainj and Tirthan Rivers, is the first stop. There's a *PWD Rest House* here and good fishing is available during March, April and October – when the Sainj River runs clear.

In the lower reaches of the Tirthan Valley is Banjar with an interesting group of temples. Continuing south you reach Shoja where there is another *PWD Rest House* with a scenic setting. From here you can make excursions to the old ruined fort of Raghupur Gahr from where there is a beautiful view, even Simla can be seen on a clear day. Another interesting day trip from Shoja is to the beautiful flower-strewn meadow of Dughu Thatch.

From Shoja you cross the 3135-metre Jalori pass. The view of the surrounding mountains from the pass crest is stunning. Khanag, at 2500 metres, is on the other side of the pass and has a *PWD Rest House*. Ani, again with a *PWD Rest House*, is the next stop and from here you can either continue straight on to the main highway from where buses run to Narkanda and Simla, or turn east to Nirmand with its temple of Devi Ambika. There is a bus service between Ani and Luhri, on the north side of the Sutlej River.

Day 1	Aut-Larji	5 km
Day 2	Larji-Banjar	20 km
Day 3	Banjar-Shoja	13 km
Day 4	Shoja-Khanag	10 km
Day 5	Khanag-Ani	20 km
Day 6	Ani-Luhri	15 km

As an alternative to this route you can branch off at Banjar and follow the Tirthan River to Narakand. Goshaini is the first day's walk from Banjar but you can get that far by bus. It's then a gentle climb to Bathad where there is a *PWD Rest House*, followed by a very hard climb to the Bashleo Pass at 3250 metres, 13 km on. A steep descent takes you to Sarahan, only three km further.

There is another beautifully situated *Rest House* here. From here it is two easy, pleasant walks to Arsu (another *PWD Rest House*) and then Rampur on the main road.

Day 3	Banjar-Goshaini	13 km
Day 4	Goshaini-Bathad	16 km
Day 5	Bathad-Sarahan	16 km
Day 6	Sarahan-Arsu	13 km
Day 7	Arsu-Rampur	13 km

Solang Valley

There are a number of treks from Manali to the Solang Valley looping back to Manali, either from the north or the south. A seven-day trek takes you to Beas Kund, the source of the Beas River, and across the remains of dying glaciers. The first day takes you to Solang Nullah where there is a mountain hut with rooms for 80 people. There are ski-runs here in the winter.

The second day's trek continues to Dhundi where you can see Deo Tibba and Indrasan from this alpine plateau and admire the many alpine flowers. The third day takes you to Beas Kund and back and the next day continues to Shagara Dugh with a good chance of seeing red bears along the way. On the fifth day you reach Marrhi over a small 4000-metre pass with views to the Kulu Valley and Rohtang Pass. Finally on day six you continue down the Keylong-Manali road to Kothi, via the Rahla waterfall, and on the last day return to Manali.

Day 1	Manali – Solang Nullah	2480 m	11 km
Day 2	Solang Nullah – Dhundi	2840 m	8 km
Day 3	Dhundi – Beas Kund & back	3540 m	10 km
Day 4	Dhundi – Shagara Dugh	3600 m	8 km
Day 5	Shagara Dugh – Marrhi	3380 m	10 km
Day 6	Marrhi – Kothi	2500 m	6 km
Day 7	Kothi – Manali		13 km

Manali Pass Treks

These two treks continue on from the Solang Valley trek but loop back to Manali from the south. They are both difficult treks involving land hard ascents over rugged terrain. The first alternative continues from Beas Kund over the Tentu Pass, an arduous and tiring climb, to

Phulangot through an uninhabited region. You then cross the Manali Pass to Rani Sui and go via Bhogi Thatch to Kalath, a little south of Manali on the Kulu-Manali road.

Day 3	Dhundi-Beas Kund	3540 m	6 km
Day 4	Beas Kund-Tentu Pass	4996 m	4 km
Day 5	Tentu Pass–camping ground	3856 m	10 km
Day 6	camping ground–Phulangot	4000 m	6 km
Day 7	Phulangot-Manali Pass	4988 m	6 km
Day 8	Manali Pass-Rani Sui	4200 m	8 km
Day 9	Rani Sui-Bhogi Thatch	2800 m	6 km
Day 10	Bhogi Thatch-Kalath	1800 m	12 km

The second alternative is to join the Manalsu Nullah from the Manali Pass and follow this straight back to Manali – up to day 8 this trek is the same as the alternative one.

An easy trek, which includes the last two days of the alternative one involves going to Rani Sui via Lama Dugh. You leave Manali bia the Hadimba Temple and climb through pleasant country to the camp site at Lama Dugh. On the second day you cross the Thanpri Tibba ridge to Rani Sui and then Day 3 and Day 4 are as Day 9 and Day 10 above.

| Day 1 | Manali-Lama Dugh | 3380 m | 6 km |
| Day 2 | Lama Dugh-Rani Sui | 4200 m | 5 km |

LAHAUL & SPITI

Only since 1977 have visitors been permitted to cross the Rohtang Pass to Keylong in Lahaul. Only 117 km from Manali this is a Tibetan region, quite unlike the Kulu Valley. The Rohtang Pass has the same 'gateway' nature as the Zoji La Pass does between Kashmir and Ladakh. The region is bounded by Ladakh to the north, Kulu to the south and Tibet to the east. All of Spiti and a large chunk of

Lahaul is off-limits to visitors. You cannot continue up the jeep road from Keylong to Leh in Ladakh, but you can make the long and difficult trek from Keylong to Padum in the Zanskar valley and from there into Ladakh. See the Lonely Planet guide *Kashmir, Ladakh & Zanskar* for information on treks in this region.

Climate

As in Ladakh little rain gets over the high Himalayan barrier so Lahaul and Spiti are dry and, for the most part, barren. The air is sharp and clear and the warm summer days are followed by cold, crisp nights. Beware of the burning power of the sun in this region – you can get burnt very quickly even on quite cool days. The heavy winter snow from September to May closes the passes except for a few months of each year.

Culture

The people of Lahaul and Spiti follow a Tibetan form of Tantric Buddhism with a panoply of demons, saints and followers. The monasteries, known as gompas, are colourful places where the monks or lamas lead lives ordered by complicated regulations and rituals. There are many similarities between these people and the Ladakhis, further north. The people of Spiti are almost all Buddhists of Tibetan stock but Lahaul is split roughly 50:50 between Buddhists and Hindus.

Rohtang Pass

The 3915-metre Rohtang Pass is the only access into Lahaul and it is open only from June to September each year, although trekkers can cross the pass a little before it opens for vehicles. During the short season it is open there are regular buses from Manali to Keylong. The Tourist Office operates a daily Rs 45 bus up to the pass, mainly for tourists to 'see the snow'. It's a very spectacular trip over the pass.

Keylong

The main town in the Lahaul and Spiti region; there are a number of interesting monasteries within easy reach of this oasis-like town. The old Kharding Monastery, formerly the capital of Lahaul, overlooks Keylong, only 3.5 km away. Other monasteries include Shashur (three km), Tayal (six km) and Guru Ghantal (11 km).

Places to Stay There is a *PWD Rest House*, a number of small hotels and the HPTDC set up tents during the summer season.

Other Places

Gondhla, with its eight-storey castle of the Thakur of Gondhla and the historically significant gompa, is a short distance before Keylong on the Manali-Keylong road. You can trek back to Gondhla from Keylong, cutting across the loop the road makes. Between Gondhla and Keylong is Tandi where the Chandrabagha or Chenab River meets the road.

Following the Chenab Valley to the north-west towards Kilar (see treks from Chamba) will bring you to Triloknath with its six-armed white marble image of Avalokitesvara. Close by is the village of Udaipur with a finely carved wooden temple from the 10th or 11th century which is dedicated to Mrikula Devi.

Spiti

The 4500-metre Kunzam Pass connects the Lahaul and Spiti valleys. Eventually a road will be completed from Kaza, the principal Spiti village, south-east through Samdoh to meet the Hindustan-Tibet road (see Kinnaur). There are few settlements in this barren, high region. Kaza (or Kaja) is the main village and slightly north-west of this is Kibar (or Kyipur) which is at 4205 metres and reputed to be the highest village in the world. Tabo Kye and Dhankhar are two of the most important gompas.

Getting There

Although the pass may be open by mid-May a safer date is mid-June. The bus trip takes eight hours and costs Rs 25. It's 475 km from Manali to Lehi via Keylong but you need special permission to use this road.

KINNAUR

Most of this region, in the valley of the Sutlej River extending up towards the Tibetan border, is off limits without permission from the Ministry of Foreign Affairs in New Delhi. You can only go as far as the Wangtu Bridge, just beyond Nachar without a permit.

Rampur

Beyond Narkanda, 140 km from Simla, Rampur is the gateway to the region. It's the site for a major trade fair in the second week of November each year. This was once a major centre for trade between India and Tibet. There are direct buses from Simla to Rampur. Rampur has a *PWD Rest House.*

Sarahan

The last village in the district before entering Kinnaur, Sarahan is a beautiful little place with the interesting Bhimkali temple which shows a curious blend of Hindu and Buddhist architecture.

Nachar

Situated on the old Hindustan Tibet road this picturesque village is four km from the Wangtu Bridge, beyond which you need a permit to continue. As in Sarahan the village is on the old road which has been replaced by the nearby new Hindustan-Tibet road. There's a *Rest House* in the orchards.

Tapri & Choltu

Only 15 km further up the valley from Nachar, three roads meet at this scenic spot. One is the main road continuing up the valley to Kalpa. The second is the old road, also continuing to Kalpa via Rogi. The third is a small road which crosses the river through Choltu and Kilba to the Sangla Valley. Choltu has a pleasant *Rest House.*

Sangla

The main village in the Sangla Valley is 18 km from Karcham, on the new Hindustan-Tibet road, and can be reached by jeep or on foot. It's a good base for trekking and there's a *Rest House.*

Kalpa

The main town in Kinnaur is close to the foot of 6050-metre high Kinnaur Khailash. This is the legendary winter home of Lord Shiva; during the winter the god is said to retire to his Himalayan home here and indulge his passion for hashish. In the month of Magha – January-February – the gods of Kinnaur are all supposed to meet here for an annual conference with Lord Shiva.

Kalpa has a *Rest House* and from here you can continue on the northern side of the river to Puh and Namgia, close to the Tibetan border. Only 14 km from Kalpa the tiny village of Pangli has a small *Rest House* and a fine view of Kinnaur Khailash. Rarang, eight km further on, is another centre for trade to Tibet.

Jammu & Kashmir

Population: 5 million
Area: 222,236 square km
Capital: Srinagar
Main languages: Kashmiri, Dogri

The state of Jammu and Kashmir, J&K for short, is a region of widely varying people and geography. In the south Jammu is a transition zone from the Indian plains to the Himalaya. Correctly the rest of the state is Kashmir but in practice this tile is reserved for the beautiful Vale of Kashmir, a large Himalayan valley in the north of the state. Here the people are predominantly Moslem and in many ways look towards Pakistan and central Asia rather than towards India.

Finally to the north-east there is the remote Tibetan plateau region known as Ladakh. Only recently opened to foreign tourists, Ladakh is primarily Buddhist and Tibetan in its culture and a very clear contrast to the rest of Kashmir, indeed to the rest of India. Sandwiched between the Kashmir and Ladakh regions is a long narrow valley known as Zanskar. This valley is even more isolated than Ladakh and has still been visited by very few westerners although this will change as a new jeep road into the valley is extended and improved.

Jammu and Kashmir has always been a centre of conflict for independent India. When India and Pakistan became independent there was much controversy over whether the region should go to one country or the other. The population was predominantly Moslem but J&K was not a part of 'British India', it was a 'princely state' and as such the ruler had to decide which way his state would move – to Moslem Pakistan or Hindu India. As *Freedom at Midnight* relates the indecisive Maharaja only made his decision when a Pakistani-prompted invasion was already crossing his borders and the

inevitable result was the first Indo-Pakistan conflict. Since that first collision Kashmir has remained a flashpoint for relations between the two countries. The region is now divided approximately two-thirds to India, one-third to Pakistan but both countries claim all of it. Furthermore Kashmir's role as a sensitive border zone applies not only to Pakistan. In 1962 the Chinese invaded Ladakh, prompting India to rapidly reassess their position in this remote and isolated region.

For visitors J&K is one of India's most popular states. Kashmir is simply beautiful and a spell on a houseboat on Dal Lake is one of India's real treats. Kashmir also offers some delightful trekking opportunities and unsurpassed scenery. Ladakh, on the other hand, offers a chance to study a region which, in today's world, is probably even more Tibetan than Tibet. It's one of the most other-worldly parts of India. No special permits are required to visit Kashmir or Ladakh today but your movements are restricted in that you are not allowed to approach within a certain distance of the border. In Ladakh this means you are not allowed more than a mile north of the Srinagar-Leh road although south of that is quite open.

Lonely Planet Guides
If you'd like a lot more information about Kashmir and Ladakh look for our guidebook *Kashmir, Ladakh & Zanskar* by Rolf & Margret Schettler. The second edition will be available soon after this book emerges. Later there will be a new trekking guide, *Trekking in the Indian Himalaya* with detailed information on many trekking routes in the state.

JAMMU (population 160,000)
Jammu is the second largest town in the state but for most travellers it is just a jumping off point for the trip north to Kashmir. Most travellers simply arrive in Jammu one evening and depart the next morning for Kashmir. If you do have time there are a number of interesting

attractions in the town. Note that Jammu is still on the plains and in the summer is a sweltering, uncomfortable contrast to the cool heights of Kashmir.

Information & Orientation
Jammu is actually two towns – the old town sits on a hilltop overlooking the river. Here you'll find most of the hotels and the Tourist Reception Centre where the Tourist Office is located and from where upper class buses depart for Kashmir. Down beside the hill is the bus station for buses to other parts of north India and for the lower class buses to Srinagar. Finally, several km away across the river is the new town of Jammu Tawi where the railway station is located.

Things to See
The Raghunath Temple is in the centre of the city, only a short stroll from the Tourist Reception Centre. This large temple complex was built in 1835 but is

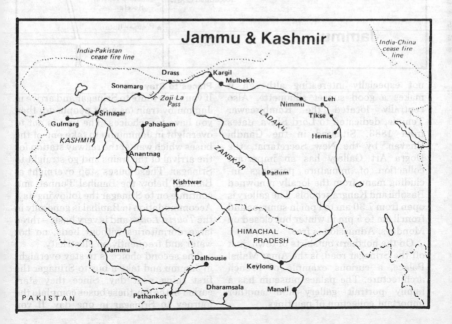

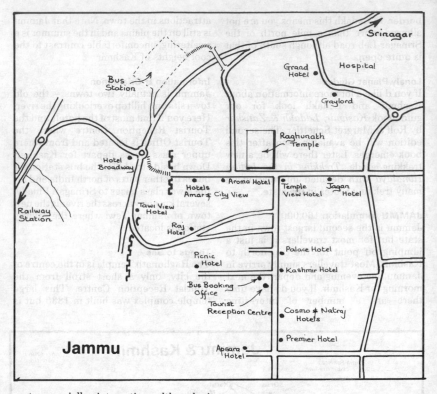

Jammu

not especially interesting although it makes a good sunset silhouette. Also centrally located the Rambireswar Temple, dedicated to Lord Shiva, dates from 1883. Situated in the Gandhi Bhavan, by the New Secretariat, the Dogra Art Gallery has an important collection of miniature paintings including many from the locally renowned Basohli and Kangra schools. The gallery is open from 7.30 am to l pm in summer and from ll am to 5 pm in winter but closed on Mondays. Admission is free.

On the northern outskirts of town, just off the Srinagar road, is the Amar Mahal Palace, a curious example of French architecture. The palace museum has a family portrait gallery and another important collection of paintings.

Places to Stay

If you're en route to Srinagar and arrive in Jammu by train (as most people do) then you have two choices. The first is not to overnight in Jammu bu to take one of the buses which wait at the railway station for the arrival of the trains and go straight to Srinagar. These buses stop overnight at Banihal, below the Banihal Tunnel, and continue on to Srinagar the following day. Accommodation in Banihal is generally in the *Tourist Lodge* and is very basic – three large dormitories without beds, no hot water and frequently no electricity.

The second choice is to stay overnight in Jammu and take a bus to Srinagar the first thing next day. Since they start earlier in the day these buses complete the journey to Srinagar in one day. If you decide to stay overnight then it's important to first find yourself a room and then book a ticket on the bus. Don't hang about as competition for both can be fierce during the tourist season. If you're coming down from Srinagar it's even more necessary to rush to find a room as you arrive late in the day, when spare rooms may be at a premium.

At the bottom of the market the *Tawi View Hotel* (tel 47301), Maheshi Gate is undoubtedly the best of the bunch and very popular with travellers. Doubles with bath are Rs 31.50 and the manager is friendly and helpful.

Another simple but clean place is the *Hotel Kashmir*, Vir Marg, where bathless doubles are Rs 30. There are many other budget hotels but there's not much to choose between them, it's usually a question of which ones have rooms available. Reasonable places include the *Hotel Aroma*, Gumat Bazaar (doubles at Rs 25 or Rs 35 with attached bath); *Hotel Raj* (bathless doubles at Rs 22) or the *Hotel Aryabhat* (overpriced and grubby – doubles at Rs 25 or Rs 45 with bath). The *Hotel Broadway* (tel 43636) on Gumat Chowk has singles with attached bath at Rs 42 to 50, doubles at Rs 60 to 75. Bathless doubles are Rs 30 to 40. They also have larger rooms available.

At the railway station there's Jammu's second *Tourist Reception Centre* (tel 8803) with doubles and dorm beds. The station also has *Retiring Rooms* at Rs 45 a double or Rs 75 with air-con, dorm beds at Rs 10. Remember that the railway station is across the Tawi River, several km from the centre. The bus station is close to the centre and has rather decrepit *Retiring Rooms* with doubles at Rs 30 and Rs 5 dorm beds.

In the middle range one of the best places is the fairly new *Hotel Jagan* (tel 42402), Raghunath Bazaar, which also has an air-con restaurant. It's spotlessly clean, pleasantly decorated and has rooms at Rs 45/60 or with air-con doubles are Rs 100 to 125. Another popular mid-

range hotels is the *Tourist Reception Centre* (tel 5421) on Vir Marg. Doubles range from Rs 50 (D block) Rs 55 (C and H Block) to Rs 60 (A block). There are also some air-cooled doubles at Rs 80. All the rooms have attatched bathrooms and there is also a restaurant.

Also on Vir Marg the *Natraj Hotel* (tel 7450) has rooms with attached bath at Rs 35/75. Down the road from the Raghunath Temple are a number of bottom and middle bracket hotels. In the middle category is the *Hotel Gagan*, Gumat Bazaar, which has clean doubles with bath for Rs 50. The *Hotel Amar* and the *Hotel City View* (tel 46120) also in Gumat Bazaar, both have doubles with attached bath for Rs 45 to 60 or with air-cooling for Rs 75. These two are both often full.

At the top end of the market is the *Hotel Jammu Ashok* (tel 46154, 42084) on the outskirts of town to the north, close to the Amar Mahal Palace. Rooms are Rs 100/150 or Rs 225/300 with air-con. The *Hotel Asia* (tel 6373-5) is in Nehru Market close to the Jammu Tawi railway station and the airport but a long way from the centre. Rooms are similarly priced to the Hotel Asia.

Hotel Cosmopolitan (tel 47561) on Vir Marg is cheaper and more convenient. Singles are Rs 50 to 80, doubles Rs 80 to 120 or with air-con doubles are Rs 150 to 200. All these upper bracket hotels have a bar and restaurant.

Places to Eat

The usual government tourist centrer menu is available at the *Tourist Reception Centre*. Reasonable sort of food. The *Cosmopolitan Hotel's* air-con restaurant is far superior to the hotel – good for a pleasant meal in cool surroundings and a cold beer. A few doors down the *Premier* has Chinese and Kashmiri food but is rather expensive.

Getting There

People generally go to Jammu simply to continue on to Srinagar. See details under

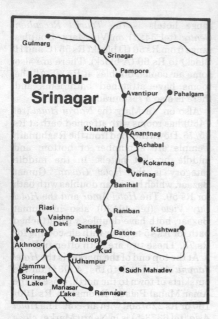

JAMMU-SRINAGAR

Although most people simply head straight through from Jammu to Srinagar there are a number of places of interest between the two centres. Some places can also be reached using Jammu as a base. Prior to the completion of the Jawarhar Tunnel into the Kashmir Valley the trip from Jammu took two days with an overnight stop at Batote.

Akhnoor

This is where the Chenab River meets the plains, 32 km north-west of Jammu. This used to be the route to Srinagar in the Moghul era. Jehangir, who died en route to Kashmir, was temporarily buried at Chingas.

Basohli

Situated fairly close to Dalhousie, which is across the border in Himachal Pradesh, this is the birthplace of the Pahari miniature painting style.

Billawar, Sukrala, Babor & Permandal

All these places have ruined and uncompleted temples of some interest.

Surinsar & Mansar Lakes

East of Jammu these lakes are picturesque and the scene for an annual festival at Mansar.

Vaishno Devi

This important cave temple is dedicated to the three mother goddesses of Hinduism. Thousands of pilgrims visit the cave each year after making a steep 12 km climb from the roadhead at Katra or a shorter and easier climb from a new road.

Riasi

Near this town, 80 km beyond Katra, is the ruined fort of General Zorawar Singh, renowned for his clashes with the Chinese over Ladakh. Nearby is a gurdwara with some interesting old frescoes and another important cave temple.

'Getting There' for Srinagar. If you're continuing on from Jammu to Srinagar the one important rule to follow is to get your bus ticket as soon as you arrive. See the Places to Stay section above for information on the 'head straight through' or 'overnight in Jammu' decision.

Southbound there are frequent buses from Jammu to Amritsar (Rs 15), Pathankot (Rs 8, three hours) and other cities. Pathankot is the jumping off point for Dharamsala, Dalhousie and the other Himachal Pradesh hill stations.

Getting Around

Jammu has metered taxis, auto-rickshaws, a minibus service and a tempo service between a number of points. From the railway station to the bus station costs Rs 1 by the new minibuses. The same trip by auto-rickshaw would be Rs 5 to 7. It's only a short distance from the Tourist Reception Centre in the town centre to the bus station, say Rs 2 or 3 by auto-rickshaw.

Ramnagar

The 'palace of colours' has many beautiful Pahari-style wall paintings. Buses go here from Jammu or Udhampur. Krimchi, 10 km from Udhampur, has Hindu temples with fine carving and sculpture.

Kud

This is a popular lunch stop on the Jammu-Srinagar route at 1738 metres. It's also popular in its own right as a hill resort and has a *Tourist Bungalow*. There's a well known mountain spring, Swamai Ki Bauli, 1.5 km from the road.

Batote

Only 12 km further on, and connected to Patnitop and Kud by a number of footpaths, this hill resort at 1560 metres was the overnight stop between Jammu and Srinagar before the tunnel was opened. There is a *Tourist Bungalow*, tourist huts and several private hotels. As in Kud there is a spring close to the village Amrit Chasma is only 2.5 km away.

Patnitop

At 2024 metres there are many pleasant walks around this popular hill station. Patnitop is intended to be the nucleus of tourist developments in this area. There are tourist huts, a *Rest House* and a *Youth Hostel* in Patnitop.

Sudh Mahadev

Many pilgrims visit the Shiva temple here during the annual July-August Asad Purnima festival which features three days of music, singing and dancing. Five km from Sudh Mahadev is Man Talai where some archaeological discoveries have been made. An eight km walking or jeep track leads to Sudh Mahadev from Kud or Patnitop.

Sanasar

At 2079 metres this beautiful valley is a centre for the Gujjar shepherds each summer. There is a *Tourist Bungalow*, tourist huts and several private hotels.

Bhadarwah

Every two years a procession of pilgrims walk from this beautiful high altitude valley to the 4400 metre high Kaplash Lake. A week later the three-day Mela Patt festival takes place in Bhadarwah. There is a rest house in this scenic location.

Kishtwar

Well off the Jammu-Srinagar road there is a trekking route from Kishtwar to Srinagar. You can also trek from Kishtwar into Zanskar. There are many waterfalls around Kishtwar and 19 km from the town is the pilgrimage site of Sarthal Devi.

Jawarhar Tunnel

During the winter months Srinagar was often completely cut off from the rest of India before this tunnel was completed. The 2500 metre long tunnel is 200 km from Jammu and 93 km from Srinagar and has two separate passages. It's rather rough and damp inside. From Banihal, 17 km before the tunnel, you are already entering the Kashmiri region and people speak Kashmiri as well as Dogri. As soon as you emerge from the tunnel you are in the green, lush Vale of Kashmir. If you take a late bus from Jammu for Srinagar you will probably overnight at Banihal and stay in the rather primitive *Tourist Lodge*.

KASHMIR

This is one of the most beautiful regions of India. The Moghul rulers of India were always happy to retreat from the heat of the plains to the cool green heights of Kashmir and indeed Jehangir's last words, when he died while en route to the 'happy valley', was a simple request for 'only Kashmir'. The Moghuls developed the art of their formal garden style to its greatest heights in Kashmir and some of their gardens are beautifully kept even to this day.

One of Kashmir's greatest attractions is undoutedly the Dal Lake houseboats.

During the Raj period Kashmir's ruler would not permit the British (who were as fond of Kashmir's cool climate as the Moghuls) to own land here. So they adopted the superbly British solution of building houseboats – each one a little bit of England, afloat on Dal Lake. A visit to Kashmir, it is so often said, is not complete until you have stayed on a houseboat. Of course Srinagar, Dal Lake and houseboats is not all there is to Kashmir. Around the edges of the valley are Kashmir's delightful hill stations. Places like Pahalgam and Gulmarg are pleasant in their own right and also good bases for trekking trips.

SRINAGAR (population 450,000)

The capital of Kashmir stands on Dal Lake and the Jhelum River and is the transport hub for the valley and also the jumping off point for trips to Ladakh. Srinagar is a crowded, colourful city with a distinctly central Asian flavour. The people indeed look different from the rest of India and when you head south from Srinagar it is always referred to as 'returning to India'.

Information & Orientation

Srinagar is initially a little confusing since Dal Lake, which is so much a part of the city, is such a strange lake. It's actually three lakes, separated by dykes or 'floating gardens' and at times it's hard to tell where lake ends and land begins. On the lake there are houseboats that are definitely firmly attached to the bottom. And houses that look like they could simply float away. Most of the houseboats are at the southern end of the lake although you will also find them on the Jhelum River and north on Nagin Lake.

The Jhelum River makes a loop around the main part of town and a canal connecting the river with Dal Lake converts that part of town into an island. Along the south of this 'island' is the Bund, a popular walk. Here you will find the GPO and the handicrafts centre. The large

Tourist Reception Centre is just north of the Bund and here the Tourist Office, Indian Airlines and the J&K Road Transport Corporation are located together with accommodation units and a rather poor restaurant. The Kashmir Tourist Office has had a very poor reputation but they claim it is now much improved.

There are many restaurants, shops, travel agents and hotels in the island part of town. The more modern part of Srinagar stretches away south of the Jhelum while the older parts of town are north and north-west of here.

Dal Lake

Much of Dal Lake is a maze of intricate waterways rather than a simple sheet of open water. The lake is divided into Gagribal, Lokut Dal and Bod Dal by a series of causeways. Dal Gate, at the city end of the lake, controls the flow of the lake water into the Jhelum River canal. Within the lake are two islands which are popular picnic spots. Silver Island (Sona Lank) is at the north end of the lake while Gold Island (Rupa Lank) is to the south. Both are also known as Char Chinar because they each have four chinar trees on them. There's a third island, Nehru Park, at the end of the main stretch of the lake side Boulevard but it is a miserable affair. North of here a long causeway juts out into the lake towards Kotar Khana, the 'house of pigeons', which was once a royal summer house.

The waters of Dal Lake are amazingly clear, considering what must be poured into them from the houseboats, and there is always something happening on the lake. Whether you're just lazing on your houseboat balcony watching the shikaras glide by or visiting the Moghul gardens around the lake there's plenty to see and do on Dal Lake. A shikara circuit of the lake is a sybaritic experience not to be missed. A leisurely cruise around will take all day, including visits to the Moghul gardens, and should cost about Rs 60.

There's hardly a more leisurely and pleasurable way of getting into the swing of Srinagar. If your budget is tight you can circuit the lake yourself by bicycle. It's also possible to ride right across the lake on the central causeway.

Jhelum River & Bridges
The Jhelum flows from Verinag, 80 km south of Srinagar, to the Wular Lake to the north. It's wide, swift flowing, muddy and picturesque as it sweeps through Srinagar. The river is famed for its nine old bridges but new bridges have popped up between them. There are a number of interesting mosques and other buildings near the river and a leisurely stroll or bicycle ride through the narrow lanes that run close to the river is very rewarding.

Museum
The Shri Pratap Singh Museum is in Lal Mandi, just south of the river between Zero Bridge and Amira Kadal, the first 'old' bridge. The museum has an interesting collection of exhibits relevant to Kashmir including illustrated titles from Harwan. It's open 10 am to 5 pm, closed on Wednesdays and admission is free.

Shah Hamdan Mosque
Originally built in 1395 the all wooden mosque was destroyed by fire in 1479 and 1731. The mosque is shaped like a cube with a pyramidal roof rising to a spire. Non-Moslems are not allowed inside.

Pather Masjid
On the opposite bank of the Jhelum is the unused Pather Masjid. This fine stone mosque was built by Nur Jahan in 1623.

Tomb of Zain-ul-Abidin
Back on the east bank between the Zaina Kadal and the Ali Kadal bridges is the slightly decrepit tomb of King Zain-ul-Abidin, the highly regarded son of Sultan Sikander. Built on the foundations of an earlier temple the tomb shows a clear Persian influence in its domed construction and glazed tiles.

Jami Masjid
This impressive wooden mosque is notable for the 300-plus pillars supporting the roof, each made of a single deodar tree trunk. The present mosque, with its green and peaceful inner courtyard was rebuilt to the original design after a fire in 1674. It has had a chequered history. First built in 1385 by Sultan Sikander it was enlarged by Zain-ul-Abidin in 1402 then destroyed by fire in 1479. Rebuilt in 1503 another fire destroyed it during Jehangir's reign. Again it was rebuilt only to burn down once more before its most recent rebuild.

Shankaracharya Hill
Rising up behind the Boulevard, beside Dal Lake, the hill was once known as Takht-i-Sulaiman, the Throne of Solomon. A temple is said to have first been built here by Ashoka's son around 200 BC but the present Hindu temple dates from Jehangir's time. It's a pleasant stroll to the top from where you have a fine view over Dal Lake – the Srinagar TV tower is also here. Alternatively there's a road right to the top.

Chasma Shahi
Smallest of the Moghul gardens at Srinagar the Chasma Shahi are well up the hillside, above the Nehru Memorial Park. The gardens were laid out in 1632 but have been recently extended. These are the only gardens with an admission charge.

Pari Mahal
Just above the Chasma Shahi is this fine old Sufi college. The ruined, arched terraces have recently been turned into a very pleasant and well-kept garden with Dal Lake – the Srinagar TV tower is also here. There's also a road right to the top.

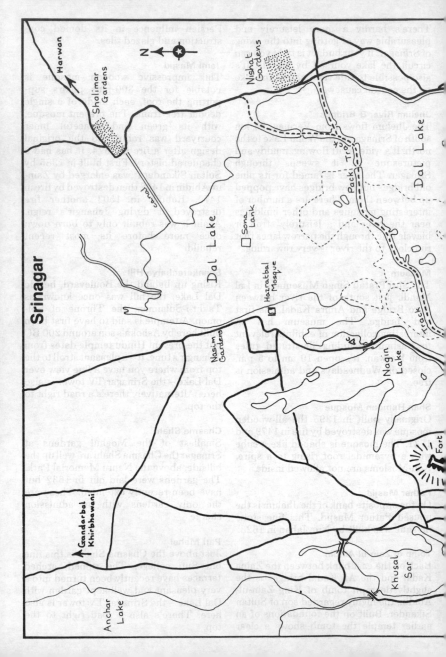

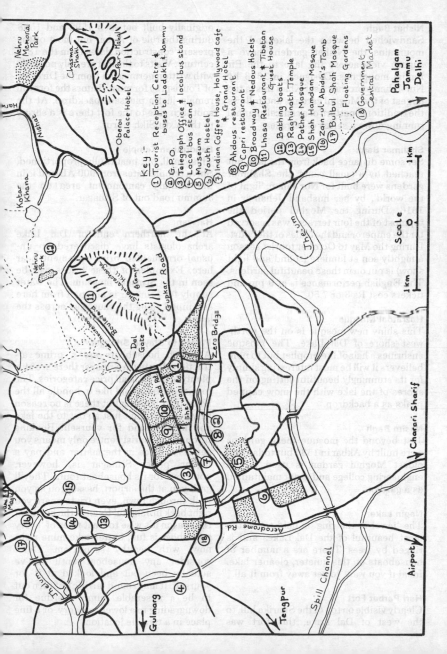

Key:-
① Tourist Reception Centre ‡ buses to Ladakh ‡ Jammu
② G.P.O.
③ Telegraph Office ‡ local bus stand
④ Local bus stand
⑤ Museum
⑥ Youth Hostel
⑦ Indian Coffee House, Hollywood café
   ‡ Grand Hotel
⑧ Ahdous restaurant
⑨ Capri restaurant
⑩ Broadway ‡ Nedous Hotels
⑪ Lhasa Restaurant ‡ Tibetan
   Guest House
⑫ Bathing boats
⑬ Raghunath Temple
⑭ Pather Mosque
⑮ Shah Hamdan Mosque
⑯ Zain-ul-Abidin's Tomb
⑰ Bulbul Shah Mosque
   Floating Gardens
⑱ Government
   Central Market

Pahalgam
Jammu
Delhi

Scale

0

1 km

1 km

Charari Sharif

Gulmarg

TengPur

Airport

Spill Channel

Nishat Bagh

Sandwiched between the lake and the mountains the Nishat gardens have a superb view across the lake to the Pir Panjal mountains. Designed in 1633 by Nur Jahan's brother Asaf Khan this is the largest of the Moghul gardens and follows the traditional pattern of a central channel running down a series of terraces.

Shalimar Bagh

Set some distance back from the lake but reached by a small canal, the Shalimar gardens were built for Nur Jahan, 'light of the world', by her husband Jehangir in 1616. During the Moghul period the topmost of the four terraces was reserved for the emperor and the ladies of the court. During the May to October tourist season a nightly son et lumiere (sound and light show) is put on in these beautiful gardens. The English performance is at 9 pm and tickets cost Rs 3 or 7.50.

Hazratbal Mosque

This shiny new mosque is on the north-west shore of Dal Lake. The mosque enshrines a hair of the prophet but to non-believers it will be most interesting simply for its stunningly beautiful setting on the shores of the lake with the snow capped peaks as a backdrop.

Nasim Bagh

Just beyond the mosque these gardens were built by Akbar in 1586 but today this oldest Moghul garden is used by an engineering college and is not maintained as a garden.

Nagin Lake

The 'jewel in the ring' is held to be the most beautiful of the Dal Lakes and is ringed by trees. There are a number of houseboats on this quieter, cleaner lake. Ideal if you want to get away from it all.

Hari Parbat Fort

Clearly visible on top of the Sharika hill, to the west of Dal Lake, this fort was originally built between 1592 and 1598 during the rule of Akbar but most of the present construction dates from the 18th century. Visits to the fort are only possible with written permission from the Director of Tourism so for most visitors the fort will remain just a pleasant backdrop. At the southern gate to the fort there is a shrine to the sixth Sikh Guru.

Pandrathan Temple

This small, but beautifully proportioned, Shiva temple dates from 900 AD and is in the military cantonment area on the Jammu road out of Srinagar.

Harwan

At the northern end of Dal Lake archaeologists have discovered an unusual ornamented brick pavement near here. Examples of these bricks can be seen in the Srinagar museum. The water supply for Srinagar is pumped from here and piped along the causeway across the lake.

Places to Stay in Srinagar

Although houseboats are a prime attraction of a stay in Srinagar there are also plenty of hotels in all price categories. The tourist centre would like to handle all the houseboat booking but there is no reason why you shouldn't just go out to the lake and look around for yourself. Booking through the tourist centre only means you get less choice in the matter and pay a higher price. Srinagar is, however, notorious for its houseboat touts. They'll grab you at the airport, hassle you as you walk through town, even try to snare you right back in Jammu! Even at the height of the season it's wise to treat tales of 'every houseboat is full, better take mine right now' with healthy scepticism. Don't consider any houseboat until you've actually been out and looked at it for yourself. It may sound terrific but turn out to be a miserable dump overdue for downgrading to a lower category, or a fine place in a terrible location.

Places to Stay – Houseboats

There is no greater escape from the noise and hassle of Srinagar, a typically noisy Asian city, than the houseboats. As soon as you get out on the lake traffic, pollution and hassles just fade away. Houseboats are superbly relaxing. Basically most houseboats are the same. You have a small verandah at one end where you can sit and watch the world pass by. Behind this is a living room, usually furnished in British '30s style. Then there is a dining room and beyond that two or three bedrooms, each with attached bathroom. Officially houseboats come in five categories each with an officially approved price for singles/doubles:

	with meals	lodging only
de-luxe or		
5-star	Rs 220/325	Rs 150/225
A class	Rs 150/220	Rs 90/140
B class	Rs 100/170	Rs 60/100
C class	Rs 65/115	Rs 30/ 40
D class or		
'donga boat'	Rs 45/ 60	Rs 45*

*for whole boat

In practice those 'official prices' are a bit meaningless. For a start there is a wide variance between boats – some are 5-star and others **5-STAR**! A good C class boat can be better than a poor A class boat. Also most houseboats are managed in groups of three or more. You can be sure the food is not going to differ materially from the best boat in the group to the worst. Plus, of course, there is competition. With so many houseboats (there are hundreds of them) a little negotiation is inevitable.

To find a houseboat go down to the shikara ghats along the lakeside and announce you want a houseboat. Either there will be somebody there with a boat available or you can hire a kid with a shikara to paddle you around the boats to ask. Generally you can get away with paying at least the price level for the category below each boat – for an A class

boat pay B class prices. If you decide to miss a meal, say lunch, each day that can generally be negotiated into a lower price. Make certain shikara trips to shore are included and if not remember it's only Rs 0.50 from ghat to boat. This is Kashmir so pin down as many details as possible. Check what breakfast is going to be for example – exactly how many eggs? Check they'll supply a bucket of hot water for washing each morning – Kashmir can be chilly.

It's virtually impossible to recommend a particular boat. There are so many, they all only have a few rooms and there are so many variable factors. A pleasant shikara man – who runs you back and forth between boat and shore, makes tea, supplies hot water and so on – can make a nondescript boat into a pleasant one. A pleasant book can be ruined by a poor cook. Or simply having some pleasant fellow houseboaters to chat with in the evening can make all the difference. Even on the best boats the food can get rather monotonous but there are plenty of 'supermarket' boats cruising by if you need soft drinks, chocolate, toilet paper, hashish or any other of life's necessities.

A peaceful life out on the lake depends, to some extent, on avoiding the attentions of the salesman who continually paddle by. If you don't want to spend your whole time going through everything from wood carvings to carpets, embroidery to papier mache, it's necessary to be very firm and decisive with these people. You can always retreat from the houseboat verandah to the more secluded roof, but why should you have to? Equally important is the attitude of the houseboat owners. Let's face it, they rake off a handy little commission from everything that gets sold on their houseboat so they have an incentive to encourage the salespeople. On some houseboats you may actually find the service, food, general attitude, takes a disastrous dip if you don't spend, spend, spend. The only answer to this policy is to move to a better houseboat, where the owners have more respect for their guests' comfort.

Places to Stay – Bottom End

There are cheap hotels scattered all around Srinagar although those in the Lal Chowk area tend to be rather noisy. The best bargains in cheap hotels are actually to be found on Dal Lake. Scattered amongst the houseboats there are a number of small hotels actually on (semi) dry land. They're cheap and also quiet but prices are very variable, depending on season and demand. Real cheapies can go as low as Rs 10 per person. Check the *Latif Guest House* or the *Hotel Sundowna* – the latter has rooms as low as Rs 20, fairly spartan but quite OK and good food. Right next door there's the *Hotel Savoy* with rooms from Rs 30 up to Rs 60. Again the food is good.

A little up market from these places – and further up the channel towards Dal Gate – is *Hotel Heaven Canal* with doubles from Rs 60 to 125. The *New Green View Hotel* (tel 76378-9) is next to the Houseboat Taj Palace, about as close as you'll get to the water without actually being on it. Doubles with bathroom with hot and cold water are Rs 40. If the weather is inclement these 'on the lake' hotels are often flooded out.

On solid ground, but still cheap, there's the friendly *Tibetan Guest House* on Gagribal Rd, parallel to the Boulevard, which you book through the Lhasa Restaurant. *Zero Inn* (tel 77904), by Zero Bridge, is also reasonably quiet but rather more expensive at Rs 75 or more a double. Kashmir is not a cheap place for accommodation by Indian standards.

The J&K tourist office operates four accommodation units in Srinagar. At the *Tourist Reception Centre* there are retiring rooms, rooms and suites with prices from Rs 80 to 125. Maximum stay is two days but they are generally full during the season. They have two hotels (*Lalla Rukh* and *Budshah*) but both are in noisy Lal Chowk. Finally there are the *Tourist Huts*

near the Chasma Shahi gardens. They come complete with kitchens and cooking equipment but you really need your own transport to get out to them. Cost is around Rs 300 a night for a double.

The *Srinagar Youth Hostel* is across the river from the town centre, near the museum. Nightly charges are just Rs 4 and reservations must be made through the Education Department. Just beyond the Nagin Lake causeway, only a short distance before the Hazratbal Mosque, there's a campsite, a good place if you have your own vehicle.

Places to Stay – Top End

On dry land the *Oberoi Palace Hotel* (tel 75641-3) is the ex-palace of the Maharaja of Kashmir and is Srinagar's top establishment. It's several km around the boulevard from Dal Gate and singles/doubles are Rs 615/875 including all meals. The actual building is rather uninspired, particularly if you've seen the sumptuous palace hotels of Rajasthan, but the gardens in front provide superb views over the lake. The more modern and more central *Broadway Hotel* (tel 71211-3) is popular and has an excellent restaurant. Singles/doubles cost Rs 290/425.

Next door is the rather run down and decrepit looking *Nedou's Hotel* (tel 73015-6) also on Hotel Rd. Singles/doubles cost Rs 200/260. Srinagar's largest hotel is the brand new *Center Lake View Hotel*, Chasme Shahi which has 281 rooms and should be open in early 1984. There are a number of more expensive hotels along the Boulevard, looking out on to Dal Lake, such as the *Shah Abbas* or the *Gulmarg*. The Shah Abbas overlooks the lake and has good, modern, well appointed, clean rooms at Rs 275 for a double. They're a bit smaller than rooms at the Broadway but the view more than compensates.

There's also a more expensive hotel right out on the lake. The *Lake-Isle Resort* (tel 78446) is on an island in the lake and has singles including breakfast for Rs 150, doubles from Rs 175 to 225.

Places to Eat

Because so many people eat on board their houseboats Srinagar is not a very exciting place for eating out. Surprisingly nobody has yet come up with a floating restaurant – a logical follow on to all those houseboats.

The *Oberoi Palace Hotel* does a very superior buffet dinner for Rs 60 and at lunch-time you can dine, or simply have a snack, on their sweeping lawn. A la carte, most dishes are in the Rs 20 to Rs 35 bracket. The *Broadway* also has a slightly cheaper buffet in their pleasantly carpet decorated restaurant. Food here (on the non-buffet nights) is quite reasonably priced and you can sample quite possibly the best kahwa tea in Srinagar – an expensive treat.

Ahdoo's, which fronts on to the Bund and backs on to Residency Rd, has been said to have some of the best Kashmiri food in Srinagar but generally fails to live up to its reputation. Most dishes are under Rs 15. Across the road the *Grand* has a similar menu. Others in this area include the *Capri Bar & Restaurant* and the *Premier*

Just off the Boulevard the Tibetan run *Lhasa Restaurant* with its 'candle-lit garden' does quite good Chinese-Tibetan food. Most dishes are Rs 10 to 25, a complete meal for two will cost Rs 50 to 75. This friendly place is very popular with travellers. Further back towards Dal Gate, on the Boulevard, there's the *Shamyana* with good vegetarian food and reasonable prices. The *Punjab Hotel & Restaurant*, on Lal Chowk opposite the Palladium Cinema, has cheap, tasty food at Rs 3 to 6 per dish plus more expensive tandoori food. Near Dal Gate the *Glocken Bakery* has good fresh brown bread and other baked goodies.

Right in the central area the *Indian Coffee House* is a good place for a coffee and a chat – the food line here is rather limited: quite good vegetable cutlets and rather so-so masala dosas. Right across the road the *Hollywood Cafe* has much, much better food than its plain appearance would suggest. Seekh kebab or kanti roast make an excellent lunch here and their french fries are superb by any standards. Plus good cakes or snacks at other times of day.

Ice cream is not bad at *Dimples*, either in the centre (opposite the Hollywood) or by Zero Bridge. The latter is known as the *Little Hut* and also has good milkshakes. There's a good selection of Indian sweets at *Shakti Sweets* also by the Hollywood. The cafe at the *Tourist Reception Centre* is terrible but you can get early morning snacks from the stalls which set up opposite the TRC for the early bus departures.

Getting There

Air Indian Airlines fly to Srinagar from New Delhi (Rs 549), Chandigarh (Rs 464), Amritsar (Rs 314), Jammu (Rs 179) and there are flights operating from Srinagar to Leh and back. Flights are more frequent during the summer tourist season, at that time there will probably be a Delhi-Chandigarh-Jammu-Srinagar flight and a Jammu Srinagar flight by 737 each day. A 737 will also fly Delhi-Amritsar-Srinagar and there will probably be another direct 737 and an Airbus. Flight time from Delhi on the direct flights is about an hour and ten minutes. As usual in India you should book your flights as early as possible.

From Srinagar airport, which is about 13 km out of the city, there's an airport bus to the Tourist Reception Centre in Srinagar which costs Rs 5. By taxi it costs about Rs 40. In Srinagar the Indian Airlines office is at the Tourist Reception Centre (tel 73538 & 73270) and is open from 10 am to 5 pm. It's also at the Tourist Reception Centre in Jammu (tel 42735 & 47577).

Rail & Bus It's 880 km from Delhi to Srinagar although almost everybody coming up from Delhi, or other Indian cities, by land will come through Jammu (591 km from Delhi) from where the buses run daily to Srinagar. By train there are about four services a day from Delhi or New Delhi to Jammu Tawi, across the river from Jammu. The trip takes nine to 13 hours, usually overnight, for the 724 km trip and costs Rs 196 in 1st class, Rs 50 in 2nd. There are also buses from Delhi but people making the trip by road will most probably be coming via Chandigarh, Amritsar or the Himachal Pradesh hill stations.

Buses leave Jammu early in the morning (between 6.30 and 7 am) for the 10 to 12 hour trip to Srinagar in the Kashmir Valley. Bus fares are Rs 28 (B class), Rs 35 (A class), Rs 67 (super de-luxe) and Rs 110 (air-con). B class buses seat two and three, A class two and two, super de-luxe two and two in individual seats with headrests. Between 11 am and 12 noon more buses depart from the Jammu Tawi railway station – take these if you don't want to overnight in Jammu. They stop for the night at Banihal on the way to Srinagar.

Although there are many buses (a veritable armada leaves Jammu each morning) you should book a seat as soon as you arrive in Jammu. The same applies from Srinagar as the day before departure all seats may be sold out. In Jammu the A class and de-luxe buses go from the town and the railway station, the B class buses go only from the bus station. There are also taxis operating between the two cities at Rs 130 per seat or Rs 520 for the whole taxi.

For information about booking trains from Jammu while in Srinagar enquire at the railways office in the Tourist Reception Centre or at N D Radha Kishen & Sons, Railway Out Agency, Badshah Chowk, Srinagar (tel 2146). Bus bookings are made at the Tourist Reception Centre (tel 2698), allow plenty of time as the booking system is archaic.

Getting Around

There is a wide choice of transport available either on the lake or out and around it, plus a variety of tours. The tour buses are generally much more comfortable than the usual run of overcrowded local buses and, since many of them offer one-way fares, they can be used for getting out to hill stations in the valley. The best known Kashmiri transport is, of course, the shikara:

Shikaras These are the graceful, long boats which crowd the Srinagar lakes. They're used for getting back and forth from the houseboats or for longer tours. Officially there is a standard fare for every trip around the lake and these are prominently posted at the main landings (ghats); in practice the fares can be quite variable. To be shuttled across to your houseboat should cost Rs 2 in a covered ('full spring seats') shikara but the kids who are always out for a little money will happily paddle you across for 50 paise or less in a basic, open shikara. Of course late at night, particularly if it is raining, the tables are turned and getting back to your houseboat at a reasonable price may require a little ingenuity! If you hire a shikara by the day or for a longer trip, count on about Rs 8 or Rs 9 per hour.

Try paddling a shikara yourself sometime – it's nowhere near as easy as it looks. You'll spend lots of time going round in circles. If your houseboat hasn't got one to spare some children passing by will find you a boat for Rs 4 or Rs 5 per day.

MAY KING
WHOPEE
LOVELY
FULL SPRING SEATS

Taxis & Auto-rickshaws There are stands for these at the Tourist Reception Centre and other strategic locations in town. Srinagar's taxi-wallahs are extremely reluctant to use their meters so you'll have to bargain hard. Count on about Rs 6 for a taxi from the Tourist Reception Centre to Dal Gate (Rs 4 by auto-rickshaw) or Rs 40 to the airport. For longer trips the official fares are all posted by the stands.

Buses The Jammu & Kashmir Road Transport Corporation buses go from the Tourist Reception Centre while private buses operate from a variety of stands in Srinagar. Certain major long distance routes are reserved for the J&K buses (Jammu, Leh, etc) but others are open for competition and there will be a great number of buses operating.

Tours The J&K Road Transport Corporation operate a number of daily tours from the Tourist Reception Centre. Private bus companies, particularly the KMDA (Kashmir Motor Drivers' Association) also have a number of tours. The J&K RTC tours are:

Pahalgam	daily	Rs 36 round trip, Rs 18 one way
Daksum	daily	Rs 36 round trip, Rs 18 one way
Gulmarg	daily	Rs 40 round trip, Rs 20 one way
Aharbal	Tues, Thur, Sun	Rs 25
Verinag	Wed, Sun	Rs 25
Wular Lake	Mon, Wed, Fri	Rs 30
Yusmarg	Tues, Thur, Sun	Rs 20 round trip, Rs 10 one way
Sonamarg	daily	Rs 28 round trip, Rs 15 one way
Moghul Gardens	twice daily	Rs 16

KMDA tours include Pahalgam (Rs 28 round trip, Rs 20 one way), Aharbal (Rs 21), Verinag (Rs 18), Wular Lake (Rs 18), Sonamarg (Rs 24) and Moghul Gardens and Shankaracharya Hill (Rs 10).

Bicycles Seeing Srinagar by bicycle is a surprisingly pleasant way of getting around – economical too. You can hire bikes for Rs 8 per day from bicycle shops. There are several along the Boulevard close to Dal Gate. Pleasant trips to be made include:

Round Dal Lake – an all day trip going by the Moghul gardens. It's particularly pleasant around the north of the lake where the villages are still relatively untouched.

Across the lake – you can ride across the lake on the causeway, a nice trip since there are no traffic problems with vehicle traffic and there is plenty of opportunity to observe the lake life without being in a boat.

Nagin Lake – you can ride out to the Hazratbal Mosque via Nagin Lake and then make a complete loop around the lake on the way back. This trip can easily be combined with a trip along the Jhelum, taking in the various mosques close to the river. The streets here are very narrow so vehicles keep away and bike riding is pleasant.

Things to Buy

Kashmir is famous for its many handicrafts and selling them is an activity pursued with amazing energy. You can visit workshops to see many of them being made. Popular buys include carpets, papier mache articles, leather and furs, wood carvings, shawls and embroidery, honey, tailor-made clothing, pleasantly coarse-knitted sweaters and cardigans, that expensive spice saffron and many other items. There are a whole string of Government Handicraft Emporiums scattered around Srinagar but the main one is housed in the fine old British Residency building by the Bund. The flashiest shops are along the Boulevard by Dal Lake. The Bund also has some interesting shops including *Suffering Moses* with high quality goods. Shikaras patrol Dal Lake like sharks, all loaded down with goodies.

A *tola* of Kashmir's finest dope should cost no more than Rs 40 but unless you've been around for awhile Rs 60 is more likely to be your price. If you pay Rs 80 then you've bought it off a friend of a friend of a friend who has an uncle whose cousin has an aunt whose sister-in-law knew Acharya Jagdish Bose and together him and Nehru knew someone in the business.

KASHMIR VALLEY

When lazing around on your houseboat beings to pall it's time to head off around the valley. There are a number of interesting places in the Kashmir Valley for day trips from Srinagar as well as several popular hill stations which serve as good bases for short or long treks into the surrounding mountains. Pahalgam and Gulmarg are the two main Kashmiri hill resorts.

SRINAGAR-PAHALGAM

The route to Pahalgam passes through a number of interesting places including, if you take the bus tour to Pahalgam, enough Moghul gardens to leave you thoroughly saturated. Only 16 km out of Srinagar is Pampore, centre of Kashmir's saffron industry. Saffron is highly prized for its flavouring and colourful properties and is consequently rather expensive. Sangram, 35 km out, is a centre for production of (would you believe) cricket bats. They're lined up by the road in their thousands.

At Avantipur there are two ruined Hindu temples which were built between 855 and 883 AD. The Avantiswami Temple, the larger of the two, is dedicated to Vishnu and still has some fine relief sculptures and columns of an almost Grecian appearance. The smaller temple to Shiva is about a km before the main temple but also close to the main road. At Anantnag the road forks, the Pahalgam road turning north from here.

Just beyond the Pahalgam turn off is Achabal, a Moghul garden laid out in 1620

by Shah Jahan's daughter Jahanara. This carefully designed garden was said to be a favourite retreat of Nur Jahan. Kokarnag, further on, is certain to give you garden overload but is famous for its rose gardens. Back on the Pahalgam route Mattan has a fish-filled spring which is an important pilgrimage spot. Above Mattan on a plateau is the huge ruined temple of Martland.

Not actually on or even close to the Pahalgam route is Verinag in the extreme south of the Kashmir Valley. The spring here is said to be the actual source of the Jhelum River. Jehangir built an octagonal stone basin at the spring in 1612 and Shah Jahan laid out a garden around it in 1620.

PAHALGAM

About 95 km from Srinagar and at 2130 metres the night time temperatures here are warmer than in Gulmarg which is higher up. The beautiful Lidder River flows right through the town which is at the junction of the Sheshnag and Lidder Rivers and surrounded by soaring, fir-covered mountains with snow-capped peaks rising behind them. This is an ideal base for short day treks or for the longer treks to the Kolahoi Glacier or the Amarnath Cave – see Kashmir Trekking. Pahalgam is also famous for its many shepherds, they're a common sight, driving their flocks of sheep along the paths all around town.

Information

The rather useless tourist office is just around the corner from the bus halt. Fishing permits have to be obtained in Srinagar but trekking supplies can be bought here.

Pahalgam Walks

Mamaleswara Only a km or so downstream and on the opposite bank of the Lidder this small Shiva temple with its square, stone tank is thought to date back at least to the 12th century.

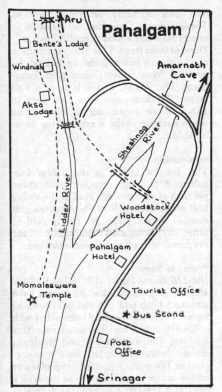

Pahalgam

equally pricey *Woodstock* (tel 27) which costs Rs 350/400 for singles/doubles. There is also a *Government Tourist Bungalow* and *Government Tourist Huts* and during the summer season the tourist office operates a number of tent sites with ready set up and furnished tents. The *Dar Camp* has been particularly recommended.

Most budget travellers head across the river to one of the lodges on the other bank. The at one time very popular riverside *Windrush* (not to be confused with another Windrush on the town side) burnt down and at last report was still in a temporary location. is the most popular.

Up the hill, a little beyond the Windrush, is the rather cheaper and more basic *Bente's Hotel*. Before the Windrush, but also slightly uphill, is the more expensive but very popular *Aksa Lodge*. It's rather more luxurious (even hot water) with doubles from Rs 50 to over Rs 100 (lower out of season). The location is superb and the food very good.

Getting There

Local buses cost Rs 7.50 and take 2½ to four hours, there are six to 10 departures a day. J&K Road Transport have tour buses which cost Rs 18 one way or Rs 36 return. The KMDA tour buses take a long time since they make many stops on the way. Taxis cost over Rs 250 return although you can sometimes find a taxi going back from Pahalgam empty and willing to bargain. If you want to get a return ticket on one of the more comfortable J&K tour buses you have to catch them when they come in around noon in order to get tickets. Get someone from your hotel to do it for you. You can get buses direct from Pahalgam to Jammu.

Ponies can easily be hired in Pahalgam for trekking trips. The fixed costs to popular destinations are all clearly posted.

Baisaran There are excellent views over the town and the Lidder Valley from this meadow, five km from Pahalgam. A further 11 km takes you to the Tulian Lake at 3353 metres. It is ice covered for much of the year.

Aru The pleasant little village of Aru makes a very interesting day walk, following the Lidder River for 11 km upstream. Unfortunately the main track also takes cars. This is actually the first stage of the Kolahoi Glacier trek.

Places to Stay

There are many hotels along the main street of Pahalgam including the expensive *Pahalgam Hotel* (tel 26) or the

GULMARG

The large meadow of Gulmarg is 52 km

from Srinagar and at 2730 metres. The name means 'meadow of flowers' and in spring it's just that. This is also an excellent trekking base and in winter it's India's premier skiing resort.

Gulmarg Walks

Outer Circular Walks A circular road, ll km in length, runs right round Gulmarg through pleasant pine forests with excellent views over the Kashmir Valley. Nanga Parbat is visible to the north and Haramukh and Sunset Peak to the south-east.

Khilanmarg This smaller valley is about a six km walk from the Gulmarg bus stop and car park. The meadow, carpeted with flowers in the spring, is the site for Gulmarg's winter ski-runs and offers a fine view of the surrounding peaks and over the Kashmir Valley. During the early spring, as the snow melts, it can be a very muddy hour's climb up the hill.

Alpather Beyond Khilanmarg, 13 km from Gulmarg at the foot of the 4511-metre Apharwat peak, this lake is frozen until mid-June, and even later in the year you can see lumps of ice floating in its cold waters. The walk from Gulmarg follows a well graded pony track over the 3810-metre Apharwat Ridge, separating it from Khilanmarg, and then up the valley to the lake at 3843 metres.

Ningle Nallah Flowing from the melting snow and ice on Apharwat and the Alpather Lake, this pretty mountain stream is 10 km from Gulmarg. The stream continues down into the valley below and joins the Jhelum River near Sopore. The walking path crosses the Ningle Nallah by a bridge and continues on to the Lienmarg, another grassy meadow and a good spot for camping.

Ferozpore Nallah Reached from the Tangmarg road, or from the outer circular walk, this mountain stream meets the Bahan River at a popular picnic spot known as 'waters meet'. The stream is reputed to be particularly good for trout fishing; it's about five km from Gulmarg.

You can continue on from here to Tosamaidan, a three day, 50 km-walk to one of Kashmir's most beautiful margs.

Ziarat of Baba Reshi This Moslem shrine is on the slopes below Gulmarg and can be reached from either Gulmarg or Tang-marg. The Ziarat, or tomb, is of a well known Moslem saint who died here in 1480. Before renouncing worldly ways he was a courtier of the Kashmir king Zain-ul-Abidin.

Information

The Tourist Office is the green/blue-coloured building complex with three patches of new wooden roof in the valley bottom about a half km beyond the golf course. Gulmarg can get pretty cold at times, even compared to Pahalgam. Come prepared with plenty of warm clothes.

Places to Stay

Hotel Highland Park (tel 30, 50) is Rs 330/450 for singles/doubles. All rooms have attached bath and hot and cold running water. There's a beautiful lounge/bar with colonial trophies and the restaurant offers English, Chinese, Indian and Kashmiri dishes both vegetarian and non-vegetarian. It's worth a visit for a cup of tea or coffee in the beautiful gardens (or even a beer in a crested silver tankard!) in this rather fine establishment.

The *Yamberzal Tourist Inn* has rooms at Rs 125/200 or Rs 200/350 including meals. All rooms have attached bath and hot and cold water and there's a bar and restaurant. It's right opposite the bus stand. *Hotel Kingsley* (tel 55) is an older place with a pleasant atmosphere. Rooms are Rs 75/90 or Rs 135/190 including meals and again the rooms all have attached bathrooms and hot and cold water.

Tourists Hotel (tel 53) is a remarkably baroque and weathered fantasy in wood, like something out of *Lord of the Rings* although it's rather dirty and grubby inside. Rooms cost Rs 20, 30 and 50 and supposedly they all have attached bath and hot water – well perhaps in the early morning and late afternoon anyway. It's right outside the horse and pony stand. The *City View* has doubles at Rs 25, a friendly manager and fine food.

Getting There

There are a variety of buses running from Srinagar to Gulmarg, many of them on day tours. On a day tour you have only a few hours at the hill resort, just long enough for one of the shorter day walks. The deluxe tour buses cost Rs 39 return or Rs 21 one-way and leave at 9 am from the Tourist Reception Centre. Ordinary buses leave hourly and cost Rs 12 return or Rs 7.50 one-way.

Until recently the road from Srinagar only ran as far as Tangmarg, seven km distance or 500 metres altitude below Gulmarg. The last stretch then had to be completed on foot or by pony. A road has now been completed over the last stretch although, there are still buses operating that terminate at Tangmarg. The winding road from Tangmarg is 13 km in length, nearly twice as far as the more direct pony track. A riding pony costs about Rs 140 from Tangmarg up to Gulmarg. Ponies, either riding or pack ponies, can also be hired from Gulmarg to other sites around the valley. Khilanmarg, for example, costs Rs 25 return. Other rates are prominently posted at the car park.

SOUTH OF SRINAGAR

Interesting places in the south-west of the valley include Yusmarg, which is reputed to have the best spring flowers in Kashmir, and is a good base for treks further afield. Chari Sharif is on the road to Yusmarg and has the shrine or Ziarat of Kashmir's patron saint. Aharbal was a popular resting place for the Moghul emperors when they made the long trip north from Delhi.

SINDH VALLEY

This is a scenic area north of Srinagar through which the road to Ladakh passes.

The Zoji La pass marks the boundary from the Sindh Valley into Ladakh. From Srinagar you pass the Dachigam wildlife reserve, once a royal game park. Anchar Lake is close to Srinagar but rarely visited and has a wide variety of water birds. There is a Moghul garden built by Nur Jahan at Manasbal Lake. The Wular Lake is possibly the largest freshwater lake in Asia and the Jhelum River flows into it.

Sonamarg, at 2740 metres, is the last major point in Kashmir and an excellent base for trekking. Its name means 'meadow of gold', which could derive from the spring flowers or from the strategic trading position it once enjoyed. There are *Tourist Huts*, a *Rest House* and some small hotels here. The tiny village of Baltal is the last place in Kashmir, right at the foot of the Zoji La. In June only you can walk to the Amarnath Cave from here. Prior to that the snow is too deep, after that the slush is too deep! The Zoji La is the watershed between Kashmir and Ladakh – on one side you have the green, lush scenery of Kashmir while on the other side everything is barren and dry.

TREKS IN KASHMIR

There are various treks both within Kashmir and from Kashmir to Ladakh or Zanskar. The short Pahalgam-Kolahoi Glacier trek is particularly popular and the Pahalgam-Amarnath Cave trek is well known not only for the natural scenery that takes place here. Porters are not used in Kashmir anywhere near as much as in Nepal. Instead ponies are used to carry the gear.

Pahalgam-Kolahoi Glacier

This short trek takes only four days Pahalgam to Pahalgam but it can be extended before returning to Pahalgam or continued up into the Sindh Valley. The first day from Pahalgam takes you to Aru along the bank of the Lidder River. This is also a very popular day trek from Pahalgam since Aru is a pretty little village. The second day's walk takes you to Lidderwat where there is a very pleasant campsite where the stream from the glacier meets the stream from the Tarsar Lake. There is also the *Paradise Guest House* here. On the third day you trek up to the lake and back to Lidderwat. The glacier, climbing from 3400 metres up to 4000 metres descends from the 5485-metre Kolahoi mountain. On day 4 you can either walk straight back to Pahalgam in one day or the trek can be extended another day by walking Lidderwat-Tarsar Lake-Lidderwat.

Instead of returning to Pahalgam three days further trek will take you to Kulan near Sonamarg in the Sindh Valley. It's only 16 km from Kulan to Sonamarg, which you can walk or travel by bus.

Day 1	Pahalgam-Aru	12 km
Day 2	Aru-Lidderwat	12 km
Day 3	Lidderwat-glacier-Lidderwat	13 km
Day 4	Lidderwat-Pahalgam	24 km
or		
Day 4	Lidderwat-Sekiwas	10 km
Day 5	Sekiwas-Khemsar	11 km
Day 6	Khemsar-Kulan	10 km

Pahalgam-Amarnath Cave

At the full moon in the month of July-August thousands of Hindu pilgrims make the 'yatra' to the Shri Amarnath Cave where a natural ice lingam, the symbol of Lord Shiva, reaches its greatest size. Although at the time of the yatra it's less a trek than a long queue, the spirit of this immense pilgrimage is quite amazing. The first day's walk out of Pahalgam is jeepable and from Amarnath it is possible to continue north to Baltal, near Srinagar although that is quite a hard trek.

Day 1	Pahalgam-Chandanwari	13 km
Day 2	Chandanwari-Sheshnag	12 km
Day 3	Sheshnag-Panchtarni	11 km
Day 4	Panchtarni-Amarnath	8 km

Sonamarg-Wangat

This 81-km trek takes five days and reaches a maximum altitude of 4191 metres. It starts from Sonamarg, reached by bus from Srinagar, then climbs to Nichinai, crosses a mountain chain and drops down to the pleasant campsite at Krishansar. Another pass has to be crossed on the third and fourth day when you reach the Gangabal Lake. From here it's a steep descent to Wangat from where you can easily bus back to Srinagar.

Day 1	Sonamarg-Nichinai	15 km
Day 2	Nichinai-Krishansar	13 km
Day 3	Krishansar-Dubta Pani	17 km
Day 4	Dubta Pani-Gangabal Lake	17 km
Day 5	Gangabal Lake-Wangat	19 km

Gangabal Trek

This trek also goes to Gangabal but approaches it from the other side. The trek commences from Errin, north of Wular Lake and takes five days in all. On the fourth day you need ropes and ice-axes to cross the glacier between the Kundsar and Gangabal Lake. The final day's trek also ends at Wangat. At Narannag, just before Wangat, there is an interesting old temple.

Day 1	Erin-Chuntimula-Poshpathri	11 km
Day 2	Poshpathri-Sarbal	11 km
Day 3	Sarbaal-Kundsar Lake	9 km
Day 4	Kundsar Lake-Gangabal Lake	11 km
Day 5	Gangabal-Wangat	19 km

Konsarnag Trek

This short trek in the south of the Kashmir Valley ascends into the Pir Panjal mountains. The first day's trek is a short walk only taking about three hours. With an early start from Srinagar you can bus to Ahrabal and complete the first walk in the same day. The Konsarnag Lake is a beautiful deep-blue stretch of water at 3700 metres.

Day 1	Ahrabal-Kungwattan	9 km
Day 2	Kungwattan-Mahinag	
Day 3	Mahinag-Konsarnag-Kungwattan	
Day 4	Kungwattan-Ahrabal	

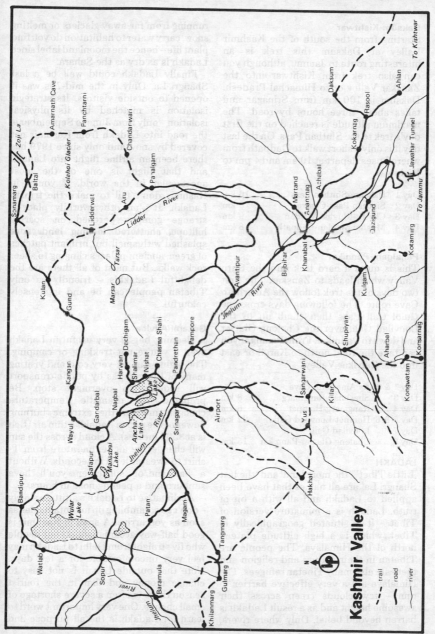

Kashmir Valley

To Kishtwar

To Jammu

Daksum
Rasool
Ahlan
Kokarnag
To Kishtwar
Jawahar Tunnel

Martand
Achibal
Anantnag
Khanabal
Dazigund
Kotamsg
Konsarnag
Kongwatam
Aharbal
Kulgam
Shupiyan
Killar
Yus
Sanjarwani
Hakhal

Zoji La
Baltal
Amarnath Cave
Panchtarni
Kolehoi Glacier
Chandarwari
Aru
Pahalgam
Lidderwet
Lidder River

Sonamarg
Tarsar
Marsar

Kulan
Gund
Kangan
Wayul
Gagardarbal
Nagbal
Safapur
Manasbal Lake
Anchar Lake
Dechigam
Harwan
Shalimar
Nishat
Chasma Shahi
Srinagar
Pandrethan
Pampore
Avantipur
Bijbihar
Jhelum River

Bandipur
Wular Lake
Watlab
Sopur
Patan
Magam
Baramula
Jhelum River
Gulmarg
Tangmarg
Khilanmarg

Airport

N

trail
road
river

Daksum-Kishtwar

Starting from the south of the Kashmir Valley at Daksum this trek is an interesting route to Jammu, although you can also trek from Kishtwar into the Zanskar Valley or to Himachal Pradesh. Daksum is 100 km from Srinagar and takes about three hours by road. The maximum altitude is reached on the first day's trek to the Sinthan Pass. On the last day it is only a short walk to Dadpath from where buses depart at 10 am and 4 pm to Kishtwar.

Day 1	Daksum-Sinthan Pass	16 km
Day 2	Sinthan Pass-Chatru	8 km
Day 3	Chatru-Mughal Maidan	9 km
Day 4	Mughal Maidan-Dadpath	8 km

Pahalgam-Pannikar

This is quite a hard trek into the Suru Valley which leads to Zanskar. The first two days of the trek follow the Amarnath Cave route. The following days cross the Gulol Gali Pass then climb up to the Lonvilad Gali, over the Chalong Glacier and down to Pannikar. From Pannikar you can take the road north to Kargil or east into the Zanskar Valley.

Day 1 & 2	As Amarnath Cave	
Day 3	Sheshnag-Rangmarg	8 km
Day 4	Rangmarg-Hampet	6 km
Day 5 & 6	Hampet-Lonvilad Gali	22 km
Day 7	Lonvilad Gali	
Day 8	Chalong Glacier-Pannikar	15 km

LADAKH

'Little Tibet', 'the moonland' and 'the last Shangri La' are all names that have been applied to Ladakh and all with a bit of truth. Ladakh is a miniature version of Tibet – it is situated geographically in Tibet, which is a high altitude plateau north of the Himalaya. The people are Tibetan in their culture and religion and there are also many Tibetan refugees. The Himalaya are a very effective barrier to rain – few clouds creep across their awesome height and as a result Ladakh is barren beyond belief. Only where rivers, running from far-away glaciers or melting snow, carry water to habitation do you find plant life – hence the moonland label since Ladakh is as dry as the Sahara.

Finally Ladakh could well be a last Shangri La. Only in the mid-70s was it opened to outside visitors. Its strategic isolation is matched by its physical isolation – only from June to September is the road into Ladakh from Kashmir not covered by snow and only since 1979 has there been an airline flight into Ladakh and that flight is one of the most spectacular in the world. If you're in Kashmir don't fail to make the trip to Ladakh. It's an other-worldly place – strange gompas perched on soaring hilltops, shattered looking landscapes splashed with small but brilliant patches of green, ancient palaces clinging to sheer rock walks. But most of all there are the delightful Ladakhis – friendly as only Tibetan people can be and immensely colourful.

General Advice

A sleeping bag is very useful in Ladakh even if you're not trekking or camping. The nights can get very cold and visiting many of the gompas by public transport will require an overnight stop. Be prepared for dramatic temperature changes and for the extreme burning power of the sun in Ladakh's thin air (Leh is at 3500 metres). A cloud across the sun will change the air temperature from T-shirt to sweater level in seconds. Without a hat and/or sunscreen you'll have sunburn and a peeling nose in hours.

Acclimatise to Ladakh's altitude slowly – don't go scrambling up mountainsides as soon as you arrive. A spell in Kashmir is good half-way acclimatisation but people who fly straight from Delhi to Ladakh may feel very uncomfortable for a few days. Note that outside Leh it is not easy to change money and that in the tourist season there is often a severe shortage of small change. One very important word to learn for Ladakh is the all purpose and frequently used greeting 'jullay'. Finally remember that this is a sensitive border region disputed by India, Pakistan and China. You are not allowed more than a mile north of the Srinagar-Leh road.

Religion

At Kargil, on the Srinagar-Leh road, the Islamic influence dies out and you are in a Buddhist region. They follow the Tibetan Tantric Buddhism with much emphasis on magic and demons. All around Ladakh are gompas, the Buddhist monasteries where the religion is carried on. They're fascinating places to visit, although they have become very commercially-minded since Ladakh's tourist boom commenced. There's a good side to this though, prior to tourists the gompas were gradually becoming more and more neglected. Today many of them are being refurbished and repaired, with the profits from visiting westerners! The monks are quite happy to have visitors wander around the gompas, sit in on ceremonies, try the appalling taste of butter tea (bring your own cup) and take photographs.

SRINAGAR-LEH

It's 434 km from the Vale of Kashmir to Ladakh and the road is surfaced most of the way. It follows the Indus River for much of the distance. Buses run along this road daily during the summer season (see Getting There) and take two days with an overnight stop at Kargil. Sonamarg is the last major place in Kashmir, shortly after Sonamarg you climb up over the Zoji La Pass (3529 metres) and enter the Ladakh region.

Zoji La

This is one of the few unsurfaced stretches on the route and it is also the first pass to snow over in the winter and the last pass to be cleared in the summer. It is not, however, the highest pass along the route. The other passes get less snow because they are across the Himalaya and in the mountain rain shadow.

Drass

This is the first village after the pass and the place from where road crews work to clear the road up to the pass for the start of the summer season. In winter Drass is noted for its heavy snowfalls and extreme cold.

Kargil

This was once an important trading post, but now it is simply an overnight halt on the way to Leh or the point where you turn south for the Zanskar Valley. The people of Kargil are chiefly Moslem and noted for their extreme orthodoxy. Already you are in a region where irrigation is vitally important.

Places to Stay *Hotel D'Zojila* is 2.5 km from the town and has doubles from around Rs 90. *Suru View*, behind the bus station, is cheaper at around Rs 50. Cheaper hotels include the reasonable *Argalia* which costs Rs 20 a double but is uncomfortably close to the town's diesel generator, fortunately it shuts down at 10 pm. The similarly priced *Yak Tail* is rather dirty. Along the Srinagar-Leh route there are also *Rest Houses* at Drass, Bodh Kharbu and Mulbekh.

There's a new *State Tourist Bungalow* near the river. It's simple, clean, adequate and has rooms at Rs 25 – good value. It's about a half km walk from the main street. The 'incredible' *Crown Hotel*, down the main street towards the river, has also been recommended as has the *Hotel Greenlands*, behind the bus stand on the way to the Suru View. Food in Kargil is rather expensive but the *Light Restaurant* on the main road has good food.

Shergol

Between Kargil and Shergol you cross the dividing line between the Moslem and Buddhist areas. The small village of Shergol has a tiny gompa perched halfway up the eastern slope of the mountain.

Mulbekh

There are two gompas on the hillside above the village of Mulbekh. As in other villages it is wise to enquire if the gompa is open before making the ascent. If not, somebody from the village may have keys and will accompany you to the gompas. Just beyond Mulbekh is a huge Chamba statue, an image of a future Buddha, cut into the rock face beside the road. It's one of the most interesting stops along the road to Leh. Those with time to spare can make a short trek from Mulbekh to the village of Gel.

Lamayuru

From Mulbekh the road crosses the 3718-metre Namika La, passes through the large military encampment of Bodh Kharbu and then crosses the 4094-metre Fatu La, the highest pass on the route. Lamayuru is the first of the typical Ladakhi gompas perched on a hilltop with its village at the foot of the hill. In its heyday the gompa had five buildings and as many as 400 monks but today there is only one building, tended by 20 or 30 monks.

Rizong

On beyond Khalsi, and a few km off the road, is the nunnery of Julichen and the monastery of Rizong. If you stay here overnight men must stay in the monastery, women in the nunnery.

Alchi

Just before Saspul this gompa is unusual in that it is built on lowland, not perched on a hilltop. It is noted for its massive Buddha statues and lavish woodcarvings and artwork. There are many *chortens* around the village. There's a hotel here, principally set up for ARTOU groups but with basic rooms available from Rs 20 and small dorm. There's also a pleasant little hotel in Saspul, it makes a good base for visiting Rizong, Alchi and Lekir.

Lekir & Basgo

Shortly after Saspul a steep road turns off to the Lekir Gompa which also has a monastery school. Closer to Leh there is a badly damaged fort at Basgo. Basgo Gompa has interesting Buddha figures but its wall paintings have suffered much water damage.

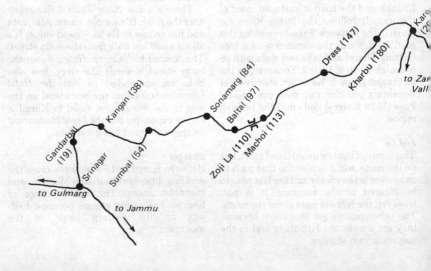

LEH (population 8500)

Centuries ago this was an important stop on the old caravan silk route from China. Today it's merely a military base and tourist centre, but wandering the winding back streets of town is still fascinating. It's situated about 10 km north-east of the Indus in a fertile side valley.

Information & Orientation

Leh is small enough to make finding your way round very easy. There's one main street with the Leh Palace rising up right at the end of it. The bus station and jeep halt is on the airport side of the town. The airport, with it's steeply sloping runway, is several km out of town near the Spitok Gompa. The Tourist Office is in the Dak Bungalow and Indian Airlines is right next door.

Leh Palace

Looking for all the world like a mini-version of the Potala in Lhasa, Tibet, the palace was also built in the 16th century. It is now deserted and badly damaged, a legacy of Ladakh's wars with Kashmir in the last century, the main reason for

making the climb up to the palace is for the superb views from the roof. The Zanskar mountains, across the Indus River, look close enough to touch. The palace is still the property of the Ladakhi royal family, although they now reside at nearby Stok. Try to get a monk to unlock the preserved, but now unused, central prayer room – dusty, spooky, with huge faces looming out of the dark. It's open 6 to 9 am and after 5 pm.

Leh Gompa

High above the palace and also over-looking the ruins of the older palace the Red Gompa was built in 1430. It contains a fine three-storey high seated Buddha image. It's open 7 to 9 am and 5 to 7 pm. The gompa above is in a very ruined condition but the views down on Leh are superb.

Sankar Gompa

It's an easy stroll to the Sankar Gompa, a couple of km up the valley from the town centre. This interesting little gompa is only open from 6 to 8 am and 6 to 7 pm but it has electric lighting so an evening visit is

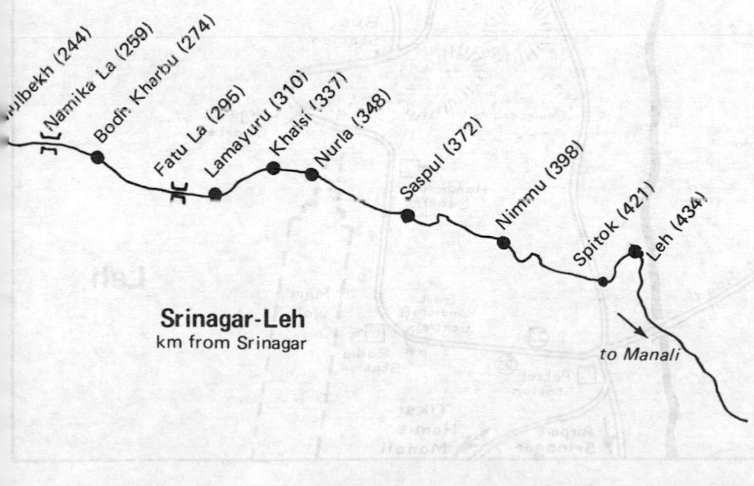

Srinagar-Leh
km from Srinagar

...lbekh (244) · Namika La (259) · Bodh. Kharbu (274) · Fatu La (295) · Lamayuru (310) · Khalsi (337) · Nurla (348) · Saspul (372) · Nimmu (398) · Spitok (421) · Leh (434)

to Manali

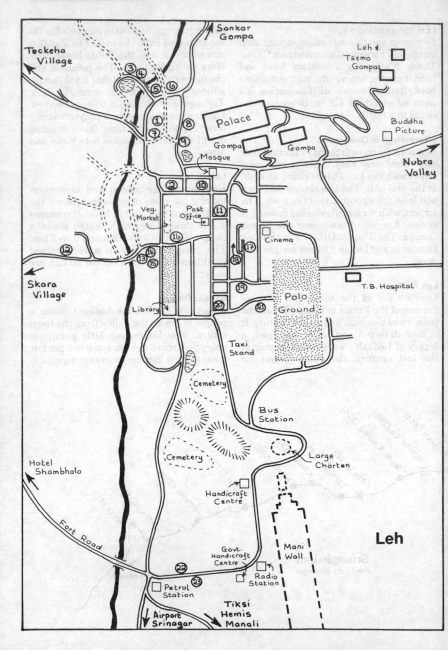

Leh

1	Police	13	Palace View Guest House
2	State Bank	14	Dreamland Hotel & Restaurant
3	Hotel Glacier View	15	Hotel Khangir & Restaurant
4	Hotel Karakoram	16	Indian Airlines
5	Hotel Shangrila	17	Apsara Guest House
6	Himalayan Hotel	18	Moonland Guest House
7	Khan Lodge	19	New Gay Time Restaurant
8	Hotel Khar Dungla	20	Barmar Restaurant
9	Ali Shah's Postcards	21	Palace View (Kidar) Hotel
10	Hilltop & Mumtaz Restaurants	22	Tibet Hotel
11	Antelope Guest House	23	Leh Motel
12	Hotel La Ri Mo		

worthwhile. Upstairs there is an impressive representation of Avalokitesvara complete with 1000 arms and 1000 heads. There is now a Rs 10 entry fee here.

Places to Stay
There are an amazing number of hotels and guest houses in Ladakh, many of which only open during the tourist season. Prices are very variable – soaring in the peak season, plummeting at other times. The cheaper guest houses are generally just rooms rented out in private homes.

Leh's top bracket hotels generally quote rates inclusive of all meals – frankly Leh is rather short of restaurants. They include the *Shambala Hotel*, some distance out of town, the *Kang-Lha-Chhen* and the *Lha-Ri-Mo*. Rooms range from Rs 350.

In the middle category the *Khangri Hotel* is close to the Tourist Office and uncomfortably close to the diesel electricity generator for Leh – which fortunately shuts down at 11 pm. Rooms cost from Rs 100, as at the side-by-side *Glacier View* and *Karakorum*, both of which have pleasant gardens, an attraction shared by many of Leh's hotels. The *Hotel Yak Tail* is in this same category. Moving down towards Rs 50 the *Dreamland* is very popular and close to the centre. The new *Kahyull Hotel* has been recommended as good value – clean, attached bathrooms and well away from the generator noise. Rooms at Rs 40/60 in season.

Down in the rock bottom bracket doubles can be found under Rs 30 (less off-season) and dorm beds at Rs 5. Bed bugs are sometimes provided at no extra cost, so take care. The *Palace View Kidar Hotel*, close to the polo ground is a very popular rock bottom choice as is the *New Antelope Guest House* on the main street. Others include the *Old Ladakh Guest House* or the *Moonland Guest House*. There are many, many cheapies.

Places to Eat
Dreamland Restaurant, near the Tourist Office, Indian Airlines office and Dreamland Hotel is the best in town. Clean, friendly and reasonably priced – most dishes around Rs 10. Tibetan kothay, various chow meins and other noodle dishes top the bill (a pleasant change from rice and more rice). Nice jasmine tea too and a terrific place for breakfast. *Chopsticks* is a good alternative to the Dreamland or the *Om Restaurant*.

The *Khangri Restaurant*, almost next door, is good, but not as good or as cheap. Good tea, not so good snacks at the *Mini Cafe* by Indian Airlines. Some of the other small cafes around town are remarkably insanitary looking – a sure ticket to stomach troubles. For breakfast buy freshly baked central Asian style bread from the little bakeries in the back streets by the mosque. Ideal with honey from Srinagar.

Try the locally made beer, chang, while

you're in Ladakh and at least sample the butter tea. The variety of locally grown vegetables and fruit in Leh is limited. It's worth bringing a few menu brighteners, like bars of chocolate or cans of apple juice, from Srinagar.

Getting There
Air Indian Airlines only started flying to Leh in 1979 but now there are flights from both Srinagar (Rs 269) and Chandigarh (Rs 387). The flight from Srinagar is very short (half an hour) and extremely spectacular (you cross right over the Himalaya), but also very problematic. Flights can only be made into Leh in the morning and only when weather conditions are good. If it's possible the conditions could deteriorate after arrival and the aircraft could not leave, the flight will be cancelled. End result is a lot of cancellations, a lot of flights that actually leave Srinagar but are not able to land at Leh (since conditions can change very rapidly) and a lot of frustrated passengers. At difficult times of the year, such as when the season is about to start but the road is still closed, the flights can be heavily overbooked. The answer is to book well ahead but be prepared for disappointment. If you're unable to get on a flight from Srinagar ask your houseboat owner for help – every Kashmiri has 'connections'.

Road The road should be open from the beginning of June through to October but in practice the opening date can be variable – sometimes mid-May, sometimes mid-June. The trip takes two days, about 12 hours travel on each day. The overnight halt is made at Kargil. There are A class buses for Rs 78 and B class buses for Rs 58. Jeeps, which take up to six passengers, will cost something like Rs 1500 but will permit additional stops and diversions along the interesting route. A complication on the return trip to Srinagar is that you may not be able to buy tickets until the evening before departure, because buses may not turn up from Srinagar. Thus you can't be certain you will be leaving until the last moment.

Before the road officially opens it is possible to cross the Zoji La on foot or by pony, although if there is still a lot of snow the Beacon Patrol will only let you through if you're properly equipped. The pass is generally physically cleared of snow before the road is repaired and ready for vehicles and there is generally transport running along the roads on both sides of the pass before the through buses start to operate. Locals cross the pass regularly on foot in these pre-season times so it is easy to tag along with a larger group or find a guide. But it can be hard work!

Getting Around
There's a bus service to Leh airport from the Indian Airlines office for Rs 2. A jeep would cost Rs 25. There is a reasonably extensive bus network around Leh, although the buses are decidedly ramshackle. Jeeps can also be hired – count on around Rs 3 or 4 per km or Rs 250 to 300 for a day. Between a half dozen people this can be a reasonable way of getting to most of the gompas around Leh. A jeep is pretty crowded with six people, four is a more reasonable number. It's also possible to hitch around Leh or you can walk from gompa to gompa.

Some bus costs from Leh include: *Kargil* – Rs 20 to 22, daily in summer, Sunday and Thursday in winter. *Choglamsar & Bridge* – 70p, fairly frequently each day. *Hemis* – there is now a daily bus leaving at 10 am and returning at 2 pm. This gives you about two hours to explore the gompa, many people prefer to stay overnight. Each way cost is Rs 7. *Spitok* Rs 1, twice daily. *Shey* – Rs 1.15, three times daily. The bus continues on to *Tikse* (Rs 1.50 from Leh) which is only a couple of km further out, you could easily bus to Shey, walk on to Tikse then bus back to Leh – or vice versa. Note that Shey Gompa is only open (officially) from 7 to 9 am. *Stok* – twice daily. *Phyang* (Fiang) – Rs

2.75, daily. *Khalsi* – Rs 7, alternate days. *Matho* – Rs 2.55, daily. *Chochot* (other bank of the Indus, between Stok and Stakna) – Rs 2 daily. In season there may be bus tours around the gompas.

Things to Buy

After a number of greedy tourists spirited important antiquities out of Ladakh the government sensibly clamped down on the sale of important older items. You must be able to prove anything you buy is less than 100 years old. Baggage is checked on departure from Leh airport. Things you might buy include chang and tea vessels, cups and butter churns, knitted carpets with Tibetan motifs, Tibetan jewellery or, for just a few rupees, a simple prayerflag. Prices in Ladakh are generally quite high – you might find exactly the same Tibetan inspired item on sale at far lower prices in Kashmir, Dharamsala or Nepal.

AROUND LEH

Spitok Gompa

On a hilltop above the Indus and beside the end of the airport runway, the Spitok Gompa is 10 km from Leh. The temple (Gonkhang) is about a thousand years old and there are fine views over the Indus from the gompa. Entry fee to the gompa is Rs 10.

Phyang

About 16 km from Leh, on the road back towards Srinagar, the gompa has 50 monks and the entry fee is Rs 10. There is an interesting little village below the gompa.

Beacon Highway

You are not allowed to visit the Nubra Valley without special permission but, if you could, it would involve taking what is probably the highest road in the world. It crosses a pass at 5606 metres! The road is only open in September and October – it takes the whole summer for the snow and ice to melt for that brief time.

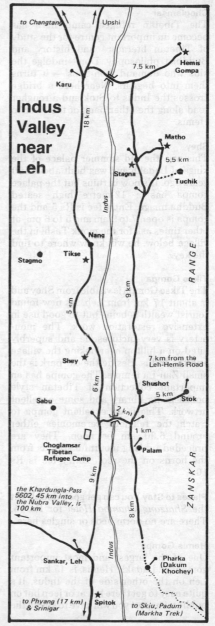

Indus Valley near Leh

to Changtang

Upshi

Hemis Gompa

7.5 km

Karu

18 km

Matho

5.5 km

Stagna

Tuchik

Indus

Nang

Stagmo

Tikse

RANGE

9 km

5 km

Shey

7 km from the Leh-Hemis Road

Sabu

6 km

Shushot

5 km

Stok

2 km

Choglamsar Tibetan Refugee Camp

1 km

Palam

9 km

the Khardungla-Pass 5602, 45 km into the Nubra Valley, is 100 km

ZANSKAR

8 km

Sankar, Leh

Indus

Pharka (Dakum Khochey)

to Phyang (17 km) & Srinagar

Spitok

to Skiu, Padum (Markha Trek)

Choglamsar

The Tibetan refugee camp here has become an important centre for the study of Tibetan literature and history and Buddhist philosophy. Don't indulge the kids who demand 'bon-bons' – it turns them into beggars. Near here a bridge crosses the Indus to Stok and a rougher road along the other bank of the river to Hemis.

Shey

This was the old summer palace of the kings of Ladakh and was built about 550 years ago. It's now in ruins but the palace gompa has a 12-metre high seated Buddha image. Entry fee is Rs 5 and the gompa is open 7 to 9 am and 5 to 6 pm, at other times ask for the monk Tashi in the village below, he will know where to find the key.

Tikse Gompa

The Tikse Gompa is visible from Shey and is about 17 km from Leh. Its new-found tourist wealth is being put to good use in extensive restoration work. The monastery is very picturesque and superbly sited on a hilltop overlooking the village and the Indus. Beside the car park is the small Zan-La temple. The gompa has an important collection of Tibetan style books in its library and some excellent artwork. This is an excellent gompa to watch the religious ceremonies either around 6.30 am or noon. They are preceded by long mournful sounds from the horns on the roof. Entry fee is Rs 10.

Places to Stay You can get good doubles at the *Shalzang Chamba Hotel* for Rs 15. There are no dorm beds or singles here.

Hemis Gompa

One of the largest and most important gompas in Ladakh, Hemis, is 45 km from Leh on the other side of the Indus. It's quite easy to get there by car or jeep but on public transport you will have to spend the night at the monastery as it is not possible to bus out there, walk the six km up from the river to the gompa, see it, walk back down and get back on one day. The Hemis Gompa is famous for its Hemis Festival, which usually falls in the second half of June or in early July. It is not only one of the largest and most spectacular of the gompa festivals, it is also virtually the only one which takes place in the summer tourist season. It is possible the business-minded monks of other gompas may switch their festivals to more lucrative dates however. The festival takes two days and features elaborate mask dances and crowds of eager spectators.

The gompa has an excellent library, particularly well preserved wall paintings and good Buddha figures. Entry is Rs 10. If instead of turning right at Karu to climb up to Hemis you had turned left you would have reached the Chemre Gompa, five km off the road and the Trak Tok Gompa, 10 km further on. Both lie in the restricted zone but tourists are allowed to visit these two gompas.

Places to Stay There's a *Tourist Hotel* with rather dirty dorm beds for Rs 10. You'll find cheaper and much cleaner rooms in local homes. The *Parachute Restaurant*, next to the bus stand, has good food.

Matho Gompa

The left bank road on the Indus is not in as good condition as the more used right bank road, but you can return from Hemis on this road and there are several interesting places to visit. Matho is five km from Stagna, in a side valley. There is an important festival held where the monks are possessed by spirits and go into a trance. Stagna, on the road, has a gompa too.

Stok Palace

Close to the Choglamsar bridge a road turns off the left bank road to the palace of Stok. The last king of Ladakh died in 1974 but his widow, the Rani of Stok, still lives in this 200-year-old palace. It is expected that her eldest son will become king when he reaches an appropriately auspicious age. You can only enter the museum here, which costs Rs 20.

Pharka Gompa

This small cave gompa is almost directly opposite the Spitok Gompa on the Stok side of the Indus. You can reach it by crossing the Choglamsar bridge but the last few km must be made on foot.

ZANSKAR

The long narrow Zanskar valley is even more recently opened than Ladakh. A jeep road is gradually being extended down the valley from Kargil towards Padum, the capital, and this will eventually open Zanskar up to more outside influence. Meanwhile it remains an area for trekkers and some of the treks are definitely hard going. You can make a number of interesting treks either down the valley or out of it to Ladakh, Kashmir or to Himachal Pradesh.

Padum

The 'capital' of Zanskar has a population of less than a thousand, of whom about 300 are Sunnite Moslems. There are a few shops in Padum and a tourist office! There are a number of interesting shorter treks that can be made from Padum. Accommodation in Padum can usually be arranged in private houses for Rs 10 to Rs 20 per person.

Zangla & Karsha Gompa

This is an interesting four-day trek around Padum. The first day takes you to Thonde on the riverbank with a monastery high above it. Since horses cannot cross the rope bridge from Padum this is the first place on this side of the river where they can be hired for treks further afield to places like Lamayuru. The second day takes you from Thonde to Zangla where the king of Zanskar has his castle. On day three you backtrack towards Thonde,

cross the river and continue to Karsha, the most important gompa in Zanskar. On the final day you can cross the river directly by ferry or continue down to the wooden Tungri Bridge and double back to Padum.

Tugri & Zongkhul Gompa

This four-day trek around Padum takes you to the Sani and Zongkhul Gompa by following the route up towards the Muni La then cutting across to the base of the Umasi La.

TREKKING IN LADAKH & ZANSKAR

Trekking in Ladakh and Zanskar can be hard going and you should be equipped for every eventuality. Srinagar is the best place to purchase stores but you will not find trekking gear like you do in Kathmandu in Nepal. Treks into Zanskar are principally down the valley from the north (from Kargil) or up the valley from the south (from Manali in Himachal Pradesh).

Drass Sanku

This is a short three-day trek into the Suru Valley joining the Kargil-Padum road at Sanku. It's simply an alternative route to the road down from Kargil.

Kargil-Padum

The seven-day trek to Padum from Kargil on the Srinagar-Ladakh road can be shortened by four days if you can get a ride all the way from Kargil to the Pensi La. When the bridges are completed the route will be open from early June to late-October. The first day's travel is mainly on a surfaced road by bus as far as Sanku. Beyond Parkutse you pass close to Kun and Nun. The Rangdum Gompa is the first gompa reached in Zanskar, the road is still reasonably good to this point. Beyond the gompa you have to cross the 4401-metre Pensi La into Zanskar proper. On the last day's walk from Phe to Padum you cross the river and pass by the Sani Gompa, one of the most important in Zanskar.

Day 1	Kargil-Namsuru
Day 2	Namsuru-Pannikar-Parkutse
Day 3	Parkutse-Parkachik-Yuldo-Rangdum Gompa
Day 4	Rangdum Gompa-Pensi La
Day 5	Pensi La-Abran
Day 6	Abran-Phe
Day 7	Phe-Padum

Manali-Padum

This 10-day trek can be very hard going at its southern end. You first have to bus across the Rothang Pass from Manali to Keylong and on to Darcha where the trek starts. On the second day you cross the Baralacha La, a double pass where even the lower side is higher than Europe's highest mountain and twice the height of Australia's highest. At the end of Day 6 you can continue north to Padum or turn back south and cross the Shingo La back to Darcha in two days. You are not, however, allowed to take the alternative route if you're heading north. On Day 7 you make a detour to the spectacular Phuctal Gompa. Continuing all the way north to Kargil on this route would take, with a few days for shorter treks around Padum, something like 20 days.

Day 1	Darcha-Mane Bar
Day 2	Mane Bar-Sarai Kilang
Day 3	Sarai Kilang-Debni
Day 4	Debni-Chumik Marpo
Day 5	Chumik Marpo-Shingsan
Day 6	Shingsan-Kargiakh
Day 7	Purni-Phuctal Gompa
Day 8	Phuctal Gompa-Katge Lato
Day 9	Katge Lato-Reru
Day 10	Reru-Padum

Padum-Lamayuru

There are a number of alternatives for this trek from Padum into Ladakh, intersecting the road at Lamayuru, about halfway from Kargil to Leh. The trek starts out from Padum to Thonde, as on the short trek to the Zangla and Karsha gompas. On Day 3 the difficult ascent to the 4500-metre Shingo La pass has to be made but on Day 4 the Nerag La, at 4900 metres, is

even more difficult and a local guide is a necessity. Photosar is a small village from where it is only two days' walk to Lamayuru. There is an alternative route, taking a day longer, from Photosar. The alternative route from Padum starts out on the opposite side of the Zanskar Rivers and takes you to the Lingshot Gompa before joining up with the first route at Day 5.

Day 1	Padum-Thonde
Day 2	Thonde-Honia
Day 3	Honia-Shingo La-Kharmapu
Day 4	Kharmapu-Nerag La
Day 5	Nerag La-Nerag
Day 6	Nerag-Yulching-Singi La-Photosar
Day 7	Photosar-Shirshi La-Hanupatta
Day 8	Hanupatta-Wanla-Shill-Prikiti La-Lamayuru

or

Day 1	Padum-Pishu
Day 2-4	Pishu-Lingshot Gompa
Day 5	Lingshot Gompa-Yulching

Padum-Kishtwar

This trek into the southern part of Kashmir is not especially difficult although it crosses the 5234 metre Umasi La, which can only be done in fine weather. You cannot use horses on this route but must take porters. On the second day you reach the Zongkhul Gompa which can also be visited on a short trek from Padum. Day 3 is a long climb and long descent over the snow covered Umasi La. On Day 4 your Zanskari porters will not continue further and you must hire local porters or a pony. The last few days are hard work with many ascents and descents but the road from Kishtwar, already extending to Galar, is gradually being lengthened.

Day 1	Padum-Ating
Day 2	Ating-Ratrat
Day 3	Ratrat-Umasi La-Bhuswas
Day 4	Bhuswas-Matsel
Day 5	Matsel-Atholi
Day 6	Atholi-Shasho
Day 7	Shasho-Galar-Kishtwar

Other Treks
Padum-Nimmu follows the Padum-Lamayuru route for most of its length then turns off eastwards to join the Srinagar-Leh road at Nimmu. Padum-Leh by the Markha Valley is a hard but rewarding trek, which goes via Zangla before turning east over the Charcha La and the Ruberung La to the Markha Gompa, and

eventually reaching Hemis near Leh. This trek can only be made in late August. Earlier than that the rivers which must be crossed are too high from melting snow and after that it is too cold. You can trek from Padum to the Phuctal Gompa by an alternative route to that described in Padum-Manali, but the trail is poor and very little used.

Uttar Pradesh

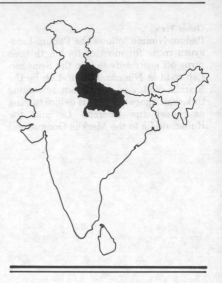

Population: 98 million
Area: 294,413 square km
Capital: Lucknow
Main Language: Hindi

In terms of population this is the largest state in India. In terms of variety, and of problems, it's also India larger than life. This is one of the great historical and religious centres of India. The Ganges River, which forms the backbone of Uttar Pradesh, is the holy river of Hinduism and there are a number of towns along the river of great importance for pilgrimages – in particular Rishikesh and Hardwar, where the river emerges from the Himalaya and starts across the plains, and Varanasi, the most holy city of all. Buddhism also has its great shrine in the state for it was at Sarnath, just outside Varanasi, that the Buddha first preached his message of the middle way.

Historically the state has also been a centre stage for great events. Over two thousand years ago this was a part of Ashoka's great Buddhist empire. More recently it was part of the Moghul Empire, and for some years Agra was its capital. Today, of course, Agra is famed for that most prfect of Moghul masterpieces, the Taj Mahal. More recently still it was in Uttar Pradesh that the Mutiny broke out in 1857 (at Meerut) and some of its most dramatic (Lucknow) and unfortunate (Kanpur) events took place here. More recently Uttar Pradesh has produced four of five Prime Ministers since independence in 1947 – Nehru, Indira Gandhi, Lal Bahadur Shastri and Charan Singh were all from UP.

Geographically and socially the state also has great variations. Most of it consists of the great Ganges plain, an area of awesome flatness which suffers great floods during the monsoon. The people of this region are predominantly backward farming peasants who scratch a bare existence from the overcrowded land. Yet the north-west corner of the state is a part of the soaring Himalayas with excellent treks, beautiful scenery and even India's highest mountain. It's a state of strong contrasts.

MATHURA (population 150,000)
On the Delhi-Agra road, 57 km north of Agra, Mathura is a site of great age. According to legends this is the place where Lord Krishna was born 3500 years ago. Today Mathura is an important pilgrimage place for followers of this popular incarnation of Vishnu. There are many places in and around Mathura with connections with the Krishna legend.

Mathura, or Muttra as it has also been known, is mentioned by Ptolemy and by the Chinese visitors Fa Hian (in India 401-410 AD) and the later Hiuen Tsang (634 AD). By that time the 20 Buddhist monasteries with 3000 monks, for this was a great Buddhist centre, had dropped to only 2000. By the time Mahmud of Ghazni arrived on his rape, burn, pillage trip from

Afghanistan in 1017 Buddhism had totally disappeared. Sikandar Lodi did further damage to the shrines of Mathura in 1500, but the town rebounded during the tolerant reigns of Akbar and Jehangir, only for fanatical Aurangzeb to do another demolition job. He destroyed the Kesava Deo temple, which had been built on the site of one of the most important Buddhist monasteries, and built a mosque in its place.

Things to See

The Jami Masjid was built by Aurangzeb's governor, Abd-in-Nabir Khan, in 1661 on the site of the Kesava Deo temple. This is the place where Lord Krishna is supposed to have been born in prison. At one time the foundations of the old temple were still visible behind the mosque but they have now been covered over with modern buildings. The modern Kesava temple has been rebuilt behind

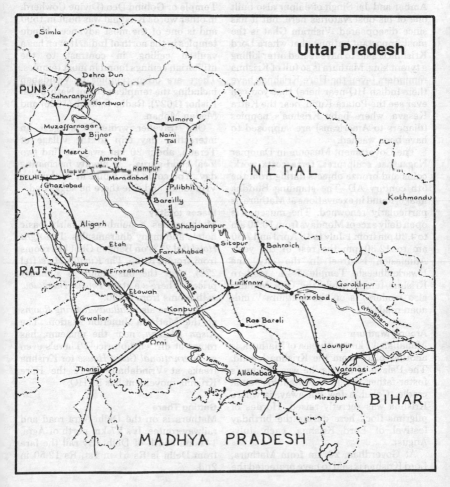

the Katra.

The 300-metre wide Yamuna River, which flows through Mathura, is lined with bathing ghats and is full of large turtles. On the banks of the river the Sati Burj is a four-storey tower built in 1570 to commemorate the sati of the builder's mother. Aurangzeb knocked down the upper storeys which have been rebuilt. The ruined Kans Qila fort on the riverbank was built by Raja Man Singh of Amber and Jai Singh of Jaipur also built one of his observatories here, but it has since disappeared. Vishram Ghat is the most important bathing ghat where Lord Krishna is said to have rested after killing a tyrant king. Mathura is so full of Krishna reminders (even the Hare Krishnas have their Indian HQ near here) that you can ever see the Potara-Kund, near the Katra Kesava, where baby Krishna's nappies (diapers to Americans) are supposed to have been washed.

The Government Museum in Dampier Nagar has sculptures, terra cotta work, coins and bronze objects dating from the 5th century AD. The standing Buddha image, found in excavations at Mathura, is particularly renowned. The museum is open daily except Mondays from 10.30 am to 4.30 pm from 1 July to 15 April and 7.30 am to 12.30 pm the rest of the year. Admission is free. In the city, the Dwarkadheesh Temple is a modern Krishna temple while the Gita Mandir, also modern, is on the Mathura-Vrindaban road.

Around Mathura

Mahaban, 11 km south-east of Mathura, is another place from the Krishna legend. The Palace of Nanda, he was Krishna's foster-father, is said to contain his actual cradle. Gokul, a few km away, is where Krishna was secretly raised. Hordes of pilgrims flock here during the birthday festival of Lord Krishna, each July-August.

At Goverdhan, 26 km from Mathura, Lord Krishna is said to have protected the inhabitants from Indra's wrath, in the form of rain, by holding the hilltops over them for seven days, neatly balanced on the top of his finger. Krishna's favourite gopi or milkmaid is said to have come from Barsana, 47 km from Mathura.

Vrindaban, 10 km north of Mathura, is the place where Krishna sported with his milkmaids and even stole their clothes while they were bathing in the river. No wonder he's so popular. The large Red Temple or Gobind Deo (Divine Cowherd, in other words Krishna) was built in 1590 and is one of the most advanced Hindu temples in the north of India. It even has a vaulted ceiling, in contrast to the utilitarian ceilings found in most temples. There are other temples in Vrindaban including the temples of Gopi Nath, Jugal Kishor (1027), Radha Ballabh (1626) and Madan Mohan.

One traveller wrote to suggest an interesting day trip to the village of Terauli, about 20 km away, to find two local child-gurus – 'a bloody fascinating day'. You could hire a bike in Mathura or Vrindaban and ride there he suggested.

Places to Stay

Mathura has a number of fairly basic hotels and many dharamsalas. The *Agra Hotel* (tel 213) on Bengali Ghat has rooms from around Rs 25. The *Kwality Hotel* (tel 272), near the bus stand, is similarly priced. There's a state *Tourist Bungalow* with rooms from Rs 30.

There are also *Railway Retiring Rooms* at the Mathura Junction station. The *Kisan Bhavan*, near the museum, has rooms at dirt cheap prices. There's even an *International Guest House* for Krishna freaks at Vrindaban, where the Hare Krishna movement has its HQ.

Getting There

Mathura is on the Delhi-Agra road and railway routes. It's 57 km north of Agra, 141 km south of Delhi. By rail the fare from Delhi is Rs 51 in 1st, Rs 12.50 in 2nd.

AGRA (population 700,000)

At the time of the Moghuls, in the 16th and 17th centuries, Agra was the capital of India and its superb monuments date from that era. In particular Agra has its magnificent fort and the building which many people have visited India solely to see – the Taj Mahal. Situated on the banks of the Yamuna River, with its crowded alleys and its predatory rickshaw riders, Agra is much like any other north Indian city, once you're away from these imposing reminders of Moghul splendour. It's quite possible to day-trip to Agra from Delhi and there's an excellent train service making this eminently practicable. Actually Agra is worth more than a day, particularly if you also intend to visit, as you certainly should, the deserted city of Fatehur Sikri. In any case the Taj deserves more than a single visit if you're going to appreciate how its appearance changes under different lights.

Agra became the capital of Sikandar Lodi in 1501 but it soon passed on to the Moghuls, and both Babur and Humayun made some early Moghul constructions here. It was under Akbar that Agra first aspired to its heights of magnificence. From 1570 to 1585 Akbar ruled from nearby Fatehpur Sikri. When he abandoned that city he moved to Lahore (now in Pakistan) but returned to Agra in 1599 and remained there until his death in 1605. Jehangir, with his passion for Kashmir, did not spend a great deal of time at Agra, but Shah Jahan is the name inevitably connected with Agra. He built the Jami Masjid, most of the palace buildings inside the Agra Fort and, of course, the Taj Mahal. Between 1638 and 1650, however, he built the Red Fort and Jami Masjid in Delhi and would probably have moved the capital there had he not been deposed and imprisoned by his son, Aurangzeb, in 1658. Aurangzeb did transfer the capital there.

In 1761 Agra fell to the Jats who did much damage to the city and its monuments, even going so far as to pillage the Taj Mahal. In turn it was taken by the Marathas in 1770 and passed through several more changes before the British took control in 1803. There was much fighting around the fort during the Mutiny in 1857.

Information & Orientation

Agra is situated on the west bank of the Yamuna River, 204 km south of Delhi. The old part of the town is north of the fort where the Kinari Bazaar, the main market place, is located in a narrow street. The cantonment area to the south is the modern part of town, known as Sadar Bazaar. Here you will find the Government of India Tourist Office (tel 72377) at 191 The Mall. The GPO and poste restante is also on The Mall and in this area you will find handicraft shops, book stores, dry cleaners, restaurants and many moderately priced hotels. De-luxe buses for Delhi and Jaipur also operate from here.

There are also some lower priced hotels and the Tourist Bungalow near the Raja Mandi railway station, but this area is rather inconveniently located. It's far from the Taj and the main hotel and restaurant area. The 'tourist class' hotels are mainly in the spacious areas of Taj Ganj, south of the Taj itself. Immediately south of the Taj there is a tightly packed area of narrow alleys where you can also find some popular rock-bottom hotels. It's a pleasant walk along the riverside between the Taj and the Red Fort.

Agra's main railway station is Agra Cantonment and it is here that trains from New Delhi arrive. The main bus station for cities in Rajasthan and for Fatehpur Sikri is Idgah. The Fort Bus Station has buses going to Mathura. Indian Airlines (tel 73434) is in the Hotel Clarks Shiraz. Agra airport is seven km out of town.

Taj Mahal

If there's a building which evokes a country – like the Eiffel Tower does for France, the Sydney Opera House for Australia – then it has to be the Taj Mahal for India. So much so that the Indian tourist office has centred an advertising capaign around the theme that there's more to India than just the Taj.

This most famous Moghul monument was constructed by the Emperor Shah Jahan in memory of his wife Mumtaz Mahal, the 'lady of the Taj'. It has been described as the most extravagant monument ever built for love for the emperor was heartbroken when Mumtaz, to whom he had been married for 17 years, died in 1629, in childbirth, after producing 14 children.

Construction of the Taj commenced in 1632 and was not completed until 1653. Workers were recruited not only from all over India but also from Central Asia and in total 20,000 people worked on the building. Experts were even brought from as far away as Europe – the Frenchman Austin of Bordeaux and the Italian Veroneo of Venice had a hand in its decoration. The main architect was Isa Khan who came from Shiraz in Iran.

The most unusual story about the Taj is that there might well have been two of them. Shah Jahan, it is said, had intended

to build a second Taj as his own tomb and this second Taj would have been in black marble, a negative image of the white Taj of Mumtaz Mahal. Before he could embark on this second masterpiece Aurangzeb deposed his father. Shah Jahan spent the rest of his life in the Agra Fort, looking out along the river to the final resting place of his favourite wife.

The Taj Mahal stands on a raised marble platform with tall white minarets at each corner of the platform. They are just for decoration, nobody is called to prayer from them. The central structure has four smaller domes surrounding the huge, bulbous, central dome. The tombs of Mumtaz Mahal and Shah Jahan are in a basement room, above them in the main chamber are false tombs, a common practice in Indian mausoleums of this type. Light is admitted into the central chamber by finely cut marble screens. The echo in this high chamber, under the soaring marble dome is superb and there is always somebody there to demonstate it.

Although the Taj is amazingly graceful from almost any angle, it's the close up

detail which is really astounding. Semi-precious stones are inlaid into the marble in beautiful patterns and with superb craftsmanship in a process known as *pietra dura*. The precision and care which went into the Taj Mahal's design and construction is just as impressive whether you view it from across the river or from arm's length.

The building, which stands right beside the Yamuna River, is in a large and formally laid out garden. Twin red sandstone mosques frame the building when viewed from the river. You enter the Taj grounds through a high red sandstone gateway inscribed with verses from the Koran in Arabic. Paths lead to the Taj, divided by a long watercourse in which the Taj would be beautifully reflected if there was water in it more often! As is so often repeated the Taj is worth more than a single visit. It's one building under the light of dawn, another at sunset. Still another under moonlight. Full moons bring people flocking to Agra in their thousands. Admission to the Taj costs Rs 2 except on Fridays when it is free. Catch is that on Fridays it can be impossibly crowded and noisy, not very conducive to calm enjoyment of this most serene of buildings. Opening hours are from sunrise to 10 pm but on full moon nights and the four nights around the full moon it stays open until midnight. A bus from Sadar to the Taj is about Rs 0.50.

A final sad note about the Taj – scientists fear that after centuries of undiminished glory the modern world may finally be shortening its life. Industrial pollution, particularly a proposed chemical plant, could cause irreparable damage to the marble before the turn of the century. Not that man hasn't damaged it in the past – in 1764 silver doors at the entrance were ripped off and carted away and raiders have also made off with the gold sheets that once lined the sub-terranean vault.

Agra Fort

Construction of the massive Agra Fort commenced with the Emperor Akbar in 1565 and additions were made right through to the time of his grandson, Shah Jahan. While in Akbar's time the fort was principally a military structure by the time of Shah Jahan the emphasis had shifted and the fort had become partially a palace. A visit to the fort is an Agra 'must' since so many of the events which led to the construction of the Taj took place here. Shah Jahan, the Taj's builder, was later imprisoned in the fort by his own son and died there in a room from which he could see his masterpiece.

There are many fascinating buildings inside the massive 20 metre walls which

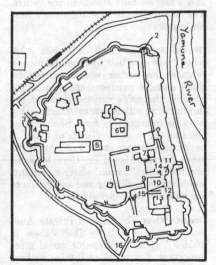

AGRA FORT

1 Jami Masjid	9 Mina Mosque
2 Northern Tower	10 Grape Garden
3 Delhi Gate	11 Octagonal Tower
4 Elephant Gate	12 Khas Mahal
5 Ladies' Bazaar	13 Jehangir's Palace
6 Moti Masjid	14 Diwan-i-Khas
7 Nagina Masjid	15 Shish Mahal
8 Diwan-i-Am	16 Amar Singh's Gate

stretch for 2.5 km, surrounded by a moat over 10 metres wide. The fort is on the banks of the Yamuna River and only the Amar Singh Gate to the south is open. Inside the fort it is really a city within the city. The fort is open from sunrise to sunset and admission is Rs 2 except on Fridays when it is free. There's an entertaining sound & light show at the fort. Some of the important buildings within the fort include:

Moti Masjid The 'Pearl Mosque' was built by Shah Jahan between 1646 and 1653. The marble mosque is considered to be perfectly proportioned and a Persian inscription inside the building compares it to a perfect pearl. The mosque's courtyard is surrounded by arcaded cloisters and a marble tank stands in the centre. The mosque has been shut for some time for 'repairs'.

Diwan-i-Am The 'Hall of Public Audiences' was also buit by Shah Jahan and replaces an earlier wooden structure. Shah Jahan's predecessors also had a hand in the hall's construction but the throne room, with its typical inlaid marble work, is indisputably from Shah Jahan. Here he sat to meet officials or listen to petitioners. Beside the Diwan-i-Am is the small Nagina Masjid or 'Gem Mosque' and the 'ladies' bazaar' where merchants would come to display and sell goods to the ladies of the Moghul court.

Diwan-i-Khas The 'Hall of Private Audiences' as also built by Shah Jahan, in 1636-37. Here the emperor would meet important dignitaries or foreign ambassadors. The hall consists of two rooms, connected by three arches. The famous 'peacock throne' was kept here before being moved to Delhi by Aurangzeb. It was later carried off to Iran and is now in Tehran.

Octagonal Tower The Musamman Burj or Octagonal Tower stands close to the Diwan-i-Khas and the small, private Mina Masjid. Also known as the Saman Burj, this tower was built by Shah Jahan for Mumtaz Mahal and is another of his finely designed and executed buildings. It was here, with its views along the Yamuna to the Taj, that Shah Jahan died in 1666, after seven year's imprisonment. Unfortunately the tower has been much damaged over the years.

Jehangir's Palace Akbar is believed to have built this palace for his son, it is the largest private residence in the fort. This was one of the first constructions within the fort where the emphasis started to change from purely military to the fort's later role as a luxurious palace. It is also interesting for its blend of Hindu and central Asian architectural styles – a contrast to the unique Moghul style which had developed by the time of Shah Jahan.

Other Shah Jahan's Khas Mahal is a beautiful white marble structure used as a private palace. The rooms underneath it were intended as a cool retreat in the summer heat. The Shish Mahal or 'Mirror Palace' was supposed to have been the harem dressing room and its walls are inlaid with tiny mirrors. The Anguri Bagh or 'Grape Garden' probably never had any grapevines but was simply a small, formal Moghul garden. It stood in front of the Khas Mahal. The Delhi Gate and Hathi Pol or 'Elephant Gate' are now closed.

In front of the Jehangir Palace is the Hauz-i-Jehangri, a huge 'bath' carved out of a single block of stone – by whom and for what purpose is a subject of conjecture. The Amar Singh Gate takes its name from a Maharaja of Jodhpur who was killed by the gate, along with his followers, after a brawl in the Diwan-i-Am in 1644! Justice tended to be summary in those days, there is a shaft leading down to the river into which those who became unpopular with the Moghuls could be hurled without further to-do!

Itmad-ud-daulah

There are a number of interesting sights on the opposite bank of the Yamuna and north of the fort. You cross the river on a narrow two-level bridge carrying pedestrians, bicycles, rickshaws and bullock carts. The first place of interest is the Itmad-ud-daulah – the tomb of Mirza Ghiyas Beg. This Persian gentleman's beautiful daughter married the Emperor Jehangir and became known as Nur Jahan, the 'light of the world'. In turn her daughter was Mumtaz Mahal, the lady of the Taj. The tomb was constructed by Nur Jahan between 1622 and 1628 and is very similar to the tomb she also constructed for her husband, Jehangir, near Lahore in Pakistan.

The tomb is of particular interest since many of its design elements foreshadow the Taj, construction of which commenced only a few years later. The Itmad-ud-daulah was the first Moghul structure totally constructed of marble and the first to make extensive use of *pietra dura*, inlay work of marble which is so much a part of the Taj. The mausoleum is small and squat compared to the soaring Taj, but the smaller, more human scale somehow makes it more attractive, and the beautifully patterned surface of the tomb is superb. There are also extremely fine marble lattice-work passages admitting light to the interior. It's well worth a visit. The Itmad-ud-daulah is open sunrise to sunset and admission is Rs 2, free on Fridays.

China-ka-Rauza

The 'china tomb' is a km north of the Itmad-ud-daulah. The squat, square tomb, surmounted by a single huge dome, was constructed in his own life-time by Afzal Khan who died in Lahore in 1639. He was a high official in the court of Shah Jahan. The exterior was covered in brightly coloured enamelled tiles and the whole building clearly displayed its Persian influence. Today it is much decayed and neglected and the remaining tilework only hints at the building's former glory.

Ram Bagh

Laid out by the Emperor Babur, first of the Moghuls, in 1528 this is the earliest Moghul garden. It is said that Babur was temporarily buried here before being permanently interred at Kabul in Afghanistan. The Ram Bagh is two to three km further north of the China-ka-Rauza on the riverside and is open from sunrise to sunset, admission is free. It's rather overgrown and neglected.

Jami Masjid

Across the the railway tracks from the Delhi Gate of Agra Fort, the Jami Masjid was built by Shah Jahan in 1648. An inscription over the main gate indicates that it was built in the name of Jahanara, Shah Jahan's daughter, who was imprisoned with Shah Jahan by Aurangzeb. Large though it is, the mosque is not as impressive as Shah Jahan's Jami Masjid in Delhi.

Dayal Bagh Temple

In Dayal Bagh, 10 km north of Agra, the white marble temple of the Radah Soami Hindu sect is currently under construction. You can see *pietra dura* inlaid marble work actually being worked on. Dayal Bagh can be reachd by bus or bicycle.

Akbar's Mausoleum

At Sikandra, 10 km north of Agra, is the tomb of Akbar. The tomb is situated in the centre of a large garden and four identical red sandstone gates lead to the tomb complex. Akbar commenced the construction of his tomb himself but it was completed by his son, Jehangir, in 1613. The tomb is a combination of Moslem and Hindu architectural styles. The building, with three-storey minarets at each corner, is built of red sandstone with white marble polygonal patterns inlaid. Like Humayun's Tomb in New Delhi it is an

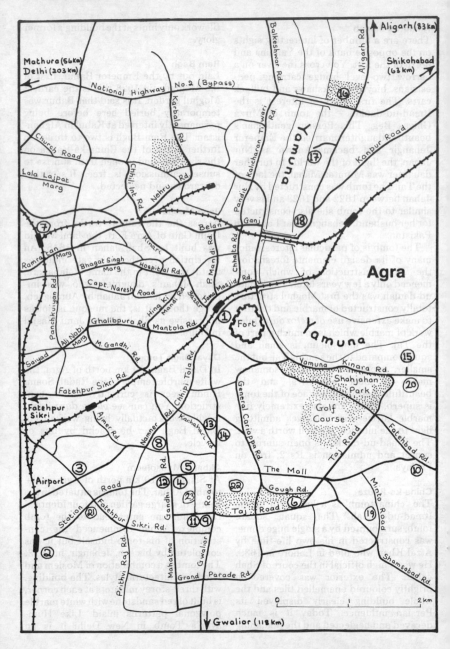

1 Agra Fort Railway Station	13 Tourist Rest House
2 Agra Cantonment Railway Station	14 Sarang Restaurant
3 Idgah Bus Station	15 Taj Mahal
4 Tourist Office	16 Ram Bagh
5 GPO	17 Chini Ka Rauza
6 Hotel Clarks Shiraz & Indian Airlines	18 Itmad-ud-Daulah's Tomb
7 Tourist Bungalow	19 Highway Inn
8 Lauries Hotel	20 Rock Bottom Hotels
9 Jaggi Hotel	21 Grand Hotel
10 Mayur Tourist Complex	22 Telegraph Office
11 Kwality Restaurant	23 Zorba the Buddha
12 Agra Caterers	

interesting place to visit to study the gradual evolution in design that culminated in the Taj Mahal. Akbar's Mausoleum is open from sunrise to sunset and entry is Rs 2, except on Fridays when it is free.

Sikandra is named after Sultan Sikandar Lodi, the Delhi ruler who was in power from 1488 to 1517, immediately preceding the rise of Moghul power on the sub-continent. The Baradi Palace, in the mausoleum gardens, was built by Sikandar Lodi. Across the road from the mausoleum is the Delhi Gate and between Sikandra and Agra are several tombs and two *kos minars* 'milestones'.

Getting There It's a fair way out to Sikandra, count on Rs 25 to 40 for the return trip in an auto-rickshaw.

Other

The Kinari Bazaar or old market place is a fascinating place to wander around. It's in the old part of Agra, near the fort, and the narrow alleys of the market start near the Jami Masjid. Girls beckon to single men from upstairs balconies of the Malka Bazaar in the old city.

Tours

The ITDC have Agra tours operating from Delhi for around Rs 160 for a day tour including breakfast. The tours include Fatehpur Sikri as well as the main sights in Agra itself. If your time is very limited these tours may be worth considering. If

you're day-tripping from Delhi to Agra, the Agra city tours operated by the UP State Road Transport Corporation commence from the railway station and tickets are sold on the tourist Taj Express from Delhi. This tour lasts from 10.30 am to 6.30 pm and covers the Taj, the fort and Fatehpur Sikri. Passengers are picked up half an hour earlier at the Tourist Office, 191 The Mall. At the Cantonment Station tickets can be bought near the Platform 1 enquiry window. Costs start from Rs 33 on an ordinary bus, Rs 42 de-luxe and go up with drinks or meals included. They are reduced by Rs 3.50 on Fridays. The ITDC also organise Agra tours – a Rs 15 morning tour covers the Taj, the fort and the tomb of Itmad-ud-daulah, while a Rs 20 afternoon tour goes to Sikandra and Fatehpur Sikri.

Places to Stay – Bottom End

The Sadar area, close to the Cantonment Railway Station, the Tourist Office and the GPO and only a Rs 2 or 3 rickshaw ride from the Taj, is a good place for reasonably cheap accommodation. There are also many good restaurants in this same vicinity. Taj Rd is the hub of the Sadar area, parallel to The Mall. Next to the Sadar there is also an area called Baluganj which has some popular budget hotels. If you're after rock bottom prices then head for the maze of small streets immediately to the south of the Taj.

There are three good places to try in the Baluganj area. The very popular *Tourist*

Rest House (tel 64961) is opposite the office of the District Board and is conveniently close to the GPO and Tourist Office. It is run by two helpful brothers, they'll even make train reservations for you. This pleasant and well kept hotel has a variety of rooms with and without attached bathroom. With bath singles/doubles are around Rs 30/40 and there are dorm beds for Rs 7, but rickshaws are unwilling to take you there as they don't get a commission.

Major Bakhshi Sardar Singh started a guest house at his home (tel 76828) conveniently situated at 33/83 Ajmer Rd. Following his death the guest house is now run by his son, Colonel Bakhshi. A double with bathroom costs Rs 75 but recently reports from travellers concering this place have been rather mixed.

Hotel Khanna is situated between the above two places. It's entirely new and doubles are Rs 60. *Hotel Ajay* in the same area is also OK. *Hotel Akbar Inn* at 21 The Mall may also be worth checking out.

In the Sadar Bazaar area *Hotel Jai Hind* is in a small street off Taj Rd, the main street of Sadar. Rooms range from Rs 20 to 40 in this recommended hotel and the management is friendly and reliable. *Hotel Akbar* is located in the top end hotel area, 25-minutes, walk from the Taj, and has rooms from Rs 25 to 60.

Camping facilities are available in Agra at the *Highway Inn* (1.5 km south of the Taj), the *Hotel Grand*, *Hotel Lauries* and the *Mayur Tourist Complex*. Agra's *Tourist Bungalow* (tel 72123) is in the Raja Mandi area, a long way from anywhere, but it does have a garden and doubles cost Rs 35.

A labyrinth of winding, narrow streets runs back from the Taj. Follow the road straight back from the main entrance and you'll find the *Hotel Shah Jahan* with doubles at Rs 15 to 22 and also a dormitory. It's fairly clean and habitable and has a quite amazing menu. Some passing traveller has put a lot of effort into this wild fantasy but the food is surprisingly good. 'Best in India!' said one traveller. Excellent breakfasts here too.

Continue into the maze and right by the tonga stand (ask) you'll find the *Hotel Mumtaz Mahal*. Doubles from just Rs 12, singles Rs 6, dorm beds only Rs 3. Again it's a reasonable place considering the rock bottom prices and is popular with many travellers. There are several other similarly cheap places in the area like the *India Guest House* with good rooms in the Rs 15 to 25 range, about 100 metres straight south of the Taj south gate. Open in late '83 the *Shanti Lodge* is on Chowk Kagjiyan, also near the Taj south gate, is reported to be clean and friendly with dorm beds for Rs 5, singles for Rs 10.

Places to Stay – Middle

In the same area as the more expensive hotels is the *Mayur Tourist Complex* (tel 64771), a smaller hotel with air-con rooms at Rs 120/160 or without air-con for Rs 60/80. It also has a small garden. Near the Cantonment Railway Station the *Hotel Grand* charges Rs 120 for doubles and has recently been completely renovated. There is parking space here for people with vehicles and they also have cheaper and more expensive rooms.

Hotel Lauries (tel 77047) on Mahatma Gandhi Rd charges Rs 75/120 for singles/doubles without air-con. There's a 'disgusting looking but surprisingly pleasant mineral-water pool and this used to be a popular place with overland groups. *Hotel Jaiwal* is also very centrally located in the Sadar area and is one of the better hotels in this price range – doubles with air-con are Rs 130. *Hotel Amar* (tel 66110, 66783, 61426) on Fatehabad Rd has rooms at Rs 80/130 up to Rs 110/160 with air-con.

A little out of town, at 6.6 km on the Shasabad Rd, the *Ekant Country Guest House* is a country hotel with camping ground. Accommodation ranges from dorm beds at Rs 15 to air-con doubles at Rs 120 and there's a garden restaurant.

Places to Stay – Top End

Agra's tourist class hotels are generally situated in the open area south of the Taj. *Hotel Mughal Sheraton* (tel 64701, 64729) has elegant, fort-like architecture and offers everything from camel or elephant rides to an in-house astrologer who will tell your fortune for Rs 50. There are 200 rooms with singles/doubles ranging from Rs 520/650.

The older *Hotel Clarks Shiraz* (tel 72421) is a long standing Agra landmark. It too is fully air-conditioned, has a swimming pool and the Indian Airlines office is also located here. Singles/doubles cost Rs 300/400. It is one of the better expensive Agra hotels.

South-east of the Taj, the *Hotel Mumtaz* is a smaller hotel with 40 rooms, all aircon. Singles/doubles are Rs 165/240. The *Hotel Galaxy Agra* (tel 64171) at Taj Ganj has rooms at Rs 350/425. The *Welcomgroup Mumtaz* (tel 64771-6) on Fatehabad Rd has rooms at Rs 165/240.

Places to Eat

The de-luxe hotels all have excellent food – for a major splurge *Clarks Shiraz* is worth considering. In the Sadar area the *Kwality Restaurant* on the Taj Rd is aircon and excellent. *Prakash Restaurant*, across the street, can also be good. 'The best tasting Indian food we had in India' wrote two New Zealanders. Opposite the Kwality in a modern shopping arcade the very clean *Brijwasi Sweet House* is very clean and helpful and all the sweets are named and priced.

On a tighter budget *Hotel Jai Hind* is good and *Hotel Jaggi*, also in the Sadar area, is alright. A good place to eat south Indian food in this area is *Laxmi Vilas* where a special masala dosa for Rs 4.50 is enough to fill you up. Two new vegetarian restaurants also provide good food in the Sadar area. *Khaji Pija* is very near the GPO and the Tourist Office and has become very popular. The *Candy Restaurant*, again in the Sadar area, is also worth a visit if you like vegetarian food. On

Gwalior Rd the *Sarang Restaurant* has been popular with travellers and they're also opening a hotel with the same name.

The *Plaza Restaurant*, on Namner Rd, round the corner from the Tourist Rest House, has good, cheap vegetarian food. At E/13 Shopping Arcade, off Gopi Chand Shivhare Rd which runs between The Mall and Taj Rd in Sadar, is *Zorba the Buddha*, another Rajneesh restaurant. The food is more expensive than usual but very good and the desserts are also delicious. In the rock bottom hotel area immediately south of the Taj you can get 'fantastic food' at *Mohamed's Good Earth Dhaba*, Taj Southgate. It's at the intersection just south of the Taj gate. Low prices and nice people.

Agra has a local speciality, the ultra-sweet candied melon called *petha*.

Entertainment

When you tire of the Taj there are various non-sightseeing possibilities in Agra. The *Hotel Galaxy* pool can be used for Rs 20 for example. There is a cinema in the Baluganj area of the city which shows English language movies every evening. The *Hotel Maurya Sheraton* has a programme of Indian folk dancing almost every evening. It costs Rs 25 for half an hour.

Getting There

Air Agra is on the touristically popular daily flight route Delhi-Agra-Khajuraho-Varanasi-Kathmandu and return. It's only a 30-minute flight from Delhi to Agra. Fare from Agra are Delhi Rs 153, Khajuraho Rs 266, Varanasi Rs 408. There is also a four times weekly Delhi-Agra-Lucknow route but at present there is no longer an Agra-Jaipur connection.

Rail Agra is on the main Delhi-Bombay broad gauge railway line, so there are plenty of trains coming through. There is a daily express train from Delhi to Agra known as the Taj Express which costs Rs

72 in 1st class, Rs 18 in 2nd. The Taj Express departs New Delhi Railway Station at 7 am daily and arrives in Agra three hours later. The return train departs Agra at 7 pm and arrives in Delhi at 10 pm – ideal for a day trip to Agra. Avoid the slow passenger trains at all costs. Take great care at New Delhi station, pickpockets, muggers and others are very aware that this is a popular tourist train and they work overtime at parting unwary visitors from their goods.

Guided tours of Agra and Fatehpur Sikri depart from the railway station as soon as the train arrives. Lucknow is about nine hours away by train.

Bus There are de-luxe buses from Delhi to Agra which cost Rs 28 and take around five hours. A similar de-luxe bus between Agra and Jaipur takes five hours and costs Rs 38. Most regular buses leave from the Idgah Bus Station, there are regular buses to Delhi about every hour for Rs 14.

Getting Around

Agra is very spread out, walking is really not on – even if you could. It's virtually impossible to walk because Agra's hordes of rickshaw-wallahs pursue would-be pedestrians with unbelievable energy and persuasive ability. Beware of rickshaw guys who take you from A to B via a few marble shops, jewellery shops and so on. Just great when you want to catch a train.

A simple solution to Agra's transport problem is to hire a rickshaw for the day. You can easily negotiate an all-in daily rate (say around Rs 10) for which your rickshaw-wallah will not only take you everywhere, he'll wait outside while you sightsee or even have a meal. Agra is so touristy that many of them speak fine English and, like western cabbies, are great sources of amusing information – like how much they can screw out of fat-cat tourists for a litle pedal down to the Taj and back to the air-conditioning. Otherwise Rs 3 to 5 will take you from pretty well anywhere in Agra to anywhere else.

If, however, you really don't want to be pedalled around, Agra is sufficiently traffic free to make pedalling yourself an easy proposition. There are plenty of bicycle hire places around. They can be rented for Rs 4 a day.

Things to Buy

Agra is well known for leather goods, jewellery and marble items inlaid like the *pietra dura* work on the Taj. The Sadar area and around the Taj itself are the main tourist shop areas although the prices here are likely to be more expensive. Around Pratapur there are many jewellery shops but if you're heading to Jaipur you'll find precious stones are cheaper here. One traveller recommended The Shalimar on Gordon Rd in Baluganj for gems. Subhas Emporium in Sadar is a good place for marble. Beware of rickshaw-wallahs taking you to shops – they'll inevitably be raking off a commission at your expense. Beware of 'marble' that turns out to be alabaster too. Alabaster will scratch, marble will not.

FATEHPUR SIKRI

Between 1570 and 1586, during the reign of the Emperor Akbar, the capital of the Moghul Empire was situated here, 40 km west of Agra. Then, as suddenly and dramatically as this new city had been built, it was abandoned. Today it's a perfectly preserved Moghul city at the height of the empire's splendour. And an attraction no visitor to Agra should miss.

The legend relates that Akbar was without a male heir and made a pilgrimage to this spot to see the saint Shaikh Salim Chisti. He foretold the birth of Akbar's son, later the Emperor Jehangir, and in gratitude Akbar named his son Salim. Furthermore Akbar transferred his capital to Sikri and built a new and splendid city. Later, however, the city was simply abandoned due, it is said, to difficulties with the water supply.

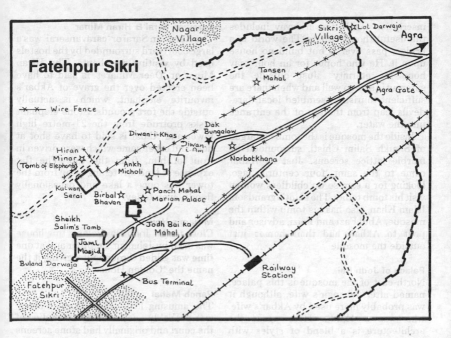

Fatehpur Sikri

Nagar Village

Sikri Village

☆ Lal Darwaja

Agra

×—×— Wire Fence

Tansen Mahal

Agra Gate

Dak Bungalow

Diwan-i-Khas

Diwan-i-Am

Hiran Minar ☆
(Tomb of Elephants)

Ankh Micholi

Norbatkhana

Kutwan Sarai

Birbal Bhavan ☆

Panch Mahal
Mariam Palace

Sheikh Salim's Tomb

Jodh Bai ka Mahal

Jami Masjid

Buland Darwaja ☆

Railway Station

Fatehpur Sikri

Bus Terminal

Akbar was known to be very tolerant towards other religions although he was Moslem, and he spent much time discussing and studying them in Fatehpur Sikri. He also developed a new religion called 'Deen Ilahi' which attempted to synthesise elements from all the major religions. Akbar's famous courtiers such as Bibal, Raja Todarmal and Abu Fazal had their houses near his palace in the city.

Information & Orientation

The deserted city lies along the top of a ridge while the modern village, with its bus stand and railway station, is down on the southern side. Fatehpur Sikri is open from sunrise to sunset and entry is Rs 0.50, free on Fridays. The Jami Masjid is outside the city enclosure.

As Fatehpur Sikri is one of the most perfectly preserved 'ghost towns' imaginable you may well decide it is

worthwhile spending a few rupees to hire a guide. When you arrive look for 'Shahi Darwaza', not 'Buland Darwaza'. Shahi Darwaza is the official entrance to the fort where officially licensed guides are available. On the other hand at the Buland Darwaza, the gateway to the mosque and shrine, unlicensed children will try to lure you into hiring them as guides. The mosque and shrine are not inside the fort, you have to go there separately.

Jami Masjid or Dargah Mosque

Fatehpur Sikri's mosque is said to be a copy of the mosque at Mecca and is a very beautiful building containing elements of Persian and Hindu design. The main entrance is through the 54-metre high Buland Darwaza, the Gate of Victory, which was constructed to commemorate Akbar's victory in south India. The impressive gateway is reached by an equally impressive flight of steps. An inscription inside the archway includes the useful thought that: 'The world is a bridge, pass over it but build no house upon it. He who hopes for an hour may hope for eternity'. Just outside the gateway is a deep well and when there are sufficient tourists assembled local daredevils leap from the top of the entrance into the water.

Inside the mosque is the tomb or dargah of Shaikh Salim Chisti, surrounded by marble lattice screens. Just as Akbar came to the saint, four centuries ago, looking for a son, so do childless women visit his tomb today. The saint's grandson, Islam Khan, also has his tomb within the mosque. Abul Fazi and Faizi, adviser and poet to Akbar, had their homes just outside the mosque.

Palace of Jodh Bai

North-east of the mosque is this palace, named after Jehangir's wife, although it was probably more used by Akbar's wife, who was a Hindu. Here again the architecture is a blend of styles with Hindu columns and Moslem cupolas. The 'Palace of the Winds' is a projecting room with walls entirely made of stone lattice work. The ladies of the court probably sat in here to keep a quiet eye on events below.

Bhirbal Bhavan

Built either by or for Raja Birbal, Akbar's favourite courtier, this small palace is extremely elegant in its design and execution. Victor Hugo, the Victorian-era French author, commented that it was either a very small palace or a very large jewellery box. Birbal, who was a Hindu and noted for his wit and wisdom, unfortunately proved to be a hopeless soldier and lost his life, and most of his army, near Peshawar in 1586. Enormous stables adjoin the Jodh Bai Palace with nearly 200 enclosures for horses and camels. Some stone rings for the halters are still in place.

Karawan Sarai & Hiran Minar

The Karawan Sarai or 'caravanserai' was a large courtyard surrounded by the hostels used by visiting merchants. The Hiran Minar or 'Deer Minaret' is said to have been erected over the grave of Akbar's favourite elephant, which is actually outside the fort grounds. Stone elephant tusks protrude from the 21-metre high tower and Akbar is said to have shot at deer and other game which were driven in front of him, from the top. The flat expanse of land stretching away from the tower was once a lake and occasionally floods, even today.

Miriam's House

Close to the Jodh Bai Palace, this house was used by Jehangir's mother and at one time was gilded throughout – giving it the name the 'Golden House'.

Panch Mahal

The amusing little 'Five Storey Palace' was probably once used by the ladies of the court and originally had stone screens on the sides. These have now been removed making the open colonnades inside visible. Each of the five storeys is stepped back from the previous one until at the top there is only a tiny kiosk, its dome supported by four columns. The lower floor has 56 columns, no two of which are exactly alike.

Ankh Michauli

The name of this building tranlates as something like 'hide and seek', and the emperor is supposed to have amused himself by playing that game with ladies of the harem! The building was more probably used for storing records although it has some curious struts with stone monsters carved into them. By one corner is a small canopied enclosure where Akbar's Hindu guru may have sat to instruct him.

Diwan-i-Khas

The exterior of the Hall of Private

Audiences is plain but its interior design is unique. A stone column in the centre of the building supports a flat-topped 'throne'. From the four corners of the room stone bridges lead across to this throne, and it is thought that Akbar sat in the middle while his four principal ministers sat at the four corners.

Diwan-i-Am

Just inside the gates at the north-east end of the deserted city is the Hall of Public Audiences. This consists of a large open courtyard surrounded by cloisters. Beside the Diwan-i-Am is the Pachchisi court-yard, blocked out like a gigantic game-board. It is said that Akbar played chess here, using slave girls as the pieces.

Other

Musicians would play from the Norbat Khana, at one time the main entrance to the city, as processions passed by beneath. The entrance road then passed between the mint and the treasury before reaching the Diwan-i-Am. The Khwabgah was Akbar's own sleeping quarters, in front of the Daftar Khana or record office. Beside that is the tiny, but elaborately carved, Rumi Sultana or 'Turkish Queen's House'.

Near the Karawan Sarai badly defaced elephants still guard the Hathi Pol or Elephant Gate. There is also a Hakim or doctor's house and a fine Hammam or Turkish Bath beside it. Outside the Dargah Mosque are the remains of the small stone-cutters' mosque. Shaikh Salim Chisti's cave was supposedly at this site and the mosque predates Akbar's imperial city.

Places to Stay

Although most people day trip from Agra you can stay at the *Dak Bungalow* for just Rs 6 for a 'suite'. Great value, book it at the Archaeological Survey of India, 22 The Mall, Agra. You get great value food in the hotel across the road from the bus station.

Getting There

The tour buses only stop for an hour or so at Fatehpur Sikri. If you want to spend longer it is worth taking a regular bus from the Idgah Bus Station for Rs 4.60. The trip takes a bit over an hour, along the way you pass milestones, known as kos minars, about every three km. There's also a train service there but it's very slow. Along the road you'll often see dancing bears, the villagers dance their trained bears out into the road to block your way while they demand money!

You can spend a day in Fatehpur Sikri and continue on to Bharatpur in the evening. The bus station restaurant will let you lock up your bags in their garage for a price Rs 5.

BETWEEN DELHI & KANPUR

Aligarh (population 280,000)

Formerly known as Koil this was the site of an important fort as far back as 1194. During the upheavals following the death of Aurangzeb and the collapse of the Moghul empire the region was scrapped over by the Afghans, the Jats, the Marathas and the Rohillas – first one coming out on top, then another. In 1776 the fort's name was changed to Aligarh (the high fort) but in 1803, despite French support for the then ruler Scindia, it fell to the British. The fort is three km north of the town and its present form dates from 1524. The ancient City of Koil has traces of Buddhist and Hindu temples of great antiquity.

Aligarh is best known today for the Aligarh Moslem University where the 'seed of Pakistan were sown'. Moslem students come here from all over the Islamic world.

Sankasya

Reached via Farrukhabad and Pakhna, from where it is 11 km, there is an Ashokan elephant capital here. A mound, topped by a ruined stupa, marks the spot where Buddha descended from heaven to earth after preaching to his mother.

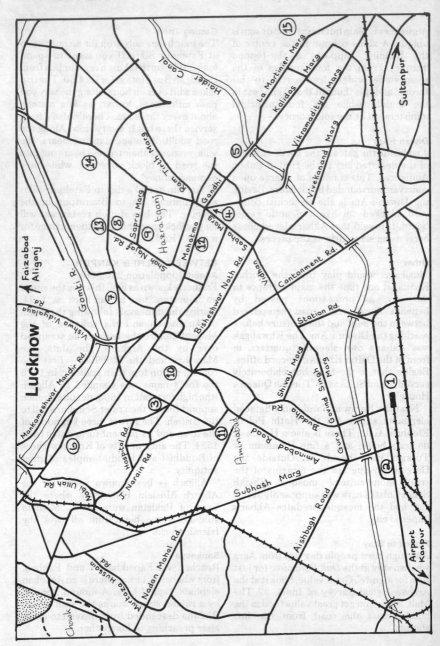

Lucknow

1	Railway Station	9	Tourist Bungalow	Chowk area—
2	Charbagh Bus Station	10	Kaiserbagh	Chotta, Bara &
3	Kaiserbagh Bus Station	11	Hotel Gulmarg	Hussainabad Imam-
4	G.P.O.	12	Hotel Capoor's	baras & Jami Masjid
5	Zoo & Museum	13	Sha Najaf	
6	Residency	14	Botanical Gardens	
7	Hotel Clarks Avadh	15	La Martiniere School	
8	Carlton Hotel			

Kanauj

Only a few dismal ruins indicate that this was once a mighty Hindu city, which quickly fell into disrepair after Mahmud of Ghazni's raids. This was the place where Humayun was defeated by Sher Shah in 1540 after which he temporarily had to leave India.

Etawah

This town rose to some importance during the Moghul period only to go through the usual series of rapid changes during the turmoil that followed the Moghuls. The Jami Masjid shows similiarities to the mosques of Jaunpur and there are bathing ghats on the riverbank, below the ruined fort.

Bareilly (population 360,000)

Former capital of the region known as Rohilkand, Bareilly came under British control when the Rohillas, an Afghan tribe, became too involved with the Marathas and the Nawab of Oudh.

Rampur (population 180,000)

This was a former Rohilla state capital. The State Library has an important collection of old manuscripts and is housed in a fine building in the old fort. There is a large Jami Masjid nearby and interesting bazaars around the walls of the palace. The library contains a fine collection of old miniatures, some of great importance, but these are normally only on view for scholars.

KANPUR (population 1,400,000)

Sometimes called 'the Manchester of India' this important industrial town attracts very few tourists, although it is not a great distance south of Lucknow. During the 1857 Mutiny some of the more tragic events took place here, at that time known as Cawnpore. Sir Hugh Wheeler defended a part of the Cantonment for most of the month of June, but with supplies virtually exhausted and having suffered considerable losses he surrendered only to have his party massacred. All Souls Memorial Church, built in 1875, has some rather moving reminders of the tragic events at Kanpur. It's two km from the station. Kanpur has a large and modern zoo.

Places to Stay

Hotel Meghdoot (tel 51141) at 17/3B Mahatma Gandhi Marg is air-conditioned and has restaurants, shops and so on. Singles are Rs 165 to 200, doubles Rs 250 to 325. The *Yatrik Hotel* (tel 60345-456) is at 65/85A Circular Rd and has air-con rooms from around Rs 80, or air-cooled from around Rs 50. There are other cheaper hotels in Kanpur.

Getting There

Kanpur can be reached daily by air from Delhi (Rs 323). It's on the main Delhi-Calcutta railway line, some express trains take less than five hours Delhi-Kanpur. From Delhi the fare is Rs 131 in 1st, Rs 34 in 2nd. From Calcutta it's Rs 248 in 1st, Rs 63 in 2nd.

LUCKNOW (population 900,000)

The capital of Uttar Pradesh, Lucknow rose to prominence as the capital of the

Nawabs of Oudh. These rulers controlled a region of north-central India for about a century after the decline of the Mogul Empire and most of the interesting monuments in Lucknow date from this period from the mid-18th century. The Nawabs were:

Sa'adat Khan Burhan–ul-mulk	1724-1739
Safdar Jang	1739-1753
Shuja-ud-daula	1753-1775
Asaf-ud-daula	1775-1797
Sa'adat Ali Khan	1798-1814
Ghazi-ud-din Haidar	1814-1827
Nasir-ud-din Haidar	1827-1837
Muhammad Ali Shah	1837-1842
Amjad Ali Shah	1842-1847
Wajid Ali Shah	1847-1856

It was not until Asaf-ud-daula that the capital of Oudh was moved to Lucknow. Safdar Jang lived and ruled from Delhi and his tomb is a familiar landmark near the Safdarjang airport. After Sa'adat Ali Khan the rest of the Oudh Nawabs were a uniformly hopeless lot and Wajid Ali Shah was so extravagant and indolent that to this day his name is regarded by many in India as synonymous with lavishness. In 1856 the British, as was their wont, pensioned him off for incompetence and exiled him to Calcutta for the rest of his life. This was one of the sparks that lit the Indian Mutiny. Lucknow became the scene for some of the most dramatic events of the Mutiny as the British residents of Lucknow held out in the Residency for 87 harrowing days, only to be besieged again for a further two months after being relieved.

The Nawabs were Shi'ite Moslems and Lucknow remains the principal Indian Shi'ite city – unlike other major Moslem cities in India like Delhi and Agra where the Moslems are mainly Sunnite. Shi'ites predominate in Iran (the Ayatollah is a Shi'ite), but in most other Islamic nations the Sunnites form the majority.

Information & Orientation

Lucknow is rather spread out and it is quite a distance between the various places of interest. It's an interesting place, but sadly neglected by tourists and the mausoleums of the Nawabs were jerry built, have generally deteriorated rather badly and are somewhat over-rated.

The historic monuments are mainly in the north-eastern part of the old city around the chowk area. The main shopping area, with its narrow alleys, is Aminabad while the modern area with wide avenues and large shops is the fashionable Hazratganj. The major bus stations, for Gorakhpur and Varanasi buses, is in Kaiserbagh. The main railway station, in the south of the city, is called Charbagh. The Tourist Office is at 21 Vidhan Sabha Marg.

Great Imambara

The Bara or Great Imambara was built in 1784 by Asaf-ud-Daula as a famine relief project. The central hall of the Imambara, containing its builder's 'pretentious' tomb, is 50 metres long and 15 metres high, it is one of the largest vaulted galleries in the world. Beneath it there are many underground passages which have now been blocked up. An external stairway leads to an upper floor laid out as an amazing labyrinth known as the bhulbhulaiya. A guide to ensure you're not lost forever, costs not more than Rs 5. There's a fine view over the city and the

A   Taj Mahal, Agra at sunset (UP)
B   Bathing ghats on the Ganges at Varanasi (UP)

Aurangzeb Mosque from the top. There is a mosque with two tall minarets in the courtyard of the Imambara. To the right of this, in a row of cloisters, is a 'bottomless' well. The Imambara is open from 6 am to 5 pm and admission is Rs 2.

Rumi Darwaza

Beside the Bara Imambara and also built by Asaf-ud-Daula, this huge and finely designed gate is a replica of one in Istanbul.

Husainabad Imambara

Also known as the Chhota or 'small' Imambara, it was built by Muhammad Ali Shah in 1837 to serve as his own mausoleum. The large courtyard encloses a raised rectangular tank with small imitations of the Taj Mahal on each side. One of them is the tomb of Muhammad Ali Shah's daughter, the other that of her husband. The main building of the Imambara is topped with numerous domes, the main one is golden, and minarets, while inside are the tombs of Ali Shah and his mother. Paying Rs 2 to the guide will also permit you to see the Nawab's silver covered throne. The watchtower opposite the Imambara is known as Satkhanda or the 'seven-storey tower', but it actually only has four storeys since construction was abandoned at that level when Ali Shah died in 1840. The Imambara is open from 6 am to 5 pm, it's six km from the Tourist Bungalow.

Clock Tower

Opposite the Husainabad Imambara is the 67-metre high clock tower and the Husainabad Tank. The clock tower was built between 1880 and 1887.

Picture Gallery

Also facing the Husainabad Tank is a baradari or summer house, built by Ali Shah. Now restored it houses portraits of the various Nawabs of Oudh. It is open from 8 am to 5 pm and admission is Rs 1.

Jami Masjid

West of the Husainabad Imambara is the great Jami Masjid mosque. One of Lucknow's few buildings of real architectural merit, it has two minarets and three domes. Construction was commenced by Muhammad Ali Shah but completed after his death. This is one of the few mosques in India, which is not open to non Moslems.

Residency

Built in 1800 for the British Resident this extensive building was to become the stage for the most dramatic events of the 1857 Mutiny – the Sieges of Lucknow. The British inhabitants of Lucknow all took refuge in the Residency with the outbreak of the Mutiny. The commander, Sir Henry Lawrence, expected to be able to hold out for as long as 15 days before relief arrived. It was 87 days later when a small force under Sir Henry Havelock broke through the besiegers to the remaining half-starved defenders. The story was still not over, for once Havelock and his troops were within the Residency the siege was recommenced and continued from 25 September to 17 November when Sir Colin Campbell broke through to the Residency for the second time.

Today the Residency is maintained in exactly the condition it was in at the time of the final relief. The shattered walls are still scarred by cannon shots and the cemetery at the nearby ruined church has the graves of 2000 men, women and children including that of Sir Henry Lawrence who died during the first siege. The area around the Residency is maintained as well kept lawns and gardens but at the time of the siege the surrounding buildings were only separated from the Residency by narrow streets and lanes. The besiegers frequently attempted to dig tunnels into the Residency.

From 1857 right up to the day India became independent in 1947 a Union Jack was flown night and day from one of the Residency's towers. Times have changed, today there is a Martyr's Memorial to the martyrs of India's independence struggle directly opposite the Residency. It was opened in 1957, the 100th anniversary of the Mutiny. There are no set opening hours for the Residency but the 'model room', where a model of the positions during the siege is on display, is only open from 8 am to 5.30 pm. Admission is Rs 4 except on Fridays when it is free.

Lakshman Tila

This high ground on the right bank of the River Gumti was the original site of the town which became known as Lucknow in the 15th century. Aurangzeb's Mosque now stands on this site.

Shah Najaf Imambara

Close to the Tourist Bungalow this mausoleum takes its name from Najaf, the town 190 km south-west of Baghdad in Iraq where Hazrat Ali, the Shi'ite Moslem leader, is buried. The Imambara is the tomb of Ghazi-ud-din Haidar Khan who died in 1827. His wives are also buried here. This was the scene for desperate fighting in November 1857 during the second relief of Lucknow. The domed exterior is comparatively plain, but inside there are chandeliers and at one time the dome was said to be covered with gold. Many precious items from the mausoleum were looted following the mutiny. The Imambara is open from 6 am to 5 pm.

Martiniere School

Outside of the town is this strange school built by the Frenchman Major-General Claude Martin. Taken prisoner at Pondicherry in 1761 he joined the East India Company's army, then in 1776 entered service with the Nawab of Oudh, while at the same time maintaining his East India Company connections. He quickly made a very substantial fortune from his dual occupations of soldiering and businessman and started to build a palatial home which he named Constantia.

He designed much of the building himself and his architectural abilities were to say the least a little mixed – Gothic gargoyles were piled merrily atop Corinthian columns to produce a finished product which a British Marquess sarcastically pronounced took its ideas from a wedding cake. Martin died in 1800, before his stately home could be completed, but left the money and the directions that it should become a school. 'Kim', the boy hero of Kipling's story of the same name, went to this school and there are similar establishments, also financed from Martin's fortune, in Calcutta and Lyons, France. The building is two km from the Tourist Bungalow and is fronted by an artificial lake with a 38-metre high column in its centre.

Other

Near the Kaiserbagh, with the palace of the last Nawab, there are the stone tombs of Sa'adat Ali and his wife. There is also a summer house in this garden. There are two museums, both closed on Mondays, and a children's museum. The Archaeological Museum is on the Kaiserbagh. The State Museum (open 10.30 am to 4.30 pm) is in the Banarsi Bagh. The zoo, founded in 1921, is also here and has a large collection of snakes. It is open from 5 am to 7 pm.

Sikandarbagh, scene of pitched battles in November 1857, is now the home of the National Botanical Research Institute. The gardens are open from 6 am to 5 pm. General Havelock, who led the first relief of Lucknow, has his grave and memorial in the Almbagh. Nadan Mahal is the tomb of the first governor of Oudh appointed by Akbar. It is one of the earliest buildings in Lucknow, dating from around 1600. Other buildings nearby include the small Sola Khamba pavilion and the tomb of Ibrahim Chisti.

Tours

There are state government operated tours starting from the Tourist Bungalow at 8 am or the railway station a little later each day. They cost from around Rs 10 and cover a number of Lucknow's spread out sights.

Places to Stay – Bottom End

The state government *Tourist Bungalow* (tel 32257) at 6 Sapru Marg in Hazratganj is good value with rooms from Rs 35 and up towards Rs 100. More expensive rooms are air-cooled or have air-con. The rooms are well furnished and have attached bathrooms. There is also a cheap dorm. Get there on a 4 bus from the station.

The popular *Hotel Capoore* (tel 43958) is also in Hazratganj and costs from Rs 40. Near the botanical gardens the *Avadh Lodge* (tel 43821) at 1 Ram Mohan Rai Marg costs from Rs 50. Like the Tourist Bungalow it has facilities for camping if you're travelling with your own vehicle. *Hotel Elora* has tiny rooms at Rs 60, but it's clean and friendly and does excellent food. The *Plaza Hotel*, just off Hewett Rd, two km from the railway station, has rooms for Rs 20.

There are *Railway Retiring Rooms* for both the Northern Railway and the North-Eastern Railway at the Charbagh Station. The Northern rooms start with a dorm and go up to rooms with air-con for about Rs

75. The North-Eastern rooms are cheaper – dorm beds or non air-con for Rs 30.

Places to Stay – Top End

Hotel Clarks Avadh (tel 40131) at 8 Mahatma Gandhi Marg is Lucknow's best hotel. It has everything from central air-conditioning to restaurants and a 24 hour coffee shop. The food here is surprisingly good. Singles/doubles cost Rs 300/450. Also in the Hazratganj area is the rather old-fashioned looking *Hotel Carlton* (tel 44021-24) on Shah Najaf Rd. Rooms here cost Rs 60/100 or Rs 160/250 with air-con. *Hotel Kohinoor* (tel 33849, 43892), 6 Station Rd, has rooms at Rs 75/100 or Rs 150/200 with air-con.

Places to Eat

The *Hotel Carlton* has the best and most expensive restaurant in Lucknow. Good Indian and western food is available at the *Kwality*, *Seem* and *Royal Cafe* restaurants. In the same area you can get good South Indian vegetarian food at low prices. On Hewett Rd, near the Plaza Hotel, the *Maduvan Restaurant* is excellent value. *Chaudhary's Place* is very popular for Indian sweets and the snacks known as *chat*.

Getting There

Air Lucknow is on a daily route Delhi-Lucknow-Patna-Ranchi-Calcutta and there is also a second direct Delhi-Lucknow flight and less frequent connections with Agra, Allahabad and Varanasi. From Delhi the fare is Rs 323, from Calcutta Rs 663. The Indian Airlines office (tel 44030, 48081) is at Hotel Clarks Avadh. Amausi Airport is 14 km out of Lucknow.

Rail By express train Lucknow is four hours from Varanasi, nine hours from Agra and only seven hours from Delhi if you travel on the Gomti Express. The Varanasi-Lucknow fare is Rs 94 in 1st, Rs 24 in 2nd.

There is only a narrow gauge line

1	Allahabad Junction Railway Station	5	YMCA
2	Allahabad City Railway Station	6	Museum
3	Tourist Office & Tourist Bungalow	7	Anand Bhawan
4	GPO	8	Fort

between Lucknow and Gorakhpur, for the Nepal border, so this trip takes eight hours by train. Both the narrow gauge North-Eastern Railway lines and the broad gauge Northern Railway lines run through the main railway station.

For Northern Railway enquiries ring 51234 or 51333. First class bookings are made on 51833, 2nd class on 51488. North-Eastern Railway enquiries are made on 51433 and all reservations are made on 51383.

Bus Charbagh bus station, by the railway station, can be phoned on 50988. The Kaiserbagh bus station number is 42503. Buses to Delhi, Agra, Allahabad, Varanasi, Kanpur, Gorakhpur (Rs 25, six hours) and so on all operate from Kaiserbagh.

To Nepal From the border at Sunauli, from where you enter Nepal to Pokhara, it is a 12-hour bus ride to Lucknow.

Getting Around

Local transport is not very frequent but a tempo will take you from the GPO to chowk, quite near the Great Imambara, for about Rs 1. There are also buses from chowk to the railway station. Or you could take a rickshaw from Hazratganj to Aminabad and then a bus to chowk. The two Imambaras and the Jami Masjid are all around the chowk area, while Shah Najaf is in Hazratganj and the Residency is about midway between the two.

Things to Buy

Lucknow is famed for its hand-woven embroidery known as *chican*. It's made into saris for women and kurtas for men. Prices are lower in Aminabad but you have to bargain.

ALLAHABAD (population 600,000)

The city of Allahabad is 135 km west of Varanasi at the confluence of two of India's most important rivers – the Ganges and the Yamuna (Jumna). This meeting point of the rivers, the 'sangam', naturally has great sin-washing powers and is an important pilgrimage site. It is even more holy since the invisible or imaginary Saraswati River is also supposed to join the Ganges and the Yamuna at this point.

Allahabad also has an historic fort built by Akbar which overlooks the confluence of the rivers and contains an Ashoka pillar. The Nehru family home, Anand Bhawan, is in Allahabad and is open for inspection. Not many western visitors pause in Allahabad, but it can be an interesting and worthwhile stop. Allahabad is built on a very ancient site since it was known in Aryan times as Prayag, and Brahma himself is said to have performed a sacrifice here. The Chinese pilgrim, Hiuen Tsang, described visiting the city in 634 AD and it acquired its present name in 1584, under Akbar. Later Allahabad was taken by the Marathas, sacked by the Pathans and finally ceded to the British in 1801 by the Nawab of Oudh. It was in Allahabad that the East India Company officially handed over control of India to the British Government in 1858, following the Mutiny.

Information & Orientation

Allahabad is less congested and more modern than its sister city, touristy Varanasi. Civil Lines, with its modern shopping centre, has broad, tree-lined avenues and the main bus station is located here. The older part of town is near the Yamuna River.

There are three railway stations – the

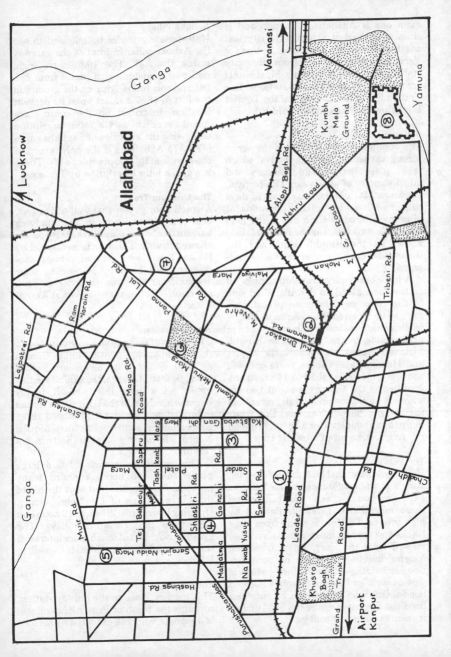

Allahabad

main one is Allahabad Junction and is situated in the central part of the city, just south of the Civil Lines area. Trains for Varanasi, however, go from the city station, about three km away. Most hotels are midway between the two stations. The Tourist Office (tel 52722) is at the Tourist Bungalow on Mahatma Gandhi Rd.

Sangam

The confluence of the rivers is the scene for a great annual bathing festival which takes place between mid-January and mid-February of each year. The festival, known as Magh Mela, lasts from 15 days to a month and attracts thousands of pilgrims who come for a dip in the holy rivers. Every 12th year the Magh Mela is known as the Kumbh Mela and the thousands grow to over a million pilgrims!

A huge temporary township springs up on the vacant land on the Allahabad side of the river and elaborate precautions have to be taken for the pilgrim's safety – in the early '50s, 350 people were killed in a stampede to the water. The Kumbh Mela alternates between Nasik, Ujjain and Hardwar every three years and will next return to Allahabad in 1989. At the confluence, the Ganges is about two km wide – it's a shallower, muddier river than the clearer, deeper Yamuna. Don't pay more than about Rs 5 for a boat trip out on the rivers, it's a bit of a tourist trap.

The Fort

Built by Akbar in 1583 the fort, which stands at the confluence on the Yamuna side, has massive walls and pillars and three magnificent gateways flanked by high towers. The fort is made from huge bricks and is at its most impressive when viewed from the river. Apart from one Moghul building there are no constructions remaining within the fort – which is just as well, as foreigners aren't allowed inside. Officially passes can be obtained from the Security Officer (tel 51370), but it seems you're just told no.

Ashoka Pillar

Unfortunately you're not allowed to see the Ashoka pillar in front of the gateway inside the fort. The 10.6 metre high, polished sandstone shaft dates from 232 BC and was found lying on the ground in the fort in 1837 and set up at its present location. Inscribed on the column are Ashoka's edicts and a later inscription eulogising the victories of Samudragupta (326-375 AD). This is the only record of the events in this Gupta ruler's life. There is a also a later inscription by Jehangir.

The Undying Tree

A small door in the east wall of the fort, near the river, leads to the 'undying banyan tree' – one place in the fort you are allowed to visit. This tree is mentioned by Hiuen Tsang who tells of pilrims sacrificing their lives by leaping to their deaths from the tree in order to seek salvation. The tree is also known as Akshai Veta.

Anand Bhawan

The Nehru family home was donated to the Indian government by Indira Gandhi in 1970. Situated in the eastern part of town, near the Ganges, the exhibits in this house show how this well-off family became involved in the struggle for Indian independence and later produced three generations of astute politicians – Motilal Nehru, Jawaharlal Nehru and Indira Gandhi.

The two-storey mansion has a large garden and the house contains many personal items connected with the life of three generations of the Nehru family. Opening hours are 9.30 am to 12 noon and 1.30 to 5 pm, closed Mondays. The exhibits would be of much more interest if they were labelled in English as well as Hindi.

Khusru Bagh

This garden, close to the railway station, contains the tomb of Prince Khusru, son of Jehangir, who was executed by his own father. Nearby are the tombs of his sister and of his Rajput mother.

Allahabad Museum

Located on Kamla Nehru Rd the museum has a fine collection of Rajasthani miniatures and terracotta figures. The museum is open from 6.30 am to 12.30 pm from 15 April to 15 July and from 10 am to 6.30 pm in other months. It's closed on Wednesdays. To the north of Alfred Park is the Municipal Museum and opposite that is a lovely Children's Park.

Other

The Bharadwaja Ashram is mentioned in the Ramayana, the Allahabad University now occupies its site. The Nag Basuki Temple on the banks of the Ganges and the subterranean Patalpuri Temple are other important shrines.

Places to Stay

Barnett's Hotel (tel 2231) is at 14 Mahatma Gandhi Marg and has rooms for Rs 80/120 or Rs 120/140 with air-con. It is fairly centrally located and all rooms in this small hotel have attached bathrooms. The *Royal Hotel* (tel 2520) at 24 South Rd has rooms at Rs 50/75 or Rs 75/125 with air-con.

The *Tourist Bungalow* (tel 53640) is at 35 Mahatma Gandi Marg and is probably the best place to stay in Allahabad. Rooms cost from Rs 40, Rs 60 if air-cooled, Rs 100 if air-con. It's about Rs 1 by rickshaw from the main railway station; there's also a cheap dormitory.

In the rock bottom bracket the *Central Hotel*, near the clock tower in the centre of the old part of town, has rooms down to Rs 20 or less. There are many other hotels around town and also *Railway Retiring Rooms* (tel 2278) at the station with doubles at Rs 30 and also dorm beds.

Places to Eat

You can get meals in the *Tourist Bungalow*. *Lucky Sweet Mart* has good Indian sweets.

Getting There

Air Allahabad is on the four-times weekly Delhi-Lucknow-Allahabad-Varanasi route. Fares are Rs 446 from Delhi, Rs 143 from Lucknow and 125 from Varanasi.

Rail Allahabad is on the main Delhi-Calcutta railway route and takes about 10 hours from Delhi or four hours from Varanasi. From Delhi fares are Rs 175 in 1st class, Rs 45 in 2nd. Allahabad is a good place to travel to Khajuraho from. If you spend the night here you can catch a morning train to Satna from where buses go to Khajuraho. If you're a backpacker beware of the police at Allahabad Railway Station – they conduct frequent drug searches.

AROUND ALLAHABAD

Bhita

On the opposite side of the Yamuna, 18 km south-west of Allahabad, are the excavated remains of this fortified city. Archaeological digs in 1910-11 revealed successive layers dating from the Gupta period (320-455 AD) right back to the Mauryan period (321-184 BC) and even earlier. There is a museum with stone and metal seals, coins from various kingdoms of the time, terracotta statues and figures and various utensils and personal possessions.

Garwha

The ruined temples in this walled enclosure are about 50 km from Allahabad. Garwha is eight km from Shankargarh and the final three km has to be completed on foot. The major temple has 16 beautifully carved stone pillars, and inscriptions reveal that the temples date back to the Gupta period at the very least. Some of the better sculptures from Garwha are now shown in the State Museum in Lucknow.

Kausambi

This ancient Buddhist centre is 63 km from Allahabad and used to be known as

Kosam. At one time this was the capital of King Udaya, a contemporary of the Buddha. A huge fortress measuring over six km around is near the village and the broken remains of an Ashoka pillar, minus any pre-Gupta period inscriptions, can be seen inside the fort. A bus runs right to the fort at Kausambi.

BETWEEN LUCKNOW & VARANASI
Bahraich & Saheth-Maheth

The nephew of that scourge of India, Mahmud of Ghazni, was killed in Bahraich in 1033. There is a shrine to him about three km from the town. At Saheth-Maheth the Buddha performed the miracle of sitting on a thouand petalled lotus and multiplying himself a million times. The town is also known as Sravasti and can be reached from Gorakhpur on the Naugarh-Gonda loop line. Gainjohwa is the nearest station and there are extensive ruins and a few modern Buddhist temples.

Faizabad (population 120,000)

This was once the capital of Oudh but rapidly declined after the death of Bahu Begam. Her mausoleum is said to be the finest of its type in Uttar Pradesh. Her husband, who preceded her as ruler, also has a fine mausoleum. There are pleasant gardens in Guptar Park, where the temple from which Rama is supposed to have disappeared, stands. Faizabad has a very spiritual feeling to it and the station has good food.

Ayodhya

Only six km from Faizabad, Ayodhya is the home town of Ramayana hero, Ram Chandra. There are numerous picturesque temples and ghats – since the town is on the Gogra (Ghaghara) River. This was also a great Buddhist centre at one time and, as usual, Hiuen Tsang dropped by to list how many monasteries there were and how many monks in residence.

Places to Stay There is a rather primitive *Tourist Bungalow* near the station, it has rooms and a cheap dormitory.

Jaunpur (population 85,000)

Founded by Firoz Shah Tughlaq in 1360 this town later became the capital of the independent Moslem Sharqui Kingdom. Eventually it fell to Sikandar Lodi and then the Moghuls. Prior to the arrival of the Moslems it had a great number of Hindu, Buddhist and Jain temples, shrines and monasteries. Many of these have been utilised by the Moslems to construct Jaunpur's architecturally unique mosques.

The more important mosques include the 1408 Atala Masjid, built on the site of a Hindu temple dedicated to Atala Devi. The massively constructed Jami Masjid was built between 1438 and 1478 during the Sharqi period. There are a half dozen other mosques worthy of note – the Jaunpur mosques are notable for their use of Jain and Hindu building materials, for their two-storey arcades and large gateways, and for their unusual minarets. The tombs of the Sharqi sultans are north of the Jami Masjid. Other important constructions include Feroz Shah's 1360 fort and the stone Akbari Bridge which was built between 1564 and 1568.

Places to Stay Jaunpur has some cheap hotels and the *Marwari Dharamsala*, near the fort, where you can get a private room for just a few rupees.

Getting There Buses and taxis are available from Varanasi, 58 km away.

Chunar

The fort here overlooks the Ganges and was captured by Humayun in 1537, but taken by Sher Shah soon after and not recovered by the Moghuls until 1575 when Akbar took it. Chunar is 37 km from Varanasi and can be reached by bus.

GORAKHPUR (population 250,000)

This is a town travellers on their way to

Kathmandu or Pokhara from Delhi or Varanasi usually pass through. Gorakhpur is situated in the centre of a rich agricultural area which has, nevertheless, remained very backward. The famous temple of Gorkahnath is found here as is the Geeta Press which specialises in publishing Hindu religious literature.

Places to Stay

In Gorakhpur the *Standard Hotel*, opposite the railway station, is a clean and comfortable place which charges Rs 35 for a double. The city centre is known as the Golghar area and here the *Hotel York* charges Rs 25/40 for singles/doubles. It's another good place to stay. The *Vivek Hotel* is a nice place, 'like a rambling old English house and very friendly'. Rooms are Rs 35/45 for singles/doubles. The *Gupta Toursit Lodge*, opposite the railway station, has doubles at Rs 20. In April, 'Gorakhpur is covered solidly in flies'.

Getting There

Buses for Nautanwa near the Nepalese border start from the bus station near the railway station. It's a three to four hour trip for Rs 12, departing from near the Standard Hotel. At Nautanwa you can charter a rickshaw to take you through customs and on to Bhairawa, six km away and on the Nepalese side of the border. There are also buses for Pokhara from Sunauli, only a couple of hundred metres over the border.

Varanasi buses go from a bus station a Rs 2 rickshaw ride away. Varanasi is five or six hours away and the fare is Rs 20.

KUSHINAGAR

The town of Kasia (Kushinagar), 55 km east of Gorakhpur, is supposed to be the site of Buddha's death and cremation. It is possible to take a local bus to Kasia, a couple of hours trip, and visit the site. There are a number of Buddhist buildings of various ages and also large seated and reclining Buddha figures.

Places to Stay

There's a small ITDC *Traveller's Lodge* (tel 38) in Kushinagar with singles/doubles at Rs 70/125 including meals.

TO LUMBINI

Lumbini is the birthplace of Buddha and also close to the 'backdoor' entrance into Nepal for Pokhara. All those going to Lumbini, even pilgrims just crossing the border for a few hours, require a Nepali visa. This can be obtained at the border check point for Rs 60 Nepalese.

Buses run from the Naugarh station on the Gonda-Gorakhpur loop line as far as the border at Kakarhwa from where you take a rickshaw (Rs 5) for the last few km to Lumbini. There is a check point in Naugarh (on the Indian side) where you must report before proceeding in either direction. Naugarh has a *Mahabodhi Society Rest House* where you can stay for a donation.

An alternative way to visit Lumbini is to cross the border into Nepal at Sunauli, stay overnight at Bhairawa and take a bus from there to Lumbini.

VARANASI (population 650,000)

Varanasi, the 'eternal city', is one of the most important pilgrimage sites in India and also a major tourist attraction. Situated on the banks of the sacred Ganges, Varanasi has been a centre of learning and civilisation for over two thousand years. It was at Sarnath only 10 km from Varanasi, that the Buddha first preached his message of enlightenment, 25 centuries ago. Later the city became a great Hindu centre, but was looted a number of times by Moslem invaders from the 11th century on. These destructive visits climaxed with the Moghul Emperor Aurangzeb, who destroyed almost all of the temples and converted the most famous one into a mosque.

Varanasi has also been known as Kashi and Benares but its present name is a restoration of an ancient name meaning the city between two rivers – the Varauana

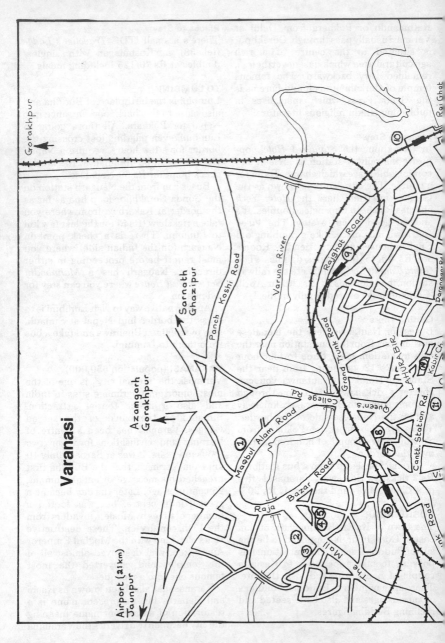

Varanasi

Gorakhpur →

Sarnath
Ghazipur →

Azamgarh
Gorakhpur →

Airport (21km)
Jaunpur →

Varuna River

Raghat Road

Panch Koshi Road

Grand Trunk Road

College Rd

Maqbul Alam Road

Bazar Road

Raja

The Mall

Queen's

Cantt. Station Rd

LAHURABIR

Kabir Ch.

Daranganj Rd

Rai Ghat

⑩

⑨

⑧

⑦

⑥

④⑤

②

③

①

⑪

⑫

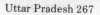

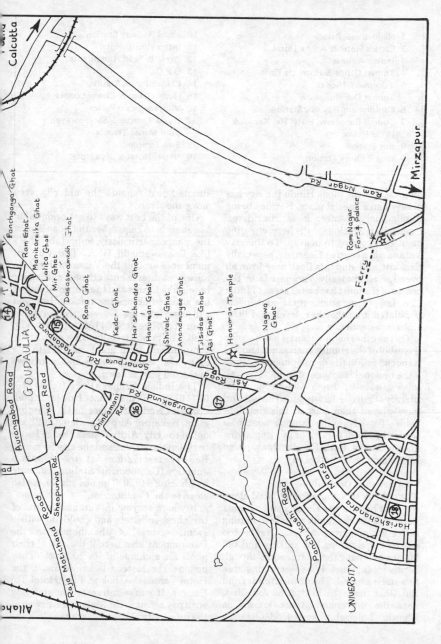

1 Nandeshwar Palace	10 Kashi Railway Station
2 Clark's Hotel & Ashok Hotel	11 International Hotel
3 Indian Airlines	12 Winfa & Tulsi Restaurants
4 Tourist Office & Hotel De Paris	13 G.P.O.
5 Telegram Office &	14 Chowk Police Station
Tourist Dak Bungalow	15 Hotel Ganga & Cheap Lodges
6 Cantonment Railway Station	16 Vijayanagaram Palace
7 Tourist Bungalow, Hotel Raj Kamal &	17 Durga Temple & Satyanarayan
Hotel Relax	Tulsi Manas Temple
8 Bus Station	18 Siva Temple
9 City Railway Station	19 Natraj Hotel & Jaya Hotel

and Asi. For the pious Hindu the city has always had a special place. Besides being a pilgrimage centre, it is considered especially auspicious to die here, ensuring an instant routing to heaven. To this day Varanasi is a centre of learning, especially Sanskrit, and students flock here from all over India. Ironically Varanasi is in the centre of the most backward areas of India – a largely agrarian, rural and over-populated area that has developed little since independence.

On the other hand Varanasi has become a symbol of the Hindu renaissance and has a special role in the development of Hindi – the national langauge of India. The well known novelist Prem Chand and the literary figure Bharatendu Harischand have played their part in this development. Tulsi Das, the famous poet who wrote the Hindi version of the Ramayana known as the Ram Charit Manas, also lived many years in this city.

Information & Orientation

The old city of Varanasi is situated along the west bank of the Ganges and extends back from the riverbank ghats in a winding collection of narrow alleys. They're too narrow for anything but walking and tall houses overhang the picturesque, though hardly clean, lanes. It's a fascinating area to wander around. The town extends from Raj Ghat, near the bridge, to Asi Ghat, near the university. Areas known as Chowk, Lahurabir and Godaulia are situated just outside the old city area along the river.

One of the best ways to get oriented in Varanasi is to remember the positions of the ghats, particularly important ghats like Dasaswamedh Ghat. The Cantonment area around the Varanasi Junction railway station is entirely new and major hotels like Clarks and the Varanasi Ashok are situated across the tracks. Here you will also find the Government of India Tourist Office (tel 64189) at 15B The Mall. The broad, tree-lined avenues of the Cantonment are a great contrast to the crowds of people, bicycles and rickshaws in the old part of town.

The Indian Airlines Office (tel 64146, 66116) is in the Mint House Motel, opposite Nadesar Palace in the Cantonment. Babatpur Airport is a lengthy 22 km out of the city. Airline buses charge Rs 20 between the airport and the city terminal. Railway reservations at the Varansia Junction (Cantonment) Station are made by phoning 64920. The bus station is also close to the Cantonment.

If you're staying in Varanasi in one of the cheaper hotels and could do with a swim, several of the hotels in the Cantonment area permit the use of their pools for a charge of Rs 20 to 25. They include the Hotel Clarks Varanasi, the Hotel Varanasi Ashok and the Hotel Taj Ganges. If you're interested in studying yoga pay a visit to the Malaviya Bhawan at the university. They offer courses in Yoga and also in Hindu philosophy. There's a good bookshop outside the Tourist Bungalow and also in the Hotel Varanasi.

The Ghats

Varanasi's principal attraction is the long string of bathing ghats which line the west bank of the Ganges. Ghats are the steps which lead down to the river, from which pilgrims make their sin-cleansing dip in the river and on which, at the two 'burning ghats', bodies are cremated. The best time to visit the ghats is at dawn, then pilgrims will be there for their early morning dip, the city will be coming alive, the light will be magical and Varanasi will seem a quite amazingly exotic place.

There are over 100 ghats in all, of which Dasaswamedh Ghat is probably the most convenient starting point. A trip from there to Manikarnika Ghat makes an interesting short introduction to the river and will cost something around Rs 5 if you hire a boat. An alternative is to hire a boat between a group of people for a longer trip

– your hotel may be able to help. Say around Rs 20 an hour.

Look out for the people on the ghats, the women bathing discreetly in their saris, the young men going through contortionist yoga exercises, the Brahmin priests offering blessings (for a price) and the ever present beggars giving others an opportunity to do their karma some good. Look for the lingams which mark each ghat, for Varanasi is the city of Shiva. Look for the buildings and temples around the ghats, often tilting precariously or in some cases actually sliding down into the river. Each monsoon causes great damage to the riverbank buildings of Varanasi. Look for the burning ghats where bodies are cremated after making their final journey to the holy Ganges swathed in white cloth and carried on a bamboo stretcher – or even the roof of a taxi. Manikarnika and the less used Harischandra Ghat are the main burning ghats. Don't try taking photos of the cremations unless you're feeling suicidal.

The Asi Ghat, the furthest ghat

upstream, is one of the five special ghats which pilgrims are supposed to bathe from in order and on the same day. The order is Asi, then Dasaswamedh, Barnasangam, Panchganga and finally Manikarnika. Much of the Tulsi Ghat has fallen down towards the river. The Bachraj Ghat is Jain and there are three riverbank Jain temples. Many of the ghats are owned by Maharajas or other princely rulers – such as the very fine Shivala or Kali Ghat owned by the Maharaja of Varanasi. The Dandi Ghat is the ghat of ascetics known as Dandi Panths and near that is the very popular Hanuman Ghat.

The Harischandra or Smashan Ghat is a secondary burning ghat. Bodies are cremated by outcastes known as chandal. Above the Kedar Ghat is a shrine popular with Bengalis and south Indians. Mansarowar Ghat was built by Man Singh of Amber and named after the Tibetan lake at the foot of Mt Kailash, Shiva's Himalayan home. Someswar or 'Lord of the Moon' Ghat is said to be able to heal diseases. The Munshi Ghat is very picturesque while Ahalya Bai's Ghat is named after the Maratha women ruler of Indore.

The Dasaswamedh Ghat's name indicates that Brahma sacrificed (medh), 10 (das) horses (aswa) here. It's one of the most important ghats and also conveniently central. Note its statues and the shrine of Sitala, goddess of smallpox. Raja Man Singh's Man Mandir Ghat was built in 1600 but has been poorly restored in the last century. Note the fine stone balcony on the northern corner of the ghat. Raja Jai Singh of Jaipur also erected one of his unusual observatories on this ghat in 1710. It is not as fine as the Jai Singh observatories in Delhi or Jaipur but its setting is unique.

The Mir Ghat leads to the Nepalese Temple with its erotic sculptures. Between here and the Jalsain Ghat, the Golden Temple stands back from the river. The Jalsain Ghat, where cremations are made, virtually adjoins one of the most

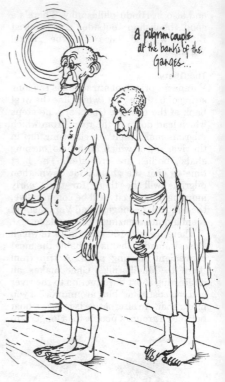

A pilgrim couple at the banks of the Ganges...

sacred of the ghats, the Manikarnika Ghat. Above the steps is a tank known as the Manikarnika Well, Parvati is said to have dropped her earring here and Shiva dug the tank out to recover it, filling the depression with his sweat! The Charandpaduka is a slab of stone between the well and the ghat, which bears footprints made by Vishnu. Privileged VIPs are allowed to be cremated at the Charanpaduka. There is also a temple to Ganesh on the ghat.

Dattatreya Ghat bears the footprint of the Brahmin saint of that name in a small temple near the ghat. Scindia's Ghat was originally built in 1830 but was so huge and magnificent a structure that it collapsed into the river and had to be rebuilt. The Ram Ghat was built by the Raja of Jaipur. As its name indicates five rivers are supposed to meet at the Panchganga Ghat. Above the ghat is Aurangzeb's smaller mosque, also known as the Alamgir Mosque, built over a Vishnu temple. The Gai Ghat has a figure of a cow made of stone upon it. The Trilochan Ghat has two turrets emerging from the river and water between them is especially holy. Raj Ghat was the ferry pier until the road and rail bridge was completed here.

Golden Temple

Dedicated to Vishveswara (Vishwanath), Shiva as Lord of the Universe, the Golden Temple is across the road from its original position. Aurangzeb destroyed the original temple and built a mosque over it – traces of the earlier 1600 temple can be seen behind his mosque. The present temple was built in 1776 by Ahalya Bai of Indore and the gold plating (3/4 of a tonne of it!) on the towers was provided by Maharaja Ranjit Singh of Lahore. Next to the temple is the Gyan Kupor well, the 'well of knowledge'. Much esteemed by the faithful, this well is said to contain the Shiva lingam removed from the original temple and hidden to protect it from Aurangzeb. Non-Hindus are not allowed into the temple but can view it from upstairs in a house across the street. Near the temple, which is interesting to visit in the evening, are narrow alleys filled with an incredible number of shops.

Great Mosque of Aurangzeb

Constructed using columns from the Biseswar Temple which Aurangzeb razed, his great mosque has minarets towering 71 metres above the Ganges. Armed guards protect the mosque as the Indian government wants to ensure there are no problems between Hindus and Moslems.

Durga Temple

The Durga Temple is commonly known as the Monkey Temple due to the many monkeys that have made it their home. It was built in the 18th century by a Bengali Maharani and is stained red with ochre. The small temple is built in north Indian Nagara style with a multi-tiered shikara. Durga is the 'terrible' form of Shiva's consort Parvati, so at festivals there are often sacrifices of goats. Although this is one of the best known temples in Varanasi it is, like the other Hindu temples, closed to non-believers. However, you can look down inside the temple from a walkway at the top. Beware of the monkeys here who are daring and vicious – they'll snatch glasses off your face.

Next to the temple is a tank with stagnant water where, as usual, pilgrims bathe.

Tulsi Manas Temple

Right next to he Durga Temple is this modern, marble shikara-style temple. Built in 1964 the walls of the temple are engraved with verses and scenes from the Ram Charita Manas, the Hindi version of the Ramayana. This tells of the history and deeds of Lord Rama, an incarnation of Vishnu, and its mediaeval author, Tulsi Das, lived here while writing this epic Hindi version. He died in 1623. On the second floor you can also watch the production of moving and performing statues and scenes from Hindu mythology. If you are at all familiar with figures from the Ramayana or Mahabharata you will find a visit here very enjoyable. Non-Hindus are allowed into this temple.

Benares Hindu University

A further 20-minute walk from the Durga Temple, or a Rs 1 rickshaw ride, is the Benares Hindu University, constructed at the beginning of the century. The large university covers an area of five square km and you can get there by bus from Godaulia or by a rickshaw for about Rs 3.

The university was founded by Pandid Malviya as a centre of education in Indian art, culture and music and for the study of Sanskrit. The Bharat Kala Bhawan or BHU at the university has a fine collection of miniature paintings and also sculptures from the 1st to 15th centuries. In a room upstairs there are some old photographs and a map of Varanasi. It's open 11 am to 4 pm (8 am to 12 noon in summer) and closed on Sundays.

New Vishwanath Temple

It's about a 30-minute walk from the gates of the university to the new Vishwanath Temple, planned by Pandit Malviya and built by the wealthy Birla family of industrialists. A great nationalist, Pandit Malviya wished to see Hinduism revived without its caste distinctions and prejudices – accordingly this temple – unlike so many in Varanasi, is open to all, irrespective of caste or religion. The interior has a Shiva lingam and verses from Hindu scriptures are inscribed on the walls. The temple is supposed to be a replica of the original Vishwanath Temple, destroyed by Aurangzeb.

Alamgir Mosque

Locally known as Beni Madhav Ka Darera this was originally a Vishnu temple erected by the Maratha chieftan Beni Madhav Rao Scindia. Aurangzeb destroyed it and erected the mosque in its place, but it is a curious Hindu-Moslem mixture with the bottom part entirely Hindu.

Bharat Mata Temple

Dedicated to 'Mother India' this temple has a marble relief map of India instead of the usual images of gods and goddesses. It was opened by Mahatma Gandhi and non-Hindus are allowed inside. The temple is about 1.5 km south of the Varanasi Junction Station.

Ramnagar Fort

On the other side of the river this 17th century fort is the home of the Maharaja of Benares. There are tours here or catch a ferry across the river to the fort with its interesting museum. The museum contains old silver and brocade palanquins for the ladies of the court, elephant howdahs made of silver, old brocades, a replica of the royal bed and an armoury of swords and old guns. The fort is open from 10 am to 12 noon and 1 to 5 pm and entry to the museum costs Rs 1.

Tours

Varanasi tours cost Rs 15 each for morning or afternoon tours or Rs 25 for both. They start from the Tourist Bungalow or the major hotels in the Cantonment area in the morning (and afternoon?) and from the Government of India Tourist Office on The Mall in the afternoon. Telephone 63233 for booking details.

The morning tour leaves at 6 am and takes you down the Ganges by the ghats, around the various temples and out to the university. The morning tour finishes at 12.15 pm and the afternoon tour commences at 2.30 pm and runs to 6.25 pm – definitely a full day. The afternoon tour takes you out to Sarnath and to the Ramnagar Fort – if there's time! In summer all times are half an hour earlier.

The Varanasi tours don't get unquestioned recommendations – 'the bus arrived late and there were more people than could fit in.....we couldn't all get on the boat so had to take a second boat, for which they tried to charge extra.......we were marched through various temples without any explanation......arrived at the university to see the miniature paintings an hour before it opened......the breakfast stop never happened.....we abandoned the afternoon tour and did it ourselves, as we were leaving the museum at the Ramnagar Fort the tour bus turned up, just before closing time!'

Places to Stay – Bottom End

There are three major areas in Varanasi if you're travelling on a budget. In the

Cantonment area, across the tracks from the railway station, you'll find the *Tourist Dak Bungalow* and *Hotel India*. These are situated in the modern area of the city away from the noise and confusion of the old city. In the station area there's the *Tourist Bungalow* and several hotels such as the *Hotel Amar* and the *Hotel Relax*. These hotels are cheaper than places in the Cantonment, but they're also closer to the centre and consequently noisier.

There are a few hotels near the city centre at Godaulia and Lahurabir which cost about the same as those in the station area. These include the *Hotel Ganges, Benares Lodge, Central Hotel* (tel 62776) and *KVM Hotel*. Finally there are a handful of places right at the rock bottom of this price range – they include the *Yogi Lodge, Tandon House Lodge* and *Om House Lodge*. Staying close to the river does have the advantage over the Cantonment places in that it tends to be cooler during the hot season. Some of the old city places charge whatever they feel you're foolish enough to pay so take care. Sometimes trishaw riders will be reluctant to take you to certain lodges because they won't get a commission – so be wary of tales that a lodge is 'closed up' or 'burnt down'.

Railway & Bus Station Area

The *Tourist Bungalow* (tel 63186) is only a five-minute walk from the station and is a popular low budget place. Rickshaws may be unwilling to take you there from the station because they do not get a commission, as they do with many of the cheap hotels. Most rooms are doubles at Rs 30 but there are some Rs 20 singles. There are some attached and some shared bathrooms but no hot showers. There is also a Rs 10 mixed dorm with big lockers. The management is helpful but there is nothing special about the food and service can be very slow, eat elsewhere.

There are several hotels around the Tourist Bungalow. The best of them is the *Hotel Amar* (tel 64044) which charges Rs 25 for a double. The rooms are clean, the service good and you often have your own (fully functioning) shower. The *Hotel Relax* is slightly cheaper and has similar facilities. There are a few other hotels in the same area, they all do good business when the Tourist Bungalow is full. *Hotel Blue Star* is popular chiefly because it is cheaper, it's only half a km from the station, down the alley from the Tourist Bungalow. Singles/doubles cost from Rs 15/20 and there's a dorm at Rs 6 – it's 'close enough to the ghats to walk and far enough away to avoid the constant sell'.

Hotel Sunite is at 712/16 B1 Bagh Baulia, Ram Kotora, just off Kabir Chaura, the main street between the station and the old city. Two hotels recommended by travellers are the *Venus Hotel*, half-way between the station and the ghats, which has large clean rooms for Rs 20 and the 'really nice' *Garden View Hotel* on Vidyapeth Rd which has good food and doubles for Rs 25. At D56/10 Aurangabad *Hotel Krishna* (tel 63260) has rooms from Rs 10 to 25 and has also been recommended. There are *Railway Retiring Rooms* at the Varanasi Junction Station.

Cantonment Area

On the other side of the station the *Hotel India* (tel 54661) is a good, clean and comfortable place. Singles at Rs 40 here are good value but this is another place not popular with touts and commission-seeking rickshaw riders. The *Tourist Dak Bungalow* (tel 56461) on The Mall is very popular with overlanders and has camping facilities. Singles/doubles cost Rs 45/75, if you're camping with your own vehicle it's Rs 5 a day. There's a beautiful garden here, ideal for relaxing but the food is poor value – 'normal prices with portions which would not suffice as hors d'oeuvres for a cockroach'.

City Centre – Godaulia & Lahurabir Area

The best hotel for budget travellers in this area is the *Hotel Ganges*. It is situated on the left side of the street betwen Godaulia and the ghats on the river. Rooms cost Rs 25/40 for singles/doubles.

On the other side of the street is the *Central Hotel* (tel 62776) – an old hotel with rooms that are OK but not that great. Singles start from Rs 25, doubles are Rs 35-50. In Godaulia itself the *Hotel KVM* is good value at Rs 20 for a single with attached bath.

In Lahurabir, between the station and Godaulia, there are several hotels where singles are in the Rs 25-35 range. These include the *International Hotel* (tel 67140) and the *Ajay Hotel*, both of which are alright.

Old City & Ghats Area This is the place to look for rock bottom hotels. Near the river and the Golden Temple, the *Yogi Lodge* (tel 53986) is the most popular place, indeed it's one of the best budget hotels in the whole of India. It's actually an old Indian house which has been converted into a hotel. There are dorm beds for Rs 7 (usually six beds to a dorm) and doubles for Rs 20 to 25 (same price for single occupancy). It's clean and well maintained and good, reasonably priced western and Indian food is available in the restaurant/ common room on the ground floor. The management and staff are very friendly and helpful and as a result the lodge has that special atmosphere that you don't come across very often. It's very popular with travellers so it's likely to be full unless you get there early in the day. Rickshaw drivers outside the station are unwilling to take you there as they do not get any commission so don't mention the lodge by name, just tell them to take you to Godaulia, the fare should be about Rs 3. The *Golden Lodge*, just opposite, is a reasonable standby with similar prices but, unfortunately, not a patch on the atmosphere. The friendly *Shiva Lodge* near the Dasaswamedh Ghat is another possibility.

Tandon House Lodge, right on the river at Gaighat, is close to the GPO from Maidagin and is somewhat difficult to find. There are excellent views of the river from the courtyard and doubles cost just Rs 15. *Om House Lodge*, in the Bansphatak area of the old city, is also quite popular with traveller's on the cheap and the owner also gives yoga lessons. *Sri Venkateshwar Lodge* on Dasaswamedh Ghat Rd is very close to the river and charges Rs 20 for a double.

Places to Stay – Top End
Varanasi has four major 'tourist class' hotels – all in the new Cantonment area near the railway station. *Hotel Clarks Varanasi* (tel 62021) is the oldest, dating back to the British era, and it is somewhat Victorian in appearance. Air-conditioned singles/doubles are Rs 200-250/300-350 and there is a swimming pool, shops and other facilities.

Cop — DIRECTING TRAFFIC, VARANASI

Hotel Varanasi Ashok (tel 52251-59) is fairly new and centrally air-conditioned although somewhat smaller in size. Rooms are Rs 190/250. *Hotel de Paris* (tel 56461-2, 56218) is also on The Mall and has singles/doubles from Rs 125/200 or slightly less without air-con. It's a wonderful old-style place in large grounds. These hotels are all about a Rs 4 rickshaw ride from the town centre.

The *Hotel Taj Ganges* (tel 54385, 54395) is an entirely new hotel in the Cantonment area and charges Rs 325/400 for singles/doubles. In the same area the *Hotel Surya* is situated just behind the *Hotel Clarks Varanasi* but is much cheaper with doubles costing only Rs 60. *Hotel Diamond* (tel 56561) at Bhelupura is situated close to the city centres and has non air-con doubles for Rs 100. This is a good place if you're looking for a medium price hotel although the service is somewhat haphazard. Their restaurant, however, is excellent.

In Lahurabir the *Gautam Hotel* (tel 54314) at Ramkatora has singles/doubles at Rs 60/100 or Rs 100/150 with air-con. It's quite a new hotel, conveniently located and has nice rooms and good service.

Places to Eat

The *Winfa Restaurant* in Lahurabir, behind the cinema, is possibly Varanasi's best Chinese restaurant – around Rs 15 for a meal. There is also a good but reasonably expensive *Kwality Restaurant* in Lahurabir. A new vegetarian restaurant in the same area is the *Tulasi Restaurant* which has become very popular because of the quality of the food.

In Godaulia the *Aces Restaurant*, right across the street from the KCM Cinema on Madanpura Rd, is a popular health food restaurant and in the evening is often packed out with travellers. In Bhelupura, near the Lalita Cinema, the *Sindhi Restaurant* does excellent vegetarian food. A very good meal here can cost just Rs 10, it's recommended.

On the right side of the street leading to the river in Godaulia is *Ayyars Cafe* where you can get a good masala dosa for Rs 2. There is also a drab-looking place in Godaulia called *The Restaurant* which is reputed to be the local meeting place for politicians. It's about 200 metres south of the main square and has excellent Bengali food and a 'racy Bengali intellectual atmosphere'. On the way to the river from Godaulia the *Sardar Restaurant*, on the left side, is also popular with low budget travellers looking for good vegetarian food. If you want to try an Indian style breakfast, known as *kachauri*, then try *Jaljog* in Godaulia, where for Rs 3 you will be served pooris and vegetables, popular food with Indians when travelling.

In the Cantonment area the *Bamboo Restaurant*, near the Tourist Information Centre, is a little expensive but serves good western food. Or at least some people say it's good, others aren't so sure! At the *Tourist Dak Bungalow* their good, Rs 12, western breakfast includes porridge, toast with butter and eggs. Varanasi's railway station restaurant also has a good reputation for all types of food. Their breakfasts are particularly good as is their 'pot tea'. The *Chinese Mandarin Restaurant* next to the Tourist Bungalow also does Chinese food although it is distinctly Indo-Chinese.

There are many small restaurants with good thalis in the alleys between Godaulia and the ghats in Dasaswamedh. Varanasi is well known for its excellent sweets and *Madhur Jalpan Grih*, on the same side of the street as the cinema in Godaulia, is an excellent place to try them. *Basant Behar* in Lahurabir is also very good. Varanasi is also supposed to have very high quality pan.

Getting There

Air Varanasi is on a number of Indian Airlines' routes including the popular daily tourist service Delhi-Agra-Khajuraho-Varanasi-Kathmandu. Four times weekly there is a Delhi-Varanasi-Bhub-

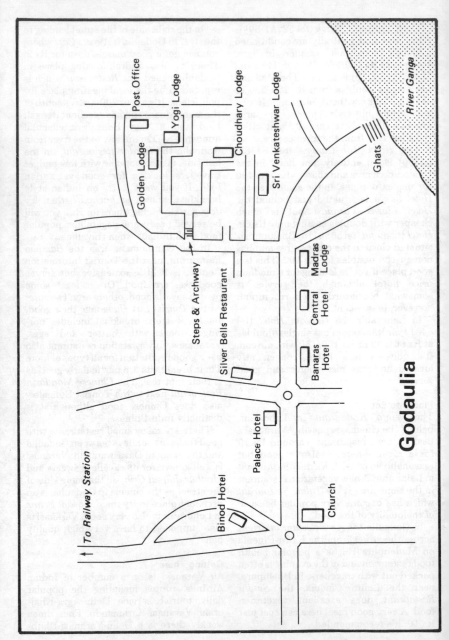

Godaulia

River Ganga

Ghats

Sri Venkateshwar Lodge

Choudhary Lodge

Yogi Lodge

Post Office

Golden Lodge

Steps & Archway

Silver Bells Restaurant

Madras Lodge

Central Hotel

Banaras Hotel

Palace Hotel

Church

Binod Hotel

To Railway Station

aneshwar service. Fares to or from Varanasi include Delhi Rs 492, Khajuraho Rs 266, Agra Rs 408 and Bhubaneswar Rs 492.

Rail There are not a great number of trains running directly between Delhi and Varanasi or between Calcutta and Varanasi, although most Delhi-Calcutta trains do pass through Moghulserai, two hours south of Varanasi by bus. Express trains between Delhi and Varanasi take 13 to 16 hours and cost Rs 215 in 1st class, Rs 55 in 2nd. From Calcutta it takes about 12 hours to Varanasi and the fare is about Rs 185 in 1st, Rs 47 in 2nd.

The Upper India Express is a direct Delhi-Varanasi train. It leaves Delhi at 8 pm and arrives in Varanasi at around 1 pm the next day. This is also a good train in the opposite direction as it departs Varanasi around 6 pm and reaches New Delhi at 10 am. Patna and Allahabad are respectively about six and four hours away by train.

If you're travelling from Varanasi to Kashmir or Himachal Pradesh you can avoid going through Delhi by taking the three times weekly overnight Himgiri Express. This originates in Howrah (Calcutta), runs through Lucknow and terminates at Jammu Tawi so you can be well on your way to Srinagar by the evening. If you want to get to the Himachal Pradesh hill stations it also stops at Chakki Bank, the little known alternative station for Pathankot, a couple of hours before Jammu Tawi. From there it's a Rs 4 rickshaw ride to the main Pathankot train and bus stations.

Varanasi has three railway stations Kashi, City and Varanasi Junction. The Varanasi Junction Station used to be known as the Cantonment Station.

Bus The bus station is next to the main railway station. If you are heading for Nepal the bus may be better than rail since there are only metres gauge trains from here to the border. Buses leave almost hourly to Gorakhpur, five hours away. A tourist bus operates from there to Sunauli on the Nepal border in eight hours. There are also direct buses operating Varanasi-Sunauli very early in the morning (4 am departure!) and costing Rs 30. De-luxe buses leave at 9 am and cost Rs 40.

Getting Around
Bus Godaulia (also spelt Godowlia and Gadaulia) is the mid-town bus stop, just an easy walk from the ghats. It's a very useful city landmark. Lanka is the bus stop closest to Benares Hindu University. Between the railway station and Godaulia a bus costs less than half a rupee, but unless you can get on at the starting point Varanasi buses tend to be very crowded. A bus from Godaulia to Sarnath, 10 km away, is about Rs 2.

Rickshaws & Bicycles Rickshaws are still comparatively cheap in Varanasi, between the railway station and Godaulia, near Dasaswamedh Ghat, is about Rs 3. You can hire a rickshaw for the whole day for Rs 15. There are a number of places to rent bicycles around Lanka – all day rates are about Rs 5.

Airport The airline bus costs Rs 20 for the trip between the airport and the airline office in the Cantonment area. Between Varanasia and the airport there's a railway crossing where the gates sometimes stay shut for 20 minutes at a time. A taxi costs around Rs 40.

Things to Buy
Varanasi is famous all over India for silk brocades and beautiful Benares saris. However, there are lots of rip-off merchants and commission men at work. Invitations to 'come to my home for tea' will inevitably mean to somebody's silk showroom where you will be pressured into buying things. There is a market near the GPO called Golghar where the makers of silk brocades sell directly to the shops in the area. You can get cheaper silk

brocade in this area compared to the big stores, but you must be careful about the quality. The big shops selling silk brocades are all located in the Chowk area of the old city.

The same care is necessary with sitars – yes Ravi Shankar does live here (or nearby) but don't believe that every sitar maker is his personal friend!

SARNATH

Only 10 km away from Varanasi, that most holy of Hindu cities, is Sarnath, one of the major Buddhist centres. Having achieved enlightenment at Bodh Gaya it was Sarnath where the Buddha came to preach his message of the middle way to final nirvana. Later Ashoka, the great Buddhist emperor, erected magnificent stupas and other buildings here. Sarnath was at its peak when those indefatigable Chinese travellers Fa Hian and Hiuen Tsang visited the site. In 640 AD, when the latter made his call, Sarnath had 1500 priests, a stupa nearly 100 metres high, Ashoka's mighty stone pillar and many other wonders.

Soon after Buddhism went into decline and by the time the destructive Moslem invasions of India had commenced Sarnath was little more than a shell. The invaders destroyed and desecrated the buildings, even Akbar built a monument to his father, Humayun, over one stupa and time did the rest. It was not until 1836 when British archaeologists commenced excavations that Sarnath regained some of its past glory. Sarnath was known as the 'deer park'.

Dhamekh Stupa

Believed to date from around 500 AD, this stupa was probably rebuilt a number of times over earlier constructions. The geometrical and floral patterns on the stupa are typical of the Gupta period, but excavations into the stupa have revealed brickwork from the Mauryan period around 200 BC.

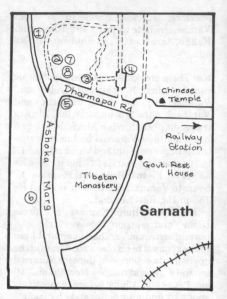

Dharmarajika Stupa

This large stupa has been comprehensively excavated by 19th century treasure seekers. Near it is the building known as the 'main shrine' where Ashoka is said to have meditated.

Ashoka Pillar

Standing in front of the main shrine is the remains of Ashoka's Pillar. At one time this stood over 20 metres high, but today the capital has been removed and can be seen in the Sarnath museum. An edict issued by Ashoka is engraved on the remaining portion of the column. The capital is the Ashokan symbol of four back-to-back lions which has now been adopted as the state symbol of modern India. On the lower portion of the column are representations of a lion, an elephant, a horse and a bull. The lion is supposed to represent bravery, the elephant symbolises the dream Buddha's mother had before his birth and the horse recalls that Buddha left his home on horseback in search of enlightenment.

Museum

Sarnath's excellent Archaeological Museum has the capital from the Ashokan pillar together with many other relics found on the site. These include many figures and sculptures from the various periods of Sarnath – Mauryan, Kushana, Gupta and later. They include the earliest Buddha image found at Sarnath, Buddha figures in various positions dating back to the 5th and 6th centuries and many images of Hindu gods such as Saraswati, Ganesh and Vishnu from the 9th to 12th centuries. The museum is open 10 am to 5 pm daily, except Fridays when it is closed. Entry is Rs 0.50.

Other

There is a modern Maha Bodhi Society temple known as the Mulgandha Kuti-Vihar. It has a series of frescoes in the interior, painted by a Japanese artist. A Bo tree growing here is a transplant from the tree in Anuradhapura in Sri Lanka, which in turn is said to be an offspring of the original tree under which the Buddha attained enlightenment. The brick remnants of the monastery or *vihara* can still be seen and amongst the mango trees you can see a deer park off to one side.

Places to Stay

Sarnath has a *Tourist Bungalow* (tel 8485) with rooms at Rs 30 or dorm beds at Rs 8.

Getting There

You can visit Sarnath on a tour from Varanasi or get there by bus from Godaulia for Rs 1.50. There are also six seater tempos which charge Rs 1.75 per person.

NORTH FROM DELHI

Meerut (population 400,000) Only 67 km north-east of Delhi this was the place where the 1857 Mutiny first broke out. There's little to remember that event by today, although the cemetery near St John's Church has the graves of, amongst

others, Sir Ochterlony whose monument dominates the Maidan in Calcutta. The Suraj Khund is the most interesting Hindu temple in Meerut.

Saharanpur (population 250,000) Situated 178 km north of Delhi the large botanical gardens here, known as the Company Bagh, are over 150 years old.

NORTHERN UTTAR PRADESH

The northern part of Uttar Pradesh, a rough rectangle bordered by Himachal Pradesh to the north-west, China to the north-east, is an area of hills, mountains and lakes. There are a number of popular hill stations such as Naina Tal and Almora, important pilgrimage centres like Hardwar and Rishikesh, where the holy Ganges leaves its Himalayan birthplace and joins the plains for its long trip to the sea. And, of course, there are many trekking routes – most of them little known and even less used.

Toll Taxes

If you're travelling up to the Uttar Pradesh hill stations (Naina Tal, Almosa, Raniket, Mussoorie) somebody will jump on the bus just as you approach the towns to charge you a Rs 1 or 2 toll tax. In Himachal Pradesh these toll taxes are included in the bus fare.

DEHRA DUN (population 250,000)

Also spelt Dehra Doon, this is the gateway to places in the Garwhal Himal such as Badrinath and Joshimath. Dehra Dun is in the centre of a forest area and has a forest research institute. The town is situated in an inter-montane valley in the Siwaliks, the southernmost and lowest of the Himalayan ranges. The high range just to the north contains the hill station Mussoorie, 22 km away.

Information & Orientation

The Tourist Office (tel 3217) is close to the bus stands and the railway station. The clock tower is the 'hub' of the town and most of the hotels are situated on the road from the railway station to the tower. There are two main bus stations – the one nearer the railway station is for buses to the hills, and the one nearer the clock tower is for other destinations.

For those lost for things to do in the evening came this card from someone who perhaps had spent a little long in India:

Got a lovely plastic relief map of India, where you can put your fingers on the mountains tops and pour water down the valleys – tho it's slightly skewed in places – I cut it down, folded it over and carry it in the top flap of my pack – got it at the Survey of India head office in Dehra Dun.

Rick Wicks

Things to See & Tours

There are a number of pleasant picnic spots around the town plus the Forestry Research Institute. The institute is the biggest research centre for forestry and forest products in India and also has a botanical garden. Popular picnic spots, with their distance from the town, include Sahastradhara (14 km) with natural sulphur springs. The Takeshwar Temple (six km) is a Shiva temple while just beyond Anarwala village (seven km) is the 'robbers' cave'. Laxman Sidh is another temple, located on the Dehra Dun-Rishikeh road. Tapovan (six km) is two km off the Dehra Dun-Raipur road and has an ashram. A sightseeing tour from the Tourist Office costs Rs 12 and goes to the institute and some of the picnic spots.

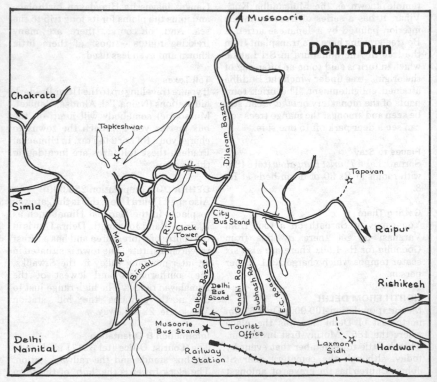

Places to Stay

Hotel Madhuban (tel 4094-97) on Rajpur Rd has air-con rooms at Rs 220/300 or non air-con at Rs 120/150. They've also got separate cottages with kitchens. *Hotel Meedo* (tel 7088), near the railway station, is a new building with good rooms from around Rs 30. In the same area the *Hotel Prince* is similarly priced. Opposite the hospital there's the slightly better *Hotel Relax* with rooms starting from Rs 45.

Places to Eat

Vaishno Restaurant, opposite the Jain dharamsala, near the station, has a bargain thali which includes the dessert known as *khir*. Good Indian dishes at *Moti Mahal*. *Kumar Sweets* has an excellent selection of sweets including their speciality, *kesar ka halwa*.

Getting There

Dehra Dun is connected with major north Indian cities by rail. There is a de-luxe bus service operating between Delhi and Dehra Dun. The trip takes about six hours and costs Rs 40. Dehra Dun-Hardwar is 54 km and takes about 1½ hours.

MUSSOORIE (population 20,000)

At an altitude of 2000 metres and 22 km beyond Dehra Dun, Mussoorie is a popular hill resort in the hot weather. It's situated on a horseshoe-shaped hill and much fruit is grown here. There is a ropeway up to Gun Hill and Municipal Gardens to the west of the town.

Places to Stay

There are a number of more expensive hotels including the large *Savoy Hotel* (tel 2510, 2620) with all inclusive prices from Rs 395/640 for singles/doubles. Or the *Roselynn Estate Hotel* (tel 201) where rooms cost from around Rs 75 to 300 depending on the standard of the room and the time of the year.

At the other end of the scale there are a great number of hotels such as the *Apsar Hotel* in Kulri Bazaar with rooms from Rs 30. The *Snow View Hotel* has singles/doubles from Rs 40/75. The *Deep Hotel* on The Mall has doubles from Rs 80, the *Mountain View Hotel* has doubles from Rs 70.

Getting There

Frequent buses operate between the railhead at Dehra Dun and Mussoorie. There is a road from Mussoorie to Simla direct but foreigners are not allowed to take it without a permit. Travelling to Mussoorie from the west or north (ie Jammu), it is best to get off the express train at Saharanpur and catch a bus (Rs 8) to Dehra Dun or Mussoorie. These buses run even in the middle of the night. Buses run from Landour to Tehri with a connection en route to Rishikesh — marvellous mountain scenery.

HARDWAR (population 85,000)

Hardwar is at the base of the Siwalik Hills, where the Ganges River, coming down from the high Himalaya, passes through a gorge and starts its slow progress across the plains to the Bay of Bengal. It is a town of great pilgrimage importance due to this propitious location and has many ashrams and itinerant sadhus. If you wish to study Hinduism you may find Rishikesh, 24 km further north, a more pleasant place. Despite its religious sanctity Hardwar is really just another noisy, north Indian city.

Every 12 years the Kumbh Mela comes to Hardwar and draws as many as half a million pilgrims. It takes place every three years, consecutively at Allahabad, Nasik, Ujjain and then here.

Information & Orientation

The main street of Hardwar is narrow and long although the suburban area is quite spread out. There is a delightful narrow street of small shops leading south from Har-ki-pauri Ghat. The bus stand and railway station are side by side, the Tourist Office (tel 19) is a little north of them. One traveller recommended buying

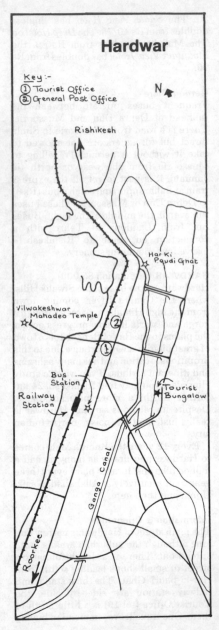

Hardwar

Key:-
① Tourist Office
② General Post Office

N

a copy of *The Gateway to the Gods, Hardwar, Rishikesh & Kankhal* for Rs 5 of guaranteed amusement.

Things to See

Although Hardwar is a very old town mentioned by the Chinese scholar-traveller Hiuen Tsang, its many temples are of comparatively recent origin and of little architectural interest, although they do have many idols and illustrated scenes from the Hindu epics. Har-ki-pairi is the most important bathing ghat as it is supposed to be at the precise spot where the Ganges leaves the mountains and enters the plains. Consequently its power to wash away sins at this spot is superlative. There is supposed to be a footprint of Vishnu in a stone at this ghat.

The Daksha Mahadev Temple, four km downstream, is Hardwar's most important temple. According to the legend Daksha was the father of Sati, Shiva's first wife. Daksha performed a sacrifice here but neglected to invite Shiva, and Sati was so angry at this disrespect to her husband that she managed to spontaneously self-immolate!

Other temples and buildings of lesser interest include the Sapt Rishi Ashram, where the Ganges divides up into a number of smaller streams, and the Parmath Ashram, six km towards Rishikesh, with fine images of the Goddess Durga. The Mansa Devi Temple is three km from the Tourist Office, while Beauty Point, in the same direction, offers fine views over the town. Chandi Devi and a number of other temples are reached by a three km walk.

'Hardwar is a far nicer place to visit than Varanasi', reported one traveller, 'there aren't the 'no entry' signs on the temples or the hard-sell salesmen. It's smaller and easier to get around, more beautiful'. 'Walking along the river is so relaxing' added another.

Places to Stay

Hardwar and Rishikesh are so close that it is quite easy to stay in the latter and day trip to Hardwar. If you want to stay in Hardwar the UP state government *Tourist Bungalow* (tel 379) costs Rs 25/55 and there's a Rs 10 dorm, but it's a little inconveniently situated across the river from the main part of town.

Near the Tourist Office is the *Hotel Gurudev* on Station Rd which costs from Rs 30. *Hotel Vikrant* is near the river and has doubles at Rs 25. It's clean, friendly and noisy but beware of the monkeys which will sneak into your room if you leave the door unlocked and will also steal clothes left outside to dry. There are many other cheaper hotels and also *Railway Retiring Rooms*.

Places to Eat

Chatewala, near the Tourist Office, does good value full thalis. The *Hotel Gurudev* has a good restaurant.

Getting There

Hardwar is 222 km from Delhi, 52 km from Dehra Dun and 24 km from Rishikesh. There are direct buses from all these places. Dehra Dun-Hardwar is about Rs 5.50 to 7, more expensive from Dehra Dun due to the tax. The 54-km trip takes about 1½ hours. From Chandigarh a bus takes about six hours for Rs 25. By train it is 14 hours from Lucknow or seven hours from Delhi. From Delhi it's 'a really excellent train' reported one letter, 'absolutely hassle-free and comfortable'.

RISHIKESH (population 22,000)

Surrounded by hills on three sides, Rishikesh is a quieter and more easy-going place than Hardwar although at an altitude of 356 metres it is only 63 metres higher. Like Hardwar, there are many ashrams and sadhus and this is an excellent place to study Hinduism.

Back in the '60s Rishikesh gained instant, and fleeting, fame as the place where the Beatles came to be with their guru, the Maharishi Mahesh Yogi. Rishikesh is also the jumping off point for treks to Himalayan pilgrimage centres like Badrinath, Kederanth and Gangotri.

Information & Orientation

The Tourist Office (tel 209) is on Railway Station Rd. The bus stand is round the corner from it on Agarwal Rd.

Things to See

The most interesting ghats and temples in Rishikesh are across the river on the left (east) bank but are connected by a free launch system. The Lakshman Jhula suspension bridge is further upstream. Interesting temples include the Parmath Temple with many images from Hindu mythology. The Lakshman Temple is by the bridge, three km from the town centre. Neel Khanth Mahadev is 12 km further on, fine views on the way up to the temple at 1700 metres.

Meditation

Studying Hinduism has, naturally, become somewhat commercialised at Rishikesh. The Divine Life Society, founded by Swami Shivanand, is an authentic place. It's on the Tourist Bungalow side of the river. You can stay there for short term study or for longer three month courses. Or simply drop by for the evening lecture at 'Satsanga'. At Ved Niketan an Indian sadhu gives lectures in English to those interested. And, of course, there's the Maharishi Mahesh Yogi's Transcendental Meditation Centre.

Places to Stay

The *Tourist Bungalow* (tel 372) is the best place in town and has rooms with attached bath for Rs 30/35 and a Rs 5 dorm. Food is also available here and there's a pleasant garden for relaxing in. The Tourist Bungalow is three km from the bus and railway station.

Hotel Indralok (tel 99) is next to the station and singles are Rs 35, doubles Rs 50 to 60 or Rs 60 to 90 with air-con. It's a

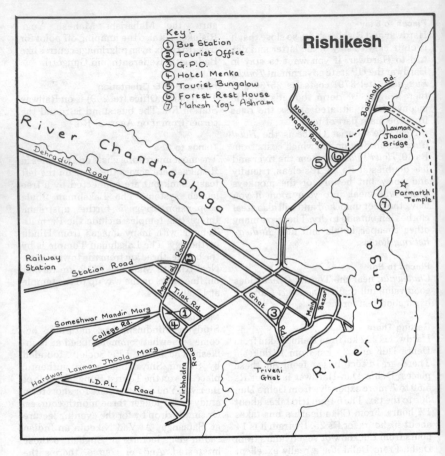

Key :-
1. Bus Station
2. Tourist Office
3. G.P.O.
4. Hotel Menka
5. Tourist Bungalow
6. Forest Rest House
7. Mahesh Yogi Ashram

Rishikesh

River Chandrabhaga

Dehradun Road

Narendra Nagar Road

Badrinath Rd.

Laxman Jhoola Bridge

☆ Parmarth Temple

River Ganga

Railway Station

Station Road

Agarwal Road

Tilak Rd.

Ghat Rd.

Main Bazar

Someshwar Mandir Marg

College Rd.

Hardwar Laxman Jhoola Marg

I.D.P.L. Road

Virbhadra Road

Triveni Ghat

new hotel with a good dining hall. Other hotels include the *Hotel Menka* (tel 285), with rooms at Rs 30/40, which is also near the bus stand. The *Janta Tourist Lodge* is on Dehra Dun Rd. As at Hardwar there are many dharamsalas offering free accommodation to pilgrims.

Getting There
There is a branch railway line from Hardwar up to Rishikesh and regular direct buses. The 24-km trip takes less than an hour by bus for about Rs 3.

CORBETT NATIONAL PARK
On the banks of the Ram Ganga River in the foothills of the Himalayas, this park is famous for its wide variety of wildlife. The park is particularly renowned for its tigers but also has elephants, several types of deer, including sambars, and panthers. The river has crocodiles and there is much birdlife. The park was established in 1935 and later renamed after Jim Corbett, who spent many years in this area and wrote the book *The Man-Eaters of Kumaon*.

Dhikala is the main accommodation

centre in the park, 51 km from Ramnagar, the nearest railhead to the park. Ramnagar is connected by train with Moradabad and by bus with Delhi and Lucknow. Most tours into the park are operated from Dhikala, although there are also three-day package tours operated from New Delhi. Entry to the park costs Rs 30 (Rs 2 for students) for three days, then Rs 6 per day. The park is open from December to May.

The park is comparatively cool and at sunrise and sunset you can go out on elephant back for Rs 12.50 for about two hours. The elephant rides are not to be missed. The elephant grass and the edge of the sal forest are searched for an hour or more and as well as spotted and hog deer, wild boar, monitor lizards, jackals and many birds there is a good chance of seeing a tiger. There are also crocodiles in the river, monkeys, sambar and other deer species in the woods and wild elephants elsewhere in the park. Corbett is also a bird watcher's paradise. During the day you can swim in the river or sit in one of the observation posts to watch for animals. They show interesting films on wildlife and expeditions in the evenings, free of charge.

Places to Stay

At Dhikala there are *Cabins* (Rs 100 per day without air-con), *New* and *Old Forest Rest Houses* (Rs 100 per day), *Tourist Hutments* (Rs 40), *Swiss Cottage Tents* (Rs 10), *Loghuts* (Rs 12 per person) and camping facilities (Rs 3 per person). One large restaurant caters for all the accommodation facilities. The meals are set price (Rs 10) but the food is good and it's eat-all-you-want. There are also *Forest Rest Houses* at Sarapduli, Bijrani, Gairal, Kanda and Sultan.

Ramnagar, which is a crossroads between the plains and the hills, has a few overpriced hotels and many restaurants with beds in the back rooms – grotty but cheap. The *Tiger Hotel* is Rs 30/45 for singles/doubles.

The park is closed at sunset, so make sure you arrive there before that time.

Getting There

Ramnagar is the nearest railhead to the park or there is a daily bus from Nainital via Ramnagar to Dhikala. It leaves Ramnagar in the mid-afternoon and the return trip from Dhikala in the morning. The trip should take six or seven hours. There are also buses just from Ramnagar to Dhikala, Rs 9. A bus from Ramnagar to the Dhangadri park entrance costs Rs 3. From there you can take an afternoon bus into the park HQ at Dhikala or try and hitch a lift.

ALMORA (population 23,000)

This picturesque hill station was taken from Nepal following the 1815 Gurkha War. It's at an altitude of 1650 metres and many travellers live in cottages in the hills around the town. There is a good walk from Almora up to the Kasar Devi temple which has excellent views. Some of the walks out of town take you to quite isolated woods, full of monkeys, if you walk far enough.

Places to Stay

There are a number of hotels and the popular *Tourist Cottage* with rooms from Rs 15.

KAUSANI

Situated 53 km north of Almora this small village is on a ridge looking out to 300 km of mountains!

Places to Stay

Excellent views from the *Hotel Prashant* about 10 minutes up the road from the bus stand. Rooms range from Rs 10 to 25. Other places include the *Tourist Rest House* with rooms at Rs 15 to 30 and also dorm beds at Rs 10. Or there's the *Gandhi Ashram* and various other private hotels.

Getting There

Buses to Ramnagar via Ranikhet pass Kausani.

NAINI TAL (population 28,000)

In this lake-dotted area of the Kumaon Hills the pretty hill town of Naini Tal was once the summer capital of Uttar Pradesh. There are many interesting walks and lakes around the town – which itself is divided into two parts, upper and lower lake (Tal). Climb up to China Peak in the early morning for the fine views over Naini Tal and the snow-clad Himalaya off in the distance. In the middle of the summer season Naini Tal is packed full of local tourists and spoilt children and the prices go up.

Places to Stay & Eat

The *Hotel Coronation*, opposite the Naini Tal Club in the old colonial part of town, is very basic with singles/doubles for Rs 20/ 35. On the other side of town, which is less 'rich tourist', *Saidar Bhawan* and the *Punjab Hotel* are two more fairly basic places. They overlook the lake and are also in the Rs 20 to 40 price range. The *Prashant* is a pleasant hotel with good food in its restaurant and doubles at Rs 45.

The *Evelyn Hotel* has spacious doubles with bath, hot water and even a separate sitting room for Rs 60 even at the height of the season. Terrific views from the top floor rooms, a good restaurant and friendly management.

There is a *Youth Hostel* with dorm beds for less than Rs 10 at the west end of the town, about three km from the bus stand. It's a 40 minute uphill walk but it's in a lovely, peaceful location. They also have good doubles for Rs 16. Otherwise most places here are rather expensive – including the *Grand Hotel* (tel 2406) on The Mall with singles/doubles at Rs 100/ 150-180. Or there's the *Royal Hotel* and the *Swiss Hotel* (tel 2603) on The Mall with singles/doubles at Rs 200/250.

The *Sharma Vaishnow Restaurant* in the Malli Tal Bazaar offers all-you-can-eat vegetarian meals for around Rs 5.

RANIKHET

North of Naini Tal and only a short distance west of Almora, this hill station offers excellent views of the snow-capped Himalaya. Only eight km away, Chaubattia is famous for its fruits.

Places to Stay

The *Moon Hotel & Restaurant* (tel 58, 182) has rooms at Rs 65/140. There are many other hotels both cheaper and more expensive.

TREKKING IN THE GARWHAL HIMAL

Although the Garwhal Himal is little known as a trekking region it boasts a number of famous peaks, including Trisul and India's highest mountain, Nanda Devi. Or at least it was the highest until Sikkim (and thus Kanchenjunga) was absorbed into India. There are also many important pilgrimage sites such as Badrinath and Kedarnath or Gaumukh, the actual source of the Ganges. The trekking routes pass through rich, green forests and across beautiful meadows that are carpeted with flowers in summer. Glistening glaciers complement the soaring Himalayan peaks and there are many excellent state government-operated *Tourist Bungalows* along the routes to simplify the question of shelter.

The best times to trek in the Garwhal Himal are May-June and Sepember-October. Some places, like the Valley of Flowers and the high altitude *bugyals* (meadows) are at their best during the July-August rainy period. The Mountaineering Division, located at the Tourist Bungalow in Rishikesh, can provide more information on trekking in the Garwhal Himal. The new Lonely Planet guide *Trekking in the Indian Himalaya* should be available during 1984.

Actually the term Garwhal Himal is something of a misnomer. There is only Garwhal (the Himal is an incorrect

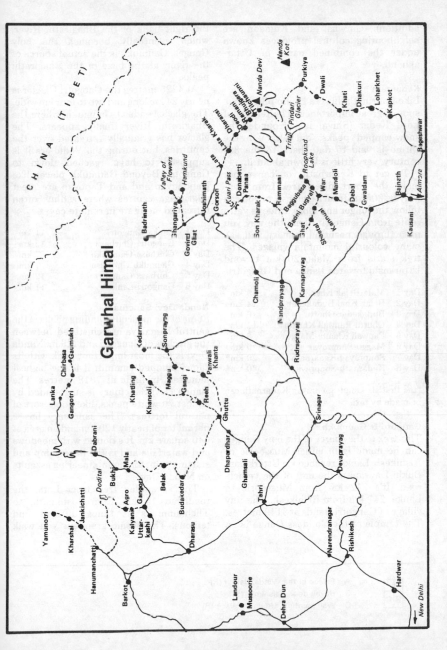

addition). Garwhal and Kumaon are neighbouring cultural provinces known under the combined name of Uttarakhand.

Kedarnath

Like Badrinath this is a Hindu pilgrimage spot of great importance. The temple of Lord Kedar (Shiva) is surrounded by snow-capped peaks, but although the shrine is said to date back to the 8th century, very little is known about it.

To get to Kedarnath you can either make the short, direct trek from Sonprayag, 205 km from Rishikesh, or you can follow the longer and more arduous yatra route from Gangotri. Along the way you pass through beautiful scenery and see many colourful mountain villages. The trek starts from Mala, 20 km beyond Uttarkashi towards Lanka and Gangotri.

Day 1	Mala-Belak Khal	15 km
Day 2	Belak Khal-Budakedar	14 km
Day 3	Budakedar-Ghuttu	16 km
Day 4	Ghuttu-Panwali Khanta	12 km
Day 5	Panwali Khanta-Maggu	8 km
Day 6	Maggu-Sonprayag	9 km
Day 7	Sonprayag-Kedarnath	20 km*
Day 8	Kedarnath-Sonprayag	20 km*

*the first six km of Sonprayag-Kedarnath can be made by taxi.

Gangotri & Gaumukh

This trek to the source of the holy Ganges can be made from either Mussoorie or Rishikesh. Lanka, reached via Uttarkashi-Bukhi-Dabrani is the end of the vehicle road. It's 212 km from Mussoorie to Lanka, 247 km from Rishikesh. The tiny village of Gangotri stands at 3140 metres. The temple of the Goddess Ganga is on the right bank of the Bhagirathi River, which eventually becomes the holy Ganges. Gaumukh is the actual source of the river, at the base of the Bhagirathi peaks.

At 4225 metres the Gangotri Glacier is nearly 24 km long and two to four km wide. The glacier ends at Gaumukh, where the Bhagirathi River finally appears. The glacier has gradually retreated over the centuries, but during the Vedic era it is supposed to have reached down to Gangotri. Beyond Gaumukh places like Nandanvan and and Tapovan are great pilgrimage centres where sadhus often retreat to meditate in remote caves.

Day 1	Lanka-Gangotri	11 km
Day 2	Gangotri-Chirbasa	12 km
Day 3	Chirbasa-Gaumukh	7 km
Day 4	Gaumukh-Chirbasa	7 km
Day 5	Chirbasa-Gangotri	12 km
Day 6	Gangotri-Lanka	11 km

Nanda Devi Sanctuary

Some of the most outstanding peaks in the central Himalaya are clustered between the glaciers of Gangotri and Milan. Nanda Devi is the most important peak with its camel-humped summit; it is the highest mountain in India at 7818 metres. The Nanda Devi Sanctuary is surrounded by almost 70 white peaks, like some sort of natural fortress. The sanctuary has a perimeter of nearly 120 km and an area of 640 square km. It's dotted with meadows and waterfalls and is the base camp and starting point for mountaineering assaults on Nanda Devi.

The seven-day trek from Lata, the roadhead 15 km from Joshimath, to Tilchaunni is at times difficult and tedious. The scenic grandeur you walk

A   Palace of the Winds, Jaipur (R)
B   Haveli door, Jaisalmer (R)
C   Wall painting, Udaipur Palace (R)

through will often compensate for weary bodies and frayed nerves. The first six km from Lata to Lata Kharak is a tiring uphill struggle of 1524 metres, but one is well rewarded by glorious views of Ronti, Nanda Ghunti and Bethartoli across the Rishi Ganga. The broad, open grassy ridge of Lata Kharak is covered with flowers in the summer but it is always windy and cold. From here there are fine views of the northern face of Bethartoli Himal and the Trisul massif to the south. Another long uphill trek crosses the 4253-metre Dharansi Pass and takes you to Dharansi. On approaching the pass you get your first glimpse of Dunagiri (7068 metres) and immediately after crossing it Nanda Devi can be seen.

From Dharansi the trail winds its way across the Malatuni Pass (4238 metres), where the western face of Hanuman (6076 metres) can be seen, then descends almost 750 metres through grass and snow slopes and dense forest to a stream. After crossing the stream you finally arrive at the hospitable meadows of Dibrugheta where a camp can be made by the river. In summer the grass is carpeted with flowers. From here to Deodi the track rises steeply at first then makes a long traverse across several ridges before you cross a bridge over the Rishi Ganga and arrive at Deodi. From Deodi it is an eight km trek through juniper and rhododendron forests to Ramani.

Nanda Devi comes ever closer as you approach Tilchaunni ('slate quarry'). It's a delightful birch clearing, the last on the Rishi gorge, but it means climbing *down* from the Bhujara trail. Hence all porters porters prefer to climb up to Patalkhan, about a km above, where there is a cave

and water. Most people would prefer to camp at Dibrugheta, four km below Dharansi, where wood is available.

There are three other routes in the sanctuary: Dunagiri and Changabang base (the ultimate mountain); Trisul base (with a new route into the inner south sanctuary discovered in 1979); and Nanda Devi north base (Rishi Tal above the Changabang Glacier).

Day 1	Joshimath – Lata	25 km*
	Lata – Lata Kharak	6 km
Day 2	Lata Kharak – Dharansi	10 km
Day 3	Dharansi – Deodi	13 km
Day 4	Deodi – Ramani	8 km
Day 5	Ramani – Bhujgara	6 km
Day 6	Bhujgara – Tilchaunni	8 km
Day 7	Tilchaunni – Nanda Devi	5 km
	base camp	
Day 8	Nanda Devi base camp –	6 km
	Bhujgara	
Day 9	Bhujgara – Ramani	6 km
Day 10	Ramani – Dibrugheta	17 km
Day 11	Dibrugheta – Dharansi	4 km
Day 12	Dharansi – Joshimath	31 km**

* by bus
** last 15 km by bus

Yamunotri & Dodital

Yamunotri is the source of the Yamuna River – it emerges from a frozen lake of ice and glaciers on the Kalinda Parvat at an altitude of 4421 metres. There is a temple of the goddess Yamunotri on the left bank of the river and, just below the temple, there are several hot springs where the water emerges at boiling point.

Two more days' walk brings you to Dodital where a dense forest of oak, pine, deodar and rhododendron surrounds a dazzling body of water. The lake is filled with fish and many colourful birds can be seen around it. Dodital is at 4024 metres and is fed by natural springs in its depths.

Day 1	Mussoorie-Hanumanchatti	81 km*
Day 2	Hanumanchatti-Jankichatti	7 km
Day 3	Jankichatti-Yamunotri–Jankichatti	14 km
Day 4	Jankichatti-Basard	14 km
Day 5	Basard-Dodital	16 km
Day 6	Dodital-Agro	15 km
Day 7	Agro-Kalyani-Gangori–Uttarkashi	17 km

*75 km by bus, 6 km by taxi

Kuari Pass

There are two routes from Joshimath to the Kuari Pass. One route goes through Auli and Gorson, Tali and Chitrakhanta and this is more rewarding than the other route via Mrig to Tugasi and Khulara then Gailgarh to Kuari. From Auli the path trails its way through rich green forests, with the mountains always in view. The camping grounds are an absolute delight – undulating slopes, carpeted in grass and set in beautiful natural surroundings. From Tali to Chitrakhanta there is only a narrow goat track which horses and mules cannot use.

At 4268 metres Kuari, reached by a narrow pass, offers a superb panorama of the Himalayas to the north-east and the vast stretches of verdant valleys to the south-east. Nanda Devi, Dunagiri, Bethartoli, Hathi Parvat and Devastan are some of the peaks which can be seen. On a clear day it is possible to sight the Nanda Devi Sanctuary. Gailgarh, just five km from Kuari, is a little gem in wonderful surroundings. Six km south-east of Gailgarh is the snow-capped 5183 metre peak of Pangarchulia. It can be easily scaled with only normal trekking gear and, from its summit, Badrinath and other snow-covered peaks can be seen.

Delisera, six km east of Gailgarh, is a little hamlet at 3354 metres. In the local dialect 'sera' means 'the rice fields' and the terraced slopes around here are thought to date back countless years. In late June the entire land is a tapestry of flowers. Bore Kund, six km noth-east of Gailgarh, is a lovely lake which is reputed to be very deep.

Day 1	Joshimath-Gorson	15 km*
Day 2	Gorson-Chitrakantha	9 km
Day 3	Chitrakantha-Kuari	8 km
Day 4	Kuari-Donabetti	7 km
Day 5	Donabetti-Panna	8 km
Day 6	Panna-Son Kharak	14 km
Day 7	Son Kharak-Rammani	6 km
Day 8	Rammani-Ghat	14 km
	Ghat-Nandprayag	29 km**

* first eight km by taxi
** by taxi

Khatling Glacier

The first four days of this trek follow the yatra route to Kedarnath, before the trail branches off north-east to the glacier. It then retraces the route to Ghuttu and continues south-west to Ghamsali from where buses run to Tehri and Rishikesh. The Khatling Glacier is a lateral glacier from the centre of which the Bhilangana River emerges. The rich pasturelands here make ideal camping sites – the summer rains make the flat land on the glacial moraines into excellent pastures. The glaciers are associated with the giant hanging glaciers of Ratangian, Jogin and Phating. Around the glacier are the snow-capped peaks of the Jogin ground (6466 metres), spectacular Sphetic Prishtwan (6905 metres), Kirti Stambh (6402 metres) and Barte Kanta (6579 metres).

The yatra route is tiring, with its constant ascents and descents, but colourful. There are many rippling streams to be crossed by improvised log bridges. Gangi, the last village before the glacier, is still very much cut off from the outside world. The people here are so isolated that they have been forced to frequently intermarry within their own community and as a result many people are sterile.

Days 1-3 as Kedarnath Trek

Day 4	Ghuttu-Reeh	10 km
Day 5	Reeh-Gangi	10 km
Day 6	Gangi-Khansoli	15 km
Day 7	Khansoli-Khatling	11 km
Day 8	Khatling-Naumuthi	9 km
Day 9	Naumuthi-Kalyani	12 km
Day 10	Kalyani-Reeh	15 km
Day 11	Reeh-Dhapardhar	15 km
Day 12	Dhapardhar-Gamsali	25 km
	Gamsali-Tehri	31 km*
Day 13	Tehri-Rishikesh	72 km*

* by bus

The Khatling Glacier trek can also be made from the Kedarnath side. In that case the first three days of the trek are like Days 6, 5 and 4 of the Kedarnath Trek. On Day 3 you reach Ghuttu and then the route is the same as from the Gangotri side.

Valley of Flowers & Hemkund
The beautiful 'Valley of Flowers' and the holy Hemkund lake can be reached in one short trek from Govind Ghat. In addition you can also visit the pilrimage centre of Badrinath, now accessible by road, on the same trip. From Rishikesh it is 252 km by bus to Joshimath and a further 44 km to Badrinath. You then have to backtrack 30 km to Govind Ghat for the start of the trek.

Badrinath Surrounded by snow-capped peaks Badrinath has been a Hindu pilgrimage centre since time immemorial. There are many temples, ashrams and dharamsalas here. The most important temple, on the left bank of the Alakananda, shows clear Buddhist influence in its architecture, indicating that in an earlier period this must also have been a Buddhist centre.

The mountaineer, Frank Smythe, is believed to be the discoverer of the Valley of the Flowers. Between mid-June and mid-September the valley is an enchanting sight with a bewildering variety of flowers fluttering in the gentle breezes.

As a backdrop snow-clad mountains stand in bold relief against the skyline. The valley is nearly 10 km long, two km wide, and is divided by the Pushpawati stream, into which several tiny streams and waterfalls merge. The huge Ghoradhungi mountain blocks one end of the valley.

From the valley you can backtrack to Ghangariya, then follow the Laxma Ganga to the lake of Hemkund. In the Sikh holy book, the Garanth Sahib, the Sikh Guru Govind Singh recounts that in a previous life he had meditated on the shores of a lake surrounded by seven snow-capped mountains. Hemkund Sahib, Sikh pilgrims have decided, is that holy lake. From Govind Ghat it is a gentle incline to the Valley of Flowers but the trek from the pretty hamlet of Ghangariya to Hemkund is rather steep.

Day 1	Govind Ghat –	
	Ghangariya	14 km
Day 2	Ghangariya – Valley of	6 km
	Flowers	
Day 3	Valley of Flowers –	
	Ghangariya – Hemkund –	
	Ghangariya	16 km

Roopkund Lake
At an altitude of 4778 metres, below the 7122-metre high Trisul massif, the Roopkund Lake is sometimes referred to as the 'mystery lake', because of skeletons of humans and horses which have been found here. Every 12 years thousands of devout pilgrims make an arduous trek when following the Raj Jay Yatra from Nauti village, near Karanprayag. The pilgrims are said to be led by a mysterious four-horned ram which takes them from there through Roopkund to the Shrine of Nanda Devi, where it disappears. A golden idol of the goddess Nanda Devi is carried by the pilgrims in a silver palanquin.

The trek commences from Gwaldom, accessible by bus from Rishikesh. It passes through delightful alpine pastureland and snow fields and offers magnificent views of peaks in the Garwhal Himal such as Trisul and Nanda Ghunti.

Day	1	Rishikesh – Gwaldom	240 km*
Day	2	Gwaldom – Debal	10 km
Day	3	Debal – Mandoli	15 km
Day	4	Mandoli – Wan	14 km
Day	5	Wan – Badni Bugyal	8 km
Day	6	Badni Bugyal – Baggubasa	8 km
Day	7	Baggubasa – Roopkund – Baggubasa	8 km
Day	8	Baggubasa – Wan	16 km
Day	9	Wan – Kannual	9 km
Day	10	Kannual – Sheetal	9 km
Day	11	Sheetal – Ghat	14 km
		Ghat – Nandprayag	30 km**
Day	12	Nandprayag – Rishikesh	192 km*

* by bus
** by taxi

Pindari Glacier

The magnificent Pindari Glacier is the most easily accessible in the region. It owes its existence to the snow sliding down from Nanda Khat and other lofty peaks. The glacier, three km long and nearly half a km wide, is at an altitude of 3353 metres. Close to the glacier there is an undulating meadow and to the east a moraine projects into the glacier.

The trek offers views of the soaring peaks all the way and passes through pine

forests, glades of ferns and wildflowers and past tumbling waterfalls. From mid-May to mid-June there are many wildflowers, while from mid-September to mid-October the air is exceptionally clear and it has not yet got too cold. Starting from Rishikesh you go by bus to Kapkot before actually starting to walk. There is an excellent view of the glacier from Purkiya and some trekkers stop here. On the return trek you can travel by road from Bajnath to Almora and Naini Tal rather than return to Rishikesh. There are PWD Inspection Bungalows at most of the night stops.

Day	1	Rishikesh – Gwaldon	240 km*
Day	2	Gwaldon – Kapkot	76 km*
Day	3	Kapkot – Loharkhet	13 km
Day	4	Loharkhet – Khati	18 km
Day	5	Khati – Purkiya	14 km
Day	6	Purkiya – Pindari	5 km
Day	7	Pindari – Khati	19 km
Day	8	Khati – Loharkhet	18 km
Day	9	Loharkhet – Bajnath	47 km*
Day	10	Bajnath – Kausani – Almora	71 km*

* by bus

Bihar

Population: 62 million
Area: 173,876 square km
Capital: Patna
Main language: Hindi

The northern state of Bihar is one of the most backward and depressed in India. Its tightly-packed population scratches a bare living from rice growing. For visitors Bihar is usually little more than a place to be crossed, with perhaps a pause in Patna if they are heading for Nepal by land. Yet 25 centuries ago this was the capital of the greatest empire in India for Ashoka ruled his kingdom from Pataliputra, where Patna is today.

Furthermore Bihar was a great religious centre for Jains, Hindus and, most important, Buddhists. It was at Bodhgaya that the Buddha sat under the Bo tree and attained enlightenment and a descendant of that original tree still flourishes there today. Nearby Nalanda was a world-famous university for the study of Buddhism in the 5th century AD, while Rajgir was associated with both the Buddha and with the Jain apostle Mahavira.

PATNA (population 550,000)

For many centuries Patna, the ancient name for which was Pataliputra, was the capital of a huge empire which ruled a large part of ancient India. Today it is the capital of the rather backward state of Bihar. The city sprawls along the bank of the Ganges, which at this point is very wide; between Varanasi and Patna three major tributaries join the Ganges and the river triples in width. The only way to cross the Ganges at Patna used to be by ferry but there is now a recently completed bridge.

Information & Orientation

The city stretches for 15 km along the south bank of the Ganges. The main railway station, airline offices and the airport are all at the western end of the town, while the older and more traditional parts of Patna are to the east. The 'hub' of the new Patna is at Gandhi Maidan. The main market area is Ashok Raj Path which starts from Gandhi Maidan. Two roads near the railway station recently changed their names: Frazer Rd is now M Haque Path, and Exhibition Rd is Braj Kishore Path respectively.

Golghar

Overlooking the maidan the huge, bee-hive-shaped Golghar was built in 1786 as a granary to store surpluses against possible famines. It stands about 25 metres high and steps wind around the outside to the top from where you have a fine view over the Patna and the Ganges. Inside there is a superb echo. The Golghar was built by Captain John Garstin at the instigation of the British administrator, Warren Hastings, following a terrible famine in 1770, but it has scarcely been used since that time.

293

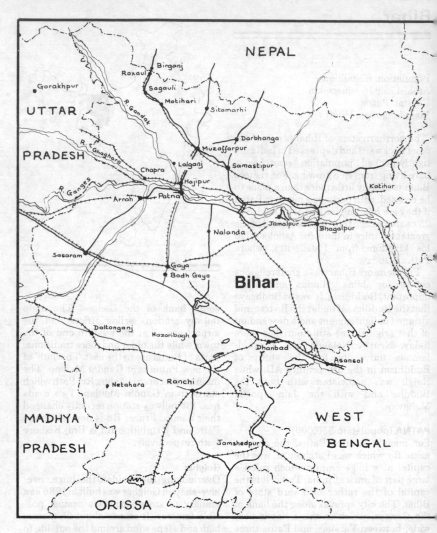

NEPAL

UTTAR

PRADESH

Gorakhpur

Raxaul Birganj

Sagauli

Motihari

Sitamarhi

R Gandak

Darbhanga

R Ghaghara

Muzaffarpur

Chapra Lalganj

Samastipur

R Ganges

Hajipur

Katihar

Arrah Patna

Jamalpur Bhagalpur

Nalanda

Sasaram

Gaya

Bodh Gaya

Bihar

Daltonganj

Hazaribagh

Dhanbad

Asansol

Netahara

Ranchi

MADHYA

WEST

PRADESH

Jamshedpur

BENGAL

ORISSA

Patna City Museum

The excellent museum contains metal and stone sculptures dating back to the Maurya (3rd century BC) and the Gupta periods, terracotta figures and archaeological finds from sites in Bihar such as Nalanda. There are also original Chinese and Tibetan scrolls and paintings. The museum is closed on Mondays.

Kumrahar

Pataliputra, Ashoka's caital in the 3rd century BC, has been excavated at the small village of Kumrahar, south of Patna.

It was earlier the capital of Chandragupta (321-297 BC), Bindusara (297-274 BC) before Ashoka ruled here between 274 and 237 BC. The main points of interest are the assembly hall with its large pillars which date back to the Mauryan period, and the remnants of the brick Buddhist monastery known as Anand Bihar.

North-west of Kumrahar is Bhikna Pahari where Ashoka built a retreat for his brother Mahinda. Kumrahar is six km from central Patna but the excavations are fairly esoteric and likely to be an attraction only for those with a keen interest in archaeology and India's ancient history.

Har Mandir
At the eastern end of the city, in the Chowk area of old Patna, stands one of the holiest Sikh shrines. Built by Ranjit Singh it marks the place where Govind Singh, the 10th and last of the Sikh gurus, was born in 1660. On the bottom floor of this dome-shaped structure there are holy Sikh scriptures and an exhibition of photos about the Sikh religion together with personal belongings of the Guru including his shoes and cradle. You must cover your head as you enter the shrine.

A tempo from Gandhi Maidan to the Chowk area only costs a few rupees. Celebrations to mark the Guru's birthday are held here in December-January of each year.

Khudabaksh Oriental Library
Founded in 1900 this library has a renowned collection of rare Arabic and Persian manuscripts, of Moghul and Rajput paintings and oddities like the Koran inscribed in a book only an inch wide. The library also contains the only books rescued from the sacking of the Moorish University of Cordoba in Spain.

Other
Gulzarbagh, to the east of the city, was the site of the East India Company's opium warehouse. Today the building houses a Bihar government printing works. The Sher Shahi, built by the Afghan ruler Sher Shah in 1545 is the oldest mosque in Patna and a heavy, domed structure. Other mosques include the squat Pathar ki Masjid and the riverbank Madrassa. Jalan's Quila houses a collection of antiques. A km west of the Har Mandir is the old cemetery, which may still bear some reminders of the British days.

Tours
Patna Tours & Travels, which has an office near the railway station, operates daily sightseeing tours around the city during the tourist season. A half-day tour costs Rs 20. The Bihar tourist office and the same travel agency also arrange day trips around the historic sites of south Bihar, such as Nalanda and Rajgir, for Rs 30.

Places to Stay – Bottom End
There are a number of reasonable hotels around the railway station and airline office area. Most travellers passing through Patna pause just for a day on their way to Kathmandu and these places are quite adequate. The *Hotel Rajasthan* (tel 25102) is near Royal Nepal Airlines. Singles run from Rs 30, doubles Rs 50 to 60. Between the station and Gandhi Maidan the *Hotel Rajdhani* (tel 23784) has singles at Rs 30 a night. *Hotel Rajkumar* on Exhibition Rd is an entirely new building and singles are just Rs 22 – good value. If you are on a tight budget *Hotel Park* on Fraser Rd and *Hotel Gayland* have spartan rooms at just Rs 15 for singles with bath.

One traveller wrote that during festivals there can be a real accommodation shortage in Patna and that many cheaper places won't take foreigners as they must then fill in forms for the police, which is a nuisance. He recommended the *Jasyim Hotel* as clean and comfortable at Rs 75 for a double.

Places to Stay – Top End

Hotel Pataliputra Ashok (tel 23467, 26270) at Beer Chand Patel Path has rooms with or without air-conditioning. Prices range from Rs 200/250 without, Rs 250/325 with, for singles/doubles.

Welcomgroup Maurya Patna (tel 22061-65) is on South Gandhi Maidan and is Patna's top hotel. All rooms are air-con, with the usual mod-cons; singles/doubles cost Rs 275-325/375-425.

The third top end hotel is the *Hotel Republic* (tel 22028) in Lawlys Building, Exhibition Rd. Singles/doubles from Rs 90/125 or Rs 140/175 with air-con.

Places to Eat

The rather expensive *Ashok Restaurant* near the railway station is good. *Hotel Rajasthan* has a clean restaurant with a good selection of Indian dishes. Masala dosas are very cheap at the *Udipi Coffee House*.

Getting There

Air There are two daily flights from Delhi through Patna, one going via Lucknow and continuing to Calcutta and the other going up into the north-east region and terminating at Imphal. Delhi-Patna costs Rs 617, Calcutta-Patna Rs 361, Lucknow-Patna Rs 333. Twice a week there's a flight between Patna and Kathmandu in Nepal.

Rail There are a number of express and mail trains daily between Delhi and Patna taking 16 to 20 hours. The distance is almost exactly a thousand km. The Delhi-Patna fare is Rs 248 in 1st class, Rs 63 in 2nd. Calcutta-Patna takes about eight to 10 hours and costs Rs 152 in 1st, Rs 39 in

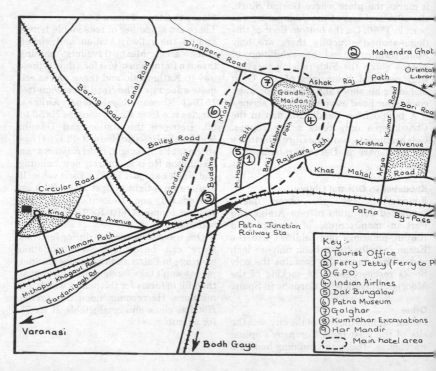

Key:-
1. Tourist Office
2. Ferry Jetty (Ferry to P
3. G.P.O.
4. Indian Airlines
5. Dak Bungalow
6. Patna Museum
7. Golghar
8. Kumrahar Excavations
9. Har Mandir

- - - Main hotel area

2nd. If the Patna-Calcutta train is full you can take a train to Dhanbad and change to a Calcutta train there. You can also also catch trains for Bhubaneswar in Orissa from here.

Arriving in Patna can be fraught – 'there was a Krishna festival and awaiting us at Patna station were 5000 devotees who stampeded the train. It was murder trying to get off and has made us super paranoid of trains ever since!'

Bus The main bus station for express buses to Muzaffarpur and Raxaul at the Nepalese border is located near the Patna Junction Station. It is only a few hundred metres west of the station, opposite the GPO and Hardinge Park.

Getting Around
As late as 1982 you still had to take

steamers to cross the river but a large bridge over the Ganges, one of the longest and most important in India, has recently been constructed. It has been named the Gandhi Bridge after the Mahatma. The bridge has not only connected the predominantly agricultural north Bihar area with Patna and the mineral rice south Bihar, but has also shortened the road distance to the Nepal border.

PATNA-NEPAL
Patna is very popular as a jumping off point for Nepal whether you are travelling by land or air. On the way to Raxaul, the Indian border town to Nepal, you can pause at a number of towns.

Sonepur
Just across the river from Patna is Sonepur. A month-long cattle fair is held

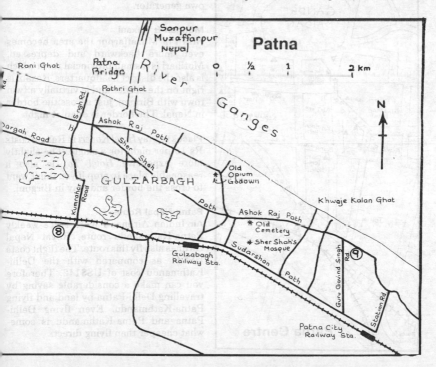

here each October-November, culminating at the full moon night of Kartika Purnima. At one time even elephants were bought and sold at this fair.

Vaisali
Only 44 km north of Patna this was the birthplace of Mahavira, one of the Jain Tirthankars. Over two thousand years ago this was the capital of a republic but very little of the city remains suspected to lie here have been excavated although an Ashoka pillar, topped by his lion symbol, has been unearthed. It was one of a series of Ashoka's pillars erected along the route between Pataliputra (Patna) and Nepal.

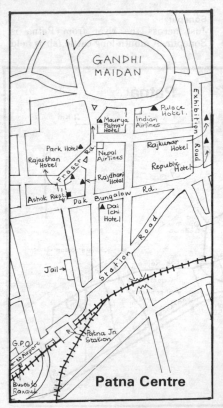

Patna Centre

Vaisali is not on the direct Patna-Muzaffarpur route but you can easily divert to make the route Patna-Hajipur-Laiganj-Vaisali-Muzaffarpur, all by bus.

Places to Stay There is a *Youth Hostel* and a *Tourist Rest House* here. The dorm costs about Rs 5. The local speciality at Vaisali is *chura*, a mixture of rice and curd.

Muzaffarpur (population 140,000)
Apart from being a bus changing point on the way to the Nepal border, Muzaffarpur is of no real interest. This is a poverty-ridden and agriculturally backward area.

Places to Stay *Hotel Deepak* has reasonable food and very spartan rooms for only around Rs 10. Most of north Bihar plunges into darkness most evenings, but this hotel is an exception because it has its own generator.

Motihari & Raxaul
North of Muzaffarpur the area becomes even more backward and depressed. Motihari is a small provincial town which is also the district headquarters. Raxaul is right on the border and is virtually a twin town with Birgunj, just across the border in Nepal. The border is open at night.

Places to Stay *Hotel Kaveri* in Raxaul costs Rs 15 per night for a single. The slightly more expensive *Hotel Taj* is also a reasonable place to stop if you don't want to cross the border and stay in Birgunj.

Patna-Nepal Routes
Air Indian Airlines have a twice weekly Patna-Kathmandu route, Royal Nepal Airlines also fly this route. The flight costs US$41 as compared with the Delhi-Kathmandu cost of US$142. Therefore you can make a considerable saving by travelling Delhi-Patna by land and flying Patna-Kathmandu. Even flying Delhi-Patna and Patna-Kathmandu is somewhat cheaper than flying direct.

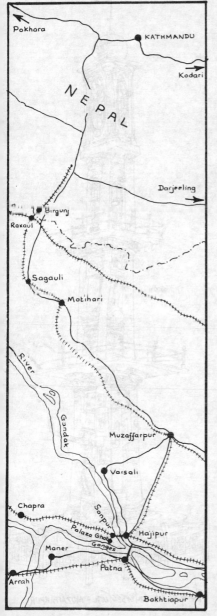

Land By land you can get from Patna to Raxaul on the India-Nepal border either by bus or train but with the opening of the Gandhi Bridge over the Ganges at Patna it does not make much sense to take a train.

Buses to Raxaul from Patna depart from Hardinge Park, across the street from the GPO, near the Patna Junction Railway Station. Look for the 'tourist bus' which departs at noon each day and costs Rs 25 to Raxaul. It may be better to buy tickets a couple of hours before departure to ensure a seat. There are now buses leaving from the main bus station at 6 or 7 am and the trip to the border takes only about three or four fours.

Some hotels and travel agencies in Patna offer a package deal to Kathmandu for Rs 110. This includes the bus transport from Patna to the border, overnight accommodation at a spartan hotel at either Raxaul or Birgunj at the border and the bus from Birgunj to Kathmandu. Although this saves a lot of hassle you can still save Rs 30 by doing it yourself.

Some trains from Delhi go all the way to Muzaffarpur via Patna. They all take a long time to reach Muzaffarpur so it's better to get off in Patna and take a bus from there to the Nepalese border.

PATNA-VARANASI
Sasaram

At the junction of the Grand Trunk Road with the road to Patna there are some fine Moslem tombs in this town, particularly that of the Afghan ruler Sher Shah who died in 1545. The dome of his tomb, visible from the railway line, rises 46 metres above the water level of the surrounding tank. The tomb of his father and the unfinished tomb of his son are also in Sasaram.

More Moslem tombs are at Maner. At Dehri, 17 km from Sasaram, the railway and the Grand Trunk Road cross the River Son on a three-km bridge. The hill fort of Rohtas is 38 km from here.

PATNA-GAYA
Nalanda
This was a great Buddhist centre over a thousand years ago until the monastery, school and library were sacked and burnt by Moslems. When Hieun Tsang, the Chinese scholar and traveller, stayed here for five years in the early 7th century AD there were 10,000 monks and students in residence.

The remains are still extensive and include the Great Stupa with steps and terraces and with a few still intact votive stupas around it. An archaeological museum houses sculpture and other remains found on the site and an international centre for the study of Buddhism was established here, in 1951. There are Burmese, Japanese and Jain rest houses at Nalanda. Buses connect Nalanda with Rajgir, Gaya and Patna; the latter is 90 km away.

Rajgir
Little remains of the Buddhist ruins at Rajgir, 19 km south of Nalanda towards Gaya. The first Buddhist council was held here after the Buddha attained nirvana. During the Buddha's life this was the capital of this part of India, and he spent 12 years here. Buy one of the locally available guidebooks to the sites – they're only Rs 1 to 3. There is a Japanese stupa on a nearby hill and three km away there are hot sulphur springs. They're over-populated. There's a Tourist Information Office at Rajgir Kund.

Places to Stay The *Tourist Bungalow Number 2* (tel 39) is convenient and has a Rs 7 dormitory. The *Tourist Bungalow Number 1* (tel 26) has Rs 20 doubles as well as a dorm. There's also a *Rest House* and *Youth Hostel* in Rajgir. The Burmese Temple has a coffee house within the grounds which specialises in South Indian food and this is also a good place to stay. It's clean and popular and handy for the Tourist Bungalow.

Triptee's Hotel has singles/doubles at

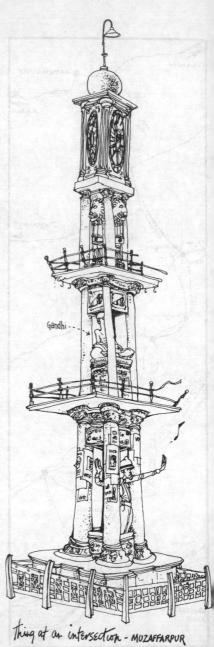

Gandhi

thing at an intersection - MUZAFFARPUR

Rs 25/35. There are a number of cheaper hotels such as the *Anand Hotel* or the *Hill View Hotel*.

Pawapuri

The Jain Thirtankar Mahavira attained nirvana here, 25 km from Nalanda. It is an important Jain pilgrimage spot.

GAYA (population 200,000)

Just as nearby Bodhgaya is a major centre for Buddhist pilgrims so is Gaya a centre for Hindu pilgrims. Gaya is second only to Varanasi in its sanctity and pilgrims believe that offering *pindas* (funeral cakes) here will free their ancestors from bondage to the earth. They must also perform a lengthy circuit of the holy places around Gaya. Gaya is about 100 km south of Patna.

Vishnupad Temple

In the crowded central part of the old town the sikhara style temple was constructed in 1787 by Queen Ahalya Bai of Indore. The temple is situated on the banks of the Falgu River, but although you can view the exterior of the temple and the picturesque bathing ghats, non-Hindus are not allowed into the temple interior. During the monsoon the river carries a great deal of water but it dries up completely during the winter.

A 30-metre high octagonal tower surmounts the temple. Inside, the 40-cm long 'footprint' of Vishnu is imprinted in solid rock and surrounded by a silver-plated basin.

Other

A temple of the Sun God stands north of the Vishnupad temple. A flight of 1000 stone steps leads to the top of the Brahmajuni Hill, a km south-west. There is a good view over Gaya from the top of the hill. At the base of the hill is the Akshyabat or immortal banyan tree, which pilrims visit to complete the cycle of rituals for their ancestors that they commenced in Varanasi.

Situated 20 km north of Gaya, the Barabar caves are very ancient, dating back to 200 BC. Two of the caves have inscriptions from Ashoka himself. These are the 'Marabar' caves of E M Forster's *A Passage to India*.

Places to Stay

There are *Railway Retiring Rooms* at Gaya station and a few other places to stay around the station – spartan but OK for a short pause. The new *Ajatsatru Hotel* (tel 1514) is on Station Rd, just across the street from the station. Singles/doubles are Rs 25/40 and it's pretty good.

The food is good there too. The *Pal Rest House* has doubles with bathroom for Rs 20. At the *Station View Hotel & Restaurant* you can get very good meals very cheaply.

Getting There

It takes eight to ten hours by train from Calcutta (Rs 135 1st class, Rs 34 2nd class) or six hours from Varanasi (Rs 72 1st class, Rs 19 2nd class) – 'pandemonium boarding and they all bloody well got off at Mughlai Sarai!' Patna to Gaya takes three to five hours by a slower train.

Getting Around

A rickshaw from the station through the narrow alleys to the Vishnupad temple will cost about Rs 2.

BODHGAYA

There are four holy places associated with the Buddha – Lumbini, in Nepal, where he was born; Sarnath, near Varanasi, where he first preached his message; Kushinagar, near Gorakhpur, where he died; and Bodhgaya where he attained enlightenment. A Bo tree growing at Bodhgaya is said to be a direct descendant of the original tree under which the Buddha sat, meditated and achieved enlightenment.

Buddhists from all over the world flock to Bodhgaya, along with many westerners who come here to learn about Buddhism

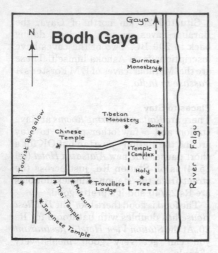

N

Bodh Gaya

Gaya

Burmese Monastery

Tibetan Monastery

Bank

Chinese Temple

Tourist Bungalow

Temple Complex

Holy Tree

Travellers Lodge

Museum

Thai Temple

Japanese Temple

River Falgu

or meditation. Bodhgaya is small and quiet but, if you are not planning a longer study stay, a day is quite sufficient to see everything.

Bodhi Tree

The sacred Bo tree growing here is said to be a direct descendant of the original tree under which the Buddha sat. Although that tree has died a sapling from the original tree was carried to Sri Lanka by Mahinda, the Emperor Ashoka's son, when he brought Buddhism to that island. That tree now flourishes at Anuradhapura in Sri Lanka and in turn a sapling from that tree was carried back to Bodhgaya where it grows today. A red sandstone slab under the tree is said to be the Vajrasan, or diamond throne, on which the Buddha sat.

Mahabodhi Temple

A pyramidal spire 50 metres high tops the Mahabodhi temple, inside of which is a large gilded image of the Buddha. You enter the temple courtyard through the east gateway with a typical Buddhist *torana* gateway. The temple is said to stand on the site of a temple originally erected by Ashoka in the 3rd century BC.

Although the current temple was restored in 1882 and earlier in the 11th century, it is said to be basically the same as a temple standing here in the 7th century, or even earlier. The Chinese pilgrim, Hiuen Tsang, describes visiting this earlier temple in 635 AD.

The stone railing around the temple, parts of which still stand, was originally thought to date from Ashoka but is now considered to be from the Sunga period around 184-172 BC. The carved and sculptured railing has been restored although parts of it now stand in the museum in Calcutta and in the Victoria & Albert Museum in London. Stone stupas, erected by visiting pilgrims, dot the temple courtyard. The Buddha is said to have bathed in the nearby lotus pond.

Monasteries

The Tibetan monastery has an interesting wheel of law, while the Japanese monastery has a very beautiful image of the Buddha brought from Japan. There is also a Burmese monastery; the Burmese attempted a restoration of the Mahabodhi in 1306-09. Since Hindus regard the Buddha as an incarnation of Vishnu, Bodhgaya is also sacred to Hindu pilgrims.

Places to Stay

The *Ashoka Travellers' Lodge* (tel 25) has singles/doubles at Rs 120/160 including breakfast. Prices are lower in the April to September off-season. It's the best place available and all rooms have bathrooms. The charges go up during the tourist season. There's also a *Tourist Bungalow* with doubles at Rs 30 or dorm beds at Rs 10 and a *Youth Hostel.*

If you're planning a longer stay and/or don't mind roughing it a little, it is possible to stay at the monasteries. The Burmese monastery has clean rooms and the management is helpful. The monastery has a garden and a library with English books. Since more Burmese visitors are now coming to Bodhgaya space is not as readily available as it used to be. If you do stay here remember that dignified conduct is expected of the guests. There is no charge for staying here but you should, of course, make a donation. Unfortunately some western visitors have abused the monasteries hospitality by smoking there or in other ways breaking the rules.

The Japanese monastery is also clean and comfortable but during the tourist season it can be packed with Japanese tour groups. Your stay there is limited to three days and, unhappily, some western visitors have made themselves unpopular here too.

You can also stay in the Tibetan restaurant tents behind the Tibetan temple or you can rent rooms in the village. Simple vegetarian meals are available at the *Kalyan Hotel* near the Mahabodhi Temple for just a few rupees.

Getting There

Bodhgaya is 13 km from Gaya and buses, minibuses and rickshaws make the trip. They start from the Kacheri in the city centre at Gaya, a rupee or two rickshaw ride from the station. Buses depart every hour but it is advisable to only travel during the daytime. At night it's better to stay in Gaya.

A tempo costs Rs 1.50 – 'what a joke, a common little auto-rickshaw with back to back seats in the rear seating three on each, a board across the driver's seat with two courageous people sitting either side of the driver, plus one out back – total 12 people and a baby and baskets of grain. Very dangerous on the narrow roads'.

SOUTHERN BIHAR
Parasnath

Just inside the Bihar state boundary from Bengal, and only a little north of the Grand Trunk Road, this is the major Jain pilgrimage centre in the east of India. Like so many other pilgrimage centres it's perched on top of a steep hill reached by a stiff climb on foot. The 24 temples,

Writer in Bihar Province ....

representing the Jain Tirthankars, stand at 1366 metres altitude. Parasnath, the 23rd Tirthankar, achieved nirvana at this spot, 100 years after his birth in Varanasi.

Hazaribagh

South of Gaya the hill resort of Hazaribagh is in the Damodar Valley. There's a wildlife sanctuary here and accommodation is available in a *Tourist Lodge* or a *Forest Rest House*. Hazaribagh is a quiet little place 67 km from the railway junction at Hazaribagh Road.

Ranchi

At the other end of the Damodar Valley, 93 km away, is Bihar's other hill resort. Ranchi is nearly as quiet as smaller Hazaribagh. At the foot of Ranchi Hill is an artificial lake flanked by two temples. Ranchi is particularly well known for its mental asylum, probably the best known one on the sub-continent.

Jagannathpur village, 10 km southwest, has the Jagannath Temple, a smaller copy of the great Jagannath Temple at Puri, which also celebrates its own, smaller, festival of the cars. See the Orissa section for more details of this great festival. The high Hundru Falls are 43 km north-east of Ranchi; there are other falls in the area. The isolated but beautiful resort of Neterahat is 150 km away, close to the border with Madhya Pradesh.

Places to Stay The new *Monarch Hotel* (tel 20440, 24827) has good doubles with bath at Rs 60 and also a good restaurant. Cheaper hotels include the *Hotel Akashdeep* which has singles/doubles at Rs 30/40. The *Palace Hotel* in Kadru has rooms from Rs 25. There is also a *South Eastern Railway Hotel* with rooms at Rs 175/235 or with air-con at Rs 235/285 including all meals.

Getting There There are through buses to Ranchi from Raxaul, Patna and Gaya. A through bus to Puri takes 15 hours. Ranchi also has good rail connections.

Calcutta

Population: 8 million
Main language: Bengali

Calcutta is capital of West Bengal

Calcutta is the largest city in India and by now may be ahead of London as the largest city in the British Commonwealth. It's an often ugly and desperate place that to many people sums up the worst of India, yet it's also one of the more fascinating centres in India and has some scenes of rare beauty. At the beginning of this century Calcutta was the capital of British India but, unlike Delhi, Calcutta is not an ancient city with a long history and many impressive relics of its past. In fact Calcutta is really a British invention dating back only 300 years.

In 1686 the British abandoned Hooghly, their trading post 38 km up the Hooghly River from present day Calcutta, and moved down river to three small villages – Sutanati, Govindpur and Kalikata. Calcutta takes its name from the last of those three tiny settlements. Job Charnock, an English merchant, who later married a Brahmin's widow whom he dissuaded from becoming a sati, was the leader of the British merchants who made this move. At first the post was not a great success and was abandoned on a number of occasions, but in 1696 a fort was laid out near present day BBD Bag (Dalhousie Square) and in 1698 Aurangzeb's grandson gave the British official permission to occupy the villages.

Calcutta then grew steadily until 1756 when Suraj-ud-daula, the Nawab of Murshidabad, attacked the town. Most of the British inhabitants escaped, but those captured were packed into an underground cellar where, during the night most of them suffocated in what became known as 'the black hole of Calcutta'. Early in 1757 the British, under Clive, retook Calcutta and made peace with the Nawab. Later the same year, however, Suraj-ud-daula, sided with the French and in the Battle of Plassey, a turning point in British Indian history, was killed. A much stronger fort was built in Calcutta and the town became the capital of British India. Much of Calcutta's most enduring development took place between 1780 and 1820. Later in the 19th century, however, Bengal became a spark point in the struggle for Indian independence, and this was a major reason for the decision to transfer the capital to New Delhi in 1911. Loss of political power did not alter Calcutta's economic control and the city continued to prosper until after WW II.

Partition affected Calcutta more than any other major Indian city. Bengal and the Punjab were the two areas of India which were both mixed in their Hindu-Moslem populations and positioned so that the dividing line would have to be drawn through them. The result in Bengal was that Calcutta, the jute-producing and export centre of India, became a city without a hinterland while across the

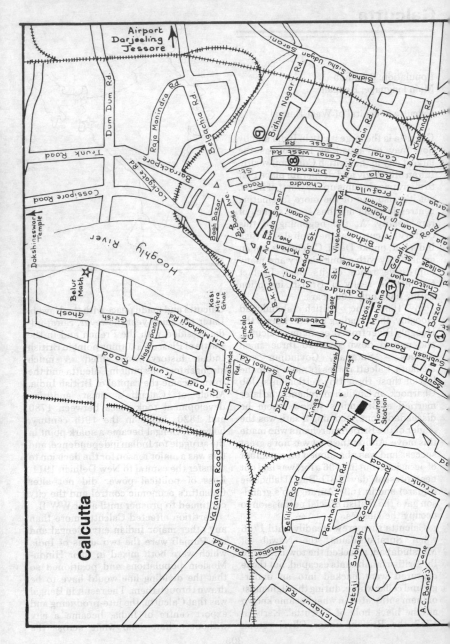

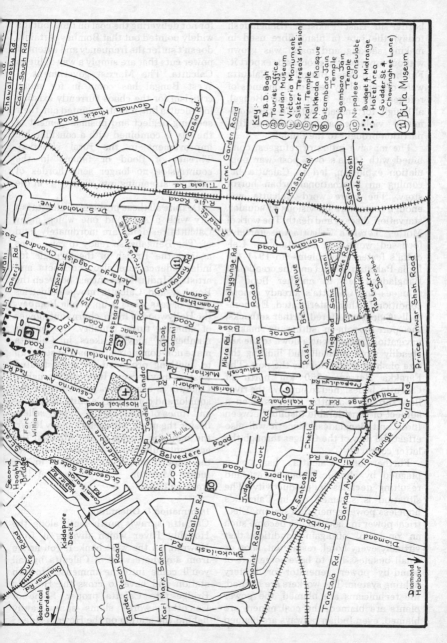

Key:-
1. B.B.D. Bagh
2. Tourist Office
3. Indian Museum
4. Victoria Monument
5. Sister Teresa's Mission
6. Kali Temple
7. Nakhoda Mosque
8. Sitambara Jain Temple
9. Digambara Jain Temple
10. Nepalese Consulate
11. Birla Museum

Budget & Midrange Hotel Area
(Sudder St. & Chowringhee Lane)

border in East Pakistan (Bangladesh today) the jute (a plant fibre used in making sacking and mats) was grown without anywhere to process or export it. Furthermore West Bengal and Calcutta were disrupted by tens of thousands of refugees fleeing from East Bengal, although fortunately without the communal violence and bloodshed that partition brought to the Punjab.

The massive influx of refugees, combined with India's own post war population explosion, led to Calcutta becoming an international urban horror story. The mere word Calcutta was enough to conjure up visions of squalor, starvation, disease and death. The work of Mother Teresa's Calcutta mission also focussed worldwide attention on Calcutta's festering problems. In 1971 the India-Pakistan conflict and the creation of Bangladesh led to another flood of refugees and Calcutta's already chaotic condition further deteriorated. Economically Calcutta suffered further setbacks, the port has been silting up making navigation from Calcutta down to the sea steadily more difficult and limiting the size of ships which can use the port. The Farakka Barrage, 250 km north of Calcutta, is designed to improve the river flow through Calcutta, but has been a subject of considerable dispute between India and Bangladesh since it will also effect the flow of the Ganges through the latter country.

Furthermore Calcutta has been plagued by chronic labour unrest and resulting declines in productivity. The situation is summed up in Calcutta's hopeless power generation system. Electrical power in Calcutta has become such an on-again, off-again condition that virtually every hotel, restaurant, shop or small business has to have some sort of stand-by power generator or battery lighting system. The workers are blamed, the technicians are blamed, the power plants are blamed, the coal miners are blamed, even Indian railways are blamed

for not delivering the coal on time, but it's widely pointed out that Bombay certainly doesn't suffer the frequency and extent of power cuts that are simply a way of life in Calcutta. The Marxist government of West Bengal has come in for much criticism for the chaos currently existing in Calcutta but, it is also pointed out, their seeming neglect and mismanagement of the city is combined with a considerable improvement in the rural situation. Threats of flood or famine in the countryside no longer send hordes of refugees streaming into the city as in the past.

Despite all these problems Calcutta is a city with a soul and one which many Calcutta residents are inordinately fond of. The Bengalis, so ready to raise arms against the British in the struggle for independence, are also the poets and artists of India. The contrast between the Bombay and Calcutta movie industries more or less sums it up. While Bombay, the Hollywood of India, churns out movies of amazing tinsel banality, the smaller number of movie-makers in Calcutta make non-commercial gems that stand up to anything produced for sophisticated western movie-goers. It carries through to Calcutta in other ways too, amongst the squalor and confusion Calcutta has places and times of sheer magic – flower sellers beside the misty, ethereal Hooghly River; the majestic sweep of the Maidan; the arrogant bulk of the Victoria Memorial; the superb collection exhibited in the Indian Museum – it's all part of this amazing city.

Information & Orientation

Calcutta sprawls north-south along the Hooghly River which divides it from Howrah, on the west bank. If you arrive from anywhere west of Calcutta by rail you'll come into the immense Howrah station and have to cross the Hooghly Bridge into Calutta proper. Some of Calcutta's worse slums sprawl away behind the station on the Howrah side.

For visitors the more relevant parts of Calcutta are south of the bridge in the areas around BBD Bag and Chowringhee. BBD Bag, as Dalhousie Square has been renamed, is the site of the GPO, the West Bengal Tourist Office and close to the American Express Office and various railway booking offices. South of BBD Bag is the open expanse of the Maidan along the river, and away from the river the area known as Chowringhee. Most of the cheap and middle range hotels (and some of the upper bracket ones) are concentrated in Chowringhee together with many of the airline offices, restaurants, travel agencies and the Indian Museum. At the southern end of Chowringhee you'll find the Government of India Tourist Office on Shakespeare Sarani and nearby the Birla Planetarium and the Victoria Memorial.

There are a number of landmarks in Calcutta and a couple of important streets to remember. The Octherlony Monument at the northern end of the Maidan is one of the most visible – it's a tall column rising from the flat expanse of the Maidan. Sudder St runs right off Chowringhee and is the core of the Calcutta travellers' scene. Most of the popular cheap hotels are along Sudder St so it is well known to any taxi or rickshaw-wallah and the airport bus runs right by it. Furthermore the Indian Museum is right on the corner of Sudder St and Chowringhee. Further down Chowringhee, which runs alongside the Maidan all the way, is Park St with a great number of more expensive restaurants and the Thai International office – an important address for people heading on to South-East Asia. On again is Shakespeare Sarani.

Street Names Like many Indian cities getting around Calcutta is slightly confused by the habit of renaming city streets, particularly those with Raj day connotations. As usual this renaming has been done in a half-hearted fashion, many streets still have the old names up, some maps show old names, others new, taxi-wallahs inevitably only know the old

PARAKEET LEAPS FROM BAMBOO CAGE AND SELECTS YOUR FORTUNE CARD

YOUR FUTURE IS FOR THE BIRDS!

Fortune teller on a Calcutta sidewalk

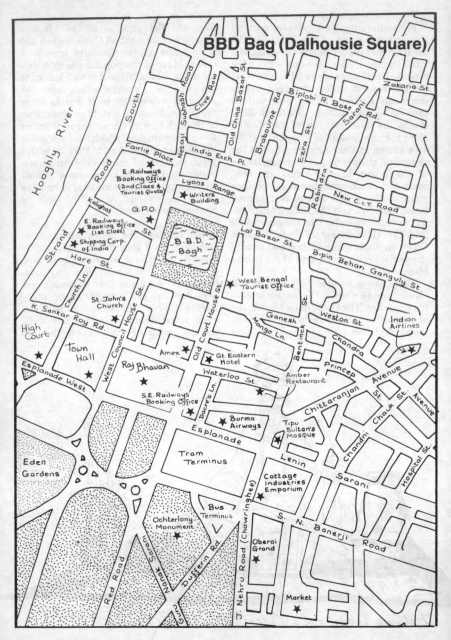

BBD Bag (Dalhousie Square)

names. It's going to be a long time before Chowringhee Rd becomes Jawaharlal Nehru Rd!

Other renamed roads include Ballyganj Store Rd (now Gurusday Rd), Bowbazar St (Bepin Behary Ganguly), Buckland Rd (Bankim Ch Rd), Harrington St (Ho Chi Minh Sarani!), Harrison Rd (Mahatma Gandhi Rd), Kyd St (Dr M Ishaque Rd), Lansdowne Rd (Sarat Bose Rd), Lower Chitpur Rd (Rabindra Sarani), Lower Circular Rd (Acharya Jagadish Bose Rd), Machuabazar St (Madan Mohan St & Keshab Sen St), Mirzapore St (Suryya Sen St), Theatre Rd (Shakespeare Sarani), Wellesley St (Rafi Ahmed Kidwai Rd) and Wellington St (Nirmal Chunder St). I've always been amused at how the street the US consulate is on was renamed Ho Chi Minh Sarani!

Offices The Calcutta GPO is on BBD Bag (Dalhousie Square) and is large and has an efficient poste restante. The Telephone Bhawan is also on BBD Bag while the Central Telegraph Office is at 8 Red Cross Place. The Foreigners' Registration Office is at 237 Acharya J C Bose Rd. American Express is nearby at 21 Old Court House (tel 236281). The Government of India Tourist Office (tel 441402, 443521) is at 4 Shakespeare Sarani. There is also a counter at Calcutta airport, but it never appears to be open when flights come in. The West Bengal Tourist Bureau is at 3/2 BBD Bag (tel 235917) – the opposite side to the post office. They, too, have a counter at the airport.

Culture Calcutta is famous for its culture – films, poetry, art and dance all have their devotees here. There are dances on at the Oberoi Grand Hotel every night at 7 pm, reduced entrance charge with a student card. At Rabindra Sadan on Cathedral Rd (tel 449936) there is a dance-drama performance, Bengali poetry readings or similar on most nights.

Books & Bookshops Geoffrey Moorhouse's classic study *Calcutta*, originally published in 1971 and out of print for some time is now once again available as a Penguin paperback. The Cambridge Book & Stationery Company at 20D Park St is a good small bookshop. Further down Park St towards Chowringhee the Oxford Book Shop is larger, but much of their stock is either very specialised or very old. Upstairs at 56D Free School St the Bookmark has a good general selection of books. There are quite a number of secondhand bookshops along Free School St and on the end of Sudder St.

Embassies & Consulates Some of the useful addresses in Calcutta include:

Bangladesh	9 Circus Ave (tel 44 5208, 445524)
Bhutan	48 Tivoli Court, Pramothesh Barua Sarani (tel 441301)
West Germany	1 Hastings Park Rd (tel 459141)
Nepal	19 Sterndale Rd (tel 454293)
Netherlands	18A Brabourne Rd (tel 225004)
Thailand	18B Mandeville Gardens (tel 460836)
UK	1 Ho Chi Minh Sarani (tel 445171)
USA	5/1 Ho Chi Minh Sarani (tel 443611)

Note that despite some reports there is no Burmese consulate in Calcutta even though Calcutta is the main gateway for flights to Rangoon. Burma Airways cannot issue visas, the nearest cities with Burmese diplomatic representation are Kathmandu, Dhaka or New Delhi.

Airline Offices Most airline offices are located around Chowringhee. Two notable exceptions are Indian Airlines on Chittaranjan Avenue and Burma Airways which is just north of the Maidan tram terminus.

Aeroflot	58 Chowringhee (tel 449831)
Air India	50 Chowringhee (tel 442356)

Bangladesh Biman	1 Park St (tel 247603)
British Airways	41 Chowringhee (tel 248181)
Burma Airways	8/2 Esplanade East (tel 231614)
Indian Airlines	39 Chittaranjan Avenue (tel 260730)
Royal Nepal Airlines	41 Chowringhee (tel 244434)
Thai International	18G Park St (tel 249696)

If you're looking for cheap airline tickets there are various places advertising their services around Sudder St. Pan Asian Tours, a tiny little office on the 2nd floor at 20 Mirza Ghalib St (Free School St), seem to know what they're on about. One traveller wrote to commend their 'friendly and efficient service'. See the Getting There section for air fare details.

Botanical Garden

On the west bank of the Hooghly, south of Howrah, are the extensive Botanical Gardens. They stretch for over a km along the river front and occupy 109 hectares. The gardens were originally founded in 1786 and initially administered by Colonel Kyd. It was from these gardens that the tea now grown in Assam and Darjeeling was first developed. Prime attraction in the gardens is the 200 year old Banyan, claimed to be the largest in the world. It covers an area of ground nearly 400 metres in circumference and continues to flourish despite having its central trunk removed in 1925, due to fungus damage. The cool and tropical tall palm house in the centre of the gardens is also well worth a visit.

The gardens are at Sibpur and can be reached by crossing the bridge – total distance 19 km from Chowringhee. More directly you may be able to get a ferry across the river from Chandpal or Takta Ghat or from the Matia Bruz Ghat further south, but finding a boat across is generally not very easy. The gardens are open from sunrise to sunset and although they tend to be very crowded on Sundays on other days they are very peaceful and make a very pleasant escape from the hassles and crowds of Calcutta. A 55 or 56 bus will take you to the gardens. The trip takes about an hour.

Indian Museum

Conveniently situated on the corner of Sudder St and Chowringhee, the Indian Museum was built in 1875 and is probably the best museum in India and one of the best in Asia. It's so convenient to the many hotels around Sudder St that if you're staying there you should not fail to drop in, if only for a few minutes. Its widely varied collection includes oddities such as a whole roomful of meteorites. Other exhibits include the usual fossils, stuffed animals, skeletons and so on, including a number of unique fossil skeletons of pre-historic animals. These include giant crocodiles and an amazingly big tortoise.

The art collection has many fine pieces from Orissan and other temples and a superb collection of Buddhist Gandharan art. This interesting meeting point between Greek artistry and Buddhist ideals was centered around the North-West Frontier Province, now in Pakistan, and produced Buddha images and other sculpture of extreme beauty.

The museum is open from 10 am to 5 pm daily except Mondays. Between December and February it closes half an hour earlier. Entry fee is Rs 0.30, except on Fridays when it is free. Almost anywhere you have been in India you will find some reminder of it in the Indian Museum, it's well worth a visit.

Octherlony Monument

Now officially renamed the Shahid (Martyr's) Minar this 48-metre high column towers over the northern end of the Maidan. It was erected in 1828 and named after Sir David Ochterlony who was credited with winning the Nepal War (1814-16). There's a fine view from the top of the column, but permission to ascend it must be obtained from the Deputy Commissioner of Police, Police HQ, Lal Bazaar. The column is a curious combination of Turkish, Egyptian and Syrian architectural elements.

Rabindra Sarobar &
Ramakrishna Mission
In the south of the city Rabindra Sarobar is a park and picnic spot with a central lake. Beside the park is the recently opened Ramakrishna Mission Institute of Culture with a library, reading rooms and lecture halls.

Maidan & Fort William
After the events of 1756 the British decided there would be no repetition and set out to replace the original Fort William, near Dalhousie Square, with a massive and impregnable new fort. First they cleared out the inhabitants of the village of Govindpur and in 1758 laid the foundations of a fort which, when completed in 1781, would cost them the awesome total, for those days, of £2 million. Around the fort a huge expanse of jungle was cut down to give the cannons a clear line of fire but, as usual, the fort has never fired a shot in anger. You can walk around the fort's massive walls with deep fortifications and trenches fronting them, but visitors are only allowed inside with special permission since the fort is still in use today.

The area cleared around Fort William became the Maidan, the 'lungs' of modern Calcutta. This huge green expanse stretches three km north to south and is over a km wide. It is bounded by Strand Rd along the river to the west and by Chowringhee Rd, lined with shops, hotels and eating places, to the east. The stream known as Tolly's Nulla forms its southern boundary and here you will also find a racecourse and the Victoria Memorial. In the north-west corner is Eden Gardens, while Raj Bhavan overlooks it from the north.

Within the gardens there are cricket

and football fields, tennis courts, ponds and trees. Cows graze there, political discussions are held there, people stroll across it or come there for early morning yoga sessions. And of course it's used, like any area of open land in India, as a public toilet.

Eden Gardens
In the north-west corner of the Maidan are the small and pleasantly laid out Eden Gardens. A tiny Burmese pagoda was brought here from Prome in Burma in 1856, it's set in a small lake and is extraordinarily picturesque. The gardens were named after Lord Auckland, the former Governor General's, sisters. The Calcutta cricket grounds, where test matches are held, are also within the gardens.

Across from the gardens there is a pleasant walk along the banks of the Hooghly. Ferries run across the river from several ghats and there are plenty of boatmen around offering to take you out on the water for half an hour.

Victoria Memorial
At the southern end of the Maidan stands the most solid reminder of British Calcutta, in fact probably the most solid reminder of the Raj to be found in India. The Victoria Memorial is a huge white marble museum, a strange combination of classical Europeaan architecture with Moghul influences or, as some have put it, an unhappy British attempt to build a better Taj Mahal. The idea behind the memorial was conceived by Lord Curzon, the money for its construction raised from 'voluntary contributions by the princes and peoples of India', the Prince of Wales (later King George V) laid the foundation stone in 1906 and it was opened by another Prince of Wales (later the Duke of Windsor) in 1921.

Whether you're interested in the British Raj period or not the memorial is an attraction not to be missed, it tells the story of the Empire in India at it's peak, just when it was about to embark on its downhill slide. The imposing statue of Queen Victoria, at her bulky and least-amused best, fronts the memorial and sets the mood for all the displays inside.

Inside you'll find portraits, statues and busts of almost all the main participants in British-Indian history – British, Indian and other nationalities. Scenes from military conflicts and events of the mutiny are illustrated. There are some superb watercolours of Indian landscapes and buildings made by travelling Victorian artists. A Calcutta exhibit includes many early pictures of the city and a model of Fort William. Of course there are many fine Indian and Persian miniatures and rare manuscripts and books. Queen Victoria appears again inside, much younger and slimmer than her statue outside. There's also a piano she played as a young girl and other memorabilia. There's a huge painting of King Edward VII entering Jaipur in a regal procession in 1876. French guns captured at the Battle of Plassey are on exhibit, and so is the black stone throne of the Nawab whom Clive defeated in that battle. To top it all there is a good view over the Maidan from the balcony over the entrance.

A Brief Guide to the Victoria Memorial is available in the building for Rs 1.50. The memorial is open from 10 am to 5 pm but closed on Mondays. Entry costs Rs 0.30.

St Paul's Cathedral

Built between 1839 and 1847, St Paul's Cathedral is one of the most important churches in India. It stands just to the east of the Victoria Memorial at the southern end of the Maidan. The steeple fell during an earthquake in 1897 and following further damage in a 1934 quake it was redesigned and rebuilt.

Birla Planetarium

This planetarium, near the Tourist Office, is one of the largest in the world and well worth the Rs 3.50 admission. It's open

from 12.30 to 6.30 pm daily, and from 10 am to 8 pm on Saturdays and Sundays. There are programmes in English several times daily.

Kali Temple

Also known as Kalighat, this temple is believed to be about 200 years old and to be the actual temple from which Kalikat (anglicised to Calcutta) takes its name. According to legend when Shiva's wife's corpse was cut up one of her fingers fell here, since when it has been an important pilgrimage site. The temple is about two km directly south of St Paul's Cathedral.

Zoo

South of the Maidan, Calcutta's 16-hectare zoo was opened in 1876. Some of the animals are displayed in near natural conditions. The zoo is open from sunrise to sunset and admission is Rs 0.50.

Howrah Bridge

Until 1943 the Hooghly was crossed by a pontoon bridge which had to be opened to let river traffic through. There had been considerable opposition to construction of a bridge due to fears that it would effect the river currents and cause silting problems. This problem was eventually avoided by building a bridge that crosses the river in a single 450-metre span with no piers at all within the river. The cantilevered bridge is similar in size to the Sydney Harbour Bridge and if anything even uglier! It carries a flow of traffic which Sydney could never dream of – it's intriguing to stand at one end of the bridge at morning rush hour time and watch the procession of double decker buses come across. They heel over like yachts due to the weight of passengers hanging on to the sides. In between there are countless rickshaws, lumbering bullock carts, hordes of bicycles and even the odd car. The bridge is also known as Rabindra Setu.

The bridge is usually horribly congested and some years ago an additional bridge was planned a couple of km downriver. Construction was commenced but the funds ran out at a very early stage and the site remained untouched for a number of years. Recently the plans have been revived and construction has commenced once again.

Dalhousie Square – BBD Bag
When Calcutta was the centre of administration for British India this was the centre of power. On the north side of the square stands the huge 'Writers Building' which dates from 1880. In those days clerical workers were known as 'writers' and the East India Company's 'writers' have been replaced by modern day ones employed by the West Bengal state government. That's where all the quintuplicate forms, carbon copies and red ink comes from. Also on Dalhousie Square is a rather more useful place – the Calcutta GPO – and on the other side of the square is the West Bengal Tourist Development Corporation's office

Until it was abandoned in 1757 the original Fort Williams used to stand where the post office now does. It stretches from there down to the river, which has also changed its course since that time. Brass markers indicate where the fort walls used to be by the post office. Calcutta's famous black hole actually stood at the north-east corner of the post office but since independence all indications of its position have been removed. The black hole was actually a tiny guardroom in the fort and 146 people were forced into the room on that fateful night when the city fell to Suraj-ud-daula. Next morning only 23 were still alive.

St John's Church
A little south of Dalhousie Square is the Church of St John which dates from 1787. The graveyard here has a number of interesting monuments including the octagonal mausoleum of Job Charnock, founder of Calcutta, who died in 1692. Admiral Watson, who supported Clive in retaking Calcutta from Suraj-ud-daula is also buried here.

Other British Buildings
The Victoria Memorial is the most imposing reminder of the British presence in Calcutta, but the city's commercial wealth resulted in quite a few other interesting buildings. Raj Bhavan, the old British Government House, is now occupied by the Governor of West Bengal and entry is restricted. The Marquess Wellesley built it between 1799 and 1805 and it is modelled on Lord Curzon's home, Kedleston Hall, in Derbyshire, England which was only completed a couple of years before it. It stands at the north end of the Maidan and there are many rare works of art and other interesting items inside including Tipu Sultan's throne.

Next to it is the Doric style Town Hall, and next to that the High Court which was copied from the Staadhaus at Ypres and completed in 1872. It has a tower 55 metres high. Just south of the zoo in Alipur is the National Library, the biggest library in India, which is housed in Belvedere House, the former residence of the Lieutenant Governor of Bengal.

Other Museums
Calcutta has a number of other interesting museums apart from the magnificent Indian Museum and the Victoria Memorial. In Calcutta University the Asutosh Museum has a collection of art objects with a particular emphasis on Bengali folk art. Admission is free and it is open from 10.30 am to 4.30 pm on weekdays, 10.30 am to 3 pm on Saturdays. At 19A Gurusday Rd there is the Birla Industrial & Technological Museum which is open from 10 am to 5 pm daily. Admission is free except on Sundays when it costs Rs 0.25. Those philanthropic (and very wealthy) Birlas have also provided the Birla Academy of Art & Culture at 109-109 Southern Avenue. That is open from 3 to 6 pm daily except Mondays and admission is Rs 0.25. It has a good

collection of sculptures and modern art. They are also building a huge new Birla temple, just round the corner from the Industrial & Technological Museum.

On Cathedral Rd, beside the cathedral, there is a permanent exhibition at the Academy of Fine Arts, which is open from 3 to 8 pm daily except Mondays. Entry is free. The Nehru Children's Museum is at 94/1 Jawaharlal Nehru Rd (Chowringhee) and is open from 1 to 8 pm daily except Mondays. Admission is Rs 0.50 for adults, Rs 0.25 for children.

On Muktaram Babu St, a narrow lane in north Calcutta, is the Marble Palace, an incongruous one-man collection of statues and paintings including works of Rubens and Sir Joshua Reynolds. It's open from 10 am to 4 pm except on Mondays and Thursdays and entry is free with a permit from the Government of India Tourist Office. Nearby is the rambling old Tagore House, a centre for Indian dance, drama, music and other arts. This was where Rabindranath Tagore, India's greatest modern poet, was born and died. It's just off Rabindra Sarani.

Sitambara Jain Temple
In the north-east of the city this temple was built in 1867 and dedicated to Sheetalnathji, the 10th of the 24 Jain Tirthankars. The temple is an ornate mass of mirrors, coloured stones and glass mosaics and overlooks a garden. It is open from 6 am to 12 noon and 3 to 7 pm daily.

Nakhoda Mosque
North of BBD Bag is Calcutta's principal Moslem place of worship. The huge Nakhoda Mosque is said to be able to accommodate 10,000 people and was modelled on Akbar's tomb at Sikandra near Agra. The red sandstone mosque has two 46-metre high minarets and a brightly painted onion-shaped dome.

Belur Math
North of the city on the west bank is the

headquarters of the Ramakrishna Mission, Belur Math. Ramakrishna, an Indian philosopher, preached the unity of all religions and, following his death in 1886, his follower Swami Vivekananda founded the Ramakrishna Mission in 1897 and there are now branches all over India. Belur Math, the movement's international headquarters, was founded in 1899. It is supposed to represent a church, a mosque and a temple, depending on how you look at it. Belur Math is open from 6.30 am to 12 noon and from 3.30 to 7.30 pm daily. Admission is free.

Dakshineshwar Kali Temple
Across the river from Belur Math is this Kali temple where Ramakrishna was a priest when he reached his spiritual vision of the unity of all religions. The Kali temple was built in 1847.

Barrackpore
There is a memorial to Gandhi called Gandhi Ghat at this point, 25 km north of Calcutta on the banks of the Hooghly.

Serampore
Across the river from Barrackpore, 25 km from Calcutta, this was a Danish centre until the Danish holdings in India were transferred to the East India Company in 1845. The old Danish Church and the Danish cemetery still stand. The missionaries Ward, Marshman and Carey operated from here in the early 1800s. Mahesh, three km from Serampore, has a large and very old Jagannath temple. In June-July of each year the Mahesh Yatra car festival takes place here and is second in size only to the great car festival of Jagannath at Puri in Orissa.

Tours
The India Tourism Development Corporation (tel 443124) at 4 Shakespeare Sarani and the West Bengal Tourist Bureau (tel 238271) at 3/2 BBD Bag both have daily tours of Calcutta except on Sundays. The morning tour from 8 am to

12.30 pm costs Rs 20 and takes in the area around BBD Bag in the city including Eden Gardens, Raj Bhavan, out to the Jain temple plus the further out sites like Belur Math, the Dakshineshwar Temple and the Botanical Gardens.

The afternoon tour operates from 1.30 to 5.15 pm and costs the same, but you can get a combined ticket for Rs 25 if you take both tours on the same day. The afternoon tour covers the Indian Museum, Victoria Memorial and the Zoo.

The morning tour is better value since it covers the further out sights while on the afternoon tour you could easily get around yourself and have more time. On Saturdays, Sundays and public holidays you can only take the whole day tour, no half day tickets are sold. In any case the number of half day tickets is restricted. Note that the tourist offices often cancel tours on short notice – check the day before if the tour will be operating.

Places to Stay – Bottom End

Sudder St, running off Chowringhee beside the Indian Museum, is Calcutta's cheap accommodation centre. Here you will find most of Calcutta's cheaper accommodation and eating places. At 2 Sudder St the *Salvation Army Red Shield Guest House* (tel 242895) now only has dormitory style accommodation – there are no longer any private rooms although the smallest dorm has only four beds, the largest nine. A bed costs from Rs 8.40 to Rs 9.40 a night depending on which room you're in. The Sally Army is still basic, although clean and well, kept but it's no longer so popular since the switch to purely dorm-style accommodation. They also no longer do meals and the water supply is decidedly erratic; a real drag to arrive after a hot, sweaty train trip to find there'll be no water available for hours to come.

Down Sudder St a bit, Stuart Lane turns off to the right and here you'll find two of Calcutta's most popular budget establishments. The *Modern Lodge* (tel

244960) is at number 1, the very popular *Hotel Paragon* at number 2. The Paragon has dorm beds at Rs 10, singles/doubles at Rs 15/25, bigger upstairs doubles at Rs 30 and doubles with bath at Rs 40. There's a pleasant courtyard upstairs but the ground floor rooms are rather gloomy. The Modern Lodge is very similar in price with four to six-bed dorms at Rs 12 a bed, singles/doubles at Rs 20/30. The latter includes breakfast – a boiled egg, two pieces of bread, a banana and tea. They're OK, clean sheets and toilets, a fan, reasonable food.

If I had to make a choice between the two I'd go for the Modern Lodge (says Geoff). The reason for this is the ground floor rooms in the Paragon are somewhat gloomy and unappealing whereas the rooms in the Modern Lodge are arranged differently and don't suffer this disadvantage. On the other hand the upstairs rooms in Paragon are every bit as good. The rooftop area at the Modern Lodge is a popular meeting place in the evening and tea and soft drinks are available. The manager of this lodge is a good person to see about airline tickets and student cards.

There are other cheap hotels around Sudder St, but many are strictly for emergency use only. 'Avoid them like the plague, you stand a good chance of getting it', reported one traveller. The *Tourist Inn* (tel 243732) at 4/1 Sudder St actually wrote to say that they didn't deserve to be placed in that category – rooms cost Rs 25/50 for singles/doubles and they offer free yoga lessons by Chowbey Baba! Other cheap Sudder St hotels are the *Shilton Hotel* at 5A at Rs 40/60 and the *Hotel Diplomat* at 10 at Rs 40-50/50-60. Or you could try the *Hilson Hotel* (tel 245283) at 4 Sudder St where dorm beds are Rs 12, singles/doubles Rs 25/35.

There are also a number of places which are up a notch, in price at least. At 6/2/3 Sudder St, opposite Stuart Lane, the *Astoria Hotel* (tel 241359, 242613) has singles/doubles at Rs 70/85 plus more

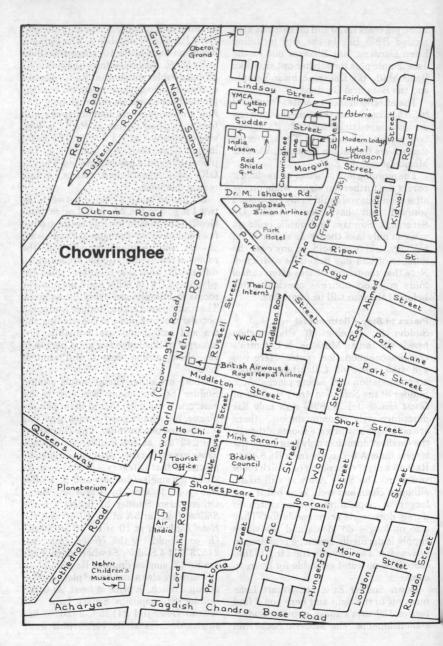

expensive rooms with attached bathroom up to Rs 150 for a double with air-con, including 'bed tea' and breakfast. The *Capital Guest House* (tel 213844) at 11B Chowringhee Lane has rooms at Rs 50/70 for singles/doubles but the singles have no windows. There are also doubles with attached bathroom for Rs 70-100. The Hotel White Hall at 5/1 Sudder St, which has had a number of uncomplimentary reports from travellers, appears to have disappeared to become the *Hotel Maria*, but it looks somewhat redundant.

Calcutta has a collection of Ys. The *YMCA* (tel 233504) is at 25 Chowringhee and takes men – a big, gloomy building but it's actually a really good place to stay. Singles are Rs 90, 105 and 110, unrenovated doubles are Rs 110 and renovated doubles Rs 120. They also have rooms for four for Rs 200. All the rooms have attached bath and the price includes breakfast (two eggs, porridge or corn-flakes, toast and butter, tea and a banana). All prices are reduced by Rs 10 for the second night onwards. They've also got some excellent full-size snooker and billiard tables in the lounge! If you're discreet it's possible to use them without being a resident.

There is a second, similarly priced YMCA (tel 240260) at 42 Surendra Nath Banerjee Rd. The *YWCA* (tel 240260) is also similarly priced at 1 Middleton Row – ladies only here. You can share a room for Rs 30 or a double costs Rs 50. Meals are Rs 10 extra, there's a good restaurant next door. 'It's fun to stay at the YWCA', reported one visitor.

The *Youth Hostel* (tel 672869) is at 10 J B Ananda Dutta Lane in Howrah. It's small and homely, take a 52 or 58 bus from Howrah Station to Shamasri Cinema or a 63 to Khirertala.

If you're transitting Calcutta by air there are *Airport Rest Rooms* (tel 572611) at the airport. Singles/doubles are Rs 50/75 and there's a reservations desk in the terminal. Finally Howrah and Sealdah Stations have *Railway Retiring Rooms*. At Howrah singles/doubles are Rs 15/30 or Rs 18/36 in the renovated rooms. Dorm beds are Rs 10. Singles/doubles at Sealdah are the same but there are also air-con doubles for Rs 50.

Places to Stay – Middle

It's said often enough that 'getting there is half the fun', well at the *Fairlawn Hotel* (tel 244460 & 241835) at 13A Sudder St, staying there is half the fun. It's a piece of Calcutta that definitely should not be missed because here the Raj doesn't just live, it's simply never ended. The terribly English couple who still, 30+ years after independence, run it look like they've been time-warped from Brighton in the '50s and their establishment is spotless, packed with memorabilia and a positive delight.

The bearer bears your gear upstairs on his head, meal times are announced with a gong (and a hissed 'Sahib, Memsahib, dinner is ready' if you dare to be late) and in mid-afternoon there's tea and biscuits. In fact you don't really stay here so much as play your part in an on-going theatre performance. At Rs 230/330 for an air-con room with all meals it's an experience not to be missed. There are also some non air-con rooms at Rs 30 less. Major plus points at Fairlawns are the open lounge areas and the garden area with tables and chairs. The land the hotel stands on was originally purchased by Europeans way back in 1781. The main building was completed in 1803 as a gentleman's residence, it was not until this century that it first became a guest house, run for many years by two English spinsters. The parents of the present owner took it over in 1936

Everything else pales into insignificance by comparison, but there are a few other places such as the *Lytton Hotel* (tel 232760, 233937, 239538 & 239794) at 14 Sudder St. The Lytton has actually been almost completely rebuilt in the past couple of years, it's now an all new centrally air-conditioned hotel, although there are also some old rooms remaining. The new rooms are Rs 250/300 for singles/doubles (room only) or the old rooms are Rs 150/200.

Round at 2 Chowringhee Place the *Carlton Hotel* (tel 233009 & 238853) costs Rs 125/150 with air-con, Rs 75/125 without including all meals. 'Excellent food' reported one traveller. There's a small sitting area here.

The *New Kenilworth Hotel* (tel 441422 & half a dozen other numbers) at 1 & 2 Little Russell St, just a stone's throw from the tourist office, is another popular middle range hotel with a spacious garden area. Singles/doubles are Rs 275/350.

Places to Stay – Top End

Calcutta does not have a great number of top class hotels. Out at the airport the *ITDC Airport Ashok* (tel 440933 & 575111) is modern and convenient for passengers in transit. Singles/doubles (all air-con) are Rs 500/600.

Most of the other hotels are centrally located. At 15 Chowringhee the *Oberoi Grand* (tel 230181) is pretty plain externally but pleasantly grand inside. In fact in that central courtyard with the swimming pool and the palm trees it's hard to think Calcutta can be so close by! Rooms cost from Rs 775/875 for singles/doubles. The *Park Hotel* (tel 248301) at 17 Park St is a more modern hotel at Rs 600/700.

Other more expensive hotels include the classic old *Great Eastern Hotel* (tel 232311) at 1-3 Old Court House St. Once again it's back to the Raj era in this large 200-room hotel; costs are Rs 300/350 with air-con, cheaper without. 'Fun to stay at and nice breakfasts' wrote one couple. The 212-room *Hotel Hindustan International* (tel 442394) is at 235/1 Acharya J C Bose Rd and costs from Rs 500/600 for singles/doubles. The *Hotel Rutt Deen* (tel 443884) is at 212B Loudon St and costs Rs 280/350-380.

Places to Eat – Less Expensive

Finding good food at reasonable prices is no problem in the Chowringhee/Sudder St area. Everyone seems to have their own favourite but some of the best include the *Taj Continental*, a very good and cheap place opposite the entrance to Stuart Lane. The *Blue Sky*, half way down Sudder St on the same side as the Salvation Army, has excellent porridge, sandwiches, fruit juices and 'the finest curd in India' according to one traveller. They've also got a sign proclaiming, in large letters, 'No Dope'!

The Sikh run *Khalsa Restaurant*, across from the Salvation Army Hostel and down the street a few doors, is a long-standing, popular place for the travellers. Turn right from Sudder St on Free School St and you soon come to the *Moghul Durbar* which is clean, has flowers on the tables, free newspapers to read and food served out with real speed. Plus big signs reassuring Hindu customers that they do not serve beef! *Cafe 48* is also not bad, a sort of Indian snack bar complete with wicker chairs and a jukebox – 'when the power is working'. You can indulge yourself in egg and chips there!

Several readers have written to recommend *Supersnax* at 55A Free School St at the corner of Ripon St (just inside and to the left of the bakery on the corner): 'run by a retired army colonel, very friendly, unusual, wholesome dishes'. *Kathleens' Restaurant & Bakery* at 12 Free School St (left from Sudder St) has very good Indian and western food from about Rs 50 for two, and fantastic baked items in the confectionery level downstair. Another reader found 'the best Chinese food in India' at the *Embassy Chinese Restaurant* across from the large cathedral near the Victoria Memorial.

At 21 Park St the *Health Food Centre* has all sorts of health foods to take away including wholemeal bread, brownies, halva, yoghurt, pizza slices and delicious (though rather expensive) bottled apple juice from Bhutan. If you like south Indian food – and who doesn't? – then just off Chowringhee on Lindsay St the *Hindustan Restaurant* (upstairs) has excellent south Indian vegetarian food – thalis for Rs 10.50, special thalis for Rs 13.50, masala dosa for Rs 3.50 and lots of other goodies at reasonable prices. It's spotlessly clean and mainly patronised by middle and upper class Indians.

Nizam's, across the street and around the corner from the Minerva Cinema, is popular among Calcuttans for mutton and chicken rolls, kebabs and Moslem food. Don't confuse it with the *New Nizam's* nearby, trying to cash in on the other's popularity although if the food's good so what?

A local speciality in Calcutta is *moghul paratha* but curiously it's all but impossible to find real Bengali food in Calcutta unless you dine at a Bengali's home. The New Market on Lindsay St has some superb cake shops near the middle including a third generation Jewish bakery, *Nahum*. 'An interesting old guy,' wrote one traveller.

Places to Eat – More Expensive

There are a number of places along Park St, in fact it's virtually solid restaurants along part of the street. There's a good *Kwality* at 17 Park St, beside the Park Hotel. On that side of the street there are half a dozen other places, some with un-Calcutta names like *Blue Fox* and *Moulin Rouge*! The *Tandoor* has a reasonably swish upstairs room with reasonably good food and fairly reasonable prices. On the other side of the road there's a *Magnolia* for ice cream, *Gupta* has thalis, a *Snack Bar*, *Silver Grill* and *Flury's* for quick snacks and take-aways.

Amber at 11 Waterloo St, behind the Great Eastern Hotel, occupies three floors and is one of Calcutta's better restaurants for Indian and western food. It's so popular that you may have to book a table or be prepared to wait.

Just off Chowringhee on Ho Chi Minh Sarani (same street as the UK and US consulates) *Jyoti Bihar* is air-con upstairs and has very good vegetarian food. On Free School St, between Sudder St and Park St the *How Hua* has good Chinese food. Most dishes are Rs 8 or 9, fancier ones generally Rs 10 to 13. They've even got northern Chinese dishes such as *jiaozi*, a bit like Tibetan mo-mo.

At the *Fairlawn Hotel* on Sudder St food is English style, but surprisingly good. If you're staying there all meals are included in the room cost. If you're not, and would like to experience that old-style service, meals can be arranged. Breakfast costs Rs 27, dinner Rs 33.

Getting There

Air Calcutta is connected by air with all the major centres and in particular it's the jumping off point for flights to the northeast region, to Darjeeling and to Port Blair in the Andaman Islands. Some fares include Madras Rs 995, flights daily; Bombay Rs 1135, flights daily; Delhi Rs 946, two flights daily; Bhubaneswar Rs 296; Varanasi Rs 492, Patna Rs 361; Bagdogra (for Darjeeling) Rs 341; Gauhati Rs 323, Port Blair Rs 966.

Air fares quoted out of Calcutta include Bangkok for Rs 1850 or Rs 1380 if you're under 30. Bangladesh Biman tickets through Dhaka to Bangkok are Rs 1350 with a free stopover. You can fly just to Dhaka for Rs 346 or via Dhaka and Rangoon to Bangkok for Rs 1930, with a student card it's Rs 1448. Burma Airways tickets to Rangoon are available for Rs 1205. Kathmandu tickets are Rs 938 but Burma Airways will take you Calcutta-Rangoon-Kathmandu for Rs 3100. You can fly with Aeroflot to most major cities in Europe for Rs 3700. Flights to the Australian east coast are available for Rs 6800. You must produce a bank receipt if paying in rupees.

Rail Calcutta has two major railway stations. Howrah on the west bank of the Hooghly handles most trains into the city, but if you're going north to Darjeeling or the north-east region then the trains will be from Sealdah Station on the Calcutta side. Beware of pickpockets and other people of similar inclination at Howrah. The Eastern Railway Book Office (tel 224025) is at 6 Fairlie Place for 2nd class and tourist quota bookings. For 1st class it's on the Strand Rd. The South-Eastern Railway Booking Office (tel 239530, 235074) is at Esplanade Mansions.

To Delhi trains take from 17 hours and cost approximately Rs 80 in 2nd class, Rs 325 in 1st. To Varanasi they take from 12 hours and cost Rs 47 in 2nd class, Rs 185 in 1st. For Darjeeling it takes about 12 hours from Calcutta (Sealdah Station) to new Jalpaiguri or Siliguri from where you take a bus or the toy train up to the hill station. Fare from Calcutta is Rs 40 in 2nd, Rs 154 in 1st.

It's a long way from Calcutta to Bombay, a 1968-km trip taking 36 hours even on the fast mail train. Fares are Rs 107 in 2nd class, Rs 415 in 1st class. The trip to Madras is nearly as long – 33 hours to cover 1662 km at a cost of about Rs 92 in 2nd class, Rs 360 in 1st. During and soon after the monsoon the railway line can be cut by the Godavari or the Krishna Rivers in north Andhra Pradesh. If this is the case the Calcutta-Madras service will make a loop inland and the trip will take rather longer. The normal service runs down the coast all the way, passing through Bhubaneswar in Orissa en route.

Bus The bus services from Calcutta are not as good an alternative as they are from a number of other Indian cities. It's generally better to travel from Calcutta by rail, although there are a number of useful routes to other towns in West Bengal.

Ship See the Andaman & Nicobar Islands section for details on the shipping services from Calcutta.

Getting Around

Airport There's an airport bus which costs Rs 10 and runs by the Indian Airlines office and down Chowringhee past Sudder St. A taxi costs about Rs 40 so between four that is as cheap as the bus, and since so many people leave India from Calcutta on the same (Thai International) flights it is quite easy to get a group together for a taxi. There is a public mini bus from BBD Bag to the airport for Rs 2. If your endurance knows no limits you can get to the airport from Howrah Station in an 11A then a 30B bus or from the Esplanade Bus Terminal in a S10 bus for just Rs 1. Incidentally Calcutta's airport takes its name, Dum Dum Airport, from the fact that this was the site of the Dum Dum Barracks, where the explosive dum dum bullet, banned after the Boer War, was once made.

Buses Calcutta's bus system is absolutely hopelessly crowded. It's an edifying sight to watch the double deckers come across Howrah Bridge during the rush hour. Fares from Rs 0.20. Take a 5 or 6 between Howrah Station and Sudder St, ask for the Indian Museum. There is also a secondary private minibus service which is rather faster and slightly more expensive. You need to be a midget to ride in these buses though. Beware of pickpockets in any Calcutta public transport.

Trams Calcutta also has a public tram service but they're like sardine tins. Take a 12A from Howrah to the Indian Museum. On Sunday it is possible to buy a ticket from the terminus for Rs 1. They're quiet, well quiet by Calcutta standards, on that day.

Underground Calcutta may eventually have an underground railway system. It's being built at minimum cost and in maximum time almost totally by hand. Calcutta's soggy soil makes digging holes by hand no fun at all and after each monsoon it takes half the time to the next monsoon simply to drain out what has already been dug. Meanwhile it simply causes Calcutta's chaotic traffic to be even worse. The first section of the underground, a short stretch along Chowringhee, is due to be opened in 1984.

Taxis Calcutta's taxi drivers are renowned not only for their passion for strikes, which in turn causes the buses to be even worse than usual, but also for their belligerent refusal to use the meters. Recently the meters finally caught up with the official fares and in early 1984 meter fares were only slightly below the real fare. If they won't use the meter it's certainly worth arguing about the price but there's no room for optimists. Sudder St to Howrah Station, for example, will cost – if you're lucky – Rs 15 but they'll often refuse to go for less than Rs 20.

Rickshaws Calcutta is the last holdout of the man-powered rickshaw. The rickshaw-wallahs would not accept the new fangled bicycle rickshaws when they were introduced elsewhere in India. After all, who could afford a bicycle? You may find it morally impossible to have a man trotting around pulling you in a carriage but they are useful for carting heavy baggage. And Calcutta's citizens are quite happy to use them. You only find these rickshaws in central Calcutta, though. Across the river in Howrah or in other Calcutta suburbs bicycle rickshaws are available.

Things to Buy

Calcutta has the usual government emporiums and quite a good Central Cottage Industries Emporium at 7 Chowringhee. New Market, formerly Hogg Market, is Calcutta's premier shopping bargain though. Here you can find a little of almost everything and it is always worth an hour or so wandering around. A particular bargain, if you're flying straight home from Calcutta, is caneware. Ridiculously cheap compared to prices in the west and, of course, very light if rather bulky.

The market is also a place to sell as well as buy. Watches and cameras are always in demand and you can also change money at a small premium over the bank rate. If nobody approaches you the uniformed porters will know where to find what you want. A litre of whisky fetches about Rs 20, a carton of cigarettes a bit less. Used Sony Walkmans go for about Rs 800 at the stores along Chowringhee. A brand new one might fetch Rs 1000 but all these deals take time. Note that 'Goodies bought from Singapore may be noted in your passport'.

Down Sudder St a tola (about 12 gm) of the best 'dreaded resin' (and it is very good reported this social deviate!) should cost Rs 60-70.

West Bengal

Population: 49 million
Area: 87,853 square km
Capital: Calcutta
Main language: Bengali

At the time of partition Bengal was split into East Bengal and West Bengal. East Bengal became the eastern wing of Pakistan and later, with the disintegration of that country, Bangladesh. West Bengal became a state of India with its largest city, Calcutta, as its capital. The state is long and narrow, running from the delta of the Ganges River system at the Bay of Bengal in the south to the heights of the Himalayas at Darjeeling in the north.

There is not a great deal of interest in the state apart from these two extremes – Calcutta, all noise, confusion and squalor at one end and Darjeeling, serene and peaceful at the other. Nevertheless the intrepid traveller will find a number of places to consider visiting, either south of Calcutta on the Bay of Negal or north along the route to Darjeeling.

SOUTH OF CALCUTTA
Down the Hooghly

The Hooghly River is a very difficult river to navigate due to the constantly shifting shoals and sandbanks. Hooghly River pilots have to continuously stay in touch with the river to keep track of the frequent changes in its course. When the Hooghly Bridge was constructed it was feared that it would cause severe alterations to the river's flow patterns. The tide rises and falls 3.5 metres at Calcutta and there is a bore, which reaches two metres in height, at the time of the rising tide. Because of the navigational difficulties and the silting up which the Hooghly is experiencing, Calcutta is losing its importance as a port.

Falta, 43 km downriver, was the site of a Dutch factory and the British retreated here in 1756 when Calcutta was captured by Suraj-ud-daula. It was also from here that Clive recaptured Calcutta. Just below Falta the Damodar joins the Hooghly. The Rupnarain also joins the Hooghly and a little up this river is Tamluk, an important Buddhist centre over a thousand years ago. The James & Mary shoal, the most dangerous on the Hooghly, is just above the point where the Rupnarain River enters. It takes its name from a ship which was wrecked here in 1694.

Diamond Harbour

A resort 51 km south of Calcutta by road, Diamond Harbour is at the point where the Hooghly turns south and flows into the open sea. Launches run from here to Sagar Island.

Places to Stay Accommodation in the *Sagarika Tourist Lodge* (doubles from Rs 60) can be booked through the West Bengal Tourism Corporation in Calcutta.

bathing festival takes place here early each January. A lighthouse marks the south-west tip of the island but navigation is still difficult for a further 65 km south.

Digha

Close to the border with Orissa, 243 km south-east of Calcutta on the Bay of Bengal, Digha is a beach resort with a six-km long beach. There are daily buses between Calcutta and Digha operated by the CSTC. The trip takes about six hours.

Places to Stay There is a *Tourist Lodge* with doubles at Rs 35 and meals are also available. Digha has a wide range of other accommodation including a *Tourist Cottage*, the *Saikatabas* and the *Hotel Sea Hawk*. These can all be booked through the West Bengal Tourist Development Corporation in Calcutta (tel 235917). Digha also has a number of private hotels and boarding houses.

Bakkhali

Also known as Fraserganj this is another beach resort, 132 km from Calcutta and on the east side of the Hooghly. Accommodation here can again be reserved through the West Bengal Tourist Corporation. From here you can get boats across to the small island of Jambu Dwip to the south-west.

Sunderbans

Spreading across the border into Bangladesh the Sunderbans is the forest at the delta where the Ganges meet the sea. Royal Bengal tigers can still be seen here, particularly on Lothian Island and Chamta Block. There are many other animals including deer, wild boar, monkeys, snakes and crocodiles.

NORTH OF CALCUTTA

Chandernagore

This was another of the French enclaves in India which were handed over at the same

Haldia

The new port of Haldia is 96 km south of Calcutta and on the west bank of the Hooghly. The port was constructed to try to regain the shipping lost from Calcutta due to the port's silting problems. There are regular buses between Calcutta and Haldia.

Sagar Island

At the mouth of the Hooghly, this island is considered to be the point where the Ganges joins the sea and a great three-day

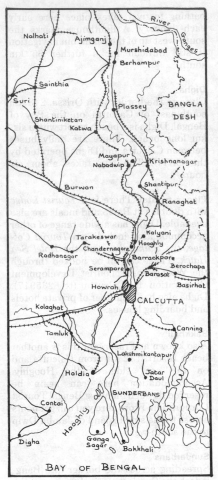

BAY OF BENGAL

Hooghly

This historic town is 41 km north of Calcutta and very close to two other interesting sites – Chinsura and Bandel. Hooghly was an important trading port long before Calcutta rose to prominence. In 1537 the Portuguese set up a factory here; prior to that time Satgaon, 10 km further north, had been the main port of Bengal but it was abandoned due to the river silting up. There are still a few traces of Satgaon's former grandeur including a ruined mosque.

The Portuguese were kicked out of Hooghly in 1632 by Shah Jahan, after a lengthy siege, but allowed to return a year later. The British East India Company also established a factory here in 1651. The Imambara, built in 1836, with its gateway flanked by lofty minarets, is the main sight in the city. Across the road from the it is an older Imambara, dating from 1776-77.

Chinsura

Only a km or so south of Hooghly, Chinsura was exchanged by the Dutch with the British for the Indonesian Island of Sumatra in 1825. The Dutch Church is octagonal and dates from 1678, there is a Dutch cemetery with many old tombs a km to the west.

Bandel

Only a couple of km north of Hooghly, Bandel is 43 km north of Calcutta. A Portuguese Church and monastery was built here in 1599 but destroyed by Shah Jahan in 1640. It was later rebuilt.

Getting There Get off the train at Naihati and take the hourly shuttle service across the river.

Bansberia

A further four km north of Bandel, Bansberia has the Vasudev temple with interesting terracotta wall carvings and also the Hanseswari Temple.

time as Pondicherry in 1951. On the banks of the Hooghly, 39 km north of Calcutta, there are still a number of buildings dating from the French era. The first French settlers arrived here in 1673 and it later became an important trading post, although it was taken by the British during conflicts with the French.

Jairambati & Kamarpukur

Ramakrishna was born in Kamarpurkur, 143 km north-west of Calcutta, and there is a Ramakrishna Mission Ashram here. Ramakrishna was a 19th century Hindu saint, who did much to rejuvenate Hinduism when it was going through a period of decline during the British rule. Jairambati, five km away, is another important point for Ramakrishna devotees.

Shantiniketan

Near Bolpur, the Vivabharati University is located here. The brilliant and prolific poet, writer and nationalist Rabindranath Tagore (1861-1941) founded a school here in 1901. It later developed into a university with an emphasis on man's relation with nature – many classes are conducted in the open air. Tagore went on to win the Nobel prize in 1913 and is credited with introducing India's historical and cultural greatness to the modern world. Despite his work for India's independence he was knighted by the British.

Places to Stay There's a small *University Guest House* and *Railway Retiring Rooms* at Bolpur station.

Nabadwip & Mayapur

Nabadwip is an ancient centre of Sanskrit culture, 114 km north of Calcutta. There are many temples here and across the river at Mayapur; both are important pilgrimage centres.

Plassey

In 1757 Clive defeated Suraj-ud-daula and his French supporters here, a turning point in British influence in India. Plassey is 172 km north of Calcutta.

Murshidabad (population 18,000)

This was once an important trading town between inland India and the port of Calcutta, 221 km south. Today it's a quiet town in central Bengal, a chance to see typical rural Bengali life, but this was once the home of Surj-ud-daula, the local sultan who put Calcutta's British residents into that infamous 'Black Hole'. A year later the British defeated his forces at Plassey and nominated a more reliable successor.

They built him a large Italian style palace, the Nizamat Kila, which was completed in 1837 and still stands right beside the Bhagirathi River (closed Fridays). Cross the river by small boat to see Suraj's tomb at Khusbagh, the 'Garden of Happiness', where the Nawabs are buried. Opposite it is the Moti Jhil or 'Pearl Lake', a fine place to view the sunsets. There are a number of other interesting buildings and ruins and this is a notable silk producing area.

Places to Stay Near the palace in Murshidabad is the *Hotel Historical*, which has rooms at Rs 15. If it's full you can sleep on the roof. Meals are also cheap. The *Tourist Lodge* in Berhampore is cleaner and more reliable, but it's 12 km away by bus. Rooms can be booked through the West Bengal Tourism Corporation in Calcutta and rooms cost from Rs 30 or there is a Rs 8 dorm.

Getting There There are seven trains daily from Sealdah Station in Calcutta and the trip takes six hours.

English Bazaar (population 70,000)

Near this town, north of the Ganges on the route to Darjeeling, there are the interesting remains of several ancient Bengali capital cities.

Gaur

Seven km south of English Bazaar, this was the capital of Bengal in the pre-Moslem days. The large city stood at the junction of the Ganges and Mahananda Rivers and was once extensively fortified. There are still many remains of the fortifications, mosques and towers.

Old Malda

At the junction of the Kalindri and Mahananda Rivers, this was once an important place as the port for the former Moslem capital of Pandua. An English factory was established here in 1656 but moved to English Bazaar in 1771.

Pandua

Gaur once alternated with Pandua as the seat of power. Many of Pandua's now ruined buildings were constructed from material taken from Gaur, which accounts for its strange blend of architectural styles. Pandua is ll km from Old Malda and 18 km from English Bazaar.

PERMITS

Before you can visit Darjeeling, Kalimpong or Sikkim special permits are required. Only in the case of Darjeeling are certain exceptions made to this rule (see below). All these places are in what the Indian Government refers to as 'sensitive border regions' and the rationale behind the permit requirements is to keep track on who goes there. Anyone having the slightest familiarity with Indian bureaucracy will know what a farce this is. As far as Darjeeling and Kalimpong are concerned it's merely a formality, but it keeps plenty of people employed pushing pens and wielding rubber stamps. Anywhere else in the world it would be called 'Job Creation'. With Sikkim obtaining a permit is more involved and you must plan ahead.

Darjeeling

The only exception to the permit rule is if you travel by air from Calcutta to Bagdogra (the nearest airport to Darjeeling), return the same way, and your stay in Darjeeling does not exceed 15 days from the date of arrival at Bagdogra. If you do this you can have your passport endorsed at Bagdogra airport checkpost for a visit to Darjeeling.

If you intend to go there by bus or train then you must obtain a permit. You can get these from any of the following places:

Indian Embassies, Consulates and High Commissions outside India.
Ministry of Home Affairs, Government of India, North Block, New Delhi.
Home Political Department, Block 2, Writers' Building, BBD Bagh, Calcutta. The office is on the first floor – ask for Mr Gautama. Or perhaps you cannot any longer – one traveller wrote that they simply referred him to the next Calcutta address:
Any Foreigners Registration Office in India. In Calcutta the office is at 237 Acharya J C Bose Rd.

There is one form to complete, no photographs are required and the permit is issued free of charge within 24 hours in India. If you apply outside India then three photographs are needed. Permits allow for a stay of seven days, extendable in Darjeeling at the Foreigners Registration Office, Laden La Rd (tel 2261). No photographs are required, and no fee charged for extensions and they are issued while you wait.

If you're planning on trekking to Sandakphu and/or Phalut a separate special permit is required obtainable, again, from the Foreigners Registration Office in Darjeeling. If you flew into Bagdogra airport then you are exempted from this requirement on condition that you report your intentions to the Foreigners' Registration Office, Darjeeling, 24 hours before leaving.

Two British travellers came up on the same train from Calcutta as I did, and they came without Darjeeling permits – nobody had told them. When I first saw them, as my permit was being checked at New Jaipalguri station, they were nearly in tears, having been told they would have to return to Calcutta for their permits. I left the desk thinking they had had it but the next day they were in Darjeeling, all grins. First the officer softened by saying that he could give them a 24-hour pass. Then he pointed out that once in Darjeeling they could extend.

Kalimpong

A permit for Darjeeling does not automatically entitle you to visit Kalimpong. To go there you must obtain a separate endorsement on your Darjeeling permit. Ask for it at the same time you apply for the Darjeeling permit or get one from the Foreigners Registration Office in Darjeeling. A three-day visit is normally allowed. If you want longer, get authorisation before you go.

Sikkim

There are no exceptions to the permit requirements for Sikkim regardless of your mode of transport. You need to apply at least six weeks in advance of your proposed visit either to an Indian Embassy/Consulate/High Commission outside India or to the Deputy Secretary, Ministry of Home Affairs (F-l), North Block, New Delhi 110001. There are three forms to complete, three photographs are required and you have to state the exact days on which you want to visit. No fee is charged for the permit.

If you apply via an Embassy/Consulate/High Commission you will receive a letter some four to six weeks after you applied which states that 'the Government of India has no objection to your visit' and that you can pick up your permit from the Deputy Commissioner's Office, Darjeeling (situated at the junction of Cutchery Rd and Cart Rd next to the Loreto Convent). The initial permitted length of stay varies between two and four days but is extendable in Gangtok at the Foreigners Regional Registration Office. Extensions are a mere formality and issued on the spot – just tell them where you want to go and how much time you require. No photographs are required and no fee charged for extensions. Your permit will be collected on leaving Sikkim at the Rangpo checkpost.

Recently permits have been changed and now only permit foreigners to go to Gangtok, Rumtek and Phodang. Pemayangtse can only be visited if you are travelling in a group with a liaison officer, so that means when making a trek to Dzongri, after you have got permission from the Indian Mountaineering Federation in New Delhi. Nobody in Sikkim seems to know why this change was made for Pemayangtse was open to individual foreign tourists for some years.

DARJEELING (population 50,000)

Straddling a ridge at 2123 metres and surrounded by tea plantations on all sides, Darjeeling has been a very popular hill station since the British established it as a rest and recreation centre for its troops in the mid-1800s. These days foreign travellers and Indian nationals come here to escape from the heat, humidity and hassle of the North Indian plain and some indication of its popularity can be gleaned from the fact that there are almost 60 hotels recognised by the West Bengal Tourist Development Corporation, apart from scores of others which don't come up to its requirements. Here you will find yourself surrounded by mountain people from all over the eastern Himalayas who have come here to work, trade or, in the case of the Tibetans, as refugees.

Outside of the monsoon season (June-September) the views over the mountains to the snowy peaks of Kanchenjunga and down to the swollen rivers in the valley bottoms are magnificent. It's a fascinating place where you can see Buddhist monasteries, visit a tea plantation and see how it's processed, go for a ride on the chair-lift which takes you down 2050 metres over eight km to the valley bottom, spend days hunting for bargains in colourful markets and handicraft shops, or go trekking to high altitude spots near the border with Sikkim. Like most places in the Himalayas, half the fun is in getting there and Darjeeling has the unique attraction of the famous 'toy train'. This miniature train which loops and switchbacks its way up the steep mountainsides from New Jalpaiguri to Darjeeling has been a favourite with travellers for many years.

History

Until the beginning of the 18th century the whole of the area between the present borders of Sikkim and the plains of Bengal, including Darjeeling and Kalimpong, belonged to the Rajas of Sikkim. In 1706 they lost Kalimpong to the Bhutanese and control of the remainder was wrested from them by the Gurkhas who invaded Sikkim in 1780 following consolidation of the latter's rule in Nepal.

These annexations by the Gurkhas, however, brought them into conflict with the British East India Company. A series of wars were fought between the two parties eventually leading to the defeat of the Gurkhas, and the ceding of all the land they had taken from the Sikkimese to the East India Company. Part of this territory was restored to the Rajas of Sikkim and the country's sovereignty guaranteed by the British in return for British control over any disputes which arose with neighbouring states.

One such dispute, which arose in 1828, led to the despatch of two British officers to this area and it was during their fact-finding tour that they spent some time at Darjeeling (then called Dorje Ling = 'Place of Thunderbolts'). The officers were quick to appreciate Darjeeling's value as a site for a sanatorium, hill station and as the key to a pass into Nepal and Tibet. The officers' observations were reported to the authorities in Calcutta and a pretext eventually found to pressure the Raja into granting the site to the British in return for an annual stipend of Rs 3000 (raised to Rs 6000 in 1846).

This transfer, however, rankled with the Tibetans who regarded Sikkim as a vassal state, and Darjeeling's rapid development as a trading centre and tea-growing area in a key position along the trade route

leading from Sikkim to the plains of India began to make a considerable impact on the fortunes of the lamas and leading merchants of Sikkim. Tensions arose and in 1849 two British travellers, Sir Joseph Hooker and Dr Campbell, who were visiting Sikkim with the permission of the Raja and the British Government were arrested. Various demands were made as a condition of their release, but the Sikkimese eventually released both prisoners unconditionally about a month later.

In reprisal for the arrests, however, the British annexed the whole of the land between the present borders of Sikkim and the Bengal plains and withdrew the annual Rs 6000 stipend from the Raja. The latter was restored to his son and raised to Rs 9000 in 1868 and raised again to Rs 12,000 in 1874. The annexations brought about a significant change in Darjeeling's status. Previously it had been an enclave within Sikkimese territory and to reach it the British had to pass through a country ruled by an independent Raja. After the take-over, Darjeeling became continuous with British territory further south and Sikkim was cut off from access to the plains except through British territory. This was eventually to lead to the invasion of Sikkim by the Tibetans and the British military expedition to Lhasa.

When the British first arrived in Darjeeling it was almost completely under forest and virtually uninhabited, though it had once been a sizeable village before the wars with Bhutan and Nepal. Development was rapid and by 1840 a road had been constructed, numerous houses and a sanatorium built and a hotel opened. By 1857 it had a population of some 10,000.

Most of the increase in the population was accounted for by the recruitment of labourers from Nepal, who were brought in to work the tea plantations which had been established in the early 1840s by the British following the smuggling of tea seeds from China. Even today, the vast majority of people speak Nepali as a first language and the name Darjeeling continues to be synonymous with tea. Although it's from here that some of the world's finest tea originates, the tea industry is presently in dire straights. The quality of the soil is deteriorating and most of the tea trees are more than 100 years old. Very little replanting has been done and, if it is to survive, it seems likely that massive government aid will be necessary.

Until the late 1800s, all supplies for Darjeeling and all exports from the town had to be moved by bullock cart along the road which connects it to Siliguri. This road, which is still known as the Hill Cart Rd, was so called because its gradient is such that even bullock carts could climb it. Naturally, this form of transportation was slow and, even by the standards of the time, expensive. Rice which sold in Siliguri for Rs 98 a tonne fetched Rs 240 a tonne by the time it reached Darjeeling. The problem was eventually overcome when an astute officer of the Eastern Bengal Railway, Franklin Prestage, came up with a scheme for constructing a miniature railway – the famous 'Toy Train'. Construction of this railway started in 1879 and was completed by 1881 at a cost of Rs 1,700,000 including the initial rolling stock, though improvements were made to it from time to time, one of the most important being the Batasia loop on the final descent into Darjeeling.

Orientation

Darjeeling is strung out over a ridge facing west and spills down the hillside in a complicated series of interconnecting roads and flights of steps, which it will take you at least several days to become familiar with. The main road is the Cart Rd running along the lower part of the town, along which are located the railway station and the bus and taxi stand. The most important route connecting this road

with Chowrasta at the top of the ridge is Laden La Rd/Nehru Rd.

Along these two roads are situated a fair number of the budget hotels and cheap restaurants, the GPO, the bus terminals for Sikkim and Kathmandu, the Foreigners Registration Office, the State Bank of India, curio shops, photographic supply shops and the Tourist Office. At the Chowrasta end of Nehru Rd and on Gandhi Rd above Laden La Rd are many of the mid-range hotels and restaurants. The bulk of the top-range hotels are clustered around Observatory Hill beyond Chowrasta. There are others along Dr Zakir Hussain Rd and A J C Bose Rd. The Youth Hostel is situated on the very top of the ride above Dr Zakir Hussain Rd.

Information

People Although the Buddhists, with their monasteries at Ghoom and Darjeeling, are perhaps the most conspicuous religious group they constitute only a minority of the population – about 14%. The majority of the inhabitants profess Hinduism reflecting their origins in the northern Indian states and Nepal. Christians and Moslems comprise little more than 3% each of the district's total population, though there are numerous churches scattered around Darjeeling.

Offices The Tourist Office is the Bellevue Hotel, Chowrasta (The address is officially 1 Nehru Rd, tel 2050). Very little literature is available except maps of Darjeeling, backed by a brief description of places of interest which cost Rs 1.50. Don't come here for information about the treks to Sandakphu and Phalut or you'll regret it once you're on your way. There's a branch of the Cambridge Bookshop on Laden La Rd.

Indian Airlines (tel 2355) is, like the tourist office, at 1 Nehru Rd, Chowrasta.

The Foreigners Registration Office, Laden La Rd is probably one of the most popular, though somewhat involuntary,

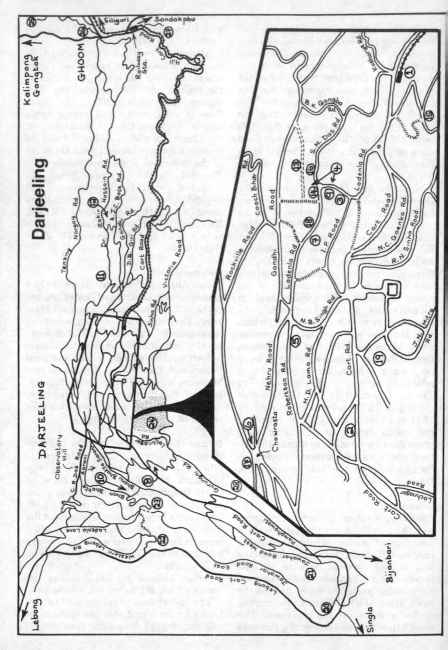

Darjeeling

1	Railway Station & Tourist Reception Centre	14	Timber Lodge
2	Bus Stand (Kalimpong, Siliguri, etc)	15	Hotels Kadambari & Nirvana
3	Buses to Gangtok (Sikkim Nationalised Transport)	16	Tibetan Restaurants (eg Solti)
4	Buses to Kathmandu	17	Chowrasta Restaurant
5	Taxi Stand	18	State Bank of India
6	Tourist Office & Indian Airlines	19	Market
7	Foreigners Registration Office	20	Ropeway (Chairlift)
8	Deputy Commissioner's Office	21	Himalayan Mountaineering Institute & Zoo
9	GPO	22	Tibetan Refugee Centre
10	Darjeeling Tourist Lodge	23	Raj Bhavan
11	Youth Hostel	24	Botanical Gardens
12	Sailabash Tourist Lodge	25	Tiger Hill
13	Several Mid-range Hotels	26	Monastery
		27	Ghoom Monastery
		28	Happy Valley Tea Estate

meeting places for travellers. Darjeeling Permit extensions take a few minutes. No photographs are required and there's no fee. Permits for Kalimpong take only 10 minutes or so. There's one form to fill in, no photographs and the permit is issued free of charge. They normally allow for a three-day stay. Remember that if you're going to Sikkim the validity of your Darjeeling permit may need extending to cover you for the return journey.

Money The State Bank of India on Laden La Rd is the usual place to change money, but it's one of the most inefficient and slowest bank branches I've ever come across. It's also unbelievably decrepit. I wouldn't bank a pair of sweaty old socks here let alone money. Be prepared for a long session changing money, snails would leave this lot standing! There's a Grindlays up the road.

Trekking The best place to hire trekking gear from is the youth hostel, but you must leave a deposit or valuables to cover the value of the articles which you borrow (deposits returnable, less hire charges, on return of the equipment). Typical charges are: sleeping bag (Rs 4.50 a day); rucksack (Rs 2 a day); air pillow (Rs 0.25 a day); air mattress (Rs 1.50 a day); bed roll (Rs 2.50 a day); two-person tent (Rs 6 a day);

aluminium camp cot (Rs 4 a day). The Youth Hostel also keeps a book where trekkers write comments and suggestions about the routes. It's well worth reading through this book if you're thinking of going trekking. The only trouble is, the entries are written in many different languages and, in many ways, you need to have been on the trek to make head or tail of what is being said. Whatever you do, don't bother asking the Tourist Office for information about trekking.

Climate The best time to visit Darjeeling is between April and mid-June and between September and November. During the monsoon months (June to September) clouds obscure the mountains and the rain is often so heavy that whole sections of the road from the plains are washed away, though the town is rarely cut off for more than a few days at a time. The average temperatures range from a maximum of $15°C$ to a minimum of $8.5°$ in summer and from a maximum of $6°C$ to a minimum of $1.5°C$ in winter. In winter it can get very cold indeed, a real surprise if you've just come up from Calcutta. If you go there during the monsoon an umbrella is more-or-less essential – cheaply bought in the market.

Viewpoints

Tiger Hill The highest spot in the area at 2590 metres, Tiger Hill is situated near Ghoom, about 11 km from Darjeeling. The hill is famous for its magnificent dawn views over Kanchenjunga and other eastern Himalayan peaks. On a clear day even Mt Everest is visible. Accommodation is available here at a Tourist Lodge.

Senchal Lake Close to Tiger Hill is Senchal Lake which supplies Darjeeling with its domestic water. It's a particularly scenic area and popular as a picnic spot with Indian holidaymakers. Entrance to the lake costs Rs 0.50.

Religious Centres

Ghoom Buddhist Monastery This is probably the most famous monastery in Darjeeling and is located about eight km from town, just below the Hill Cart Rd and railway near Ghoom. It enshrines an image of the Maitreya Buddha (the coming Buddha). Foreigners are allowed to enter the shrine and take photographs. A small donation is customary and the monks here are very friendly. There is another monastery nearby in Ghoom itself.

Aloobari Monastery Nearer Darjeeling, on Tenzing Norgay Rd, this monastery is still in the process of construction. Visitors are welcome and the monks often have Tibetan and Sikkimese handicrafts and religious objects (usually hand bells) for sale.

Dhirdham Temple The most conspicuous Hindu temple in Darjeeling, it is just below the railway station and built along the lines of the famous Pashupatinath temple in Kathmandu.

Museums, Parks & Gardens

Himalayan Mountaineering Institute On Jawahar Rd West, about two km from the town, the institute is the only one of its kind and exists to train mountaineers. It also has a museum containing an interesting collection of mountaineering equipment, specimens of Himalayan flora and fauna (though not one of the Abominable Snowman!) and a relief model of the Himalayas. It is open from 9 am to 5 pm during summer and from 9 am to 4 pm during winter, except between 1 pm and 2 pm. Except during the tourist season it is closed on Tuesdays. The entrance fee is Rs 0.50 and another Rs 0.50 to the Everest Museum.

Zoological Park Adjacent to the Himalayan Mountaineering Institute, the park has a collection of high-altitude fauna including the Siberian tiger, Himalayan black bear, deer, panda and a bird collection. The entrance fee is Rs 0.50.

Botanical Gardens Below the bus and taxi stand near the Market, these gardens contain a representative collection of Himalayan plants, flowers and orchids. The hot houses are well worth a visit. The gardens are open between 6 am and 5 pm, entrance is free.

Handicraft Centres

Tibetan Refugee Self-Help Centre The centre was established in October 1959 to help rehabilitate Tibetan refugees who had fled from Tibet with the Dalai Lama following the Chinese invasion. Religious importance is attached to this place as the 13th Dalai Lama (the present is the 14th) stayed here during his visit to India in 1919-22. The centre produces superb carpets, woollens, wood carvings and leather work and has various Tibetan curios for sale (coins, banknotes, jewellery, etc).

You can wander at leisure through the various workshops and watch the work in progress. The weaving and dying shops and the wood carving shop are particularly interesting and the people who work there very friendly. Their prices, however, are on a par with those in the curio shops of Chowrasta and Nehru Rd. It's an interesting place to visit apart from the workshops and the views en route are magnificent.

Curio Shops The majority of these are located on Chowrasta and along Nehru Rd. All things Himalayan are sold here – *thankas*, brass statues, religious objects, jewellery, wood carvings, woven fabrics, carpets, etc – but if you're looking for bargains you have to shop judiciously and be prepared to spend plenty of time looking through various shops. Thankas in particular are nowhere near the quality which was usual 10 years ago. They may look impressive at first sight but on closer inspection you will find that little care has been taken over the finer detail. The brocade surroundings (said to originate from China) are often of much finer quality.

Wood carvings tend to be excellent value for money. Most of the shops accept international credit cards. In addition to the curio shops themselves there is the market off the Cart Rd next to the bus and taxi stands. Here you can find excellent and relatively cheap patterned woollen sweaters. If you need an umbrella these can be bought here for around Rs 12. Made out of bamboo, they are collectors' items themselves!

Bengal 'Manjusha' Emporium Located on the Cart Rd about two km from town on the way to Ghoom and opposite the Ava Art Gallery, this emporium sells Himalayan handicrafts, silk and handloom products from West Bengal. It's open on all working days from 8 am to 5 pm.

Tea Plantations
Tea is, of course, Darjeeling's most famous export. From its 78 gardens are produced 10.5 million kgs annually – 2% of India's total. It employs over 46,000 people in the area. The most convenient garden to visit is the Happy Valley Tea Estate only two km from the centre of town where tea is still produced by the

'orthodox' method as opposed to the 'Curling, Tearing and Crushing' (CTC) method adopted in the plains. The process is a fascinating one to observe and you should set aside a half day to visit the estate.

After picking, the fresh, green leaves are placed 15 to 25 cm deep in a 'withering trough' where the moisture content is reduced from 70 to 80% to 30 to 40% using high velocity fans. When this is complete the withered leaves are rolled and pressed so as to break the cell walls and express their juices onto the surface of the leaves. Normally two rollings at different pressures are undertaken and in between rolls the leaves sifted to separate the coarse from the fine. Next the leaves, coated with their juices, are allowed to ferment on racks in a high-humidity room, a process which develops their character-istic aroma and flavour. This fermentation must be controlled carefully since either over– or under-fermentation will ruin the tea.

The process is stopped by feeding the fermenting leaves onto a conveyor belt which passes through a chamber into which is forced dry air at 115-120°C and which reduces the moisture content further to around 2 to 3%. The last process is the sorting of the tea into grades. In their order of value they are; Golden Flowery Orange Pekoe (unbroken leaves), Golden Broken Orange Pekoe, Orange Fannings and Dust (the latter three all consisting of broken leaves).

In the last few years modern agri-cultural practices have been brought to the tea estates to maintain and improve their viability. They were one of the first agricultural enterprises to use clonal plants in their replanting schemes, though very little of this has been done and, as was mentioned earlier, most of the tea trees are at least 100 years old. The fact that most of them are getting towards the end of their useful or even natural lives is causing grave concern to the growers and government assistance has already started in an attempt to save the gardens from extinction. This is important not just because of the value of the tea exported, but because of the large numbers of people in this area who would be made redundant if the gardens were to close.

The Happy Valley Estate is open daily from 8 am to 12 noon and between 1 pm and 4.30 pm except on Mondays and Sunday afternoons.

The Passenger Ropeway

At North Point, about three km from town, this was the first passenger ropeway to be constructed in India. It is five km long and connects Darjeeling with Singla Bazaar on the Little Ranjit River at the bottom of the valley. This is a superb excursion though not one for vertigo sufferers. The return fare costs Rs 16. Before you go there ring 2731 to enquire about the availability of chairs.

Places to Stay

The places that follow are only a limited selection of the scores of hotels and lodges available in Darjeeling. You will find plenty of others along virtually any road you choose. The object of this list is to see you through the first couple of days. After that you may well find others that are more appealing than these and decide to move. In the cold winter 'off season' prices will often be discounted.

Places to Stay – Bottom End

Hotel Kadambari, situated below the railway station, has concrete box rooms with attached 'bathroom' (buckets of hot water delivered) and toilet, clean sheets and blankets from Rs 35 to 45 per person. It's clean and run by very friendly staff. Lounge and dining room on the top floor with excellent views across the valley.

Hotel Nirvana, next door to the Hotel Kadambari on S K Pal Rd, is similar in quality and facilities to the Kadambari. Rooms cost from Rs 30 to 60 per person. Front rooms are more expensive than those at the back. Friendly people. *Timber*

Lodge is at the back of Laden La Rd – to get there take the stone steps on the left hand side of the restaurants opposite the top end of the GPO and take the first turning on the right. The place is very popular with budget travellers, though definitely on the decrepit side of rustic. The manager is very pleasant and eager to please but there's no hot water available. Rooms here cost from as little as Rs 10.

Shamrock Hotel is 100 metres further along the dirt track from the Timber Lodge. Rooms here cost from Rs 15, the upstairs rooms are more expensive than the downstairs. Communal facilities and no hot water. *Hotel Pagoda* (tel 2143) is on Upper Beechwood Rd, three minutes walk from the railway station, with fine views over the town and of Mt Kanchenjunga.

There are numerous guest houses around Darjeeling. Some which travellers have recommended include *Puri Villa* (Springburn Hotel) at 70 Gandhi Rd which has doubles with bath from Rs 40 and a friendly, family atmosphere. Opposite the Rink Cinema the *Stuart Lodge* has just two rooms. There's another small Tibetan run private hotel on Tenzing Rd. *Nabins Lodge* is a small guest house just below the Youth Hostel, between Zakir Hussain Rd and A J C Bose Rd. It has rooms for Rs 25 and you get a pot of excellent Darjeeling tea in in the morning. It's a bit cold because it's on the shadowed side of the hill.

The *Youth Hostel*, above Dr Zakir Hussain Rd (tel 2290), is very popular with trekkers and other budget travellers. There are rooms (for less than Rs 20) and a dormitory (Rs 5 members, Rs 8 non-members). Couples can't get a room together because the manger, 'doesn't want to have to ask people if they are married'! The hostel is clean and well-maintained and there's a friendly manager. Meals can be provided, there are cooking facilities and there are excellent views across the mountains. A book is kept here with trekkers' comments about the route to Sandakphu and Phalut, and if you're thinking of doing the trek you'd be well advised to spend an hour or two reading through it (there are sections in every language under the sun!). Trekking gear is available for hire.

At Tiger Hill near Ghoom there is the *Tourist Lodge* where you can stay if you want to watch the sunrise over Kanchenjunga. Rooms here cost from Rs 40 and there's a dormitory. Advance booking is advisable – either ring the Lodge direct (tel 2813) or contact the Tourist Office at the junction of Nehru Rd and Chowrasta.

Places to Stay – Middle

The *Tourist Lodge*, Bhanu Sarani (The Mall) (tel 2611-13) is managed by the West Bengal Tourist Department. Rooms here cost Rs 75 to 150 a double (there are no singles) but note that breakfast and dinner is compulsory. It's not a particularly inviting building but many tourists stay here. *Maple Tourist Bungalow* is a cheaper subsidiary of the Tourist Lodge. Check at the Tourist Lodge first, there is plenty of hot water, splendid views towards the Happy Valley tea estate and rooms as cheap as Rs 25, doubles from Rs 50.

Ambassador Hotel, 1B Chowrasta (tel 2781) has rooms from Rs 50. *Capital Hotel*, 1A Gandhi Rd (tel 2860) costs from Rs 50 per person. *Kundu's Hotel*, 2A Rockville Rd (tel 2867) costs from Rs 50. There is another Kundu's Hotel at 1 Gandhi Rd (tel 2146) which has rooms for Rs 60 to 75 per person. Also on Gandhi Rd the *Tara Hotel* looks better than it actually is. Doubles are Rs 60, the hot water is unreliable.

Meghdoot Hotel, 4 Laden La Rd (tel 2975) has rooms from Rs 50 to 150. *Mayfair Hotel*, 6 Gandhi Rd costs Rs 30-55 a single and Rs 55-110 a double. *Rex Hotel*, 1A Gandhi Rd (tel 2571) costs from Rs 50.

Places to Stay – Top End

The top-range hotels includes the *Oberoi Mt Everest*, 29 Gandhi Rd (tel 2616) where rooms cost Rs 475/725 for singles/doubles with full board. There is a bar and foreign money can be exchanged here. *Windamere Hotel* (tel 2841), Bhanu Sarani (The Mall) costs Rs 200/300 with full board. Facilities are similar to the Oberoi.

Central Hotel (tel 2033), Robertson Rd costs Rs 130/260 including all meals. *New Elgin Hotel*, H D Lama Rd (tel 2182) costs from Rs 100 for singles and from Rs 200 for doubles with full board. *Pine Ridge Hotel*, 19 Nehru Rd (tel 2094) costs from Rs 100 a double. Meals are extra and they have no single rooms. *Hotel Bellevue*, Nehru Rd (tel 2129) costs from Rs 150 a double. Meals are extra.

Places to Eat

Most of the cheaper restaurants are along Laden La Rd, Nehru Rd and Cart Rd. Many of them are Tibetan restaurants and popular with budget travellers, but there's little to choose between them. Among the better ones is the *Himalaya Restaurant*, Laden La Rd, opposite the State Bank of India. A good Tibetan restaurant which serves porridge, omelettes and other Tibetan food including great Tibetan bread. Porridge, omelettes and tea costs less than Rs 10. Friendly management and run by an old man who chants mantras all morning!

Chowrasta Restaurant, Chowrasta, is an open-air restaurant which serves excellent South Indian food (vegetarian only) including masala dosas and special dosas. The *Solti Restaurant* is on Laden La Rd, opposite the top end of the GPO and below the Timber Lodge. They offer Tibetan, Chinese and 'European' food. The omelettes, chips and pancakes are excellent but avoid the chicken like the plague unless you're bent on being buried with botulism. Near the Himalaya Restaurant you can get good steak, onion and chips at the *Washington Restaurant* for just Rs 6.

Glenary's Restaurant is near the junction of Laden La Rd and Nehru Rd. An excellent mid-range cafe with surprisingly reasonable prices. Come here for a minor splurge and to get a glimpse of the ghost of the Raj – the waiters all wear white uniforms with cummerbunds and frilly turbans!

Getting There

Air The nearest airport to Darjeeling is at Bagdogra down on the plains near Siliguri, about 90 km from Darjeeling. From Bagdogra you can get to Darjeeling either by rail or road. There are daily flights by Indian Airlines between Calcutta and Bagdogra. The fare is Rs 341 and the journey takes 55 minutes. There's also a daily flight from Delhi to Bagdogra via Patna. The Delhi-Bagdogra fare is Rs 927.

Indian Airline offices in the Darjeeling area are at Siliguri (tel 20692), Kalimpong (tel 241), Darjeeling (tel 2355) and Bagdogra Airport (tel 20366).

If you fly into and out of Bagdogra then you are exempted from the permit requirements for Darjeeling. On arrival at Bagdogra your passport will automatically be endorsed for a 15-day visit to Darjeeling. Flying into and out of Bagdogra does not exempt you from the permit requirements for Sikkim. If you're intending to go there you must apply for one of these in advance.

Rail One of the quickest way to get from Calcutta to Darjeeling (or vice versa) is to take the daily 'Darjeeling Mail' from Sealdah Station, Calcutta to New Jalpaiguri and then a bus or taxi from there to Darjeeling. But the most interesting way of doing the last stage of the journey from New Jalpaiguri to Darjeeling is to take the 'Toy Train', even though this will add hours to the journey.

From Calcutta to New Jalpaiguri takes a little over 12 hours overnight. It's also an overnight journey from New Jalpaiguri

back to Calcutta (Sealdah Station). The fares are Rs 154 in 1st class and Rs 40 in 2nd class. Second class sleeping berths can be booked at the Eastern Railways Booking Office, Fairlie Place, Calcutta; New Jalpaiguri Station between 8.30 am and 10.30 am and between 2.30 pm and 4.30 pm; or the Darjeeling Railway Station. If you intend to go by 2nd class rail all the way between Calcutta and Darjeeling (or vice versa) you can book a ticket all the way there. If you're booking in Darjeeling, a sleeping berth can be booked for you on the night mail train from New Jalpaiguri.

Another train which might be of use to you along the main line if you're heading west is the Siliguri-Moghulserai train. Moghulserai is only a few km from Varanasi (Benares). This train departs Siliguri daily at 6.30 pm and takes 23 hours to Moghulserai. Again you can get a ticket which includes the journey on the 'Toy Train' from Darjeeling to Siliguri.

The Toy Train The journey to Darjeeling from New Jalpaiguri or Siliguri by this miniature railway is a superb experience and one which shouldn't be missed even though it does take three hours longer than the buses.

The idea for a railway to Darjeeling was put forward by Franklin Prestage, an agent working for the Eastern Bengal Railway, in 1870. The scheme was accepted and construction begun in 1879. It was completed in 1881 and in 1885 a further km extension was added to take the line into the market area (now in disuse). Later on, in 1914, it was further extended south towards Kishanganj close to the Nepalese border to cope with the transport of jute and, in 1915, from Siliguri to 15 km beyond Sevok on the way to Kalimpong. The initial cost of the original section to Darjeeling was Rs 1,700,000 including rolling stock. The whole line is an ingenious feat of engineering and includes four complete loops and five switchbacks some of which were added after the initial construction had been completed to ease the line's gradient at certain points. Altogether, there are 132 unmanned level crossings!

Officially there are two or three departures in either direction daily, but in practice there can be more and the departures from New Jalpaiguri don't necessarily follow the official timetable (though they usually do from Darjeeling). The fares are approximately Rs 60 in lst class and Rs 12 in 2nd class and the journey takes seven hours. Meals are available on the train. If you fly in to Bagdogra from Calcutta, you can travel just to Ghoom on the toy train in order to experience it, then get a share jeep back to Darjeeling! Darjeeling-Ghoom is about Rs 12 in 1st class.

Your permit for Darjeeling will be checked at New Jalpaiguri Station both on entering and leaving. There is also a Tourist Reception Office at the station.

Buses Most of the buses from Darjeeling depart from the Bazar Bus Stand (Cart Rd). Most jeeps and taxis depart from the Motor Stand, Robertson Rd/Laden La Rd. There are many different companies operating buses, jeeps and taxis. Take your pick.

Calcutta/Siliguri (and vice versa). Daily departures in either direction at 8 pm arriving at 7 am the following morning by 'Rocket Service'. The fare is Rs 75 and bookings can be made with North Bengal State Transport Corporation at Esplanade Bus Stand, Calcutta (tel 23 1854); Bazar Taxi Stand, Darjeeling, or at Siliguri Bus Stand (tel 20531). This bus is much faster than the train and has fairly comfortable seats. This company also runs buses from Siliguri to Patna and vice versa. The buses leave Siliguri daily at 11 am and arrive in Patna at 10 pm. The fare is Rs 38.

New Jalpaiguri/Siliguri-Darjeeling (and vice versa). There are numerous buses, jeeps and taxis in either direction daily

between 6 am and 10 pm. The journey takes 3½ to four hours (sometimes less) and costs Rs 9 to 19 from Siliguri and Rs 11 to 21 from New Jalpaiguri depending on the quality of the bus and whether you go by bus, jeep or taxi (the cost in order of cheapness is: bus, jeep, taxi).

Bagdogra-Darjeeling (and vice versa). Minibuses and jeeps connect the airport with Darjeeling. The fare is Rs 29 to 33 and the journey takes three hours approximately.

Darjeeling-Kalimpong Many buses, jeeps and taxis in either direction daily from 6 am to 10 pm. Buses depart from the Bazar Motor Stand. Jeeps and taxis depart either from the Bazar Motor Stand or from the Robertson Rd/Laden La Rd taxi stand. The fare is Rs 12 to 17 and the journey takes 2½ hours. The Kalimpong Motor Transport Syndicate, for example, at the Bazar Motor Stand runs jeeps for Rs 15 in the back seats and Rs 16 in the front seats. Your permit for Kalimpong will be checked by military at Teesta bridge. The road as far as Teesta is pretty rough in parts but from there to Kalimpong it's in good shape.

Darjeeling-Gangtok If you don't want to go by taxi or jeep there is only one bus line to Gangtok. This is run by Sikkim Nationalised Transport (SNT) which has its Darjeeling office in the first building below the GPO on Laden La Rd (it's unmarked). There is one minibus daily in either direction and as there are few seats available, early booking is essential. The bus departs at 8 am, takes five hours and costs Rs 40. Your permit will be inspected before you cross the bridge at Rangpo and at Rangpo itself you will have to visit the Police Station to fill in the visitors' book. On the way out your permit will be collected at Rangpo.

Darjeeling-Kathmandu There are a number of companies operating buses between Darjeeling and Kathmandu. Tickets can be booked directly with the bus companies or through the tourist office. Typically you might start from

Darjeeling at 7.30 am, arrive at the border (Kakarbitta) around 5 pm, drive through the night and arrive Kathmandu around 7 am the next morning. There are also some services which overnight in Kakarbitta and travel to Kathmandu by day. Fare vary with the company, the bus and with day and night services. Typical fares are between Rs 90 and 110.

Some of the companies are Indiana, Kankai, Shabnam Travel, Railly Mai and Rajdoot. With some services you take a bus to Siliguri (Rs 11), a jeep from there to the border (Rs 8) and then the bus to Kathmandu (around Rs 75). Hotels are available at the border town from Rs 4 upwards but these days most buses travel overnight. There is no Nepalese Consulate in Darjeeling, the nearest one is in Calcutta. Seven-day visas are available at the border and can be extended in Kathmandu.

Avalanches can sometimes delay the bus. A traveller's experience of the Darjeeling-Kathmandu trip during the monsoon: 'took us three days to do the trip due to the landslides and bridges being destroyed. Got some incredible shots of us wading through thigh-deep water in swirling, full flowing rivers to get across and hopefully find another bus to the next disaster. Never again!'

TREKS IN THE DARJEELING REGION

The best months to trek in this region are April, May, October and November. There may be occasional showers during April and May but, in a way, this is the best time to go as this is the season when many shrubs are in flower, particularly the rhododendrons. There may also be occasional rains during the first half of October if the monsoon is prolonged. November is generally dry and visibility excellent during the first half of December, though it's usually rather cold by then. After the middle of December there are occasional snow falls.

In planning what clothes to take with you bear in mind that you will be passing through valley bottoms as low as 300 metres and over mountain ridges as high as 4000 metres, so you'll need clothing for low, tropical climates and high mountain passes. No matter what time of year you go it's a good idea to take a light raincoat which can be folded up and put inside your rucksack since the weather may be unpredictable, particularly at high altitudes.

Trek 1

Darjeeling – Manaybhanjang – Tonglu – Sandakphu – Phalut and return (118 km to Sandakphu and 160 km to Phalut return).

This is the most popular of the treks and the best one for those with limited time at their disposal. It offers excellent views of Kanchenjunga and of Everest, and passes through superb tropical countryside.

On the first day either walk or take a jeep or taxi to Manaybhanjang, 26 km from Darjeeling. The first day's walk to Tonglu is a fairly steep climb of ll km via a succession of zig-zags all the way up to the bungalow. Tonglu looks directly on Darjeeling and commands an excellent view of Kanchenjunga.

The next day's walk to Sandakphu covers 22 km and initially passes through bamboo thickets with many ascents and descents until Kalapokhri is reached. About five hours should be allowed for this part of the trek. The last part up to Sandakphu bungalow involves a steep climb and should take about three hours. On a clear day you can see both Kanchenjunga and Everest from Sandakphu – the latter is only 144 km from Sandakphu as the crow flies. You can either continue on to Phalut from Sandakphu or return to Darjeeling. If you decide to continue the trek starts with a steep descent and then levels out for the next 13 km or so finishing up with a steep zig-zag ascent to Phalut bungalow. Phalut is at the trijunction of Nepal, Sikkim and West Bengal and the views from here are similar to those from Sandakphu.

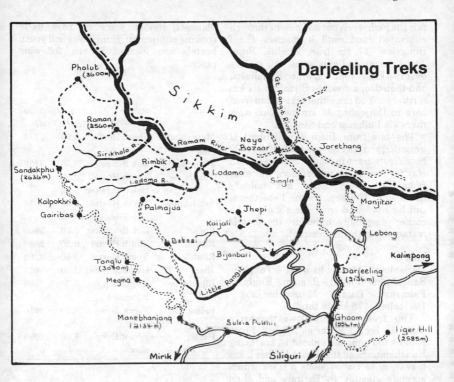

It's possible to return to Manaybhanjang from Phalut in one day if you start out early enough (allow about eight hours continuous walking) or you can return in two days at a more leisurely pace by breaking the journey at Tonglu.

Due to disrepair of the accommodation at Tonglu, most people now turn west from Megma and walk the extra five km to Javbari in Nepal – no problems about the border.

Trek 2

Darjeeling – Manaybhanjang – Tonglu – Sandakphu – Phalut – Ramam – Rimbik – Jhepi – Darjeeling via Bijanbari (153 km in total).

The first part of this trek up to Phalut follows the same route as in Trek 1.

Leaving Phalut there is a steep descent along a forest bridle path for about 11 km to Ramam River which is crossed by a bridge. A further three km brings you to Ramam Youth Hostel, 14 km from Phalut. This part of the journey takes you through dense forests of rhododendrons, silver firs, chestnuts, oaks, magnolias and hemlocks. On the next day's walk to Rimbik the road stays more or less level for nine km, crosses the Shirikhola River, and then rises steeply for a km before levelling out again in the vicinity of Rimbik Forest Bungalow and the Youth Hostel. If you need supplies there is a small bazaar at Rimbik.

The next day's walk begins with a fairly steep descent over about eight km to the bridge across the Lodoma River. After this the path levels out and passes through cultivated land until it reaches Jhepi Bungalow, 17 km from Rimbik. From Jhepi the road climbs some 150 metres over two km to a spur on which Kaijali sits, and then drops down to Bijanbari six km further on. You can either take a jeep from here to Darjeeling 36 km away, or walk there via Pulbazar and Singtam.

The bus from Jhepi to Bijanbari is irregular, you may have to walk. If the only hotel/restaurant in 'town' is full you can stay for free at the government *Haryana Bhawan* – very basic but nobody complains. The key, no-one lives there, can be borrowed from the shop on the corner diagonally opposite the hotel/ restaurant in the main street.

Trek 3

Darjeeling – Manaybhanjang – Tonglu – Sandakphu – Phalut – Ramam – Rimbik – Palmajua – Batasi – Manaybhanjang – Darjeeling (178 km in total).

This trek initially follows the same route as Trek 2 as far as Rimbik. From Rimbik to Palmajua is about 14 km facing Kanchenjunga all the way. A further ll km takes you to Batasi along a track which ascends steadily to Deoraly and then descends, gradually at first and steeply towards the end, to Batsi. The next day's walk takes you over the final 14 km to Manaybhanjang from where you can either take a jeep or walk to Darjeeling.

Places to Stay

There is an adequate number of bungalows and youth hostels along the trekking routes though, if possible, advance reservation should be made for the bungalows before you leave Darjeeling. This isn't necessary with the youth hostels. The bungalows are fairly well furnished and have cooking equipment, sheets and blankets. Firewood can be bought from the chowkidar. The youth hostels provide, as you might expect, somewhat more basic accommodation and usually only have mattresses and blankets, though some do have basic cooking equipment. Bungalows and youth hostels are located in the following places:

Place	accommodation	charge (Rs)	altitude (m)
Manaybhanjang	Youth Hostel	0.50	2134
Jorepokhri	Dak Bungalow	3.50	2256
Tonglu	Youth Hostel	0.50	3070
	Dak Bungalow	3.50	
Sandakphu	Youth Hostel	0.50	3636
	Dak Bungalow	3.50	
Phalut	Dak Bungalow	3.50	3600
Ramam	Youth Hostel	0.50	2560
Rimbik	Youth Hostel	0.50	2286
Jhepi	Dak Bungalow	2.00	1624
Bijanbari	Inspection Bungalow	3-5	762
Palmajua	Forest Bungalow	3.00	2210
Batasi	Forest Bungalow	3.00	2098

Reservations for the Dak Bungalows should be made with the Deputy Commissioner, Darjeeling Improvement Fund Department, Darjeeling, except in the case of the Bungalow at Jhepi which can be reserved through the District Land Revenue Officer, Darjeeling. Reservations for the Inspection Bungalows should be made with the Divisional Engineer, State Electricity Board, Siliguri. Reservations for the Forest Bungalows should be made with the Divisional Manager, West Bengal Forest Development Corporation, Darjeeling.

Rice, dhal, eggs, chicken, onions and

potatoes can be bought at most places en route, though they're likely to be more expensive than in Darjeeling. In addition there are small chai shops en route at Sandakphu, Meghma, Garibas, Rimbik, Jhepi, Lodoma and Bijanbari. If you would be happy with this kind of diet then you need carry no food with you. If not, then take your own supplies from Darjeeling.

Before you go on any of these treks you're advised to browse through the book at Darjeeling Youth Hostel where trekkers write their comments about the routes.

KALIMPONG

Kalimpong is a quiet, little bazaar town set amongst the rolling foothills and deep valleys of the Himalayas at an altitude of 1250 metres. It was once part of the lands belonging to the Rajas of Sikkim until the beginning of the 18th century when it was taken from them by the Bhutanese. In the 19th century it passed into the hands of the British and thus became part of West Bengal.

Though its name conjures up images of a really fascinating Himalayan outpost, it doesn't have a great deal of interest other than the two Buddhist monasteries and the fine views over the surrounding countryside. The most interesting part of Kalimpong is the journey there from Darjeeling via the Teesta River bridge. If you have no permit for Sikkim then it's worth visiting just for the journey, but if you do have a permit then you could by-pass Kalimpong without missing a great deal. The market here is over-rated.

Information & Orientation

Though it's a much smaller town than Darjeeling, Kalimpong has a similar kind of lay-out, straddling a ridge and consisting of a series of interconnected streets and flights of steps. Life centres around the Motor Stand and Chowrasta, and it's here that most of the cheap cafes and budget hotels are located, though

very few of the latter can be recommended since they're all pretty dilapidated affairs. The nearest decent hotels are the Crown Lodge below the Motor Stand and the Himalayan Hotel and Shangri La Tourist Lodge out beyond the junction of Main Rd and the road from Darjeeling. There are other fairly decent hotels out on Rishi Rd but they're quite a walk from town. The Tharpo Choling Monastery on Tirpai Hill and the Bhutanese Monastery are both a long, but pleasant, walk from town.

There is no Tourist Office in Kalimpong. There is a Railway Out-Agency Booking office on the Motor Stand where you can make reservations.

Tharpa Choling Monastery

This monastery belongs to the Yellow Hat sect (Sakya-pa) which was founded in Tibet in the 14th century and is the one which the Dalai Lama belongs to. This particular monastery was founded in 1937 though it looks like it has been on the decline for centuries. It's worth a visit if only for the walk.

Bhutanese Monastery (Thongsa Gompa)

This is the oldest monastery in the area and was founded in 1692. Unlike the Tharpo Choling Monastery it obviously has some enthusiastic benefactors as it's looking very prosperous and has been repainted and restored.

Flower Nurseries

Kalimpong is an important orchid-growing area and flowers are exported from here to many cities in northern India. The Sri Ganesh Moni Pradhan Nursery, the Standard Nursery and the Sri L B Pradhan Nursery are among the most important in the area.

The Market

Though of some interest, the market here is over-rated. It's worth a look if you've come to Kalimpong anyway, but it's not worth making a special journey to Kalimpong just to see it. There's nothing

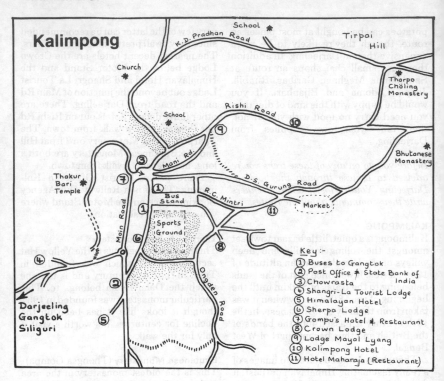

Kalimpong

Key:-
1. Buses to Gangtok
2. Post Office & State Bank of India
3. Chowrasta
4. Shangri-La Tourist Lodge
5. Himalayan Hotel
6. Sherpa Lodge
7. Gompu's Hotel & Restaurant
8. Crown Lodge
9. Lodge Mayal Lyang
10. Kolimpong Hotel
11. Hotel Maharaja (Restaurant)

for sale here that you can't find in either Darjeeling or Gangtok.

Places to Stay – Bottom End

There are quite a number of these on the far side of the Motor Stand but the majority of them look like the ceiling would fall on your head if you raised your voice, and can't really be recommended. They're certainly cheap but before you try them ask at *Gompu's Hotel & Restaurant* on Chowrasta. They have a few rooms above the restaurant with good views of the street life outside. They'll ask Rs 40 a double initially but will settle for less if you eat there (it's a good restaurant).

The *Himalayan Hotel* (tel 248) is on the right hand side up the hill just past the Post Office. Singles cost Rs 40 to 60, doubles Rs 125 to 150. *Shangri La Tourist Lodge* (tel 230) is in grounds off the road leading to Darjeeling. Rooms here cost Rs 45 a double or Rs 10 in the dormitory. It's popular with travellers.

Crown Lodge is a few metres down a side street off Ongden Rd and visible from the Motor Stand. Rooms here cost Rs 25 – double bed, fan, clean sheets and own bathroom. It's very clean and the rooms are pleasantly furnished and decorated (the wiring is the most immaculate I've seen anywhere in India!). The management is very friendly and morning tea is included in the room charges. Recommended.

Sherpa Lodge overlooks the playing field. Rooms here cost Rs 30 a single. It's of similar quality to the Crown Lodge. The *Kalimpong Hotel* is another mid-range hotel located on Rishi Rd but it's quite a long walk from town. A traveller recommended the *Venus Hotel* above Mira's Restaurant as being 'unbelievably clean; you get a sheet, pillow case and a heavy blanket, there's a common shower and a double costs Rs 20'. *Deki Lodge*, run by a Tibetan woman, has also been recommended.

Places to Stay – Top End
The *Himalayan Hotel* (tel 248) is the most expensive hotel in town. Rooms cost Rs 200/360 including meals.

Places to Eat
Gompu's Restaurant, Chowrasta is a pleasant restaurant with friendly staff. They serve Tibetan food (Rs 6 to 10 on average per dish) and western breakfasts (omelettes, toast and so on). Good food but 'stick to the Chinese dishes' recommended one traveller.

Hotel Maharaja, R C Mintri Rd has excellent South Indian vegetarian food. A masala dosa will cost you just a couple of rupees. *Nizam Restaurant* is a tiny and very friendly chai shop between the Crown Lodge and the Motor Stand with simple food. There are plenty of other cafes along Main Rd.

Getting Around – Buses, Jeeps & Taxis
Kalimpong-Darjeeling Frequent departures daily in either direction by bus, jeep and taxi. The journey takes about three hours and costs Rs 12 to 14 depending on what form of transport you take. All the transport leaves from the Motor Stand.
Kalimpong-Siliguri Frequent departures daily in either direction by bus, jeep and taxi. Takes about three hours and costs Rs 10. The views are magnificent.

Kalimpong-Gangtok (Sikkim) There are several bus companies which do this run, the main one being Sikkim Nationalised Transport, which has two buses daily at 8.30 am and 2 pm costing Rs 14. The journey takes four hours. 'Jayshree' (sometimes spelt 'Joy Shree') also has one bus daily at 2.30 pm which costs Rs 14. Both these companies have offices on the Motor Stand. The companies are fond of calling their buses 'luxury', which is a joke and should be treated as such. The other company which runs buses to Sikkim is Mintri Transport Ltd which has an office on Main St in the same building as Indian Airlines. The bus leaves daily at 9.30 am and costs Rs 12.

Kalimpong-Bagdogra Mintri Transport Ltd operates one bus daily to Bagdogra at 8.30 am.
Kalimpong-Phuntsholing If you're one of those rare and lucky people with a Bhutanese visa, then transport is available from Kalimpong to Phuntsholing on the Bhutanese border.

Siliguri – Places to Stay
If you want to pause in Siliguri the *Airview Hotel*, directly opposite the bus station, has singles/doubles at Rs 20/30. It's a typical, huge Indian hotel with loads of rooms – most of them very grubby and dirty. Other places include the *Hill View Hotel*, *Hotel Broadway* and the *Tourist Lodge* where doubles cost from Rs 35 and there's a dorm with beds at Rs 12.

Hotel Sinclairs (tel 22674-5) is Siliguri's most expensive hotel with singles/ doubles at Rs 80/120 or Rs 175/250 with air-con.

Good food can be found at only slightly above normal prices at places like the *Saliya* and other classier hotels further down Hill Cart Rd.

Coping with India – Beggars

Beggars are a problem which face most travellers in India face. During the emergency a determined effort was made to stamp out begging – beggars were rounded up, trucked a long way out of town and left to make their own way back. Despite various official statements about how people don't need to beg, India is a country with only limited social services and a place where being down and out is no fun at all. Beggars are a way of life and after all giving is good for the giver as well as the receiver.

For the traveller it's worth remembering a few ground rules and then doing whatever you feel best. First of all beggars in the tourist areas are there because that's where the money is, and they're taking a professional outlook on extracting it from you. The real poverty in India

is not in the cities but out in the country, which tourists don't get to. Secondly if you start handing it out to all and sundry outside your hotel entrance, you'll soon find a lot more alls and a lot more sundries waiting for you. Thirdly however much you hand out you're only going to be adding a drop to the ocean.

Nevertheless cold hard reality doesn't rule out how you and your conscience are going to feel. So if you want to do something but keep things within bounds you can always decide I'm going to hand out so much per day and then stop, I'm only going to hand out to particularly desperate cases, or, and probably most sensibly, I'm not going to give a damn thing, but I'll make a donation to one of the aid organisations which work in India.

Sikkim

Population: 250,000
Area: 7214 square km
Capital: Gangtok
Main Language: Nepali

Until fairly recently Sikkim ('New House') was an independent kingdom, though in treaty relations with the Indian government which allowed the latter to control Sikkim's foreign affairs and defence. In 1975, however, following a period of political crises and riots in the capital, Gangtok, India annexed the country and Sikkim became the 22nd Indian state. The move was far from universally popular at the time, though tensions have now cooled and the central government has been spending relatively large amounts of money to subsidise road building, electrification, water supply, and agricultural and industrial development. India's motivation for much of this activity was undoubtedly its fear of Chinese military designs in the Himalayan region, and even today you'll see a lot of military activity going on along the route from Darjeeling to Gangtok.

For many years, Sikkim was regarded as one of the last 'Shangri Las' in the Himalayan region because of its remoteness, its spectacular mountain terrain, varied flora and fauna and its ancient Buddhist monasteries. It was never easy to get there and even now a special permit must be obtained from the central government before a visit can be made. It's likely that this requirement will continue for the foreseeable future, but its becoming more and more a formality as tourism is promoted. Foreign visitors are now permitted to trek up into the remote Dzongri region of western Sikkim but further permission is needed from Delhi and, for the present at least, much of eastern Sikkim along the Tibetan border remains out of bounds.

History

The country was originally peopled by the Lepchas, a tribal people who are thought to have migrated from the hills of Assam around the 13th century. The Lepchas were forest foragers and small patch cultivators who worshipped nature spirits and were a pacific people in temperament. They still make up some 18% of the total population of Sikkim, though their ability to lead their traditional life style has been severely limited due to immigration from Tibet and, more recently, from Nepal.

The Tibetans started to emigrate into Sikkim during the 15th and 16th centuries due to religious strife between the various Lamist sects at that time. In Tibet itself the yellow hat sect – the Sakya-pa to which the Dalai Lama belongs – gradually gained the upper hand whereas in Sikkim the red hat sect – Nying-ma-pa – remained in control and was, until the country became a part of India, the official state religion. Though the Lepchas originally retreated to the more remote regions in the face of the waves of Tibetan immigrants a blood brotherhood was eventually engineered

347

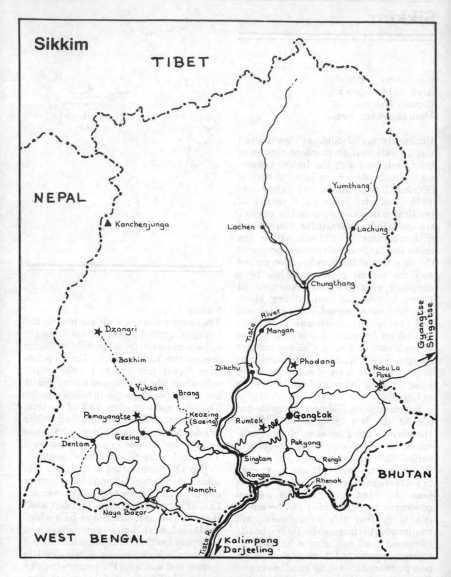

Sikkim

TIBET

NEPAL

▲ Kanchenjunga

Yumthang

Lachen • • Lachung

Chungthang

Tista River

• Dzongri

• Bakhim

• Yuksam • Brang

Pemayangtse ★ • Keozing
(Sosing)

• Gezing

• Dentam

Mangan

• Phodang

Dikchu

Rumtek ★ ● Gangtok

Pakyong

Singtam

Rangli

Rangpo • Rhenok

Namchi

Naya Bazar

BHUTAN

Gyangtse
Shigatse

Natu La
Pass

WEST BENGAL

Tista R.

↓ Kalimpong
Darjeeling

between their leader, Thekong Tek, and the Bhutyas leader, Khye-Bumsa, and the heavy hand of spiritual and temporal authority imposed on the anarchistic Lepchas. The union generated a good deal of suspicion between the two groups, particularly when the Lepchas were persuaded to bring all their literature and totems to a ceremony where it was destroyed by the Tibetans. Having imposed their control over the Lepchas, the Dalai Lama in Lhasa appointed Penchoo Namgyal as the first king of Sikkim in 1641. At this time the country included the whole of the area bounded by the present state plus a part of eastern Nepal, the Chumbi Valley (Tibet), the Ha Valley (Bhutan) and the Terai foothills from the present border down to the plains of India, including Darjeeling and Kalimpong.

Between 1717 and 1734, during the reign of the fourth king, a series of wars were fought with the Bhutanese which resulted in the loss of much territory in the southern foothills including Kalimpong, then a very important bazaar town on the trade route leading from Tibet to India. More territory was lost after 1780 following the Gurkha invasion from Nepal, though the invaders were eventually checked by a Chinese army with Bhutanese and Lepcha assistance. Unable to advance into Tibet, the Gurkhas turned south and came into conflict with the British East India Company. A series of wars were fought between the two parties ending in the treaty of 1817 whereby the borders of Nepal were delineated, and the Gurkhas ceded to the British all the Sikkimese territory they had taken. A substantial part of this territory was returned to the Raja of Sikkim in return for control by the British of all disputes between Sikkim and its neighbours. The country thus became a buffer state between Nepal, Tibet and Bhutan.

In 1835, the British, seeking a hill station as a rest and recreation centre for its troops and officials, persuaded and pressured the Raja into ceding the Darjeeling area in return for an annual stipend. The Tibetans objected to this transfer of territory as they continued to regard Sikkim as a vassal state, and Darjeeling's rapid growth as a trade centre began to make a considerable impact on the fortunes of the leading lamas and merchants of Sikkim. Tensions rose and in 1849 a high ranking British official and a botanist, who were exploring the Lachen region with the permission both of the Sikkimese Raja and the British government, were arrested. Following threats of intervention, the two prisoners were unconditionally released a month later, but the British annexed the whole of the area between the present Sikkimese border and the Indian plains and withdrew the Raja's stipend (the latter was eventually restored to his son).

Further British interference in the affairs of this area led to the declaration of a protectorate over Sikkim in 1861 and the delineation of its borders. The Tibetans however continued to regard all these actions as illegal and in 1886 invaded Sikkim to reassert their authority. They were thrown back by the British, and a military expedition sent to Lhasa in 1888 as a punitive measure. The powers of the Sikkim Raja were further reduced and high-handed treatment by the British officials prompted him to flee to Lhasa in 1892, though he was eventually persuaded to return.

Being keen to develop the area, the British encouraged immigration from Nepal, as they had done in Darjeeling, and a considerable amount of land was brought under rice and cardamom cultivation. As a result of this influx of labour, which was still going on right up until the 1960s, the Nepalese constitute some 75% of the population of Sikkim. The subject became a heated topic of discussion in the late '60s and the Raja was constrained to prohibit further immigration. Further steps were taken to placate those of non-Nepalese origin in the form of new laws regarding the rights of citizenship, but these inflamed the opposition parties.

The Raja's American-born wife was also active in stirring up resentment against the Nepalese, and matters eventually reached a head with demonstrations in Gangtok and the flight of the

Raja to India. Though India had inherited the treaties with Sikkim from the British at independence they were in no mood to be seen propping up the regime of an autocratic Raja in Sikkim, while doing their best to sweep away the last traces of princely rule in India itself. Their response to this instability in a very sensitive border region with China was to pension off the Raja and annex the country. Though there was much resentment over this action at the time and international protests, the political situation has cooled down and Sikkim is now governed by its own democratic congress with representatives in the central government in New Delhi.

The current population make-up of Sikkim consists of approximately 18% Lepcha, 75% Nepalese and the rest Butyas and Indians from various northern states. About 60% of the population is Hindu and 28% Buddhist, although the two religions exist, as in many parts of Nepal, in a syncretic form. The ancient Buddhist monastaries, of which there are a great many, are one of the principal attractions of any visit to Sikkim.

GANGTOK (population 14,000)

Gangtok, the capital of Sikkim, occupies the west side of a long ridge flanking the Ranipool River. Scenically, it has a very spectacular setting and excellent views of the entire Kanchenjunga range can be obtained from many points in the vicinity. On the other hand, it's not, as many people expect it to be, a smaller version of Kathmandu overflowing with ancient temples, palaces, monastaries and narrow, colourful bazaars. Gangtok only became the capital in the mid-1800s, the previous ones being sited at Yoksam and Rabdantse. It has undergone rapid modernisation in recent years.

Information & Orientation

To the north is Raj Bhavan, the former British and later Indian Residency, and above it the Tourist Lodge and Enchen Monastery. Lower down along the ridge is the palace of the former Raja (known as the Chogyal) and the large and impressive Royal Chapel (the Tsuk-La-Khang). The chapel, but not the palace, is open to visitors. Nearby is the huge Secretariat complex, built in traditional style, was damaged during a recent earthquake.

On a continuation of this ridge but much lower is the Namgyalk Institute of Tibetology established in 1958 and, like the Secretariat building, built in the traditional style. The library here can be visited and a collection of objects relating to Tibetan Buddhism, including some unique and very beautiful silk embroidered *thankas*, is on permanent display. An orchid sanctuary surrounds the institute, which itself is enclosed in a peaceful forest. Not too far beyond the institute is a large white stupa and adjoining it a Buddhist monastery and school for young lamas. Inside the temple here are huge images of Guru Padma Sambhava, the Indian teacher of Buddhism in Tibet, and his manifestation, Guru Snang-Sid Zilnon.

All the other main facilities – hotels, cafes, bazaars, bus stand, post office, tourist information centre and the Foreigners Registration Office – are either on, or very near to, the main road from Darjeeling. The Tourist Office is staffed with friendly and exceptionally helpful people but their leaflets are all rather out of date. Just below the office is a display of some of the main crafts produced by the Cottages Industries Emporium located much higher up on the main road.

Extending Your Permit You might think that after all the effort and waiting that was required to get your permit for Sikkim (see Darjeeling) that extensions would be dificult to come by. Not so! In fact, it's remarkably uncomplicated. You merely go along to the Foreigners Registration Office on the national highway, tell them

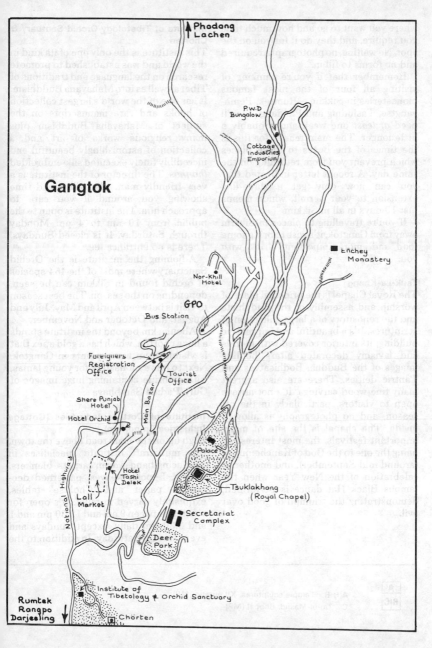

Gangtok

Phodang
Lachen

P.W.D.
Bungalow

Cottage
Industries
Emporium

Enchey
Monastery

Nor-Khil
Hotel

GPO

Bus Station

Foreigners
Registration
Office

Tourist
Office

Shere Punjab
Hotel

Hotel Orchid

Main Bazar

Palace

Hotel
Tashi
Delek

Tsuklakhong
(Royal Chapel)

Lall
Market

National Highway

Secretariat
Complex

Deer
Park

Institute of
Tibetology & Orchid Sanctuary

Chörten

Rumtek
Rangpo
Darjeeling

where you want to go and how much time you require, and they do it for you on the spot. No waiting, no photographs required and no forms to fill in.

Remember that if you're thinking of visiting all four of the most famous monasteries in Sikkim – Rumtek, Pemayangtse, Tashiding and Phodang – you'll need *at least* one week and probably a little longer. The main reason for this is the times of the buses to these places which prevent you from returning on the same day. A recent letter indicated that you can now only get a three-day extension to your permit, which means just 10 days in all in Sikkim.

If you're travelling to places in Sikkim away from Gangtok, it's wise to bring some food and, more important, drink with you.

Tsuk-La-Khang

The Royal Chapel is the principal place of worship and assembly of the Buddhists and the repository of a large collection of scriptures. It's a beautiful and impressive building; its interior covered with murals and lavishly decorated altars holding images of the Buddha, Bodhisatvas and Tantric deities. There are also a great many fine wood carvings. It's not always open to visitors, particularly in the off season, and no photography is allowed inside. The chapel is the site of many important festivals, the most interesting being the one to the God of Kanchenjunga (around mid-September), and another in celebration of the New Year when the famous Black Hat dance is performed, demonstrating the triumph of good over evil.

Institute of Tibetology Orchid Santuary & Chorten

This institute is the only one of its kind in the world and was established to promote research on the language and traditions of Tibet as well as into Mahayana Buddhism. It has one of the world's largest collection of books and rare manuscripts on the subject of Mahayana Buddhism plus many religious works of art and a collection of astonishingly beautiful and incredibly finely executed silk-embroided *thankas*. The director of the institute is a very friendly man, who will spend time showing you around if you care to approach him. The institute is open to the public from 10 am to 4 pm Monday through Saturday. It is closed Sundays. There is no entrance fee.

Adjoining the institute is the Orchid Sanctuary where most of the 454 species of orchid found in Sikkim can be seen, depending on the season. The best season to visit is between April and May, July and August, and October and November.

About a km beyond the institute stands a huge chorten, which has a gold apex that is visible from many points in Gangtok. Next to it is a monastery for young lamas, with a shrine containing huge images of Guru Padma Sambhava.

Institute of Cottage Industries (Cottage Industries Emporium)

High up on the main road above the town, this multicraft institute specialises in producing hand-woven carpets, blankets, shawls, Lepcha weaves, patterned decorative paper and 'Choktse' tables, exquisitely carved in relief. It's open for visiting between 9 am and 12.30 pm and 1 and 3.30 pm daily, except Sundays and every second Saturday. In addition to the

A & B   Temple sculptures, Khajuraho (MP)
C   Taj-ul-Masjid, Bhopal (MP)

shop here, there is a smaller display of craftwork on the ground floor of the Tourist Office which is well worth a visit.

Deer Park

This a popular viewpoint right on the edge of the ridge next to the Secretariat building. In it, as you might expect, are deer and an image of the Buddha which is a replica of that standing at Sarnath in India.

Enchey Monastery

Situated next to the Tourist Lodge, about three km from the centre of town, is the 200-year old Enchey Monastery. It's well worth a visit, particularly if you're in Gangtok during December when annual religious dances are performed here.

Lall Market

If you've been to Kathmandu or Darjeeling, then this market will come as a disappointment. It has none of their colour, magic or range of products and is of marginal interest only.

Tours

The Department of Tourism offers tours of the various points of interest in Gangtok and of Rumtek Monastery daily from February to May and from October to December. For reservations on these tours, contact the Department of Tourism, Gangtok Bazaar (tel 292).

Gangtok city tour This tour includes visits to Tashi View Point, the Deer Park, Enchey Monastery, the Royal Chapel, Secretariat, Cottage Industries Institute, the Institute of Tibetology and the nearby chorten and orchid sanctuary. It runs 9.30 am to 12.30 pm, costs Rs 18.

Places to Stay – Bottom End

The *Shere Punjab* is just below the Hotel Orchid. Rooms here cost Rs 14 a single room with common bathroom and Rs 25 a double with own bathroom. The *Doma Hotel* costs Rs 10 a single and Rs 24 a double both with common bathrooms.

The *PWD Bungalow* is high up on the National Highway beyond the Cottage Industries Emporium. There are only two rooms available here so book in advance if possible. The double-bedded rooms cost Rs 12 per bed. Reservations from the Executive Engineer, CPWD North, Sikkim Highway, Gangtok.

Places to Stay – Middle

The *Gangtok Tourist Lodge* (tel 292/664) costs Rs 35 a single and Rs 50 a double. The hotel is managed by the Government of Sikkim Tourist Department. Transport is available from the Tourist Office above the Bus Stand.

Hotel Orchid (tel 381) costs Rs 50 for a double or Rs 60 with own bathroom. Prices are much lower in the low season. The place is clean, has attractive rooms with excellent views of Kanchenjunga, hot water when the electricity is on (there are frequent power cuts in Gangtok) and a restaurant and bar on the top floor. The restaurant serves excellent food (chicken curry, vegetables, fried dhal and so on). Beer is cheap, a tot of Sikkimese spirit even cheaper. The staff are friendly and the place is secure. Avoid getting a room on the top floor at the back – someone has economised on glazing and facilities are communual though the prices are the same.

The *Green Hotel* (tel 254) is a little way up the main bazaar from the Tourist Office on the same side of the road. Rooms here cost Rs 20 a single with a common bath (Rs 15 in the off season) and Rs 40 to 60 a double with own bathroom (Rs 20 to 40 in the off-season). The rooms are possibly even slightly better than the Orchid's. There's an attached restaurant with very good food although not quite up to the standard of the Orchid. The *Karma Hotel* costs Rs 35 a single and Rs 40 to 50 a double both with attached bathroom. There is no reduction during the off-season.

The *New Hotel Quality* (tel 619) costs Rs 30 a single and Rs 50 a double, both with attached bathroom. There are no reductions during the off-season. The *Deeki Hotel* costs Rs 30 a single with common bathroom and Rs 40 a double with own bathroom, again prices are cheaper in the off-season.

Places to Stay – Top End

The *Nor-Khill Hotel* (tel 386, 618) has rooms at Rs 250/350 for singles/doubles including all meals. *Hotel Tashi Delek* (tel 311, 458) has singles for Rs 120 to 180 and doubles for Rs 200 to 320. There are plans to open a new Tibetan run three-star hotel called the *Hotel Tibet* (tel 833) on Stadium Rd.

Places to Eat

There are very few good restaurants in Gangtok which are not attached to hotels, and you'll probably find that most of the time you'll eat at your own hotel. The restaurant at the *Hotel Orchid* is popular with the middle-class local people and open to non-residents. Their food is excellent.

Other than this, there are a number of simple vegetarian cafes around the bus stand and along the main bazaar where you can obtain basic food at very low prices (Rs 2 to 4 on average). About half a km uphill from the bus stand on the National Highway, where a road branches off to the stadium and Nor-Khill Hotel, there is a cafe which serves snacks and tea or coffee, and also sells cheese. If you have

a yen for some of this wonderful stuff then come here.

Try *thungba* from a chang shop in the market – a large bamboo mug full of millet to which you add hot water to get fresh chang.

Getting There

There is no airport in Gangtok and no rail connection. The nearest airport is at Bagdora and the nearest railheads at Ghoom (on the 'Toy Train' from Siliguri to Darjeeling) or Siliguri (on the main line). Bus transport is nationalised so the only buses available are those operated by Sikkim Nationalised Transport (SNT). There is a fee for reservations of Rs 0.50, except on the Gangtok-Siliguri and Gangtok-Kalimpong routes.

Gangtok-Siliguri Buses three times daily at 7 am, 8.30 am and 1 pm. From Siliguri to Gangtok the buses depart at 7 am, 9.30 am and 1 pm. The journey takes about five hours (the fastest bus is the first one in the morning) and costs Rs 20.

Another company which covers this route is: Aspara (Agents: Janata Auto Agency, New Market, Gangtok and near the Armadeep Hotel, Siliguri). It has one bus daily in either direction at 1.30 pm from Gangtok and 7.30 am from Siliguri. Sikkim Beauty (Agents: M/S Punchshed, New Market, Gangtok, and near Armadeep Hotel, Siliguri) also has one bus daily in either direction at 2 pm from Gangtok and 8.30 am from Siliguri. North Bengal Transport's daily bus in either direction departs at 12.30 pm from Gangtok and 6 am from Siliguri. The journey takes five hours.

Gangtok-Bagdogra SNT bus once daily in either direction departs at 8 am from Gangtok and from Bagdogra after arrival of the plane. The journey takes five hours.

Gangtok-Darjeeling SNT bus once daily in either direction at 8.30 am. The journey takes five or six hours and costs Rs 40. This bus is heavily over-subscribed so it's advisable to book in advance. SNT use what is probably its best minibus for this trip. If you need to get to Darjeeling but the bus is booked out, then take a bus first to Kalimpong and then another bus from there. The road house at Rangpo, on the West Bengal-Sikkim border, is the only place you can get food between Sikkim and Darjeeling. The service is impossibly slow so perhaps it's better to bring some food with you.

Gangtok-Kalimpong SNT buses twice daily in either direction at 8.30 am and 1.30 pm. The journey takes four hours and costs Rs 14. Other companies which cover this route are: Sangam Transport with one bus daily in either direction at 2 pm from Gangtok and 7 am from Kalimpong. The journey takes about four hours.

AROUND GANGTOK

Rumtek Monastery

Rumtek is visible from Gangtok on the other side of the Ranipool Valley at about the same elevation, yet it's 24 km away by road. The monastery is the seat of the Gyalwa Karmapa, the head of the Kagyupa sect of Tibetan Buddhism. The sect was founded in the 11th century by Lama Marpa who was the disciple of the Indian guru, Naropa. It later split into several sub-sects, of which the most important are Duk-pa, Kangyupa and Karma-pa. The teachings of the sect are orally transmitted to the disciples.

The main monastery here is a recent structure, which was built by the Gyalwa Karmapa strictly according to the traditional architectural designs on which the monastery he came from in Tibet was constructed. Visitors are welcome at the monastery and there's no objection to you sitting in on the prayer and chanting sessions. They'll even bring you a cup of salted butter tea when it's served to the monks. Mural work is still being done and if you're interested in the Tibetan style of religious painting then Rumtek is a must for you. It's a very interesting place and well worth a visit. The old monastery can

still be seen just beyond the new structure, though it's not obvious as it's hidden by trees.

If you follow the tarmac road beyond Rumtek for two or three km there is another interesting, but smaller, monastery off to the left through a gate.

Places to Stay If you wish to stay at Rumtek for the night, there is a lodge opposite the monastery with about 20 rooms available. Most of them have two to three single beds in them. It's basic but clean and blankets and candles are provided (there's no electricity most of the time), and it's beautifully quiet and peaceful. The price of the rooms is negotiable but you shouldn't have to pay much more than Rs 5 for a bed. Just below the lodge is a small chai shop which serves eggs and fresh bread in the morning (two fried eggs, bread and tea cost Rs 4 or 5), and chow-chow in the evening. Friendly people.

Getting There There's a daily bus at 4.30 pm which returns from Rumtek the next day at 7.30 am. This means you have to spend at least two nights at Rumtek. The journey takes about two hours and costs Rs 6. You have to get off the bus at the Ranipool River and walk across the bridge as it's structurally weak and won't take the weight of a fully-laden bus. In fact, it looks like it would plummet into the river if you raised your voice!

There are also jeeps and Ambassador taxis available, count on around Rs 175 return per car, the return journey takes half a day.

Pemayangtse & Tashiding Monasteries

Pemayangtse Monastery, situated at a height of 2085 meteres, is the second oldest monastery in Sikkim and belongs to the Nyingma-pa sect. This Tantric sect was established by the Indian teacher, Padma Sambhava, in the 8th century. All monasteries of this sect are characterised by a prominent image of this teacher,

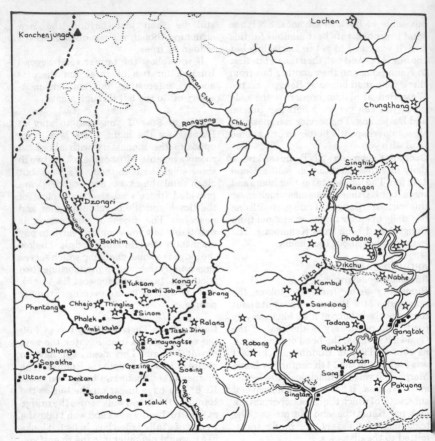

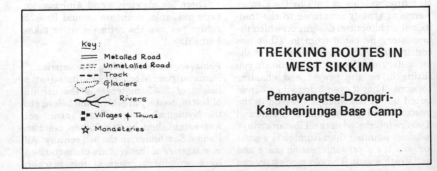

Key:

═══	Metalled Road
┅┅┅	Unmetalled Road
‒ ‒ ‒	Track
∙∙∙∙∙	Glaciers
〰〰	Rivers
■▪	Villages & Towns
☆	Monasteries

TREKKING ROUTES IN WEST SIKKIM

Pemayangtse-Dzongri-Kanchenjunga Base Camp

together with two female consorts. The followers of the sect wear red caps and the monastery here is the head of all others in Sikkim. It appears that you may now need a special permit from Delhi to go out to Pemayangtse.

Pemayangtse is about six km from the bus terminus at Gezing but Tashiding is a full day's hike from Pemayangtse up along a ridge. The hike starts with a 1½ hour walk to Tashiding village, going uphill all the way. The monastery itself is further up the hill near the summit but hidden by pine trees. Sangacholing monastery is also in the vicinity.

At present it appears that permits to visit Pemayangtse are very restricted. See the Sikkim permits section under Darjeeling.

Places to Stay For accommodation there is a choice of at least four basic lodges at Gezing for around Rs 12 a room – any number of people can share a room. Food is also available there and a typical meal of rice, dahl and eggs would cost about Rs 6.

If you want something slightly better there is the *PWD Rest House* about two km up the hill from Gezing towards Pemayangtse. It's excellent value at Rs 12 per room, but prior booking is necessary from the CPWD in Gangtok between 9.30 am and 4.30 pm. The chowkidar here cooks excellent meals for a further charge.

At Tashiding there is a *Forestry Department Bungalow* where you can stay for Rs 12 per room, but you must bring your own blankets and sheets. To stay here you need authorisation from the Tourist Office in Gangtok or the Forestry Department in Gezing. The monastery is some 15 minutes' walk from the village. Good meals are available in the village chai shop and if you go there to eat you'll have the whole village for company!

If you're looking for luxury accommodation then there is the *Pemayangtse Tourist Lodge* (tel 73). Rooms here with full board cost Rs 175 a single and Rs 240 a double. For reservations contact the Tourist Office in Gangtok.

Getting There There's one bus daily in either direction at 9.30 am from Gangtok and 7.30 am from Gezing (sometimes spelt Geyshing). The journey takes about seven to eight hours and costs Rs 24. Pemayangtse is about six km from Gezing but basic accommodation is available in Gezing if the bus is late. It's clear that a trip to Pemayangtse will take at least three days. Make sure your permit covers you for this period.

As with Rumtek you can hire a car or jeep for around Rs 700 to 800 depending on the route taken. The trip takes two days.

Phodang Monastery

This is the furthest you are permitted to go in eastern Sikkim without further entanglement with bureaucracy. Phodang Monastery at Thumlong, 40 km north of Gangtok, has recently been rebuilt, but just above it is Labrang Gompa where the original construction is still intact. Labrang is accessible only by bridle path and you should allow about half an hour to get there from Phodang. If you're allowed to go further up the road to Mangan and Singhik a clear, unobstructed view of Kanchenjunga can be had. The Phodang Monastery is sometimes closed.

Places to Stay The *Yak & Yeti*, along the highway to Mangan, has big, clean rooms for Rs 10 per bed. The food here – rice, dhal, vegetables, momos and so on – is excellent and so is the *chang* and *raksi*. The people are very friendly and don't charge you any more than the locals.

Getting There There are daily buses to Phodang at 8.30 am, 1.30 and 4.15 pm. The two earlier buses continue on to Mangan. There are also three daily buses on the return journey, the first leaving at 8 am. the trip takes around 2½ hours and the fare is Rs 7. Allow plenty of time if you want to see anything of Phodang and the other monasteries in the area.

A car or jeep will cost about Rs 250 for the return trip. Travel time for the return trip is about half a day.

TREKKING IN SIKKIM

Trekking is now being allowed in western Sikkim but you need a further endorsement on your permit to do this at present. Though the regulations are somewhat elastic (depending on how you put yourself across), officially you're allowed to trek up to Dzongri for up to 10 days so long as you're accompanied by a travel agent recognised by the Indian Tourist Development Corporation and a liaison officer or guide provided by the government of Sikkim, that you travel by air from Calcutta to Bagdogra, and that you follow one of either of the following routes: Nayan Bazaar-Pemayangtse-Yaksum-Dzongri or Rangpo-Gangtok-Yaksum-Dzongri.

In other words, you have little choice than to go with an organised tour at present, unless you have political clout in the Sikkimese bureaucracy. The travel agents which organise these treks are: Yak & Yeti Travels, Gangtok; Snow Lions Travels, Gangtok and Sikkim Himalayan Adventure, Gangtok. The best time to go trekking is from mid-February to late May and from October to December. Trekking gear can be hired at the agencies in Gangtok.

North-East Frontier

State	capital	area (sq. km)	population
Assam	Gauhati	79,500	19,200,000
Manipur	Imphal	22,300	1,400,000
Meghalaya	Shillong	22,400	1,300,000
Negaland	Kohima	16,500	700,000
Tripura	Agartala	10,400	2,000,000
Arunachal Pradesh	Itanagar	83,600	500,000
Mizoram	Aizawi	21,000	400,000

The north-east region is the most varied and at the same time the least visited part of India. Prior to independence the whole region was known as Assam Province, but it was finally split into five separate states and two Union Territories – Mizoram and Arunachal Pradesh. In many ways the north-east is quite unlike the rest of India. It is the chief tribal area of India with a great number of tribes who speak many different languages and dialects – in Arunachal Pradesh alone over 50 distinct languages are spoken! In many ways these tribal people are similar to the hill tribes found right across the sweep of the country at the eastern end of the Himalaya, which extends from India through Burma and Thailand into Laos. Also the north-east has a high percentage of Christians, particularly in the more isolated areas where the population is predominantly hill tribespeople.

For a number of reasons India has always been touchy about the north-east and this attitude has increased dramatically in 1980-81, making a visit to the north-east a tricky proposition at present.

For a start the north-east is a sensitive border zone where India meets with Bhutan, China, Burma and Bangladesh. Equally important the region is physically remote from the main Indian land mass – only the narrow Siliguri corridor connects it to the rest of India and prior to independence the usual route to Assam would have been through Bangladesh. Today, reaching the north-east by train involves a long journey by metre gauge rail. Roads have been dramatically improved but there are still very few of them compared to the rest of India. For these reasons the Indian government has been sensitive about visitors and only permitted them to go to Assam and Meghalaya; the other five regions, all bordering with China or Burma, were for all practical purposes off-limits. Even a visit to Assam and Meghalaya required a special permit, although this was readily available, at least for certain distinct tourist attractions.

Dramatic events since 1980 have virtually shut the region off completely. The north-east has developed into the

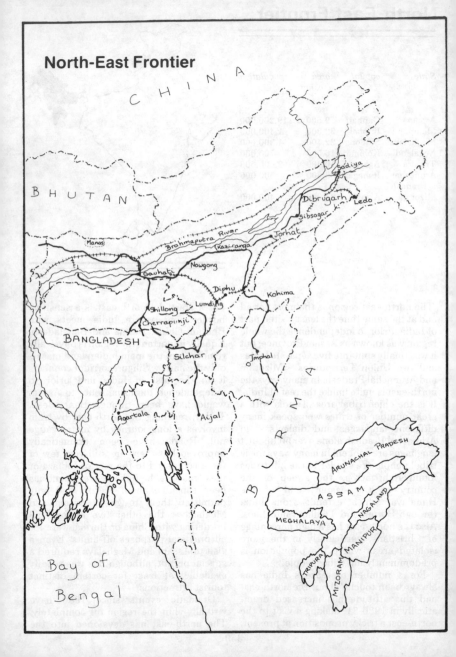

North-East Frontier

most troubled part of India and the central government has experienced great difficulty in asserting its authority there. Strikes, riots, violence and terrorism have all been a part of the story, and at times even the Indian Airlines' flights to the north-east have had to be suspended.

There are a number of reasons for this unrest including a feeling of neglect by the central government – poor transport links and lack of infrastructure development are the main complaints. This feeling has become increasingly strong with the rising price of oil since Assam pumps a substantial part of India's small, but important, oil output. Very little of this oil wealth finds it's way back to improve Assam's industrial development and the whole region remains overwhelmingly agricultural.

WORLD NEWS

India to fence off Bangladesh

NEW DELHI, 14 Aug. — The Government said today it would build a $A513 million barbed-wire fence along India's 2000-kilometre border with Bangladesh to keep out illegal alien settlers.

The decision was taken after the issue of alien settlers led to mass killings in the north-eastern Indian State of Assam earlier this year.

Native people of Assam, which borders Bangladesh, complain they are economically and culturally swamped by millions of immigrants from Bangladesh, most of them illegal.

Assamese resorted to violence when the Prime Minister Indira Gandhi called elections in Assam last February. The natives complained that illegal settlers could vote.

Officials said the barbed-wire fence would begin as soon as possible and would be completed in different phases, with the Assam-Bangladesh border sealed in two years and the rest in five years. — AAP-AP

Neglect may be a minor issue, but the number one complaint has been about 'foreigners'. The cycle of events in Bangladesh, just to the south-east of the region, combined with that tightly packed country's undiminished birthrate has pushed thousands of Bengalis over the lightly policed borders into the north-east region. This influx of 'foreigners' has resulted, in some cases, in the indigenous population actually becoming outnumbered. Demands that 'foreigners' be repatriated has been a major part of the unrest. Of course, such a wholesale repatriation is an impossibility, particularly since many of thse Bengali 'foreigners' have been resident in the region for generations – legally or not. In 1983 the unrest led to wholesale massacres in some villages and, as long as the strife in the region continues, visits to the north-east are far from easy.

Permits

Normally permits are required for the two accessible states of the region – Assam and Meghalaya. These would usually be granted with the minimum of formality. You can approach these states either through Bangladesh, by looping noth of Bangledesh through the Siliguri corridor, or by air.

Assam Permits for Assam actually only permit you to visit Gauhati (the capital) and the game reserves at Manas and Kaziranga. Permits can be applied for at India consular offices overseas. In India the Foreigner's Registration Office, Hans Bhavan (near Tilak Bridge), Bahadur Shah, Zafar Marg, New Delhi 110002 or the Trade Adviser, Government of Assam, 8 Russel St Calcutta 700071 issues them.

Normally the permit allows a maximum stay of 15 days but this could be extended in Assam. If you fly to Gauhati and follow a specified route to Kaziranga and back you are allowed to visit Assam without a permit. For places in Assam apart from

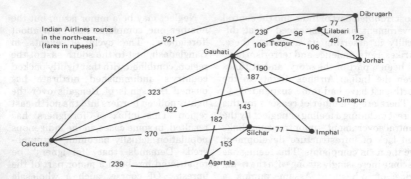

Indian Airlines routes
in the north-east.
(fares in rupees)

Dibrugarh
77
Lilabari
239   96   49   125
521   106 Tezpur 106
Gauhati   Jorhat
190
187
323   Dimapur
492   143
182
370   Silchar 77   Imphal
Calcutta   153
239   Agartala

Gauhati, Manas and Kaziranga permission must be requested from the Home Ministry, Government of India, North Block, New Delhi at least six weeks in advance. In Calcutta you must apply to the Trade Adviser 'sufficiently in advance'.

Meghalaya The Meghalaya Information Centre in Calcutta is right next to the Assam office at 9 Russel St, and they issue permits with equal ease for a seven-day visit. Shillong, the capital of Meghalaya, is approached via Guahati or through Bangladesh. As in Assam permits are usually extendable after you arrive.

ASSAM

The largest and most easily accessible of the north-east states, Assam is a major tea-producing area (60% of India's tea comes from here) and also produces a large proportion of India's oil. The main attractions for the visitor are the Manas and Kaziranga wildlife reserves, which are home for India's rare one-horned rhinoceros.

GAUHATI (population 140,000)

Capital of the state, Gauhati is on the banks of the Brahmaputra River. It has many ancient Hindu temples but its main importance is as a gateway to the north-east and a jumping off point for visits to the wildlife reserves.

Information

The Tourist Office (tel 24475) is on Station Road.

Temples

Umananda Temple is a Shiva temple on Peacock Island in the middle of the river. There's a pleasant ferry across the river. The Navagrah Temple is the Temple of the Nine Planets. In ancient times this was a centre for the study of astrology. It is situated on the Chitrachal Hill, near the city. Gauhati's best known temple is the Kamakshya on the Nilachal Hill, 10 km from the city. it attracts pilgrims from all over India, especially during the Ambuchi festival in August. The temple is the centre for Shakti (energy) worship and Tantric Hinduism due to the fact that when Shiva was sorrowfully carrying away his first wife's (Sati's) corpse her *yoni* fell here! The temple was rebuilt in 1665 after being destroyed by Moslem invaders. In the centre of Gauhati the Janardhan Temple has an image of the Buddha, indicating how Buddhism was assimilated back into Hinduism.

Other

The Assam State Zoo has tigers, lions, panthers and, of course, Assam's famous rhinos – plus African two-horned ones for comparison purposes. It's open from 6 am to 6 pm in summer, 7 am to 5 pm in winter, and admission is Rs 0.50.

There is an Assam State Museum with exibits pertaining to Assam and its history. The museum is open from 9.30 am to 3.30 pm daily except on Sundays when it closes at 12.30 pm, and Monday when it is shut. The Assam Government Cottage Industries Museum is open the same hours on the same days and entry is also free.

Tours

There are government-operated tours to Kaziranga from Saturday at 12 noon to Sunday at 5 pm for Rs 150. Manas tours operate at the same times and for the same price.

Places to Stay

The *Hotel Belle Vue* (tel 24225) is on Mahatma Gandhi Rd and costs Rs 100/150 for air-con singles/doubles, Rs 80/120 without air-con. It's 'a bit spartan but satisfactory'. *Hotel North-Eastern* (tel 25314) is on G N Bordoloi Rd and costs Rs 75/120 including breakfast. *Hotel Nova* (tel 23258) in Fancy Bazaar is cheaper at Rs 80/120 with air/con, Rs 40/60 without.

Cheaper hotels include the *Hotel Ambassador* (tel 25587) in the Paltan Bazaar with singles/doubles at Rs 25/35. The *Hotel Alka* (tel 24205) in Fancy Bazaar and the *Happy Lodge* (tel 23409) in Paltan Bazaar are similarly priced.

There's a government *Tourist Bungalow* (tel 24475) on Station Rd with accommodation at Rs 15 per person. There are also *Railway Retiring Rooms* (tel 26688) with very cheap doubles, triples and dormitory accommodation.

Getting There

Air See the chart on the previous page for the details of air routes to the north-east – these mainly run from Calcutta.

Rail & Bus There are also buses and a number of train services. A change from broad gauge to narrow gauge is necessary to reach the north-east from other parts of India. From Calcutta it's 991 km to Gauhati and takes about 24 hours with fares of Rs 248 in 1st class, Rs 63 in 2nd. It's about 19 hours to Dibrugarh, 1552 km from Calcutta with fares of Rs 345 in 1st class, Rs 88 in 2nd. New Delhi is over 1900 km and nearly 40 hours away, even on the fastest train. There are also a number of services from Lucknow, which is 1400 km away.

AROUND GAUHATI

Hajo

On the north bank of the Brahmaputra, 24 km away from Gauhati, Hajo is an important pilgrimage centre for Buddhists and Moslems. Some Buddhists believe that it was here that the Buddha attained nirvana and they flock to the Hayagriba Madhab temple. For Moslems the Pao Mecca mosque is considered to have one quarter (pao) the sanctity of the great mosque at Mecca.

Sualkashi

Also across the river from Gauhati, 20 km away, this is a famous silk weaving centre where the Endi, Muga and Pat silks of Assam are made in a small household weaving centre. There is a regular ferry service across the river and a bus service several times daily.

Other

Basistha Ashram is 12 km south of Gauhati, and the rishi or sage, Basistha, once lived here. It's also a popular picnic spot. The beautiful natural lagoon at Chandubi is 64 km from Gauhati. Darranga, 80 km away on the Bhutan border, is a great winter trading area for the Bhutia mountain folk. Barpeta, with a monastery and the shrine of a Vaishnavaite reformer, is 145 km north-west of Gauhati.

WILDLIFE PARKS

Assam is famous for its rare one-horned Great Indian Rhinoceros – when Marco Polo saw them he thought he had found

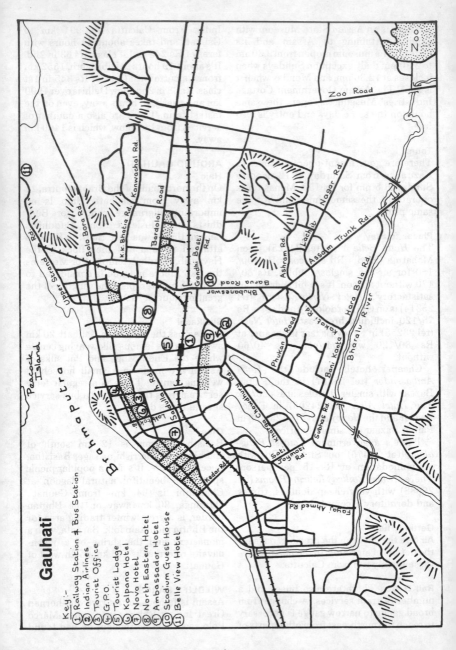

Gauhati

Key:-
1. Railway Station & Bus Station
2. Indian Airlines
3. Tourist Office
4. G.P.O.
5. Tourist Lodge
6. Kalpana Hotel
7. Nova Hotel
8. North Eastern Hotel
9. Ambassador Hotel
10. Stadium Guest House
11. Belle View Hotel

the legendary unicorn! Kaziranga and Manas are the two well-known parks in Assam although there are also smaller parks at Orang and Sonai.

Kaziranga

North-east of Gauhati, Kaziranga wildlife reserve is on the banks of the Brahmaputra River and is famous as the last major home of 'Rhinoceros Unicornis'. The 430 square km park is thought to have a rhino population approaching a thousand, but in 1904 they were on the verge of extinction here. The park became a game sanctuary in 1926 and by 1966 the numbers had risen to about 400.

The park also has wild buffaloes, deer, elephants, tigers, bears and a wide variety of water birds, including pelicans which breed here. One of the standard ways of observing the wildlife is from elephant back and the rhinos are said to have become quite used to elephants toting camera-packing tourists.

Information The park is at its best from February to May. There is a Tourist Information Centre (tel 23) at Kaziranga, but you're supposed to give 10 days' notice for booking accommodation or transport. They have a minibus and a jeep and also organise those elephant rides into the long grass. There's a Rs 5 entry charge to the park and an additional Rs 5 charge for a still camera, higher charges for telephoto lens (!) or movie cameras.

Places to Stay There is a wide variety of accommodation around the park:

Kaziranga Forest Lodge – singles/doubles Rs 160/160 with air-con, Rs 70/100 without.
Tourist Bungalow No 1 – Rs 40/50 or dorm beds at Rs 6.
Tourist Bungalow No 2 – Rs 22/28.
PWD Inspection Bungalow, Kaziranga – Rs 6 per person.
Forest Inspection Bungalow, Beguri – Rs 45 a double but bedding and mosquito nets are not included.
Forest Inspection Bungalow, Arimarh – actually within the park, Rs 40 a double, no electricity.
Forest Inspection Bungalow, Kohora – Rs 45 a double.
Soil Conservation Inspection Bungalow – Rs 50 a double.

Getting There
There are flights from Calcutta to Jorhat which is 84 km from the park. By rail Furketing is the most convenient station, 72 km away, from where the buses run to Kaziranga. Gauhati is 233 km away on Highway 37. There are state transport buses from Gauhati.

Jorhat

A little beyond Kaziranga this is the gateway to the north-eastern part of Assam. Sibsagar, 55 km away, has the huge Jay Sagar tank and many temples in the environs. This way was the old capital of the Ahom kingdom. There's a small *Tourist Bungalow* by the tank.

Manas

In the foothills of the Himalaya, north-west of Gauhati, Manas wildlife sanctuary is right on the border with Bhutan. Three rivers run through the sanctuary which has a wide variety of bird and animal life. The rare pygmy hog and the golden langur (monkey) are amongst the most notable animals here, although you may also see rhinos.

Information Manas is best between January and March, there is excellent fishing in November-December. Mothangiri is the main town in the park but the Tourist Information Centre (tel 49) is at Barpeta Road. Park entry charges and camera charges are the same as Kaziranga. Boats can be hired for excursions or fishing trips on the Manas River.

Places to Stay *Manas Tourist Lodge* has two rooms in the Upper Bungalow for Rs

15 per bed, Rs 25 per room on the ground floor or Rs 15 per bed, Rs 30 per room on the 1st floor. At the Lower Bungalow it's Rs 12 per bed, Rs 20 per room. You can also camp for Rs 5 if you have a tent. The *Forest Bungalow* costs Rs 10 per room, including bedding and mosquito nets but no electricity. There is a *Rest House* at the Barpeta Road Tourist Centre with doubles at Rs 45.

Getting There Gauhati, 176 km away, is the nearest airport. Barpeta Road, 40 km from Mothangiri, is the nearest railway station. Transport from here to Mothangiri must be arranged in advance.

MEGHALAYA

Created in 1971, this state is the home for Khasia, Jantia and Garo tribespeople. The hill station of Shillong is the state capital while Cherrapunji, 58 km away, is said to be the wettest place on earth with an average annual rainfall of 1150 cm, nearly 40 feet! In one year 2300 cm (75 feet) of rain fell. It's no wonder Meghalaya means 'abode of clouds'.

Other places of interest around the state include Jakrem with its hot springs, Kayllang Rock at Mairang, the Mawjymbuin Cave at Mawsynram and the Umiam Lake. Recently Mawsynram had an annual rainfall total that even surpassed the record at Cherrapunji.

SHILLONG (population 16,000)

This pleasant hill station, standing at 1496 metres, is renowned for its climate and breathtaking views; it's even had the label 'Scotland of the East' applied to it! Around town you can pass the time observing the tiny red light district behind the Delhi Hotel as there's really not a lot to do apart from pass through. The people around Shillong, the Khasias, are matrilineal, passing down property and wealth through the female rather than the male line.

The State Museum covers the flora, fauna, culture and anthropology of the

state. It's open Monday to Saturday from 10 am to 4.30 pm, half an hour earlier in winter. The town has a number of parks and gardens and a Botanic Garden and Botanical Museum beside the central Ward Lake. The Crinoline Waterfalls are near the Lady Hydari Park and there are various other waterfalls around Shillong. The town takes its name from the 1960-metre high Shillong Peak from where there are fine views. It's 10 km from the centre.

Information

There is a Government of Meghalaya Tourist Office (tel 6054) in Police Bazar where there is also a Government of India Tourist Office on G S Rd. The GPO is also on G S Rd.

Tours

There are morning tours of the city area (Rs 12), and day tours to Cherrapunj (Rs 20) and the hot springs at Jakrem (Rs 24).

Places to Stay & Eat

There's a good *Tourist Bungalow* near the polo grounds with singles for Rs 10 to 12, doubles at Rs 20 to 24 and dorm beds (supply your own bedding) at Rs 3. There are many other middle-price hotels around and cheap accommodation can be found in the Police Bazaar where there is also a tourist office. Good food at the *Lhasa Restaurant*; there are a number of other restaurants around town.

The *Hotel Pinewood Ashok* (tel 23116, 23765) is Shillong's premier hotel (and Ashok's worst said a visitor) with singles/doubles at Rs 95-105/150-205. Damp and mouse infested.

Getting There

A good road runs the 100 km from Gauhati in Assam to Shillong. Cherrapunji is 58 km south of Shillong, if it's not raining the views from here over Bangladesh are superb. Permission is required from the Commissioner of Police to visit the area, but it's given readily. Coming from Bangladesh you cross the border at Dawki from where it's a 1½ km walk to the town, and then a 3½ hour trip to Shillong.

OTHER STATES & TERRITORIES
The other north-eastern regions are generally hard to get permission to visit even at the best of times. All of them border either with China or Burma. The following information is for interest only.

Arunachal Pradesh
The furthest north-east of the regions, this was known as the North-East Frontier Agency under the British. Arunachal Pradesh borders with Bhutan, China and Burma and is a mountainous, remote and predominantly tribal area. The old 'Stillwell Road' used to run from Ledo in the south of Arunachal Pradesh to Myitkyinya in the north-east of Burma. Built in 1944 by General 'Vinegar Joe' Stillwell, it must rate as one of the most expensive roads in the world. The 400 km cost US\$137 million way back then, and after just a few months' use has hardly been used since. All roads routes into Burma are closed.

Nagaland
South of Arunahal Pradesh and north of Manipur, the remote and hilly state of Nagaland is bordered by Burma. Kohima, the capital of Nagaland, was the furthest point Japanese troops advanced into India during WW II.

Manipur
South of Nagaland and north of Mizoram,

Manipur also borders with Burma. The state is inhabited by over two dozen different tribes, many of them Christians. The state is famous for its Manipuri dances and its handloomed textiles. Imphal (population 110,000) is the capital, surrounded by wooded hills and lakes, and with the golden Shri Govindaji temple. During WW II a road was built from Imphal to Tamu on the Burma border but, as with the Stillwell road further north, this route into Burma is also closed.

Mizoram
This finger-like extension in the extreme south-east of the region pokes down between Burma and Bangladesh. The name means hill people's land – Mizo (man of the hill) and ram (land). It's a picturesque place where the population is both predominantly tribal and overwhelmingly Christian.

Tripura
The tiny state of Tripura is almost totally surrounded by Bangladesh. It's a wooded and lush region with many beautiful waterfalls. Agartala is the capital near where is the lake palace of Nirmahal. Here too the population is largely tribal.

Transport in the Region
The only railway to these states and territories terminates at Ledo, but the roads have been much improved of late. Indian Airlines operates a comprehensive service to the region from Calcutta.

Rajasthan

Population: 29 million
Area: 342,214 square km
Capital: Jaipur
Main language: Rajasthani

Rajasthan, the 'Land of the Kings', is India at its exotic and colourful best. This is the home of the Rajputs, a group of warrior clans who have controlled this part of India for a thousand years with a code of chivalry and honour akin to that of the mediaeval European knights. The Rajputs were never a united force, like the Marathas of central India; when they were not warring against outsiders they were generally squabbling amongst themselves. Thus they were never a real opposition to the Moghuls, but their bravery and sense of honour were unparalled.

The Rajput warriors would fight on against all odds and, when no hope was left, the women and children would commit suicide by marching into a funeral pyre in a ritual known as *jauhar*. Meanwhile the men would don the saffron robes of rejoicing worn at weddings and ride forth to certain death. Over and again, this grim tale would unfold as stronger forces attacked the Rajputs. In Chittorgarh's long history three times the women consigned themselves to the flames while the men rode out to their martyrdom. It's hardly surprising that Akbar persuaded Rajputs to lead his army or that Aurangzeb clashed unsuccessfully with them.

Under the British, Rajasthan continued as a collection of princely states under the collective name of Rajputana, each with its own Maharaja. Independent India combined them with Ajmer to make Rajasthan. Huge, often battle-scarred, forts dominate almost every town in Rajasthan. They're a clear reminder of the state's warlike past. And what forts they are – battlements, turrets, massive walls and inside palaces of amazing luxury and whimsical charm. They're redolent of that impossibly romantic Rajput sense of honour and bravery above all.

Rajasthan's exotic atmosphere extends to far more than just splendid forts for the Rajasthanis themselves are a brilliant splash of colour. The men top their outfit with a huge, pastel-coloured turban and almost without exception sport fierce 'soup strainer' moustaches. The bright, mirrored-skirts of the women are equally colourful. They complement it with chunky jewellery worn from head to toe – Rajasthani jewellery is a favourite purchase for visitors to the state.

Geographically Rajasthan is a somewhat dry and inhospitable place, but it's very varied. A line drawn south-west to north-east divides the state into the hilly and rugged south-east region and the barren north-east Thar Desert, which extends across the border into Pakistan. Apart from historic cities, colourful people and superb scenery Rajasthan also has some popular travellers' centres –

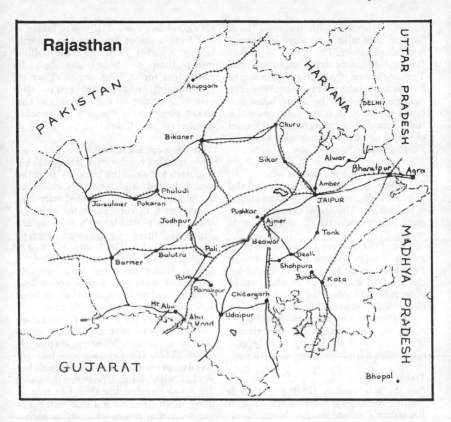

Rajasthan

peaceful Pushkar with its holy lake and the exotic desert city of Jaisalmer, like some fantasy from the Thousand and One Nights. It's a fascinating state.

Art & Architecture

Rajasthan has a school of miniature painting, derived from the Moghul style but with some clear differences – in particular, the palace and hunting scenes are complemented by religious themes, particularly relating to the Krishna legends. This art carried through to the elegant palaces the Rajputs built when they were freed of confrontation with the Moghuls. Many of them are liberally covered with colourful frescoes.

Most of Rajasthan's early architecture was damaged or destroyed by the first waves of Moslem invasions. Fragments remaining from that period include the Adhai-din-ka-jhonpra mosque in Ajmer, which is basically a converted Hindu temple of great elegance, or the ruined temples at Osian, near Jodhpur. There are many buildings from the 10th to 15th century, including the superb Jain temples at Ranakpur, Mt Abu and Jaisalmer. Most of the great forts date, in their present form, from the Moghul period.

Festivals

Rajasthan has the usual Indian festivals,

some celebrated with especial local fervour, and also a number of special festivals of its own. The harvest festival of Gangaur is particularly important and Teej, at the end of August or beginning of September, is also very popular. When the monsoon rains fill the many lakes and tanks the state is at its most beautiful. Rajasthan also has many fairs, best known of which is the immense and colourful Pushkar cattle fair.

Palaces & Tourist Bungalows

Rajasthan is famous for its delightful palace hotels – in these harder times many of Rajasthan's Maharajas have had to turn their palaces into hotels to make ends meet.

Two of the best are the beautiful Lake Palace Hotel in Udaipur and the Rambagh Palace in Jaipur. At a rather more day-to-day level the state has an excellent series of government operated Tourist Bungalows in almost every big town. They're very often the best value in town, have a restaurant and, usually, the local tourist office. For real shoestringers they also often offer dormitory accommodation.

Trains

See the introductory Gricing section in Getting Around for more information on Rajasthan's often unique locomotives. The 'Palace on Wheels' is a special tourist train service which operates three and seven-day tours out of Delhi, but principally around Rajasthan. The carriages used to belong to various maharajas and the cost includes your accommodation on the train plus all meals. It's a hefty US$141 a day and the name may be changed to 'Adventure on Wheels', as there were complaints that it wasn't really luxurious enough to rate the initial title. One visitor commended it as 'a good way of seeing the sights without having to make all the arrangements oneself'.

Buses

Rajasthan has an extensive and reason-ably good bus system. If you're taking a bus from a major bus stand it's worth buying a ticket from the ticket office rather than on board the bus. It guarantees (or at least comes closer to guaranteeing) a seat and you're also certain of getting on the right bus as the ticket clerk writes the bus registration number on your ticket.

JAIPUR (population 650,000)

The capital city of the state of Rajasthan is popularly known as the 'pink city' from the pink-coloured sandstone with which the buildings in its old, walled city are constructed. In contrast to the cities on the Ganges plain, Jaipur's avenues are broad and there is a harmony which is quite remarkable. The town is situated in a desert-like landscape, surrounded by barren hills. Rajasthan is a sparsely populated state and Jaipur seems less crowded and more relaxed than its large size and population would indicate.

Jaipur owes its name, its foundation and its careful planning to the great warrior-astronomer Maharaja Jai Singh II (1699-1744). His predecessors had enjoyed good relations with the Moghuls but in 1727, with Monghul power on the wane, Jai Singh decided the time was ripe to move down from his hill side fortress at nearby Amber to a new site on the plains. He laid out the city with its surrounding walls and six rectangular blocks by principles of town planning set out in the *Shilpa-Shastra*, an ancient Hindu treatise on architecture. In 1728 he constructed the remarkable observatory which is still one of Jaipur's central attractions.

Information & Orientation

The walled 'pink city' is situated in the north-east of Jaipur while the new parts have spread away to the south and west. The main shopping centre in the old city is Johari Bazaar or the jeweller's market. Unlike other shopping centres in narrow alleys in India and Asia this one is broad and open.

Mirza Ismail Rd (M I Rd) is the main street of the new part of Jaipur and the modern shopping centre. Most of the hotels and restaurants frequented by budget travellers are located around the railway station and bus stand to the south-west. There is also an area opposite the GPO on M I Rd which has become a popular centre for travellers on a really tight budget. There are many souvenir shops and cheap restaurants here.

Jaipur's tourist attractions are mainly concentrated in the old city. The state Tourist Office is in the bus and railway stations while the Government of India Tourist Office is in the Rajasthan State Hotel. The State Bank of India has a very quick and efficient foreign exchange counter on the first floor of its branch in M I Rd at the Sanganeri Gate. It's open six days a week too.

Old City
The old city is encircled by a crenollated wall with seven gates – the major gates are Chandpol, Sanganeri and Ajmeri. The broad (over 30 metres wide) avenues of the pink city divide it up into neat rectangles. It's an extremely colourful city – in the evening light the pink and orange buildings have a magical glow which the brightly-clothed Rajasthanis comple-ment. The strange looking camel-drawn carts are part of the passing scene in Jaipur and black-faced monkeys peer out from some of the buildings. The Iswari Minar Swarga Sul, the 'minaret piercing heaven', near the Tripolia Gate, was built to overlook the city.

Palace of the Winds
Built in 1799 the Hawa Mahal or Palace of the Winds is Jaipur's central landmark, although it is actually little more than a facade. The five-storey building looks out over the main street of the old city. Its pink sandstone windows are semi-octagonal in shape and delicately honeycombed. It was originally built to enable ladies of the royal household to watch the everyday life and

processions of the city. You can climb to the top of the Hawa Mahal and get an excellent view over the city. The palace was originally built by Maharaja Sawaj Pratap Singh and is part of the City Palace complex.

Entrance to the Hawa Mahal is from the rear of the building and is a little difficult to find. It's open from 9 am to 4.30 pm and it's worth spending Rs 0.60 to enjoy the views of the snake charmers and camels down below. 'We always found the camel carts amusing, very rarely did we see them actually pulling anything on those silly little carts.'

City Palace
In the heart of the old city the City Palace occupies a large area divided into a series of courtyards, gardens and buildings. The outer wall was built by Jai Singh but other additions are much later, some right up to the start of this century. Today the palace is a blend of Rajasthani and Moghul architecture, the former Maharaja still lives in part of the palace.

The centre of the palace is the seven-storey Chandra Mahal with fine views over the gardens and the city. The ground and first floor of the Chandra Mahal forms the Maharaja Sawai Man Singh II Museum. The apartments are maintained in luxurious order and the museum has an extensive collection of art, carpets, enamelware and old weapons. The paintings include miniatures of the Rajasthani, Moghul and Persian schools. The armoury has a collection of guns and swords dating back to the 15th century plus many of the ingenious and tricky weapons which the warrior Rajputs were famous for. The textile section contains dresses and costumes of the former Maharajas and Maharanis of Jaipur.

Other points of interest in the palace include the Diwan-i-Am or Hall of Public Audiences with its intricate decorations and manuscripts in Persian and Sanskrit, the Diwan-i-Khas or Hall of Private Audiences with a marble paved gallery.

1 Central Bus Station	16 Museum
2 G.P.O.	17 Govt. of Rajasthan
3 Indian Govt. Tourist	Tourist Office
Office, Circuit House	18 Nehru Bazaar
4 Indian Airlines	19 City Palace & Museum
5 Youth Hostel	20 Jantar Mantar
6 Achrol Lodge	21 Hawa Mahal
7 Gangaur Tourist	22 Vidyadharji ka Bagh
Bungalow	23 Sisodia Rani Palace
8 Teej Tourist Bungalow	& Garden
9 Jaipur Ashok Hotel	24 Swagat Tourist Bungalow
10 Jaipur Inn	25 Chandralok Hotel
11 Rambagh Palace Hotel	26 Shalimar Hotel
12 Man Singh Hotel	27 Bissau & Khetri Hotel
13 Niros Restaurant	28 Haldiyon Restaurant
14 LMB Restaurant	29 Gopal Restaurant
15 Rajasthan Handicraft	30 Hotel Arya Niwas
Emporium	

There is also a clock tower and the newer Mubarak Mahal.

Outside the buildings you may see a large silver vessel which a former Maharaja used to take drinking water with him to England. Being a devout Hindu he could not drink the English water! The palace and museum are open daily except on holidays and entry is Rs 5 (Rs 2 for students). Hours are 9.30 am to 4.40 pm.

Observatory

Across from the City Palace is the observatory or Jantar Mantar which Jai Singh began in 1728. In all he built about five of these curious complexes. Jai Singh's passion for astronomy was even more notable than his prowess as a warrior and before commencing construction he sent scholars abroad to study foreign observatories. Of the five he built, the Jaipur observatory is the largest and the best preserved – it was restored in 1901. The others are in Delhi (the oldest, dating from 1724), in Varanasi, Ujjain and there was one in Muttra, but it has now disappeared.

At first glance the observatory appears to be just a curious collection of sculptures but in fact each construction has a specific purpose such as measuring the positions of stars, altitudes and azimuths, or to calculate eclipses. The most striking instrument is the sundial with its 30-metre high gnomon. This casts a shadow which moves up to four metres an hour! It's very accurate but on Jaipur local time! Admission to the observatory is Rs 1, free on Mondays, open 9 am to 5 pm.

Central Museum

Situated on the Ram Niwas Gardens, south of the old city, the museum is housed in the architectually impressive Albert Hall. The upper floor contains portraits of the Jaipur Maharajas and many other miniatures and works of art. The ground floor has a collection of costumes and woodwork from different parts of Rajasthan and a description of the people and life in the rural areas of the state. The collection, which started in 1833, is also notable for its brassware, jewellery and pottery. Entry to the

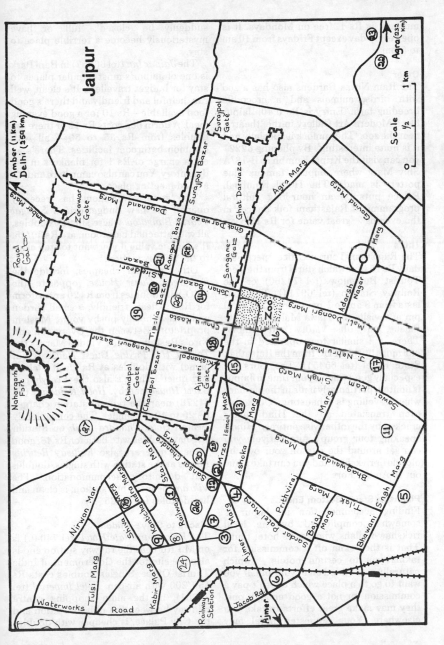

Jaipur

Scale

0   ½   1 km

Agra (232 km)

Amber (11 Km)
Delhi (359 km)

Amber Marg

Zorawar Gate

Royal Gaitor

Nahargarh Fort

Surajpol Gate

Surajpol Bazar

Dhadwand Marg

Ghat Darwaza

Ghat Darwaza

Agra Marg

Govind Marg

Adarsh Nagar

Sangane Gate

Zoo

Moti Doongri Marg

Sireedeori Bazar

Ramganj Bazar

Johari Bazar

Johari Bazar

Tripolia Bazar

Chaura Rasta

Hanganri Bazar

Kishanpol Bazar

Chandpol Gate

Chandpol Bazar

Ajmeri Gate

J. Nehru Marg

Sawai Ram Singh Marg

Sansar (Chandra) Marg

Mirza Ismail Marg

Ashoka Marg

Bhagwaandas Marg

Station Marg

Govind Marg

Kanti Chandra Marg

Rajwanj

Ramlowiji Marg

Sardar Patel Marg

Tilak Marg

Prithviraj Marg

Bajaj Marg

Bhawani Singh Marg

Nirwan Marg

Shiva Marg

Tulsi Marg

Kabir Marg

Waterworks Road

Railway Station

Jacob Rd.

Ajmer

museum is Rs 1, free on Mondays. It is open every day except Fridays from 10 am to 5 pm.

Other

The Ram Niwas Gardens also has a zoo with birds, animals and a crocodile breeding farm. Entry is Rs 0.40. Jaipur has a Modern Art Gallery in the 'theatre' near the zoo. 'They unlock it specially and it is quite interesting'. By phoning 62227 you can visit the Kripal Kumbh at B-18/A Shiv Marg where Jaipur's famous blue pottery is made. The Hotel Rambagh Palace puts on an hour-long cultural programme of Rajasthani folk dances in the evening – 'great value for Rs 15'.

Tours

The Rajasthan Tourist Office operates a daily Rs 15 tour which starts from the Teej Tourist Bungalow (tel 74260) or the Railway Station (tel 69714). The tour lasts from 8 am to 1 pm or from 1 to 6.30 pm and visits the Hawa Mahal, the City Palace, the observatory and Amber. There is a similar tour operated in the mornings by the ITDC from the Rajasthan State Hotel (tel 65451). The tours are especially good value if your time in Jaipur is limited, particularly if it's in the summer when travelling is exhausting. 'Our guide even translated all the Hindi jokes cracked by the (otherwise entirely) Hindi-speaking tour group'. Alternatively you can get around the city on your own by bicycle or rickshaw and you can take a bus out to Amber Fort.

Places to Stay – Bottom End

Finding accommodation in Jaipur is somewhat complicated by the local rickshaw-wallahs who act as hotel touts. That is they skim off a commission for taking you to certain hotels – which naturally gets added on to your bill. If you want to go to a place which doesn't pay a commission, or not a good enough one, they may make great efforts to take you elsewhere. Your requested hotel may suddenly be 'closed', 'full' or have mysteriously become a terrible place to stay.

The *Jaipur Inn* (tel 66057) in Bani Park is one of Jaipur's most popular places to stay for budget travellers. It's clean, well run, helpful and friendly and there's good food available – Rs 10 for a good evening meal. A dorm bed costs Rs 12 or there are doubles from Rs 35 to 50 – all with common bathroom facilities. There's an extra charge of Rs 1 for blankets in the dormitory. You can also camp here and it's a good meeting place.

The state government has recently opened the new budget-priced *Swagat Tourist Bungalow* where singles/doubles, all with attached bathroom, are Rs 30/45. It's terrific value if you want to stay close to the railway station.

Other popular cheapies, include the *Evergreen Guest House*, opposite the GPO, with doubles from Rs 20 and a dorm for Rs 7. Clean, friendly, a small garden and a 'delightfully pushy young Moslem proprietor'. Between the Evergreen and Niro's Restaurant at 4 Vindoa Marg is the *Tourist Hut Paying Guest House* (great name) with doubles at Rs 15, it's 'clean and quiet'. There's also the *Everyhappy Guest House* nearby. *Hotel Rajdhani* (tel 61276) near the railway station charges Rs 25 to 40 for singles. The conveniently located *Hotel Chandra Loak* on Station Rd, has doubles with bath for Rs 45, good value. There are also *Railway Retiring Rooms* at the station with singles, doubles and dormitory accommodation. The *Vikram*, near the bus station, is clean and has doubles for Rs 25.

Places to Stay – Middle

The *Rajasthan State Hotel* (tel 74040) is on M I Rd near the railway station and is also the site for the Government of India Tourist Office. Singles/doubles costs Rs 150/200 with air-con. *Hotel Imperial* (tel 78651), in the main shopping centre midway between the railway station and the City Palace, is cheaper with doubles from Rs 80 (non air-con) and Rs 125 (air-con). The *Achrol Lodge & Tourist Camp* (tel 72254) at Civil Lines costs Rs 90 to 110 for a double, but also has good camping facilities. The *Satya Mahal*, next door, has also been recommended. Large singles with bath and hot water cost Rs 40 and the food is good and cheap.

An excellent budget priced hotel is the *Hotel Bissau* (tel 74191) at Chandpol Gate. This was the palace of one of the princes of Rajasthan but has since been converted into a hotel. All rooms have hot showers and there's even a garden and swimming pool, all for the non-princely sum of Rs 80/100. In the same area *Hotel Khetri House* (tel 69183) has large rooms and is popular with some overland groups. Singles/doubles cost Rs 75/120. *Hotel Shalimar* (tel 61187) is one of the new hotels opened near the bus station. It's a reasonably good place with rooms, some of them rather dirty, at Rs 65/85.

Several travellers have written to recommend the new *Hotel Arya Niwas* (tel 73456) which is behind the Amber Cinema on Sansar Chandra Marg, near the GPO. The hotel only opened in mid-83 and there are singles from Rs 50 to 100, doubles from Rs 60 to 120, all with attached bath and air-cooling in the summer. It's clean and well run by a helpful family, the food is excellent and you get bed tea!

There are two more expensive tourist bungalows, both close to the railway station. The *Gangaur Tourist Bungalow* (tel 74373) is on M I Rd and costs Rs 120/140 with air-con, Rs 90/110 without. The *Teej Tourist Bungalow* (tel 74260) in Bani Park is cheaper at Rs 100/120 with air-con, Rs 50/60 without, just Rs 30/40 for bathless rooms. It also has a Rs 10 dormitory. Because of the wide variety of accommodation alternatives available in Jaipur, the tourist bungalows are not the standout bargains they are elsewhere in Rajasthan but they're good places.

Places To Stay – Top End

Jaipur is a major tourist centre and conveniently close to Delhi, so it has a wide variety of hotels in all categories. The *Rambagh Palace* (tel 75141) on Bhawani Sangh Marg, was the palace of the Maharajas of Jaipur after the City Palace. Situated to the south of the town, it is a charming old building, fully air-con and with a luxurious indoor swimming pool. Singles/doubles cost Rs 415/500. The Polo Bar is one of the hotel's main attractions. Polo is still a big deal in Jaipur, the previous Maharaja died while playing!

Welcomhotel Mansingh (tel 78771) is on Sansar Chandra Rd, close to the railway and bus stations. It is a part of the Welcomhotel group, looks like a huge red sandstone palace and costs Rs 350/450. The *Hotel Jaipur Ashok* (tel 75171) is also centrally located in Bani Park. Part of the ITDC chain, it costs Rs 200/300. *Hotel Clarks Amer* (tel 82216) is on Jawahar Lal Nehru Marg, an uncomfortably long way from the town, and costs Rs 350/450.

The *Narayan Niwas Hotel* is a lovely, old building, recently converted into a hotel. Lots of beautiful old furniture, some of it quite unusual.

Places to Eat

Niro's, on M I Rd, is one of Jaipur's best and most expensive restaurants – pleasant decor, soft music, chicken specialties and about Rs 35 for a meal. *LMB*, in Johari Bazaar near the palace, is well known for its vegetarian food – try the excellent sweet dish known as *rasmali*. There is also a *Kwality* on M I Rd.

For a real splurge have lunch at the *Rambagh Palace Hotel*. It's a fine experience, there's a set menu (the menu itself is leather-bound) for Rs 75 and that covers as much as you eat.

Chandralok, near the GPO on M I Rd, is a good place for very cheap vegetarian food. A thali costs just Rs 6. Basic, all-you-can eat thalis are also available at *Krishna Bhojnalaya* at the top of the stairs between 63 and 64 Johri Bazaar.

The *Circuit House*, near the Government of India Tourist Office, is a good place for breakfast. For Rs 10 you get corn flakes, two eggs, toast and coffee – good value. Along the road from there to the right there are several nice places to eat. Jaipur has a number of good Chinese restaurants. In the Ram Niwas gardens there are open air restaurants with good masala dosas and other south Indian food.

Getting There

Air There are two direct flights daily from Delhi to Jaipur and on to Bombay (and vice versa). The Jaipur-Bombay sector goes, on different days of the week, via different combinations of Jodhpur, Udaipur and Ahmedabad. Fares to or from Jaipur are Delhi (Rs 190), Bombay (Rs 701), Jodhpur (Rs 239), Udaipur (Rs 247) and Ahmedabad (Rs 398). The Indian Airlines office (tel 72940 or 74500) is on Ajmer Rd. The airport is 15 km out of town.

Rail The train services from Jaipur are generally not as fast as buses because they are on a metre gauge. The Pink City Express leaves old Delhi Railway Station at 6 am and reaches Jaipur at 11 am. The Jaipur-Delhi service leaves at 5 pm and arrives at 10 pm. Fares are Rs 109 in 1st class, Rs 25 in 2nd. An overnight train leaves Delhi in the late evening and arrives in Jaipur at around dawn. All Jaipur trains leave from the old Delhi station.

The Chetak Express continues through Jaipur to Ajmer and Udaipur. There is now a 'superfast' train from Jaipur to Agra which only takes five hours, it leaves Jaipur at 5 am and costs Rs 19. Six days a week there's a train to Jodhpur which arrives there just over seven hours later.

Bus From Delhi or Agra de-luxe buses operated by the Rajasthan State Transport take five hours to Jaipur. The 306-km trip costs Rs 45 from Delhi. Regular express buses from Delhi are Rs 33. There are also de-luxe buses from Agra for Rs 40.

Tours ITDC operate a one-day conducted tour to Jaipur from Delhi. The tours depart from the Hotel Janpath, Ashok or Akbar or the ITDC office in L Block, Connaught Place and cost about Rs 200 per person.

Getting Around

Jaipur has taxis (unmetered), auto-rickshaws and a city bus service which also operates out to Amber. A cycle rickshaw from the station to the Jaipur Inn will cost Rs 2 or from the station to Johari Bazar Rs 5. Cycle rickshaws in Jaipur are notorious for their commission gathering activities – an especially low fare to a hotel from the station probably means he's planning on an especially big commission at your expense. It is also possible to share 'four seaters' or 'six seaters', larger auto-rickshaw-like devices which go from the station to the main gates of the city (ie Sanganer) for Rs 1 or 1.50. You can hire bicycles from near the railway station and the city bus service is quite useful and cheap.

Things to Buy

Jaipur is well-known for precious stones which seem to be cheaper here than anywhere else in India. It is even better known for semi-precious stones. For precious stones find a narrow alley called Haldion ka rasta of Johari Bazaar (near the Hawa Mahal). For semi-precious stones there's another alley on the opposite side of the street called the Gopalji ka rasta. There are many shops here which offer bargain prices.

Shops around the City Palace and Hawa Mahal are likely to be more expensive, although they do have many interesting items including miniatures and clothes. Marble statues, jewellery and textile prints are other Jaipur specialties. The Rajasthan Government Emporium in

M I Rd is reasonably priced, and also has a branch in Amber.

AMBER

Situated on the Jaipur-Delhi road, 11 km out of Jaipur, Amber was the ancient capital of Jaipur state before the move was made to Jaipur. The fortress-palace was constructed from 1592 by Raja Man Singh, the Rajput commander of Akbar's army. It was later extended and completed by the Jai Singhs before the shift to Jaipur on the plains below. The fort is a superb example of Rajput architecture, stunningly situated on a hillside overlooking a lake which reflects its terraces and ramparts.

From the road you can climb up to the fort in 10 minutes but it's a popular activity to ride up on elephant back – count on a rip off Rs 50. 'The elephants have been nationalised and now cost only Rs 5', reported a more recent visitor. 'Elephant rides Rs 65', said another! Within the palace you can get cold drinks, should the climb have been a hot one, before exploring the palace.

An imposing stairway leads to the Diwan-i-Am or Hall of Public Audiences with a double row of columns and latticed galleries above. Steps to the right lead to the small Kali temple. There is also the white marble Sila Devi Temple.

The Maharaja's apartments are on the higher terrace – you enter through a gateway decorated with mosaics and sculptures. The Jai Mandir or Hall of Victory is noted for its inlaid panels and glittering mirror ceiling. Opposite the Jai Mandir is the Sukh Niwas or Hall of Pleasure with an ivory inlaid sandalwood door, and a channel running right through the room which at one time carried cooling water. From the Jas Mandir you can enjoy the fine views from the palace ramparts over the lake below.

Amber palace is open from 9 am to 4.30 pm and entry costs Rs 1.

Getting There

A bus to Amber from the Hawa Mahal in Jaipur costs Rs 0.80 and the trip takes half an hour. Buses depart every few minutes.

AROUND JAIPUR

There are a number of other attractions around Jaipur, including several on the road between Jaipur and Amber. Jaipur tours usually stop at some of these sites on the way to or from Amber.

Gaitor

The cenotaphs of the royal family are at Gaitor, 6.5 km from Jaipur on the road to Amber. The white marble cenotaph of Maharaja Jai Singh II is the most impressive and is decorated with carved peacocks. Next to it is the cenotaph of his son. Opposite the cenotaphs is the Jal Mahal water palace in the middle of a lake, and reached by a causeway. Or at least it was in the middle of a lake, the water is now all but squeezed out by the infamous weed, water-hyacinth. There is another Royal Gaitor, just outside the city walls.

Galta

If you leave the city by the Surya Gate it's a 2.5 km climb to the temple of the Sun God at Galta, 100 metres above the city to the east and with fine views over the surrounding plain. A deep temple-filled gorge stands behind the it.

Tiger Fort

The Nahargarh Fort looks out over the city from a sheer ridge 6.5 km away. It's reached by a jeepable road from Amber through the hills. You can get there by rickshaw too but it's a km and a half of zigzag path to actually reach the top. The views fully justify the effort and the Rs 1 entry fee. There's a small and all but deserted restaurant on the top. The fort was initially built in 1734 and extended in 1868.

Jaigarh Fort

The imposing Jaigarh Fort, built by Jai Singh in 1726, was only opened to the public in mid-83. It's near Amber and there's a fine view over the plains from the *Diwa Burj* watchtower. The fort, with its water reservoirs, residential areas, puppet theatre and the cannon *Jaya Vana* is open from 9 am to 4.30 pm and there is an admission charge.

Sisodia Rani Palace & Gardens

Eight km from the city on the Agra road, the palace was built for the second wife of Maharaja Jai Singh, the Sisodia Princess. The outer walls of the palace are illustrated with murals of hunting scenes and the Krishna legend, and the palace is surrounded by terraced gardens.

Vidyadhar's Garden

Nestled in a narrow valley, this beautiful garden was built in honour of Jai Singh's

chief architect and town planner.

Sanganer

Situated 16 km south of Jaipur, this small town is entered through the ruins of two 'Tripolias' or triple-gateways. The town has a ruined palace and a group of Jain temples with fine carvings. Entry to the temples is restricted. The town is noted for hand-made paper and block printing.

BHARATPUR

This small town is best known for its bird sanctuary – a must if you are interested in bird watching. Bharatpur also has an 18th century-fort with a small museum. It is 55 km from Agra and 180 km from Delhi via Mathura. Bring your mosquito repellant, there are plenty of them.

Bird Sanctuary

No less than 328 kinds of birds have been sighted at the sanctuary, 117 of which are

Jaigargh Fort near Amber

migrants, which come from as far away as Siberia or China. It takes about a week to fly from Siberia to India! The sanctuary was the duck-shooting preserve of the Maharajas of Bharatpur when this was a princely state. Shooting has not been permitted since 1964 and today there are 80 types of ducks seen in the sanctuary.

October to February is the best time to visit the sanctuary when there are many migratory birds to be seen. There is an entry fee per car or bus plus charges for photography or for taking boats onto the waters. The sanctuary covers 52 square km of low lying marshland. Entrance to the park costs a hefty Rs 10 for foreigners and a boat with guide will cost about Rs 20 an hour – 'well worth it to have a closer look at the birds'. The tourist bungalow does a dawn minibus tour at Rs 7.50, so long as there are enough seats sold.

Two travellers reported that 'even for those with no interest in ornithology, Bharatpur is a must. See the sun rise over the lakes and the enormous Siberian cranes weighing down the branches of the tiny trees'.

Lohagarh Fort

The 'Iron Fort' was built in the early 18th century and took its name from its supposedly impregnable defences. Maharaja Suraj Mal, the fort's constructor and the founder of Bharatpur, built two towers within the ramparts, the Jawahar Burj and the Fateh Burj, to commemorate his victories over the Moghuls and the British. The fort is open from 9 am to 5 pm daily and admission is free. The museum is closed Fridays; it has sculptures, inscriptions and works of art from the region.

Places to Stay

There is an ITDC operated *Ashok Forest Lodge* (tel 2260) in the sanctuary, near the entrance. Singles/doubles cost from Rs 115/175 or Rs 180/240 with air-con. There is also the cheaper *Sarus Tourist Bungalow* (tel 2169) on the Agra road just

200 metres from the sanctuary entrance. Rooms there are Rs 50/65 or with air-con 75/90 all with hot showers, or Rs 10 for the dormitory. The rooms are excellent and the restaurant food is very good too. It's also known as the *Travellers' Lodge*.

A cycle rickshaw from town will cost Rs 3 to 4 to the Tourist Bungalow which is some distance out. If you're told it's full, a little polite persistance may well solve the problem. Near the bus station the *Tourist Lodge* has rooms from Rs 10 for a single, but the food is not good value. In the town, a km from the park, the *Govind Niwas Guest* (tel 3347) has rooms at Rs 75/100, all with attached bath and balconies.

Getting There

It is only three hours by train from Delhi to Bharatpur. It's on the Agra-Jaipur road, just two hours by bus from Agra or an hour from Fatehpur Sikri – five buses a day for Rs 3.10. The Agra and Fatehpur Sikri buses run right by the front door of the Tourist Bungalow and will stop if you ask. By bus it's about 4½ hours from Jaipur and the fare is about Rs 20. 'The Rajasthan bus company seem to select their most decrepit bus for this run, beware holes in the floor almost big enough to fall through. Our bus had no starter motor or seat back cushions', wrote one visitor. Travel time and fare from Delhi is similar.

Getting Around

There are tongas and cycle rickshaws for getting around the town and the Rajasthan Tourist Office has a minibus (see the tourist officer in the Tourist Bungalow). You can also hire bicycles for Rs 5 a day, a good way to make a dawn visit to the sanctuary.

DEEG

This small town, 35 km from Bharatpur or Mathura, contains the summer palace of the Maharaja of Bharatpur. Built two centuries ago, it seems like a 'modest' palace for a 'modest' Maharaja but in

1762 the Maharaja of Bharatpur had the temerity to attack the Red Fort! Some of the booty he carried off included an entire marble building which can still be seen. Deeg has palaces and gardens laid out with foundations in the Moghul style. The palace is open from 8 am to noon and 1 to 7 pm, and admission is free.

SARISKA WILDLIFE SANCTUARY

Situated 107 km from Jaipur and 200 km from Delhi, the sanctuary is in a valley surrounded by barren mountains. The sanctuary, which covers 480 square km, has blue bulls, sambhar, spotted deer, wild boar and, above all, tigers. The sanctuary can be visited year-round, except during July/August when the animals move to higher ground.

The best time to see the wildlife is in the evening or at night; night outings are arranged at a rather steep cost of Rs 37 per person. A better game run can be had for only a rupee by taking the daily bus to the Kaligati ranger post. Nilgai, spotted deer, sambar, wild boar and other animals can be seen on the way. At Kaligati there is a 'watch tower' – a pill-box affair beside a waterhole which is an excellent hide from which to watch and photograph animals. You can stay overnight for Rs 10 but take a sleeping bag, food and drink although mattresses are provided. If you don't want rats for company it would pay to block up the windows at night!

Places to Stay

The *Tiger Den Tourist Bungalow* at the sanctuary is very good but rather expensive at Rs 60/90 for singles/doubles but there is also a Rs 10 dormitory. There is also a cheaper *Forest Rest House*.

Getting There

Sariska is 35 km from Alwar, which is a convenient town from which to approach the sanctuary.

AJMER (population 280,000)

South of Jaipur, Ajmer is a green oasis on the shore of the Ana Sagar Lake and hemmed in by barren hills. Ajmer always had great strategic importance and in its time it was sacked by Mahmud of Ghanzi on one of his periodic forays from Afghanistan. Later it became a favourite residence of the great Moghuls. Sir Thomas Roe met with Jehangir in Ajmer in 1616 – one of the first contacts between the Moghuls and the British.

Later the city was taken by the Scindias, then handed over to the British in 1818 – it was thus one of the few places in Rajasthan which was controlled directly by the British rather than being a part of a 'princely state'. Ajmer is a major pilgrimage place for Moslems during the fast of Ramadan. Today it is an easy-going and quite interesting town, although for many travellers it is just a stepping stone to nearby Pushkar.

Information

The Tourist Office is in the Tourist Bungalow (tel 20430).

Orientation

The bus stand is on the Jaipur side of town and close to the Tourist Bungalow, while the railway station, and most of the other hotels, are on the other side of town. The lake is more-or-less between the two, but slightly to the north.

Ana Sagar Lake

This artificial lake was created in the 12th century by damming the River Luni. On its bank is a fine park, the Dault Bagh, with a series of marble pavilions which were erected by Shah Jahan in 1637. It's a popular site for an evening stroll. Because the lake tends to dry up if the monsoon is poor, the city's water supply is taken from the Foy Sagar Lake, five km further up the valley. Good views from the hill beside the Dault Bagh.

Dargah

In the old part of town, at the foot of a barren hill, this is one of India's most

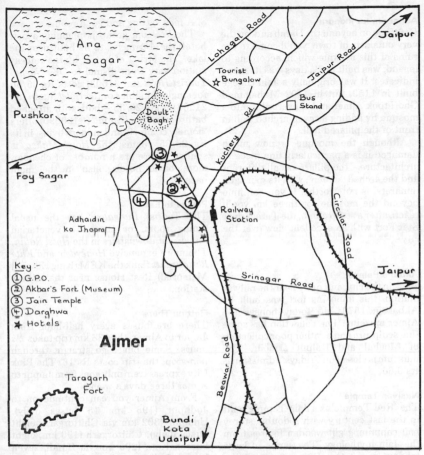

important places of pilgrimage for Moslems. The Dargah is the tomb of a Sufi saint who came to Ajmer in 1192. Construction of the shrine was completed by Humayun and the gate added by the Nizam of Hyderabad. Akbar used to make the pilgrimage to the Dargah from Agra once a year.

As you enter the courtyard, removing your shoes at the gateway, there is a mosque constructed by Akbar on the right. The large iron cauldrons are for offerings which are customarily shared amongst families connected with the

shrine's upkeep. On an inner court there is another mosque built by Shah Jahan. Constructed of white marble it has 11 arches and a Persian inscription running the full length of the building.

The saint's tomb is in the centre of the second court with a marble dome and inside the actual tomb is surrounded by a siver platform. The shrine doors have horseshoes nailed on them, offerings from successful horse dealers! Beware of 'guides' hassling for donations around the Dargah, with the standard fake donation books, all donations over Rs 50!

Adhal-din-ka-jhonpra

Continue on beyond the Darah and, on the very outskirts of town, you'll come to the ruins of this mosque which, according to legend, was built in 2½ days – as its name indicates. It was originally a Jain college built in 1153, but in 1192 Muhammad Ghori took Ajmer and converted it into a mosque by adding a seven-arched wall in front of the pillared hall.

Although the mosque is now much damaged it is a particularly fine piece of architecture – the pillars are all different and the arched 'screen', with its damaged minarets, is noteworthy. If you continue beyond the mosque for three km you'll reach, after a steep climb, the Taragarh or Star Fort with an excellent view over the city.

Akbar's Palace

Back in the city, and quite near the railway station, this imposing fort was built by Akbar in 1570 and today houses the Ajmer museum. The collection has some fine sculpture and a rather poor collection of Moghul and Rajput armour. The museum is closed on Fridays, admission is Rs 0.60.

Nasiyan Temple

The 'Red Temple' is a Jain Temple built in the last century with a double-storey hall containing gilt wooden figures from the Jain mythology. The series of large models depict the Jain concept of the ancient world. Admission is Rs 0.25, it's certainly worth a visit.

Places to Stay

Although there are a number of hotels along the road opposite the railway station, the *Khadim Tourist Bungalow* (tel 20490) is the best place to stay. It's only a few minutes walk from the bus stand, from the railway station it's just Rs 1 or 2 by trishaw. Singles/doubles cost Rs 30/40 (ordinary), Rs 45/60 (de-luxe) and Rs 75/100 (air-con). There is also a dorm for Rs

8. A nice setting and good rooms.

The Welcom group is planning a new hotel, the *Ajaymeru*, to be built near the lake. The string of hotels by the railway station vary from dismal to OK. *Nagpal Tourist Hotel* (tel 21603) costs Rs 35/50 for singles/doubles or the *Hotel Ratan* (tel 21238) is Rs 20/35 – both with attached bathrooms. *Hotel Anand* (tel 20090) offers 'homely comforts and modern living' in its Rs 25/35 rooms; the *Hotel Malwa* is similar. There are a number of cheaper, more basic hotels, also in the main bazaar.

Places to Eat

The *Tourist Bungalow* has the usual dining room, or there's a vegetarian restaurant downstairs in the *Hotel Ratan*. The more expensive *Honeydew* and *Elite Restaurants* flank the KEM (King Edward Memorial) Rest House near the railway station.

Getting There

There are buses every half-hour from Jaipur to Ajmer, the 138 km trip takes 2½ hours. Some buses go straight through non-stop, the trip costs Rs 16. The Pink City express train only goes from Jaipur to Ajmer three days a week.

From Ajmer you can continue on to Jodhpur (198 km, 15 buses daily), Udaipur (302 km via Chittorgarh, eight buses daily), Chittorgarh (190 km, eight buses), Kota (200 km via Bundi, seven buses). Jodhpur takes 4½ hours and costs Rs 24 but you can also travel direct between Pushkar and Jodhpur. There are also some buses to Abu Road, Agra, Delhi and Ujjain.

Getting Around

Ajmer is compact enough to get around on foot and by trishaw. Buses to Pushkar go from outside the railway station.

PUSHKAR

Like Goa or Dharamsala, Pushkar is one of those travellers' centres where people go for a little R&R from the hardships of life on the Indian road. It's a delightful little village, only 11 km from Ajmer, but separated from it by Nag Pahar, the 'Snake Mountain', and right on the edge of the desert.

The town clings to the side of the beautiful Pushkar Lake with many bathing ghats, for Pushkar is also an important pilgrimage centre for Hindus. It's a really nice, laid back place, but in October-November each year it comes alive with the huge Pushkar Cattle Fair.

Cattle Fair

At the full moon of Kartik Poornima each year up to 200,000 people flock to Pushkar, bringing with them 50,000 cattle for several days of pilgrimage, horse dealing, camel racing and colourful festivities. The Rajasthan Tourist Office has promoted it as an international attraction by adding Rajasthan dance programmes and other cultural events, and putting up a huge tent city for foreign visitors. It's one of India's biggest and most colourful festivals. The fair will take place from 4 to 8 November 1984. It generally takes place in early November each year.

Temples

Pushkar is packed with temples, although many were destroyed by Aurangzeb. The most famous is that of Brahma, which is said to be the only temple to Brahma in India. It's marked by a red spire and over the entrance gateway is the *hans* or goose symbol of Brahma, who is said to have personally chosen Pushkar as its site. The Rangji temple is also important.

Places to Stay & Eat

The *Sarovar Tourist Bungalow* (tel 40) is on the opposite side of the lake from the Brahma Temple. It's an exotic looking old palace once owned by the Maharaja of Jaipur. Built around a courtyard there are five very pleasant de-luxe rooms overlooking the lake for Rs 30/40 (single/

double), other rooms are Rs 25/30, dorm beds are Rs 8, or you can camp for Rs 3. A catch – the Tourist Bungalow is full all the time, you just have to hang around in Pushkar until a room comes vacant. A new 20-room extension, due in early-84, may help to meet demand.

There are plenty of small hotels and guest houses around town like the *Krishna Hotel* for Rs 15 a double – a friendly little place with a restaurant downstairs. Next door to the Tourist Bungalow the *Hotel Pushkar* has doubles for Rs 20 and dorm beds at Rs 5, or you can sleep on the roof for Rs 4. It has a lovely courtyard and rooms overlook the lake but mosquito coils are a must.

The *Gopal Rest House* is Rs 10 for a double with common bathroom, it's a nice family-run place up a side street off the bazaar. There are lots of little places around for less than Rs 10, if you wander around looking lost a kid, looking for a commission from some lodge or other, will grab you!

During the Cattle Fair, which attracts several thousand foreign visitors, the tourist office tent city costs Rs 150 per day, including food or Rs 35 in a dormitory tent. Prices everywhere skyrocket at this time of year.

Places to Eat

There are also plenty of small food stalls. The *Sun Set Cafe* by the Tourist Bungalow, right by the water, is popular. This is also a good place to go swimming and the sunset views over the lake are spectacular. *Sri Venktesh* at the start of the main street is a friendly place with excellent and cheap food. Across the road the chai shop does local cheese with garlic and herbs. 'Take care with the bhang lassi' reported one traveller, 'it will blow your head off'. *The Fruit Juice Bar* in the main street has great fruit juices.

Getting There

Buses run frequently from Ajmer, outside the railway station, for Rs 2.25. They also go, less frequently, from the bus stand. It's quite a spectacular climb up and over the hills, but the bus is likely to be too crowded to offer much of a view. The private minibuses are like little old hot rods.

You can continue straight on from Pushkar to Jodhpur without having to backtrack to Ajmer. A direct bus costs Rs 21 or take a bus to Meta Road, the junction town, for Rs 8 and then a train to Jodhpur for Rs 6.50 or 9.50 in 2nd class. Meta Road is a friendly little place where foreigners are still a strange and unusual sight.

Things to Buy
Like any good, freak centre there are lots of travellers' clothes tailors in town. During the Cattle Fair there are many artisans selling locally-made jewellery and other items.

KISHANGARH
Noted for its school of painting which is still produced today, this small town is 27 km from Ajmer.

KOTA (population 240,000)
Kota was the capital of an independent state of the same name, which was integrated into Rajasthan after independence. Today Kota is the industrial centre of Rajasthan (mainly chemicals), due principally to the hydro-electric power plants on the Chambal River. There is also an atomic power plant near Kota.

Information & Orientation
The Tourist Office is at the Chambal Tourist Bungalow. Kota is strung out along the east bank of the Chambal River. The railway station is well to the north, the tourist bungalow and bus stand in the middle and the Chambal Garden, the Fort and the Kota Barrage to the south.

Fort
The Kota Fort has two museums, the government museum (open 10 am to 5 pm, daily except Friday) is only of mild interest, but the Rao Madho Singh Museum (open 11 am to 5 pm, daily except Friday) is superb. It is entered by a gateway topped by rampant elephants like the fort at Bundi. Inside, having paid your Rs 1 entry fee, you'll find exhibits of weapons, clothing and more fine murals

A   Ferry at Daman (Gu)
B   Unloading the fish at dawn, Sasoon Dock, Bombay (M)
C   Buddha statue in Ajanta Caves (M)

like those at nearby Bundi. Indeed until 1572 Kota was part of the state of Bundi.

Chambal Gardens

The gardens south of the fort at Amar Niwas, are popular for picnics, and have a pond well stocked with garwhal crocodiles. The pond also has some flamingoes, which appear remarkably unbothered by their companions. At Bhitariya Kund, upstream from the Chambal Gardens, there is a popular swimming spot in the suprisingly clear waters of the Chambal River.

The Kota Barrage acts as a control over the river's waters and feeds an irrigation canal system. It's also used to cross the river when the 'Irish' bridge from Bundi is flooded. A little upstream from Kota the Chambal runs through a spectacular gorge.

Jag Mandir

Near the tourist bungalow this large tank has a building on a small island in the centre. Beside the tourist bungalow, there is a curious collection of somewhat neglected, but imposingly large, royal tombs.

Close to Kota

There are a number of interesting sites around Kota. At Baroli, 40 km from Kota, on the way to Pratap Sagar, there is one of the oldest temple complexes in Rajasthan. Many sculptures from these 9th century temples are displayed in the Kota government museum. The Pratap Sagar Dam is the Chambal's second dam.

At Jhaira Patan, 60 km from Kota on the Jhalawar road, are the ruins of an old Surya or sun temple. Ramgarh, 64 km

from Kota on a jeepable road, has some notable temples. Only eight km out of Kota there's a bridge built by Colonel Tod, a notable British 'Political Agent' of the Raj days, and the author of the *Annals & Antiquities of Rajasthan.*

Places to Stay

The *Chambal Tourist Bungalow* (tel 6527) is conveniently close to the bus stand. There are singles/doubles at Rs 30/40, 45/60 and 75/100 with air-con. Plus dorm beds for Rs 8. Another pleasant tourist bungalow. There are a number of other hotels in Kota including the *Payal Hotel* (tel 5401) at Nayapura and the *Navrang Hotel* (tel 3294) at Civil Lines with rooms from Rs 25 to 120. There are also *Railway Retiring Rooms* at the station.

The *Brij Raj Bhawan Palace Hotel* (tel 3071) is mainly used by Kota's not too frequent tourist groups. The palace is not particularly special although lots of hunting pictures decorate the walls, including one of the local Maharaja hunting moose in Canada.

Getting There & Around

Kota is connected by buses to Bundi, Ajmer (Rs 20), Chittorgarh (Rs24, sic hours), Udaipur (Rs 30) and other centres in Rajasthan. The Chittorgarh and Udaipur buses only depart at very inconvenient times. If you're heading into Madhya Pradesh a through bus to Gwalior takes 10 to 12 hours. Kota is a junction town on the Bombay-Delhi broad gauge line.

Around town there are trishaws, autorickshaws, buses and tempos. The tempos run a regular service between the railway station, bus stand and main part of town.

A   Colva Beach, Goa
B   Rice fields near Pandua, Goa
C   A mini-sadhu in Pondicherry (TN)

BUNDI (population 35,000)

Bundi is a picturesque little town, well off the beaten tourist track, 142 km to the south-east of Ajmer and only 39 km west of Kota. The town is beautifully sited in a narrow valley, brooded over by the gloomy Taragarh Fort. The road into Bundi comes in along the other side of the valley so you have a good view over the town and across to the fort as you arrive.

A word of warning – Bundi is almost too unspoilt. So few tourists pass through that most things are kept under lock and key. If you want to see the famous palace murals you must either make enquiries beforehand to ensure the keys are there, or else be prepared to 'persuade' the chowkidar to let you into whatever is open.

Orientation

The bus station is at the Kota, eastern end of town. Since accommodation is limited you can best see Bundi by stopping, looking around and then continuing on rather than planning to stay overnight. Simply walk into the town and you'll see the Taragarh Fort and palace up the hill on your right. The town is surrounded by a walled fortification with four gateways.

Taragarh Fort

The Star Fort was built in 1372 and is reached by a steep road up the hillside to its enormous gateway, topped by rampant elephants. Inside the palace is the Chitrashala or picture gallery covered with in murals of hunting, historical and religious scenes painted in Bundi style. There's a fine view over Bundi from the fort ramparts. Directly below are the Ratan Daulat or horse stables.

Naval Sagar

Also visible from the fort is the square artificial lake of Naval Sagar. In the centre is a temple to Varuna, the Aryan god of water.

Other

Bundi's other attractions are all out of

town and difficult to reach without transport. The modern palace is at Phool Sagar, with its beautiful artifical tank and gardens several km out of town on the Ajmer side. Shikar Burj is a small hunting lodge and picnic spot near Bundi. Cenotaphs of Bundi's rulers are near here at Khshar Bagh. Another small palace, the Sukh Niwas, is located at the Jait Sagar tank.

Places to Stay

Bundi's accommodation is of the 'government-officials-only-tourists-not-welcome' variety. There's a *Circuit House* (Rs 20) and a much less luxurious *Dak Bungalow* (Rs 5) near the bus stand.

Getting There & Around

It takes about five hours by bus from Ajmer to Bundi and costs Rs 16. From Bundi it's only an hour or so to Kota and costs Rs 6. Buses also to Chittorgarh and Udaipur from Bundi. Around town, you've got a choice of walking or taking a tonga.

CHITTORGARH (population 30,000)

The hilltop fortress of Chittorgarh sums up the whole romantic, doomed ideal of Rajput chivalry. Three times in its long history Chittor was sacked by a stronger enemy, and on each occasion the end came in textbook Rajput fashion. The men donned the saffron wedding robes of martyrdom and rode out from the fort to certain death. Meanwhile the women built a huge funeral pyre and marched in to the flames in the form of ritual suicide known as *jauhar*.

Chittor's first defeat took place in 1303 when Ala-ud-din Khilji, the Pathan king of Delhi, besieged the fort in order to capture the beautiful Padmini who was married to Bhim Singh, uncle of the Rana. When defeat was inevitable the Rajput noblewomen, including Padmini, commited *jauhar* and Bhim Singh led the orange-clad noblemen out to their deaths.

In 1535 it was Bahadur Shah, the Sultan of Gujurat, who besieged the fort and once

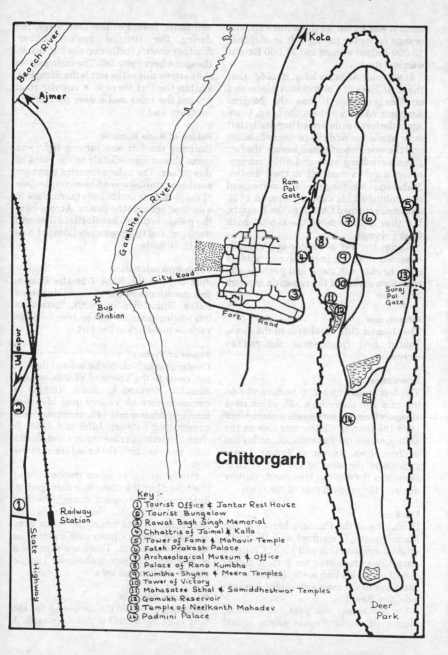

Chittorgarh

Key:-
1. Tourist Office & Jantar Rest House
2. Tourist Bungalow
3. Rawat Bagh Singh Memorial
4. Chhattris of Jaimal & Kalla
5. Tower of Fame & Mahavir Temple
6. Fateh Prakash Palace
7. Archaeological Museum & Office
8. Palace of Rana Kumbha
9. Kumbha-Shyam & Meera Temples
10. Tower of Victory
11. Mahasatee Sthal & Samiddheshwar Temples
12. Gomukh Reservoir
13. Temple of Neelkanth Mahadev
14. Padmini Palace

again it was *jauhar* for the women and the orange robes for the men. It is said that 13,000 Rajput women and 32,000 Rajput warriors died.

It was only 33 years later, in 1568, that the final 'Sack of Chittor' took place, and on this occasion it was the Moghul Emperor Akbar who took the town. Once again the fort was defended heroically, but once again the odds were overwhelming and the women performed *jauhar*, the fort gates were flung open and 8000 orange-robed warriors rode out to their deaths. Maharana Udai Singh fled to Udaipur and re-established his capital there. In 1616 Jehangir returned Chittor to the Rajputs, but they did not move the capital back from Udaipur.

Today the fort of Chittor is a virtually deserted ruin, but impressive reminders of its heyday still stand and perhaps you can catch a whiff of the romantic heroism in the air.

Information
The Tourist Office (tel 9) is in the *Janta Tourist Rest House* near the railway station.

Orientation
The fort stands on a 280-hectare site on top of a 180-metre high hill, which rises abruptly from the surrounding plain. Until 1568 the town of Chittor was also on the hilltop, within the fort walls, but today the modern town, known as Lower Town, sprawls to the west of the hill. A river separates it from the bus stand, railway line and the modern part of the town.

The Fort
Bhim, one of the Pandava heroes of the Mahabharata, is credited with the fort's original construction and all of Chittor's attractions are within the fort. A zigzag ascent over a km long leads through seven gateways to the main gate on the western side, the Ram Pol.

On the ascent you pass two *chattris*, memorials marking spots where Jaimal

and Kalla, heroes of the 1568 siege, fell during the struggle against Akbar. Another chattri, further up the hill, marks the spot where Patta fell. The main gate on the eastern side of the fort is the Suraj Pol. Within the fort there is a circular road around the ruins and a deer park at the southern end.

Palace of Rana Kumbha
Entering the fort and turning right you come almost immediately to the ruins of this palace. The palace contains elephant and horse stables and a Shiva temple. One of the jauhars is said to have taken place in a vaulted cellar in the palace. Across from the palace is the archaeological office and museum, and the treasury building or Nau Lakha Bhandar.

Fateh Prakash Palace
Just beyond the Rana Kumbha Palace, this much more modern palace (Maharana Fateh Singh died in 1930), houses an interesting museum with statues found in various buildings in the fort.

Tower of Victory
Continuing anti-clockwise around the fort you come to the Tower of Victory or Jaya Stambh. Erected by Rana Kumba to commemorate his victory over Mahmud Khilji of Malwa in 1440, the tower was constructed between 1458 and 1468. It rises 37 metres in nine storeys and, for Rs 0.50, you can climb the broad stairs to the top.

Hindu sculpures adorn the outside of the tower but the dome was damaged by lightning and repaired during the last century. Close to the tower is the Mahasati, an area where the *ranas* were cremated during Chittorgarh's period as the Mewar capital. There are many *sati* stones here. The Sammidheshwar Temple stands in the same area.

Gaumukh Reservoir
Walk down beyond the temple and at the very edge of the cliff is this deep tank. A

spring feeds the tank from a carved cow's mouth in the cliff side – from which the reservoir get its name. The opening here leads to the cave in which Padmini and her compatriots are supposed to have commited jauhar.

Padmini's Palace

Continuing south you come to Padmini's Palace, beside a large pool with a pavilion in its centre. Legends relate that Padmini stood in this pavilion and that Ala-ud-din was permitted to see her reflection in a mirror in the palace. This glimpse was the spark that convinced him to destroy Chittor in order to possess her.

The bronze gates in this pavilion were carried off by Akbar and can now be seen in the fort at Agra. Continuing round the circular road you pass the deer park, the Bhimlat Tank, the Suraj Pol Gate, the Neelkanth Mahadev Jain temple and reach the Tower of Fame.

Tower of Fame

Chittor's other famous tower, the Kirti Stambha or Tower of Fame, is older (probably built around the 12th century), and smaller (it stands 22 metres high), than the Tower of Victory. Built by a Jain merchant it is dedicated to Adinath, first Jain Tirthankar, and is decorated with nude figures of the various Tirthankars – thus indicating that it is a Digambara or 'sky clad' monument. A narrow stairway leads through the seven storeys to the top.

Other Buildings

Close to the Fateh Prakash Museum is the Meera Temple, built in the ornate Indo-Aryan style during the reign of Rana Kumbha, and associated with the mystic-poetess Meerabai. The larger temple in this same compound is the Kumbha Shyam Temple or Temple of Vriji. The Jain, but Hindu influenced, Singa Chowri Temple, is also nearby.

Across from Padmini's Palace is the Kalika Mata Temple, an 8th century Surya or Sun God temple, which was later converted to a temple to the Goddess Kali. At the northern tip of the fort is another gate, the Lokhota Bari, while at the southern end there is a small opening from which criminals and traitors were hurled into the abyss.

Tours

There is a daily Rs 12 tour which takes in all the main sites on the fort. The tour operates from the Tourist Office and Tourist Bungalow from 8 am to 1 pm daily and also from 3 pm to 6 pm during the cooler winter months.

Places to Stay

Accommodation possibilities in Chittor are limited. The *Panna Tourist Bungalow* (tel 273) is close to the railway station and the Udaipur road. It's a fairly modern building with singles at Rs 30 to 35 or doubles at Rs 35 to 45. Rooms with air-con are Rs 70/90 and there's also a dormitory with beds at Rs 8.

Closer to the railway station is the *Janta Tourist Rest House* (Avas Griha) (tel 9) where the Tourist Office is also located. Dormitory beds cost Rs 8 or there are spartan doubles at Rs 14 or Rs 20 with bath. Also close to the railway station is the very basic, and not so special, *Hotel Savaria* where the doubles cost Rs 20. There are other similar hotels and there are also *Railway Retiring Rooms* at Rs 12/22 for singles/doubles. The Tourist Bungalow has a dining hall.

Getting There & Around

Chittor is on the main bus and rail routes. It's 182 km from Ajmer or 115 km from Udaipur by road. Bus fare to Udaipur is Rs 15, it takes three hours. Bundi is 156 km away.

It's six km from the railway station to the fort and the fort itself sprawls quite a bit – so if you're not taking a tour you'll need transport. There are tongas or unmetered auto-rickhaws for hire or you can rent a bicycle.

AROUND CHITTORGARH
Menal

On the Bundi-Chittorgarh road, 48 km from Bundi, Menal is a complex of Shiva temples built during the Gupta period. Bijolia, 16 km from Menal, was once a group of a hundred temples but today only three are left standing. One has a huge figure of Ganesh. A diversion between Menal and Bijolia takes you to Mandalgarh the third fort of Mewar built by Rana Khumbha – the others are the great fort of Chittorgarh and the fort at Kumbalgarh.

Nagri

One of the oldest towns in Rajasthan, Nagri is 14 km north of Chittor. Hindu and Buddhist remains from the Mauryan to the Gupta period have been found here.

UDAIPUR (population 225,000)

The lake city of Udaipur is a cool oasis in the dry heart of Rajasthan. It's probably the most romantic city in a state where every city has some romantic or exotic tale to tell.

Udaipur has several palaces, two of which should not be missed. The Lake Palace, now converted into a luxury hotel, is simply delightful – if you can afford to stay there don't miss the opportunity. Even if you can't, it's worth the expense of the boat trip out there to have a look around. The huge City Palace on the lake side has been converted into a museum and is well worth a visit. Udaipur also has gardens, fountains, museums and temples and there are a number of interesting excursions around Udaipur.

The Maharana of Udaipur is the highest ranking of the Rajput rulers and head of the 'Solar' Rajput clan. Udaipur is also known as the 'City of Sunrise' and the Maharana's standard bears an image of the sun. Udaipur was founded in 1567 by Maharana Udai Singh, following the third sack of Chittor.

Information & Orientation

The old city, bounded by the remains of a city wall, sprawls away on the east side of Lake Pichola. The railway station and bus station are both just outside the city wall to the south-east. The Tourist Office (tel 3509) and the Tourist Bungalow are also outside the city walls, to the north-east and only a km or so from the bus stand. There are also tourist information counters at the railway station and airport. The GPO is directly north of the old city, behind the movie theatre at Chetak Circle but the poste restante is at the post office at the junction of Hospital Rd and the road north from Delhi Gate.

Pichola Lake

The beautiful Pichola Lake was enlarged by Maharana Udai Singh after he founded the city. He built a masonry dam known as the Badi Pol and the lake now stretches for four km in length by three km wide. The City Palace extends for a considerable distance along the east bank of the lake, while south of the palace a pleasant garden runs down to the lake side. North of the palace is very interesting to wander along the lake side where there are some beautiful scenes of bathing and dobhi ghats. Out in the lake there are two islands – Jagniwas and Jag Mandir.

Islands

Jagniwas is the Lake Palace island, about 1.5 hectares in size. The palace was built by Maharana Jagat Singh II in 1754 and covers the whole island. Today it has been converted into a luxury hotel with courtyards, fountains, gardens and a swimming pool. It's a quite delightful place and, even if you can only dream of staying there, it's worth the trip out to have a look around. A launch crosses to the island from Bhansi Ghat, just south of the Palace Museum. The trip out and back, including coffee, tea or a soft drink and biscuits in the hotel, costs Rs 20. You might even manage a swim in the hotel pool.

The other island palace, Jag Mandir, may also eventually become a hotel. It was commenced by Maharana Karan Singh, but takes its name from Maharana Jagat Singh (1628-1652) who made a number of additions to it. It is said that the Moghul Emperor Shah Jahan derived some of his ideas for the Taj Mahal from this palace, after he stayed here in 1623-24, while leading a revolt against his father, Jehangir. Looking across the lake from the southern end, with the city and its great palace rising up behind the island palaces, is a scene of rare beauty.

City Palace & Museum

The huge City Palace towers over the lake, it's the largest palace complex in Rajasthan. The palace is actually a conglomeration of buildings added by various Maharanas, but it manages to retain a surprising uniformity of design. It was originally commenced by Maharana Udai Singh, the city's founder. The palace is surmounted by balconies, towers and cupolas, and there are fine views over the lake and the city from the upper terraces.

The palace is entered from the northern end through the Bari Pol of 1600 and the triple Tripolia Gate of 1725 with its eight carved marble arches. It was once a custom for Maharanas to be weighed under the gate and their weight in gold or silver to be distributed to the populace.

The main part of the palace is now preserved as a museum with a large and varied, although somewhat run down, collection. The museum includes the Mor Chowk with its beautiful mosaics of peacocks, the favourite Rajasthani bird. The Manak or Ruby Mahal has glass and porcelain figures. Krishna Vilas has a remarkable collection of miniatures. In the Bari Mahal there is a fine central garden. More paintings can be seen in the Zanana Mahal. The Moti Mahal has beautiful mirror work, the Chini Mahal is covered in ornamented tiles. Other exhibits even include the princely Rolls-Royces.

The City Palace Museum is entered through the Ganesh Deori to the Rai Angam or Royal Courtyard. The museum is open from 9.30 am to 4.30 pm but closed on Fridays. Entry is Rs 3 plus Rs 3 for a camera. There's also a government museum (entry Rs 0.60) within the palace complex. Exhibits here include a stuffed kangaroo and Siamese-twin deers.

Jagdish Temple

Only 150 metres north of the entrance to the City Palace, this fine Indo-Aryan temple was built by Maharana Jagat Singh in 1651 and enshrines a black stone image of Vishnu as Jagannath, Lord of the Universe. A brass image of the Garuda is in a shrine in front of the temple, and the steps up to the temple are flanked by elephants.

Lake Fateh Sagar

North of Lake Pichola this lake was originally built in 1678 by Maharana Jai Singh, but heavy rains destroyed the dam and it was reconstructed by Maharana Fateh Singh. There is a pleasant lakeside drive that winds along the east bank of the lake and a number of hills and parks overlook it. Nehru Park is a popular garden island with a restaurant in the middle of the lake. You can get to it for Rs 1 by a boat service from the bottom of Moti Magri Hill.

Pratap Samak

Atop the Moti Magri or 'Pearl Hill' overlooking Fateh Sagar Lake is a statue of Rajput hero, Maharana Pratap, who frequently defied the Moghuls, astride his charger Chetak. A visitor commented that his growth in popularity since independence owes much to the fact that he was a Hindu and the Moghuls Moslem! He added that the regard paid to his horse contrasts strongly with the ill-treated tonga ponies below the hill. The path to the top goes through elegant gardens including a Japenese rock garden. The park is open from 9 am to 6 pm and admission is Rs 1.

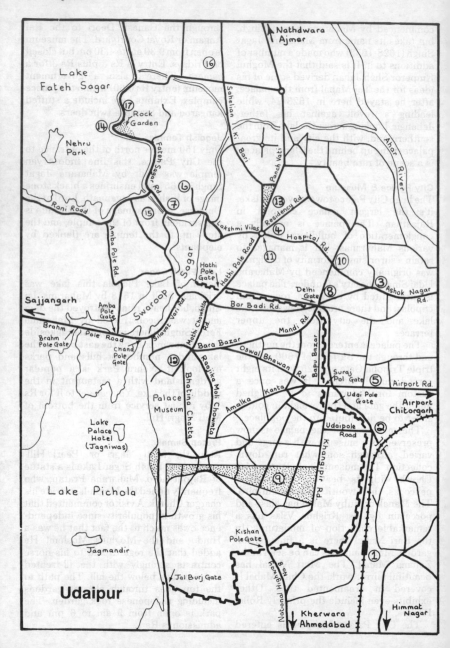

Udaipur

1	Railway Station	10	Poste Restaurant
2	Long Distance Bus Terminal	11	Chetak Circle
3	Tourist Office &	12	Jagdish Temple
	Tourist Bungalow	13	Lok Kala Mandal Museum
4	G.P.O.		(Folk Museum)
5	Keerti Hotel	14	Lake boat moorings
6	Lake View Hotel	15	Hotel Hill Top
7	State Hotel	16	Saheliyon ki Bari
8	Indian Airlines	17	Bhul Restaurant
9	Sajjan Niwas Garden		

Bhartiya Lok Kala Museum

This small museum and foundation for the preservation of folk arts has an interesting collection including dresses, dolls, masks, musical instruments, paintings and, the high point of the exibits, puppets. There are regular puppet shows in the museum. Opening hours are 9 am to 6 pm and admission is Rs 1.

Saheliyon ki Bari

In the north of the city, the 'Garden of the Maids of Honour' is a small ornamental garden with fountains, kiosks, marble elephants and a delighful lotus pool. It's open 9 am to 6 pm, entry is Rs 0.50; Rs 2 to have the fountains turned on.

Ahar Museum

East of Udaipur there are the remains of an ancient city with a small museum and the cenotaphs of the Maharanas of Mewar.

Other

Patel or Sukhadia Circle is north of the city – in the centre is a huge fountain, illuminated at night. Sajjan Niwas Gardens have pleasant lawns, a zoo and a children's train ride. Admission is free, a toy train ride costs Rs 1. Basically, however, the area is a guava and mango orchard! Beside it is the Rose Garden or Gulab Bagh. Don't confuse the Nehru Park opposite Bapu Bazaar with the island park of the same name in Lake Fateh Sagar. The city park has some strange topiary work, a giant cement teapot, and children's slides incorporating an elephant and a camel.

Tours

There's a daily tour, starting from the Tourist Bungalow, from 8.30 am to 1.30 pm each day. It costs Rs 15 and takes in all the main city sights. A Rs 35 afternoon tour from 2 to 7 pm goes out to Eklingi, Haldinghati and Nathdwara.

Places to Stay – Bottom End

The *Kajri Tourist Bungalow* (tel 3509) is conveniently situated, but it's not one of the better tourist bungalows in Rajasthan. The Tourist Office is also here, at the traffic circle on Ashoka Rd, and there is a restaurant. Singles/doubles start from Rs 30/40 without bath, 40/50 with bath, Rs 60/76 air-cooled or Rs 80/100 air-con. There is also a Rs 8 dormitory.

The *Keerti Hotel* (tel 3639) on Sarsvati Marg is very popular with travellers. There are rooms at all sorts of prices from Rs 15 for the most basic up to de-luxe rooms at Rs 40 or Rs 75 with air-con. There is also a Rs 6 dormitory. Recently, however, we have had a number of comments that the Keerti Hotel is not as clean and well run as it might be, although another letter warned that it should not be confused with the nearby Keerti Tourist Hotel, so named to cash in on the Keerti's popularity.

Behind the Keerti on College Rd, the *Ghunghnu Guest House* has been recommended by a traveller. 'Good rooms from Rs 30 or with attached bathroom at Rs 55, plus a pleasant garden and friendly staff'.

Near the bus stand there is a string of hotels, all with low prices and most of them offering reasonable accommodation. *Apsara Hotel* (tel 3400), *Manta Hotel* (tel 3927), *Sonika Hotel* (tel 5353) all on the City Station Rd, and *Alka Hotel* (tel 3611) on Shastri Circle all have rooms from about Rs 15. The *Hotel Raj* near the bus station is good value with doubles at just Rs 16. Udaipur also has *Railway Retiring Rooms* with rooms and a dormitory.

Round on Lake Palace Rd by the Sajjan Niwas Gardens and near to the zoo, the *Rang Niwas Hotel* (tel 3891) is a relaxed, pleasant place, built around a green courtyard. Singles cost from Rs 20 to 50, doubles from Rs 40 to 80. It's 'clean, management is friendly and helpful but food is slightly expensive'. In a calm and peaceful area, overlooking the Rose Garden and close to the lake, is the *Hotel Ratnadeep* with rooms from Rs 20 to 75.

Finally there's one interesting place situated just outside Udaipur. The *Pratap Country Inn* is operated by the same people as the Keerti, so go there first and they'll arrange transport out there for you. It's at Titadha village, about six km out of the city. City buses run there every hour for about a rupee. They have tents and rooms at prices from as low as Rs 15 to as high as Rs 100, as well as a Rs 6 dormitory. There's a swimming pool, free horse riding, camels, slightly expensive food, beautiful surroundings and a very laid back atmosphere. Since the first edition of this book we've had a number of complaints indicating that it's not always a great place to stay – 'no water in the pool and no horses' was one comment, 'run down' and 'a positive freeway of mice scampering back and forth' were others. Then just recently we've had a whole series of letters about it, some loudly proclaiming how good it is, others complaining about it equally loudly.

Those in favour run about two to one against those not in favour but it's obviously a place you love or hate!

Places to Stay – Top End

Udaipur's top hotel is one of the most delightful in India. It's the luxurious *Lake Palace Hotel* (tel 3241-45), in the middle of Pichola Lake. Singles/doubles are Rs 350/450, and it's the very image of what a Maharaja's palace should be like, with the additional touch that it occupies its own little island. Even if you can't stay here it's worth taking the boat trip out to see how the other half lives. The restaurant is quite good but reasonably expensive.

The *Shikarbadi Hotel* (tel 3200) is about three km out of town on the Ahmedabad Rd and has singles/doubles at Rs 325/450. It's a small but pleasant hotel set in beautiful grounds with swimming pool, lawns and a small lake. There's also a deer park and a stud farm – horse and elephant rides are available. The food here is really excellent Between Pichola and Fateh Sagar Lakes there are two upper notch hotels side by side. The ITDC operated *Lamix Vilas Palace Hotel* (tel 4411) has rooms at Rs 300/375 with air-con, Rs 125/175 without. Right beside it is the *Hotel Anand Bhavan* (Anand Bhavan, tel 3257) with air-con rooms at Rs 125/165 – big rooms with big bathtubs!

A number of hotels span the top to bottom bracket. *Hotel Chandralok* on Saheli Marg has singles/doubles at Rs 70/120 or Rs 120/175 with air-con. *Lake End Hotel* (tel 3841) is by Fateh Sagar Lake and has rooms at Rs 100/125 with air-con, Rs 80/100 without. *Hotel Hill Top* (tel 3708) also overlooks Fateh Sagar from 5 Amba Mata Marg. Rooms cost from Rs 60/80 and at that price it's excellent value with good food and service and fine views over the lake. Other rooms cost up to Rs 100/150 or Rs 175/200 with air-con.

Places to Eat

Udaipur is not over-endowed with good places to eat, although you can get good

Chinese food here. The *Tourist Bungalow* has a restaurant with the usual menu and variable results – sometimes the food is surprisingly good, sometimes it is not. There are a number of places by Chetak Circle including a so-so (bad in fact reported one traveller) *Kwality*, the *Chetak Restaurant* and *Berry's Restaurant*. The vegetarian *Green Cafe*, next to Berry's is good.

A number of vegetarian places around Suraj Pol include the *Jagdish Hindu Lodge* and the *Krishna Gujrati Lodge*. The *Parkview Restaurant*, on a road parallel with Bapu Bazaar but outside the walls, is 'a good place to eat, on a par with the LMB in Jaipur'. *Patel's Soda Factory* near the Suraj Pol gate is a clean and friendly spot for a cold drink – they've even got an autographed picture of Roger Moore having a drink there during the filming of the James Bond 007 epic *Octopussy* in Udaipur in late '82.

Opposite the Nehru Park and close to the Bank of Baroda is the *Parkview*, quite a good restaurant. The rooftop *Bheel* restaurant has Indian, Chinese and western food as well as fine views over Lake Fateh Sagar. It's above the bay, just beyond the lake boat moorings

Getting There

Air There are two daily flights from Delhi to Udaipur and on to Bombay, and vice versa. One goes Delhi-Jaipur-Jodhpur-Udaipur, then direct to Bombay. The other goes Delhi-Udaipur direct then continues to Bombay via Aurangabad. Air fares are Delhi Rs 417, Jaipur Rs 247, Jodhpur Rs 182, Aurangabad Rs 455 and Bombay Rs 503. Dabok Airport is 25 km out of the city, the Indian Airlines office (tel 3952) is at Delhi Gate.

Rail The daily Chetak Express between Delhi and Udaipur takes nearly 21 hours. Fares are Rs 198 in 1st class, Rs 50 in 2nd. The train goes via Jaipur and Ajmer. The daily express between Udaipur and Ahmedabad takes nine to 10 hours.

Bus There are frequent buses from Udaipur to other regional centres such as Ahemedabad (about six times daily), Mt Abu (twice), Ajmer (once), Jodhpur (once), Bundi-Kota (three times), Jaipur (seven buses daily), Chittorgarh (approximately hourly). The three-hour trip to Chittor costs Rs 12. Jodhpur is a gruelling 10 hours away, the trip costs Rs 38. If you're going to Mt Abu note that some buses go all the way there, some stop at Abu Road (the railhead for Mt Abu). Fare to Abu Road is Rs 18.

Getting Around

There's a reasonably OK city bus service, taxis are unmetered, auto-rickshaws are metered, but the drivers won't use them. Udaipur is small enough and vehicle traffic slow enough to make getting around on a bicycle quite enjoyable. You can hire bicycles all over town (quite a few places just by the Tourist Bungalow) at a cost of around Rs 0.40 per hour, Rs 3 per day.

AROUND UDAIPUR
Eklingi (22 km)

This interesting little village with a number of ancient temples is only a short bus ride north of Udaipur. In the village itself there is a Shiva temple which was originally built in 734 AD, although its present form dates from the rule of Maharana Raimal, who ruled from 1473 to 1509. The walled complex includes an elaborately pillared hall under a large pyramidal roof. There is a four-faced Shiva image of black marble. The temple is only open rather odd hours – 4.45 to 7.30 am, 10.30 am to 1.30 pm, 5.30 to 7.30 pm.

At Nagada, about a km off the road and a km before Eklingi, there are three old temples. The Jain temple of Adbudji is fairly well ruined, but its architecture is interesting and this is a very old temple. Nearby is the Sas Bahu or 'Mother and Daughter-in-Law' group. It's quite a little complex with some very fine and intricate

Around Udaipur

architecture and carvings, including some erotic figures.

Getting There You can get out to these temples most conveniently by hiring a bicycle in Eklingi itself. There are buses from Udaipur to Eklingi every half hour to an hour and the cost is Rs 3. One visitor wrote that the buses weren't that frequent and they couldn't find a bicycle to hire, so the round trip ended up taking a whole day. There is a small Rs 10 guest house in the village.

Haldighati (40 km)
This is where Maharana Pratap valiantly defied the superior Moghul forces of Akbar in 1576. The site is a battle field and the only thing to see is the *chhatri* to

his horse, Chetak, a few km away. There's a *Tourist Bungalow* here – clean, with good food and in a lovely setting.

Nathdwara (48 km)
The important 18th century Vishnu temple of Sri Nathji stands here. It's a popular pilgrimage site but non-Hindus are not allowed inside. The black stone Vishnu image was brought here from Mathura in 1669 to protect it from Aurangzeb's destructive impulses. According to legend when an attempt was later made to move the image, the getaway vehicle, a wagon, sunk into the ground up to the axles – indicating that the image would prefer to stay where it was!

Kankroli & Rajsamand Lake (65 km)
At Kankroli, Dwarkadhish (an incarnation of Vishnu) is similar to Nathdwara and, like that temple, is open for extremely erratic hours. Near here there is a lake created by the dam constructed by Maharana Raj Singh in 1660. There are many ornamental arches and chhatris along the huge bund. Raj Singh tangled with Aurangzeb on a number of occasions.

Kumbhalgarh Fort (84 km)
This is the most important fort in the Mewar region after Chittorgarh, and was built by Maharana Kumbha in the 15th century. The seven great gates of the Badal Mahal lead to the Cloud Palace. The fort, with its many temples and palaces, was renovated in the last century.

Jagat (58 km)
The 10th century Ambika Mata Temple here is not as good as some tourist literature would indicate. It is not in very special condition.

Jaisamand Lake (48 km)
This is the second largest artificial lake in Asia and was built by Maharana Jai Singh in the 17th century. There are beautiful marble chhatris around the embankment,

each with an elephant in front. The summer palaces of Udaipur queens are also located here and nearby is a wildlife sanctuary.

Rikhabdeo (65 km)
The Jain temple to Adinath is on the Ahmedabad road. Major offerings are made every day in this architecturally elegant temple, parts of which date back to the 14th century.

Ranakpur (98 km)
One of the most important, and biggest, Jain temples in India the extremely beautiful Ranakpur complex is situated in the remote and peaceful Aravalli Valley. The main temple in the complex is the Chaumukha or 'Four-Faced' temple, dedicated to Adinath. This huge, beautifully crafted and well kept marble temple was built in 1439. It has 29 halls, supported by 1444 pillars, no two of which are alike. Within the complex there are two other Jain temples to Neminath and Parasnath and a little distance away, a Sun Temple. A km away from the main complex is the Amba Mata Temple.

The temple is open to non-Jains from noon to 5 pm.

Places to Stay Ranakpur has a *Tourist Bungalow* with a particularly good dormitory. There is also a dharamsala within the complex where you can stay for a donation. If you arrive at a meal time you can get a good thali in the dining hall just inside the main entrance to the complex on your left, again for a donation. Staying overnight at Ranakpur breaks up the long trip between Udaipur and Jodhpur.

Getting There Ranakpur is 39 km from Palna (or Falna) Junction on the Ajmer-Mt Abu rail and road routes. From Udaipur there are half a dozen buses a day to Ranakpur and you can continue on from here to Jodhpur or Mt Abu on the same day – but the trip to Ranakpur can be a real, time consuming bore. The Rs 8 trip

can take five to six hours, an average of well under 20 kph!

MT ABU (population 12,000)
Rajasthan's only hill station spreads out along a 1200-metre high plateau in the south of the state. It's a pleasant hot season retreat from the plains, but you won't find many western travellers here – visitors are predominantly Indians, including many honeymooners. Mt Abu is a popular hill station for Gujarat as well as Rajasthan and its pace is easy-going and relaxed. There is more than simply lower temperatures to attract visitors up here – Mt Abu has a number of important temples, particularly the superb Dilwara group of Jain Temples.

Information & Orientation
Mt Abu stretches along a plateau about 22 km long by six km wide. It is 27 km from Abu Road, the railway station for Mt Abu. The main part of the town extends along the road in from Abu Road, down to the Nakki Lake. Coming in by bus you pass first the Tourist Bungalow, up a hill to your right, then a string of hotels before you arrive at the bus stand, opposite which is the Tourist Office (tel 51). The office is open 8 to 11 am and 4 to 8 pm.

Continuing from here you pass more hotels and restaurants, the small market to your right, and eventually arrive at the lake front. The GPO is on Raj Bhavan Rd, opposite the Art Gallery and Museum.

Nakki Lake
Virtually in the centre of Mt Abu, the small lake takes its name from the legend that it was scooped out by a god, using only his nails or *nakk*. It's a short and easy stroll around the lake – look for the strange rock formations around it. Best known is Toad Rock which looks just like a toad about to hop into the lake. Others, like Nun Rock, Nandi Rock or Camel Rock, require rather more imagination to picture them. You can hire boats and row (or be rowed) out on the lake. The 14th

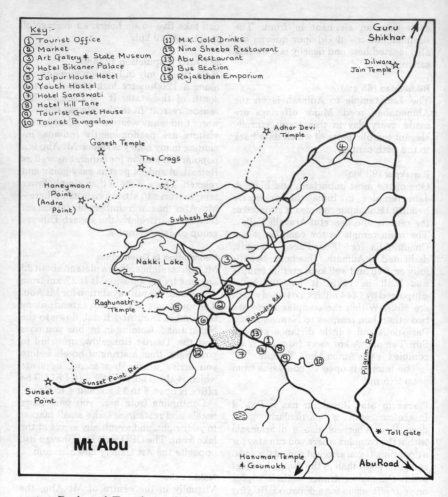

Key:-
1. Tourist Office
2. Market
3. Art Gallery & State Museum
4. Hotel Bikaner Palace
5. Jaipur House Hotel
6. Youth Hostel
7. Hotel Saraswati
8. Hotel Hill Tone
9. Tourist Guest House
10. Tourist Bungalow
11. M.K. Cold Drinks
12. Nina Sheeba Restaurant
13. Abu Restaurant
14. Bus Station
15. Rajasthan Emporium

Guru Shikhar

Dilwara Jain Temple

Adhar Devi Temple

Ganesh Temple

The Crags

Honeymoon Point (Andra Point)

Subhash Rd.

Nakki Lake

Raghunath Temple

Rajendra Rd.

Pilgrim Rd.

Sunset Point Rd.

Sunset Point

Mt Abu

Toll Gate

Hanuman Temple & Gaumukh

Abu Road

century Raghunath Temple stands beside the lake.

Viewpoints
There are various viewpoints around the town, best known of which is Sunset Point. Hordes stroll out here every evening to catch the setting sun and there are food stalls and all the usual entertainments. Other popular points include Honeymoon Point, which also offers a view of the

sunset, the Crags and Robert's Spur.

Museum & Art Gallery
The small museum is on Raj Bhavan Rd and is open from 9.30 am to 4.30 pm daily, except Fridays. Admission is free. There is also a Rajasthan Emporium further back towards the market.

Adhar Devi Temple
Three km out of the town, there are 200

steep steps to climb to this Durga temple in a natural cleft in the rock. You have to stoop down to get through the low entrance into the temple. Good views over Mt Abu from up here.

Dilwara Temples (5 km)

These Jain temples are Mt Abu's main attraction and amongst the finest examples of Jain architecture in India. The complex includes two temples where the art of carving marble has been carried to unsurpassed heights. The older of these temples is the Vimal Vasahi which is dedicated to the first Tirthankar, Adinath, and was built in 1031. The central shrine has an image of Adinath, while around the courtyard are 52 identical cells, each with a Buddha-like cross-legged image. The entrance to the courtyard is formed by 48 elegantly carved pillars. In front of the temple stands the 'House of Elephants' with figures of elephants marching in procession to the temple entrance.

The later Tejpal temple is dedicated to Neminath, the 22nd Tirthankar, and was built in 1230 by the brothers Tejpal and Vastupal. Like Vimal they were ministers in the government of the ruler of Gujarat. Although the Tejpal temple is important as an extremely old and complete example of a Jain temple, its most notable feature

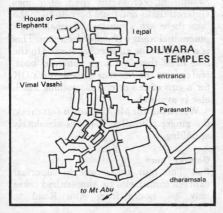

is the fantastic intricacy and delicacy of the marble carving. In places the carving is so fine that the marble becomes almost transparent. In particular, the lotus flower which hangs from the centre of the dome is an incredible piece of work. It's difficult to believe that this huge lace-like filigree actually started as a solid block of marble. The temple employs several full-time stone carvers to maintain and restore the work.

There are three other temples in the enclosure but they all pale beside the Tejpal and Vimal Vasahi. The complex is open from 12 noon to 6 pm and there is a Rs 5 camera change. Note that no leather at all is permitted in the complex – apart from removing shoes or sandals you must take off belts and even camera cases if they are leather. You can stroll out to Dilwara in less than an hour from the town, or take a taxi for about Rs 10.

Achalgarh (11 km)

The Shiva temple of Achaleshwar Mahandeva has a number of interesting features including a toe of Shiva, a brass Nandi, and, where the Shiva lingam would normally be, a deep hole said to extend all the way to the underworld. Outside, by the car park, is a tank beside which are three stone buffaloes and the figure of a king shooting them with a bow and arrows. A legend states that the tank was once filled with ghee but demons, in the form of buffaloes, came down and drank it each night – until the king shot them. A path leads up the hillside to a group of colourful Jain temples with fine views out over the plains. Entry is Rs 0.25.

Guru Shikhar (15 km)

At the end of the plateau is 1721-metre Guru Shikhar, the highest point in Rajasthan. There is now a road almost up to the summit. On the top there is the Atri Rishi Temple, and there are good views all around.

Gaumuckh Temple (8 km)

Down on the Abu Road side of Mt Abu a small stream flows from the mouth of a marble cow, giving the shrine its name. There is also a marble figure of the bull Nandi, Shiva's vehicle. The tank here, Agni Kund, is said to be the site for the sacrificial fire made by the sage Vasishta from which four of the great Rajput clans were born. An image of Vasishta is flanked by figures of Rama and Krishna.

Tours

There are daily tours from the bus stand costing Rs 15. They run from 8 am to 1 pm and 2 to 7 pm and visit the Dilwara Temples, Achalgarh, Guru Shikhar, Adhar Devi and other places. In the season they tend to be heavily booked so plan ahead.

Places to Stay

Back from the bus stand, and up a steepish path, the *Shikar Tourist Bungalow* (tel 69) is the biggest place in Mt Abu with about 100 rooms. Rooms vary widely in price and also from the high season to low season. Off-season singles/doubles start from Rs 25/40, in season they start at Rs 45/55. With air-con prices start from Rs 70. Dorm beds are Rs 12 in season. The Tourist Bungalow also has a bar and a rather poor restaurant.

Amongst the lower-priced places there is a pleasant *Tourist Guest House* (tel 160) at the foot of the driveway to the Tourist Bungalow. Built around a courtyard this clean, well run place has doubles at Rs 30 with bath and mosquito nets, Rs 20 without bath. Off-season rates are lower. *Saraswati Lodge* (tel 7) is a clean, bright place with similar prices to the Tourist Guest House.

Other similarly priced cheapies include the *Bharati Hotel* (tel 61) just before the market and the *Navjivan Hotel* (tel 53) and *Hotel Tourist* (tel 53 also) directly across the road from the Bharati. The Navjivan has rooms from Rs 45 to 100. Good vegetarian food at these three places too.

The *Youth Hostel* is also central and has dorm beds at Rs 8.

Mt Abu has a quite amazing number of hotels at all sorts of prices. More expensive places include the *Mount Hotel* (tel 55), which is a little inconveniently situated but very pleasant. Singles/ doubles cost Rs 140/180. The centrally located *Hotel Hill Tone* (tel 137) has singles/doubles at Rs 180/230 and an intriguing sign outside announcing that they have honeymoon suites: 'cave and bamboo type'!

Places to Eat

Mt Abu also has a wide selection of eating places although there are no real standouts. The *Tourist Bungalow* has the usual Tourist Bungalow menu in its restaurant and it becomes (as usual) fairly boring after a couple of meals. The Hotel Hill Tone has the flashier *Madhuban Restaurant* where the food is sometimes quite good – around Rs 40 for two. The *Nina Sheeba Restaurant*, on the Sunset Point road, has even better Chinese food and at slightly lower prices.

Good Gujarati thalis for Rs 7 are available at the *Tourist-Navjivan-Bharati Hotel* trio between the bus stand and the market. At the corner of the road down to the lake *MK Cold Drinks* has excellent ice cream and also does thalis. The *Bharti Restaurant*, across the road, also does Gujarati thalis and from here down to the lake there are a number of small snack places including a *Havmor Icecream*. This is a popular for an evening stroll. On the lake itself there's a large concrete 'boat' restaurant, the *Sarovar Cafe*, but it's OK for a cup of tea or coffee, nothing much else is available.

Watch out for Mt Abu's own soft drink, the ginger Rim Zim. It tastes absolutely appalling.

Getting There

Rail The four times weekly superfast express from Delhi to Ahmedabad takes only 3¼ hours from Abu Road to

Ahmedabad – a 187 km metre gauge journey. Fares are Rs 64 in 1st, Rs 16.50 in 2nd, plus a compulsory reservation fee.

Bus Abu Road, the railhead for Mt Abu, is a small place with the bus station right by the railway station. There are regular buses making the 27-km climb up to Mt Abu. It takes about an hour and costs Rs 4 or Rs 5 by 'express' bus. A taxi will cost Rs 70. There's a toll gate as you enter Mt Abu where bus passengers are charged Rs 2.50. People arriving by taxi or other forms of transport are charged Rs 3.50.

There's an extensive bus schedule from Mt Abu and to many destinations you will find it faster and more convenient to go straight there by bus rather than going down to Abu Road and waiting for a train. For example there are four buses daily to Ahmedabad, the trip takes about seven hours and costs Rs 24. To Udaipur it takes seven hours, depending on the route taken, and costs Rs 24 to 35. Coming to Mt Abu note that some buses go all the way there, some terminate at Abu Road.

Getting Around

There are buses from the bus stand to the various sites in Mt Abu, but it takes a little planning to get out and back without too much hanging around. Some buses go just to Dilwara (Rs 1.20) others out to Achalgarh (Rs 1.50), so it's a matter of deciding which to go to first, depending on the schedule. It takes about 40 minutes to Achalgarh and the last bus back is at 5 pm.

There are also plenty of taxis with posted fares to anywhere you care to mention. Mt Abu's unique form of transport is large 'baby prams' in which you can sit and be wheeled around! They're all seemingly operated by 'Abu Enterprises', but are mainly used by parents who dump their children in them.

Things to Buy

The Rajasthan Emporium is on Raj Bhavan Rd but there are also quite a few shops on the road down to the lake front. Jewellery shops have a good selection. Here, as in most of India, jewellery is usually sold by weight.

JODHPUR (population 400,000)

The largest city in Rajasthan after Jaipur, Jodhpur stands at the edge of the Thar Desert. The massive fort, topping a sheer rocky hill which rises right in the middle of the town, totally dominates the city. Jodhpur was founded in 1459 by Rao Jodha, a chief of the Rajput clan known as the Rathores. His descendants ruled not only Jodhpur, but also other Rajput princely states. The Rathore kingdom was once known as Marwar, the 'Land of Death'.

The old city of Jodhpur is surrounded by a wall 10 km long, which was built about a century after the city was founded. From the fort you can clearly see where the old city ends and the new begins. The old city is a fascinating jumble of winding streets of great interest to wander around. Eight gates lead out from the walled city. It's one of the more interesting cities in India and, yes, it was from here that those baggy/tight horse riding trousers, jodhpurs, took their name. Today you're more likely to see them actually worn in Saurashtra in Gujarat than here.

Orientation & Information

The Tourist Office, railway stations and bus stand are all outside the old city. High Court Rd runs from the Raika Bagh railway station, directly across from the bus stand, round by the Umaid Gardens, the Tourist Bungalow and Tourist Office, and round beside the city wall towards the main station and the GPO. Most trains from the east stop at the Raika Bagh station before the main station – quite handy if you want to stay at the Ghoomar Tourist Bungalow.

The GPO is right by the main station, the Tourist Office (tel 21900) is at the Tourist Bungalow. You can use the

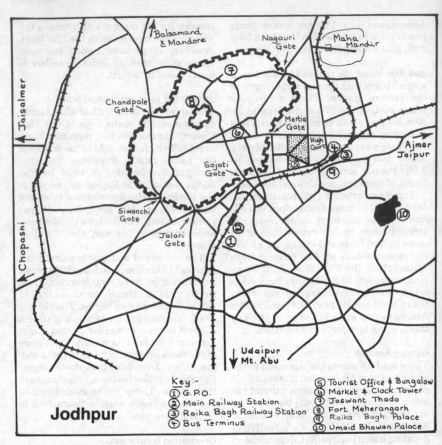

Jodhpur

Key:-
1. G.P.O.
2. Main Railway Station
3. Raika Bagh Railway Station
4. Bus Terminus
5. Tourist Office & Bungalow
6. Market & Clock Tower
7. Jaswant Thada
8. Fort Meherangarh
9. Raika Bagh Palace
10. Umaid Bhawan Palace

subterranean swimming pool at the Umaid Bhawan Palace Hotel (tel 22316) for Rs 15. Zinc water bottles are a good buy in Jodhpur; they're covered in felt which you can soak so the evaporation keeps the water cool.

Meherangarh Fort The 'Majestic Fort' is just that, sprawled across the 125-metre high hill this is the most impressive and formidable fort in fort-studded Rajasthan. A winding road leads up to the fort entrance from the city below. The first gate is still scarred by cannon balls –

indicating that this was a fort that earned its keep. The gates include the Jayapol, built by Maharaja Man Singh in 1806 following his victory over the armies of Jaipur and Bikaner, and the Fatehpol or Victory Gate, erected by Maharaja Ajit Singh in 1907 to commemorate his defeat of the Moghuls. The final gate is the Lahapol or Iron Gate beside which there are 15 handprints, the sati marks of widows of Maharaja Man Singh who threw themselves upon his funeral pyre in 1843.

Inside the fort, which is still run by the

Maharaja of Jodhpur, there are a whole series of courtyards and palaces. The palace apartments have evocative names like the Moti Mahal or Pearl Palace, the Sukh Mahal or Pleasure Palace, the Phool Mahal or Flower Palace. They house a fantastic collection of the trappings of Indian royalty. There's an amazing collection of elephant howdahs, used when the Maharajas rode on elephant back in glittering processions through their capitals. Miniature paintings of a variety of schools hang on the walls. There's a superb collection of folk music instruments and the inevitable Rajput armoury, palanquins, furniture and costumes. One room even has a collection, of often humorous, baby cradles! The palace apartments are beautifully decorated and painted and have delicately carved, red sandstone, latticework windows.

At the southern end of the fort there's a collection of old cannons on the ramparts, looking out over the sheer drop down to the old town below. There's no guard rail and you can clearly hear voices and shouts carrying up from the houses far below you – it's magical. Note the many blue houses – painted that colour to distinguish them as belonging to Brahmins. The Chamunda Temple, to Durgra, stands at this end of the fort.

The fort is open from 9 am to 5 pm and admission is Rs 10 for the complete museum including a guide to open the locked doors. 'All the best things are in the locked rooms' wrote one visitor. There's an additional Rs 10 charge to use a camera – Rs 15 for a flash and Rs 20 for a movie camera. The guided tour ends with an audio-visual presentation of the history of the fort and its rulers. A couple of musicians will usually stand just inside the entrance and strike up a merry Rajasthani number to herald your arrival – it helps to set the mood for a visit to this superb fort.

Jaswant Thanda

Part way down from the fort, just off the fort road, is this white marble memorial to Maharaja Jaswant Singh II. The cenotaph was built in 1899, and the royal crematorium and three later cenotaphs are near to it. Inside there is a collection of portraits of the various Jodhpur rulers.

A traveller wrote 'About 200 metres down that winding road from the fort there's an interesting old chap who has set up a tea and water stall. He speaks fluent English and is full of local knowledge and wisdom!'

Clock Tower & Markets

The clock tower is a popular landmark in the old city. The colourful Sardar Market is close to the tower and narrow alleys lead from here to bazaars for textiles, silver and handcrafts. See the note in Places to Eat about Makhania Lassi in the cafe in the gateway to the market.

Umaid Gardens & Museums

The Tourist Bungalow is on the edge of this garden on High Court Rd. The Government Museum is within the gardens and has a unique and amusing collection. Scarcely a thing has been added (or maintained) since the British departed, consequently it's a frozen-in-time Raj era display. There are lots of badly moth-eaten stuffed animals including two glass cases of birds, each with a thorn bush and a number of almost featherless desert birds, some of which have toppled off their perches and now lie stiffly on the ground with their feet pointing at the ceiling! The military section includes cumbersome wooden biplane models and an extraordinary brass battleship. The museum is open from 10 am to 5 pm and admission is Rs 0.30.

Umaid Bhawan Palace

Maharaja Unmaid Singh, who died in 1947, lived at first in the Raika Bagh Palace, but in 1928 commenced construction of the Umaid Bhawan Palace on the outskirts of town. Constructed of marble and red sandstone this immense palace was designed by the president of the British Royal Institute of Architects and not finally completed until 1943. It is also known as the Chhittar Palace because of the local Chhittar sandstone used.

Probably the most surprising thing about this grandiose palace is that it was built so near to independence. Surely the Maharaja, or even more to the point his British advisers, could see that the upheavals of independence were just around the corner and that Maharajas, princely states and the grand extravagances would all soon be a thing of the past? Some say it was built as a sort of royal job-creation programme!

Today most of the palace has been turned into a hotel, but it's a gloomy, sepulchral place – devoid of that zany, whimsical charm that the Udaipur and Jaipur palace have in such abundance. Even the basement swimming pool is a dark clinical sort of place. The Maharaja still has quite a circle of fiercely protective

servants and retainers who not only closely guard the Maharaja but also his Mercedes – number plate 'Rajasthan 1'. The palace is open 9 am to 5 pm and admission is Rs 2.

Tours

There are daily tours starting from the Tourist Bungalow. Cost is Rs 15 and they cover the Umaid Bhawan Palace, Meherangarh Fort, Jaswant Thada, Mandore Gardens and the museum.

Places to Stay – Bottom End

The *Ghoomar Tourist Bungalow* (tel 21900) is on High Court Rd by the Umaid Gardens. Singles/doubles cost from Rs 40/50 or Rs 70/90 with air-con, de-luxe doubles are Rs 75, dorm beds are Rs 10. The rooms in the new wing are quite good. The Tourist Office and the Indian Airlines desk are located here. There are very clean *Railway Retiring Rooms* (tel 22741) with singles/doubles at Rs 10/20 near the main railway station.

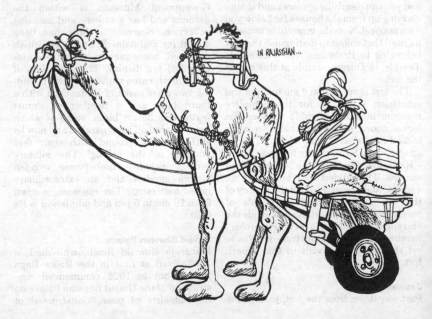

IN RAJASTHAN...

There is a string of cheaper hotels near the railway station with rooms in the Rs 15 to 25 bracket. Best of them is probably the *Adarsh Niwas Hotel* (tel 23936) which also has a very good restaurant. Others include the *Agarwal Lodge* (tel 20837), the *Charli Bikaner* (tel 23985), the *Alpana Hotel* (tel 24504), *Raghunath Das Dharamshala* (tel 20386) and the *Shanti Bhawan Lodge* (tel 21689). The *Arun Hotel* (tel 20238) is at Sojati Gate and is 'good, clean and handy' with doubles at Rs 20.

Places to Stay – Top End

The *Umaid Bhawan Palace Hotel* (tel 22316) is Jodhpur's premier hotel. It's fairly small, just 58 rooms, but has all the palatial luxuries from a theatre to squash and tennis courts, an underground swimming pool and a bar. Singles/doubles cost Rs 350/450. There are fine views across to the fort from the terrace.

The *Ajit Bhawan Palace* (tel 20409) on the Airport Rd is used for groups but also welcomes independent travellers. They have 20 new, separate cottages (they call them pavilions), good value at Rs 150/250, and the food here is good too. It's rather like being a guest in a stately home, the Maharaja is even likely to check that you're comfortable.

Hotel Ratanada International (tel 25911) is a new place on Residency Rd. Singles/doubles, all air-con, are Rs 275/375 in this well run new hotel.

Places to Eat

Very good non-vegetarian food at the *Kalinga Restaurant* in the Adarsh Niwas Hotel near the railway station. *Pankaj* at Jalori Gate has good vegetarian food or you could try the *Coffee House* at Sojati Gate which has excellent and cheap masala dosas, but very little else. There is also a restaurant at the *Tourist Bungalow* and the *Renuka Restaurant*, opposite the Kalinga behind the trees. Overall Jodhpur is no gastronomic paradise.

While you're in Jodhpur try Makhania Lassi, a delicious thick cream variety of that ultra-refreshing drink. You can find a terrific example at *Agra Sweet Home*, right opposite the Sojati Gate, but also at the place in the gateway to the central market. It's so popular here that they claim to sell 1500 glasses a day, at Rs 2.50 each! Other popular specialties in Jodhpur include the baclava like desert known as *mawa kachori* and *mawa ladoo*, another popular desert.

In *Dimples Snack Bar*, round the corner from the Agra Sweet Home, 'try the Bombay Special Butter Pav Bihaji' (whatever that may be) wrote a traveller.

Getting There

Air Indian Airlines have two flights a day in each direction through Jodhpur. One goes Delhi-Jaipur-Jodhpur-Ahmedabad-Bombay while the other goes Delhi-Jaipur-Jodhpur-Udaipur-Bombay. Fares are Delhi Rs 398, Jaipur Rs 239, Udaipur Rs 182, Ahmedabad Rs 323 and Bombay Rs 617. The Indian Airlines office (tel 20909) is in the Tourist Bungalow.

Rail There are now superfast expresses between Delhi and Jodhpur which take about 10 hours. On other trains from Delhi it takes about 16 hours to Jodhpur and costs Rs 174 in 1st class, Rs 45 in 2nd class. Not many people would make that trip straight through. The direct trains go via Bikaner, alternatively you can change at Jaipur for a direct train from there. Jaipur-Jodhpur takes 10 or 11 hours at a cost of Rs 94 in 1st class, Rs 24 in 2nd. There are overnight and day trains to Jaisalmer – see the relevant sections for details.

Bus There are bus services operated by Rajasthan State Roadways from the bus stand at Raika Bagh to other major centres in Rajasthan. Some road distances from Jodhpur include Barmer 220 km, Bikaner 240 km, Jaipur 340 km, Jaisalmer 290 km, Mt Abu 264 km, Ranakpur 175 km, Udaipur 275 km. There are daily buses to Jaisalmer, the trip takes seven to

10 hours and costs Rs 32. Udaipur takes
10 hours and costs Rs 38, Ajmer takes 4½
hours and costs Rs 24. Jodhpur-Mt Abu
takes about 10 hours. The overnight bus
from Jaipur is a hard, uncomfortable
trip.

Getting Around

Jodhpur has unmetered taxis and metered
(but not very metered) auto-rickshaws as
well as tongas. You'd have difficulty
getting through the narrow lanes of the old
city in anything wider than an auto-
rickshaw. There are regular city buses to
places around Jodhpur like Mandore,
Balsamand and Mahamandir. The airport
is 24 km out of the city, a long way. The bus
costs Rs 20, taxis may start at Rs 75 but
can be knocked down to less than Rs 50.

Things to Buy

The ususal Rajasthani handicrafts are
available in Jodhpur but this is a good
place to look for antiques. There are many
little shops in the convoluted streets of the
old town but Abani Handicrafts, next door
to the Tourist Bungalow, has a large and
varied collection. They also have a branch
in the Palace Hotel.

AROUND JODHPUR

Mahamandir (2 km)

The 'Great Temple' is a small walled town
north-east of the city. It is built around a
100-pillared Shiva temple but is not of
great interest.

Balsamand Lake & Palace (7 km)

Originally constructed in 1159 this lake
and garden is to the north of the city. A
palace, built in 1936, stands by the lake
side and this is a popular excursion spot.
The gardens are open 8 am to 6 pm and
entry is Rs 1. The larger Pratap Sagar
Lake and Kailana Lake (where there is
also a garden), west of Jodhpur, provide
the city's water supply.

Mandore (9 km)

Further north, this was the capital of

Marwar prior to the foundation of
Jodhpur. Today it is a popular local
attraction due to its extensive gardens
with high rock terraces. The gardens also
contain the cenotaphs of Jodhpur rulers,
including Maharaja Jaswant Singh and,
largest and finest of all, the soaring
temple-shaped memorial to Maharaja Ajit
Singh.

The 'Hall of Heroes' contains 15 figures
carved out of a rock wall. The brightly
painted figures represent Hindu deities or
local heroes on horseback. The Shrine of
33 Crore (330 million) Gods has painted
figures of gods, spirits and divinities.
There are regular buses to Mandore from
Jodhpur.

Other

Sardar Samand Lake is a wildlife centre
55 km from Jodhpur. The route passes
through a number of colourful villages and
there is a summer palace of the Maharaja
here – accommodation can be arranged.
Dhawa or Doli is another wildlife
sanctuary with many antelopes, 45 km
from Jodhpur on the road to Barmer.

Osian is an ancient Thar Desert town 58
km out. The ruins of 16 Jain and
Brahmanical temples from the 8th to 11th
centuries stand here and the town is
inhabited by hundreds of peacocks. The
architecturally interesting temples are in
a beautiful area of small hills and sand
dunes. At Soyala, 74 km out on the Nagaur
road, there is an interesting Shiva temple.
Nagaur is 135 km from Jodhpur and has
an historic fort and palace – it's an
interesting site in an otherwise dull
stretch of desert.

JAISALMER (population 20,000)

Jaisalmer is one of Rajasthan's, indeed
India's, most exotic and unususal towns.
It's so remote that few people have even
heard of it. Yet travellers who make the
effort to get there are never disappointed
in this mediaeval-looking place, something
right out of tales of the Arabian Nights. A
'living museum' and the 'golden city' are

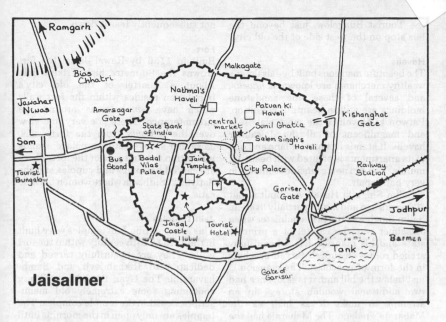

Jaisalmer

just two descriptions which have been applied to the desert outpost.

Centuries ago its strategic position on the camel train routes between India and central Asia brought great wealth to Jaisalmer. The merchants and townspeople built magnificent houses and mansions – all exquisitely carved from a golden yellow sandstone. From the humblest shop to the palace and the temples in the fort the whole town glows in the same golden colour. Even today new buildings must be designed to blend in with the old.

The rise of shipping trade and the port of Bombay pushed Jaisalmer into decline. Partition, and the cutting off of the trade routes through to Pakistan, after WW II, seemingly sealed the town's fate, and water shortages could have pronounced the death sentence. But the '65 and '71 Indo-Pakistan wars revealed Jaisalmer's strategic importance, paved roads and a railway linked it to the rest of Rajasthan, even electricity finally reached out to the

remote town. Today military bases are the pillar of the town's economy but increasing numbers of travellers are waking up to the fascination of this exotic place.

Orientation & Information

Finding your way around Jaisalmer is not really necessary – it's a place you simply wander around and get lost in. Within the old city walls the streets are a tangled maze but it's small enough not to matter. You simply head off in what seems like the right direction and eventually you'll get there. The old city is completely surrounded by a lofty fort wall and, within this, a hill rises with more fortified walls. The Jain temples and the old palace are on this hilltop.

The central market area is directly below the hill while the bank, the new palace and several other shops and offices are near the Amar Sagar Gate to the west. Just outside the gate is the bus stand while the railway station is outside the city walls at the other side. The Tourist Office is at the Tourist Bungalow, just beyond the bus stop on the west side of the old city.

Havelis

The beautiful mansions built by Jaisalmer's wealthy merchants are known as *havelis*, and several of these fine sandstone buildings are still in beautiful condition. Patwon ki Haveli is the most elaborate and magnificent of all the Jaisalmer havelis. It stands in a narrow lane and one of its apartments is painted with beautiful murals. You can now go inside it but it is in very bad repair.

Salim Singh ki Haveli was built about 300 years ago and is still partially lived in. Salim Singh was the prime minister when Jaisalmer was the capital of a princely state and his mansion has a beautifully arched roof with superb carved brackets in the form of peacocks. The mansion is just below the hill and, it is said, once had two additional wooden storeys in an attempt to make it as high as the Maharaja's palace. The Maharaja had the upper storeys torn down!

The late 19th century Nathmal ki Haveli was also a prime minister's house. The left and right wings of the building were carved by brothers and are very similar, but not identical. Yellow sandstone elephants guard the building and the front door alone is a work of art.

Gadi Sagar Tank

This tank, south of the city walls, was once the water supply of the city and there are many small temples and shrines around the tank. In winter a wide variety of water birds flock here. The beautiful arched gateway across the road down to the tank is said to have been built by a famous prostitute. When she offered to pay to have this gateway constructed the Maharaja refused permission since he would have to pass under it on going down to the tank and that, he felt, would be unseemly. While he was away she built the gate anyway – and added a Krishna temple on the top of it so the king could

not subsequently tear it down.

Fort

Built in 1156 by Rawal Jaisal the fort crowns the 80-metre high Trikuta hill. About a quarter of the old city's population resides within the fort walls which have 99 bastions around the circumference. There is a very fine view over the old city from the fort walls. Jaisalmer's seven-storey palace stands just within the first gate of the fort. There are carved balconies and cupolas and the Satiyon ki Sidhiyan where women became satis.

Jain Temples

This group of fine Jain temples were built in the 12th to 15th century within the fort walls. They are beautifully carved and dedicated to Rikhabdevji and Sambhavanthji. The Gyan Bhandar, a library containing some extremely old manuscripts, is within the temple complex. The temples are only open in the morning until 12 noon but the library is only open from 10 to 11 am. There is also a Shiva and a Ganesh temple within the fort.

Outside the Walls

Outside the town walls the Jawahar Niwas, opposite the Tourist Bungalow, is a splendid guest house for private guests of the Maharaja. It even features a grand billiard room, alas unused! At the road intersection is a war memorial from the '71 Indo-Pak conflict. Almost every military man involved, or at least those of officer rank, manages to get a mention in an exceedingly long and tedious inscription.

Places to Stay – Bottom End

There is quite a travelling community in Jaisalmer these days and a number of cheap hotels have sprung up to cater for them. Right in the central market area there's the *Sunil Bhatia Rest House* with rooms from Rs 10. Continue on a hundred or so metres towards the Amar Sagar Gate and a small sign will direct you to the right to the *Rama Guest House*. You can 'see both sunrise and sunset from the roof' and sleep there for just Rs 5. The staff are very helpful.

Others in this same Rs 10 to 20 price bracket include the *Tourist Hotel* on the south side of the city behind the municipality, the small *Sunray Hotel* behind the Bank of India building right by the Amar Sagar Gate, and the new palace, or the friendly *Golden Rest*. The *Prince Hotel*, Rs 15 a double, offers free jeep transport from the station. They are all as basic as their prices would indicate but OK. Local musicians sometimes visit the lodges, stay overnight and can be persuaded to do an encore the next morning, on the flat roof.

The *Fort View Hotel* got a rave recommendation from a traveller. Doubles are Rs 30 and it's centrally located with an excellent view of the fort. The food is vegetarian and quite OK, and the manager is helpful and speaks good English. When the writer became ill and had to leave Jaisalmer at short notice the manager retrieved money he had paid for train reservations and a camel safari and sent him the money in Delhi.

The *Hotel Swastika* is another new place which has been recommended. It's a short walk up a side street approximately opposite the State Bank of India. Rooms range from Rs 20/40 (some have bathrooms) and there's a Rs 8 dorm. There are tea making facilities availble to guests and the Gaylord Restaurant is nearby.

Places to Stay – Top End

Jaisalmer's 'top end' places are really more middle than top. The *Moomal Tourist Bungalow* (tel 92) is just outside the city walls to the west. It's very close to the bus halt, but quite a distance from the railway station which is right on the other side of the walled town. Singles/doubles cost from Rs 40/50 here or Rs 70/90 with air conditioning, there's also a Rs 10 dormitory. It's a modern building with a restaurant and a bar and it's quite comfortable although V S Naipaul tore into it in *India – A Wounded Civilisation*.

Jaisalmer's other upper bracket hotel is the *Jaisal Castle Hotel* (tel 62), which is situated right on the ramparts of the fort, by the Jain temples. Singles/doubles are Rs 50/75 and there's also a restaurant but several people have complained about the food and service here. The hotel is in a traditional old Jaisalmer house with large rooms, all with attached bath. Sunsets from the roof of the hotel are superb, and the hotel is 'out of this world' according to one visitor. It can get chilly at night in winter, the wind whistles through the rooms. One catch is you have a long walk up to the hotel, tough work if you're toting much baggage.

Up the lane by the Gaylord Restaurant (across from the State Bank of India) the *Narayan Niwas Hotel* is a new hotel with expensive accommodation. A new hotel, the *Rawal Jaisal*, is being built near Kadi Bundar, north of the town.

On Station Rd at the west edge of the city *Hotel Neeraj* is another new hotel. Rooms are Rs 45/80 and the cook, formerly with a maharaja, is 'excellent, he turns out some of the best food we had in India (outside of the Taj Hotel in Bombay) at a price of about Rs 10 a meal'.

Places to Eat

There are a number of cold drink and food places around the market area and near the Golden Rest and some good special lassi places. The small (and basic) *Gaylord Restaurant* is across from the State Bank of India and has friendly sparrows and pretty good food. Near here, by Mahendra Travel, there is also the small *Ghoonghat Restaurant*.

The *Tourist Bungalow* has a restaurant (with slightly higher prices) as does the *Jaisal Castle Hotel*. However, the Tourist Bungalow's 'extensive menu proved to be a fiction on our sole evening visit, when we were served a very poor meal for an outrageous Rs 70!' reported a traveller.

'Jaisalmer is even more gastronomically limited than Jodhpur' he continued. Nor does the Jaisal Castle get much good said about its food. At the *Narayan Niwas Hotel* the food is good but somewhat expensive.

Getting There

Rail Jaisalmer is 290 km from Jodhpur via Pokaran, Dechu and Balesar or 330 km from Bikaner via Pokaran and Phalodi. There are two buses daily to Bikaner, a 10-hour trip, and one bus daily to Jodhpur. It is easier to get to Jodhpur by train, there is a day train and a night train in each direction and the trip takes about 10 hours. Fares are Rs 94 in 1st class, Rs 24 in 2nd. In Jaisalmer, the reservations office is open only from 8 to 11 am and in the chaotic period just before departure.

Note the comments in the introductory section on Gricing about the unique engines used on this run. The Maharaja of Jodhpur's personal railway carriage takes 20 people and it costs Rs 11,000 (including meals) to have the carriage hooked on to the regular train.

The train journey from Jodhpur, at least by day, can be rather gruelling due to dust and the coal smuts, which swirl in and turn your hair to wire! Still, fleeting glimpses of gazelles, or the still rarer bustard, compensate. At Pokaran, which until 1968 was the rail terminus, the train goes into reverse – the engine is switched from front to rear for the leg out to Jaisalmer.

Bus Buses from Jodhpur take 10 hours and cost Rs 32.

Getting Around

Unmetered taxis and jeeps are available, about Rs 14 from the railway station to the Tourist Bungalow. Around the city the tourist office's jeep can be hired for sightseeing for Rs 30 for up to 10 km locally, Rs 2 a km for more than 10 km out of the city. You can also hire bicycles in Jaisalmer and ride out to nearby places.

For camel hire and camel safaris contact the Narayan Niwas Hotel or Mahendra Travel.

Things to Buy

Jaisalmer is famous for embroidery, Rajasthani mirror work, rugs blankets, old stone work and antiques. At Kadi Bundar, north of the city, tie dye and other fabrics are made.

Festivals

The recently commenced Desert Festival is intended to take place in January/February of each year. Camel races and dances, folk music, desert ballads, puppeteers are all part of the activity. However, a disgruntled visitor wrote that it 'is not a festival at all, it is basically a tourist trap and not worth seeing. All the prices in town go up.' At the full moon night of Purnima a sound and light drama is performed at Sam.

AROUND JAISALMER

There are some fascinating places in the area around Jaisalmer, although it soon fades out into a barren sand-duned desert which stretches across the lonely border into Pakistan.

Camel Safaris

The most interesting way of exploring the desert around the town is on a camel safari – check with Mahendra Tours or the Narayan Niwas Hotel about the camel safaris they organise. The Golden Rest and Hotel Fort View has also been recommended for good low price camel safaris.

Mr Singh at the Narayan Niwas used to organise his trips through the Jaisal Castle. He has been operating trips a long time and a number of overseas tour operators use him. Although the trips are arranged principally for group tours, other arrangements can be made at a cost of around Rs 150 per day depending on what you want to do. Although that is relatively expensive (it does include food), the

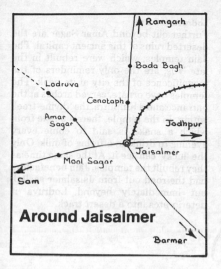

Around Jaisalmer

camels are excellent and his Hindu camel men are friendly and speak some English.

The usual tours take four days and three nights in a circuit around Jaisalmer via Mool Sagar, the Sam sand dunes and back via Lodruva passing through Hindu, Moslem, Rajput, tribal and abandoned villages. You can also do longer, seven-day safaris to Pokran or 11 days to Bikaner. October to February is the best time for the camel safaris.

Mahendra Travel tends to offer shorter trips such as a half-day to Bada Bagh for Rs 40 for two people on one camel. Or a one-day trip covering Bada Bagh, Ram Kunda, Rupsi, Lodruva and Amar Sagar for Rs 50 per person without lunch. Or two days and one night for Rs 100 per person. Both operators have books with tourist's comments on their trips, well worth reading. Check what you're getting in terms of food, blanket and sights before signing up.

If you are contemplating a long trip, take a short one first as some people experience stiff muscles and saddlesore behinds from the unaccustomed rocking

motion. This can rapidly detract from a pleasant trip. Take a cushion perhaps and certainly bring tangerines as the desert is very parching. An individual waterbottle is a good idea too – you can hang it off the front saddle prong; sunburn cream and a head-cloth (Arab style) are also advisable. Normally the tourist sits in front with feet in stirrups with a camelman/boy behind, perched on top of a large fodder bag. The reins are fastened to the camel's nose peg and they are easily steered. At resting points the camels are completely un-saddled and then hobbled. They limp away to browse on nearby shrubs while the camelmen brew sweet chai or prepare basic food – rice, chappatis and the inevitable dhal. The whole crew rests in the shade of thorn trees by a tank or well.

It's a great way to see the desert, which is surprisingly well-populated and sprinkled with ruins. You constantly come across tiny fields of millet, girls picking berries or boys herding flocks of sheep or goats. The latter are always fitted with tinkling neckbells and in the desert silence it sounds like beautiful music. Camping out at night in the Sam sand dunes, huddled around a tiny fire, beneath the stars and listening to the camelmen's yarns can be quite romantic. You may hear tales of their alternative income to tourists – smuggling trips over the border into Pakistan, running the gauntlet of patrols for Rs 300 profit a night. They take over *beedis*, betel pan and whisky; return with gold and electronic goods!

Anatomically, the camels are interesting. They have strange calloused pads on knees and chest, appallingly bad breath and an uncomfortable-looking sitting position with back legs tucked under. Nevertheless, 'you can rapidly get fond of them,' reported two visitors. Not if you're 'on an female pursued by several amorous males' reported another. 'Two days, preferable to the west of Jaisalmerm would be interesting and quite long enough', was another comment. Your camelman will probably expect a tip or gift in addition to the money paid to the tour agent.

Amar Sagar

North-west of Jaisalmer, this used to be a very pleasant formal garden but it has now fallen into ruins. The lake here dries up several months into the dry season. A beautifully carved Jain temple is being painstakingly restored by craftsmen brought in from Agra. Commenced in the late '70s this monumental task is expected to take many years.

Lodruva (15 km)

Further out beyond Amar Sagar are the deserted ruins of this ancient capital. The Jain temples, which were rebuilt in the late '70s, are the only reminders of the magnificence of the city at its peak. The temples have ornate, carved arches at the entrance and a Kalputra, the 'divine-tree', within. In the temple, there's a hole from which a snake is said to come every evening to drink an offering of milk. Only the 'lucky' can see it. At the same time as they rebuilt the temples, Jain benefactors had the road out from Jaisalmer sealed, but immediately beyond Lodruva it deteriorates into a desert track.

Bikaner, Rajasthan

A SIDEWALK HOT MILK VENDOR ON A GRAND SCALE. HOT MILK, SUGAR & CURD MIXED UP WITH A FLOURISH FOR 75 PAISA (9¢) A GLASSFULL. ENTERTAINMENT FREE.

Mool Sagar (9 km)

Directly west of Jaisalmer this is another pleasant small garden and tank. Continuing in this direction you reach the Sam sand dunes, about 40 km from the town. This is the nearest point to Jaisalmer for the real Sahara-like desert.

Khuri

About 40 km southwest of Jaisalmer, out in the desert, it's a delightfully peaceful place with houses of mud and straw decorated like Persian carpets. There is a small guest house with good food.

Bada Bagh & Cenotaphs

North of the town Bada Bagh is a fertile oasis with a huge old dam. Much of Jaisalmer's vegetables and fruit is grown here and carried into the town by colourfully-dressed women each day. Above the gardens are royal cenotaphs with beautifully carved ceilings and equestrian statues of the former rulers. This is a popular place to come in the early evening to watch the setting sun turn Jaisalmer a beautiful, golden brown.

Other

Three km off the road to Barmer, at a point 14 km from Jaisalmer, the 180-million-year-old fossils of old trees can be seen. A desert national park is intended to be established in the Thar Desert near the road to Barmer.

POKRAN

The junction where the Jaisalmer-Bikaner and Jaisalmer-Jodhpur roads split is the site for another magnificent Rajasthan fortress. The yellow sandstone fort rises from the yellow desert sands and shelters a tangle of narrow streets with balconied houses decorated with parrots, elephants and Rajasthan's inevitable peacocks. The usually quiet town springs to life at its annual cattle fair. It must also have sprung to life in May 1974 when a nuclear explosion was made near here!

BARMER

This desert town is a centre for wood carving, carpets, embroidery, block printing and other handicrafts. Barmer is 153 km from Jaisalmer and 220 km from Jodhpur. At Kiradu, 35 km west of Barmer, there are 11th century Kathiawar-style temples with Gupta elements in their design.

BIKANER (population 200,000)

This desert town in the north of the state was founded in 1488 by Rao Bikaji, a descendant of the founder of Jodhpur, Jodhaji. Like many other Rajasthan cities it is surrounded by a high, battlemented wall and, like its smaller sister to the south, Jaisalmer, it was once an important staging post on the great caravan trade routes. The city is chiefly interesting for its superb large fort, but it is also noted for the fine camels bred here. There is a government camel breeding farm near the city. The Gang Canal, built between 1925 and 1927, has irrigated a great area of previously arid land around Bikaner.

Information & Orientation

The city is encircled by a seven-km long city wall with five entrance gates, built in the 18th century. The fort and palace, built of Bikaner's same reddish-pink sandstone, is within the city walls. The GPO is at the collectorate, the city post office is inside Kot Gate. The Tourist Office is located in the Junagarh Fort.

Junagarh Fort

Constructed between 1588 abd 1593 by Raja Rai Singh, a general in the Moghul Emperor Akbar's army, the fort has a 986-metre long wall with 37 bastions and two entrances. The Suraj Pol or Sun Gate is the main entrance to the fort. The palaces within the fort are at the southern side – they're a picturesque ensemble of courtyards, balconies, kiosks, towers and windows.

Among the places of interest are the Chandra Mahal or Moon Palace with paintings, mirrors and carved marble panels. The Phool Mahal or Flower Palace is also decorated with glass and mirrors. The Karn Mahal was built to commemorate a notable victory over the Moghul Aurangzeb. Other palaces include the Rang Mahal, Bijai Mahal and Anup Mahal. The Durga Niwas is a beautifully painted courtyard while the Ganga Niwas, another large courtyard, has a finely carved red sandstone front. Har Mandir is the royal temple, dedicated to Lord Shiva.

The fort is open from 9.30 am to 5 pm, closed on Wednesdays, and admission is Rs 3 (plus Rs 10 for a camera) including a Hindi-speaking guide. 'Stay with him and he'll try to speak some English!' There is a museum, library of Persian and Sanskrit manuscripts and armoury in a corner of the fort; closed on Fridays.

Lalgarh Palace

The 'Red Fort' was built by Maharaja Ganga Singh (1881-1942) in memory of his father Maharaja Lal Singh. The Bikaner royal family still lives in part of the palace, which is made of red sandstone and has beautiful lattice work. There is a collection of old photographs and the usual exhibition of half of India's wildlife, shot and stuffed, inside. The Shri Sadul Museum, to the glory of the maharajas is open 10 am to 5 pm, closed Wednesdays. Entry to the palace costs Rs 2.50 (plus Rs 10 for a camera) and it is open from 9 am to 6 pm.

Ganga Golden Jubilee Museum

Said to be one of the best museums in Rajasthan, it contains pre-Harrapan, Gupta and Kushan pieces and a wide collection of terracottas, pottery, paintings, particularly miniatures of the Bikaner school, and weapons. It is open from 10 am to 5 pm but closed on Fridays. Entry is Rs 0.50, the museum is near the Circuit House.

Places to Stay

Unusually, accommodation is often fully booked in Bikaner – you may have to search around. The new *Dhola-Maru Tourist Bungalow* is on Pooran Singh Circle and has singles/doubles from Rs 40/50 or with air-con at Rs 70/90. There are *Railway Retiring Rooms* at the station and nearby, there is a *Dak Bungalow* (tel 151) with doubles at less than Rs 10.

If that fails there is a string of low-priced hotels near the station on Station Rd. The *Delight Hotel*, the *Deluxe Hotel* (tel 192), the *Green Hotel* (tel 296) and the *Roopan Hotel* (tel 373). At the Deluxe rooms range from around Rs 12 to 24. The rooms are good, as in the Delight which is next door and has the same manager. There's a dharmasala opposite, and two km away there is a *Circuit House* with rooms at Rs 15.

The *Lalgarh Palace Hotel* (tel 312) has singles/doubles at Rs 250/350 including meals.

Places to Eat

Chhotu Motu Joshi Restaurant is just down from the Green Hotel towards the station and has good and cheap vegetarian food and icy cold lassi. The *Green Hotel* also does smooth, cold lassi. More great lassi on the street near the bus stand, also good yoghurt for Rs 4 a kilo! There is also the *Ambar Restaurant* on Station Rd and the *Delight* and *Deluxe Hotels* have good south Indian food, but a limited menu.

Getting There

Rail There are day and night trains from Delhi to Bikaner and the 46-trip takes 11 to 12 hours. Fares are Rs 110 in 1st class, Rs 28 in 2nd. There is a daily overnight train to and from Jodhpur and the 277-km trip takes eight hours and costs Rs 58 in 1st, Rs 15 in 2nd. The 379-km trip between Jaipur and Bikaner takes 10 to 11 hours, and again there is an overnight train with fares of Rs 116 in 1st class, Rs 30 in 2nd class.

A cheap way of travelling Jaisalmer-Bikaner is to take a night train to Pokran, sleep in the waiting room and then catch a bus for the five hour ride to Bikaner, arriving around noon. Total cost is around Rs 28 and this way you get some sleep on the way. Continuing on from Bikaner to Amritsar by rail can be hard work.

Bus On the edge of the Thar Desert, Bikaner is connected by rail and road with the rest of Rajasthan. There is a national highway to Jaipur (320 km) and to Jaisalmer (330 km). The bus from Jaisalmer takes a weary 10 to 12 hours and costs Rs 35. Jodhpur is 240 km away. There are regular bus services.

Getting Around

Taxis are unmetered, Bikaner also has auto-rickshaws and tongas.

AROUND BIKANER
Bhand Sagar Temple (5 km)
The 16th century Jain temple to the 23rd Tirthankar, Parasvanath, is the most important of the complex, but others include the Chintamani Temple of 1505 and the Adinath Temple. There is a fine view of the city wall and surrounding countryside from the park behind the temple.

Devi Kund (8 km)
This is the site of the royal *chhatris* or cenotaphs of many of the Bika dynasty

rulers. The white marble chhatri of Maharaja Surat Singh is among the most imposing.

Camel Breeding Farm (10 km)
This government-managed camel breeding station is probably unique in Asia. There are hundreds of camels here and rides are available. It's a great sight at sunset as the camels come back from grazing. The British army had a camel corps drawn from Bikaner during WW I.

Gajner Wildlife Sanctuary (32 km)
A number of animals can be seen in this reserve on the Jaisalmer road. In winter imperial sand grouse migrate here. The old royal summer palace stands on the bank of the lake and is sometimes used as a hotel.

Karni Mata Temple (33 km)
At Deshnok on the Jodhpur road this temple is dedicated to the mystic Karni Mata. The huge silver gates to the temple and the marble carvings were donated by Maharaja Ganga Singh and a golden umbrella tops the temple, but the main interest here is the rats. The temple is infested with holy rats, which are fed and cared for in the belief that they will reincarnate as mystics or holy men.

The Indian passion for labelling and logging things is never better illustrated than in the Rajasthan Tourist Bungalows where every moveable item, and a good few that aren't, is coded and numbered. And doubtless listed in some giant register somewhere. In one room I spotted this notation: TBGL-Ju-TP Stand 8 (R No 8), that is to say Tourist Bungalow Jodhpur-Toilet Paper Stand 8 (in room number 8)!

Tony Wheeler

After a short time in Rajasthan you soon realise why the peacock is the state bird. They're everywhere. Peacocks stroll parks and gardens, sit on top of roofs, wander around hotels. If it's not real ones, then there are mosaic ones in palaces, painted ones on walls, glass ones in windows. And they're every bit as colourful as Rajasthan itself.

Gujarat

Population: 29 million
Area: 195,984 square km
Capital: Gandhinagar
Main language: Gujarati

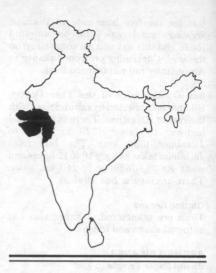

The west coast state of Gujarat is not one of India's busiest destinations. Although it is quite easy to slot Gujarat in between Bombay and the cities of Rajasthan, few people pause to explore this interesting state. Yet Gujarat has a long and varied history and a great number of interesting places to visit. If you want to go right beyond history into the realms of legend, then the Temple of Somnath was actually there to witness the creation of the universe! And along the south coast are the sites where many of the great events in Lord Krishna's life took place.

On more firm historic footing, Lothal was the site of a Harappan or Indus Valley Civilisation city over 4000 years ago. The main sites from this very ancient culture are now in Pakistan, but it is thought Lothal may have survived the great cities of the Sind by as much as 500 years. Gujarat also featured in the exploits of the great Buddhist Emperor Ashoka and one of his rock edicts can be seen near Junagadh.

Later Gujarat was to suffer Moslem incursions from Mahmud of Ghanzi on through the Moghuls and was to be a battlefield between the Moghuls and the Mahrattas. It was an early contact point with the west and at Surat the first British commercial outpost was established. The Portuguese enclaves of Daman and Diu survived within the borders of Gujarat right up to 1961. More recently Gujarat had a close tie with the life of the father of modern India, Mahatma Gandhi. It was in Gujarat that the Mahatma was born and spent his early years and it was to Ahmedabad, the great city of Gujarat, that he returned to wage his long struggle with

the British for independence.

Gujarat has always been a centre for the Jains and some of its most interesting sights are Jain temple centres like those at Palitana and Girnar. The Jains are an influential and energetic group and as a result Gujarat is one of the wealthier states of India with a number of important industries, particularly textiles. Apart from the Jain temples other major attractions of Gujarat include the last Asian lions in the Gir Forest and the fascinating Indo-Saracenic architecture of Ahmedabad.

Geographically, Gujarat can be divided into three areas. The mainland region includes the major cities of Ahmedabad, Surat and Baroda. The Gulf of Cambay divides the mainland strip from the flat, often barren, plain of the Kathiawar Peninsula, also known as Saurashtra. This was never incorporated into British India, but survived as more than 200 princely states right up to independence. In 1956 they were all amalgamated into the state of Bombay but in 1960 this was in turn split, on linguistic grounds, into Maharashtra and Gujarat. Finally the Gulf of Kutch divides Saurashtra from Kutch which is virtually an island cut off from the rest of Gujarat, to the east, and Pakistan, to the north, by the low-lying 'Ranns' of Kutch.

Gujarat is much less touristed than neighbouring Rajasthan and you'll also notice, in comparison with that state, how much less fluent the people are in English. Gujarat has provided a surprisingly large proportion of India's emigrants particularly to the UK and USA. More than half of the 100,000 Indians in the New York area are Gujaratis and the name Patel, a popular Gujarati surname, has become commonly identified as Indian.

Gujarati Food

The strict Jain vegetarianism has contributed to Gujarat's distinct regional cuisine. Throughout the state you'll find the Gujarati variation of the thali – it's the traditional all-you-can-eat vegetarian meal with an even greater variety of dishes than usual. But with the drawback, if you're not sweet-toothed, that it can be overpoweringly sweet. Popular dishes include *kadhi*, a savoury curry of yoghurt and fried puffs, flavoured with spices and finely chopped vegetables. *Undhyoo* is a winter speciality of potatoes, sweet potatoes, broad beans and aubergines roasted in an earthenware pot which is buried, *undhyoo*, upside down, under a fire. In Surat there's a local variation on this which is more spicy and curry hot. *Sev Ganthia* is a crunchy fried chickpea flour snack, which you buy from *farsan* stalls.

In winter, in Surat, you can try *paunk*, a curious combination of roasted cereals, or *jowar*, garlic chutney and sugar. Then there's *khaman dhokla*, a salty, steamed chickpea flour cake. Or *doodhpak* which is

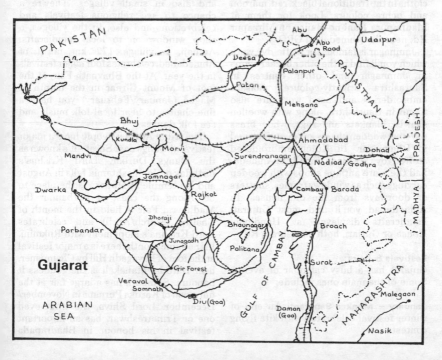

a sweetened, thickened milk-based dessert with nuts. *Srikhand* is a dessert made from yoghurt spiced with saffron, cardomom, nuts and candied fruit. *Gharis* are another rich sweet made of milk, clarified butter and dried fruits – it's another specialty of Surat. In summer *am rasis* is a popular mango juice drink.

Things to Buy

With its busy modern textile works, it's not surprising that Gujarat has a number of interesting buys in this line. At the top end of this field there are the extremely fine, and often extremely expensive, Patola silk saris still made by a handful of master craftsmen in Patan. From Surat comes the *zari* or gold thread embroidery work. Surat is also a centre for silk saris. At a more mundane, but still beautiful, level there are the block prints of Ahmedabad where you will also find hand painted cloths in the traditional black, red, maroon and ochre colours. Look for them at Madhupura Rani-no-Hajiro on Mirzapur Rd, near the Ahmedabad GPO.

Jamnagar is famous for its tie-dye work which you'll find in the other bazaar shops in Jamnagar and other centres in Saurashtra. Brightly-coloured peasant embroideries and bead work are also found in Saurashtra, along with woollen shawls, blankets and rugs, while brass covered wooden chests are manufactured in Bhavnagar. In Kutch embroidered stuffed toys are made. Finally in Ahmedabad there are antique shops with wooden carvings such as windows frames, shutters or doorways from the old houses. In Ahmedabad you'll find most Gujarati handicrafts displayed at Handloom House or Gurjari, both on Ashram Rd.

Festivals & Fairs

Gujarat has a busy calendar of events. Some of the main ones include:

January – Mankar Sankranti An end of winter festival celebrated with kite flying contests.

January/February – Muharram Tazias, large replicas of the tombs of two Moslem martyrs are paraded in the evening, particularly in Surat, Junagadh and Ahmedabad.

September/October – Navarati Nine nights of music and dancing celebrate this festival of the mother goddess Amba. The Dandiya Ras, which Lord Krishna danced with his milkmaids or *gopis*, is featured. Champaner celebrates this festival with particular fervour.

October – Dussehra The 10th day of Navarati culminates in the celebration of Rama's victory over the evil Ravana in the Ramayana.

October/November – Sharad Purnima Song and dance celebrates the end of the monsoon on the full moon night of the month of Sharad.

Gujarat has many fairs in temple towns and also in small villages. They're a chance to see religious festivals and celebrations and also, in the villages, a shop window on to local handicrafts. Ambaji, a village 177 km north of Ahmedabad, celebrates four major festivals in the year. At the Bhavnath Fair, at the foot of Mount Girnar in the month of Magha (January/February) you have a fine chance to hear local folk music and see folk dances.

The tribal Adivasi people have a major festival at Dangs near Surat – it's known as the Dangs Durbar. Lord Krishna's birthday or Janmashtamia falls in August and his temple at Dwarka is the place to be. Along the coast at Porbandar the Madhavrai Fair is held in the month of Chaitra (March/April) and celebrates Lord Krishna's elopement with Rukmini. In the same month there is a major festival at the foot of Pavagadh Hill by Champaner, near Baroda. Mahakali is the goddess it honours. Somnath has a large fair at the full moon of Kartika Purnima in November/December. Lord Shiva, the three-eyed one or Trinetreshwar, has an important festival in his honour in Bhadrapada

(August/September) in Ternetar village – a chance to see colourful local tribal costumes.

AHMEDABAD (population 1,750,000)

The principal city of Gujarat, Ahmedabad is also one of the major industrial cities of India, it has been called the 'Manchester of the East' due to its many textile industries. Today it is destined to be the earth station for India's satellite TV project, but it's also a rather noisy and polluted city. Over the centuries Ahmedabad has had a number of periods of grandeur followed by decline. It was originally founded in 1411 by Ahmed Shah and in the 1600s was thought to be one of the finest cities in India. Sir Thomas Roe, the noted English ambassador, judged it, in 1615, to be: 'a goodly city, as large as London' but in the 1700s it went through a period of decline. Its industrial strength once again raised the city up, and from 1915 it became famous as the site for Gandhi's ashram and from where he launched his famous march to break the Salt Law.

Today this comparatively little visited city has a number of attractions for travellers. Gandhi's ashram at Sabarmati can be visited and there is a small museum. In the city there are some of the finest examples of Islamic architecture in India and a number of other interesting buildings both religious and secular. Ahmedabad is one of the best places to study the blend of Hindu and Islamic architectural styles known as the Indo-Saracenic. The new capital of Gujarat, Gandhinagar, is 23 km from Ahmedabad. Visitors in the hot season should bear in mind the Moghul emperor Jehangir's, derisive title for Ahmedabad: Gardabad, 'the city of dust'.

Orientation

The city sprawls across the Sabarmati River. Two main roads run back from the river to the railway station, about a km away. They are Relief Rd (Tilak Rd) and Gandhi Rd. The city walls are now virtually all demolished but some of the gates remain. The airport is off to the north-east of the city. The Gandhi Ashram is on the west bank of the Sabarmati River, to the north of the city.

Information

The state Tourist Office is across the river from the centre, just off Sri R C Rd. Indian Airlines is close to the Nehru Bridge, behind and across the road from the Siddi Saiyad Mosque. For some strange reason you cannot conduct transactions of more than Rs 10 in the main section of the GPO. For these you must go to a single special counter right at the rear and outside!

Bhadra & Teen Darwaza

The ancient citadel, the Bhadra, was built by Ahmed Shah in 1411 and later named after the goddess Bhadra, an incarnation of Kali. It is now used for government offices and is of no particular interest. There is a post office in the former Palace of Azam Khan within the citadel. In front of the citadel stands the triple gateway or Teen Darwaza, from which sultans would watch processions from the palace to the Jami Masjid

Jami Masjid

The Friday Mosque is beside Gandhi Rd, a short distance down from Teen Darwaza. This large mosque was built in 1424 by Ahmed Shah, the city's founder. There are 260 columns supporting the roof with its 15 cupolas but in the great earthquake of 1819 the two 'shaking' minarets lost half their height and another tremor in 1957 completed the demolition. In this early Ahmedabad mosque much of the building was made from items salvaged from demolished Hindu and Jain temples. It is said that a large black slab by the main arch is actually the base of a Jain idol, buried upside down for the Moslem faithful to tread on!

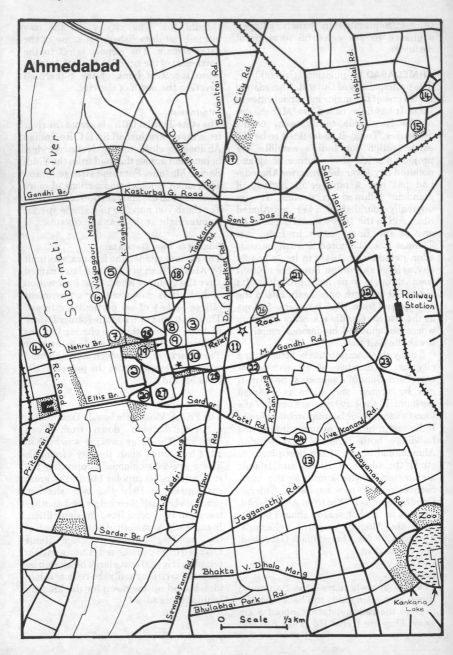

Ahmedabad

1	Tourist Office	15	Dada Hari's Well
2	Local Bus Terminal	17	Hathee Singh Temple
3	GPO	18	Rani Rupmati Mosque
4	ITDC Hotel	19	Siddi Saiyad Mosque
5	Hotel Sabar	20	Azam Khan's Mosque
6	Cama Hotel	21	Swami Temple
7	Ritz & Ambassador Hotels	22	Jami Masjid & Market
8	Gulmarg & Esquire Hotels	23	Shaking Minarets
9	Chetak, Capri, Metropole & Plaza	24	Rani Sipri Mosque
	Hotels & Kwality Restaurant	25	Indian Airlines
10	Hotel Ashiana	26	Chetna Restaurant
11	Gokul Hotel	27	Bhadra
12	Hotel Moti Mahal	28	Teen Darwaza
13	Long Distance Bus Station	☆	Havmor Ice-Cream Bar
14	Mata Bhawani's Well	★	Gandhi Cold Drinks Bar

Tombs of Ahmed Shah & His Queens

The Tomb of Ahmed Shah stands just outside the east gate of the Jami Masjid. His son and grandson, who did not long survive him, also have their cenotaphs in this tomb with its perforated stone windows. Women are not allowed into the central chamber. Across the street is the tomb of his queens on a raised platform – it's now really a market and in very poor shape compared to Ahmed Shah's tomb.

Sidi Saiyad's Mosque

This small mosque once formed part of the city wall, it is close to the river end of Relief Rd. Constructed by Sidi Saiyad, a slave of Ahmed Shah, it is noted for its beautiful carved stone windows in which the branches of a tree are intricately interwined to form the complete window.

Ahmed Shah's Mosque

Dating from 1414 this was one of the earliest mosques in the city and was probably built on the site of a Hindu temple, using parts of that temple in its construction. It is located in the south-west of the Bhadra and the front of the mosque is now a garden.

Rani Rupmati's Mosque

A little north of the centre, this mosque

was built between 1430 and 1440 and named after the Sultan's Hindu wife. The minarets were partially brought down by the disastrous earthquake of 1819. Note how the dome is elevated to allow light in around its base. The mosque, as so many of Ahmedabad's early mosques, displays elements of Hindu and Islamic design.

Rani Sipri's Mosque

A little south-east of the centre this small mosque was built in 1514 and is also known as the Masjid-e-Nagira or 'jewel of a mosque' due to its extremely graceful and well executed design. Its slender, delicate minarets are again a blend of Hindu and Islamic styles. The mosque is said to have been built by a wife of Sultan Mehmood Begada after he executed their son for some minor misdemeanour.

Sidi Bashir Mosque – shaking minarets

Just south of the railway station, outside the Sarangpur Gate, the Sidi Bashir Mosque is famed for its shaking minarets or *Jhulta Minar*. When one minaret is shaken, the other rocks in sympathy, this was said to be a protection against earthquake damage. Unfortunately this mosque is generally closed and the opening hours posted outside appear to bear no relation to reality.

The Raj Babi Mosque also had shaking minarets, one of which was dismantled by an inquisitive Englishman in an unsuccessful attempt to find out how it worked. Within the railway station area, a little to the north, are minarets lacking a mosque which was destroyed in a battle between the Moghuls and Mahrattas in 1753.

Hathee Singh Temple

Just outside the Delhi Gate, to the north of the old city, this is a Jain temple in typical style and, as so often with Jain temples, made of white marble. Built in 1848 the temple is dedicated to Dharamanath, the 15th Jina or Jain apostle.

Step Well of Dada Hari

Step wells or *baolis* are a strange construction unique to Gujarat and this is one of the best. The curious well has a series of steps leading down to the lower and lower platforms, eventually terminating with a small octagonal well. Built in 1499 the depths of the well are cool, even on the hottest day, and it must have been quite beautiful in its prime. Today it is completely neglected but it's an eerie, interesting place with galleries above the well and a small portico at ground level. Behind the well is the equally neglected Mosque and Tomb (Rauza) of Dada Hari. The mosque has a tree-motif like the windows of Sidi Saiyad's Mosque.

There is a second step well, that of Mat Bhawani, a couple of hundred metres north of Dada Hari's. Ask children to show you the way. It's thought to be several hundred years older, is much less ornate and is now used as a crude Hindu temple.

Kankaria Lake

South-east of the city this artificial lake was constructed in 1451 and has 34 sides, each 60 metres long. It is now a local picnic spot but was once frequented by the Emperor Jehangir and his Empress Nur Jahan. The zoo and children's park by the lake are outstanding. The Ghattamendal pavilion in the centre houses an aquarium.

Other Mosques & Temples

It's very easy to get mosque-ed out in Ahmedabad. If your enthusiasm for mosques is limited, then don't go further than Sidi Saiyad's and the Jami Mashid. If you have real endurance then you could continue to Dastur Khan's Mosque, near the Rani Sipri Mosque, or Haibat Khan's Mosque, Saiyad Alam's Mosque, Shuja'at Khan's Mosque, Shaikh Hasan Muhammed Chisti's Mosque and Muhafiz Khan's Mosque.

Then for a complete change you could plunge into the narrow streets of the old part of town and seek out the brightly painted Swami Narayan Temple. Enclosed in a large courtyard, it dates from 1850. To the south of this Hindu temple are the nine tombs known as the Nau Gaz Pir or 'Nine Yard Saints'.

Around the Town

Ahmedabad can be quite an interesting place to wander around. The bazaar streets are narrow, crowded and colourful with many houses having ornately carved wooden fronts. There are Jain birdfeeding places known as *parabdis* in many streets. Children catch pigeons then release them just for fun. The older parts of the city are divided into totally separate areas known as *pols*. It's easy to get lost!

Across the river there are many more modern buildings, including the Ahmedabad Mill Owner's Association building and the museum, both designed by Le Corbusier who also had a hand in the new capital of Gandhinagar. There's little evidence of the British period in Ahmedabad, unlike so many large cities. The chief landmarks of the era are the tall smokestacks that ring this industrial city. On the sandy bed of the Sabarmati River traditional block printed fabrics are still stretched out to dry, despite the 70-plus large textile mills. The river dries up to a mere trickle in the hot season.

Other places of interest in and around the town include the ruined tomb of Darya Khan (1453) north-west of the Hathee Singh Temple. It has a particularly large dome. Near it is the Chhota Shahi Bagh and across the railway line is the Shahi Bagh. Ladies of the harem used to live in the chhota (small) garden. In Saraspur, east of the railway line, the Temple of Chintaman is a Jain temple originally constructed in 1638, but converted by Aurangzeb into a mosque.

Museums

Ahmedabad has a number of museums including the Calico Museum of Textiles (tel 5100), which has a display of antique and modern textiles including rare tapestries, wall hangings and costumes and displays of old weaving machines. It is open 8.30 to 10.30 am from April to June and from July to March it is open 11 am to 12 noon and 3 to 5 pm. Admission is free and it has 'great antique fabrics and is the best laid out museum I've seen', according to one traveller.

The N C Mehta Museum of Miniatures (tel 78369) is at Sanskar Kendra, Paldi and has an excellent exhibit of the various schools of Indian miniature paintings. It is open 9 to 11 am and 4 to 7 pm, daily except Mondays. The building was designed by Le Corbusier.

There is also the Shreyas Folk Museum with exhibits of the folk arts and crafts of Gujarat, the National Institute of Design, the Tribal Research and Training Institute Museum and a Philatelic Museum. The Institute of Indology on the university campus (tel 78295) has an important collection of illustrated manuscripts and miniatures and one of the finest collections relating to Jainism in India. It is open from 11.30 am to 5.30 pm weekdays, 11.20 am to 2.30 pm on Saturdays, closed Sundays. Admission is free.

Sabarmati Ashram

Situated six km from the centre of town, on the west bank of the Sabarmati River, this was Gandhi's headquarters during his long struggle for Indian independence. His ashram was founded in 1918 and still makes handicrafts, handmade paper and spinning wheels. Gandhi's spartan living quarters are preserved as a small museum and there is a pictorial exhibit of the major events in his life.

CHAI (TEA) VENDOR AT ANY RAILWAY STATION

The ashram is open from 8.30 am to 12 noon and from 2 to 6.30 pm (to 7 pm April to September), admission is free. On Sundays, Tuesdays, Thursdays and Saturday evening there is a son et lumiere show in English at 8.15 pm. There is a small admission fee for this performance. An auto-rickshaw from the city centre side of Nehru Bridge to the ashram at Sabarmati will cost around Rs 8. Buses 81, 82, 83 or 84 will get you there for Rs 0.80.

Tours

There are tours operated from the Lal Darwaza bus stand each day which cost Rs 10. The Tourism Corporation of Gujarat have a Rs 30 tour each Sunday which departs at 8 am and returns at 2.15 pm and includes the Gandhi Ashram, the Adalaj Vav step-well and the Calico Museum of Textiles and Shreyas Folk Museum. They also have longer (four or five days) tours around north Gujarat, south Gujarat and Saurashtra.

Places to Stay – Bottom End

If you don't mind being out of town a bit there's the modern *Gandhi Ashram*, close to the river. There are just nine rooms (so it's wise to book ahead), each with attached bath and balcony. Singles/ doubles are Rs 30/60, phone 86 7652 or contact the tourist office, 44 9683.

Other cheap hotels are scattered, mainly around the centre. There's nothing very special or any great bargins to be found. Right behind the big Capri Hotel and the Kwality Restaurant on Relief Rd is the *Plaza Hotel* where singles/doubles with attached bathroom are Rs 30/50. Habitable but little more. Close by, in the small alleys off Relief Rd, are the *Chetak Hotel* (Rs 35/60) and the *Metropole Hotel* (Rs 40/70). A couple of hundred metres along Relief Rd the *Apna Ghar Guest House* is OK at Rs 24/30.

The *Hotel Ashiana* is also central, doubles cost Rs 30 without bath, Rs 40 with, it's very basic. The *Hotel Sabar* is just beyond the big Cama Hotel, but back from the river and has doubles at Rs 50 to Rs 100 with air-con. Good food too in this quieter location. Behind the Bhadra citadel, right next to the Ahmed Khan Mosque, is the *Hotel Natraj* with singles/ doubles at Rs 30/45. It's a modern building, close to the centre but fairly quiet – it is also close to the Lal Darwaza bus station.

For emergencies more than anything, there's the *Alankar Hotel* at Kapasia Bazaar near the railway station. There are many other hotels (like the *Hotel Moti Mahal*) close to the railway station and *Railway Retiring Rooms* at Rs 30/50 for singles/doubles. Or the *Hotel Gulmarg* and *Hotel Esquire* both in Lal Darwaza, near the river end of Relief Rd. Both relatively expensive and the Gulmarg is also rather drear.

Places to Stay – Top End

The *Cama Hotel* (tel 25281-85) is on Khanpur Rd, centrally located and pleasantly situated overlooking the river. Singles/ doubles, air-con, are Rs 320/395. It's got a good restaurant (excellent breakfast), and is probably the best top end place in Ahmedabad. Out of town at the Kandla Highway Crossing on Narol Rd is the *Hotel Ahmedabad International* (tel 87282) with rooms at slightly lower rates.

There are a number of other upper notch places close to the Cama Hotel and the river. The *Ritz Hotel* (tel 24373-75) is pleasantly secluded in a garden well back from the road. Singles/doubles are Rs 80/ 120 or Rs 110/160 with air-con, all rooms have attached bathrooms. Almost next door to it is the *Hotel Ambassador*.

Moving away from the river there is the *Hotel Capri* (tel 24643-44) on Relief Rd, almost next door to the Kwality Restaurant. Singles/doubles cost Rs 90/125 without air-con, Rs 125/175 with it. Opposite Piramshah Roza, near the Regal Cinema on Pankore Nama, is the 'Indian-modern' *Gokul Hotel* (tel 382770-80) with singles/

doubles at Rs 140/180, all with air-conditioning.

The *Hotel Kingsway* near the Relief Cinema (tel 26806-07) spans the middle to upper bracket with singles from Rs 75 to 100 and doubles at Rs 100 to 150. There are rooms with and without air-conditioning. Or there's the *Hotel Capital* at Chandanwadi, Mirzapur (tel 26396-97), where again there are air-con rooms and prices range from around Rs 50 to Rs 150 – it's not very good according to one traveller.

Across the river on Ashram Rd is the *Hotel Nataraj* (tel 44 8647-48) with singles/doubles at Rs 180/225. Again all rooms are air-con. On the same road is the new *Hotel Karnavati* (tel 76351) with singles/doubles for Rs 360/390. Note that top end places may charge a 10% luxury tax on top of a 10% service tax.

Places to Eat

A number of hotels, like the *Cama Hotel*, have pleasant dining rooms, often with air-con, a near necessity in the hot weather. On Relief Rd there's a *Kwality Restaurant*, it's one of the better class Kwality's with an extensive English-Chinese-Indian menu. Further down the road, on the opposite side, is a *Havmor* ice cream parlour where, apart from good quality ice cream, you can also get snacks and cold, flavoured milk. There are a number of clean milk bars where you can get bottles of (curiously) flavoured milk. Across the road from the Kwality there's a second *Havmor* parlour 'with a waiter who is a compulsive changer of water – every time you have a sip from your glass he takes it away and refills it!'

Very close to the Teen Darwaza Gate is the tiny *Gandhi Cold Drinks Bar* with more good ice cream and cold drinks. The Capri Hotel has a '60s space age' style restaurant called the *Gold Coin*, complete with mirrors and spiral staircase; OK food.

Opposite the Gujarat College, the *Collegian Restaurant* is popular with college students. The food is mainly Punjabi with lots of variety and reasonably priced too. A pulao plus a meat dish will cost Rs 15 to 20. Near Teen Darwaja the *Neelam Hotel* and the *Paramount* are both good for western food – 'the best in the city'. The Paramount is much less expensive than the somewhat pretentious Neelam where you can easily spend Rs 60 for a meal.

Ahmedabad is, of course, a good place to sample a Gujarati thali, see the Gujarat food section. One of the best thali specialists in Ahmedabad is the *Chetna Restaurant* on Relief Rd where you may have to queue to get in for its Rs 11, all-you-can-eat thali. It can be a little hard to locate since the sign is not in Roman script, but it almost adjoins Krishna Talkies (well their sign is not in our script either) and is directly across the road from the Oriental Building. It's so popular that you may have to queue to get in and a special waiter is provided to ply the waiting customers with water. 'We ate all we could', reported one gourmand, 'and had to lie down in a park to recover'.

Other good places for a thali include the *Hotel Sabar* where the thalis are Rs 12 and you can follow it up with fruit salad for dessert. Slightly more expensive again at the flashy *Gokul Hotel*.

One traveller recommended 'the little hole-in-the-wall *Vepari Hotel* between Teen Darwaja and Manek Chowk'. It's back from the street along a narrow lane, up flights of stairs and it's crowded, you always have to wait 15 minutes for a table. 'The thalis are great and it's also a good place for a real taste of old Ahmedabad and its bustle and energy'.

Getting There

Air Indian Airlines have two daily flights Delhi-Ahmedabad-Bombay and often an additional flight just Bombay-Ahmedabad. One of the Delhi flights goes either via Jaipur or via Jaipur and Jodhpur. Fares: from Bombay Rs 333, Delhi Rs 568, Jaipur Rs 398, Jodhpur Rs 323.

Rail Ahmedabad is not on the main broad gauge line between Delhi and Bombay, although there is a broad gauge line running south to Bombay and a metre gauge line runs north to Delhi via the major towns of Rajasthan. Delhi-Ahmedabad is 939 km and takes nearly 24 hours except for the twice weekly Sarbodaya Express which only takes 17 hours but this train takes the broad gauge line from Delhi via Kota and Ratlam to Baroda then turns north to Ahmedabad. Fares between Delhi and Ahmedabad are Rs 236 in 1st class, Rs 60 in 2nd.

There are plenty of daily trains between Ahmedabad and Bombay, the 491-km trip takes 10 to 15 hours with the fastest mail trains making the trip in around nine hours. Fares are Rs 143 in 1st class, Rs 36.50 in 2nd. The Delhi trains taking the metre gauge line north will get you to Abu Road in about five hours (186 km), to Ajmer in 12 hours (491 km), and to Jaipur in 15 hours (626 km).

Bus There are also plenty of buses both around Gujurat and to neighbouring states. If you're heading north into Rajasthan the direct bus to Mt Abu (seven hours) will probably be faster than a train to Abu Road and a bus from there.

Getting Around

There are the usual buses and taxis around Ahmedabad and hordes of reckless auto-rickshaw drivers. In Ahmedabad's frantic traffic conditions venturing out in an auto-rickshaw is a nerve-shattering experience. On the plus side the auto-rickshaw wallahs use their meters 100% and without argument. The meters may be well away from the correct fare, but they do use them. The bus stand is known universally as Lal Darwarja. The routes, destinations and fares are all written in Gujarati.

OUTSIDE OF AHMEDABAD

Sarkhej

Only eight km out of Ahmedabad the suburb of Sarkhej is noted for its elegant group of buildings. They're possibly the finest group of buildings in Ahmedabad. The architecture here is interesting in that the style is almost purely Hindu, with little evidence of the Saracenic influence felt so strongly in Ahmedabad. The buildings include the Mausoleum of Azam and Mu'azzam – built in 1457, they are the brothers who were responsible for Sarkhej's architecture.

As you enter Sarkhej you pass the Mausoleum of Mahmud Begara and, beside the tank and connected to his tomb, that of his queen, Rajabai (1460). Also by the tank is the tomb of Ahmad Khattu Gaj Buksh, a renowned Moslem saint and spiritual adviser of Ahmed Shah. The saint is said to have died in 1445 at the age of 111. Next to this is the fine mosque – 'the perfection of elegant simplicity'. Like the other buildings it is notable for the complete absence of arches, a distinct feature of Moslem architecture. Also around the tank is the palace with pavilions and a harem. The Dutch established a factory in Sarkhej in 1620 for the indigo grown here.

Batwa

South-east of Ahmedabad, the suburb of Batwa has tombs of a noted Moslem saint (himself the son of another saint), and the saint's son. Batwa also has an important mosque.

Adalaj Vav

Situated 19 km north of Ahmedabad, this is one of the finest of the Gujarati step wells or *baolis*. Built by Queen Rudabai in 1499, it provided a cool and secluded retreat during the hot summer months.

Cambay

The old sea port of Ahmedabad is situated to the south-west, at the northern end of the Gulf of Cambay. At the height of Moslem power in Gujarat the entire region was known as Cambay and when, in 1583, the first ambassadors arrived from

England they bore letters from Queen Elizabeth addressed to Akbar, the 'King of Cambay'. The Dutch and Portuguese had established factories in the port before the British arrived, but the rise of Surat eclipsed Cambay and when its port silted up the city's decline was inevitable.

Nal Sarovar

From November to February this 116 square-km lake is home for vast flocks of indigenous and migratory birds. Particularly early in the morning and in the evening you may see ducks, geese, pelicans, and flamingoes. There is a *Holiday Home* with accommodation near the lake, it has to be booked through the tourist office in Ahmedabad.

Lothal

About 80 km south of Ahmedabad, towards Bhavnagar, this site is of great interest to archaeologists as the city which stood here, 4500 years ago was clearly closely related to the Indus Valley cities of Mohenjodaro and Harappa – both in Pakistan. It has the same neatly laid out street pattern, the same carefully assembled brickwork and the same scientific drainage system.

The name Lothal actually means 'mound of the dead' in Gujarati, just as Moenjodaro does in Sindhi. At its peak, this was probably one of the most important ports on the sub-continent and trade was possibly carried on with the civilisations of Mesopotamia, Egypt and Persia.

Getting There Lothal is a day trip from Ahmedabad. You can reach it by rail, disembarking at Bhurkhi on the Ahmedabad-Bhavnagar railway line, from where you can walk or take a bus. Or you can bus straight there from Ahmedabad.

Places to Stay Cheap accommodation is available at the *Tourist Centre*.

Modhera

The ruined Sun Temple of Modhera was built by King Bhimdev I (1026-27) and bears some relationship to the later, and far better known, Sun Temple of Konarak in the state of Orissa. Like that temple it was designed so that the sun shone on the image of Surya, the Sun God, at dawn at the time of the equinoxes. The main hall and shrine is reached through a pillared porch. The exterior of this fine temple is intricately and delicately carved. As at Somnath, it was Mahmud of Ghanzi who did the ruining.

Getting There Modhera is 106 km north-west of Ahmedabad. There are buses direct to Modhera or you can take the train to Mehsana from where buses make the 40-km trip to Modhera.

Unjha

A little north of Mehsana, the station for visits to the Modhera Temple, the town of Unjha is interesting for the marriage customs of the Kadwakanbis who live in this region. Marriages occur only once every 11 years and on that day every married girl over 40 days old must be wed – if no husband can be found a proxy wedding takes place and the bride immediately becomes a 'widow' and later remarries when a suitable husband shows up. Further north again is Sidhpur with the very fragmented ruins of an ancient temple. This region was an important centre for growing opium poppies.

Patan

Situated about 120 km north-west of Ahmedabad, this was an ancient Hindu capital before being sacked by Mahmud of Ghanzi in 1024. Now a pale shadow of its former glory it still has over 100 Jain temples and is a centre for the manufacture of beautifully designed Patola silk saris. There's another step well here.

Getting There Patan is 25 km north-west of the Mehsana railway station, which also serves as a jumping off point for Modhera.

GANDHINAGAR (population 25,000)

The old state of Bombay was split into Maharashtra and Gujarat in 1960 and a new capital was planned for the state of Gujarat. Situated on the west bank of the Sabarmati, 32 km north-east of Ahmedabad, Gandhinagar is named after Mahatma Gandhi, who was born in Gujarat. It is India's second planned city, after Chandigarh, and like that city is laid out into numbered sectors. Construction of the city commenced in 1965 and the secretariat was moved there in 1970.

Places to Stay

Gandhinagar has an excellent *youth hostel* in sector 16, and in sector 11 there is the *Panthik Ashram* government rest house. Other rest houses and guest houses are located at Pethapur and opposite Sachivalaya. The Tourist Information Centre (tel 2211/479-82) is also at Sachivalaya but it's a 'dead loss'. Buses from Ahmedabad cost Rs 1.75.

BARODA (population 500,000)

Also known as Vadodara, this was the capital of the princely Gaekwad state prior to independence. Today, it is a pleasant, medium-sized city with some interesting museums and art galleries and a fine park. A good place for a short pause.

Orientation & Information

The railway station, bus stand and a cluster of cheaper hotels are all off to one side of the city. The tourist office is in a small, upstairs room across from the station to the left. A road runs straight out from the station, across the river by the Sayaji Bagh and into the main part of town.

Sayaji Bagh & Baroda Museum

This extensive park is a popular spot for an evening stroll and also has a small zoo. A mini-railway encircles the park. Within the park is the Baroda Museum and Art Gallery which is open 9.30 am to 4.45 pm daily, except Saturday when it opens at 10 am. Admission is 20p. The museum has a varied collection, while the gallery has Moghul miniatures and also a collection of European masters. Also within the park grounds is the relatively new planetarium where there is an English language performance at 6 pm each evening, admission is Rs 2.

Maharajah Fateh Singh Museum

A little south of the centre this royal art collection includes European works by Raphael, Titian and Murillo and exhibits of Graeco-Roman, Chinese and Japanese art as well as Indian exhibits. The museum is open 9 am to 12 noon and 3 to 6 pm from July to March, 4 to 7 pm April to June. It is closed on Mondays and admission is 75p. The museum is in the palace grounds.

Other

The flamboyant Lakshmi Vilas Palace has a large collection of armour and sculptures, but is not normally open to the public. The Naulakhi Well, a fine *baoli* or step well, is 50 metres north of the palace. These interesting multi-level wells are unique to Gujarat. Others you may visit are the Dada Hari well in Ahmedabad and the Adalaj well just outside that city.

The Railway Staff College now occupies the Pratap Vilas Palace; there are a number of other palaces in the city. The Gaekwad rulers' family vault, the Kirti Mandir, is decorated with murals by Indian artist Nandial Bose. The centre of town is built around a lake swarming with fish – vendors sell food to throw to them.

Tours

From the railway station, book at the tourist office opposite, there is a daily tour from Tuesdays to Saturdays departing at 2 pm and returning at 6 pm. Tour cost is Rs 7.

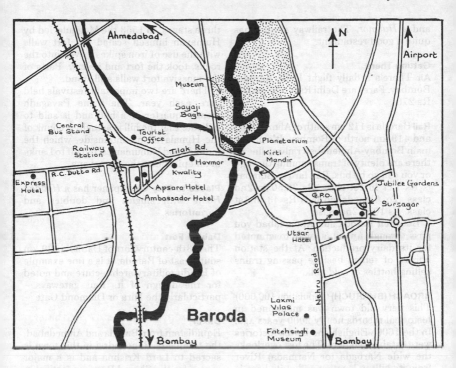

Ahmedabad

N

Airport

Museum

Sayaji Bagh

Central Bus Stand

Tourist Office

Railway Station

Tilak Rd.

Haymor

Kwality

Planetarium

Kirti Mandir

R.C. Dutta Rd

Express Hotel

Apsara Hotel

Ambassador Hotel

Jubilee Gardens

Sursagar

G.P.O.

Utsav Hotel

Baroda

Nehru Road

Laxmi Vilas Palace

Fatehsingh Museum

Bombay

Bombay

Places to Stay – Bottom End

There are a lot of cheaper hotels within walking distance of the railway station. If you head straight out from the station and take the second road right you'll find the *Laxmi Lodge* where doubles cost Rs 40. The pleasant and well kept *Apsara* is Rs 50 for small, but comfortable, doubles with attached bathroom. Across the road and a little further down is the big *Ambassador* where singles are Rs 50 and doubles Rs 70. Finally right down on the corner is the *Chandan Mahal* at Rs 60 with bath, Rs 50 without. There are other cheap hotels along this road (like the *Baroda Guest House*), but they're not so good.

The *Municipal Corporation Guest House*, or Pravashi Gruh, is directly opposite the railway station and has rooms from around Rs 25 to 60. It's

conveniently situated but rather drab and grey. *Railway Retiring Rooms* are Rs 30/50. The new *Motel Suren* has small rooms for Rs 45/60.

Places to Stay – Top End

The *Utsav Hotel* (tel 51415) on Professor Manekrao Rd, near the centre, is centrally air-conditioned and has singles/doubles at Rs 150/225. It also has the Tana Restaurant. Other top end hotels include the *Express Hotel* on R C Dutt Rd (tel 67051-54) with air-con singles/doubles for Rs 250/300.

Places to Eat

The *Ambassador Hotel* is popular for its excellent Rs 8 thalis. Along the main road from the station towards the gardens and the river, there's a reasonable *Kwality*, good lunch-time snacks on its verandah, and a *Havmor*. The railway station has quite a good restaurant.

Getting There
Air There's a daily flight Delhi-Baroda-Bombay. Fares are Delhi Rs 635, Bombay Rs 276.

Rail Baroda is 112 km south of Ahmedabad and 419 km north of Bombay. It's on the main Bombay-Ahmedabad railway line so there are plenty of trains running through or you can go by bus. Rail fare to Bombay is Rs 127 in 1st class, Rs 32.50 in 2nd class. To Ahmedabad it is Rs 43 in 1st class, Rs 10 in 2nd class.

Between Baroda and Ahmedabad you pass through Anand, a small town noted for its dairy production. At the station hordes of sellers besiege passing trains selling bottles of *cold* milk.

BROACH (BHARUCH) (population 100,000) This very old town was mentioned in historical records nearly 2000 years ago. In the 1600s English and Dutch factories were established here. The fort overlooks the wide Narbada (or Narmada) River from its hilltop location and at its base is the Jami Masjid which was constructed from a Jain temple. On the riverbank, outside the city to the east, is the Temple of Bhrigu Rishi, from which the city took its name of Bhrigukachba, later shortened to Bharuch. Near Broach the town of Suklatirtha has a holiday home and at the nearby island of Kabirwad, in the river, there is a gigantic banyan tree which covers a hectare.

AROUND BARODA
Champaner
North-east of Baroda, 47 km along the main broad gauge railway line to Delhi, Champaner was taken by Saltan Mahmud Begara in 1484. The Jami Masjid in this city is one of the finest mosques in Gujarat and is similar in style to the Jami Masjid of Ahmedabad. The hill of Pavagadh, with its ruined fort, rises beside Champaner, in

three stages. In 1553 the Moghuls, led by Humayan himself scaled the fort walls with the use of iron spikes driven into the rocks, took the fort and its city. Parts of the massive fort walls still stand.

There are two important festivals held here each year. The name Pavagadh means 'quarter of a hill' and is said to indicate that the hill is actually a chunk of the Himalayan mountainside, which the monkey god Hanuman carted off to Lanka in an episode of the Ramayana.

Places to Stay Champaner has a *Holiday Home* with singles and doubles and dormitories.

Dabhoi Fort
The 13th century fort of Dabhoi is 29 km south-east of Baroda. It is a fine example of Hindu military architecture and noted for the design of its four gateways – particularly the Hira or Diamond Gate.

Dakor
Equidistant from Baroda and Ahmedabad, the temple of Ranchodrai in this town is sacred to Lord Krishna and is a major centre for the Sharad Purnima festival in October or November.

SURAT (population 500,000)
Standing on the banks of the River Tapti this was once one of the major ports and trading towns of western India. Two hundred years ago it had a bigger population than it does today and was far more important than Bombay. In the 12th century Parsis first settled in Surat; they had earlier been centred 100 km south in Sanjan, where they had fled from Persia five centuries before. In 1573 the city fell to Akbar after a prolonged siege, and became an important Moghul trading port and also the departure point for Moslem pilgrims bound for Mecca.

Surat soon became a wealthy city and in 1612 the British established a trading factory in Surat followed by the Dutch in 1616 and the French in 1664. Portuguese

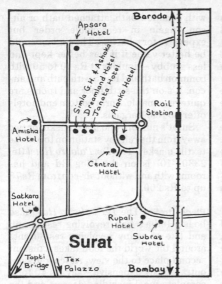

Apsara Hotel

Baroda

Simla G.H. • Ashoka Hotel
Dreamland Hotel
Janata Hotel
Alanka Hotel

Rail Station

Amisha Hotel

Central Hotel

Satkara Hotel

Rupali Hotel

Subraq Hotel

Surat

Tapti Bridge

Tex Palazzo

Bombay

Orientation An eight km long wall encircled Surat on its land side, while the Tapti River forms the other side. Until the sack of the city by Shivaji the walls were made of mud, but they were then reconstructed in brick. The railway station, with many cheaper hotels in its immediate vicinity, is connected to the old fort beside the river by one of Surat's few wide roads.

Castle Built in 1546, the castle is beside the Tapti Bridge on the river bank. It is of no great interest today since most of it is given over to offices but there is a good view over the city and river from the bastions. Ask for the Tapti Bridge if you want to get to it.

Factories Without a guide you would have difficulty finding the remains of the factories, and in any case there is little to indicate their former importance. They are near the IP Mission High School. The English Factory is about midway from the castle to the Kataragama Gate out of the old city. Standing close to the river the Portuguese Factory, French Lodge and Persian Factory were also close by. From the river bank you can see the Tapti Bridge to your left, and across the river to your right you'll see the mosque studded suburb of Rander. There's a small temple to Hanuman by the river.

Cemeteries Just beyond the Kataragama Gate, to the right of the main road, is the now very run down, overrun and neglected English Cemetery. Note how many of the tombstones are for children under five years of age. As you enter the cemetery the huge mausoleum to the right is that of Sir George Oxenden, who died in 1669. The structure is actually a tomb within a tomb since his brother was buried here 10 years earlier, then a larger mausoleum constructed over that tomb. Another large tomb next to it is said to be that of Gerald Aungier, the next President of the English Factory. Like any scrap of waste ground in

power on the west coast had been severely curtailed by a crashing naval defeat at the hands of the British settlement in India. In 1664 Moghul power and prestige suffered a severe blow when the Mahratta leader Shivaji sacked the town. In a classic display of British stiff upper lip, Sir George Oxenden, sent a message to Shivaji, from the strongly defended English Factory, that he should 'save the labour of his servants running to and fro on messages and come himself with all his army'. Perhaps Shivaji took him seriously because the English Factory was not attacked.

Although the English Factory later transferred its 'Presidency' to Bombay, Surat continued to prosper and in 1720 a dock was built followed by two British shipyards. In 1759, by which time Moghul power was long past its prime, the British virtually took full control over the ruler of the city and by 1800 the city was in British hands. Today Surat is no longer of any importance as a port, but it is an important manufacturing town with a major textile industry.

India the English Cemetery has become a public toilet and the imposing mausoleums are in a sorry state.

Backtrack towards the city and about half a km after the Kataragama Gate, and a hundred or so metres off the road to the left (to the right if you are coming from the centre) is the Dutch Cemetery. The mausoleum of Baron Adriaan van Reede, who died in 1691, is a massive structure and at one time was decorated with frescoes and wood carvings. Note the inscription on the wall where 'Souratta' rates capital letters while lesser 'bombai' is in lower case. Adjoining the Dutch Cemetery is the Armenian Cemetery.

Other Surat has a number of mosques and Jain, Hindu and Parsi temples. Cotton, silk and the manufacture of bangles are important industries in Surat. The nearby town of Rander, five km across the Hope Bridge, was built on the site of a very ancient Hindu city after it had been taken by the Moslems in 1225. Swally (Suvali) was the old port for Surat, situated 19 km to the west. It was off Swally, in 1615, that Portuguese colonial aspirations in India were ended by the British navy.

Places to Stay There are lots of hotels near the railway station but no standouts. They're all within reasonable walking distance. In the basic cheapie bracket the *Subras* has dorm beds and cell-like singles/doubles at Rs 15/25 with common bath and Rs 20/35 with attached bath. The next door *Rupali* is Rs 6 (dorm), Rs 12 (single) and Rs 30 (double with bath), but it's a grubby little place.

The *Central* is slightly higher class as is the pleasant enough *Hotel Dreamland* (singles Rs 35 to 40, doubles Rs 55 to 65) – the Rs 10 difference gets you a carpet on the floor! Close by are two basic cheapies – the *Hotel Ashoka* and the *Simla Guest House* – the latter has doubles at Rs 30, fair value and reasonably clean.

Just a bit further down is the *Hotel Anishna* with singles from Rs 30 to Rs 100

with common bath, attached bath or air-con. Again in reasonable order but expensive for what it is. The *Satkar* would be better value if it was better kept and less grubby – doubles at Rs 40 to 50 with common bath and Rs 75 with bath and air-con. It's on the sixth floor and rooms are quite reasonable. Surat bottom end hotels offer no real bargains.

Surat's numero uno hotel is a km or two away from the railway station on top of the textile market. The *Tex Palazzo Hotel* (tel 23301-10) is on the Ring Rd and has rooms with and without air-con from Rs 75 up to Rs 200.

Places to Eat The *Tex Palazzo Hotel* also boasts India's first revolving restaurant, and like so many revolving restaurants around the world the food takes a distant second place to the view. At least it's not outrageously expensive – say Rs 40 for a complete meal including dessert and tea or coffee. But the splendours of Surat unfold below you through windows nearly as grubby and dirty as those on the average Indian bus! In fact it's rather the way you'd imagine an Indian revolving restaurant to be. The ride to the top costs Rs 1.

Back at ground level you can get a Gujarati thali for Rs 9 in the same hotel. You pay a similar price in the good air-con restaurant upstairs in the otherwise rather grotty *Subras Hotel* near the railway station. Downstairs the thalis are cheaper but you pay extra for second helpings.

AROUND SURAT

There are a number of beaches near Surat. Only 16 km out, Dumas is a popular health resort. Hajira is 28 km from the city, Ubhrat is 42 km out, while Tithal is 108 km away and only five km from Valsad on the Bombay-Baroda rail line. Navsari, 29 km south of Surat has been a headquarters for the Parsi community since the earliest days of their settlement in India. Udvada, which is only 10 km north of Vapi, the station for Daman, has the oldest Parsi sacred fire in India. It is said that the fire was brought from Persia to Diu, on the opposite coast of the Gulf of Cambay, in 700 AD. Sanjan, in the extreme south of the state, is the small port where they first landed.

DAMAN

Right in the south of Gujarat the tiny enclave of Daman was, along with Diu, taken from the Portuguese at the same time as Goa. It is still, officially, governed from Goa along with Diu. Its main function seems to be as a place to get a drink as Gujarat is completely 'dry'. Lots of 'Finest scotch whisky – Made in India' and the streets are lined with bars!

The Portuguese seized Daman, which totals 380 square km in area, in 1531 and were officially ceded the region by Bahadur Shah of Gujarat in 1559. There is still some Portuguese flavour to the town with a fine old fort and a number of churches and other imposing Portuguese buildings. The town is split in two by the Damao Ganga River. A ferry shuttles back and forth for 10p and a bridge is under slow construction. The northern part of the town, with the hotels, restaurants, bars and so on is known as 'little' Daman while the southern part, with government buildings and churches, all enclosed within an imposing wall, is known as 'big' Daman.

Although Daman is, like Goa, beside the sea, its beaches bear no relation to those glowing, golden stretches further south. Daman's beaches are grey, drab, dirty and dismal – quite apart from their function as the local toilet.

Places to Stay The *PWD Rest House* is very well kept and rooms at Rs 8 are a great bargain, but it is often full up. Right across the road is the *Brighton Hotel* which is a reasonable second best with rooms from Rs 20, but this too is often full. A little further back up the road from the beach the *Sovereign Hotel* is big and also well kept with rooms at a variety of prices

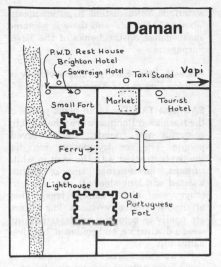

from Rs 20 and up. Some of them are rather cubical like, but there is also a popular upstairs restaurant – a good place for a beer on the verandah.

Back beyond the taxi stand the *Hotel Tourist* is a dump to avoid – a newish building but totally neglected and miserable at Rs 15 per person. Daman has lots of bars but not a great variety of places to eat.

Getting There Vapi Station, on the main railway line, is the jumping off point for Daman. Vapi is about 170 km from Bombay and 90 km from Surat. Take care, not all trains stop at Vapi so be very certain yours will be halting there or you'll sail straight by (as we did – Tony). From Vapi it's 10 or so km into Daman and there are plenty of share taxis for a couple of rupees per person. Or buses at less than Rs 1.

SAPUTARA

In the south-east corner of the state, this cool hill resort stands at 1000 metres and is a popular base for excursions to Mahal Bardipara forest wildlife santuary 60 km waterfalls, 52 km distant. Saputara means 'abode of serpents' and there is a sacred snake image on the banks of the River Sarpagana.

Places to Stay Sarutara has a variety of *Holiday Homes* and *Tourist Bungalows*.

SAURASHTRA The often bleak plains of the Kathiawar Peninsula are inhabited by colourful and friendly, but reserved, people. The country people are distinctively dressed with the men in white turbans, laced-across smocks (short-waisted and long-sleeved) and jodhpurs (baggy seat and drainpipe legs). They often sport golden ear-studs. The women are nearly as colourful as Rajasthan but wear a distinctive, embroidered, backless halter-top.

It's a pleasant area to travel around and there is an extensive network of metre-gauge railway lines to make that travel much easier although the trains are very slow. Most people travel by bus – there are limited stop de-luxe buses. Saurashtra is rather out on a limb and pretty much off the main tourist routes. A severe cyclone in late '82 caused extensive damage and more than 600 deaths in the Veraval, Amreh, Bhavnagar region.

The peninsula took its name from the Kathi tribespeople who used to roam the area stealing whatever was not locked into the many village forts or *kots* at night. You may notice, around Kathiawar, long lines of memorial stones known as *palias* – men are usually shown riding on large horses while women ride on wheels, which shows that they were in carriages.

BHAVNAGAR (population 250,000)
Founded as a port in 1723, Bhavnagar is still an important trading post for the cotton goods manufactured in Gujarat. The Gandhi Smitri is a library, small museum, gallery and memorial to the founder of India. Bhavnagar also has the Gaurishankar Lake, a popular picnic spot, and the Takhteshwar Temple with fine

views from its hilltop location. The Bhavnagar lock gate keeps ships afloat during low tides in the city's port.

Places to Stay Basic hotels include the *Evergreen Guest House* (tel 4605), the *Kashmir Hotel* near the Pathik Ashram and *Geeta Lodging & Boarding* (tel 3985). Bhavnagar also has the *Pathik Ashram* with rooms around Rs 15 and *Railway Retiring Rooms*. The *Mahavir Lodge*, near the station has good thalis for Rs 6.

The *Natraj Guest House*, Nirmalnagar, Diamond Market is an eight minute walk from the bus station and has singles/doubles for Rs 15/30. It's a good place and there's also a Rs 7 dorm. It doesn't (or didn't) have a sign but everyone knows the diamond market and once there it's easy. Yes there really are lots of little shops that sell diamonds. Why in Bhavnagar? Their first ever western guest, who wrote to tell us about this hotel, says his photograph was going up in the reception area!

Bhavnagar has two better hotels, both with air-con rooms. They are the *Apollo Hotel* (tel 5251-52) opposite the Central Bus Stand and the *Hotel Takte-Khurshid* (tel 6881) on Waghawadi Rd, near Takhteshwara. The Apollo has rooms at Rs 80/105 or Rs 130/150 with air-con.

Places to Eat There's nowhere much to eat around the bus station apart from the expensive Apollo. Take an auto-rickshaw (Rs 2 or 3) to the *Nataraj Restaurant* which has good food and a two page menu of ice cream goodies! Outside the *Vadilal Ice Cream* sign is more prominent than *Nataraj*. Tell rickshaw wallahs it's opposite Ganga Devi.

There's also a *Havmor Restaurant* diagonally across from the main covered food market and on the edge of the extensive shopping area.

Getting There Bhavnagar is 244 km by road from Ahmedabad or about 270 km by rail. The rail trip takes about seven hours and costs Rs 86 in 1st class, Rs 22 in 2nd.

There are also buses connecting Bhavnagar with Ahmedabad amd other centres in the region. There's a daily flight connection with Bombay which costs Rs 247.

PALITANA

Situated 56 km from Bhavnagar, Palitana is a gateway to Shatrunjaya, the 'place of victory'. From here you have a two-km walk, up 600 metres to the hilltop where, over a period of 900 years, 863 temples have been constructed. The hilltop is dedicated entirely to the gods, at dusk even the priests depart from the temples and leave them deserted.

Almost all the temples are Jain and this hill, one of the holiest pilgrimage places for Jains, is another indication of the merit Jains belive is derived from constructing temples. The hilltops are bounded by sturdy walls and the temples are grouped into nine enclosures or *tuks* – each with a central major temple and many minor ones clustered around. Some of the earliest temples were built here in the 11th century, but in the 14th and 15th centuries those spoilsport Moslems knocked them down, so the current temples date from the 1500s down to the present time.

The hilltop affords a very fine view in all directions, on a clear day you can see the Gulf of Cambay beyond Bhavnagar. The most notable of the temples is that to Shri Adishwara, the first Jain Tirthankar. Note the frieze of dragons around the temple. Adjacent to this temple is the Moslem shrine of Angar Pir. Women wanting children make offerings of miniature cradles at this shrine.

Built in 1618 by a wealthy Jain merchant the Chaumukh, or 'four faced' shrine, has images of Adinath facing out in the four cardinal directions. Other important temples are those to Kumar Pal, Sampriti Raj and Vimal Shah. The marble temples are so thick on the hill summit that it looks like some giant, glistening white wedding cake from a distance. The temples are open from 7 am

Palitana

to 7 pm. Temple jewels are shown at 9 am to 3 pm, image washing is at 9.45 am, puja at 10.45 am.

If you're taking a camera up the hill you'll need a photography permit. The Hotel Sumeru Toran will fix these up for you if you're staying there – they're issued three permits daily as a matter of course so ask at reception in advance. You will only be asked for the permit at the main entrance, which you get to by taking the left hand fork as you near the top. If you enter the complex by taking the right hand fork there's no one there to ask for the permit.

A horse cart to the base of the hill costs Rs 3 per person or Rs 5 if you're by yourself. The walk is not strenuous although it's time consuming. For Rs 40 round trip (one-way up Rs 30) you can take a *dooli* swing chair!

Valabhipur North of Palitana this ancient city was once the capital of this part of India. Extensive ruins have been located and archaeologial finds exhibited in a museum, but there's little to see apart from scattered stones.

Places to Stay Palitana has scores of *choultries* (pilgrims' rest houses) but unless you're a Jain it's unlikely any of them will allow you to stay. That leaves only one place for foreigners, the *Hotel Sumeru Toran* (tel 227) on Station Rd. This is a Tourism Corporation of Gujarat enterprise which offers excellent accommodation at reasonable prices. Doubles with spotless, tiled bathrooms with hot and cold water, clean sheets and a balcony are Rs 45. Single occupancy is Rs 25, depending on demand and the season. There are also two 13-bed dormitories and one with eight beds where you can get a bed for Rs 6.

The manager of this hotel is extremely friendly and helpful and speaks perfect English. If you want a photo permit, want to know which is the best bus to take out of Palitana, in fact anything like that, then just ask him. The hotel also has an excellent restaurant with very reasonable prices, Rs 5 for a thali.

Getting There If you're coming from the north there are plenty of state transport authority buses from Bhavnagar. They cost Rs 5 and take half an hour to 45 minutes (or more) but it's advisable to buy a seat reservation ticket for Rs 1 as they tend to be very crowded. Pay your fare on the bus.

Between Palitana and Diu, which is the route most travellers take, the route is Palitana-Talaja-Mahuva-Una-Diu. If you're going in that direction then it's advisable to travel early in the day (before 10 am). As soon as the heat gets up local people behave as though there were a pack of lepers advancing down the main street intent on mischief. Getting on to public transport in Kerala is a battle royale but this is something else! By comparison, Keralan buses are like a vicarage tea party!

The first part of the journey isn't too trying even if you set off late. If you're interested in Jain temples Talaja also has hill-top monuments though they're nowhere near as extensive as those at Palitana. Most of the buses which come through Talaja, however, originate elsewhere (usually at Bhavnagar, Mahuva or Una) and they are always full to bursting when they arrive. Despite the obvious impossibility of getting anyone else on a good percentage of those who have been waiting do achieve this feat. Including one of the writers of this book (it was Geoff) though it cost him 2½ hours of hanging from a roof rail with a pack on his back and a shoulder bag in one hand being jostled like crazy everytime the bus stopped (which was frequently) because nobody could get past him. And then there was no connecting bus from Mahuva.

In brief Palitana-Talaju has frequent buses which cost Rs 3 and take one hour along the rough road. Take the 7 am bus if you're heading for Diu. Talaja-Mahuva has fairly regular buses through the morning and early afternoon but very few in the late afternoon. The fare is Rs 3.50 and it takes about 1½ hours. The 7 am bus from Palitana continues to Una and you won't have to change. Note that Mahuva is pronounced 'Mauwa'.

For Mahuva-Una there are frequent buses all day until 5 pm. They cost Rs 8.40 and take about 3½ hours. There are few buses Una-Ghogla but most people take a shared auto-rickshaw, motorcycle-rickshaw or a pickup truck. The locals pay Rs 2 for this trip but you'll be asked for Rs 10 to 15, even Rs 25 to 50 in some cases! Tell them firmly where to go! The journey takes about 20 minutes and you may well be asked for your passport as you cross from Gujarat to Diu. The auto-rickshaws and so on for Ghoghla don't leave from outside the bus stand in Una but from another street about three minutes' walk away. Rickshaw drivers will, naturally, offer to take you there for Rs 2 to 3.

Ghoghla-Diu is by ferry. You'll be dropped off at the entrance to Ghoghla from where you must walk about a km down the main street to the ferries. They cross when full throughout the day and evening. The crossing takes three or four minutes and costs Rs 0.25.

DIU (population 30,500)

Diu is one of India's undiscovered gems. Like Daman and Goa it was a Portuguese colony until taken over by India in 1961 and it is still governed as part of the Union Territory of Goa, Daman and Diu rather than as a part of Gujarat. Most of the ex-colony consists of the island of Diu itself, which is about 11 km long by three km wide, separated from the coast by a narrow channel, but there are also two tiny mainland enclaves. One of these, on which the village of Ghoghla stands, is the entry point to Diu if you come in through the town of Una. Diu's crowning glory is the huge fort which was constructed by the Portuguese in 1547. It's a sight which rewards all the trials and tribulations of

getting here on public transport.

These days its hard to understand why the Portuguese should have been interested in capturing and fortifying such an apparently unimportant and isolated an outpost as Diu but in the 14th, 15th and 16th centuries it was an important trading post and naval base from which the Ottoman Turks controlled the shipping routes in the northern part of the Arabian Sea.

After an unsuccessful attempt to take the island in 1531, during which the Sultan of Gujarat was assisted by the Turkish navy, the Portuguese finally secured control in 1534 by taking advantage of a quarrel between the Sultan and the Moghul Emperor, Humayun. He had sent an army into the Sultan's territory in search of Mirza Zamal, who had made an attempt on the emperor's life. Not wanting to fight on two fronts, the Sultan concluded a treaty with the Portuguese which allowed them to stay in Diu in return for providing 500 infantry men for service with the Sultan. The treaty was soon cast to the wind and although both Bahadurshah, the Sultan of Gujarat, and his nephew, Sultan Mahmad III, attempted to contest the issue a peace treaty was eventually signed in 1539 in which the island of Diu and the mainland enclave of Ghoghla were ceded to the Portuguese. Soon after this treaty was signed the Portuguese began constructing their virtually impregnable fortress.

The northern side of the island, facing Gujarat, is tidal marsh and salt-pans while the southern coast alternates between limestone cliffs, rocky coves and sandy beaches, the best of which is at Nagoa. The somewhat windswept and arid island is riddled with quarries where vast quantities of limestone have been removed during the Portuguese era to construct huge monuments and buildings. The interior of the island reaches a maximum height of just 29 metres and is either rocky or sandy, so agriculture is limited although there are extensive stands of coconut and

Diu Island

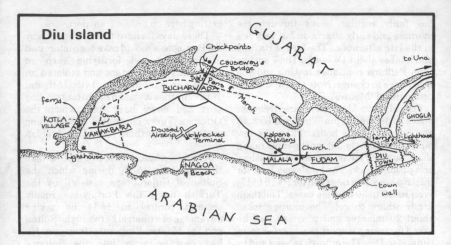

other palms. Branching palms (Hyphaene species) are very much a feature of the island and were originally introduced from Africa by the Portuguese.

The Indian government appears to have an official policy of playing down the Portuguese era. A memorial commemorates the seven Rajput soldiers (six of them Singhs) killed in Operation Vijay which liberated the island. A few civilians were also killed. The Indian Air Force bombed the airstrip terminal, near Nagao and it has still not been repaired! The old church in Diu Fort was also bombed and is now a roofless ruin. It's said the Portuguese blew up Government House to prevent it falling into 'enemy' hands.

Diu Town

The main industry of the island would have to be fishing, followed by booze and salt! A distillery at Malala produces rum from mainland-grown sugar cane. The town boasts quite a few bars, where visitors from the 'dry' mainland can enjoy a beer (or stronger IMFL – 'Indian Made Foreign Liquor'). The town is sandwiched between the massive fort to the east and a huge city wall to the west. An old gateway in the wall has some nice carvings of lions,

angels and a priest – just inside the gate is a miniature chapel with an icon, dating to 1702. Diu Town has two churches – St Paul's and St Francis of Assisi. It's said that there are now only 15 Christian families left on the whole island!

The town is a maze of meandering and often leafy lanes. Many of the houses are well ornamented and brightly painted, a legacy of the Portuguese era. The main 'town square' is on the northern shore and all the buses operate from here, the post office and banks (three of them) are nearby along with Goa Travels, customs, a few bars and a (useless) tourist info office. A gateway with a bell leads off the square down to the ferry quay. Diu also has a tiny, but beautiful, bazaar.

The massive fort is well worth a couple of hours. It must have been virtually impregnable in the past with its double moat – one tidal. Sea erosion and neglect are leading to its slow, inevitable collapse. Piles of cannon balls litter the place and the ramparts have a superb array of cannons, many old and in good condition. One dates from 1624, built by Don Diego de Silva Conde de Porta Legre in the reign of Don Philippe, Rex d'Espana – all legible. The cannons have all been catalogued by the Archaeological Survey of India and bear ASI numbers. But who has been responsible for cementing out many of the old inscriptions – an unforgiveable act of vandalism! Diu urgently deserves a museum, but it's hardly probable given the lack of official imagination here.

Other Villages

Diu town is the main centre but there are also a number of interesting villages:

Fudam has a huge abandoned church, Our Lady of Remedies. A large, old, carved wooden altar with Madonna and child remains inside but the vestry has become a manger, full of straw!

Vanakbana at the extreme west has another church, Our Lady of Mercy, a fort, a lighthouse and a post office. A sailing ferry operates across to Kotla village on the mainland from here. You can get a bus

from Kotla to Kodinar.

Bucharwada is the village on the northern side, not far from the mainland. There is a checkpoint either side of the bridge, where vehicle drivers have to sign a book.

Nagoa has a beautiful palm-fringed beach, safe for swimming. One of the two island buses leaves Diu for Nagoa at 7 and 11 am, returning at 7.45 am and 1 pm daily.

Places to Stay & Eat

There's a *PWD Rest House*, towards the fort, which is clean, quiet and well run. It's excellent value at Rs 12 a double, but it's often full. Meals, other than breakfast, have to be ordered in advance. Lunch is a thali and good fish and prawn dishes are available on request. Alternatively there's the *Nilesh Guest House* with rooms with common bath at Rs 15/20 or Rs 25 for the solitary double with attached bath. There's a bar and a mediocre restaurant

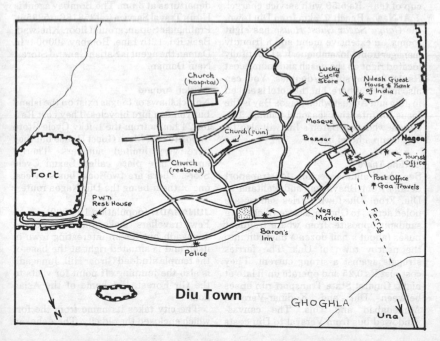

and extensions are underway. Diu town has nowhere that could be called a restaurant – just a few chai shops and stalls.

The PWD Rest House and the Nilesh Guest House are OK but if you've made so much effort to get to Diu it's worth paying a little more to stay somewhere special. *Baron's Inn* (previously the Municipal Guest House and before that the Pensoa Beira Mar) is also on the Old Fort Rd, halfway between the ferry quay and the PWD Rest House and offers accommodation in an old Portuguese villa. It's right by the sea, overlooking the channel between Diu town and Ghoghla. The management are very friendly and keen to retain the ambience of the place. Spacious rooms with fan and attached bathroom are Rs 45/60. Good meals, Indian or seafood, can be provided on request – fried fish, dhal/chips and roti costs Rs 14. The only complaint is how they can justify Rs 5 for a cup of tea – Rs 5.50 with service charge!

At Nagoa Beach, 7½ km from Diu town, the *Ganga Sagar Guest House* has eight rooms, an extensive menu and a friendly manager from Mozambique. It's beautifully located right on the beach and rooms cost Rs 18/20 for singles/doubles. You can also hire bikes here, but the hotel is closed in July and August when Nagoa Bay is the focus for intensive seasonal fishing. The people who own Baron's Inn will also be setting up a hotel here.

Getting There

See the Palitana section for transport details from Bhavnagar and Palitana to Diu. From Diu town ferries sail or are poled across to Ghogla, a large village on a sandspit opposite, from where frequent buses (about a half dozen a day) run into the nearby town of Una. The ferries struggle against a strong current. They cost just Rs 0.25 and operate until late at night. Gujarat State Transport run buses between Diu and Kodinar-Veraval, Ahmedabad and Una. The canvas-windowed bus from Veraval to Diu costs Rs 8.50.

If, en route to Diu, you get into Mahuva after 5 pm at night, you'll have to stay there overnight as there will be no connecting bus to Una. You can try the *Rupam Guest House* where hardboard partitioned cubicles cost Rs 10/15 for singles/doubles. There's a fan, common showers, lots of mosquitoes but no bed bugs. It's a bit Dickensian but OK for a night. As you come out of the bus stand you'll see a cinema opposite. Go straight down that road in front of you with the cinema on your right hand side and take the third road on the right. The Rupam is about three doors down.

Goa Travels operates a 'luxury' coach service about six times a week on a somewhat flexible itinerary between Diu and Bombay via Bhavnagar, Anand and Vapi (for Daman). The trip takes 20-plus hours and costs Rs 145 all the way. Diu departures are at 11.30 am, Bombay departures at 3 pm. The Bombay agent is Hirup Travel Service (tel 358186, 359856), Prabhakar Sadan, ground floor, Khetwadi Back Rd, 12th Line, Bombay 400004. In Daman the agent is Satish General Stores, Nani Daman.

Getting Around

No rickshaws or tongas exist on the island but you can hire bicycles. They cost Rs 5 for 24 hours from the Lucky Cycle Store opposite the Nilesh Guest House but they have very limited numbers. There's another hire place called Laxmi Cycle Store. There are two local bus services, one of them being the Diu-Nagoa route.

JUNAGADH (population 100,000)

Few travellers make the trip out to Junagadh but it's an interesting town in itself and is situated right at the base of the temple studded Girnar Hill. Junagadh is also the jumping off point for visits to the Gir Forest, last home of the Asian lion.

The city takes its name from the fort which enclosed the old city. The Ashokan edicts, dating from 250 BC, near the town indicate the great antiquity of this site. At the time of partition the Nawab of Junagadh opted to take his tiny state into Pakistan, but the inhabitants were predominantly Hindu and the Nawab soon found himself in exile.

Tourists are a very unusual sight here. 'We changed money at the Bank of India', wrote one of those rare visitors, 'it only took 90 minutes'. You can find out more about the city in the booklet *Junagadh & Girnar* by S H Desai.

Uparkot

The old fort, from which the city derived its name, stands on the eastern side of Junagadh. It is very old and has been rebuilt and extended many times in its history. In places the fort walls are 20 metres high and the fort is entered by an ornate, triple gateway. It's said that the fort was once besieged, unsuccessfully, for a full 12 years and in all it was besieged 16 times! It is also said that the fort was completely abandoned from the 7th to 10th centuries and was rediscovered, completely swamped by the jungle. The top of the old fort forms a plateau-like area covered in lantana scrub. Paths go from one point of interest to the next.

Inside the fort is a mosque, the Jami Masjid, built from a demolished Hindu temple. Other points of interest include the Tomb of Nuri Shah and two fine wells known as the Adi Chadi and the Naughan. The Adi Chadi was named after two slave girls who fetched water from it. The Naughan is reached by a magnificent circular staircase. Close to the mosque there are also some very old Buddhist caves, thought to be more than 1500 years old, cut into the hillside. The double-storey cave has six pillars with very fine carvings. There are other caves in Junagadh including some, thought to date back to the time of Ashoka. The soft rock on which Junagadh is built encouraged the construction of caves and wells.

Apart from the amazing wells and caves

another point of interest is the colossal five-metre long cannon called *Nilam*. It was cast in Egypt in 1531 and left behind by a Turkish admiral, who was assisting the Sultan of Gujarat against the Portuguese at Diu in 1538.

Maqbara

The mausoleums of the Nawabs of Junagadh feature silver doors and intricate architecture, including minarets with spiralling stairways. The keys can be obtained from the adjacent mosque. The Maqbara badly needs maintenance work.

Durbar Hall Museum

In the Durbar Hall and Sileh Khana of the palace the usual weapons and armour from the Nawabs are displayed along with their collection of silver chains and chandeliers, settees and thrones, howdahs and palanquins, a few cushions and gowns, a portrait gallery of the Nawabs and local petty princes, including photos of the last Nawab with his various beloved dogs. It's open 9.30 to 11.45 am and 3 to 5.30 pm and admission is 20 paise.

Other

Junagadh's zoo in the Sakar Bagh has Gir lions, should you be unable to visit the Gir Forest. It's surprisingly good with well kept lions, tigers, leopards and crocodiles as main attractions. The garden also has a fine museum. Junagadh has a number of other lovely gardens. Narsi Mehta, a Gujarati 'poet-saint', has a shrine in the city.

Ashoka Edicts

On the way to the Girnar Hill temples you pass a huge boulder on which the Emperor Ashoka inscribed 14 edicts around 250 BC. His inscription is in the Pali script. Later inscriptions were added in Sanskrit around 150 AD by Rudradama and 450 AD by Skandagupta, the last emperor of the Mauryas. The 14 edicts are moral lectures, while the other inscriptions mainly refer to recurring floods destroying

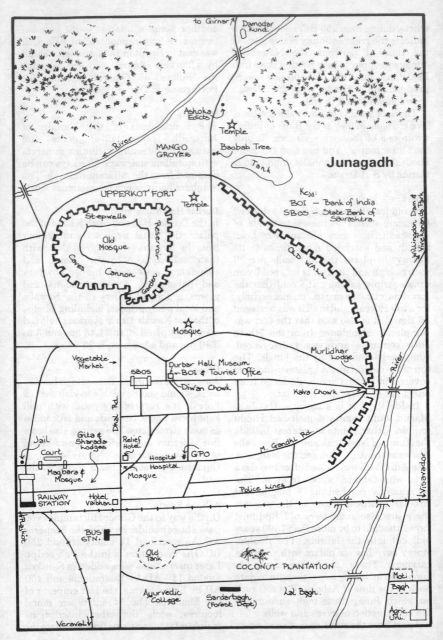

to Girnar / Damodar Kund

Ashoka Edicts

Temple

Baobab Tree

MANGO GROVES

River

Tank

Junagadh

UPPERKOT FORT

Temple

Step-wells

Reservoir

Old Mosque

Caves

Cannon

Garden

OLD WALL

Willingdon Dam & Vivekananda Park

Key:—
BOI — Bank of India
SBOS — State Bank of Saurashtra.

River

Mosque

Vegetable Market

SBOS

Dhol. Rd.

Durbar Hall Museum
BOI & Tourist Office

Diwan Chowk

Kalva Chowk

Murlidhar Lodge

Jail

Court

Gita & Sharada Lodges

Relief Hotel

Magbara & Mosque

Mosque

Hospital
Hospital

GPO

M. Gandhi Rd.

Wosavador

RAILWAY STATION

Hotel Vaibhav

Police Lines

to Rajkot

BUS STN.

Old Tank

COCONUT PLANTATION

Moti Bagh

Agric. Uni.

to Veraval

Ayurvedic College

Sardarbagh (Forest Dept)

Lal Bagh

the embankments of Sudershan Lake which was nearby, it no longer exists. The boulder is actually housed in a small roadside building, on the right if you're heading towards Girnar.

Girnar Hill

It's a 600-metre ascent, up 10,000 stone steps, to the 1118-metre high summit of Girnar. The steps are well-built and maintained and were constructed between 1889 and 1908 from the proceeds of a lottery! The start of the climb is a km or two beyond the sacred Damodar Kund in a scrubby teak forest. There are frequent refreshment stalls on the ascent which takes 2½ to three hours. You'll see monkeys by the path and eagles soaring by. At the summit sadhus may lecture you on the virtues of reading the Gita and practising yoga! It's best to make the climb early in the morning, preferably at dawn.

Like Palitana the temple-topped hill is of great significance to the Jains. The sacred tank of Damodar Kund marks the start of the climb to the temples. The path ascends through a wood to the marble temples near the summit. Five of them are Jain temples, including the largest and oldest of them – the 12th century temple of Neminath, the 22nd Jain Tirthankar. There is a large black image of Neminath in the central shrine and many smaller images around the temple.

Nearby is the triple temple of Mallinath, the 19th Tirthankar, which was erected by two brothers in 1177. During festivals this temple is a favourite gathering place for sadhus. A great fair is held here during the Kartika Purnima festival in November or December. On top of the peak is the temple of Amba Mata, where newly-weds are supposed to worship at the shrine of the goddess in order to ensure a happy marriage.

Information

The Tourist Office is near the Durbar Hall museum but it's completely useless.

There's an excellent map of Junagadh on the wall behind the counter in the GPO.

Places to Stay & Eat

Junagadh has *Railway Retiring Rooms* and a number of rather basic hotels such as *Sharada Lodge* where there is a dormitory (Rs 4) as well as rooms from Rs 10. Other places include the *Gita Lodge, Jai Shri Guest House* and the *Tourist Guest House*. *Sharada Lodge*, which is only a couple of hundred metres from the railway station, offers fairly standard thalis.

The *Hotel Vaibhav*, close to the bus station, is a rather better place with singles from Rs 22 to 40, doubles at Rs 40, 60 and 110. It's a bit expensive and on a noisy intersection. Downstairs they have an amazingly flashy, air-con, mirrored dining hall where you can get the 'ultimate' all-you-can-eat thali for Rs 10.

Hotel Relief on Dhal Rd is also good and has doubles at Rs 40 to 50. It has a good dining hall with vegetarian and non-vegetarian food and is run by a friendly Singaporean. The staff are an equally friendly bunch of young Moslems who enjoy a joke.

Junagadh is famous for its fruit, especially *kesar* mangoes and *chiku* (sapodilla). The latter are popular in milkshakes around town in November-December.

Getting There

Air There is a daily flight from Bombay to Keshod, 47 km from Junagadh. The flight takes one hour and 20 minutes and the fare is Rs 284. The flight continues to Porbandar for Rs 86.

Rail The Somnath Mail runs between Ahmedabad and Veraval via Junagadh and the 37-38 Mail runs between Rajkot and Veraval via Junagadh. Ahmedabad-Junagadh takes about 13 hours and costs Rs 116 in 1st, Rs 29.50 in 2nd for the 380 km journey. The Somnath Mail is a multi-part train so make sure you get in the right part.

VERAVAL

Only a few km from Somnath, this was once the major seaport for Mecca pilgrims before the rise of Surat. It still has some importance as a port. This is one of India's major fishing ports, over a thousand boats work out of here. Dhows are still being built and some run across to Bombay – you could probably get a ride by asking around. There's not a lot to see in Veraval, despite its size. Pigs abound in the streets. Between Veraval and Somnath, a large ship lies (spectacularly) wrecked on the shore.

Information

You may have trouble changing travellers' cheques here – except (surprisingly) at the State Bank of Saurashtra!

Places to Stay

Accommodation in Veraval can be hard to find, places are often full and prices get jacked up. Veraval has a *Tourist Bungalow* and a *Circuit House* located near the lighthouse – fine views of the sunset over the sea. The Tourist Bungalow is quiet and has doubles for Rs 35. Meals have to be ordered in advance.

The *Satkar Hotel* (tel 120) near the bus stand is clean and well maintained. They have all sorts of rooms from dorm beds at Rs 12 to singles/doubles at Rs 22/25 up to Rs 120/140 with air-con and a wide variety of prices in between. There prices may tend to rise when there's an accommodation squeeze on.

There are *Railway Retiring Rooms* at the station with doubles for Rs 20. Close by is the *Chandrani Guest House* while a little further away is the *Sri Niwas Guest House* and the *Hotel Supreme*.

In Somnath about half way between the bus stand and the temple, about 100 metres north of the road, the *Sri Somnath Temple Trust* has a vast guest house. There are 100 double rooms, a bit dingy but not very old and good value at Rs 10. The signs for the guest house are only in Hindi and Gujarati but you can ask directions.

Places to Eat

There's not much choice in eating places in Veraval. *Hotel Satkar*, near the bus station, does good Gujarati thalis with plenty of refills for Rs 16. *Hotel La'Bela* is actually a restaurant, which does (hot) thalis. The *New Apsara*, not far from the station, does vegetarian thalis and dosas downstairs and non-vegetarian (including local fish) upstairs, but it's fairly basic.

Street stalls all over town sell drinking coconuts for Rs 1.50.

Getting There

Air The nearest airport is Keshod but there is no Indian Airlines office in Veraval. Somnath Travels (tel 162) in Satta Bazaar will obtain tickets for a fee of Rs 16. The Bombay-Keshod fare is Rs 284. Keshod-Porbandar costs Rs 86. There is a good road to Keshod and the bus takes only an hour for Rs 5.

Rail It's about 15 hours from Ahmedabad to Veraval. Fares are Rs 135 in 1st class, Rs 34 in 2nd.

Bus From the bus station buses run to Diu daily via Kodinar for Rs 9. Buses also go along the coast road to Porbandar via Chorwad and Mangrol. Bhavnagar is nine hours away, the trip costs Rs 21.

Getting Around

An auto-rickshaw to Somnath, six km away, costs about Rs 9 or 10. There are municipal and local buses to Somnath – Rs 0.75 to 1.25.

AROUND VERAVAL

Chorvad

On the coast, 70 km from Junagadh and just 20 km from Veraval, Chorvad is a popular beach resort. This was the site of the summer palace of the Junagadh Nawabs and it has now been converted into a guest house.

Somnath

The Temple of Somnath, at Somnath

Patan which is near Veraval and about 80 km from Junagadh, has had an extremely chequered history. The earliest history of the temple fades into legend. It was said to have been originally built by Somraj, the Moon God himself, out of gold, only to be rebuilt by Ravana in silver, then by Krishna in wood, then by Bhimdev in stone. What is more certain is that a description of the temple by Al Biruni, an Arab traveller, was so glowing that it prompted a visit in 1024 by a most unwelcome tourist – Mahmud of Ghanzi. At that time the temple was so wealthy that it had 300 musicians, 500 dancing girls and even 300 barbers simply to shave the heads of visiting pilgrims.

Muhmud of Ghanzi, who was to gain quite a reputation for his raids on the riches of India from his Afghan kingdom, descended on Somnath and after a two-day battle took the town and temple and, having carted off its fabulous wealth, destroyed it for good measure. He started a tradition of Moslems destroying the temple and Hindus rebuilding it, for in the following centuries it was razed again in 1297, 1394 and finally in 1706 by Aurangzeb, that notorious Moghul spoilsport.

It was rebuilt in 1169 after Mahmud's visit and again in 1325 and soon after 1394. But after the 1706 demolition it was not finally rebuilt until 1950. The temple is currently being extended. Outside, opposite the entrance, is a large statue of S V Patel (1875-1950) who was responsible for the restoration. It costs Rs 0.75 to go up to the second floor inside the temple, from where there are fine views, as well as a photo collection with English commentary on the archaeological excavations on the seven temples and restoration work.

The current temple was built to traditional patterns on the original site by the sea. The temple is one of the 12 most sacred Shiva shrines, or Jyotorlingas, in India but despite its long history and its holiness it's not really very interesting. Hardly anything of the original temple

remains and the new one is an unimaginative monstrosity and dead boring. There's a simple dining hall in the temple compound, north of the main gate, where you can get lunch. The grey sand beach is right outside the temple and it's OK for a swim although there's no shade.

Down the lane from the temple is a museum, open 9 am to 12 noon and 3 to 6 pm, closed Wednesdays and holidays. Admission is 20 paise plus 20 paise for each photograph you take. They don't count very seriously. Remains of the old temple can be seen here, a jumble of old carved stones which litter a courtyard. There are pottery shards, a seashell collection and a (strange) glass case of water bottles containing samples from the Danube, Nile, St Lawrence, Tigris, River Plate and the Murray in Australia! Together with seawater from Hobart and New Zealand.

Other Somnath Sites

The town of Somnath Patan is entered by the Junagadh Gate from Veraval. This was the gate through which Mahmud finally broke through to take the town and the triple gate is very ancient. Close to the second is an old mosque dating from Mahmud's time. The Jami Masjid, reached through the town's picturesque bazaar, was constructed using parts of a Hindu temple and has interesting Bo tree carvings at the four corners. It is now a museum with a collection from many of these temples.

About a km before the Junagadh Gate, coming from Veraval, is the finely carved Mai Puri which was once a Temple of the Sun. This Hindu temple was converted into a mosque during Mahmud's time and there are thousands of tombs and *palias* around it. Close by are two old tombs and on the shore is the Bhidiyo Pagoda which probably dates from the 14th century.

To the east of the town is the Bhalka Tirth where Lord Krishna was mistaken for a deer (he was sleeping in a deerskin) and wounded by an arrow. The legendary

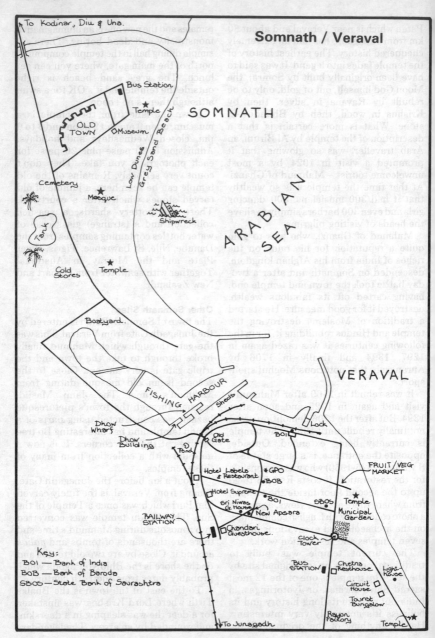

Somnath / Veraval

To Kodinar, Diu & Una.

SOMNATH

Bus Station

OLD TOWN

Temple

Museum

ARABIAN SEA

Low Dunes
Grey Sand Beach

Cemetery

Mosque

Shipwreck

Tank

Cold Stores

Temple

Boatyard.

FISHING HARBOUR

VERAVAL

Dhow Wharf

Dhow Building

Sheds

Old Gate

Lock

BOI

Pond

FRUIT/VEG MARKET

Hotel Labela & Restaurant

GPO

BOB

Hotel Supreme

BOI

Sri Niwas G. House

New Apsara

SBOS

Temple

Municipal Garden

RAILWAY STATION

Chandari Guesthouse

Clock Tower

Chetna Resthouse

Light House

BUS STATION

Circuit House

Key:
BOI — Bank of India
BOB — Bank of Baroda
SBOS — State Bank of Saurashtra

Tourist Bungalow

Rayon Factory

Temple

To Junagadh

spot is at the confluence of three rivers. You get to it through the small Sangam (confluence gate), which is simply known as the Nana (small gate). North of this sacred spot is the Temple of the Sun or Suraj Mandir which Mahmud also had a go at knocking down. This very old temple probably dates from the same time as the original Somnath Temple. Around the walls is a frieze of lions with elephants' trunk. Back inside the small gate is a temple which Ahalya Bai of Indore built as a replacement for the Somnath Temple.

Sasan Gir Forest

The last home of the Asian lion is 54 km from Junagadh via Keshod. There are less than 200 lions left. The sanctuary covers 1400 square km and the best time to visit this dry scrubland is between October and June. Apart from the lions there are also bears, hyenas, foxes and a number of species of deer and antelope. The deer include the largest Indian antelope, the *nilgai*, the graceful *chinkara* gazelle, the *chousingha* and the barking deer. You may also see parrots, peacocks and monkeys. The tourist office in Junagadh will have details about visiting the park – you need a jeep. You can wait in Sasan in the early morning for a group to form, a jeep, if one is available, will cost about Rs 100 to 150 and will carry up to eight people.

Places to Stay

The State Forest Department has a *Guest House*, very spaciously laid out in a garden. Chalets with bathroom cost Rs 20 per person and meals cost about Rs 4. There's also the modern, two storey, ITDC operated *Forest Lodge* (tel 21, 28). This costs Rs 115/180 or Rs 175/240 with air-con.

Tulsi Shyam

In the Gir Forest, 165 km from Junagadh, there is a scenic hot spring together with a temple to Bhim and a *Holiday Home*.

Getting There

It's around a two to 2½ hour trip on a very crowded bus from Junagadh. The fare is Rs 6.40. To or from Veraval takes a little under two hours by bus for Rs 3.50. There is also a train service costing Rs 3 in 2nd class.

JAMNAGAR (population 350,000)

The princely state of Jamnagar was ruled by the Jadeja Rajputs prior to independence. The city is built around a lake with an island in the middle reached by a bridge. On this island, the Lakhota Fort is a museum with a good collection of sculptures and archaeological finds from surrounding villages – particularly Ghumli in the Bardo Hills to the south.

Also on the island, the Kotha Bastion was an old well from which water can be drawn by blowing into a small hole in the floor. Jamnagar has two local ports, Rosi and Bedi. The town also has a long history of pearl fishing and there is a local variety of tie dyeing.

Places to Stay

There are a number of hotels along Station Rd and also the *Lal Bungalow*.

Getting There

There are direct trains from Ahmedabad 308 km away, via Rajkot, and from Mehsena. The fare from Ahmedabad is Rs 97 in 1st, Rs 24.50 in 2nd. There is a daily flight from Bombay to Bhavnagar, continuing to Bhuj. The fare from Bombay is Rs 370.

DWARKA

On the extreme western tip of the Kathiawar Peninsula, Dwarka is one of the four holiest pilgrimage sites and is closely connected to the Krishna legend. It was here that Krishna set up his capital after his flight from Mathura. Dwarkanath, the name of the temple, is a title of Lord Krishna.

The temple is only open to Hindus (you can sign a form and go in one visitor reported), but the exterior, with its tall five-storey spire supported by 60 columns, is far more interesting than the interior. Archaeological excavations have revealed five earlier cities at the site, all now submerged. Dwarka is the site for an important festival at Janmashtami which falls in August or September.

Island of Bet

A little north of Dwarka you can ferry across from Okha to the island of Bet where Vishnu is said to have slain a demon. There are modern Krishna temples on the island. There are other important religious sites around Dwarka.

Places to Stay

Dwarka has *Railway Retiring Rooms*, a *Rest House* and a number of small hotels.

Getting There

Dwarka is 145 km from Jamnagar and connected by rail.

PORBANDAR

On the south coast, about mid-way between Veraval and Dwarka, the town is today chiefly noted as the birthplace of Mahatma Gandhi. In ancient times the city was known as Sudamapuri after Sudama, a compatriot of Krishna, and at one time there was a flourishing trade from here to the Persian Gulf and Africa. The Africa connection seems to be apparent in the number of Indianised blacks around, called Siddis, who form a virtually separate caste of Harijans.

Porbandar has several large cement and chemical factories and a textile mill. A massive breakwater has been constructed recently to shelter a deepwater wharf and

fishing harbour. Dhows are still being constructed here. Fish drying is an important activity and lends a certain 'aroma' to the town!

Swimming is not recommended near the Tourist Bungalow. The shore there, called Chopatty, is used as a local toilet and there is a factory drain outlet by the Hazur Palace. Swimming is said to be OK a few km down the coast towards Veraval.

Kirti Mandir

As in so many places in India there is a collection of Gandhian memorabilia in the Kirti Mandir, his birthplace. A swastika on the floor in a small room marks the actual spot! Admission is 25 paise and there is also a collection of photographs, *some* of which have English captions, and a small bookshop.

Planetarium

Across the muddy creek, spanned by the Jynbeeli (once Jubilee) Bridge, are the Nehru Planetarium and the Bharat Mandir (Hall of India). Flocks of flamingoes are an (unexpected) sight along the creek. The planetarium has afternoon sessions in Gujarati. Men and women enter by separate doors from the verandah where panels celebrate Indian 'non-alignment' – on one side showing Shastri with Kosygin and the other Nehru with JFK! The projection equipment is a little antiquated and stars cross the domed roof to the sound of whirring machinery. machinery.

Bharat Mandir

Opposite the planetarium, in a charming irrigated garden, is the large Bharat Mandir hall. Inside there's a huge relief

A   Dhobi Ghats at Halebid (Ka)
B   Temple carvings on the Hoysala Temple at Halebid (Ka)
C   Gol Gumbaz Mausoleum at Bijapur (Ka)

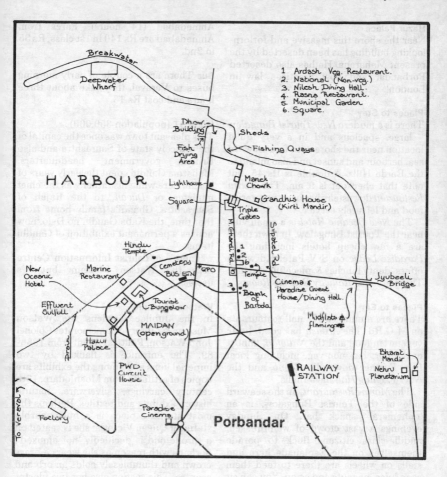

1. Ardash Veg. Restaurant.
2. National (Non-veg.)
3. Nilesh Dining Hall.
4. Rasne Restaurant.
5. Municipal Garden
6. Square

Breakwater

Deepwater Wharf

HARBOUR

Dhow Building

Sheds

Fishing Quays

Fish Drying Area

Lighthouse

Manek Chowk

Square

Gandhi's House (Kirti Mandir)

Triple Gates

Hindu Temple

New Oceanic Hotel

Marine Restaurant

Cemetery

BUS STN

GPO

Temple

Cinema & Paradise Guest House/Dining Hall

Jyubeeli Bridge

Effluent Outfall

Tourist Bungalow

MAIDAN (open ground)

Hazur Palace

PWD Circuit House

Mudflats & flamingos

Bharat Mandir

Nehru Planetarium

RAILWAY STATION

Factory

Paradise Cinema

Porbandar

To Verovol

Bank of Baroda

map of India on the floor. The pillars of the building have brilliantly painted bas reliefs of over a hundred legendary persons from Hindu epics and religious figures. The verandah has six distorting mirrors, popular with kids.

Hazur Palace

Near the shore this massive and forlorn-looking building has been deserted by the present Maharana. He has also deserted Porbandar and now practises law in London!

Places to Stay

There is a modern *New Tourist Bungalow* – large, spacious and in a very quiet location near the shore with fine views of sea, harbour and sunset and also inland to the Barda Hills. A double is Rs 45, but note that checkout is 9 am. The *Toran Restaurant* downstairs has basic vegetarian food and leisurely service.

The *New Oceanic Hotel* is a small villa near the Tourist Bungalow. In town there are a few cheap hotels including the *Paradise Lodge* on S V Patel Rd which offers 'denty lunches & piecefull staying'. There are also *Railway Retiring Rooms*.

Places to Eat

There are a number of small restaurants on M G Rd. The *Ardash* has good, basic vegetarian food and the *National*, almost next door, has non-veg, including local fish. Further down the *Rasna* and the *Nilesh Dining Hall* have thalis.

The *Marine Restaurant*, on the seaward side of the Tourist Bungalow, is an 'ephemeral' snack bar. On Sunday evenings a vast crowd of well-dressed, middle-class citizens flock to parade themselves on the Esplanade here and stalls on wheels are there to feed them cane juice, peanuts and so on. You can sit on the room of the Marine 'Rest' and enjoy excellent samosas or an ice cream.

Getting There

Air There's a daily flight from Bombay to Porbandar via Keshod. The fare from Bombay is Rs 341.

Rail Porbandar is the terminus of a rail line, the main services are the Kirti Express to and from Rajkot (6½ hours) and the 45/46 Express to and from Ahmedabad (14 hours). Fares from Ahmedabad are Rs 140 in 1st class, Rs 35 in 2nd.

Bus There are a couple of early morning buses to Veraval, they take about three hours and cost Rs 13.

RAJKOT (population 350,000)

This pleasant town was once the capital of the princely state of Saurashtra and also British government headquarters. Mahatma Gandhi spent the early years of his life here while his father was the chief minister, or *Diwan*, to the Rajah of Saurashtra. Ghandi's family home from that time, the Kaba Gandhi no Delo, now houses a permanant exhibition of Gandhi items.

There's a Tourist Information Centre near the Watson Museum but it's useless.

Watson Museum

In the Jubilee Gardens the Watson Museum & Library commemorates Colonel John Watson, Political Agent from 1886-89. The entrance is flanked by two imperial lions and among the exhibits are copies of artifacts from Moenjodaro, 13th century carvings, silverware, natural history exhibits and textiles. Perhaps the most startling piece is a huge marble statue of Queen Victoria; she is seated on a throne and is decidedly 'not amused', perhaps with reason as she wears a brass crown and thumblessly holds an orb and sceptre. This section also has two plaster Venuses and many splendid portraits of colonial heroes. The Raj lives! Admission is 20 paise.

Wankaner

Situated about 50 km from Rajkot the Royal Palace of Wankaner is now, like so many Indian palaces, a hotel and holiday resort. The regal palace has a swimming pool, museum and game reserve, not to mention the Maharana's collection of vintage cars. From here those who can

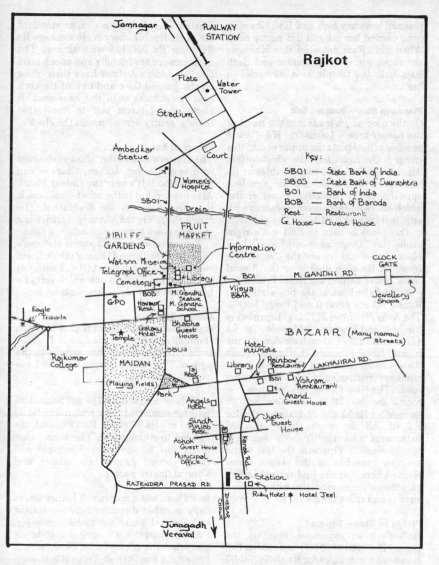

Rajkot

Key:
- SBOI — State Bank of India.
- SBOS — State Bank of Saurashtra
- BOI — Bank of India
- BOB — Bank of Baroda
- Rest. — Restaurant
- G. House — Guest House

afford it can make excursions to the Little Rann of Kutch or to the palace and monuments of Halvad.

Wadhwan (Surendrangar)

On the route to Rajkot from Ahmedabad this town has the very old temple of Ranik Devi, who became involved in a dispute between local rulers Sidh Raja (who planned to marry her) and Rao Khengar (who carried her off and did marry her). When Sidh Raja defeated Rao Khengar she chose sati over dishonour and Sidh Raja built the temple as a memorial to her.

Places to Stay – Bottom End

On the road which leads into the heart of the bazaar area – Lakhajiraj Rd – are a number of hotels. At the upper end of this group is the *Hotel Intimate* which offers 'laxurious living' (sic) with doubles at Rs 60 or Rs 110 with air-con. More or less opposite is the *Himaliya Guest House* which offers budget accommodation with attached bath at Rs 18/33. The entrance to this place is hard to find – it's right inside the shopping complex. Others places you could try are the *Jyoti Guest House* at Rs 40 a double or the *Anand Guest House* behind the Hotel Intimate.

Around the back of the bus station on Kanak Rd are several mid-range hotels. The *Ruby Hotel* (tel 31722-3) is probably the best and has singles/doubles for Rs 44/69 or Rs 120/150 with air-con. All the rooms have attached bathrooms and there's also a restaurant. There are also a number of bottom end places on this same road. The *Hotel Jeel* has window-less rooms for Rs 20/30, doubles with a window for Rs 35 and de-luxe doubles for Rs 40. All the rooms have attached bathrooms and the friendly manager speaks English. Opposite the bus stand are two branches of the *Ashok Guest House* where you can find typical Indian guest house accommodation with attached shower and toilet for Rs 15/35.

Places to Stay – Top End

Rajkot's most expensive hotel is the *Galaxy Hotel* (tel 31781-7) on Jawahar Rd. It has singles/doubles for Rs 45-70/60-90 or with air-con for Rs 120-230/160-270. All rooms have attached bath but the management are not excessively friendly and it's not the best hotel in town.

Angel's Hotel (tel 22026, 32016),

Dhebar Chowk, is of a similar standard but considerably cheaper. Rooms are Rs 34/66 or Rs 100/125 with air-con. The management are friendly and speak good English. Indian Airlines have their office on the ground floor and one of Rajkot's best restaurants is in the basement. It might also interest you to know that there's 'pentry service round the clock'.

Places to Eat

The *Havmor* is a better class restaurant with veg, non-veg, Indian, Chinese and western food. It's near the Galaxy Hotel. Also nearby, but in the other direction, is the vegetarian only *Taj Restaurant*. The *Sindh Punjab* in the Municipal Office is a cheaper place for veg and non-veg food.

Try the basement restaurant at *Angel's Hotel* for a really good Gujarati thali. It will cost you Rs 15 with sweet (Rs 12 without) but if you can find a place which serves a better one we'd like to know about it.

Getting There

Air There are daily direct flights between Bombay and Rajkot, the fare is Rs 323. Indian Airlines have a bus service to the airport. Their office is open 9 am to 1 pm and 2 to 3.35 pm.

Rail The overnight (broad gauge) Saurashtra Express connects Rajkot with Ahmedabad – fares are Rs 86 in 1st, Rs 22 in 2nd. It's 216 km to Ahmedabad. There are other fast trains to and from Jamnagar and Hapa (broad gauge), Porbandar and Veraval (metre gauge).

Bus There are a number of luxury buses daily in either direction between Rajkot and Veraval and Rajkot and Jamnagar. For either service it's advisable to buy a seat reservation ticket for Rs 1 beforehand. Pay on the bus. Rajkot-Veraval is about a five hour trip via Junagadh costing Rs 15. Rajkot-Jamnagar takes about two hours and costs Rs 14.10. There are three morning luxury buses among others but it's simply not worth the effort of fighting your way on to the ordinary buses.

In addition to these state buses there are a number of private buses which run to places such as Ahmedabad. Eagle Travels, Moti Tati Shop (10 minutes' walk from the bus station) has daily luxury buses to Ahmedabad (Rs 60) and Bombay (Rs 120).

KUTCH (KACHCHH)

The western-most part of Gujarat is virtually an island, indeed during the monsoon period from May it really is an island. The Gulf of Kutch divides Kutch from the Kathiawar Peninsula while to the north Kutch is separated from the Sind region of Pakistan by the Great Rann of Kutch.

This low-lying marsh area is virtually completely barren due to the salt in the soil, only on scattered 'islands' which rise above the salt level is there vegetation. During the dry season the Rann is a vast expanse of hard, dried mud. Then, with the start of the monsoon in May, it is flooded by sea water, then flooded deeper again by the fresh water from rivers as they fill up. Kutch is also separated from the rest of Gujarat to the east by the Little Rann of Kutch.

The Gulf of Kutch is a breeding ground for flamingoes and pelicans during the winter. In the Little Rann of Kutch the rare Indian wild ass roams. Because of their isolation the people of Kutch have maintained their local customs and traditions.

BHUJ (population 50,000)

The major town of Kutch, Bhuj is an old walled city – until very recently the city gates were still locked each night from dusk to dawn! It's one of those places which leaps right out of the pages of Rudyard Kipling (or Salman Rushdie, whichever you happen to have read lately). It's the Bikaner of Gujarat, a walled city surrounding a lake and enclosing one of the most colourful and lively bazaars you're likely to come across

anywhere in India. You can get lost for hours inside the maze of streets and alleyways of this town without ever having a clue where you are or how you're going to find your way out. There are walls within walls, crenellated gateways, old palaces with intricately carved wooden pavilions the equal of any of those at the Topkapi in Istanbul, Hindu temples decorated with that gaudy, gay abandon which only tribal people seem capable of, equally colourful tribespeople and camels pulling huge cartfuls of produce into the various markets. In short, never a dull moment. And all this right next to one of the largest Indian Air Force bases in the country. A war plane takes off from here on average every 20 minutes yet you wouldn't know any of this was going on inside the city.

Bhuj is like a lot of India was before the tourist invasion. You can expect to get stared at by just about everyone because they don't get many westerners through here. On the other hand, because people remain largely unaffected by what goes on outside the area you're much more likely to come across that disarming hospitality which was once the hallmark of rural India. Where else would someone offer you a lift on their bicycle?

Around Bhuj

The city is connected by road with the old port of Mandvi to the south-west and by road and rail to the new port of Kandala. It is intended that Kandala should substitute for Karachi as a port for this area. There is a boat service from Kandala to Navlakhi, which is on the Kathiawar Peninsula and connected to Morvi and Wankaner by rail.

Gandidham, near Kandala, is a new town which was established to take refugees from the Sind, following partition. About 150 km north-east of Bhuj the remains of Indus Valley Civilisation fortifications have been discovered.

Places to Stay – Bottom End

The *Hotel Ratrani* (tel 1607) on Station

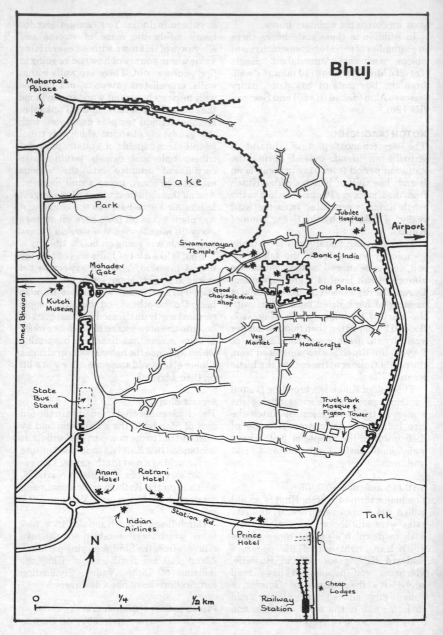

Bhuj

Maharao's Palace

Lake

Park

Jubilee Hospital

Airport

Swaminarayan Temple

Bank of India

Mahadev Gate

Old Palace

Kutch Museum

Good chai/soft drink shop

Umed Bhavan

Veg Market

Handicrafts

State Bus Stand

Truck Park Mosque & Pigeon Tower

Anam Hotel

Ratrani Hotel

Indian Airlines

Station Rd.

Prince Hotel

Tank

N

Cheap Lodges

0   ¼   ½ km

Railway Station

Rd between the Hotel Prince and Hotel Anam is a good budget hotel. Rooms with common bath and fan are Rs 15/25. With attached bath you can have a triple for Rs 35, or a room for four for Rs 50. The manager can be surly but the rest of the staff are very friendly. There's an air-con restaurant where you can get a Gujarati thali for Rs 10 plus Rs 3 for sweet.

There are one or two other, even cheaper, places to stay such as the *Umed Bhavan* (the Government Rest House) which costs Rs 10 per bed and comes complete with imbecilic staff. There are a couple of similarly priced rest houses behind the bus station.

Places to Stay – Top End
At the top end of the market is the *Hotel Park View* (tel 344) on Hospital Rd, Camp Corner, which has air-con rooms with attached bath, an air-con dining hall and other facilities.

Closer to the old city are two somewhat less expensive hotels which are perfectly adequate for most people's requirements. The *Hotel Prince* (tel 1095, 1370, 1371), Station Rd, is a very pleasant, well maintained place with friendly and helpful staff. Singles/doubles with attached bath and hot water are Rs 60/100 or there are air-con rooms from Rs 128 to 180. There's a restaurant with vegetarian and non-vegetarian food but no Gujarati thalis!

The *Hotel Anam* (tel 1390-3, 1397) is also on Station Rd and is of similar standard and has equally pleasant staff. Rooms with attached bath are Rs 48/76 or Rs 112/146 with air-con. The hotel restaurant is open daily except Sundays and a Gujarati thali costs Rs 12, plus Rs 3 for dessert.

Getting There
Air Indian Airlines have daily flights from Bombay to Bhuj via Jamnagar. Three days a week it returns to Bombay via Jamnagar, the other days it goes direct.

Fares are Rs 435 from Bombay, Rs 96 from Jamnagar.

Rail There is a daily rail connection with Ahmedabad, 310 km away. Fares are Rs 97 in 1st, Rs 24.50 in 2nd. There are also three trains in either direction daily between Bhuj and Kandla Port.

Bus There are daily luxury buses between Bhuj and Bombay which cost Rs 150 and also between Bhuj and Rajkot for Rs 22.25. The latter depart from the state bus stand. Alternatively you can take taxis between Bhuj and Rajkot. These depart from near the state bus stand and cost Rs 25 per seat.

Getting Around
When you're not just wandering around the bazaars there are plenty of auto-rickshaws which will get you from A to B – they'll go anywhere including down some of the narrowest streets in the bazaar. Going to or from the airport, taxis and auto-rickshaws appear to charge the same. The fare should be only about Rs 5 for the four km trip but Rs 10 to 12 is the normal quote although some drivers ask Rs 25. It's worth waiting for a driver who will accept a reasonable fare.

If you're flying out of Bhuj the airport security check takes offence at cameras. They'll tell you that they are 'prohibited' and should have gone into the hold in your baggage. They don't appreciate it if you point out that the notices say 'photography prohibited' not 'cameras prohibited'. Just apologise and say it won't happen again!

Things to Buy
If you're looking for handicrafts in Bhuj it's worth getting in touch with Ramnik K Shah, Gopiani St, Shroff Bazaar. He's a very friendly person, speaks English and is involved in the import/export trade. His shop is on the map.

Madhya Pradesh

Population: 46 million
Area: 442,841 square km
Capital: Bhopal
Main Language: Hindi

The large state of Madhya Pradesh is the geographical heartland of India. Most of the state is a high plateau and in summer it can be very dry and hot. The size and geographical isolation of Madhya Pradesh, historically known as Malwa, kept it relatively immune from outside invaders, but virtually all the phases of Indian history have left their mark on the state. There are still many pre-Aryan Gond and Bhil tribal people in the state, but Madhya Pradesh is overwhelmingly Indo-Aryan with the majority of the people speaking Hindi and following Hinduism.

The state's history goes right back to the time of Ashoka, the great Buddhist emperor whose Mauryan empire was powerful in Malwa. At Sanchi you can see the Buddhist centre founded by Ashoka, the most important reminder of Ashoka in India today. The Mauryans were followed by the Sungas, and the Sungas by the Guptas before the Huns swept across the state. Around a thousand years ago the Parmaras ruled in south-west Madhya Pradesh – they're chiefly remembered for Raja Bhoj who gave his name to the city of Bhopal and also ruled over Indore and Mandu.

Between 950 and 1050 AD the Chandellas constructed the fantastic series of temples at Khajuraho, in the north-east of the state. Today Khajuraho is one of India's main attractions. Between the 12th and 16th century the region saw continuing struggles between Hindu and Moslem rulers or invaders. Often the fortified city of Mandu in the south-west was the scene for these battles, but finally the power of the Moghuls overcame Hindu resistance and controlled the region, only to fall to the rise of the Marathas who, in turn, were to fall to the advance of British power.

Two of Madhya Pradesh's attractions are remote and isolated – Khajuraho is off to the north-east, a long way from anywhere and most easily visited by travelling between Agra and Varanasi. Jabalpur, with its marble rocks, is in the south-east of the state and can be reached if you are travelling between the west of India and Calcutta, or Orissa on the east coast.

Most of the state's other attractions are on, or close to, the main Delhi-Bombay rail line. From Agra, just outside the state to the north, you can head south through Gwalior, with its magnificent fort, Sanchi, Bhopal, Ujjain, Indore and Mandu. From there you can head east to Gujurat or south to the Ajanta and Ellora caves in Maharashtra.

GWALIOR (population 450,000)
In the extreme north-west of Madhya Pradesh, only a few hours from Agra by train or road, Gwalior is famous for its very

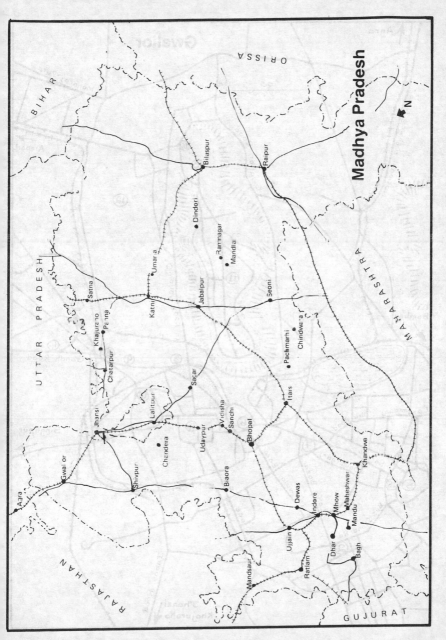

Madhya Pradesh

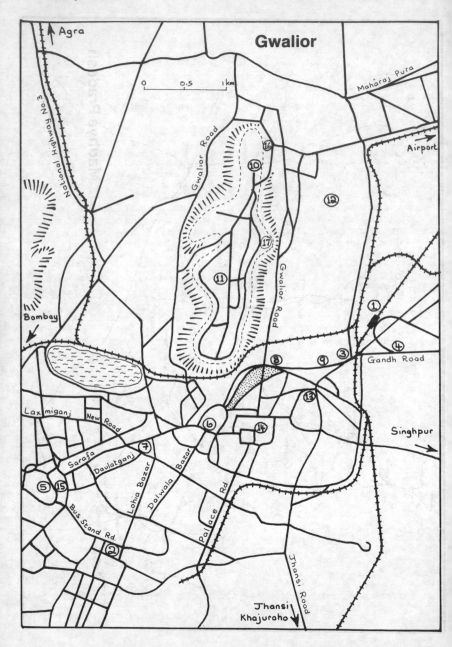

1 Railway Station	10 Man Mandir & Gujri Mahal Museum
2 Bus Station	11 Teli Ka Mandir
3 Indian Airlines	12 Tansen & Muhammad Gaus Tombs
4 Tourist Office & Tourist Bungalow	13 Moti Mahal
5 GPO	14 Palace Museum
6 Usha Kiran Hotel	15 Jayaji Chowk
7 Gujri Mahal Hotel	16 Archaeological Museum
8 Kwality Restaurant	17 Sasbahu Temple
9 Wengier's Restaurant	

old and very large fort. Within the fort walls there are a number of interesting temples and ruined palaces. The dramatic and colourful history of the great fort certainly goes back over a thousand years.

Gwalior's legendary beginning stems from a meeting between Suraj Sen and the hermit Gwalipa, who lived on the hilltop where the fort stands. The hermit cured Suraj Sen of leprosy with a drink of water from the Suraj Kund, which still remains in the fort. Then he gave him a new name, Suhan Pal, and said his descendants would remain in power so long as they kept the name Pal. His next 83 descendants did just that, but number 84 changed his name to Tej Karan and, you guessed it, good-bye kingdom.

What is more certain is that in 1398 the Tomar dynasty came to power in Gwalior and, over the next several centuries, Gwalior fort was a scene of continual intrigue and clashes with neighbouring powers. Man Singh, who came to power in 1486, was the greatest of these Tomar rulers but in 1516, after earlier repelling an assault by Sikander Lodi of Delhi in 1505, the fort was besieged by Ibrahim Lodi. The siege had no sooner started than Man Singh died, but his son held out for a year before finally capitulating. Later the Moghuls, under Babur, took the fort and held it, despite an assault by Man Singh's grandson during the time of Akbar, until the Mahrattas took it in 1754.

For the next 50 years the fort changed

hands on several occasions including being taken twice by the British. It finally passed into the hands of the Scindias, although behind the scenes the British retained control. At the time of the Indian Mutiny in 1857 the Maharaja remained loyal to the British but his troops didn't, and in mid-1858 the fort was the scene for some of the final, and most dramatic, events of the mutiny. It was near here that the British finally defeated Tantia Topi and it was in the final assault on the fort that the Rani of Jhansi was killed. See Jhansi for more details on this heroine of the mutiny. There is a memorial to her in Gwalior.

The area around Gwalior, particularly between Agra and Gwalior, was well known until recent years for the dacoits who terrorised travellers and villagers. They were especially concentrated in the valleys along the Chambal River, which forms the boundary between Rajasthan and Madhya Pradesh. In that area you still see many men walking along the roads carrying rifles.

Information & Orientation

The Tourist Office is located in the Tourist Bungalow, about a half km west of the railway station. Old Gwalior town is off to the north of the fort which, topping the long hill to the north of the newer part of the town, totally dominates the area. The newer town is known as Lashkar and stands to the south-west of the fort. The railway station and the modern town is to the south-east. There are regular tempos running along the main route from the railway station to Lashkar.

Fort

You can approach the fort from the south-west or the north-east. The north-east path, starting from the Archaeological Museum, follows a wide, winding slope to the doors of the Man Singh Palace. The south-west entrance is a long gradual ascent by road, passing cliff-face Jain sculptures on the climb. The climb up to the fort can be hot and sweaty work in the hot season. A taxi or auto-rickshaw up the south-west road is probably the easiest way in, you can then walk down from the palace to the museum when you've looked around the fort. Note that there are no refreshments available in the fort at all. Come prepared in the summer.

The fort hill rises 100 metres above the town and is about three km in length. It's width varies from nearly a km to less than 200 metres. The fort walls, which continue around almost the entire hilltop, are 10 metres high and imposingly solid. Beneath the walls, the hill face drops sheer away to the plains. On a clear day the view from the fort walls is superb, the crowded streets of the older part of the town, known as Lashkar, is off to the south-west while the more spacious part of the town lies to the south-east. Old Gwalior itself clings to the northern and north-eastern end of the fort hill. The view extends far out over the surrounding plains.

There are a number of things to see in and around the fort, although most of the enclosed area is simply open space and fields. Entry to the fort costs 25 paise.

Archaeological Museum

The museum is within the Gujari Mahal palace, at the start of the north-east ascent to the fort. The palace was built in the 15th century by Man Singh for his favourite queen, Mrignayani. The building is now rather deteriorated but the museum has a collection of Hindu and Jain sculptures and copies of the Bagh

Caves frescoes. The museum is open 10 am to 5 pm daily, closed on Mondays, admission is just 25p.

North-East Entrance

There is a whole series of gates as you ascend the path to the Man Singh palace. At one time the path had steps in it but it has now been smoothed into one long ascent, though still more suitable for feet than wheels. The first of the six gates is the Alamgiri Gate, dating from 1660. It was named after Aurangzeb, who took the title of Governor of Alamgiri in this region. The second gate dates from the same period as the Gujari Mahal and is known as the Badalgarh, after Badal Singh, Man Singh's uncle, or as the Hindola Gate after a swing or *hindol* which used to stand here. The third gate, the Bansur or archer's gate, has disappeared.

The interesting fourth gate was built in the 1400's and named after the elephant-headed god, Ganesh. There is a small pigeon house or Kabutar Khana here and a small four-pillared Hindu temple to the hermit Gwalipa, after whom the fort and town was named. Next you pass a Vishnu shrine dating from 876 AD known as Chatarbhujmandir, shrine of the four-armed. A tomb near here is that of a nobleman killed in an assault on this gate in 1518. From here a series of steps lead to rock-cut Jain sculptures at the north-east of the fort. They are not of the same size, quality and importance as the sculptures on the south-west side. There are other Hindu sculptures along this same face.

The Hathiya Paur, or Elephant Gate, forms the entrance to the palace. Within the palace was the final gate, the Hawa Gate, but this has also been removed.

Man Singh Palace

The palace, or Man Mandir, which forms the entrance to the fort is a delightfully whimsical building, also known as the Chit Mandir, or Painted Palace, because of the tiled and painted decorations of ducks, elephants and peacocks. Painted blue, with hints of green and gold, it still looks very good today. The palace was built by Man Singh between 1486 and 1516 and repaired in 1881. The palace has four storeys, two of them underground and all of them now deserted. The subterranean ones are cool, even in the summer heat, and were used as prison cells during the Moghul period. The east face of the fort, with its six towers topped by domed cupolas, stands over the fort entrance path.

The museum in the palace is open from 8 am to 5 pm from Tuesday to Sunday.

Other Palaces

There are a number of other palaces clustered within the fort walls at the northern end. None of them are as interesting or as well preserved as the Man Singh Palace. The Karan Palace or Kirti Mandir is a long, narrow, two-storey palace on the western side. At the northern end are the Jahangiri and Shah Jahan Palaces with a very large and deep tank. The Jauhar Tank, north-west of the palaces, was named after the *jauhar*, or ritual Rajput suicide, that took place here in 1232.

Sasbahu Temples

The 'mother-in-law' and 'daughter-in-law' temples stand close to the eastern wall about mid-way along that side of the fort. The two temples are similar in style and date from the 9th to 11th centuries. The larger temple has an ornately-carved base and figures of Vishnu over the entrances. Four huge pillars carry the heavy roof.

Teli-ka-mandir

On the opposite side of the fort, beyond the Suraj Kund tank, this temple probably dates from the 9th century and has a peculiar plan and design. The roof is Dravidian while the decorations, the whole temple is covered with sculptures, are Indo-Aryan. A Garuda tops the 10-metre high doorway. This is the highest structure in the fort.

South-West Entrance

The long ascent on the south-west side climbs up through a ravine to the fort gate. Along the rock faces flanking this road are a large number of Jain sculptures, some of impressively large size. Originally cut into the cliff faces in the mid-1400's, they were mutilated by the forces of Babur in 1527 but were later repaired.

The images are in five main groups and are numbered. In the Arwahi group, image 20 is a 17-metre high, standing image of Adinath, while 22 is a 10-metre high seated figure of Nemnath, the 22nd Jain Tirthankar. The south-eastern group is the most important and covers nearly a km of the cliff face with more than 20 images.

Jai Vilas Palace

Located in the 'new town', which actually dates from 1809, this was the palace of the Scindia family. Although the current Maharaja still lives in the palace, a large part of it is used as a museum. It's full of the erratic sort of items Hollywood Maharajas are supposed to collect – like Belgian cut glass furniture, including a rocking chair. Or what looks like half the tiger population of India, all shot, stuffed and moth-eaten. Then there's a little room full of erotica, including a life-size marble statue of Leda having her way with a swan. But the *piece-de-resistance* is a model railway that carried brandy and cigars around the dining table after dinner.

It's a long way from the palace entrance around the part still in use to the museum section. If you go there by auto-rickshaw get it to drop you off at the museum, not at the palace entrance. The museum is open daily, except Mondays, from 10 am to 5 pm, admission Rs 4.

The palace is in Lashkar, which took its name 'camp' from the camp which Daulat Rao Scindia set up here in 1809, when he took control of Scindia. The Moti Mahal Palace is also in Lashkar and there is another museum.

Old Town

The old town of Gwalior lies to the north and north-east of the fort hill. The 1661 Jami Masjid mosque is a fine old building, constructed of sandstone quarried from the fort hill. Muhammad Ghaus, a Moslem saint who played a key role in Babur's acquisition of the fort, has his fine, large tomb on the eastern side of the town. It has hexagonal towers at its four corners, and a dome which was once covered with glazed blue tiles. It's a very good example of early Moghul architecture. Close to the large tomb is the smaller Tomb of Tansen, a singer much admired by Akbar. Chewing the leaves of the tamarind tree near his grave is supposed to do wonders for your voice.

Places to Stay – Bottom End

There's nothing much close to the railway station, but only a minute or so walk from there (turn left) there's the very (very) basic *Hotel Ashok* with accommodation at Rs 10 per person. Straight across the road there's the rather better, but at Rs 30/40 for singles/doubles rather more expensive, *Hotel India*. Both are rather noisy but there are plenty of eating places around. The station has *Railway Retiring Rooms*, but a women traveller suggested that the 2nd class ladies' waiting room is almost as comfortable and free – so long as you can manage the mosquitoes and the constant comings and goings.

About a half km from the station, it's possible to walk there or get there by auto-rickshaw for a couple of rupees, is the *Tourist Bungalow* (tel 22491). It's comfortable and has reasonably well kept rooms with attached bathrooms at Rs 50/60 for singles/doubles. It's also possible to camp in the garden here and the food is good and reasonably priced. It's a popular place with foreign visitors.

None of Gwalior's accommodation is concentrated in one area – there's nothing much around the bus station in Lashkar either. *Hotel Gujri Mahal* (tel 23492-93) on High Court Lane has singles/doubles

as low as Rs 25/35, although there are others at much higher prices (Rs 80 and up with air-con). The rooms are quite reasonable rooms, the food is very good, and all-in-all it's quite a pleasant hotel. On M L B Rd in Lashkar the *Regal Hotel* has rooms from Rs 20 to 40 or with air-con at Rs 110/130 for singles/doubles.

Places to Stay – Top End

Gwalior's top end hotel is the *Usha Kiran Palace Hotel* (tel 22049 & 23453) at Jayendragunj, Lashkar. It's right behind the Jai Vilas Palace. The 32 rooms are all air-con or air-cooled and singles/doubles are Rs 225/350.

Places to Eat

There's the usual selection of places to eat including a *Kwality* and a *Wengier's Restaurant*, both between the station and Lashkar. The Kwality has air-conditioning of Arctic intensity.

Getting There

Air There are daily flights from Delhi to Gwalior. On some days they continue to Bhopal, on others to Bhopal, Indore and Bombay. Reverse schedules are the same. Fares are Delhi Rs 228, Bombay Rs 741, Bhopal Rs 276 and Indore Rs 398.

Rail Gwalior is on the main Delhi-Bombay rail line, 317 km from Delhi, 118 km from Agra and 1225 km from Bombay. From Delhi the express or mail trains take about six hours to Gwalior, and the fare is Rs 99 in 1st class, Rs 25 in 2nd class. It's only two hours between Agra and Gwalior and the fares are Rs 44 in 1st class, Rs 10 in 2nd class.

Bus There are also regular bus services from Gwalior to Delhi, Agra, Ujjain, Indore, Bhopal, Jabalpur and Khajuraho, as well as to nearby centres like Shivpuri.

Getting Around

There are taxis, rickshaws, auto-rickshaws

and tempos. Auto-rickshaw drivers in Gwalior will not use their meters – arrange the fare before you depart. Tempos run regular services around the city, from the railway station to Bada, the main square in Lashkar, is Rs 1.

AROUND GWALIOR

The old summer capital of Shivpuri is 117 km south-west of Gwalior or 51 km east of Jansi. The road runs through a national park where you sometimes see animals on the road. The *Chinkara Motel* (tel 297) in Shivpuri has rooms from Rs 40.

Near Shivpuri there's a pleasant lake with gardens around the perimeter. The road from Gwalior passes through Narwar with a large old fort. Between Gwalior and Agra, actually on a finger of Rahasthan that separates Madhya Pradesh and Uttar Pradesh at this point, is Dholpur, near where Aurangzeb's sons fought a pitched battle to determine who would succeed him as emperor of the rapidly declining Moghul empire. The Shergarh fort in the old Dholpur state is very old but now in ruins. Near Bari is the Khanpur Mahal, a pavilioned palace built for Shah Jahan but never occupied.

To the east of the railway line, 61 km south of Gwalior towards Jhansi, a large group of white Jain remples are visible scattered along a hill. They're one of those strange, dream-like apparitions that so often seem simply to materialise in India. Sonagir is the nearest railway station. Only 26 km north of Jhansi is Datia with the now deserted seven-storey palace of Raj Birsingh Deo. The town is surrounded by a stone wall and the palace is to the west of the town.

CHANDERA

At the time of Mandu's greatest power this was an important place as the many ruined palaces, *sarais*, mosques and tombs, all in a Pathan style similar to Mandu, indicate. The Koshak Mahal is a ruined Moslem palace, still maintained. Today the town is chiefly known for its gold brocadas and saris. Chandera is 33 km west of Lalitpur which in turn is 90 km south of Jhansi, on the main railway line.

JHANSI (population 225,000)

Situated 101 km south of Gwalior, Jhansi is actually in Uttar Pradesh – a finger of that state extends into Madhya Pradesh, but for convenience we'll include it here. Although Jhansi has played a colourful role in Indian history, most visitors to the town today go there simply because it's a convenient jumping off point for Khajuraho. This is the closest point the Delhi-Bombay rail line runs to Khajuraho and there are regular buses.

Orchha, only 11 km south of Jhansi, was once the capital of a powerful state in this area. Bir Singh Deo ruled from Orchha between 1605 and 1627 and built the Jhansi fort. A favourite of the Moghul Prince Salim, he feuded with Akbar and in 1602 narrowly escaped the emperor's displeasure; his kingdom was all but ruined by Akbar's forces. Then in 1605 Prince Salim became the Emperor Jehangir, and for the next 22 years Bir Singh was a powerful figure. In 1627 Shah Jahan became emperor, Bir Singh once again found himself out of favour, and his attempt to revolt was put down by 13-year-old Aurangzeb.

In the 18th century Jhansi rose to power, eclipsing Orchha, but in 1803 the British East India Company got a foot in the door and gradually assumed control over the state. The last of a string of none too competent rajas died without a son in 1853 and the British, who had recently passed a neat little law allowing them to take over any princely state under their patronage when the ruler died without a male heir, pensioned the Rani off and took full control.

The Rani of Jhansi, who wanted to rule in her own right, was unhappy about this enforced retirement and when, four years later, the Indian Mutiny burst into flame she was in the forefront of the rebellion at

Jhansi. The British contingent in Jhansi were all massacred, but next year the rebel forces were still quarrelling amongst themselves and the British retook Jhansi. The Rani fled to Gwalior and, in a valiant last stand, she rode out against the British, disguised as a man, and was killed. She has since become a heroine of the Indian independence movement, a sort of Joan of Arc of central India.

The Jhansi fort, now much modernised, still offers excellent views from its ramparts. The British ceded the fort to the Maharaja of Scindia in 1858, then exchanged it for Gwalior in 1866.

Orchha

The former capital of this region is now just a village, but the old fort still stands and contains Bir Singh Deo's fine palace and another palace built for, but never used by, Jehangir. The fort is on an island in the Bekwa River.

Places to Stay

There are dorm beds in the *Railway Retiring Rooms* and a handful of low-price places close to the station. Turn left out of the station and head straight a few hundred metres to half a km. The *Central Hotel* and *Hotel Sipri* are both close to the junction and have rooms for Rs 20. The Central is simple, but clean and pleasant, with a friendly manager and quite reasonable food. Rooms up on the roof have good views and there are lots of clean showers. *Hotel Ashok*, near the Natraj Cinema, is a little more expensive.

The *Jhansi Hotel* on Shastri Marg has rooms at a variety of prices from Rs 40 to 100, some with attached bath, some without.

Getting There

Jhansi is on the main Delhi-Agra-Bhopal-Bombay railway line and is a jumping off point for Khajuraho. Buses to Khajuraho leave at 6, 7 and 8 am and the fare is Rs 20.

SANCHI

Beside the main railway line, 68 km north of Bhopal, a hill rises from the plain. It's topped by some of the oldest and most interesting Buddhist structures in India. Although this site had no direct connection with the life of Buddha himself, it was the great Emperor Ashoka who built the first stupas here in the third century BC, and a great number of stupas and other religious structures were added over the succeeding centuries.

Then, with the decline of Buddhism, the site decayed and was eventually completely forgotten. In 1818 a British officer rediscovered the site, but in the years that followed amateur archaeologists and greedy treasure hunters did immense damage to Sanchi, before a proper restoration was first commenced in 1881. Finally, between 1912 and 1919, the structures were carefully repaired and restored to their present condition by Sir John Marshall.

Information & Orientation

Sanchi itself is little more than a tiny village at the foot of the hill. At the base of the hill, where you pay admission to enter the site, there is a small museum. You can get a copy of the guidebook *Sanchi*, published by the Achaeological Survey of India, here.

The Great Stupa

Stupa 1, as it is listed on the site, is the main structure on the hill. Originally constructed by Ashoka in the third century BC, it was later enlarged and the original brick stupa enclosed within a stone one. In its present form it stands 16 metres high and 37 metres in diameter. A railing encircles the stupa and there are four entrances through magnificently carved gateways or *toranas*. These toranas are the finest works of art at Sanchi and amongst the finest examples of Buddhist art in India.

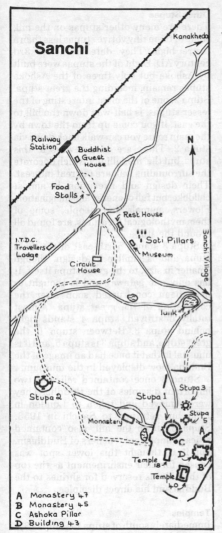

Sanchi

Kanakheda

Railway Station

Buddhist Guest House

Food Stalls

Rest House

I.T.D.C. Travellers Lodge

Sati Pillars

Museum

Circuit House

Sanchi Village

Tank

Stupa 2

Monastery

Stupa 1

Stupa 3

Stupa 5

Temple 18

Temple 40

A Monastery 47
B Monastery 45
C Ashoka Pillar
D Building 43

Toranas

The four gateways were erected around 35 BC and had all fallen down at the time of the stupta's restoration. The scenes carved onto the pillars and their triple

architraves are mainly tales from the *jatakas* – the episodes of the Buddha's various lives. At this stage in Buddhist art the Buddha was never represented directly. His presence was always alluded to through symbols such as the Bo tree, the wheel of law or his footprint. Even a stupa is itself a symbol of the Buddha.

Go round the stupa clockwise, as one should around all Buddhist monuments:

Northern Gateway The north gateway, topped by an unfortunately broken wheel of law, is the best preserved of the gateways. It shows many scenes from Buddha's life both in his last incarnation and in earlier lives. Scenes include a monkey offering a bowl of honey to the Buddha, whose presence is indicated by a Bo tree. In another panel he ascends a road into the air (again represented by a Bo tree) in the 'miracle of Sravasti'. This is just one of several miraculous feats he performs on the north gateway – all of which leave his spectators stunned. Elephants, facing in four directions, support the architraves above the columns, while horses with riders and more elephants fill the gaps between the architraves.

Eastern Gateway This gateway includes scenes of the Buddha's entry to *nirvana* on a pillar. Across the front of the middle architrave is the 'great departure', where the Buddha (symbolised by a riderless horse) renounces the sensual life and sets out to find enlightenment. Maya's dream, of an elephant standing on the moon, which she had when she conceived the Buddha, is also shown on one of the columns. The figure of a *yakshi* maiden, hanging out from one of the architraves, is one of the best known images of Sanchi.

Southern Gateway The oldest of the gateways, this includes scenes of the Buddha's birth and also events from Ashoka's life as a Buddhist. As on the western gateway the tale of the Chhaddanta Jataka features on this gateway.

Western Gateway The western gateway,

with the architraves supported by dwarves, has some of the most interesting scenes. The rear face of one of the pillars shows the Buddha undergoing the temptation of Mara, while demons flee and angels cheer that he manages to resist. Mara also tempts on the back of the lowest architrave. The top front architrave shows the Buddha in seven different incarnations but since he could not, at the time, be represented directly he appears three times as a stupa and four times as a tree. His six incarnations prior to the seventh, Gautama Buddha, are known as the Manushi Buddhas.

The colourful events of the Chhaddanta Jataka are related on the front face of the bottom architrave. In this tale the Buddha, in a lower incarnation, took the form of a six-tusked elephant, but one of his two wives became jealous and managed to re-incarnate as a queen and then arranged to have the six-tusked elephant hunted and killed. The sight of his tusks, sawn off by the hunter, was sufficient for the queen to die of remorse! Pot-bellied dwarves support the architraves on this gateway.

Pillars

Scattered around the site are a number of pillars or the remains of pillars. The most important is pillar 10 which was erected by Ashoka and stands close to the south entrance to the great stupa. Only the base of this beautifully proportioned and executed shaft now stands, but the fine capital can be seen in the museum. The three back-to-back lions, which once topped the column, are an excellent example of the Graeco-Buddhist art of that era at its finest. They now form the state emblem of India and can be seen on every bank note.

Pillars 25 and 35, both dating from the 5th century AD, are not as fine as the earlier Ashoka pillar. Pillar 35, also broken, stands close to the north gateway of the great stupa and again the capital figure is in the museum.

Other Stupas

There are many other stupas on the hill, some of them tiny votive stupas less than a metre high. They date from the 3rd century AD. Eight of the stupas were built by Ashoka but only three of the Ashoka stupas remain, including the great stupa. Stupa 2, one of the most interesting of the lesser stupas, is half-way down the hill to the east. If you come up from the town by the main route you can walk back down via stupa 2. There are no gateways to this stupa, but the 'medallions' which decorate the surrounding wall are of great interest. Their design and execution is almost childlike, but full of energy and imagination. Flowers, animals and people, some of them mythological creatures, are found all around the stupa.

Stupa 3 stands north-east of the main stupa and is similar in design, though smaller in size, to the great stupa itself. It has only one gateway and is thought to have been constructed soon after the completion of the great stupa. Almost totally destroyed, stupa 4 stands right behind stupa 3. Between stupa 1, the great stupa, and stupa 3 is stupa 5, and it is unusual in that it once had an image of the Buddha, now displayed in the museum.

Stupa 3 once contained relics of two important disciples of the Buddha. They were removed and taken to London in 1853 but returned to Sanchi in 1953. Stupa 2, down the hill, also contained relics of important teachers of Buddhism, but it is thought this lower spot was chosen for their enshrinement as the top of the hill was reserved for shrines to the Buddha and his direct disciples.

Temples

Immediately south of stupa 1 is stupa 18, a *chaitya* hall which in style is remarkably similar to the classical Greek-columned buildings. It dates from around the 7th century AD but traces of earlier, wooden buildings have been discovered beneath it. Beside this temple is the small temple 17 which is also Greek-like in style. The large temple 40, slightly south-east of these two temples, dates, in part, right back to the Ashokan period.

Temple 6 stands between 40 and 18. It is known as the Gupta Temple and dates back to the 4th century AD. The flat-roofed structure is made of stone slabs. It,too, shows a Greek influence, probably stemming from the use of Bactrian craftsmen. This temple is interesting in that it shows the style of Indian temple, where a porch leads to the central shrine, which later developed into classical Hindu temples at Khajuraho and in Orissa.

Monasteries

The earliest monasteries on the site were made of wood and have long since disappeared. The ususal plan is of a central courtyard surrounded by monastic cells. Monasteries 47 and 45 stand on the higher, eastern edge of the hilltop. They date from the later period of building at Sanchi and show the strong Hindu elements in their design during this transition period from Buddhism to Hinduism. There is a good view of the village of Sanchi and away to Bhilsa (Vidisha) from this side of the hill. Monastery 51 is part way down the hill on the western side toward stupa 2.

Other Buildings

The modern *vihara* (monastery) on the hill was contructed to house the returned relics from stupa 3. The design is a poor shadow of the former artistry of Sanchi. Close to monastery 51 is the 'great bowl' in which food and offerings were placed for distribution to the monks. It was carved out of a huge boulder. The Sanchi guidebook describes all these buildings, and many others, in much greater detail.

Places to Stay & Eat

Best value for money in Sanchi is probably (and suprisingly) the *Railway Retiring Rooms*. There are just two of them at Rs 20 double or Rs 10 single. They're big, spacious, spotlessly clean (in fact the whole Sanchi station is most un-Indian like – clean, prim and proper). Crowning touch is the toilets though – you've got a western and Asian toilet side by side! Almost beside the station is the *Buddhist Guest House*, which is rather more spartan – doubles Rs 20, dorm beds at Rs 8, supposedly you should make reservations in advance, but in practice you can just drop in.

Continue on to the main road and turn right 250 metres to the *Ashok Traveller's Lodge* (tel 23). Singles here cost Rs 115, doubles Rs 210, including meals. Without meals they cost from Rs 60/90. Air-con costs an extra Rs 45 but the rooms are neither as nice as the railway's nor anywhere near as well kept. Pleasant lounge though. If you crossed the main road towards the hill you'd come to the Gothic-looking *Rest House* on the left just before the museum (doubles Rs 10 but only two of them and mainly for government people) or the very pleasant looking *Circuit House* (tel 22) on the right (Rs 25 double and again usually unavailable).

To eat you've got a choice of the *Traveller's Lodge*, where the food is both terribly bland and very overpriced or the cluster of food stalls on the main road – most of them remarkably insanitary looking.

Getting There

Rail Sanchi is on the main Delhi-Bombay railway line only 68 km north of Bhopal. Note that certain mail and express trains do not stop at Sanchi. First class passengers who have travelled a minimum distance to Sanchi can request that the train be halted for them. It is necessary to arrange this in advance.

Bus There are also buses from Bhopal to Sanchi. There are two routes there, a 69 km route which takes three hours and costs Rs 7.50 or a 47 km route which takes 2¼ hours and costs Rs 5. You can get everywhere in Sanchi on foot.

AROUND SANCHI

In the immediate vicinity of Sanchi there are a number of other Buddhist sites, although none are of the scale or in the state of preservation of Sanchi itself. They include Sonari, 10 km south-west of Sanchi where there are eight stupas, two of them quite important. At Satdhara, west of Sanchi on the bank of the Beas River, there are two stupas, one 30 metres in diameter. Another eight km south-east is Andher where there are three small, but well preserved, stupas. These stupas around Sanchi were all discovered in 1851, after the discovery of Sanchi itself.

Other places of interest around Sanchi include:

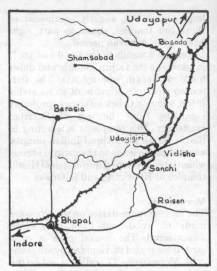

Vidisha (Bhilsa or Besnagar)

Vidisha was an important town in Ashoka's time, his wife came from here. Today the city is known as Besnagar, and Bhilsa railway station has an important collection of antiques discovered in the area. The Khamb Baba pillar is one of the more interesting attractions. It was erected by Heliodorus, a Greek ambassador to the city from Taxila (now in Pakistan). The pillar celebrates his conversion to Hinduism and is dedicated to Vishnu. Also in town is the Bija Mandal, a mosque built from the remains of Hindu temples.

Udayigiri

The Gupta caves here date from 320 to 606 AD, two of them are Jain, the other 18 are Hindu. In cave 5 there is a superb image of Vishnu in his boar incarnation. Cave 7 was cut out for King Chandragupta II's personal use. The caves are seven km west of Vidisha.

Raisen

On the road to Bhopal, 23 km south of Sanchi, the huge and colourful hilltop fort has temples, cannons, three palaces, 40 wells and a large tank. This Malwa fort was built around 1200 AD, but was later dependent to Mandu. Raisen declared its independence at one time, but was conquered by Bahadur Shah.

Gyaraspur

There are tanks, temples and a fort at this town, 51 km north-east of Sanchi. The town's name is derived from the big fair which used to be held here in the 11th month, Gyaras.

Udaypur

Reached through Basoda and Gyaraspur, Udaypur is 90 km north of Sanchi. The large Neelkantheswara Temple is thought to have been built in 1059 AD. It's profusely and very finely carved with four, prominent, decorated bands around the *shikara*. The temple is aligned so that the first rays of the morning sun shine on the Shiva lingam in the sanctum. It's a particularly fine example of Indo-Aryan architecture and is reached via the railway station at Bareth, seven km away.

BHOPAL (population 425,000)

The capital of Madhya Pradesh takes its name from its legendary 11th century

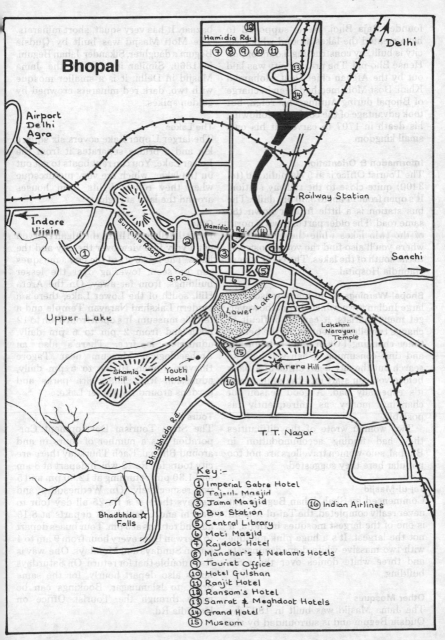

Bhopal

Key:-

1) Imperial Sabre Hotel
2) Tajul Masjid
3) Jama Masjid
4) Bus Station
5) Central Library
6) Moti Masjid
7) Rajdoot Hotel
8) Manohar's & Neelam's Hotels
9) Tourist Office
10) Hotel Gulshan
11) Ranjit Hotel
12) Ransom's Hotel
13) Samrat & Meghdoot Hotels
14) Grand Hotel
15) Museum
16) Indian Airlines

founder Raja Bhoj. He is supposed to have created the lakes around which the city is built, by constructing a dam or *pal*. Hense Bho-pal. The present city was laid out by the Afghan chief Dost Mohamed Khan. Dost Mohamed had been in charge of Bhopal during Aurangzeb's reign, but took advantage of the confusion following his death in 1707 to carve out his own small kingdom.

Information & Orientation

The Tourist Office is at 5 Hamidia Rd (tel 3400) quite close to the railway station. It's open from 11 am to 5.30 pm daily. The bus station is a little further down the same road. The older part of town is north of the twin lakes while the newer part, where you'll also find the youth hostel, is to the south of the lakes. The GPO is near Hamidia Hospital.

Bhopal Warnings As in many reasonably large Indian town, which do not, however, get many tourists, it can be difficult to change travellers' cheques. At the best of times changing TCs in India is laborious and time-consuming. When you have to search out the city head office of a bank before you can start into the paperwork, it's especially bad. A good reason for changing money as infrequently as possible.

Two women wrote of the difficulties they had finding accommodation in Bhopal, solo-women travellers are not too popular here they suggested.

Taj-ul-Masjid

Commenced by Shah Jahan Begum, but never really completed, the Taj-ul-Masjid is one of the largest mosques in India, if not the largest. It's a huge pink mosque with two massive white-domed minarets and three white domes over the main building.

Other Mosques

The Jama Masjid was built in 1837 by Qudsia Begum and is surrounded by the bazaar. It has very squat, short minarets. The Moti Masjid was built by Qudsia Begum's daughter, Sikander Jahan Begum, in 1860. Similar in style to the Jama Masjid in Delhi, it is a smaller mosque with two, dark red minarets crowned by golden spikes.

The Lakes

The larger Upper Lake covers six square km and a bridge separates it from the Lower Lake. You can rent boats to get out on the lakes, which are very picturesque when they reflect lights from houses around the lake at night.

Other

From the Shamla Hill or the Idgah Hill you get a very fine view over the city and the lakes. The minarets of the city's mosques can be seen, towering over the lesser buildings, from far away. On the Arera Hill, south of the Lower Lake, there's a modern Lakshmi Narayan Temple and a temple museum. It's open from 8 am to 12 noon and from 2 pm to 6 pm daily, admission is free. There's also an Archaeological Museum near Tagore Bhavan – open 10 am to 5 pm daily, admission free. There are parks and gardens around the Lower Lake.

Tours

The State Tourism Development Corporation has a number of tours in and around Bhopal. Each Thursday there are city tours for Rs 12 which depart at 8 am and 1.30 pm, returning at 12.30 pm and 5 pm respectively. On Wednesdays and Fridays there is a Rs 25 all-day tour to Sanchi and Udayigiri. It departs at 8.15 am and returns at 5 pm. Tour buses depart to Kerwan Dam every hour from 9 am to 4 pm on Sundays and Mondays. One-way is Rs 3, double that for return. On Saturdays buses also depart hourly, for the same price, to Islamnagar. Bookings can be made through the Tourist Office on Hamidia Rd.

Places to Stay – Bottom End

There are a lot of hotels along Hamidia Rd which runs between the railway station and the bus station, and on which the tourist office is located. If you come out the front of the railway station you'll have to get an auto-rickshaw down alongside the line and over the railway lines on a flyover. If you cross the other way, there's a footbridge which brings you out right on the Hamidia Rd corner. Hotels along Hamidia Rd include the older, basic, but reasonable *Grand Hotel* (tel 4070) with singles at Rs 15 to 20 and doubles at Rs 25 to 50, depending on facilities. The *Hotel Ranjit* (tel 3641) is also on Hamidia Rd and has singles/doubles from Rs 30/50. Similar prices at the adjacent *Gulshan Lodge*.

Still on Hamidia Rd, the *Hotel Samrat* is newish and in not bad condition – Rs 25/35 for singles/doubles. Ditto for the *Hotel Meghdoot*. The *Rajdoot Hotel* (tel 2797) is also new but rather grubby. Singles range from Rs 30 to Rs 50, doubles from Rs 50 to over Rs 100 with air-con. There are plenty of other places along this popular hotel road.

Bhopal has *Railway Retiring Rooms* at the station with air-con rooms from Rs 50, non air-con from Rs 20 and dorm beds at Rs 10. The *Youth Hostel* (tel 63671) is in North TT Nagar, to the south of the lakes. It costs about Rs 1 for an auto rickshaw there from the station. Dorm beds cost Rs 10.

Places to Stay – Top End

Also on the Hamidia Rd hotel strip is Bhopal's number one location, *Hotel Ramsons International* (tel 2298, 2299) with singles/doubles at Rs 66/100 non air-con, Rs 138/182 air-con. Other more expensive hotels in Bhopal include the *Pagoda* (tel 3949) still on Hamidia Rd and the *Imperial Sabre*, out of town in the old palace grounds.

Places to Eat

There are a lot of places to eat along Hamidia Rd of course. *Neelam's* and *Manohar's* are both vegetarian places, side by side. Good fruit juice drinks in *Manohar's*. The *Ranjit Hotel* has a good air-con restaurant and it's open late at night. There's also a restaurant, though not so good, in the *Rajdoot*.

Getting There

Air There are a surprising number of flights into and out of Bhopal. A daily flight operates either Delhi-Bhopal-Indore-Bombay or Delhi-Gwalior-Bhopal-Indore-Bombay. There's another daily flight Delhi-Bhopal, via Gwalior on some days of the week. There are also daily flights Bhopal-Jabalpur, continuing on some days of the week to Raipur and on others to Nagpur. There are similar flights in the opposite direction. Fares are Bombay Rs 503, Delhi Rs 446, Gwalior Rs 276, Indore Rs 143 and Jabalpur Rs 228.

Rail Bhopal is on the main Delhi-Bombay railway line. It's 705 km from Delhi, takes about 11 to 13 hours and costs Rs 188 in 1st, Rs 49 in 2nd. From Bombay it's 837 km and takes 13 to 16 hours. The fare is Rs 217 in 1st class, Rs 55 in 2nd. Sanchi is only 68 km north of Bhopal, but note the warning in the Sanchi section on non-stop trains.

Bus There is a direct bus from Khajuraho to Bhopal, the trip takes nearly 12 hours (overnight) and the fare is Rs 45. There are regular buses to Sanchi from Bhopal. They leave every couple of hours and take two to three hours to get there, depending on the route.

AROUND BHOPAL

Neori, only six km from Bhopal, has an 11th century Shiva temple, and is a popular picnic spot. Islampur, 11 km out, was built by Dost Mohamed Khan and has a hilltop palace and garden. It's on the Berasia road. At Ashapuri, six km north of Bhopal, there are ruined temples and Jain palaces with statues scattered on the ground. Chiklod, 45 km out, has a palace in a peaceful sylvan setting.

Bhojpur

Raja Bhoj built not only the dam at Bhopal but also a dam here, which created the largest lake in Asia. Hoshang Shah, the ruler of Mandu, destroyed it. A massive, but never completed, Shiva temple dating from the 11th century overlooks the lake. Bhojpur is 28 km from Bhopal.

Ginnorgarh Fort

This hilltop fort is 61 km from Bhopal and reached its peak in the 13th century during the reign of Udayavarman. It's famous for its parrots.

Bhimbetka

Neolothic caves and cave paintings discovered in this village, 40 km from Bhopal, are one of the earliest traces of man in India.

UJJAIN (population 225,000)

Only 80 km from Indore, on the right bank of the River Sipra, Ujjain is a very holy city for Hindus. It is also the site for the triennial Kumbh Mela, which comes to Ujjain every 12 years – next time in 1992.

The city has a long and distinguished history. It was an important city in the kingdom ruled by Ashoka's father, when it was known as Avanti. Later it was so attractive to Chandragupta II (380-414 AD), one of the Gupta kings, that for a long period he ruled from here rather than his actual capital, Pataliputra. His court supported the 'nine gems' of Hindu literature, including the important poet Kalidasa.

Later Ujjain became a centre for much turmoil and although it was, for a time, capital of the Malwa region it passed between the Rajputs and Moghuls before eventually falling to the Scindias of Gwalior.

Temples

The Mahakala Temple, later restored by the Scindias, was destroyed by Altamish of Delhi in 1235. An ancient gateway, known as the Chaubis Khanba Ghaj, is said to date from the original temple. It stands near the palace of Maharaja Scindia. The riverside temples and ghats are west of here.

Other temples include the small Bridh Kaleshwar, south of the Mahakala. The marble-spired Gopal Mandir was built by Jai Singh of Jaipur, but is so buried in the bazaar that it's easy to miss. The Temple of Nine Planets is on the Indore road where two other rivers join the Sipra.

Other

Out of the city, which was once bounded by a stone wall, to the south-west, is the Jantar Mantar – another of those strange observatories constructed by Maharajah Jai Singh. This is in poor condition and not as impressive as the Jantar Mantars of Jaipur or New Delhi. Eight km north of the town is the water palace of the Mandu Sultans. Known as Kaliadah, it stands on an island in the Sipra River. River water is diverted over stone screens in the palace, and the bridge to the island uses carvings from the sun temple which once stood on the island.

Places to Stay

The Ujjain Motel (tel 1862) has singles/doubles at Rs 40/50. There are also Railway Retiring Rooms and a variety of hotels opposite the railway station such as the Hotel China (Rs 20/25, OK), but avoid the bed-bugged although slightly cheaper Hotel Vikram.

INDORE (population 600,000)

Indore is not of itself of great interest but does make a good jumping off point for visiting Mandu. It's an affluent-looking town, a major textile producing centre, with plenty of new houses and flats. The rivers Khan and Sarasvati run through the town. From 1733 the town was ruled by the Holdar dynasty who were firm supporters of the British, even at the time of the mutiny.

Information & Orientation

The older part of town is on the western side, the newer part on the east. The railway line forms a rough north-south dividing line, while Mahatma Gandhi Rd bisects the town in an east-west direction. The railway and bus stations are quite close together but separated by a complicated flyover system. Curiously, there seem to be as many pigs congregating in the bus and train stations as the ever present cows. Rupayana, by the Central Hotel, is a reasonably good bookshop.

The Tourist Office (tel 38888), where you can find out about tours to Mandu, is on R N Tagore Marg behind the R N

mongoose →

Tagore Natya Griha. 'They have an excellent map of Indore with pictures and titles of all the tourist spots in English and Hindi, but they are very reluctant to part with them. It was the best city guide I saw in India and excellent for auto-rickshaw drivers who can understand the pictures or the Hindi'.

Palaces

In the old part of town the multi-storey gateway of the Rajwada or 'old palace' looks out onto the main square in the crowded streets of the Kajuri Bazaar. It's now given over to government offices, while the 'new palace' has become a hospital. The bazaar streets are busy and picturesque with deep verandahs on to the road. The Manik Bagh, to the south of the city, and the Lal Bagh, to the south-west, also have palaces. Daly College, a public school for the sons of Maharajas, is worth seeing – it's more like a palace than a school.

Kanch Madir

On Sunday St (Jawahar Rd), close to the Rajwada, is the Kanch Mandir or Seth Hukanchand Temple. This Jain temple is very plain externally, but inside is completely mirrored with pictures of sinners being tortured in the after-life as light relief.

Museum

Near the GPO, the museum has a car park which was a 'battlefield in the Independence War of 1857'. It specialises in sculptures and coins excavated in the Malwa region. In particular, there are over 700 pieces from Mandsaur. It has the biggest collection of antiques in Madhya Pradesh. Admission is free, it's closed on Mondays.

Chattris

The *chattris* or memorial tombs of the region's former rulers are now neglected and forgotten. They stand in the Chattri Bagh on the banks of the River Khan. The cenotaph of Malhar Rao Holkar I, founder

1	Railway Station	6	Central Hotel
2	Bus Station	7	Indian Airlines
3	GPO	8	Hotel Samrat
4	Kanch Mandir	9	Ashoka & Janata Hotel
5	Museum		

of the Holkar dynasty, is the most impressive.

Tours

There are a number of conducted tours from Indore. From Wednesday to Sunday there is a Mandu tour. On Monday the tour goes to Omkareshwar and on Tuesday to Ujjain. Tours start at 8.30 am from the bus and cost Rs 35.

Places to Stay – Bottom End

The railway station and the Sarwate Bus Station are only a few minutes' walk apart, and there's a reasonable selection of places directly opposite the bus station on Nasia Rd. There are *Retiring Rooms* in the bus station at Rs 15/20 for singles/doubles.

The *Janta Hotel*, across from the bus station, (tel 37695 & 36691) is OK – fairly clean, fans in the rooms, singles/doubles at Rs 12/15 or Rs 22/28 with their own bathroom. Flanking it on one side is the *Standard Lodge* (tel 37370 & 36889) with singles from around Rs 15 to Rs 25, doubles from Rs 18 to Rs 30. The *Ganesh Hind Lodge* in Chhotgwaltoli Rd is friendly and clean and has Rs 18 doubles with common bathroom.

On the other side is the newish *Hotel Ashok* (tel 37391-5), which is rather more expensive with rooms from Rs 35. Pleasant, clean, well-kept – the front rooms are a little noisy, due to the bus station. *Hotel Neelam* at 33/2 Chhoti Gwaltoli (tel 37161 & 37274) is also close to the railway and bus stations – rooms from Rs 15 (no bath) or from Rs 24 (with bath).

A little further away from the bus/train

centres on Mahatma Gandhi Rd, there are a number of more expensive places to choose from. The *Central Hotel* (tel 32131, 32041) in the Rampurawala Buiding at number 27, is a little old-fashioned and has big, fairly well kept rooms. Fan-cooled rooms are Rs 50-75/75-110, air-con Rs 100-150/140-200. If you cross the railway tracks on M G Rd you'll find the *Hotel Sheba* (tel 7720 & 7750) at 562, right by the statue of the Mahatma. Prices start from Rs 30/40 and head up with air-con.

Places to Stay – Top End

Further down Mahatma Gandhi Rd is the *Hotel Samrat* (tel 30758-59) at 18/5 M G Rd with slightly higher prices. These latter two hotels are both quite new – of the Indian 'rapidly deteriorating as soon as it's completed' variety. Indore's top hotel, the *Suhag Hotel* (tel 36580-9, 33270-9), is four km out of the city on the Bombay-Agra road, towards Dewas Rd. Air-con rooms cost from Rs 250/350.

Places to Eat

There are a number of good places to eat close to the bus stand. The *Janta* and *Standard Restaurants*, in the hotels of the same name, are both good value. The former has a surprisingly long list of Indian beer varieties, cold. The *Volga Restaurant*, near the Mahatma Gandhi statue on M G Rd, has good vegetarian food and aggressive air-conditioning.

Getting There

Air There's a daily flight through Indore either Delhi-Bhopal-Indore-Bombay or Delhi-Gwalior-Bhopal-Indore-Bombay. A similar schedule operates in reverse.

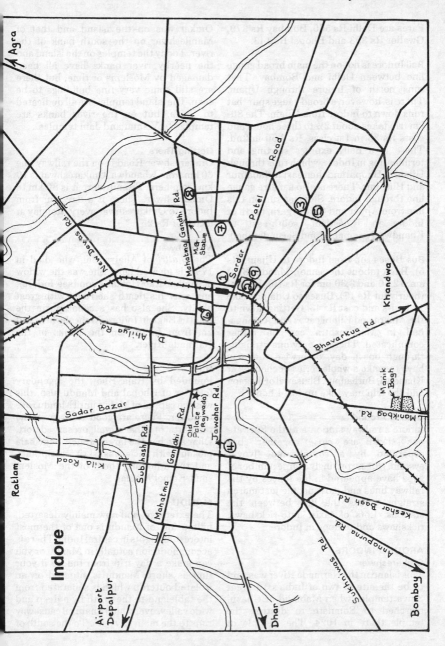

Indore

Fares are Delhi Rs 560, Bombay Rs 379, Gwalior Rs 398 and Bhopal Rs 143.

Rail Indore is not on the main broad gauge line between Delhi and Bombay. That runs north of Indore through Ujjain. There is, however, a broad gauge spur that runs down to Indore from Ujjain. The 80-km trip takes about 2½ to three hours and costs Rs 33 in 1st class, Rs 7.50 in 2nd. There is a daily express starting and terminating in Indore, which runs through Ujjain to Bhopal and then east to Jabalpur and Bilaspur. There is also a metre gauge line through Indore. Services run on this line from Ajmer and Chittorgarh, north of Indore in Rajasthan, south-east to Khandwa, Nizamabad and Secunderabad.

Bus Buses run from Indore to Ujjain (Rs 5), Bagh (about the same), Mandu (8.30 am, 12.30 and 3.30 pm for Rs 10), Bhopal (hourly for Rs 17). Buses to Udaipur take 12 hours and cost Rs 43. Getting down to the Ajanta and Ellora caves and Aurangabad in Maharashtra can be rather complicated. There is only one straight-through bus a day, otherwise you may have to make a whole series of changes at Khandwa, Burhanpur, Bhusawal or Jalgaon and the trip may take up to 14 hours.

Getting Around
Indore's railway station and the Sarwate bus stand are close together, but separated by a complicated flyover system. Not surprisingly a large number of gaps have appeared in the fences by the railway lines and most people just march straight across the line between the stations. Lots of taxis, auto-rickshaws, rickshaws and tempos in Indore.

AROUND INDORE
Omkareshwar
This island in the Narmada River was said to be the site of two of India's 12 great Shiva temples when Mahmud of Ghazni marched to Somnath to destroy the temple there in 1024. The Temple of

Omkar was on the island and that of Manileshwar on the south bank of the river. Today the temples on the island and the nearby river banks have all been damaged by Moslems or time, but there are still some very fine buildings to be seen. The island temples are all dedicated to Shiva, but on the river banks are temples to Vishnu and Jain temples.

Getting There
Omkareshwar Road is on the railway line 60 km from Khandwa. Omkareshwar is 10 km from here. From Indore it is 80 km to Omkareshwar. There is a day-tour from Indore to Omkareshwar every Monday at a cost of Rs 25.

Maheshwar
The *chattri* of Ahalya Bai, who died in 1795, is located here. She was the widow of Malhar Rao Holkar's son (see Indore), and after his death she ruled with great ability. She also has a cenotaph in the Chattri Bagh in Indore. Maheshwar is 100 km from Indore on the banks of the Narmada River.

Dhar
Founded by Raja Bhoj, the legendary founder of Bhopal and Mandu also, this was the capital of Malwa until Mandu rose to power. There are good views from the ramparts of Dhar's well preserved fort. Dhar also has the large, stone Bhojashala mosque with ancient sanskrit inscriptions, and the adjoining tomb of the Moslem saint Kamal Maula.

MANDU
The extensive, and now mainly deserted, hilltop fort of Mandu is one of the most interesting sights in central India. There is accommodation actually in Mandu or you can make a day-trip from Indore if your time is short. Mandu is situated on an isolated outcrop which is separated from the tableland to the north by a deep and wide valley, over which a natural causeway runs to the main city gate. To the south of

Mandu the land drops steeply away to the plain far below and the view is superb. Deep ravines cut into the sides of the 20-square-km plateau which the fort occupies.

History

Mandu, known as the 'city of joy', has had a chequered and varied history. Founded as a fortress and retreat in the 10th century by Raja Bhoj (see Bhopal), it was conquered by the Moslem rulers of Delhi in 1304. But when the Mongols invaded and took Delhi in 1401 the Afghan Dilawar Khan, governor of Malwa, set up his own little kingdom and Mandu embarked on its golden age. Even after it was added to the Moghul empire by Akbar Mandu it retained a considerable degree of independence, until the declining Moghuls lost control of it to the Marathas. The capital of Malwa was then shifted back to Dhar and Mandu became a ghost town. For a ghost town it's a remarkably grandiose and impressive place, and worth a day's inspection at the very least. Mandu has one of the best collections of Afghan architecture to be seen in India.

Although Dilawar Khan first established Mandu as an independent kingdom it was his son, Hoshang Shah, who shifted the capital from Dhar to Mandu and raised it to its greatest splendour. Warlike as he was, Hoshang's rule, from 1405, was marked by the construction of the Delhi Gate, the Jami Masjid, his own fine tomb and the extensive and complex fortifications.

His son ruled for only a year before being poisoned by Mahmud Shah, who became king himself and ruled for 33 years, during which Mandu was in frequent, and often bitter, dispute with neighbouring powers. There are few architectural remains of his reign for his most imposing structures, such as his own tomb, were poorly designed and built, and soon collapsed. Nevertheless his constant war-making raised Mandu to great importance and prosperity.

In 1469 his son, Ghiyas-ud-Din, ascended the throne and spent the next 31 years devoting himself to women and song – if not wine, for he was reputed to be teetotal. His son, Nasir-ud-Din, became so fed up with waiting for over-indulgence to finish off his father that he poisoned him in 1500, when he was 80 years old. The son lived only another 10 years before dying, some say, of guilt. In turn his son, Mahmud, had an unhappy reign during which his underlings, like Gada Shah and Darya Khan, often had more influence than he did. Finally, in 1526, Bahadur Shah of Gujarat conquered Mandu.

In 1534 Humayun, the Moghul, defeated Bahadur Shah but, as soon as Humayun turned his back, an officer of the former dynasty took over. Several more changes of fortune eventually led to Baz Bahadur taking power in 1554, but his chief pursuits were not conquest or building, like his predecessors, but music. In 1561 he fled from Mandu rather than face Akbar's advancing troops, and Mandu's period of independence ended. Although the Moghuls maintained the fort for a time and even added some new, minor, buildings its period of grandeur was over.

Information & Orientation

The buildings of Mandu can be divided into three groups. When you enter through the Delhi Gate at the north, a road branches off to the west almost immediately. This leads to the group of buildings known as the Royal Enclave. If you continued straight on from the entrance you'd pass the Tourist Bungalow and come to the tiny village which is all that Mandu is today. The buildings here are known as the village group. Continuing on beyond here, you'll eventually reach the Rewa Kund group at the extreme south of the fort. You can get a copy of the Archaeological Survey of India's excellent guidebook *Mandu* from the Taveli Mahal in the Royal Enclave. There are many other buildings in Mandu apart from those described below.

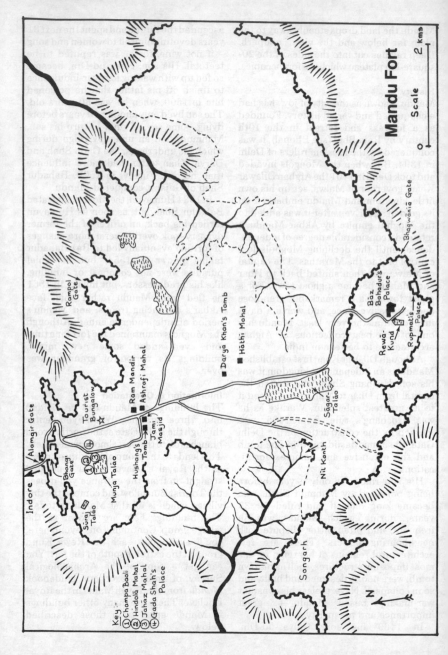

Mandu Fort

Scale

0 ____ 2 kms

Bhagwānā Gate

Bāz Bahadur's Palace

Rūpmati's Palace

Rewā-Kund

Rāmpol Gate

Daryā Khan's Tomb

Hāthī Mahal

Sāgar-Talāo

Ram Mandir

Ashrafi Mahal

Tourist Bungalow

Jāmī Masjid

Hushang's Tomb

Munja Talāo

Sūraj Talāo

Bhangi Gate

Alamgir Gate

Indore

Nīl Kanth

Songarh

N

Key:-
① Champa Baoli
② Hindolā Mahal
③ Jahaz Mahal
✛ Gada Shah's Palace

Royal Enclave – Jahaz Mahal

The 'Ship Palace' is probably the most famous building in Mandu, it really is ship-like being far longer (110 metres) than it is wide (15 metres), and the illusion is completed by the two lakes that flank it to the east and west. It was built by Ghiyas-ud-Din, son of Mahmud Shah. Ghiyas had become thoroughly fed up with his father's warring ways and decided to dedicate himself to more pleasurable pursuits. The Jahaz Mahal is his magnificent harem. At the northern end of the 'ship' is a beautifully-tiered bath where one can easily imagine the ladies of the harem lolling around seductively.

Hindola Mahal

Just north of Ghiyas' stately pleasure dome this church-like hall is known as the 'swing palace', because the inward slope of the walls is supposed to create the impression that the walls are swaying. 'Supposed' to anyway. A wide, sloping ramp in the northern end of the building is said to be for the ruler to be conveyed upstairs by elephant. The building is massively constructed, quite strong enough to handle the odd elephant.

Champa Baoli

To the west of the first two Royal Enclave buildings is this interesting building on the north shore of the lake. Its subterranean levels featured cool wells and baths and it was obviously a popular hot weather retreat. There are a number of other buildings in the enclave, including the 'house and shop' of Gada Shah and the 1405 Mosque of Dilawar Khan, one of the earliest Moslem buildings in Mandu. Just south of the Jahaz Mahal is the Taveli Mahal, which is used as a rest house.

Village Group – Jami Masjid

The huge, 1454 mosque dominates the village of Mandu. It is claimed to be the finest and largest example of Afghan architecture in India. Construction of the mosque was commenced by Hoshang Shah, who patterned it on the great mosque in Damascus, Syria. The mosque features an 80-metre square courtyard.

Hoshang's Tomb

Immediately behind the mosque is the imposing marble tomb of Hoshang, who died in 1435. The tomb is entered through a domed porch and the interior is lit by stone *jali* screens – typical of the clear Hindu influence on the fine design of this tomb. You enter the tomb through a double arch and the squat, central dome is surrounded by four smaller domes. It is said that Shah Jahan sent his architects to Mandu to study this tomb before they embarked upon the design of the Taj Mahal. To one side of the tomb enclosure is a long, low colonnade with its width divided into three by rows of pillars. Behind is a long, narrow hall with a typically Moslem barrel-vaulted ceiling. This was intended as a shelter for pilgrims visiting Hoshang's tomb.

Ashrafi-Mahal

The ruin of this building stands in front of the Jami Masjid, directly across the road from it. Originally built as a *madrasa* (religious college), it was later extended by its builder, Mahmud Shah, to become his tomb. But the design was simply too pretentious for its builders' abilities and it later collapsed. The seven-storey, circular tower of victory, which Mahmud Shah erected, has also fallen. A great stairway still leads up to the entrance to the empty shell of the building.

Rewa Kund – Palace of Baz Bahadur

It is about three km south from the village group, past the large Sagar Talao tank, to the Rewa Kund group. Baz Bahadur was the last independent ruler of Mandu. When he fell to Akbar and the Moghuls, Mandu became a mere shadow of its former glory. His palace, constructed around 1509, is beside the Rewa Kund and there was a water-lift at the northern end of the tank to supply water to the palace. The palace is a curious mix of Rajasthani and Moghul styles, and was actually built well before Baz Bahadur came to power.

Rupmati's Pavilion

At the very edge of the fort, perched on the hillside over the plains below, is the pavilion of Rupmati. The Malwa legends relate that she was a beautiful Hindu singer, and that Baz Bahadur persuaded her to leave her home on the plains by building her this pavilion. From its terraces and domed pavilions Rupmati could gaze down on the Narmada River, winding across the plains far below.

It's a romantic building, the perfect setting for a fairytale romance – but one with an unhappy ending. Akbar, it is said, was prompted to conquer Mandu partly due to Rupmati's beauty. And when Akbar marched on the fort Baz Bahadur fled, leaving Rupmati to poison herself.

Darya Khan's Tomb & Hathi Mahal

To the east of the road, between the Rewa Kund and the village, are these two buildings. The Hathi Mahal or 'elephant palace' is so named because the pillars supporting the dome are of massive proportions – like elephant legs. Nearby is the tomb of Darya Khan, which was once decorated with intricate patterns of mosaic tiles.

Nilkanth Palace

Situated at the end of one of the ravines which cuts into the fort, this palace is actually below the level of the hilltop and reached by a flight of steps down the hillside. At one time this was a Shiva shrine as the name, the god with the blue throat, suggests. Under the Moghuls it became a pleasant, water palace with a typical Moghul water cascade running down the middle. It was a favourite place for the Emperor Jehangir, but today it has once again become a Shiva temple, and a favourite playground for monkeys. Although it is of no great architectural merit, it's a very pretty and pleasant place.

Places to Stay

There is an *Archaeological Rest House* with accommodation at Rs 15 per person. It's situated by the Jahaz Mahal in the Royal Enclave. Or, on the main road into the fort to the village group, there's the *Ashok Travellers' Lodge* with rooms at Rs 60/90 or Rs 115/200 including all meals.

The *Tourist Bungalow* (tel 35) is Rs 25 a double. Rooms at the Tourist Bungalow can also be booked through the Tourist Office in Indore. There are a number of small eating places in the village and a *dharamsala* (less than Rs 10) near the bus stop, but it's not very good value.

Getting There

There are buses from Bhopal, Mhow, Ujjain, Dhar and Indore to Mandu. From Indore buses depart at 8.30 am, 12.30 and 3.30 pm and the trip costs Rs 10. Going back it's only Rs 9 because there's a Rs 1 entry charge to Mandu. It's 115 km from Indore to Mandu, the bus takes about four hours. There are tours from Indore to Mandu on most days of the week departing at 8.30 am, they cost Rs 35.

BAGH CAVES

The Bagh Caves are seven km from the village of Bagh and three km off the main road. Bagh is about 50 km west of Mandu,

A Backwater trip from Allepey to Quilon (Ke)
B Statue of Gomateshvara, Sravanabelagola (Ka)
C Reading the book, Brihadeshwara Temple, Tanjore (TN)

on the road between Indore and Baroda in Gujarat. The caves date from 400 to 700 AD and are Buddhist, but are all in very bad shape. Cave-ins, smoke and water damage have reduced them to such a poor condition that restoration work is barely worthwhile. Compared to the caves of Ajanta or Ellora, the Bagh Caves are hardly worth the not-inconsiderable effort of getting to them.

In the Archaeological Museum in Gwalior you can see reproductions of the wall paintings from Cave 4, known as Rang Mahal or the Painted Hall, when they were in much better condition than today. There is a *PWD Dak Bungalow* at the caves.

KHAJURAHO

The temples of Khajuraho are one of India's major attractions – close behind the Taj and up there with Varanasi, Jaipur and Delhi. The temples, of course, are superb examples of Indo-Aryan architecture, but it's the decorations with which the temples are so liberally embellished that has made Khajuraho so famous. Around the temples are bands of sculptures of exceedingly fine and artistic stone work. The sculptors have shown many aspects of Indian life a thousand years ago – gods and goddesses, warriors and musicians, animals real and mythological. But two elements appear over and over again and in greater detail than anything else – women and sex. Stone figures of *apsaras* or 'celestial maidens' appear on every temple. They pout and pose for all the world like Playboy models posing for the camera. In between are the *mithuna* couples – couples, on some of the temples even larger groups, running through a whole Kama Sutra of positions

and possibilities. Some obviously require amazing athletic contortions, some just look like good fun!

These temples were built during the Chandella period, a dynasty which survived for five centuries before falling to the onslaught of Islam. Khajuraho's temples almost all date from one century-long burst of creative genius. These magnificent structures were almost all built between 950 and 1050 AD. Almost as intriguing as the sheer beauty and size of the temples themselves is the question of why and how they were built here. Khajuraho is simply a long way from anywhere and was probably just as far off the beaten track a thousand years ago as it is today. There is nothing of great interest or beauty to recommend Khajuraho as a building site, there is no great population centre here and during the hot season Khajuraho is very hot, very dry, very dusty and very uncomfortable.

Having chosen such a strange site how did the Chandellas manage to recruit the labour to turn their awesome dreams into stone? To build so many temples of such monumental size in just 100 years must have required a huge amount of manpower. Whatever their reasons, we can be thankful they built Khajuraho where they did, because its very remoteness must have helped to preserve it from the desecration Moslem invaders were only too ready to inflict on 'idolatrous' temples elsewhere in India.

Information & Orientation

The modern village of Khajuraho is a cluster of hotels, restaurants, shops and stalls around the bus station. A little north of this, there are three government-run hotels and by the bus stand there is also

A Meenakshi Temple, Madurai (TN)
B Tirikkalikundram (TN)
C The Rahtas, Mahabalipuram (TN)

the museum, the tourist office (tel 47) and the post office. The temples are in three groups. Right by this modern part of Khajuraho is the western group, most of the temples in this group are in a well kept enclosure, and it includes the largest and most important temples at Khajuraho.

A km or so east of the bus stand is the old village of Khajuraho, and around the village are the temples of the eastern group. Finally, there are the two southern group temples, further to the south. Apart from everything else Khajuraho is a delightful place to lie around in, restful, interesting and easy-going. Small images of the gods can be bought from the shops in Khajuraho – plus lots of post cards.

Terminology

The Khajuraho temples follow a fairly consistent design pattern and it's pretty well unique to Khajuraho. Understanding the architectural conventions here, and some of the terms used to describe it, will help you enjoy the temples more. Basically the temples all follow a five-part or three-part plan.

You enter the temples through an entrance porch, known as the *ardhaman-dapa*. Behind this is the hall or *mandapa*. This leads into the main hall or *mahaman-dapa*, supported with pillars and with a corridor around it. A vestibule or *antarala* then leads into the *garbhagriha*, the inner-sanctum where the image of the god to which the temple is dedicated is displayed. An enclosed corridor, the *pradakshina*, runs around this sanctum. The simpler three-part temples delete part 2 (the *mandapa*) and part 5 (the *pradakshina*), but otherwise follow the same plan as the five-part temples.

Externally the temples consist of successive waves of higher and higher towers culminating in the soaring *sikhara*, which tops the sanctum. While the lower towers, over the *mandapa* or *mahaman-dapa*, may be pyramid-shaped, the *sikhara* is taller and curvilinear. The ornate, even baroque, design of all these

vertical elements is balanced by an equally ornate horizontal element from the bands of sculptures that run right around the temples. Although the sculptures are so superbly developed in their own right, they are also a carefully integrated part of the overall design – not some tacked on afterthought.

The interiors of the temples are as ornate as the exteriors. The whole temple sits upon a high terrace, known as the *adisthana*. Unlike temples in most other parts of India there is no enclosing wall but the temples often had four smaller shrines at the corners of the terrace – many of these have disappeared today. The finely-carved entrance gate into the temple is a *torana*. The lesser towers around the main sikhara are known as *urusringas*.

The temples are almost all aligned east-west with the entrance facing east. Some of the earliest temples were made of granite, or granite and sandstone, but all the temples from the classic period of Khajuraho's history are completely made of sandstone. At this time there was no mortar, so all the blocks are simply fitted together. The sculptures and statues play such an important part in the total design that many have their own terminology:

apsaras – heavenly nymphs, the beautiful dancing women who adorn the temples.
salabhanjikas – women figures with trees, which together act as supporting brackets in the inner chambers of the temple. Apsaras also perform this bracket function.
surasundaris – when a surasundari is dancing she is an apsara. Otherwise they attend to the gods and goddesses by carrying flowers, water, ornaments, mirrors or other offerings. They also engage in everyday activities like washing their hair, applying make-up, taking a thorn out of their foot, fondling themselves, playing with pets and babies, writing letters, playing musical instruments or simply posing seductively.
nayikas – it's really impossible to tell a

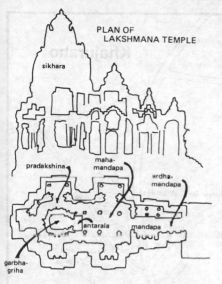

PLAN OF
LAKSHMANA TEMPLE

sikhara

pradakshina

maha-
mandapa

ardha-
mandapa

antarala

mandapa

garbha-
griha

nayikas from a surasundari, since the only difference is that the surasundari is supposed to be a heavenly creature while a nayika is human.

mithuna – Khajuraho's most famous images, the sensuously-carved, erotic figures which adorn so many of the temples. They're reputed to have been shocking people from Victorian archaeologists to blue-rinse tourists, but no one is really certain about their purpose. Some say they represent the sexual side of the path to final deliverance, others that they are simply another part of life and that the sculptors were trying to include all of life in the temples. Whatever the reason they're certainly an important part of what makes Khajuraho so interesting.

sardulas – a mythical beast, part lion, part some other animal or even man. Sardulas, usually carry an armed man on their back, and can be seen on many of the temples. They all look like lions but the faces are often different. They may be demons or *asuras*.

Western Group

The western group of temples is the most conveniently situated to the tourist part of Khajuraho, and also has the most interesting temples. Most of them are contained within a fenced enclosure, which is kept as a very well-maintained park. The enclosure is open from sunrise to sunset and your Rs 0.50 admission covers you for multiple entries for one day. It also permits entry to the archaeological museum across the road, so don't lose your ticket. Admission is free on Fridays. The enclosure temples are described below in a clockwise direction.

Lakshmana Temple

The large Lakshmana Temple is dedicated to Vishnu, although in design it is similar to the Kandariya Mahadev and Vishvanath temples. It is one of the earliest of the western enclosure temples, dating from around 930 to 950 AD, but also one of the best preserved since it has not only the full five-part floor plan, but also still retains its four subsidiary shrines. Around the temple are two, rather than the usual three, bands of sculpture, and the lower one has some fine figures of *apsaras* and some erotic scenes.

On the subsidiary shrine at the southwest corner you can make out an architect working with his students – it is thought this may be the temple's designer, including himself in the grand plan. Right around the base of the temple there is a continuous frieze with scenes of battles, hunting and processions. The first metre or two of the frieze consists of a highly energetic orgy, including one gentleman proving that a horse can be man's best friend, while a stunned group of women look aside in shock.

Lakshmi & Varah Temples

Facing the large Lakshmana Temple are these two small shrines. The Varah Temple, dedicated to Vishnu's boar incarnation or Varah Avatar, actually faces the Matangesvara Temple which is

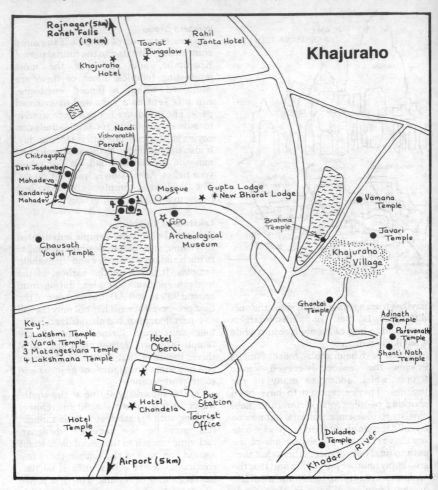

Khajuraho

Rajnagar (5km)
Raneh Falls
(19 km)

Tourist
Bungalow

Rahil
Janta Hotel

Khajuraho
Hotel

Nandi
Vishvanath
Parvati

Chitragupta

Devi Jagdambe

Mahadeva

Kandariya
Mahadev

Mosque

Gupta Lodge
New Bharat Lodge

Vamana
Temple

Brahma
Temple

Javari
Temple

GPO

Archeological
Museum

Khajuraho
Village

Chausath
Yogini Temple

Ghantai
Temple

Adinath
Temple

Parsvanath
Temple

Key:-
1 Lakshmi Temple
2 Varah Temple
3 Matangesvara Temple
4 Lakshmana Temple

Hotel
Oberoi

Shanti Nath
Temple

Bus
Station

Hotel
Chandela

Tourist
Office

Hotel
Temple

Duladeo
Temple

Khodar River

Airport (5km)

outside the enclosure. Inside this small, open shrine is a huge, solid and intricately-carved figure of the boar.

Kandariya Mahadev

The first of the temples on a common base – at the back of the western enclosure – is the one temple to see in Khajuraho above all others. The Kandariya Mahadev is not only the largest of the temples, it is also artistically and architecturally the most perfect. Built between 1025 and 1050, it represents Chandella art at its most finely-developed phase. Although the four subsidiary shrines which once stood around the main temple have long disappeared, the central shrine is in superb condition and shows the typical five-part design of Khajuraho temples.

The main spire soars 31 metres high and the temple is lavishly carved. The English archaeologist Cunningham counted

226 statues inside the temple and a further 646 outside – 872 in total with most of them nearly a metre in height. The statues are carved around the temple in three bands and include gods, goddesses, beautiful women, musicians and, of course, some of the famed erotic groups. The *mithuna* on the Kandariya Mahadev include some of the most energetic eroticism to be seen at Khajuraho. In the sexual olympics there would definitely be some gold medal winners here.

Mahadeva

This small, and mainly ruined, temple stands on the same base as the Kandariya Mahadev and the Devi Jagadamba. Although it is so small and insignificant by comparison to its mighty neighbours, it houses one of Khajuraho's best sculptures – a fine figure of a person (man or woman, observers have been unable to decide), caressing a lion.

Devi Jagadamba

The third temple on the common platform is slightly older than the Kandariya Mahadev and of a simpler, three-part design. The temple was probably originally dedicated to Vishnu, but later changed to Parvati and then Kali. Some students believe it may still be a Parvati temple and that the Kali image (or Jagadamba) is actually an image of Parvati, painted black. The sculptures around the temple are again in three bands. Many of the two lower band images are of Vishnu with *sardulas* in the inner recesses. But on the third and uppermost band the *mithuna* again come out to play, and some feel that this is Khajuraho's most erotic temple.

Chitragupta

The fourth temple at the back of the western enclosure does not share the common platform with the other three. Similar in design to the Devi Jagadamba, this temple is probably slightly later and is unique, at Khajuraho, in being dedicated to Surya, the Sun God. The temple has

obviously been much restored and is not in such good condition as other temples. Nevertheless it has some very fine sculptures including processions, dancing girls, elephant fights and hunting scenes. In the inner sanctum Surya can be seen driving his chariot and seven horses, while on the central niche in the south facade you can see an 11-headed statue of Vishnu. The central head is that of Vishnu himself, the 10 others are of his incarnations.

Parvati

Continuing around the enclosure you come to the Parvati temple on your right. The name is probably incorrect since this small, and not so interesting, temple was originally dedicated to Vishnu and now has an image of Ganga riding on the back of a crocodile.

Vishvanath Temple & Nandi

Believed to have been built in 1002, this temple also has the complete five-part design of the larger Kandariya Mahadev temple, but also has two of its four subsidiary shrines still standing. That it is a Shiva shrine is made very clear by the large image of his vehicle, the bull Nandi, which faces the temple from the other end of the common platform. Steps lead up to this high terrace, flanked by lions on the northern side and elephants on the southern side. The sculptures around the temple include the usual Khajuraho scenes, but the sculptures of women are particularly notable here. They write letters, fondle a baby, play music and, perhaps more so than any other temple, simply languish around in provocative poses.

Matangesvara Temple

Standing next to the Lakshmana Temple, this temple is not within the fenced enclosure because it is still in everyday use, unlike all the other old Khajuraho temples. It is one of the older temples at Khajuraho, dating from around 900 to 925

AD. The temple is rather simpler in floor plan than the later, more highly developed temples and does not have the same profusion of carvings. Inside the shrine is a highly polished 2.5-metre high lingam.

Chausath Yogini

Standing beyond the tank, some distance from the other western group temples, this ruined temple is probably the oldest at Khajuraho, dating from 900 AD or earlier. It is also the only temple constructed entirely of granite and the only one not to be aligned east-west. Chausath means 64 – the temple once had 64 cells for figures of the 64 yoginis who attended the goddess Kali. A 65th cell sheltered Kali herself. A further half km west is the Lalguan Mahadev Temple, a small, ruined shrine dedicated to Shiva and constructed of granite and sandstone.

Archaeological Museum

Close to the western enclosure, across the road from the post office, the museum has a fine collection of statues and sculptures rescued from around Khajuraho. It's quite small and definitely worth a visit. The museum is open from 9 am to 5 pm daily except on Fridays, and the western enclosure entrance fee also includes the museum. Opposite the museum, in the Archaeological Survey of India's compound beside the Matangesvara Temple, there are many more rescued sculptures – but it's off limits.

Eastern Group

The eastern group of temples can actually be subdivided into two groups. The first is the walled enclosure which contains an interesting group of Jain temples. The other four temples are scattered through the small village of Khajuraho. The easiest way to see these temples is to take a rickshaw out to the Jain enclosure, and then walk back to your hotel through Khajuraho village. Alternatively you can visit all these temples en route to the southern group.

Parsvanath Temple

The largest of the Jain temples in the walled enclosure is also one of the finest temples at Khajuraho. Although it does not approach the western enclosure temples in size, or attempt to compete in the sexual activity stakes, it is notable for the exceptional skill and precision of its construction, and for the beauty of its sculptures. Some of the best-known figures at Khajuraho can be seen here, including the classic figures of a woman removing a thorn from her foot and another of a woman applying eye make-up. Although it was originally dedicated to Adinath, an image of Parsvanath was substituted about a century ago and the temple takes its name from this newer image.

Adinatha

Adjacent to the Parsvanath Temple, the smaller Adinatha has been partially restored over the centuries. It has fine carvings on its three bands of sculptures and, like the Parsvanath, is very similar to the Hindu temples of Khajuraho. Only the Jain image in the inner sanctum indicates that it is Jain rather than Hindu.

Santinatha

This temple is a relatively modern one built about a century ago, but it contains many components from older temples around Khajuraho and a fine collection of Jain sculpture. The Jain compound also contains a small museum.

Ghantai Temple

Walking back from the eastern Jain temple group towards Khajuraho village you come to this small ruined temple. Only the pillared shell of this Jain temple remains, but it is interesting for the delicate columns with their bell and chain decoration and for the figure of a Jain goddess astride a Garuda which marks the entrance.

Javari Temple

You walk right through the village, a typical small Indian settlement, to this temple. Dating from around 1075 to 1100 AD it is dedicated to Vishnu, and is a particularly fine example of Khajuraho architecture on a small scale. The exterior has more of Khajuraho's delightful women.

Vamana Temple

About 200 metres north this temple is dedicated to Vamana, the dwarf incarnation of Vishnu. Slightly older than the Javari Temple, the Vamana Temple stands out in a field all by itself. It's notable for the relatively simple design of its *shikara*. The bands of sculpture around the temples are, as usual, very fine with numerous 'celestial maidens' adopting numerous interesting poses.

Brahma Temple

Turning back towards the modern village you pass this granite and sandstone temple, one of the oldest at Khajuraho. It was actually dedicated to Vishnu and the definition of it as a Brahma temple is incorrect. Taking the road directly from the modern village to the Jain enclosure, you pass a temple to Hanuman with a large image of the monkey god.

Southern Group

There are only two temples in the southern group, one of which is several km south of the river.

Duladeo Temple

A dirt track runs to this isolated temple, about a km south of the Jain enclosure. This is the latest temple at Khajuraho, and experts say that at this time the skill of Khajuraho's temple builders had passed its peak and that the sculptures are more 'wooden' and 'stereotyped' than on the earlier temples. Nevertheless, it's a fine and graceful temple with figures of women in a variety of pin-up poses and a number of *mithuna* couples.

Chaturbhuja Temple

South of the river, about three km from the village and quite a healthy hike down the dirt road that leads to it, this ruined temple has a fine large (three metre high) image of Vishnu.

Tours

There are a number of walking tours available around the western group of temples. Sometimes the Archaeological Survey of India in Khajuraho provides cheap tours by competent guides. Licensed private guides cost Rs 25 for a half-day.

Places to Stay – Bottom End

The *Rahil (Janata Hotel)* (tel 62) is fairly close to the Khajuraho Hotel. Run by the state government it costs Rs 40 single, Rs 60 double, with hot showers. In the dormitory there are beds at Rs 10 each. A less than enthusiastic traveller complained that it is 'not new, clean or comfortable', and that not only did she get 'apathetic (barely existent) service', but her 'toothpaste was eaten by rats'!

The recently opened *Hotel Payal* is under the same management as the Rahil, but is slightly more expensive with singles from Rs 75. In the nearby *Tourist Bungalow* (tel 64) the rooms are all four-bedded and cost Rs 80. The Rahil and the Tourist Bungalow both have parking places so they're good for people with vehicles.

Near the bus station there are a number of cheap local hotels. Rooms in these hotels are all from around Rs 15 or Rs 20, and some of them are quite reasonable. Try the *New Bharat Lodge*, popular with travellers, or the *Jain Lodge* (tel 52). Doubles in those two cost Rs 35 or 40. *Hotel Sunset View* has doubles with bath for just Rs 30 in the low season and is very clean and modern. It's on the main road from the airport, just before the town.

Places to Stay – Top End

The *Hotel Chandela* (tel 54) is south of the modern village, towards the airport. It's the number one hotel at Khajuraho and its rooms are all air-con, costing Rs 450/600 for singles/doubles. You can use the Chandela's swimming pool, if you are not a guest there, for Rs 20.

Hotel Khajuraho Ashok (tel 24, 42), a short walk north of the modern village, is a somewhat cheaper at Rs 300/375 for singles/doubles with air-con, Rs 150/200 without. Both have restaurants, reasonably good food at the Khajuraho. At the Khajuraho 'the staff hang around like vultures waiting for tips'. The *Jass Oberoi* (tel 66), on By Pass Rd, has only recently opened. Singles/doubles there are Rs 425/575.

Places to Eat

Opposite the entrance to the western enclosure, *Raja's Cafe* is run by a Swiss woman. It's a popular gathering spot under the large shady tree in the restaurant's courtyard. They also operate a free book swap system here. The *New Bharat Lodge* does good thalis and other food plus really good tea – if you're heartily sick of the usual over-milky, over-sweet tea in India.

Getting There

Getting to Khajuraho can be a major pain. Khajuraho is really on the way from nowhere to nowhere, and is not near any railway station. Although many travellers slot Khajuraho in between Varanasi and Agra it involves a lot of travelling to cover not particularly great distances. If you can afford to fly, then do, you'd save a lot of time.

Air Indian Airlines have a daily flight which operates Delhi-Agra-Khajuraho-Varanasi-Kathmandu, then returns by the same route to Delhi. It's probably the most popular tourist flight in India and can often be booked solid for days by tour groups. Delhi-Khajuraho costs Rs 379, Agra-Khajuraho Rs 266 and Varanasi-Khajuraho Rs 266.

Rail & Bus From the west there are bus services from Agra (412 km), Gwalior (293 km) and Jhansi (192 km). Jhansi is the nearest approach to Khajuraho on the main Delhi-Bombay rail line, and there are at least three buses a day on the Jhansi-Khajuraho route. This is the most popular route to Khajuraho by public bus. It's a seven hour trip costing Rs 17.50.

There is no direct route to Varanasi from Khajuraho. Satna, 120 km from Khajuraho, is the nearest railhead for visitors from Varanasi, Calcutta or Bombay. It's on the Bombay-Allahabad line. From Varanasi it takes about nine hours to Satna on the Sarnath Express or the Ganga-Cauvery Express which leaves early morning on Tuesday, Thursday, Saturday and Sunday.

Once there, you walk up the road and to the left to the local bus station. A bus leaves around 3.30 or 4 pm for Khajuraho and costs about Rs 12. The trip takes about four hours if you get a straight-through bus, longer if you have to change on the way. So an early morning departure from Varanasi should get you to Khajuraho by evening at an all-up cost of about Rs 40. In the opposite direction you could take a bus from Khajuraho, then a train around midnight would get you to Varanasi early in the morning.

In Satna the *Park Hotel* has clean singles/doubles at Rs 25/40 and is a reasonable distance from the bus stand. Directly opposite the stand is the *India Hotel*, which is not so clean but rather cheaper – may be OK for one night. *Hotel Natraj* is also marginally cheaper and there is the *Motel Satna* which is slightly more expensive. You can also sleep in the 1st class waiting room.

There is a direct night bus from Khajuraho to Bhopal, good for moving on to Sanchi. Another alternative from Khajuraho to Varanasi is to take a bus to Mahoba and a train from there but it's a rather slow passenger train. Harpalpur is much closer to Khajuraho than Satna wrote another visitor.

Getting Around

The airport bus into town costs Rs 5 but a taxi only costs Rs 15. The western temples are all for viewing on foot. To the eastern or southern group take a rickshaw. You can go out to the Jain enclosure and walk back from there, or for Rs 4 or 5 make a round-trip to Duladeo. All the rickshaw-wallahs have 'fixed rates' to any temple or group of temples you care to name, but it's all for show. The rates are round trip for two people. Bicycles can be hired in Khajuraho for Rs 4 a day.

AROUND KHAJURAHO

'Masochists', suggested one writer, 'might enjoy the four-hour, 63-km bus trip from Khajuraho to Mahoba where there is an under-used 12-room *Tourist Bungalow* with singles at Rs 25. A trip out to the ruined Surya temple five km from Mahoba is a worthwhile excursion'. Another suggestion was a jeep trip to 'an amazing, undiscovered fort called Kalinjer. On the way you cross the lovely Ken River, itself worth a visit and a picnic. It is about half an hour by bus from Khajuraho, and there is even a *Dak Bungalow* nearby'.

The people who run the Raja Cafe in Khajuraho are opening a *Tree Top Restaurant*, complete with accommodation, about 45 km from Khajuraho. En route you can visit the Panna Safari Park, 30 km from Khajuraho, and, a little further on, the famous Panna diamond mines, the Pandwa Falls and the Rajgarh Palace.

JABALPUR (population 550,000)

Almost due south of Khajuraho and due east of Bhopal the large town of Jabalpur, the second largest town in the state, is principally famous today for the gorge of the Narmada River known as the Marble Rocks. A century ago Jabalpur was the centre for the long British effort to suppress the practice of 'Thuggee'. The practitioners of this strange activity were known as 'Thugs', from which the word comes. They engaged in ritual murders, strangling their victims with a silken cord,

in order to please the goddess Kali.

In 1829 Colonel Sleeman was appointed to wipe out this bizarre activity and the 'School of Industry', where at one time suspected Thugs were interned, can still be seen in Jabalpur. Today it is used as a boys' reform school. It took the best part of 50 years to totally wipe out the Thugs. Today Jabalpur also has the Rani Durgavati Museum.

Information

At the station there is a Tourist Office (tel 2211).

Marble Rocks

Known locally as Bhera Ghat, the marble rocks are white limestone cliffs rising 30 metres above the water of the Narmada River. The gleaming rocks have a magical effect, especially by moonlight. If you wait for a group to form it will cost just a few rupees to boat up the gorge. The water falls down the Dhuandhar or 'smoke cascade' at the top of the gorge, and on the trip down the gorge you can see the Hathi-ka-paon or 'elephant's foot', a group of curiously-shaped rocks, the ledge known as 'monkey's leap' and an inscription cut by Madho Rao Peshwa.

It's about 24 km to the marble rocks, you can take a bus, or, if you're feeling fit, cycle out and back in a day. The road is fairly flat, and there are plenty of stalls to stop at along the way. You can buy cheap marble carvings there.

Madan Mahal & Chausath Yogini Temple

This ancient Gond fortress is on the route to the marble rocks, perched on top of a huge boulder. The Gonds, who worshipped snakes, lived in this region even before the Aryans arrived, and kept their independence until the arrival of Akbar.

Above the lower end of the gorge a flight of over 100 stone steps leads to the Chausath Yogini or Madanpur Temple. The circular temple has damaged images of the 64 yoginis, or attendants of the goddess Durga.

Places to Stay

The *Raja Gokuldass Dharamsala*, near the railway station, is very good for just Rs 3 on the first day, Rs 2 for succeeding days in a private room. *Rajhans Hotel* at Naudera Bridge has rooms from Rs 15/25 for singles/doubles. Also at Naudera Bridge the *Sawhney Hotel* is marginally more expensive. There are numerous other hotels around the station area.

At the top end of the scale there's *Jackson's Hotel* (tel 21320) in Civil Lines. Singles/doubles costs from Rs 30/40 or 60/100 with air-con. The Tourist Department's *Marble Rocks Inn* (tel 38) has just four rooms at Rs 40/60 for singles/doubles.

Getting There

There are daily flights between Bhopal and Jabalpur, continuing on some days of the week to Napgur, on others to Raipur. The fare to or from Bhopal is Rs 228.

There are buses to Jabalpur from Allahabad, Khajuraho, Varanasi, Bhopal and other main centres. Jabalpur is on the Bombay-Allahabad-Calcutta railway line. It's 1183 km from Calcutta, 369 km from Allahabad and 990 km from Bombay.

OTHER PLACES – East & South-East
Pachmarhi

At an altitude of 1100 metres this is Madhya Pradesh's hill station. It's near Itarsi on the Bombay-Jabalpur-Allahabad railway line. There are fine views out over the surrounding red sandstone hills and some interesting walks to be made.

Places to Stay

The Tourist Department has a variety of accommodation at Pachmarhi. The *Satpura Forest Lodge* (tel 97) has singles/doubles at Rs 50/70, while in the *Holiday Homes* (tel 99) there are rooms at Rs 20 and Rs 40. The more expensive Holiday Homes have cooking facilities.

Bandhavgarh National Park

In the Vindhyan Mountain Range in central Madhya Pradesh, there is a wide variety of wildlife in this national park although you'd have to be lucky to see a tiger. If you want to explore by elephant it costs Rs 20 an hour – for the whole elephant. Umaria, on the Katni-Bilaspur rail line, is the nearest railhead. It's also accessible from Satna on the Bombay-Allahabad rail line.

Places to Stay

White Tiger Forest Lodge in the park has singles/doubles at Rs 40/60. The manager is friendly and the food good although not dirt cheap. Accommodation can be booked in advance in Bhopal or Jabalpur.

Mandla & Ramnagar

On the route to Nagpur in Maharashtra, 100 km south of Jabalpur, is the fort of Mandla, which is situated in a loop of the Narmada River so that the river protects it on three sides and a ditch on the fourth. Built in the late 1600s, the fort is now subsiding into the jungle although some of the towers still stand. About 15 km away is Ramnagar with a ruined three-storey palace overlooking the Narmada. The palace, and then the fort, were both built by Gond kings, retreating south before the advance of Moghul power. Near Mandla there is a stretch of the Narmada where many temples dot the riverbank.

Kanha National Park

There are rest houses and watchtowers in this park, 77 km from Mandla and 173 km from Jabalpur.

Places to Stay

There is a variety of accommodation possibilities, including the *Kisli Youth Hostel* with dorm beds at Rs 8 and *Forest Bungalows, Forest Lodges* and *Log Huts* with rooms from Rs 25 to 75.

Bilaspur & Raipur

There are larger towns in the east of the state on the Bombay-Calcutta railway line. Ratanpur, 25 km north of Bilaspur, was the capital of the old kingdom of Chattisgarh, the 'kingdom of 36 forts'.

OTHER PLACES – North-West
Indore/Ujjain-Chittorgarh

The railway line passes through Ratlam, capital of a former princely state whose ruler died in one of those tragically heroic Rajput battles against the might of the Moghuls. At Mandsaur, north of Ratlam, a number of interesting archaeological finds were made in a field three km from the town. Some others are displayed in the museum at Indore. Two 14-metre high sandstone pillars are on the site, an inscription commemorates the victory of a Malwa king over the Huns in 528 AD. In the fort there are some fine pieces from the Gupta period.

Orissa

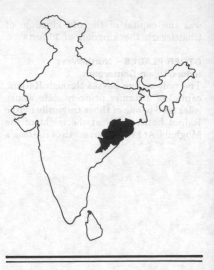

Population: 24 million
Area: 155,842 square km
Capital: Bhubaneswar
Main language: Oriya

The State of Orissa lies along the eastern seaboard of India, south of Bengal. The main attractions of Orissa are the temple towns of Puri and Bhubaneswar and the great Sun Temple at Konarak. These three sites make a convenient and compact little triangle and Bhubaneswar is on the main Calcutta-Madras railway route. The state is predominantly rural with fertile green plains along the coast rising up to the hills of the Eastern Ghats.

Orissa's hazy past comes into focus with the reign of Kalinga. In 260 BC he was defeated by Ashoka, the great Indian emperor, but the bloody battle left such a bitter taste with Ashoka that he converted to Buddhism and spread that gentle religion far and wide. Buddhism soon declined in Orissa, however, and Jainism held sway until Buddhism reasserted itself in the 2nd century AD. By the 7th century AD Hinduism had, in turn, supplanted Buddhism and Orissa's golden age was in full swing.

Under the Kesari and Ganga kings the Orissan culture flourished and countless temples from that classical period still stand today. The Orissans managed to defy the Moslem rulers in Delhi until the region finally fell to the Moghuls during the 16th century. Many of Bhubaneswar's temples were destroyed at that time. Today Orissa is tapping the hydro-electric potential of its many rivers and fledgling industries are being started but the state is still a region of green fields and small villages.

Temple Architecture
Orissan temples, whether it is the mighty Lingaraj in Bhubaneswar, the Jagannath in Puri, the Sun Temple at Konarak, or the many smaller temples all follow a similar pattern. Basically there are two structures – the *jagamohan*, or entrance porch, and the *duel*, where the image of the temple deity is kept and above which the temple tower rises. The design is complicated in larger temples by the addition of one or more entrance halls in front of the *jagamohan*. These are the *bhoga-mandapa* or 'hall of offering' and the *nata-mandir* or 'dancing hall'.

The whole structure may be enclosed by an outer wall and within the enclosure there may be other smaller subsidiary temples and shrines. The most notable aspect of the temple design is the soaring tower and the intricate carvings that cover every surface of the temple. These may be figures of gods, men and women, plants and trees, flowers, animals and every other aspect of everyday life, but to many visitors it is the erotic carvings which create the greatest interest. They reach their artistic and explicit peak at Konarak where the close up detail is every bit as

deul   jaga-mohana   nata-mandira   bhoga-mandapa

PLAN OF LINGARAJA TEMPLE

style. At one time the Bindusagar tank had over 7000 temples around it. Today there are about 500, but most of these are just decayed fragments. Perhaps a dozen are of real interest including the great Lingaraj Temple, one of the most important temples in India. The Puri temples are in a variety of Orissan styles and date from the 8th to the 13th century AD.

interesting as the temple's sheer size and imagination.

Information & Orientation
Bhubaneswar is a sprawling town divided

Things to Buy
Orissan handicrafts include the applique work of Pipli and the filigree jewellery of Cuttack. In Sambalpur tie die fabrics are produced and there are a variety of Orissan handloom fabrics. At Puri you can buy strange little wood carved replicas of Lord Jagannath and his brother and sister. At Balasore lacquered children's toys are manufactured.

Tribal People
Orissa has no less than 62 distinct tribal groups, aboriginal people who date from prior to the Aryan invasion of India. They live mainly in the hilly area of central Orissa. Amongst the better known tribes are the Kondh's who still practise colourful ceremonies, although animal sacrifices have now been substituted for the human ones which the British took so much trouble to stop – particularly around Russelkonda (Bhanjanagar). The Bondas are known as the 'naked people' and are renowned for their wild ways, and the dormitories where young men and women are encouraged to meet for night-time fun and frolics. Other major tribes are the Juangs, the Santals, the Parajas, the colourful and primitive Godabas and the Koyas.

BHUBANESWAR (population 125,000)
The capital of Orissa is known as the temple town due to its many temples in the extravagant, Orissan architectural

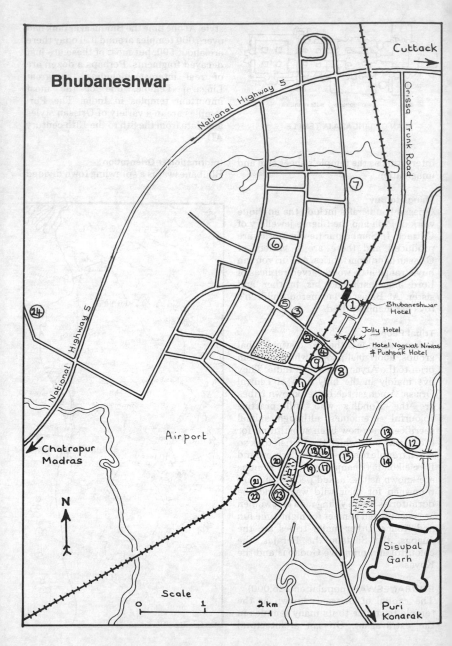

Bhubaneshwar

Cuttack

Orissa Trunk Road

National Highway 5

National Highway 5

① Bhubaneshwar Hotel

Jolly Hotel

Hotel Vaqwat Niwas & Pushpak Hotel

⑦

⑥

⑤ ③

④

⑨

⑧

⑪

⑩

⑬

⑱ ⑯

⑳

⑲ ⑰

⑮

⑫

⑭

㉑

㉒ ㉓

㉔

Chatrapur
Madras

Airport

Sisupal
Garh

N

Scale

0   1   2 km

Puri
Konarak

1 Railway Station	13 Bhaskareswar
2 Rajmahal Hotel	14 Brahmeswar
3 Market	15 Rajrani
4 Hotel Konark	16 Siddheswar & Mukteswar
5 Bus Stand	17 Kedareswar
6 State Guest House	18 Parasurameswar
7 Prachi Resort	19 Kotitirtheswar
8 State Museum	20 Vaital & Sisneswar
9 Hotel Ashok Kalinga	21 Bakeswar
10 Tourist Bungalow & Tourist Office	22 Jameswar
11 Lakshamaneswar	23 Lingaraj
12 Megheswar	24 Khandagiri & Udayagiri Caves

into old and new parts – the railway line forms the approximate dividing line. The bus stop and the Indian Airlines office are both in the new town as are most of the hotels. The Tourist Bungalow (and Tourist Office) and the ITDC Ashoka Hotel are both across the tracks. Most of the temples are within reasonable walking distance of the Tourist Bungalow. The airport is very close to the centre.

Lingaraj Temple

The great temple of Bhubaneswar is off limits to all non-Hindus. Close to the wall, on the northern side, is a viewing platform, originally erected for Lord Curzon during the days of the Raj. It's the best view you'll get of the temple and you really need binoculars to see anything.

The temple is dedicated to Tribhuvaneswar or 'Lord of the Three Worlds', also known as Bhubaneswar. In its present form the temple dates from 1090 to 1104 AD, although parts of it are over 1400 years old. The granite block which represents Tribhuvaneswar is said to be bathed daily with water, milk and bhang (hashish). The temple compound is about 150 metres square and dominated by the 40-metre high temple tower.

The ornately carved tower is intricately sculptured, from the viewing platform you can easily see the lions crushing elephants, said to be a representation of the re-emergence of Hinduism over Buddhism. More than 50 smaller temples and shrines crowd the enclosure. In the north-east corner a smaller temple to Parvati is of particular interest.

Bindusagar

The 'Ocean Drop' tank is just north of the great temple and is said to contain water from every holy stream, pool and tank in India. Consequently when it comes to washing away sin this is the tank which washes whitest. There are a number of temples and shrines scattered around the tank, several of them with towers in imitation of the Lingaraj Temple's. In the centre of the tank is a water pavilion where, once a year, the Lingaraj Temple's deity is brought to be ritually bathed.

Siddharanya

Close to the main Bhubaneswar-Puri road, on the same side as the Lingaraj Temple, the 'Grove of the Perfect Beings' is a cluster of about 20 smaller temples, including some of the most important in Bhubaneswar. Right by the road the small, 11-metres high, Mukteswar Temple is finely detailed with some excellent carving, but unfortunately much of it is defaced. The dwarves are particularly nice. The Mukteswar features an arched *torana*, a gateway showing clear Buddhist influence.

Also by the road, across the path from the Mukteswar, the Kedareswar is one of the older temples at Bhubaneswar and has a small tank. Close to the Mukteswar is the Siddeswar Temple, an interesting old temple with a fine, standing Ganesh figure. If you follow the path from these temples towards the Lingaraj you soon come to the Prashurameswar on your right. It's the best preserved of the early (7th century AD) temples and has interesting bas reliefs of elephant and horse processions. All its fine carvings are vigorous and alive.

If you work up a thirst while temple hunting, the shop beside the cinema near the junction has the coldest and cheapest soft drink in town.

Raj Rani

Across the road and about a hundred metres to the right, the Raj Rani stands alone in a green field. It's one of the latest of the Bhubaneswar Temples and particularly finely sited. Statues of nymphs, embracing couples, elephants and lions fill the niches and decorate the pillars.

Brahmeswar

About a km east of the main road, the Brahmeswar Temple stands in a courtyard flanked by four smaller structures. It's notable for its very finely detailed sculptures, with an erotic element and some quite amusingly carved – such as the young lady with the surprised look on her face, no doubt due to her lover's hand in her pants! The temple dates from the 9th century.

Close by are two other temples which are not of such great interest. The Bhaskareswar has an unusual 'stepped' design in order to accommodate an unusually large (three-metre) lingam it once contained. The Megheswar is in a courtyard and its shrine entrance is topped by a figure. Beside it there is a tank.

Other Temples

Close to the Bindusagar Tank, the Vaital has a double-storey 'wagon roof', an influence from Buddhist cave architecture. The Lakshamaneswar is a very plain temple, dating from the 7th century it is one of the earliest specimens of Orissan architecture and acts as a gateway to the city.

Museum

The museum is opposite the Hotel Ashok Kalinga and has an interesting collection relating to Orissan history, culture and architecture and to the various Orissan tribes. The Tribal Research Bureau is also located here. The museum is open 10 am to 5 pm daily except Mondays and entry is Rs 0.25.

Tours

During the season there are various tours operated from the Tourist Bungalow, including a tour of temples and caves of Bhubaneswar for Rs 12 or a Puri-Konarak tour for Rs 35. The latter tour takes from 8 am to 6 pm. The Bhubaneswar tour 'spends too long at a zoo/nature reserve, not long enough at the caves and temples'.

Discrimination

Two of the main attractions in Puri and Bhubaneswar (the Temple of Jagganath and the Lingaraj Temple) are 'off limits' to foreigners (non-Hindus). Nowhere in the tourist office's Orissa brochures is this ban mentioned – should tourist attractions be promoted if the tourists are not allowed into them?

Even more to the point should you pay for the places you're banned from? At the Lingaraj Temple there'll be someone waiting for you near the viewing platform to ask for not one but two donations – one for upkeep of that temple you're not fit to enter and a second for 'upkeep' of the viewing platform; which has clearly had no upkeep at all since the British built it. You'll also be asked for a donation for viewing the Jagganath Temple from the Raghunandan Library. Fair enough, since it's a private building, but Rs 1 is quite enough. Just because all the names in the visitors' book have Rs 25 written after them doesn't mean for a moment that's what they've 'donated'!

Places to Stay – Bottom End

Many of Bhubaneswar's middle range hotels are close to the museum, behind the railway station. The popular *Panthnivas Tourist Bungalow* (tel 54515), where you will also find the Tourist Office, is only a couple of hundred metres from the Hotel Ashok Kalinga and conveniently near to the many temples. Rooms with attached bath are Rs 50, more expensive with air-con. There are also a couple of four-bedded rooms which can be used as dormitories at Rs 10 per bed. The state government-run Tourist Bungalows are all similarly priced throughout Orissa and offer very similar standards. They're well kept, all rooms have attached bathrooms, and there's also a reasonably priced restaurant. Food can get a little monotonous though.

Most other accommodation is in the new town part of Bhubaneswar, nearer the railway station. There are a lot of hotels; most of them of similar standard to the Tourist Bungalow or below. A particularly good value hotel is the *Bhubaneswar Hotel* (tel 51977) directly behind the railway station with singles/doubles at Rs 30/50 or with air-con at Rs 90/115. There's a 5% service charge even though the hotel rules state 'No room service'. It's a big, well kept and clean place and has a restaurant.

Also good value, *Hotel Pushpak* has singles/doubles with attached bath for Rs 30/35 and also has a restaurant. Another very pleasant place to stay is the *Hotel Vagwat Niwas* (tel 54481), very close to the Pushpak, which has good clean doubles with fan and attached bath for Rs 35.

The centrally located *Rajmahal Hotel* (tel 52448) has its own bar and restaurant and is excellent value at Rs 25/30 for singles/doubles with attached bath. If you're looking for something cheaper, try the *Jolly Lodge*, Cuttack Rd, opposite the Pushpak, which has small but clean rooms with sheets provided for Rs 15, or for Rs 20 with attached bath. There are a lot of other small cheap lodges between the

Rajmahal and the expensive Hotel Konark. They include the *Gajapali Hotel, Samita Lodge* and *Ratna Lodge*. The Government of Orissa has an *Inspection Bungalow* on Old Station Bazaar, Satyanagar, which costs Rs 6.50 for singles, Rs 10 for doubles.

The railway station has *Retiring Rooms* (tel 52233) as does the bus station – upstairs at Rs 25 a double. Out at the Udayagiri-Khandagiri hills there's a very run down building claiming to be the *Khandagiri Youth Hostel*.

Places to Stay – Top End

Bhubaneswar's ritziest hotel is the recently completed *Hotel Konark* (tel 54382, 53330) – not Konarak. It's centrally air-conditioned, all rooms have attached bath, there's a restaurant, bar, swimming pool and bookshop. Singles/doubles cost Rs 300/400.

Nearby is the *Hotel Ashok Kalinga* (tel 50745), opposite the museum. It's also modern, centrally air conditioned and has a good restaurant and bar. Singles/doubles cost Rs 250/300. There are also some cheaper non air-con rooms. The *Prachi Resort* (tel 52521) at 6 Janpath is a little cheaper and also has rooms without air-con. There's also the *Hotel Gajapati* (tel 52371) at 77 Budha Nagar with rooms at Rs 40/50 or Rs 100 for an air-con double.

Places to Eat

The *Tourist Bungalow* has a reasonably priced, if monotonous, dining hall. Amongst the eating places in town you could try the *South Indian Hotel*, close to the Rajmahal, for a thali. The restaurant at the *Hotel Pushpak* offers reasonable and inexpensive food but the service is agonisingly slow.

The *Ashok Kalinga* is an excellent place for an escape to air-con comfort and good food – say Rs 30 to Rs 50 per person for a complete meal. The service is good but very slow. They also have a nice bar with free peanuts.

Getting There

Air There's a daily flight from Calcutta to Bhubaneswar, continuing on four days a week to Visakhapatnam and on the other days to Hyderabad and Bangalore. Four times a week there's a Delhi-Varanasi-Bhubaneswar service. The reserve schedules are the same. Fares are Calcutta Rs 296, Visakhapatnam Rs 296, Hyderabad Rs 682, Delhi Rs 927 and Varanasi Rs 492.

Rail Bhubaneswar is 469 km from Calcutta and 1222 km from Madras. Since it is on the main Calcutta-Madras railway line there are plenty of trains to Bhubaneswar as well as the trains terminating at Puri. The crack Coromandel Express departs Calcutta at 5.40 pm and arrives in Bhubaneswar just over six hours later, just before midnight. Other trains are rather slower, the Madras Mail leaves at 8 pm and takes 8½ hours. Other trains can take as long as 10 hours. Fares are Rs 138 in 1st class, Rs 35 in 2nd.

From Madras the Coromandel Express takes about 19 hours, the Madras Mail about 24 hours and other trains 30 or more hours. Fares from Madras are Rs 289 in 1st class, Rs 74 in 2nd. Trains terminating in Puri take 1½ hours to two hours longer from Calcutta or Mandras.

Five days a week there are trains from Delhi to Bhubaneswar and Puri. The once weekly Kalinga Express takes about 37 hours, but other trains take closer to 48 hours. Delhi-Bhubaneswar is 2063 km and the fares are Rs 420 in 1st, Rs 109 in 2nd.

Bus to Puri & Konarak There are frequent private buses from Bhubaneswar to Puri. The trip takes 1½ to two hours and costs Rs 5 or 6. It's a similar time and Rs 5 to Konarak. See Konarak for Puri-Konarak information. If it is not possible to get a direct bus to Konarak any Puri bus will go through Pipli where the Konarak road branches off.

Getting Around

The Indian Airlines airport bus costs Rs 5 but only to the IA office. A taxi costs about Rs 20 but you could also get a rickshaw for less than Rs 10, rather uphill from the town though. From the Tourist Bungalow a rickshaw to town or the Lingaraj Temple would be Rs 2 to Rs 3.

If you're planning on staying at one of the hotels along Cuttack Rd, at the back of the station, it isn't worth getting a rickshaw all the way round there – simply cross the railway tracks at the southern end of the station and walk through. It's much quicker.

AROUND BHUBANESWAR

There are two interesting sites close to Bhubaneswar, both dating from the Buddhist period.

Udayagiri & Khandagiri Caves

About five km out of Bhubaneswar these two hills, flanking the road on each side, are riddled with caves. On the right of the road the Udayagiri or Sunrise Hill has the most interesting caves, scattered at various levels up the hill. All the caves are numbered. At the base of the hill, round to the right, is the two-storey Rani ka Naur or Queen's Palace cave (1). Both levels have eight entrances and the cave is extensively carved.

Return to the road via the Chota Hathi Gumpha (3) with carvings of elephants coming out from behind a tree. The Jaya Vijaya Cave (5) is again double-storeyed and a Bo tree is carved in the central compartment. Back at the entrance ascend the hill to cave 9, the Swargapuri, and 14, the Hathi Gumpha or 'Elephant Cave'. The latter is quite plain but an inscription relates, in 117 lines, the exploits of its builder, King Kharaveli of Kalinga who ruled from 168 to 153 BC.

Circle round the hill to the right to the Ganesh Gumpha (10), which is almost directly above the Rani ka Naur. The carvings here tell the same tale as in the lower level cave but are better drawn. The

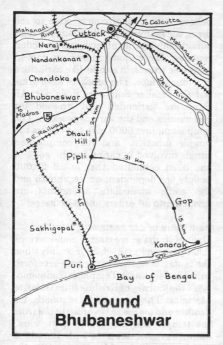

**Around
Bhubaneshwar**

women, elephants and geese carrying flowers. The right path leads to a series of Jain temples. At the top of the hill is an 18th century Jain temple.

Getting There
There are only a few buses specifically to the caves but there are plenty going by the nearby road junction. It's less than a rupee into town or by rickshaw you can get there for less than Rs 10.

Dhauli Edicts
About eight km south of Bhubaneswar, to the right of the Puri road, King Ashoka carved his famous edicts into a rock five metres by three metres. The famous Buddhist emperor related the horrors he experienced in the Kalinga wars, which he won, and his subsequent conversion to Buddhism. These 13 inscriptions are still remarkably clear after over 2000 years and the site is also marked by a new Peace Pagoda.

Other
The only partly excavated ruins at Sisupal Garh are thought to be the remains of an Ashokan city. At Nandankanan, 30 km from Bhubaneswar, there is a garden divided into a wildlife sanctuary, botanical garden and lake. You can rent boats on the lake.

PURI (population 75,000)
On the coast, 61 km from Bhubaneswar, Puri is one of the four holiest cities in India. The city revolves around the great Jagannath Temple and its famous Rath Yatra or Car Festival. It is thought that Puri was the hiding place for the Buddha tooth of Kandy before it was spirited away to Sri Lanka. There are similarities between the Rath Yatra and the annual Kandy procession.

Information & Orientation
There is only one wide road in Puri, the Baradand or Grand Road which runs from the Jagannath Temple to the Gundicha

cave is only single-storey. Retrace your steps to cave 14, then on to the Pavana Gumpha 'Cave of Purification' and the small Sarpa Gumpha or 'Serpent Cave', the tiny door to which is surmounted by a three-headed cobra.

Only 15 or so metres from this is the Bagh Gumpha (12) or Tiger Cave, entered through the mouth of the beast. The hill is topped by the foundations of some long-gone building. The oldest of these various caves date back to the 2nd century BC. Some are of Jain origin.

Across the road the Kandagiri hill is not so interesting, apart from the fine view back over Bhubaneswar from its summit. You can see the airport, the tower of the Lingaraj Temple rising behind it, and further away the Dhauli Stupa. The steep path divides about a third of the way up the hill. The right path goes to the Ananta Cave (3) with carved figures of athletes,

Mandir. Buses stop along this road. Most of the hotels are along the seafront. The Tourist Office is in the Panthnivas Tourist Bungalow.

Jagannath Temple

The temple of Jagannath, 'Lord of the Universe', is not open to non-Hindus, but amongst Hindus its considerable popularity is partially due to the lack of caste distinctions – all are welcome before Jagannath. Non-believers can look down into the temple from the roof of the Raghunandan Library, opposite the main entrance to the temple. You'll be asked for a donation.

The temple enclosure is nearly square, measuring almost 200 metres on each side. The walls of the enclosure are six metres high. Inside there is a second wall enclosing the actual temple. The conical tower of the temple is 58 metres high and is topped by the flag and wheel of Vishnu. It is visible from far out of Puri. The temple was built in its present form in 1198. In front of the main entrance is a beautiful pillar, topped by an image of the Garuda, which originally stood in front of the temple at Konarak. The main entrance is known as the Lion Gate from the two stone lions guarding the entrance.

Balabhadra, Subhadra &
Lord Jagannath

In the central Jagmohan, pilgrims to the temple can see the images of Lord Jagannath and his brother, Balbhadra, and sister, Subhadra. Although non-believers are not, of course, able to see them, the many shop stalls along the road outside the temple all sell small wooden replicas. The curious images are carved from tree trunks, in a child-like caricature of a human face. The brothers have arms but the smaller Subhadra does not. All three are garlanded and dressed for ceremonies and the various seasons. The temple employs 6000 men to perform the temple functions and the complicated rituals involved in caring for the gods. It has been estimated that in all 20,000 people are dependent on Jagannath and the god's immediate attendants are divided into 36 orders and 97 classes!

Rath Yatra or Car Festival

One of India's greatest annual events takes place in Puri each June or July when the fantastic festival of the cars sets forth from the Jagannath Temple. It commemorates the journey of Krishna from Gokul to Mathura. The images of Jagannath, his brother and his sister are brought out from the temple and dragged in huge 'cars', known as *raths*, down the wide Baradand to the Gundicha Mandir or 'Garden House' over a km away.

The main car of Jagannath stands 14 metres high, over 10 metres square and rides on 16 wheels, each over two metres in diameter. It is from these colossal cars that our word 'juggernaut' is derived and, in centuries past, devotees were known to have thrown themselves beneath the wheels of the juggernaut in order to die in the god's sight. To haul the cars takes over 4000 professional car-pullers, all employees of the temple. Hundreds of thousands of pilgrims (and tourists) flock from all over India to witness this stupendous scene. The huge and unwieldy cars take an enormous effort to pull, are virtually impossible to turn and once moving are nearly unstoppable.

Once they reach the other end of the road the gods take a week long summer break, then are loaded back onto the cars and trucked back to the Jagannath

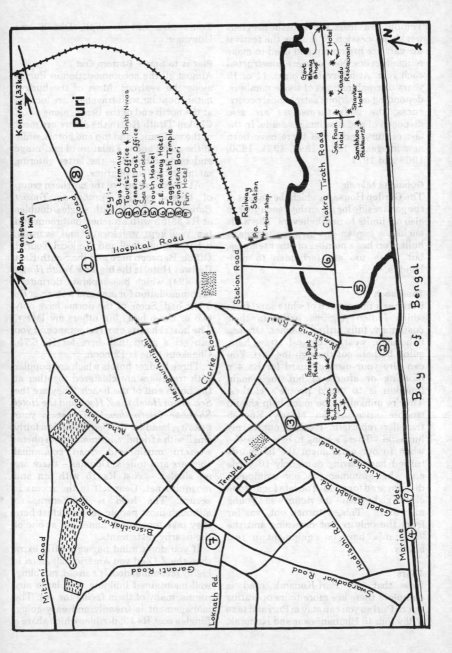

Puri

Key:-
1 Bus terminus
2 Tourist Office ★ Panth Nivas
3 General Post Office
4 Sea View Hostel
5 S.E. Railway Hostel
6 Youth Hostel
7 Jagganath Temple
8 Gundicha Bari
9 Puri Hotel

Kenarak (33km)
Bhubaneswar (c1 km)
Grand Road
Hospital Road
Station Road
Chakra Tirath Road
Bay of Bengal

Railway Station
P.O.
Liquor shop

Z Hotel
Govt. Bhang Shop
Xanadu Restaurant
Shankar Hotel
Sea Foam Hotel
Sambhoo Restaurant

Armstrong Road
Clarke Road
HerbanchariSahi
Athar Nola Road
Biseichakuro Road
Forest Dept. Rest House
Inspection Bungalow

Kutchery Road
Temple Rd.
Gopal Ballabh Rd.
Gopal Ballabh Rd.
Hodisahi Rd.
Swargadwar Road
Marine Pde.

Mitiani Road
Garanti Road
Loknath Rd.

Temple, in a virtual repeat of the previous week's procession. Following the festival the cars are broken up and used to make religious relics. New cars are constructed each year. At intervals of eight, 11 or 19 years or combinations of those numbers, depending on various astrological occurrences, the gods themselves are also disposed of and new images made. In the last century and a half there have been new images in 1863, 1893, 1931, 1950, 1969 and 1977.

Gundicha Mandir

The Garden House, in which the images of the gods reside for seven days each year, is also off-limits to non-believers. The walls enclose a garden in which the temple is built. Puri has a number of other temples, but these too are forbidden to non-Hindus.

The Beach

Puri has a fine stretch of white sand from which Indian pilgrims bathe in their customary, fully attired manner. Orissan fishermen, wearing conical straw hats, guide bathers out through the surf. You can hire your own lifeguard for Rs 4 a morning or afternoon but their main function is to guard people's clothes. They're unlikely to be much help should trouble arise as an elderly English traveller reported: 'I called out to my husband – There's going to be a rescue! – when to our amazement the lifeguards turned back having done only 10 yards and the swimmer (or non-swimmer?) disappeared for good. Too late for anyone else to go by then – the victim was a young man of 19'. This, it turned out, was far from the only recent drowning and the 'lifeguards' have no equipment or real ability.

Tours

Now that the Puri-Konarak road is complete there are more tours operating out of Puri so you can stay in Puri and take a day tour to Bhubaneswar and Konarak.

Tours also run to Pipli, Dhauli and Udayagiri.

Places to Stay – Bottom End

Almost all the accommodation in Puri is along the seafront. Most of the budget hotels popular with travellers are located at the north end of the beach, along or off Chakra Tirath Rd. In the centre are most of the mid-range and top end hotels, while at the south end is a mixture of mid-range and budget hotels – the latter catering mainly to Indian pilgrims.

At the sound end of the northern group of hotels is the *Panthnivas Tourist Bungalow* (tel 131) with singles/doubles at Rs 35/55 with attached bathroom and fan. Well kept, well located and, as usual, it has a dining hall and the local Tourist Office. Between here and the South-East Railway Hotel is the big, new *Youth Hostel* (tel 424) which has separate dormitory accommodation for men and women at Rs 5 per bed. Some of the dorms have only two or three beds but others are larger. The hostel has its own restaurant and you can get a good thali here for Rs 6.75. Checkout time is 12 noon.

Three budget hotels which are popular with travellers are clustered together at the north end of the beach. They are the *Sea Foam Hotel*, the *Z Hotel* and the *Hotel Shankar International*. If cost is your priority, head for the *Sea Foam*. It's fairly small with a friendly, intimate atmosphere, western music and clean communal showers and toilets. Doubles – there are no singles – cost Rs 15 with fan and mosquito net. Gear left in the rooms is secure. The food is indifferent, so although most people eat breakfast here they take lunch and dinner out at one of the nearby restaurants.

If you don't mind paying a little extra then the *Z* (Zed you Americans!) *Hotel* is highly recommended. It's an old, rambling, well-maintained building with large airy rooms, many of them facing the sea. The management is friendly and easy-going. Singles cost Rs 15; doubles which share a bathroom with one other room are Rs 30, with attached bath they're Rs 50. You can also get a dorm bed for Rs 10, the beds are in an open area on the top floor. There's a 'terrific ocean view' and it's 'quiet and pleasant and has good seafood'. If both these places are full then try the *Shankar International* next to the Sea Foam. A few of the rooms facing the sea are good value at Rs 35 for a double with attached bathroom, but others tend to be a little spartan. The restaurant at this hotel is not very good.

Down at the main bathing beach, about a km south of the northern group, is the *Puri Hotel*, which was renovated in mid-1983, and the cheaper *Sea View Hotel* (tel 117) on Marine Parade. The Sea View advertises on its cards as commanding a 'Full View of Refreshing Sea – Rubberised Coir Mattress Beds – Attached Baths & Homely Living' (all true!). Full board is Rs 32 to 35 per person per day depending on the room. It's excellent value and includes bed tea (6 am), breakfast (7-8 am), lunch (12 noon-1 pm), tiffin (4-5 pm) and dinner (8.30-9.30 pm). The only disadvantage is that checkout time is *6 am*!

There are also *Railway Retiring Rooms* and a 'railway camping coach' which costs Rs 1.50 per night.

Places to Stay – Top End

At the north end of the northern group of hotels is the delightfully 'olde worlde' *South-East Railway Hotel* (tel 63) with air con singles/doubles including all meals at Rs 180/405. Non air-con singles are Rs 125-175, doubles Rs 250-275, again with all meals. It has a pleasant lounge, bar, dining hall and an immaculate stretch of lawn. Non-residents can also eat here, lunch or dinner costs Rs 45 and the food is good.

Places to Eat

Puri is nowhere near as 'developed' as those other popular travellers' beaches in Goa, Kovalam (Kerala) and Mahabalipuram (Tamil Nadu) which is one reason why it's so pleasant. If you're looking for good seafood you're in luck, there are two places which offer consistently excellent seafood in pleasant and congenial surroundings complete with a good selection of western music. The more popular is the *Xanadu*, although those who have lived in Puri for a long time claim that the *Sambhoo Restaurant* is actually better. The distinction is academic, both offer lobsters, prawns, fish, chips and a range of salads as well as a variety of sweets. Most dishes cost Rs 3 to 4 although, naturally, you pay more for a lobster or a whole fish.

If you're looking for a cup of tea and/or a snack at other times of the day then the best chai shop in Puri is two doors up the hill from the Xanadu, right on the road side. It's run by a very friendly, oldish guy and his young son.

Getting There

All trains into and out of Puri pass through Bhubaneswar, the Orissa state capital. If you want to travel between these two places the buses are faster and more convenient than the trains, although more expensive. By train it's about two hours for Rs 4.20 in 2nd class. Buses, which run every half hour throughout the day, take about 1½ hours and cost Rs 5 or 6.

Trains out of Puri are as follows:

Tirupathi Express Don't take this train if you're heading to Madras as it involves you in a lot of unnecessary hassle at the other end. Go to Bhubaneswar first and take a more convenient train from there.
Howrah Express & Jagganath Express These daily trains both run to Calcutta, taking 12 or 13 hours.
Utkal Express & Nilachal Express Between these two trains they provide a daily service to New Delhi.

The Puri Railway Booking Office is open daily from 9 am to 1 pm and 1.30 to 4.30 pm.

There are State Transport buses to

Calcutta daily at 6.15 am and 4.45 pm and a number of private buses also go to Calcutta, most of them departing around 6.30 pm. See Konarak for Puri-Konarak transportation details. Puri doesn't really have a bus station – just a stretch of street where buses depart and arrive. It can be rather chaotic.

Getting Around

A rickshaw from Puri bus stand to the hotels along the beach is around Rs 3. There are lots of rickshaws in Puri.

Things to Buy

Puri is one of those delightfully eccentric Indian towns where the use of ganja and bhang is not only legal, but also the government very thoughtfully provides for smokers' requisites in the form of shops selling high quality weed comparable to Mullumbimy Madness at the very reasonable price of around Rs 10 a *tola* (about 12 gm). Should you be unfortunate enough to be suffering from Delhi Belly, they also do a nice medicinal line in opium at slightly more than double the price. There are at least two of these shops, one of them close to the railway station and the other just beyond the Z Hotel, but I was told by afficionados that there are three altogether. Life is full of pleasant surprises.

You'll come across quite a few craftsmen/salesmen offering fabric, bead and bamboo work. Some of it is well worth a second look. Prices are negotiable as always with this sort of thing. There are also plenty of people trying to sell snake and animal skins. The snake skins are certainly the best you will find in India (in terms of the care that has been taken in curing and finishing them), but the people who sell them always seem to have hundreds and they're all large. I dread to think what is happening to the wildlife in the Orissan forests. Still, at least you can have one on your living room wall or part of one keeping your dollar bills warm when they're all extinct.

KONARAK

Situated on the coast, 64 km from Bhubaneswar and only about 30 km north of Puri, the site consists of little more than the mighty temple and a handful of shops, stalls and places to stay. The Temple of the Sun was constructed at some time in the 13th century, but remarkably little is known about its early history. It is thought it was built by an Orissan king to celebrate a military victory. It has been in ruins for centuries but until the early 1900's, it was simply an interesting ruin of impressive size.

Then in 1904 debris and sand was cleared from around the temple base and the sheer magnitude of its architect's imagination was revealed. The entire temple was conceived as a chariot for the Sun God, Surya. Around the base of the temple are 24 gigantic, carved stone wheels, seven mighty horses haul at the temple and the immense structure is covered with carvings, sculptures, figures and bas reliefs. It is not known if the construction of the temple was ever actually completed. If the tower was completed it would have soared to 70 metres high and archaeologists wonder if the sandy foundations could have supported such a structure. Part of the tower was still standing in 1837 but by 1869 it had collapsed and today the interior of the temple has been filled in to support the ruins.

The main entrance, from the Tourist Bungalow side, is guarded by two stone lions, crushing elephants. Steps ascend to the main entrance, flanked by the straining horses. The entrance porch or *jagamohan* still stands, but the *duel*, behind it, has collapsed. The three images of Surya, the Sun God, still stand and are designed to catch the sun at dawn, at noon and at sunset. Between the main steps up to the *jagamohan* and the enclosure entrance there is an intricately carved 'dancing hall' or *nata-mandir*. To the north is a group of elephants and to the south a group of rearing horses, trampling

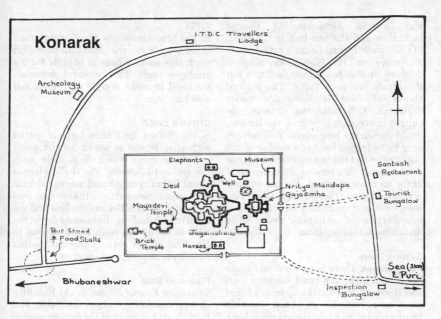

down men.

All around the base of the temple and up the walls and roof is a continuous procession of carvings. Many are in the erotic style for which Konarak, like Khajuraho, is so famous. These erotic images of entwined couples, or solitary exhibitionists, can be minute images on the spoke of a temple wheel or life-size figures higher up the walls.

Outside the temple enclosure there is a museum (open 9 am to 5 pm) containing many sculptures and carvings found during the temple excavation. The sea is a couple of km from the temple, you can walk there or hire a bicycle rickshaw. The temple was once known as the Black Temple by sailors, in contrast to the whitewashed temples of Puri. It was said to contain a great mass of iron which would draw unwary ships in to the shore.

Places to Stay

Now that there is a direct, sealed road along the coast between Puri and Konarak there's no real need to stay here. If you take an early morning bus from Puri and a late bus back (or on to Bhubaneswar) in the afternoon then you're going to get all the time in the word to have a look at the temple. Of course there are always people who disagree with anything and a couple of people have written to recommend staying in Konarak and visiting Puri from there!

The *Tourist Bungalow* (tel 21) is very close to the main entrance to the temple. As usual singles/doubles are Rs 35/55 with attached bathroom and fan. It's well kept, pleasantly located and has a dining hall and the Tourist Office. Many people coming from Puri for the day use the dining hall for meals, but although the food is OK the service is very slow and you should take note of the prices as a meal can work out quite expensive. Close to it is the basic *Santosh Restaurant*.

Half-way between the village and the beach is the new *Labanya Lodge* – clean and isolated. Between the Tourist Bungalow and the bus halt is the small ITDC *Ashok Tourist Lodge* – rather more expensive at Rs 60/90 for singles/doubles. It also has dining facilities but the meals are poor value. The limited choice of food is Konarak's major drawback. Otherwise the sunsets, the superb beach and, of course, the temple, could encourage long stays. You can get very basic Indian food at a couple of the shacks down at the beach. Sun bathing or swimming at this very pleasant beach is likely to draw a crowd. For emergency accommodation there's the *Inspection Bungalow*, and around the bus halt there's a collection of extremely basic little 'boarding & lodging' huts.

Getting There

Puri-Konarak There is now a direct route the 33 km along the coast between Puri and Konarak. Prior to the opening of that road you had to go back towards Bhubaneswar to Pipli, then double back to the coast – total distance 85 km. Now there is plenty of transport running along the coast, although they don't really leave to any schedule. None of the buses/minibuses/jeeps will leave until they're packed to the gunwales, so you may find yourself with at least an hour's wait at Puri bus station until the driver decides he can't possibly get anyone else into the vehicle. (In the short wheelbase jeep that I took there were 30 adults and five children at one point! – Geoff) If you offer to pay more than the standard Rs 3 to 4 fare, the drivers will naturally be content with fewer passengers. Well, they will until they see someone further up the road who might add to their takings. Coming back from Konarak is no problem – simply flag down any bus/minibus/jeep at any point along the road.

Konarak-Bhubaneswar There are buses fairly regularly to Bhubaneswar, including at least one express bus at 1.30 pm. Fare is Rs 5.

PIPLI

At the junction, where the Konarak road branches from the Bhubaneswar-Puri road, this small village is notable for it's applique craft. The colourful materials are used to make temple umbrellas and wall hangings.

CHILKA LAKE

South of Puri the Chilka Lake is dotted with islands and is noted for the many migratory birds which flock here each December to January. The shallow lake is about 70 km in length and averages 15 km wide, it is separated from the sea only by a narrow sand bar. The railway line and the main road run along the inland edge of the lake. It is 130 km from Bhubaneswar to Rambha at the lake. There is another Ashokan rock edict at Jangada.

Places to Stay

There are *Tourist Bungalows* at Rambha, at the southern end of the lake, and Barkul, six km north of the railway station of Balugaon and 32 km north of Rambha. The *Barkhul Tourist Bungalow* is very small with just two rooms. At both locations singles/doubles cost Rs 35/55.

GOPALPUR-ON-SEA

This popular little beach resort is 18 km from Berhampur where there is a railway station. There are regular buses between Berhampur and Gopalpur. From here you can also make excursions to the hot springs at Taptapani, 45 km away.

Places to Stay

At the top end there is the 21-room *Oberoi Palm Beach Hotel* with rooms from Rs 385/515 including meals while at the other end of the scale there is a 16-bed *Youth Hostel* (Rs 8) and a selection of local hotels. The *Hotel Sea Breeze* has doubles from Rs 30 while the *Hotel Holiday Home* is marginally more expensive. The *Wroxham House Tourist Lodge* is similarly priced.

CUTTACK (population 200,000)

Only 35 km north of Bhubaneswar, this riverine city was the capital of Orissa until the new city was constructed at Bhubaneswar. Only a gateway and the moat remains of the 14th century Barabati Fort. The stone revetment on the Kathjuri River, which protects the city from seasonal floods, dates from the 11th century.

Places to Stay

The *Hotel Anand* (tel 21936) on Canal Bank Rd has rooms from Rs 50 to 90, with and without air-con. The *Hotel Ashoka* (tel 21942) on Ice Factory Rd and the *Hotel Orienta* (tel 24509) in Buxi Bazaar are both a little more expensive. There are also the *Asian Hotel*, the *Cuttack Hotel* and a number of other small hotels, but if you wish to visit Cuttack it is probably easier to day-trip from Bhubaneswar.

BALASORE & CHANDIPUR

Balasore is the first major town on the railway line from Calcutta in north Orissa. It was once an important trading centre with Dutch, Danish, English and French factories. It was, in 1634, the first British East India Company factory in Bengal. Remina, eight km away, has the Gopinath Temple, an important pilgrimage centre. Chandipur, 16 km away on the coast, is a beach resort where the beach retreats six km at low tide! There are buses twice a day from Balasore.

Places to Stay

There are a few small hotels in Balasore such as the *Hotel Sagarika* or the *Hotel Moonlight*. The new and very pleasant Municipal Tourist Bungalow known as *Deepak Lodging* has doubles with bath and mosquito net for Rs 30. Walk from the station to the main road, turn left and it's on the right hand side, two blocks from the corner and across the street from the cinema. In Chandipur there is a *Tourist Bungalow*.

OTHER PLACES

In the north of Orissa, about 200 km inland from the coast, Khiching was once an ancient capital and has a number of interesting temples, temple ruins and a small museum. Further inland is the important industrial city of Rourkela with a major steel plant. North-east of Cuttack, about 100 km from Bhubaneswar, there are Buddhist relics and ruins at the three hilltop complexes of Ratnagiri, Lalitgiri and Udayagiri. The Ratnagiri site has the most interesting ruins. At Lalitgiri craftsmen make replicas of stone sculptures.

In the extreme west of the state the twin villages of Ranipur-Jharial are 30 km from Titlagarh and are noted for the extensive collection of temples on an outcrop of rock. They include a circular 64-yogini temple, similar to the one at Khajuraho. Harishankar, near Bolangir in the west, has a number of temples and a waterfall. The Similipal National Park is in the north-east of the state, near Khiching. The Ushakothi Wild Life Santuary is in the north-west. In the south-west of the state is the Gupteswar Cave, this is the region of the Bonda tribespeople. A little north-west of Cuttack is the Shiva temple of Kapilas.

Entry Prohibited

One clear contrast to the general Indian mood of tolerance is the way westerners are not allowed into Hindu temples. This chiefly applies to the temples in Orissa, in Varanasi and in some temples in the south. It's in complete contrast to Jain and Buddhist temples or to Moslem mosques where you are almost always allowed to wander at will. There is nothing much you can do about it, although these regulations have been much relaxed over the years and there are today far fewer places where an outright ban applies. An irritation is that in many cases the national or state tourist boards expound at length about the glories of these temples, and never mention even in the smallest print that if you're a westerner you will not be allowed inside.

Bombay

Population: 9 million
Main language: Marathi

Bombay is the capital of Maharashtra

Bombay is the economic powerhouse of India. It's the fastest moving, most affluent, most industrialised city in India. It also has India's busiest airport for international arrivals and departures and India's busiest port, handling nearly 50% of India's total foreign trade. It's the stronghold of free enterprise in India, a major manufacturing centre for everything from cars and bicycles to pharmaceuticals and petrochemicals. It's the centre for India's important textile industry. Bombay is the financial centre of India, an important base for overseas companies and Nariman Point is rapidly becoming a mini-Manhattan with India's tallest buildings. Yet once upon a time it was nothing more than a group of low-lying, swampy and malarial mud flats and was passed on to the British by its Portuguese occupiers as a wedding dowry!

When the Portuguese arrived on the scene Bombay consisted of seven islands occupied by simple fisherfolk known as Kolis. In 1534 the seven islands, from Colava in the south to Mahim in the north, were ceded to Portugal by the Sultan of Gujarat in the Treaty of Bassein. The Portuguese did little with them and in 1661 the major island of the group, Mumbadevi, was part of the wedding dowry when Catherine of Braganza married England's Charles II in 1661. In 1665 the British took possesion of all seven islands and in 1668 the British government leased them to the East India Company for an annual £10 in gold.

Soon after the British takeover Bombay started to develop as an important trading port. One of the first signs of this was the arrival of the Parsis who settled in Bombay in 1670 and built their first Tower of Silence in 1675. In 1687 the Presidency of the East India Company was transferred from Surat to Bombay and by 1708 it had become the trading headquarters for the whole west coast of India.

Although Bombay grew steadily for the next century it was around the middle of the 1800s that Bombay's most dynamic development took place. The first railway was laid out of Bombay in 1854 and one of the effects of the Mutiny of 1857 was to further improve the city's image as a 'safe' place, far from the insurrections of the north. Then the American Civil War provided Bombay's young cotton and textile industries with an enormous boost as supplies of cotton from the US dried up. In 1862 a major land reclamation project joined the original seven islands into a single land mass and a year later the governor, Sir Bartle Frere, dismantled the old fort walls and thus sparked off a major building boom.

During this century Bombay has further extended its position as the major commercial, industrial, financial and trading centre of India. It's an active, alive city, full of interest in its own right and yet also an ideal gateway to the states around it.

Orientation

Bombay is an island, connected by bridges with the mainland. At one time it was actually a number of islands and low swampy areas indicate where these divisions once were. The principal part of the city is concentrated at the southern end of the island and the northen end is comparatively lightly populated. The airport, Santa Cruz, is 26 km to the north. There are three main railway stations in the city centre. Churchgate and Victoria Terminus are conveniently central, but Bombay Central is some distance further out.

Orientation in Bombay is relatively simple. The southern promontory is Colaba Causeway and the northern end of this promontory is known as Colaba. Most of the cheap hotels and restaurants, together with a number of Bombay's top notch establishments, are located here. Bombay's two main landmarks – the Gateway of India and the Taj Mahal Hotel – are at Colaba.

Directly north of Colaba is the area known as Bombay Fort since the old fort was once here. Most of the impressive buildings from Bombay's golden period during the last 40 years of the last century are located here, together with the GPO, offices, banks, the Tourist Office and the two main railway stations. To the west of the fort is Back Bay around which sweeps Marine Drive. The southern end of this drive is marked by Nariman Point. This is the modern business centre of Bombay with more international class hotels, skyscrapers, airline offices (including Indian Airlines and Air India) and banks. The other end of the drive is Malabar Hill, a classy residential area.

Information

The Government of India Tourist Office is at 123 Maharashi Karve Rd, Churchgate (tel 293144) directly across from the Churchgate Station. It's open from 8.30 am to 5.30 pm weekdays and every other Saturday, and 8.30 am to 12.30 pm every second Saturday and on public holidays. It's closed on Sundays. They also have a counter at the airport and in the Taj Inter-Continental Hotel. The main office has a comprehensive leaflet and brochure collection and can be quite helpful.

There is also a Maharashtra Tourism Development Corporation Office (tel 296241) at CDO Hutments, Madame Cama Rd. They also operate city and suburban tours of Bombay; long distance buses to Mahabaleshwar, Aurangabad and Panaji; and make bookings on the ferry to Panaji.

The GPO, with its efficient poste restante service, is an imposing building on Nagar Chowk near Victoria Terminus Station. The American Express office is on Dadabhoy Naoroji Rd (tel 269421). Many airline offices can be found in the big Air India building on Nariman Point. The airport buses depart from here, and there are a number of shops and fast money changers in the building. Nalanda bookshop in the Taj Hotel is excellent. There is also a good pharmacy here. An indication of Bombay's relative affluence and fast moving nature is the city even has its own fortnightly 'what's on' magazine, Bombay.

Travel Agents Two recommended travel agents for discounted airline tickets are Spaceways (tel 242269), Kulsum Terrace (1st floor), Walton Rd, Colaba and Travel Corner Ltd, Marine Drive, near the Ambassador Hotel. The former is associated with Tripsout Travel in New Delhi and with Spaceways at Calangute Beach, Goa.

If you're staying in the Colaba area of Bombay and want to make bookings/reservations with either Air India or

Indian Airlines, you don't have to go all the way to Nariman Point. It's just as quick, and much easier, to book at the Taj Mahal Hotel. The woman who runs the Air India office here is very helpful and pleasant.

Airlines Offices Some of the airlines with offices in Bombay include:

Aeroflot	87 Stadium House, Veer Nariman Rd (tel 221682, 221743)
Air France	Taj Mahal Hotel, Apollo Bunder (tel 245021)
Air India	Air India Building, Nariman Point (tel 233747, 234142)
Alitalia	Industrial Assurance Building, Veer Nariman Rd (tel 220613)
Alyemda	Oberoi Towers, Nariman Point (tel 244292, 234343)
Bangladesh Biman	Airlines Hotel, 199 J Tata Rd (tel 221339, 220676)
British Airways	Vulcan's Building, Veer Nariman Rd (tel 220888)
Cathay Pacific	Taj Mahal Hotel, Apollo Bunder (tel 244112, 244113, 244561)
Egypt Air	Oriental House, 7 J Tata Rd (tel 221415, 221489, 221562)
Ethiopian Airlines	Taj Mahal Hotel, Apollo Bunder (tel 244525, 243366)
Gulf Air	Air India Building, Nariman Point (tel 231777, 231441)
Indian Airlines	Air India Building, Nariman Point (tel 233031, 233521)
Iran Air	Sunder Mahal, Marine Drive (tel 253524)
Iraqi Airways	79 Mayfair, Veer Nariman Rd (tel 221217, 221399)
Japan Air Lines	No 2 Raheja Centre, Nariman Point (tel 233348, 233136)
Kenya Airways	Airlines Hotel, 199 J Tata Rd (tel 220064)
Kuwait Airlines	86 Veer Nariman Rd (tel 312393, 298394, 298351)
Lufthansa	Express Towers, Nariman Point (tel 2333430)
PIA	Oberoi Towers, Nariman Point (tel 231373, 231480, 231455)
Pan Am	Taj Mahal Hotel, Apollo Bunder (tel 244020, 244434)
Qantas	Oberoi Towers, Nariman Point (tel 2020343, 2029297)
Sabena	Nirmal Building, Nariman Point (tel 233240, 233284)
Saudia	Express Towers, Nariman Point (tel 230199, 230298)
Singapore Airlines	Air India Building, Nariman Point (tel 233259, 233316)
Swissair	90 Veer Nariman Road (tel 293535)

Consulates Due to Bombay's importance as a business centre many countries maintain consulates or embassies in Bombay as well as in the capital, New Delhi. They include:

Germany (West)
    10th floor, Hoechst House, Nariman Point (tel 296023)
Netherlands
    16 M Karve Rd (tel 296840)
UK
    2nd floor, Mercantile Bank Building, Mahatma Gandhi Rd (tel 259981)
USA
    Lincoln House, Bhulabhai Desai Rd (tel 363611)

The honorary Irish consul can be found in the Royal Bombay Yacht Club!

Movies

Quickly, which is the biggest film producing city and country in the world? Hollywood and the USA? Wrong twice, Bombay and India! The Indians turn out 500 to 600 full-length feature films a year and, of these, nearly half get made in Bombay. Calcutta makes some arty, intellectual films; Madras some family comedies or musicals but for extravaganzas, action dramas, the 'starcast' A features, it's Bombay all the way.

A visit to the film studios in Bombay is easy to arrange – just tell the tourist office you'd like to see a film being made and they'll fix it all up for you. It's a real education, as we found when we turned up at Famous Film Studios. For a start the film production company and the studios are totally separate. Bombay has about 12 studios and far more film-makers. When they want to make a film they simply hire the studio by the day. Nor are Indian films made one-at-a-time as in the west. A big star could be involved in a number of films simultaneously – shooting a day on one, a week on another, a morning on a third. This involves phenomenal scheduling problems and also means that Indian films generally take a long time to make.

A glance at Indian film posters or film

magazines gives you the impression that Indian movie actors are a band of escapees from weight-watchers. Well there's no glamour in being thin in India. Every beggar in the street is skinny; it's the well-padded look which appeals. It's amusing to see how this works on western films shown in India – familiar European and American film stars become remarkably rotund when they're repainted for the Indian posters.

Our image of these chubby, smug actors was quickly shattered when we were asked into the dressing room to meet the star of the film we went to see. He was friendly, very open about the problems involved in making films in India – and not a kilo overweight! Life for a lot of Indians is not all that much fun and illiteracy is still widespread. Bombay film-makers are not trying to produce something for a sophisticated and intellectual audience. It's pure, straight-forward, down-to-earth entertainment. Escapism and nothing more.

Indian films are always a bit of everything – drama, action, suspense, music, dancing, romance – all mixed together into one extravagant blend. They've even got a name for them – 'masala films', since masala is the all-purpose word for spices, something you add to make it tasty.

Within their commercial constraints Indian movie-makers often do a surprisingly good job, particularly the cameramen and technicians, who manage to produce reasonable standard films from hopelessly outdated equipment. Apart from the restrictions on importing new equipment, a large slice of the proceeds goes to the Indian government. Film admission prices may be only Rs 3, 4 or 5, but the government gulps down about 75% of that figure. To make an Indian movie and make money out of it, you really have to know what you're about.

Gateway of India

In the days when most visitors came to India by sea and when Bombay was India's principal port, this was indeed the 'gateway' to India. Today it's merely Bombay's principal landmark. The gateway was conceived following the visit of King George V to India in 1911 and officially opened in 1924. Architecturally it is a conventional Arch of Triumph with elements in its design derived from the Moslem styles of 16th century Gujarat. It is built of yellow basalt and stands on the

Apollo Bunder, a popular Bombay meeting place in the evenings. The Taj Mahal Inter-Continental Hotel overlooks the Apollo Bunder and launches run from here across to Elephanta Island. Close to the gateway are statues of the Maratha leader, Shivaji, astride his horse and of Swami Vivekananda.

Colaba Causeway

The streets behind the Taj Mahal Hotel are the travellers' centre of Bombay. Here you will find most of the cheap hotels and restaurants. Colaba Causeway, now renamed Shahid Bhagat Singh Rd, extends down to the end of the Colaba promontory, the southern end of Bombay Island. Sassoon Dock is always interesting to visit around dawn when the fishing boats come in and unload their catch in a colourful scene of intense activity. There's an old lighthouse at the end of the promontory, although the actual lighthouse used today is further south still on a rocky island.

St John's Church

The Afghan Church was built in 1857 and is dedicated to the soldiers who fell in the Sind campaign of 1838 and the First Afghan War of 1843.

Prince of Wales Museum

Beside the Wellingdon Circle, close to the Colaba Causeway hotel enclave, the Prince of Wales Museum was built to commemorate King George V's first visit to India in 1905, while he was still Prince of Wales. The first part of this interesting museum was opened in 1914. It was designed in the Indo-Saracenic style and has sections for art, art and paintings, archaeology and natural history. Among the more interesting items is a very fine collection of miniature paintings, images and bas reliefs from the Elephanta Caves, Buddha images and models of the Parsi Towers of Silence.

The museum is open from 10 am to 6.30 pm March to June, to 6 pm July to

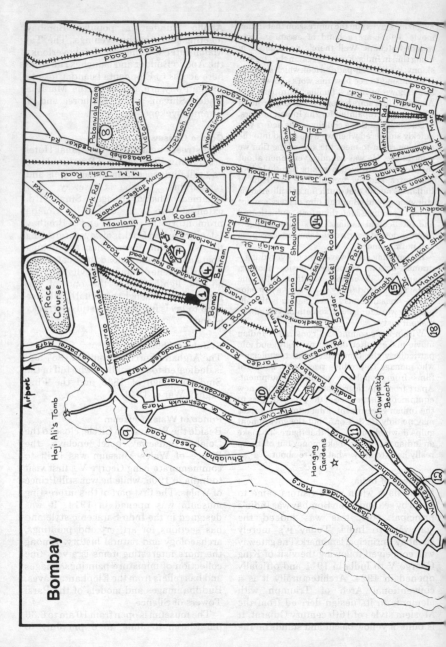

Bombay

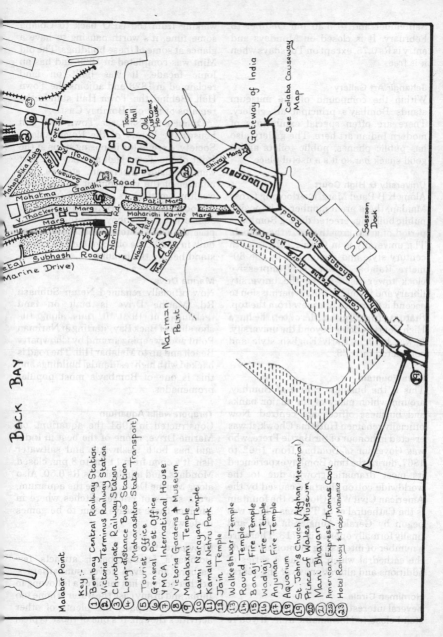

BACK BAY

Malabar Point

Marine Drive)
(etaji Subhash Road

Mahatma Gandhi Road

V. Thackersey Marg

Mahapalika Marg
Somnath
Noroji

Fort St.

Town Hall

Old Customs House

Gateway of India

See Colaba Causeway Map

Shivaji Marg

K.B. Patil Marg

Maharishi Karve Marg

Wacla Rd.

Mint Road

Nariman Point

N Patell Marg

Sprott Road

Cape B.P.M. Marg

Shahid Bhagat Singh Road

Sasson Dock

Key:-
① Bombay Central Railway Station.
②a Victoria Terminus Railway Station
③ Churchgate Railway Station
④ Long-distance Bus Station
　(Maharashtra State Transport)
⑤ Tourist Office
⑥ General Post Office
⑦ YMCA International House
⑧ Victoria Gardens & Museum
⑨ Mahalaxmi Temple
⑩ Laxmi Narayan Temple
⑪ Kamala Nehru Park
⑫ Jain Temple
⑬ Walkeshwar Temple
⑭ Round Temple
⑮ Banaji Fire Temple
⑯ Wadiaji Fire Temple
⑰ Anjuman Fire Temple
⑱ Aquarium
⑲ St. John's Church (Afghan Memorial)
⑳ Prince of Wales Museum
㉑ Mani Bhavan
㉒ American Express/Thomas Cook
㉓ Hotel Railway & Hotel Manama

September and to 5.30 pm October to February. It is closed on Mondays and entry is Rs 0.75, except on Tuesdays when it is free.

Jehangir Art Gallery
Within the compound of the museum stands Bombay's principal art gallery. There are often special exhibitions of modern Indian art here. The gallery also has public phones, public toilets and a good snack bar so it's a useful place.

University & High Court
Along K B Patel Marg, overlooking Cross Maidan, there are a number of imposing public buildings erected during Bombay's period of great growth under the British. The university is in Gothic 14th to 15th century style and dominated by the 80-metre Rajabai Tower. This impressive clock tower rises above the university library and if you can obtain permission to ascend it there is a fine view from the top. Statues of Justice and Mercy top the huge High Court building beyond the university. It was built in Early English style and completed in 1878.

Flora Fountain
This is the business centre of Bombay, around which many of the major banks and business offices are centred. Now officially renamed Hutatma Chowk, it was erected in honour of Sir Bartle Frere, who was Governor of Bombay from 1862 to 1867, during the time Bombay experienced its most dramatic growth due to the worldwide cotton shortage caused by the American Civil War. Close to the fountain is the Cathedral of St Thomas which was begun by Gerald Aungier in 1672 and finally formally opened in 1718. There are a number of interesting memorials inside the cathedral which has had a series of additions and alterations over the years.

Horniman Circle
Several interesting old Bombay buildings stand close to Horniman Circle. If you're walking from the GPO back to Colaba some time, it's worth pausing to have a glance at some of these buildings. The old Mint was completed in 1829 and has an Ionic facade. It was built on land reclaimed in 1823 and adjoins the Town Hall. Behind the Town Hall stands the remains of the old Bombay Castle.

Opened in 1833, the Town Hall still houses the library of the Royal Asiatic Society. Ascend the imposing steps at the front of the Town Hall and have a short wander inside. There are statues of a number of the government officials and wealthy benefactors of Bombay's golden period, including Sir Bartle Frere and Sir Jamsetjee Jeejeebhoy. Continuing, you pass the Old Customs House which was built in 1720. The old Bombay dockyards stand behind the building.

Marine Drive
Now officially renamed Netaji Subhash Rd, Marine Drive is built on land reclaimed in 1920. It runs along the shoreline of Back Bay, starting at Nariman Point and sweeping around by Chowpatty Beach and up to Malabar Hill. The road is backed with high residential buildings and this is one of Bombay's most popular promenades.

Taraporewella Aquarium
Constructed in 1951 the aquarium, on Marine Drive, is one of the best in India and has both freshwater and saltwater fish. It's open from 11 am to 8 pm, closed Mondays, and admission is Rs 0.50. Also along Marine Drive, before the aquarium, are a series of cricket pitches where in summer there always seem to be games underway.

Chowpatty Beach
Bombay's famous beach attracts few bathers and even fewer sunbathers – neither activity has much of a following in India, and in any case the water is none too healthy. Chowpatty has plenty of other activities though. It's one of those typical

Indian slices of life where anything and everything can happen, and does. Sand-castle sculptures make elaborate figures in the sand, contortionists go through equally elaborate contortions and family groups stroll around. In between there are kiosks selling Bombay's popular snack, *bhelpuri*, and *kulfi* ice cream.

Chowpatty Beach is also the scene for the annual Ganesh Chaturthi festival, during which large images of the elephant-headed god are immersed in the sea.

Mani Bhuvan

At 19 Laburnum Rd, near August Kranti Maidan, is the building where Mahatma Gandhi stayed on his visits to Bombay between 1917 and 1934. Today it has a pictorial exhibit of incident's in Gandhi's life and contains a library of books by or about the Mahatma. It is open from 9.30 am to 6 pm.

Malabar Hill

At the end of Back Bay, Marine Drive climbs up to Malabar Hill. This is an expensive residential area, for not only is it a little cooler than the sea-level parts of the city, but there are also fine views over Back Bay and Chowpatty Beach to the town. At the end of the promontory is Raj Bhavan, the old British govern-ment headquarters. Close to this is the temple of Walkeswar, the 'sand lord', an important Hindu pilgrimage site. According to the Ramayana, Rama rested here on his way from Ayodya to Lanka to rescue Sita. He constructed a lingam of sand at the site. The temple is about a thousand years old.

Jain Temple

This marble temple was built in 1904 and is dedicated to the first Jain Tirthankar, Adinath. It's typical of modern Jain temples in its gaudy, mirrored style. The walls are decorated with pictures of incidents in the lives of the Tirthankars.

Hanging Gardens

On top of Malabar Hill, these gardens were laid out in 1881 and are correctly known as the Pherozeshah Mehta Gardens. They take their name from the fact that they are built on top of a series of reservoirs that supply water to Bombay. The formally laid out gardens have a notable collection of hedges cut into the shape of animals and there are good views over the city from here.

Kamala Nehru Park

Directly across the road from the Hanging Gardens, this park offers more superb views over Bombay. It was laid out in 1952 and was named after Nehru's wife. An unusual feature is a large nursery rhyme 'old woman's shoe' which children love to play in.

Towers of Silence

Beside the Hanging Gardens, but carefully shielded from viewers, are the Parsis' Towers of Silence. The Parsis hold fire, earth and water as sacred and thus will not cremate or bury their dead. Instead the bodies are laid out within the towers to be picked clean by vultures.

Elaborate precautions are taken to keep ghoulish sightseers from observing the towers, despite which a Time-Life book on Bombay provided a bird's eye view of one of the towers. The Parsis power in Bombay is sufficiently strong that the book was black-ink censored. Tour guides, always fond of a tall story for tourists, like to tell you that the reason the Hanging Garden reservoirs were covered over was that the vultures had an unpleasant habit of dropping the odd bit in the water supply.

Mahalaxmi Temple

Descending from Malabar Hill and continuing around the coastline you come to the Mahalaxmi Temple, the oldest in Bombay and, appropriately for this city of business and money, dedicated to the goddess of wealth. The images of the goddess and her two sisters were said to have been found in the sea.

Near here is the Mahalaxmi Racecourse, said to be the finest in India, where horse races are held each Sunday from November to March. The road along the seashore by the racecourse was once known as the Hornby Vellard, and was constructed in the 18th century to reclaim the swampland on which the course is now constructed.

Haji Ali's Tomb

This tomb and mosque are devoted to a Moslem saint who was drowned here. The buildings are reached by a long causeway which can only be crossed at low tide. A scene of typical Indian ingenuity and resourcefulness takes place along this pathway. Hundreds of beggars line the length of the causeway waiting for the regular stream of pilgrims. At the start of the causeway is a small group of money-changers who, for a few paise' commission, will change a one rupee coin into 100 one paise coins. Thus a pilgrim can do his soul the maximum amount of good for the minimum expenditure.

No doubt at the ebb tide the mendicants can change their one paise coins into something a little more manageable, thus giving the money-changers their small change for the next low tide and, no doubt, probably providing them with another commission rake off.

Victoria Gardens

These gardens, which contain Bombay's zoo and the Victoria & Albert Museum, have been renamed the Veermata Jijabai Bhonsle Udyan. The museum has some interesting exhibits relating to old Bombay. Just outside the museum building there is the large stone elephant which was removed from Elephanta Island in 1864, after which the island was named.

The museum is open 10.30 am to 5.30 pm, the zoo from sunrise to sunset. Both charge Rs 10 admission.

Other

The Nehru Planetarium is on Dr Annie Besant Rd at Worli near the Haji Ali Tomb. There are shows in English at 3 and 6 pm daily and also at 12 noon on Saturdays and Sundays. The planetarium is closed on Mondays, admission is Rs 5.

Falkland St is the centre for Bombay's notorious red light district known as 'the cages'. The ladies stand behind metal-barred doors, hence the name. A 130 bus from the museum passes through this fascinating area.

Tours

There are numerous tours of Bombay but they tend to be more expensive than in most Indian cities. Daily city tours are operated by the ITDC and the Maharashtra Tourist Development Council. The ITDC tours can be booked at the Tourist Office and leave from there at 10 am and from the Taj Mahal Hotel at 10.15. The tour covers the main city sights, finishes at 2 pm and costs Rs 25. It does not operate on Mondays. The MTDC tour costs Rs 35, lasts from 9 am to 1 pm and also does not operate on Mondays.

In the afternoons there are MTDC tours from 2.30 to 6.30 pm for Rs 22. Again the tours are daily except Mondays. There are also privately operated tours leaving the Tourist Office at 2.15 pm and the Taj Mahal Hotel at 2.30. The tour finishes at 6.30 pm and costs Rs 35. It operates daily including Mondays.

There are also a variety of suburban tours which basically go to the Aarey Milk Colony, Kanheri Caves and Juhu Beach. The Sanghi Travels tour departs the Tourist Office at 8.45 am and the Taj Mahal Hotel at 9 am. The tour returns at 1.30 pm and costs Rs 50. On Sundays and holidays the MTDC have a tour which leaves at 11.45 am and returns at 7.30 pm. Cost is Rs 35. There is also a Sunday tour in a normal public transport bus (all other tours are in air-con buses). This leaves the Gateway of India at 8.45 am and the

Tourist Office at 9 am and returns at 5.30 pm. Cost is Rs 15, but there is no guide.

Launch services and tours to Elephanta leave regularly from Apollo Bunder and can be booked at the kiosk there. The round-trip takes four hours. The ITDC and the MTDC have some tours further afield such as a Friday-to-Monday tour to Aurangabad and the Ajanta and Ellora Caves. Check at the Tourist Office for details.

Places to Stay

Bombay is India's most expensive city as far as accommodation goes, so if your funds are limited you should plan on spending as little time as possible here. Not only that, but it's a magnet for Middle East and Gulf Arabs, who come here for their holidays, on shopping expeditions and for business. They invariably bring with them their entire harem. Not all of these visitors are super-rich oil sheikhs who can afford to stay in the Taj Mahal Inter-Continental, so the pressure for accommodation – even at the bottom end of the market – is intense.

Because of this, there is no guarantee that you will be able to find a room in the price range that you expected to pay and, at least for the first night, you may well have to settle for something considerably more expensive. As though that were not enough, the standard of accommodation you get at the bottom end of the market is often poor.

The only way to give yourself a fighting chance, not only for a room, but for something half-way decent, is to arrange to get into Bombay as soon as possible after dawn. Luckily, most international flights into Bombay arrive in the early morning. The same is true of the ferry from Panaji (Goa) to Bombay.

It's also a distinct advantage to be part of a small group (impromptu or otherwise), since if the first place you try is full, then one or two of you can look after the baggage, while the rest fan out in search of somewhere else. If you should be unlucky

enough not to find anything in the price range that you can afford on the first day, try making a booking for the following day. It's wise to remember though, that even budget accommodation is expensive in Bombay. The Tourist Office can sometimes be helpful in finding an empty room.

Places to Stay – Bottom End

Colaba Area The majority of the budget hotels are to be found in the Colaba area directly behind that useful landmark, the Taj Mahal Inter-Continental. Best known are the *Rex* and *Stiffles* (tel 231518, 230960), 8 Ormiston Rd and it's here that many travellers start their search for a room. The Rex is on floors 3 and 4, the Stiffles on 1 and 2. A great deal has been said and written over the years about the standard of accommodation at these two places – some of it good, most of it bad.

Personally, I don't know what all the fuss is about, since I've always managed to get a reasonable room here with clean sheets, a fan and an attached toilet and shower – as well as a window – and they've never known that I have had a hand in this book, so there's no favouritism involved. Certainly, every centimetre of available space has been converted into rooms, so some are rather cramped, and there are some weird and wonderful ways of getting into some of the rooms, but otherwise it's OK. The only problem is that unless you get here early in the morning, the chances are that it will be full. The management is pleasant and gear left in your room is secure. Prices start at Rs 60 a single and Rs 90 a double for a room with attached bath. Larger rooms and those with air-con cost more.

Across the road on the corner of the street is another old favourite, the *Salvation Army Red Shield Hostel* (tel 241824), 30 Mereweather Rd. Full board here costs Rs 40 in the dormitory and Rs 100 a double. Safe deposit lockers can be hired for a returnable deposit of Rs 30 plus Rs 1 for the first day and 50p for subsequent days. Checkout time is 9 am and you need to be there early in the morning in order to be well up the line when 9 am rolls round. Some say that there's usually more room for women than men.

There's another *Salvation Army Hostel* in the Social Service Centre, 122 Maulana Azad Rd North, Byculla, which costs only Rs 7 for a bed in the dormitory (four beds per dorm), but it's for men only. It's a 15-minute walk from either Bombay Central or Byculla railway stations.

Another cheapie in the Colaba area is the *Carlton Hotel* (tel 230642), 12 Mereweather Rd, an interesting old place with singles/doubles including breakfast for Rs 55/80-100 with common bathrooms and four-bed rooms for Rs 160. If you don't want breakfast it's Rs 5 less. Not everybody is impressed, however. 'The grottiest place I saw in *all* of India', wrote one traveller. 'Basic but clean', wrote another!

Others include *Hotel Prosser* (tel 241715), corner of Henry Rd and P J Ramchandani Marg, which has doubles with share bath and hot and cold running water for Rs 70 (no singles). *Whalley's Guest House*, Mereweather Rd, is a nice old place with rooms with common bath for Rs 55/115 including breakfast. *Cowie's Guest House* (tel 240232), Walton Rd, offers full board and lodging for Rs 100/200 with attached bath, or Rs 150/230 with air-con and attached bath.

Then there's the *Royal Guest House* (tel 221758), 1st floor, 5 Shahid Bhagatsingh Rd, opposite the Delhi Durbar Restaurant. It's a small place with a friendly proprietor which has singles/doubles for Rs 50/80. Opposite Cowie's Guest House on Walton Rd is the *Oliver Guest House*. It's cheap and clean at Rs 35/70 with common bathrooms, but the management is surly and the checkout time is 10 am. Another place you might like to try is the *Moti Hotel International* (tel 225714), 10 Ormiston Rd, right next door to the Rex and Stiffles. Double rooms with attached bath and air-con cost Rs 150, but they also have double rooms with common bath and air-con for Rs 100. There are no singles.

There is also a whole collection of small hotels on various floors along Arthur Bunder Rd. They include the *Seashore Hotel, Janata Guest House, Imperial Guest House, India Guest House, Hotel Mukund, Gateway Guest House, Gulf Hotel* and the *Hotel Al-Hijaz*. Many of them look like they ought to be cheap, but don't let appearances fool you. Even though most offer only airless, windowless, hardboard partitioned boxes for rooms, prices can vary from as little as Rs 35 to 45 for singles with attached bath and no window – (Gateway Guest House) – to as much as Rs 175 a double with bath, window and air-con – (Hotel Mukund, tel 214753). Have a look at them if you can't find anything else in the area, but don't take the first you come across as prices and standards vary considerably.

Elsewhere Away from the Colaba area, one of the most popular places – deservedly so – is the *Lawrence Hotel* (tel 243618), Ashok Kumar Lane (sign-posted as Rope Walk Lane) off K Dubash Marg at the back of the Prince of Wales Museum. It's often full since it only has nine rooms, but it's excellent value with singles/doubles with common bathroom at Rs 50/90. Some of the rooms also have balconies.

Three other cheapies are grouped together on P D'Mello Rd at the eastern end of the GPO/Victoria Terminus Station. The first is the *Railway Hotel* (tel 266705), 249 P D'Mello Rd, which has singles/doubles for Rs 35-40/60-70 with common bathroom and 24-hour checkout. It's definitely for those who don't care too much about windows and hardboard partitioned rooms. The second is the *Rupam Hotel* (tel 267103/4), which has non-air-con doubles for Rs 70 with share bathroom, and Rs 150 with attached bath.

The third is the *Hotel Manama* (tel

264149), 221/225 P D'Mello Rd, previously known as the Sea View Hotel, although there's no way it could ever have had sea views. This is the best of the three, and presently costs Rs 85 a double with common bath and Rs 95 with attached bath – no singles. There's a lot of upgrading going on here, so prices will doubtless rise steeply when it's completed.

The Ys Like other Indian cities, Bombay has its share of YMCAs and YWCAs, and although they are very good value for money, they're invariably full. The most popular is the *YWCA International Guest House* (tel 230445), 18 Madame Cama Rd, which takes both men and women, and offers bed and breakfast for Rs 71/139 plus 10% tax and Rs 10 membership charges (valid for one month). It's generally booked out three months in advance.

Around the corner is the *YMCA International Guest House* (tel 230445), Mayo House, Cooperage Rd, which has bed and breakfast for Rs 88/156 plus 10% tax and Rs 20 membership charges, but if you can find a way of getting in there during the day, I'd like to know what it is!

There's also a *YWCA* (tel 372744) at 34 Mostibai St, Byculla, which has beds for Rs 16.50 plus 10% tax and a *YMCA* (tel 891191, 377573) at Club Back Rd, Central, which has accommodation at similar rates to the YMCA International Guest House, but both of these are a long way from the centre.

Other There are no purpose-built Youth Hostels as such in Bombay, but during university/college vacations you may be able to find cheap accommodation at *Bhavan's College* (tel 572192), Versova Rd, Bhavan's Camp, Andheri; or *University Hostel* (tel 472425), L A Kidwai Rd; and *Podar College of Commerce Hostel* (tel 472414), 193 Sion Koliwada Estate.

Lastly, there are *Railway Retiring Rooms* at both Bombay Central and Victoria Terminus Railway Stations. The former cost Rs 35 to 40 per bed and the latter Rs 20 per bed for 24 hours. And, yes, I did once spend several nights on the concrete of the 3rd class waiting room in Victoria Terminus, and although nothing was stolen from me – I only had a passport and £15 to my name – I can't seriously recommend it, even though these days it's called 2nd class.

Places to Stay – Middle

Many of the middle bracket hotels along with the Taj Inter-Continental and most of the cheapies – are in the Colaba area. The other main group is clustered along Marine Drive (Netaji Subhash Rd) between Madame Cama Rd and Veer Nariman Rd, and along Veer Nariman Rd itself. The ones in the Colaba area tend to be less expensive in general than those along Marine Drive.

Three popular ones in the Colaba area can be found along Garden Rd. The *Ascot Hotel* (tel 240020), 38 Garden Rd, has air-con singles/doubles with attached bath for Rs 279/328 as well as a number of double rooms with common bathrooms for between Rs 204 and 236. A few doors down the *Godwin Hotel* (tel 241226), 41 Garden Rd, offers accommodation of a similar standard for Rs 269/330. It's possible you may be offered a discount of up to 15%, depending on the season. The *Garden Hotel* (tel 240895) at 42 Garden Rd has air-con singles/doubles with attached bath for Rs 235/297 as well as two very ritzy de-luxe rooms at Rs 350. This hotel also has its own bar and restaurant.

Another in this price bracket is the *Hotel Diplomat* (tel 231661), 24 Mereweather Rd on the corner of Ormiston Rd. This is a relatively new place with its own bar and restaurant, which has rooms for Rs 280/330. An extra bed in either costs Rs 62.

Still in the Colabar area, but less expensive, are five more hotels. The first is the *Sea Palace Hotel* (tel 241828), 26 P J

1 Hotel Fariyas	16 Carlton Hotel
2 Hotel Ascot	17 Laxmi Vilas
3 Godwin Hotel	18 Leopold Restaurant
4 Garden Hotel	19 Apollo Restaurant
5 Cowie's Guest House	20 Olympic Coffee House
6 Shelley's Guest House	21 Delhi Durbar
7 Strand Hotel	22 Majestic Dining Hall
8 Sea Palace Hotel	23 YWCA International Guest House
9 Whalley's Guest House	24 Cafe Mondegar
10 Pure Drinks	25 Regal Cinema
11 Ananda Punjabi	26 Nanking Restaurant
12 Dipti's Pure Drinks	27 Maharashtra State Emporium
13 Salvation Army Red Shield Hostel	28 Mandarin & Hong Kong Restaurants
14 Rex & Stiffles Hotel	29 Oliver Guest House
15 Hotel Diplomat	30 Hotel Prasser

Ramchandani Marg (Strand Rd), a large building with air-con singles/doubles with attached bath for Rs 180/280. The hotel has its own restaurant. Next door is the *Strand Hotel* (tel 241624), which has air-con singles/doubles for Rs 137/186 and non-air-con singles/doubles for Rs 98/150. 'Everything the more expensive hotels have including a view of the sea', wrote one happy visitor but writer was far less impressed. At the end of the same block is *Shelly's Hotel* (tel 240229), 30 P J Ramchandani Marg, which offers air-con singles/doubles for Rs 97/131.

Back from the harbour front are the last two. *Bentley's Hotel* (tel 241733), Oliver Rd, has air-con singles/doubles for Rs 120/175-210 respectively and non-air-con singles/doubles for Rs 75/130-165 including breakfast. The *Hotel Apollo* (tel 230223), M Bhushan Marg (Landsdowne Rd), has its own bar and restaurant. Air-con singles/doubles cost Rs 275/340 including taxes and service charges. There is another *Bentley's Hotel* (tel 250693), 'D' Rd, Netaji Subhash Rd, which offers non-air-con singles/doubles for Rs 75/110 including breakfast.

Moving to the Marine Drive (Netaji Subhash Rd) area, you can try the *Sea Green Hotel* (tel 222294), 145 Netaji Subhash Rd, which has air-con singles/doubles for Rs 190/265 and non-air-con singles/doubles for Rs 130/200. Next to it

is the *Sea Green South Hotel* (tel 221662), which offers air-con singles/doubles for Rs 235/325 and non-air-con singles/doubles for Rs 175/265. These charges include taxes and meals.

Nearby is the *Chateau Windsor Guest House* (tel 293376), 86 Veer Nariman Rd, which has large singles/doubles with attached bath for Rs 235/295 (air-con) or Rs 195/245 (non-air-con). They also have a number of smaller rooms with common bathroom for Rs 120 to 150 a single, and Rs 160 to 195 a double. These charges do not include taxes, but do include morning tea. Another hotel of similar standard in the same area is the *Astoria Hotel* (tel 299121), 4 Jamshedji Tata Rd.

Places to Stay – Top End

Hotels in this category will usually have 10% service charge and 7% state 'luxury' tax tagged on top of the room charge – as do some of the middle range places.

Bombay has the hotel reputed to be the best in India. It's certainly a place with an air of glamour about it, and since most of Bombay's cheap hotels cluster right behind it – and it has a comfortable air-conditioned lounge and one of the best bookshops in the city – you'll also find a fair number of backpackers around it too! The *Taj Mahal Hotel* is an elegant turn-of-the-century building on Apollo Bunder near the Gateway of India. Not long ago the *Taj*

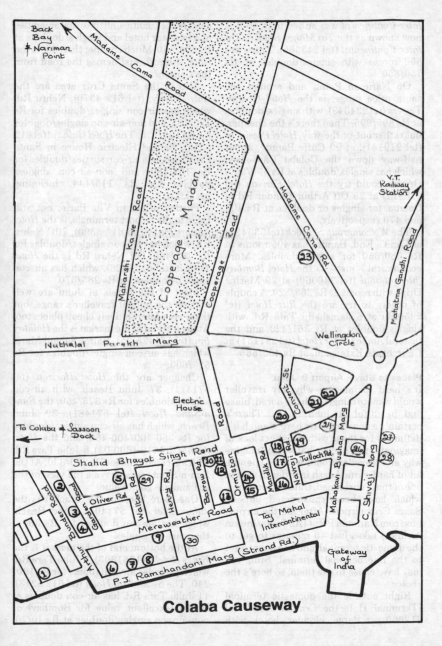

Back Bay
Nariman Point

Madame Cama Road

Cooperage Maidan

Madame Cama Rd

V.T. Railway Station

Maharshi Kave Road

Cooperage Road

Mahatma Gandhi Road

23

Nuthalal Parekh Marg

Wellington Circle

Convent St

Electric House

To Colaba & Sassoon Dock

21 22

20

Ormiston Road

Barrow Rd

Mandlik Rd

Navroji Rd

Tulloch Rd.

24

27

Shahid Bhayat Singh Road

5
29

Garden Rd

Oliver Rd

Walton Rd

Henry Rd

10 11
12

19

18
17

Mahakavi Bushan Marg

26

28

Arthur Bunder Road

2

3

4

14
15

13

16

Mereweather Road

9

30

Taj Mahal Intercontinental

C. Shivaji Marg

1

6 7 8

P.J. Ramchandani Marg (Strand Rd.)

Gateway of India

Colaba Causeway

Inter-Continental was added to it, so it is now known as the *Taj Mahal Hotel & Taj Inter-Continental* (tel 243366). There are 650 rooms with singles/doubles at Rs 750/850.

On Nariman Point, and around the same price range, is the *Hotel Oberoi-Towers* (tel 234343), with singles/doubles at Rs 895/995. Then there's the cheaper, but rather out-of-the-way, *Hotel President* (tel 219141), at 90 Cuffe Parade, about half-way down the Colaba Causeway, which has singles/doubles at Rs 550/650. Or you could try the *Hotel Fariyas* (tel 215911) at 25 Off Arthur Bunder Rd in Colaba, for singles or doubles at Rs 400 and 470 respectively.

The *Welcomgroup Searock* (tel 535421) at Land's End, Bandra has 405 rooms at Rs 550/650 for singles/doubles. More economical – just – is the *Hotel Bombay International* (tel 240060) at 29 Marine Drive with rooms at Rs 365/520. A couple of others to try are the *Ritz Hotel* (tel 295061) at 5 Jamshedji Tata Rd, with singles/doubles at Rs 361/420 and the tasteful *Ambassador Hotel* (tel 291131) at Churchgate Extension, at Rs 485/565.

Places to Stay – Airport & Juhu

It's hard to imagine why any traveller would want to mingle with the bored, blasé and beautiful at Juhu Beach. There's certainly a beach of sorts here, though it's definitely for those with a distinct lack of imagination. It's even harder to imagine why any traveller would want to spend a lot of hard-earned cash in order to stay in one of those cushioned, transient cocoons, which have been constructed outside Santa Cruz airport. After all, the airport bus from Nariman Point (Air India/Indian Airlines) takes just 40 minutes to get to the domestic terminal, and one hour to get to the international terminal. Still, you may have cause to use them, so here's the choice.

Right outside the domestic terminal (Terminal 1) is the *Centaur Hotel* (tel 612660), a large circular hotel with conference facilities, all the usual amenities of a five-star hotel and singles/doubles at Rs 500/550. Much cheaper than this is the *Hotel Aircraft*, just across the road from the Centaur.

Also in the Santa Cruz area are the *Hotel Lovely*, (tel 612 4370), Nehru Rd, which has air-con singles/doubles for Rs 130/165, and non-air-con singles/doubles for Rs 105/130. The *Hotel Galaxy* (tel 612 5315), behind Electric House in Santa Cruz East, has air-con singles/doubles for Rs 152/180, and non-air-con singles/doubles for Rs 115/144, including breakfast.

Further afield in Vile Parle, but still close to the airport terminals, is the *Hotel Airport Plaza* (tel 612 3390), 70C Nehru Rd, which has air-con singles/doubles for Rs 385/460. Off Nehru Rd is the *Hotel Transit* (tel 6129326), which has air-con singles/doubles for Rs 285/370.

Most of the hotels at Juhu are well outside the budget traveller's range, but there are a few relatively cheap places too. At the top end of the market is the *Holiday Inn* (tel 571425-35), Balraj Sahani Marg, which has air-con singles/doubles for Rs 525/600.

Cheaper are the *Hotel Horizon* (tel 571411), 37 Juhu Beach, with air-con singles/doubles for Rs 375/450; the *Sun-n-Sand Hotel* (tel 571481), 39 Juhu Beach, which has air-con singles/doubles for Rs 350-400/400-450; and the *Hotel Ajanta* (tel 612 4890-91), 8 Juhu Tara Rd, with air-con rooms for Rs 260/330. At the Sun-n-Sand rooms have a full view of the sea and are good value.

One more hotel in this bracket is the *Juhu Hotel* (tel 571401), Juhu Beach, which has air-con doubles for Rs 300 – there are no singles.

At the bottom end of the market is the *Kings Hotel* (tel 561803), 5 Juhu Tara Rd, which provides air-con rooms for Rs 190/240. The *South End Hotel* (tel 612 5213), 11 Juhu Tara Rd, has air-con doubles at Rs 90 (excellent value for Bombay) or non-air-con singles/doubles at Rs 40/70.

There's also the *Sea Side Hotel* (tel 561972), 39/2 Juhu Beach, which offers air-con singles/doubles for Rs 70/100.

Other places to try at the bottom end of the market are the *Sea View Hotel* and the *Purnima Guest House* (tel 541215). There's even a Krishna Consciousness hotel, the *Iskcon* (tel 566860), which looks expensive, but is relatively cheap.

Incidentally, if you're thinking of swimming in the sea at Juhu, don't get too enthusiastic about it. Once you've taken a good look at the neat, untreated sewage which slithers sluggishly out to sea from the vast slum encampments from Dada to Juhu, you will probably change your mind. The stench alone will knock you out.

Places to Eat

The accommodation shortage certainly doesn't spill over into restaurants. Bombay probably has the best selection of restaurants of any major Indian city. As in other cities a meal in a better class restaurant can be one of India's bargains. A foray into the more expensive places is a worthwhile investment, even for back-packers.

Cheaper Restaurants There are plenty of places to eat around Colaba. *Dipti's Pure Drinks*, near the Rex and Stiffles, is popular for its fruit juices (a bit expensive at Rs 2.50 to 5), fruit salads and ice cream (Rs 5). The high prices don't put people off this tiny establishment.

Round the corner on Nawroji Furounji Rd, *Laxmi Vilas* has excellent vegetarian thalis for Rs 5. On Wodehouse Rd (alias Shahid Bhagat Singh Rd alias Colaba Causeway) the *Ananda Punjabi* is more expensive but tasty, say Rs 30 to 40 for two.

The *Leopold Restaurant* is a very popular place, not only for breakfast, lunch and dinner, but for somewhere to hang around and enjoy a cold beer. And it's not only travellers, there are plenty of Gulf Arabs doing just the same. Indeed, some of them seem to spend all day and all night here. Tut, tut! All good Moslems too! The Leopold has a very pleasant, unhurried, olde worlde atmosphere. The service is fast, the food is good, the place is hygienic and the prices are very reasonable. What's more, you'll never be short of someone to chat with.

Very similar is the *Cafe Mondegar*, a pleasant coffee bar place in the next block towards Wellingdon Circle. Across the road, the *Majestic Dining Hall* is a big vegetarian, plate-meal specialist. You may also like to try the *Gokul*, in the same area. The *Samovar*, in the Jehangir Art Gallery, is a good place for a cold drink or a quick snack. The *Naval & Military Restaurant*, a couple of doors up from the Nanking, has good snacks at low prices. At the top of Garden Rd, next to the garage, the *Edward VIII Restaurant* is a well kept little place with good fruit juices.

Colaba is renowned for fine prawns and seafood. You can get fish and chips in a few places, including right beside the Marine Drive aquarium! *Bhelpuri* is a Bombay speciality – a tasty snack of crisp noodles, spiced vegetables and other mysterious ingredients for a rupee or less. It's available from stalls all over town, but particularly on Chowpatty Beach.

Away from Colaba at Churchgate is the *Sahyadi*, 117 Maharshi Karve Rd, which serves excellent vegetarian food at reasonable prices. In the same area, next to the Sterling Cinema, Victoria Terminus, is the *Waikiki*, a kind of snack bar, which specialises in that Bombay dish, *panbhaji* – a tasty, hot mixture of different vegetables.

Two good places to hang around and have a snack, coffee or cold drink while you read that mail you've just picked up from poste restante are the *Kohinoor Restaurant*, opposite the GPO, and the *New Empire Restaurant*, on the corner of Nagar Chowk, opposite the main entrance to Victoria Terminus Railway Station.

More Expensive Restaurants The Taj Mahal has a whole range of restaurants and snack bars including the *Sea Lounge*, a good place for a snack or beer overlooking the waterfront. The *Shamiana* has light meals, the *Rendezvous* on the rooftop caters for western tastes, but the *Tanjore* is probably the best place for a splash-out meal – traditional Indian food (most dishes Rs 20 to 50) accompanied by sitar music and classical Indian dancing. The thought of a Rs 35 *thali* will probably bring a smile to the face of backpackers though! ('good value, included a live band', said a traveller who tried it and I found one in an Indian restaurant in Melbourne recently for $15!! – Tony) There's also a 'wonderful pastry shop' here and the views from the 20th floor *Apollo Bar* are terrific.

There is a string of restaurants along K Dubash Marg, just across from the Jehangir Art Gallery and Prince of Wales Museum. Close to the junction with Mahatma Gandhi Rd the *Khyber Restaurant* has a varied menu with particularly good tandoori dishes and kebabs. Try the chicken tikka kebab. Most dishes are around Rs 10 to 25. A complete meal including dessert (and they offer 'leeches & cream' as a possibility!) will probably come to about Rs 40 to 50 per person. A bit further along there's the similarly priced *Copper Chimney* – not so extensive a menu though. In between you'll find the *Chinese Home* with good Chinese food.

The *Delhi Durbar* on Falkland St is reputed to have excellent curries, but you're advised to take a taxi there. There's a second *Copper Chimney* branch at Worli. The *Kabab Corner* in the Hotel Natraj on Marine Drive has excellent food and a sitar player. There's a second *Delhi Durbar* too, on Colaba Causeway (Shahid Bhagat Singh Rd) near Wellingdon Circle with a similar menu to the Khyber at slightly lower prices. They have very good milkshakes and ice cream here (try the pista kulfi). There are branches of *Kwality* at Colaba, Worli and Kemps Corner. Good ice cream desserts.

Bombay has a particularly good selection of Chinese restaurants and some say the *Nanking*, on Shivaji Marg in Colaba, has the best Chinese food in India. Most dishes average Rs 18, tasty and well prepared. Directly across the road, the *Mandarin* is marginally more expensive.

Daba Lunches

Mr Bombay Business-Wallah sets off from home, boards his train or bus and heads into the city every morning – just like his office worker counterpart in Australia, England or America. Just like many of his overseas office-wallah brothers he'd like to take his lunch with him and eat in the office. But an Indian lunch isn't as simple as a couple of sandwiches and an apple. A cut lunch could never satisfy an Indian – there has to be curry and rice and parathas and spices and a lot of things that take a lot of time to prepare and would hardly slip into a brown paper bag in the briefcase.

Naturally there's a supremely complex, yet smoothly-working, Indian solution to this problem – it's called the daba lunch system. After he's left for work his wife – or more likely the cook or bearer – sets to and fixes his lunch. When it's all prepared it's packed into a metal bucket about 15 cm in diameter and about 30 cm high. On the lid there's a mysterious colour-coded notation. The container is then carried down to a street corner pick-up point where it meets up with lots of other little lunch buckets and heads towards their city office destination. From the pick-up point they're conveyed to the nearest train station where they're transported to the appropriate city station.

In the city they're broken down to their separate destinations, and between 11 and 12 in the morning thousands upon thousands of individually-coded lunches pour out of Victoria Terminus, Churchgate, Bombay Central and other stations. On the heads of porters, carried in carts, slung from long poles, tied on bicycle handlebars those lunch buckets then scatter out across the city. Most of the daba-wallahs involved in this long chain of events are illiterate, but by some miracle of Indian efficiency when Mr Business-Wallah opens his office door at lunchtime there will be his lunch by the door. Every day, without fail, they never lose a lunch.

Getting There

Air There is a very extensive network of

flights operating into and out of Bombay's Santa Cruz airport. The domestic terminal is now quite separate, and some distance away, from the international terminal. Bombay is the main international gateway to India with far more flights than New Delhi, Calcutta or Madras. It also has the busiest domestic network of flights.

Between Delhi and Bombay there are more than 10 flights daily including a number of direct Airbus connections. There are a couple of daily flights to and from Calcutta and Madras and connections with numerous other cities in India. Examples of fares include Ahmedabad Rs 333, Aurangabad Rs 239, Bangalore Rs 635, Calcutta Rs 1135, Cochin Rs 776, Dabolim (Goa) Rs 323, Delhi Rs 833, Hyderabad Rs 521, Madras Rs 786, Pune Rs 125, Trivandrum Rs 899 and Udaipur Rs 503.

Rail Two railway systems operate out of Bombay. Central Railways handles services to the east and south, plus a few trains to the north. The booking office (tel 264321) is at Victoria Terminus, and is a vast and bewildering collection of different ticket windows on two floors. It takes time to locate the right ticket window for the train you want, so don't go there in a hurry if you can avoid it.

The best thing to do is to go to the tourist kiosk in the main concourse first – that's the one on the right hand side as you enter from the GPO – since it's here that the tourist quota is held. The man who works there is one of those rare discoveries – the answer to every traveller's Indian Railways' nightmare. Not only does he have the entire timetable, journey times and prices at his fingertips, but he will patiently explain all manner of esoteric connections between Bombay and anywhere else you want to go. He'll tell you precisely which ticket window to go to, what your chances of getting a sleeper are on a certain train on a certain date, and if you have any problems, he'll shut up shop and sort them

out for you. Unfortunately, because he's so good, he'll probably be offered a better job before long.

The booking offices are open daily from 9 am to 1 pm and 2 to 4.30 pm.

The other railway system which operates out of Bombay is Western Railways. This has services to the north from Churchgate and Central Stations. Bookings in 1st class can be made at Churchgate (tel 291952) between 9 am and 4 pm or at the booking office, next to the Government of India Tourist Office opposite Churchgate, between 8 am and 8 pm. It's closed for lunch between 1.45 and 2.15 pm. This is also the place where they hold the tourist quota for 1st and 2nd classes. With the exception of the tourist quota, 2nd class has to be booked from Central Station (tel 395757) between 9 am and 4 pm.

Note that there are four Central trains that do not depart from either Central or Churchgate but from Dadar Station, which is further north of Central. These trains are the Amritsar Express, the Varanasi Express, the Dadar-Nagpur Express and the Dadar-Madras Express. The latter is the fastest train to Madras.

From Bombay it is 1588 km and from 17 hours to Delhi and the fare is about Rs 350 in 1st class, Rs 90 in 2nd. The Rajhani Express is the fastest train, it's a special all 2nd class train much more luxurious than usual. It costs Rs 200 in a chair car and this includes tea, dinner, coffee and breakfast on board.

Bombay-Calcutta is a lengthy 1968-km trip taking 36 hours and costing Rs 415 in 1st class, Rs 105 in 2nd class. Bombay-Madras is 1279 km and takes from 26 hours at a cost of Rs 300 in 1st class, Rs 76 in 2nd.

Bus Long distance buses depart from the State Transport Terminal opposite Bombay Central Station. The state bus companies of Maharashtra, Gujarat, Karnataka and Madhya Pradesh all have offices here and bookings can be made (tel

374272 or 376622) between 8 am and 11 pm. Some travel times and approximate costs include:

Aurangabad	11 hours	Rs 54
		Rs 75*
Bangalore	25 hours	Rs 125
Indore	16 hours	Rs 75
		Rs 110*
Surat	9 hours	Rs 36
Hyderabad	16 hours	Rs 95
Ganeshpuri	3 hours	Rs 12
Mahabaleshwar	8 hours	Rs 35
Mangalore	25 hours	Rs 122
Nasik	5 hours	Rs 22
		Rs 26*
Baroda	10 hours	Rs 75
Panaji (Goa)	17 hours	Rs 75
		Rs 105*
Pune (Poona)	5 hours	Rs 18

*de-luxe buses

Boat See Goa for more details on the popular Mogul Lines' Bombay-Goa ferry, a very pleasant alternative to taking a bus or train. Departures are every day except Tuesday, but the service is suspended during the monsoon between June and September. Cabins cost Rs 220, 235, 260 and 300. Upper deck-class is Rs 72, lower deck-class is Rs 48.

The Maharashtra Tourist Development Corporation (tel 296241) at CDO Hutments, Madame Cama Rd make bookings for deck class only between 11 am and 3 pm daily, except Mondays. You can also book passages on this ferry, both for deck and cabin classes, direct from Mogul Lines' headquarters at 16 Bank St, near the Horniman Circle.

Getting Around

Airport The airport bus service operates between Air India/Indian Airlines headquarters at Nariman Point and Terminals 1 (Domestic) and 2 (International). The journey from Nariman Point to Terminal 1 takes about 40 minutes and costs Rs 15. To Terminal 2, it takes about an hour and costs Rs 20. From Nariman Point departures are at 4 am, 6.30 am, 8 am,

then every hour on the hour until midnight, plus a last bus at 1.30 am.

From Terminal 2 (International), they depart at 3 am, 5 am, then every hour on the hour until 11 pm. Tickets for the buses are bought either on the buses themselves, at Air India headquarters or at the Terminals.

For those die-hards who are determined to get there on the el cheapo regardless of inconvenience, it is possible to get from the International Terminal to central Bombay for a mere Rs 6.60. First take the airport bus from the International to the Domestic Terminal – Rs 5 – then an ordinary bus to Vile Parle (number 321) or Santa Cruz, followed by a suburban train to Churchgate – Rs 1.60 in total. If you're carrying anything more than a toothbrush, avoid doing anything as defiant as this in rush-hours.

A taxi to the airport will cost you at least Rs 80 even outside rush-hours. During rush-hours you won't find anyone who's prepared to use the meter so expect to pay considerably more. Coming from the airport there is a police operated taxi booth where you pay a set fare and are then assigned to a taxi. You give the driver your slip and there's no further fuss. You do, however, pay about twice what the fare would be if you went by meter (plus adjustment card). An alternative is to walk down the line of taxis until you get to one far enough back that he will be willing to take less to go now rather than wait to get to the front of the line.

Taxis Bombay has a large fleet of metered taxis, and you won't have any trouble finding one. As usual the meters are out of date, so you pay according to a fare conversion card which all drivers carry, regardless of how reluctant they are to pull them out when they'd prefer to tell you the first figure that comes into their head.

You probably won't have any difficulties about drivers re-setting the meters – Colaba to Victoria Terminus, for example, should cost Rs 4 to 5 – from dawn until late evening. But between midnight and dawn, they're reluctant to take you anywhere on the meter, so you'll have to negotiate a price – Colaba to Nariman Point, for instance, might cost you Rs 8 to 10 at this time – but it's still cheaper in the long run than staying in one of the expensive hotels around Nariman Point, if you have to get to the airport the next day.

Rail Bombay has an extensive system of electric trains, and it's virtually the only place in India where it's worth taking trains for intra-city travel. But *avoid* rush-hours.

The main suburban route of interest to travellers is Churchgate-Bombay Central-Dadar with many other stops in between There's a train every 10 to 15 minutes in either direction between 4.30 am and 10.30 pm. The fare between Churchgate and Central is Rs 1 (2nd class) and Rs 8 (1st class).

A taxi over the same distance would cost you about Rs 15 on the meter. Note that if you arrive at Bombay Central on the main railway system, your ticket covers you for the journey from there to the more convenient Churchgate station.

Bus Bombay has probably the best public transport system of any major Indian city. There are lots of well kept double-decker buses with fares ranging from Rs 0.40. They tend to be crowded, especially during rush hours and Bombay's pick pockets are notoriously adept. Take care. The buses are operated by BEST (Bombay Electric Supply & Transport) and they have separate route maps for their extensive city and suburban services. From the Victoria Terminus Railway Station take a 1, 6 Ltd, 7 Ltd, 103 or 124 to 'Electric House' which is a useful landmark in Colaba. From Bombay Central take a 70 or a 124. Ltd means 'limited stops'.

Things to Buy
Bombay has a number of intriguing

markets. Chor Bazaar is Bombay's thieves' market. It's off Grant Rd (Maulana Shaukatali Rd) and here you'll find a phenomenal collection of 'antiques', jewellery, wooden items, leather and general bric-a-brac. Mutton St has a particularly interesting collection of shops for miscellaneous 'junk'. Shops are generally open from 10 am but are closed on Fridays.

Crawford Market, officially renamed Mahatma Phule Market, is the centre for flowers, fruit, vegetables, meat and fish in Bombay. This is the place to look for Bombay's two famous fish – the pomfret and the 'Bombay duck'. The market building was constructed in 1867 and it's one of the most colourful and photogenic places in Bombay. Near here is Javeri Bazaar, the jewellery centre off Mumbadevi Rd. There is some fantastic stuff here, especially silver belts and old statues and charms. Nearby is the brass bazaar on Kalbadevi Rd.

There are all sorts of places selling handicrafts, artifacts, antiques and art around the Colaba area. Shops in the Taj Hotel specialise in high quality – and high prices. Check the Jehangir Gallery by the Prince of Wales Museum too. The evening stalls along S B Singh Rd in Colaba are good places to buy things; as are Kheedi House and the Rajasthan Emporium at 286 and 230 D Naoroji Rd respectively. You can find some real bargains in the Khadi Village Industries Emporium.

AROUND BOMBAY
Elephanta Island
The island of Elephanta is about 10 km north-east from Apollo Bunder and is Bombay's major tourist attraction due to the four rock-cut temples on the island. They are thought to have been cut out between 450 and 750 AD, and at that time the island was known as Gharapuri, the 'fortress city'. When the Portuguese arrived they renamed it Elephanta after the large stone elephant near the landing place. This figure collapsed in 1814 and

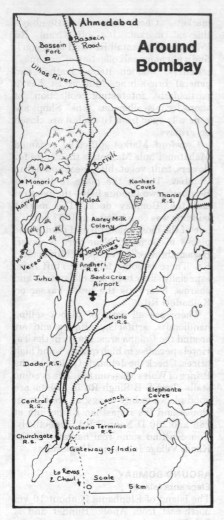

Around Bombay

is not as impressive as the rock-cut temples of Ellora the size, beauty and power of the sculptures is unexcelled.

The caves are reached by a stairway up the hillside from the landing place. Palanquins are available for anybody in need of being carried up. There is one main cave with a number of large sculptured panels, all relating to Shiva, and a separate lingam shrine.

The most interesting of the panels includes one of Trimurti, or the three-headed Shiva, where he also takes the role of Brahma, the creator, and Vishnu, the preserver. In other panels Shiva appears as Arddhanariswar where he unites both sexes in one body, one side of the sculpture is male, one side female.

There are figures of Shiva and his wife Parvati and of their marriage. In another panel Shiva dances the Tandava, the dance that shakes the world. Parvati and their son, Ganesh, look on a little astonished. One of the best panels is that of Ravana shaking Kailasa. The demon king of Lanka decided to carry Shiva and his companions off by the simple expedient of removing their Himalayan home, the mountain Kailasa. Parvati became panic-stricken at his energetic attempts to jerk the mountain free, but Shiva calmly pushed the mountain back down with one toe, trapping Ravana beneath it for ten thousand years.

Getting There Launches leave regularly from Apollo Bunder by the Gateway of India. The economy boats cost Rs 13, de-luxe ones Rs 25, more with air-con. The more expensive trips also include a guide. A good guide, and there are some excellent ones, can considerably increase your enjoyment and understanding – even, as one tubby little gentleman with glasses does, show you how Shiva danced the Tandava. During the monsoon there are no boats to the island since the water is too rough. Elephanta gets very crowded on weekends.

the remaining pieces were removed to the Victoria Gardens in Bombay in 1864 and reassembled in 1912.

Unfortunately the Portuguese took their traditional disdain for other religions to its usual lengths at Elephanta and did considerable damage to the sculptures. Although some people feel that Elephanta

Juhu

Close to Bombay's international airport, Santa Cruz, Juhu is 18 km north of the city centre. It's the nearest beach to the city and has quite a collection of upper notch hotels, but it's no place for a pleasant swim. On weekdays it is fairly quiet, but on weekends there are donkeys, camels, dancing monkeys, acrobats and every other type of Indian beach entertainment. From Santa Cruz station you can get there on a 182, 231 or 253 bus.

Aarey Milk Colony

Fresh milk, something of a rarity in cow-infested India, is produced at this model milk production centre. It's notable also for its hilltop viewpoint with a fine view over the island.

Krishnagiri Upavan National Park

Reached via the Borivli station, the Kanheri Caves and the lakes, which act as reservoirs for much of Bombay's water supply, are in the national park. The lakes are Vihar, Tulsi and Powari.

At the entrance to the park there's a huge outdoor movie lot, including a fort frontage, partly constructed from old oil drums. Also near the park entrance is, believe it or not, a Lion Safari Park. Open from 9 am to 5 pm, daily except Mondays (Tuesdays if Monday is a public holiday), a half-hour trip through the park in a 'safari vehicle' costs Rs 6.

Kanheri Caves

Within the national park, about 42 km from Bombay, there are 109 caves along the side of a rocky ravine. The caves are Buddhist and date from around the 2nd to 9th century AD. Although there are so many of them, most are little more than holes in the rock and only a handful are of real interest. The most important is cave 3, the 'Great Chaitya Cave', which has a long colonnade of pillars around the *dagoba* at the back of the cave. Further up the ravine there are some good views right out to the sea.

Kanheri can be visited on the regular suburban tours or you can take a train to Borivli station and then a taxi the 10 km or so to the caves. On Sundays and holidays there is a bus service from the station to the caves. Entrance to the caves is Rs 0.50.

Other Beaches

Bombay's best known beach, Juhu, is too close to the city and not sanitary enough for a pleasant swim, but there are more remote beaches on the island. Marve and Manori beaches are near to each other, about 40 km out of the city. You can get to them via the station at Malad, 32 km out. Marve is a stretch of unspoilt and lightly populated beach. There's an interesting fishing village and an old Portuguese church nearby.

A nice place to stay near the village of Manori is the *Manoribel Hotel* (tel 241707), which has double rooms with attached bath from Rs 55. To get there, take the suburban electric train to Malad, then a bus to Marve ferry, cross on the ferry and walk to the Manoribel. It's a km and a bit walk from where the ferry stops at Manori to the beach

Other beaches around Bombay include Madh, 45 km out and also reached via Malad. Versova is 29 km from the city, reached via Andheri station. Getting to Uran involves a 74-km trip, the last 10 km by sea. Launches leave from the New Ferry Wharf.

Montpezir & Jogeshvari Caves

There are a few Hindu caves, one of which was converted into a Portuguese church, at Montpezir, near Borivli. The Jogeshvari Caves are near the Andheri station.

Bassein

Just across the river which separates the mainland from Bombay island is Bassein, a Portuguese fortified city from 1534 to 1739. The Portuguese took Bassein at the same time as Daman, further north in Gujarat. They built a fort containing a city of such pomp and splendour that it came to be known as the 'Court of the North'. Only the Hidalgos or aristocracy were permitted to live within the fort walls, and by the end of the 17th century there were 300 Portuguese and 400 Indian-Christian families here, with a cathedral, five convents and 13 churches.

Then in 1739 the Marathas besieged the city and the Portuguese surrendered after three months of appalling losses. Today the city walls are still standing and there are the ruins of some of the churches and the Cathedral of St Joseph.

Bassein is ll km from the Bassein Road (Vasai Road in Marathi) railway station. Sopara, near Bassein Road, is thought to be the Biblical Ophir. About an hour by bus from the station are the Vajreshwari hot springs.

Chaul

South of Bombay this was another Portuguese settlement, although not as important as Bassein. They took it in 1522 and lost it to the Marathas at the same time as Bassein. There are a few remains and old ruined churches within the Portuguese fortifications. Looking across to the Portuguese fort from the other side of the river is the hill top Moslem Korlai Fort.

Ferries run to Revas from the New Ferry Wharf, a 1½ hour trip. From there you've got a 30-km bus trip to Chaul. It's possible to continue on from here by road to Mahabaleshwar or to join the Bombay-Pune Rd.

Maharashtra

Population: 56 million
Area: 307,762 square km
Capital: Bombay
Main language: Marathi

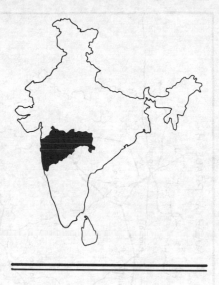

The state of Maharashtra is one of the largest in India, both in terms of population and area. Its booming capital, Bombay, makes it not only one of the most important states economically, but also a major arrival point for overseas visitors. From Bombay you can head off into India in a number of directions but most travellers will either be heading south through Pune (Poona), with its famous ashram, to Goa or north-east to the amazing cave temples of Ajanta and Ellora. Most of the state stands on the high Deccan plateau, and historically this was the main centre for the Maratha empire which defied the Moghuls for so long and under the fearless rule of Shivaji carved out a large part of central India as their own domain.

Cave Architecture

The rock-cut caves in Maharashtra all have several distinct design elements. All the Buddhist caves, which are generally the older ones, are either *chaityas* (temples) or *viharas* (monasteries). Chaityas are usually deep and narrow with a stupa at the end of the cave. There may be a row of columns down both sides of the cave and around the stupa.

The viharas are usually not as deep and narrow as the chaitya caves. These caves were usually intended as living and sleeping quarters for the monks and often have rows of cells along both sides of the cave. In the back there is a small shrine room, usually containing an image of the Buddha. At Ajanta the cliff face the caves are cut into is very steep and there is often a small verandah or entrance porch in front of the main cave. At Ellora the rock face is more sloping and the verandah or porch element generally becomes a separate courtyard.

The cave temples reach their peak of complexity and design in the Hindu caves at Ellora, in particular the magnificent Kailasa temple. Here they are hardly caves any longer for the whole enclosure is open to the sky. In design they are much like other temples of that era – except that instead of being built up from the bottom they were cut down from the top. They are an imitation of conventional architecture of that period.

The caves are notable for their sculptures and paintings but the famous Ajanta 'frescoes' are not, technically speaking, frescoes at all. A fresco is a painting done on a wet surface where the colour is absorbed into the surface. The Ajanta paintings are more correctly tempera since they were painted on a dry surface. The rough-hewn rock walls were coated with a cm-thick layer of clay and cow-dung mixed with rice husks. A final coat of lime was then applied to produce the finished surface on which the artist

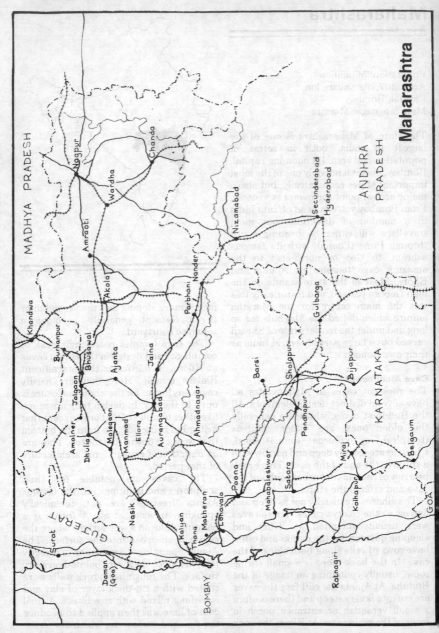

Maharashtra

MADHYA PRADESH

ANDHRA PRADESH

KARNATAKA

GUJERAT

GOA

Nagpur

Wardha

Chanda

Amraoti

Akola

Parbhani

Nander

Nizamabad

Secunderabad

Hyderabad

Gulbarga

Bijapur

Belgaum

Khandwa

Burhanpur

Bhusawal

Jalgaon

Amalner

Dhulia

Malegaon

Manmad

Ajanta

Jalna

Ellora

Aurangabad

Ahmadnagar

Barsi

Sholapur

Pandharpur

Miraj

Kolhapur

Satara

Mahableshwar

Paona

Nasik

Kalyan

Thana

Matheron

Lonavala

Surat

Daman (Goa)

BOMBAY

Ratnagiri

painted. The final surface was then polished to produce a high gloss.

MATHERAN

The nearest hill station to Bombay, Matheran is 171 km from the city via Neral on the Bombay-Pune railway line. The name means 'jungle topped' or 'wooded head' which is just what it is – an undulating hill top, cloaked in shady trees. It's the abundance of shade as much as the 700 to 800-metre altitude which makes Matheran a slightly cooler place than Bombay. Matheran became a popular hill station during the days of the Raj, Hugh Malet is credited with its discovery in 1850.

Getting to Matheran is half the fun; from Neral you take a tiny, narrow gauge toy train up the 21-km route to the hill. It's a choice of train or walk, there are no motor vehicles in Matheran and the trekking route is an 11-km long climb. The train twists, turns and winds on its steep, two-hour ascent. Food and drink vendors cling to the outside and at one point you pass through 'one kiss tunnel'.

On the top Matheran sprawls north-south along the hill top. There are many km of walking tracks leading to the viewpoints that ring the station. At many of the points the ground drops sheer to the plains, far, far below. On a clear day the view can be fantastic and even in the hazy pre-monsoon air the eerie views of surrounding hills are very fine.

From Porcupine, Monkey or Hart Points on the north-west of the hill you can see the lights of Bombay on a clear night. Porcupine is also a good place for catching the sunset but Panorama Point, at the extreme north, is said to have the finest views. The western side, from Porcupine to Louisa Point, is known as Cathedral Rocks and Neral can be seen far below, straddling the Central Railway line. At the south, near One Tree Hill, a trail down to the valley below is known as Shivaji's Ladder, so called because the Maratha leader is said to have used it.

Places to Stay

Most of the more expensive places provide boarding and lodging only – you must take all your meals at the guest houses. These include the *Lord's Central House* (tel 28) (also called just Central Hotel) and the *Regal Hotel*, which costs around Rs 100 to 130 per person. The *Royal Hotel* (tel 47, 75) costs Rs 150 for a double including all meals.

At *Brightlands* (tel 44) per person cost is Rs 90. Somewhat cheaper – but still quite comfortable is the *Alexander Guest House* (tel 51) at Rs 50 per person (more with air-con). The *Silvan Guest House* (tel 74) has rooms at Rs 100/150 or room-only accommodation at Rs 25 per person. All these places have attached bathrooms and small verandahs with chairs and tables.

Moving down a notch you could try *Laxmi Hotel* with double rooms at Rs 35, still with your own bathroom. *Khan's Cosmopolitan Hotel* (tel 40) is very close to the centre but rather primitive, Rs 15 to Rs 25. For the real economisers there is dormitory accommodation at the *Holiday Camp* (the train stops at the camp, a km or two before Matheran) or at *Maneklal Terrace*, two km south of the railway station. There are rooms at Rs 30 to 40 at the Holiday Camp, while at Maneklal Terrace a mat on the floor, plus all meals, costs Rs 12 per day.

Places to Eat

Away from the hotels and guest houses there is a string of snack style eating places in the town centre. Good fruit juices at the *Kwality Fruit Juice House*. Matheran is famed for its honey and for *chikki* – a toffee-like confectionery made of gur sugar and nuts. Chikki is sold at many shops in Matheran.

There are many monkeys in Matheran, watch out for them if you buy bananas in the market!

Getting There

From Bombay, the Pune expresses or the

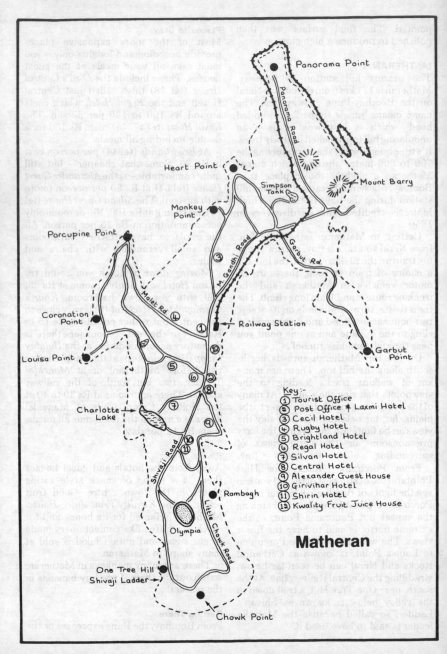

Matheran

Key:-
1. Tourist Office
2. Post Office & Laxmi Hotel
3. Cecil Hotel
4. Rugby Hotel
5. Brightland Hotel
6. Regal Hotel
7. Silvan Hotel
8. Central Hotel
9. Alexander Guest House
10. Girivihar Hotel
11. Shirin Hotel
12. Kwality Fruit Juice House

Panorama Point

Mount Barry

Heart Point

Monkey Point

Porcupine Point

Simpson Tank

Panorama Road

Garbut Rd.

M. Gandhi Road

Malet Rd.

Coronation Point

Railway Station

Louisa Point

Garbut Point

Charlotte Lake

Shivaji Road

Little Chowk Road

Rambagh

Olympia

One Tree Hill
Shivaji Ladder

Chowk Point

Karjat local trains will take you to Neral from where the toy train runs up to Matheran. It's about two hours from Bombay to Neral and two hours again up to Matheran. The Matheran train generally connects with the Pune expresses. Fare from Bombay is Rs 17 in 2nd class, Rs 66 in 1st – the Matheran toy train has pink curtains on the 1st class carriage!

Trains depart from Matheran for Neral at 6 am, 12.45 and 2.35 pm. There's a Rs 4 'capitation tax' on each arrival at Matheran, you pay it as you leave the station. During the monsoon the Neral-Matheran train service is suspended.

Getting Around

In Matheran itself the only transport is rickshaws – one man pulls, two push (or hold it back on the descents). If your gear is too heavy to carry very far, and you're staying a long way from the station, you may want to use one to get your bags to the hotel. Ponies can also be hired for riding on the many trails that wind around Matheran.

KARLA & BHAJA CAVES

Situated 126 km south-east of Bombay on the main rail line to Pune, Lonavla (sometimes spelt Lonavala) is the place from which to visit the Karla and Bhaja caves. If, however, your interest in archaeological sites is such that you intend to spend more than a day exploring the caves then it would be more convenient to stay either at the Government Holiday Camp, near the Malavli railway station, or at the Karla Hotel, since there's little of interest in Lonavla itself. The Karla Cave is about 12 km from Lonavla, about 1½ km off the main road. The Bhaja caves are about three km off the main road. If you plan on walking to the latter then take a train to Malavli first of all.

The Tourist Office at Lonavla Station is completely useless.

Karla Cave

It's a steep climb over about half a km up the hillside to the Karla Cave. The cave is Hinayana Buddhist and was completed around 80 BC. It's one of the best preserved cave temples of its type in India and also dates from the time when this style of temple was at its height in terms of design purity.

A beautifully carved 'Sun Window' filters the light in towards the small stupa at the inner end of the deep, narrow cave. Unfortunately an ugly little modern temple has been erected just outside the cave entrance. Inside the pillars are topped by figures of two kneeling elephants with two seated figures with their arms over each other on the elephants. Generally the figures are male and female, but sometimes they are of two women. The roof of the cave is ribbed with teak beams which are said to be original; at Ajanta and Ellora the wooden beams that may once have been there are now all gone. On the sides of the vestibule there are carved elephant heads which once had real ivory tusks.

Other carvings can also be seen along the sides. A pillar topped by four back-to-back lions, an image usually associated with Ashoka, stands outside the cave. It may be older than the cave itself.

There are some small monastery or *vihara* caves at Karla, further round the hillside. Some of these have been converted into Hindu shrines.

If possible avoid going to the Karla Cave at weekends or on public holidays when it is invaded by the transistor radio and picnic mobs from Bombay. The noise and mess which they create isn't going to do anything for your appreciation of this beautiful site. Bhaja is too far from the main road for this to happen on the same scale but it does get its fair share too. Entry to the Karla Cave now costs Rs 0.50.

Bhaja Caves

It's a fairly rough route from the main road to the 18 Bhaja Caves. They're in a rather lusher, green setting than the dry hillside

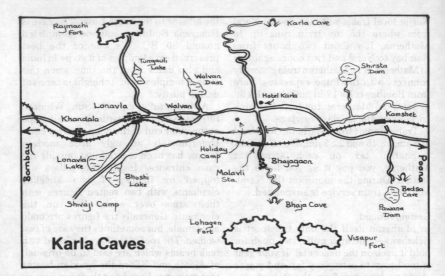

Karla Caves

with the Karla Cave. The caves are thought to date from around 200 BC and cave 12, a *chaitya* cave similar in style to the Karla Cave, is the most important. South of this is a strange group of 14 stupas, five inside and nine outside the cave. The last cave on the south side has some fine sculptures.

Other

Further along the line, six km south-east of Kamshet station, are the Bedsa Caves. They are thought to be newer than the better executed Karla Cave. At one time the roof of the main cave was probably painted. There are a number of old forts in the vicinity including the hill-top Lohagen Fort, six km from Malavli, which was taken twice by Shivaji, and lost again on each occasion. Above the Bhaja Caves is the Visapur Fort.

Khandala, before Lonavla, is picturesquely situated overlooking a ravine. In the wet season there is a fine waterfall near the head of the ravine.

Places to Stay – Lonavla

Like Khandala and Mahabaleshwar, Lonavla is seen as a kind of hill station by people from Bombay so there's quite a range of accommodation here. It's a compact town and there are a number of places close to the bus and railway stations. At the top of the market is the *Adarsh Hotel* (tel 2353), close to the bus station. Rooms cost Rs 50, 80, 125, 150, 200 and 250. There's a vegetarian restaurant although the food is somewhat expensive – Rs 12 for a thali, for instance.

Hotel Girikunj (tel 2529) is less expensive with singles/doubles for Rs 45/60, plus more expensive doubles at Rs 70 and 95. All rooms have their own bathroom and there is a vegetarian restaurant but note that checkout time is 9 am. The *Hotel Purohit* (tel 2695) is similar in standard with rooms at Rs 20 or Rs 50 to 60 with attached bath. *Pitale Boarding & Lodging* (tel 2657) is similar again; doubles with attached bath are Rs 40. The Pitale is a charming old stone and wood colonial-style bungalow, encircled by a verandah, and it has a restaurant and bar.

At the cheaper end of the market is the friendly *Hotel Chandralok* (tel 2294) with doubles at Rs 40 (no singles) and a vegetarian restaurant. The *Dinesh Hotel* (tel 2561) has doubles with attached bath at Rs 55 (no singles again). Cheaper still is the *Janata Hotel* (tel 2689), opposite the Girikunj, which has doubles at Rs 30 but is a somewhat drab place. If you don't mind dormitory accommodation you can find a bed for just Rs 15 at the *Highway Lodge* (tel 2321). It's run by a nice old Persian guy.

There are a number of other places out along the main road to the Karla Cave. They include the *Shamian Lodge* and the *Maharaja Inn*, as well as the *Hotel Filmstar* near the Walvan Lake.

There are a number of eating places along the Bombay-Pune road through Lonavla and others across the railway

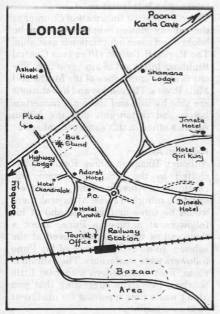

tracks in the main parts of this small town.

Places to Stay – Khandala

Khandala is the station before Lonavla and can be used as an alternative jumping off point for the caves. The *Hotel Mount View* (tel 746) on Khandala Rd is reasonably cheap. The *Khandala Hotel* (tel 239) and *Hotel on the Rocks* (tel 690) are at the luxurious end of Khandala's scale.

Places to Stay – Karla

The most convenient location for a cave visit is the government operated *Holiday Camp* (tel 30) just off the Bombay-Pune road near the caves. There are two types of accommodation blocks from Rs 20 and 25 per day plus a couple of dormitories. From the Holiday Camp you can get to both the Karla and Bhaja caves relatively easily, but during the monsoon you can't get to the camp from the Malavli railway station because a river blocks the way. At that time you must leave the train at Lonavla and bus to the camp. Food is available at the camp – Rs 6 for a vegetarian thali.

You can also find similarly priced rooms at the *Karla Hotel* at the junction where the road to Karla turns off from the main road. They're not as pleasant as those at the Holiday Camp.

Getting There

It's possible to see the Karla and Bhaja caves comfortably in a day from either Bombay or Pune so long as you're prepared to hire an auto-rickshaw in Lonavla to take you there and back. There is a choice of both trains and buses to Lonavla from either of the cities but you can give up the idea of a bus *from* Lonavla to Bombay or Pune because they invariably turn up full and if anyone does get off you can be sure that someone has booked the seat in advance.

Bombay-Lonavla takes about three hours and convenient trains are the

Deccan Express, the Bombay-Bangalore Udyan Express or the Bombay-Miraj Koyna Express. These trains all go through in the morning but they can all be up to an hour late. The 2nd class fare is Rs 11.50 for the 126 km trip. Back to Bombay the same trains pass through in the afternoon.

From Pune there are the long-distance express trains and the commuter shuttles which run between Pune and Lonavla. The Madras-Dadar Express, the Sinhagad Express, the Deccan Express, the Sahyadri Express and the Hyderabad-Bombay Express all make the hour to hour and a half trip in the morning. Suitable commuter shuttles leave Pune at 5.50 and 8 am and take about two hours. Pune-Lonavla is 64 km. Travelling to Pune you could take the Dadar-Madras Express, the Sinhagad Express, the Bombay-Trivandrum Express, the Deccan Express or the Sahyadri Express. Shuttle trains go at 4, 6 and 9 pm.

Getting Around

In theory there are local buses 10 times a day in either direction between Lonavla and Karla but not only is the timetable a figment of the imagination but they turn up at Lonavla full and leave even fuller. Plus everybody fights like crazy to get on and you never know which buses are going where because there are no signs. Likewise for the, in theory, 12 buses a day to the Rajmachi Fort. If you're determined to go by bus practise saying 'Karla zanarkhai?' – Marathi for 'is this going to Karla' – since no one speaks English.

You can save a lot of time and frustration by hiring an auto-rickshaw. The prices are fairly standard: Lonavla-Karla (Rs 15), Lonavla-Karla-Lonavla (Rs 40 including waiting time), Lonavla-Karla-Bhaja-Lonavla (Rs 50 to 60 including waiting time at both sites). It would, of course, be cheaper to stay at the Holiday Camp overnight and walk to the caves.

PUNE (POONA) (population 950,000)

Shivaji, the great Maratha leader, was raised in Pune which was granted to his grandfather in 1599. Later it became the capital of the Peshwas, but in 1817 went to the British, under whom it became the capital of the region during the monsoon. It has a rather more pleasant climate at that time than muggy Bombay.

Although Pune has a number of points of interest and can be conveniently visited if you're heading from Bombay to Aurangabad (for Ajanta and Ellora) or to Goa, its major attraction to western visitors was the Shree Rajneesh Ashram. The ashram became so well known that it was even included on the city bus tour, where, in a superb reversal of roles, Indians flocked to view westerners. Rajneesh, however, has now shifted his ashram to Oregon in the USA and the Pune ashram is a mere shadow of its former self.

Information & Orientation

There's a Tourist Information Counter at the railway station where tours can be booked and some information is available. The Regional Tourist Office is in Central Buildings but is not of any great use. The city is at the confluence of the Mutha and Mula Rivers. The railway and bus stations are side by side and there are numerous hotels and restaurants and the Indian Airlines office in this same central area.

Rajneesh Ashram

Although Bhagwan Shree Rajneesh has shifted to the US, his ashram still continues in Koregoan Park, a relatively spacious suburb of Pune. At its peak there would be three or four thousand of his followers at a time in Pune, about a thousand of whom actually lived at the ashram. In all 90% or more of his Pune followers were westerners. The ashram is clean, neat and modern with neat little touches, like signs suggesting that you 'don't waste time queueing for mail, rent your own mailbox'.

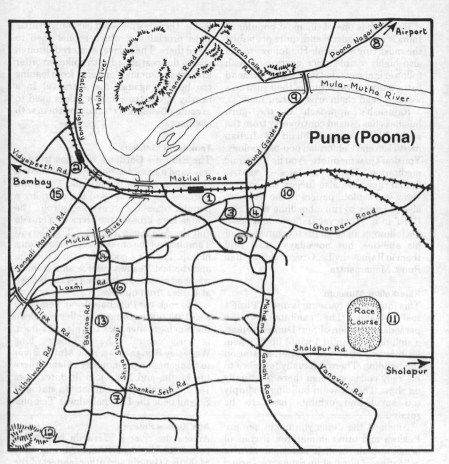

Pune (Poona)

Legend:

1 Poona Railway Station, State & Municipal Bus Terminals
2 Shivajinagar Railway Station
3 Tourist Office (Central Buildings)
4 Indian Airlines
5 G.P.O.
6 City Post Office
7 Swargate State & Municipal Bus Terminal
8 Kasturba Samadhi (Aga Khan's Palace)
9 Bund Gardens
10 Rajneesh Ashram
11 Empress Gardens
12 Parvati Temple
13 Raja Kelkar Museum
14 Shanwarwada
15 Panchaleshwar Temple

Rajneesh is one of the most popular of India's 'export gurus' and, quite probably, the most controversial. His followers are also highly visible since every Rajneesh follower is always clad in orange from head to toe and wears a picture of their guru on a wooden bead chain around their neck.

Rajneesh's approach to the guru business has caused controversy from the start. It's a curious blend of Indian mysticism and Californian pop-psychology. You don't just meditate – you do 'dynamic meditation'. Hyped up tales of tantric sexual rites have also fuelled the controversy and tabloid papers in the west are always happy to run a headline with 'Sex Guru' in it. Whatever the pros and cons, his followers all seem pretty convinced of his abilities, but nowadays you'll find them in Rajneeshville, Oregon rather than Pune, Maharashtra.

Raja Kelkar Museum
This interesting museum is one of Pune's real delights. The exhibits are the personal collection of Shri Dinkar Kelkar, a smiling old man in a white dhoti whom visitors will often see wandering around the building. There's actually far more to his zany collection than there is actually on show. The museum building is simply too small and exhibits have to be rotated.

Amongst the items you might see are Peshwa and other miniatures, a coat of armour made of fish scales, a bizarre collection of musical instruments, carved doors and windows, hookah pipes, strange locks, oil lamps and a superb collection of betel nut cutters. The museum is housed in a quaint purple, red and green Rajasthani-style building.

Shanwarwada Palace
In a section of the town where narrow and winding streets form a maze stands the imposing fortress-like Shanwarwada Palace. Built in 1736 the massive walls enclosed the palace of the Peshwa rulers – until it was burnt down in 1827. Today,

inside, there is a pleasant garden and little signs proclaiming which rooms used to stand there. The palace is entered through sturdy doors studded with spikes in order to dissuade enemy elephants from leaning too heavily against the entrance! In a nearby street the Peshwa rulers used to execute offenders by trampling them with elephants.

Temples & Gardens
The Empress Gardens, with fine tropical trees and a small zoo nearby, has a moated Ganesh temple in the middle. The Bund Gardens, on the banks of the river, are a popular place for an evening stroll. The bridge here crosses the river to Yeravda and the Aga Khan's Palace. The Parvati Temple is on the outskirts of the town on a hilltop. There's a good view from the top, and the last Peshwa ruler is said to have watched his troops defeated by the British at Kirkee from up here.

The rock-cut Panchaleshwar Temple, a small 8th century temple similar in style to the much grander rock temples of Ellora, is fairly central. The 150-metre long Wellesley Bridge crosses the Mutha River to Sangam, the promontory of land where the Mutha and Mula join. It dates from 1875. There's a fine equestrian statue of Shivaji near the Panchaleshwar Temple.

Aga Khan's Palace
Across the river in Yeravda is the fine palace of the Aga Khan. At one time Mahatma Gandhi and other leaders of the movement for Indian independence were interned here and today it is maintained as another memorial to Gandhi. Kasturba Gandhi, the Mahatma's wife, died here while interned and her memorial tomb stands in the palace grounds.

Tours
There are two tours daily from the railway station in Pune – the morning tour departs at 8 am, the afternoon tour at 3 pm and they last 3½ hours. The tours cost Rs 14 and go to all the main sights in Pune.

Places to Stay – Bottom End

Since the Rajneesh ashram departed, there's probably a lot more hotel space available in Pune. There is the usual collection of grubby, drab and/or dismal places close to the railway station. *Green Hotel* in Wilson Garden is reasonable at Rs 35 double. Next door the *Samrat* is similarly priced, across the road the *Central Lodge* is cheaper at Rs 25 a double and next door again the *Alankar Hotel* (tel 20670) is rather better at Rs 50 a double. Wilson Gardens start directly opposite the railway station, beside the *National Hotel* which is Rs 40 a double.

There are quite a few others in the immediate vicinity if you draw a blank at all of the above – but some are of extremely poor quality, quite uninhabitable. If you follow the road in front of the station to the left you'll soon come to Connaught Rd. The Indian Airlines office is here, at the bigger flashier Amir Hotel. Down a little from the Amir is the *Gulmohr* and then the *Shalimar* (tel 20290-91) at 12A Connaught Rd. The latter is clean enough but very rundown, drab grey, dismal and poorly cared for. Rooms cost from Rs 30 all the way to Rs 75.

There are *Railway Retiring Rooms* at the station – dorm beds at Rs 10 each or rooms at Rs 15 a head. *Hotel Saras*, (tel 448499) run by the state tourist office, is actually built into the Nehru Stadium, about a Rs 5 or 6 auto-rickshaw ride from the railway station but very close to the Swargate Bus Station. Singles/doubles cost Rs 50/75 and it's quite pleasant. Other cheaper hotels include the *Ellora Hotel* (tel 40714) at 2156 Sadashiv and rooms from Rs 20 per person. The *Metro* at 14 Connaught Rd (tel 24145) runs from Rs 25.

Places to Stay – Top End

The *Hotel Amir* (tel 27371) is very close to the railway station at 50 Connaught Rd. This is one of the best places in Pune with air-con rooms at Rs 200/275 and non air-con at Rs 120/160. It has the usual mod cons, a vegetarian restaurant and a good (and fairly reasonably priced) snack bar, if you're in need of something non-Indian.

The *Blue Diamond* (tel 27334, 28735) is in Koregoan Park. Rooms here are from Rs 400/475 for air-con singles/doubles and again it's all mod cons including a swimming pool, restaurants and coffee bar.

Places to Eat

The food scene is pretty good in Pune. The *Amir* and *Blue Diamond* have more expensive restaurants, but there are several good cheap places right in front of the station to the left. *Neelam Restaurant* is pleasant and the *Hotel Madhura* (only a very small sign in English but it's in the big Hotel Metro building) has excellent thalis from Rs 5, good lassi and super-cool drinks. A couple of doors further down there's the *Savera Restaurant*, also with good food.

Getting There

Air There are two daily flights Bombay-Pune, which cost Rs 125.

Rail Pune is 192 km from Bombay and the trains take four or five hours and cost around Rs 64 in 1st class, Rs 17 in 2nd.

Bus There are daily air-con buses between Bombay and Pune for Rs 45 and you can also get taxis between the two cities for around Rs 65 per seat. Buses run from Pune to Mahabaleshwar, Panjim (Goa), Aurangabad (via Ahmednagar). Pune-Aurangabad takes about six hours. From Pune they operate from the Pune taxi stand in front of the railway station.

Pune has three bus stations:

Railway Bus Stand – points south including Goa – Belgaum, Panjim, Kolhapur, Mahabaleshwar, Ratnagiri, Panchgani, Satara and Sholapur.
Shivaji Nagar Bus Stand – points north and north-east – Ahmednagar, Amravati, Aurangabad, Belgaum, Dehu, Jalgaon,

Lonavla, Murud, Nanded, Nasik.
Swargate Bus Stand – Baneshwar, Bhorgar, Daund, Khodakwasla, Morgaon, Purandar, Saswad, Shivapur and Sinhagad.

Getting Around

Lots of taxis and auto-rickshaws – from the railway station to the Swargate Bus Stand or the Saras Hotel costs about Rs 5 to Rs 6, to Shivaji Nagar Bus is about Rs 5. Pune is packed with bicycles and lots of places rent bicycles.

AROUND PUNE

Simhagad, the 'lion fort', is 25 km southwest of Pune and was the scene of another of Shivaji's daring exploits. The fortress stands on top of a sheer-sided hill at 1270-metres altitude. In 1670 Shivaji's general, Tanaji Malusre, led a force of men who scaled the steep hillside in the dark and defeated the unprepared forces of Bijapur.

Legends about this dramatic attack relate that the Maratha forces used trained lizards to carry ropes up the hillside! Tanaji died in the assault and there are monuments at the spot where he died, and also at the place where he lost his left hand before his death. Purandar is another old fortress, it's 27 km south-east of Pune, further by road.

MAHABALESHWAR

This popular hill station was the summer capital of the Bombay presidency during the days of the Raj. At an altitude of 1372 metres, Mahabaleshwar has pleasant walks, good lookouts (the sea, 30 km away, is visible on a clear day) and the area has interesting historical connections with Shivaji. Mahabaleshwar was founded in 1828 by Sir John Malcolm.

Elphinstone Point, Babington Point, Bombay Point, Kate's Point and a number of other lookouts around the wooded plateau offer fine views over the plains below. Arthur's Seat, 12 km out, looks over the coastal strip between the ghats and the sea known as the Konkan, a sheer drop of 600 metres. There are pleasant waterfalls such as Chinaman's Waterfall (2½ km out), Dhobi Waterfall (three km) and Lingmala Waterfalls (six km).

Venna Lake, within Mahabaleshwar, has boating and fishing facilities. In the village of Old Mahabelshwar there are three old temples. The Krishnabai or Panchganga ('Five Streams') Temple is said to contain five streams including the Krishna River.

Pratapgarh Fort

Built in 1656 this fort is about 24 km, and 500 steps, from Mahabaleshwar. It's connected with one of the more notable feats in Shivaji's dramatic life. Outnumbered by the forces of Bijapur, Shivaji arranged to meet with the opposing General Afzal Khan. Neither would carry any weapon or wear armour but neither, it was to turn out, could be trusted.

When they met Afzal Khan pulled out a dagger and stabbed Shivaji, but the Maratha leader had worn a shirt of mail under his white robe and concealed in his left hand was a deadly set of 'tiger claws'. This nasty weapon consisted of a series of rings to which long, sharpened, metal claws were attached. Shivaji drove these claws into Khan and disemboweled him. Today a tomb marks where their encounter took place and a tower was erected over the Khan's head. There is a statue of Shivaji in the ruined fort. There is another Shivaji fort at Raigarh, 80 km from Mahabaleshwar.

Places to Stay

There are a lot of hotels at Mahabaleshwar. More expensive hotels, with tariffs over Rs 100, include the *Race View Hotel* (tel 238-76), *Dina Hotel* (tel 246) and the *Fredrick Hotel* (tel 240). These more expensive places generally quote all-inclusive prices in the Rs 120 to 250 per person range.

Other hotels go down to less than Rs 30. The *Ripon Hotel* (tel 257) is Rs 50, the *Bharat Hotel* (tel 233) is around Rs 35.

There is also a state government-operated *Holiday Camp* (tel 318) with rooms from Rs 20 to 60 and a Rs 10 dorm. Reservations can be made through the Maharashtra Tourism Development Corporation at Express Towers, Nariman Point, Bombay (tel 234522-482).

There are tourist information centres at the bus stand (tel 271) and at the Holiday Camp (tel 318).

Getting There

Pune is the normal departure point for Mahabaleshwar. Pune is also the nearest railhead. It's 120 km from Pune, via Panchgani which is 19 km before Mahabaleshwar. From Pune the ordinary bus fare is Rs 12, there are also state transport de-luxe buses and taxis. From Bombay it's 286 km via Pune or 259 km via Mahad.

PANCHGANI

'Five Hills' is just 19 km from Mahabaleshwar and, at 1334 metres, just 90 metres lower. It's a popular hill station but overshadowed by better known Mahabaleshwar. On the way up to Panchgani you pass through Wai, a site which featured in the Mahabharata.

Places to Stay

As in Mahabaleshwar, there are various hotels from the Rs 150/200 *Amir Hotel* (tel 211, 346) on down. Here too there is a *Holiday Camp* with rooms from Rs 35 to Rs 55 and a Rs 10 dorm.

SATARA

On the main road from Pune to Belgaum and then Goa, but 15 km off the railway line from Satara Road, this town houses a number of relics of the Maratha leader Shivaji. Situated near the new palace a building contains his sword, the coat he wore when he met Afzal Khan and the Waghnakh or 'tiger's claws' with which he killed him. The Shivaji Maharaj Museum is opposite the bus station.

The Fort of Wasota stands on the south of the town – it has had a colourful and bloody history, including being captured from the Marathas in 1699 by the forces of Aurangzeb, only to be recaptured in 1705 by means of a Brahmin who befriended the fort's defenders then let in a band of Marathas.

OTHER PLACES IN THE SOUTH

Kolhapur, with a population of nearly 300,000, was once the capital of an important Maratha state. The old palace contains some interesting items including a collection of swords. One of Kolhapur's maharajas died in Florence, Italy, and was cremated on the banks of the Arno where his *chhatri* (cenotaph) now stands.

Ratnagiri, on the coast 130 km west, was the place where Thibaw, the last Burmese king, was interned by the British from 1886 until his death in 1916. Panhala and Pawangarh are interesting hill stations – at Panhala there is a fort with a long and interesting history, it was originally the stronghold of Raja Bhoj II in 1192. The Pawala Caves are near here plus a couple of Buddhist cave temples.

AHMEDNAGAR (population 130,000)

On the road between Pune (82 km away) and Aurangabad, Ahmednagar has had a colourful history. It was here that the Emperor Aurangzeb died in 1707, aged 97. The town's imposing fort was erected in 1550, and at one time Nehru was imprisoned here by the British.

Places to Stay

There are various hotels including the *Ashoka Tourist Hotel* and the *Hotel Sablok*. The Ashoka (tel 3607-8) is at Kings Gate, about a km from the centre, and has rooms at Rs 40/50 plus more expensive rooms with air-con.

NASIK (population 200,000)

This interesting little town with its picturesque bathing ghats makes a good stopover on the way from Bombay to Aurangabad. The town is actually about eight km north-west of the station, which is 187 km from Bombay. Nasik stands on the Godavari River, one of the holiest rivers of the Deccan. Like Ujjain, this is the site for the triennial Kumbh Mela which comes here every 12 years. The riverbanks are lined with steps above which stand temples and shrines. Although there are no particularly notable temples in Nasik the Sundar Narayan Temple, to the west of the city, is worth seeing.

Other points of interest in Nasik include the Sita Gupha cave from which Sita was supposed to have been carried off to the island of Lanka by the evil king Rawana, according to the Ramayana. Near the cave, in its grove of large banyan trees, is the fine house of the Panchavati family. Also near here is the temple of Kala Rama or 'black Rama', in a 96-arched enclosure. The Kapaleswar temple is upstream and is said to be the oldest in the town.

Kumbh Mela

Aeons ago the gods and demons, who were constantly at odds, fought a great battle for a *kumbh* or pitcher, drinking the contents of which would ensure immortality. They had combined forces to raise the pitcher from the bottom of the ocean, but once safely in their hands Vishnu grabbed it and ran. After a struggle lasting 12 days the gods eventually defeated the demons and drank the nectar – it's a favourite scene in illustrations of Hindu mythology. During the fight for the pitcher's possession four drops of nectar spilt on the earth – at Allahabad, Hardwar, Nasik and Ujjain. Thus each holds its own Kumbh Mela over a 12-year (for a god's day is a human's year) span – the *mela* span – the mela is held each three years, rotating between the four cities.

Pandu Lena

About eight km south-west of Nasik, close to the Bombay road, are these 21 Hinayana Buddhist caves. They date from around the 1st century BC to the 2nd AD. The most interesting caves are 3, 10 and 18. Cave 3 is a large *vihara* with some interesting sculptures. Cave 10 is also a vihara and almost identical in design to cave 3, although it is much older and finer in its details. It is thought to be nearly as old as the Karla Cave. Cave 18 is a *chaitya* cave and thought to date from the same time as the Karla Cave. It too is well-sculpted and its elaborate facade is particularly noteworthy. Cave 20 is another large vihara, but the other caves are not of great interest.

Trimbak

The source of the Godavari River is here, 33 km from Nasik. From its source high on a steep hill the river virtually dribbles into a bathing tank reputed to perform the usual washing duties upon one's sins. From this tiny start, the Godavari eventually flows right down to the Bay of Bengal, clear across India.

Places to Stay

The *Dwarka Tourist Hotel* on the Eastern Express Highway has rooms at Rs 30/40 plus more expensive suites. Singles/doubles are Rs 40/50 at the *Hotel Siddhartha* on the Nasik-Pune road.

On Trimbak Rd, two km from the centre, the *Green View Hotel* (tel 2231-4) is more expensive at Rs 60/100 for non air-con rooms. There are also air-cooled and air-con rooms. There are many other places to stay in Nasik including a *Tourist Bungalow*.

AURANGABAD (population 175,000)

It's easy to think of Aurangabad simply as a place to stay when visiting the cave temples of Ajanta and Ellora. In fact Aurangabad has a number of attractions in its own right and could easily stand on its own were it not so overshadowed by the famous caves. The city is named after Aurangzeb, but earlier in its history it was known as Khadke.

Information & Orientation

The railway station, tourist office and a

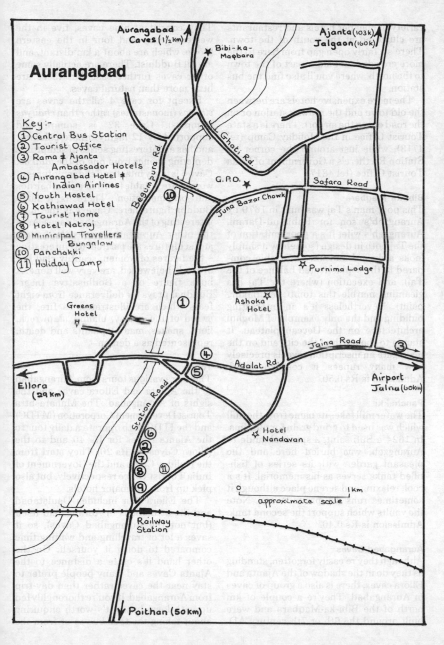

variety of cheaper hotels and restaurants are clustered at the south of the town. There's a fairly open gap from here to the more crowded and older part of the town to the north, where you'll also find the bus station.

The more expensive hotels are between the old town and the railway station or on the road out to the airport. There is a state Tourist Office in the Holiday Camp (tel 4713), while just around the corner on Station Rd there's a Government of India Tourist Office (tel 4817).

Bibi-ka-Maqbara

This poor man's Taj was built in 1679 by Aurangzeb's son for Rabia-ud-Darani, Aurangzeb's wife. It's a poor imitation of the Taj both in design (somehow it simply looks awkward and uncomfortable compared to the sophisticated balance of the Taj), and execution (where the Taj has gleaming marble this tomb has flaking paint). Nevertheless it's an interesting building and the only example of Moghul architecture on the Deccan plateau. It stands to the north of the city and on the main gate an inscription reveals precisely how many rupees it cost to build. Admission is Rs 0.50.

Panchakki

The water mill takes its name from the mill which was used to grind grain for pilgrims. In 1624 a Sufi saint, a spiritual guide to Aurangzeb, was buried here and the pleasant garden with its series of fish-filled tanks serves as his memorial. It's a cool, relaxing and serene place although it sometimes runs dry pre-monsoon. Note the vaults which support the second tank. Admission is Rs 0.40.

Aurangabad Caves

Although they're easily forgotten, standing as they do in the shadow of the Ajanta and Ellora caves, there is also a group of caves in Aurangabad. They're a couple of km north of the Bibi-ka-Maqbara and were built around the 6th or 7th century AD.

They consist of nine caves, five in the western group and four in the eastern group, which are about a km distant, and are all Buddhist. There are actually some other caves further east, but these are little more than natural caves.

Except for cave 4 all the caves are *viharas* (monasteries) rather than *chaityas* (temples). Cave 32 is square and supported by 12 highly ornate columns, and has an interesting series of sculptures depicting scenes from one of the *jatakas*. Cave 6 is fairly intact and the sculptures of women are notable for their exotic hairdos and ornamentation. There is a large Buddha figure here. Cave 7 is the most interesting of the Aurangabad caves. As in the other Aurangabad caves the figures and sculptures are particularly interesting – the figures of women, scantily clad but ornately bejewelled, are very well done. A huge figure of a Bodhisattva (near-Buddha) prays for deliverance from eight fears which are illustrated as fire, the sword of the enemy, chains, shipwreck, lions, snakes, mad elephants and death, represented as a demon.

Tours

There are various tours from Aurangabad to the Ajanta and Ellora caves and the sights of Aurangabad. The Maharashtra Tourist Development Corporation (MTDC) and the ITDC both operate a daily tour to the Ajanta Caves for Rs 40 and to the Ellora Caves for Rs 20. They start from the Holiday Camp and the Government of India Tourist Office respectively, but also pick up from the major hotels.

The Ellora tour includes Daulatabad and the attractions in Aurangabad itself (but not the Aurangabad Caves), so it saves a lot of travelling and waiting time compared to doing it yourself. On the other hand it's quite a distance to the Ajanta Caves and many people prefer to stay near the caves rather than day-trip from Aurangabad. If you're thoroughly fed up with local buses it's worth enquiring about taking the tour bus to or from the caves – much faster than the stop-start-stop-start local bus service. As well as the MTDC and ITDC tours the state transport system also runs daily tours which start from the railway station. At Rs 12 for Ellora and Rs 24 for Ajanta, they are much cheaper than the other tours and from all reports they're quite OK.

Places to Stay – Bottom End

Most of Aurangabad's cheaper hotels are close to the railway station. The notable exception is the excellent *Youth Hostel* which is mid-way between the railway station and the main part of town. Dorm beds cost Rs 8 (Rs 1 less for YHA members) and it's spotlessly clean, has hot and cold water; breakfast and evening meals (Rs 5 for a thali) are available.

A hundred metres or so from the station is the *Government Holiday Camp* where you'll also find the state government Tourist Office. There are several wings in this large accommodation complex with doubles from Rs 35 to Rs 45. Rooms have mosquito nets and bathrooms and they're excellent value.

There are lots of other possibilities around. On the other road out from the station there's the *Kathiawad Hotel* with doubles at Rs 25 and a helpful manager. The *Tourist Home* is Rs 25 a double with your own bathroom – fair to reasonable. The *Hotel Natraj* costs Rs 35 but is not so special. The *Ambrika Lodge* near the railway station has doubles with bathroom for Rs 15, it's good and clean.

Back round the corner towards the Holiday Camp you'll find the *Hotel Ashok* or *Ashok Lodging* which is dirt cheap – Rs 15 a double and with standards to match the price. Or the *Arnanda Lodge* with doubles at Rs 20 (without bath), Rs 25 (with).

Places to Stay – Top End

There are two new 'international standard' hotels situated a couple of km out of town towards the airport. The *Welcomgroup Rama International* (tel 8241-44) has all mod-cons from air-con, restaurants, swimming pool to tennis courts and costs from Rs 350/450 for singles/doubles. The *Ajanta Ambassador* (tel 8211-5) is virtually beside it in Chikalthana and is similarly equipped. Rooms here cost Rs 230 to 300.

The *Aurangabad Ashok* (tel 4521-29) is more centrally located on Dr Rajendra Prasad Marg and costs Rs 250/325 for air-con singles/doubles, or Rs 175/225 for rooms without air-con. Along Station Rd, towards the railway station and a cluster of cheaper hotels, is the *Nandavan* (tel 3571) with singles/doubles at Rs 75/125 and the *Printravel* (tel 2707) at Rs 100/200.

Places to Eat

There are a string of places to eat near the railway station. The *Hotel Guru* has good food, including breakfast cornflakes. The *Holiday Camp* has a dining hall which serves the usual state government menu – when it's open. The *Aurangabad International* has a good Rs 40 buffet, including entertainment.

Getting There

The cave groups at Ajanta and Ellora are off the railway lines and are usually approached from either Aurangabad (Ellora 30 km, Ajanta 106 km) or from Jalgaon (Ajanta 59 km). Jalgaon is on the main broad gauge line from Bombay to Allahabad, but Aurangabad is off the main line and getting there requires a change to metre gauge line at Manmad. On the other hand Aurangabad is the access point from Pune (by road) or Hyderabad (by rail). Plus it has the airport.

Air There's a daily flight connection Bombay-Aurangabad-Udaipur-Delhi and the reverse – it's another popular tourist route flight. Fares to or from Aurangabad are Bombay Rs 239, Delhi Rs 711 and Udaipur Rs 455.

Rail Jalgaon is 420 km from Bombay, the

trip takes about eight hours by rail and costs Rs 127 in 1st class, Rs 32.50 in 2nd. From Jalgaon there are frequent buses to Ajanta and Aurangabad. By rail direct to Aurangabad you change train at Manmad, 261 km from Bombay for the 113-km trip to Aurangabad. Travelling time is about eight hours, plus the time changing trains and the cost is Rs 114 in 1st class, Rs 29 in 2nd. From Hyderabad (Secunderabad), which is on the same metre gauge line as Manmad, it's 510 km, takes 12 hours and costs Rs 146 in 1st class, Rs 37 in 2nd.

Bus There are also bus connections to and from Aurangabad, in particular if you're coming north from Pune or south from Nagpur and Madhya Pradesh.

Getting to the Caves

Aurangabad is a good base for visiting either cave. Unless you're planning on doing a day-tour from Aurangabad to Ajanta, you'll probably find it more convenient to actually stay at Ajanta though. Bus fares from Aurangabad are Rs 4 to Ellora (every half hour), Rs 10 to Ajanta, Rs 14 to Jalgaon, Ajanta-Jalgaon is Rs 7. Most of the Ajanta accommodation is actually at Fardapur, about five km from the caves – Rs 1.50 or so by the reasonably frequent buses. You can negotiate round trip-rates to the caves by taxi – say Rs 150 for Ellora, Rs 400 for Ajanta.

AURANGABAD TO ELLORA
Daulatabad

Situated between Aurangabad and the Ellora Caves is the magnificent hilltop fortress of Daulatabad. The fort is surrounded by five km of sturdy wall, while the central bastion tops a two hundred-metre high hill. In the 14th century the slightly nutty Muhammed Tughlaq, Sultan of Delhi, conceived the crazy plan of not only building himself a new capital, but marching the entire population of Delhi 1100 km south to populate it. His unhappy subjects proceeded to drop dead like flies on this forced march and 17 years later, he turned round and marched them all back to Delhi. The fort remained.

It's worth making the climb to the top for the superb views over the surrounding country. Along the way you'll pass through a complicated series of defences including multiple doorways so that elephants could not charge them, and spike studded doors, just in case they did. A magnificent tower of victory, the Chand Minar, soars 60 metres high. It was built in 1435 and the Qutb Minar in Delhi, five metres higher, is the only loftier victory tower in India. On the other side of the entrance path is a mosque built from the remains of a Jain temple.

Higher up is the blue-tiled Chini Mahal palace where the last king of Golconda was imprisoned for 13 years until his death. Finally you climb the central fort to a huge six-metre cannon, cast from five different metals and with Aurangzeb's name engraved upon it. The final ascent to the top goes through a pitch-black, spiralling tunnel down which the fort's defenders could hurl burning coals at any invaders. Of course, your guide may tell you, the fort was once successfully conquered despite these elaborate precautions – by the simple expedient of bribing the guard at the gate.

The hill the fort stands on was originally known as Devagiri, the 'hill of the gods', but Muhamad Tughlaq renamed it Daulatabad, the 'city of fortune'.

Rauza

Also known as Khuldabad, the 'heavenly abode', this walled-town is only three km from Ellora. This is the Karbala or holy shrine of Deccan Moslems and a number of historical figures are buried here including Aurangzeb, the last great Moghul emperor. Aurangzeb built the battlemented wall around the town which was once an important centre, although today it is little more than a sleepy village.

The emperor's final resting place is a

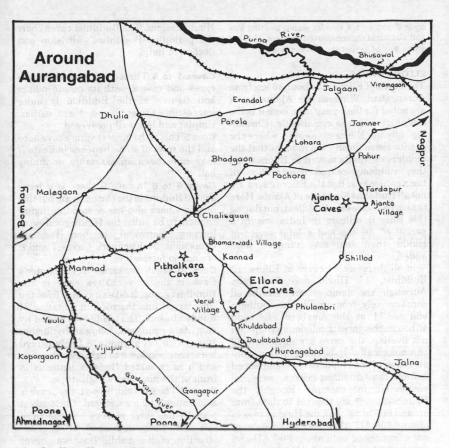

Around Aurangabad

Purna River

Bhusawal

Jalgaon

Viramgaon

Erandol

Dhulia

Parola

Jamner

Lohara

Bhadgaon

Pahur

Pachora

Fardapur

Malegaon

Ajanta Caves

Ajanta Village

Chalisgaon

Bhamarwadi Village

Kannad

Shillod

Manmad

Pithalkara Caves

Ellora Caves

Verul Village

Phulambri

Yeula

Khuldabad

Vijapur

Daulatabad

Aurangabad

Kopargaon

Jalna

Godavari River

Gangapur

Poona

Ahmednagar

Poona

Hyderabad

Nagpur

Bombay

simple affair of bare earth in a courtyard of the Alamgir Dargah in the centre of the city. Aurangzeb's pious austerity extended even to his own tomb for he stipulated that his mausoleum should be paid for with money he earned himself by copying out the Koran. Within the building there is also supposed to be a robe worn by the Prophet Mohammed, it is only shown to the faithful once each year. Another shrine across the road from the Alamgir Dargah is said to contain hairs of the Prophet's beard and also lumps of silver from a tree of solid silver, which miraculously grew here after a saint's death.

Guidebooks

At many places in India there are excellent locally produced guidebooks which you can buy very cheaply at the sites, and which will help to give you a deeper appreciation of what you are seeing. The caves of Ajanta and Ellora are no exception, and both *Aurangabad, Daulatabad, Ellora & Ajanta* by Professor Dr S Siddiqui and *Ajanta, Ellora & Aurangabad Caves – an Appreciation* by T V Pathy are worthwhile investments. The former has good black and white pictures, which help in the identification of the actual sculpture or painting being described. The latter guide has more examples of the delightful way Indians have with English. The author describes a statue as being a 'semi nude dryad with a slender waist, pouting lips and abundant mammalian equipment....' What a fine way of saying she had big boobs.

ELLORA CAVES

The caves of Ellora are about 30 km from Aurangabad. Whereas the Ajanta caves are noted for their paintings, here it is the sculpture which is remarkable. Chronologically the Ellora caves start where the Ajanta caves finish – it's thought that the builders of Ajanta moved to Ellora when they suddenly ceased construction of their earlier site. But the Ellora caves are not all Buddhist like those of Ajanta. Here the earliest caves are Buddhist, but during this time Buddhism in India was in a period of decline and a later series of Hindu, then Jain cave temples were added.

In all there are 34 caves at Ellora: 12 Buddhist, 17 Hindu and five Jain. Although the temples are numbered consecutively, from one at the southern end to 34 at the northern end, and although the various religious groups do not overlap, the caves are not arranged chronologically. It is thought that construction of the Hindu caves commenced before the Buddhist caves were all completed, for example. Roughly the Buddhist caves are thought to date from around 600 to 800 AD, the Hindu caves to around 900 AD, while the Jain caves were not commenced until about 800 AD and were completed by 1000 AD.

The caves are cut into a hillside running north-south. The hill slopes down rather than drops steeply as at Ajanta. Therefore many of the caves have elaborate entrance halls to the main shrines. From south to north, the caves cover about two km.

Buddhist Caves

Apart from cave 10 all the Buddhist caves are *viharas* (monasteries) rather than *chaityas* (temples). They are not as architecturally ambitious as the Hindu caves, although 11 and 12 show signs of attempting to compete with the complex Hindu designs. The Buddhist caves chart the period of Buddhism's division and decline in India.

Caves 1 to 4 These caves are all vihara caves and cave 2, with its ornate pillars and figures of the Buddha, is quite interesting. Caves 3 and 4 are earlier, simpler and less well preserved.

Cave 5 This is the biggest vihara cave here and the rows of stone benches indicate it may have been an assembly or dining hall.

Caves 6 to 8 In cave 6 there is a large seated Buddha in the shrine room, but this ornate vihara also has a standing figure thought to be either the Hindu goddess of learning, Saraswati, or her Buddhist equivalent, Mahamayuri. Caves 7 and 8 are not so interesting.

Cave 10 The Viswakarma or Carpenter's Cave is the only chaitya cave in the Buddhist group. It takes its name from the ribs carved into the roof, in imitation of wooden beams. The temple is entered by steps to a courtyard, followed by further steps to the main temple. A finely-carved horseshoe window lets light into the cave and a huge seated Buddha figure is in front of the nine-metre high stupa.

Cave 11 The Do Thal, 'two-storey', cave is also entered by a courtyard. Curiously it actually has three storeys but the third was not discovered until 1876. Construction of the middle floor was never completed.

Cave 12 The Tin Thal, 'three-storey', cave also has three storeys and is entered through a courtyard. There is a very large seated Buddha and a number of other figures in the cave, and the walls are carved with relief pictures, just like in the Hindu caves.

Hindu Caves

The Hindu caves are the most dramatic and impressive of the Ellora cave temples. In size, design and energy they are in a totally different league to the Buddhist or Jain caves. If calm contemplation des-

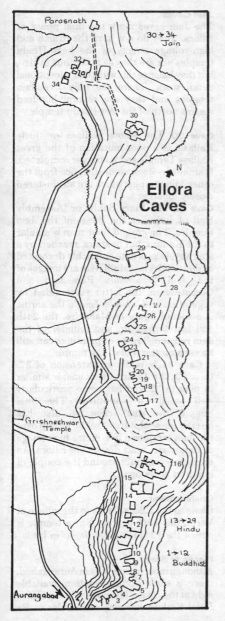

cribed the Buddhist caves, then dynamic energy is the description for the Hindu caves. The sheer size of the Kailasa Temple (cave 16) is overwhelming. It covers twice the area of the Parthenon in Athens and is 1½ times as high. Remember that this whole, gigantic structure was cut out of solid rock! It has been estimated that carving out the Kailasa entailed removing 200,000 tonnes of rock! All these temples were cut from the top down, so that it was never necessary to use any scaffolding – their builders started with the roof and moved down to the floor. It's worth contemplating the skill and planning that must have gone into such a process – there was no way of adding a panel or a pillar if things didn't work out quite as expected.

Cave 14 The first Hindu cave, cave 13, is not impressive but cave 14, the Rava Kakhai, sets the scene for the other Hindu caves. Like all the others it is dedicated to Shiva, and it is Lord Shiva who appears in many of the carvings around the cave. You can see Shiva dancing the *tandava*, a victory dance over the demon Mahisa, or playing chess with his wife Parvati, or defeating the buffalo demon. Parvati also appears in the form of Durga, while Vishnu also makes several appearances including one as Varaha, his boar incarnation. The seven 'mother goddesses' can also be seen, and Ravana makes yet another attempt to shake Kailasa.

Cave 15 The Das Avatara cave is one of the finest at Ellora, and the two-storey temple is reached by a long flight of steps. Inside there is a modern image of Shiva's mount, the bull Nandi. Many of the familiar scenes involving Shiva can be again found here, but you can also see Vishnu resting on a five-hooded serpent or rescuing an elephant from a crocodile. Vishnu also appears as the man-lion, Narsimha, while Shiva emerges from his symbolic lingam and in another panel he marries Parvati.

Cave 16 The mighty Kailasa Temple is the

central attraction at Ellora. Here Indian rock-cut temple architecture reaches its peak. Kailasa is, of course, Shiva's Himalayan home and the Kailasa Temple is a representation of that mountain. The temple consists of a huge courtyard, 81 metres long by 47 metres wide and 33 metres high at the back. In the centre, the main temple rises up and is connected to the outer enclosure by a bridge. Around the enclosure are galleries, while towards the front are two large, stone elephants with two massive stone 'flagstaffs' flanking the Nandi pavilion, which faces the main shrine.

As in the previous two caves, there is a variety of dramatic and finely carved panels, the most impressive being the image of Ravana shaking Kailasa. In the *Ramayana* the demon king Ravana flaunted his strength by lifting up Shiva's mountain home. Unimpressed Lord Shiva simply put his foot down on the top and pressed the mountain and the upstart Ravana back into place. Vishnu also appears along one gallery as Narsimha once again – in this legend he defeats a demon, who could not be killed by man or beast by the simple expedient of becoming a man-lion, neither man nor beast.

Other Caves The other Hindu caves pall beside the majesty of the Kailasa, but several of them are worth at least some study. Cave 21, known as the Ramesvara, has a number of interesting interpretations of scenes also depicted in the earlier temples. Shiva once again marries Parvati and plays dice with her, and the goddesses Ganga and Yamuna once again appear. The figure of Ganga, standing on her crocodile or *makara*, is particularly notable.

The very large Cave 29, the Dumar Lena, is similar in design to the Elephanta Cave at Bombay. It is thought to be a transitionary model as the designers moved from the simpler hollowed-out caves towards the fully developed temples exemplified by the Kailasa.

Jain Caves

The Jain caves mark the final phase of Ellora. They do not have the drama and high-voltage energy of the best Hindu temples nor are they as ambitious in size, but they balance this with their exceptional detail work. There are only five Jain temples and they are several hundred metres north of the last Hindu temple.

Cave 30 The Chota Kailasa or 'little Kailasa' is a poor imitation of the great Kailasa Temple and was never completed. It stands by itself some distance from the other Jain temples which are all clustered closely together.

Cave 32 The Indra Sabha or 'Assembly Hall of Indra' is the finest of the Jain temples. The ground floor plan is similar to the Kailasa, but upstairs, reached by a stairway, is as ornate and richly decorated as downstairs is plain. There are images of the Jain *tirthankars* Parasnath and Gomatesvara, the latter surrounded by vegetation and wildlife. Inside the shrine is a seated figure of Mahavira, the 24th and last *tirthankar*, and founder of the Jain religion. Traces of paintings can still be seen on the roof of the temple.

Cave 31 is really an extension of 32. Cave 33, the Jagannath Sabha, is similar in plan to 32 and has some particularly well preserved sculptures. The final temple, the small cave 34, also has interesting sculptures. On the hilltop over the Jain temples a five-metre high image of Parasnath looks down over Ellora. An enclosure was built around it a couple of hundred years ago.

Grishneshwar

Close to the Ellora Caves in the village of Verul, this 18th century Shiva temple is one of the 12 Shiva *jyotorlingas* in India.

Places to Stay

Although most people stay in Aurangabad, there is some accommodation available right at the caves. The relatively expensive *Hotel Kailasa* has singles/doubles at Rs

40/60 – all rooms with attached bath and it's very close to the caves. There is also a restaurant attached to the hotel and it's cheaper than the other government restaurant here – intended for tour groups.

AJANTA CAVES

The caves of Ajanta pre-date those of Ellora, so if you want to see the caves in chronological order you should visit here first. Although the Ellora caves are easily visited using Aurangabad as a base, it's much easier to stay near the Ajanta caves rather than make a day trip to them. Unlike the Ellora caves, which are Buddhist, Hindu and Jain, the Ajanta caves are all Buddhist and, whereas at Ellora the caves are masterpieces of sculpture, at Ajanta it's the magnificent paintings for which the caves are famous.

The caves, after their abandonment with the move to Ellora and the decline of Buddhism, were gradually forgotten and their rediscovery was dramatic. In 1819 a British hunting party stumbled upon them, and their remote beauty was soon unveiled. Their isolation had contributed to the fine state of preservation in which some of the paintings remain to this day. The caves are cut into the steep face of a deep rock gorge. There are 29 caves in a curve of the gorge, and there is a good viewpoint from across the ravine. The caves date from around 200 BC to 650 AD. They do not follow the chronological order that the Ellora caves generally do; here the oldest caves are mainly in the middle and the newer ones to each end.

The cave paintings initially suffered some deterioration after their rediscovery and some heavy-handed restoration also caused damage. Between 1920 and 1922 two Italian art experts conducted a meticulous restoration process and the paintings have been carefully preserved since that time. Many of the caves are quite dark and without a light the paintings are hard to see – it's worth paying for a lighting ticket which will ensure the cave guards turn the lights on for you. Or you could try tagging along with a tour party, although normally the doors are shut after each party enters a cave.

Five of the caves are *chaityas* or temples while the other 24 are *viharas* or monasteries. Caves 8, 9, 10, 12 and 13 are the older Hinayana caves, while the others are Mahayana. In the simpler, more austere Hinayana school the Buddha was never represented directly – his presence was always alluded to by a symbol such as the footprint or wheel of law. The Ajanta paintings are not, strictly speaking, frescoes but tempera paintings – a difference purely of technique. Although the Ajanta paintings are particularly notable, there are also many interesting sculptures here.

Cave 1 This vihara cave is one of the most recent and also most fully developed of the Ajanta caves. A verandah at the front leads to a large square hall with elaborate carvings and paintings and a huge Buddha statues. Cave 1 is notable both for its sculpture and its paintings. Amongst the interesting sculptures is one of four deer sharing a common head. There are many paintings of women, some remarkably similar to the paintings at Sigiriya in Sri Lanka. Notable paintings include those of the 'black princess' and the 'dying princess'. Other paintings include scenes of the *jatakas* (events from the Buddha's previous lives), and portraits of the Bodhisattvas (near-Buddhas), Padmapani (holding a lotus flower) and Vajrapani.

Cave 2 Also a more recent vihara cave, this one also has a number of important paintings, although some of them are unfortunately damaged. As well as murals, there are paintings on the ceiling. Scenes include a number of jatakas and events connected with the Buddha's birth, including his mother's dream of the six-tusked elephant which heralded the Buddha's conception.

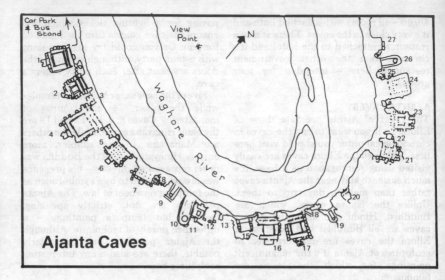

Ajanta Caves

Cave 4 This is the largest vihara cave at Ajanta and is supported by 28 pillars. Although it was never completed, the cave has some fine sculptures including scenes of people fleeing from the 'eight great dangers' to the protection of the Buddha's disciple Avalokitesvara. One of the great dangers is an angry-looking elephant in pursuit of a man and woman. Caves 3, 5 and 8 were never completed.

Cave 6 This is the only two-storey cave at Ajanta, but parts of the lower storey have collapsed. Inside there is a seated figure of the Buddha with an intricately-carved door to the shrine. Upstairs the hall is surrounded by cells with fine paintings on the doorways.

Cave 7 This cave is of unusual design in that the verandah does not lead into a hall with cells down the sides and a shrine room at the rear. Here there are porches before the verandah which leads directly on to the four cells and the elaborately-sculpted shrine. Cave 8 is used solely for the generating equipment which lights the caves.

Cave 9 This is a chaitya cave and one of the

earliest at Ajanta. Although it dates from the Hinayana period, there are two Buddha figures flanking the entrance door which were probably later, Mahayana, additions. Similarly the paintings inside, which are not in excellent condition, show signs of being refurbished at some time in the past. Columns run down both sides of the cave and around the three-metre high *dagoba* at the far end. At the front, there is a horseshoe-shaped window above the entrance and the vaulted roof has traces of wooden ribs.

Cave 10 is thought to be the oldest cave and was also the cave first spotted by the British soldiers who rediscovered Ajanta. It is also the largest chaitya cave and is similar in design to cave 9. The facade of the cave has collapsed and the paintings inside are rather damaged, in some case by graffitists soon after the caves' rediscovery. Caves 11, 12 and 13 are not of great interest – they are all relatively early, either Hinayana or from the early periods of the Mahayana period. Cave 14 is an incompleted vihara, standing above cave 13. Cave 13 is also an early

Mahayana vihara.

Cave 16 Some of Ajanta's finest paintings can be seen in this, one of the later vihara caves. It is thought that cave 16 may have been the original entrance to the entire complex, and there is a very fine view of the river from the front of the cave. Best known of the paintings here is the 'dying princess'. Sundari, wife of Buddha's half-brother Nanda, is said to have expired at the hard news that her husband was renouncing the material life (and her) in order to become a monk. This is one of the finest paintings at Ajanta. Nanda features in several other paintings, including his conversion by Buddha.

Cave 17 This is the cave with the finest paintings at Ajanta. Not only are they in the best condition, they are also the greatest in number and variety. They include beautiful women flying overhead on the roof while carved dwarfs support the pillars. A popular scene shows a woman, surrounded by attendants, applying make-up. In another there is a royal procession, while in another a couple engage in a little private love making. The Buddha returns from his enlightenment to his own home to beg from his wife and astonished son in another panel. A detailed panel tells the story of Prince Simhala's expedition to Ceylon. With his 500 companions he is shipwrecked on an island where ogresses appear as beautiful women, only to seize and devour their victims. Simhala escapes on a flying horse and returns to conquer the island. (A recent report indicates that this cave may be shut for renovations for some time).

Cave 19 The facade of this chaitya cave is remarkably detailed and includes an impressive horseshoe-shaped window as its dominant feature. There are two very fine standing Buddha figures flanking the entrance. Inside this excellent specimen of a chaitya cave there is a tall dagoba with a figure of the Buddha on the front. There are some fine sculptures and paintings in this cave, but one of the most important is outside the cave to the west where there is an image of the Naga king with seven cobra hoods arrayed around his head and his wife, topped by a single cobra, seated beside him.

Caves 20 through 25 are either incomplete or not of great interest, although cave 24 would have been the largest vihara at Ajanta, if finished. You can see how the caves were constructed from this example – long galleries were cut into the rock and then broken across to each other.

Cave 26 The fourth chaitya cave's facade has fallen and almost all trace of its paintings have disappeared. Nevertheless there are some very fine sculptures

Electric spotlight in the darkened caves

far out!

Tour guide & freak • AJANTA CAVES •
MARVELLING AT THE NATURAL WONDERS...

remaining. On the left wall there is a huge figure of the 'reclining Buddha', lying back as he prepares to enter Nirvana. Other scenes include a lengthy depiction of the Buddha's temptation by Mara. In one scene Mara attacks the Buddha with demons, then his beautiful daughters tempt him with more sensual delights. The Buddha's resistance is too strong however, and the final scene shows a glum and dejected-looking Mara having failed to deflect the Buddha from the straight and narrow.

Cave 27 is virtually a vihara connected to the cave 26 chaitya. Caves 28 and 29 are higher up the cliff face and relatively hard to get to.

Places to Stay & Eat

There is a *Forestry Rest House* right by the caves, but it only has two rooms and it's not much good. You can't get in until late afternoon either. Most people stay at Fardapur, five km from the caves, where there is an excellent *Holiday Camp* run by the state government, rooms along the pleasant verandah cost from Rs 30; they are supposed to be cheaper in the June to September off-season. All rooms have attached bathrooms and there is a restaurant at one end.

You can also get simple food from the stalls along the road through Fardapur. Right behind the Holiday Camp is the *Fardapur Travellers Bungalow* with rooms with bathroom for just Rs 10 (in the off-season at least). Rs 15 for rooms with common bath, Rs 30 with own bath in the season. There's no sign or name, just follow the path next to the Holiday Camp. The small village of Fardapur, set back from the road, is worth wandering around.

Getting There

It's about Rs 14 from Aurangabad to Ajanta. The caves are a couple of km off the main road from Aurangabad to Jalgaon and Fardapur is a little further down the main road towards Jalgaon.

There are regular buses between Fardapur and the Ajanta caves, costing a bit less than a rupee – the fare seems to vary with every bus! On from Ajanta (or Fardapur) it's Rs 15 to Edalbad and Rs 26 on from there to Indore, 10 hours in all.

There's a 'cloak room' at the Ajanta caves where you can leave gear, so that it is possible to arrive on a morning bus from Jalgaon, look around the caves, and continue to Aurangabad in the evening. Or vice versa.

NAGPUR (population 950,000)

Situated on the River Nag, from which the town takes its name, Nagpur is the orange-growing capital of India. This was once the capital of the central province, but was later incorporated into Maharashtra. Long ago it was a centre for the aboriginal Gond tribes who remained in power until the early 18th century. Many Gonds still live in this region. Later it went through a series of changes before eventually falling to the British. About 40 km north-east of Nagpur is Ramtek with a number of picturesque 600-year-old temples surmounting the 'Hill of Rama'. In summer this is one of the hottest places in India.

Wardha & Sevagram

About 80 km south-west of Nagpur, near Wardha station, is Sevagram, the 'Village of Service', where Gandhi established his ashram in 1933. For the 15 years from then until India achieved independence this was in some ways the alternative capital of India.

The Centre of Science for Villages (Magan Sangrahalaya) is a museum intended to explain and develop Gandhi's ideals of village level economics. The huts of his ashram are still preserved in Sevagram and at Mahadev Bhawan, beside the Sevagram hospital, there is a photo exhibit of events in the Mahatma's life. Only three km from Sevagram is the ashram of Vinoba Bhave, Gandhi's follower who walked throughout India persuading rich landlords to hand over tracts of land for redistribution to the landless and poor.

Places to Stay

There are all sorts of hotels in Nagpur from cheapies like the *Hotel Shyam* (tel 24073) on Pandit Malviya Rd with rooms at Rs 30/50 to a number of middle price places.

Sometimes the frustrations of trying to do things in India soar far beyond the merely annoying into the realms of grand comedy. In New Delhi I wanted to phone a friend at his office, my hotel room had a phone, but no phone directory. I contacted the hotel operator and asked her to get me A F Fergusson. Twenty minutes passed and I called her back, directory enquiries had been unable to get the number, she would now look it up in the directory herself. After another half hour had passed I realised that this was one of those cases of being unable to do it, but not wanting to lose face by telling you.

I went down to the front desk and asked for a phone directory. We haven't got one. Nor has the girl at the switchboard. Nor has the manager. But you have one in your room. No I don't. Yes you do. I go upstairs again, search the room, look under the bed. No directory. Back downstairs to report there is definitely no directory, how about getting me one. OK. Time passes, is there anywhere else I can find a directory I finally ask. The restaurant upstairs they suggest. Meanwhile the lift operator has disappeared and the steps, of course, are locked.

Eventually I get to the restaurant where my request for a phone directory is met with a table and, 10 minutes later, a menu. No, a p-h-o-n-e d-i-r-e-c-t-o-r-y please! Not even a drink? No. Eventually a phone directory is found. It's in Hindi. Someone comes to my rescue, but although it's easy to look up Kumara or Ashoka or Akbar in a Hindi directory, A F Fergusson proves difficult. Others also come to the rescue and long discussions develop on how to transliterate F or FER. Eventually, they give in and I trek back to the front desk and suggest that if they cannot find me a phone directory, perhaps they could change my room to a room with a phone directory. This amazing suggestion works, one of the half dozen lackeys who are always hanging around hotel front desks in India is despatched to another room, and promptly returns with a phone directory. Ten seconds later I've looked the number up. Total time to make one call about an hour and a half. I could have walked the km or two to his office in ten minutes.

Tony Wheeler

Goa

Population: 9 million*
Area: 3813 square km*
Main languages: Marathi, Konkan &
Gujarati

*including Daman & Diu

The small former Portuguese enclave of
Goa is still one of India's most touristically
important places. It combines old Portuguese architecture with a Portuguese
flavour to the lifestyle which somehow
manages to exist even 20 years after India
took Goa over. Most important, to many
travellers, there are the superb beaches
and the 'travellers' scene' which so many
of them offer. Officially Goa is governed
together with two other Portuguese
coastal enclaves, Daman and Diu, which
were taken over at the same time. The
latter two are both in the state of Gujarat
and are covered in the Gujarat section of
this book.

Goa has a long history stretching back
to the 3rd century BC when it formed part
of the Mauryan Empire. It was later ruled
by the Satavahanas of Kolhapur at the
beginning of the Christian era and
eventually passed to the Chalukyans of
Badami who controlled it from 580 to 750
AD. Over the next few centuries it was
ruled successively by the Shilharas, the
Kadambas and the Chalukyans of Kalyani.
The Kadambas are credited with constructing the first settlement on the site of
Old Goa in the middle of the 11th century
when it was called Thorlem Gorem.

Goa fell to the Moslems for the first time
in 1312, but they were forced to evacuate
it in 1370 by Harihara I of the Vijayanagar
Empire whose capital was at Hampi in
Karnataka state. The Vijayanagar rulers
held on to Goa for nearly 100 years and
during this time its harbours were
important as places where Arabian horses
were landed on their way to Hampi to
strengthen the Vijayanagar cavalry. In
1469, however, Goa was reconquered, this
time by the Bahmani Sultans of Gulbarga.
When this dynasty broke up the area
passed to the Adil Shahis of Bijapur who
made Goa Velhaa their second capital.
The present Secretariat building in
Panjim is the former palace of Adil Shah,
later taken over by the Portuguese
Viceroys as their official residence.

The Portuguese arrived in Goa in 1510
under the command of Afonso de
Albuquerque after having been unable to
secure a base on the Malabar coast further
south due to opposition from the Zamorin
of Calicut and stiff competition from the
Turks who, at that time, controlled the
trade routes across the Indian Ocean.
Blessed as it was by natural harbours and
wide rivers, Goa was the ideal base for the
seafaring Portuguese, bent on their quest
for control of the spice route from the east
and the spread of Christianity. For a while,
their control was limited to a small area
around Old Goa but by the middle of the
16th century they had expanded to
include the provinces of Bardez and

Salcete.

Goa reached its present size in the 18th century as a result of further annexations, first in 1763 when the provinces of Ponda, Sanguem, Quepem and Canacona were added and later in 1788 when Pednem, Bicholim and Satari were added. The Marathas nearly vanquished the Portuguese in the late 18th century and there was a brief occupation by the British during the time of the Napoleonic Wars in Europe. It was not until 1961, when India ejected the Portuguese in a near bloodless operation, that the Portuguese finally disappeared from the sub-continent. The other enclaves of Daman and Diu were also taken over at the same time. Despite the 20 intervening years of Indian rule, Goa still maintains its distinctively Portuguese flavour and easy-going ways.

Goan Food

Although food in Goa is much like anywhere else in India there are a number of local specialties including the popular pork *vindaloo*. Other local pork specialties include the Goan sausage *chourisso*, and the pig's liver dish known as *sarpotel*. Seafood of all types is, of course, plentiful and fresh in Goa. There are the usual travellers' menu items at the beach restaurants. Although the ready availability of alcohol is a contrast to some other parts of India the Goans also brew their local *feni* spirits, made from coconut or cashews.

PANJIM (PANAJI)

Panjim is one of India's smallest and pleasantest state capitals. Situated on the south bank of the wide Mandovi River, it became the capital of Goa in 1843, though the Portuguese Viceroys had shifted their residence from the outskirts of Old Goa to the former palace of Adil Shah at Panjim as early as 1759. The town has preserved its Portuguese heritage remarkably well and parts of it still consist of narrow winding streets, old houses with overhanging balconies, red-tiled roofs and numerous small bars and cafes. Signs in Portuguese over shops, cafes and administrative buildings are still visible in many places.

People are friendly and the atmosphere is easy-going. The main attraction for travellers is, of course, Old Goa, nine km east of Panjim and the former capital founded by Alfonso de Albuquerque in 1510. Nevertheless, Panjim, apart from the services and facilities which it offers, is well worth a visit for its own sake.

Panjim's main attraction is the narrow winding streets, small cafes and bars and the occasional old stone buildings dating from the 16th and 17th centuries. Its 'sights' are few, but among those worth visiting are the old **Church of the Immaculate Conception** built on the hillside at one end of the Municipal Gardens and the **Mahalaxmi Temple**. If you're staying in Panjim rather than on the beaches of Goa, then the nearest beach to Panjim is at Miramar, three km along the road to Dona Paula.

Information & Orientation

The town has a wide range of hotels, many excellent restaurants, old churches and monuments and is well served by transport facilities connecting it to the rest of India. It not only has its own State Tourist Office but also tourist offices for the states of Karnataka and Andhra Pradesh and an Indian Railways Out-Booking Office (the railhead is at Vasco da Gama on the other side of the Zuari River). The airport is at Dabolim near Vasco.

Tourist Offices The Tourist Office, Tourist Home (a kind of Youth Hostel with dorm-type accommodation) and the South Central Railway Out-Agency Booking Office are all in a new complex between the bus stand and Ourem creek – turn left when you get to the bridge which leads into town (it's signposted).

There are also Tourist Offices for Andhra Pradesh (Rua de Ourem); Karna-

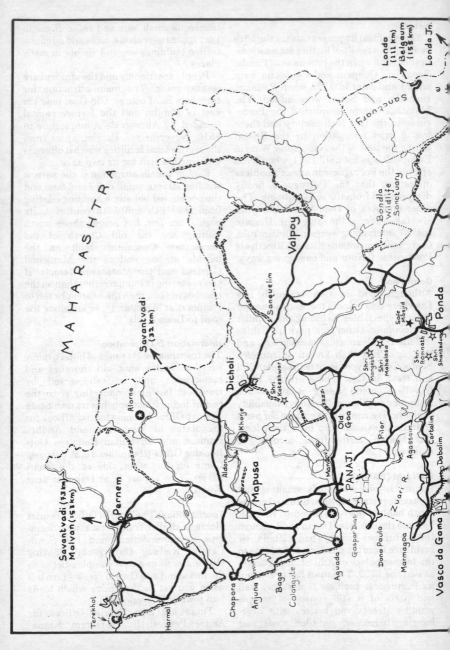

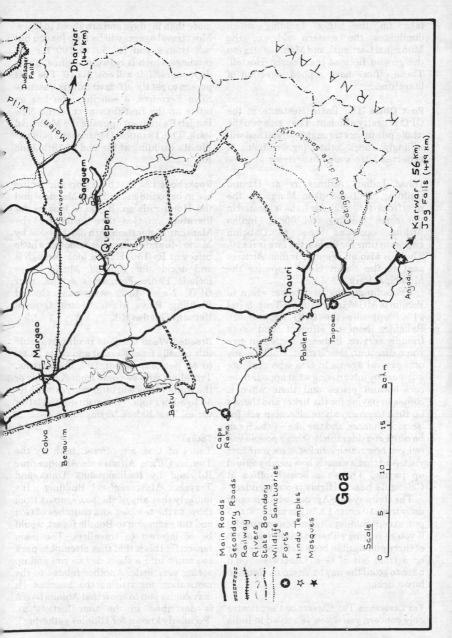

taka (in the office building which dominates the eastern side of the Municipal Gardens), and Maharashtra (on the ground floor of the Tourist Hostel). These offices have a good selection of literature.

Post Office The Poste Restante at the GPO is pretty efficient. They give you the whole pile to sort through yourself and will willingly check other pigeon holes if expected letters are not arriving.

Travel Indian Airlines is at Dempo Building, D Bandodkar Marg, on the riverfront (tel 3822). Air India is located in the same building (tel 3081). Indian Airlines operates buses to Dabolim airport in time for flights, the fare is Rs 10. There is also an agent of Indian Airlines next to the Safari Hotel opposite the Municipal Park.

Undoubtedly the best travel agent in Panjim is MGM International Travels (tel 2150) opposite the GPO (first floor). Reliable, honest, efficient and very friendly service. If these people can give you a discount, they'll do it. Unlike many other travel agents in Goa who generate business by advertising what appear to be rock-bottom prices and then, when it comes to paying for the ticket and there's no time to go anywhere else, slap you for 'service charges' and the like – (which can be quite considerable!) – these people will tell you how much a ticket is on your first visit. And that's exactly how much you end up paying. There's a branch office at Calangute beach. Highly recommended.

The Railway Out-Agency, which is open daily from 10 am to 12.30 pm and 2.30 to 5 pm, except Sundays, is particularly useful if you're staying either in Panjim or north of there and want to book a seat or sleeper on a train out of Goa. Otherwise you'd have to go all the way to Vasco da Gama to buy a ticket.

Tax Clearance Tax Clearance Certificates only concern you if you've stayed in India

more than 90 days and are about to leave. Most travel agents will fix it up for you but will charge you Rs 50 to 100 for the privilege which is ridiculous since, if you do it yourself, it will cost Rs 10. The best person to get the affidavit from is Vasco de Silva Ferreirra, a solicitor who has an office on the first floor next to the New Punjab Restaurant opposite the Municipal Park. The Taxation Department is in the Shanta Building at the end of 18th June Rd.

Bookshops The best bookstores in Panjim are to be found at the Hotel Mandovi and the Hotel Fidalgo. If you're looking for literature on Goa then *Inside Goa* by Manshar Mulgastion with illustrations by Mario Miranda is excellent, though a little pricey at Rs 150. Have a look through it and decide for yourself. Music stores include Pedro Fernandes & Cia, near GPO; New Music Art, near Govind Building; Paiva Music Centre, General Bernard Guedes Rd.

Dreaded Weed Ganja is readily available (it's usually from Kerala) and costs Rs 60 to 80 per *tola* (about 10 gm) for resin. Travellers who've come from Kashmir or the Kulu Valley will offer you resin for Rs 40 to 50 per tola. The quality of the latter varies. Test before buying.

Tours
Tours of Goa are offered both by the Tourist Office, Alfonso de Albuquerque Rd, and by Radhakrishna Tours and Travels, Mascarenhas Building. It's unlikely that any of the tours, apart from those to the temples and churches of Goa and the excursion to Bondla forest, would be of interest to travellers. The main reason for this is that they attempt to pack too much into a short day so you end up seeing very little. Another relates to the motivation for visiting the beaches. (It may amuse you to know that Anjuna beach is described in the tour leaflets as, 'Popularly known for Hippies gathering').

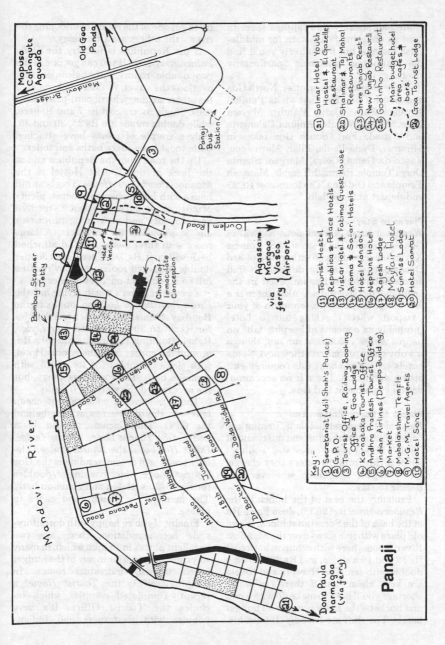

Panaji

Key:-
1. Secretariat (Adil Shah's Palace)
2. G.P.O.
3. Tourist Office, Railway Booking Office ≠ Goa Lodge
4. Ka-nataka Tourist Office
5. Andhra Pradesh Tourist Office
6. Indian Airlines (Dempo Building)
7. Market
8. Mahalaxshmi Temple
9. M.G.M. Travel Agents
10. Hotel Sona
11. Tourist Hostel
12. Republica ≠ Palace Hotels
13. Vistar Hotel ≠ Fabima Guest House
14. Aroma ≠ Safari Hotels
15. Hotel Mandovi
16. Neptune Hotel
17. Rajesh Lodge
18. Mayfair Hotel
19. Sunrise Lodge
20. Hotel Samrat
21. Solmar Hotel, Youth Hostel ≠ El Gazelle Restaurant
22. Shalimar ≠ Taj Mahal Restaurants
23. Shere Punjab Rest.
24. New Punjab Restaurant
25. Godinho Restaurant
26. Main budget hotel area, cafes, bars
27. Goa Tourist Lodge

Mapusa
Calangute
Aguada

Old Goa
Ponda

Mandovi Bridge

Panaji Bus Station

Ouem Road

Agassim
Margao
Vasco
Airport
via ferry

Church of Immaculate Conception

Bombay Steamer Jetty

Mandovi River

Secretariat Road
Pissurlem Col.
Rood
June Road
Altua Vee ave
Dr. Dada Vaidya Rd.
18th June Road
Dr. Bocho
Ovel Pestana Road
Alfonso
Dr. Dada Vaidya Rd.

Dona Paula
Marmagoa
(via ferry)

Nude and scantily-clad hippies seem to hold an enduring fascination for middle-class Indians, but it's unlikely you'll find the supposed spectacle particularly rivetting.

There are two tours on offer: North Goa and South Goa. The first visits Panjim, Arvalem Falls, Datta Mandir, Mayem Lake, Mapusa, Vagator, Anjuna, Calangute and Aguada Fort. South Goa takes in Miramar, Dona Paula, Pilar, Marmagoa, Vasco da Gama, Colva, Margao, Shanta Durga Temple, Ramnath Temple, Mangesh Temple and Old Goa. The tours cost Rs 25 and depart at 9 am daily.

Places to Stay

Whenever there is a religious festival in Goa – especially the festival of St Francis Xavier (several days on either side of 3rd December) – it can be difficult to find accommodation in Panjim, even in the small inexpensive lodges. Also, there is a law which demands presentation of your passport when checking into a hotel (probably as a means of keeping tabs on people whose visas have run out, though it's obviously of limited efficiency). Some hotels are strict about this requirement; others don't care. There is no accommodation available at Old Goa.

Places to Stay – Bottom End

Most of the budget hotels in Panjim are very definitely at the dim and dusty end of 'basic', but in many cases you wouldn't suspect this from the prices they charge. Don't expect too much wherever you decide to stay.

Probably the best of the bunch is the *Republica Hotel* (tel 2638), Jose Falca Rd at the back of the Secretariat block. It's an old place with fine views over the Mandovi River. Rooms here with common bath cost Rs 12 and 15 a single, and Rs 20 and 25 a double with fan. The showers and toilets are kept clean, but if there's a water shortage you'll have to make do with a cup and bucket – the same goes for all budget hotels. The staff are friendly. If possible,

try to get one of the rooms overlooking the river – the others are a bit dingy.

If the Republica is full, try the *Hotel Palace*, next door. If you can get one of the two double rooms with balconies that overlook the street, you're in luck; most of the others are dingy, hardboard-partitioned cells. Single rooms cost Rs 7 and 10 here, while double rooms are Rs 25, 30 and 35. Only a couple of rooms have attached bath; most have share baths and toilets.

Up the road from the Republica and at the back of the Tourist Hostel is the *Mandovi Pearl Guest House*. This is an old house with large, spacious rooms, plenty of mosquitoes and no nets, but it's run by a very friendly and easy-going proprietor and is popular with travellers. A large room with three beds, fan and attached bath will cost Rs 70. There are cheaper double and single rooms, but they're often full so if you want one, get here early.

Two other places worth trying are the *Kiran Boarding & Lodging*, opposite the Bombay steamer jetty, which has doubles for Rs 25 to 30; and the *Glemar Lodge*, Rebelo Building, D Antao de Noronha Rd, around the corner from the Aroma Hotel, with singles/doubles for Rs 15/25 with common bath. The rooms are dingy, but it's secure and the staff are friendly.

There is a whole collection of cheap hotels in the old, narrow streets behind the GPO. They include the *La Vista Lodge, Goa Tourist Lodge, Deluxe Lodge, Daluz Hotel* and the *Bharat Lodge*. The only one worth recommending is the Goa Tourist Lodge, which has singles/doubles for Rs 15/20 with fan and common bath. The manager is friendly and eager to please.

Finally, if you're happy with dormitory-style accommodation, there are two excellent places in Panjim which, in many ways, are far superior to any of the budget hotels offering individual rooms. In Panjim itself is the *Tourist Home*, a recently-completed complex which includes the Tourist Office. It's very popular with westerners and Indians alike, and costs Rs 8 per bed per night. There is a restaurant and bar.

Out at Miramar Beach is the *Youth Hostel* (tel 5433), which not only has dormitory accommodation for Rs 8 per night, but also one or two double rooms with attached bath for Rs 30 – there are no single rooms. Officially the hostel is closed between 1 pm and 4 pm, but they're not strict about it. The hostel has a superb location right next to the beach. Its only drawback is the distance from the centre of town if you have things to do there, but there are regular buses which will get you there within five minutes.

Places to Stay – Middle

The *Tourist Hostel* (tel 2303) is the bargain among the mid-range hotels. The only trouble is, it's often booked solid for up to eight weeks in advance! It's clean, cheap, semi-western in style and on the ground floor there's the Maharashtra State Tourist Office and a whole complex of shops selling photographic supplies, postcards and souvenirs. Rooms here cost Rs 30 a single and Rs 60 a double, both with attached bathrooms. There is a restaurant on the first floor.

The next best place to try is the *Hotel Aroma* (tel 3519), Cunha Rivara Rd, facing the Municipal Gardens. In the last edition we included this hotel in the top end section, but it doesn't really belong there any more as they appear to have invested all their money in the two restaurants – Indian and Chinese – and none in room maintenance. Nevertheless, it's the best of the mid-range places. Rooms cost Rs 35 for the solitary single, Rs 70 for a double. Most of the rooms have attached bath with hot water in the mornings and evenings. It's clean, friendly, very popular and highly recommended.

If the Aroma's full, or you want something cheaper, the *Safari Hotel*, two doors up, is worth trying. It's only a small place and often full, but it does have rooms for just Rs 20/30. It isn't really any better than a lot of bottom end hotels.

Another hotel which just squeezes into this bracket, not on account of its standards, but because of its prices which are unjustifiably high, is the *Hotel Mandovi Palace*, Rua de Ourem, just up from the Hotel Sona. It's an old building with its own rustic restaurant and bar, and offers doubles for Rs 40 to 50. There are no singles.

Out at Miramar Beach there is another selection of mid-range hotels. At the top end of the range is the *Hotel Mayur* (tel 3174), off Bandodkar Marg. This is a relatively small place with a homely atmoshpere, restaurant and bar, quiet surroundings and only two minutes' walk from the beach. Double rooms – no singles – cost Rs 60 to 80 with attached bath and hot and cold running water. There are no service charges. Cheaper is the rustic *Belvila Lodge* (tel 364)) right on the main road opposite the turn-off for the Youth Hostel. Good, clean rooms here cost Rs 15 a single without bath, and Rs 30 and 40 a double with attached bath.

Places to Stay – Top End

The most expensive hotel in Panjim, and the one where all the rich Indians from Bombay book in, is the *Hotel Fidalgo* (tel 3023, 3025), 18th June Rd. Rooms here cost Rs 275/375 with central air-conditioning, bathroom and all the facilities you would expect in a hotel of this nature. The hotel has its own restaurant – Indian, Chinese and continental food – bar and an excellent bookshop. It's certainly the most expensive, but I found it somewhat soulless, and there always seems to be hordes of spoilt brats rampaging around the place.

The *Mayfair Hotel* (tel 5952, 5772), Dr Dada Vaidya Rd, has heaps more character, and this is the one I'd give top rating to. In the high season – October to February inclusive – rooms with balcony cost Rs 70/95 non air-con, and rooms without balconies cost Rs 65/90 non air-con and Rs 90/120 air-con. In the shoulder season – March to June inclusive – rooms with balcony cost Rs 55/75 non air-con, and rooms without balcony cost Rs 50/70 non air-con or Rs 85/100 air-con. In the low season – July to September inclusive – rooms cost Rs 60/70 with air-con and Rs 35/50 without air-con. All the rooms have their own bath with hot and cold water, and the hotel has its own restaurant – Goan, continental, Indian vegetarian and non-vegetarian – and bar.

Other hotels in the upper end of this bracket include the *Hotel Mandovi* (tel 4481), Bandodkar Marg overlooking the Mandovi River, which has singles Rs 110 to 115, doubles for Rs 200 to 250. All the rooms are air-conditioned and have their own bath with hot and cold water. There is a roof garden, two restaurants – Indian, Chinese, western – a bar, money-changing facilities and an excellent bookshop.

Cheaper is the *Hotel Sona* (tel 4426), Rua de Ourem, which has singles for Rs 65, doubles for Rs 75 (back rooms) and Rs 85 (front rooms), and triples for Rs 110. All the rooms have attached bath with hot and cold water. The hotel has its own restaurant and bar.

Away from the centre of town on the way to Miramar Beach and at Miramar Beach itself, there are one or two other top end hotels. Opposite the Children's Park off Bandodkar Marg is the *Hotel Campal* (tel 4230-3), which has rooms at Rs 70/90 or Rs 100/150 with air-con. There is a roof garden, restaurant – vegetarian and non-vegetarian – and car rental facility. At Vainguinim Beach, Dona Paulo, the *Welcomgroup Cidade-de-Goa* has rooms at Rs 450 a swimming pool and other mod-cons.

Places to Eat

If you're looking for a splurge without burning a hole in your pocket, try the *Godinho*, which offers a good range of Goan and other Indian non-vegetarian dishes. It's a new place with a very pleasant atmosphere, and is about as close as you'll get to anything with a Portuguese flavour in the whole of Panjim.

Lunchtime is probably the best time for food as most of the evening clientele come here to talk over bottles of beer (beer is pleasantly cheap in Goa) or spirits, not to eat. It's highly recommended. Also recommended are the restaurants in the *Hotel Aroma* on the municipal gardens.

The *New Punjab Restaurant*, on the same side of the Municipal Gardens as the Hotel Aroma, serves excellent Punjabi food and is not only very popular, but also cheap. Tandoori specialities are naturally more expensive (average Rs 20 to 30). The restaurant is open between 12 noon and 3 pm and again between 7 pm and 11 pm. Closed on Saturdays.

The *Hotel Venite* is in the narrow streets behind the GPO (see map for location). This is a beautiful old place on the first floor with polished wood floor and balconies overlooking the street and bags of atmosphere. It has a limited menu, but it's a great place to sit and have a drink. It's also friendly and even has a sound system. *Jesmal Cafe* has excellent milkshakes (particularly mango). Good thalis at the *Tourist Hostel* for Rs 5.50.

Other good restaurants if you're looking for a minor splurge are the *Shere Punjab Restaurant* on 18th June Rd and the *Shalimar* and *Taj Mahal Restaurants* situated next to each other on Afonso de Albuquerque Road. The former is a non-vegetarian restaurant and the latter a vegetarian restaurant. All three restaurants have prices similar to those of the New Punjab Restaurant. The *Goenchin* is an excellent, but expensive, new Chinese restaurant just off Dr Dada Vaidya Rd, the *A Pasteria* cake shop is on the corner. If you're looking for a night out rather than just a meal, take a taxi to the *El Gazelle Restaurant* at Miramar but be prepared to spend some money! It's an elegant Portuguese restaurant set in a flower-drenched garden.

Getting There

Air The airport is at Dabolim near Vasco da Gama. Indian Airlines runs special buses from their office in the Dempo Building, Panjim, to the airport. The buses cost Rs 20 per person which is pretty absurd when you can take a whole taxi for Rs 20. There is a daily Airbus to and from Bombay plus a 737 six days a week. The fare is Rs 323. There is also a daily flight Belgaum-Dabolim-Bangalore and reverse. Fares are Belgaum Rs 96 and Bangalore Rs 370. Indian Airlines' office here is a complete chaotic shambles.

Rail The railhead in Goa is at Vasco da Gama (it actually continues on to Marmagoa but very few of the main trains start from there). See the Getting Around section for details of getting to Vasco from Panjim. The other main station in Goa is at Margao. Seats and sleepers on the trains can be booked at Vasco, Margao or at the South Central Out-Agency Booking Office (part of the Tourist Office) in Panjim. If you're staying north of Panjim and planning on leaving by train, this Out-Agency office saves you the trouble of having to go to Vasco.

Apart from the main trains from Vasco and Margao there are also some local trains which ply between Kolamb (another Goan town further up the line) and Marmagoa, but they're of little interest to travellers.

Bangalore To Bangalore the trip takes from 20½ hours to 25 hours depending on the train you take. Fastest is the Vasco Miraj 'Mandovi Express' then the Miraj-Bangalore 'Karnataka Express'. There are now some through carriages from Margao so you do not have to change trains at Londa. Fares for the 689 km trip are Rs 186 in 1st class, Rs 48 in 2nd class.

New Delhi Getting to New Delhi from Goa involves several changes of train. Fastest is to take the 205 (Vasco-Miraj 'Gomantak Express'), 308 (Miraj-Bombay 'Konya Express'), 177 (Poona-Jammu Tawi 'Jheelam Express'). Total journey time is 46½ hours. The total trip is about 2400 km

with fares of about Rs 484 in 1st class, Rs 123 in 2nd.

Bombay Trains to Bombay involve a change at Miraj and take from 21 to 25 hours for the 788 km trip. Fares are Rs 208 in 1st, Rs 53 in 2nd.

You can book 2nd class sleeping berths on any of these routes at the South Central Out-Agency Booking Office in Panjim. You cannot book 1st class here. This must be booked either at Vasco or Margao, where you can also book 2nd class. The Out-Agency office is open daily except Sundays from 10 am to 12.30 pm and from 2.30 to 5 pm. On public holidays it's open from 9.30 am to 12.30 pm only.

Long Distance Buses There are several private companies which offer 'super luxury' buses to places like Bombay and Bangalore. Most of them are also video coaches and have night departure times. The only drawback to these coaches – as one exhausted traveller I bumped into related it – was that if you're placed at the front of the coach and it's a lousy film, you can't sleep. On the other hand, if you're at the back, it's just as difficult to sleep because the roads are rough, and you don't even have the compensation of being able to see/hear the video, if it happens to be a good one. It's up to you. These companies have offices in Panjim, Mapusa and Margao. The coach to Bombay costs Rs 110 to 115 depending on the company. The trip takes about 16 hours.

Slightly cheaper buses are operated by the Karnataka State Road Transport Corporation, the Maharashtra State Road Transport Corporation and Goa's own bus company, Kadamba Transport Company. The Karnataka and Maharasthra offices are next to each other on the Mandovi River waterfront, close to the Bombay steamer jetty. Kadamba buses can be booked at the long distance part of the Panaji bus station.

If you're heading down into Karnataka,

you might well be interested in the buses to Londa (from where you can get a direct railway carriage to Mysore every day), Hubli (a railway junction on the main Bombay-Bangalore line, where you can also get trains to Gadag for both Bijapur/Badami and Hospet/Hampi) and Belgaum. A bus to Hubli takes seven hours and costs Rs 18.50, from there to Hospet is Rs 16 and another 4½ hours. There's a daily bus to Mysore for Rs 60, takes 16 hours. Mangalore is an 11 hour trip costing Rs 65 in a luxury bus, Rs 45 in a KSRTC bus.

Goa-Bombay Steamer The boat departs daily at 9.45 am except on Wednesdays from Panjim and Tuesdays from Bombay. The service is suspended during the monsoon and at other times when the weather is very rough. The steamer is a far pleasanter way of getting to or from Bombay than the train, and highly recommended by many travellers. If you're travelling in deck class, make sure you get to the quay about an hour before departure as when the gates are opened it's the usual panic. If you're right at the back, and therefore one of the last on, you'll have a very limited choice about where to sleep. An alternative plan is to buy a deck cloth and get a coolie to rush on board and use it to claim a patch of deck for you. The trip takes 22 hours.

Fares are as follows: Owner's Cabin (two-berth cabin, shower and toilet) Rs 300; De-luxe A (four-berth cabin, shower and toilet) Rs 260; De-luxe B (four-berth cabin) Rs 235; 1st class (20-berth cabin) Rs 220; Upper Deck (deck space for 290) Rs 72; lower deck (deck space for 700) Rs 48. Bedding is available for hire in both deck classes for Rs 15. In theory, there's nothing to stop you paying for Lower Deck and then going to sleep in Upper Deck. The front and back of the upper deck is actually classified as lower deck so that's a good place for lower deck ticket holders to head for. Lunch and dinner are available on board – fairly good food at reasonable prices (vegetarian and non-vegetarian).

The booking office in Panjim is V S Dempo & Co (tel 3842), opposite the steamer jetty in Panjim. You can book any number of days ahead for 1st class and above, but only six days ahead for deck class. Advance bookings can be made daily except Wednesdays from 10 am to 12.30 pm (cabin classes only), and from 2.30 pm to 5 pm (cabin classes and deck class). If you want a ticket on the day of sailing these go on sale at 8 am. Cabin classes are usually booked out several weeks in advance.

The most convenient place to buy tickets in Bombay is at the Maharashtra Tourist Development Corporation Offices, The Hutments, Madame Cama Rd, daily except Mondays between 11 am and 3 pm. You can also buy them from Mogul Lines, 16 Bank St near the Horniman Circle, and at New Ferry Wharf, Mallet Bunder (tel 334042), opposite Wadi Bunder Railway Goods Depot, Gate No 11.

Getting Around

Buses If you've done much travelling by bus in Karantaka, Kerala or Tamil Nadu for instance, you're in for a pleasant surprise in Goa. Most of the buses here are privately owned, and they're pretty good as far as maintenance and standards of comfort go. There's not the same mad scramble for seats as there is in other states, and people will make room for you instead of trying to squeeze you out. There is no timetable of buses, but services to most places in Goa are frequent. The conductors of the buses holler out their destinations and buses go when approximately full. Some of the more popular routes you're likely to use include:

Panjim-Vasco da Gama/Marmagoa There are two ways of getting there. You can either go via the ferry from Dona Paula to Marmagoa or by road via Agassaim and Cortalim. Unless you know there will be a ferry waiting for you on arrival at Dona Paula, the route via Agassaim and

Cortalim is the quicker of the two. Either way it will cost about Rs 3 to 4 and take about one hour – the exact cost depends on the sort of bus you take.

Panjim-Margao You can get to Margao either via Agassaim/Cortalim or Ponda. The former is the more direct route and will take about 1½ hours. It's Rs 3 to 4 depending on what type of bus you take. Via Ponda it will take about an hour longer and cost a little more.

Panjim-Old Goa To get here you can take one of the frequent buses going straight to Old Goa or any bus going to Ponda. The journey costs Rs 0.90 and takes 20 to 30 minutes.

Panjim-Calangute There is a frequent service thoughout the day and evening. The journey takes about 35 to 45 minutes and costs Rs 1.30.

Panjim-Mapusa Buses cost Rs 1 and take about 25 minutes. Frequent service. There are also three buses daily direct to Chapora Village which go via Mapusa. Note that Mapusa is pronounced 'Mapsa', and this is what the conductors shout.

Local Ferries One of the joys of travelling around Goa are the ferries across the many rivers in this small state. Almost without exception they are combined passenger/car ferries. The main ferries are:

Dona Paula-Marmagoa This ferry runs between September and May only. There are regular crossings, but they are somewhat infrequent and at certain times of the day you could find yourself waiting about two hours for a ferry. The crossing takes 30 to 45 minutes and costs Rs 1.20. Buses wait on either side for the arrival of boats. This is a passenger ferry only but it's the best way of getting from Panaji to Vasco da Gama.

Old Goa-Piedade Ferries every 30 minutes between 7.15 am and 9 pm.

Other Other ferries include: Aldona-Corjuem; Colvale-Macasana; Pomburpa-Chorao; Ribander-Chorao; Siolim-Chopdem, and St Estevam-Tonca. There are also launches from the central jetty in Panjim to Aldona (once daily), Britona (twice daily), Naroa (twice daily) and Verem.

Bicycles It's quite easy to hire bicycles (Rs 4 to 5) at most of the major Goan towns or beaches. You can also hire motorcycles (if you've ever wanted to try a Rajdoot) from around Rs 50 or Rs 60.

OLD GOA (Goa Velha)
Even before the arrival of the Portuguese, Old Goa was a thriving and prosperous city and the second capital of the Adil Shahi dynasty of Bijapur. At that time it was surrounded by fort walls, towers and a moat, and contained many temples, mosques as well as the large palace of Adil Shah. Today, nothing of these former structures remain except a fragment of the gateway to the palace. What is there dates from the Portuguese period.

Under the Portuguese the city grew rapidly in size and splendour eventually coming to rival Lisbon itself, despite an epidemic in 1543 which wiped out a large percentage of the population. Many huge churches, monasteries and convents were erected by the various religious orders which came to Goa under royal mandates, the Franciscans being the first to arrive. Old Goa's splendour was short lived, however, as by the end of the 16th century Portuguese supremacy on the seas had been replaced by that of the British, Dutch and French. The city's decline was accelerated by the activities of the Inquisition and a devastating epidemic which struck the population in 1635. Indeed had not the Portuguese been in treaty relations with the British it is probable that Goa would either have passed to the Dutch or been absorbed into British India.

The city muddled on into the early 19th century as the administrative capital of Portugal's eastern empire (Goa, Daman and Diu in India; Timor in Indonesia, and

Macau in China) but, following the transfer of the seat of power to Panjim in 1843 and repressive religious orders in 1835, the city was deserted. Today, it's a small village surrounded by the huge churches and convents which were built during its heyday, and which attract visitors from many parts of the world. Some of them remain in active use, though others have become museums maintained by the Archaeological Survey of India – a maintenance very necessary since unless the lime plaster which protects the laterite structure is renewed frequently, the monsoons soon reduce such buildings to ruin.

Information

The Archaeological Survey of India publishes an excellent booklet about the monuments at Old Goa which is well worth buying for background material and further detail. It's entitled, *Old Goa* by S Rajagopalan (New Delhi 1975). The booklet costs Rs 3.25 from the Archeological Museum at Old Goa.

Se Cathedral

The largest of the churches at Old Goa, the Se Cathedral was begun in 1562 during the reign of King Dom Sebastiao (1557-78) and substantially completed by 1619, though the altars were not finished until 1652. The cathedral was built for the Dominicans and paid for by the Royal Treasury out of the proceeds of the sale of the Crown's property.

Architecturally, the building is Portuguese-Gothic in style with a Tuscan exterior and Corinthian interior. There were originally two towers, one on either side of the facade, but the one on the southern side collapsed in 1776. The existing tower houses a famous bell, one of the largest in Goa and often referred to as the 'Golden Bell' on account of its rich sound. The main altar is dedicated to St Catherine of Alexandria and old paintings on either side of it depict scenes from her life and martyrdom.

The Convent & Church of St Francis of Assisi

This is probably one of the most interesting buildings in Old Goa. It contains gilded, carved woodwork, old murals depicting scenes from the life of St Francis and a floor, substantially made of carved gravestones, complete with family coats of arms dating back to the early 1500s. The origins of this church date back to the humble beginnings made by eight Franciscan friars who arrived here in 1517 and constructed a small chapel consisting of three altars and a choir. This was later pulled down and the present building constructed on the same spot in 1661.

The convent at the back of this church is now the Archaeological Museum but it's closed indefinitely for 'repairs'. It houses many portraits of the Portuguese Viceroys – most of them inexpertly touched-up – fragments of sculpture from Hindu temple sites in Goa which show Chalukyan and Hoysala influences, stone Vetal images from the animist cult which flourished in this part of India centuries ago, and a model of a Portuguese caravelle minus the rigging (surely someone could get it together to do the rigging?!).

The Professed House & Basilica of Bom Jesus

The Basilica of Bom Jesus is famous throughout the Roman Catholic world since it contains the tomb and mortal remains of St Francis Xavier who, in 1541, was given the task of spreading Christianity among the subjects of the Portuguese colonies in the east. A former pupil of St Ignatius Loyola, the founder of the Jesuit Order, St Francis Xavier's missionary voyages in the east became a legend and, considering the state of communications at the time, are nothing short of miraculous.

Arriving in Goa in 1542, St Francis Xavier spent the next few years spreading the Christian faith along the Malabar and Coromandel coasts, until news reached him that Christianity had begun to make inroads in the Molucca Islands (now part of Indonesia). Wishing to make sure that the converts properly comprehended their new faith he set out on a voyage to those islands, returning to Goa in 1548. He stayed in Goa only a short time, however, and soon embarked on a voyage to Japan where he sought permission to teach Christianity from the King of Yamaguchi. Though permission was granted, Francis made little headway due to the opposition of the Bonzes and so, disappointed, he boarded a ship bound for Goa but got off at Sancian Island just off the coast of China. There he fell ill and died in December 1552 at the age of 46.

His body was buried on Sancian, but subsequently taken to Melaka (Malacca) and placed in the Church of Our Lady of the Mount there. Four months later Francis' successor had the grave opened in order to pay his respects, finding that the body was still fresh and life-like, had it sent to Goa in 1554. It was first kept in St Paul's College but transferred to the Professed House in 1613. After canonisation the body was removed to the Basilica of Bom Jesus. The body is exposed to public view once every 10 years (1984 then 1994) on the anniversary of St Francis' death; but is no longer whole having been through some weird and wonderful mutilations at the hands of relic seekers, both lay and ecclesiastical.

While in Melaka, the body was kept in too small a grave which resulted in the neck being broken. One of the toes was bitten off in 1554 by a Portuguese woman who wanted a relic of the saint. In 1615 part of the right hand was cut off and sent to Rome where it is venerated in the Church of Gesu, and in 1619 the remaining part of the hand was removed and sent to the Jesuits in Japan. Portions of the intestines have been removed from time to time and distributed to various places.

Apart from the 10 year cycle of expositions, there is a festival held in Old Goa every year on the anniversary of the Saint's death (3rd December), at which time the normally sleepy little village becomes a mad-house of pot and pan stalls, food and beer tents, trinket sellers, balloons, firecrackers, buses from all over Goa and even further afield, and thousands of pilgrims, many of whom doss down in the cloisters of the Basilica. When mass is said there isn't a square cm of space left in the church. It's like a sardine tin!

Apart from the richly gilded altars, the interior of the church is remarkable for its simplicity and is the only one which is not plastered on the outside. It was commenced in 1594 and completed in 1605. The point of interest inside the church is, of course, the tomb of St Francis, the construction of which was underwritten by the Duke of Tuscany and executed by the Florentine sculptor, Giovanni Batista Foggini. It took 10 years to build and was completed in 1698. The remains of the body are housed in a silver casket which at one time was covered in jewels and, on the walls surrounding it, are murals depicting scenes from the saint's journeys including one of his death on Sancian Island.

The Professed House next door to the Basilica is a two-storeyed laterite building covered with lime plaster which was completed in 1585 despite much opposition to the Jesuits. Part of the building was burnt down in 1663 but rebuilt in 1783. There's a modern art gallery attached to the basilica.

Church of St Cajetan

Modelled on the original design of St Peter's Church in Rome, the Church of St Cajetan was built by Italian friars of the Order of Theatines, who were sent by Pope Urban III to preach Christianity in the Kingdom of Golconda (near Hyderabad). The friars were not permitted to work in Golconda and so settled down at Goa in 1640. The construction of the church was begun in 1655. Historically, it's of much less interest than the other churches.

Ruins of the Church of St Augustine

All that is left of this church is the enormous 46-metre high tower which served as a belfry and formed part of the facade of the church. What little is left of the other parts of the church is choked with creepers and weeds, and access is difficult. The church was constructed in 1602 by Augustinian friars who arrived in Goa in 1587.

It was abandoned in 1835 as a result of repressive policies followed by the Portuguese government, which resulted in the eviction of many religious orders from Goa. The church fell into neglect and the vault collapsed in 1842. Many years later in 1931 the facade and half the tower fell down, followed by more parts in 1938.

The Church & Convent of St Monica

This huge, three-storeyed laterite building was commenced in 1606 and completed in 1627, only to be burnt down nine years later. Reconstruction started the following year and it's from this time that the buildings date. Once known as the Royal Monastery, on account of the royal patronage which it enjoyed, the building is now used by the Mater dei Institute as a nunnery which was inaugurated in 1964. Visitors are not allowed inside.

Other Buildings

Other monuments of minor interest at Old Goa are the **Viceroy's Arch**, the **Gate of Adil Shah's Palace**, **Royal Chapel of St Anthony**, the **Church of St John of God**, the **Chapel of St Catherine**, the ruins of the **Church of the Carmelites**, and the **Church of Our Lady of the Mount**.

Getting There

You need the best part of a day to wander around the churches and other monuments of Old Goa. 'An afternoon is quite enough', wrote a non-believer. 'I needed the best part of an hour and a half', said another. There are frequent buses to Old Goa from the bus stand at Panjim, but as all the

buses from Panjim to Ponda also pass through Old Goa you can use these buses too. Buses take 20 to 30 minutes and cost Rs 0.90. Whenever there is a festival at Old Goa (such as the Festival of St Francis Xavier at the end of November/beginning of December) boats ply between Panjim (from the Bombay Steamer Jetty) and Old Goa. This is a very pleasant way of getting there. It costs Rs 2.50 and takes about 45 minutes.

MARGAO (MADGAON)

The capital of Salcete province, Margao is the main population centre of southern Goa and a pleasant provincial town, which still displays many reminders of its Portuguese past. In itself it's not of great interest to travellers, though the old Margao church is well worth a visit and the covered market is definitely the best of its kind in the whole of Goa. Its importance is as a service and transport centre for people staying at Colva beach. If you're planning on staying at Colva you must first head for Margao which is connected to the rest of Goa and to the neighbouring states by bus, train and taxi.

If you're coming to Margao from outside Goa, note that the last bus to Colva beach leaves at 8 pm. After that you will either have to hire a taxi (or motorbike) to get to Colva or stay overnight in Margao.

Information & Orientation

The Tourist Office is housed in the Secretariat building on the bottom side of the Municipal Gardens. The staff are friendly and helpful though, like elsewhere in India, they're limited in what they can offer because of lack of funds.

The Post Restante is not in the GPO on the top side of the Municipal Gardens but in a separate office about 300 metres from the GPO – see the map of Margao.

The covered market here is the best in Goa and a fascinating place to wander through, even if you don't want to buy anything. If you'll be staying at Colva for some time and renting a house, the other,

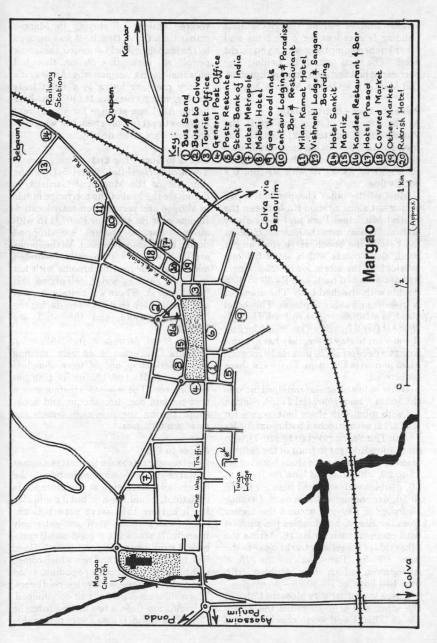

Key:

1. Bus Stand
2. Buses to Colva
3. Tourist Office
4. General Post Office
5. Poste Restante
6. State Bank of India
7. Mabai Hotel
8. Goa Woodlands
9. Centaur Lodging # Paradise
   Bar # Restaurant
10. Milan Kamat Hotel
11. Vishranti Lodge # Sangam
    Boarding
12. Hotel Sankit
13. Marliz
14. Kandeel Restaurant # Bar
15. Hotel Prasad
16. Covered Market
17. Other Market
18. Ruknish Hotel

Margao

smaller market behind the Secretariat building is excellent for pots, pans and other kitchen equipment which you might need. The taxi stand is behind the Secretariat building. Rau Raje Deshprabhu, Old Market is an Indian Airlines Agent.

Places to Stay – Bottom End
At the top end of this bracket is the *Woodlands Hotel* (tel 3121), which has friendly staff, its own bar and restaurant – closes at 10 pm – and singles/doubles for Rs 25/35 or Rs 60/70 with air-con. It's good value.

Most of the other cheaper hotels are strung out along Station Rd between the central Municipal Park and the railway station. I'd nominate the *Rukrish Hotel* as the best of the bunch. Here you can get good, clean rooms with a small balcony overlooking the street for Rs 25 a single without attached bath, and Rs 30 to 40 a double with attached bath. The manager is friendly and eager to please. This hotel also has an offshoot, the *Rukrish Holiday Home* at Betul Beach, 14 km from Margao. If you want to stay there, they have rooms with two beds for Rs 20 plus Rs 10 for each extra person in the room. There are share bathrooms.

Other hotels of similar standard include the *Milan Kamat Hotel* (tel 2715), Station Rd with room with share bathroom – for Rs 14/18; with attached bathroom for Rs 16/20. The *Sanrit Hotel* (tel 3226-7), also on Station Rd right in front of the railway station, has singles with share bath for Rs 15 to 20, with attached bath for Rs 30 to 40, doubles with attached bath for Rs 40 to 50, depending on the season. *Centaur Boarding & Lodging*, around the corner from the Sanrit, has doubles (no singles) with common bath for Rs 16. Across the other side of the railway tracks close to the turn off for Benaulim is the *Hotel Annapurna*, which has doubles with attached bath for Rs 30.25 – no singles.

There is another very pleasant lodge at the other end of town called the *Twiga Lodge*. This is well worth checking out if you're thinking of staying in Margao rather than Colva Beach – I was assured by the manager, Abel Lourenco, that some people do make this choice, though I personally can't imagine why. Anyway it's a very pleasant lodge in a quiet leafy setting, which costs Rs 15/30 with share baths. Abel can arrange for you to rent bicycles to get to Colva beach or wherever else you want to go nearby.

Places to Stay – Top End
The *Mabai Hotel* (tel 3653-4-5-7), on the top side of the Municipal Gardens, is definitely the best of the top range hotels in Margao and very conveniently located. Rooms cost Rs 45/75 or Rs 75/115 with air-con. Service charges are dropped during the monsoon season. All the rooms are large and airy, pleasantly decorated and have their own bathrooms with hot and cold running water, telephone and piped muzak. There's a restaurant, bar and roof garden (latter closed during the monsoon season) and the staff are friendly.

The *Hotel Metropole* (tel 3552-6-7), Avenida Concessao is an ugly building and a little way out of town. Singles/doubles are Rs 100/135 or Rs 150/200 with air-con. There are two restaurants, a roof garden, bar, discotheque and bookshop. During the monsoon season the rates are 50% less.

Places to Eat
Hotel restaurants aside, the best restaurant in Margao is the *Kandeel* (or Icandeel – the orange and black sign at the entrance is indistinct, it could be a 'k' but it could also be 'Ic'). Here they serve superb Goan-style food and the staff are extremely friendly. If you want a good meal, come here. I would suggest you try their Goan fish, masala chicken and rice which comes complete with chappati, papadum, salad and pickles. They also have ice-cold beers. The restaurant is partially air-conditioned.

La Marina Cafe, a few metres from the Colva bus stand, is also a very reasonable restaurant, but although they have an extensive menu there are very few items available except in the evenings. Prices average Rs 4 to 6 per dish. There is a bakery next door. If you're looking for a vegetarian restaurant, the *Hotel Prasad*, opposite the covered market, serves typical south Indian vegetarian meals. It's cheap and popular with local people.

For snacks and breakfasts, the *Marliz* on the top side of the Municipal Gardens is an extremely popular cafe and has been for many, many years. It's always crowded – and for very good reason as its snacks are excellent. They include sandwiches, vegetarian and non-vegetarian pasties, cakes and coffee. You can eat well here for Rs 2 to 4

Getting Around

To Colva Beach Buses run to Colva on an approximately hourly basis and go via Benaulim. The first bus from Margao leaves at about 7.30 am and the last at 8 pm. The fare is Rs 0.60 and the journey takes 20 to 25 minutes. If you'd prefer a taxi these cost at least Rs 2 per person – they usually take six people though, sometimes more. There are a few drivers who demand Rs 10 or more, even when the taxi is shared but fortunately they're an objectionable exception. Obviously, if you want a taxi to yourself this will cost a minimum of Rs 12.

An alternative to taxis are the motorbikes which you can pick up on the road outside the bus stand. This is the quickest way of getting to the beach and costs Rs 6. They have no objection to taking people with rucksacks. A bus to Betul, way down at the south of the beach which Colva is in the centre of, costs Rs 1.75.

To Panjim The bridge across the Zuari River between Cortalim and Agassaim was completed a little while ago, so these days you can get a bus all the way from Margao to Panjim. (It takes about 1½ hours and costs Rs 3.50 to 4). I'm sure the bus companies and many local people who

commute into Panjim daily will be very pleased with this development, but using the ramshackle ferries to cross the rivers in the territory was one of the great pleasures for the visitor to Goa years ago.

Sadly, this is all disappearing rapidly as bridges are thrown across the various rivers, but even so the journey between Margao and Panjim is still one of the best in Goa. All along the road you will see many old, whitewashed churches and monasteries, along with small roadside shrines. There must be a lot of people who are hoping that the Indian government doesn't get too carried away in its zeal to Indianise Goa.

Other buses You can find buses to most towns in Goa from the bus stand in Margao. There is no timetable as such as the buses are all privately owned and go when full, but they are frequent. You'll rarely have to wait more than a few minutes for a bus, if at all.

Trains Since most travellers who come to Goa arrive by rail (the other main route is via the steamer from Bombay), trains are dealt with under the Panjim section.

MAPUSA

Mapusa (pronounced locally as 'Mapsa') is the main centre of population in the northern provinces of Goa and the main town for supplies if you are staying either at Anjuna or Chapora. If you're staying at Calangute or Baga then you have a choice of Panjim or Mapusa as a service centre. In itself, there's nothing to see in Mapusa, though the Friday market is perhaps worth a visit. You may, however, need to stay here overnight if you're catching a bus to Bombay the following day.

Places to Stay

I've never met anyone who has stayed overnight in Mapusa as there's no need to – accommodation at the nearby beaches of Anjuna, Vagator and Chapora is far

Woodlands Bar & Restrnt

Safari Lodge

Bookshop

Janki Shankar Lodge

Market

Sanman Boarding

Hotel Bardez

State Bank of India

Imperial Bar

Bus Stand

Taxi & Motorbike Stand

Panjim

Tourist Hostel

Post Office

Mapusa

Church

Anjuna & Chapora

Calangute Aguada

Places to Eat

The *Imperial Bar & Restaurant* serves good non-vegetarian food which averages Rs 2 to 5 for egg dishes and Rs 5 to 8 for meat dishes. It's clean, easy-going, popular with local people and they have cold beers.

Getting Around

Buses As at Panjim, there's no schedule, but services are frequent. Buses to Anjuna and Chapora can be very crowded – mostly with westerners staying on the beaches. Mapusa-Panjim takes about 25 minutes and costs Rs l. There are also buses to Calangute, Anjuna and Chapora as well as to other population centres in northern Goa.

As an alternative to the buses you can take either a taxi or a motorbike to wherever you want to go. A motorbike to Anjuna will cost Rs 6 to 7 and take about 15 minutes (taxis ask for considerably more).

THE BEACHES

Goa is justifiably famous for its beaches and westerners have been flocking to them since the early '60s. They occasionally suffer from a bad press both in the western and Indian media, because of the real or imagined nefarious activities of a small minority of visitors. If you were to believe these outrageously exaggerated and one-sided reports you might be tempted to give the beaches a miss thinking that they're dens of iniquity. Don't, because Goan beaches are still magnificent and most people find them extremely difficult to leave.

The only problem is deciding which one to head for. Calangute became almost a travellers' cliche in the '60s and early '70s and tourist literature is fond of referring to it as the 'Queen' of Goa's beaches, but it isn't the best or the most beautiful. It certainly isn't the most serene and has been somewhat over-developed in the last few years. Baga, a little further north, is far superior.

preferable. All the same, if you want to/ have to stay at Mapusa, you have a choice of the *Hotel Bardez* (tel 2607), or the *Tourist Hostel*. The Bardez is the best hotel in Mapusa and offers double rooms at Rs 49.50 with attached bath – Rs 38.50 for single occupancy.

The Tourist Hostel is a large, newly-constructed place on the roundabout at the entrance to Mapusa and has rooms for Rs 20 a single, Rs 30 a double, Rs 36 for a room with four beds and Rs 48 for a room with six beds. There is a large dining hall here, but the food is rather expensive – a pot of coffee costs Rs 5 (for three small cups!), though the fixed-menu breakfast (fried eggs, plain omelette or vegetable cutlet, two slices of bread and butter, tea or coffee) cost Rs 5.

You might also consider the *Janki Shankar Lodge* (tel 401), which has double rooms with attached bath for Rs 25 – there are no singles – but it's a bit grim.

The vast majority of travellers these days head for either Anjuna or Chapora. At any one time there will be thousands of travellers staying here, many of them on a long-term basis in rented houses scattered among the coconut plantations which reach right up to the beach. Other than the Vagator Beach Resort complex, there are no hotels as such at Chapora and only two or three semi-permanently full ones at Anjuna, but finding accommodation is no problem. Simply ask around in the cafes. On the other hand, if you want to rent a whole house you'll have to talk in terms of renting on at least a monthly basis – often longer. Naturally, with a floating population of several thousand you won't find any deserted beaches but you will find plenty of action, and despite the numbers both places have retained their charm. This isn't Kuta beach!

If any beach deserves the title of 'Queen' it is Colva. This beach is without equal in India. It's nothing short of paradise. Forty km of uninterrupted white sand fringed with coconut palms along the whole of its length and a warm, calm sea. It's very laid-back and there are rarely more than 50 to 100 travellers here at any one time. Go a little way in either direction from Colva village and you will find the nearest thing to a deserted beach. For accommodation you have the choice of either an instant roof in a hotel or a restaurant/hotel or renting a house on a long-term basis. It's wise to be at least a little security conscious on the Goa beaches. Things do get stolen both on the beach and from rooms.

The other main beaches at Aguada and Bagmalo are largely for the jet-set and sport five-star hotels and the like. Few travellers go there.

COLVA

Fifteen years ago Colva stretched sun-drenched, palm-fringed and deserted for km after km. Precious little disturbed its soft, white sands and warm, crystal-clear, turquoise waters, except the local fisher-men who pulled their catches in by hand each morning, and a few of the more intrepid hippies who had forsaken the obligatory drugs, sex and rock and roll of Calangute for the soothing tranquility of this corner of paradise. Since there were only two cottages for rent and one cafe (Vincy's), most people stayed either on the beach itself or in palm-leaf shelters, which they took over from departing travellers or constructed themselves.

Those days are gone forever, and even in the days of yore, the property speculators and developers had begun to sniff around in search of a fast rupee. Today, you can see the results of their efforts – three-storey, air-conditioned resort complexes, serried ranks of tourist cottages, discotheques, trinket stalls and cold drink places. You'll be lucky if you see a fisherman around the main area and, anyway, they all appear to have acquired motorised trawlers which stand anchored in a line off-shore. Likewise, you won't come across anyone sleeping out on the beach these days or throwing up a palm-leaf shelter: the determination of the average Indian day-tripper to catch a glimpse of a scantily-dressed, preferably female, body put paid to all that.

It's only fair to point out that this development is concentrated into a relatively small area at the end of the road from Margao, and that it's simplicity itself to get away from it. Walk two km either side of here, and you'll get close to what it used to be like before the cement mixers began chugging away. When you're there, if you're tired of wearing clothes, take them off. Everyone else does.

It could be said we have only ourselves to blame for making the beach so popular in the first place. This is partly true of course, but it ignores a lot of other factors. I certainly never encouraged the construction of air-conditioned resort complexes!

So Colva has changed, but it has quite a long way to go before it gets as developed as Calangute, or a lot of other beaches I could think of around the world. It's still the best of the Goan beaches and, if you like a quiet life, you can always head further south to Benaulim or Betul.

Information & Orientation

The nearest post office is in Colva village. Letters can be sent post restante to there rather than Margao if you like. At present there is no bank in the village, but the Hotel Silver Sands may be prepared to change travellers' cheques.

Bicycles can be hired from a place half-

way between the Tourist Nest and the Umita Corner Restaurant & Bar (see map).

Places to Stay

The best deal – if you're going to stay here for a while – is to rent a house with a number of other people. If you're not already part of a large enough group, ask around in the cafes at Colva and Benaulim, or take a walk along the road which runs parallel to the beach from Colva village in both directions and ask

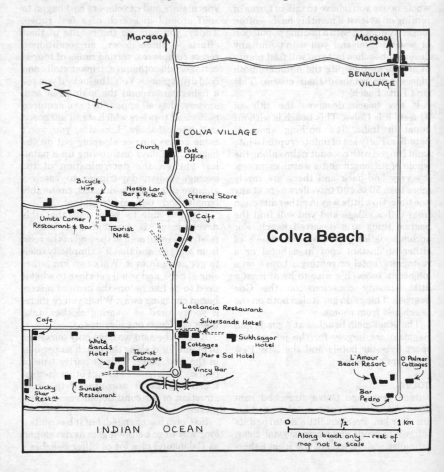

every time you see a likely-looking place. It shouldn't take more than a few days. Obviously you get what you pay for, but prices vary from Rs 200 to 400 per month. Between November and March competition is stiff, so get there before then if possible. Note that there are very few places to rent on a long-term basis on the beach itself. Most houses are a good 15 to 20 minutes' walk from the beach.

For short-term accommodation there is a wide choice. At the top end of the market is the *Hotel Silver Sands* (tel 3645-6), which has 55 air-con rooms, three de-luxe suites, air-con public areas, restaurant (Goan, Indian and western food), bar, coffee shop, 24-hour room service, money-changing facilities and free transport to and from the airport. Rooms with attached bath and hot and cold running water cost Rs 150 a single, Rs 200 a double and Rs 250 for a suite. There is a 20 to 35% discount in the off-season (monsoon months).

Next comes the *Whitesands Hotel* (tel 3253), a Goa Tourist Development Corporation enterprise, which has five luxury suites, eight duplex suites and 14 double rooms all within 100 metres of the beach. It also has a good restaurant – the *Dolphin* – which has Goan and Portuguese food as well as seafood. If you're looking for this kind of place to stay in while you're here, this is very good value at Rs 100 a luxury suite, Rs 80 for a duplex suite, and Rs 65 a double. A third person in any of the above is charged an extra Rs 16. There's a 40% discount during the monsoon – June to mid-September. All the rooms have attached bath.

If the Whitesands is full, you can find accommodation of a similar standard at the *Mar e Sol Hotel* at the back of the Vincy Bar, which has double rooms with attached bath and fan for Rs 45. There is also a restaurant here. Another good value, super-clean hotel with air-con doubles, clean sheets and attached bath for Rs 125 and non air-con doubles, sheets, fan and attached bath for Rs 60 is

the *Sukhsagar Beach Resort*. There is a discount of Rs 5 per night if you're staying for more than a few days. Note there are no single rooms. Cheaper still are the *Sea View Cottages* in front of the Silver Sands Hotel which cost Rs 40 a double with attached bath and fan. A little over-priced I think.

Back up the road which runs parallel to the beach from Colva village is the *Tourist Nest*, a rambling old place in traditional Goan style, which is very popular despite its distance from the beach. It has a range of different rooms from Rs 20 a double with common bath, Rs 30 a double with attached bath. All the rooms have fans and clean sheets. The hotel has its own restaurant and bar with prices on the lower side of average and excellent food.

At the cheaper end of the market are various places strung out along the beach, north of the main area. They're all much the same price – Rs 20 a double for back rooms and Rs 25 a double for front rooms with share bath and toilet – and perfectly adequate for most people's purposes. Probably the best at present is the *Lucky Star*, followed by the *Sunset Restaurant*. They both have good attached restaurants, but the Lucky Star is the more popular of the two and has a sound system with a wide selection of tapes.

Three years ago, the Sunset Restaurant was the most popular place on the beach, but it's changed hands and the present proprietors seem totally bewildered about what to do with it. Agnel, who used to own it, has moved further north to another place beyond the Lucky Star. If he runs it like he used to run the Sunset Restaurant, it will be worth checking out. Another more basic place to stay in this area is the fisherman's cottage next door to the Sunset Restaurant.

If you hanker after the more tranquil aspects of Colva Beach, think instead of Benaulim Beach less than two km south of Colva. Here you can find excellent accommodation at the *L'Amour Beach Resort* for Rs 30 a double with own bath and toilet, clean top sheet and fan. Most of the rooms are cottages aligned so that they catch the sea breezes. The staff are very friendly and eager to make you welcome. The attached restaurant offers some of the finest food to be found in Goa, and it's very popular. Try the garlic fish or tomato fish – Rs 12 for huge fish steaks with salad and French fries. Highly recommended.

More-or-less opposite are the *O Palmar Beach Cottages*, which offer a similar standard of accommodation at Rs 35 a double with own bath and toilet, fan and clean top sheet. Ask for Joseph at *Pedro's Bar & Restaurant*, just opposite and right next to the beach.

North of Colva, nearly at the airport, is Bogmalo where the *Hotel Oberoi Bogmalo Beach* (tel 2191-2) has rooms at Rs 350/425.

Places to Eat

It's in the nature of beach life that everyone has his/her own favourite restaurant, but some places are definitely better than others, not only because the food is consistently good and the prices reasonable, but because they've got the surroundings right too. In many ways it doesn't matter how good the food is, if it's spoilt by having to eat it inside glass and concrete and away from the sight and sound of the very things which have attracted you to Goa in the first place. You might as well eat to the accompaniment of a video in an hermetically sealed room.

There is one place which offers you the best of both worlds – though you have to walk down the beach to get there – and it's *Pedro's Bar & Restaurant* at Benaulim Beach. Excellent seafood, friendly management, good sound system with a wide variety of tapes and usually an interesting collection of people to talk to. While you're down this end of the beach, you might like to check out the *L'Amour Beach Resort* restaurant too.

At the Colva end of the beach one of the most popular places is the *Lucky Star*

restaurant which offers very good food, and has a good sound system – all within sight and sound of the beach. Another extremely popular place you must check out is the *Lactancia Restaurant*, next door to the Silver Sands Hotel. This has been most people's favourite meeting point for years and hardly a night goes by that it's not packed out. *Vincy's Bar* was, of course, Colva's original restaurant and, although it now occupies about three times its former space and still attracts a fair share of customers, it appears to have lapsed into a kind of middle-aged smugness. Apart from these places, it's worth trying the *Dolphin* if you're looking for a change – this is part of the Whitesands Hotel.

Away from the beach, the *Umita Corner Restaurant & Bar* is popular with travellers who are renting in the area and, as you might expect, the atmosphere is quite different from any restaurants on the beach. If you want a splurge in a restaurant with a Portuguese flavour, give the nearby *Nosso Lar Bar & Restaurant* a try.

Getting There

Buses run to Margao about every hour and take 25 minutes. The fare is Rs 0.65. The first bus from Colva to Margao leaves at 7.30 am. The last bus back to Colva from Margao leaves at 8 pm.

A shared taxi from Colva to Margao will cost you about Rs 2 – assuming the driver can find six to 10 people to pack into the taxi. If you're hiring one for yourself, expect to pay around Rs 12. If you like the wind through your hair the easiest way to get between the two places is to take a motorcycle. The standard fare is presently Rs 6. They have no objections to rucksacks.

VASCO DA GAMA

Close to Marmagoa Harbour and Dabolim Airport, Vasco da Gama is the terminus of the railway line to Goa – apart from a few local trains which continue to the harbour. If you arrive by train you can get down at

Margao, near Colva Beach, but if you arrive by air it is possible to arrive in Goa too late to get much further than Vasco da Gama. There are a number of hotels in this not very exciting town.

Places to Stay

The *Hotel Rebelo* (tel 2620), Vadem has singles from as little as Rs 25 to air-con doubles at Rs 100. *Lapaz Hotel* (tel 2121), Swatentrya Path is rather more expensive with rooms from Rs 60 or from Rs Rs 100 with air-con. The *Hotel Zuari* (tel 127) is similarly priced. There are a number of cheaper local hotels.

CALANGUTE & BAGA

Until very recently, Calangute was the beach which all self-respecting hippies headed for, especially around Christmas when all psychedelic hell broke loose and the beach was littered with more budding rock stars than most people have hot dinners. If you enjoyed taking part in those mass *nights* with their endless half-baked discussions about 'when the revolution comes' and 'the vibes, man', then this was just the ticket. You could frolic around with not a stitch on, be ever so cool and liberated and totally disregard the feelings of the local inhabitants. You could get totally out of your head every minute of the night and day on every conceivable variety of ganja from Timo to Tenochtitlan, exhibit the most bizarre behaviour, babble an endless stream of drivel and bore everybody shitless. Naturally, John Lennon or The Who were always about to turn up and give a free concert. Ah, Woodstock! Where did you go!

Calangute's heyday as the Mecca of all expatriate hippies has passed and the place has settled down to the more bourgeois pursuits of selling handicrafts, jewellery and woven fabrics to the tourists. It no longer provides the Indian press with a permanent shock-horror story about decadent, drug-crazed fiends and naked bodies who were supposed to be rotting the moral fibre of Indian youth. Indeed, it isn't that popular anymore – except with middle-class Indian holiday-makers.

There are those who will continue to swear by it though it's difficult to fathom why, since it's one of the least attractive of the beaches. Unlike Colva, Anjuna and Chapora, there are hardly any swaying palms to grace the shoreline, much of the sand is contaminated with red soil and the beach drops pretty rapidly into the sea. It's also become quite expensive. Still its fame lingers on.

Baga, about two km north, is far superior and still a pleasant place to stay despite its proximity to Calangute. It still clings to its charm, the beach is much better and it remains fairly laid-back. If you're thinking of staying at Calangute, try Baga first.

Information & Orientation

The Tourist Office and the post office are next to each other where the road forks to Baga and Calangute beach. Half-way between these two places and Calangute village is a branch of the State Bank of India where you can change travellers' cheques and cash. Calangute has a useful little tourist 'lending library' in the stalls 50 metres on the sea side of the square; Rs 0.25 a day to borrow books. Once a week there's a soccer match between the western visitors and the local Calangute team – who usually win!

Close to the Tourist Office are two travel agents – MGM Space Travels – which offer discount tickets to others parts of the world at similar rates to those you can get in Bombay. There's also a branch of Spaceways – another travel agent – next to the Sea View Restaurant. They also have a branch in Colaba, Bombay and is associated with Tripsout Travel in New Delhi.

There are numerous stalls all the way from the crossroads to the beach selling genuine and repro Tibetan and Rajashtani crafts. Most of it is very well made and

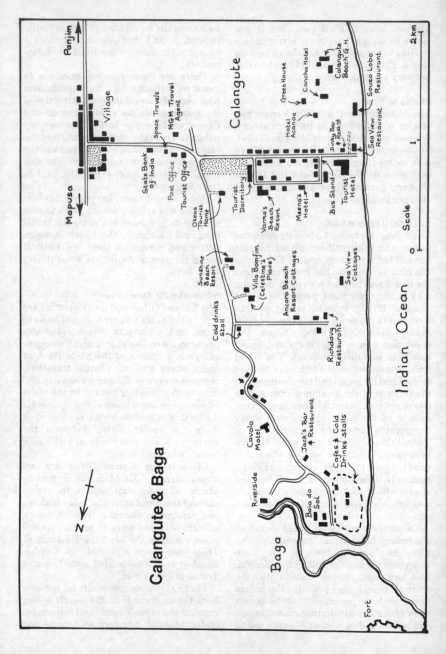

Calangute & Baga

Panjim

Mapusa

Village

MGM Travel Agent

Space Travels

State Bank of India

Post Office

Tourist Office

Oseas Tourist Home

Tourist Dormitory

Sunshine Beach Resort

Villa Bomfim (Celestine's Place)

Varma's Beach Resort

Ancora Beach Resort Cottages

Cold drinks Stall

Richdavy Restaurant

Calangute

Green House

Concha Hotel

Calangute Beach G.H.

Souza Lobo Restaurant

Sea View Restaurant

Hotel Acanoa

Dinky Bar & Restnt

Bus Stand

Tourist Hotel

Meena's Hotel

Sea View Cottages

Indian Ocean

Scale

0   1   2 km

N

Cavola Motel

Jack's Bar & Restaurant

Cafes & Cold Drinks stalls

Riverside

Baia do Sol

Baga

Fort

some of it stunningly beautiful but it isn't cheap! There is also a number of stalls in the street below the Sea View Restaurant, which sell some interesting jewellery, bangles and other ethnic trinkets (usually Tibetan, Kashmiri and Indian tribal in origin) at reasonable prices. Bargaining is obligatory.

Places to Stay – Calangute

It's hard to pick out bargains in the middle range as a lot depends on what sort of room you get and what's available. The *Calangute Beach Guest House* is good value. It's a modern, partly western-style hotel, which looks a lot more expensive than it is. In season, doubles with bath cost Rs 65 or Rs 35 without bath. Out of season they cost Rs 55 with bath and Rs 25 without bath. There are no singles, but in the off-season a double room with bath costs Rs 45. The rooms are spacious, clean and provided with mosquito nets and clean sheets. The management is very friendly and the place has its own restaurant.

Another good place is the *Tourist Hostel* – that big, ugly, uncompromising building right on the beach front, though they now have some more attractive cottages which were completed recently. Rooms in the main building cost Rs 40/55 with attached bath. There are also dormitory beds for Rs 8 per night. The cottages cost Rs 35/50. There is an attached bar and restaurant. Also right on the beach front are the rooms at the *Souza Lobo Restaurant*, which cost Rs 35 whether you're on your own or you're with someone. There is no increase in the rates during the high season. The rooms are attractively constructed out of bamboo matting. They're clean and a table fan is provided. The restaurant here is excellent.

Meena's Lodge, at the back of the Tourist Hostel, has doubles at Rs 90 to 100 with attached bath and singles/doubles without attached bath for Rs 40/45 during the high season. In the low season it has doubles with attached bath for Rs 65 and singles/doubles without attached bath for Rs 30/35. The *Hotel A Canoa*, at the back of the Souza Lobo, has rooms during the high season for Rs 40/75 and for Rs 30/60 in the low season, though the manageress was very reluctant to be pinned down on prices and I got the distinct impression that she'd attempt to charge you as much as she thought you'd be prepared to pay. Another place you can try if you're looking for dormitory accommodation is the *Tourist Dormitory & Annapurna Restaurant*, next to the sports ground, which offers eight-bed dormitory accommodation for Rs 8 per bed per night. There are a number of other lodges and private houses where you can find relatively cheap accommodation – some of it excellent.

At the top end of the market you can stay in what I think is one of the pleasantest and most thoughtfully designed hotels anywhere in India, *Varma's Beach Resort*. This is a brand new hotel with rooms facing on to a shady courtyard, polished wood furniture, as clean as a new pin and popular with travellers, who can afford the extra. It costs Rs 150/175 during the high season and Rs 100/120 during the low season. All the rooms have attached bath and toilet.

Similarly priced is the *Concha Hotel*, which has air-con doubles for Rs 330 and non air-con doubles for Rs 220 during the high season, or Rs 165 air-con and Rs 90 non air-con during the low season. There are no singles, and the hotel does not have its own restaurant. Just why the Concha should be so highly priced is a mystery as it's nothing special. Indeed, it isn't a patch on Varma's.

Places to Stay – Calangute to Baga

Moving away from Calangute itself and along the road to Baga, the first place you come to is the *Overseas Tourist Home*. This is a quiet, shady place, managed by people who are keen to please. It has double rooms with attached bath and clean sheets for Rs 25 per person and double rooms without attached bath for Rs 20 per person. The place has its own restaurant and bar.

Next comes the *Sunshine Beach Resort* (otherwise known as the Bamboo Hut), which has recently been converted for guest accommodation. Big, airy rooms with attached bathrooms cost Rs 66 a double in the high season, Rs 50 in the low season. There are also one or two smaller rooms, also with attached bathrooms which cost Rs 45 out of season. The rooms surround a large, shady courtyard and the place has a very relaxing atmosphere.

A little further on, just before you get to the turn-off to the beach, is *Vila Bomfim* (formerly Celestine's Place). If you're not staying in a privately rented house, this place gets my nomination for best hotel at Calangute/Baga. Run by an exceptionally friendly family who can't do enough to make sure you're happy and relaxed, it offers large, airy rooms for Rs 60 a double in the high season and Rs 50 a double in the low season, plus Rs 10 for each extra bed in a double room. Most of the rooms have attached bathrooms, except the two enormous front rooms, which would be spoilt by such additions – the family wishes to retain the traditional atmosphere of the place. There are also cottages at the back with attached bathrooms for the same price. The place is given a face-lift every year and is kept spotlessly clean. Meals can be arranged on request, it's an excellent place and very popular with discerning travellers.

Down the road to the beach on the left-hand side is the *Ancora Beach Resort*, a somewhat grandiose name for what is essentially a few cottages. It's OK as it goes, but is a lot to pay for somewhere to lock up your gear while you're down at the beach or relaxing in one of the cafes. It costs Rs 50 a double with attached bath – no reduction for single occupancy – plus Rs 10 for each extra person with a mattress or Rs 5 without a mattress. There is a sort of restaurant and bar attached, but I've never seen anyone in

there.

Back on the road to Baga, there is the *Cavala Hotel*, (tel Calangute 90), a middle range hotel constructed in traditional Goan style. It's good value at Rs 85 to 95 for a double cottage with attached bath between December and February inclusive, and Rs 70 to 80 between March and November inclusive. The room rates include breakfast. Bathrooms have hot and cold showers. There is a bar and restaurant and, during the monsoon months, you can stay here for Rs 30 to 40 including breakfast.

Places to Stay – Baga

As you come into Baga you will see *Jack's Bar & Restaurant* on the left-hand side. At the back are a row of cottages with attached bathrooms which cost Rs 50 a double in the high season and Rs 35 a double during the low season. They're clean, pleasantly decorated and very close to the sea. Ask at the restaurant.

Lastly, there are the *Baia do Sol* and the *Riverside*. The former is a modern, top range hotel set in an attractive flower garden, which offers a range of rooms in the main block as well as a number of self-contained cottages. During the high season, rooms in the main block cost Rs 150 a double – no reduction for single occupancy – and the cottages cost Rs 200. In the off-season, rooms in the main block cost Rs 100 a double (Rs 80 for single occupancy) and the cottages cost Rs 150 (Rs 100 for single occupancy). If you want air-con this costs an extra Rs 50. There is a restaurant and bar.

The Riverside is slightly less expensive than the Baia do Sol, and a very pleasant place to stay. It consists largely of a number of cottages set in leafy surroundings, which cost Rs 70 a double during the high season, Rs 50 in the low season. All the rooms have attached bath and the hotel has its own restaurant and bar. If you're travelling alone, there are also a number of single cottages across the river which the hotel owns. You can rent these for Rs 30. There is a ferry service across the river via dug-out.

Places to Eat

There are any number of small restaurants serving both Indian food and seafood all the way from Calangute village to the beach especially around the bus stand and a whole collection of them on the beach at Baga. The *Sea View Restaurant* has reasonably good food, but unless you pay a lot of money, the portions are tiny, so if you're really hungry, you'll end up having to buy two meals. It has an extensive menu which includes various kinds of eggs from Rs 2 to 4.50; fried eggs, liver, bacon and chips for Rs 6; fried fish, chips and salad for Rs 6; fried prawns, chips and salad for Rs 7; whole, fried pomfret fish, chips and salad for Rs 18. There's a sound system with a good collection of rock music tapes.

Souza Lobo Restaurant is much the same as far as food is concerned but the setting is far superior. A perfect place to watch the sunset or relax in the afternoons. *Richdavy Restaurant* is halfway between Calangute and Baga and is popular with travellers. Good food at reasonable prices and the management is very friendly. Fresh fruit juices cost Rs 6 here; prawns, chips and salad Rs 22 to 24; various fish dishes Rs 12 to 14 and sweets Rs 4. There's a free notice board here where you can leave messages or for sale notices.

Getting There

There are frequent buses to Panjim and Mapusa from Calangute throughout the day. The fare is Rs 1.30 from Calangute to Panjim and the trip takes 35 to 45 minutes.

There are no regular buses between Calangute and Baga, but there are minibuses which run between the two places. It's often easier to hitch. Bikes can be hired in Calangute for Rs 6 a day, a great way of exploring the area.

AGUADA

South of Calangute, near the mouth of the Mandovi River, Aguada is Goa's jet set beach. Its chief attraction is the 16th century Portuguese Aguada Fort in which the hotel is built.

Places to Stay

Fort Aguada Beach Resort (tel 3404) is built within the ramparts of the old fort and has rooms or individual cottages with prices from around Rs 360/425 for singles/doubles. The resort has a swimming pool, tennis courts, shops, boats and canoes to rent, or bicycles.

ANJUNA

If you want to know where everyone went when Calangute had been filmed, recorded, reported and talked about into the sand, this is the beach to head for. It's one of the world's weirdest and most wonderful collections of overlanders, monks, defiant ex-hippies, gentle lunatics, 'orange' people, artists, craftspeople, seers, searchers and peripatetic expatriates who normally wouldn't be seen out of the organic confines of their health-food emporia in San Francisco or London.

There's no point in trying to define what Anjuna is or what it's like , it's many different things to many different people. The only way to find out is to stay here for a while and make some friends. Full moon is a particularly good time to be here when there's usually a mass party with psychedelics freely available. Unlike Calangute, the place has retained its charm. Nude bathing is de rigeur with the added satisfaction that you're unlikely to attract the voyeuristic attentions of any but the most intrepid holidaymaker.

Information & Orientation

There is a post office here to which you can have mail sent post restante but there is no bank.

Places to Stay

It isn't easy to find a place to stay between

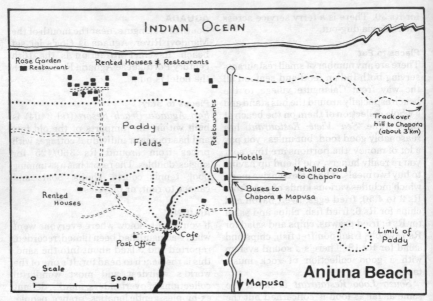

Anjuna Beach

INDIAN OCEAN

Rose Garden Restaurant

Rented Houses & Restaurants

Paddy Fields

Rented Houses

Post Office

Cafe

Scale

0   500m

Restaurants

Hotels

Metalled road to Chapora

Buses to Chapora & Mapusa

Track over hill to Chapora (about 3 km)

Limit of Paddy

↓ Mapusa

November and March. Most of the available houses are rented on a long-term basis, often six months to a year, by people who come back here again and again. There are only two or three hotels which are located near the junction where the road from Chapora meets the road to the beach, but they're more-or-less permanently full. If you want to stay here you may initially have to make do with a very primitive shack or even sleep outside a restaurant, leaving your gear with the owner until you've made some friends or had a good scout around for a house. It's not a beach to head for if you're expecting immediate comforts in the shape of a hotel. This beach is definitely for people with plenty of initiative. If you're only planning on staying a few days then it's not really worth comming here.

Places To Eat

There are any number of restaurants and cafes strung out along the road to the beach and all along the beach front. Which one you choose as your favourite will depend largely on what sort of person you are and who you meet, though one of the best for seafood (but not the most popular) is the *Rose Garden Restaurant*. The prices here are higher than elsewhere, but the food is excellent and size of the helpings impressive. Fish steak, chips and salad – beautifully presented – costs Rs 7 to 9. They also have cold beers.

The Flea Market

After a lapse of about two years the Wednesday flea market at Anjuna beach is back in business and attracting the sort of nonsense comment from newspaper hacks that should have been laid to rest when Noah left the Ark. Try this gem from Cheryl D'Souza:

Panjim Nov 1 (1983) – Today is Wednesday – the day of the famous – or notorious? – flea market on the beautiful Anjuna beach. All roads lead to this market where hippies, 'respectable' foreign tourists, Indian tourists from all parts of the country and locals congregate to buy and sell wares ranging from electronic goods to used panties.

It is here more than anywhere else in the Union Territory that the lure for things 'phoren' is brazenly exploited. Anything with a foreign tag commands a premium. Gone are the days when foreigners used to dispose of their things for whatever price they could get easily. The foreigner today is a tough negotiator who more often than not drives a good bargain in the Indians' rush for foreign things.

A pair of used mocassins used to be priced at nothing more than Rs 70. Now they cost nothing less than Rs 250. And yet Indian buyers take them.

A Herald team visited the flea market last Wednesday for a survey. It was indeed astonishing to spot a well-known underworld personality of Ulhasnagar supervising the flea market operation. Discreet enquiries revealed that Indian things bearing the 'Made in the USA' tag, meaning things made by Ulhasnagar counterfeiters, were in great demand. Unwary buyers who thought the 'USA' goods to be genuine were getting fooled – and were paying for it.

The flea market which has become part of the Anjuna beach scene provides a perfect platform for the disposal of over-used, highly-prized, third-rate Indian goods which are often marketed as things foreign. Of course, a few genuine foreign goods find their way into the market.

Inquiries showed that some smugglers were using the market to dispose of smuggled goods, using the needy hippies as showroom boys. And wherever hippies go drugs cannot lag behind. Charas hashish toffees and 'chelums' are available too for the jing-bang groovy crowd to go on a 'trip'.

So widespread is the reputation – notoriety – of the flea market that foreigners coming to stay in Goa for a long time load themselves with all kinds of foreign goods which in times of need can be sold in the market.

It was this direct encouragement to smuggling and drugs that forced the then Superintendent of Police, Mr P V Sinari, to ban the flea market in 1979. The ban order remained in force for two years during which extreme co-ordination was witnessed among the police, the excise, the customs and the magistracy.

But the same fate that befalls all good things met the ban and it could not continue subsequently. The result was that the Flea market bounced right back with a vengeance.

Panjim Herald

Actually the market is colourful and great fun with everyone from Tibetan traders to rapacious and rich Gujarati ladies. For Rs 1 you can set up your own stall and sell unwanted gear.

Getting There

There are buses every one to two hours to Chapora and Mapusa, they can be very crowded at certain times of the day. There are also plenty of motorcycles available, they cost Rs 8 to Mapusa and take about 15 minutes.

CHAPORA

This is one of the most beautiful, interesting and unspoilt areas of Goa and a good deal more attractive than Anjuna either for a short or a long stay. Much of the inhabited area nestles under a canopy of dense coconut palms and the village is dominated by a rocky hill on top of which sits an old Portuguese fort. The fort is fairly well preserved and worth a visit and the views from its ramparts are excellent. Secluded, sandy coves are to be found all the way around the northern side of this rocky outcrop, though the main beaches all face west towards the Indian Ocean.

It shares with Anjuna the distinction of being the most popular beach in Goa and at any one time there will be thousands of westerners staying here, many of them, as at Anjuna, on a long-term basis. Indeed there is probably one westerner to every Goan in Chapora village itself. If this sounds a little bit too much like a ghetto you can rest assured that it doesn't feel that way. Local people remain friendly and surprisingly unaffected by it all, and since the houses which are available for rent are scattered over quite a large area and there are many beaches and coves to choose from, it's rare to see more than a hundred travellers together in one place.

Places to Stay

There are very few places where you can find instant accommodation in Chapora. This is one of the things which makes it

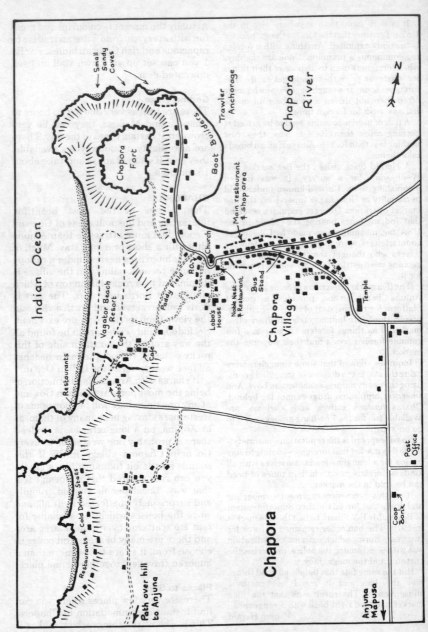

such a pleasant place to stay, particularly as most people who do go here, stay for a long time. However, you need somewhere to stay until you can find a house or room to rent. At the top end of the market is the *Vagator Beach Resort* (tel Siolim 41) which is right on the beach in its own palm-shaded grounds. It comprises a main block containing the restaurant (Indian and seafood), bar and reception area and two types of cottages. The staff are very friendly and eager to please and, as far as beach 'resorts' go in Goa, I'd give this top billing. It's very relaxing. The cottages cost Rs 120/80 a single (in A and B respectively), and Rs 180/130 a double (in A and B). An extra person in an A cottage costs Rs 50, Rs 90 in a B cottage. All the cottages have attached bathrooms.

Down at the bottom end of the market you can find a room, either at *Dr Lobo's* house for Rs 10 to 15 (this is a very friendly family who will make you welcome, but the facilities are somewhat basic), or at the *Noble Nest Restaurant & Boarding*, opposite the church at the bottom of the track which leads to Dr Lobo's. Here you can find accommodation for Rs 15 a single and Rs 30 a double in the off-season. Prices are negotiable in the season.

Most people who stay in Chapora come on a long-term basis and find a house or room to rent. If you're particular about where you want to stay, this can take some time. It helps if you get here before most of the others – try September and October when there are only a few people about. On the other hand it isn't particularly difficult to find somewhere to live – just make it your top priority and keep asking around in the stores and cafes. Wherever you decide to live, make sure you have a torch (flashlight) handy. This isn't a commercialised holiday resort and there are no street lamps. Finding your way along the paths through coconut palms late at night when there's no full moon is a devil of a job without a light! As at the other beaches, houses for rent cost between Rs 150 to 400 a month depending on their size and location.

Places To Eat
For food, there are any number of restaurants all the way up to the main street of Chapora village, opposite the church, at the back of the Vagator Beach Resort and along the beach south of the road which leads to Vagator. Many of them are really pleasant and serve good seafood and it's hard to recommend one as opposed to another, except *Lobo's* (not to be confused with Dr Lobo's house in the village). Here you'll get the best seafood in Goa expertly presented. No-one else quite makes it up to their standard. King prawns, salad and chips will cost you Rs 9; fish a little less. They have cold beers too. It's a superb little restaurant and very friendly, but if you want to be sure of getting a meal there turn up early. The place is well known for its excellent food and seating is limited. They're closed on Sundays.

Forget about the two 'restaurants' at the end of the tarmac road to Vagator – they're a waste of time.

Getting There
There are frequent buses to Mapusa throughout the day for Rs 0.75, and three direct buses to Panjim daily (via Anjuna and Mapusa). The bus stand is near the road junction in Chapora village. There are also motorcycles here which will take you to Mapusa or Anjuna.

HARAMBOL
Perhaps this is the last of the Goan beaches. By the bus stop there is a chai shop and a few tiny shops. A road takes you to the village by the sea where kids will offer you a room for around Rs 10 a day. All you get is bare walls and no beds apart from in an old hotel/house which is always full in any case. You can rent mattresses, cookers and all the rest from two shops at the village – obviously one comes here for at least a week. In the village there are 10

or so chai shops that serve 'westernised-Indian' food for around Rs 6. The seashore is beautiful, the village quiet and friendly – just a few hundred locals, mostly fishermen, and a couple of hundred western residents in the November to February high season. Over a rocky hill, 10 minutes walk from the village beach, there's another beach with the last of the hippies, young people living in huts made of palm leaves on the slopes of a jungle valley with a river that makes an inland lake, just 20 metres from the sea. Some mutter that the lake is being polluted by people who come, stay two days, and use soap....

Getting There

To get to Harambol, near Harmal on the maps, is a near three hour bus journey from Mapusa.

OTHER ATTRACTIONS IN GOA
Bondla Wildlife Sanctuary

Up in the foothills of the Western Ghats, Bondla is being promoted by the Department of Tourism and is a good place to see sambar and wild boar among other things. It's the smallest of the Goan Wildlife Sanctuaries but the only one at present which has accommodation for those wishing to stay more than a day. The larger sanctuaries are Molem Wildlife Sanctuary and Cotigao Wildlife Sanctuary.

You can get to Bondla bus via Ponda or on a tourist bus trip if they are being run. Accommodation is available at Bondla at the *Tourist Cottages* where rooms cost Rs 12/18 from October to May and Rs 8/12 between June and September. There is also dormitory accommodation available for Rs 5 a bed.

Temples

When the Portuguese arrived in Goa they destroyed every Hindu temple and Moslem mosque they could lay hands on, so temples in Goa are generally back from the coast and comparatively new. Despite their earnest attempts to spread Roman Catholicism only 38% of Goans today are Christian. In Ponda itself is the Safe

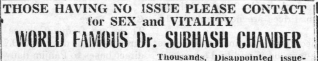

Masjid mosque which was built in 1560 and for some reason the Portuguese neglected to knock it down.

Most of the Hindu temples of interest are close to Ponda, on the inland route between Panaji and Margao. The Shiva temple of Shri Mangesh is at Priol-Ponda Taluka, about 22 km from Panaji. The tiny temple with its white tower, a local landmark, is situated on top of a small hill. Only a km further down the road is Shri Mahalsa, a Vishnu temple.

About five km from Ponda are Shri Ramnath and Shri Mahalakshmi and nearby is the Shri Shantadurga temple. Dedicated to Shantadurga, the goddess of peace, it has a strange, almost pagoda-like, tower in the temple compound. To get to these temples get off the bus about a km on the Old Goa side of Ponda and take the turn on your right (if travelling towards Ponda, left if travelling away).

Forts

There are quite a number of old Portuguese forts dotted around Goa, most of them on the coast. Most of them are in a reasonable state of preservation and are worth a visit if you have the time. The one at Chapora is particularly recommended. Only one of them has been converted into hotel accommodation. This is the one at Terekhol on the coast at the extreme northern tip of Goa. Rooms here cost Rs 15/25 between October and May and Rs 10/15 between June and September. Dormitory accommodation is also available.

Festivals

The Christian festivals in Goa take place on the following dates:

6 January	Feast of Three Kings at Reis Magos, Cansaulim and Chandor.
2 February	Feast of Our Lady of Candelaria at Pomburpa.
February/March	Carnival.
Monday after 5th Sunday in Lent	Procession of the Franciscan Order at Old Goa.
1st Sunday after Easter	Feast of Jesus of Nazareth at Siridao.
16 days after Easter	Feast of Our Lady of Miracles at Mapusa.
24 August	Festival of Novidades.
1st fortnight of October	Fama de Menino Jesus at Colva.
3rd Wednesday of November	Feast of Our Lady of the Rosary.
3 December	Feast of St Francis Xavier at Old Goa.
8 December	Feast of Our Lady of Immaculate Conception at Panjim and Margao.
25 December	Christmas.

The old adage that 'many hands make light work' certainly gets its come-uppance in India. Every job has at least twice as many people doing it as necessary, and inevitably the result is it takes twice as long. Indian hotel employees always seem to be scurrying around cleaning things up, but as often as not that simply means sweeping everything under the bed.

Karnataka

Population: 32 million
Area: 191,773 square km
Capital: Bangalore
Main language: Kannada

The state of Karnataka, formerly known as Mysore, is one of the more easy-going Indian states. It's a state of strong contrasts with the modern, industrialised city of Bangalore at one extreme and the expanses of rural farming areas at the other. Karnataka also has some of the most interesting historic architecture in India, and a varied and tumultous history.

It was to Sravanabelagola in Karnataka that Chandragupta Maurya, India's first great emperor, retreated after he had renounced worldly ways and embraced Jainism. Later the mighty statue of Gomateshvara was erected at Sravanabelagola and it celebrated its 1000th anniversary in 1981. At Badami, in the north of the state, the Chalukyans built some of the earliest Hindu temples in India, 1500 years ago. All later south Indian temple architecture stems from the Chalukyan designs at Badami and the Pallavas at Kanchipuram and Mahabalipuram in Tamil Nadu.

Other important Indian dynasties, such as the Cholas and the Gangas, have also played their part in Karnataka's history, but it was the Hoysalas, who ruled between the 11th and 14th centuries, who left the most vivid evidence of their presence. The beautiful Hoysala temples at Somnathpur, Belur and Halebid are gems of Indian architecture with intricate and detailed sculptures rivalling anything to be found at Khajuraho or Konorak.

In 1327 Hindu Halebid fell to the Moslem army of Mohammed bin Tughlaq and in the succeeding centuries Karnataka was held by first the followers of one religion, then the other. Founded in 1336,

the Hindu kingdom of Vijayanagar, with its capital at Hampi, is one of the least visited and thus most surprising of India's ruined kingdoms. Vijayanagar reached its peak in the early 1550s, but in 1565 it fell to the Deccan Sultans and Bijapur became the most important city of the region. Today Bijapur is just a small city surrounded by an imposing wall and packed with an amazing collection of mosques and other reminders of its glorious past.

Finally Hyder Ali took control in 1761 and the seat of power moved back south to Srirangapatnam near Mysore. His son, Tipu Sultan, with help from the French, further extended his father's kingdom and put the British in their place on more than one occasion before being finally defeated and killed in 1799.

The British installed a Hindu ruler when they brought the region under their control and a series of enlightened and progressive rulers held power right through to independence. The Maharaja at that time was so popular that he became the first governor of the state.

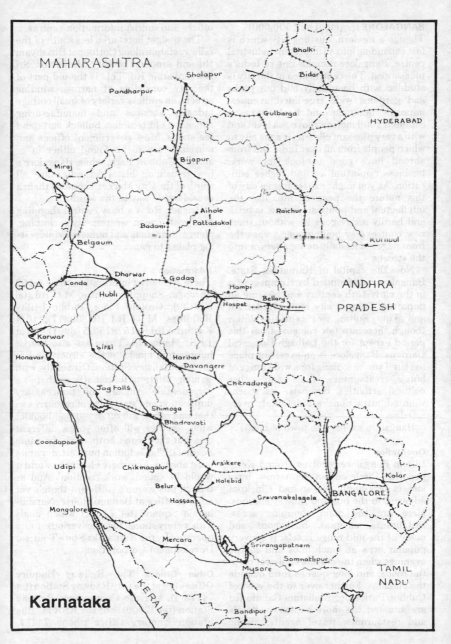

MAHARASHTRA

Sholapur

Pandharpur

Bhalki

Bidar

Gulbarga

HYDERABAD

Miraj

Bijapur

Belgaum

Aihole

Badami

Pattadakal

Raichur

Kurnool

GOA

Londa

Dharwar

Gadag

Hampi

Bellary

ANDHRA

PRADESH

Hubli

Hospet

Karwar

Sirsi

Honavar

Harihar

Davangere

Chitradurga

Jog Falls

Shimoga

Bhadravati

Coondapoor

Udipi

Chikmagalur

Arsikere

Kolar

Belur

Halebid

BANGALORE

Mangalore

Hassan

Sravanabelagola

Mercara

Srirangapatnam

Somnathpur

TAMIL
NADU

Mysore

KERALA

Bandipur

Karnataka

BANGALORE (population 2,500,000)
Though a modern, bustling city which is fast expanding into an important industrial centre, Bangalore remains one of India's pleasantest. The central area of the city is studded with beautifully laid out parks and gardens, wide tree-lined avenues, imposing buildings and lively bazaars. Situated 1000 metres above sea level and with a very pleasant climate, it's the city to which people from all over India and from abroad have gone to look for work, business opportunities and higher education. As you might expect from a city of this nature the pace of life, like the intellectual and political climate, is brisk and hardly a day goes by without some new controversy boiling over across the front pages of its daily newspapers or into the streets.

Now the capital of Karnataka State, Bangalore was founded by Kempegowda in the early 16th century and became an important fortress city under Hyder Ali and Tipu Sultan two centuries later, though there are few remains from this period except for the Lalbagh Botanical Gardens. Bangalore is an excellent place to visit if you're looking for a wide range of hotels, restaurants, films and other cultural activities, otherwise its much-vaunted 'attractions' are definitely over-rated.

Bangalore means 'the town of beans'.

Orientation

Life in Bangalore revolves around Kempegowda Circle and in the narrow, busy streets of Gandhi Nagar and Chickpet adjacent to the bus and railway stations. Here are the main shopping areas, restaurants, cinemas, bookshops and many of the mid-range hotels. It's a very popular area at lunchtimes and in the evenings when the crowds spill over on to the roads, and long queues form outside the cinemas. Further over to the west of Cubbon Park along Mahatma Gandhi Rd are situated the more expensive hotels and restaurants, travel agents, airline offices and tourist information centres.

The budget hotel area lies south of the railway station along Cottonpet Bhashyam Rd and around the City Market on Sri Narsimharaja Rd. This is the old part of the city consisting of narrow, winding streets, an endless variety of small cottage industry services and manufacturing concerns, old temples, bullock carts and tea shops. Most government offices and museums are to be found either in or around Cubbon Park, while Bangalore's few remaining historical relics are all south of the City Market – some of them a considerable way to the south.

Brigade Rd is a busy central shopping area with cheap western-style clothing, plenty of cinemas and numerous interesting places to eat.

Information

There are tourist information offices at 52 Shrungar Shopping Centre, M G Rd (tel 579139); Ground Floor, Public Utility Buildings, M G Rd (tel 52377); 10/4 Kasturba Rd (tel 578753/578901) and at 19 St Marks Rd. There are also tourist information kiosks at the airport and at the City Railway Station. Obviously, with so many different tourist offices, there's a considerable amount of unnecessary duplication and stretching of resources so that one office will offer you one booklet while another will offer you a different one, but they won't both stock the same booklets. This is Indian bureaucracy at its most absurd. Anywhere else in the world it would be called 'work creation'. And as though this weren't sufficient there's yet another office at Badami House, Narsimharaja Square (tel 74711) which deals with reservations for the various tours operated by the Karnataka State Tourism Development Corporation!

Other Offices The Railway Enquiry Offices are at the City Railway Station (tel 74173-4), and the Cantonment Railway Station (tel 27000). For the KSRTC Bus Station Enquiry Office phone 73377.

Indian Airlines (tel 79431) is at the CBAB Buildings, K G Rd. Air India (tel 77222, 76396) is at Unity Buildings J C Rd. Thomas Cook (tel 51729) is at M G Rd, Bangalore I. The British Libary, near Oxford University Press at the Cubbon end of M G Rd, has lots of British newspapers and magazines.

Vidhana Soudha

This is Bangalore's – and indeed one of India's – most spectacular buildings. Built of granite in the neo-Dravidian style of architecture and located at the northern end of Cubbon Park, it houses both the Secretariat and the State Legislature. The cabinet room is famous for its massive door made of pure sandalwood. The building is floodlit on Sunday evenings and on public holidays. If you want to pay a visit join the queue at the top of the main front entrance staircase at 5.30 to 6.30 pm.

Cubbon Park

One of the main 'lungs' of the city, this beautiful shady park, full of flowering trees, covers an area of 120 hectares and was laid out in 1864. In it are to be found the red Gothic building which houses the Public Library, the High Court, the Government Museum and the Technological and Industrial Museum.

The Government Museum, one of the oldest in India, was established in 1886 and houses sections on geology, art, numismatics and relics from Moenjodaro (one of the cradles of Indian civilisation, dating back 5000 years). 'I think the curator must have died 50 years ago and not been replaced', wrote a museum-goer. 'The caption on one stuffed fish stated that the flesh was somewhat insipid and eaten only by the lower classes of natives!' Admission costs Rs 0.20 and the museum is open daily except Wednesdays and public holidays from 8 am to 5 pm.

The Technological and Industrial Museum, also on Kasturba Rd adjacent to the Government Museum, is open daily except Mondays and public holidays between 10 am and 5 pm. Admission costs Rs 0.20. Its theme is the application of science and technology to industry and human welfare. It's full of exciting exhibits reflecting India's justified pride in its technological progress and full of happy children pressing buttons.

Lalbagh Botanical Gardens

Again, a beautiful and popular park located in the southern suburbs of Bangalore. It covers an area of 96 hectares and was laid out in the 18th century by Hyder Ali and his son Tipu Sultan. It contains many centuries-old trees (most of them labelled), lakes, lotus ponds, flower beds, a deer park and one of the largest collections of rare tropical and sub-tropical plants in India. Refreshments are available at several places within the park.

The Fort

Located on Krishnarajendra Rd close to the City Market, this was originally a mud-brick structure built in 1537 by Kempegowda. It was later rebuilt in stone in the 18th century by Hyder Ali and Tipu Sultan, but much of it was destroyed during the wars with the British and you would be missing little if you left it out of your itinerary. It is supposed to be open daily from 8 am, but this isn't always the case.

Tipu Sultan's Summer Palace

Situated on Albert Victor Rd near the junction with Krishnarajendra Rd, this palace was begun by Tipu Sultan's father, Hyder Ali, and completed by Tipu in 1791. It resembles the Daria Daulat Bagh at Srirangapatnam near Mysore City, but has been sadly neglected and is falling into disrepair. You may well find the temple next to it of far greater interest. The palace is open daily from 6 am to 6 pm. Admission is free.

1 City Railway Station
2 Central Bus Station
3 Vidhana Soudha
4 GPO
5 Government Museum &
   Technological Museum
6 City Market

7 The Fort
8 Tipu Sultan's Palace
9 Bull Temple
10 Sudha Lodge
11 Kaveri Arts & Crafts Emporium
12 Cantonment Railway Station

Top End hotels & restaurants
(Mahatma Gandhi Rd)

Bottom End hotels
(City Market)

Mid Range hotels & restaurants
(Kempegowda Circle & Gandhi Nagar)

The Bull Temple

Situated on Bugle Hill at the end of Bull Temple Rd, this is one of Bangalore's oldest temples. Built by Kempegowda in the Dravidian style, it contains a huge monolith of Nandi similar to the one on Chamundi Hill at Mysore. Non-Hindus are allowed to enter and the priests are friendly. You will be offered jasmine flowers and expected to leave a small donation.

Other

The remains of the four watch towers built by Kempegowda are worth a visit if you're in the vicinity of the Bull Temple. They are situated about 400 metres to the west of the temple. Ulsoor Lake, to the east of Cubbon Park, has boating facilities and a swimming pool.

Tours

The Karnataka State Tourism Development Corporation offers the following tours:

Bangalore City Daily except Sundays from the City Railway Station. The tour starts at 8 am and ends at 7 pm and includes visits to Tipu's Palace, Bull Temple, Lalbagh Botanical Gardens, Ulsoor Lake, Government Soap Factory, Vidhana Soudha, Cubbon Park, Government Museum, Technology Museum and Art Gallery. The tour costs Rs 25.

Srirangapatnam, Mysore City & Brindavan Gardens Daily tours beginning at 7.15 am and returning at 10.45 pm. The tour includes visits to the Ranganathaswamy Temple, the Fort, Gumbaz and Daria Daulat Bagh at Srirangapatna and St Philomena's Cathedral, Chamundi Hill, the Palace, Art Gallery and Cauvery Arts and Crafts Emporium at Mysore. The tour costs Rs 65 by de-luxe and Rs 80 by air-con bus.

Nandi Hills Daily tours in the season – from March to June – as well as Sundays and holidays throughout the year, which depart at 8 am and return at 6 pm. Nandi Hills is the nearest hill station to Bangalore at 1479 metres, and was once the summer retreat of Tipu Sultan. The tour costs Rs 35.

Hampi & Tungabhadra Dam This is a two-day tour, which departs on Fridays at 10 pm and returns to Bangalore at 9.30 pm on Sunday. It includes visits to Mantralaya, the village associated with the Hindu saint, Raghavendra Swami, to the Tungabhadra Dam and to Hampi. Overnight accommodation is at the *T B Dam Hotel*. The cost of the tour is Rs 160, including accommodation.

There is also a three-day tour to Srirangapatnam, Mysore, Ooty and the

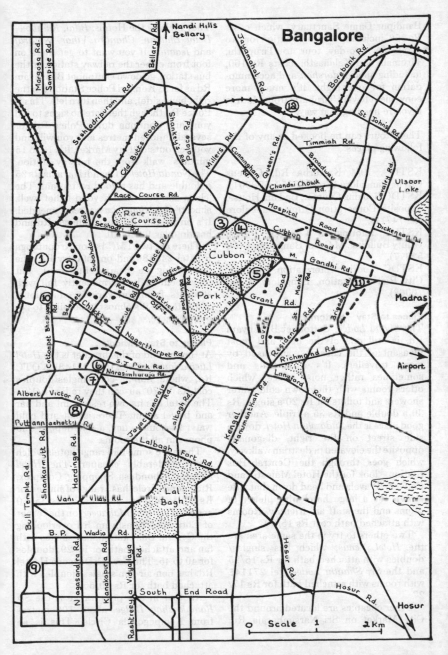

Bangalore

Nandi Hills
Bellary

Nandi Hills
Bellary Rd.

Margosa Rd.
Sampige Rd.

Jaganmath Rd.

Borebank Rd.

St John's Rd.

Seshadripuram

Shankey's Palace Rd.

Old Butts Road

Millers Rd.

Cunningham Rd.

Queen's Rd.

Timmiah Rd.

Broadway

Chandni Chowk Rd.

Cavalry Rd.

Ulsoor Lake

Race Course Rd.

Race Course

Hospital Road

Dickenson Rd.

Seshadri Rd.

③ ④

Cubbon

Cubbyon Road

M. Gandhi Rd.

① ②

Subahdar

Palace Rd.

Post Office Rd.

Upachchapp Rd.

Park

⑤

Markt Rd.

St. Marks Rd.

⑪

Madras

Kemplegowda Rd.

District Office

Kempegowda

Grant Rd.

Residency Rd.

Brigade Rd.

⑩

Salpet

Cottonpet Bhasyan

Chickpet Rd.

Nagarthpet Rd.

Lavelle

Airport

⑥

S.T. Park Rd.

Narasimharaja Rd.

Richmond Road

Lansford Rd.

⑦

Albert Victor Rd.

Jayachamaraja Rd.

Fallbagh Rd.

Kengal Hanumanthiah Rd.

⑧

Puttannachetty Rd.

Shankarmtt Rd.

Hardinge Rd.

Lalbagh Fort Rd.

Lal Bagh

Vani Vilas Rd.

Wadia Rd.

Bull Temple Rd.

B.P.

Nagasandra Rd.

Kanakapura Rd.

Rashtreeya Vidyalaya Rd.

South End Road

Hosur Rd.

Hosur Rd.

Hosur

⑨

N

Scale

0 1 2 Km

Bandipur Game Sanctuary, which costs Rs 250, including accommodation for two nights. A two-day tour to Tirupathi, Tirumala and Kalahasthi, costs Rs 160, including special *darshan* and accommodation for one night. It's much more convenient to visit Tirupathi from Madras if you're heading that way.

These tours can be booked at any of the following places:

KSTDC, 10/4 Kasturba Rd, Queens Circle, Bangalore 1 (tel 578753, 578901).
KSTDC Booking Counter, Badami House, opposite Corporation Office, Bangalore (tel 74711).
KSTDC Information Counter, Public Utility Building, M G Rd, Bangalore 1 (tel 52377).
KSTDC Tourist Information Counter, City Railway Station, Bangalore 2 (tel 70068).

Places to Stay – Bottom End

The *Sudha Lodge*, Cottonpet Bhashyam Rd, is still one of the best and most pleasant of the cheapies, and used by many travellers. It's a no-frills and sometimes rather noisy place, which offers rooms with their own cold water showers and toilets for Rs 20 a single, Rs 30 a double and Rs 35 a triple. Another good place is the *Sudarshan Hotel*, down a side street on the right, diagonally opposite the elevated pedestrian walkway, which goes through the Central Bus Station – look for the Hotel Majestic and Cauvery Travels and head down that side street. It's a large hotel with plenty of rooms and the staff are friendly. Rooms with attached bath cost Rs 15/30.

Two others to try in the same area are the *Hotel Venus*, which has singles/doubles with attached bath for Rs 15/25 and the *Sri Shanthi Lodge* (tel 27114), with rooms with attached bath for Rs 17/27.

Other cheapies are located around the City Market on Sri Narsimharaja Rd.

They include the Hotels: *Bilal, Rainbow, Delhi Bhavan, Chandra Vihar, Nataraj* and *Isaquia*. If you want to get there on foot from either the railway station or the bus station, go down Cottonpet Bhashyam Rd as far as Kengeri Police Station (on the right hand side), and then turn left. This is Police Rd though there are no signs to tell you this. Continue down Police Rd for several hundred metres and you will find yourself outside City Market. It's 10 to 15 minutes' walk from the railway station. The *Nanda Hotel* in Ghandi Nagar is Rs 25 a double and has a good restaurant. The 'clean and luxurious beyond belief (well, almost)' *Hotel Sumukha* was recommended. It's on Double Rd near Lalbagh Rd and has doubles for Rs 50.

There are two *YMCAs* – on Nrupatunga Rd (tel 24848) and on Infantry Rd (the latter being the cheaper of the two) – but they seem to be permanently full with students from the various educational institutes, so it's almost impossible to get a room there.

Places to Stay – Middle

At the top end of this bracket is the *Hotel Luciya International* (tel 224148), 6 OTC Rd, where non-air-con singles/doubles cost Rs 50/70, air-con they're Rs 75/125. The hotel has its own restaurant and bar and travel agent. There is hot and cold water 24 hours a day, a safe deposit and phones in all the rooms.

There are some mid range hotels which are considerably cheaper. The *Hotel Nataraj*, Dhondusa Shopping Complex, Richmond Circle, has a range of singles for Rs 40, 45 and 60, doubles for Rs 55, 60 and 80. The *Hotel Mahaveer*, on the corner of Cottonpet Bhashyam Rd overlooking the Central Bus Station, has singles with fan and attached bath for Rs 29, doubles for 40 to 45. The *Geo*, 11 Devanga Hostel Rd, has non-air-con singles/doubles with attached bath for Rs 40/55.

Another in this price range is the *Sri Ramakrishna Lodge*, about 100 metres from Kempegowda Circle. This is an enormous Hindu-style hotel where you can always find a room if other places are full. Rooms here – all with attached bath – cost Rs 30/50. Rooms facing the street cost slightly more. The hotel has its own restaurant.

Also in this bracket is *Gupta's Board & Lodging* (tel 75131, 75136), 1st floor, Gupta Market, Kempegowda Rd. Gupta Market is the shopping complex right next to Kempegowda Circle and the hotel is on the same floor as the Aishwarya Restaurant. This place has been recommended by quite a few travellers. All rooms have attached bath and they cost Rs 37/40 or Rs 60 for a de-luxe double – Rs 45 for single occupancy of the latter.

The *Hotel Tourist*, Race Course Rd near the junction with Subahdar Rd, is a huge place, but it's often full. Rooms with attached bath cost Rs 25/40. The *Suprabhatha Hotel* (tel 71821, 71241), Sri Krishna Complex, 32 Sheshadri Rd near the Ananda Rao Circle, has rooms for Rs 28/50. Another huge Hindu style boarding house is the *Hotel Hindustan*, Gandhi Nagar just off Kempegowda Circle, which has singles/doubles for Rs 25/45 with attached bath, fan and clean sheets.

Places to Stay – Top End

The *ITDC Hotel Ashok* (tel 79411) at Kumara Krupa, High Grounds is close to central Bangalore and has all mod-cons from tennis courts, shops and a swimming pool to full air-conditioning. Singles/ doubles cost from Rs 300/400. The *Bangalore International* (tel 26011) is at 2A-B Crescent Rd, High Grounds and is rather smaller than the large Hotel Ashok. Singles/doubles here are available with air-con from Rs 190/285, or without from Rs 140/210.

The *West End* (tel 29281-89) is on Race Course Rd, High Grounds and is again fully air-con with singles/doubles from Rs 350/450. This hotel has a particularly pleasant garden and pool area and an excellent, though expensive, restaurant. The new *Taj Residency* (tel 563566) on M G Rd has rooms from Rs 300/400. The new, swish and spacious Welcomgroup *Windsor Manor* at 25 Sankey Rd has rooms at Rs 425/625. It's a good place for a splash out buffet lunch. Other more expensive hotels in Bangalore include:

Shilton (tel 54471), St Mark's Rd – singles/ doubles Rs 150/200 air-con, Rs 100/140 non-air-con. There's a good cellar restaurant but it's a little out of town, Rs 4 by rickshaw from the bus station.
Rama (tel 53381), Levelle Rd – singles/doubles Rs 110/140 non-air-con.
East-West (tel 53265), Residency Rd – singles/ doubles Rs Rs 165/225 non-air-con, Rs 180/ 250 air-con.
Harsha (tel 74071), Shivajinagar – singles/ doubles Rs 150/175 non-air-con, Rs 200/225 air-con.

Places to Eat

In the Gandhi Nagar and Chickpet areas of Bangalore, it's impossible to walk more than a few metres without coming across a restaurant. There are literally thousands. The only trouble is that most of them offer just the standard south India fare of dosa, idlil, rice and vegetables and coffee, but they are clean and extremely cheap – a masala dosa and coffee costs on average Rs 2.50.

If you'd like something more substantial than this there are several *Kamat Hotels* (for example, on S C Rd and on Sri Narsimharaja Rd) where you can get a good 'plate meal' (thali) for Rs 4, consisting of three different curry sauces, fried vegetables, curd, pickles, three puris and rice. These cafes are always good value. If you'd like more choice, an excellent place is the *Hotel Blue Star* opposite the Tribhuvan Cinema in Gandhi Nagar at the back of Kempegowda Circle. It has an extensive menu (both vegetarian and non-vegetarian) which includes curried dishes, omelettes, chicken, fish (and chips!), tandoori. Chicken mughlai, nan, salad, lassi and tea cost Rs 14.

A place which can be highly recommended for a night out, and one that's very popular with local people, is the *Aishwarya Restaurant* (tel 79143), 1st floor, Gupta Market, Kempegowda Rd. The food in this restaurant is excellent, service is good, and they have an extensive range of vegetarian and non-vegetarian dishes. There is an attached bar – Rs 12 for a big bottle of Kingfisher beer. Mutton mughlai, allu gobi and nan came to Rs 15 – large helpings. On Lalbagh Rd near Double Rd the *Hotel Olympia* has good western and Indian food at reasonable prices; as does the locally popular *Elite Restaurant* opposite the bus station.

In Cubbon Park the KSTDC run *Mayura Cubbon Park Restaurant*, near the State Library, has good and very economical food. At the top of the price range the *Mandarin*, on the 6th floor of the Ashok Hotel, has excellent Chinese food.

Getting There

Air Indian Airlines have twice daily flights between Bangalore and Hyderabad or Bombay, daily flights to and from Delhi, Calcutta, Cochin, Madurai or Dabolim (Goa), plus less frequent connections to Bhubaneswar and other centres. Madras-Bangalore flights are up to four times daily. Fares include Bombay Rs 635, Cochin Rs 284, Delhi Rs 1174, Hyderabad Rs 398, Dabolim Rs 370, Madras Rs 228 and Madurai Rs 276.

Rail Bangalore is connected by direct daily express trains with all the main cities in southern and central India and with New Delhi. But, as elsewhere in India where there is more than one express per day, you should be careful to choose the right train if speed is your priority as journey times vary considerably from one express to the next. Naturally, the fastest night express trains are often booked out days in advance so your choice may be limited. Also note that no tourist quota is available for sleeping berths at Bangalore Station. They do have a VIP quota but they are very reluctant to release these to

tourists. If you're stuck it's worth a try – contact the Station Superintendant on Platform 1. One writer reported getting an 'emergency quota' without difficulty.

The express train to New Delhi (Karnataka Express) departs twice a week on Wednesdays and Sundays and takes 38 hours to make the 2491-km trip. The fare in 1st class is Rs 502, in 2nd class it's Rs 129.50 plus sleeping berth charges. The Bangalore-Trivandrum Express leaves daily at 8.20 pm and costs Rs 220 in 1st, Rs 56 in 2nd plus berth charges. The 791-km trip takes about 20 hours.

Bangalore to Bombay (Udyan Express) departs daily at 4.10 pm and costs Rs 288 in 1st class, Rs 73.50 in 2nd. If it's full, take either the Mahalaxmi Express (daily at 6 am), or the Kittur Express (7.25 pm every day), and get another train from Miraj to Bombay. Bombay-Bangalore is 1221 km and the trip takes around 27 hours.

To Madras you have a choice of the fast Brindavan Express at 1.50 pm each day, the Bangalore-Madras Express, 7.50 am daily, or the Bangalore-Madras Mail at 9.50 pm daily. The fare is Rs 110 in 1st, Rs 29 plus berth charges (if necessary) in 2nd class, and the 358-km journey takes about seven hours.

From Bangalore to Hyderabad, there is the daily express train at 9.25 pm and it costs Rs 206 in 1st class, or Rs 63.50 in 2nd class, plus berth charges. The 646-km trip takes about 18 hours.

There are five daily trains to Mysore, some of them faster than others – three hours is about the average. They are the Mysore Express, Kaveri Express, Chamundi Express, Mysore Mail and Tippu Express. Most people take the buses between these two cities.

Bus Bangalore has a well-organised central bus station for all long-distance buses. It's situated directly in front of the City Railway Station. Some of the more important routes include:

Bijapur Two buses daily at 5.15 am and 6.30 pm

Bombay Three buses daily at 8 am, 2 pm and 7 pm. The state bus costs Rs 120 and takes 24 or more hours. Luxury video buses, departing from near the railway station, cost Rs 160.

Calicut Two buses daily at 9 am and 1 pm

Ernakulam Three buses daily at 5 am, 7 am and 6 pm

Hassan Nine buses daily, the first at 7.30 am and the last at 7 pm

Hospet Three buses daily at 6.30 am, 10.30 am and noon

Jog Falls One bus daily at 6.30 pm

Madras Three buses daily at 7 am, 2 pm and 10 pm. The trip takes about nine hours. Ordinary buses cost Rs 30, de-luxe are Rs 35.

Mangalore 12 buses daily, the first at 6.45 am and the last at 11 pm

Mysore 17 buses daily, the first at 5.30 am and the last at 10 pm. Takes 3½ hours and costs around Rs 14.

Ooty Two buses daily at 6.30 am and 8 am

All the above buses are operated by the Karnataka State Road Transport Corporation. Andhra Pradesh State Road Transport Corporation and Tiruvalluvar Transport Corporation also run buses from the same terminal. Of interest is the twice-daily APSRTC bus service to Hyderabad; the first departing at 6 pm and costing Rs 66.50, the second at 8 pm – a super de-luxe – costing Rs 72.50. Tiruvalluvar has buses running to Madras eight times a day, starting at 8.10 am and finishing at 11 pm. The fare is Rs 37 (super de-luxe) and Rs 51 (air-con). The buses go via Chittor or Vellore. Tiruvalluvar also has buses to Madurai daily at 6 pm, 8 pm and 9 pm, which go via Dindigul and cost Rs 44.50.

In addition to the various state buses detailed above, there are numerous private companies which offer buses between Bangalore and the other major cities in central and southern India. You'll find them all over the central area. Their prices are higher than the state service, but their buses are better and there's more leg room – important on long journeys.

The thing you need to watch out for is that recent Indian fad – 'video coaches'. We know you've travelled on these buses in South-East and North-East Asia and found them pleasant enough, but this is India. By the time you've reached Bangalore, you'll be well aware of what Indians do with the volume control on any sound equipment. If you think you're going to get any sleep in the back seats of these buses because you're a long way from the TV screen, forget it. If that's what you want, don't take a 'video coach' – the ones without video are also cheaper!

Getting Around

Taking a taxi or auto-rickshaw from the airport be careful you don't get stuck with the parking fee which a sign clearly states is the driver's responsibility. Since the airport is outside the city limits you'll probably have to agree an over the meter fee.

Things to Buy

The Cauvery Arts and Crafts Emporium, 23 Mahatma Gandhi Road (tel 51418), like its sister establishment at Mysore, stocks a huge range of superb handcrafted tables, carvings (many of them in sandalwood), ivory ware, jewellery, ceramics, carpets and *agarbathis*. Few things are cheap as such, but this emporium stocks some of the best craft work in India and they're good at packing and posting.

AROUND BANGALORE
Nandi Hills

This hill station is 68 km from Bangalore and was a popular summer retreat even in Tipu Sultan's days. Tipu's drop, a 600-metre high cliff face, provides a good view over the surrounding country. There are two ancient temples here and cheap

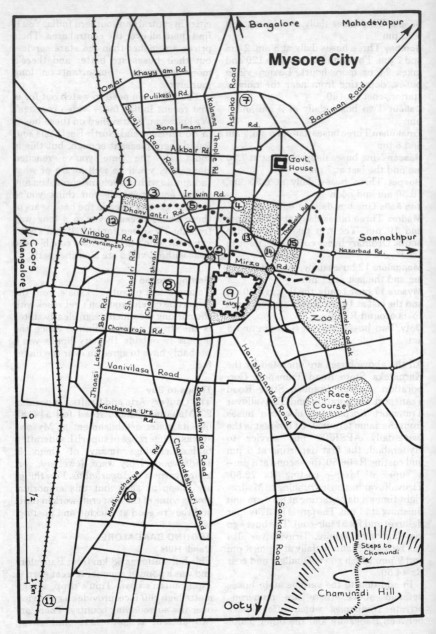

Mysore City

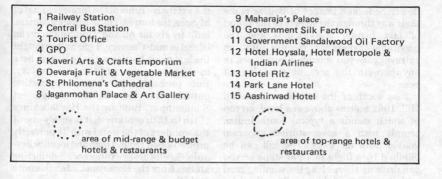

1 Railway Station
2 Central Bus Station
3 Tourist Office
4 GPO
5 Kaveri Arts & Crafts Emporium
6 Devaraja Fruit & Vegetable Market
7 St Philomena's Cathedral
8 Jaganmohan Palace & Art Gallery

9 Maharaja's Palace
10 Government Silk Factory
11 Government Sandalwood Oil Factory
12 Hotel Hoysala, Hotel Metropole &
   Indian Airlines
13 Hotel Ritz
14 Park Lane Hotel
15 Aashirwad Hotel

area of mid-range & budget
hotels & restaurants

area of top-range hotels &
restaurants

accommodation is available through the Horticulture Department in Bangalore (tel 602231).

Kolar Gold Fields

The mines here, 100 km east of Bangalore, are the major gold producers for India and are said to have the deepest mine shafts in the world, reaching over 3000 metres below the surface. Visits to the mine can be arranged.

MYSORE (population 400,000)

Sandalwood City! Everywhere you go in this beautiful city you'll find yourself enveloped with the lingering aromas of sandalwood, jasmine, rose, musk, frangipani and a hundred others. Whenever you smell them again, you'll be reminded of this place. It's one of the major centres of incense manufacture in India and scores of small, family-owned *agarbathi* (incense) factories are scattered all over town, their products exported all over the world.

Every one of those incense sticks is hand-made – usually by women and children – and a good worker can turn out at least 10,000 a day! They are made with thin slivers of bamboo, dyed red or green at one end, on to which is rolled a sandalwood putty base. The sticks are then dipped into small piles of powdered perfume and laid out to harden in the shade. You can see them being made if you visit the Government Sandalwood Oil

Factory or enquire at any of the small firms you come across.

Mysore is also a craft centre and there are numerous shops selling an incredible range of ivory, sandalwood, rosewood and teak carvings and furniture. Probably the most stunning display of these can be seen at the Cauvery Arts and Crafts Emporium in the centre of town. Their rosewood tables and elephants intricately inlaid with ivory and other woods are perhaps the best you will see anywhere in the world. Hardly anyone comes here and leaves empty-handed. It's impossible to visit the post office without seeing at least two or three travellers going through the motions of sending a package back home!

As if this were not enough, there are plenty of other reasons why you would not want to miss Mysore. Until independence, the city was the seat of the Maharajas of Mysore, a princely state covering much of present day Karnataka, and their walled Indo-Saracenic palace in the centre of the city draws visitors from all over the world. Its silhouette in many ways typifies what you would expect of Indian architecture. The ex-ruler still lives here (though the palace is open to visitors) and during the 10-day festival of Dussehra, held in the first and second week of October each year, he leads one of India's most colourful processions. Richly caparisoned elephants, liveried retainers, cavalry, the gaudy and flower-bedecked images of deities make their way through the streets to the sound of jazz bands, brass bands and the inevitable clouds of incense. It's an extravaganza you shouldn't miss if you're anywhere in the area at this time of year.

Just south of the city lies Chamundi Hill, 1062 metres above sea level, on top of which stands a typical south Indian temple with a seven-storied gopuram visible from far away. The hill can be climbed by a flight of 1000 steps or you can drive up there along the winding road with its many switchbacks. Two-thirds of the way up the hill is the famous Nandi (Shiva's Bull), a huge monolithic image always garlanded with flowers and a pilgrimage spot for Hindus.

Outside of the city to the north-west lie

the extensive ruins of the former capital of Mysore, the fortress city of Srirangapatnam, built by Hyder Ali and Tipu Sultan on an island in mid-Cauvery. Tipu Sultan fought the last of his battles with the British here in the closing years of the 18th century. But probably the biggest attraction outside the city is the temple of Somnathpur. Built by the Hoysala kings (11th to 13th centuries), it is surely one of the wonders of the world with its perfectly proportioned ground plan and its unbelievable sculptural exuberance depicting stories from the Ramayana, Mahabharata and Bhagavata epics.

Mysore is a travellers' Mecca and it's easy to see why. Apart from the attractions mentioned above, it's a friendly, easy-going city with plenty of shady trees, well-maintained public

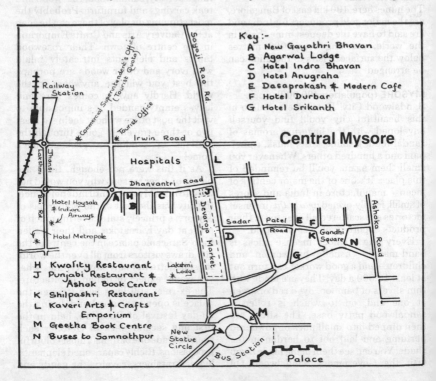

Key:-
A New Gayathri Bhavan
B Agarwal Lodge
C Hotel Indra Bhavan
D Hotel Anugraha
E Dasaprokash & Modern Cafe
F Hotel Durbar
G Hotel Srikanth

Central Mysore

H Kwality Restaurant
J Punjabi Restaurant & Ashok Book Centre
K Shilpashri Restaurant
L Kaveri Arts & Crafts Emporium
M Geetha Book Centre
N Buses to Somnathpur

buildings, clean streets, a good climate, and yet small enough not to overwhelm (you can walk from one end to the other in 20 minutes).

Orientation

The railway station and bus station are located conveniently close to the centre of the city and only a few minutes walk from all the main hotels and restaurants. The main shopping street is Sayaji Rao Rd which runs from New Statue Square on the north side of the Maharaja's Palace, across Irwin Rd to the north of the city. The budget hotels are mostly located along Dhanvantri Rd and around Gandhi Square. The mid-range and top end hotels are mostly to be found south of Government House along Nazarbad Rd and at the railway station end of Jhansi Lakshmi Bai Rd.

Information

The Tourist Office (tel 23251) is in the Old Exhibition Building, Irwin Rd. Tourist literature is available if you ask for it, and they have a breakdown of all the information you're like to need pinned to a number of boards. Most of this is sufficient, but the hotel prices are all way out-of-date. This is the sort of complaint we get about these travel guides, so it's heartening to know they can't keep up-to-date when the information is right on their doorstep!

Indian Airlines (tel 21486) is in the Hotel Mayura Hoysala on Jhansi Lakshmi Bai Rd. It's open from 10 am to 5.15 pm daily, but is closed for lunch between 1.30 to 2.15 pm. Don't miss Mysore's eccentric evening newspaper the *Star of Mysore*.

Bookshops Two very good bookshops in Mysore are the Geetha Book House, New Statue Square (at the bottom of Sayaji Rao Rd) and the Ashok Book Centre, Dhanvantri Rd (near the junction with Sayaji Rao Rd). Both have plenty of English-language paperbacks and Penguin books.

Festivals During the 10-day Dussehra festival in early October each year accommodation prices can zoom to the sky, if you can even find a room. Mysore also has an active horse race course, patronised by the Maharaja.

Wildlife Sanctuaries If you're planning a visit to the wildlife sanctuaries of Bandipur (80 km from Mysore) or Nagarhole (93 km from Mysore), it's advisable to book accommodation and transport in advance with the following people:

Bandipur Field Director, Project Tiger, Government House, Nazirbad, Mysore (tel 20901).

Nagarhole Assistant Conservator of Forests, Wildlife Preservation, Chamarajendra Circle, Vanivilas Rd, Mysore (tel 21159). At present there are two travellers' bungalows at Nagarhole – *Kaveri* and *Gangothri*. They both cost Rs 25 a double but *Kaveri* is the better of the two. There's also dormitory accommodation available. Contact the range officer there, Mr Chinappa, if you want to go for a ride in their safari van (24 km ride for Rs 5 per person. If you have your own van the entrance fee is Rs 14). No elephant rides are available at present.

Maharaja's Palace

The beautiful profile of this walled, Indo-Saracenic palace, the seat of the Maharajas of Mysore, dominates the city's skyline. It was built in 1911-12 at a cost of Rs 4.2 million to replace the former palace which was burnt down. Internally it reminds one of an Afghani waistcoat – an extravaganza of stained glass, mirrors, gilt and gaudy colours. But there are some beautiful, carved wooden doors and mosaic floors as well as a whole series of mediocre, though historically interesting, paintings depicting life in Mysore during the Edwardian Raj. Note the beautifully carved mahogany ceilings, solid silver doors, white marble floors and superb columned Durbar Hall.

The palace even has its own Hindu temple inside the walls, complete with gopuram. On Sunday nights the palace is spectacularly illuminated. The Maharaja is still in residence at the back of the palace.

It's certainly worth a visit though, depending on how many tourist coaches there are outside in the parking lot, it can rival the departure lounge of a major international airport. Check this out before you go in! Entry is from the south gate only and the palace is open daily from 10.30 am to 5.30 pm. Tickets cost Rs 2 and you must leave your shoes at the shoe deposit (there's a 10 paise charge for this). 'For once we forgot our scruples and used our status as foreigners to jump the three hour queue,' reported a visitor. Booklets about the palace are on sale inside. Outside in the parking lot there's a permanent gaggle of snakeskin sellers and postcard vendors. The postcards are abysmal; the snakeskins are better but you have to haggle for at least 20 minutes before the price gets reasonable.

Chamundi Hill
You can spend a very pleasant half day walking up the 1000 steps to the top of this hill where the temple to Sri Chamundeswari stands. It's a fairly strenuous climb but there are plenty of trees on the way up. The views over the surrounding countryside and Mysore City, even from half-way up, are superb. Two-thirds of the way up you come across the famous Nandi (Shiva's bull) carved out of solid rock and, at five metres high, perhaps the largest in India. It's always garlanded in flowers and constantly visited by bevies of pilgrims offering *prasad* to the priest in attendance there.

Sri Chamundeswari temple on the summit is a huge structure with a seven-storey gopuram 40 metres high. Visiting hours (non-Hindus are allowed inside) are 9 am to 12 noon and 5 pm to 9 pm. The priests are quite enthusiastic to show you around. If you don't walk up the hill or,

having walked up, you don't want to walk back down again, there are buses approximately every half hour from the central bus station. The terminus on the hill is about 300 metres from the temple. Demand for buses can be very heavy on Sundays (I've seen 500 people waiting for a bus!). Refreshments, snacks and south Indian plate meals are available at cafes around the temple. Note that local guide books and tourist literature will tell you that the summit is 13 km from the city. This refers to the road only. Going via the steps it's about four km.

Devaraja Fruit & Vegetable Market
This market stretches almost the whole length of Sayaji Rd from Dhanvantri Rd to New Statue Square and is one of the most colourful in India. Well worth a visit and, if you have a camera, excellent subject material for photographs.

Cauvery Arts & Crafts Emporium
Even if you're not going to buy anything this place is worth a visit – more details under 'What to Buy'.

Other
The **Government Sandalwood Oil Factory**, where sandalwood oil is distilled and incense sticks are made, used to be a really interesting place to visit but these days they tend to rush you round ('timed it at four minutes', reported a visitor) and quickly shepherd you into the sales office. Visiting hours are 9 am to 11 am and 2 to 4 pm daily except Sundays. Excellent sandalwood oil is on sale here at Rs 32 per 25 gm bottle. They also have some good incense.

The **Government Silk Weaving Factory**, where pure silk saris are made, is also worth a visit. It's a short walk back down the road from the sandalwood factory. Hours are 7.30 to 11.30 am and 12.30 to 4.30 pm daily except Sundays.

Other places worth a visit in town are the **Sri Chamarajendra Art Gallery** housed in the Jaganmohan Palace. Not only does it display paintings, particularly by Ravi Varma, but also handicrafts, historical objects of interest and rare musical instruments. Visiting hours are 8 am to 5 pm daily. Entrance costs Rs 1. **St Philomena's Cathedral** is of interest if you want to see what the Christians got up to here in the last century. It's one of the largest churches in India, built in neo-Gothic style.

Tours

There are a number of tours available from Mysore which include:

Mysore City, Somnathpur, Srirangapatnam, Brindavan Gardens, Ranganathittu Bird Sanctuary (latter only in season). Daily tour starting at 7.30 am and finishing at 8.30 pm. Costs Rs 25. Frankly, this tour attempts to do too much in one day but if you're in a hurry....

Belur, Halebid & Sravanabelagola – the other two Hoysala temples and the Jain pilgrimage centre where the immense statue of Lord Gomateshvara stands. Tours on Fridays and Sundays between December and April starting at 7.30 am and finishing at 9 pm. Costs Rs 50.

Ootacamund – the hill station in the Nilgiris. Daily tours in season starting at 7 am and finishing at 9 pm. Costs Rs 50.

You can book these tours at the following places:

Mysore Tourist Centre, 2 Jhansi Lakshmi Bai Rd.
Tourist Office, Cauvery Arts & Crafts Emporium, Sayaji Rao Rd.
Tourist Office, opposite Shalimar Hotel round the corner from the New Gayathri Bhavan Hotel, Dhanvantri Rd.
Many other places especially around Gandhi Square.

Places to Stay – Bottom End

Virtually all the budget hotels are located either along Dhanvantri Rd or around Gandhi Square. There are literally scores

of them but one of the best is the *New Gayathri Bhavan* (tel 21224), Dhanvantri Rd where rooms cost Rs 18 to 20 a single and Rs 30 to 40 a double, both with attached bathroom and fan. (If they try to give you room 20 tell them you want a different one – it's incredibly small!). The rooms are secure and the staff are pleasant. There's hot water in the mornings and evenings and a 'meals' cafe downstairs.

The *Agarwal Lodge* (tel 22730), Dhanvantri Rd has rooms for Rs 22/30 for singles/doubles, both with attached bathroom. The quality and facilities are the same as the Gayathri. *Hotel Indra Bhavan* (tel 23933), Dhanvantri Rd (tel 23033) has rooms for Rs 25/35 both with attached bathroom.

Over in Gandhi Square, check out the *Hotel Satkar*, opposite the Hotel Dasaprakash. It only has a few rooms, but they're very reasonably priced at Rs 20/35, both with attached bath. The *Hotel Dasapraksh* (tel 24444) itself is a huge place with a wide choice of rooms spanning the division between bottom end and middle range. Singles cost Rs 35 to 40 and doubles Rs 60, 70, 80, 100 and 125. All rooms have attached bath and the higher priced double rooms include aircon. The hotel has a vegetarian restaurant.

Close by is the *Hotel Durbar*, which has rooms for Rs 15/25 with common bath, and Rs 40 a double with attached bath – a little over-priced for rooms with common bath and it's rather noisy at night. The hotel has a rooftop restaurant. On Ashoka Rd near Gandhi Square the *Balaji Lodge* has doubles at Rs 30 and very friendly management. Better than the Durbar wrote a Danish traveller.

One very good budget hotel which is not in the Dhanvantri Rd or Gandhi Square areas is the *Lakshmi Lodge* (tel 22316), Shivarampet (Vinoba Rd). This is a new place, clean and tidy with hot water and pleasant staff. It costs Rs 25 a single and Rs 40 a double. Outside Mysore City there is accommodation available at

Somnathpur, Srirangapatnam and the Brindavan Gardens. See Around Mysore.

Places to Stay – Middle

For value for money the KTDC *Hotel Mayura Hoysala*, (tel 25349), Jhansi Lakshmi Bai Rd, opposite the Hotel Metropole, is excellent. It offers spacious, pleasantly decorated rooms all with attached bath for Rs 50 a single and Rs 70 a double. There are also a few suites for Rs 80. The checkout time is noon and there is a bar and restaurant. Indian Airlines has its Mysore office here.

Of similar standard is the *Hotel Aashirwad*, (tel 23210), 3 Nazarbad Rd, which has an air-con bar and restaurant, money-changing facilities, laundry service and car rental counter. Air-con singles/ doubles cost Rs 60/90 while non-air-con singles are Rs 35 to 45, double Rs 50 to 60. They all have attached bathrooms and hot and cold running water. It's used mainly by Indian middle-class holiday-makers and businessmen.

Another good place in this bracket is the *Park Lane Hotel* (tel 30400), 2720 Curzon Park Rd, next to the KEB Building on the top side of the palace and close to Gandhi Square. It offers non-air-con rooms for Rs 30/50. All rooms have attached bath, and there's a very pleasant restaurant/bar on the ground floor. The *Hotel Ritz* (tel 22668), on the Bangalore-Ooty road, has rooms at the same price as the Park Lane Hotel. It's an older building with very pleasant staff, who display a remarkably sardonic sense of humour about the hotel's facilities. There's a good restaurant offering Indian, Chinese and western food and a bar.

The *Srikanth Hotel* (tel 22951), Gandhi Square, has rooms at Rs 25 a single and Rs 50 to 60 a double, both with attached bath. *Hotel Anugraha* (tel 20581), Sayaji Rao Rd, is a popular place with travellers and Indians alike as it's right in the centre of the city, and very good value for money. Rooms with attached bath cost Rs 30/50. There is no reduction for single occupancy of a double room.

Hotel Athithya (tel 25466), Dhanvantri Rd has been recently re-decorated and has well-maintained rooms with attached bathrooms – with hot and cold running water – for Rs 25/45. The management is very pleasant and tries hard to please. There is a rooftop restaurant with Indian vegetarian food and 'meals' at lunch time for just Rs 3.50.

Places to Stay – Top End

Mysore offers one of those rare Indian opportunities of staying in an ex-Maharaja's palace, so if you can afford it try the *Lalithamahal Palace* (tel 23650, 23033), a huge, gleaming white structure on the eastern outskirts of town. Rooms vary from Rs 225 to 425 although if you want the 'Viceroy Suite' you can shell out Rs 2000! The less expensive rooms are worth it for a night, even if you can't afford to stay longer, although the standards inside aren't as good as the external appearance would lead you to believe.

The *Hotel Rajendravilas* (tel 22050), at the top of Chamundi Hill, is similar and has rooms from Rs 165 to 300 and superb views over the city, particularly at night. You can drop in for a pot of coffee and biscuits in the sumptuous Canopy Restaurant for around Rs 10.

In Mysore itself the top two hotels are the *Hotel Metropole* (20681, 20871), 5 Jhansi Lakshmi Bai Rd, and the *Hotel Highway* (tel 211117), New Bannimantap Extension-7. The Metrople is tucked away in its own spacious and well kept grounds, and has air-con rooms for Rs 150 to 210, and non air-con rooms for Rs 120 to 180. All rooms have their own bathroom with hot and cold running water. There is a restaurant serving Indian, Chinese and western food, a bar, barbecue, money-changing facilities and a laundry service. The Highway offers double rooms with attached bath – hot and cold water – for Rs 145 to 215. Like the Metrople it has a restaurant, bar and other facilities.

The *Hotel Dasaprakash Paradise* (tel

26666, 25555) at 105 Yadavagiri has
singles/doubles at Rs 160/200, a good
restaurant and a swimming pool. Slightly
cheaper than these is the *King's Court
Hotel* (tel 25250), Jhansi Lakshmi Bai Rd,
which has a range of double rooms from Rs
110 to 170. All the rooms have their own
bathroom with hot and cold water.

Places to Eat

There are any number of reasonably good
'meals' restaurants where you can get
standard south Indian vegetarian food for
Rs 3.50. They include the *New Gayathri
Bhavan* and *Hotel Indra Bhavan* (Dhanvantri Rd); *Bombay Indra Bhavan* and
Indra Cafe (Sayaji Rao Rd), and the *Hotel
Durbar* (Gandhi Square). You may
occasionally find one or another of these
closed due to a strike by the employees
(the workers in these cafes earn a mere Rs
95 to 100 per month!).

If you're looking for something more
interesting than a 'meals' cafe, go to the
Shilpashri Restaurant & Bar, Gandhi
Square, in the evening. It's on the first
floor above a liquor store and includes an
open-air rooftop section. It's very popular
with travellers and for good reason as the
food – both vegetarian and non-vegetarian
– is excellent and prices are very
reasonable. One ecstatic traveller wrote in
recently to say that this restaurant's
chicken tikka masala 'is what they eat in
heaven'. I can't vouch for that, of course,
but I did meet a lot of satisfied customers.
They also have some of the coldest beers
in Mysore.

Similar to the Shilpashri, but considerably more expensive, is the *Punjabi
Restaurant & Bombay Juice Centre*,
Dhanvantri Rd near the junction with
Sayaji Rao Rd. They serve excellent
Punjabi food here and you do see a lot of
people eating there, but a full meal is going
to cost you more than your accommodation
for the night. Likewise, the fruit juices are
good, but they're top dollar.

Kwality Restaurant, Dhanvantri Rd,
serve both vegetarian and non-vegetarian

food as well as 'Chinese' and tandoori
specialities, but their vegetarian dishes all
taste the same regardless of what they are
and the waiters have an annoying habit of
obviously hovering around for a tip when
the bill comes. You can eat here for Rs 15
(three vegetarian dishes plus nan or
chappatis). They also serve spirits and
beers. In the evenings it can be really noisy
as it fills up with Indian families whose
kids kick up an incredible racket. *Gun
House Imperial* is located close to the
south-east corner of the Maharaja's
Palace at the start of the Ooty road. This is
a fairly select lunch and night spot with
live music in the evenings plus silver
candelabras, incense burning under the
tables and turbanned waiters. Nice for a
treat.

The *Durbar Hotel* in Gandhi Square has
a rooftop restaurant. Travellers have
recommended the *Kalpaka* on Dhanvantri
for good sandwiches and good ice cream.
The *Akshaya* at the Hotel Dasaprakash
has 'wonderful tiffins and thali for Rs 4 or
5'. The *Hotel Metropole's* garden is a good
place for dinner out in the open. At 1487
Shivarampet (Vinoba Rd), a little distance
from the centre, the *Shanghai Chinese
Restaurant* has also been recommended.
Look for the street stalls selling steamed
chick peas, puris stuffed with potatoes,
dahl and raw carrots all for a rupee.

The de-luxe *Lalithamahal Palace Hotel*
has an excellent evening buffet meal.

Getting There

Air There are no Indian Airline flights to
Mysore. The nearest airports are Bangalore, Mangalore or Coimbatore.

Rail The enquiry office at Mysore station
is very good and rarely has more than two
or three people in it.

If you're heading for Bombay but don't
want to go through Bangalore the quickest
route is to take the 4.50 pm Arsikere
Passenger which has one coach going all
the way to Miraj arriving there at 1.15 pm
the next day. From Miraj there is an

express train to Bombay the same day at 3.10 pm arriving in Bombay at 6 am the next morning. Other trains include:

Bangalore There are six express trains to Bangalore (140 km away) daily: Chamundi Express (6.15 am); Tipu Express (8 am); Bangalore Express (10.35 am); Nandi Express (2.20 pm); Bangalore Mail (5.45 pm); Kaveri Express (8.30 pm). In addition there are two passenger trains to Bangalore at 8.15 am and 10.55 pm and a passenger train to Maddur at 6.40 pm. These last three can be used to get to Srirangapatnam. The trip usually takes around 3½ hours at a fare of Rs 49 in 1st class, Rs 12 in 2nd.

Arsikere There are three passenger trains daily to Arsikere via Hassan at 7.10 am, 2.15 pm and 4.50 pm. If you're planning on visiting the Hoysala temples of Belur and Halebid and the Jain centre of Sravanabelagola and you're going to use Hassan as a base, these are the trains to take. To Hassan the journey takes 4½ hours and costs Rs 44 in 1st, Rs 10.50 in 2nd; only Rs 7.40 in 2nd on an ordinary pasenger train.

Chamarajanagar There are five passenger trains to Nanjangud daily and three passenger trains to Chamarajanagar daily but they're of little use to travellers. If you were heading for Bandipur it is more convenient to take a bus.

Goa The No 964 train which leaves Mysore daily at 3 pm includes a 2nd class sleeping carriage as far as Londa Junction, where it arrives at 9.30 am the next day. Here you change and take another train to Margao/Vasco da Gama which departs at noon. A 2nd class sleeper ticket all the way from Mysore to Goa will cost Rs 42.50 plus the overnight fee. In 1st class it will cost Rs 168. You can, if you like, take the train all the way, but this isn't the quickest method of getting there as you have to wait 2½ hours at Londa for a connection.

If you don't want to do this, book as far as Londa and take a bus from there. There are buses from Londa to several centres in Goa. To Panaji (via Ponda) buses depart at 8.30 am, 10 am, 10.05 am, 12.45 pm, 1 pm and 4.30 pm. The fare is Rs 9 and the journey takes about 3½ hours. To Margao departures are at 9 am, noon, 1 pm, 3 pm and 4.30 pm. To Marpusa departures are at 11 am and 2 pm.

To get to the bus station from Londa railway station cross the tracks to your right and walk uphill until you reach the main street of Londa – it's essentially a one-street town. Turn left when you get to this street and keep going until you pass the bulk of the buildings. About 100 metres past that point, head up one other of the paths on your right. The bus stand is just a patch of tarmac. You can't miss it.

If you're trying to book sleeper tickets on trains from Mysore and you're told that the quota is full for the day you're hoping to leave on, buy a ticket anyway and go to the Commerical Superintendent's Office, Irwin Rd – that's the entrance just before you cross the road and come to the Tourist Office. Find the office marked, 'Concession Orders Issued Here' – it's on your right as you enter – and ask for the 'Tourist Quota'. Have your ticket handy – you can't do this without a ticket for the journey – fill in a form, wait for five minutes, and you'll get that sleeper. The quota which they have here has precedence over the official waiting list compiled at the station ticket office.

Bus Apart from the Somnathpur bus all the buses below depart from the Central Bus Station.

Somnathpur First get a bus from the Suburban Bus Stand (Gandhi Square) to the village of Tirarasipura (tell the conductor you want to go to Somnathpur). This part of the journey costs Rs 3.25. At Tirarasipura take another bus to Somnathpur. You'll have no trouble locating this bus as all the local kids and the bus conductors will make sure you know when it arrives. These buses are frequent and this part of the journey costs Rs 1. An alternative route is to take a bus to Bannur (Rs 2.25) and change there for Somnathpur (Rs 1).

You can either return to Mysore via the same route or continue to Srirangapatnam. There is a direct bus from Somnathpur to Srirangapatnam at 1.10 pm. If you want to go before or after this, take a bus from Somnathpur to Bannur (Rs 1) and then another bus from there to Srirangapatnam (Rs 2.75). The buses from Bannur to Srirangapatnam can get incredibly crowded. The bus I was on had 202 people on board and I ended up with a child on my knee and two pails of milk in each hand!

Srirangapatnam There are plenty of buses all day and night from the Central Bus Stand. Some go only as far as Sriranga-patnam; others pass through on their way to somewhere else. The fare is Rs 1.60. There's no problem getting back to Mysore along the same route. As an alternative to the bus it's also possible to get there by taking the Bangalore passenger train from Mysore station. If you want to visit Somnathpur from Srirangapatnam use the route indicated above under 'Somnathpur' in the reverse direction.

Other Places To Arsikere buses depart 14 times daily from Platform 4. First bus at 6.30 am and the last at 11.30 pm. (You can use Arsikere as a base from which to visit Belur, Halebid and Sravanabelagola though Hassan is the more usual base).

To Bandipur, there are three buses daily at 6.30 am, 2.30 pm and 3.15 pm. To Bangalore, non-stop buses depart every 20 to 30 minutes from 5.40 am to 9.20 pm. Ordinary stopping services go every 30 minutes throughout the day starting at 6 am. To Bellary there's one bus daily at 9 pm from Platform 4. This is the bus to take if you want to visit the Vijayanagar ruins at Hampi direct from Mysore.

To Calicut, there are six buses daily from Platform 3. First bus at 6 am and the last at 6.30 pm. To Cannanore, two buses daily at 10.45 am and 11.15 am from

Platform 3. To Chikmagalur, seven buses daily. First bus at 6 am and the last at 4 pm. (This bus goes via Belur.) To Coimbatore, three buses daily at 7.15 am, 3 pm and 3.20 pm from Platform 3.

To Hassan, 15 buses daily from Platform 8. First bus at 5.30 am and the last at 9.30 pm. Hassan is the usual base from which to visit Belur, Halebid and Sravanabelagola. There are other buses to Hassan from Platform 4 (six times daily) and Platform 6 (once daily). To Ernakulam, two buses daily at 8.30 am and 10.30 am from Platform 3. The buses go via Calicut. To Mangalore, 11 buses daily from Platform 7. First bus at 6 am and the last at 10.40 pm. To Nagarhole, two buses daily at 6.30 am and 1.00 pm.

To Ootacamund, seven buses daily from Platform 3. First bus at 6.15 am and the last at 3 pm. You can use these buses to get to the wildlife sanctuaries of Bandipur and Mudumalai. The trip takes five hours and costs Rs 18. To Sravana-belagola, five buses daily. First bus at 7.30 am and the last at 3.45 pm. To Udipi, three buses daily at 8.30 am, 12 noon and 9 pm.

To Panjim (Goa) there is one bus daily at 5.30 pm which arrives next day at 9 am. The fare is Rs 65.

Getting Around

Local buses which you may find useful include 1 and 1A (to the Sandalwood Oil Factory) and 4 and 5 (to the Silk Weaving Factory). For buses to Chamundi Hill go to the Suburban Bus Stand at the eastern end of Gandhi Square. They run approximately every 30 minutes and cost Rs 1.60. There are plenty of auto-rickshaws if you prefer this form of transport (Sayaji Rd to the Sandalwood Oil Factory will cost Rs 4 to 5). The drivers use the meters.

Things to Buy

Mysore is famous for carved sandalwood and ivory articles, inlay works, silk saris and incense (*agarbathi*). The best place to see the whole range of what is available is the Cauvery Arts and Crafts Emporium on Sayaji Rao Rd. It's open daily except Thursdays from 10 am to 2 pm and 3.30 pm to 7.30 pm (Sundays from 10 am to 2 pm). They won't take credit cards, but they will take foreign currency or travellers' cheques and will arrange packing and export of anything except ivory for you (government regulations stipulate that ivory has to be carried personally). They do a very good job of packing things up.

Few of the larger things are cheap by Indian standards (eg the smallest of the inlaid tables cost about US$100), but the place is worth a visit even if you're not going to buy anything. One traveller commented, however, that the selection was better and the prices comparable at the Cottage Industries Emporium in New Delhi. There are many other craft shops along Dhanvantri Rd with similar prices. Some of them specialise in ivory chess sets, but a 10-cm set can cost you anywhere between US$1000 to 1500! The best bargains are the carved sandalwood images of Indian deities. They retain their scent for years. There are always a number of street hawkers outside the Cauvery Emporium. They sometimes have some interesting and cheap bangles, rings and old coins.

AROUND MYSORE
Srirangapatnam
16 km from Mysore on the Bangalore road stands the ruins of Hyder Ali and Tipu Sultan's capital from which they ruled much of southern India during the 18th century before being finally defeated by the British, allied with local disgruntled leaders and with the help of a traitor, in 1799. Tipu's defeat marked the real beginning of British territorial expansion in southern India. There isn't a great deal left of Srirangapatnam as the British did a good job of demolishing the place, but the extensive ramparts and battlements and some of the gates still stand and the dungeon where Tipu held prisoner a

number of British officers has been preserved. Inside the walls there's also a mosque and the Sri Ranganathaswamy temple, a popular place of pilgrimage with Hindus.

Across the other side of the road from Srirangapatnam stands the Daria Daulat Bagh, Tipu's summer palace, and the Gumbaz, Tipu's mausoleum. These are perhaps the most interesting part of a visit to Srirangapatnam. The Daria Daulat Bagh stands in well-maintained ornamental gardens and is now a museum, which houses some of Tipu's belongings as well as many ink drawings of him and his family and 'artists' impressions' of the last battle, executed by employees of the British East India Company. All around the internal walls of the ground floor are paintings depicting Tipu's campaigns against the British with French mercenary assistance.

Ten years ago this summer palace was graced with ornamented leather awnings to keep out the sun, but they have now disappeared and it's obvious that maintenance of the building has been seriously neglected – a pity when they look after the garden so well. The Daria Daulat Bagh is open daily until 5 pm and entry is Rs 0.50.

Places to Stay Contact the Assistant Engineer, PWD, Srirangapatnam for accommodation at the *Travellers Bungalow*, close to the Sri Ranganathaswamy temple.

Getting There There are scores of buses everyday in either direction from the central bus station in Mysore. The fare is Rs 1.50.

Somnathpur
45 km east of Mysore stands the Sri Channakeshara temple at Somnathpur, built around 1260 AD during the heyday of the Hoysala kings. It's one of the most beautiful and interesting buildings in the world. The walls of the star-shaped

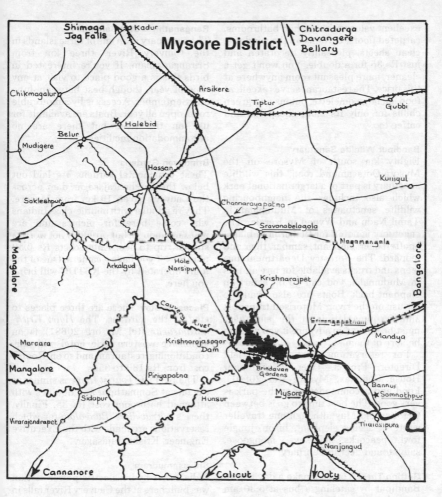

temple are literally covered with superb sculptures in stone depicting various scenes from the Ramayana, Mahabharata, Bhagavata and the life and times of the Hoysala kings. No two friezes are alike.

If you like this place then don't miss the other Hoysala temples at Belur and Halebid, north of Mysore. The temple is open daily between 9 am and 5 pm and entry costs Rs 0.50. There is no fee for cameras.

Information A booklet, *The Hoysalas* by P K Mishra, is on sale at the temple for Rs 6. As Indian booklets on these places go, it's pretty good and worth buying. For details on how to get to Somnathpur by public transport see the 'Getting Around' section.

Places to Stay Just outside the temple compound is a KSTDC *Tourist Home & Restaurant*. The rooms, rarely full, are excellent value with attached bathrooms, carpeted floors, curtains on the windows, clean sheets, pleasantly decorated and just Rs 35 for a double. You won't get a cleaner, more pleasant room anywhere at this price. The restaurant serves excellent food – a large omelette, onions and green chillis for only Rs 2.50, cheap tea and coffee too.

Bandipur Wildlife Sanctuary

Eighty km south of Mysore on the Mysore-Ootacamund road, this wildlife sanctuary is part of a larger national park which also includes the neighbouring wildlife sanctuaries of Mudumalai in Tamil Nadu and Wynad in Kerala. The sanctuary is noted for its herds of bison, spotted deer, elephant, sambar, tiger and leopard. The Forestry Department has jeeps and trucks available for hire and, as in Mudumalai, you can go on safari on elephant-back. Boats are also available for use on the river. Motorised transport and accommodation in the sanctuary must be booked in advance if you want to be sure of them.

For reservations contact the Field Director, Project Tiger, Government House Complex, Mysore (tel 20901). Food and accommodation at the park is very good. The best time to go is between October and May although one traveller wrote of seeing elephant, bison, jungle fowl, peacocks, monkeys, mongoose, sambar and deer in February!

Getting There You can make a day trip to Bandipur by catching a bus at 5.30 am towards Ooty. You'll arrive at the Bandipur office two or three hours later and you can take a jeep trip (Rs 110 for up to nine people) or hire an elephant and guide (Rs 15 for two hours) without any advance reservation. Doing both you'll still be in time to catch the last bus back to Mysore around 5.30 pm. Jeeps are better than trucks which tend to be crowded and noisy.

Ranganathittu Bird Sanctuary

The sanctuary is on one of three islands in the Cauvery River, three km from Srirangapatnam. If you're interested in birds this is a good place to visit at any time of year, though best between June and September. Access is by a motorable road, open all year. Boats are available for use on the river but there are no accommodation facilities.

Brindavan Gardens

These ornamental gardens are laid out below the Krishnarajasagar dam across the Cauvery River, 19 km from Mysore. They're popular with middle-class Indians who come here for picnics and are pleasant enough, but probably not worth a special trip to see. Entry costs Rs 0.50 plus Rs 4 if you have a camera. One of the tours operated by the KSTDC will bring you here.

Places to Stay There are three places to stay at the gardens. The *Hotel Krishnarajasagar* (tel Mysore 20681) is an expensive western-style hotel with air-conditioning, restaurant and so on. Rooms cost from Rs 180 to 350.

The KSTDC *Tourist Home* is similar to the one at Somnathpur and doubles with attached bathroom cost Rs 35. Finally, there's a *Travellers' Bungalow* for which reservations are made with the Executive Engineer, Krishnarajasagar.

Shivasamudram

India's first hydro-electric power station was built here at the Cauvery River falls in 1902. Shivasamudram is 80 km east of Mysore, beyond Somnathpur. The twin falls known as Gaganachukki and Bharchukki drop nearly 100 metres in a series of cascades.

Hunsur

Outside of Hunsur, to the west of Mysore, there's a Tibetan refugee settlement called Rabgayling – which means 'Good Progress Place' although nobody calls it that! There are 15 villages scattered over low, rolling hills in a grid pattern – they're quite lovely to see against the green cornfields. There are two monasteries, one of them a Tantric college, both quite involved in the village life.

Two carpet factories make Tibetan carpets here and they'll produce them to your own design. Thankas are painted at the Tantric college. There's no commercial accommodation in the area although there are two small cafes serving momos, noodles and curd. You can approach Hunsur, from where it's Rs 0.25 on an auto-rickshaw, from Mysore or from other centres.

BELUR & HALEBID

The temples at Belur and Halebid along with that at Somnathpur, east of Mysore, are the cream of what remains of one of the most artistically exuberant periods of Hindu cultural development. These temples are superb and, as far as their sculptural decoration goes, even rival the temples of Khajuraho and Konarak. They also rival the best of Gothic art to be found anywhere in Europe. Amazing though they all are, the wealth of sculptural detail found on the Hoysaleswara temple at Halebid makes it easily the most outstanding example of Hoysala art. Every cm of the outside walls of this temple and much of the interior is covered with an endless variety of Hindu deities, sages, stylised animals and birds and friezes depicting the life and times of the Hoysala rulers. No two are alike. Scenes from war, hunting, agriculture, music, dancing and some very sensual sculptures explicitly portraying the apres-temple activities of the dancing girls are all represented here, together with a huge Nandi (Shiva's bull) and a monolithic Jain statue of Lord Gomateshvara.

The Hoysala temples are squat and low, more human in scale than the soaring temples found elsewhere in India. What they lack in size they make up in the sheer intricate detail of their sculptures. They

were carved from a soap stone which is relatively soft and easily cut when first quarried, but with age and exposure gradually hardens. The Hoysaleswara Temple at Halebid was constructed about 10 years after the temple at Belur, but despite 80 years' labour it was never finally completed. There is also a smaller temple, the Kedareswara, at Halebid.

At Belur the Channekeshava Temple is the only one at the three Hoysala sites which is still used as a functioning temple. Non-Hindus are allowed inside. In design it is very similar to the others. Here much of the decoration has gone into the internal supporting pillars and lintels and larger, but still very delicately carved, images of deities and guardian beasts. As at Halebid the external walls are covered in friezes. The other, lesser, Hoysala temples here are the Channigaraya and the Viranarayana.

The Hoysalas, who ruled this part of the Deccan between the 11th and 13th centuries, had their origins in the hill tribes of the Western Ghats and were for a long time feudatories of the Chalukyas. They did not become fully independent until about 1190 AD, though they first rose to prominence under their leader Tinayaditya (1047-78 AD) who took advantage of the waning power of the Gangas and Rashtrakutas. Under Bittiga (1110-52 AD), better known by his later name of Vishnuvardhana, they began to take off on a course of their own and it was during his reign that the temples of Belur and Halebid were built.

The times were one of great religious upheaval with the Jain faith being predominant due to the patronage of the Chalukyas and the Gangas and, although tolerance of other sects was usually practised, religious persecution was not unknown. Bittiga's predecessors and he himself in his earlier years was a devout Jain, who encouraged one of his generals, Gangaraja, to restore the Jain temples destroyed by the Shaivite Chola invaders from the south-east. Later in his reign he came under the influence of the famous saint, Ramanuja, who converted him to faith in Vishnu. As a result of this conversion he adopted the name of Vishnuvardhana and devoted himself to erecting temples honouring his new creed, but continued to show tolerance for other religious sects. Indeed, there are records of him making grants to Shaivite and Jain temples and of his making a pilgrimage to Sravanabelagola even after his conversion.

Vishnuvardhana's conversion was one of the main factors which led to a decline of Jainism, but it was not the only one. Corruption among the priesthood and the public defeat of the Jain texts by Ramanuja also undermined its influence, but it was by no means extinguished and at least one of Vishnuvardhana's wives and a daughter continued to practise that faith. Later Hoysala rulers also continued to patronise the religion. This normally easy co-existence between Shaivite, Vaishnavites and Jainas explains why you will find images of all these various sects' gods, their consorts and associated companions in Hoysala temples.

The early temples of this dynasty naturally closely followed the style of those of their Chalukyan overlords, but by Bittiga's time they had developed a distinctive style of their own. Typically, it is a relatively small star-shaped structure set on a platform to give it some height and in which most of the attention is devoted to sculptural embellishment.

It's quickly apparent from a study of these sculptures that the arts of music and dancing reached a high point in grace and perfection during their time. As with Kathakali dancing in Kerala, this was used to express religious fervour, the joy of a victory in battle or simply for domestic pleasure, but there the similarity ends as it's obvious these were times of a relatively high degree of sexual freedom and prominent female participation in public affairs. Most books written by Indians which describe these temples and the ones at Khajuraho bend over backwards to play down the sensuality of these sculptures. Quite why they're so embarrassed about them is hard to fathom. Perhaps it just reflects the repressed attitudes of the average urban Indian today regarding all matters physical. Of course a century ago our Victorian ancestors were also slightly shocked by some Indian temples!

Both temples are open every day. Entry to Belur costs Rs 0.50 plus a 10 paise tip for the shoe minder. There is no charge for photography. A spotlight is available inside to enable you to see the sculptural work (it's quite dark otherwise) but, if it's not already turned on you'll be charged Rs 2 for the privilege. Entry to Halebid is free although, as at Belur, it's customary to tip the shoe minder. This temple is now maintained by the Archaeological Survey of India. There is a small museum adjacent to the temple but it's of little interest. It does, however, sell excellent postcards of the temple and the one at Belur for Rs 0.50 each. The attendant who works here will attempt to waylay you before you get to the museum and sell you the same postcards for Rs 1 each. Where else but India?!

Places to Stay

Though Halebid was once the capital city of the Hoysala rulers it is now little more than a rural village. Belur is just a small town. Accommodation facilities are available in both places. At Halebid there are KSTDC *Tourist Cottages* adjoining the temple where rooms cost Rs 20 a single and Rs 24 a double with attached bathrooms and clean sheets. It's a very pleasant place to stay and there are catering facilities. There is nowhere to stay in the village. Note that there is a sign in the centre of the village which indicates the temple as being 1.6 km away. Someone obviously can't measure since it's only 500 metres.

At Belur there are KSTDC *Tourist Cottages* 200 metres from the temple at the same price as the Halebid Cottages, but they have no catering facilities (there are plenty of small cafes in the town). In addition to these there is a *Travellers' Bungalow* and two fairly basic hotels, the *New Hotel Gayatri* and the *Tourist Hotel*. Both have attached restaurants and are two minutes' walk from the bus stand.

Though it's obviously possible to stay in either place – and this would be a good idea if you wanted to spend a day at each temple – most people use Hassan as a base. Arsikere is another possibility. Accommodation and transport facilities at both of these places are covered later in this section.

SRAVANABELAGOLA

This is one of the oldest and most important Jain pilgrimage centres in India and site of the huge statue of Lord Bahubali (Gomateshvara) which, at 17 metres high and carved out of a single piece of rock, is said to be the world's tallest monolithic statue. It stands on top of the rocky hill known as Indragiri, below which the small town of Sravanabelagola nestles, and is visible even at a distance of 25 km. Its simplicity is in complete contrast to the complexity of the sculptural work at the temples of Belur and Halebid.

Sravanabelagola has a long historical pedigree going back to the 3rd century BC when Chandra Gupta Maurya came here with his guru, Bhagwan Bhadrabahu Swami, after renouncing his kingdom. In the course of time Bhadrabahu's disciples spread his teachings all over the region and thus firmly established Jainism in the south. The religion found powerful patrons in the Gangas who ruled the southern part of what is now Karnataka between the 4th and 10th centuries, and it was during this time that Jainism reached the zenith of its influence. Indeed it was during the reign of the Ganga king Rachamalla that the statue of Lord Bahubali was created. It was commissioned by a military commander in the service of Rachamalla and executed by the sculptor

Aristanemi in 981 AD.

Legend has it that Bahubali was the youngest son of the Jain Emperor, Adi Thirthankara Vrishabha Deva, who ruled over a kingdom in northern India and later became the first Jain saint. When Vrishabha Deva renounced his kingdom and retired to the forest to perform penance, a bitter struggle for succession broke out between his two sons, Bahubali and Bharatha. The battle culminated in a duel between the two brothers in which Bahubali emerged the victor, but in his moment of triumph he realised the futility of worldly success, gave his kingdom and all his worldly possessions to Bharatha, and retired to the forest to begin a 1000-year penance.

The statue is the subject of the spectacular Mahamastakabhisheka ceremony, which takes place once every 12 to 14 years when the small town of Sravanabelagola (population 5000) becomes a Mecca for thousands of pilgrims and tourists from all over India and abroad. The 1981 festival coincided with the 1000th anniversary of the erection of the statue and because of this attracted over one million people!! Seven satellite towns had to be constructed to accommodate the extra people and transport was diverted from all over the state. The climax of the Mahamastakabhisheka involves the annointing of Lord Bahubali's head with thousands of pots of coconut milk, yoghurt, ghee, bananas, jaggery, dates, almonds, poppy seeds, milk, gold coins, saffron and sandalwood from the top of a scaffolding erected for the purpose. There must be a lot of work for cleaners after this event!

The rest of the time, Sravanabelagola reverts to a quiet little country town which is a very pleasant place to stay for a few days. The people are friendly, the pace is unhurried and the place is full of cosy little chai shops.

In addition to the statue of Lord Bahubali – which to get to you have to climb 614 steps carved out of the sheer rock face of Indragiri Hill – there are several very interesting Jain *bastis* (temples) and *mathas* (monasteries) both in the town and on Chandragiri Hill, the smaller of the two hills between which Sravanabelagola nestles. Two of these – the Bhandari Basti and the Akkana Basti – are in the Hoysala style and a third – the Chandragupta Basti – is believed to have been built by the Emperor Ashoka the Great. They're all well worth a visit.

Information

There is a tourist office in Sravanabelagola a few metres to the left of the entrance to Indragiri Hill. The staff are friendly and helpful and have a good selection of leaflets. Postcards of the statue of Lord Bahubali are on sale here for Rs 1. You can leave your belongings safely in the tourist office while you climb up the hill. There's no charge for this but, they're closed between 1 and 2.15 pm.

Places to Stay

There are only two hotels as such in the town and they are usually full, and not at all cheap considering the standard of accommodation they offer. There is a *Tourist Bungalow* at the foot of Indragiri Hill but this too is often full, so if you want to stay here for a few days it's best to ask around in the chai shops for a room. There are plenty of people willing to put up travellers for a few rupees or even for nothing. Accommodation is usually a floor, or a bed if you're lucky.

The alternative to this is to stay at one of the pilgrims' rest houses, all of which are two to three km from the town itself. A room in one of these costs Rs 6. As was pointed out in the section on Belur and Halebid, most people use Hassan as a base.

Getting There

Belur and Halebid are only 16 km apart and can be seen in one day using public transport and starting from Hassan around 9 am. On returning to Hassan

there's still time to catch the 6.30 pm bus to Sravanabelagola or a bus to Mysore, Bangalore or Arsikere. It is *not* possible to see Belur, Halebid *and* Sravanabelagola all in one day using public transport. If you don't have a lot of time at your disposal, and want to see them all in one day, the best thing to do is to go on one of the tours organised by the KSTDC in Mysore City.

HASSAN

Hassan is probably the most convenient base from which to explore Belur, Halebid and Sravanabelagola. In itself it has little of interest – it's simply a place for accommodation and transport.

Information

The Tourist Office is friendly and helpful and has a good selection of leaflets on places of interest in the area. If you want to stay at the KSTDC Tourist Cottages at either Belur or Halebid book them in advance here.

Places to Stay

Although there are quite a few hotels in Hassan many of them appear to be semi-permanently full. An early check-in is advisable. The alternative is to check with the Tourist Office about the KSTDC *Tourist Cottages* at Belur and Halebid and, if there's room, to go there.

The *Hassan Ashok* (phone 8731) is the best hotel in town and one of the chain of ITDC hotels you will find all over India. Rooms with attached bath cost Rs 110/140 for singles/doubles, Rs 125/160 with air-con. There is a restaurant attached.

At the other end of the scale *Hotel Dwaraka* is a very popular hotel which fills up rapidly. Singles/doubles here cost Rs 9/17 with common bathroom, Rs 12/20 with attached bathroom. You're very unlikely to get a room here later in the day. The *Sathyaprakash Hotel* (above the Shanbag Cafe) next door is of a very similar quality. *Prashanth Tourist Home* is a very pleasant little place where rooms

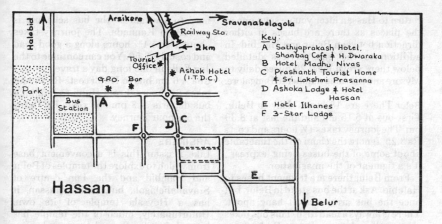

Key:
A Sathyaprakash Hotel,
  Shanbag Cafe ≄ H. Dwaraka
B Hotel Madhu Nivas
C Prashanth Tourist Home
  ≄ Sri Lakshmi Prasanna
D Ashoka Lodge ≄ Hotel
  Hassan
E Hotel Ilhanes
F 3-Star Lodge

with attached bathroom cost Rs 11/20. Another popular hotel which fills up rapidly. Watch the steps on the way down to the street – they're hazardous!

Hotel Madhu Nivas is the place to come if you can't find a room at the hotels above. Here rooms cost Rs 11/18 with attached bathroom. Mosquito nets are provided but clean sheets are not. The upstairs rooms are by far the best and are light and airy. The downstairs rooms are a fair imitation of the Black Hole of Calcutta. All the same, although they may look like they harbour every nasty creepy-crawly under the sun, there are no bugs. There's a passable 'meals' cafe in the basement, but it's better to eat at the Shanbag. Other hotels you could try include *Sri Lakshmi Prasanna*, *Hassan Hotel*, *Ilhanes Hotel* and, as a last resort, the *Ashoka Lodge*, (which is about as basic as you can get).

Places to Eat

Undoubtedly the best place to eat is the *Shanbag Cafe* next to the bus stand. For Rs 3 you'll get one of the best set meals in India – a huge plate of rice, chappatis, masala sauces, pickles, curd and as much mixed vegetable as you can eat. They also serve excellent masala dosa and coffee. The cleanest place in town.

You can also get a vegetarian set meal in the *Madhu Nivas Hotel* for about the same price, but it's nowhere near as good. For non-vegetarian food, a good place is the *Three Star Lodge* (mutton curry Rs 3.50, chappatis Rs 2.25, onions and lime Rs 1). This is the only place which is open until late – the manager says he stays open until 1.30 am. It's popular with Indian students and young men late at night, friendly staff and good teas. If you want to have a beer, there are several bars but you won't find a *cold* beer anywhere. A lukewarm beer will cost you between Rs 9 to 12 depending on where you go.

Getting There

Rail Hassan to Mysore (passenger train), departures at 6.30 am, 9.14 am and 4.50 pm. The 119 km journey takes 4½ hours and costs Rs 7.40. Hassan to Arsikere (passenger train), departures at 11.30 am, 6.30 pm and 9.35 pm.

Note there are no express trains. The station at Hassan is about two km from the centre of town so if you want a choice of hotels when you get there, hire an autorickshaw.

Bus If you're planning on visiting Belur and Halebid in one day, there's no need to return to Hassan after you've seen one of the places as there are buses in either direction between Belur and Halebid. In addition to the bus services detailed below there are at least 20 buses daily to Mysore and the same number to Bangalore.

Belur There are 18 buses daily to Belur. First bus at 6.15 am and the last at 8.30 pm. The journey takes 1½ hours and costs Rs 3.25. Ignore the claim on the timetable about some of the buses being 'express', it's a figment of the imagination.

From Belur there are frequent buses to Halebid. Ask at the bus stand in Belur, but once the bus arrives don't hang about. There is always a mad rush. This bus takes about half an hour and costs Rs 1.10.
Halebid There are nine buses daily to Halebid. First bus at 7.30 am and the last bus at 7 pm. The journey takes two hours and costs Rs 2.40 (it's a dirt-track most of the way hence the two-hour journey).

If you went to Belur in the morning and Halebid in the early afternoon, there's a bus back to Hassan from Halebid at about 3.30 pm. Just hang around in the centre of the village – several chai shops.
Sravanabelagola There are three buses daily to Sravanabelagola at 5.30 am, 9 am and 6.30 pm. It costs Rs 4.50 going there and Rs 4 on the way back. They must reckon that having made the effort you deserve a bonus. The journey takes 1½ hours. Going back to Hassan, there is a bus at 3.30 pm. Late in the afternoon bus paranoia sets in and the usual chaos results.

If you miss the direct buses you can travel between Hassan and Sravana-belagola via Channarayapatna – there are frequent buses until late. Hassan-Channarayapatna takes 1½ hours and costs Rs 3.25. Channarayapatna-Sravanabelagalo takes half an hour and costs Rs 1. There is also a direct bus from Sravanabelagola to Mysore at 1 pm (among others).
Arsikere Buses to Arsikere depart many times daily, though the exact times are

hard to acertain as the bus schedule is entirely in Kannada. The journey takes about 1¼ to 1¾ hours along a good road and costs Rs 3.50. You can continue to the Jog Falls in one long day's travel.
Goa A 6 am bus to Hubli costs Rs 35 and takes 8½ hours. From Hubli to Panjim a bus departs at 3 pm and costs Rs 18 for the 5½-hour journey.

ARSIKERE

Like Hassan, this is a convenient base from which to explore the temples of Belur and Halebid and the Jain centre of Sravanabelagola but, unlike Hassan, it has a Hoysala temple of its own. Unfortunately, much of the temple has been defaced and vandalised, and many contemporary structures have been added so it's no longer very representative. Arsikere is also a railway junction where express trains to Bangalore and Bombay (via Miraj) can be taken.

A man pummeling a slice of melon rind with implements of torture. To what end I cannot say, but he could 'do' 300 an hour.

Places to Stay

Fairly basic accommodation only is available in Arsikere. The *Tourist Lodge* is on B H Rd, one minute from the bus stand and about five minutes from the station, and is probably the best of the hotels in Arsikere. Rooms here cost Rs 10 a single and Rs 15 a double with attached bathroom, fan and clean top cover on the bed. Possessions left in the rooms are secure. The rooms are pleasantly decorated and the bathrooms are clean, though decorated with amusing graffiti from aspiring Indian romantic poets, who seem to have read too much Shelley. Coffee is brought round at about 7 am. Friendly management, though they seem perplexed at the sight of a westerner in this backwater.

The *New Gayitri Lodge*, on B H Rd directly in front of you as you come to the end of the road leading from the station, has rooms for Rs 7/14. It's not as pleasant as the Tourist Lodge. *Janatha Hotel* is next door to the Gayitri Lodge and the same price, pretty basic. *Sri Raghavendra Lodge* is the first building on the left after leaving the railway station. A quiet, pleasant place which costs the same as the Gayitri and has a vegetarian cafe downstairs.

Places to Eat

Prasanna Hotel is probably the best of the vegetarian places. They serve standard 'meals' and tiffin. Masala dosa and two coffees cost Rs 3. *Rathin Hotel* is next door to the Prasanna. Their 'meals' are OK, but they won't give you extra vegetables – a very unusual occurrence in southern India. *Hotel Majestic* is a Moslem non-vegetarian cafe which serves food at very reasonable prices. Open late – at least until 11.30 pm – for food and tea.

Getting There

Rail There is no sleeping accommodation quota on the Bangalore-Miraj Mail at Arsikere. Arsikere-Bangalore is about Rs 95 in 1st class, Rs 24 in 2nd. If you're

heading for Mysore there are several passenger trains daily, Rs 10.50. If you're trying to get from Arsikere to Hospet (for the Vijayanagar ruins at Hampi), take the passenger trains as far as Harihar and then a bus from there. The bus station at Harihar is just opposite the railway station.

Bus The bus schedule here is entirely in Kannada which is bad news if you've just mastered the rudiments of Tamil or Hindi (or Malayalam or Telugu or ....) but there are plenty of buses. Just ask. People here are very friendly!

COORG & THE SOUTH-WEST

Until 1956, when it was included in Karnataka, Coorg was a mini-state in its own right. A mountainous area, Coorg is in the south-west of Karnataka, bordering with Kerala.

Mercara (population 25,000)

The small town of Mercara is the capital of Coorg and stands 124 km west of Mysore. There is a fort here which has played an important part in Karnataka's tumultuous history and also the Omareswara Temple. This region, where the Western Ghats start to tumble down towards the sea, is green, scenic and fertile and an important coffee-growing area. The view from the Raja's Seat is wonderful.

Places to Stay Mercara is a very pleasant hill station and a double room at the KSTDC *Tourist Lodge* costs Rs 25.

Nagarhole

This 18-square-km wildlife sanctuary is in the south-east of Coorg. Elephant rides are available in the early morning and the best time to visit the sanctuary is from October to May. Accommodation can be booked in Mysore, see the Mysore Information section.

Mangalore (population 250,000)

The west coast railway line through

Kerala crosses the border into Karnataka and terminates at this port. At one time Mangalore was a port of great importance and was the major seaport and shipbuilding centre of Hyder Ali's kingdom. Even today it is a major centre for the export of coffee and cashew nuts. The Sultan's Battery, the old lighthouse and nearby St Aloysius College Chapel are all worth seeing. There's a good view from Kadri Hill and temples such as Shri Yogeshwar Math are nearby. There may still be a shipping service which makes its way, with many stops, along the coast between Mangalore and Bombay.

Places to Stay *Nirmal Lodge*, near the bus stand, has single rooms at Rs 14. The government *Tourist Home* at Kadri Hills, about three km away and just opposite the All India Radio Station, has rooms at Rs 14/20 for singles/doubles and also a Rs 6 dorm. There are *Railway Retiring Rooms* at the station.

At the other end of the scale there's the *Motimahal Luxury Hotel* (tel 25611) on Falnir Rd and the *Summer Sands Beach Resort* (tel 6400) at Ullal, five km from Mangalore. At Summer Sands singles/doubles are Rs 80/100 or Rs 120/170 with air-con. Good vegetarian meals are served upstairs at the *Taj Mahal Restaurant* near the bus stand for Rs 3.50.

The newish *Hotel Navaratna* on K S Rao Rd has singles/doubles at Rs 45/70 or with air-con at Rs 60/90 but it looks like it may be subject to rapid deterioration due to lack of maintenance.

Getting There

Air Indian Airlines has daily flights to and from Bombay and Bangalore. Fares to Mangalore are Bangalore Rs 247, Bombay Rs 541.

Rail The twice weekly Bangalore-Mangalore fast passenger train takes about 16 hours for the 447 km trip. Fares are Rs 132 in 1st, Rs 34 in 2nd. Trivandrum-Mangalore takes about 14 to 16 hours for the 635 km

trip via Calicut, Ernakulam and Quilon. Fares are Rs 175 in 1st, Rs 45 in 2nd.

Madras-Mangalore is a 900 km trip taking around 18 hours with fares of Rs 229 in 1st, Rs 58.50 in 2nd. Five days a week there's a direct train between Delhi and Mangalore, the 3036 km trip takes 2½ days at a fare of Rs 588 in 1st, Rs 150 in 2nd, plus appropriate berth charges.

Bus There is a Goa government bus (Kadamba) to Panjim which leaves the main bus stand at 11.30 am but beware – it leaves earlier if full. It takes nearly 10 hours at a fare of around Rs 55. This is a super luxury bus and the trip is pretty reasonable. It would be possible to do the journey for less by taking an ordinary bus from Mangalore to Karwar, crossing by ferry and then taking another bus to Panjim. Only for those desperate to save rupees. The trip will be speeded up when the bridge is completed at Karwar. Southern Travels have a slightly more expensive night bus.

Near Mangalore
If you liked Sravanabelagola (near Mysore) and would like to visit other famous Jain pilgrimage centres there are several of them fairly close to Mangalore.

Dharmastala Situated a little south of the Mangalore-Belur road, about half-way between the two, there are a number of Jain *bastis* including the famous Manjunatha temple. There is also a 14-metre high statue of Lord Bahubali which was erected in 1973. **Venur** Mid-way between Mangalore and Dharmastala, 41 km from the latter, there are eight *bastis* here and the ruins of a Mahadeva temple. An 11-metre high statue of Lord Bahubali stands on the south bank of the Gurupur River, where it was installed in 1604.
Mudbidri There are 18 *bastis*, the oldest of which is the Chandranatha Temple with its 1000 richly carved pillars, at this site 22 km from Venur.
Karkala A further 31 km north of Mudbidri

there are several important temples and a 13-metre high statue of Lord Bahubali, which was completed in 1432.

JOG FALLS

Near the coast, 348 km north-west of Mysore at the terminus of the Birur railway line, the Jog falls are the highest falls in India. The Shiravati River drops 253 metres in four distinctly separate falls known as the Rani, the Rocket, the Raja and the Roarer. During the dry season the falls are less impressive and during the wet they may be totally obscured by mist. The best time to see them is just after the monsoon finishes. The most exciting view seems to be from the top of the Raja where you can see the Raja fall over the Roarer! Even in the dry season the ever changing fans of rainbows over the falls are superb.

To get to the falls take the road towards Sirsi, cross the bridge, turn left and take the second path on you left. Don't fall off the cliff!

Places to Stay *Hotel Woodlands* (tel 22) or the Karnataka Government *Youth Hostel*, which has dormitory accommodation. There is also an electricity board *Guest House* and a Power Corporation *Guest House* since there is a major hydro-electric power plant nearby.

UP THE COAST

There are a number of good beaches and interesting small ports along the coast from Mangalore to Goa. Ullal beach is only five km from Mangalore itself.

Udipi

Further up the coast from Mangalore is Udipi, where the 13th century Shri Krishna temple is located. There's also a *Tourist Bungalow* here.

Malpe

Only five km from Udipi, Malpe has a good beach, swimming and fishing.

Marvanthe

There's another good beach here, nine km from Coondapur.

Gokarna

This is an important pilgrimage place due to the Mahabaleshwara Temple.

Karwar

Only a short distance south of Goa, 56 km north of Gokarna, Karwar has excellent beaches. You can make trips up the Kali River from Karwar and there's an *Inspection Bungalow* (tel 305) for accommodation. Between 1638 and 1752 there was an English factory involved in the pepper trade at Karwar.

Inland from Karwar

Near Yallapur on the Hubli-Karwar road are the Magod Falls (*Tourist Home* nearby) and the Lal Guli Falls.

OTHER PLACES IN CENTRAL KARNATAKA

Chitradurga

On the Bangalore-Hampi road Chitradurga has a famous fort of the Naik Pallegars (chieftains) of the 17th and 18th centuries.

Harihar

On the Bangalore-Hubli railway line, Harihar has a Hoysala temple dating from 1223. Shri Harihareswara was later added to in 1268 by Soma, who built Somnathpur near Mysore. The image in the temple is of Harihar, half-Shiva, half-Vishnu. There is a *Travellers Bungalow* here.

Gadag

There are a number of interesting temples in this cotton-growing town south of Badami. The Shiva temple of Trimbakeswar (or Trikuteswar) the 'Lord of the Three Peaks' is elaborately carved, and in the back of the enclosure is the Temple of Saraswati with a porch supported by extremely elegant pillars.

Lakkandi

Only 13 km south-east of Gadag,

Lakkandi also has a number of interesting temples including the fine Kashi Vishwanath Temple, the Nandeswar Temple and the partially ruined, but very finely carved, Iswara Temple. Near the latter temple, which is thought to have been built by the architect and sculptor of Halebid, is a fine *baoli* or well. Beyond this is a temple to Manikeswar, another name for Krishna.

HAMPI – THE VIJAYANAGAR RUINS

Hampi (Vijayanagar) was once the capital of one of the largest Hindu empire in Indian history. Founded by the Telugu princes, Harihara and Bukka, in 1336 it reached the height of its power under Krishnadevaraya (1509-29) when it controlled the whole of the peninsula south of the Krishna and Tungabhadra Rivers, except for a string of commercial principalities along the Malabar coast. Comparable to Delhi in the 14th century, the city covered an area of 33 square km, was surrounded by seven concentric lines of fortification and was reputed to have had a population of about half a million. It maintained a mercenary army of over one million according to the Persian Ambassador, Abdul Razak, which included Moslem mounted archers to defend itself from the Moslem states to the north.

Its wealth was based on control of the spice trade to the south and the cotton industry of the south-east. Its busy bazaars, described by such European travellers as Nunez and Paes, were centres of international commerce. The religion was a hybrid of current Hinduism with the gods Vishnu and Shiva being lavishly worshipped in the orthodox manner though, as in the Hoysala kingdom, Jainism was also prominent. Brahmins were privileged, *sati* (the burning of widows on the funeral pyres of their husbands) was widely practised and temple prostitution was common. Brahmini inscriptions, which have been discovered on the site, date the first settlement here back to the lst century AD and suggest

that there was a Buddhist centre nearby.

The empire came to a sudden end in 1565 after the disastrous battle of Talikota when the city was ransacked by the confederacy of Deccan Sultans (Bidar, Bijapur, Golkonda, Ahmadnagar and Berar), thus opening up southern India for conquest by the Moslems.

Hampi is set in a strange and beautiful landscape – hill country strewn with enormous, rounded boulders – with the Tungabhadra River running through the centre of it. It has a magic quality to it and the ruins are superb, though scattered over quite a large area. It is possible to see all the main sites in one day on foot if you start early, but a hired bicycle makes life a lot easier. Signposting on the site is somewhat inadequate and a lot of the land between the ruins is planted out with sugar cane and other crops. All the same, even where the trail is indistinct, there are plenty of cattle and goat tracks so you can't really get lost.

Probably the most interesting sites are the Vittala Temple with its famous stone chariot, musical pillars and incredible sculptural work; the Purandara Dasara Mandapa (the riverside temple) with the ruined stone bridge nearby which used to span the Tungabhadra River; the Sule and Hampi Bazaars (the latter partially occupied by squatters – a surreal sight!); Achutaraya Temple; the Palace area with its Dasara Platform, Lotus Mahal, Elephant Stables and Watchtower; the Hazarama Temple, and the Queen's Bath.

Information

There are no booklets for sale about Hampi or the Vijayanagar Empire anywhere at Hampi or Hospet. The only thing that's available is a very vague coloured sketch map of the ruins which costs Rs 0.50. There are good maps of the area (put out by the Archaeological Survey of India) in Hampi Bazaar, next to the Lotus Mahal in the Palace area and

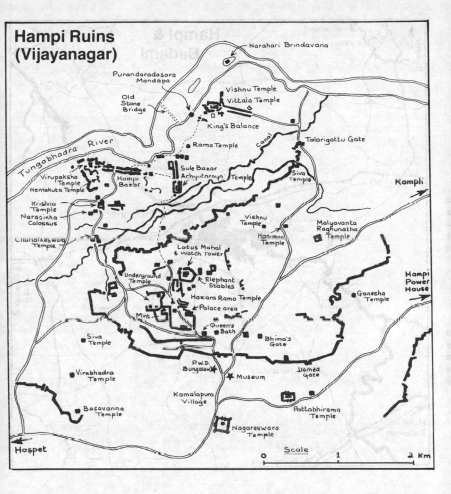

Hampi Ruins (Vijayanagar)

outside the Archaeology Office at Kamalapuram.

Places to Stay

If you'd prefer to stay near the ruins rather than in Hospet there is the *Hampi Power Station Inspection Bungalow*, three km from Kamalapuram. The chances are that you'll get in without prior reservation, but if you want to make sure contact the Superintending Engineer, HES, Tungab-

hadra Board, Tungabhadra Dam, Hospet (tel 8272). A pleasant, carpeted double with fan and a rather grubby bathroom costs just Rs 5. If you want a meal (veg or non-veg) you must order it before 5 pm as they go down to the village to buy the ingredients. The PWD Inspection Bungalow has reportedly gone but there are plenty of suitable places where you could camp among the ruins.

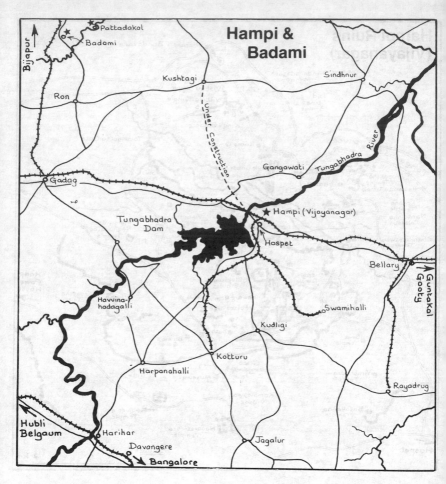

Places to Eat

There are several simple cafes in Kamalapuram where you could get a meal. Elsewhere there is a *Government Tourist Canteen* between the Hazarama Temple and the Palace site which has a *very* limited menu – omelettes are the only thing available – although they do have ice-cold beers. There is also a simple cafe in Hampi Bazaar and a chai shop next to the Varaha Temple near Sule Bazaar – a

very friendly little place. Fruit sellers usually hang around between the King's Balance and the Vittala Temple.

Getting Around

Hampi is 13 km from Hospet, the town which most people use as a base. There are two main points of entry to the ruins – Hampi Bazaar and Kamalapuram – and buses run to these two points from Hospet frequently. As an alternative to the buses you can hire a bicycle in Hospet which definitely makes the going easier since there is no transport between the various sites. 'Not if you get five punctures', reported one unhappy bicyclist! If you're walking, expect to cover at least seven km just to see the main sites. It is possible to see most of the ruins in a day, though two days would allow a more leisurely pace.

HOSPET

Most people who come to see the Vijayanagar ruins at Hampi use Hospet as a base. It's a fairly typical Karnataka country town with dusty roads, plenty of bullock carts, bicycles and dilapidated buses. There's an unobtrusive industrial area near the Tungabhadra Dam.

For much of the year it's not a particularly interesting place in itself but, because it has a large Moslem population, it comes alive during the festival of Moharam. If you're here at this time don't miss the firewalkers, who walk barefoot across the red-hot embers of a bonfire that's been going all day and night. Virtually the whole town turns out to watch or take part and excitement gets to fever pitch around midnight. The preliminaries which go on all day appear to be a bewildering hybrid of Moslem and Hindu ritual and quite unlike any other festival I've ever seen in the Moslem world. It's well worth staying up half the night to witness.

Information

The Tourist Information Office, Station Rd, is run by friendly people with a good selection of information. Their duplicated handout on Hospet, Hampi and Tungabhadra is pretty comprehensive but the map of the Vijayanagar ruins on the back page is a joke.

Places to Stay

Malligi Tourist Home (tel 8377), off Hampi Rd, is definitely the pleasantest hotel in town and, for the price, a bargain. Rooms – all with attached bathrooms, fan and mosquito nets – cost Rs 14/27 and there are also larger rooms for three or four. The rooms are pleasantly decorated, there's running hot water between 6 and 10 am and the management is very friendly. They also have two air-con rooms. A rickshaw from the station costs about Rs 2.

Hotel Sandarshan (tel 8574), Station Rd has singles/doubles with attached bathroom for Rs 15/25 and it has a vegetarian restaurant. It's convenient for the railway station and bus station, but the rooms are not as pleasant as the Malligi. *Hotel Mayura* (tel 8418), Gandhi Chowk, opposite the GPO, has rooms at Rs 8 for a single with common bathroom, Rs 10 for a single and Rs 18 for a double with attached bathrooms. There is a vegetarian restaurant downstairs.

Lokare Lodge (tel 8447), Station Rd, is a pleasant lodge but somewhat overpriced at Rs 8 to 10 for a single with common bathroom, Rs 15/24 for singles/doubles with attached bathrooms. *MRK Lodge* (tel 8780), opposite the old bus stand, costs Rs 7/13 for rooms with attached bath rooms, but there's no hot water and the management won't fetch you a bucketful even if you offer to pay. Fairly basic rooms with indifferent decor but there are good views from the roof. The *Shanbag Hotel*, New Bus Stand, costs Rs 9/18 with common bathroom or Rs 20 for a double with attached bathroom. There is also a Rs 5 dormitory.

Then there are *Railway Retiring Rooms* (Rs 10 a double); the *Pampa Lodge*, Station Rd (Rs 10/18 for rooms with attached bath); *Janatha Lodge* (Rs 6/10 for rooms with with common bath) and the *Naga Lodge*, which is down a side street off Main Bazaar (Rs 8/20, the doubles have attached bath).

Remember that if you want to stay near the ruins at Hampi it is possible to stay at Kamalapuram. There is also the *Tourist Home* near the Tungabhadra Dam.

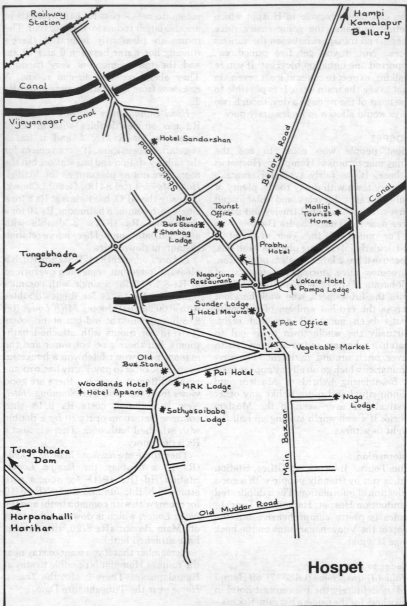

Hospet

Places to Eat

For vegetarian set meals you can't beat those at the restaurant in the *Malligi Tourist Home*, it's open to non-residents. They serve excellent meals – rice, puris (6), papadums (3), masala sauces (2), vegetables (2), curd and two coffees comes to Rs 5, a bargain.

Another restaurant where you can get very good vegetarian set meals is the *Pai Hotel* near the MRK Lodge. For non-vegetarian food try the *Nagarjuna Bar & Restaurant* at the junction of Gandhi Chowk and Station Rd. It also sells ice-cold beer. If you like *plenty* of ginger in your food, try the *Prabhu Hotel*, Hampi Rd (not to be confused with the restaurant at the Malligi which has the same name)

Getting There

Rail The railway station in Hospet is a long walk (about 15 minutes) from the centre of town. Rickshaws quote Rs 1 to 2. The station has a healthy quota allotted them for express trains between Hubli and Bangalore and they are rarely booked up more than one day in advance.

If you're heading for Bijapur after Hospet note that there are no direct buses. You can get there by rail by taking any of the trains going west and changing at Gadag. The journey from Gadag to Bijapur (via Badami) by rail is very slow, but there's usually plenty of entertainment en route in the form of buskers! If you're heading for Badami take the same route. It takes about four hours to Badami and costs about Rs 10.50.

Bus To Badami there is one bus daily at 7 am, it's quicker than the train. Hospet-Bagalkot takes five hours and costs Rs 16, it's another hour from there to Badami for Rs 3.50. To Bangalore there are eight express buses daily, first bus at 6.30 am and the last at 11.45 pm. There is also a 'Tourist Bus' to Bangalore daily at 8.15 pm, which is bookable from the agent next door but one to the MRK Lodge.

To Bellary there are buses approxi-

mately every hour from 6.45 am until 8 pm. To Davangere there are six buses daily, first bus at 5 am and the last at 3.35 pm. To Hubli, two buses daily at 2.15 am and 4.45 pm. To Hyderabad, one express bus daily at 1.30 pm. To Karwar, one bus daily at 9 am. To Shimoga, three buses daily at 6.15 am, 12.45 pm and 3.15 pm. The last two are expresses.

Getting Around

Hampi Frequent buses from Platform 10 at the New Bus Stand. Costs Rs 1.50 and takes around 30 minutes. The terminus is at Hampi Bazaar but you can also get down at Kamalapuram and walk into the ruins from there (in which case the bus fare is Rs 1.10). Taxis from Kamalapuram to Hospet cost Rs 1.25 per person and go when full (they take four or five people).

Tungabhadra Dam Frequent buses from Platform 12 at the New Bus Stand. (The buses have 'TB Dam' on the front). Costs Rs 0.50 and takes 15 minutes. If you find yourself waiting a long time for a bus back to Hospet from the dam, walk down to the junction at the bottom. There are more frequent buses to and from there.

Tungabhadra Dam

If you've ever spent any time browsing through Indian tourist literature you'll know that Indians love their dams and will go into the most breathless eulogies to put them on the tourist map and project their unsurpassed potential as 'picnic spots'. Possibly it comes from living in a country where famine was always just around the corner when there were no facilities to compensate for a failed monsoon. Whatever the reason Tungabhadra gets the same treatment, but if you've seen dams before this one isn't going to radically alter your appreciation of them. If you've already visited Hampi and have time to spare then it's worth a visit as there's very little else of note to see in Hospet.

The literature makes the dubious claim that it's the largest masonry dam in the world. It is 2421 metres long and 49 metres high and has created a lake some 370 square km in surface area. It was begun in 1945 and completed in 1953 at a cost of over Rs 1,080,000,000. It's used to generate electricity and to irrigate Bellary and Raichur in Karnatka and Cuddapa and Kurnool districts in Andhra Pradesh.

Places to Stay Naturally, a *Tourist Home* has been built below the dam where tourists are encouraged to stay but it's very inconvenient for anything other than the dam. Rooms here cost Rs 14 a single, Rs 24 a double and Rs 35 a triple, all with attached bathroom. There's also a multi-star western-style hotel, the *Vaikunta Guest House*, overlooking the dam on the hill top. There are frequent buses to the dam from the bus station in Hospet.

THE CHALUKYAN CAVES & TEMPLES
Set in beautiful countryside amongst red sandstone hills, rock-hewn 'tanks' (artificial lakes) and peaceful farmlands, these three small rural villages were once the capital cities of the Chalukyan Empire which ruled much of the central Deccan between the 4th and 8th centuries AD. Here you can see some of the earliest and finest Dravidian temples and rock-cut caves with forms and sculptural work that provided inspiration for the later Hindu empires which rose and fell in the southern part of the peninsula before the arrival of the Moslems. Though principally promoters of the Vedic culture, the Chalukyans were tolerant of all sects, and elements of Shaivism, Vaishnavism, Jainism and even Buddhism can be found in many of their temples, especially in the rock-cut caves at Badami.

Aihole
At Aihole, the capital between the 4th and 7th centuries, can be seen Hindu temple architecture in its embryonic stage from the earliest Ladkhan Temple to the later and more complex structures like the Kunligudi and Durgigudi Temples. The Durgigudi is particularly interesting,

probably unique in India, being circular in shape and surmounted by a primitive gopuram – those structures which typify the temples throughout Tamil Nadu. There are over 70 structures in and around this village which stand witness to the vigorous experimentation in temple architecture undertaken by the Chalukyans. Most are in a good state of preservation.

Badami
Badami, magnificently nestled in a canyon and the later capital from about 540 until 757 AD when the Chalukyans were otherthrown by the Rashtrakutas, is famous for its rock-cut temples. Cut into the cliff-face of the red sandstone hill and overlooking the picturesque tank of Agastyatirtha (itself constructed in the 5th century), these caves display the full range of religious sects which have grown up on Indian soil. There are five caves altogether, four of them artificial and one natural, all connected by flights of steps. Of the rock-cut temples, two are dedicated to Vishnu, one to Shiva and the fourth is a Jain temple. The natural cave is a Buddhist temple. Fragments of a fresco in the upper Vaishnavite temple show that the art of painting had reached a similar stage of perfection as sculpture, and it's probable that most of the images in these caves were painted at the time of their creation.

The caves are only one of the many things to be seen at Badami. All over the sides and tops of the hills, which enclose the tank on three sides, are temples and fortifications, carvings and inscriptions dating not just from the Chalukyan period but from other times when its value as a fortress site has been appreciated. After it fell to the Rashtrakutas, Badami was occupied successively by the Chalukyans of Kalyan (a separate branch of the Western Chalukyans), the Kalachuryas, the Yadavas of Devagiri, the Viyanagar Empire, the Adil Shahi kings of Bijapur and the Marathas.

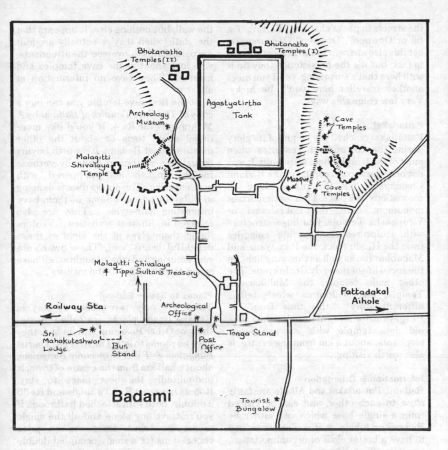

Bhutanatha Temples (II)

Archeology Museum

Malagitti Shivalaya Temple

Bhutanatha Temples (I)

Agastyatirtha Tank

Cave Temples

Mosque

Cave Temples

Malagitti Shivalaya Tippu Sultans Treasury

Railway Sta.

Places to Stay. Badami

Sri Mahakuteshwar Lodge

Bus Stand

Archeological Office

Post Office

Tonga Stand

Pattadakal Aihole

Badami

Tourist Bungalow

All these various rulers have left their mark at Badami, and there's even a Pallava inscription dating back to 642 AD when their king Narasimhavarman briefly overwhelmed the Chalukyans and occupied Badami for 13 years, before being driven out again. Of these other monuments, some of the most beautiful are the two groups of lake-side temples (known as the Bhutanatha temples). Reflected in the water of the tank they're a most enchanting sight and have the simplicity and freshness found also in the very early Pallava temples at Mahabalipuram, south

of Madras. The Archaeological Museum, on the north side of the tank, is also well worth a visit. It houses some superb examples of sculpture collected locally, and some remarkable images of a fertility cult which flourished in the area – the Lajja-Gauri images.

Badami is a small town and, off the main street, full of narrow, winding lanes, old houses, the occasional Chalukyan ruin and tiny squares. It's a pleasant place and people are friendly, but the street kids can be incredibly persistent in hassling you for pens and money. They'll follow you down the streets in packs chanting 'Ta, ta!', 'Ta, ta!' or 'One pen!', 'One pen!'. Of course you get this elsewhere in India. In most places, in fact, but it's the persistence they do it with here that's surprising, yet if you meet another traveller here you'll be lucky. Very few come this way.

Pattadakal

Pattadakal reached the height of its glory during the 7th and 8th centuries when most of the temples here were built. It was not only the second capital of the Badami Chalukyans, but the place where all coronations took place. The most important monument here, the Lokeshwari or Virupaksha Temple, is a huge structure with sculptures that narrate episodes from the Hindu epics, the Ramayana and Mahabharata, as well as throwing light on the social life of the early Chalukyans. The other main temple, the Mallikarjuna Temple, has sculptures which tell a different story – this time from the Bhagavata, the story of Lord Krishna. The old Jain temple with its two stone elephants, about a km from the centre, is also worth visiting.

Information & Orientation

Badami, Pattadakal and Aihole are fairly close to each other, and can be visited from a single base which can either be Badami or Aihole or, if you're concerned to have a better class of accommodation, from Bagalkot. There are no accommodation facilities at Pattadakal. Both Badami and Bagalkot are on the railway line which runs from Gadag to Bijapur. Service buses connect Badami, Pattadakal and Aihole, but you deserve a medal for tenacity and endurance if you can locate the right bus.

There are no charges for visiting the monuments or the Archaeology Museum but the attendants at the cave temples won't allow flash photography. The so called Archaeological Office on the main road in Badami has a painted sketch map of the Badami-Pattadakal-Aihole area on the wall, but nothing else. It appears that the staff (when they're actually around) are paid simply to 'oversee' the attendants, who loaf about at the cave temples and museum. They have no information at all.

At the first cave temple you can buy a copy of *The Cave Temples of Badami* by A M Annigeri for Rs 4. If you'd like more detail about them or about the other monuments at Badami, it's worth buying though it's written in typically verbose Indian English and peppered with nonsense like, 'This shows dwarfs dancing in different poses ....Some of them have interesting hair-styles ....They are also engaged in different activities ....Visitors forget themselves at the sight of these delightful dwarfs', and, 'These dwarfs are very amusing and create laughter ....These arrest the attention of the visitors'.

Places to Stay – Badami

There are only two places to stay in Badami (many places are called 'Something or Other Boarding' but, in fact, they have no rooms to let). The *KSTDC Tourist Bungalow & PWD Inspection Bungalow*, about a half km from the centre of town, is undoubtedly the best place to stay. Rooms here cost Rs 15 a single and Rs 30 a double, both with attached bathroom. If you're travelling alone and all the single rooms are taken, there are no price concessions for a singly-occupied double room (as there is in most other places).

Sri Mahakuteshwar Lodge, next to the bus stand, is run by a reincarnation of The Mekon (Dan Dare fans). Rooms cost Rs 8/15 for rooms with common bathroom, Rs 15/28 with attached 'bathroom'. The downstairs rooms are another determined attempt to recreate the Black Hole of Calcutta, but all the rooms have been painted in the most ugly and depressing combination of colours I've seen anywhere in India. Mosquito nets are provided, but since they don't reach the mattress, are useless. The locks they provide are a joke (by this time of course you will have acquired one of your own in which case possessions left in the room are secure).

There is also a *Travellers Bungalow* close to the railway station, but it's very inconvenient for anything other than the trains. *Sri Laxmi Lodging* in the town centre has very good food.

Places to Stay – Aihole

If you'd like to stay at Aihole accommodation is available at the *KSTDC Tourist Bungalow*. Rooms here cost Rs 15 a single and Rs 30 a double, both with attached bathroom. It's of a similar standard to the Tourist Bungalow at Badami.

Places to Eat

Probably the best place to eat in Badami is the *Hotel Sanman*, next to the Sri Mahakuteshwar Lodge. It has a la carte vegetarian and non-vegetarian meals, cold beers, other alcoholic drinks and loud music from current Indian films which the proprietor is loathe to turn down.

There are plenty of small cafes, especially around the tonga stand on the main road, but most of them serve only tiffin. If you want a vegetarian set meal go to either *Sri Veera Bhadreshwar Boarding* or *Sri Raghuvendra Bhavan* which has excellent masala dosa and not very friendly people. These two stand opposite one another at the tonga stand and serve meals for Rs 3. One of the friendliest tiffin places is the *Udaya Vilas* on the main road.

Getting There

Rail All the trains from Badami station are passenger trains. There are no express trains. On the other hand, although the trains are slow, the journeys I made on this line were the liveliest I came across in India. Virtually the whole of the way from Gadag to Bijapur buskers board the train and entertain the passengers. Some of them are excellent, particularly the two women (very unusual to see this in India) who sing Kannada folk songs in harmony to the accompaniment of a harmonium.

Judging by the way people delved into their pockets for small change and quietly sang along with them, they must have been singing some very popular songs.

The schedule of the trains is as follows: Hubli-Sholapur, daily at 1.04 am, 10.38 am and 3.18 pm. Sholapur-Hubli, daily at 2.33 am, 11.08 am and 4 pm. Gadag-Sholapur, daily at 5.14 am. Sholapur-Gadag, daily at 9.43 pm. Bijapur-Hubli, daily at 7.32 am. Hubli-Bijapur, daily at 7.22 pm.

If you're heading for Bijapur you can take either the trains for Bijapur or Sholapur. Similarly, if heading for Gadag, you can take either the trains for Gadag or Hubli. The journey from Badami to Bijapur takes 9½ hours and costs about Rs 7.

Bus To Bijapur there is one bus daily at 7 am – four hours, Rs 12. To Bagalkot, 13 buses daily, first bus at 7.30 am and the last bus at 7.45 pm. To Hospet, one bus daily at 11 am. To Hubli, four buses daily at 7.30 am, 10 am, 1 pm and 5.15 pm. To Bangalore, two buses daily at 5.30 pm and 7.30 pm. To Gadag, five buses daily, first bus at 7.30 am and the last at 4.50 pm.

Getting Around

Badami railway station is five km from the village itself and a tonga from outside the station will cost you Rs 2 to 3. The locals pay less than a rupee but you need brown skin, black hair, brown eyes and fluency in Kannada to get it for that! There are also service buses which run between the station and village approximately hourly. It takes a whole day to see the cave temples, ruins and fortifications at Badami. You could see Pattadakal and Aihole on the following day if you start out as early as possible.

It's convenient and pleasant to hire a bicycle to explore these places but bear in mind that the round trip will involve cycling about 100 km. If you're not up to this then you'll need two days. The bicycle shop opposite the tonga stand on the main road in Badami hires bicycles for Rs 5 a day plus a deposit. I was asked for Rs 300 deposit, but managed to persuade them that my student card was a passport and left that.

If you can locate the service bus which will take you to either Pattadakal or Aihole at the bus stand in Badami then you deserve a medal for tenacity and endurance. Either that or you speak fluent Kannada. Every enquiry will produce a different response. In theory you take the Iikal buses, of which there are nine daily. The first bus at 8 am and the last at 7.30 pm. Badami-Aihole takes two hours and costs Rs 4 reported a tenacious traveller!

Service buses connect Aihole with Bagalkot and Badami (latter via Pattadakal). The nearest railway stations to Aihole are at Bagalkot (46 km) and Badami (51 km).

BIJAPUR (population 120,000)

Bijapur is the Agra of the south, full of ruined and still intact gems of 15th to 17th century Moslem architecture – mosques, mausoleums, palaces and fortifications – and, like Agra, it has its world-famous mausoleum, the Golgumbaz. This enormous structure with its vast hemispherical dome, said to be the world's second largest, dominates the landscape for miles around, and was built during the reign of Mohammed Adil Shah (1626-1656). The austere grace of the monuments in this city is in complete contrast to the sculptural extravaganza of the Chalukyan and Hoysala temples further south. The Ibrahim Roza mausoleum, in particular, is one of the most beautiful and finely-proportioned Islamic monuments anywhere in the world.

Bijapur was the capital of the Adil Shahi kings (1489-1686), one of the five splinter states formed when the Bahmani Moslem kingdom broke up in 1482. The others, formed at roughly the same time, were Bidar, Golkonda, Ahmednagar and Berar. Like Bijapur, all these places have their own collection of monuments dating from

this period, though the ones at Bijapur are definitely more numerous and generally in a better state of preservation. The rulers of these states spent their days fighting each other and the Hindus further south, with any spare resources being used to build palaces and tombs for themselves and to pay for entertainers at their courts. They did, however, occasionally act in consort and it was a confederacy of these states which in 1565 overthrew the Hindu Vijayanagar Empire at the battle of Talikota, thus eclipsing Hindu rule in the south.

Bijapur is well worth a visit. It's a pleasant garden city, still strongly Moslem in character, and small enough not to be overwhelming. You will need at least two days to see the monuments in a fairly leisurely manner since they are spread out right across the city.

Information

The Tourist Office is attached to the KSTDC Tourist Home. They have sketch maps of the city for Rs 0.60 and verbose leaflets which don't tell you a great deal, take up lots of paper and cost Rs 1.20. If you want a guide book to the city, pick up a copy of *Tourist Guide to Bijapur* by H Padmaraj, on sale at many stationers and bookshops.

The best place to change money is at the State Bank of India in the public offices in the Citadel. They have the current exchange rates and are fast. Avoid the banks in the old part of the city on the north side of Gandhi Rd (especially the Canara Bank). They'll keep you waiting all morning, tell you a lot of unadulterated garbage and then offer you a rate well below par.

Golgumbaz

The most famous and the largest though not the most beautiful monument in Bijapur, the Golgumbaz is a simple building, which has four walls that enclose a majestic hall 1704 square metres in area, and are buttressed by octagonal seven-storied towers at each of the corners. This basic structure is capped by an enormous dome which is said to be the world's second largest (St Peter's in the Vatican City, Rome, has the largest). St Peter's dome diameter is 38 metres, St Paul's in London is 33 metres, the Golgumbaz is 42 metres. It was built in 1659.

All the way around the base of the dome at the top of the hall is a three metre wide gallery known as the 'whispering gallery', since the acoustics here are such that any sound made is repeated 10 times over (some guide books claim it's repeated 12 times over). Fortunately you won't have the chance to get embroiled in that controversy as the 'whispering gallery' is permanently full of kids running amok up there and screaming at the top of their voices. Bedlam gallery would be a more appropriate name. Access to the gallery is via a narrow but, for most of the way, well-lit staircase up the left-hand tower. There's a notice on the wall just before you enter the gallery from outside the dome. It says, 'Silence please'.

The views over Bijapur from the base of the dome are superb. You can see virtually every other monument and almost the whole of the city walls from here. You can also ascend the south-east tower, the right tower as you enter from the south.

The Golgumbaz is the mausoleum of Mohammed Adil Shah (1626-56), two of his favourite wives – Rambha and Arusbib, one of his daughters and a grandson. Their caskets stand on a raised platform in the centre of the hall, though their actual graves are in the crypt, accessible by a flight of steps under the western doorway.

It's open 6 am to 6 pm and entrance costs Rs 0.50 except on Fridays when it's free. Shoes have to be left at the entrance. There's also an archaeological museum in the front which opens at 10 am and is free.

Ibrahim Roza

Constructed at the height of Bijapur's prosperity by Ibrahim Adil Shah II (1580-1626) for his queen Taj-Sultana, the Ibrahim Roza is one of the most beautiful Islamic buildings you will see anywhere in the world. Unlike the Golgumbaz, which is impressive only for its immensity, here the emphasis is on elegance and delicacy. Its minarets, which rise 24 metres from the ground, are said to have inspired those of the Taj Mahal. It's also one of the few monuments in Bijapur with substantial stone filigree and other sculpturally decorative work.

Buried here are Ibrahim Adil Shah, his queen, Taj-Sultana, his daughter, two sons, and his mother, Haji Badi Sahiba. There is no entrance charge, but shoes should be left on the steps up to the platform on which the mausoleum stands.

Jami-e-Masjid

This is another finely-proportioned building with graceful arches, a fine dome and a large inner courtyard containing fountains and a reservoir. It's quite a large monument covering an area of 10,800 square metres and has space for 2250 worshippers. Spaces for them are marked out in black on the polished floor of the mosque. There's very little ornamentation here, the whole concept being one of simplicity. The flat roof is accessible by several flights of stairs. This mosque was constructed by Ali Adil Shah I (1557-80), who was also responsible for erecting the fortified city walls, Gagan Mahal and installing a public water system. There is no charge for entry here.

Asar Mahal

Standing to the east of the citadel, the Asar Mahal was built by Mohammed Adil Shah in about 1646 to serve as a Hall of Justice. The rooms on the upper storey are profusely decorated with fresco paintings, many of them using foliage and flower motifs, but some portraying male and female figures in various poses. These latter have all been defaced. The building

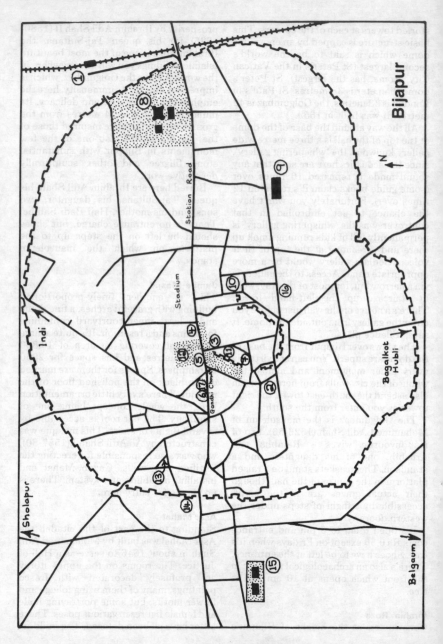

1 Railway Station	10 Asar Mahal
2 Bus Station	11 Citadel (Gagan Mahal, Sat Manzil,
3 Tourist Home & Tourist Office	Anand Mahal & Mecca Masjid)
4 Travellers' Lodge	12 Bara Kaman (Ali Roza II)
5 Hotel Midland & Mysore Lodge	13 Upli Buruj
6 Hotel Tourist	14 Mailik-i-Maidan Cannon
7 State Bank of India	15 Ibrahim Roza
8 Gol Gumbaz	16 Mehtra Mahal
9 Jami Masjid	17 Post Office

was also used to house two hairs from the Prophet's beard. The front of the building is graced with a square tank still fed by conduits from Begum Tank.

The Citadel

Located in the centre of the city and surrounded by its own fortified walls and wide moat, this once contained the palaces, pleasure gardens and Durbar Hall of the Adil Shahi kings. Unfortunately, most of them are now in ruins but some superb fragments remain, and it's well worth spending some time wandering around this area.

Of the most important fragments, the Gagan Mahal probably gives the best impression of the scale on which things were built here. This monument was built by Ali Adil Shah I around 1561 to serve the double purpose of a royal residence and a Durbar Hall. Essentially it's an enormous hall which was left completely open to the north, so that an audience outside the hall would have a full and unobstructed view of the proceedings on the raised platform inside. The hall was flanked by small chambers used to house the families of the royal household. Through suspended screens which enclosed the projecting balconies overhanging the Durbar on all sides, the ladies of the harem were able to witness the proceedings down below. Most of this has now been destroyed, but the immense arch which spanned the whole front of the Durbar still stands.

Nearby, the Sat Manzil, Muhammed

Adil Shah's seven-storied palace, is now substantially in ruins and the remaining parts of it are used for public offices, but just across the road from this stands one of the most delicate pieces of architecture in Bijapur. This is the Jala Manzil or Jala Mandir, a water pavilion no doubt intended as a cool and pleasant place to relax in the days when it was surrounded by secluded courts and gardens within the palace precincts. Opposite the Citadel on the other side of Station Rd are the graceful arches of Bara Kaman, the ruined mausoleum of Ali Roza, which is also worth visiting.

Malik-e-Maidan

This huge cannon must be one of the largest mediaeval guns ever made. It measures over four metres long and almost 1.5 metres in diameter, and is estimated to weigh 55 tonnes! It was cast by Mohammad-bin-Hasan Rumi, a Turkish officer in the service of the King of Ahmednagar, in 1549 from an alloy of copper, iron and tin. It was brought to Bijapur as a trophy of war and set up here with the help of 10 elephants, 400 oxen and hundreds of men. Its outer surface is polished dark green and adorned with inscriptions in Persian and Arabic, one of them attributed to the Moghul Emperor Aurangzeb saying that he subdued this gun, the name of which means Monarch of the Plains.

Upli Buruj

This watch tower, 24 metres high and

located on high ground near the western walls of the city, was built by Hyder Khan, a general in the service of Ali Adil Shah I and of Ibrahim II, in about 1584. The tower can be climbed by a flight of steps which winds around the outside of the building. The top commands a good view of the city and is well furnished with guns, powder chambers and water cisterns. The guns are much longer than the Malik-e-Maidan (nine metres and 8.5 metres respectively), but of much narrower bore – only 29 cm.

Other

There are a number of other monuments worth visiting in Bijapur, the most important of them being the **Anand Mahal** and the **Mecca Masjid**, both in the Citadel, and the **Mehtar Mahal**. This much-photographed latter building is typical of the architecture of Bijapur and has been richly decorated with sculptural work. It serves as an ornamental gateway leading to a small mosque.

Places to Stay

The literature will have you believe that the *Ashok Travellers Lodge* (tel 401), on Station Rd, is the best place to stay in Bijapur. It's certainly the most expensive, but as the KSTDC Tourist Home, just across the road, offers a similar quality of accommodation at a fraction of the cost, it's far from the best bargain. Rooms at the Travellers Lodge cost Rs 50/80 for singles/doubles with attached bathroom. The building is pleasantly situated in well-maintained flower gardens and has an attached restaurant and bar.

The *KSTDC Tourist Home* is located at the entrance to the Citadel, just off Station Rd. This is the best deal you'll come across in Bijapur. Rooms cost Rs 25/35 with attached bathrooms – spotless, tiled and with constant hot water – clean sheets, carpeted rooms, fan, mosquito nets, very friendly staff and a quiet, pleasant courtyard ablaze with bougainvillea. There's a restaurant and bar and

room service (tea and coffee is remarkably expensive!). The Tourist Office is attached to this hotel.

The very basic *Hotel Midland*, Station Rd, costs Rs 10 a single with common bathroom, Rs 12 a single with own shower but common toilet, Rs 15 a single or Rs 20 a double with own bathroom and toilet. There is a good vegetarian restaurant downstairs. *Hotel Tourist*, Gandhi Rd (a continuation of Station Rd) charges Rs 20 a single, Rs 30 a double and Rs 35 a four-bedded room, all with attached bathrooms. There is a good 'meals' cafe downstairs, but it's not actually part of the hotel.

Mysore Lodge, Station Rd, is next door to the Hotel Midland. If you want basic accommodation, come here. Rooms cost Rs 7/12 for singles/doubles with common bathroom, Rs 15 a double with attached bathroom. Extra people can occupy any of the rooms for Rs 3 per person extra. It's a no-frills hotel.

Places to Eat

Good vegetarian set meals can be found in the restaurant attached to the *Hotel Tourist* (lunch and dinner for Rs 3.50. Excellent curd!). There are plenty of other such places along Gandhi Rd. If you're looking for an excellent non-vegetarian meal, try the restaurant about two doors up from the Hotel Tourist. Popular with local middle-class people.

The *KSTDC Tourist Home* offers breakfasts (omelette and toast) for Rs 3 but beware their pots of tea which cost a staggering Rs 3.50 (unheard of anywhere else). Even the *ITDC Travellers Lodge* will serve you a pot of tea for less and put it in a delightful pewter tea service!

Getting There

Rail Bijapur station has a healthy quota of sleeping berths allotted to it on all the main trains which pass through Sholapur and Gadag. These are rarely taken up more than one day in advance. Note that the line from Bijapur to Gadag though slow is one of the most entertaining rides you will find in India. It's the permanent pitch of at least three lots of buskers.

Bijapur to Hubli takes nine hours (it's usually late) and costs about Rs 12 in 2nd class. If you're getting on at Sholapur the quotas available at Bijapur are: Sholapur-Bombay (10 UP), 10 berths; Golgumbaz Express, four berths; Minar Express (Secunderabad-Bombay), four berths; Minar Express (Bombay-Secunderabad), two seats. Getting on at Gadag the Vijayanagar Express (Bangalore-Hubli), 12 berths; Karnataka Express (Miraj-Bangalore), two berths.

Bus Some of the main bus service from Bijapur are:

Aurangabad – two buses daily at 6.15 am and 6.30 pm.

Badami – two buses daily, both at 4 pm (one goes via Kerur).

Bagalkot – six buses daily, first bus at 9 am and the last at 10 pm. Use this as an alternative way of getting to Badami, Aihole and Pattadakal.

Bangalore – two buses daily at 4 pm and 6 pm.

Belgaum – seven buses daily, first bus at 12.45 am and the last at 11.45 pm.

Bellary – one daily express bus at 7.45 am. Use this bus to get to Hospet and the Vijayanagar ruins at Hampi as there are no direct buses from Bijapur to Hospet.

Bidar – one bus daily at 12.55 am.

Bombay – one bus daily at 8 am.

Gadag – one bus daily at 10 am.

Hubli – six buses daily via Jamkhandi. First bus at 2.30 am and the last at 9.30 pm. There is also a luxury bus once daily via Belgaum at 4.30 pm.

Hyderabad – 11½ hour trip costing Rs 40.

Miraj – one bus daily at 4.30 pm.

Poona – three buses daily at 11 am, 3 pm and 5 pm.

Sholapur – eight buses daily, first bus at 2.45 am and the last at 5.30 pm. It takes two to three hours and costs Rs 14.

Getting Around

The most convenient forms of local transport are the auto-rickshaw and the tonga (horse-drawn cart). From the railway station to the Tourist Home will cost Rs 2 to 2.50 (local people pay less than a rupee). From the Tourist Home to Ibrahim Roza will cost about Rs 3.50 per person in a tonga (these take four or five people). Haggling is a must.

HUBLI

Hubli is important to the traveller principally as a major railway junction on the routes from Bombay to Bangalore, Goa, and north Karnataka. Other than this it's an industrial city and there's precious little to see. It's included since you may have to spend the night here on your way somewhere else. All the main services – hotels, restaurants, etc – are situated conveniently close to the railway station.

Places to Stay

Hotel Ajanta (tel 2216), Jaichamarajanagu, is a short distance off the main street and visible from the railway station. It's a huge place and you'll always be able to find accommodation here. Rooms cost Rs 16 a single and Rs 30 a double, both with their own bathroom, fan, clean sheets, etc. The rooms are pleasantly decorated, provided with mosquito nets, there is room service and the staff are friendly. On the ground floor there is a 'meals' cafe (meals cost Rs 3). Highly recommended.

Modern Lodge is located on the main street before you get to the Ajanta. This is a typical one-night stand hotel with basic facilities. Rooms here cost Rs 15 a single and Rs 25 a double, both with attached bathroom and fan, but you must provide your own sheets. There is a 'meals' cafe on the ground floor where meals cost Rs 3.

Further down the street from the Modern Lodge on the opposite side of the road is the *Udipi Hotel* which offers similar accommodation to the Modern Lodge. There is a meals cafe on the ground floor.

Places to Eat

The *Kamat Hotel*, close to the Modern Lodge, offer fairly good plate meals for Rs 3 at lunch time and in the early evening. During the rest of the day coffee and tiffin are available. *Bombay Restaurant* is next door to the Kamat. It provides plate meals similar to the Kamat for the same price. There is a juice bar/ice cream parlour opposite the Kamat Hotel which is excellent.

Getting There

Hubli is a major rail junction on the Bombay-Bangalore route and for trains to Bijapur and Hospet. If you're heading for Goa (either Vasco da Gama or Margao) note that on the 237 Hubli-Miraj 'Link Express' there is one 2nd class three-tier sleeping coach and another combined lst class/2nd class two-tier sleeping coach attached to the train which goes all the way to Vasco, so avoiding the need to change at Londa.

At Londa these coaches are detached from the 237 and added to the 206 Miraj-Vasco Express at about 3.30 am. There's a quota of 20 berths in the three-tier sleeper, six in the two-tier sleeper plus four seats, and a quota for lst class at Hubli station. The full quota is rarely taken up even on the day of departure, but booking closes at 4 pm. After that time you have to apply for reservations at the Ticket Collector's Office between 6.30 and 7 pm, but don't count on getting a reservation at that time – you get no priority unless you have a calling card and look presentable. There's also baksheesh flying around for these unbooked sleepers.

If you're setting out from Hubli early in the morning and heading for Goa, the best train to get is the 207 Bangalore-Miraj 'Karnataka Express' which gets into Londa in plenty of time to let you have breakfast there at the station (the restaurant at Londa station is very good), and then catch the Miraj-Vasco Express which leaves Londa at 11.45 am. This train arrives at Margao or Vasco in time for you to get to Colva beach or to Panjim respectively.

BELGAUM (population 250,000)

In the north-west corner of the state and on the Bombay-Pune-Goa bus and rail route, Belgaum was a regional capital in the 12th and 13th centuries. It has an old oval-shaped stone fort, a mosque, the Masjid-Sata, dating from 1519 and two interesting Jain temples. One has an extremely intricate and complicated roof, while the other has some fine carvings of musicians. A little north of Belgaum, and eight km off the railway line from Gokak Road, are the Gokak Falls where the Ghataprabha River takes a 52-metre drop.

THE NORTH-EAST

Bidar

This little-visited town in the extreme north-east corner of the state was the capital of the Bahmani kingdom from 1428 and later of the Barid Shahi dynasty. It's a pleasant town with a splendid old 15th century fort containing the Ranjeenmahal, Chini Mahal and Turkish Mahal palaces. The impressive Khwaja Mahmud Gawan Madrasa and the tombs of the Bahmani and Barid kings are also worth seeing.

Places to Stay The *KSTDC Tourist Home* near the bus station costs Rs 15 single, Rs 25 double or you can try the *Sri Venkateshwara Lodge* on the main street. The adjoining *Kalpana Hotel* has good food.

Gulbarga (population 160,000)

This town was the Bahmani capital from 1347 until its transfer to Bidar in 1428. Later the kingdom broke up into a number of small kingdoms – Bijapur, Bidar, Berar, Ahmednagar and Golconda. The last of these, Golconda, finally fell to Aurangzeb in 1687. Gulbarga's old fort is in a much deteriorated state, but has a number of interesting buildings inside.

The Jami Masjid, inside the fort, is reputed to have been built by a Moorish architect during the late 14th or early 15th century in imitation of the great mosque in Cordova, Spain. The mosque is unique in India with a huge dome covering the whole area, four smaller ones at the corners and 75 smaller still, all around. The fort itself has 15 towers. Gulbarga also has a number of imposing tombs of Bahmani kings, a shrine to an important Moslem saint and the temple of Sharana Basaveshwara.

Places to Stay There are a number of hotels in the town and a *KSTDC Tourist Home*.

Raichur

The town of Raichur was part of the 13th century Kakatiyas kingdom, then part of the Bahmani kingdom, became the first capital of Bijapur when the Bahmani kingdom fragmented in 1489, and later came under the rule of Vijayanagar. The fort, with its impressive gate, has a citadel with a fine view from the top.

Places to Stay Raichur has *Inspection* and *Tourist Bungalows* as well as hotels such as the *Uma Hotel*, near the railway station, and the *Ashok Hotel*, near the bus stand.

Indian hotels often have amazingly complicated switch panels with switches for fans, bells, lights in bathrooms, entrance-ways, over the beds, mirrors and so on. Generally three-quarters of them don't work, since failed light bulbs are rarely replaced as long as there is at least one still working.

Why, when Indians are so keen on writing everything down in triplicate, will waiters never (at least initially) write orders down? Trying to remember everything inevitably results in at least one item failing to appear.

Andhra Pradesh

Population: 49 million
Area: 276,754 square km
Capital: Hyderabad
Main language: Telegu

The large state of Andhra Pradesh was created by combining the old princely State of Hyderabad with the Telegu speaking portions of the former State of Madras. Most of the state stands on the high Deccan plateau, sloping down to the low-lying coastal region to the east where the mighty Godavari and Krishna Rivers meet the Bay of Bengal in wide deltas.

Andhra Pradesh was once a major Buddhist centre and part of Ashoka's large empire until it broke apart. Traces of that early Buddhist influence can still be seen in several places. Later the Chalukyas held power in the 7th century but they in turn fell to the Chola kingdom of the south around the 10th century. In the 14th century Moslem power finally reached this far south, and for centuries the region was an arena for Hindu-Moslem power struggles. Finally it was taken over by a general of the Moghul Emperor Aurangzeb in 1713. His successors, the Nizams of Hyderabad, ruled the state right down to independence.

The final Nizam of Hyderabad was reputed to be one of the richest men in the world but Andhra Pradesh itself is one of the poorest and least developed states in India. New dams and irrigation projects are improving the barren, scrubby land of the plateau but much of the state remains economically backward. There is not a great deal of interest in Andhra Pradesh apart from the capital, Hyderabad. Visitors with a keen interest in architecture or archaeology may wish to visit some of the excavations or old temple sites but otherwise Hyderabad is the only real attraction.

HYDERABAD (population 1,800,000)

Like Bijapur, further to the west in neighbouring Karnataka state, Hyderabad is an important centre of Islamic culture and offers central India's counterpart to the Moghul splendours of the northern cities of Delhi, Agra and Fatehpur Sikri. Consisting of the twin cities of Hyderabad and Secunderabad, it is the capital of Andhra Pradesh state and famous as the former seat of the fabulously wealthy Nizams of Hyderabad. Here, lively crowded bazaars surround huge and impressive Islamic monuments dating from the 16th and 17th centuries. The city – India's fifth largest – was founded in 1590 by Mohammed Quli, the fourth of the Qutab Shahi kings who ruled this part of the Deccan from 1512 until 1687 when the last of their line was defeated by the Moghul emperor Aurangzeb, following suspension of the annual tribute due to their nominal suzerain in Delhi.

Before the founding of Hyderabad, the Qutab Shahi kings had ruled from the fortress city of Golconda, 11 km west. The extensive ruins of this fort, which has

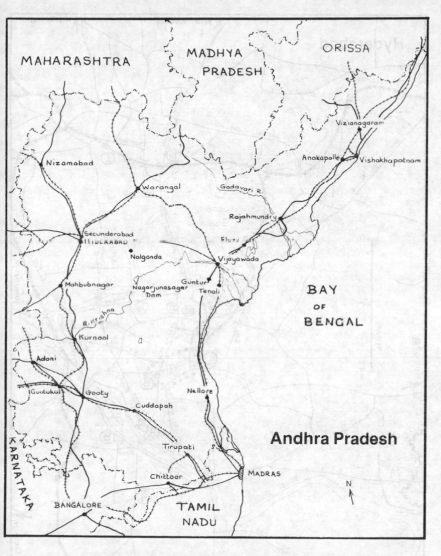

roots going back to the earlier Hindu kingdoms of the Yadavas and Kakatiyas, together with the nearby tombs of the Qutab Shahi kings, are the principal attractions of any visit to Hyderabad.

Following Aurangzeb's death in 1707,

Moghul control over this part of India rapidly waned and the viceroys who had been installed to look after the interests of the empire broke away and established their own independent state taking the title, first, of Subedar and, later, that of

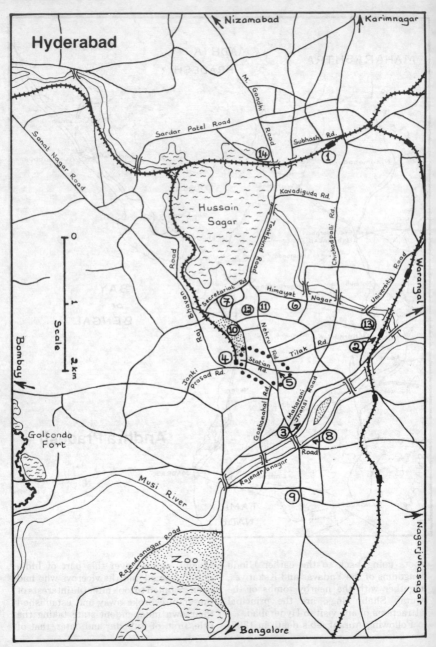

1	Secunderabad Railway Station	8	Salar Jang Museum	
2	Kacheguda Railway Station	9	Charminar and Mecca Masjid	
3	Bus Station	10	Public Gardens and	
4	Hyderabad Railway Station		Archaeological Museum	
5	GPO (Abids)	11	Hotel Nagarjuna	area of budget &
6	Tourist Office (ITDC — Lidcap	12	Hyd-Inn and Ritz Hotel	mid-range hotels
	Building)	13	Tourist Home & Tourist Hotel	around Abids &
7	Birla Mandir Temple	14	Youth Hostel	Nampally High Rd

Nizam. These new rulers became embroiled in the rivalry between the French and British for control of India during the latter half of the 18th century as allies of the French but, after the defeat of the French and subsequent Maratha raids which seriously weakened their kingdom, they were forced to conclude a treaty with the British and relinquish most of their power.

When independence came to India in 1947, the Nizam toyed with the idea of declaring independence and went so far as to allow an Islamic extremist group to seize control. This however led to his downfall as the Indian government, mindful of Hyderabad's Hindu majority of around 85% and unwilling to see the creation of an independent and possibly hostile state in the centre of the Deccan, used the insurrection as an excuse to occupy Hyderabad in 1948 and force its accession to the Union.

This dusty city retains much of its 19th century atmosphere and is quite unlike any cities further south. Lovers of graffiti should make a point of visiting Osmania University where every available square inch of stone and brickwork is plastered with political slogans. Though this is fairly common in many Indian cities, nothing quite so extreme as this can be seen elsewhere.

Orientation

The old city of Hyderabad itself lies on either side of the River Musi and south of the lake, Hussain Sagar, which effectively divides the twin cities of Hyderabad and Secunderabad. In this part are located most of the historical monuments, the bulk of the hotels and cafes used by travellers, the city bus depot, Salar Jang Museum and the zoo. Most of the budget hotels are situated in the area known as Abids between the GPO and Hyderabad railway station. The more expensive hotels are, in general, clustered around the Secretariat building at the south end of Hussain Sagar.

The ruins of Golconda Fort and the tombs of the Qutab Shahi kings lie about 11 km to the west of the city. The more recent city of Secunderabad is situated on the north side of Hussain Sagar and, if you are coming by train, you will get off at Secunderabad railway station (the main station). The YMCA, YWCA and the Youth Hostel are all here, but few travellers stay in Secunderabad itself. To get to Hyderabad you will have to take a bus, auto-rickshaw or taxi (about 10 minutes' journey). Note that few trains pass through Hyderabad railway station.

Information

There are tourist information kiosks at both Secunderabad and Hyderabad railway stations but you'd be advised not to waste your time going there. They have no literature, no city maps and will even direct you to the former address of the main tourist office. Incredible that they could be so out of touch!

Other than these, there are two tourist offices, both of them on Himayatnagar,

Hyderabad. Andhra Pradesh Travel & Tourism Development Corporation (tel 36252), 2nd Floor, Diamond House, Himayatnagar stocks hardly any literature and seems to exist solely to promote its sight-seeing tours of Hyderabad and Nagarjunasagar.

The India Tourism Development Corporation (tel 220730), Lidcap Building, 3-6-150 Himayatnagar are the people to go to if you're looking for literature on Hyderabad and the rest of Andhra Pradesh or a street plan of the city. They also promote their own tours of the city and to Nagarjunasagar.

Air India and Indian Airlines are both in Saifabad near the Secretariat building. The telephone numbers are 222747 and 36902/72910 respectively. Hyderabad has an incredibly active bazaar.

Charminar

Standing in the heart of the old walled city, this huge triumphal arch was built by Mohammed Quli Qutab Shah in 1591 to commemorate the end of the plague in Hyderabad. It's surrounded on all sides by lively bazaars and the views from the top are superb. An image of this building graces every packet of *Charminar* cigarettes, which hoardings all over India assure you are the only brand to 'satisfy a man like you'. The monument is open every day and entry costs Rs 0.50. No guides are necessary.

Mecca Masjid

Situated next to the Charminar, this is one of the largest mosques in the world and is said to accommodate up to 10,000 worshippers. Construction began during the reign of Mohammed Quli Qutab Shah in 1614 but was not finished until 1687, by which time the Moghul Emperor Aurangzeb had annexed the Golconda kingdom. The colonnades and door arches are made out of single slabs of granite, which history records were quarried ll km away and dragged to the site by a team of 1400 bullocks! The minarets were originally planned to have been much higher than they are, but the enormous cost of erecting the main part of the building apparently forced the ruler to settle for something less grand.

It's definitely a very beautiful and impressive building but disfigured by huge awnings of chicken wire, which have presumably been erected to stop birds nesting in the ceiling and liming the floor. Nevertheless, they still get in and the steel supports which have been carelessly cemented into the tiled and patterned floor to hold this netting are nothing short of vandalism.

To the left of the mosque is an enclosure containing the tombs of the Nizams.

Birla Mandir (Naubat Prahad) Temple

This stunningly beautiful modern Hindu temple, built out of white marble, graces the rocky hill which overlooks the south end of Hussain Sagar. It's a very popular Hindu pilgrimage centre but non-Hindus are allowed inside. There's no entry fee and the priests make no efforts to press you for contributions. There are excellent views over the city from the summit. The temple is only open from 8 am to 12 noon and 4 to 8 pm.

Salar Jang Museum

This is India's answer to the Victoria and Albert Museum in London. The collection was put together by Mir Yusaf Ali Khan (Salar Jang III), the Prime Minister of the Nizam. It contains 35,000 exhibits drawn from all corners of the world including sculptures, wood carvings, religious objects, Persian miniature paintings, illuminated manuscripts, armour and weaponry, the swords, daggers and clothing of the Moghul emperors and of Tipu Sultan, and many other objects. All of this is housed in one of the ugliest buildings imaginable.

Open daily except Fridays from 10 am to 5 pm. Entrance costs Rs 2 (Rs 1 if you have a student card). All bags and cameras have to be deposited in the entrance hall –

there's no charge for this and it's secure. Refreshments are available inside. Avoid going there on Sundays as it's bedlam (seems half the population of Hyderabad are there on this day!).

Archaeological Museum
Situated in the public gardens between Nampally High Rd and the branch railway line which leads to Hyderabad railway station, the museum has a small collection of archaeological finds from the area together with copies of the Ajanta frescoes. They've also got an Egyptian mummy. It's supposed to be open daily except Mondays from 10.30 am to 5 pm but appears to be semi-permanently 'under construction'. Entry is Rs 0.50.

Golconda Fort & the Tombs of the Qutab Shahi Kings
To see the ruins of this extensive fort thoroughly, or with any degree of ease, you need to put aside at least half a day. The bus tours of Hyderabad organised by the Tourist Office bring you here for just one hour which is a ridiculously short period of time – sufficient only to quickly climb to the summit and, equally quickly, come back down again.

Though the bulk of the ruins date from the time of the Qutab Shahi kings (16th-17th centuries), the origins of the fort have been traced back to the earlier Hindu periods of Deccan history when the Yadavas and, later, the Kakatiyas ruled this area of India. In 1512, Sultan Quli Qutab Shah, a Turkoman adventurer from Persia who had risen to be Governor of Telangana under the Bahmani rulers, declared independence and made Golconda his capital.

It remained the capital until 1590 when the court was moved to the new city of Hyderabad, but subsequently came into its own again on two separate occasions in the 1600s when Moghul armies from Delhi were sent against the kingdom to enforce payment of tribute. Abul Hasan, the last of the Qutab Shahi kings, held out in the fort

of Golconda against a Moghul army commanded by the emperor Aurangzeb for seven months before losing it by treachery in 1687. Following Aurangzeb's death, early in the next century, the viceroys whom he had installed to look after Moghul interests rapidly became sovereign princes (soon to be known as the Nizams). They chose Hyderabad as their capital and abandoned Golconda.

The citadel itself is built on a granite hill 120 metres high and surrounded by battlemented ramparts constructed of large blocks of masonry, some of them weighing several tonnes. The massive gates are studded with large pointed iron spikes intended to prevent elephants from battering them and further protected by a cordon wall to check direct attack. Outside of the citadel stands another battlemented rampart with a perimeter of 11 km. All of these walls are in an excellent state of preservation.

Unfortunately, many of the structures inside the citadel – the palaces and harem of the Qutab Shahi kings, assembly halls, arsenal, stables and barracks – have suffered a great deal from past sieges and the ravages of time but enough remains to give a good impression of what the place must once have looked like. Restoration work is underway on the buildings around the Balahisar Gate (the main entrance) – even the wrought iron work is being replaced – but it will be many years before this is anywhere near completion.

One of the most remarkable features of this fort is its system of acoustics whereby the sound of hands clapped in the Grand Portico can be heard in the Durbar Hall at the very top of the hill – a fact not lost on tour guides (or their charges) who do their utmost competing with each other to make as much noise as possible! There is also supposed to be a 'secret' underground tunnel leading from the Durbar Hall to one of the palaces at the foot of the hill but, predictably, you are not allowed to investigate this.

The tombs of the Qutab Shahi kings lie

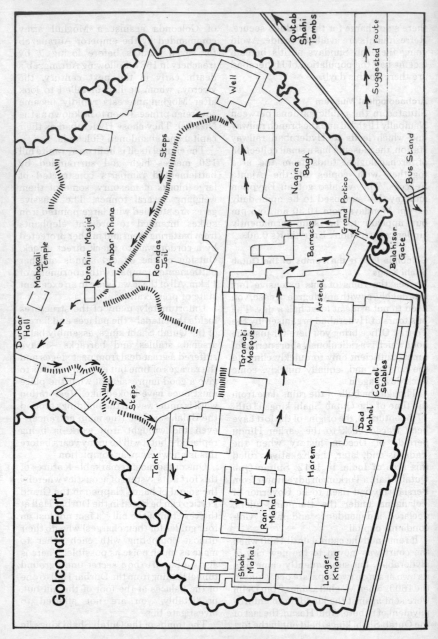

Golconda Fort

Qutab Shahi Tombs

Suggested route

Bus Stand

Well

Steps

Mahakali Temple

Ibrahim Masjid

Ambar Khana

Ramdas Jail

Nagina Bagh

Grand Portico

Balahisar Gate

Durbar Hall

Steps

Barracks

Arsenal

Taramati Masque

Camel Stables

Dad Mahal

Tank

Harem

Rani Mahal

Shahi Mahal

Langer Khana

about a km north of the outer perimeter wall of Golconda. They are fairly small, but graceful, structures surrounded by landscaped gardens. A number of them display beautifully carved stonework. Entrance to these tombs cost Rs 0.25 plus Rs 2 if you have a camera or Rs 10 (!!) if you have a movie camera. A small guide book, *Guide to Golconda Fort & Qutub Shahi Tombs*, is on sale at both the tombs and the fort. How much you pay for it depends on your bargaining power, but Rs 2 should be sufficient. It's worth getting hold of if you're going to spend the day here.

If you want to make your own way to the fort, take service bus 142 or 119 from Nampally High Rd opposite Hyderabad Railway Station. These will take you to the main entrance at Balahisar Gate. The trip takes about an hour and costs Rs 1.75. Otherwise taxis are available – negotiate the cost before setting off.

Nehru Zoological Park

One of the largest in India, the zoo is spread out over 120 hectares of landscaped gardens with the animals contained in large, open enclosures. They don't look any less bored than animals in zoos anywhere else in the world, but at least here an effort has been made which is more than can be said for most other zoos in India.

The park is open from 9 am until 6 pm daily except Mondays and entry costs Rs 0.50. There's also a Lion Safari Park which you can go around in a minibus for Rs 1 and a toy train for children. It's a very popular park with local people.

Other

Tourist literature on Hyderabad raves on about various 'lovely picnic spots', such as the lake of Osmansagar (Gandipet) from which the city receives its water supply, but it's as well to take this with a pinch of salt. They're nothing special and a definite case of over-enthusiasm.

Tours

Andhra Pradesh Travel & Tourism Development Corporation, Diamond House, Himayatnagar, Hyderabad, offers a daily tour of the city which includes visits to Osmania University, Birla Mandir, Qutan Shahi Tombs, Golconda Fort, Gandipet, Salar Jang Museum, Charminar, Mecca Masjid and the Zoological Gardens. The tour starts at 8 am and ends at 6 pm and tickets cost Rs 25. You have to pay your own entrance fees to the zoo, Museum and Qutab Shahi Tombs. The lunch stop is at Gandipet Lake.

The India Tourism Development Corporation, Lidcap Building, Himayatnagar, Hyderabad, also offer daily tours of the city visiting the same places as above but in a different sequence. The tour starts at 8 am and ends at 6.30 pm but the time allowed for each sight is ludicrously short. Five and 10 minute stops are the order of the day. Tickets cost Rs 25 by deluxe coach and entry fees are extra.

Both these tours allow insufficient time for visiting Golconda Fort and the Tombs of the Qutab Shahi kings (60 minutes on the former and 70 minutes on the latter), and a lot of time is wasted on an inconsequential visit to Gandipet lake. If there is anything to choose between them, then the ITDC tour would be the better of the two as the lunch break is in Abids, in the centre of Hyderabad, where there is a choice of restaurants. At Gandipet there is no choice and facilities are very limited.

Places to Stay – Bottom End

Other than the Youth Hostel, YMCA and YWCA, the best of these are located on Nampally High Rd, opposite Hyderabad railway station. There are others around the Charminar in the old part of the city, but they're very basic.

The *Super Lodge*, Nampally High Rd, opposite Hyderabad Railway Station, was once the best and one of the cheapest of the budget hotels, but at present it's closed for renovations. If it's open when you get there, let us know what it's like these days.

A few doors down from the Super Lodge, near the junction with Station Rd, is the *Royal Lodge*, Nampally High Rd. This is a huge place, and you'd be very unlucky if you found it full. Singles with share bath cost a bargain Rs 12 here. Rooms with attached bath cost Rs 20 a single and Rs 30 to 50 a double.

Other budget hotels to try are the *Sri Anu Hotel*, Nehru Rd near the junction with Station Rd, the *Metro Lodge* and the *Everest Lodge*, which are both on Tilak Rd, near the junction with Nehru Rd.

The *Youth Hostel*, behind the Boat Club at the north-eastern end of Hussain Sagar, Secunderabad, is recommended by quite a few travellers, because it offers the cheapest dormitory-type accommodation. There are 51 beds and the cost is Rs 5 per night.

In addition to the above there are the *YMCA* (tel 57850) and *YWCA* but they are often semi-permanently full with students. Only Secunderabad railway station (tel 70144/5) has *Railway Retiring Rooms*, but you would be lucky to get one since they have only one double room (Rs 16) and one dormitory (four beds at Rs 10 per bed).

Places to Stay – Middle

The best place to head for if you're looking for a mid-range hotel is Station Rd, which runs between Hyderabad Railway Station and the GPO. There's a choice of several along this road. One of the largest in the city is *Sri Brindavan Hotel* (tel 220820), and you're sure to get a room here. A few years ago it was very good value for money, but they've put the prices up. Large, airy singles/doubles cost Rs 40/60 with fan, clean sheets and attached bath. Most of the rooms are built around a quiet courtyard well off the road. Avoid the noisy rooms over the main road. Room service is available, the staff are friendly (but watch out for extra charges) and a newspaper is pushed under your door every morning. The restaurant here is very

good, see Places to Eat, below. Baggage can be left securely at the reception if necessary.

Another mid-range hotel of similar quality is the *Hotel Palace* (tel 52011), Station Rd, which has non-air-con rooms with attached baths for Rs 35, 40 and 45 a single, and Rs 60 and 65 a double. It also has a few more expensive air-con rooms. Then there's the *Hotel Apsara*, also on Station Rd, with singles/doubles with attached baths for Rs 40/60. Another popular mid-range hotel is the *Hotel Taj Mahal* (tel 221167), King Kothi Rd, which costs Rs 45/65 with attached bath.

At the cheaper end of this bracket is the *Hotel Imperial* (tel 53071), once again on Station Rd, which has singles for Rs 22 and doubles for Rs 32 to 35. Rooms on the roof are unbearably hot in summer. All rooms have attached baths and there is a restaurant which serves vegetarian and non-vegetarian food. One other hotel in this bracket is the *Tourist Hotel* (tel 44491), Kachiguda, Hyderabad, close to the railway station there, which makes it convenient if you're heading for Guntakal, Bangalore or Madras by rail – otherwise it's rather out-of-the-way. Rooms here cost Rs 18 a single and Rs 25 a double.

Places to Stay – Top End

The *Ritz Hotel* (tel 33571) on Hill Fort Rd, Basheer Bagh, between Nampally High Rd and J Nehru Rd, is one of Hyderabad's more expensive hotels. Rooms cost Rs 225/275 for singles/doubles and there are all the usual mod cons from air-conditioning to swimming pool and tennis courts. The much larger *Welcomgroup Banjara* (tel 222222) is at Banjara Hills, overlooking the lake and 15 minutes from the railway terminal by car. Rooms here run from Rs 475/575 for singles/doubles and again there are all the usual facilities and luxuries.

Bluemoon Hotel (tel 30136) on Rajbhavan Rd, Begumpet is rather more central and has singles/doubles from Rs 125/175. *Hotel Siddhartha* (tel 57481, 57421) on

Bank St has rooms at Rs 80/110 or Rs 45/65 without air-con. *Hyd-Inn*, Lake Hill Rd, Basheer Bagh (tel 38481) is a smaller, more pleasant and friendlier hotel than the Ritz. Air-con rooms cost Rs 80/140, non-air-con they're Rs 50/80.

Hotel Jaya International, Abids (tel 223444) is situated just off to the left on J Nehru Rd as you face the GPO. A very pleasant modern hotel where rooms cost Rs 100 for an air-con single and Rs 130 a double, or Rs 50 a single and Rs 70 to 85 a double for non air-con rooms. All rooms have an attached bath and the hotel has its own restaurant.

Places to Eat

Most travellers eat in their respective hotels since there are few good restaurants, as such, in Hyderabad. Good cheap vegetarian meals can be found at any *Kamat Hotel* where the standard fare costs Rs 3. While there are several of these hotels around Hyderabad, the most convenient one – if you're staying in Abids – is on Station Rd near the junction with Nampilly High Rd.

The *Emerald Restaurant* has 'wonderful' vegetarian food. The *Ruby Restaurant*, in the centre of Hyderabad's very active bazaar, is a large Moslem restaurant where, if you are a women, you may find yourself sitting in a room full of women, traditionally separated from the menfolk in the party! There are any number of cheap vegetarian cafes along Nampally High Rd, Station Rd and around the GPO on Nehru Rd.

At the Sri Brindavan Hotel the *Shalimar Bar & Restaurant* has south Indian vegetarian food and a more expensive air-conditioned restaurant, only open in the evenings. The air-con restaurant has Chinese and western dishes as well as Indian and is 'easily the best in Hyderabad and as good as any in Delhi – but cheaper' according to a traveller. Another added that its non-vegetarian food is 'decidedly welcome in oh-so vegetarian Hyderabad'. They also have a range of beers including locally brewed Kingfisher at Rs 14.

Getting There

Air There are flight connections between Hyderabad and Delhi (Rs 899), Calcutta (Rs 966), Madras (Rs 408), Bangalore (Rs 398) and Bombay (Rs 521). Calcutta flights are daily, Delhi, Madras and Bangalore flights twice daily, Bombay flights two to three times daily. Beware of officious security guards at the airport who may insist on inspecting your camera from the inside. The airport is surprisingly well appointed and less frantic than most other Indian airports.

Rail Note that the main railway station is at Secunderabad. Hyderabad Railway Station is only a branch line, but if you're heading south to Guntakal, Bangalore or Madras and staying in Abids you can board the train at Kacheguda station instead of going all the way up to Secunderabad. As elsewhere, the fastest night express trains are booked up days in advance, so reserve your seat or sleeper as early as possible.

New Delhi-Secunderabad can take less than 24 hours on the Andhra Pradesh Express. It's a 1675-km trip costing Rs 365 in 1st class, Rs 93 in 2nd class. It's 6½ hours on the Golconda Express between Hyderabad and Vijayawada (this train does go from Hyderabad). The fare is Rs 119 in 1st class, Rs 30 in 2nd class. The quickest route from Calcutta is to take the Madras Mail from Howrah Station (daily) and change at Vijayawada. If you're coming from Nagpur, change at Kazipet – just west of Warangal.

Bombay-Secunderabad, a distance of 800 km, takes as little as 15 hours on the Minar Express, fares are Rs 209 in 1st, Rs 53 in 2nd. Madras to Secunderabad is a 510 km trip taking about 15 hours. The fare is Rs 144 in 1st, Rs 36.50 lin 2nd. It's a 19-hour trip to Bangalore costing Rs 175 in 1st, Rs 45 in 2nd.

The line from Secunderabad to

Aurangabad is metre gauge – the 517-km trip takes 12 hours at a cost of Rs 151 in 1st class, Rs 38 in 2nd. The express continues through Aurangabad to Manmad which is on the Bombay-Delhi line via Bhopal and Agra. The Secunderabad-Ajmer line is also metre gauge. This route goes through Khandwa, Mhow, Indore, Ratlam and Chittorgarh. All the way to Ajmer is a 1818-km trip, taking 39 hours at a cost of Rs 386 in 1st class, Rs 98 in 2nd.

Bus The bus to Aurangabad departs at 4 pm, takes 16 hours and costs Rs 80.

Getting Around

Local transport is available by service bus, auto-rickshaw and taxi. Getting on to any service bus, other than at the terminus, in Hyderabad is (as one traveller put it) 'like staging a banzai charge on Guadalcanal'. He wasn't exaggerating! Useful ones which you might be able to get on to include No 2 – Secunderabad Railway Station to Charminar & vice versa. No 7 – Secunderabad Railway Station to Afzalganj & vice versa. This is one to catch if you're heading for Abids as it goes down Tankbund Rd and J Nehru Rd via the GPO. Nos 119 or 142 – Nampally High Rd (opposite Hyderabad Railway Station) to Golconda Fort & vice versa.

Auto-rickshaws are the cheapest alternative during the day. Unlike many other cities in India, the drivers here appear to need no prompting about use of meter. Some sample fares are Secunderabad Railway Station to Himayatnagar: Rs 4.25 to 4.50. Abids to Charminar: Rs 3.50 to 4. Himayatnagar to Abids: Rs 3.25. Secunderabad to GPO: Rs 6.40.

An auto-rickshaw from the airport will cost about Rs 10 to Abids – the meter fare plus a dubious rupee or two for the airport car park. There is no airport bus.

NAGARJUNAKONDA & NAGARJUNA-SAGAR

Nagarjunakonda, 150 km south-east of Hyderabad on the Krishna River, was once one of the largest and most important Buddhist centres in southern India, spanning a period from the 2nd century BC until the 3rd century AD. In those days known as Vijayapur, it takes its present name from Nagarjuna, one of the most revered of Buddhist monks and founder of the Madhyamika school, who governed the *sangha* for nearly 60 years around the turn of the 2nd century AD. The school which he established attracted students from as far afield as Sri Lanka and China.

The site was discovered in 1926 and subsequent excavations, particularly in the '50s and '60s, have unearthed the remains of stupas, viharas, chaityas and mandapas, as well as some outstanding examples of white marble carvings and sculptures depicting the life of the Buddha. These have been moved to a museum on the site, following a decision to create the Nagarjunasagar dam which will eventually submerge the whole of this area. The dam is one of the largest masonry constructions in the world and India claims that it will create the world's third largest artificial lake.

The Nagarjunakonda panels lack the more elaborate sculptural features of those found further down river at Amaravati – 32 km north of Guntar – but are the best you will find in this part of India today. Amaravati itself, once the capital of Andhra during the Buddhist period but now described in tourist literature as 'a squalid little village', contained over 20 monasteries with more than 1000 monks and a huge marble stupa unrivalled elsewhere in the world.

Every cm of this stupa and the rail which surrounded it was richly carved and the whole decorated with lamps on festive occasions, but before you rush off to see it you should know that it was largely destroyed at the end of the 18th century by local people in their quest for building material. Marble is excellent raw material for a lime-kiln. The fragments which remained were spirited off to the Madras Museum and the British Museum in London during the 19th century.

Places to Stay
At Nagarjunasagar there is a choice of accommodation maintained by the Andhra Pradesh Travel & Tourism Development Corporation (tel Hyderabad 36252) which includes the *Soundarya Guest House, Project House, Sethu Sadan*, a number of separate cottages, and the *Konda Guest House*, at Nagarjunakonda. They're all very reasonably priced – the Project House, for instance, costs Rs 25 a double – and for budget travellers, there's also a *Youth Hostel*, which is Rs 5 per night in dormitory accommodation. Other accommodation can also be arranged through the Executive Engineer, R&B Division, Nagarjunasagar Dam, Hill Colony.

Getting There
Probably the easiest way to visit Nagarjunakonda and Nagarjunasagar is to take the tourist coach from Hyderabad organised by the India Tourism Development Corporation, Lidcap Building, 3-6-150 Himayatnagar, Hyderabad (tel 220730) on Sundays and public holidays. It departs at 7.30 am, returning at 9.30 pm and costs Rs 55 by de-luxe coach. The tour includes visits to the Nagarjunakonda Museum, Pylon (an engraved granite monolith from the Buddhist period), Nagarjunasagar dam, and the working model of the dam.

If you'd prefer to make your own way there, regular buses connect Hyderabad, Vijayawada and Guntur with Nagarjunasagar. The nearest railway station is at Macherla – a branch line running west from Guntur and ending at Macherla. If coming from Hyderabad, head first for Guntur. There are regular buses from Macherla to Nagarjunasagar.

Local sight-seeing tours of Nagarjunakonda and Nagarjunasagar are organised by the Tourism Department, Project House, Hill Colony, Nagarjunasagar and costs Rs 5 per head.

If you're not part of one of the local tours or those organised from Hyderabad, launches to Nagarjunakonda Museum, which is situated on an island in the lake, depart at 9.30 am and 1.30 pm. The fare is Rs 4 return.

WARANGAL (population 160,000)
This was once the capital of the Kakatiya kingdom, which ruled the greater part of present-day Andhra Pradesh from the latter half of the 12th century until the early 14th century when it was conquered by the Tughlaqs of Delhi. The Hindu Kakatiyas were great builders and patrons of the arts, and it was during their reign that the Chalukyan style of temple architecture and decoration reached the pinnacle of its development.

If you have an interest in the various streams of Hindu temple development and have either visited or intend to visit the early Chalukyan sites at Badami, Aihole and Pattadakal in neighbouring Karnataka state, then an outing to Warangal would be worthwhile.

The Fort
Warangal's main attraction is the enormous deserted mud-brick fort which has a terrific atmosphere and many interesting features including carved stones from wrecked Chalukyan temples which have been indiscriminately set in the massive stone walls. These walls form a distinct fortification almost a km inside the outer mud walls. The construction and defences of the gateways are very interesting. The fort was built by the Kakatiyas, these same rulers were also responsible for the first fort at Golconda – also constructed from mud-brick but later converted to masonry by the Qutab Shahi kings.

Chalukyan Temples
The most notable Chalukyan temples which remain today are the Thousand-Pillared Temple on the slopes of Hanamkonda hill (one shrine of which is

still in use), the Bhadrakali Temple situated on a hillock between Warangal and Hanamkonda, and the Shambu Lingeswara or Swayambhu Temple (originally a Shiva temple). The thousand-pillar temple is, however, much inferior to those found further south and the Bhadrakali Temple is not really very interesting.

There is also the Ramappa Temple at Palampet, 77 km from Warangal, which represents a combination of the Chalukyan and the later Hoysala styles. It's hard to get to but reputed to be one of the finest examples of Deccan architecture.

Places to Stay

Accommodation facilities are modest but the new *Vijaya Lodge* (tel 4142, 4345) on Station Rd is excellent value for Rs 45 for a double with bath although there is no restaurant here. Most of the hotels and lodges are located on R N Tagore Rd and on Chowrasta. They include *Hotel Nataraj* (about a km from the railway station) and *Krishna Lodge* (both on R N Tagore Rd), *Annapurna Lodge, Ganesh Lodge, Hotel Kohinoor, Ananda Lodge* and the *Venkatarama Lodge* (all on Chowrasta).

There are plenty of vegetarian restaurants in town. Good non-vegetarian meals can be found at the *Kohinoor Hotel*.

Getting There

Rail The daily Warangal Express connects Warangal with Hyderabad. It departs Secunderabad railway station at 6 pm and takes three hours. There are also good rail connections to Vijayawada so you can visit Warangal quite easily if travelling that way. If you're coming from outside the state, Kazipet, a few km west of Warangal, is the most convenient point to alight. Regular buses connect Kazipet with Warangal.

Bus Regular buses connect Warangal with Hyderabad, Nizamabad and other major centres of population. Local buses connect Warangal with Kazipet and Hanamkonda.

TIRUPATHI & TIRUMALA

The town of Tirupathi and the 'holy hill' of Tirumala, 13 km away in the extreme south of Andhra Pradesh, are two of the most important pilgrimage centres in the whole of India on account of the temple of Sri Balaji at Tirumala. Balaji is the god whose picture you will find in the reception area of most lodges and restaurants in southern India. He's the one with his eyes covered up (since his gaze would scorch the world) and garlanded in so many flowers that the only part of him visible is his feet.

Amongst his attributes is the belief ('realisation' would be a better word as far as his devotees are concerned) that any wish made in front of the idol at Tirumala is granted. Naturally, with a legend like that, pilgrims flock in from all over India and there are never less than 5000 here at any one time. Such numbers also ensure that the temple is one of the richest in India though it's fair to say that a lot of its income is ploughed back into schemes to help the poor and into providing shelter for pilgrims on their way to Tirumala. It's considered auspicious to have your head shaved when visiting the temple so if you see people with shaved heads in south India then you can be pretty sure they've recently been to Tirupathi – this applies to men, women and children.

In order to cope with this army of pilgrims everything at Tirupathi and Tirumala is organised to keep them moving, keep them fed and keep them sheltered. Most of the hotels and lodges are in Tirupathi. There's only one place to stay in Tirumala unless you're prepared to bed down in the vast dormitories with thousands of others. A whole fleet of buses (known as the Tirumala Link Buses) constantly ferries pilgrims to and fro between Tirupathi and Tirumala. To get back down again you'll have to join the wire cages just like everyone else.

The temple is one of the few in India

which will allow non-Hindus into the sanctum sanctorum but before you can do this you must go to the 'Complaints Office' and sign a statement which says, 'I........am of the..........religion and have reverence for Sri Balaji'. They will expect you to say you're a Christian and that Tamil Nadu Tourist Development Corporation is your sponsor. After that you pay Rs 25 for 'Special Darshan' and then you're allowed into the temple. Special darshan allows you to jump the queue ahead of all those who have paid only Rs 5 for ordinary darshan and who have to queue up – often for up to 12 hours – in the wire cages which ring the outer wall of the temple.

In some ways it's commercialism gone mad. There are a whole series of darshans which range from the simplest at Rs 5 up to ones costing thousands of rupees. A huge signpost outside the temple details what is available. Then there are the trinket stalls and the prasad stalls. The laddha prasad, round sweets made with chickpea flour and raisins, are actually quite delicious. And, lastly, the wig stalls. Having had your hair shaved off you can now buy it back (or rather you can buy someone else's). All the same, it's well worth coming here.

Places to Stay

Tirupathi is chock a block full of hotels and lodges so there's no problem finding somewhere to stay. *Bhima's Deluxe Hotel* (tel 2501-4) at 42 G-Car St, has excellent doubles at Rs 70 – the marble continues from the lobby to every room, there are hot showers, comfortable beds and even phones in every room! You can see it from the walkway over the tracks at the railway station. Tirumala only has one hotel offering private rooms – most of the pilgrims stay in vast dormitories which ring the temple.

Getting There

Unless you particularly want to stay in Tirupathi overnight you can get there and back from Madras easily in one day so long

as you make an early start. Tiruvalluvar have express buses from the Esplanade bus station at 9.30 am, 2.30 pm and 8.30 pm as well as many other ordinary buses (the latter are not particularly recommended as they take circuitous routes).

Andhra Pradesh state transport also have buses from the same depot 16 times daily, the first at 4.30 am and the last at 8 pm. Fares are Rs 17.50 (super de-luxe), Rs 16 (Asiad bus) and Rs 13.50 (express). Getting back to Madras is simplicity itself – just wait at the express bus terminal until a Madras bus arrives and get on. They're very frequent. The journey takes 3½ to four hours.

Although it's easy to get there under your own steam most people who visit Tirupathi do so on one of the tour buses operated by Tamil Nadu Tourist Development Corporation, Andhra Pradesh TDC or Karnataka TDC. If you're going to take one of these tours then Madras is the most convenient place to do it from as the journey is only 3½ hours. Taking a tour bus works out about twice as expensive as doing it yourself but if you're that keen to save $5....... See the Madras section for details.

Getting Around

Tirumala Link Buses operate from the state bus stand next to the express bus stand and from the Sri Venkateshwara bus station near the tank in Tirupathi. They operate from dawn till well past dusk. The fare is Rs 4.20 going up and Rs 3.20 coming down. Getting a bus back down can take time so bear this in mind.

SOUTH OF HYDERABAD

Other places south of Hyderabad include:

Kurnool (population 150,000)

Situated 240 km south of Hyderabad, Kurnool has fragments of its old fortress still standing and a number of mosques and mausoleums. The Mallikarjuna temple near here is an important Shiva shrine and a major pilgrimage centre.

Tadpatri

Fifty km south-east of the junction town of Gooty, there are the remains of two temples which date from around 1485 when they were built by the rulers of Vijayanagar. The riverbank Rameswara-swami temple was never completed, but is more imposing than the Chintalaraya-swami.

Kalahasti & Tiruttani

Kalahasti is another important pilgrimage centre, east of Tirupati. Almost on the border with Tamil Nadu, 60 km south of Tirupati, Tiruttani is another very old hill top temple.

Konai Waterfalls

These waterfalls are 90 km north-west of Madras on the Madras-Uthukottai-Tirupati road. Get down after Nagalapuram at Narayanawanam and walk two km the quiet, lonely and unspoilt falls. October to January, after the monsoons, is the best time to go but avoid weekends or public holidays when people come in droves from Madras. There is accommodation in a small cottage for Rs 5 per person.

EAST COAST

Although the main Calcutta-Madras railway line runs along the east coast of Andhra Pradesh few travellers stop south of Orissa. During the monsoon the extensive deltas of the Godavari and Krishna Rivers may flood, forcing the Calcutta-Madras trains to take an alternative route further inland through Raipur, Nagpur and Hyderabad.

Waltair & Visakhapatnam (population 400,000)

These two towns have really merged into one and the local people do not observe any distinction between them. The northern residential area can be thought of as Waltair and the booming southern business and industrial area towards the docks as Visakhapatnam (abbreviated as Vizag). The railway station, roughly in the centre, is called Waltair Junction.

Waltair, a popular seaside resort, has rocks and pools as well as kms of sand. The beach must be one of the best in India, unused except by some Russians building a steel works. Simhachalam Hill, about 10 km north of Waltair, has an 11th century Vishnu temple in fine Orissan style.

Places to Stay Vizag has plenty of hotels right up to 5-star level. The *Ocean View* is near the best (northern) end of the beach and is very comfortable, peaceful and friendly with doubles for Rs 80. The *Dolphin Hotel* (tel 64811, 66660) has rooms at Rs 125/160 or Rs 225/300 with air-con. The *Park Hotel* (tel 64333, 63081) on Beach Rd is even more expensive with rooms at Rs 400/500. The excellent bus station has *Retiring Rooms*.

Cheap hotels include the *Hotel Poorna* (tel 62344) on Main Rd with rooms at Rs 20/35. *Hotel Apsara* (tel 64861) on Waltair Main Rd has rooms at Rs 60/95 or Rs 100/125 with air-con.

Getting There Vizag is connected by broad gauge railway line to Raipur and by Indian Airlines directly to Bhubaneswar and Hyderabad. There's a new and well organised bus station in Vizag, quite different from the usual bus station confusion. Good services run to and from Puri and Vijayawada.

Rajamundry (population 200,000)

A three-km long railway and road bridge, the second longest in India, crosses the Godavari River at Rajamundry. This delta region of the Godavari is very flat but 100 km inland, where the Deccan plateau drops away to the delta, the scenery is very fine. Yanam, on the coast near Rajamundry, is another portion of the former French enclave of Pondicherry.

Vijayawada (population 380,000)

On the banks of the equally mighty Krishna River, only 149 km south of

Rajamundry and the Godavari River, Vijayawada is the junction for the railway line to Warangal and Hyderabad. Two thousand years ago this was an important Buddhist area and there are interesting excavations upstream at Amaravati (now much damaged) and Nagarjunakonda. See the Nagarjunakonda section for more information.

To reach Amaravati you have to continue south to Guntur then turn back north, a distance of about 65 km. Kondapalli, only 20 km from Vijayawada, is renowned for the wonderful small toys which have been made here for many years. Only a few km from Vijayawada, but across the river, are the ancient Hindu cave temples of Undavalli. There is also a museum in Vijayawada itself. Masulipatam, 80 km from Vijayawada on the coast, once had English, Dutch and French factories and was the subject of violent dispute between the English and French.

Places to Stay In Vijayawada the *Ashok*, near the bus station, is very comfortable with doubles with bath at Rs 45 and a helpful manager. There's no restaurant but they will serve meals in your room – a good vegetarian thali with nine side dishes is Rs 6. *Hotel Manorama* at 27-38-61 Bunder Rd has rooms at Rs 55/80 or Rs 80/115 with air-con.

At the top of the price scale the *Hotel Kandhari International* (tel 61311) at Labbipet, Bunder Rd is also very good with air-con rooms at Rs 190/240.

Tolerance

For all the aggravations and annoyances India can throw in your path, there's one factor which almost every visitor praises about the country and that is its tolerance. In part it's related to the Hindu religion – it makes no effort to go out and convert people, it already has so many gods that other people's gods are quite welcome to join the happy band. In India anything seems to go down. If an Indian wants to leave his job, family and comfort to don a loincloth and wander the country as a sadhu that's considered quite normal. Similarly if western visitors want to dress up in '60s flower power gear and wander the country they're quite welcome. If they want to take all their clothes off and lie on the beach at Goa it's considered strange, but that's OK too. Basically anything goes.

Hotel Quirks

Why is it, wrote an India visitor, that so many hotels have this mania for collecting deposits in excess of the prospective room rate? If it was to facilitate a deduction in the event of damage I could understand it, but invariably the excess is returned the following morning without any check being made of the room and its contents. Is it to create an artificially high cash flow figure at the end of each day for some obscure purpose?

Kerala

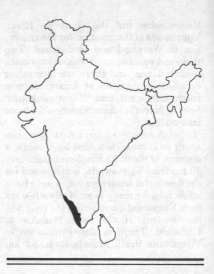

Population: 23 million
Area: 338,864 square km
Capital: Trivandrum
Main language: Malayalam

Kerala, the land of 'green magic', is a narrow, fertile coastal strip bordered by the Western Ghats on the south-west coast of India. These high mountains have sheltered Kerala from invaders from the rest of India, but at the same time Kerala has a very long history of contact with the outside world. In Cochin there is still a small community, descendants of Jewish settlers who fled from Palestine 2000 years ago. Kerala has also had Christians for as long as Christianity has been in Europe! The Portuguese were more than a little surprised to find Christianity already established along the Malabar coast when they arrived here 500 years ago. And more than a little annoyed that these Christians had never heard of the Pope.

Long before Vasco de Gama led the Portuguese to India the coast had been known to the Phoenicians who came in search of spices, sandalwood and ivory. Kerala was not only a spice centre in its own right but also a trans-shipment point from the Moluccas. The Biblical Ophir, visited by King Solomon, is also thought to be in Kerala at the site of the small village of Puvar, south of Trivandrum. The Arabs and Chinese also made their mark on Kerala and fishermen still use Chinese fishing nets to this day.

The present day state of Kerala was created in 1956 from Travancore, Cochin and Malabar, which was formerly part of Madras State. The people speak Malayalam which hundreds of years ago was derived from Tamil. In 1957 Kerala became the first place in the world to freely elect a communist government. Although the communists are currently in power they

have not always held power since that initial election success. The princely state of Travancore had, however, carried out a far-sighted policy of land distribution over a century ago. Today Kerala has a more equitable distribution of land ownership than almost anywhere else in India, and this has resulted in unusually intensive cultivation and a much more even distribution of income than is found elsewhere in India. Although Kerala, predominantly agricultural and with little industry, is far from top of the per capita income scale in India it has remarkably little real poverty.

This distribution of wealth applies also to education and health. The literacy rate in Kerala is 60%, twice the all-India average, and is actually growing faster than the rest of India despite the already high literacy level. Similarly infant mortality in Kerala is relatively low and both these achievements have been made without spending a higher proportion of the state's income on education or health than other states.

For visitors Kerala offers one of the best

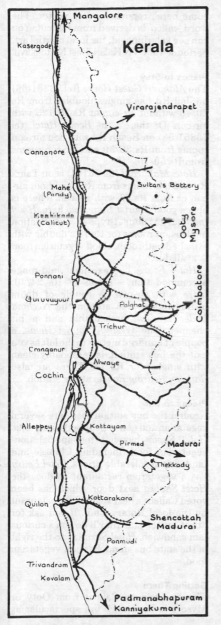

Kerala

Mangalore

Kasergode

Virarajendrapet

Cannanore

Mahé
(Pandy)

Sultan's Battery

Kembikade
(Calicut)

Ooty
Mysore

Ponnani

Guruvayoor

Palghat

Coimbatore

Trichur

Cranganur

Alwaye

Cochin

Alleppey

Kottayam

Pirmed

Madurai

Thekkady

Kottarakara

Quilon

Shencottah
Madurai

Ponmudi

Trivandrum

Kovalam

Padmanabhapuram
Kanniyakumari

beaches in India at Kovalam, a unique wildlife sanctuary at Periyar, its intriguing blend of cultures and some unusual ways of getting around. Perhaps more than anywhere else in India getting there can be half the fun, particularly on the backwater trips along the coastal lagoons. Best of all Kerala has an easy going, relaxed atmosphere quite unlike the bustle you find elsewhere in India.

Things to Buy
Kathakali dance masks, sandalwood carvings, rush mats, handloomed cottons and brass temple lamps and figurines. There are Kerala Cottage Industries Emporiums in Trivandrum and Cochin.

Religions in Kerala
Kerala has an amazing mixture of religions, 24% of the population today are Christians and Christianity has been longer established here than almost anywhere in the world. St Thomas the Apostle, 'doubting Thomas', is supposed to have landed on the Malabar coast in 52 AD near Cranganore and in that town there is a church, with carved Hindu-style columns, supposed to date from the 4th century AD. Further south there is the 9th century Syrian church of Vallia Palli. Kerala's Syrian Christians were here at least as early as 190 AD for a visitor at that time reports seeing a Hebrew copy of St Matthew here.

Kerala's now disappearing Jewish population also made a very early appearance on the sub-continent. The 'black Jews' are supposed to have fled here in 587 BC when Nebuchadnezzar occupied Jerusalem. Their descendants have now intermarried with the Hindu population, but there are still a small number of the later 'white Jews' in Cochin.

NORTH OF CALICUT
Mahe, 60 km north of Calicut, was a small French dependancy made over to India at the same time as Pondicherry. Today

Mahe's main function is to supply passing truck drivers with cheap Pondicherry beer. It's still part of the Union Territory of Pondicherry. Only eight km north of Mahe is Tellicherry with some interesting houses and a fine bazaar. The English factory established here in 1683, to purchase pepper and cardamom, was set up by the Surat Presidency and was the first permanent English factory on the Malabar coast. The East India Company had a fort here in 1708.

Directly east of here, in the Western Ghats, is Sultan's Battery, a fort built by Tipu Sultan. Cannanore, 88 km north of Calicut, was another port where Vasco da Gama dropped in. The Portuguese built their Fort St Angelo here in 1505, but it later passed to the Dutch and was eventually taken by the British.

CALICUT (Kozhikode) (population 360,000) Vasco da Gama first landed in India at Calicut in 1498. He was the first European to reach India via the sea route around the southern cape of Africa, and his arrival heralded the period of Portuguese supremacy in India. The history of Calicut after that time was certainly dramatic. The Portuguese attempted to conquer the town, a centre of Malabar power under the Zamorins or 'Lords of the Sea', but their attacks in 1509 and 1510 were both repulsed, although in the latter assault the town was virtually destroyed.

In 1513 the Zamorins and Portuguese reached an agreement which permitted the Portuguese to build a factory here. The British followed in 1616, but in 1766 the Zamorins were defeated and a period of local turmoil followed with Tipu Sultan adding to the damage in 1789 when he laid the whole region waste and destroyed the coconut, sandalwood and pepper tree plantations. In 1792 the British arrived and established their rule.

Despite its colourful past Calicut does not have a great deal to see. 'Auto-rickshaws use their meters without prompting – which proves no tourists come here', reported a rare visitor. The word 'calico' is derived from Calicut. You can see kalarippayat, the local martial art, performed at CVN Kalari, East Naddakavu.

Places to Stay

The *Alakpuri Guest House* (tel 73361-66) on Jail Rd has singles/doubles from Rs 30/40 without air-con or Rs 75/125 with air-con. Or there's the *Beach Hotel* (tel 73851-53) on Beach Rd with non air-con rooms from Rs 30/50 and air-con rooms from Rs 50/75.

Hotel Maharani (tel 76161) is on Taluk Rd and has rooms from Rs 25 without air-con or from Rs 75 with air-con. There is also a good *Tourist Bungalow* here. *Hotel Imperial* has budget-type accommodation in pleasant rooms for Rs 15 a double with attached bathroom. Good vegetarian food is available.

Hotel Foura has excellent mid-range accommodation – rooms at Rs 24/40, more with air-con. A couple of doors nearer to the bus station the *Neelima Lodge* is new, presentable and a bit cheaper. The *Western Tourist Home*, a couple of hundred metres to the left as you exit the bus station, is reasonably clean with singles for Rs 15. There are also *Railway Retiring Rooms* at the station.

Places to Eat

Around the bus station there are several vegetarian and non-vegetarian restaurants. *Hotel Sagar* has not too special non-vegetarian food (including Chinese and tandoori) at tolerable prices. *Hotel Foura* has a vegetarian restaurant as does the *Hotel Shobra* next door, which has been voted Calicut's best vegetarian restaurant by the local Rotary Club. If you ask for 'toast-butter-jam' they'll do you a curious jam sandwich. *Hotel Sarovar*, to the right of the state bus stand, has non-vegetarian food.

Getting There

The bus trip to Calicut from Ooty or Mysore is hard work but spectacular as the bus climbs up and over the Western Ghats. From Mysore it's a painful 5½ hour trip with amazing views down to the sea from the top of the range.

TRICHUR

Situated 74 km north of Ernakulam, Trichur has the old temple of Vadakkunnathan (Hindus only), a museum and a zoo with a notable collection of snakes. In April-May of each year the Pooram festival is one of the biggest in the south with fireworks and colourful processions including brightly-decorated elephants. The Kerala Kala Mandalam at Cheruthuruthy, north of Trichur, is an important centre for training Kathakali dancers.

Places to Stay

Trichur has a comfortable *Tourist Bungalow* or *Jaya Lodge*; costs Rs 10/20 for singles/doubles.

COCHIN & ERNAKULAM

Cochin population 480,000
Ernakulam population 130,000

With its wealth of historical associations and beautiful setting on a cluster of islands and narrow peninsulas, Cochin is one of India's most interesting cities. It reflects the eclecticism of Kerala perfectly. Here you can see the oldest church in India, winding streets crammed with old houses constructed by the Portuguese 500 years ago, cantilevered Chinese fishing nets, a Jewish community with roots going back to 1000 AD and a 16th century synagogue, a palace built by the Portuguese and given to the Raja of Cochin which was later renovated by the Dutch and contains perhaps the most beautiful murals to be seen anywhere in India, a performance of the world-famous Kathakali dance-drama and many other things.

This unlikely pastiche of mediaeval Portugal, Holland and an English country village somehow grafted on to the tropical Malabar coast, which you find in the older parts of Fort Cochin and Mattancherry, contrasts wildly with the bright neon lights, dimly-lit seamen's bars and big hotels of mainland Ernakulam. A strange contrast perhaps but Port Cochin is one of India's largest ports. On any day of the year the misty silhouettes of huge merchant ships can be seen anchored off the point of Fort Cochin waiting their turn for a berth in the docks of Ernakulam or Willingdon Island. This man-made island was created with material dredged up when the harbour was deepened. It also provides a site for the airport. As you might expect in a major port, there's a lot of wheeler-dealing going on so don't be too surprised if, when staying in Ernakulam, you get approached with offers for things which are not easy to acquire in India such as cameras, watches, tape recorders and the like.

Orientation

Cochin consists of mainland Ernakulam, the islands of Willingdon, Bolgatty and Gundu in the harbour, Fort Cochin and Mattancherry on the southern peninsula and Vypeen Island north of Fort Cochin. All these separate parts are connected by ferry. In addition there are bridges and a road connecting Ernakulam with Willingdon Island and the Fort Cochin/Mattancherry peninsula. The railway station, bus station, Tourist Reception Centre and the bulk of the hotels and cafes are located in Ernakulam.

Mahatma Gandhi Rd is the locale of most of the top range hotels while the road connecting the railway station to Mahatma Gandhi Rd and Shanmughan Rd on the waterfront has most of the mid-range hotels. The budget hotels are situated mainly on Press Club Rd and Canon Rd off Broadway with a few just outside the railway station.

Almost all the historical sites are in Fort Cochin or Mattancherry but hotel and restaurant facilities are very limited – there are only four budget-type hotels in this area. The GPO (including the Poste

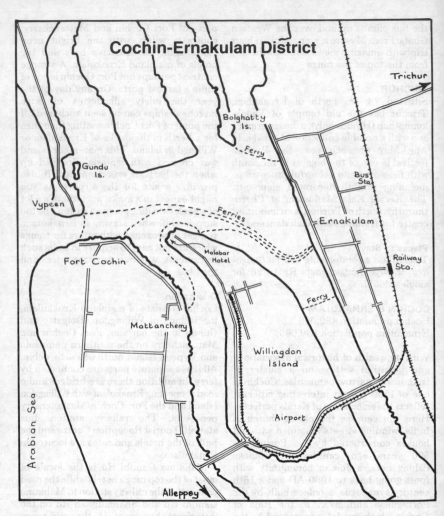

Cochin-Ernakulam District

Trichur

Bolghatty Is.

Ferry

Gundu Is.

Vypeen

Ferries

Ernakulam

Bus Sta.

Malabar Hotel

Fort Cochin

Railway Sta.

Ferry

Mattancherry

Willingdon Island

Arabian Sea

Airport

Alleppey

Restante) and Chinese fishing nets are also in Fort Cochin. On Willingdon Island is the airport and, at the tip of the island opposite Fort Cochin, the main Tourist Office and Cochin's top hotel, the Malabar.

One of the best hotel bargains in Cochin, the Bolgatty Palace Hotel, a former palace built by the Dutch in 1744,

is situated on Bolgatty Island. To get there first go to the Tourist Reception Centre outside the shopping precinct where Shanmughan Rd meets Broadway in Ernakulam. They operate a launch to the island, Vypeen Island is only of interest if you want to see the nearest surviving Portuguese fort, which is situated on the northern end of the island at Pallipuram.

Information

The Tourist Reception Centre (tel 33234), Shanmughan Rd, Ernakulam has friendly, helpful staff but not a lot of literature. They'll fix you up with accommodation at the Bolgatty Palace Hotel and with the conducted boat cruise around the harbour.

The Tourist Office headquarters is attached to the Malabar Hotel on Willingdon Island. This is the best tourist office in southern India, it's friendly, helpful and has a whole range of leaflets and maps. Indian Airlines are now in Durbar Hall Rd. Ernakulam's poste restante is not very efficient, sort through letters yourself if possible.

You can use the Malabar Hotel's swimming pool for Rs 10 (Rs 5 for children). Coconut products like bowls or placemats, teak bowls and coir products are good buys in Cochin.

Fort Cochin – St Francis Church

This is the oldest church constructed by Europeans on Indian soil. Vasco da Gama, first European to reach India by sailing around Africa, died in Cochin in 1524 and his tomb is here. It was built in 1503 by Portuguese Franciscan friars who accompanied the expedition led by Pedro Alvarez Gabral. The original structure was one of wood but the church was later rebuilt in stone around the middle of the 16th century – the earliest Portuguese inscription found in the church dates back to 1562. In 1663 it passed into the hands of the Protestant Dutch with their capture of Cochin and they later restored it in 1779. After the occupation of Cochin by the British in 1795 it became an Anglican church and is at present used by the Church of South India.

Although it's the earliest church constructed by Europeans in India, Christianity has a much longer history on the Malabar coast. Tradition has it that St Thomas the Apostle landed here in AD 52, though there's no archaeological evidence to support this and the first documentary evidence of churches in Kerala comes from the accounts of a Byzantine monk who travelled here in the 6th century. By the middle of the 9th century the Christian communities were playing an important part in the trade and commerce of this area and there are records of substantial gifts of property to the Church of Teresa (no longer in existence) during the reign of Sthanu Ravi (844-85).

These earlier Christian communities were all Syrian Orthodox and, until the 16th century when the Portuguese put a stop to the practice in their efforts to enforce the supremacy of Rome, all the Keralan bishops were brought from Persia and Mesopotamia. This suppression of the Syrian Church was only partially successful, however, and even today there are many Syrian Orthodox churches to be found in Kerala.

Also in Fort Cochin is the much later Cathedral of Santa Cruz, which is worth a visit.

Chinese Fishing Nets

Strung out along the tip of Fort Cochin opposite Vypeen Island, these cantilevered fishing nets were introduced by traders from the court of Kublai Khan. You can also see them along the backwaters between Cochin and Kottayam and between Alleppey and Quilon.

Mattancherry – Mattancherry Palace

The 'Dutch' Palace was built by the Portuguese in 1557 and presented to the Cochin Raja, Veera Kerala Varma (1537-61), as a gesture of goodwill (and probably as a means of securing trading privileges). It was substantially renovated by the Dutch after 1663, hence its other name, the 'Dutch' Palace. It's a double-storied quadrangular building surrounding a central courtyard containing a Hindu temple. The central hall on the first floor was the Coronation Hall of the Rajas of Cochin and there is a display there of dresses, turbans and palanquins which

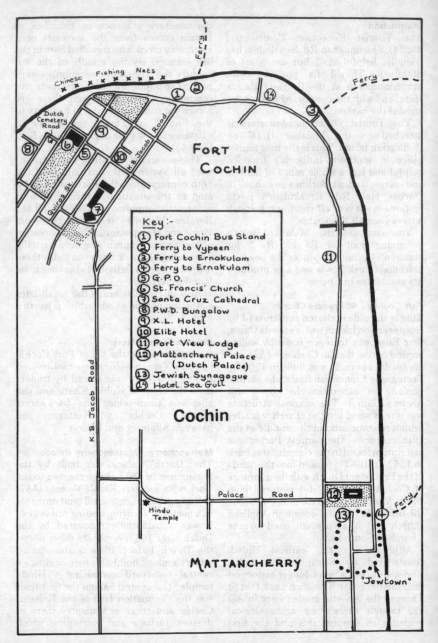

Chinese Fishing Nets

Dutch Cemetery Road

FORT
COCHIN

K. B. Jacob Road

Quiros St.

Key :-
(1) Fort Cochin Bus Stand
(2) Ferry to Vypeen
(3) Ferry to Ernakulam
(4) Ferry to Ernakulam
(5) G.P.O.
(6) St. Francis' Church
(7) Santa Cruz Cathedral
(8) P.W.D. Bungalow
(9) X.L. Hotel
(10) Elite Hotel
(11) Port View Lodge
(12) Mattancherry Palace
      (Dutch Palace)
(13) Jewish Synagogue
(14) Hotel Sea Gull

Ferry

Ferry

Cochin

K. B. Jacob Road

Hindu
Temple

Palace   Road

MATTANCHERRY

"Jewtown"

Ferry

once belonged to these rulers.

The most important aspect of this palace, however, is the astonishing murals in the bed-chambers and other rooms, depicting scenes from the Ramayana and Puranic legends connected with Shiva, Vishnu, Krishna, Kumara and Durga. These are without doubt some of the most beautiful and extensive you will see anywhere in India. You can pick up pamphlet after pamphlet of Indian tourist literature containing breathless eulogies of the murals at Ajanta and Ellora but never see a mention of these, yet they are one of the wonders of India. It's worth coming to Cochin just to see these murals alone! There are similar murals at the Shiva temple in Ettumanur (a few km north off Kottayam).

The palace is open Monday to Saturday between 9 am and 5 pm; closed Sundays. Entrance is free but flash photography is prohibited (effectively precluding photography altogether), which is a great pity since there are no books or postcards for sale here. They can be photographed quite well by holding your camera on the railing wrote one visitor. There are three black and white photographs of the murals in the Archaeological Survey of India's booklet, *Monuments of Kerala* by H Sarkar (1978, Rs 3.25). Other books where you will find them illustrated are, *Cochin Murals* by V R Chitra & T N Srinivasan (Cochin, 1940) and, *South Indian Paintings* by C Sivaramamurti (New Delhi, 1968).

The Jewish Synagogue

Built in 1568, this is the oldest synagogue in the Commonwealth. It was preceded by an earlier one at Kochangadi, built in 1344, which has since disappeared, although a stone slab inscribed in Hebrew from this earlier building can be found on the inner surface of the wall which surrounds the present synagogue. The present building was destroyed by shelling during a Portuguese raid in 1662 and rebuilt two years later when the Dutch

took over Cochin. It's an interesting little place with handpainted, willow-pattern floor tiles (no two alike) brought from Canton, China, in the mid-18th century by Ezekial Rahabi who had trading interests in that city. He was also responsible for the erection of the clock tower which surmounts the building.

The synagogue is open daily from 10 am to 12 noon and from 3 pm until 5 pm except Saturdays and Jewish holidays. Entrance is free. The synagogue guardian is very friendly, keen to tell you about the history of the place and the Jewish community here, and to talk about what's happening in the rest of the world. He speaks fluent English.

This unexpected and isolated Jewish community has roots going back to the time of St Thomas the Apostle's voyage to India in AD 52. They had their first settlement at Cranganore, north of Cochin. Like the Syrian Orthodox Christians, they became involved in the trade and commerce of the Malabar coast, and a number of copper plates, inscribed in an ancient script, recording the grant of the village of Anjuvannam (near Cranganore) and its revenue to the Jewish merchant, Joseph Rabban, by King Bhaskara Ravi Varman I (962-1020), are preserved in the synagogue to this day. You may view these plates if you ask the synagogue guardian for permission.

The concessions given by Ravi Varman I included permission to use a palanquin and parasol – in those days the prerogative of rulers – and so, in effect, gave sanction for the creation of a tiny Jewish kingdom. On Rabban's death his sons fought amongst themselves for control of the 'kingdom' and this led to its break-up and the move to Mattancherry.

Quite a lot of research has been done on this community, and one particularly interesting study, which was done by an American professor of ethnomusicology, found that the music of the Cochin Jews contained strong Babylonian influences and that their version of the Ten

Commandments was almost identical with a Kurdish version housed in the Berlin Museum Archives. Naturally, there's also been a lot of local influence and many of the hymns are similar to ragas.

The area around the synagogue is known as Jewtown and is one of the centres of the spice trade in Cochin. Scores of small firms huddle together in old dilapidated buildings and the air is filled with the pungent aromas of ginger, cardamom, cumin, turmeric and cloves. Many Jewish names are visible on business premises and houses but the community has diminished rapidly since Indian independence and now numbers only 45. Most of the young people have gone to Israel, and few people under 50 years of age remain. When they die the community will probably go the same way and the synagogue be turned into a museum. As a mark of its decline, there has been no rabbi within living memory so all the elders are qualified to perform religious ceremonies and marriages. All the same, it's an interesting area and well worth a visit. There are many curio shops on the street leading up to the synagogue where you might pick up something interesting.

There is another synagogue in Ernakulam at the junction of (predictably) Jews St and Market St, but it appears not to be used any longer.

Ernakulam – Kathakali Dancing

This is India's most spectacular dance-drama and you must go to see a performance while you're here. The origins of the dance go back around 400 to 500 years, when open-air performances were held in a temple courtyard or on the village green. There are over a hundred different arrangements, all of them based on stories from the Ramayana and Mahabharata, those two epics of Indian mythology, and they were designed to continue well into the early hours of the morning. Since most visitors don't have the inclination to stay up all night, the centres which put on the dance in Ernakulam offer shortened versions lasting about two hours. I personally felt this was too abbreviated.

Kathakali isn't simply another form of dancing, incorporates elements of yoga and ayurvedic medicine – traditional Indian medicine. All the props are fashioned out of natural materials – powdered minerals and the sap of certain trees for the bright facial make-up; wigs made from the beaten bark of certain trees, dyed with fruits and spices; coconut oil for mixing up the colours; burnt coconut oil for the black paint around the eyes; and egg-plant flowers tucked under the eyelids to turn the whites of the eyes deep red. Usually you're welcome to see the make up process before the dance, quite a show in its own right. The dancers are accompanied by two drummers and another musician, who plays finger cymbals.

Each one of the three companies which put on performances kick off the evening with an explanation of the symbolism involved in the dance drama – the facial expressions, hand movements and ritualistic gestures. This is then followed up by an actual dance drama lasting about one hour. The centres which offer Kathakali are:

The Cochin Cultural Centre (tel 37866), Durbar Hall Ground, Durbar Hall Rd. There are daily performances from 6.30 to 8 pm and entry costs Rs 15. There's usually no need to book in advance. This is a beautiful little theatre constructed in traditional style and set in the grounds of Durbar Hall next to the Cochin Museum. *Art Kerala*, Menon & Krishna Annexe, near the junction of Chittoor Rd and Church Landing Rd, opposite the Devi Temple. Daily performances at 7 pm. Entry costs Rs 15.

See India Foundation (tel 31871), Kalathiparambil Lane. Daily performances except on Thursdays from 7 to 8.30 pm. Entry costs Rs 15.

Cochin Museum

The museum is housed in what was previously the Durbar Hall on Durbar Hall Rd – an enormous building constructed in traditional Keralan style. It contains collections of 19th century oil paintings, old coins, sculptures and Mughal paintings as well as exhibits from the Cochin royal family. It's open daily except Mondays and public holidays from 9.30 am to noon, and 3 pm to 5.30 pm. Entry is free.

Gundu Island

The smallest island in Cochin harbour is close to Vypeen Island. There is a coir factory here – the only building on the island – where attractive doormats are made out of coconut fibre. You come across their mats all over Cochin. The only way to get there is on the boat tour organised by the Kerala Tourist Development Corporation.

Tours

The Kerala Tourist Development Corporation offers two conducted boat cruises daily around Cochin harbour and includes visits to Willingdon Island, Mattancherry Palace and the Jewish Synagogue at Mattancherry, Fort Cochin including St Francis Church and Bolgatty Island. The first tour is 9 am to 12.30 pm and the second tour is 2 to 5.30 pm. The morning tour is better because the afternoon one leaves out the Mattancherry Palace. Cost of the tour is Rs 12 and it's very worthwhile. There's also a Sunset Tour from 5.30 to 7 pm every day for Rs 5. The tourist department also has backwater tours around Cochin (three hours for Rs 10) and trips to the Periyar Wildlife Sanctuary.

For reservations contact either the Tourist Reception Centre, Shanmughan Road, Ernakulam (tel 33234) or the Manager, Bolgatty Palace Hotel, Bolgatty Island (tel 35003). The tour starts and finishes at the boat jetty in front of the Sealord Hotel, Shanmughan Rd, Ernakulam. You can also board the boat at the Tourist Office Jetty, Willingdon Island, 20 minutes after the start of each tour from the Sealord boat jetty. They seem to put foreigners on the roof of the boat and crowd the locals below decks.

Places to Stay

If you want top-range hotels then you have a choice of Ernakulam and Willingdon Island. For mid-range hotels, the choice is Ernakulam and Bolgatty Island plus a solitary place in Fort Cochin. If you want a budget hotel you can stay in Ernakulam, Bolgatty Island or Fort Cochin.

Places to Stay – Bottom End

If you want the sleepy, laid-back atmosphere of the old part of the city then head for Fort Cochin. If you want the beer, drugs and city action of an international port, stay in Ernakulam.

Fort Cochin In Fort Cochin the *PWD Bungalow*, Dutch Cemetery Rd, is the best value in budget accommodation in the whole of Cochin. It has a superb location looking out over the Indian Ocean and the rooms are a bargain at Rs 12/16 with common bathrooms and toilets. Despite the size of the building there are only three rooms in this place and since it's very popular with travellers it's usually full although well worth trying to get in. The *XL Hotel*, on the same street as the GPO, only accepts long-term lets of a month or more these days. It's invariably full but there is a cafe and bar downstairs.

The *Elite Hotel*, very close to St Francis Church (see map), has rooms with common bathroom and toilet for Rs 6/12. It's an old building, so expect the floorboards to creak. The non-vegetarian cafe on the ground floor is excellent value (egg biriyani, papadum and coffee for Rs 3.50) and popular with local young people and students. The *YWCA* is a few metres from the GPO, overlooking the green in front of St Francis Church. It's a very small place and often full but worth enquiring about if you're in the area.

Port View Lodge is about half-way between Fort Cochin and Mattancherry (see map) and is one of the very few places in that area that can be classified as a budget hotel (there are a few incredibly decrepit doss-houses along this road). It's an old place with beautifully carved stairways and bannisters which has been allowed to go to seed, but it still retains a lot of character and the views from the roof are excellent. However, I'd be reluctant to leave anything valuable 'locked up' in a room here (I can't substantiate that, it's just a feeling). Rooms cost Rs 8 for an ordinary single and Rs 12 for a single which looks like an Indian impression of an *Anthony & Cleopatra* film set – all with common bathrooms and toilets. Recommended by those travellers who swear by BIT Information travel guides.

Ernakulam Of the budget hotels in Ernakulam, I'd single out the *Basoto Lodge*, Press Club Rd, as one of the best. It's a small, simple, friendly place, which is popular with travellers and has singles with common bath for Rs 10 and doubles with attached bath for Rs 20. Get there early if you want a room.

If it's full, try the *Hotel National*, Cannon Shed Rd, just up from the main boat jetty, which has rooms at a similar price. The rooms here are built around a quiet, pleasant courtyard and the management is friendly. If you prefer to stay near the railway station, the *Central Lodge*, just outside the station compound, is a good bet at Rs 12/18 for singles/doubles with common bath, and Rs 16/22/32 for singles/doubles/triples with attached bath. The *Premier Tourist Lodge* near the station is similarly priced.

Places to Stay – Middle

Undoubtedly the best of the mid-range hotels is the *Bolgatty Palace Hotel* (tel 35003), on Bolgatty Island. Formerly a palace built by the Dutch in 1744 and later a British Residency, it is now run by the Kerala Tourist Development Corporation as a hotel. It's set in six hectares of lush green lawns with a golf course, bar and restaurant. Rooms here are a bargain at Rs 35/62 with attached bathroom, but no air-conditioning. Air-con doubles cost Rs 120. The hotel is often very full and some reports indicate that it's on a downhill slide due to neglect.

For the ferry service to the island contact the Tourist Reception Centre, Shanmughan Rd, Ernakulam, or ring the hotel itself. Ferries to the island run on a definite schedule, but if you want to get there or leave there at any other time, rowing boats are available (price negotiable). If you'd like to stay there make sure the KTDC union isn't about to call a strike. Two days after I got there all the personnel connected with the Tourist Offices, the Bolgatty Palace Hotel and the ferry service to Bolgatty Island went on strike and everyone had to leave! It doesn't happen often. There's also a regular ferry, every 20 minutes from 6 am to 10 pm, from the 'Bolgatty Ferry Station'. On the island turn left, walk to the hotel gate (uniformed guard) and across the golf course. The ferry costs 20 paise.

Some other very pleasant mid-range hotels include the *Hotel Blue Diamond* (tel 33221), Br Market Rd. Singles/doubles are Rs 30/58; air-con doubles with attached bathroom are Rs 90 to 150. It also has a roof garden, restaurant (vegetarian, non-vegetarian and Chinese food), and an air-con bar. The rooms are nice, it's very good value and the staff are very friendly. *Hakoba Hotel*, Shanmughan Rd, is on the waterfront with excellent views over the harbour from the front rooms. Non air-con rooms are Rs 20/30 and there are also five rooms with air-conditioning. It's secure, there's a restaurant and bar and even a lift!

Another good place to stay in this bracket is the *Bijus Tourist Home* (tel 39881), Cannon Shed Rd, near the

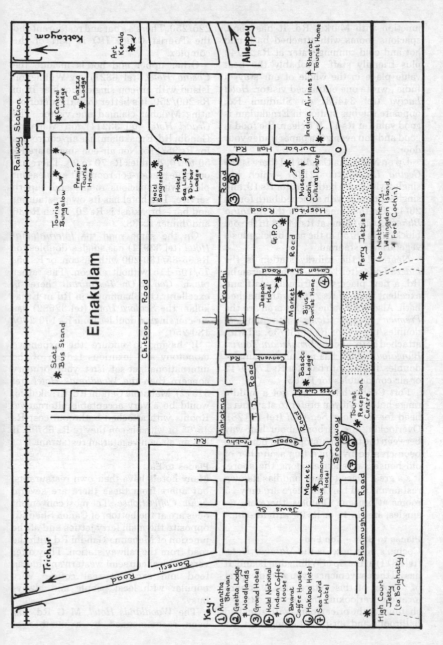

Ernakulam

Key:
1 Anantha Bhavan
2 Geetha Lodge
★ Woodlands
3 Grand Hotel
4 Hotel National
★ Indian Coffee House
5 Bharat Coffee House
6 Hakoba Hotel
7 Sea Lord Hotel

junction with Market Rd. It has good, spacious rooms with attached bath and hot and cold running water at Rs 25/40 plus friendly staff. 'Probably the best value place in the whole of our stay in India', wrote one entranced visitor. *Hotel Luciya* (tel 34433) on Stadium Rd, opposite the bus station in Ernakulam is good value at Rs 47. It's clean, the food is good and you even get a paper under your door.

Up on Mahatma Gandhi Rd there is the *Geetha Lodge* (tel 32136), which has singles with share bathroom for Rs 19, and singles/doubles with attached bath for Rs 26/42. On the same road is the *Anantha Bhavan*, with rooms at Rs 14/28 in the old block or Rs 26/50 in the new block, plus a vegetarian restaurant.

Nearer to the railway station is the *Piazza Lodge* (tel 37408), Kalathiparambu Rd, a new place with friendly staff and excellent value at Rs 20/30 with attached bath. Also good value in this area are the *Premier Tourist Home* with singles/doubles/triples for Rs 20/30/35, all with attached bath; and the *Ernakulam Tourist Bungalow*, which has non air-con single/doubles/triples with bath for Rs 17/29/42 or air-con doubles for Rs 65.

Fort Cochin has, at last, got a middle range hotel, so if you prefer to stay there, head for the *Hotel Sea Gull* (tel 28128). Overlooking the harbour about half-way between the two ferry stops, this hotel has been created by converting a number of old houses/warehouses along the shore. It's a great place to stay, and has its own restaurant and bar, but there are only 15 rooms at present. Doubles, there are no singles, are Rs 45 or Rs 90 with air-con.

Places to Stay – Top End

Cochin's best hotel is the *Malabar Hotel* (tel 6811) at the tip of Willingdon Island. It has all the conveniences you would expect of a hotel of this nature plus a superb location overlooking the harbour. Rather shabby (for the price) rooms with attached bathroom and air-conditioning cost Rs 225/250. There's a bar and restaurant and the Tourist Office HQ is part of the complex.

Other upper end hotels include the *Casino Hotel* (tel 6821) on Willingdon Island with air-con singles/doubles from Rs 200/250. It's better than the deteriorating Malabar claimed one visitor. The *Grand Hotel* (tel 33211), on Mahatma Gandhi Rd, Ernakulam, has air-con rooms for Rs 95/115. Non air-con singles are Rs 50 to 70, doubles Rs 70 to 90. There are only five non air-con rooms. It's a pleasant place with spacious rooms and superb service. The hotel has its own restaurant and bar – breakfast is Rs 20, lunch Rs 36 and dinner Rs 38.

On the same road the *International Hotel* (tel 33911) has singles/doubles for Rs 65-85/130-200 with air-con, or Rs 55-75/105-115 without air-con. The rather plush *Coq d'Or Restaurant* here is excellent. On Shanmugham Rd in Ernakulam the *Sealord Hotel* (tel 32682) has air-con singles/doubles from Rs 140-200/180-250.

If having to endure the expensive monotony and luxurious tedium of the international jet-set isn't your primary concern then the *Woodlands Hotel* (tel 31372), Mahatma Gandhi Rd, Ernakulam, would be a very acceptable alternative. Rooms with attached bathroom cost Rs 45/65 or with air-con they're Rs 65/90. It has an air-con vegetarian restaurant.

Places to Eat

Many hotels have their own restaurants, but apart from these there are several *Indian Coffee Houses*. The most convenient ones are at the bottom of Canon Shed Rd opposite the main ferry jetties and at the junction of Mahatma Gandhi Rd with the road from the railway station. They offer very good, cheap semi-western and Indian food and excellent real coffee. Very popular with local people and always busy.

The *Woodlands Hotel*, M G Rd, has been recommended by a number of travellers. *Ranjim Vegetarian Restaurant* on Chittoor Rd is part of the Sangeetha Hotel. Excellent food and a varied menu with an air-conditioned room upstairs if you need it. *Bharat Coffee House*, on Broadway next door to Indian Airlines, is similar to the Indian Coffee Houses. Good, cheap, Indian vegetarian food and excellent coffee. *Arul Jyothi*, 50 metres from the Hakoba Hotel, has good masala dosas. Fish filled with grapes and baked cheese at the *Sealord Restaurant* on Shanmughan St is delicious. The *Mughal Durbar* is nearby.

In Fort Cochin the very popular *Elite Hotel*, near St Francis Church, is recommended for good non-vegetarian meals. One traveller reported in glowing terms that the *Golden Dragon Restaurant*, oppsite the Park Hotel, was an experience not to be missed. Good Chinese food and excellent music and decor – 'quite alien to India' in fact.

There are many lively, dimly-lit bars along Mahatma Gandhi Rd and Shanmughan Rd in Ernakulam if you're looking for some light entertainment. Non-stop Abba music with the occasional Beatles' song thrown in for a little variety in most of them (half of Abba's income must come from India). Beers are the same price in all the bars – Rs 12 to 15 a large bottle.

The airport restaurant is OK for snacks.

Getting There

Air Indian Airlines has three flights daily between Bombay and Cochin (Rs 776). There are also four flights each week Trivandrum-Cochin and a daily flight Madras-Bangalore-Cochin. Fares to or from Cochin are Trivandrum Rs 153, Madras Rs 492 and Bangalore Rs 284.

Rail Twice a week the Karnataka-Kerala runs from New Delhi to Ernakulam, the 2833-km trip takes 43 hours and costs Rs 558 in 1st class, Rs 141 in 2nd. On the other days of the week it runs from Hazrat Nizamuddin, just outside New Delhi and goes to Cochin but is considerably slower.

The 201-km trip to Trivandrum takes four to five hours at a cost of Rs 66 in 1st, Rs 17 in 2nd. Bangalore is a 629-km trip taking 14 hours and costing Rs 174 in 1st, Rs 44.50 in 2nd on the Island Express. It's 1841 km and 38 hours to Bombay and the Jayanti Janata Express only has 2nd class which costs Rs 100. This train continues on right down to Trivandrum.

The Malabar Express makes a daily run from Mangalore to Trivandrum right along the Kerala coast through Calicut, Trichur, Ernakulam, Cochin, Kottayam, Quilon to Trivandrum. Other trains also follow part of this coastal route. The Ernakulam-Kottayam daily service at 7 am and 5.30 pm and the Ernakulam-Quilon service at 11.30 am are local passenger trains which you might find useful.

Bus Buses depart from the KSRTC Bus Stand in Ernakulam. Since Ernakulam is almost in the middle of the state, there are obviously a lot of buses which start in places north and south of here, but pass through Ernakulam en route. It's often possible to get a seat on these buses, but you cannot make advance reservations. You simply have to join the scrum when it turns up. Buy a priority ticket (Rs 0.50) and wave this in front of the conductor's nose when the bus turns up. In theory, if there are more passengers than seats and standing room allows, those with these tickets are taken on first.

Even with buses which start out of Ernakulam, it isn't always easy to make an advance reservation. Unless you speak Malayalam, you're not going to be able to make head or tail of the timetable at the bus stand. Fortunately, there is a way round this, and that is to buy the monthly booklet, *Time Table (Travel Guide)*, published by Jaico. It costs Rs 1 and is available at the bus stand, or at bookshops in the city. In it – in readable form – are the schedules, journey times and fares of all

KSRTC bus routes, together with details of which buses it's possible to make advance reservations for. It also contains train and air shedules, and a list of the better hotels.

Buses which originate from Ernakulam are as follows:

Going South
Alleppey 14 buses daily, the first at 8 am and the last at 9.20 pm. There are limited stop buses at 9.20 am and 8.35 pm. The fare is Rs 6.40 and the journey takes 1½ hours.

Quilon One express bus daily at 4 pm. The fare is Rs 16.20 and the journey takes 3½ hours. You can get to Quilon at other times of the day by taking a Trivandrum bus via Alleppey.

Trivandrum There are two routes to Trivandrum, one via Alleppey and the other via Kottayam. Via Alleppey, there are nine buses daily, the first at 1 am and the last at 11 pm, with an express bus at 2 pm. Via Kottayam there are five buses daily, the first at 12.45 am and the last at 8 pm. The fare is Rs 22.60 by fast passenger – 6½ hours – and Rs 24.40 by express – about five hours.

Going East
Kottayam 10 buses daily, the first at 7 am and the last at 9 pm. The fare is Rs 7.50 and the journey takes 2¼ hours.

Thekkady (Kumily) Three buses daily, two via Kottayam at 6.30 am and 2.45 pm, and one via Kattappana at 2 pm. The fare is Rs 20.60 and the journey takes 6¾ hours.

Going North
Cannanore Six buses daily, the first at 2 am and the last at 10.30 pm. All the buses, apart from those at 6.45 am and 10 am, are limited stop. The fare is Rs 34.90, and the trip takes about 8½ hours.

Kozhikode (Calicut) Five buses daily, the first at 5.15 am and the last at 7.30 pm. The fare is Rs 21.10 and it takes 6½ hours.

Palghat Four buses daily, the first at 1.30

am and the last at 7.10 pm. It costs Rs 15 and it takes 4½ hours.

Trichur Five buses daily, the first at 7 am and the last at 6.25 pm. The fare is Rs 8 and the journey takes 2¼ hours. From there buses connect to Mysore, a further seven hour trip costing Rs 32.

Getting Around
Ferries These are the main form of transport between the various parts of Cochin. If you're going to be making your own way around the sights of Cochin and Mattancherry (especially if you're staying in Ernakulam), then you need to think about the sequence you're going to do it in, since there are no ferries or convenient bus connections between Fort Cochin and Mattancherry. Also, there are two Fort Cochin ferry jetties and they too are not connected with each other (it's a 10 to 15-minute walk between the two). In some ways it's easier to get to the main part of Fort Cochin from Ernakulam by taking the ferry to Vypeen and then another ferry from there to Fort Cochin. There are no ferry connections between Fort Cochin and Willingdon Island so if you want to do this you have to hire a row boat (costs Rs 2 per person).

If you're taking the ferry from Ernakulam to Fort Cochin note that the boarding arrangements are ridiculously chaotic. It's the typical Indian mass hysteria trip. You often have to scramble across three boats to get to the ferry you want, and there are no indications as to which boat is going where. It's suggested you don't attempt this with a rucksack! It's only this ferry on which you get all the chaos – all the others are well organised. It doesn't make sense of course, except perhaps in an Indian context. 'It helps being a woman', wrote one visitor, 'as the ladies' ticket queue never has so many people'.

Perumanoor-Willingdon Island 35 times daily in either direction. First ferry at 6 am and the last at 10 pm. Costs Rs 0.15 and takes 10 minutes. Not a very useful ferry since the jetty on Willingdon Island is a long way from the Tourist Office and Malabar Hotel.

Ernakulam-Mattancherry Goes via Willingdon Island. This is the ferry to take if you want to go to the Tourist Office or to the Mattancherry Palace and the Jewish Synagogue. Twenty nine times daily in either direction. From Ernakulam the first ferry is at 6.30 am and the last at 9.40 pm. From Mattancherry the first ferry is at 6 am and the last at 9 pm. Costs Rs 0.65 and takes 20 minutes.

Ernakulam-Fort Cochin 18 times daily in either direction. From Ernakulam the first ferry is at 6.30 am and the last at 8.40 pm. From Fort Cochin the first ferry is at 6.50 am and the last at 9 pm. Costs Rs 0.05 and takes 10 to 15 minutes.

Ernakulam-Vypeen Island 40 times daily in either direction. From Ernakulam the first ferry is at 5.30 am and the last at 10.30 pm. From Vypeen the first ferry is at 6 am and the last at 10 pm. Costs Rs 0.65 and takes 15 minutes.

Mattancherry-Willingdon Island Willingdon Island is known as 'Terminus' on the timetable board at Mattancherry. Two ferries every hour (on the hour and the half hour as a rule). The first ferry is at 6 am and the last at 9 pm. Costs Rs 0.35 and takes 5 to 10 minutes.

Fort Cochin-Vypeen Island Every 10 minutes approximately in either direction throughout the day and evening. Costs Rs 0.25 and takes three to four minutes. There is also a drive on-drive off car ferry between these two points which operates 15 times daily in either direction.

Buses & Auto-Rickshaws There are no convenient bus services between Fort Cochin and the Mattancherry Palace/Jewish Synagogue. Buses do run from Fort Cochin down K B Jacob Rd to South Mattancherry but it's a 15-minute walk back to the Palace from where you get off. If you're planning on walking between the two (a pleasant half an hour walk) you can go either along K B Jacob Rd and then

Palace Rd or along the port-side road. It's probably best to take an auto-rickshaw, but none of the drivers are willing to use the meter so expect to pay at least Rs 3 (they won't take you unless you agree to the price asked).

In Ernakulam, auto-rickshaws are the most convenient form of transport and drivers use the meters. The trip from the bus station to the Tourist Reception Centre, Shanmughan Rd costs between Rs 3 and 3.50. The buses are fairly good and quite cheap – minimum fare is Rs 0.50 for quite a long journey, such as Hotel Hakoban to the airport.

Taxis charge round trip fares between the islands, even though you only go in one direction.

AROUND COCHIN

High in the Western Ghats, 137 km inland from Cochin, Munnar is a cool retreat amongst the tea plantations. Kaladi is 48 km north-east of Cochin and was the birthplace of the 8th century philosopher and monotheist Shankaracharaya. Cranganore is only 35 km north of Cochin by ferry but 77 km north by road. There's a Portuguese Fort and Hindu temples here plus the oldest mosque in India. St Thomas first set foot in India in 52 AD at nearby Kottapuram.

KOTTAYAM

There is a regular ferry service (more than 10 boats a day) through the lagoons from Alleppey to Kottayam. This was a centre for the Syrian Christians of Kerala and there are several of their churches, including Cheria Pallia and Valia Palli, about five km north-west of the railway station. Today Kottayam is also a centre for Indian rubber production. Kottayam is a good base for visits to the Periyar Wild Life Sanctuary and its two km long main street is busy and colourful.

Idukki District

Kerala's best ganja is grown in the Idukki district, between Kumily and Mumar.

Idikki, a town 100 km east of Cochin, is the main centre. The town has a good bank and small game and forest reserves. You can visit Idikki from Kumily, 2½ hours away by bus. Between Kumily and Thekkady the attractive *Hotel Ambadi* is good value with dorm beds at Rs 10 and rooms at Rs 40.

Places to Stay

The *Anjali Hotel* (tel 3661) on K K Rd has singles/doubles from Rs 50/75 with air-con. At the *Hotel Ambassador* (tel 3755, 3293-94), also on K K Rd, prices are similar but there are also some slightly cheaper non air-con rooms. Opposite the bus stand the *Anurag Lodge* is reasonably clean and acceptable at Rs 15/25. Kottayam also has a *Tourist Bungalow*.

Getting There

Kottayam has two bus stations – a local one for town buses and a chaotic state one for longer distance beasts. As the boat jetty is at the bottom of a steep hill and over a km from the state bus stand it's best to take an auto-rickshaw. Buses to Thekkady for the Periyar Wildlife Sanctuary go about every two hours and cost around Rs 12. Some go right through to Madurai.

PERIYAR WILDLIFE SANCTUARY

This 800-square-km sanctuary in the Thekkady district on the border of Tamil Nadu is one of the most important in India. In it you can see elephants, bison, antelope, sambhar, wild boar, monkeys and, if you're very lucky, one of those elusive tigers. The park is centred around a large artificial lake, and there's a choice of either private or KTDC accommodation. Unfortunately, you won't see much in the way of wildlife if that's how far you get, as there's too much human activity and traffic noise around the lodges. Indeed, at weekends they get inundated by day trippers and tourist coaches, and the only thing you will hear is transistor radios and ape-like noises made by fellow human

beings.

Elephants are the animals you're most likely to see although as with any wildlife sanctuary it's quite possible to see nothing at all. It's worth checking if it's a good time of year/good season.

If you really want to see Periyar, you must plan on spending at least four or five days here, and staying in one of the self-catering look-outs/observation huts that are scattered through the park, for some of that time. If possible, try to book these in advance through the Forest Department, but if you can't, make enquiries at the Park Office down by the boat jetty below the Aranya Nivas as soon as you can after arrival. You have to hire a ranger to take you to these places anyway. The forest *rest houses* cost Rs 5 a double and offer a superb jungle experience.

If you don't have four or five days to spare, you'll have to take one of the launch trips down the lake. These are good value as far as they go, and you'll probably see a variety of game, but it doesn't equal the experience of being alone in a small hut in the middle of the night engulfed by the noises of the jungle. 'As soon as a shy animal sticks its head up', reported one visitor, 'all aboard shout and scream until it goes again'.

It's advisable to bring warm clothes and waterproof clothing to Periyar. These cannot be hired when you get there. Kumily is the nearest place to buy supplies if you're going to stay in one of the forest rest houses/observation towers.

Places to Stay

The Kerala Tourist Development Corporation runs three different places inside the park. They are:

Periyar House (tel Kumily 26), which is the cheapest of the three, and very popular, so unless you get there early or make advance reservations it may be full. Dormitory accommodation costs Rs 7.50 per bed – there are two dorms which take 10 people each – single rooms with share bath cost Rs 20 and double rooms with attached bath cost Rs 40. The bathrooms have hot (very hot!) and cold running water. There is a restaurant here which serves good vegetarian and non-vegetarian food at reasonable prices, considering you have no choice. A breakfast of omelette, toast, butter, jam and a pot of coffee costs Rs 12.75, including service charge.

Aranya Nivas (tel Kumily 23), is considerably more expensive and offers ordinary rooms at Rs 80/100 for singles/doubles, de-luxe rooms for Rs 95/145, and VIP suites for Rs 160/240. There is a restaurant, bar, postal and banking facilities and a handicrafts showroom. The Aranya Nivas is located at the end of the road which leads into the park from Kumily. Periyar House is about half a km back from there.

Lake Palace is the most expensive of the three, but is on the lake shore, a long way into the park. If you can afford the extra money, it's well worth staying in this delightful place. Rooms with full board cost Rs 170/295. You can actually see animals from your room. There is a restaurant, bar, postal and banking facilities and a handicrafts showroom. To get to the Lake Palace you have to arrange to be at the Aranya Nivas launch jetty by 5 pm at the latest. The ferry costs Rs 10.

If possible you should try to book accommodation at Periyar in advance. This can be done at any Kerala Tourist Office. If you haven't done this, make sure you call at the Tourist Office in Kumily before catching a bus into the sanctuary. The man there will ring up and find out what rooms are available.

If the KTDC places are all full or you can't afford the more expensive ones, try the *Ambadi* at the checkpost, just as you enter the sanctuary. This recently-built hotel offers beautiful cottages with clean sheets, hot and cold running water and teak furniture for Rs 40 a double. They also have four-bed dorms which cost Rs 10 per bed. Indian and Chinese food is available between 7.30 am and 10.30 pm.

There's also a good selection of cheap hotels in the pleasant small town of Kumily itself. Try the *Mini Lodge* – Rs 6 a single – or the *Kavitha Lodge* – Rs 7 a single. The only drawback to these places outside the sanctuary is that they're a long way from the launch.

Getting There
Although there are bus connections between Kumily and Cochin, Idikki, Kottayam, Madurai, Quilon and Trivandrum, it's best to come in from Cochin, Kottayam or Madurai. The bus from Quilon takes all day and may involve confusing changes in what seems like the middle of nowhere. The bus from Trivandrum takes even longer, and it will take you half the morning to find the right bus at the terminal. From Kumily there are the following buses:

Cochin Daily at 5.45 am, 9.15 am and 2.40 pm
Idikki Daily at 6 am and 9.15 am.
Kottayam Nine times daily, the first at 4.30 am and the last at 6.40 pm with express buses at 8.30 am, 12.40 pm and 4 pm. The journey takes about four or five hours and costs Rs 14.70 by express bus. There are plenty of connecting buses to Cochin/Ernakulam which take about two hours and cost Rs 8.30.
Madurai Three daily express buses at 7 am, 1.30 pm and 6.30 pm. **Quilon** One bus daily at 5 am.
Trivandrum Two buses daily at 8 am and 1.30 pm.

All the express buses and many of the others come down to the Aranya Nivas and Periyar House before leaving Kumily, so you can catch them there rather than go up to the bus stand in Kumily.

Getting Around
There are local buses between Kumily and Periyar House/Aranya Nivas about 15 times a day. The fare is Rs 1. It's also possible to hitch.

There are two different launches on the lake. One is run by the Aranya Nivas on a charter basis (ie you must hire the whole launch), and the other is run by the Forest Department. The latter takes all comers and costs Rs 6 each, but it doesn't leave until it's full – this can take up to two hours. There are several departures every day.

ALLEPPEY (population 175,000)

Like Quilon, a pleasant, easy-going market town surrounded by coco-palm plantations and built around canals which service the coir industry of the backwaters. There's precious little to see in Alleppey, when I got there a bunch of medical students at St George's Lodge said to me, 'Why have you come here? There's nothing in Alleppey!'

While that may be true for most of the year, there is one event which you should not miss if you're anywhere in the vicinity on the second Saturday of August. This is the snakeboat races which take place here for the Nehru Cup. On this day scores of long, low-slung dug-outs with high decorated sterns and up to 100 rowers compete for the cup watched by thousands of spectators on the banks. It's the biggest event of the year.

The other reason you might pass through here on any other day of the year is, of course, to make the backwater trip to Quilon (or, if you're coming from that place, to stay here overnight before heading further north). For fuller details on this unforgettable trip, refer to the section on Quilon.

Information & Orientation

The bus station and boat jetty are located conveniently close to each other on the canal but are some distance from the main hotels so, if you have a lot of baggage, it's worth taking an auto-rickshaw. If you don't want to do this, St George's Lodging – Alleppey's best bargain in hotels – is a good 15 minutes' walk from the boat jetty. There is no rail connection with Alleppey.

Things to See

The Hindu temple, opposite the Indian Coffee House, is worth a look although, as a non-Hindu, you won't be allowed inside. It's a fine example of an elaborately-carved wooden south Indian temple somewhat reminiscent of those in Nepal. Alleppey has a lengthy beach.

Places to Stay

St George's Lodging is magnificent value.

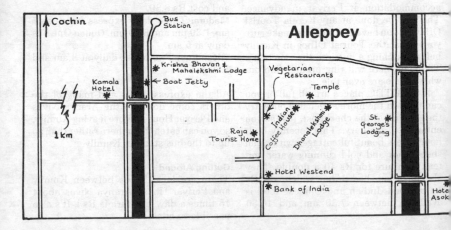

It's spotlessly clean, pleasantly decorated, has curtained windows, provides clean sheets and the staff are very friendly. There's even a Gideon's Bible on the desk! (The only time I've ever come across one in India.) ('I found four in just four weeks', replied a traveller!) Rooms cost Rs 12 a single, Rs 20 a double and Rs 24 a triple. Double and triple rooms have attached bathrooms. Single rooms share clean common baths. There's nothing to compare with it in Alleppey.

Dhanalekshmi Lodge, diagonally opposite the Hindu temple, is an older building than St George's Lodging and not as well-maintained. Rooms cost Rs 9 a single with common bathroom and Rs 15 a double with attached bath. *Raja Tourist Home* is probably the next best after St George's. Rooms here cost Rs 9 a single and Rs 15 a double, both with attached bathroom.

There are several other budget hotels opposite the boat jetty such as *Krishna Bhavan* and *Mahalakshmi Lodge* but they look decidedly scruffy. Near the Komala Hotel the modern *Sheeba Lodge* has singles for Rs 15.

Outside of town, close to the beach is the *PWD Bungalow.* It's a very pleasant place to stay and cheap at Rs 7.50 per person but you must add the cost of getting there by auto-rickshaw or taxi. Also, there are no restaurants nearby and meals at the PWD are expensive. Nevertheless, it's recommended by many travellers and is near the beach.

Places to Eat

One of the pleasantest places to eat is the *Indian Coffee House* opposite the Hindu temple. It serves cheap non-vegetarian food and is divided up into several rooms furnished with comfortable chairs and coir matting on the floor. The waiters display a touch of the Raj in their white uniforms, cummerbunds and frilly turbans. Prices are very reasonable and they serve excellent real coffee – of course. The cafe is popular with students and the local intelligentsia.

The *Komala Hotel,* on the other side of the canal bridge, has been recommended as having 'the best food in south India' by one traveller. 'We were not impressed', reported a later visitor! If you're looking for vegetarian plate meals (standard south Indian menu), there are a number of vegetarian cafes near the Raja Tourist Home. The restaurant on the top floor of *St George's Lodging* gets mixed reports, some say it is good another traveller reported that – 'half of the items on the menu are unavailable, the waiters are pretty clueless and the cashier is absurdly particular about the bills he accepts'. There's a rose garden up there too.

Getting There

Buses The main express services north and south are as follows:

Going South To Quilon there are eight buses daily. First bus at 7.20 am and the last at 9.05 pm. To Trivandrum there are 29 buses daily. First bus at 12.50 am and the last at 11.10 pm.

Going North To Ernakulam there are 38 buses daily. First bus at 1.50 am and the last at 10.35 pm. Takes 1½ to two hours and costs Rs 6.40. If you are heading for Fort Cochin as opposed to Ernakulam, you can get off this bus just before the bridge which connects Cochin and Willingdon Island (see the district map of Cochin and Ernakulam) and take a service bus or auto-rickshaw from there into either Mattancherry or Fort Cochin. This will save you a lot of messing about with ferries when you get to Ernakulam.

To Cannanore daily at 9.17 pm. To Calicut (Kozhikode) daily at 5.30 pm. To Palghat daily at 8.15 am, 10.05 am, 1.20 pm and 4 pm.

Boats

To Quilon (the backwater trip) The boats depart daily at 7.30 am and 10.30 pm. The trip takes about 8½ hours and costs Rs 4. For more details on this incredible trip refer to the Quilon section.

To Kottayam These boats cross Lake Vembanad, taking 2½ hours and cost Rs 2.25. There are 14 boats daily, the first at 5 am and the last at 9.30 pm. It's a good short taste of the backwaters.

QUILON (population 140,000)

Buried amongst coconut palms and cashew tree plantations on the edge of Ashtamudi Lake, this small market town of old wooden houses with red-tiled roofs overhanging winding streets is perhaps the most typical of Keralan towns. If you're coming up from the south, it's also the gateway to the backwaters of Kerala. The trip by boat to Alleppey through these backwaters is a fascinating and unique experience not to be missed.

Quilon has roots going back centuries and its history is interwoven with the rivalries between the Portuguese, Dutch and English for control of commodities grown in this part of the sub-continent and the trade routes across the Indian Ocean. Only three km from the centre of town at Thangasseri stand the ruins of a fort originally constructed by the Portuguese and later taken over by the Dutch. In Ashtamudi Lake are many Chinese fishing nets of the type more usually associated with Cochin, further north.

Information & Orientation

The transport facilities are at opposite ends of the town, three km apart, so if you arrive by rail and want to get to the bus station or the boat jetty you will need to take an auto-rickshaw (costs approximately Rs 3.50). Other than the Tourist Bungalow (not to be confused with the Travellers' Bungalow) which is a long way from the centre of town (Rs 10 auto-rickshaw ride), most hotels are located in the central area between the Clock Tower and the Post Office. There is no Tourist Office in Quilon. The GPO is open until 8 pm from Monday to Saturday and until 6 pm on Sundays and public holidays.

Things to See

Apart from the miserable ruins of the Portuguese/Dutch fort at Thangasseri, there are few 'sights' in Quilon. It's just a pleasant place to stroll around for a day or so and soak up the atmosphere of a Keralan market town. Most travellers come here to take the boat through the backwaters or, if coming from Alleppey, are en route to Trivandrum. As such it's an overnight stop.

Places to Stay

The most interesting place to stay is the *Tourist Bungalow* – a former British Residency converted to a hotel. The tourist literature is fond of telling you that 'Lord Curzon slept here'. It's a beautiful place overlooking the lake but rather a long way from town. Rooms cost Rs 15 per person but there are only eight of them and although meals are available they're on the expensive side. On the surface, it seems a cheap place to stay, but you have to add on the cost of getting there by auto-rickshaw (about Rs 10 one-way).

The best place to stay in the centre of Quilon itself is the *Hotel Karthika*, (tel 3760, 3764), a large newly-completed hotel, which is very clean and pleasantly decorated. It's excellent value at Rs 14 a single and Rs 27 a double for non air-con and Rs 52 a double for air-con. All the rooms have their own bathroom and the hotel has a restaurant.

Before the Karthika was constructed the *Hotel Sudarsan*, Parameswar Nagar between the Post Office and the boat jetty, used to be the best hotel in town, but it's been allowed to run down over the last few years and some rooms are decidedly tatty at the edges. Rooms with attached bath cost Rs 26 to 30 for singles, Rs 40 to 52 for doubles. The hotel has two restaurants, one air-con, the other non air-con, and its own bar. The food is good but the service haphazard, room service is also very poor. Better than the Sudarsan is the *Iswarya Lodge*, another fairly new building, but quite a way from the centre

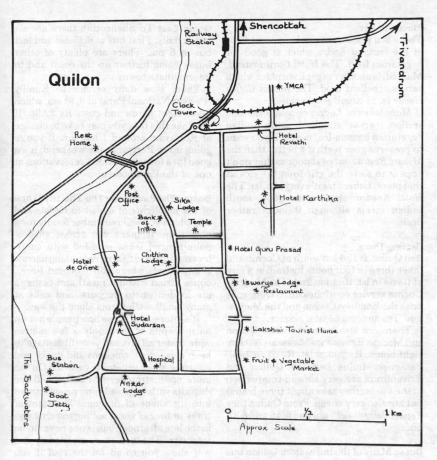

Quilon

Railway Station

Shencottah

Trivandrum

Clock Tower

YMCA

Hotel Revathi

Rest Home

Post Office

Sika Lodge

Bank of India

Temple

Hotel Karthika

Hotel de Orient

Chithira Lodge

Hotel Guru Prasad

Iswarya Lodge & Restaurant

Hotel Sudarsan

Lakshmi Tourist Home

Bus Station

Hospital

Fruit & Vegetable Market

The Backwaters

Boat Jetty

Anzar Lodge

0   ½   1 Km
Approx. Scale

of town. Rooms here cost Rs 20/40 with attached bath and there is a good restaurant on the ground floor.

If you're looking for something cheaper, try the *Sika Lodge/Hotel Apsara* (tel 7096), which is about 100 metres down the road, opposite the bridge across the river. This place is good value at Rs 15/20 with attached bath and fan. On the ground floor there is a reasonable vegetarian restaurant. *Samos Lodge*, also 100 metres from the Sudarsan, has rooms at Rs 10/15 and lots of mosquitoes. Another place to

try is the *Rest House*, just across the bridge from the Post Office. You can get rooms here for Rs 15 a double with attached bath and lots of mosquitoes, but it's often full.

The *Hotel de Orient*, half-way between the Post Office and the Hotel Sudarsan is mainly a flop house and drinking spot for men, which is unfortunate as it's set in beautiful grounds. You can get a scruffy cell-like room here for Rs 10 a single. There are no doubles.

Places to Eat

There is a restaurant on the ground floor of the *Iswarya Lodge* which is good for vegetarian food. The *Hotel Guru Prasad*, Main St, is another vegetarian place which serves excellent food. The *Indian Coffee House* is, as usual, good value.

Mahalakshmi Lodge, opposite the bus station, serves standard south Indian vegetarian banana-leaf meals. If you want to preserve your teeth it's better than the *Mysore Restaurant* next door as they don't appear to sieve the grit from the rice at that place. Otherwise it's very similar. The *Hotel Apsara* also serves good south Indian meals although it looks rather drab.

Getting There

Rail Quilon is 156 km south of Cochin and takes three or four hours by train at a fare of Rs 54 in 1st, Rs 14 in 2nd. The Madras-Cochin service continues on to Quilon, as does the Bombay-Cochin and the Mangalore-Trivandrum coastal service.

There are also trains between Quilon and Madras Egmore via Madurai (760 km, eight hours, Rs 200 in 1st, Rs 51 in 2nd). Passenger trains between Quilon and Trivandrum are very slow in comparison to the buses (they take about three hours) but are also very cheap. From Quilon they depart daily at 6.25 am and 5.45 and 8.15 pm.

Buses Many of the buses from Quilon bus station do not originate from there but are en route from somewhere else. Along the most important routes they depart as follows:

Going South To Trivandrum at least 23 times daily. First bus at 3.10 am and last bus at 10.40 pm. The trip takes about two hours and costs Rs 7.50.

Going North To Alleppey there are six buses daily. First bus at 5.30 am and last bus at 6.30 pm. To Ernakulam there are 15 buses daily. First bus at 1 am and last bus at 11.10 pm.

Going East To Shencottah there are six buses daily. First bus at 6.15 am and last bus at 8 pm. There are plenty of other buses going further up the coast and to intermediate towns.

There is a daily service to Kumily (Periyar National Park) at 8.30 am, which takes eight hours and costs Rs 22.30. If you take this bus, you may have to change at Kottayam around 10.30 am. If you're going up to Periyar at the weekend, it's a good idea to make advance reservations at one of the Park hotels.

Boats – The Backwater Trip This trip is one of the highlights of a visit to Kerala and one which you will remember fondly for a long time. It takes you across shallow palm-fringed lakes studded with canti-levered Chinese fishing nets, along narrow shady canals where coir (coconut fibre), copra (dried coconut meat) and cashews are loaded on to dugouts, and calls at many small settlements along the way.

It's interesting to see how people live on narrow spits of land only a few metres wide, water all around, yet still manage to keep cows, pigs, chickens and ducks and cultivate small vegetable gardens. On the more open stretches of canal, you'll see dugouts with huge sails and prows carved into the shape of dragons. The sight of three or four of these sailing towards you in the late afternoon sun is one never to be forgotten. The boat crews are friendly and will allow you to sit on the roof if you exchange a little conversation with them. It gets kind of hot up there, though.

There are two 10-minute 'chai stops' along the way where snacks and tea can be bought, but you may decide it's worth bring some food with you. Beware of jacked up prices for food and drink at these stops. Daily departures from Quilon are at 10 am and 8.30 pm. From Alleppey at 7.30 am and 10.30 pm. The trip takes approximately 8½ hours and costs only Rs 4 per person. If you're pushed for time you can take a bus from Ernakulam to Alleppey, make the trip to Quilon and get a bus back to Ernakulam all in the same day.

Other, shorter boat trips are possible from Quilon if, for some reason, you can't make the trip to Alleppey. They are Quilon-Kapapuzha daily at 9.30 am and 9.45 pm. Quilon-Guhanandapuram daily at 7.30 am, 11 am, 1.30 pm, 5.30 pm, 8 pm and 10.30 pm. It's not necessary to book any of the boat trips in advance. There's always plenty of room and no problems with rucksacks or other gear.

Getting Around
The hills in Quilon are too steep for bicycle rickshaws. An auto-rickshaw from the station to the Hotel Sudarsan will be about Rs 3.

VARKALA
Only 19 km south of Quilon, 55 km north of Trivandrum, Varkala is a seaside resort with a mineral water spring on the beach and the Janardhana Temple. Near here at Anjengo one of the earliest British East India Company trading posts was established in 1684.

TRIVANDRUM (population 460,000)
Strolling around this friendly, relaxed city built over seven luxuriously forested hills, it's hard to imagine this is a state capital. The 'City of the Sacred Snake' is quite unlike any other state capital in India and has managed to retain the magic ambience that is so characteristic of Kerala in general. Low sky-line, red-tiled roofs, narrow winding lanes, intimate corner cafes, beaten-up municipal buses and necessary business accomplished in a friendly manner with a relatively high degree of efficiency.

At least, this is how it is when political tensions between the various factions haven't got to the stage where they spill out into violence on the streets. Political slogans, emblems and flags, especially those of the communist parties, dominate the urban landscape of Kerala. Luckily, even when there's violence, it rarely affects the traveller or tourist and is generally an indication that you'll be drawn into some very lively discussions in the cafes and restaurants.

On the other hand, there isn't a great deal to see in Trivandrum itself other than the museum, art gallery and zoological gardens. The famous Sri Padmanabhaswamy Temple, though a magnificent example of south Indian architecture, isn't an 'attraction' as such (though the tourist literature will have you believe otherwise), since it's not open to non-Hindus. The main reason people come to Trivandrum is to stay at Kovalam beach, 16 km south of the city and one of the finest in all India. You also might find yourself staying here a day or so if you're planning on flying to Sri Lanka or to the Maldive Islands.

Orientation
Trivandrum is spread out over quite a large area but most of the services and places of interest are on, or very near to, Mahatma Gandhi Rd which is the main road running through the centre of the city from the zoological gardens to the Sri Padmanabhaswamy Temple. The long-distance bus terminal, railway station and Tourist Reception Centre are all to be found within a few metres of each other, as are many of the budget hotels, though very few of the latter can be recommended as pleasant places to stay.

The municipal bus stand is five minutes' walk from the railway station opposite Sri Padmanabhaswamy Temple. From here bus No 15 runs to Kovalam beach 25 times daily, the first at 6.20 am, the last at 9 pm, and takes approximately half an hour. (Even if you have to take the last bus to Kovalam there's no problem finding accommodation when you get there). The post office in Trivandrum is a good half-hour walk from the railway station, so to get to it, as well as to the museum, art gallery and zoological gardens you will need to take either an auto-rickshaw or taxi.

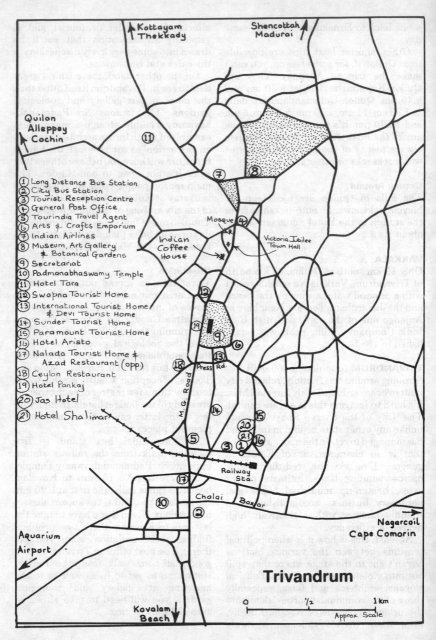

↑ Kottayam
Thekkady

↑ Shencottah
Madurai

Quilon
Alleppey
Cochin

① Long Distance Bus Station
② City Bus Station
③ Tourist Reception Centre
④ General Post Office
⑤ Tourindia Travel Agent
⑥ Arts & Crafts Emporium
⑦ Indian Airlines
⑧ Museum, Art Gallery
   & Botanical Gardens
⑨ Secretariat
⑩ Padmanabhaswamy Temple
⑪ Hotel Tara
⑫ Swapna Tourist Home
⑬ International Tourist Home
   & Devi Tourist Home
⑭ Sunder Tourist Home
⑮ Paramount Tourist Home
⑯ Hotel Aristo
⑰ Nalada Tourist Home &
   Azad Restaurant (opp.)
⑱ Ceylon Restaurant
⑲ Hotel Pankaj
⑳ Jas Hotel
㉑ Hotel Shalimar

Mosque

Indian
Coffee
House

Victoria Jubilee
Town Hall

M.G. Road

Press Rd.

Railway
Sta.

Chalai   Bazar

Aquarium
Airport

Kovalam
Beach

Nagarcoil
Cape Comorin

Trivandrum

0   ½   1 km

Approx Scale

Information

The Tourist Reception Centre is situated between the railway station and Mahatma Gandhi Rd (right hand side) and is open daily. They have maps of Trivandrum but precious little else that isn't 20 years out-of-date. It's here that you book tours of Trivandrum City, Cape Cormorin and Thekkady Wildlife Sanctuary. The headquarters of the Kerala Tourist Development Corporation is on the north-east side of the Secretariat building.

Dr Matthai at the Fatima Clinic on Statue Rd has been recommended if you need a doctor in Trivandrum. There are some good bookshops along the main street. You can see the local martial art kalarippayat performed at CVN Kalari at East Fort.

Museum, Art Gallery & Zoological Gardens

These are all located in the same area in the park at the north end of the city. They are open daily, except Monday and Wednesday mornings, between 8 am and 6 pm.

Museum Housed in an attractive building, it offers a good collection of bronzes, historical and contemporary ornaments, temple carts, ivory carvings and life-size figures of Kathakali dancers in full regalia.

Sri Chitra Art Gallery Here are displayed paintings of the Rajput, Mughal and Tanjore schools together with works from China, Tibet, Japan and Bali. In addition, there are many modern Indian paintings, especially those of Ravi Varma.

Zoological Gardens This is one of the best laid-out zoos in Asia set amongst woodland, lakes and well-maintained lawns. It includes a botanical garden where there are examples of almost every tropical tree. About a half km beyond the zoo the ex-Maharaja's palace (palace is probably too grand a word for it) is now a state government building and you can

see the conference room and banqueting/ballroom from the Maharaja's time and admire the fine view from the terrace.

Aquarium

Situated quite a distance from the city centre near the airport. It houses what you would expect of an aquarium plus many rare species of aquatic animals. Open daily except Mondays between 9.30 am and 6 pm.

Padmanabhapuram Palace

Although it is actually in Tamil Nadu this fine palace is easily visited from Trivandrum. See the Kanyakumari section in Tamil Nadu for more details. To get there you can either take a service bus from Trivandrum (or Kovalam beach) or go on one of the tours organised by the Kerala Tourist Development Corporation. Closed Mondays.

Tours

Trivandrum City Tour Daily except Mondays at 8 am returning at 7 pm. The tour costs Rs 25 per person and includes visits to Sri Padmanabhaswamy Temple (for Hindus only), museum, art gallery, aquarium, Kovalam beach, the zoo and Neyyar Dam.

Cape Cormorin Daily at 7.30 am. The tour costs Rs 35 and includes visits to Padmanabhapuram Palace and Cape Cormorin.

Thekkady Wildlife Sanctuary This tour to the wildlife sanctuary in the mountains of Kerala near the border with Tamil Nadu departs every Saturday at 6 am and returns the following day at 9 pm. The tour costs Rs 85 excluding board and lodging. If you're staying at Kovalam, you will miss the last bus back from Trivandrum. This must be one of the silliest tours in India, since there's no way you're going to have the time to see any wildlife at all – even if it were that easy!

Places to Stay – Bottom End

One of the best of the cheapies is the

Nalanda Tourist Home, M G Rd on the right hand side after you have crossed the bridge which goes over the railway. It's a modern building – clean, convenient and well organised with singles/doubles at Rs 25/30 with attached bath. Similar in standard is the *Streevas Tourist Home*, Station Rd, which has singles, doubles and triples for Rs 17.50, 28 and 40, all with attached bath. Near the Nalada is the *Ritz Lodge* – dim, spartan, clean, singles at Rs 10.

Cheaper still is the *MGM Lodge*, across the other side of the railway from Station Rd near the bridge, which has singles and triples without attached bath for Rs 10 and 20, and singles and doubles with attached bath for Rs 12 and 20. It's often full, so if you want a room get there early.

There are many other cheap lodging houses along Station Rd, but they're often full and a lot of them are very basic. This road is very busy and noisy. A few hundred metres from the railway and bus stations, is the relatively new and very well kept *Hotel Shalimar* (tel 67578) with rooms from Rs 25 to 65. All except the cheapest singles have attached bathrooms and many rooms have balconies.

Further away from the bus and railway stations, going up Mahatma Gandhi Rd, is the *International Tourist Home*, Press Rd (United Bank of India Building). This is a pleasant, quiet and clean hotel with friendly staff. Singles, doubles and triples with attached bathrooms cost Rs 12, 20 and 30 here. Nearby on the same road is the cheaper, but more basic, *Devi Tourist Home*, which has a choice of small rooms with and without attached bath.

Off to the right at the bottom end of the Secretariat block is the *Kerala Hotel*. This is used by the Kerala Tourist Development Corporation for their tour buses so it can be booked out at times, but it's good value at Rs 14/28 with attached bath. There is a 'meals' restaurant downstairs where you can get a banana leaf thali for Rs 4.50 or a Bombay-style meal for Rs 7.

Places to Stay – Top End

If comfort, air-conditioning and the facilities and conveniences of a modern five-star hotel are your priorities (let alone its incomparable setting), you would do yourself a disservice if you didn't head for the ITDC *Kovalam Beach Resort* at Kovalam Beach (quarter of an hour away by taxi). It's one of the best hotels in India – and comparatively cheap for what it offers. Details under the Kovalam Beach section which follows.

If you want to stay in Trivandrum itself the *Hotel Pankaj* (tel 66557), is conveniently situated opposite the Government Secretariat. It has two restaurants, one on the roof-top overlooking the city, with a choice of Mughlai, Tandoor, Chinese and western cuisine, banking and travel facilities and 24-hour room service. All the rooms have en suite bathrooms with hot and cold running water, and cost Rs 130 to 175 a single and Rs 160 to 200 a double with air-con. Without air-con the rooms cost Rs 65 a single and Rs 90 a double.

Another hotel of a similar standard in the centre of town is the *Rajdhani* (tel 3353), East Fort. Further to the north and west of the Botanical Gardens are two other top end hotels – the *Hotel Tara* (tel 61373) and the *Hotel Belair* (tel 3402-3), Agricultural College Rd in the Vellayani area. At the Belair rooms cost Rs 300/360 including meals.

The *Hotel Luciya Continental* (tel 3443) is a new top end hotel at the East Fort. Singles/doubles are Rs 75/100 or Rs 135/175 with air-con and in this category it's very good value. There are two good restaurants and the travel bureau here has also been recommended.

Places to Eat

If you're looking for a better class of restaurant try the *Azad Restaurant*, on Mahatma Gandhi Rd between the railway bridge and the Sri Padmanabhaswamy Temple. Popular with office workers in the area although it's not much good for breakfast. Or there's the *Capri Hotel*, on the opposite side of the road from the municipal bus stand. The restaurant is upstairs and is air-conditioned. On the ground floor there is a 'meals' cafe where standard south Indian plate meals are served for Rs 3.50. The *Jas Hotel* is also good for a splurge meal in air-con comfort or even a cold beer.

A good low-priced non-vegetarian restaurant is the *Ceylon Restaurant* on the opposite side of Mahatma Gandhi Rd from Press Rd. They serve meat, fish and egg curries as well as omelettes and other breakfast foods. *New Agra Sweets*, between the Nalada and the bridge is very good for snacks and has exceptionally good lassi. *Mukkadans Restaurant* near the GPO has also been recommended.

Getting There

Air Trivandrum is a popular place from which to fly to Colombo (Sri Lanka) and Male (Maldives). Fares are Rs 479 to Colombo, Rs 572 to Male, and you can pay in rupees so long as you have bank receipts showing you changed at least that much in a bank. There are two Indian Airlines flights a week to Male and two a week to Colombo plus two more flights to Colombo with Air Lanka.

One traveller reported how somebody at Trivandrum airport tried to charge him Rs 100 airport tax on his flight to Colombo because he was only transitting Sri Lanka and therefore it was not an 'adjacent country' Rs 50 flight. Lies! Another claimed that Trivandrum airport was the most chaotic he'd experienced in 20 years of travel and checking in for the 45 minute flight to Colombo took over two hours!

Domestically there are daily flights Bombay–Trivandrum and Madras–Tiruchirappalli–Trivandrum plus four flights a week Cochin-Trivandrum. Fare to or from Trivandrum are Bombay Rs 899, Madras Rs 464, Trichy Rs 239 and Cochin Rs 153.

Rail Although buses are much faster than the trains, Kerala State Road Transport buses, like most others in southern India, make no concessions to comfort and the drivers are pretty reckless. If you like to keep your adrenalin levels down the trains are a pleasant alternative, so long as you're not going too far.

The trains through Trivandrum are the same as those right down the coast through Cochin/Ernakulam and Quilon. The same twice weekly Karnataka/Kerala Express departs from New Delhi and arrives at Trivandrum 48 hours later. The 3054-km trip costs Rs 591 in 1st class, Rs 151 in 2nd class. Madras-Trivandrum is a 921-km trip costing Rs 233 in 1st class, Rs 59 in 2nd class. It takes 18 hours on the Trivandrum Mail.

The Mangalore-Trivandrum coastal route takes 11 hours from end to end on the Yercaud Express. Trivandrum-Quilon is just 65 km (Rs 27 in 1st, Rs 6.50 in 2nd), Trivandrum-Ernakulam is 201 km (Rs 66 in 1st, Rs 17 in 2nd) and Trivandrum-Calicut is 414 km (Rs 125 in 1st, Rs 32 in 2nd).

Trivandrum-Bangalore takes 19 hours on the Island Express. Fares for the 950-km trip are Rs 237 in 1st, Rs 60.50 in 2nd. From Bombay it's a lengthy 45 hours on the 2nd class only Jayanti Janata Express. The 2062-km trip costs Rs 109. To Mettuppalaiyam (for Ooty) is a 14-hour trip involving changes of train at Shoranur and Coimbatore – not a bad trip though.

Bus The bus station at Trivandrum opposite the railway station is total chaos. There is a timetable of sorts, but nothing in English. Even so, it's largely a fiction and as there are no bays, you have to join the scrum every time a bus arrives just in case it happens to be the one you want. It's the law of the jungle every time one of the battered old buses comes to a screeching halt in a cloud of dust, but it does help if you buy a 'priority ticket' (Rs 0.50). In theory, this entitles you to a seat on the bus of your choice so wave it above your head as you're fighting to get on. If the conductor sees it, he'll generally pull you on, but don't count on that seat.

There are frequent buses to all the main cities in Kerala and to Kanyakumari. Long distance buses are also available to Madras, Mysore and Bangalore, but it would be better to take a private bus company if you're going as far as that as the State Transport buses are very tatty and often hopelessly overcrowded.

Getting Around

For local transport around the city and to Kovalam beach there are state government buses (very crowded), auto-rickshaws and taxis. For transport around the city itself auto-rickshaws are probably your best bet. The drivers need no prompting about using the meters and fares are cheap.

For Kovalam beach, bus No 15 runs 25 times daily from the Fort Bus Depot. The first departs at 6.20 am and the last at 9 pm (don't pay too much attention to the timings posted at the bus stop!). The journey takes about half an hour. Note that the bus starts out ridiculously overcrowded but rapidly thins out. A taxi from Trivandrum to Kovalam beach will cost Rs 4 to 5 per person – they leave when they have seven passengers – though it is sometimes possible to get it for Rs 3 each.

Bus 14 goes to the airport, about Rs 0.60.

KOVALAM

Kovalam is not only one of India's best beaches – perhaps *the* best – but the favourite watering hole of travellers in the south of India. Just south of Trivandrum, it consists of a number of small, palm-fringed bays separated by rocky headlands. There is good surf on most days, although, unless you are a strong swimmer, you should approach the water cautiously until you're familiar with the rip as one or two people get drowned here every year. There are plenty of cheap places to stay and a choice of simple restaurants, many of which stand right on the water's edge,

and most of which offer excellent seafood. If anything, the atmosphere at Kovalam is even more mellow than it is on the beaches of Goa, and many people who turn up here intending to stay for a few days find themselves staying considerably longer. It can become very difficult to leave.

Back from the beach and on either side of the two main coves, life goes on as it always has. The local people continue to cultivate their rice, coconuts, bananas, pawpaws and vegetables; the fishermen still row their dug-outs out to sea and pull the nets in by hand. The influx of westerners here over the past few years hasn't radically affected the life-styles of the people who live at the back of the two main coves. What it has meant is that extra income can be earned by selling fruit and other produce to the sun and waves worshippers and, anyone who can is offering rooms for rent or doing something to make this possible. Otherwise the place is, as yet, unspoiled.

It requires some effort and time to get to Kovalam. You can't do it within a day of arriving at Bombay by 'plane from London, Sydney or wherever, so by the time you do get there you've given India a chance to seep into your veins. This is one of the reasons why you get such an interesting collection of people on the beach here.

Information & Orientation

The nearest post office is in Kovalam village. There is a bank which will change travellers' cheques without fuss or form-filling at the ITDC Kovalam Beach Resort. Suntan lotion, Nivea cream, pain-killers and other general store commodities can be bought from the chai stalls at the bus stop.

Note that the paths through the coconut palms and around the back of the paddy field are difficult to negotiate at night without a full moon unless you're familiar with them. If you're not, and want to try Silent Valley or Sreevas House for an evening meal, go there before dark. This

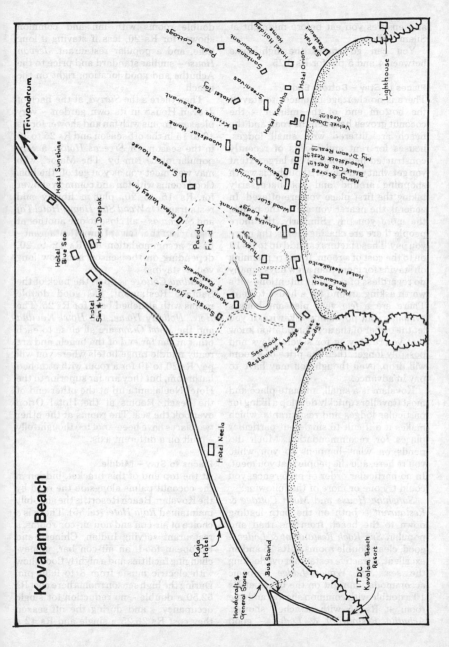

also ensures you eat before midnight at Silent Valley.

You can go round the lighthouse between 4 and 5 pm for Rs 0.25.

Places to Stay – Bottom End

There is no shortage of places to stay at the bottom end of the market – the coconut groves between the road and the beach are littered with small lodges, houses for rent and blocks of recently constructed bedrooms. To a large extent you get what you pay for, though it is worth shopping around and not necessarily taking the first place you are offered. In general, the nearer you are to the beach, the more you pay. Similarly, the more people there are chasing rooms, the more you pay. These factors can add up to Rs 10 on to the cost of a room. If you're planning on staying for more than a few days – many do regardless of previous intentions – it's worth asking around for a house to rent. There are a *few* very pleasant houses available, but not many. Likewise, if you let the owner of the accommodation know that you're staying for several days and possibly longer, then the price of a room will drop, even though you may have to pay in advance.

Kovalam is a small, intimate place and most travellers quickly develop a liking for particular lodges and restaurants, which makes it difficult to single out particular places for recommendation. Much depends on what happens to you while you're here, and the people that you meet. In no particular order of preference, you could try one or more of the following:

Sunshine House and *Moon Cottage & Restaurant* – both on the path leading down to the beach from the road and popular. *Sea Rock Restaurant & Lodge* – good, clean double rooms at Rs 15 and an excellent, attractive restaurant overlooking the sea. *Sea Waves Lodge* – basic accommodation right on the beach at Rs 10 a double with common shower and one room at Rs 15 with attached shower. *Achutha Restaurant & Lodge* – good

double rooms with fan and common shower for Rs 20, less if staying a long time, and a popular restaurant. *Jeevan House* – similar standard and price to the Achutha and good location, right on the beach.

Then there's the *Suriya*, at the back of Jeevan House in its own garden – very pleasant rooms with fan and shower for Rs 12 to 15 in the off-season and Rs 25 to 30 in the season. Or *Sreevas House*, a very popular place run by 'The Major', who may well meet you as you get off the bus. Good rooms with fan and common shower for Rs 15 to 20, plus a library and restaurant. Or *Wood Star Home, Hotel Taj* and *Sreenivas* – all close to one another at the back of the Velvet Dawn Restaurant – basic accommodation for Rs 12 to 20, depending on the season and how long you're staying.

Padma Cottage is up at the back of the Santana Restaurant, has good double rooms with attached bath for Rs 25. The *Hotel Holiday Home*, the *Hotel Kavitha* and the *Hotel Orion* are all close to each other at the far end of the beach, and are really middle range hotels where you will pay Rs 20 to 40 for a room with attached bathroom, but they are far superior to the Hotel Neelakanta up at the other end of the beach. Rooms at the Hotel Orion overlook the sea. The rooms at the other two places have been – not too thoughtfully – built on a different axis.

Places to Stay – Middle

At the top end of this bracket, hidden in the coconut palms alongside the road by the Kovalam Beach Resort, is the shabbily maintained *Raja Hotel* (tel 55). There is a choice of air-con and non air-con rooms, a restaurant serving Indian, Chinese and European food, an air-con bar, money-changing facilities and a nightly floor show with electric music from 8 to 9.30 pm. During the high season rooms here cost Rs 52.50 a double – no reduction for single occupancy – and during the off-season they cost Rs 26.25 a single and Rs 42 a double, inclusive of all taxes.

Considerably cheaper and a lot more pleasant is the *Hotel Blue Sea* (tel 21), back up the road towards Kovalam village. If you want to stay in a hotel rather than a beach hut while you're here, this is the place to head for. It's a beautiful, old period mansion built in traditional style with polished wooden staircases, window frames, doors and the like, and newly whitewashed inside and out. The two brothers who run it are very friendly and conscientious about keeping up standards. Very good food is available in the restaurant, the *Padma*, which is also open to non-residents. Try the garlic fish. There are numerous different kinds of rooms here, all with fan and attached bathrooms. Prices vary depending on what you take and on the season, but they're all reasonable.

The *Hotel Neelakanta*, right on the beach, offers rooms which are slightly more expensive at Rs 35 to 40 a double with attached bath. However, the management is unpleasant, the hotel an ugly concrete box and I didn't meet anyone who seemed particularly satisfied with the place. Other mid-range hotels to try if the Hotel Blue Sea is full include the *Hotel Depak*, opposite the Hotel Blue Sea, which has rooms with shower, toilet, fan and clean sheets for Rs 10 to 35 – can be more in the high season depending on demand. The *Hotel Palm Garden* and the *Hotel Sunshine*, are both close to the Blue Sea and Deepak, and have rooms with shower and toilet for Rs 20 to 35. Note the latter only has two rooms available at present.

You can give the *Neela Hotel*, opposite the Raja Hotel, a miss as it's outrageously priced at Rs 25/45 with only bucket showers available. This place has an air of dereliction about it, and nobody seems to give a damn. The same can be said for the *Hotel Sun & Waves* which, judging from the attitude of the manager, seems to have no interest in attracting custom. I did hear other stories about it, but can't sub-stantiate them, though they did fit into the general picture.

Places to Stay – Top End
The most luxurious place to stay is the ITDC *Kovalam Beach Resort* (tel 3031, 3331), on the headland just above the bus terminal. Studio rooms, double rooms and cottages are Rs 450 to 500 for single occupancy. Doubles and double suites are Rs 675. There are also suites in the old Maharaja's Lodge (Halcyon Castle) for Rs 450. It comes complete with every facility you would expect including air-conditioning, swimming pool, bar, craft shop and boats for hire. It's a beautiful place and it's obvious that a lot of effort has been put into its design and construction. It has facilities for yoga and Ayurvedic massage, both of which are open to non-residents at a cost of Rs 15 per session. For an international five-star hotel it's cheap. For Kovalam beach it's outrageously expensive. If you're planning on a night out bear in mind that a beer will cost you Rs 30 or so these days, over three times what it will cost you virtually anywhere else! There is a bank here which will change travellers' cheques with no fuss or form filling.

The KTDC *Hotel Samudhra* is a pleasant, modern building, nicely placed on the beach 15 minutes walk north of the Kovalam Beach Resort. Non air-con rooms are Rs 65/90 but the service is grudging and poor. In contrast the service is excellent at the superbly situated *Rockholm* which is about 100 metres south of the lighthouse. It hangs on a cliff overlooking two small, clean and fairly private beaches with fine surf. Rooms are Rs 140/165. There's an excellent restaurant on a palm-shaded terrace, most meals Rs 15 to 20.

Places to Eat
Restaurants have sprung up all over the place at Kovalam. Most of them line the beach front but there are others – just as good – which are scattered among the coconut palm groves. Almost all of them

cater for that international palate – western-style breakfasts (porridge, omelettes, toast, jam, pancakes, etc), seafood (fish, prawns with French fries, lobster, etc), a variety of fruit salads and custard-based sweets. Everyone has his/her own favourite, though there isn't a great deal to choose between them in terms of quality – they all tend to be pretty good. They do, however, vary quite a lot in terms of the size of helpings, how long you have to wait before a meal arrives, distractions in the meantime (music or no music) and lighting facilities.

Some places have definitely bitten off much more than they can chew and will attempt to cater for up to two dozen customers on one primus stove. This isn't just a commendable case of over-enthusiasm, it's clearly impossible which is why you'll still be waiting for the first course three hours after you ordered it. Prices are much the same – eg a meal consisting of omelette, toast, tea/coffee is around Rs 5 to 6; grilled/fried fish is Rs 8 to 12 depending on size; French fries are Rs 3.50 to 4; lime soda is Rs 1.50.

Some of the most popular restaurants which are capable of catering simultaneously for more than just a few people are the *Moon Restaurant, Sea Rock Restaurant, Achutha Restaurant, Sreevas House, Silent Valley Inn, Woodstock, Velvet Dawn* and *Santana Restaurant.* This is by no means an exhaustive list of possible eating places – others are indicated on the map – nor is it given in any order of preference. You may also find that one year after this is written some of the places will have folded, others been renamed and new ones opened. While I was there the *Sea Mother* changed its name to *Black Cat*, the *Woodstock* was busy putting up a new sign reminding customers that it was formally the *Wood Star* because an upstart shack nearby had purloined that name, and I didn't see the *Krishna Restaurant* open once.

In addition to the restaurants, there are a number of local women who do the rounds of the sun worshippers on the beach selling fruit. The familiar ring of, 'Hello, baba. Mango? Papaya? Banana? Coconut? Pineapple?' all delivered with a seductive pout of the lips and a flashing of bright, brown eyes from under lowered eyelids will soon become part of your day. Naturally, they'll sell you fruit for any price you're willing to pay, so on your first few encounters you have to establish what you think is a fair price for certain fruits. After that they'll remember your face and you don't have to repeat the performance. They rarely have any change, but are reliable about bringing it to you later on.

Toddy (coconut beer) and *feni* (spirits made by distilling the fermented mash of either coconuts or cashew nuts – the two varieties taste quite different) are available from shops in Kovalam village. Beers are available at both the ITDC Kovalam Beach Resort or the Raja Hotel, but at a price likely to singe the hair on the back of your hand as you reach for your wallet. Buy them in Trivandrum at a wine store and ask the restaurant manager to put them in the fridge for you. They're happy to do this, so long as you eat there. Cigarettes are sold in most of the restaurants down on the beach. Otherwise there are stores at the bus stop.

Getting There

The local bus to Trivandrum runs 25 times daily but the schedules are not too believable. The first bus is at 6.15 am the last at 10 pm. The depot is right outside the Kovalam Beach Hotel. It costs Rs 1.20 or 1.60 depending on the type of bus. If you want to get to Kovalam from Trivandrum, there are plenty of taxis hanging around the bus stop there. They'll take you to the beach for Rs 4 to 5 per person – Rs 3 if you're lucky. They leave when they have seven passengers.

There are also direct services to Ernakulam and Kanyakumari (Cape Cormorin), which are a good way of avoiding the crush at Trivandrum – see Trivandrum for details.

Things to Buy

Apart from the fruit sellers there are men who come around selling *lungis*. It seems batik has arrived in Kovalam because there are some fine bargains to be picked up in this line, so have a look through what they've got. You may also come across a local artist who sells exquisite and subtly-executed leaf paintings. He started doing these about a year ago and occasionally brings his work down to the beach, if you see him have a look as they're brilliant. Prices are reasonable and well within the range of a tight budget.

Also there is usually plenty of excellent ganja for sale, and there are no problems about smoking it. A *tola* (about 10 grams) should cost about Rs 8 to 10. Most of it comes from Idukki District in the mountains east of Cochin, though you may well be told that is comes from 'around Thekkady'.

Madras

Population: 3.5 million
Main language: Tamil

Madras is the capital of Tamil Nadu

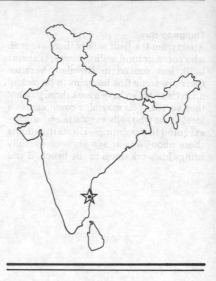

Madras is India's fourth largest city and capital of Tamil Nadu state, but despite its size it is an example of how pleasant other Indian cities might be if they were not so overcrowded. Madrassis are not only zealous guardians of Tamil culture, which they regard as inherently superior to the hybridised cultures further north, but they also appear to know the meaning of relaxation and efficiency with regard to public services – a remarkable combination, to be found only in isolated pockets elsewhere in India! Here it's possible to use public buses without undue discomfort and the urban commuter trains without a second thought. There are, it is true, slums and beggars, as there are in other Indian cities, but they are far less obtrusive and smaller in number. The city also has the advantage of a long beach front on the Bay of Bengal, which ensures a good supply of refreshing sea air and provides a popular place to relax in the evening.

Madras was the site of the first important settlement of the East India Company – founded in 1639 on land given by the Raja of Chandragiri, the last representative of the Vijayanagar rulers of Hampi. A small fort was built in the settlement in 1644 and a town which subsequently became known as George-town, in the area of Fort St George, arose north of it. The settlement became independent of Batnam in Java in 1683 and was granted its first municipal charter in 1688 by James II. It thus has the oldest Municipal Corporation in India, a fact which Tamil Nadu state governors are only too keen to point out at every available opportunity.

During the 18th and early 19th century rivalry between the British and French for supremacy in India, its fortunes waxed and waned, being briefly occupied by the French on one occasion. It was also the base from which Clive set out on his military expeditions during the Wars of the Carnatic. During the 19th century it was the seat of the Madras Presidency, one of the four divisions of British Imperial India.

Though it has long been important for textile manufacture, a great deal of industrial expansion has taken place in recent years and its concerns now include motor assembly plants, railway coach and truck works, engineering plants, cigarettte factories, film studios and educational institutes.

Orientation

The city may be conveniently divided into two parts. The older section of the city is west of the dock area and north of Poonamallee High Rd. In these narrow, busy streets and bazaars are the offices of shipping and forwarding agents, the bulk of the cheaper hotels and cafes, other large office buildings and the GPO and American Express. Its main focal point is Parry's Corner/Popham's Broadway which runs alongside the High Court Buildings. The official name of this road is Netaji Subhash Bose Rd, but everyone knows it simply as Parry's Corner. Along this road are the municipal bus terminals and just off it, along Esplanade Rd, is the Tamil Nadu State Bus Stand and the Tiruvalluvar Bus Stand, the two long-distance bus terminals.

The other main part of the city is south of Poonamallee High Rd. Through it runs Madras' main road, Anna Salai, which is still generally known as Mount Rd. Along it are situated most of the airline offices, theatres, banks, bookshops, craft centres, consulates, the tourist offices and the bulk of the top-range hotels and restaurants. It's the Janpath of Madras.

Egmore and Central, Madras' two main railway stations, are close to Poonamallee High Rd. If you're arriving from anywhere other than Tamil Nadu or Kerala you'll come into Central Station. Egmore is the arrival point for most Tamil Nadu and Kerala trains apart from the principal Kerala expresses and the Nilgiri Express from Ootacamund.

Information

The Indian Government Tourist Office (tel 88520 & 89672) is at 154 Anna Salai and is open daily except Sundays from 9 am to 6 pm. As tourist offices in India go, this one on Mount Rd is good and the staff friendly and helpful. Leaflets and city maps are apparently in short supply, two people in front of me were offered maps without even requesting them whereas I was refused a copy until a calling card was produced. Indian officials fall over themselves over business cards, get some printed before you go!

A bus 11 or 18 from Parry's Corner or Central Station will take you to the Tourist Office. There is also an information counter at the airport, open daily from 9 am to 9 pm. The Tamil Nadu Government

Tourist Office (tel 840752) is at 143 Anna Salai (Mount Rd) and they too have an airport counter. Various other state tourist departments have information centres in Madras.

Liquor permits are no longer issued, so you don't need one to buy alcoholic drinks in the bars and stores – until recently Tamil Nadu was a 'dry' state, and without such a permit you couldn't buy a drink in a bar.

The Automobile Association (tel 86121) is at 38A Anna Salai. Apart from route information the organisation has accommodation available for members of any foreign automobile association at Rs 25/35 for singles/doubles. They also have car parking facilities on the premises for between Rs 3 and 10. *Hallo Madras* is a monthly tourist guide to the city with hotels, restaurants, tourist attractions, bus routes both local and further afield and lots of addresses. It's available from newstands.

Offices Immigration is at 9 Village Rd just off Nungambakkan Rd and before the junction with Sterling Rd – bus route No 10. Visa extensions can be obtained here and, if you're planning to visit the Andaman and Nicobar Islands, you can arrange a permit from here. Permits to these islands take about three days to issue – no photos are required – but you must know the exact date you intend going there, so arrange aircraft or boat tickets before you apply for the permit.

Banks American Express is at Binny Ltd, 7 Armenian St (PO Box 66). This Amex office is unable to cash travellers' cheques, including their own. It's also suggested that if you lose or have your Amex cheques stolen, you should have alternative sources of finance available if you report the loss here. Whilst I was there they told a German that he would have to wait six weeks for cheque replacement, despite the fact that he had reported the loss to the local police within 24 hours. So

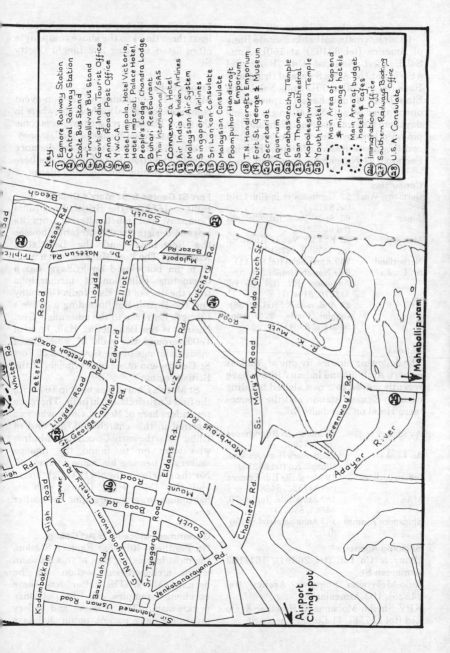

Key:
1. Egmore Railway Station
2. Central Railway Station
3. State Bus Stand
4. Tiruvalluvar Bus Stand
5. Govt. of India Tourist Office
6. Anna Road Post Office
7. Y.W.C.A.
8. Hotel Impala, Hotel Victoria, Hotel Imperial, Palace Hotel, Peoples Lodge Chandra Lodge, Buhari Restaurant
9. Thai International/SAS
10. Connemora Hotel
11. Air India ★ Indian Airlines
12. Malaysian Air System
13. Singapore Airlines
14. Sri Lankan Consulate
15. Malaysian Consulate
16. Poompuhar Handicraft Emporium
17. T.N. Handicrafts Emporium
18. Fort St George ★ Museum
19. Secretariat
20. Aquarium
21. Parathasarathy Temple
22. San Thome Cathedral
23. Kapaleeshwara Temple
24. Youth Hostel
25. Immigration Office
26. Southern Railways Booking Office
27. U.S.A. Consulate

○ Main Area of top end ★ mid-range hotels

○ Main Area of budget hotels ★ cafes

Mahaballipuram →

Airport Chingleput →

much for same-day replacement!

Other international banks include Bank of America (tel 82103) at 150B Anna Salai; First National City Bank (tel 810756) at 153 Anna Salai and Grindlay's Bank (tel 87474) at 36D Anna Salai. The State Bank of India has an airport office open from 6.30 am to 12 midnight on any day there is an international flight and to 8 pm on other days. Income tax clearance certificates are available from the Foreign Section, 121 Nungambakkam High Rd.

Consulates

Germany, West	22 Commander-in-Chief Rd (tel 82125)
Japan	60 Spur Tank Rd, Chetput (tel 665594)
Malaysia	23 Khader Nawaz Khan Rd (tel 443989, 443810)
Netherlands	739 Anna Salai (tel 86411)
Sri Lanka	9-D Nawab Habibullah Ave, Anderson Rd (tel 85316, 812270, 810831)
UK	24 Anderson Rd (tel 83136)
USA	Gemini Circle, 220 Anna Salai (tel 83041)

Airlines

The following airlines fly out of Madras airport. Air India and Indian Airlines have recently moved to a new shared building close to Egmore station and the Connemara Hotel on Marshalls Rd.

Air India	19 Marshalls Rd, Egmore (tel 847799)
Air Lanka	Connemara Hotel Annexe, Binny's Rd (tel 86315)
Indian Airlines	19 Marshalls Rd, Egmore (tel 847522, 848879)
MAS	189 Anna Salai (tel 88970, 88525, 88675)
Singapore Airlines	167 Anna Salai (tel 86156-8)

Shipping Agents

Binny & Co Ltd (tel 26894), 101/102 Armenian St
Indo-Malaysian Shipping Agency (tel 24525), 103 Armenian St
KPV Sheikh Mohammed Rowther & Co Ltd (tel 25756), 41 Linghi Chetty St

Linghi Chetty St has been renumbered at least three times so the above company is often listed as being 202 Linghi Chetty St.

Things to See

Madras is something of a non-event compared to the real marvels elsewhere in the state. The main reason travellers come here is to transact business (mail, money, tickets, visas) or to make a long distance travel connection. But while you are here it's worth visiting the following places:

Fort St George & St Mary's Church

Built in 1653 by the British East India Company, but much altered from its original design, the fort presently houses the Secretariat and the Legislative Assembly. The Fort Museum, open 9 am to 5 pm but closed on Fridays, has a fascinating collection of memorabilia from the days of the East India Company and the British Raj, including a 'Clive's Corner'. Entrance to the museum is free. Nearby is the Banqueting Hall, built in 1802, around the walls of which hang many paintings of the Governors of Fort St George and other high officials of the British regime.

St Mary's Church was built in 1678-80, the first English church in India. There are reminders here of Robert Clive, who was married in this church in 1753, and of Elihu Yale, the early Governor of Madras who went on to found the famous university bearing his name in the US. North of the fort is the old 1844 lighthouse and the 1892 High Court, with its lighthouse tower superseding the earlier one.

Government Museum & Art Gallery

On Pantheon Rd, near Egmore Station, the most interesting part of this museum is the archaeological section and the bronze gallery. The latter has some excellent examples of Chola bronze workmanship. The museum and gallery are open daily except public holidays between 8 am and 5 pm. Entrance is free.

Kapaleeshwara Temple

Off Kutchery Rd, in the southern part of the city, this is an ancient Shiva temple with a typical Dravidian gopuram. It's worth a visit if your time is limited and you won't be visiting the more famous temple cities of Tamil Nadu. As with other functioning temples in this state, non-Hindus are only allowed into the outer courtyard.

San Thome Cathedral

Near the Kapaleeshwara Temple at the southern end of South Beach Rd, close to the sea front, this Roman Catholic church is said to house the remains of St Thomas the Apostle. It was originally built in 1504 but rebuilt in 1893.

Parathasarathy Temple

Located on Triplicane High Rd, the temple is dedicated to Lord Krishna. Built in the 8th century during the reign of the Pallavas, it was subsequently renovated by the Vijayanagar kings in the 16th century.

The Marina & Aquarium

The sandy stretch of beach known as the Marina extends for 13 km, as far south as the San Thome Cathedral. The aquarium is on the sea front near the junction of Pycroft's Rd and South Beach Rd and is open daily between 2 and 8 pm except on Sundays when it is open from 8 am. Entrance costs Rs 0.25. Near the aquarium is the 'ice house', this relic of the Raj era was used, 150 years ago, to store enormous blocks of ice, cut from lakes in the northern USA and sent out to India by sailing boat. If you wanted a cold drink that was how you got it in the days before refrigerators and air-conditioners. There was once a similar building in Calcutta. Watching the fishing boats come ashore in the evenings always provides an interesting hour.

Guindy Deer Park & Snake Park

Situated close to Raj Bhavan at Guindy, on the southern outskirts of Madras, this is the only place in the world where it is still possible to see fairly large numbers of the fast-dwindling species of Indian antelope (black buck). It also has small numbers of spotted deer, civet cats, jackals, mongoose and various species of monkeys.

The reptile house is open daily between 9 am and 6 pm and entrance costs Rs 0.50. Probably the best way of getting to Guindy is to take the urban commuter train from either Beach Railway Station, opposite the GPO, or from Egmore Station. There are also regular service buses from the centre of Madras (15 or 45B from Anna Square).

Other

The Ramayana dance performances in December/January are worth attending. They take place in the dance school featured in the film *Phantom India*. It takes two hours to get there on a bus 19M from Parry's Corner and tickets to the evening concert cost Rs 5 to 25. You can sit on the floor in front of the stage for Rs 10.

Tours

Both the India Tourism Development Corporation (ITDC) and Tamil Nadu Tourism Development Corporation (TNTDC) offer the following three tours:

City Sightseeing Tour This includes visits to Fort St George, Madras Museum & Art Gallery, Valluvar Kottam, Gandhi Madapam, Snake Park, Kapaleeshwara Temple and Marina Beach. The tours are daily, start at 2 pm and end at 6 pm and cost Rs 25. Fairly good value.

Kanchipuram, Tirukkalikundram and Mahabalipuram Includes visits to three of the four ancient temples at Kanchipuram, the famous hill top temple of Tirukkalikundram and the 7th century Pallavan antiquities

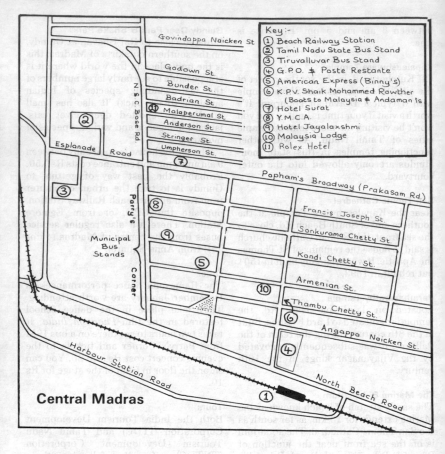

Central Madras

Key:-
1. Beach Railway Station
2. Tamil Nadu State Bus Stand
3. Tiruvalluvar Bus Stand
4. G.P.O. & Poste Restante
5. American Express (Binny's)
6. K.P.V. Shaik Mohammed Rowther (Boats to Malaysia & Andaman Is)
7. Hotel Surat
8. Y.M.C.A.
9. Hotel Jayalaxshmi
10. Malaysia Lodge
11. Rolex Hotel

at Mahabalipuram. A stop is made at the Crocodile Farm on the way back to Madras. There's a breakfast halt at the ITDC Travellers Lodge in Kanchipuram, and a lunch halt at the ITDC Restaurant in Mahabalipuram. The tours are daily, start at 7.30 am and finish at 6 pm, and cost Rs 40 (de-luxe coach) or Rs 55 (air-con coach). Good value if you're strapped for time, but otherwise a breathless dash around too many places.

Tirupathi This all-day return tour to the famous temple of Sri Balaji at Tirumalai in southern Andhra Pradesh is good value if

you don't have the time or the inclination to get there under your own steam. Going on a tour bus works out at about double what it would cost by public transport, but it's a long trip and the convenience is perhaps worth the extra. The daily tours depart at 6 am (TNTDC) or 6.30 am (ITDC) and return at 8.30 pm (ITDC) or 9 pm (TNTDC). The fare is Rs 105 (de-luxe bus) and Rs 130 (air-con), and includes the 'special darshan' fee at Tirumalai (Rs 25).

The tours by TNTDC can be booked

either at 143 Anna Salai (tel 88806) or at the Express Bus Stand, Esplanade Rd (tel 21835). Those by ITDC can be booked at 29 Victoria Crescent off Commander-in-Chief Rd (tel 890672, 88520) or at the Government of India Tourist Office, 154 Anna Salai (tel 88520/89672).

Places to Stay

There are three main areas for hotels in Madras. The top-range hotels are mainly along Anna Salai (Mount Rd) and on the roads off this principal highway. Around Egmore Station and along the section of Poonamallee High Rd between Egmore and Central Station are mid-range places interspersed with a few budget places. The cheaper hotels are in the old part of the city between Mint Rd, Netaji Subhash Bose Rd (Parry's Corner/Popham's

Broadway) and North Beach Rd.

Egmore Station is the most popular area for travellers these days, but places like Broadlands in the Anna Salai area and the Malaysia Lodge in the old part of town continue to be firm favourites.

Hotels in the middle and top end brackets will often have service charges and luxury tax tagged on to the regular room rate.

Places to Stay – Bottom End

There is one hotel in this category which is far and away the best in Madras, and judging by the number of travellers who stay there, many other people feel the same way. It's *Broadlands* (tel 845573, 848131), 16 Vallabha Agraharam St, off Triplican High Rd, opposite the Star Cinema. It's a beautiful, whitewashed

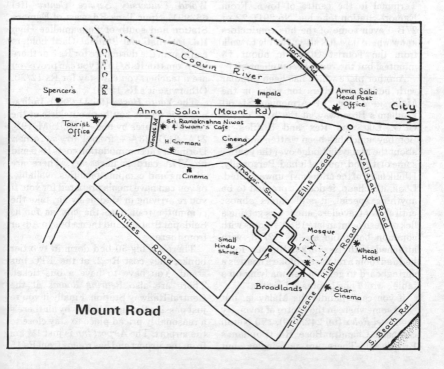

Mount Road

place with rooms on two floors set around three inter-connected shady, quiet, leafy courtyards. You'll be hard-pressed to find anywhere else in India with an atmosphere as tranquil as here. Most of the praise for this must go to the friendly and unassuming management and staff. Clean sheets are provided, the toilets and showers are scrubbed out daily with disinfectant, and the rooms, though simple, have a table and chair, two wicker easy chairs, a coffee table, and beds, of course. There is a comprehensive library, a good notice board, and you can hire bicycles here. Definitely the nicest hotel in India.

Rooms with attached bath are Rs 17/34 for singles/doubles. To get there take an auto-rickshaw – most of them know where it is – or bus No 30, 31 or 32 from Esplanade Rd outside the Express Bus Terminal in the centre of town. From Egmore Station take bus No 29D, 22 or 27B – even some of the bus conductors know where it is! It's also possible to walk from the Tourist Office in about 15 minutes, but the route is complicated.

Another place which has been popular with budget travellers for years is the *Malaysia Lodge*, 44 Armenian St off Popham's Broadway, at the back of the GPO. Like the Rex and Stiffles in Bombay, much has been written and said about the Malaysia Lodge over the years – some of it good, most of it bad. Personally, I think most of the criticism is unwarranted. Look, it's cheap, it doesn't pretend to be anything special, it still caters almost entirely for travellers, and it was getting a lick of fresh paint in late 1983. Rooms with common bathroom are Rs 12/18, with attached bath Rs 15/22. 'In our four-bedded room a rat used a bloke's head as a springboard to get to a banana lying on a table', wrote one impressed visitor.

If you can't handle the Malaysia, but want somewhere in the centre of town, try the *Hotel Rolex* (tel 24236-9), 190 Netaji Subhash Chandra Bose Rd (Popham's Broadway). There are no singles, but doubles are a reasonable Rs 35 with attached bath. Get there early in the day, otherwise it could be full.

Away from the centre of town a cheap, popular place to stay is the *YWCA Guest House & Camping Ground* (tel 34945), 1086 Poonamallee High Rd, which takes both men and women, and has its own restaurant serving western food. Single rooms here cost Rs 23 to 30 plus Rs 2 transient membership fee per head. The camping ground costs Rs 3 per person, Rs 2 per tent and Rs 5 per vehicle, if you have one. The rooms are clean and well kept and there's a big garden where you can sit and relax. It's right at the back of the Egmore Station. The *YMCA*, Netaji Subhash Chandra Bose Rd in the centre of town, is closed until further notice for renovations.

Another cheap place to stay is the *World University Service Centre* (tel 663991), Spur Tank Rd, west of Egmore Station and south of Poonamallee High Rd. International Student Card holders can stay in the dorm here for Rs 5 or there are rooms for Rs 8/15. If you can prove you are a teacher, you can stay for Rs 12/20. Otherwise it's Rs 15/30.

The *Youth Hostel* (tel 412882), Indiranagar, is on the southern outskirts of the city, 30 minutes by bus – 19B, 19M, 19S, 21A, 21D, 23A – from Parry's Corner. Dormitory accommodation costs Rs 5 and no YHA card is necessary. There are cooking and camping facilities available, or you can have meals prepared for you. If you're arriving in Madras by air, take the commuter train into the city as far as Saidapet Station, and then a bus to Adyar from there.

There's a big 50-bed dorm in two tier bunks, they cost Rs 2, at the TTC bus stand. You have to have a bus ticket. There are also *Retiring Rooms* at the Central Railway Station. Finally if you're just passing through Madras by air there's a reasonably priced place to stay close to the airport. The *Airport Inn* is just 1½ km from the airport and has rooms from Rs 15 per person up to air-con singles/doubles at Rs 100/120.

Places to Stay – Middle

Hotel Imperial (tel 847076), 14 Whannels Rd, right in front of Egmore Station, is one of the better mid-range place. Non-air-con singles/doubles are Rs 70/125, with air-con they're Rs 125/175. The Imperial is an enormous place with many different buildings surrounding a garden and courtyards. It has three restaurants, a bar, nightclub, disco and a good bookshop. There's also a travel agent, but I can't imagine how the man gets any business at all, as he knows absolutely zilch about the most basic of things.

There are a couple of other mid range places which are excellent value. The *Hotel President* (tel 842211), Dr Radhakrishnan Rd, has non-air-con singles/doubles for Rs 45/110, with air-con they're Rs 70-90/135-175. The *New Woodlands Hotel* (tel 83111, 83161), 72-76 Dr Radhakrishnan Rd, with non-air-con rooms for Rs 27-57/40-75, with air-con they're Rs 55-90/95-120. *Hotel Kanchi* (tel 83101) is at 21 Commander-in-Chief Rd, just down from the Connemara. It's also good value at Rs 60/90 without air-con, Rs 85-100/120 with air-con. At 69 Marshalls Rd, Egmore the *Hotel Guru* (tel 87939) has singles/doubles at Rs 40/75 or Rs 100/125 with air-con. It's reasonably clean, the staff are helpful and it's conveniently located.

If you're searching for something at the cheaper end of the middle bracket, the best place to head for is Egmore Station. Clustered around this station are several hotels which fall into this category. The cheapest of them are almost always booked out, unless you get there first thing in the morning. Also, at present, there's a lot of competition for rooms from Sri Lankan Tamils, who have fled from the violence in that country.

The best of these is the *Hotel Vagai* (tel 844031), 3 Gandhi Irwin Rd, a new place with pleasantly-decorated double rooms

for Rs 75 – no singles. It also has a reasonably priced vegetarian restaurant. After that, try the *Tourist Home* (tel 844079), 21 Gandhi Irwin Rd, which has friendly staff and rooms with attached bathroom for Rs 38/60. Or there's the *Hotel Ramprasad*, also on Gandhi Irwin Rd, a couple of doors up from the Tourist Home, which has rooms with attached bath for Rs 40/50-70 and its own air-con restaurant.

If both of these are full, try the *Hotel Impala Continental*, directly opposite the station on Gandhi Irwin Rd. The latter could be very nice – could being the operative word – as it has rooms overlooking a quiet, leafy courtyard in what is otherwise a fairly noisy area. But in the last few years the management and staff have got even slacker than they were before, and the room service has always been slack. It's a pity to see a place with such potential slide downhill. So get off your butts you idle bludgers and clean the place up! A coat of paint would go down well too! And some insecticide! Rooms with attached bath at the Impala cost Rs 18 to 35 – the singles are usually booked out.

Two other places to try are the *People's Lodge*, Whannels Rd, around the corner from the Imperial, which has singles/doubles with attached bath for Rs 30/60, and a gruff manager; or the *Hotel Majestic* (tel 842679), 20 Kennets Lane, opposite the Hotel New Victoria. The Majestic offers rooms with common bath for Rs 15/30, with attached bath for Rs 25/35. You'll be lucky to get a room in either of these places if you try later in the day.

There are a number of similar quality hotels on Poonamallee High Rd between Central and Egmore stations. There are, however, two major drawbacks to this area: the noise and pollution are horrendous. You can't get away from it by getting a room at the back of the hotels as they look out onto the suburban and main line railway tracks. Two you could try are *Everest Boarding & Lodging* (tel 30772-3), which has dorm beds for Rs 14, singles for Rs 19.50, doubles for Rs 39 and triples for Rs 54; or the *Hotel Devi*. The latter has singles/doubles/triples with common bath for Rs 15/28/40, with attached bath for Rs 19/33/45.

Also close by is the *Hotel Blue Diamond* (tel 665981), 934 Poonamallee High Rd, which offers non-air-con singles/doubles for Rs 60/90 and air-con singles/doubles for Rs 90/125

Places to Stay – Top End

The *Hotel Taj Coromandel* (tel 848888), 17 Nungambakkam High Rd, is probably Madras' most luxurious hotel with air-con singles/doubles at Rs 400-450/475-525. Others in the same price and quality bracket include the *Hotel Chola Sheraton* (tel 82091), 10 Cathedral Rd, with air-con singles/doubles at Rs 405-535/480-610. The *Adyar Gate Hotel* (tel 444676), 132 Mowbrays Rd, has air-con singles/doubles for Rs 350/400. *Hotel Sudarsan International* (tel 812061), 53 Montieth Rd, combines singles/doubles at Rs 325-340/400-430 with excellent food, friendly and efficient service, but somewhat run down and tatty rooms and facilities.

The old fashioned, but elegant *Hotel Connemara* (tel 810051) is on Binny's Rd, off C-in-C Rd, near the Tourist Office on Anna Salai. Air-con singles and doubles cost Rs 360 and 450 respectively and there's an excellent bookshop in this hotel. If you feel like a splurge, it also has excellent buffet lunches at Rs 50, recommended by a number of travellers.

The *Welcomhotel Chola* (tel 82091) is at 5 Cathedral Rd and has singles for Rs 170-190, doubles for Rs 220-240. The *Hotel Savera* (tel 810031), 69 Dr Radhakrishnan Rd, Mylapore, has air-con rooms for Rs 300/350.

Other, cheaper, hotels in this category include the *Hotel Atlantic* (tel 810561), 2 Montieth Rd, Egmore with air-con singles/doubles for Rs 65/110; and the *Hotel New Victoria* (tel 847738), 3 Kennet Lane, Egmore, with air-con singles/

doubles for Rs 114/170, and non air-con singles/doubles for Rs 90/144. The latter is probably somewhere between the top end and the middle range in quality and price. It has a working lift, good restaurant and helpful staff.

Places to Eat

If you'd like air-con comfort (so cold you should bring a sweater), a live soft-rock band (quite good on some numbers, totally untogether on others) then try the *Hotel Imperial's* restaurant on Gandhi Irwin Rd, opposite Egmore Station. The menu is fairly extensive but the food is often indifferent despite the relatively high prices. The waiters also have an annoying habit of hanging around like hungry vultures to see if you're going to leave a tip. Count on around Rs 30 for a meal including tea or coffee. The bar is open until 10 pm and beers are Rs 20 a bottle!

Also opposite Egmore Station the *Impala*, at the junction of Kennet Lane and Gandhi Irwin Rd, is an excellent vegetarian and tiffin restaurant. It's popular with travellers and locals. Typical south Indian vegetarian meals are served at lunch and dinner or you could have a masala dosa and coffee for Rs 3.50. They also have a similar place on Anna Salai near to Anna Salai Head Post Office. *Vega Vasanta Bhavan* is also good – tasty thalis and fine lassi. Remember that in south India 'meals' means lunchtime, ask for 'tiffin' at other times. The *Matsya*, in the Udipi Home at the corner of Gandhi Irwin Rd and Harris Rd has good masala dosas and air-con – when they switch it on.

In the Mount Rd area the *Buhari Hotel* at 3/17 is probably the best non-vegetarian restaurant. Excellent food, reasonable prices and again the air-con can be fierce. It's been popular with travellers for many years. For a delicious treat try the Rs 60 buffet lunch at the *Connemara Hotel*. The restaurant here is very good, try the lobster.

In the old part of the town there are

many vegetarian restaurants but few shine out. *Rama Krishna*, next door to the YMCA on Netaji Subhash Chandra Bose Rd (Parry's Corner), looks good but in fact it's overpriced, pretentious and the bureaucracy is astounding even by Indian standards. Your order passes from the person who takes your order, to a money taker, rubber stamper, order maker and finally to a waiter. And they call this self-service! *Madras Cafe*, off China Bazaar, two blocks from Popham's Broadway, has excellent Rs 5 thalis.

Another good place to have a meal along Anna Salai - or preferably a cold drink and a snack as the meal prices are quite high - is the *Fiesta Restaurant* at the front of Spencer's Building, diagonally opposite the Tourist Office. You can either eat outdoors under the fans or inside with air-con, and they're open every day until 11 pm. Both western and Indian food is available, the latter being better value. If you decide on western food, try the 'lamburgers'. Soup, bread and a main course will cost you Rs 20 to 25, including a cold soft drink.

At *Madras Farm Agencies*, 23 Poonamallee High Rd, you can get a respectable glass of milk. It's on the left hand side of the road walking towards the YWCA from the main station, close to the Everest Boarding & Lodging.

Since the state government relaxed the laws about permits for buying alcoholic drinks, the price has rocketed - apparently that is the compromise which was reached; no permits, higher prices. You should expect to pay a hefty Rs 20 for a bottle of cold beer in any bar these days, sometimes more. If you buy beer from a liquor store, it should cost around Rs 11 to 12 a bottle.

Getting There

Air Madras is an international arrival point for India as well as an important domestic airport. There are flights from Singapore (Singapore Airlines and Air India), Penang (MAS) and Colombo (Air Lanka and Indian Airlines).

There are frequent domestic connections between Madras and Bombay Rs 786, Calcutta Rs 995 and Delhi Rs 1183. Other Indian Airlines connections include Bangalore Rs 228, Cochin Rs 492, Coimbatore Rs 379, Hyderabad Rs 408, Madurai Rs 323, Nagpur Rs 645, Trichy Rs 239 and Trivandrum Rs 464.

Rail The rail journey to Delhi is 2188 km in length, taking from 40 hours and costing Rs 450 in 1st class, Rs 114 in 2nd. Calcutta is 1662 km away and takes from 27 hours at a cost of Rs 363 in 1st, Rs 93 in 2nd. The Coromandel Express is the fastest Calcutta train. Bombay trains take from 26 hours to cover the 1279 km at a cost of Rs 300 in 1st, Rs 76 in 2nd. The Bombay, Calcutta and Delhi trains all depart from Madras Central Station.

There are daily trains from Central to Ernakulam/Cochin - a 700-km trip taking 12 hours and costing Rs 187 in 1st, Rs 48 in 2nd. This train continues on to Quilon and Trivandrum. The daily Yercaud Express, also from Central, takes 10½ hours to make the 530-km trip to Mettuppalaiyam from where you continue by the rack train up to Ooty. Fares are Rs 152 in 1st, Rs 38.50 in 2nd.

Bangalore, 356 km away, is connected by frequent trains from Central. The fast Brindavan Express and Bangalore Mail take just seven hours at a fare of Rs 109 in 1st, Rs 28 in 2nd. Also from Central the daily Hyderabad Express whisks you to Hyderabad, a 794-km journey, in 16 hours for Rs 209 in 1st, Rs 53.50 in 2nd.

From Egmore there are a number of daily trains to Trichy - 337 km direct, eight hours, Rs 105 in 1st, Rs 27 in 2nd. They continue on to Madurai - 492 km, 11 hours, Rs 143 in 1st, Rs 36.50 in 2nd. The new Vagai Express takes only eight hours, it's all 2nd class but comparatively luxurious. Starting from Madras Beach Station on some days and Egmore Station on others, the Ganga Kaveri takes 18 hours to make the 666-km trip to

Rameswaram at a fare of Rs 182 in lst, Rs 46 in 2nd. There are also trains from Egmore to Pondicherry (a five hour, 200 km trip costing Rs 66 in lst, Rs 17 in 2nd), Chidambaram and Tanjore.

Apart from the two main railway stations, there is also a Southern Railway Booking Office on Mount Rd (tel 85642) which is open 10 am to 6 pm but can only reserve 2nd class. If you want tourist quota sleeping berths it's best to check first with the Southern Railway booking office next to Central Station (tel 39101). The booking hours at Egmore and Central are 8.30 am to l pm and l.30 to 4.30 pm for both classes.

Bus Both the Tamil Nadu State Transport and the privately-run Tiruvalluvar Transport Corporation have their terminals off Esplanade Rd. The schedule at the State Transport depot is entirely in Tamil (as elsewhere in the state) except for the Mhabalipuram buses. This does not present any real difficulties since an army of young boys attach themselves to every foreigner who enters the terminal and for 10 to 20 paise (though, naturally, they try for more) find you your bus. Services to most large towns in the state are frequent. The Tiruvalluvar schedule is in English.

There are ll daily State Transport buses (19A) to Mahabalipuram from 6.20 am to 8.15 pm. There are also ll number 19C buses from 6 am to 8.30 pm and five number 68 buses from 9.30 am to 7.40 pm. The 2½ hour journey costs Rs 4 to 5 depending on whether the bus takes the shorter coast route or goes via Chingleput.

Tiruvalluvar buses include:

Bangalore Five buses daily via Kanchipuram and Vellore from 7 am to 11 pm. There are also three other buses daily by KSRTC between 10 am and 10 pm. The journey time is between 7¾ and 9¼ hours depending on the bus. Fares range from Rs 27.90 to 36, up to Rs 50 with air-con.

Madurai Six buses daily between 7.30 am and 10.30 pm. It takes 11¾ hours and the fare is Rs 35.50. There are other buses bound for Shenkottah, Nagercoil and Trivandrum which pass through Madurai.
Nagapattinam 10 buses daily via Pondicherry – some also via Karaikal – between 5.30 am and 10.30 pm. The journey takes nine hours and costs Rs 26.10.
Pondicherry Six buses daily between 6.30 am and 11.30 pm. It takes about four hours and costs Rs 12.20 to 15.50, depending on the type of bus.
Tanjore 12 buses daily from 6 am to 11 pm. The journey takes about 8½ hours and

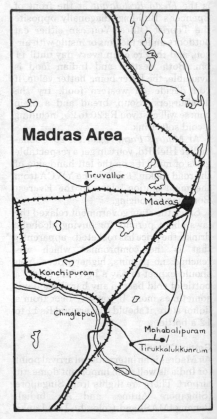

Madras Area

Tiruvallur

Madras

Kanchipuram

Chingleput

Mahabalipuram

Tirukkalukkunrum

costs Rs 24.10 to 30.50, again depending on the type of bus.

Rameswaram These buses go via Tiruchirappalli and terminate at Mandapam. There are three buses daily at 9 am, 5.45 pm and 7.45 pm. The journey takes 14 to 15 hours, and costs Rs 41.20 to 51.40, depending on the type of bus.

Trivandrum Two buses daily at 2 pm and 4 pm, which go via Trichy, Madura and Nagercoil. The journey takes about 17½ hours, and costs Rs 71.50 – Rs 109 by aircon coach.

Vellore Seven buses daily between 9 am and 4 pm.

Tiruvaluvar also has many daily buses to Tirupathi, but some of them take circuitous routes to get there, so make sure you get an express bus. There are at least three daily in either direction. The journey takes about 3¾ hours and costs Rs 13.50 to 16.

Andhra Pradesh State Road Transport Corporation (APSRTC) also operates buses out of the Tiruvalluvar terminal, but this service is mainly of interest if you're heading for Tirupathi. There are 17 buses daily between Madras and Tirupathi from 5 am to 9 pm.

While you're at the Tiruvalluvar terminal, it's worth picking up a copy of the *Bus Route Map*, which not only lists all the Tiruvalluvar services, journey times and fares – but not the schedules – but provides you with an excellent map of Tamil Nadu and Kerala. It costs Rs 2.50.

Boat The Shipping Corporation of India has two interesting services out of Madras. Their agents are K P V Shaikh Mohammed Rowther & Co, 202 Linghi Chetty St (tel 25756-7-8). Linghi Chetty St has been renumbered several times and their address is sometimes quoted as 41. The services are:

Andaman & Nicobar Islands See the Andaman & Nicobar Islands section for details.

Malaysia & Singapore The usual route is Madras–Nagappattinam–Penang–Singapore-Port Kelang-Penang-Nagappattinam-Madras but some sailings also include Trincomalee in Sri Lanka.

The ship is the *MV Chidambaram* and the journey takes 4½ days to Penang and 6½ to Singapore including a one-day stop at Penang. Singapore passengers can disembark while the ship is in Penang. On the return journey Penang-Madras takes 3½ days. There is a sailing about every 21 days. There are two classes of accommodation available to westerners: A grade and B grade. The former consists of a two or three-berth cabins with attached bathroom. B grade is similar to A. Dormitory and bunk classes also exist, but westerners are not permitted in any of them.

	Penang	Singapore
A grade	Rs 2574	Rs 3343.50
B grade	Rs 1778	Rs 2187.50

Fares include all surcharges and port taxes but there is an extra charge for staying on board in Penang if you are bound for Singapore. Student concessions are allowed only for nationals of Malaysia, India and Singapore.

Going to Penang or Singapore by ship might seem like a very pleasant alternative to flying, but before you get too excited about the prospect you should know that we've never heard anything but shock-horror stories about the trip. Typical of these is the following:

Tourist Class 1, which is two grades below deluxe is down among the migrant workers, most of whom sleep literally in cages, who are not toilet-trained and were prone to use the corridor outside our cabin. We had been told in advance by KPV Sheikh Mohammed Rowther (no relation if you add a 'C' – Geoff) that we would be sharing a four-berth cabin, the toilet would be shared with another similar cabin, and would have only Indian food.

We thought this well worth putting up with for three days to save Rs 800 each. What they didn't tell us was that (a) the food would be disgusting, (b) we would be sharing with Indians who didn't know what to do with a western toilet, and (c) we would be down amongst the cages. We chickened out and changed to first class before the boat sailed. But we did meet some westerners who survived the trip. Their advice to anyone who absolutely can't afford to spend the extra is to bring three days' food with them and to ignore the ship's notices regarding segregation of classes . . . . The food in first class was dreadful, and being a first class passenger is no help at all in getting through immigration.

On the other hand Gavin Young's book *Slow Boats to China* has a chapter on travelling Madras-Penang-Singapore on the *Chidambaram* and he doesn't make it sound too bad.

Getting Around

Airport There is an airport bus for Rs 10, one to three times per hour from 4.20 am to 10.10 pm. It stops at the major hotels and at Egmore Station and terminates at the Indian Airlines office on Marshall Rd after dropping off at the bigger hotels. A taxi will cost Rs 30 plus.

For those on a very tight budget the cheapest way of getting from the airport at Meenambakkam to the city is to walk to Ninambakkan railway station (about 10 minutes) and take a commuter train into the city. The train passes through Egmore Station and the last stop is Beach Station, opposite the GPO. There are frequent trains from 4 am to midnight. If you're heading for the Youth Hostel then get off the train at Saidapet Station and take a bus from there to Adyar.

Bus If you're spending long in Madras and will be using city buses then a copy of *Madras City Tourist Guide* (Rs 2.50) will be useful as it contains a full list of all the city bus routes. Some of the more useful buses include:

9 & 10 – Parry's Corner to Central and Egmore Stations. Other buses which pass through Egmore include 4D, 16, 17, 17D, 17E, 22, 23A, 27, 27B, 27D, 29A, 29D, 38B, 40, 43 & 71A.

11A & 18 – Parry's Corner to Mount Rd (Anna Salai). Other buses which run along the city end of Mount Rd include 3A, 4G, 5A, 11D, 11E, 17A, 17C, 18, 18B, 18C, 18D, 18E, 19S, 23, 23B, 23C, 25, 25B, 27A, 27D, 36 & 36A.

27D – Mount Rd to Egmore Station.

Taxis Taxis take up to five people and cost Rs 3 for the first 1.6 km followed by Rs 1.70 for each subsequent km. Waiting costs Rs 2.40 per hour. Most drivers will use the meters without being reminded of their existence.

Auto-rickshaws & Bicycle-Rickshaws Auto-rickshaws take up to two people and cost Rs 1.70 for the first 1.6 km, followed by 90 paise for each subsequent km. A little persuasion may be required for them to use the meter. The cycle-rickshaw wallah's are inclined to ask for more than the agreed fare on arrival – they may often ask for more than the equivalent taxi fare. You have to be firm.

Tamil Nadu

Population: 46 million
Area: 130,069 square km
Capital: Madras
Main language: Tamil

The southern state of Tamil Nadu is the most 'Indian' part of India. The Aryans never brought their meat-eating influence to the extreme south so this is the true home of Indian vegetarianism. The early Moslem invaders and the later Moghuls never made more than a fleeting incursion into the region, so Hindu architecture here is at its most vigorous and the Moslem architecture virtually non-existent. Even the British influence was a minor one, although Madras was their earliest real foothold on the subcontinent. There were a number of early Dravidian kingdoms in the south. The Pallavas, with their capital at Kanchipuram, were the earliest and they were superseded by the Cholas, centred at Tanjore. Further south the Pandyas ruled from Madurai while in the neighbouring region of Karnataka the Chalukyans were the main power.

Tamil Nadu is the home of Dravidian art and culture, characterised best by the amazingly ornate temples with their soaring towers known as *gopurams*. A trip through Tamil Nadu is very much a temple hop between places like Kanchipuram, Chidambaram, Tirichurippalli, Tanjore, Madurai and Rameswaram. There are also earlier temples in Tamil Nadu, particularly the ancient shrines of Mahabalipuram, and the state also has an important group of wildlife reserves, some fine beaches and a number of pleasant hill stations like the well known Ooty.

The people of Tamil Nadu, the Tamils, are familiar faces far from their home state. Many Tamils have immigrated to Singapore, Malaysia and Sri Lanka. Despite their reputation as hard workers Tamil Nadu is an easygoing, relaxed state.

Things drift by here and even Madras, India's fourth largest city, is a laid back, unhurried and uncrowded place compared to the northern cities of Calcutta and Bombay.

For the traveller Tamil Nadu offers excellent value, particularly in accommodation. Prices are generally lower than they are further north and in addition standards are often higher. There are many modern, low price hotels in Tamil Nadu. Food in Tamil Nadu is also good, you may get heartily sick of thalis while you're here, but they are consistently good and consistently low priced.

Architecture

The Dravidian temples of the south, found principally in Tamil Nadu, are quite unlike the classic temple designs found further north. The central shrine is topped by a pyramidal tower of several storeys known as the *vimana*. One or more entrance porches, the *mandapams*, lead to this shrine. Around the central shrine there are a series of courts, enclosures, even tanks. Many of the larger temples have

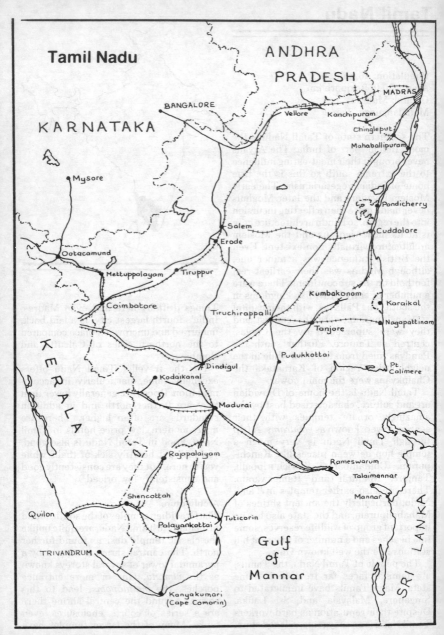

Tamil Nadu

ANDHRA
PRADESH

KARNATAKA

MADRAS

BANGALORE

Vellore Kanchipuram

Chingleput

Mahaballipuram

Mysore

Pondicherry

Salem

Cuddalore

Erode

Ootacamund

Mettuppalayam Tiruppur

Kumbakonam

Karaikal

Coimbatore

Tiruchirappalli

Nagapattinam

Tanjore

Pudukkottai

Pt.
Calimere

Dindigul

Kodaikanal

KERALA

Madurai

Rajapalaiyam

Rameswarum

Talaimannar

Mannar

Quilon

Shencottah

Tuticorin

Palayankottai

SRI LANKA

TRIVANDRUM

Gulf
of
Mannar

Kanyakumari
(Cape Comorin)

'thousand-pillared halls', although rarely are there actually a thousand pillars. At Madurai there are 997, at the Sri Ranganathaswamy Temple in Trichy there are 940, at Tiruvarur there are only 807.

The whole complex, which often covers an enormous area, is surrounded by a high wall with entrances through towering gopurams. These rectangular, pyramidal towers are the most notable element of Dravidian design. They are often 50 or more metres high, but size alone is not what makes them so interesting – they are generally completely covered with sculptures of gods, demons, mortals and animals. The towers positively teem with life, they're as crowded and busy as any Indian city street. Furthermore, many of them are painted in such a technicolor fashion that the whole effect is like some sort of Hindu Disneyland. This is no recent innovation – like classical Greek statues they were all painted at one time.

Tourist Bungalows

As in other states the tourist bungalows are good value but the Tamil Nadu Tourist Development Council (TTDC) have renamed all their various Tourist Bungalows as *Hotel Tamil Nadu*. One traveller reported that on several occasions in Tamil Nadu she was told that no rooms were available in Tourist Bungalows. Only for vacant rooms to mysteriously appear after she'd stood around and complained for a while!

VELLORE (population 150,000)

Almost the only reason to come to Vellore, 145 km from Madras, is to see the 16th century Vijayanagar fort and the Jalakanteshwara Temple inside it. Both the moated fort and the temple are in an excellent state of preservation. Other than the fort and temple, Vellore is a fascinating semi-rural bazaar town, full of bullock carts and street markets. It's a photographer's paradise. It also has, surprisingly, one of the best hospitals in India.

The Fort

The fort is constructed out of granite blocks and has a moat supplied from a subterranean drain fed by a tank. It was built by Sinna Bommi Nayak, a vassal chieftain under the Vijayanagar kings Sada Sivaraja and Sriranga Maharaja, in the 16th century. It later became the fortress of Mortaza Ali, the brother-in-law of Chanda Sahib, who claimed the Arcot throne, and was taken by the Adil Shahi Sultans of Bijapur in 1676. It then passed briefly into the hands of the Marathas until they in turn were displaced by Daud Khan of Delhi in 1760.

The British were next to occupy the fort, following the fall of Srirangapatnam and the death of Tipu Sultan, and they used it as a prison for Tipu's sons and daughters. It's the Windsor Castle of southern India and the only one of its kind in Tamil Nadu. There is no entry charge to the fort and it is open daily. It is now occupied by various public buildings and private offices.

Jalakanteshwara Temple

The Jalakanteshwara Temple was constructed about the same time as the fort (around 1566) and is a gem of late Vijayanagar architecture. The stone carvings are superb and in an excellent state of preservation. You won't see Vijayanagar relics like this outside of Hampi. It ceased to be used following the invasions by the Adil Shahis of Bijapur, the Marathas and the Carnatic Nawabs when it was occupied as a garrison and desecrated.

For many years it was maintained by the Archaeological Survey of India as a museum but in 1981 it was rededicated as a Shiva temple. The idol, which had been removed when Vellore was threatened by a Moslem army, was moved back into the fort. Non-Hindus are still, however, allowed to enter the sanctum sanctorum

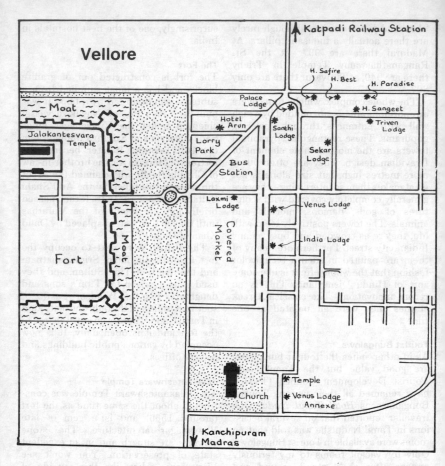

Vellore

Katpadi Railway Station

H. Safire
H. Best
H. Paradise
H. Sangeet
Triven Lodge
Palace Lodge
Hotel Arun
Santhi Lodge
Lorry Park
Sekar Lodge
Bus Station
Laxmi Lodge
Venus Lodge
Covered Market
India Lodge
Temple
Church
Venus Lodge Annexe
Kanchipuram Madras

Moat
Jalakantesvara Temple
Fort
Moat

and in any case the best carvings are outside. The temple has an elephant which you can often see walking around the market area, making collections from shops and stalls.

Christian Medical College Hospital
This hospital is a surprising find in such a small town. There are over a thousand beds in the main buildings alone and patients come from as far away as Malaysia, Sri Lanka and the Middle East. It was founded by an American missionary

in 1900 and has a staff of nearly 300 and over 1000 students and trainees. It is supported by 74 churches and organisations worldwide.

Church
The modern church, see map, is built in an old British cemetery. There is the tomb of a captain who died in 1799 'of excessive fatigue incurred during the glorious campaign which ended in the defeat of Tipoo Sultaun'. There is also a memorial to the victims of the little-known 'Vellore

Mutiny' of 1856, the year before the great Indian Mutiny. It was instigated by the second son of Tipu Sultan, who was incarcerated in the fort at that time, and was put down by a task force sent from Arcot.

Places to Stay

Hotel Sangeet, about three minutes' walk from the bus stand, has singles/doubles with attached bathrooms for Rs 14/28. There are basic lodges around the bus stand, along the main bazaar street and near the Sangeet, all similar in quality and price. The India Lodge, opposite the clock tower (built for George V!) over the covered market, is perhaps one of the best with rooms with attached bathrooms for Rs 10/20 for singles/doubles. It's secure, the management is friendly, but don't bother asking staff to wake you up if you have to get up early. Downstairs there's a vegetarian restaurant with typical meals on a banana leaf for Rs 3.

Other similar lodges include the Laxmi Lodge, Venus Hotel, Palace Lodge, Sekar Lodge, Hotel Safire and the Triven Lodge. Near the Sekar Lodge the Hotel Solai has rooms at Rs 16/32 – basic but acceptable. If you want something really cheap, try the Hotel Best, opposite the hospital.

Places to Eat

Hotel Paradise, opposite the hospitals, has good non-vegetarian food. Egg biriyani and coffee will cost Rs 5. There are any number of south Indian vegetarian places like the Palace Cafe or the Hotel Susil, just opposite the CMC Hospital, which has the best dosais in town. Good ice creams and ice-cold drinks are available from the Simla Ice Cream Parlour on the road opposite the fort entrance.

Getting There

Rail Vellore has two stations on the metre gauge line from Katpadi to Villupuram, the larger cantonment one is about a hundred metres from the Hotel Tamil Nadu. The nearest main line railway station to Vellore is at Katpadi on the main Bangalore-Madras line. Buses wait for the arrival of trains outside the station. The fare into Vellore is Rs 0.50 and the journey takes 10 to 15 minutes. Katpadi to Bangalore costs Rs 75 in 1st class, Rs 19 in 2nd class and an express train takes about five hours. If you're coming from Villipuram or Tiruvannamalai, however, Vellore Cantonment will be the nearest railway station.

Bus As elsewhere in Tamil Nadu there are the state buses and those run by the Tiruvalluvar Transport Corporation. The former are cheaper but the latter are generally faster and a good deal less degenerate.

There are 12 buses daily to Madras from 12.47 am to 6.30 pm. They go via Arcot, Kanchipuram and Poonamallee. There is also a non-stop air-con bus at 5 am daily, but you must get a 'priority booking ticket' the day before and be at the depot at 4.30 am at the latest for this bus at least in theory. The bus I was on was not only empty but stopped for a (very welcome) chai break at Kanchipuram. The buses cost Rs 9 and the journey takes about three hours.

There are five buses daily to Bangalore, departing at 2.25 and 10.25 am, 12.55, 4.25 and 10.25 pm. They go via Ambu, Thirupathur, Natrampalli and Krishnagiri and the fare is Rs 24 for the 5½ hour journey.

THE NORTH-WEST

Thali

This sleepy little village is 20 km from Hosur and 45 km from Bangalore. Hosur is on the Bangalore-Krishnagari-Salem route. Thali is noted for its pleasant climate and there's a tourist bungalow here.

Hogenekkal

This beautiful and quiet waterfall is 25 km from Dharampuri and 80 km from

Bangalore on the Bangalore-Salem route. Here the Cauvery River enters the plains and it's a great sight where the river dashes against the rocks. It's most impressive in July-August. A huge weekly fair is held in the nearby village of Pennagaram.

Places to Stay The *Hotel Tamil Nadu* (tel 47) in Dharmapuri has rooms at Rs 30 and dorm beds at Rs 6.

Yercaud

This quiet and low-priced hill town with its many coffee plantations is 33 uphill km from Salem. It's a good place for trekking and boating.

Places to Stay The *Hotel Tamil Nadu* has singles/doubles at Rs 35/50 and dorm beds at Rs 6. The *Hotel Shevaroy* is more expensive.

KANCHIPURAM (population 125,000)
Sometimes known as Siva Vishnu Kanchi, this is one of the seven sacred cities of India and was successively the capital of the Pallavas, Cholas and the Rajas of Vijayanagar. During Pallava times it was, on occasion, briefly occupied by the Chalukyans of Badami and the Rashtrakutas when the battle fortunes of the Pallava kings hit a low spot.

Kanchipuram is one of India's most spectacular temple cities and its many gopurams can be seen from miles away. Many of the temples are the work of the later Cholas and of the Vijayanagar kings. They're spread out all across the city and you'll need at least a whole day to see them. The best way to do this is to hire a bicycle for the day or to take on a rickshaw driver for the whole day (this should cost around Rs 15). There are no taxis or autorickshaws.

You should have plenty of small change handy when visiting the temples to mollify various demands for baksheesh by 'temple watchmen', 'shoe watchers', 'guides' and assorted priests. As it's a famous temple city plenty of pilgrims and tourists come here and the army of hangers-on is legion. Almost to a man, the people who attach themselves to you as 'guides' are a complete waste of time and will bore you shitless. They'll hustle you round at the speed of light, fill your ears with nonsense and then demand you pay them up to Rs 10 for the unsolicited pain of their tedious company. Give them a miss!

Kanchi is also famous for its handwoven silk fabrics. This industry has roots going back to the Pallava times when the weavers were employed to produce clothing and other fabrics for the kings.

Kailasanatha Temple

Dedicated to Shiva, this is one of the earliest temples and was built by the Pallava king, Rayasimha in the late 7th century, though its front was added by the later king, Mahendra Varman III. It's the only one of the temples at Kanchi which hasn't been cluttered with more recent additions by the Cholas and Vijayanagar kings, and so reflects the freshness and simplicity of early Dravidian architecture of which other examples can be seen at Mahabalipuram.

A few fragments of the 8th century murals which used to grace the alcoves are still visible and a reminder of how magnificent the temple must have looked when it was first built. If you have any interest in archaeology, the Archaeological Survey of India has an office opposite the temple and the staff are most willing to tell you more about the history of Kanchipuram.

Vaikuntaperumal Temple

Dedicated to Vishnu, this temple was built between 674-800 AD, shortly after the Kailasanatha Temple by Parameshwara and Nandi Varman II. The cloisters inside the outer wall consisting of lion pillars represent the first phase in the evolution of the grand 1000-pillared halls of later temples.

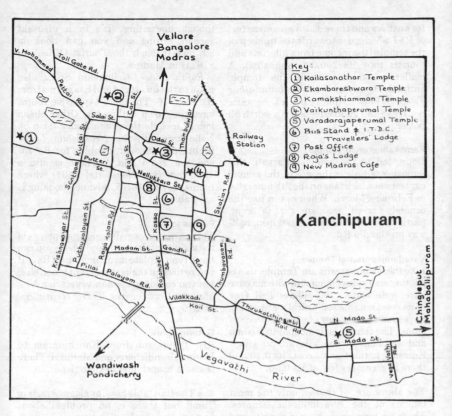

Kanchipuram

Key:
1. Kailasanathar Temple
2. Ekambareshwara Temple
3. Kamakshiamman Temple
4. Vaikunthaperumal Temple
5. Varadarajaperumal Temple
6. Bus Stand & I.T.D.C. Travellers' Lodge
7. Post Office
8. Raja's Lodge
9. New Madras Cafe

Ekambareshwara Temple

Dedicated to Shiva, this is one of the largest temples in Kanchipuram and covers nine hectares. Its huge gopuram, 59 metres (192 ft) high, and massive outer stone wall were constructed by Krishna Devaraja of the Vijayanagar Empire in 1509, though construction was originally started by the Pallavas and later added to by the Cholas. Inside are five separate enclosures and a 1000-pillared hall.

The name of the temple is said to be a modified form of Eka Amra Nathar – the Lord of the Mango Tree – and in one of the enclosures is a very old mango tree with four branches representing the four Vedas. The fruits of these four branches are said to have different tastes and there is a plaque nearby which claims that the tree is 3500 years old. Wishful thinking though this might be, it's revered as a manifestation of the god and is the only 'shrine' you'll be allowed to walk around as a non-Hindu and partake of the sacred ash (modest contributions gratefully accepted). You will not be allowed into the sanctum sanctorum as this is still a functioning Hindu temple but you may be able to go up inside the gopuram, good views from the top. There's a temple elephant kept here which suffers from the worst boredom-induced eczema and running sores that I've ever seen in India.

This is undoubtedly the worst temple

for hustlers and there's also a 'camera fee' of Rs 1 which goes towards the upkeep of the temple (the income from pilgrims and tourists tops Rs 200,000 annually!). A leaflet is on sale inside the temple entitled, *History of Sri Ekambaranathar Temple*. For a quick hit of esoteric nonsense and gobbledegook it's worth 80 paise!

Kamakshiamman Temple

Dedicated to the goddess Parvati, this imposing temple is the site of the annual car festival which falls on the 9th lunar day in February/March. When not in use the ornately-carved wooden car is kept, partially covered in corrugated iron, halfway up Gandhi Rd.

Varadarajaperumal Temple

Like the Ekambareshwara Temple, this is another enormous monument with massive outer walls and a 1000-pillared hall. One of its most notable sculptural features is a huge chain carved out of a single piece of stone. The temple is dedicated to Vishnu and was built by the Vijayanagar kings. Entrance to this temple costs Rs 0.10 and there is a 'camera fee' of Rs 0.50.

The above are, of course, only the most famous of the Kanchipuram temples. There are many more both in the city and outside it. Walk in any direction and you will come across others. The small Kailasanatha Temple, for example, is run by the archaeology department and is very interesting. It's closed between 12.30 and 4 pm.

Places to Stay

The *ITDC Travellers' Lodge* (tel 2561), 78 Kamakshi Amman, Sannathi St, is close to the bus stand, railway station and the Kamakshiamman Temple. This is the only middle or upper bracket place in Kachi and rooms (there are only three) cost Rs 115/240 for singles/doubles including meals. There is an attached restaurant where the food is 'healthy and copious

though unexciting'. It's in a pleasant garden setting and you can book in advance through the Tourist Office (tel 87621) in Madras.

Raja's Lodge, Nellukkara St, is also close to the bus stand and has rooms from Rs 10 to 30. The more expensive rooms have their own bathrooms. Other cheap lodges include the *Rama Lodge* (also on Nellukkara St), the *Neokrishna Lodge* (right opposite with doubles for Rs 15) and the *Town Lodge*. There is also a *Municipal Rest House* (tel 2301) where rooms cost Rs 10/15, advance booking is advisable.

Places to Eat

There are many small vegetarian places in the vicinity of the bus stand where you can buy a typical plate meal for around Rs 3. If you're tired of thalis there's not much else, but you could try the non-vegetarian *New Madras Cafe* or the *ITDC Travellers' Lodge*.

Getting There

Rail Trains run from Kanchipuram to Madras, Pondicherry and Madurai. There is also a branch line to Chingleput.

Bus The timetable here, as elsewhere, is in Tamil but there is no problem about finding a bus in the direction you want to go. There are frequent services to Madras, Pondicherry, Vellore, Chingleput and so on. Direct buses to Madras (2½ hours to three hours) cost Rs 6.50 (bus 141) but going via Poonamallee, where you change, costs less. To Mahabalipuram take a bus to Chingleput and then change. Vellore-Madras buses run through Kanchi, Vellore-Kanchi is about two hours for Rs 6.

MAHABALIPURAM (Mamallapuram)

Mahabalipuram was the second capital and sea port of the Pallava kings of Kanchipuram, the first Tamil dynasty of any real consequence to emerge after the fall of the Gupta Empire, and is world famous for its shore temples. Though their origins are lost in the mists of legend they were at the height of their political power and artistic creativity between the 5th and 8th centuries AD, during which time they established themselves as the arbiters and patrons of early Tamil culture. Most of the temples and rock carvings here were completed during the reigns of Narasimha Varman I (630-668 AD) and Narasimha Varman II (700-728 AD) and are notable for the delightful freshness and simplicity of their folk-art origins in contrast to the more grandiose monuments left by the larger empires, such as the Cholas, which succeeded them. The shore temples in particular strike a very romantic theme and are some of the most photographed monuments in India.

The wealth of the Pallava kingdom was based on the encouragement of agriculture as against pastoralism, and thus the increased taxes and surplus produce which could be raised from this settled lifestyle. Their early kings were followers of the Jain religion but this came to an end when Mahendra Varman I (600-630 AD) was converted to Shaivism by the saint, Appar. This conversion was to have disastrous effects on the future of Jainism in Tamil Nadu and explains why the majority of the temples at Mahabalipuram (and Kanchipuram) are dedicated either to Shiva or Vishnu.

Today, Mahabalipuram is just a small, but very pleasant and easy-going, village consisting of essentially two streets standing at the foot of a low lying, boulder-strewn hill where most of the temples and rock carvings are located. It's gradually becoming a travellers' haunt, though still in the formative stages, as people begin to rent houses and stay here for some time and cafes are set up catering to western tastes – usually seafood. After the noise, fumes, bustle and severely limited personal space of Madras and other large cities, Mahabalipuram is like coming to another planet. It's very relaxing and there is, of course, a long stretch of superb beach. Nowhere else in southern India will you will find this combination of an excellent beach, cheap accommodation, good seafood *and* the fascinating remains of an ancient Indian kingdom.

The sculpture here is particularly interesting because it shows scenes of day to day life – women milking buffaloes, portentous city dignitaries, young girls primping and posing at street-corners, swinging their hips in artful come-ons. By contrast other carvings throughout the state represent gods and godesses and any images of ordinary folk are conspicuous by their absence. Stone carving is still very much a living craft in Mahabalipuram, as a visit to the School of Sculpture will show. It's diagonally opposite the bus station and is open from 9 am to 1 pm and 2 to 6 pm, closed Tuesdays.

Information

There is a Tourist Office in Mahabalipuram though they only have a leaflet on the expensive tourist beach complexes further up the coast. They are open from 9.30 am to 1 pm and from 2 to 5 pm daily. There are good views over the whole town from the lighthouse. It's open from 2 to 4 pm and they charge a Rs 0.25 entry fee. No photography for 'security reasons'.

There is one bank is Mahabalipuram (Indian Overseas Bank) a few doors away from the Mamalla Bhavan where you can change travellers' cheques. The library near the Tourist Office here has a surprising little collection of English-language novels, history ooks, Hindu philosophic treatises, biographies of Gandhi and current Indian daily newspapers. An excellent little place if you need something to read.

Mahabalipuram even has a resident guru, the Guruji Thapas Yogi, who does yoga lessons daily at his ashram on Five Rathas Rd and is only too happy to have western visitors. If you get ill try the Anna Ashram Christian Dispensary.

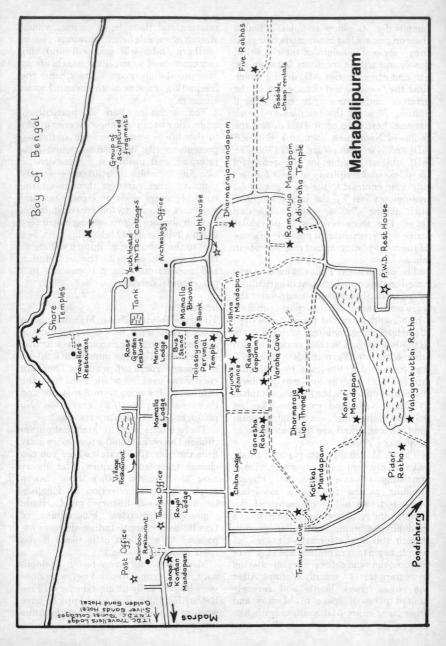

Mahabalipuram

Arjuna's Penance

This is one of the most interesting sights of Mahabalipuram. Here on the face of a huge rock, has been carved in relief the mythical story of the River Ganges issuing from its source high up in the Himalayas. The panel depicts animals, deities and other semi-divine creatures, fables from the Panchatantra, and Arjuna doing a penance to obtain a boon from Lord Shiva. It's one of the freshest, most realistic and unpretentious rock carvings to be seen anywhere in India.

Krishna Mandapam

This is one of the earliest rock-cut temples with carvings of a pastoral scene depicting Lord Krishna lifting up the Govardhana mountain to protect his kinfolk from the wrath of Varuna, the god of rain, on its wall.

Mandapams

In all there are eight *mandapams* (shallow, rock-cut halls) scattered over the main hill which are of interest for their internal figure sculptures. Two of the mandapams have been left unfinished.

Rathas

Here are the architectural prototypes of all the Dravidian temples with their imposing gopurams and *vimanas*, multi-pillared halls and sculptured walls which dominate the landscape of Tamil Nadu. The Rathas (literally temple chariots) are named after the Pandavas, the heroes of the Mahabharata epic, and are full-size models of different kinds of temples known to the Dravidian builders of the 7th century AD. With one exception, the Rathas depict structural types which recall the earlier architecture of the Buddhist temples and monasteries. Though they are popularly known as the 'Five Rathas', there are in fact eight of them altogether.

Shore Temples

These beautiful and romantic, wind and sea-ravaged temples are unique in India and one of its finest sights. They represent the final phase of Pallava art and were built in the late 7th century during the reign of Rajasimha. The two spires of these temples, containing a shrine for Vishnu and one for Shiva, were modelled after the Dharmaraja Ratha but with considerable modification.

The temples are approached through paved forecourts with weathered perimeter walls supporting long lines of bulls and entrances that are guarded by mythical deities. Most of the detail of the carvings has, of course, disappeared over the centuries yet a remarkable amount remains, especially inside the shrines themselves.

Saluvan Kuppan

This cave temple complex is about a half hour's walk along the beach, north of the TTDC resort and beyond the fishing village. There are two cave temples, one with a tiger's head carved over it and a relief cut in the rock. They're worth seeing.

Places to Stay — Bottom End

Mahabalipuram is a small village and cheaper accommodation is in limited supply. Depending on the season you may have little choice about where to stay for the first night or two. The other thing to bear in mind here is that very few of the hotel rooms face the sea, so they miss out on the cooling effects of the sea breezes. The top rooms in some of the smaller lodges can, as a result, become stifling by evening, even with the fan on. Beware, however, of thieving monkeys taking advantage of open windows. One woman wrote of losing all her tampons (difficult to replace in India!) that way.

A very popular place to stay is the new *TTDC Youth Hostel & Cottages*, off the road to the Shore Temples. The dormitories consist of two very large rooms, one for women and the other for men, and cost Rs 7.50 per night. Lock-up cupboards are available (Rs 10 deposit for the key). The only trouble with the dorms is that they're full of mosquitoes and there are no nets, so you'll be eaten alive unless you have repellent and a sheet sleeping bag. The cottages are much better in this respect and they face the sea, so you get the benefit of sea breezes. They're excellent value at Rs 30 a double with attached bath. There's a restaurant at the Youth Hostel, but there's no atmosphere to it. The food is expensive and you have to order it two hours in advance. Very few people eat there.

Another very good place is the *Mamalla Bhavan* (tel 50) facing the bus stand. The rooms here are cool, clean and well maintained, and you'll be made to feel very welcome by the affable Raju, who has worked here for a number of years. It's largely as a result of his influence that the hotel is so popular with travellers. Double rooms cost Rs 20 with attached bath, clean sheets and a fan. The whole of the ground floor is taken up by the best south Indian vegetarian restaurant in the village.

If the Mamalla Bhavan is full, the next best place is the *Mamalla Lodge*, which is run by the same people. Rooms here cost Rs 10/20 for singles/doubles with common showers and toilets. The staff here are pretty lethargic, but somehow they manage to keep the place reasonably clean. There are also some rooms in the new extension with attached baths, which cost more.

Apart from the above there are at least five other small lodges in Mahabalipuram – the *Merina Lodge* (singles/doubles for Rs 15/25), the *Pallava Lodge* (singles/doubles for Rs 15/25), the *Royal Lodge (singles/doubles for Rs 15/30), and the Chitra Lodge* (singles/doubles for Rs 15/25 and singles without fan for Rs 10). Their room charges are much the same as the Mamalla Bhavan and the Mamalla Lodge, but their standards are abysmal. It would be generous, but dishonest, to describe them as 'very basic'. In fact, most

of them are filthy, depressing hovels with walls that are blathered with the dessicated spittle of what appears to be generations of slobs; the beds have the appearance of tussocks of paspalum grass and the sheets (where they exist) bear the indelible stains of numberless nuptials and execrable practices. How much does a new sheet and a can of whitewash cost you idle, money-grabbers? Certainly no more than two nights' rent.

If you don't want to stay in a hotel at all, but prefer to rent a room in one of the houses of the local people, you'll have no difficulty finding one. You'll pay around Rs 50 a week, but don't expect electricity, fans and toilets for this. Most rooms of this type are in the Five Rathas village.

Places to Stay – Top End

Scattered over several km, north of Mahabalipuram, is a string of beach resorts ranging from the very expensive to the remarkably cheap. They all offer fairly similar facilities – swimming pool, bar, restaurant catering to both western and Indian tastes, games, sometimes a discotheque – but vary a lot in terms of the quality and siting of the rooms. Some are obviously pitched at those whose major concern is sun-n-sand activities; others more for the businessman in search of a congenial place to relax away from the city or somewhere to conclude a deal. Occasionally, you get remarkable mixtures of people at some of the resorts. I came across a bunch of very reserved Russian functionaries on annual leave, a group of American college kids from the mid-West out for a good time, and an Indian table tennis team!

Going north from Mahabalipuram, the first of the resorts is the *ITDC Temple Bay Beach Resort* (tel 51). This is the most expensive of them all. In fact, it's excessively expensive as it doesn't offer much more than any of the other places. Rooms in the main building cost Rs 300/375. Rooms in the separate cottages cost Rs 250/325. All the rooms and cottages are air-conditioned and there's a restaurant, bar (fiercely expensive!), swimming pool, tennis court and a lounge with daily newspapers.

Next to it is the *TTDC Beach Resort Complex* (tel 35, 36) a Tamil Nadu Government enterprise. I'd nominate this one as being the best value for money. Accommodation here costs Rs 65/75 or Rs 82/100 with air-con. All the rooms are in groups of beautiful and thoughtfully-constructed cottages facing the sea. Many of them are split-level with a toilet and lounge downstairs and a bedroom upstairs. They are kept spotlessly clean and the staff are very friendly. Like the other resorts there is a swimming pool, restaurant and bar.

Further up the coast is the *Silver Sands Beach Village* (tel 28), about two km from Mahabalipuram and the largest of all the resorts. There's a wide range of different cottages here; many of them constructed in such a way as to reflect local building styles, and certainly the widest range of facilities. What you pay depends on the season. In order of increasing cost they are: Season (15 April to 30 June); Low Season (1 July to 30 September); High Season (1 October to 15 December/1 February to 14 April) and Peak Season (16 December to 31 January). Non air-con cottages cost Rs 70 to 80 a single and Rs 100 to 120 a double; standard air-con cottages are Rs 100 to 160 a single and Rs 140 to 210, and de-luxe air-con cottages cost Rs 160 to 240 a single and Rs 200 to 325. There are some more expensive cottages right on the seafront. De-luxe air-con cottages include a refrigerator and a stereo. All rooms have mosquito nets. Facilities here include bar and restaurant (western, Chinese, Mughlai and South Indian), a discotheque, films, mini-golf, volley ball, a catamaran, table tennis and a minibus, which will pick you up from Madras free if you're staying at least three nights.

Next up the coast is the *Golden Sun Hotel & Beach Resort* (tel 45, 46), which has a total of 35 rooms. Lodging only costs Rs 120/155 or Rs 155/200 with air-con. The rates for meals are Rs 20 (breakfast), Rs 40 (lunch or dinner). If you stay here in the off-season there's a discount of a little less than 10%.

The last of the resorts is the *Ideal Beach Resort* (tel 40). This is the smallest of them with only 15 rooms (10 more are planned), and the owner wants to keep it that way in order to preserve the intimate atmosphere. Accommodation here costs Rs 50/70 or Rs 100/135 with air-con. There is a restaurant and swimming pool but no bar. This place has a very pleasant atmosphere.

Places to Eat

Wherever travellers congregate on a beach, you can be pretty sure that sooner or later a number of restaurants will be set up offering good seafood. Mahabalipuram is no exception and currently there is a choice of four. All of them turn out excellent, attractively presented seafood, as well as a range of sweets; all of them charge about the same price; all of them have thought carefully about the sort of ambience which they want the restaurant to project, so although they've all come up with different ideas, they're equally *muy tranquillo*. All but one has a good selection of contemporary western music and they all fall over backwards to cater for your every whim. Naturally, everyone has his/her favourite, but it would be unjust to single out one as opposed to another, since so much depends on the mood on a certain evening, and the people you meet that night.

Mahabalipuram is too small and too easy-going to inject that sort of big-city rivalry bias into it. Try them all and decide for yourself which ones you like best. They are the *Rose Garden Restaurant, Village Restaurant, Sea View Restaurant* and the *Bamboo Restaurant*, which is the 'meeting place' these days. The Village Restaurant has a particularly nice garden setting.

If you're looking for south Indian

vegetarian food, the place to go is *Mamalla Bhavan*, opposite the bus stand. You can eat well and cheaply here. Round the back of the main restaurant is the special thali section. They have different thalis every day for Rs 6 and they're really excellent – but *lunchtime only*. The 'best vegetarian food I had in India', said one happy traveller. When all the seafood restaurants are pulling down the shutters, and even the 'Wine Store' has closed, you'll find many travellers and local people gathering for a final nightcap at the chai stall at the top of the road which leads down to the Shore Temples.

Getting There
Bus Buses 19A, 19C and 68 go to Madras. The 2½ hour journey costs Rs 5.50 or 6.50 depending on whether you go by the coast route or the Chingleput route and there are frequent departures. Direct buses leave for Pondicherry at 7.30 am and 6.30 pm. The 2-1/2 hour journey costs Rs 5.50. Get there early if you want a seat. Every one to two hours a bus departs for Chingleput, the one-hour journey costs Rs 2.50. This is the bus to take if you want to go to Tirukkalikundram.

It's theoretically possible to get to Pondicherry via Chingleput rather than taking the direct bus, but you should resist the temptation. The buses all arrive full from Madras and most of them don't even stop. You'll be stuck there for hours. The Mahabalipuram Tourist Office will tell you, with gay abandon, that it's possible and even give you bus numbers and arrival times at Chingleput. Don't try it. If, however, you're a glutton for punishment, the buses are 188 and 188A and times scheduled are 7.30 am, 8 am, 10.30 am, 6 pm and 7.30 pm. The fare is Rs 7.50. But don't do it!

Getting Around
Bicycles are available for hire in the village if you want to visit Tirukkalilkundram or the Crocodile Farm. The cycle shop is about half-way between the Mamalla Lodge and the Mamalla Bhavan (you can't miss it – it's the only likely looking shop) They cost Rs 6 per day or less, if you hire by the hour. There's no fuss, no deposit. Just write your name and passport number in the book.

Things to Buy
Mahabalipuram has revived the ancient crafts of the Pallava stone masons and sculptors, and the town awakes every day to the sound of chisels chipping away at pieces of granite. There are several places where this is being done and there is some excellent work turned out. The yards here have contracts to supply images of deities and restoration pieces to many temples throughout India and Sri Lanka. Some of the smaller works are available for sale in the craft shops which line the road from the bus stand to the Rose Garden Restaurant.

Also for sale in these shops are soapstone images of Hindu gods, wood carvings, jewellery and bangles made from sea shells and other similar products. This is one of the best places to buy soapstone work. Prices are very reasonable (although you must bargain), and there are few other places in southern India where you'll find such work.

OTHER PLACES AROUND MADRAS
Chingleput & Kovelong
Chingleput is on the Mahabalipuram-Madras road and has the ruins of an ancient Vijayanagar fort which had a chequered history during the British period. On the coast, Kovelong is a fishing settlement with a fine beach.

Tirukkalikundram (Tirukazhukundram)
This pilgrimage centre, 14 km from Mahabalipuram, with its hill-top temple is famous as the place where two eagles come to be fed by a priest every day. Legend has it that they come from Varanasi (Benares). India, of course, is full of such legends. What most guide books ignore about this place, however, is the

amazing temple complex with its enormous gopurams at the base of the hill. It's very impressive and seemingly little visited but well worth the effort. You can get here from Mahabalipuram either by bus or by bicycle.

Crocodile Farm

Located about 15 km from Mahabalipuram on the road to Madras, this farm is engaged in breeding crocodiles to augment their population in the wildlife sanctuaries of India. There are now only several hundred of these reptiles left. They welcome visitors and you can see all sizes from the newly-hatched to the adults. The farm is signposted so you can't miss it. Probably the best way of getting there is by bicycle, although you can take any Madras bus from Mahabalipuram.

Vedanthangal

This is one of India's major bird sanctuaries, 80 km from Madras. There's a Rest House and an observatory tower here. Peak time is immediately after the end of the rainy season when great numbers of aquatic birds flock here. Between 3 and 6 pm is the best time to see them.

Tiruvannamalai

Further south towards Pondicherry, a 66 km detour inland from Tindivanam will bring you to this temple town. There are over 100 temples here but the Shiva-Parvati temple of Arunachaleswar is said to be the largest in India. The main gopuram is 66 metres high and has 13 storeys and there is a 1000-pillared hall. The splendid old fortress of Gingee can be visited between here and Pondicherry.

Places to Stay You can stay at the *Park Hotel* or the *Modern Cafe* in Tiruvannamalai.

Gingee

About 150 km south-east of Madras, Gingee (pronounced 'shingee') is on the road to Tiruvannamalai. There is an interesting complex of forts, built mainly around 1200 AD by the Vijayanagar empire. On three separate hills, the fort is joined by three km of fortified walls. The buildings – a granary, audience hall, Shiva temple, a mosque in memory of a favourite general – are fairly ordinary but the landscape is impressive. The mountains are all covered by huge boulders. Gingee is pleasantly free of postcard sellers and the like; in fact it's quite deserted.

PONDICHERRY (population 400,000)

Formerly a French colony which was settled in the early part of the 18th century, Pondicherry became part of the Indian Union in the early '50s when the French voluntarily relinquished control. Together with the other former French enclaves of Karaikal (also in Tamil Nadu), Mahe (Kerala) and Yanam (Andhra Pradesh), it now forms the Union Territory of Pondicherry.

The tourist literature about this place will give you the impression that it's an enduring pocket of French culture on the Indian sub-continent, but it's really nothing of the sort. The only visible French influence which remains are the red *kepis* and belts worn by the local police, the huge French Consulate-General which, together with the predictable Hotel de Ville, dominates the waterfront, and a few streets around the central square which exude a Mediterranean ambience. Apart from that, it's as Indian as anywhere else in India although it is relatively well lit, paved and laid out. It certainly doesn't compare with Goa's Portuguese or Darjeeling's English flavour. English is spoken everywhere, even the signs are in English or Tamil – not French. The name Pondicherry itself may soon disappear to be replaced by the older name, Puducherry, if a recent state government resolution is put into effect.

The main reason people visit Pondicherry is to see the Sri Aurobindo Ashram and its off-shoot, Auroville, 10 km outside

1 Government Square	12 International Guest House
2 Bus Station	(Ashram accommodation)
3 State Bank of India	13 Ellora Hotel
4 GPO	14 Amala Lodge (main building)
5 Sri Aurobindo Ashram	15 Amala Lodge (annexe)
6 Ashram Beach Office & Auroville	16 Geekay Lodge
Information Centre	17 Market
7 French Consulate-General	18 Aristo Hotel
8 French Institute	19 Venus Bar
9 Foreigners' Registration Office	20 Tourist Informaiton Office
10 Government Tourist Home	21 Air India
11 Park Guest House	
(Ashram accommodation)	

of town. The ashram, founded by Sri Aurobindo in 1926, is one of the most popular with westerners in India, and also one of the most affluent. Its spiritual tenets are based on a synthesis between yoga and modern science. After Aurobindo's death, spiritual authority passed to one of his devotees, a French woman known as 'The Mother', who herself died in 1973, aged 97. Although the Ashram underwrites and promotes a lot of cultural and educational activities in Pondicherry, it's very unpopular with local people since it owns virtually everything worth owning in the union territory but refuses to allow local participation in the running of the society.

Orientation

The town is constructed on a grid plan surrounded by a more-or-less circular boulevard so it's easy to find your way around. The Aurobindo Ashram, its offices, educational institutes and guest houses are all clustered around the streets between the waterfront and the drain to the left of the central Government Square. The French Consulate-General is also in this area. The streets in this part of town are very attractive and strongly reflect French influence.

Most of the hotels are to be found along Rangapillai St, which connects West Boulevard with the Government Tourist Home (the best of the mid-range) and the

super-cheap Youth Hostel next door. These are on the southern edge of town close to the railway station. Auroville lies 10 km to the north-west of town. If you're planning on having a look around there, it's best to rent a bicycle for the day since everything is very spread out.

Note there's a good deal of Indianisation of street names taking place in Pondicherry, so these may change slightly. For example, Rangapoulle has been changed to Rangapillai.

Information

The Tourist Information Centre has moved and is now in the Directorate of Information & Publicity (tel 398, 278), 19 Goubert Avenue (now Nehru St?). It has booklets about Pondicherry and street maps, but the Ashram Beach Office has a better street map for Rs 1.

The Ashram Beach Office and Auroville Information Office, Goubert Avenue, has information about the Sri Aurobindo Ashram and Auroville. They have maps of Pondicherry, backed with one of Auroville which has a descriptive outline of the latter, cost is Rs 1. Handicrafts made at Auroville, such as incense, jewellery, hand-made paper, are sold here.

The Auroville Information & Reception Centre is part of the Promesse settlement on the main road to Madras, outside town. There's very little printed information about Auroville here – they mostly seem to

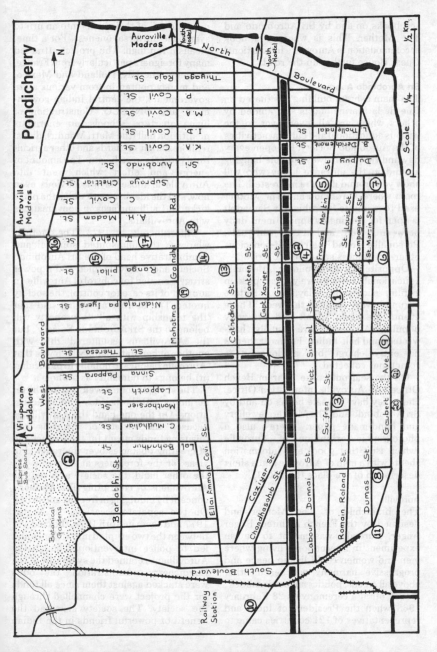

Pondicherry

N

Auroville
Madras

Youth
Hostel

North

Boulevard

Youth
Hostel

Scale

1/2 km
1/4
0

Auroville
Madras

West   Boulevard

Botanical Gardens

Express Bus Stand

Viluppuram
Cuddalore

Thiyaga Raja St.
P. Cavil St.
M.A. Cavil St.
I.D. Cavil St.
K.A. Cavil St.
Sri Aurobindo St.
Suproyu Chettiar St.
C. Cavil St.
A.H. Madam St.
T. Nehru St.
Ranga pillai St.
Nidaraja pa Iyers St.
St. Theresa
Sinna Pappara St.
Lapporth St.
Monthorsier St.
C. Mudholiar St.
Bohadhur St.
Barathi St.

A.H. Rd.
Gandhi
Mahatma
Cathedral St.
Canteen St.
Capt Xavier St.
Gingy St.

Vict. Simonel St.

Ellai Ammon Cavi St.
Chandhasohib St.
Caziyar St.
Labour St.
Domai St.
Romain Roland St.
Dumas St.

Su fren St.
Vict. Simonel St.
Francois Martin
St. Louis St.
Compagnie St.
St. Martin St.
Dupuy St.
B. Derichemont St.
L. Tholleindal St.

South Boulevard

Railway Station

Goubert Ave.

sell books on and by Sri Aurobindo and The Mother. This is where you book accommodation in Auroville's International Guest House further up the road.

Sri Aurobindo Ashram

The main ashram building is situated on Rue de la Marine and is surrounded by others which are all given over to the various educational and cultural activities of the Aurobindo Society. It's open every day and there are always people hanging around in the entrance lobby who will show you around if you're interested. The room where Aurobindo and The Mother used to meditate (Aurobindo's Samadhi) is open for viewing by appointment daily between 11.30 and 11.45 am only. Personally, I found its air of self-conscious other-worldliness somewhat contrived.

Opposite this main building is the main educational centre where you can pick up a film, slide-show, play, or a lecture virtually every night of the week. These events are open to all and are very popular. Audiences are usually half-western and half-Indian. For most there's no entry charge but a donation is sometimes collected.

On the seafront is the Ashram Beach Office and Auroville Information Office. Here they have for sale books on and by Sri Aurobindo and The Mother, jewellery and hand-made paper. There's also a photographic exhibition of Auroville (which isn't that good) and information sheets with a map of Auroville and a short description of the place (cost Rs 1).

Auroville

The brainchild of The Mother and designed by the French architect Roger Anger, Auroville was meant to be 'an experiment in international living where men and women could live in peace and progressive harmony with each other above all creeds, politics and nationalities'. It took off at a ceremony on 28 February 1968 when the President of India and representatives of 121 countries came to pour the soil of their lands into an urn to symbolise universal oneness. For a time, idealism ran high. The project attracted many foreigners particularly from France, Germany, the UK, Holland and Mexico, and money poured in from various state governments, the central Indian government and UNESCO. Construction of living quarters, schools, an enormous meditation hall (the Matri Mandir), dams, reafforestation, orchards and other agricultural projects were begun. The amount of energy and effort which went into Auroville in those days is obvious even now, and the idealism with which the place kicked-off still surfaces in conversations with Aurovillians.

Unfortunately in 1973, The Mother, who was the undisputed spiritual and administrative head of the Sri Aurobindo Society and Auroville, died and a power struggle ensued for control of Auroville. In support of its case for control, the society quoted The Mother as having said that 'the township with all its property will belong to the Sri Aurobindo Society', but the Aurovillians countered this with another of her statements which was that 'Auroville belongs to nobody in particular, (it) belongs to humanity as a whole'.

The struggle soon developed into bitter acrimony with both sides trading accusations. On the one hand the Aurovillians accused the society of diverting and misusing funds meant for the project and of creating obstacles over the renewal of visas for the foreigners at Auroville. On the other hand, the society accused the Aurovillians of corrupting The Mother's concept by indulging in free sex and drugs. On two separate occasions, in August 1977 and again in April 1978, the cold war between the two erupted into violence and led to police intervention. Though the Aurovillians retained the sympathy of the Pondicherry adminstration, the odds were stacked against them since all funds for the project were channelled through the society. The society also had the benefit of powerful friends in the Indian

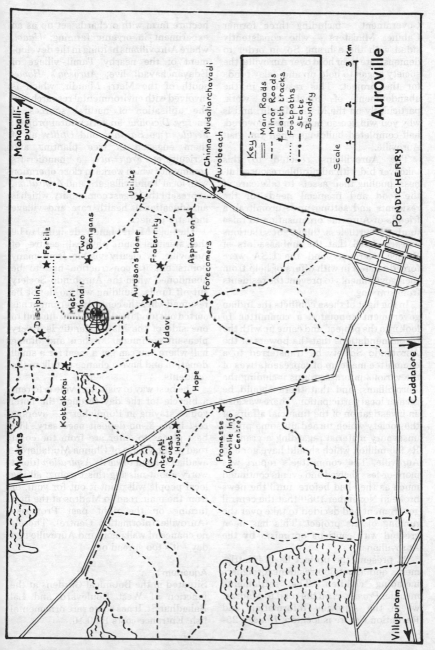

Government – including three former Cabinet Ministers – who consistently sided with the ashram. So, in order to demonstrate their hold over Auroville, the society began to hold up and delay funds for the project. This resulted in the abandonment of construction work, particularly on the Matri Mandir, and is why you will see so many moss-covered, half-completed buildings when you visit Auroville.

The Aurovillians reacted to this takeover bid with admirable resourcefulness, pooling their assets to take care of the food and financial needs of the residents and setting up 'Auromitra', a friends-of-Auroville organisation to raise funds. Nevertheless, things got so serious in early 1976 that the ambassadors of France, Germany and the USA were forced to step in with offers of help from their governments to prevent the residents from starving.

In the light of these conflicts the Indian government appointed a committee to look into the project, and came up with the recommendations that the powers of the Aurobindo Society be transferred to a committee made up of representatives of the various interest groups including the Aurovillians, and that there should be greater local participation. There was also an investigation of the financial affairs of the society which turned up some pretty unsavoury material regarding a grant of Rs 9.6 million which should have gone to Auroville. The committee's report was more-or-less shelved and events continued much as they had before, until the news broke in November 1980 that the central government had decided to take over the running of the project. This has been greeted with cautious optimism by the Aurovillians.

At present, the project has 14 settlements and about 550 resident foreigners including children. The settlements include: *Promesse*, on the road to Madras, where the Auroville Information and Reception Centre is located; *Hope*, a 25-hectare farm with orchards set up as an experiment in organic farming; *Udavi*, where Aurovillians helping in the development of the nearby Tamil village of Edayanchavadi live; *Auroson's Home*, south of the Matri Mandir, which is involved with environmental research and the utilisation of natural sources of energy; *Dicipline*, an agricultural project; *Fertile, Two Banyans* and *Utility*, all of them engaged in tree planting and agriculture; *Fraternity*, a handicrafts community which works in close operation with local Tamil villagers, and *Aspiration*, at present the largest community, which is an educational, health care and village industry project.

The huge Matri Mandir, designed to be the spiritual and physical centre of Auroville, is clearly visible from many points but its construction had to be abandoned when the Aurobindo Society cut off funds. Building will no doubt be resumed when the central government has sorted out funds for the project. Just off to one side of the Matri Mandir is a very pleasant communal kitchen and dining hall where you can get a meal for a small donation and have a chance to talk to the residents.

The best way to visit Auroville is to rent a bicycle for the day through the hotel you're staying in Pondicherry – average cost is Rs 3, no deposit necessary. The best places to enter are from the coast road at the village of Chinna Mudaliarchavadi and head towards *Aspiration* (don't worry about missing this turning: all the local people will point it out for you), or from the main road to Madras at the first turning on the right past Promesse (Auroville Information Centre). There's no chance of walking round Auroville in a day – it's too spread out.

Aquarium

Situated in the Botanical Gardens at the junction of West Boulevard and Lal Bahadhur St. It has some rare ornamental fish. Entrance costs Rs 0.10.

French Institute

Located on Dumas St it was established in 1955 primarily as a research centre for Indian culture. Its vegetation maps are universally acclaimed.

Tours

The Tourist Information Centre and Excursion Centre (tel 398, 278), 19 Goubert Avenue, runs local sightseeing tours of Pondicherry and Auroville when there are at least 10 tourists wanting to go. They depart from the Government Tourist Home at 9 am and return at 6 pm. The tour costs Rs 7 and can be booked either at the Tourist Home (tel 694, 958, 968) or at the Directorate of Information, Publicity and Tourism, 19 Goubert Avenue (tel 398, 278).

Places to Stay

Whatever the locals may think about the Sri Aurobindo Ashram, they do have the best hotel in Pondicherry. And there are always a lot of travellers staying there (though tobacco smokers will have to severely curtail their filthy habit – there are not only people breathing here, but notices in all the public areas saying 'No Smoking'). It's the *Park Guest House* at the south end of Goubert Avenue in a superb location right next to the beach, and large enough to virtually guarantee you a room at any time of year. Double rooms cost Rs 40 to 50 with attached bath. The place has its own restaurant.

The other hotel owned by the ashram is the *International Guest House*, Gingy Salai St (tel 2200), but it's often full due to long-term group bookings. If there is room, singles cost Rs 18, doubles Rs 25, 30 and 50 and triple rooms Rs 45. There is a 10% discount for ashram members. The only thing I want to know about this place is who was the petulant, other-worldly wanker who was responsible for pinning to the notice board the following sign: 'Cleanliness is the first indispensible step towards the supramental manifestation. We cannot shelter hippies in our guest house'.

I probably wouldn't even have noticed it had it not been done in gold-tinted paint in a virtually illegible and pretentious pseudo-artistic scrawl. Wake up you people! It's 1984.

If the ashram guest houses are full or you want somewhere cheaper to stay, head for the *Government Tourist Home* (tel 694), Uppalam Rd, which is excellent value at Rs 8 a single, Rs 15 a double with a few air-con doubles for Rs 35. It's quiet, surrounded by lawns and gardens, well maintained and there's an attached canteen, which offers standard south Indian vegetarian food at normal prices. All the rooms have attached bath. Get there early in the day if you want a room.

There's a wide range along Rangapillai St. At the top end of the market is the *Hotel Ellora* (tel 2111) near the junction with Cathedral St, which offers singles with attached bath for Rs 15 to 20, doubles for Rs 50 and air-con doubles with attached bath for Rs 90. The *Hotel Seker*, 48 Rangapillai Street, has rooms with attached bath for Rs 25/40. *Hotel Aristo* has air-con doubles at Rs 125 and is well appointed and very clean.

Similar in standard, but with fewer pretensions, are the *Ajantha Lodge*, 144 Rangapillai Street, which is good value and secure at Rs 20/35 with attached bath, and the *Hotel Raj* with clean rooms for Rs 15 a single without bath, Rs 20 a single with attached bath and doubles with attached bath for Rs 35, 40 and 45. The *Amala Lodge*, opposite the Hotel Raj, is also good with singles/doubles without bath for Rs 15/25, with attached bath for Rs 20/35-40.

There are other similarly priced hotels along West Boulevard (eg *Geekay Lodge* and *RSK Lodge*) and Mahatma Gandhi Rd (eg *Hotel Swagath* and *Hotel Palace*), but regard them as emergency crash-pads as they're either outrageously over-priced or disgustingly filthy.

The cheapest place in town – and one which I highly recommend – is the *Youth*

Hostel (tel 3495) out at Solaithandavan-kuppam in the northern suburbs, which has dormitory rooms with beds at Rs 6, lock-up cupboards, bedside tables with lamps, a restaurant and cooking facilities for those who want to put their own food together. Not only that, but it's situated right on the seashore, so you get the benefit of cooling sea breezes. The only problem with this place is its distance from town – and perhaps the pronunciation of the name of the suburb! – but it's easy enough to get there on a rented bicycle. If you're only staying overnight, it's probably not worth the adventure.

There are nine guest houses attached to the villages at Auroville. They cost Rs 30 to 40.

Places to Eat

Hotel Aristo is probably the best restaurant in town. It has a 207-item menu with everything made to order so expect to have to wait at least 20 minutes before your food arrives. They put a lot of effort into the preparation and presentation of the food. Unfortunately, food here works out quite expensive. Fish masala, allu gobi and one nan costs Rs 20. They've also got very good ice cream.

Hotel Bilal, West Boulevard opposite the junction with Rangapillai St, is a good, cheap, non-vegetarian cafe where a meal will cost you Rs 5. Outside of meal times they serve tiffin. *Hotel Dhanalakshmi*, Rangapillai St, is a good vegetarian restaurant. *Hotel Liberty*, near the Tourist Home, is also good.

Although prohibition has gone out of style in Tamil Nadu and you no longer need a liquor permit to buy beer and spirits, this has only taken place against a background of steeply rising prices. So it's with a sense of relief that the quaffer of ale crosses the state border into either Pondicherry or Karaikal where the cheapest brands (Burtons of Bangalore) sell for a mere Rs 5.75 per cold 750 ml bottle. Even Golden Eagle and Kingfisher are only Rs 7.50 (bottles of the latter can

cost up to Rs 20 in hotel bars in Tamil Nadu and Rs 11 to 12 from a 'wine store'). Pondicherry is full of bars, but many of them would be at home in a Charles Dickens' novel. However, there are a few reasonable places; places where you won't feel an immediate and urgent need for penicillin after visiting. Try, for instance, the *Venus Bar* on Mahatma Gandhi Rd near the junction with Rangapillai St.

Getting There

Rail There is one direct train to Madras each day (the Pondicherry Express) but, since the line to Pondicherry is a branch line, all other journeys by rail involve changing at Villupuram. There are severall trains to Villupuram each day from Pondicherry. If you're heading south or coming back from there, you can avoid having to back-track from Villupuram by going via Thiruppapuliyar Railway Station, a short Rs 1 bus journey from Pondi.

Bus there are two bus stations in Pondicherry: the local bus stand is at the back of the roundabout where West Boulevard Rd becomes South Boulevard Rd opposite the Botanical Gardens, the express bus stand is about half a km out on the Villupuram Rd, past the Botanical Gardens.

It is possible to get buses to quite a few places from the local bus stand (and cheaply too), if you have a penchant for wasting time. Unfortunately, the timetable is entirely in Tamil, but that's of little consequence since it's a complete fiction. Every enquiry will produce a different response. In theory, there are buses to Bangalore (by VDS Travels at 9.30 pm; by TPTC at 7.25 am, and by RVS Travels at 11 am), to Madras (every 10 minutes from 4 am to 9 pm), and to Mahabalipuram (at 5.50 am, 9 am and 2.05 pm – Nos 188/188A). You'll probably be able to find a bus to the last two without wasting all day, but if you're heading south forget about this place, and go to the express bus terminal. The Mahabalipuram bus trip is a pleasant ride along the coast.

Tiruvalluvar operates out of the express bus stand as well as a few other private carriers. Here you can find buses to the following places:

Coimbatore No 591 at 9.30 am and 7.30 pm.

Kanyakumari No 533 at 2.45 pm via Madurai and Nagercoil.

Madras No 583 six times daily, the first at 2 am and the last at 10.15 pm. There also 17 other daily buses which call at Pondy en route to Madras between 12.10 am and 11.40 pm (mainly No 508).

Nagercoil No 550 at 8 am and 7 pm via Madurai and Trichy. There is also a No 523 at 9 pm.

Palani No 531 at 7.45 am and 8.30 pm via Tanjore and Trichy.

Tanjore No 557 at 10.05 am and 3.05 am. This takes about six hours and costs Rs 14.

Tirupathi No 593 at 10.30 pm.

A new express bus terminal is under construction a little further down the road, so things may change in the near future.

TANJORE (Thanjavur) (population 160,000) Tanjore was the ancient capital of the Chola kings whose origins, like those of the Pallavas, Pandyas and Cheras with whom they shared the tip of the Indian peninsula, go back to the beginning of the Christian era. Power struggles between these groups were a constant feature of their early history with one or another gaining the ascendant from time to time. The Chola's turn for empire building came between 850 and 1270 AD and, at the height of their power, they controlled the greater part of the Indian peninsula south of a line drawn between Bombay and Puri, including parts of Sri Lanka and even, for a while, the Srivijaya kingdom of the Malay peninsula and Sumatra.

Probably their greatest emperors were Raja Raja (985-1014 AD), who was responsible for building the Brihadesh-wara Temple (Tanjore's main attraction), and his son Rajendra I (1012-1044 AD), whose navies competed with the Arabs for control of the trade routes across the Indian Ocean and who was responsible for bringing Srivijaya under Chola control. Most of the Chola emperors were generous patrons of the arts and it was during their rule that Dravidian culture reached the pinnacle of its development. The temples, forts and palaces of Tanjore are all superb examples of this cultural explosion which had its roots in the early folk-art traditions originally developed by the Pallavas at Kanchipuram and Mahabalipuram. The wealth which underwrote all this seemingly endless construction came originally from the rich, fertile rice growing area of the Cauvery River delta which, even today, is the rice bowl of southern India. It was later augmented by the profits which accrued from control of the lucrative trade between China and India, following Rajendra I's conquest of Srivijaya.

But Tanjore wasn't the only place which was graced with Chola patronage and there are numerous other places, all within easy reach of Tanjore, with enormous Chola temples, the main ones being at Kumbakonam (45 km), Thiruvaiyyaru (13 km), Thirukandiyur (10 km) and Gangaikondacholapuram (71 km). There is also the enormous temple complex at Srirangam near Tiruchirappalli – probably India's largest – in which the Cholas had a hand. It's well worth putting aside several days to see Tanjore and its surrounding temple towns.

Orientation & Information

Tanjore is dominated by the enormous gopurams of the Brihadeshwara Temple. The temple itself is surrounded by fortified walls and a moat, and located between the Grand Anicut Canal and the old town. The old town, consisting of winding streets and alleys and containing the vast labyrinthine ruins of the palace of the Nayaks of Madurai, stands between

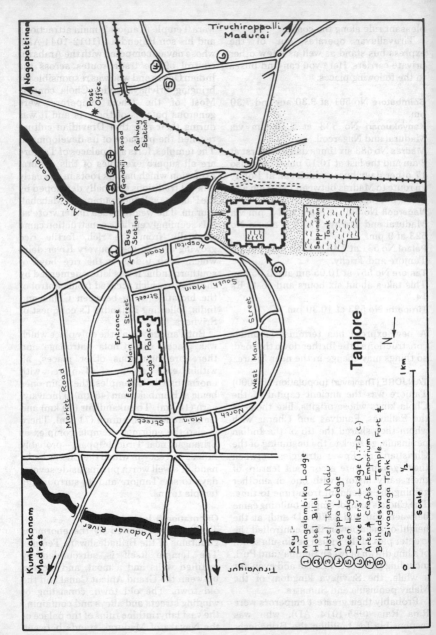

Tanjore

Key:-
① Mangalambika Lodge
② Hotel Bilal
③ Hotel Tamil Nadu
④ Yagappa Lodge
⑤ Deen Lodge
⑥ Travellers' Lodge (I.T.D.C.)
⑦ Arts & Crafts Emporium
⑧ Brihadeswara Temple, Fort
   Sivaganga Tank

N

Scale

0   ½   1 km

the Grand Anicut Canal and the Vadavar River. It was at one time surrounded by a fortified wall and moat, though most of this has now disappeared. Between the bus stand at the edge of the old city and the railway station runs Gandhiji Rd along which are located most of the hotels, a number of restaurants, the State Arts and Crafts Emporium and the GPO. Most of the other hotels are at the back of the railway station on Trichy Rd.

The Tourist Office (tel 613001) is in front of the Hotel Tamil Nadu on Gandhiji Rd. It is open daily except Wednesdays and Fridays between 8 am and 8 pm. On Wednesdays and Fridays, the hours are 8 am to 11 am and 4 pm to 6 pm. The Tourist Bungalow on Gandhiji Rd has good maps of Tamil Nadu showing all the main places of interest. If you're going to be spending any amount of time visiting the numerous temple cities of this state it's a good idea to get hold of a copy of this map which costs Rs 2.

Brihadeshwara Temple & Fort

Built by Raja Raja (985-1014 AD), this is the crowning glory of Chola temple architecture. It's a superb and fascinating monument, which you could spend several days exploring and still not feel that you'd seen enough. The dome on top of the apex of the 63-metre (206 ft) high temple, which encloses an enormous Shiva lingam (Hindus only!), is a single piece of granite weighing an estimated 81 tonnes. It was put in place by hauling it along an earthwork ramp six km long in a similar manner to which the Egyptian pyramids were built.

The gateway to the inner courtyard is guarded by a huge Nandi (Shiva's bull), also carved out of a single piece of rock. This Nandi is second only in size to India's largest at the Lepakshi Temple in Andhra Pradesh. The carved stonework of the temple, the gopurams and the adjoining structures is rich in detail and reflect not only Shaivite influences, but also Vaishnavite and Buddhist themes. Recently

discovered frescoes adorn much of the walls and ceilings of the inner courtyard surround. They have been dated to Chola times and were executed using the same techniques as were used in European fresco work.

Inside the inner courtyard off to the left is an Archaeological Museum, which is well arranged and has some interesting exhibits as well as wall charts and maps detailing the history of the Chola empire. It's well worth a visit and is open daily from 9 am to 12 noon and 4 to 9 pm. You can get a copy of an interesting little booklet titled *Chola Temples* for Rs 2.

The temple and fort are open every day and there is no charge for entry, but as this is still a functioning Hindu temple non-Hindus may not enter the sanctum sanctorum. This is really no great loss.

The Palace, Art Gallery & Saraswati Mahal Library

This vast, labyrinthine building of huge corridors, spacious halls, observation towers and shady courtyards in the centre of the old town was built partly by the Nayaks of Madurai around 1550 and partly by the Marathas. Some sections of it are now in ruins, but a substantial amount remains intact. Housed in this building is the Art Gallery containing granite and bronze statues from the 9th to 12th centuries and the Saraswati Mahal library established around 1700 AD. The library contains a collection of over 30,000 palm leaf and paper manuscripts in Indian and European languages and set of prints of Chinese tortures of prisoners on its walls!

All the above are open daily from 10 am to 1 pm and 3 pm to 5 pm, entry to the museum is Rs 0.50.

Other Temples

The Brihadeshwara Temple, though undoubtedly the most impressive and interesting, is only one of more than 70 temples in Tanjore! Many of these may be seen by walking around the old town.

Places to Stay

Many of the hotels are either along Gandhiji Rd between the bus station and the railway station, or at the back of the railway station itself along the Tiruchirappalli Rd – otherwise known as Vallam Rd. You're not going to find better value in Tanjore than the *Hotel Tamil Nadu* (tel 57 or 601), Gandhiji Rd. Run by the State Government Tourist Corporation, it's spacious, spotless, very pleasantly decorated and the rooms have curtains, fan, desk, wardrobe, comfortable beds with clean sheets, blankets and your own bathroom with hot water in the mornings. The rooms surround a quiet, leafy courtyard, and room service is available until 9.30 pm. The staff here bend over backwards to make you feel happy and comfortable. All this for just Rs 35 a single – you'll often be given a double for the same price – or Rs 50 a double. There are a few air-con doubles at Rs 100. There is an attached restaurant and recent reports indicate that the food there has improved of late. There's also a 'permit room' but at Rs 22 a bottle of beer, it has that air of being permanently deserted. Give yourself a treat and stay here. It's one of the best hotels in southern India. An easy five minutes' walk from the bus station.

Similar in standard, but more expensive is the *Ashok Traveller's Lodge* (tel 613007). Like the Hotel Tamil Nadu, it's situated in its own pleasant gardens, but costs Rs 50 a single and Rs 100 a double, both with attached bath and hot and cold water. An extra bed in a room costs Rs 30. The restaurant normally only prepares food for groups, the food is not so good anyway. Slightly cheaper is the *Ashoka Lodge* (tel 593-4), Abraham Panjithar Rd, which has singles/doubles with common bath for Rs 12/18, and singles/doubles/triples with attached bath for Rs 18/30/40. There are also two rooms with air-con, which cost Rs 66 a double. This is a large hotel with 76 rooms. There is no attached restaurant.

Towards the bottom end of the market,

there is the *Hotel Bilal*, Gandhiji Rd, which has singles/doubles without attached bath for Rs 6/12, and rooms with attached bath for Rs 12/30. Note there is a curious notice in reception here which states, 'Family cannot stay here except foreigners'. It's usually the other way round! 'It means that it is full of single Indian men who spent the better part of two nights peering in through the window, opening the shutters and banging on the door' wrote one visitor!

Another in this bracket is the *Sri Rajeswari Lodge* (tel 1476), 17 Pillaiyar Koil St, which has dorm beds for Rs 5 and singles/doubles with attached bath for Rs 10/15. You can also try the *Eswari Lodge*, 1338 South Rampart Rd near the bus station, which has no singles, but does have doubles with attached bath for Rs 20.

If you're looking for the really cheap end of the market, you could try *Raja's Rest House* (tel 501), right at the back of the Hotel Tamil Nadu, which has 30 single rooms with common bath for Rs 7, and a cottage with attached bath for Rs 13. Also in this bracket are the *Sri Krishna Lodge* (tel 1149), which costs Rs 7 a single with common bath and Rs 12 a double with attached bath, and the *Ajanta Lodge* (tel 736), 1306 South Main St, which has singles with common bath for Rs 7 and singles/doubles with attached bath for Rs 8/12. There are also four *Municipal Bungalows*, all of them around the bus terminal, which cost Rs 7/15, some of them with attached bath, others without.

Places to Eat

There are plenty of simple vegetarian restaurants around the bus stand and along the beginning of Gandhiji Rd with plate meals for Rs 3 to 4. One good vegetarian restaurant is the *Ananth Bhavan*, Gandhiji Rd, which has mid-day banana leaf thalis with curd for Rs 3.50. In the evenings it's a good place for tiffin (no meals in the evenings). *Sri Vasavi Cafe* at 1367 South Rampart does excellent thalis for Rs 3.50. The *Hotel Tamil Nadu's* restaurant has improved of late but in general in Tanjore it's thalis or nothing.

Getting There

Rail It's 8½ hours and 351 km between Tanjore and Madras (Egmore) at a fare of Rs 108 in lst class, Rs 27.50 in 2nd class. It only takes 1½ hours for the 50 km trip to Trichy at a cost of Rs 5 in 2nd class in a passenger train. To Villupuram takes 4-1/2 hours at a cost of Rs 66 in lst, Rs 17 in 2nd. Tanjore to Madurai is a 205 km trip which takes seven hours and costs Rs 68 in lst class, Rs 17.50 in 2nd. To Coimbatore is Rs 88 in lst, Rs 22.50 in 2nd.

Bus As usual the bus timetables are in Tamil, but (also as usual) it's no real problem since conductors shout out their destinations and most people speak some English and will direct you to the right bus. There is a sign in English announcing 'Can I help you?' A traveller reported that a traffic policeman 'escorted us to the bus for Trichy! Buses to most places within the state are frequent, the main destinations being Courtallim, Madras, Madurai, Nagarcoil, Palani, Shencottah, Trichy and Vellore.

Buses to Trichy depart approximately every 10 minutes from bay 11. The journey takes one to 1½ hours and costs Rs 4.50. Buses to Kumbakonam, where there are more huge Chola temples, also depart approximately every 10 minutes. The trip takes one hour and costs Rs 2.50.

Things to Buy

Tanjore is famous for *repousse* (metal work with raised relief) and copper work inlaid with brass and silver. Bronze images are made at Samimalai, 72 km from Tanjore, by traditional craftsmen.

The best place to see the range of crafts made in and around Tanjore is the Poompuhar Handicrafts Emporium on Gandhiji Rd, just beyond the Hotel Tamil Nadu. It's closed from 1 to 3 pm daily.

They not only stock repousse and inlaid copper work, but also excellent wood carvings like those on temple carts (the type which are drawn through the streets at festivals). These carvings are particularly cheap, and it's well worth spending some time sorting through them. Old brass betel boxes and cutters and Chola bronze pots are also interesting.

AROUND TANJORE

There are many smaller towns in the Tanjore area famous for their huge and impressive Chola temples. Their distances from Tanjore are in brackets.

Thirukandiyur (10 km)

The temples here are dedicated to Brahma Sirakandeshwara and Harsaba Vimochana Perumal and are noted for their fine sculptural work.

Thiruvaiyaru (13 km)

The famous temple here is dedicated to Shiva and known as Panchanatheshwara. Every January there is an eight day music festival held here in honour of the saint, Thiagaraja. Accommodation is completely booked out at this time.

Thiruvarur

The Shiva temple at this town, between Tanjore and Nagapattinam, was gradually extended over the years. Its 1000-pillared hall actually has just 807 pillars!

Kumbakonam (36 km)

There are four enormous temples here, of which the most important are Sarangapani, Kumbeshwara and Nageshwara. The largest of these is second only to the Meenakshi Temple at Madurai. The semi-erotic sculptural work is a feature of these temples. Once every 12 years a festival is held here at the Mahamaham tank. Thousands of devotees flock here as the waters of the Ganges are said to flow into the tank at that time! The next festival will take place in 1992.

Of all the temple towns around Tanjore

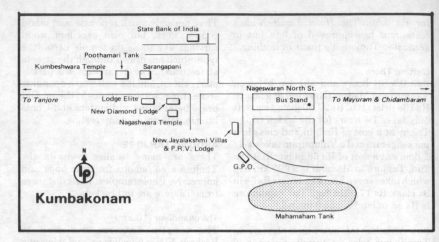

Kumbakonam

(map labels:)
State Bank of India
Poothamari Tank
Kumbeshwara Temple
Sarangapani
Nageswaran North St.
To Tanjore
Lodge Elite
New Diamond Lodge
Nagashwara Temple
Bus Stand
To Mayuram & Chidambaram
New Jayalakshmi Villas & P.R.V. Lodge
G.P.O.
Mahamaham Tank

this is perhaps the best to visit if your time is limited and it makes an excellent base to visit the nearby, and very interesting, towns of Dharasuram and Gangakondacholapuram. Kumbakonam is a typical, small south Indian town and well worth staying in. Get a copy of *Chola Temples* by C Sivaramamurti, published by the Archaeological Survey of India and costing just Rs 2. It describes the three temples in Tanjore, Dharasuram and Gangakondacholapuram. You'll find it in the Brihadeshwara Temple museum in Tanjore or in the Fort St George museum in Madras.

Places to Stay The *New Diamond Lodge* at 93 Nageswaran North St is very clean with doubles with shower and toilet for Rs 20. The *P R V Lodge* and *Lodge Elite* at 106 Nageswaran North St are comparable. Really excellent vegetarian meals are available at the *New Jayalakshmi Vilas*.

Getting There A bus from Tanjore, there are plenty of them, takes about an hour and costs Rs 3.50. There are few direct buses from Trichy, it may be easier to go first to Tanjore. The bus stops by the temples, they are all a couple of blocks from each other. To avoid full buses on the

return take a rickshaw to the bus stand further on. There are plenty of places to hire bicycles in Kumbakonam including one just opposite the New Diamond Lodge.

Dharasuram

Dharasuram is a small town four km west of Kumbakonam and the Dharasuram or Airatesvara Temple is a superb example of 12th century Chola architecture built by Rajaraja II (1146-1163). The temple is set back, behind the village, and is in a fine state of preservation and fronted by columns with unique miniature sculptures. In the 14th century the row of largest statues around the temple was replaced by brick and concrete statues similar to those found at the Tanjore temple – many of these have been removed to the art gallery in the Raja's Palace in Tanjore but are scheduled to be returned to Dharasuram in the near future. The sculptures representing Shiva as Kankala-murti (the mendicant) and a number of wives of sages who stand by, dazzled by his beauty, are remarkable.

The temple is little used at present but there's a helpful and knowledgeable priest here who speaks good English. This 'wrinkled, old retainer must be the only guide in India who is truly in love with his treasure,' was one report. The town is also a silk weaving centre.

Gangakondacholapuram (71 km)

The gopurams of this enormous temple dominate the landscape for miles around. It was built by the Chola emperor Rajendra I (1012-1044) in imitation of the style of the Brihadeshwara Temple at Tanjore, built by his father, and is dedicated to Shiva. There are many beautiful sculptures on the walls of the temple and its enclosures and a huge tank into which vessels containing the water of the River Ganges, brought by vassal kings to the court of the Cholas, were emptied. Like the temple at Dharasuram few tourists come to visit this temple and it is no longer used for Hindu worship.

Gangakondacholapuram is 35 km north of Kumbakonam and, like Dharasuram, easily visited from there as a day trip.

Chidambaram

South of Pondicherry, towards Tanjore, is another of Tamil Nadu's gems of Dravidian architecture – the temple complex of Chidambaram with the great temple of Nataraja, the dancing Shiva. The complex is said to be the oldest in the south and covers 13 hectares. There are four gopurams, the north and south ones towering 49 metres high. Two of the gopurams are carved with the 108 classical postures of Nataraja, Shiva in his role as the cosmic dancer.

Other notable features of the temple include the 1000-pillared hall, the Nritta Sabha court which is carved out like a gigantic chariot, and the image of Nataraja himself in the central sanctum. There are other, lesser, temples in the complex including ones to Parvati, Subrahmanya, Ganesh and a newer Vishnu temple. Chidambaram was a Chola capital from 907 to 1310 and the Nataraja temple was erected during the reign of Vira Chola Raja (927-997).

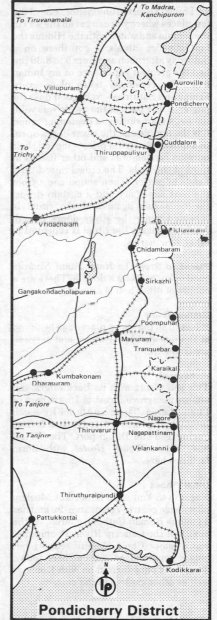

Pondicherry District

'This is', reported one visitor, 'one of the few places where you can get all the way in the temple and watch with the Hindus the fantastic fire rituals. I got there on a Saturday afternoon and from 6 to 8.30 pm had the greatest experience of my Indian trip'. The ceremony takes place every Friday and Saturday – very good days for prayer. '...the pace of the music was wild, the bells start ringing, a deafening sound fills the temple and the silver doors open. In a quick succession priests moved their burning candelabras and other flames in front of the idols. The crowd raised their hands in prayer. Then sound came from the next sanctuary and a curtain drops, the bells ring again and the ritual is repeated while the silver doors closed. Again and again the ritual is repeated in other sanctuaries'.

Places to Stay The *Hotel Tamil Nadu* is good value at Rs 32 a double. There are a couple of other hotels around.

Getting There
Buses to all the above places can be found at the bus stand in Tanjore and services are frequent.

Pichavaram
This sea resort with its backwaters and unique mangrove forest is 15 km east of Chidambaram. There is a Marine Research Institute at nearby Porto Novo, a former Portuguese and Dutch port. The TTDC has built a *Youth Hostel* with dorm facilities here.

Other Places
Nagore (45 km) is an important Moslem pilgrimage centre. Velankanni (90 km) has a famous Roman Catholic church. At the mouth of the Cauvery River, Poompuhar was a major Chola Empire seaport but only a small village stands there today. Trade was once carried on with Rome as well as other centres in the east.

TIRUCHIRAPPALLI (population 340,000)
Usually known by its shortened names of Trichy or Tiruchy, the city's most famous landmark is the Rock Fort Temple. This spectacular monument is perched on top of a massive outcrop of rock which rises abruptly from the plain and towers over the old city. There are a few other such outcrops on the way to Tanjore, one of which has a temple built on it, but none are as large or as tall as the one at Trichy. The Rock Fort Temple is reached by a seemingly endless, steep flight of steps cut into a tunnel through the rock and the views from the summit are magnificent.

The other landmark at Trichy is much less well-known, which is surprising since it's probably the largest – and one of the most interesting – temple complexes in India. This is the Srirangam Temple, built on an island in the middle of the River Cauvery, which covers a staggering 250 hectares! As though this were not enough there is another huge temple complex nearby – the Sri Jambukeshwara Temple. Both of these temples are visible from the summit of the Rock Fort Temple, shrouded in coconut palms. Each one of these temples is worth spending a whole day exploring. Very few travellers seem to find their way to Srirangam probably because of the fame of the other Tamil Nadu temples at Tanjore, Madurai and Rameswarum, which is a pity since the temples at Trichy are fascinating and deserve far more recognition. Don't miss them!

Trichy itself has a long history going back to the centuries before the Christian era when it was a Chola citadel. In the first millenium AD, it changed hands many times between the Pallavas and Pandyas until taken by the Cholas in the 10th century AD. When the Chola Empire finally decayed it passed into the hands of the Vijayanagar kings of Hampi, and remained with them until they were defeated by the forces of the Deccan Sultans in 1565 AD. The town and fort, as it stands today, was built by the Nayaks of

THE DEVOTIONAL BELL AT SOME TEMPLES DOES NOT FAVOR THE DIMINUTIVE DEVOTEE...

Madurai, and it was one of the main centres around which the wars of the Carnatic were fought in the 18th century when the British and French were struggling for supremacy in India.

Other than the monuments, it's a pleasant place to stay with a good range of hotels and facilities and, though spread out over a large area, it has an excellent local bus system which doesn't demand the strength of an ox and the skin of an elephant to make use of.

Orientation & Information

Trichy is spread out over a considerable area and you will need transport to get from one part to another but most of the hotels, restaurants, the bus stand and railway station, the Tourist Office, airline offices and GPO are all within two or three minutes' walk of each other in the so-called cantonment area. The Rock Fort Temple is situated several km north of this area near the banks of the River Cauvery. Further north, still on an island in the Cauvery, stand the temples at Srirangam. These latter lie on opposite sides of the main road to Madras and Salem.

The Tourist Office is situated at the front of the Hotel Tamil Nadu within sight of the bus terminal. It's open daily except Sundays and public holidays between 10.30 am and 5 pm. Both Indian Airlines and Air Lanka have their offices in the same building on Dindigul Rd. The telephone numbers are 23116 and 27951 respectively.

If you're thinking of flying to Sri Lanka, a good travel agent to approach is *Durga Travels* (tel 24501) in the grounds of the Hotel Ajanta, Junction Rd. They're agents for Indian Airlines and Air Lanka, and are friendly people to do business with. Note that Trichy is now the cheapest place from which to fly to Sri Lanka as there are no longer any flights from Madurai. (Other places you can fly to Sri Lanka from are Bombay, Madras and Trivandrum).

1 Rock Fort Temple	7 Selvam Lodge
2 Teppakulam Tank	8 Guru Hotel & Vijay Lodge
3 Bus Stand (State Transport)	9 Hotel Anand
4 Tourist Office & Hotel Tamil Nadu	10 Hotel Aristo
5 Tiruvalluvar Bus Stand	11 Hotel Sangam
6 GPO	

Rock Fort Temple

This monument, which can be seen for miles around, stands on top of a massive outcrop of rock, 83 metres (273 ft) high and is reached by climbing up 437 steps cut into a tunnel through the rock. It's a stiff climb but well worth it for the views from the top. Non-Hindus are not allowed into the sanctum sanctorum at the summit or into the Sri Thayumanaswamy Temple, dedicated to Shiva, half-way up, so a visit here tends to be a brief affair.

It's open daily from 6 am until 8 pm and costs Rs 0.10 entrance fee plus an outrageous Rs 5 if you have a camera (the only photographically interesting vista is the one to the north over the temples at Srirangam). You must leave your shoes at the entrance. There are no guidebooks for sale. At the entrance you can amuse yourself by offering the temple elephant a coin, which he takes in the tip of his trunk and passes to his keeper. You're rewarded by a tap on the head with the elephant's trunk.

Apart from the climb up to the summit there are a few rock-cut cave temples nearby which are worth visiting. They date from the Pallavas (6th to 7th centuries).

Srirangam – Sri Ranganathaswamy Temple

This superb temple complex is probably the largest in India. It's surrounded by seven concentric walls and has 21 gopurams in total. Many peoples have had a hand in its construction including the Cheras, Pandyas, Cholas, Hoysalas and the Vijayanagar kings, though the bulk of it dates from the 14th to 17th centuries. It's very well preserved and has excellent carvings throughout with numerous shrines to various gods, though the main temple is dedicated to Vishnu. Even the Moslems are said to have prayed here after the fall of the Vijayanagar empire. Non-Hindus are, of course, not allowed into the sanctum sanctorum but this is really no loss since the whole place is fascinating.

Bazaars and Brahmins' houses fill the space between the outer four walls, and you don't have to take your shoes off until you get to the fourth wall (it's customary to tip the shoe minder 10 paise on leaving). If you have a camera with you, you'll be charged Rs 5 at this point. Opposite the shoe deposit is the 'Art Gallery' which is hardly worth a second thought, but it's here that you buy Rs 0.50 tickets and go on top of the wall for a look over the complex. A guide will go with you to unlock the gates and make sure you don't take photographs of the golden Vinanan Temple. You can spend all day wandering around this complex with never a dull moment. The inner temple complex is open daily from 6.15 am to 1 pm and from 3.15 to 8.45 pm.

There is an annual car festival held here in the last week of December and the first week of January which draws pilgrims from all over India. If you're in the area at the time, make sure you see it.

There is a book for sale in certain shops within the temple complex called *Sri Ranga Kshetra Mahatmyam* by R Narasimhan Praveen, which costs Rs 1.50. The intention of the author was probably to create a guidebook and collection of legends about the temple, but it's full of the most prosaic Indian-English and

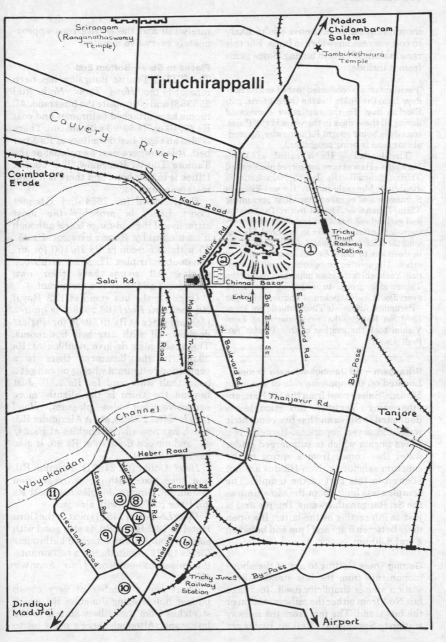

Tiruchirappalli

Srirangam
(Ranganathaswamy Temple)

Madras
Chidambaram
Salem

Jambukeshwara Temple

Cauvery River

Coimbatore
Erode

Karur Road

Madura Rd.

Trichy Town
Railway Station

Salai Rd.

Chinna Bazar

Entry

E. Boulevard Rd.

Big Bazaar St.

Shastri Road

Madras Trunk Rd.

W. Boulevard Rd.

By-Pass

Channel

Thanjavur Rd.

Tanjore

Woyakondan

Heber Road

Lawson's Rd.

Warner's Rd.

Birds Rd.

Convent Rd.

Cleveland Road

Madurai Rd.

Dindigul
Madurai

Trichy Junc.
Railway Station

By-Pass

Airport

incomprehensible nonsense you're likely to come across anywhere in India. For this reason alone it's worth buying. Some gems from it include:

'Pavithrotsava is conducted to the Lord for nine days from the Sukla-Paksha (bright fortnight) Ekadasi day. To the negligence committed during all these days in the years in the Pujas, remedy is being sought for otherwise Aparad-akshanpana is being sought for.'

'Thondar-Adi – He is called as Vipra Narayana – He was born in a sacred place called Thirumadangudi. His Janma Nakashatra is Jyeshta in Margazhi month. He was living in Srirangam and engaged himself in presenting Thiru Thuzhai or Thulasi to Sri Tanganatha and garlands of beautiful and scented flowers were daily offered by him to the Lord. He has sung the famous Thirumalai, which is especially in devotion to Lord Sri Ranganatha and no others. His another prabandha named Thiruppalli Yezhuchi is the most important part of the Thirumozhi group to wake up the Lord everyday. It is also spoken as Thirumalai Ariyar – Perumalai Ariyar – ie Those who do not know Lord Sri Ranganatha. Sri Vanamal of Lord Vishnu took the avathar of this Tondar Adi Podi Alwar.'

Srirangam – Sri Jambukeshwara Temple

Located on the opposite side of the main Madras/Salem road from the Sri Ranganathaswamy Temple, this temple is dedicated to Shiva and has five concentric walls and seven gopurams. Its deity is a Shiva lingam which is submerged under water that comes from a spring in the sanctum sanctorum. Non-Hindus are not allowed in this part of the temple. The complex was built about the same time as the Sri Ranganathaswamy Temple and is just as interesting as the latter. It's open daily between 6 am and l pm and between 4 and 9.30 pm.

Getting There Getting to any of the above monuments from the bus stand/railway station area is simplicity itself. Just take bus No 1 from either the railway station or the bus stand. The fare from the railway station to Srirangam is Rs 0.90. Buses are

rarely full and the service runs approximately every five minutes.

Places to Stay – Bottom End

The TTDC Tourist Bungalow has been renamed the *Hotel Tamil Nadu* (tel 253383) and is opposite the bus stand. All rooms have attached bathrooms and cost Rs 30/40 or Rs 60/90 with air-con. There is also an eight-bed dormitory at Rs 5 per bed. It is nowhere near as palatial as the Tanjore Tourist Bungalow. The Tourist Office is in this hotel and there is a good restaurant and bar.

Hotel Anand (tel 26545), 1 Racquet Court Lane, is probably the most attractive of the mid-range hotels although it's a bit grubby. Rooms here cost Rs 25/45 without air-con or Rs 75/100 for air-con doubles/triples. There are no air-con singles. All rooms have their own bathrooms and there is a restaurant.

Opposite the bus stand at 13A Royal Rd the *Guru Hotel* (tel 25298) is quite a pleasant place at Rs 19.50/30 for singles/doubles, all with attached bathrooms. There are also de-luxe doubles at Rs 39.50. In the basement there is a vegetarian restaurant where you can get a good thali with curd for Rs 2.50. Just beyond the Guru is the slightly more expensive, but also pleasant, *Hotel Lakshmi* (tel 25298), at 3A Alexander Rd, which has non air-con doubles at Rs 24/45, and air-con doubles at Rs 95. It also has a restaurant.

Hotel Ajanta (tel 24501), Junction Rd, is a huge place with its own vegetarian restaurant. Singles/doubles here cost Rs 25/40 or Rs 60/70 with air-con.

Vijay Lodge (tel 24511) next to the Guru Hotel at 13B Royal Rd, is also good with singles/doubles with attached bathrooms for Rs 19/30. Again there's a restaurant – the pleasant outdoor *Uma Shankar Hotel*.

There are a number of very cheap budget hotels along Junction Rd which stretches from the railway station to the bus stand. Although there's not a lot to choose between them the *Selvam Lodge* (tel 23114) has been the most popular with travellers for years. The rooms are very basic and cell-like and sheets are not provided. Costs are Rs 12/20 for singles/doubles with common bath, or Rs 17/27 for with attached bath. The lodge is secure and has a rooftop restaurant which is an excellent place for south Indian food in the evenings. There is also a south Indian vegetarian restaurant on the ground floor and a dimly-lit, prison-like air-conditioned restaurant on the first floor.

If you'd prefer to stay near the Rock Fort, try the *City Lodge* (tel 23452), 69 West Boulevard Rd, which has singles/doubles for Rs 7/15.

Places to Stay – Top End
Sangam Hotel (tel 25202) on Collector's Office Rd is the best hotel in town although it is not all that well appointed or maintained. Rooms here cost Rs 210/265 for air-con singles/doubles or Rs 130/180 without air-con. The hotel has one of the few bars in Trichy but beers are mite expensive and the restaurant is too. Other hotels with bars are the Hotel Tamil Nadu, the ITDC Lodge and the Ashby.

The *ITDC Travellers' Lodge* (tel 23498) on Race Course Rd is south of the railway station on the way to the airport. Rooms here are Rs 50/80 for non air-con singles and doubles. The lodge is somewhat inconveniently situated.

Rooms at the *Hotel Aristo* (tel 26565), 2 Dindigul Rd, are Rs 35/55 or Rs 65/90 with air-con. There are also air-con cottages at Rs 140/220. It's good value and has it's own restaurant.

The *Hotel Ashby* (tel 23652), 17A Junction Rd, merits description as Trichy's only faded touch of the Raj. If you like the Fairlawn in Calcutta, try this place. Non air-con rooms are Rs 40/50 or Rs 80/95 with air-con. All the rooms have their own bath and the hotel has its own restaurant and bar.

Places to Eat
There are plenty of vegetarian meals cafes around the bus stand and along Junction Rd. One of the best is at the *Guru Hotel*, and another good one is the rooftop of the *Selvam Lodge*, both mentioned above. If you're looking for something other than a thali, then try the non-vegetarian restaurant at the *Vijay Lodge* or the vegetarian *Hotel Anand* where the food is good. Almost opposite the Hotel Anand is the *Karitha*, a vegetarian restaurant that does excellent, highly elaborate thalis for Rs 5, and has an air-con room. The *Ashby* also has good thalis and drinks and excellent service.

Getting There
Air Trichy has an airport and is connected with Madras and Trivandrum by Indian Airlines. The Madras-Trichy-Trivandrum (and back) flights operate daily and fares to Trichy are from Madras or Trivandrum are Rs 239. Indian Airlines and Air Lanka each have two flights to Colombo each week. The fare is Rs 503.

If you're going to Sri Lanka it's worth considering the flights. The Rameswarum ferry is cheaper and you get the chance to see the magnificent temple but accommodation there is very tight. If you are heading for Rameswarum try to make advance bookings through the Tourist Office in the Hotel Tamil Nadu. Remember that the Rameswarum ferry service to Sri Lanka is suspended during the monsoon in November and December.

Rail Trichy is on the main Madras-Madurai rail line. Some trains run directly from Madras (337 km, five to eight hours, Rs 105 in 1st, Rs 27 in 2nd) while others go via Chidambaram and Tanjore, 64 km further. The Rockfort Express (No 178) departs Trichy daily at 9 pm and arrives at Madras at 5 am.

Another useful train is the Vaigai Express which leaves Madurai daily, except Tuesdays, at 6 am arriving in Madras at 1.30 pm. This train goes via Trichy. In the opposite direction it departs Madras at 2 pm and arrives in Madurai at 10.10 pm. The Ganga Kaveri, operating Madras-Rameswarum, also passes through Trichy. It's seven hours Trichy-Rameswarum.

From Trichy it's 155 km on to Madurai, taking 2½ to four hours at a cost of Rs 54 in 1st, Rs 14 in 2nd. There are many passenger trains as well as express services Trichy-Madurai but during the day you cannot reserve 2nd class seats so it's the usual battle for a space.

Bus Trichy has a state transport bus stand and a Tiruvalluvar bus stand only two minutes' walk away. As usual the state bus stand timetables are only in Tamil. Express buses are distinguished from ordinary buses by the word 'Fast' (in English) on the direction indicator at the front. Services to most places are frequent and tickets are sold by the conductor as soon as the bus arrives. Just buy your ticket and hop on.

One useful service is a direct bus departing daily to Kodaikanal at 9.15 am, which arrives there at 2.45 pm and costs Rs 14.20. Trichy to Madurai takes three or four hours and costs Rs 11. The 'Fast' bus only stops twice, once at Dindigul for chai. There is a service about every half hour,

Tiruvalluvar bus company has the following (theoretical schedule):

Madras & Villapuram – hourly 5 am to 9 pm then up to six buses per hour from 10 pm to 5 am.

Nagarcoil & Madurai – hourly 7 am to 12 midnight then up to five buses per hour from midnight to 6 am.

Coimbatore – 15 buses spread fairly evenly throughout the day but with gaps between midnight and 5 am and between 9 and 11 pm.

Getting Tiruvalluvar buses in Trichy is a hopeless, complicated mess. Most buses are just 'passing through' from other places and tickets for the few empty seats are only sold by the conductor when the

bus arrives. The scramble for tickets is far worse than on the state bus stand and there's no guarantee of success. On some routes 'priority tickets' are sold for Rs 0.50 which gives you priority for a ticket when the bus arrives. Getting hold of one of these, however, is an equally hopeless task as the ticket windows are hardly ever manned and when they are it's almost impossible to get their attention. 'To their sloppy incompetence', wrote one disgruntled visitor, 'you can add insolence'.

Getting Around

Trichy has an excellent privately run local bus service. It's comparatively easy to use and uncrowded. Take a bus 7, 63, 63A, 122 or 128 to the airport. Allow about half an hour to get there.

MADURAI (population 600,000)

This bustling city of over half a million people – packed with pilgrims, beggars, businessmen, bullock carts and legions of under-employed rickshaw wallahs – is one of southern India's oldest, and has been a centre of learning and pilgrimage for centuries. Its main attraction is the famous Shree Meenakshi Temple in the heart of the old town, a riotously baroque example of Dravidian architecture with gopurams covered from top to bottom with a breathless profusion of multi-coloured images of gods, goddesses, animals and mythical figures. Nothing quite like it exists outside Disneyland! The temple seethes with activity from dawn till dusk and its many shrines attract pilgrims from all over India and tourists from all over the world. On any one day it's been estimated that there will be 10,000 visitors here!

Madurai's history falls into roughly four periods beginning over 2000 years ago when it was the capital of the Pandyan kings and known to the 4th century BC Greeks via Megasthenes, their ambassador at the court of Chandragupta Maurya. In the 10th century AD it was taken by the Chola emperors and remained with them

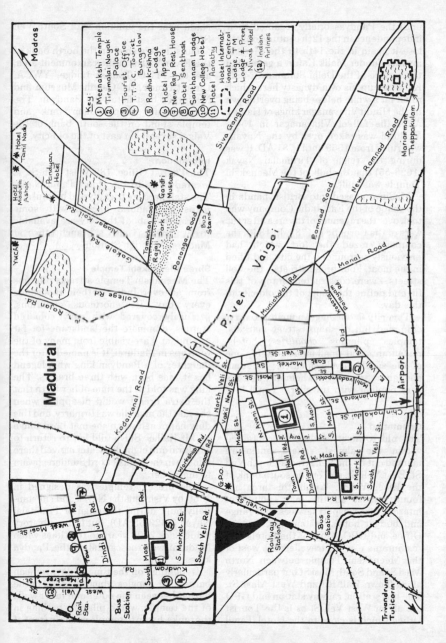

Madurai

Key:
1. Meenakshi Temple
2. Tirumalai Nayak Palace
3. Tourist Office
4. T.T.D.C. Tourist Bungalow
5. Radhakrishna Lodge
6. Hotel Apsara
7. New Raja Rest House
8. Hotel Senthosh
9. Santhanam Lodge
10. New College Hotel
11. Hotel Aarathy
    Hotel International, Central Lodge, TM Lodge & Prem Nivas Hotel
12. Indian Airlines

until the Pandyas briefly regained their independence in the 12th century, only to lose it again in the 14th to the Moslem invaders under Malik Kafur, a general in the service of the Delhi Sultanate. Malik Kafur set up his own dynasty here which ruled for a while before being overthrown by the Hindu Vijayanagar kings of Hampi. After the fall of Vijayanagar in 1565, Madurai was taken over by the Nayaks who ruled from 1559 until 1781 AD. It was during the reign of Tirumalai Nayak (1623-55) that the bulk of the Meenakshi Temple was built.

Madurai passed into British hands in the shape of the East India Company who took over the revenues of the area after the wars of the Carnatic in 1781. In 1840, the company razed the fort which had previously surrounded the city and filled in the moat. Four broad streets – the Veli streets – were constructed on top of this fill and define the limits of the old city to this day.

This city is one huge, non-stop bazaar crammed full of shops, street markets, temples, pilgrims' *choultries*, hotels, restaurants and small industries. It's one of the south's liveliest cities, yet small enough not to be overwhelming, and it's very popular with travellers. You'll love it!

Orientation

The old town of Madurai is contained within the almost square enclosure marked out by the Veli streets (South Veli St, East Veli St, etc) on the south bank of the River Vaigai. Within this area are found almost all the main points of interest, the transport services, mid-range and budget hotels, restaurants, Tourist Office and GPO. Most of the hotels and restaurants used by travellers are west of the Meenakshi Temple between North Masi St and South Masi St but particularly along Town Hall Rd and West Masi St. The bus station, railway station and GPO are all on West Veli St as is the Tourist Office which is close to the Hotel Tamil

Nadu near the junction with South Veli St.

Outside this area, on the north bank of the River Vaigai in the cantonment area, are the ITDC Tourist Lodge, YWCA, Circuit House, the Gandhi Museum and Madurai's best hotel, the Pandyan. The Mariammam Theppakulam tank and temple stand on the south bank of the Vaigai several km east of the old city.

Information

The Tourist Office, 180 West Veli St, is located close to the Hotel Tamil Nadu. The staff here are friendly and helpful and maps of Madurai backed with some information about the city are available (free). There is also a branch office at Madurai Junction Station.

Shree Meenakshi Temple

The Meenakshi Temple attracts pilgrims from all over India in their thousands every day. Its enormous gopurams, profusely covered with gaily coloured statues, dominate the landscape for far around, and are visible from many of the rooftops in Madurai. It is named after the daughter of a Pandyan king who, legend has it, was born with three breasts. The king was told at the time of her birth that the extra breast would disappear when she met the man she was to marry, and this duly happened when she met Lord Shiva on Mt Kailas. Shiva told her to return to Madurai and eight days later arrived there himself in the form of Lord Sundareshwara to marry her.

The present temple was designed in 1560 by Vishwanatha Nayak and substantially built during the reign of Tirumalai Nayak (1623-55 AD), but it has a history going back 2000 years to the times when Madurai was the capital of the Pandya kings.

Depending on the time of day, you can bargain for bangles, spices or saris in the bazaar between the outer and inner walls of the temple, watch pilgrims bathing in the tanks, listen to temple music in front of the Meenakshi Amman shrine (which is relayed through the whole complex on a PA system), wander through the interesting museum or climb to the top of a gopuram. It's a city within a city and many travellers spend days exploring its labyrinthine corridors and halls. There's even a railway timetable posted on the wall near the Meenakshi shrine!

Part of the temple complex has been converted into a museum – the Temple Art Gallery – which is well worth a visit, even though it's decidedly dilapidated these days and many labels are missing. It contains some beautiful stone and brass images, examples of ancient south Indian scripts, friezes and various attempts to explain the Hindu pantheon and the many legends associated with it. Entrance to the Art Gallery costs Rs 0.50 plus (officially) Rs 5 for a camera if you intend to use it, though I wasn't even asked about mine.

You can climb to the top of the south facing gopuram between 6 am and 5.30 pm. Buy a Rs 0.50 ticket from the office on the left as you enter the temple. A guide takes you up there via the many winding, grimy and gradually narrower and narrower stairways. If you suffer from vertigo this climb is not for you since you emerge on the very top of the gopuram and there are no restraining rails and very little else to hold on to, but the views are excellent! On the way down the guide will hassle you for a 'tip'.

On most evenings between 6 and 7.30 pm and between 9 and 10 pm temple music is played outside the Meenakshi Amman shrine – mantras, fiddle, squeeze box, tabla and bells. It's well worth making a point of going there to hear this as there are some excellent musicians among those who play.

The temple in general is open between 5 am and 12.30 pm and again between 4 and

10 pm. Photography is allowed inside only between 12.30 and 4 pm on payment of Rs 5. You can leave your shoes at any one of the four entrances where they will be looked after for Rs 0.15. Many of the priests inside are very friendly and will take the trouble to show you around and explain what's happening if you'd prefer that.

Tirumalai Naick Palace

About a km from the Meenakshi Temple (Rs 2 by rickshaw), this palace was built in 1636 by the ruler of the same name in the Indo-Saracenic style. Much of it has fallen into ruin and the pleasure gardens and surrounding defensive wall have disappeared but it was partially restored by Lord Napier, the Governor of Madras, in 1866-72 and further restoration work is in progress at present. Only the entrance gate and the main hall remain today but they're well worth a visit.

The palace is open daily between 8 am to 12.30 pm and 2 to 5 pm and entrance costs Rs 0.40. You can get there on an 11, 11A or 17 bus from the Central Bus Stand. There's no charge for photography. There is a *son et lumiere* in English at 6.45 pm daily. Tickets cost Rs 1, Rs 2 and Rs 3 and it's excellent entertainment telling the history of the city with sound and coloured lights on the temple carvings.

Gandhi Museum

Housed in the old palace of the Rani Mangammal, this oddly moving museum tells a few little known facts about the Mahatma although the only real Gandhi memorabilia is the blood stained dhoti from the assasination, behind a bullet-proof screen. There's also a library and an exhibition of crafts produced by village industry concerns in south India. Not to mention an 'everything you want to know about latrines' display. Part of the museum is also used for lectures and seminars. It's open daily between 10 am and 1 pm, 2 to 4 pm, except Wednesdays. Get there on a bus number 3 from the Central Bus Stand.

Mariamman Teppakkulam Tank

This tank, several km east of the old city, covers an area almost equal to that of the Meenakshi Temple and is the site of the Teppam Festival (Float Festival) in January and February when images of Meenakshi and Lord Sundareshwara are mounted on floats and taken in procession to the tank. Here they are pulled back and forth across the water to the island temple in the centre of the tank. The festival attracts thousands of pilgrims from all over India. The tank was built in 1646 by Tirumalai Nayak and is connected to the River Vaigai by underground channels.

Other Temples

Besides the Meenakshi temple there are several other important temples worth visiting in Madurai, all of them built in the typical late Dravidian style. Try the two along South Masi St between Kundram Rd and West Masi St. One of them has a temple elephant, the other offers some fine music in the evening. The Femina Fabric Store at 10-12 West Chitrai St will let you view the temples from their roof.

Places to Stay – Bottom End

Madurai is another town where finding a room can sometimes be difficult. In a pilgrim city the size and importance of Madurai, there are lots of cheap hotels and lodges offering basic accommodation. Many of them are just flop houses which bear the scars of previous occupants' bad habits. They're OK for a night, but not for much longer. On the other hand, there are a few – mostly along Town Hall Rd and Dindigul Rd – which are clean and very good value. Along Town Tall Rd between West Masai St and West Veli St you can try any one of the following:

Hotel Krishna: singles/doubles with attached bath at Rs 10/25.

Santhanam Lodge: singles/doubles with attached bath at Rs 10/25.

New College Hotel: an enormous place where you'll always be able to find a room. Singles/doubles all with attached bath for Rs 15-18/30-35 and few air-con doubles for Rs 60. The hotel has an attached vegetarian restaurant, bookshop and general store. Ask for a room on the top floor – excellent views of Meenakshi Temple.

Another hotel which is reasonably good value is the *New Raja Rest House*, off Dindigul Rd. It's a huge place, which caters mainly for pilgrims. Note that the 'bathrooms consist of a tap, bucket and toilet. A few years ago the *Rahakrishna Lodge*, Koodalalagarkoil St, used to be popular with travellers though it's hard to see why, other than the price at Rs 10/15 for singles/doubles. Fine if you don't mind dingy, hardboard-partitioned rooms, which aren't too clean, although the staff are friendly.

Places to Stay – Middle

There are three hotels at the top end of the middle range. The *Hotel Prem Nivas* (tel 625 001), 102 West Perumal Maistry St, has been recommended by a lot of travellers. It's fairly new and very well-maintained and all the rooms have their own bath with hot and cold running water. Rooms without air-con cost Rs 25/46; with air-con they are Rs 86 a double – there are no singles. It's less than five minutes' walk from the railway station.

The new *Hotel Aarathy* (tel 31571), 9 Perumalkoil West Mada St is similar in standard to the Prem Nivas and is just a few minutes' walk from the bus station. It has a choice of air-con and non air-con rooms all with their own bath and hot and cold running water and there's also a restaurant. Rooms here are Rs 35/60 or Rs 75/110 with air-con. You even get a complimentary paper in the morning.

The last of the three, the *Hotel Tamil Nadu* (tel 31435), is on West Veli St, opposite the bus terminal. It's a State Tourist Development Corporation undertaking and good value at Rs 35/50 or Rs 70/100 with air-con. All the rooms have their own bathroom and the hotel is conveniently situated directly opposite the bus station. On the other hand, it's often full, and even if you have made a booking you shouldn't rely on having a room there when you arrive.

At the cheaper end of this bracket, the best is undoubtedly the *TM Lodge*, West Perumal Maistry St, which has beautifully clean rooms for Rs 21 a single and Rs 45 a double, both with attached bath. The staff are attentive and it's excellent value.

Next would come the *Hotel Apsara* (tel 31444-5), 137 West Masai St. This place is popular with travellers – possibly because we recommended it in the last edition – but it's definitely gone downhill, and is no longer the good value it used to be. There are no singles, and doubles with attached bath are Rs 34 – clean sheets provided. This is a bit steep for peeling plaster, broken furniture, erratic water supplies, an obscure view of the toilet opposite plus late-night kitchen noises. If you're the lucky owner of this place, it's time to get off your butt and clean it up. The Apsara has its own bar and restaurant. The *Gurney Lodge* at 18 Town Hall Rd has doubles at Rs 18.

Places to Stay – Top End

Madurai's three best hotels are clustered together well out of the centre of town across the Vaigai River, along Alagarkoil Rd. If you haven't got too much luggage, you can get there by city bus Nos 2, 16 or 20 (among others) for Rs 0.50. Otherwise take an auto-rickshaw. This should cost around Rs 6 to 7, but as soon as they hear where you want to go the price doubles.

The two best hotels are the *Hotel Madurai Ashok* (tel 42531), and the *Pandyan Hotel* (tel 42471), both on Alagarkoil Rd. Both are centrally air-conditioned, all the rooms have their own baths with hot and cold water 24 hours, telephone and room service. Both have their own bar and restaurant offering a variety of cuisine (Indian, Chinese and western). The Ashok costs from Rs 250/325 for singles/doubles and claims to be Madurai's best hotel. The Pandyan Hotel has rooms for Rs 225/275. Both are large hotels and you're almost certain to get a room.

Also on Alagarkoil Rd but cheaper than these is the second state government operated *Hotel Tamil Nadu* (tel 42461). Having two different hotels with the same name is somewhat confusing. It's a slightly smaller hotel with a choice of air-con or non air-con rooms. They all have attached bath, hot and cold running water and a telephone. Rooms are Rs 75/100 or Rs 100/150 with air-con. There is a bar and restaurant (Indian, Chinese and western cuisine) and the staff and pleasant and friendly.

Places to Eat

There are many typical south Indian vegetarian restaurants all around the Meenakshi Temple, along Town Hall Rd, Dindigul Rd and West Masai St which serve thalis for Rs 3 to 43 and masala dosa and coffee for Rs 1.50 to 2.50. Some of the best are the restaurants at the junction of Dindigul Rd and West Masi St, the *New Arya Bhavan* on West Masi St (air-con) and another on Dindigul Rd about 200 metres from the junction with West Masi St. It only has a Tamil name ( ), but serves the biggest masala dosa you'll get in Madurai.

For non-vegetarian food try the restaurant in the *Hotel Tamil Nadu*, West Veli St, which has a variety of dishes including western breakfasts (toast and jam, omelettes, fried and scrambled eggs, etc). The *Indo-Ceylon Restaurant*, Town Hall Rd, very close to New College House, has vegetarian and non-vegetarian meals and excellent curd, as does the *Taj Restaurant*, Town Hall Rd. The *Sri Ram Mess Restaurant* has excellent all-you-can-eat vegetarian meals at lunchtime for Rs 8. The *Railway Station Restaurant* has good food and is conveniently located.

If you want really good non-vegetarian food then plan on a night out at the *Pandyan Hotel* where the *Jasmine Restaurant* has fairly good food, 'proper' service and decor and rather high prices.

Getting There

Air There is a daily flight Madras-Bangalore-Madurai and return. Fares to Madurai are Madras Rs 323, Bangalore Rs 276.

Rail It's 492 km from Madras to Madurai and takes eight hours via Trichy, longer via Chidambaram and Tanjore. Fares are Rs 143 in 1st class, Rs 36.50 in 2nd. The new all 2nd class Vagai Express is particularly fast and comparatively luxurious. To Rameswaram it takes six hours to cover the 164 km. Fares are Rs 57 in 1st class, Rs 14.50 in 2nd. It's a nice journey across the Western Ghats to Quilon, takes about eight hours. The train schedule is as follows:

Madras 6 am (No 136), 7 am (No 138); 2.50 pm (No 104); 7.25 pm (No 118) and 9.40 pm (No 120).
Quilon 6.40 am (No 165) and 9.05 pm (No 137).
Rameswaram 5.15 am (No 165); 1.15 pm (No 783); 5.40 pm (No 785) and 10.45 pm (No 769).

If you're heading for Kerala, the best train to take is the morning Madras-Quilon Mail as the line goes through some spectacular mountain terrain, and there are some superb gopurams to be seen at Srivilliputur (between Sivaksi and Rajapalaryam) and Sankarankovil. This train takes eight hours and costs Rs 86 in 1st class, Rs 22 in 2nd for the 268-km journey. It gets into Quilon in plenty of time for you to make it to Trivandrum or Kovalam Beach later in the afternoon.

Sleeping berths and seats can only be booked on the night trains out of Madurai. You cannot book a seat on a day train which does not start from Madurai, but it's easy to get one from the compartment attendant when a train arrives. Many of the through trains are half-empty. You can book trains and the ferry from Madurai right through to Colombo in Sri Lanka.

Bus The Central Bus Stand and the Tiruvalluvar Bus Stand are adjacent to each other on West Veli St, but Madurai is one of the few places in Tamil Nadu where Tiruvalluvar has got around to putting English as well as Tamil above the various arrival/departure bays, so it's relatively easy to find the bus you want. Also, the enquiry office here is very helpful and the people who work there speak fluent English. There's a third bus stand (the Anna Stand) on the far side of the river, five km from the town centre. If you bus terminates there (some from Trichy certainly do) then you'll have to take a bus 3 or 3A to the Central Bus Stand.

Note that if you're heading for Kanyakumari the best buses to take are at 6 am, 7.30 am and 9 am. These all start from Madurai, so you're more-or-less assured of a seat. There are plenty of others after that (eg 9.20 am, 12.12 pm, etc), but they all start from other places and go via Madurai, so you can't be sure of a seat until the bus arrives. The super de-luxe buses cost Rs 34 and take six hours.

There are four Tiruvalluvar buses daily to Kottayam in Kerala. It's a pleasant, scenic trip taking about 8½ hours. The 9 am departure may stop for lunch in the new and very attractive *Hotel Ambadi* between Kumili and Thekkady.

Getting Around
Some useful local buses include 3 and 4 to the Gandhi Museum, 4 to the Mariammam Theppakkulam Tank, 5 to the Tiruparankundram rock-cut temple (eight km outside Madurai) and 44 to the Alagarkoil Vaishnavite shrine (21 km from Madurai). See the note above about the three bus stations in Madurai.

Festivals
Madurai's principal festivals are:

Teppam Festival (Float Festival) This is a very popular festival which attracts pilgrims from all over India. The images of Shree Meenakshi and Lord Sundareshwara (Shiva) are mounted on floats and taken to the Mariammam Theppakkulam Tank, where they are pulled back and forth across the waters of the tank for several days before being taken back to Madurai. The festival takes place between January and early February.
Chithirai Festival This festival takes place in late April/early May and celebrates the marriage of Shree Meenakshi to Lord Sundareshwara.
Avanimoola Festival Another popular festival which takes place in late August/early September. Temple cars are drawn round the streets of Madurai.

RAMESWARAM (population 11,000)
Rameswaram is the Benares of the south and a major pilgrimage centre both for Saivaites and Vaishnavites. The Ramanathaswamy Temple is one of the most important temples in the south. This is also the port from which the ferry to Talaimannar (Sri Lanka) departs except during November and December when it is normally suspended due to rough seas.

Information & Orientation
Rameswaram is an island in the Gulf of Mannar which is connected to the mainland at Mandapam by rail only. Though a road bridge is being constructed, it will be some time before it is completed and until then the only access to Rameswaram is by rail. It's a small town and most of the hotels, restaurants, the ferry jetty, railway station and post office are clustered around the Ramanathaswamy Temple.

It is often very difficult to find accommodation here, especially if you arrive late in the day. If at all possible you should make an advance booking for the TTDC Hotel Tamil Nadu if you want to be sure of a reasonable place to stay.

Ramanathaswamy Temple
The town's most famous monument is the Ramanathaswamy Temple which is a gem of late Dravidian architecture. Its most renowned features are the magnificent corridors lined with massive sculptured pillars, which are noted for their elaborate design, style and rich carving. One of these corridors is an incredible 1220 metres (4000 ft) in length! – the longest in India.

Legend has it that Rama (of the Indian epic, the Ramayana) sanctified this place by worshipping Lord Shiva here after the battle of Sri Lanka. Rama sent his most devout disciple, Hanuman (the monkey god), to Mt Kailas to bring a lingam but the monkey god was delayed and as Shiva had to be worshipped at a certain time, Rama's wife, Sita, moulded one herself which subsequently became known as the Ramanatha. On Hanuman's return, Rama was forced to console the monkey god by having the lingam which he had brought from Mt Kailas installed near the Ramanatha, and decreeing that the Hanuman lingam should have precedence over the Ramanatha.

The temple as it stands today was begun in the 12th century AD and added to by various rulers over the succeeding centuries. Its gopuram is 53.6 metres (176 ft) high.

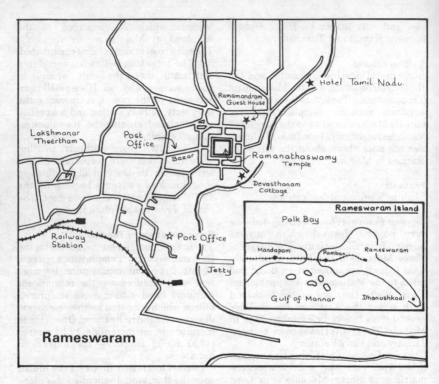

Rameswaram

(Map labels:)
Hotel Tamil Nadu
Ramamandram Guest House
Lakshmanar Theertham
Post Office
Bazar
Ramanathaswamy Temple
Devasthanam Cottage
Railway Station
Port Office
Jetty

Rameswaram Island
Palk Bay
Mandapam
Pamban
Rameswaram
Gulf of Mannar
Dhanushkodi

Kothandaraswamy Temple

There is another famous temple at Dhanushkodi on the extreme tip of the island known as the Kothandaraswamy Temple. This temple was the only structure to survive the 1964 cyclone which washed the rest of the village away. Legend has it that Vibishana, brother of Ravana, the kidnapper of Sita, surrendered to Rama at this spot. Dhanushkodi can be reached by road from Rameswaram, buses go there every two hours, the last one back at 8 pm.

Other

Rameswaram's other attractions are its coral reefs and beaches fringed with swaying coconut palms and tamarind trees. From Gandhamathana Parvathum, a hillock to the north of Rameswaram and

the highest point on the island, an excellent view over the whole island can be had. At Dhanushkodi, at the very tip of the peninsula, is a lovely bathing pool. There's nobody there except friendly fishermen.

Places to Stay

As mentioned above accommodation can be a real problem at Rameswaram and you should try to make advance bookings at the *Hotel Tamil Nadu* (tel 77) if you want a reasonable place to stay. If you cannot do this then you must be prepared to take whatever is available. This TTDC operated place is without doubt the best place to stay but is almost always full. The rooms are quite luxurious at Rs 70 a double with their own bathroom and balcony overlooking the sea. The food, on the other hand, is ghastly and you should eat elsewhere. A rickshaw from the railway station to the hotel should cost Rs 4 to 5.

Nadar Mahajana Sangam Lodge, New St, is about 15 minutes' walk from the railway station. Rooms here cost Rs 15 a double with own bathroom. It's clean and quiet and the next best place after the Tourist Bungalow. The *Alanka Tourist Home* is a new hotel near the temple entrance on the town side with doubles at Rs 25. The new *Hotel Maharaja* (tel 71) has singles for Rs12 to 25, doubles for Rs 25 to 40 and air-con doubles at Rs 75. Except for the cheapest singles they're all with bath.

Railway Retiring Rooms at the station cost Rs 15/20 for singles/doubles or Rs 7.50 for a dorm bed. Other places to stay include the *Lakshmi Lodge, Meenakshi Lodge, Devasthanam Cottage, Vivekananda Illam, Rama Mandiram Guest House* and the *Tirupati Devasthanam Bungalow*. The prices of these places range from Rs 8 to 12 for singles, Rs 15 to 25 for doubles. If you're really stuck there is a covered roof at the *Lakshmi Lodge*, near the temple, where you can sleep for Rs 5 a night.

Places to Eat

There are a number of vegetarian restaurants which serve typical south Indian thalis. They're all of a similar quality, none of them is outstandingly good and worth particular recommendation.

Getting There

There are trains from Madras and Madurai which arrive pre-dawn, ideal for the Sri Lanka ferry departures, but the main mail-express train is the Ganga-Kaveri Express which arrives from Madras daily at 1.20 pm and departs for Madras at 1.50 pm.

Sri Lanka Ferry

See the introductory Getting There section for full details on the Rames-

waram-Talaimannar ferry service. You can book from Madurai right through to Colombo including the ferry. Or at least you can get ticketed for it – the Talaimannar-Colombo train ticket will be unreserved and the ferry is pretty much first come, first served and is sometimes completely full. Still it's worth avoiding doing things in Rameswaram which can be a real madhouse.

TIRUCHENDUR

South of Rameswaram and Tuticorin there is a *Hotel Tamil Nadu* here with singles/doubles at Rs 20/30.

KANYAKUMARI (Cape Cormorin)

Kanyakumari is the 'Land's End' of India where the Bay of Bengal meets the Indian Ocean, and where it's possible to enjoy the unique experience of seeing the sun set and the moon rise over the ocean simultaneously at full moon. It's also a popular pilgrimage destination for Hindus and dedicated to the goddess Kanyakumari, an incarnation of Parvati, Shiva's consort.

Other than that it's highly over-rated – trinket stalls, a lousy beach and one of those places with megaphones at the end of each street which rip your ear drums apart between 4 am and 10 pm. Do Indians collectively suffer from some congenital disability, which makes them incapable of understanding the excruciating level of noise pollution, which is found in some places in this country, or is it some perverse form of merit-garnering penance? No, you can safely give this place a miss if your time is limited or you have better things to do. The real show is the pilgrims from all over, a good cross section of India.

Information

There is a Tourist Office about half-way between the Bus Stand and the Gandhi Mandapam – but what could you possibly want to know?

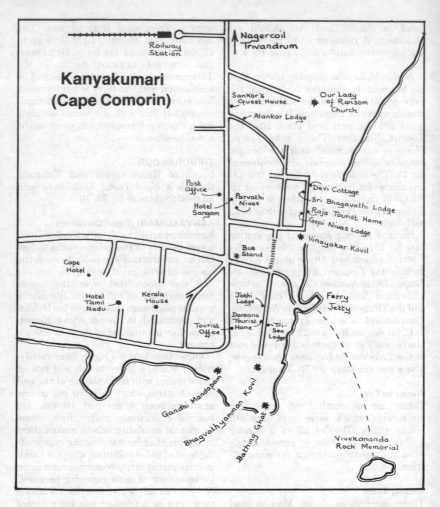

Kanyakumari (Cape Comorin)

Railway Station

↑ Nagercoil Trivandrum

Sankar's Guest House

Our Lady of Ransom Church

Alankar Lodge

Post Office

Parvathi Nivas

Hotel Sangam

Devi Cottage

Sri Bhagavathi Lodge

Raja Tourist Home

Gopi Nivas Lodge

✳ Vinayakar Kovil

Bus Stand

Cape Hotel

Hotel Tamil Nadu

Kerala House

Jothi Lodge

Darsana Tourist Home

Tri-Sea Lodge

Ferry Jetty

Tourist Office

✳ Gandhi Mandapam

✳ Bhagvathyamman Kovil

✳ Bathing Ghat

Vivekananda Rock Memorial

Kanyakumari Temple

Picturesquely located overlooking the shore, pilgrims from all over India come here to worship and to bathe at the Kumari Ghat. Legend has it that Parvati, in one of her incarnations as Devi Kanya, did penance here to secure Shiva's hand in marriage but was unsuccessful, and so vowed to remain a virgin (Kanya). The temple is open daily from 4.30 to 11.30 am and from 5.30 to 8.30 pm. Non-Hindus are not allowed into the inner sanctum.

Vivekananda Memorial

This memorial is located on two rocky islands which project from the sea about 200 metres from the shore line. The Indian philosopher, Swami Vivekananda came here in 1892 and sat on the rock meditating before setting out as one of

India's most important religious crusaders. The mandapam which stands here in his memory was built in 1970 and employs architectural styles from all over India. There's a ferry service to the island every few minutes for Rs 2 per person plus an entry fee of Rs 1 to the Rock Temple. The islands are open to visitors between 7 and 11 am and 2 to 5 pm.

If you're looking for a quiet beach, one of the finest in Tamil Nadu, before heading north into Kerala, try the one at Kolachal about half-way between Kanyakumari and Trivandrum.

Suchindram Temple

This temple to Indra is about 10 minutes from Kanyakumari by auto rickshaw and can be visited by non-Hindus. It's very interesting with, reported one visitor, 'marvellous carved pillars, some depicting extremely rude scenes'! If you go there immediately after the sunset-bathing ceremonies at the cape you can watch the evening sacred flame ceremonial.

Padmanabhapuram

Near Nagarcoil this was once the capital of the state of Travancore. There's an old fort and a pagoda-shaped palace with fine 17th and 18th century murals on the topmost floor. Even finer than those at Matancherry in Cochin reported one visitor. They are 'less restored, in better condition and staggeringly beautiful'. It was once the seat of the rulers of Travancore – a princely state during the days of the Raj which included a large part of present-day Kerala and the western littoral of Tamil Nadu.

It's actually close to the Kerala border, 55 km south of Trivandrum, and conveniently visited between Kanyakumari and Trivandrum. It's closed Mondays.

Courtallam

Further north, three km from Tenkasi Junction on the Madurai-Trivandrum railway route, there are seven sparkling waterfalls here, amongst the best in India.

It's best from June to September but avoid Sundays.

Places to Stay

Hotels can be heavily booked here and prices, as a result, can be pushed up. At the bottom end of the market there's a whole bunch of cheap hotels clustered together at the back of the bus stand close to Vinayakar Koil. They include the *Raja Tourist Lodge* and the *Gopi Nivas Lodge*, both of which have singles/doubles with attached bathroom for Rs 15/30. Close to them and of similar standard is the *Sri Bhagavathi Lodge*.

Cheaper still is the *Devi Cottage*, opposite the Sri Bhagavathi, which has rooms with three, four and five beds, but no singles. You need to bargain here, as they quote whatever they think you're silly enough to pay. Lastly, there is the *Township Lodge*, near the bus stand, which has singles/doubles/large doubles with common bathroom for Rs 8/10/15, as well as a large hall – no beds which will fit 50 people.

The *Tri-Sea Lodge*, opposite the Darsana Tourist Home, is largely for families and groups, who are going to share large rooms, and it's not at all cheap.

Right in the centre of town, the best middle range hotel is the *Darsana Tourist Home*, which is newly decorated and offers double rooms with attached, tiled bath, clean sheets and fan for Rs 35. There are no singles. Similar in standard, but not quite as good is the *Jothi Lodge*, two or three doors up from the Darsana. Again, there are no singles.

Also in this bracket, you might like to try the *Parvathi Nivas Lodge*, very close to the Hotel Sangam. There is only one single room here at Rs 20, all the others are doubles at Rs 40. All rooms in this pleasant, older-style building have attached bath.

The hotels that overlook the sea to the west of the bus stand are particularly pleasant. They include *Hotel Tamil Nadu* (tel 22, 57) which offers really pleasant rooms with balcony – some of which overlook the sea – and attached bath. A double room costs Rs 50 – there are no singles. There is an attached restaurant and bar but a traveller complained that: 'my vegetable fried rice was rice, three peas and two slivers of carrot, honest, I counted'. Also overlooking the sea *Kerala House* (tel 29) is a huge building, but actually contains only eight rooms which cost Rs 21 a double, plus Rs 8 for each additional person. Again, there is an attached restaurant.

At the top end of the market is *Sankar's Guest House*, one of the first hotels you will come to on your way from the railway station to the centre of town. Rooms with attached bathrooms are Rs 31.50/52.

The most expensive place to stay is the new *Hotel Sangam* (tel 62), opposite the post office, 200 metres from the bus stand, on Main Rd. Air-con doubles with attached bathroom are Rs 60 and 75, similar rooms with four beds are Rs 100. There are no singles but all the rooms are well fitted out. The more expensive doubles have a verandah.

Getting There

Rail There is now a railway line direct to Kanyakumari and the following trains are available:

Nagarcoil Junction Daily at 2.30 pm and 9.10 pm.
Trivandrum Daily at 6.25 am, 10.25 am and 7.15 pm. The fare is Rs 37 in 1st class and Rs 8 in 2nd class.
Tirunelvelli Daily at 1.45 pm.

Reservation times are 8 am to 12 noon and 2 to 4 pm. Sleeping quotas are available to Bangalore (two three-tier 2nd class).

Bus There are the following buses from Kanyakumari:

Coimbatore Six times daily, the first at 6.15 am and the last at 9.30 pm. The journey takes 11½ hours and costs Rs 36.10 (ordinary) and Rs 45.70 (super de-luxe).
Madras Daily at 9.45 am, 12.45 pm, 4.45 pm and 9.45 pm. The last three are super de-luxe buses. The journey takes 16 hours, and costs Rs 52.50 (ordinary) and Rs 66.50 (super de-luxe).
Madurai Daily at 8.45 am. The trip takes six hours and costs Rs 19 (ordinary) and Rs 34 (super de-luxe).
Pondicherry Daily at 2.50 pm, taking 14 hours and costing Rs 43.80.
Rameswaram Six times daily, the first at 3.45 am and the last at 10.35 pm. This trip takes 7½ hours and costs Rs 22.20 (ordinary) and Rs 28.20 (super de-luxe).
Trivandrum Four buses daily at 4.15 am, 6 am, 12 noon and 6.30 pm. There are all super de-luxe buses. The journey takes 2½ hours and costs Rs 10.70.

KODAIKANAL (population 16,500)

Of the three main hill stations of the south – Ootacamund, Kodaikanal and Yercaud – Kodaikanal is undoubtedly the most beautiful and has the advantage over Ooty that the temperature – even in winter – never drops to the point where you need to wear thick woollen clothing. It's located on the southern crest of the Palani Hills, about 120 km north-west of Madurai among thickly wooded slopes, waterfalls and precipitous rocky outcrops. Some of the views to the south are the most spectacular you will find anywhere in India, and are within a few minutes' walking distance of the centre of town – unlike Ooty where you have to walk km to find them.

Kodaikanal isn't just for those who want to get away from the heat of the plains during the summer months, but for those who are looking for a relaxing place to put up their feet for a while, and do some hiking now and again. Like Ooty, Kodaikanal has its own landscaped, artificial lake and there are the usual boating facilities. Having said that, once you've rowed around the lake, admired

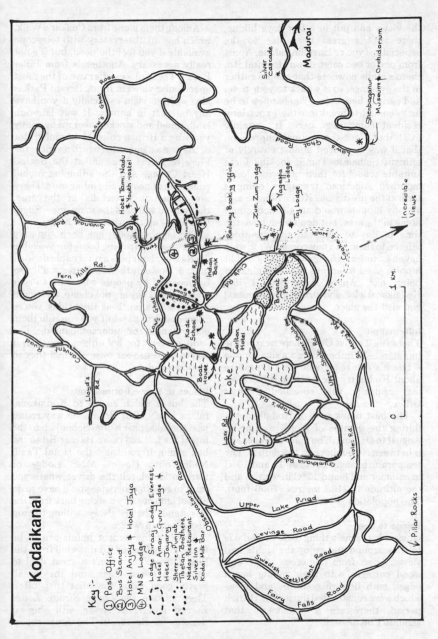

Kodaikanal

Key :-
① Post Office
②️ Bus Stand
③ Hotel Anjay   ✦ Hotel Jaya
✦ MNS Lodge

the views and put in a few days hiking, there isn't a great deal else to do, especially if you're travelling alone. Apart from one or two cafes down Hospital Rd, there's really nowhere that people gather in the evenings, so it's back to your hotel and early to bed, unless you happen to be lucky enough to break into the 'expatriate' resident community here. It certainly exists but I got the distinct impression that it was composed almost entirely of affluent Sinhalese Tamils looking for a suitable school for their offspring; loud-mouthed American teenagers doing a term at the prestigious Kodai School; and snobby hippies who'd set up house and home in the area, but don't even have the time of day to reply to the greetings offered to them by a newcomer. Well, well, haven't times changed. That's what hippies used to accuse the 'straights' of being like. Apart from that, I like Kodaikanal a lot, and strongly recommend you visit the place.

Information
There is a Tourist Office here next to the bus stand – or rather there's a sign for one – but it's a joke. If you want literature about Kodai, try the bookshop more-or-less opposite this so-called Tourist Office.

The best times to visit Kodaikanal is during the months of April to June or August to October. The main rainy season is between November and December. The temperature ranges between 11 and 20°C in summer and 8 and 17°C in winter, and the altitude is 2133 metres (7000 feet). The population is 16,500.

Things to See
Obviously the main thing to do in Kodai is to walk around and enjoy the sights and views. Apart from numerous stone and wood cottages with their rolling lawns edged with flowering shrubs and trees which were constructed during the British period, there are a few views that shouldn't be missed.

Among them is one from Coaker's Walk, which has an observatory with telescope available if you feel the need, but it's not really necessary. Another is from Pillar Rocks. These places offer two of the most spectacular views in India. Bryant Park is also worth a visit, especially if you have any interest in botany. It was laid-out, landscaped and stocked over many, many years by a British colonial administrator of the same name. Also worth a visit is the Flora & Fauna Museum at the Sacred Heart College and the adjoining orchid collection at nearby Shembaganur. There are numerous waterfalls in the area, though you will pass the main one – Silver Cascade – on the road up to Kodai.

The lake at Kodai has been superbly landscaped, and rowing boats are available for Rs 2 per hour plus a returnable deposit of Rs 5. Down by the boathouse you'll also be accosted by people who want to rent you horses. They are not cheap, and you'll be quoted as much as they think you're silly enough to pay, but you can ride them accompanied or unaccompanied. The saddles aren't too hot either, especially if you're used to your own – in fact they're bloody awful.

Places to Stay – Bottom End
The buses which go up to Kodaikanal follow Law's Ghat Rd all the way round past the lake, past Kodai School up to the top of the hill and down Bazaar Rd to the bus stand. If you want the Hotel Tamil Nadu/Youth Hostel, MNS Lodge or Carlton Hotel, tell the driver where you want to get off, otherwise you'll have to do a lot of unnecessary walking back from the bus stand. They're always willing to stop just about anywhere.

Many of the budget hotels are to be found along Bazaar Rd downhill from the Post Office. There isn't a great deal to choose between them and they're all pretty good value for what they offer. They include the *Lodge Siraaj, Lodge Everest* and *Hotel Amar* with singles/doubles for Rs 12/20. The Amar rooms have with attached bath – hot water extra at Rs 1 per bucket. The *Guru Lodge* has rooms at Rs 12/20 with common bath and toilet – pleasant, clean little rooms.

Another place, popular with travellers, is the *MNS Lodge* off Law's Ghat Rd below the Hotel Jaya. It's one of the cheapest at Rs 15 a double or Rs 12 for single occupancy with common showers (cold) and toilets. The staff are friendly but it's in need of a major rehabilitation job, let alone a clean-up and not really worth it at half the price. How come I know? Because I stayed there. Blankets are provided. Until the MNS gets itself together I'd suggest you stay at the *Zum Zum Lodge* at the top end of Bryant Park where Coaker's Walk starts. The rooms are just as primitive and the staff just as friendly, but you can get buckets of hot water for Rs 1 and there's a sort of common room with a log fire going in the evenings. Rooms with two beds and attached bath cost Rs 15 here. The price is negotiable if you're staying longer.

Nearby, but more expensive, are the *Yagappa Lodge* and *Taj Lodge*. The Taj is *the* place to stay if you want a room overlooking that fantastic view from Coaker's Walk but, as you might imagine, it's often full. Rooms are also available in private homes, usually with full board either by the day or for longer periods – you'll get a few offers while you're here.

Places to Stay – Top End

Kodaikanal's most prestigious hotel is the *Carlton Hotel* (tel 252) Boathouse Rd, which overlooks the lake and has its own restaurant and bar. During the high season (April, May, June, August, September and October) double rooms with dressing room and bath cost Rs 105, and double suites with sitting room, dressing room, verandah and bath cost Rs 160. In the off-season (July, November, December, January, February, March) double rooms cost Rs 72 (Rs 50 for single occupancy), and double suites cost Rs 160 (Rs 100 for single occupancy). Meals can be served in

your room, but are subject to a 10% service charge and Rs 2 per head. Bundles of firewood are available at Rs 10 each. All rooms have hot and cold running water.

Less expensive than the Carlton, but without the advantage of lake views, is the *Hotel Tamil Nadu & Youth Hostel* (tel 481), Fern Hill Rd. Like the other Hotel Tamil Nadus this is a state government project. In the high season (April, May, June) rooms cost Rs 60/110 for singles/ doubles, Rs 110 for a double cottage and Rs 150 for a family room with five beds. In the low season (July to March) rooms cost Rs 40/70. The attached Youth Hostel offers beds in dormitory-style accommodation for Rs 10.50 in the high season and Rs 8 in the off-season. The hotel has a restaurant and bar.

Similar in standard, but without the cheap hostel beds is the *Hotel Jaya* (tel 462). This is a modern hotel within a stone's throw of the bus stand. All the rooms have attached bath, clean sheets and hot and cold running water. From 1 April to 30 June, double rooms cost Rs 80, and double de luxe rooms Rs 100. From 1 July to 31 March they're Rs 50 and 70. If you need extra blankets, these can be hired for Rs 3.

Also worth considering in this bracket is are the *Hotel Anjay*, Bazaar Rd, next to the bus stand, which has doubles (no singles) for Rs 55, including your own bathroom with hot and cold running water. The *Hotel Jayaraj* (tel 348), Bazaar Rd opposite the Post Office has singles/doubles for Rs 36/ 72 betwen 16 April and 15 June; and for Rs 14/28 between 16 June and 15 April. All the rooms have attached bath and hot and cold running water. The Hotel Anjay has its own restaurant, but there is no restaurant at the Jayaraj.

Places to Eat

Kodaikanal is full of signs advertising restaurants which offer the 'best' food in town, but there's never any indication of where they are. Fortunately, most of them are on, or just off Hospital Rd. Walk down this road from the five-cornered junction at the end of Bazaar Rd and just opposite the main gate of the Kodai School are at least five places for taste sensations.

The first is a *baba* who offers French fries – nothing else – for Rs 2. You won't find them better cooked than this – anywhere! – and he has salt and vinegar too. It's closed in the evenings. Another is the *Tibetan Brothers Restaurant*, which is popular, run by friendly people and the food is good. They have good chow mein, chop suey, soups, curries and certain western food like omelettes. Try the noodle soup for Rs 6 and the fried rice here.

The third is the *Silver Inn Restaurant*, which is similar to the above, but not as popular. Then there's the *Kodai Milk Bar* which is good and sells what you'd expect, so long as you can get through to the surly shits who work here. At the *Shere-e-Punjab* very good Punjabi food is available at reasonable prices. The restaurant is just off Hospital Rd to the right as you go down the road.

You can find excellent vegetarian thalis at lunch times at the *Pakia Deepam*, right opposite the bus stand between the Hotels Anjay and Jaya, but they're more expensive than similar thalis down on the plain.

One last place that's worth mentioning is the chai stall next to the Zum Zum Lodge. The guy who runs it is very friendly and it's worth stopping for a chai, snack and conversation.

Getting There

There is no railway to Kodaikanal, so you must go by road. Madurai is perhaps the most convenient place from which to get a but to Kodaikanal, but if you are coming down from the north there are buses from Tiruchirappalli (via Dindigul). There is also a bus link with Thekkady in Kerala state. A list of bus services is printed below.

Madurai Seven buses daily in either direction. From Kodaikanal the first is at 7 am and the last at 4.15 pm. The journey takes about four hours and costs Rs 9.50.

Tiruchirappalli One direct bus daily in either direction. From Trichy it departs at 9.15 am and arrives at 2.45 pm. The fare is Rs 14.20. This bus goes via Dindigul, so it's also possible to catch it from there.

Thekkady (Kumily) One bus daily in either direction. It departs Kodaikanal at 1 pm.

OOTACAMUND (Ooty) (population 78,000)

Known as Udagamandalam in Tamil, this hill station in the Nilgiri mountains near the tri-junction of Tamil Nadu, Kerala and Karnataka was founded by the British in the early part of the 19th century to serve as the summer headquarters of the government of Madras. Before that time it was inhabited by the Todas, a tribal people, who still live in the area and whose animist shrines can still be seen at various places.

Though it stands at a height of 2268 metres amongst some of the most spectacular mountains in southern India it's not, as you might expect it to be, similar to the Himalaya since it lacks the fascinating cultures which make those mountains so interesting. Indeed, it's more a faded touch of the Raj and suffers from a bad case of over-enthusiasm on the part of the Indian tourist organisation. There's precious little to see here as such and not a great deal to do unless you're fond of long walks and boating on the lake. The whole place has a run-down feeling about it and, although this isn't unusual in India, you are led to expect something special when really there isn't anything. The best part of Ootacamund is the journey there along a narrow, winding and very steep mountain road which passes first through luxuriant rain forest and then through tea plantations.

Having put the tourist literature into a more realistic perspective Ooty is, nevertheless, a very pleasant and relaxing

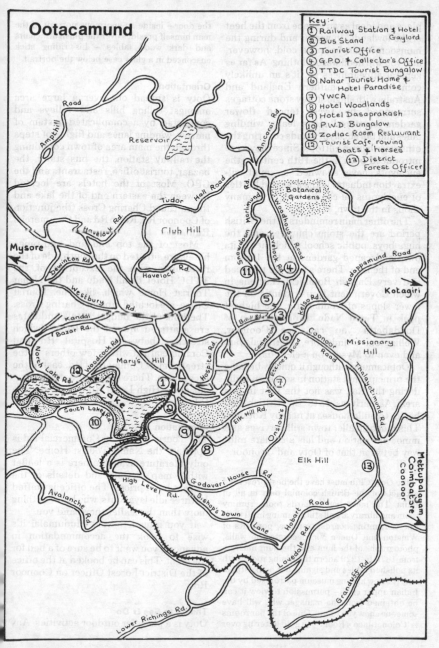

Ootacamund

Key:-
1. Railway Station & Hotel Gaylord
2. Bus Stand
3. Tourist Office
4. G.P.O. & Collector's Office
5. TTDC Tourist Bungalow
6. Nahar Tourist Home & Hotel Paradise
7. YWCA
8. Hotel Woodlands
9. Hotel Dasaprakash
10. P.W.D. Bungalow
11. Zodiac Room Restaurant
12. Tourist Cafe, rowing boats & horses
13. District Forest Officer

Ampthill Road

Reservoir

Tudor Hall Road

Club Hill

Havelock Rd.

Dewinton Rd.

Havelock Rd.

Westbury Rd.

Kandal

Bazar Rd.

North Lake Rd.

Woodcock Rd.

Mary's Hill

Lake

South Lake Rd.

Hospital Rd.

Anticorai Rd.

Botanical Gardens

Snowdown Marlimund Rd.

Woodhouse Road

Havelock Rd.

Kelso Rd.

Kodappamund Road

Kotagiri

Commercial Rd.

Bank Rd.

Missionary Hill

Coonoor Road

Etimes Road

Onslows Rd.

Thalaikatmund Rd.

Mysore

Elk Hill Rd.

Godavari House Rd.

High Level Rd.

Bishop's Down

Avalanche Rd.

Hobart Road

Lane

Lovedale Rd.

Granduff Rd.

Lower Richings Rd.

Elk Hill

Mettupalagam Coimbatore Coonoor

place and ideal as an escape from the heat of the lowlands. In winter and during the monsoon it can be quite cold, however, and you will need warm clothing. As far as general appearances go, it's an unlikely combination of southern England and Australia with single storey stone cottages surrounded by twee, fenced flower gardens scattered along leafy, winding lanes and tall eucalypt stands covering the otherwise barren hill tops. Since they were introduced back in the 19th century, the eucalypts have spawned a small oil-extraction industry in the area and bottles of eucalyptus oil can be bought in many shops in the town.

The other main reminders of the British period are the stone churches and the huge boys' public school which sits in its own landscaped gardens at the bottom end of the lake. There's also the terraced and very English Botanical Gardens in which Government House stands on the lower slopes of Doddabetta, the highest peak in Tamil Nadu. From the top of Doddabetta you can see Coonoor, Wellington, Coimbatore, Mettupalayam and even to Mysore on a clear day.

Ootacamund, although it quickly became the principal hill station in southern India during the Raj, was not the first in this area. As early as 1819 the British had begun to build houses at nearby Kotagiri. This much smaller town still survives as a minor hill station and has a climate midway between that of Ooty and Coonoor.

....the Ooty Club must have the best preserved artifacts of the British colonial past in all of India. The mens bar, billiards room, rummy room and library are all still gleaming in all their finery. Hunting boards, trophies, portraits of Winston and Queen Vic decorate the walls, photographs of the hunt and the hunt masters from 1870 to 1929 adorn the dining room with its polished tables and signing out book, still in use. It's now a living museum patronised by the Indian upper class – permission to view it can be obtained from the manager who will have someone show you round. One of the bar rooms is 'Colonel Jaco's Room' – in gold lettering over the door – inside an enormous portrait of the man himself presides over the plush armchairs and dark wood tables – his riding stick ensconced in a glass case below the portrait.

Orientation

Ooty is spread out over a large area amongst rolling hills and valleys and connected by a complicated system of narrow, winding lanes and flights of steps through the main area of town containing the railway station, the bus stand, the bazaar, tourist office, restaurants and the GPO. Most of the hotels are located between the eastern end of the lake and the so-called Charing Cross (the junction of Coonoor Rd, Kelso Rd and Commercial Rd).

Most of the top end and mid-range hotels are situated on the south side of the racecourse with the exception of the TTDC Hotel Tamil Nadu and the Nahar Tourist Home which, like the Tourist Office, are located around Charing Cross. The bulk of the budget hotels and cafes are scattered around the bazaar which stretches between Hospital Rd and Commercial Rd with a few others in the streets below Commercial Rd, east of the racecourse. There are other hotels strung out along High Level Rd and Avalanche Rd.

Information

The Tourist Office on Commercial Rd is opposite the Nahar Tourist Home. The only literature available here is a leaflet with a map of Ooty and details of the current hotel prices. The office is staffed by three idle layabouts, who know nothing more than the leaflet they hand you.

If you intend to visit Mudumalai it's wise to book the accommodation in advance if you want to be sure of a bed for the night. This can be booked at the office of the District Forest Officer on Coonoor Rd.

Things to See & Do

Ooty is a place for outdoor activities. Any

number of long walks can be made, just head out in any direction you like. Some superb views over Ooty and the Nilgiris can be found. If you'd prefer to go on horseback, horses can be rented next to the boathouse on the north side of the lake for about Rs 15 per hour. They can be delivered to your hotel for no extra charge. You can take them off on your own or hire one of the owners as a guide. Rowing boats and motor boats can be hired for use on the lake. Costs depend on the boat and the season but rowing boats are Rs 4 to 15 per hour, motor boats are rather more expensive.

The off-season is July-August and November-February, the high season is March-June and September-October. The notice board which used to be here included this gem of Indian-English: 'Rowers are available for rowing capacity including rower's rowing cooly charges extra'. Work that one out! If you want to go out on the lake do it soon, water hyacinth has already claimed half of it and will soon take over completely.

In the town itself the bazaar is worth a visit and you may come across some interesting crafts produced by the hill tribes in the area. See Chellaram's Department Store for literally dozens of reminders of British occupancy. Other oddities around Ooty include the police's 'Single Digit Finger Print Section' and the 'Co-operative Society of Ooty — Potato Chip Division'.

If you'd like a day or two's outing then take a bus to Kotagiri, a much smaller and quieter hill station about 28 km from Ooty. From this town you can visit Catherine Falls (eight km), Elk Falls (eight km) and Kodanad View Point (16 km). From the latter place there is a fine panoramic view over the eastern slope of the Nilgiris and on to the plains. There are a few basic lodges in Kotagiri such as the *Hotel Ram Vihar* where singles/doubles are Rs 18/30. In Coonoor the *Hampton Manor Hotel* (tel 244, 961-4) has singles at Rs 100, doubles at Rs 140 to 190. In

Mettupalayam there's a very pleasant two-bed *Retiring Room* spanning the width of the platform so you can hear the steam engine on one side and the Nilgiri Express on the other in the evening.

Tours

Kings Travel (tel 3137), c/o Nahar Tourist Home, Commercial Rd, offer two tours. The first covers Doddabetta Peak, Kotagiri, Kodanad View Point, Coonoor, Dolphin's Nose, Lamb's Rock and Sims Park. The tour runs from 8 am to 7 pm and costs Rs 60.

The other tour goes to Doddabetta Peak, the Botanical Gardens and Ooty Lake in the morning, then to the Mudumalai Wildlife Sanctuary in the afternoon. This tour runs from 9 am to 8 pm and costs Rs 60.

Charges include a vegetarian lunch, snacks, entrance fees, a guide and a group photograph (!). If you're hoping to see very much of Mudumalai, forget the second tour as you spend precisely 2¼ hours there.

Places to Stay

During the high season budget hotel prices may double or even triple. On the other hand the mid and top end places may offer considerable reductions in the off-season.

Places to Stay — Bottom End

The *Hotel Tamil Nadu* (tel 2543-4) is on the hill above the Tourist Office. It's a reasonably pleasant and modern building although not up to the standard of other TTDC places. In the 15 April to 15 June high season rooms cost Rs 60/100 but drop to Rs 40/60 in the low season. There is also a Rs 12 dormitory. The rooms are pleasantly furnished with table and chair, balcony, bathroom (hot water from 6 am to 9 am only). The radio doesn't work though, and a heater in the room will cost an extra Rs 15. Vegetarian and non-vegetarian meals are available in the dining room on the top floor and there is a coffee bar and games room (table tennis). The staff are friendly and most of the rooms have excellent views over Ooty.

Hotel Dasaprakash (tel 2460, 2680), on the hill south of the bus station, was once a grand building but has now gone to seed. Mouldy old moth-eaten photographs of the Maharaja of Mysore being shown around in better days attempt to recapture that old grandeur, but it's no longer in that bracket. Rooms start at Rs 30/60 and go on up to Rs 160 for de-luxe twin suites. There are also some cheaper doubles without attached bathrooms. There is a vegetarian restaurant.

On Commercial Rd, opposite the Tourist Office, the *Nahar Tourist Home* occupies a modern building. Singles/doubles, all with attached bathrooms and 24-hour hot water are Rs 50/60. The vegetarian restaurant downstairs is a bit expensive, Rs 9 for a thali with coffee.

The *YWCA* (tel 2218) on Anandagiri Ettines Rd takes both men and women and costs Rs 55 (in season), Rs 25 (out of season) for a double with bathroom. It's quite luxurious – carpeted floors, spacious lounge upstairs with a log fire, and good food. Bland and tasteless food reported a not so impressed visitor. Highly recommended – but beware of extra charges for blankets, hot water, even for the fire in the off season!

Hotel Gaylord (tel 2378) is on the hill behind the railway station and costs Rs 18/30.50. All the rooms have attached bathrooms and hot water but it's somewhat run down and dingy although it is very friendly. The attached restaurant purports to offer Punjabi, Bengali, Gujarati, continental and Chinese food if ordered in advance.

On South Lake Rd the *PWD Bungalow* is superbly located on the south shore of the lake and is one of the best mid-range places although accommodation is very limited. If it's early in the day then it's worth trying, otherwise you can make an advance reservation and stay elsewhere in the meantime. It's a good 15 minutes' walk from the bus stand and railway station. On Ettines Rd, *Hotel Nataraj* (tel 2772) costs from Rs 50/120 for singles/doubles, from only Rs 25 in the low season.

Rock bottom places vary widely in quality and prices can increase dramatically in the high season. Do some shopping around, prices don't necessarily equate with quality – many of them are very dingy, some of them revoltingly filthy.

Sri K R Bhavan Boarding & Lodging costs Rs 8 for a double with common bathroom. It's small, friendly and has good food but you must provide your own bedding. *Green Lands Hotel* is another small cheapie with Rs 6 doubles.

On the second street on the left, off the road along the top side of the racecourse as you leave the bus stand or railway station, is the dirty, dingy doss house known as *Nataraja Lodge*. There is no hot water and singles/doubles cost an overpriced Rs 8/18 but it's an interesting place and the manager is a practising astrologist.

Places to Stay – Top End

The *Fernhill Palace* (tel 2055, 3097-8) has singles from Rs 150, doubles from Rs 200. Costs are lower in the off season and there are also cottages. It seems the hotel is now mainly patronised by the Bombay film set.

The *Hotel Savoy* (tel 2572, 2463) costs Rs 225/350 for singles/doubles including all meals. The cheaper *Hotel Brindavan* (tel 2061-2-3) on Woodcock Rd, costs from Rs 60/120 in the high season.

The Fernhill Palace is decorated with hunt photographs (of the hunt assembled on the lawn outside). The ballroom, now the restaurant, is a huge grand affair, bordered by a balcony on which the old snooker table sits, balls cracked with age, and hung with decidedly moth-eaten velvet drapes. The bookcase is not to be missed, housing gems such as *Juvenile Crime in Southern India* by J W Combes in 1890, condoning flogging as the best form of punishment and comparing the physical features of young criminals with apes. Others of interest are *Polo in India* from 1907, *Lord*

Curzon in India 1898-1905 and so on. You can have coffee here for Rs 6, served in solid silver by uniformed waiters.

Places to Eat

Many hotels have their own restaurants which are open to non-residents, but if you want a change you could try the *Hotel Paradise* on Commercial Rd. It's diagonally opposite the co-operative supermarket and Tourist Office and has Punjabi and north Indian food of excellent quality and at reasonable prices. *Ghobi* (cauliflower & potato), curd, three chappatis and two coffees cost Rs 8.

Nahar Tourist Home has excellent, if slightly expensive, thalis in the ground floor restaurant. The Chinese *Zodiac Room* close to the GPO and State Bank has excellent meals for around Rs 8 to 10.

Getting There

Rail Like Darjeeling and Matheran, Ooty has its own miniature railway connecting it with the lowlands. The trains, with their quaint yellow and blue carriages, are not quite as small as the Darjeeling toy train, but they're nowhere near as big as those on the main lines. The unique feature of this line is the toothed central rail which the locomotives lock into on the steeper slopes.

Wellington, just above Coonoor, is a good place to watch the train climb one side of the valley, cross it by bridge and then double back to climb the opposite side. Like the journey up to Darjeeling by train, this is an excellent way of getting to Ooty and affords some spectacular views of the precipitous eastern slopes of the rain-forest covered Nilgiris. Highly recommended!

The miniature railway starts at Mettupalayam, north of Coimbatore and goes via Coonoor to Ooty. The departures and arrivals at Mettupalayam connect with the Nilgiri Express, which runs between Mettupalayam and Madras. If you're heading for Ooty, the Nilgiri Express departs Coimbatore at 6.35 am and arrives at Mettupalayam at 6 pm. The miniature trains depart Mettupalayam for Ooty at 8 am and Ooty at 11.20 am and 2 pm, the latter to connect with the Nilgiri Express. There are also trains from Ooty to Coonoor at 7.30 am and 5.40 pm. The 46 km journey takes about 4½ hours up to Ooty, about 3½ hours going down.

Bus – Local

Kotagiri – hourly from 7.30 am to 6.30 pm, journey takes 1¼ hours and costs Rs 2.50.

Coonoor – 11 buses from 7.20 am to 7 pm, journey takes one hour and costs Rs 1.50.

Bus – Long Distance

Bangalore – daily at 6.30 and 10.30 am, the journey takes nine hours and costs Rs 20.

Calicut – eight buses from 5.30 am to 3.15 pm. This is a very fine bus trip, 'our favourite journey in the whole of southern India (sit on the left side)' wrote a traveller.

Gudalur – five buses from 7.15 am to 7 pm.

Gundulpet – buses at 8.30, 9.50, 10.50 am and 2.15 pm.

Hassan – buses at 8 and 11.30 am, 2.30 and 5 pm.

Mysore – buses at 8 and 9 am, 1.30 and 3.30 pm. The 5½ hour trip costs Rs 15. This is the bus to take if you're heading for the Mudumalai Wildlife Sanctuary under your own steam. Get off at Theppukady where the reception centre is located. The journey this far from Ooty takes about 2½ hours and costs Rs 8.

COIMBATORE (population 380,000)

Coimbatore is a large and busy city at the foot of the Nilgiri mountains, full of 'shirting & suiting' shops. Its only interest for travellers is as a way station to Ootacamund and the other Nilgiri hill stations.

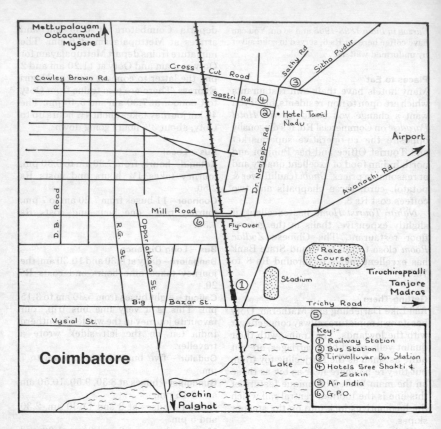

Coimbatore

Key:-
① Railway Station
② Bus Station
③ Tiruvalluvar Bus Station
④ Hotels Sree Shakti & Zakin
⑤ Air India
⑥ G.P.O.

Orientation

The bus station and railway station are a considerable distance from each other and both are well outside the centre of the city. You'll need an auto-rickshaw to get from one to the other. There are a number of mid-range and budget hotels clustered around the bus station—they are adequate for a night's stay.

Places to Stay

Hotel Sree Shakti, ll/148 Sastri Rd (tel 34225, 34229) is a large modern hotel opposite the bus station. The rooms cost Rs 30/45 for singles/doubles and are pleasantly decorated, reasonably clean and have attached bathrooms. The rooms have a fan, the staff are very friendly and room service is available.

Zakin Hotel, Sastri Rd, is a few doors up from Shakti and also opposite the bus station. Rooms here cost Rs 20/30 with attached bathrooms, Rs 15 for a bathless single. It's of similar quality to the Shakti.

There is now a *Hotel Tamil Nadu* on Dr Nanjappa Rd, across from the bus station. Rooms are Rs 60/90 or Rs 90/120 with air-con. All rooms have bath and running hot and cold water (well sometimes). There is also restaurant and bar.

Places to Eat

The *Zakin Hotel* has an attached restaurant on the ground floor which serves excellent non-vegetarian food. A large meat and vegetable stuffed paratha, mutton curry with very tender meat and a coffee cost Rs 12. A traveller wrote that it had not only gone seriously downhill but they had written themselves a Lonely Planet recommendation in their guest book! Untrue. There are also a number of other vegetarian and non-vegetarian restaurants where you can get a good meal, opposite the bus station along Sastri Rd. There's also a cheap cafe in the bus station itself.

Getting There

Air There are flights between Coimbatore and Madras (Rs 379) and twice daily flights to and from Bangalore (Rs 190).

Rail Coimbatore is a major rail junction and there are services to most major centres. The direct Karnataka Kerala Express operates twice a week from New Delhi and makes the 2627-km trip in 38 hours at a cost of Rs 522 in 1st, Rs 133 in 2nd. There are numerous daily trains between Madras (Central) and Coimbatore. The 494-km trip takes seven to nine hours and costs Rs 143 in 1st, Rs 36.50 in 2nd.

The daily trains to Madurai take from seven hours for the 229-km trip and costs Rs 75 in 1st, Rs 19 in 2nd. One of them goes on to Rameswaram, a 14-hour trip for 393 km at a cost of Rs 120 in 1st, Rs 31 in 2nd. Bangalore is 424 km away, the eight-hour trip costs Rs 128 in 1st, Rs 33 in 2nd. Direct trains to Bombay take 33 hours for the 1635-km trip and cost Rs 358 in 1st, Rs 92 in 2nd.

Take the Nilgiri Express if you're heading for Ooty, it connects with the miniature railway at Mettupalayam. Coming from Ooty you can take the toy train to Mettupalayam and then a bus the rest of the way – it may be faster than continuing by train.

Bus There's a huge and well organised bus station in Coimbatore. As elsewhere timetables are only in Tamil except for buses to Ooty and some interstate buses.

Bangalore – buses at 6.30 and 8.30 am and 8 pm. There's also a Conti Travels air-con bus at 7 am.

Guruvayur – buses at 4.40 and 10 am, 3.30 and 8 pm. The journey takes four hours.

Kanyakumari – buses at 5.30 am and 10.15 pm via Dindigul and Madurai.

Madras – six buses from 5 pm to 11 pm. The first and last buses go via Vellore and Kanchipuram.

Madurai – seven buses from 6 am to 11 pm, they go via Palani, Dindigul and Kodai Road.

Mysore – daily at 6 am, takes 6½ hours.

Naggapattinam – four buses from 5.30 am to 10.30 pm, they go via Trichy and Tanjore.

Nagarcoil – six buses from 5 am to 8.30 pm via Dindigul and Madurai.

Ootacamund – 26 buses from 5 am to 7.20 pm. The three-hour journey costs Rs 8.50 and is one of the most spectacular bus journeys in southern India. Don't expect to get on the first bus which arrives, because even in the off-season there will be a long queue for the buses. You generally can expect to get on the second or third bus to arrive after you join the queue.

Palghat – one to four buses hourly from 4.45 am to 7.25 pm. The 1¼ hour journey costs Rs 4.50.

Pondicherry – buses via Cuddalore at 9 am and 9.30 pm.

Tanjore – buses via Trichy at 9.30 am and 7.30 pm.

Trichy (Tiruchirappalli) – six buses from 6 am to 11 pm, the 5-1/2 hour trip costs Rs 22.

Trichur – buses at 5.30 and 9 am, 12.45 and 5.15 pm. The journey takes 3¼ hours.

Getting Around

Useful buses around Coimbatore include

bus 20 to the airport, bus 25 and 32A to
the GPO and bus lA, 7, 65 and 75 to Indian
Airlines. There are numerous buses
between the bus and railway stations.
Coimbatore's local buses are not too
crowded.

WILDLIFE SANCTUARIES IN TAMIL NADU

There are six wildlife sanctuaries in Tamil
Nadu, three close to the east coast and the
others in the richly forested mountains on
the borders of Kerala and Karnataka.
Mudumalai, at the foot of the Nilgiris in
the extreme north-western tip of the state,
is the largest and is contiguous with
Bandipur Wildlife Sanctuary in Karnataka
and Wynad Sanctuary in Kerala. The
smallest is Guindy Deer Park within the
metropolitan boundaries of Madras.

All the sanctuaries, except Guindy,
have accommodation and transport
facilities and although it's possible to turn
up at any of them without prior arrangements having been made, it's advisable to
book in advance. The reason for this is
that rooms in sanctuary lodges and rest
houses cannot be allocated to unannounced
guests until very late in the afternoon
when there's no further possibility of
anyone with a booking arriving.

There's also the question of arranging
motorised transport to the more remote
parts of the sanctuaries where you're far
more likely to see animals, which don't
often venture too close to areas of human
settlement or main roads. Some of the
sanctuaries offer elephant rides through
the forest and, although these needn't be
booked in advance and are great fun as far
as they go, you're unlikely to see many of
the animals which live in these sanctuaries
from the back of an elephant.

At present, most of the sanctuaries are
geared to groups who arrive with their own
transport and who have pre-booked at
least a few days ahead. If you're alone and
haven't booked, you could find that a lot of
your time is taken up waiting for a group to
arrive that you can attach yourself to.

Without transport, too, your choice of
accommodation is limited unless you can
get a lift. It's time the Indian tourist
organisation gave some thought to
catering for visitors without their own
transport and who can't, because of the
way they travel, make bookings weeks in
advance. All the same, don't let this put
you off visiting at least one of the
sanctuaries as it can be a very rewarding
experience.

Mudumalai Wildlife Sanctuary

In the luxuriously forested foothills of the
Nilgiris, Mudumalai is part of a much
larger sanctuary which includes those of
Bandipur and Wynad in neighbouring
Karnataka and Kerala respectively. The
main attractions here are the herds of
spotted deer, gaur (Indian bison) and
elephant, tiger, panther, wild pig, sloth
and the otters and crocodiles which live in
the River Moyar. It's possible to see all of
these if you have made arrangements with

the forest department for a vehicle to take you to the more remote parts of the sanctuary.

Even around Theppukadu, where the Reception Centre is located, you will see spotted deer, elephant and wild pig and at night, if you're lucky, tiger. The Reception Centre has a board on which they keep a record of which animals were sighted and where. There's also a visitors' book which makes interesting reading, especially the accounts of those who (perhaps foolishly) have gone out walking at night and met tigers!

The main service area in this sanctuary is the village of Theppukadu on the main road between Ootacamund and Mysore where the Wildlife Sanctuary Reception Centre, Sylvan Lodge, chai shops and elephant camp are. Any of the service buses which run between Ooty and Mysore will take you there. From Ooty it's a 2½ hour journey and costs Rs 8. It's advisable to book accommodation and transport in the sanctuary in advance, either with the Forest Officer in Ooty on Coonoor Rd or at a Tamil Nadu Tourist Office. Charges are as follows:

Entrance fees:
  adults Rs 1, children Rs 0.50
  car Rs 5, jeep Rs 5, van Rs 7.50
  cameras Rs 2, movie cameras Rs 10

Hire charges for transport:
  jeep (up to six people): Rs 2 per km
  van (up to eight people): Rs 3 per km
  elephant rides (up to four people): Rs
    20 per elephant

Elephant rides are available between 6 and 10 am and again between 4 and 6 pm. If you're on your own, there's no problem about finding space with another group. The elephants go crashing through the bush over a four to five km circuit and are great fun but you'll be lucky to see anything other than spotted deer, warthogs, buffaloes and monkeys.

As far as places to stay are concerned, if you're relying on public transport, you'll have to stay either at Theppukadu or at Abhayaranyam which are both on the bus route. In any event, you first have to call at the Reception Centre whether you have a booking or not. The following accommodation is available:

Abhayaranyam Rest House There are two suites here which cost Rs 20 for the first person and Rs 10 for each additional person. There is also a dormitory at the Range Office a short way from the Rest House for Rs 12 per person. Catering facilities are available.

Theppukadu Village The main place here is the *Sylvan Lodge* which has four suites at Rs 30 a single, Rs 50 a double. They also have a log house with three suites and a dormitory at Rs 12 per person. Meals are available here whether you are staying there or not (good meals).

The Reception Centre has a dormitory attached to it with eight beds (four per room) which costs Rs 12 per person. There is an attached toilet and shower but no catering facilities. If you're staying here you can eat at the two chai shops in the village or at the Sylvan Lodge. Baggage can be left safely at the Reception Centre whether you have a booking or not, if you're planning on staying for the night.

There's also a dorm at Kargundi, three km south of Theppukadu (about 25 beds) at Rs 4. Dinner and breakfast are availabel but you still must get permission from Theppukadu to stay there. There's a watchtower half a km from Kargundi on the river and two others about seven km into the park.

Masinagudi Village There are three possibilities here: *Masinagudi Rest House* which has three suites costing Rs 10 a single plus Rs 5 for each additional person, catering facilities are available. *Bamboo Banks Farm* (tel 22), accommodation here costs Rs 90 a single and Rs 150 a double with full board or Rs 50 a

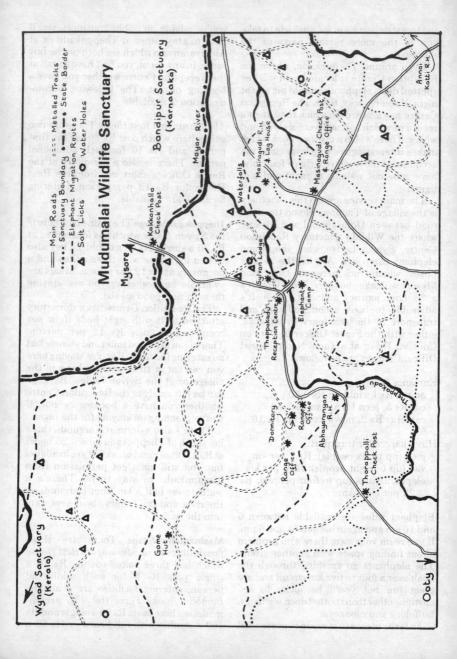

Mudumalai Wildlife Sanctuary

Main Roads
Sanctuary Boundary
Elephant Migration Routes
Solt Licks
Metalled Tracks
State Border
Water Holes

Mysore

Bandipur Sanctuary (Karnataka)

Moyar River

Annai Katti R.H.

Kakkanhalla Check Post

Waterfalls

Masinagudi R.H.
Log House

Masinagudi Check Post & Range Office

Sylvan Lodge

Thappakadu Reception Centre

Elephant Camp

Thorappalli Check Post

Thorappalli R.

Dormitory

Abhayaranyan R.H.

Range Office

Range Office

Game Hut

Wynad Sanctuary (Kerala)

Ooty

single and Rs 75 a double for bed and breakfast. *Mountania Rest House* (tel 37) where you can rent a de-luxe cottage with six beds for Rs 150 in the high season or Rs 125 in the low season; cheaper with just two or three beds. All the cottages have attached bathrooms.

They also have a log cabin with 10 beds and common bathroom for Rs 10 per person in the low season. Meals are available and the food is excellent. There is also a bar where you can get a drink without a liquor permit. Bookings can be made in advance at Safari Travels (tel 3141), opposite Union Church, Ooty.

Note that the Ooty-Mysore and Ooty-Hassan buses both stop at Theppukadu if there's anyone getting off or if they have spare seats. If not, they tend to drive straight through. If you're leaving the sanctuary, you have to make a determined effort to flag the bus down. On the other hand, it's relatively easy to have a word with people who arrive in their own transport and get yourself a lift back to Ooty or Mysore, or even to Masinagudi if you don't want to stay at Theppukadu for the night. Ooty-Gundalpet buses also pass through the sanctuary and they're more easily flagged down.

You can visit the sanctuary on tours from Ooty. A writer reported seeing two herds of elephants, Indian bison, deer and peacocks from his perch on the roof of the tour minibus.

The best time to visit the sanctuary is between February and May, though you can visit at any time of the year except possibly in the dry season when it may be closed. Heavy rain is common in October and November.

Vedanthangal Water Birds Sanctuary

This is one of the most spectacular breeding grounds in India. Water fowl gather here for about six months of the year from October/November to March, depending on the monsoons, and peaks in December and January. At the height of the breeding season it's possible to see up to 30,000 birds at one time. The best time to visit is in the early morning or late afternoon.

The main types of birds which come here to breed and nest include cormorants, egrets, herons, storks, ibises, spoonbills, grebes and pelicans. Many other species of migratory birds also visit the sanctuary.

The best way to get there is via bus from Madras to Chingleput, but you will have to hire transport to take you to the Forest Rest House. The only place to stay here is the *Forest Rest House* which has four suites at Rs 20 a single and Rs 30 a double.

Calimere Wildlife Sanctuary

Located on the east coast just south of the Pondicherry territory of Karaikal in Tanjore district, Point Calimere is noted for its congregation of black buck, spotted deer, wild pig and vast flocks of migratory waterfowl especially flamingoes. Every year in winter the tidal mud flats and marshes are covered with masses of birds – teals, shovellers, curlews, gulls, terns, plovers, sandpipers, shanks and herons. It's possible to see up to 30,000 flamingoes at any one time. In the spring a different set of birds – the koels, mynas and barbets – are drawn here by the profusion of wild berries.

The best time to visit is between November and January. From April to June there is very little activity. The main rainy season is from October to December. You can get to Point Calimere either by rail on the Mayavaram-Thiruthuraipoondi section or by regular bus from either Tanjore or Mayavaram. A *Forest Rest House* with two suites is available which costs Rs 8 per person. Facilities are very basic and no meals are available.

Mundanthurai Tiger Sanctuary

One of the most recently created sanctuaries, Mundanthurai is in the mountains near the border with Kerala. The nearest railway station is at Amabasamudram and there are regular buses from there to the sanctuary. As the name implies, this is principally a tiger sanctuary and the best time to visit is between January and September, though you can visit at any time of year. The main rainy season is between October and December. Since you're most likely to see tigers in the very early morning or late evening you should stay here for the night. The Forest Department will arrange to take you around the sanctuary.

Accommodation is in a *Forest Rest House* which has two suites costing Rs 15 a single, Rs 25 a double. There is also a small charge for electricity.

Anamalai Wildlife Sanctuary
This is the third of the wildlife sanctuaries in the mountains along the Tamil Nadu-Kerala border. Anamalai is south of Coimbatore and can be reached either by regular bus from Coimbatore or by rail to Pollachi and then by bus to the sanctuary. The Reception Centre is at Parambikulam dam. The major attractions at Anamalai are elephant, gaur, tiger, panther, spotted deer, wild boar, bear, porcupine and civet cats. The Nilgiri tahr, commonly known as ibex, can also be seen here. Transport through the sanctuary can be arranged by the Forest Department.

Accommodation is available at three places: *Forest Rest House* at Topslip, six suites are available here. *Varagaliar Rest House*, this is deep inside the forest and offers basic accommodation but you must take your own provisions as there are no catering facilities. *Mount Stuart Rest House*, two suites are available here and meals can be provided. The sanctuary can be visited at any time of the year but the best time of day to go is in the very early morning or late evening.

Guindy Deer Park
Within the metropolitan boundaries of Madras city, this is the only place in the world where it is still possible to see fairly large numbers of the fast-dwindling species of Indian antelope (black buck). It also has small numbers of spotted deer, civet cats, jackal, mongoose and various species of monkey. There is a reptile house within the park.

The Deer Park is adjacent to Raj Bhavan at Guindy and you can get there either by catching a commuter train from Beach Railway Station opposite the GPO or from Egmore Railway Station and getting off at Guindy Station. There are also regular service buses from Madras to Guindy.

Andaman & Nicobar Islands

Population: 130,000
Area: 8293 square km
Capital: Port Blair
Main languages: various tribal

In the middle of the Bay of Bengal half-way between India and Burma lies this string of over 300 richly-forested, tropical islands which reach almost to the tip of Sumatra. Ethnically, they are not a part of India and were, until fairly recently, peopled by several distinct tribes having different physiognomies and speaking different languages.

The tribes fall into three main groups. The Onges, concentrated mainly on Little Andaman, are a small, dark-complexioned tribe of hunters and gatherers, who wear no clothes other than tassled genital decorations and are fond of colourful make-up. The Nicobaris, whose home is on Car Nicobar are a fair-complexioned people, who have begun to adapt to contemporary Indian society. They live mainly on fish, coconuts and pigs and are organised into villages controlled by a village headman. The last group, the Shompens, are found on Great Nicobar. So far they have resisted integration into Indian society and tend to shy away from areas occupied by Indian immigrants from the mainland, preferring to lead their lives according to their own traditions.

The Indian Government is fond of eulogising its efforts to bring civilisation to these islands but, reading between the lines, it's obvious it regards these indigenous tribes as stone-age people and its attitude towards them is very condescending. In an effort to develop the islands economically, the Indian government has completely disregarded the needs and land rights of the tribes and has encouraged massive immigration from the mainland – mainly of Tamils who were expelled from Sri Lanka – which has pushed the population of these islands from 50,000 to 150,000 in just 15 years. It is little wonder that the islanders' culture is about to be swamped so, if you want to see anything of it, you will have to go there soon. This isn't as easy as you might imagine, as not only is a permit required (in addition to any visa requirement for India as a whole), but there are numerous restrictions as to which parts you can visit on arrival.

The Andaman and Nicobar Islands were annexed by the Marathas from the mainland of India in the late 17th century. In the early 18th century they were the base of the Maratha admiral, Kanhoji Angre, whose navy harrassed British, Dutch and Portuguese merchant vessels at that time, frequently capturing them. Angre even managed to capture the British Governor of Bombay's yacht in 1713 and released it only after a ransom of

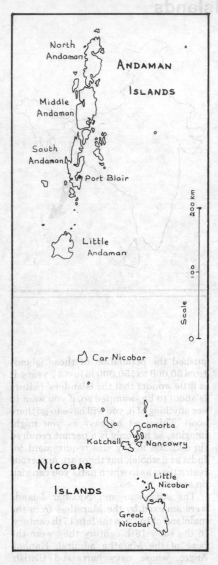

North
Andaman

ANDAMAN

ISLANDS

Middle
Andaman

South
Andaman

Port Blair

200 km

Little
Andaman

100

Scale

0

Car Nicobar

Camorta

Katchall   Nancowry

NICOBAR

ISLANDS

Little
Nicobar

Great
Nicobar

The islands were finally annexed by the British in the 19th century and used as a penal colony for Indian freedom fighters. The notorious 'cellular jail', one of the 'tourist attractions' of Port Blair, where many of the inmates were executed either judicially or clandestinely, was begun in the last decade of the 19th century and finished in 1908. During WW II the islands were occupied for a time by the Japanese, but they were not welcomed as liberators and the local tribes took up guerrilla activities against them. When independence came to India they were incorporated into the Indian Union.

At present, a big effort is being made to develop the islands and vast tracts of forest have been cut down. There has been some replanting with 'economic' timber like teak, but much of it has been turned over to rubber plantations. As for the climate, there is little seasonal variation. Continuous sea breezes keep the temperatures within the range of 23 to 31°C, but humidity stays around 80% all year. The south-west monsoons come to the islands between mid-May and October and the north-east monsoons between November and January. The best season to visit is between mid-November and mid-May.

Permits

All foreigners need a special permit before they can visit the Andaman and Nicobar Islands. You can, if you like, get this before you leave home by applying at least six weeks in advance either to: The Secretary, Government of India, Ministry of Home Affairs, New Delhi, India, or to your nearest Indian Embassy or Consulate.

If you apply at the latter they will pass your application on to New Delhi. It's only worth doing this if you intend to fly to the islands, since you have to state the dates you intend being there. It's almost impossible to do this if you are planning to go by ship from Madras, as they only run on an *irregular* schedule. If you are going by ship, wait until you get to Madras, and

powder and shot was delivered. Though attacked by the British, and later by a com-bined British-Portuguese naval task force, Angre remained un-defeated right up to his death in 1729.

then as soon as you arrive, find out when the next sailing is and make a booking. Having done this, you can go to the Chief Immigration Officer, 9 Village Rd, just off Nungambakkan Rd , before the junction with Sterling Rd (bus route No 10), and have your permit issued in three days. No photos are needed.

Things to See

For the sightseer, these islands don't offer a great deal, and probably the only reason you would come here would be to relax and/or visit the various tribes who live here. The Indian Tourist organisation runs daily tours of the sights around Port Blair (the main settlement). These cost Rs 4.50 and include visits to the Cellular Jail, Chatham saw mills, the Anthropology Museum, the Fisheries Museum, Marina Park, Corbyn's Cove and the Cottage Industries Emporium.

Corbyn's Cove is the nearest beach to Port Blair (10 km), but is used by Air India package tours.

Places to Stay

Other than accommodation at Corbyn's Cove, South Andaman, all the available places to stay are controlled by various Indian Government departments (mostly the PWD and Forestry Departments), and the standard is fairly basic. Meals are available at standard prices and the charges for accommodation and meals at these places are standardised as follows:

Accommodation type	Single	Double
Dak Bungalows	Rs 20	Rs 20
Circuit Houses	Rs 15	Rs 20
Tourist Homes	Rs 10	Rs 20
Government of India Guest Houses	Rs 10	Rs 20
Inspection Bungalows	Rs 10	Rs 20

Government accommodation is available as follows:

South Andaman

Tourist Home, Haddo, Port Blair; *Tourist Home*, Corbyn's Cove, Port Blair; *Circuit House*, Haddo, Port Blair; *Government Guest House*, Haddo, Port Blair; *Dak Bungalow*, Haddo, Port Blair; *Inspection Bungalow*, Ferragunj; *Inspection Bungalow*, Milletilak; *Guest House*, Hamfregunj; *Guest House*, Havelock Island; *Rest House*, Neil Island.

Apart from the above there are the more expensive places which cater largely to package tourists from the mainland:

Megapore Nest, Port Blair, rooms cost Rs 50 a single and Rs 100 a double for non air-con rooms and Rs 75 a single and Rs 150 a double for air-con rooms.

Nicobari Huts, Port Blair: These cost Rs 160 a double for non air-con and Rs 200 a double for air con. There are no single rooms.

Andaman Beach Resort, Corbyn's Cove, Port Blair, rooms here cost Rs 200 a single and Rs 240 a double with air-con. This is the place that Air India uses for its package tours.

Welcomgroup Bay Island, Marine Hill, Port Blair, is a new place with singles for Rs 225 (Rs 275 with air-con), doubles for Rs 325 (Rs 375 with air-con).

In addition to the above there are *rest houses* at Chidiatapu, overlooking the sea on the southernmost tip of the island, and the *Wright Myo Rest House* on the fringe of the forest. The Forestry Department also has a number of *rest houses* in the forest. Contact the Forestry Department, Port Blair, for details of these.

Middle Andaman

Rest House, Betapur; *Rest House*, Kandamtala; *Rest House*, Rangat.

North Andaman

Rest House, Aerial Bay; *Rest House*, Diglipur; *Rest House*, Kadamtala; *Rest House*, Mayabunder; *Circuit House*, Mayabunder; *Rest House*, Parangara; *Rest House*, Tugapur.

Nicobars

Circuit House, Car Nicobar; *Inspection Bungalow*, Car Nicobar; *Guest House*, Kamorta Island.

Foreign exchange facilities are available at either the Cooperative Bank, near Aberdeen Bazaar, Port Blair, or the State Bank of India, near the Deputy Commissioner's Office, Port Blair. The nearest hospital is Gobinda Ballabh Pant Hospital, Port Blair. Note that total prohibition is in force in these islands and alcoholic drinks are not available. It's definitely BYO.

Getting There

Air Indian Airlines connect Port Blair with Madras twice weekly and Calcutta twice weekly. The Madras flight takes just over two hours and costs Rs 976. The Calcutta flight takes exactly two hours and costs Rs 966.

Boat The Shipping Corporation of India (13 Strand Rd, Calcutta 1) and its agents in Madras, K P V Sheikh Mohammed Rowther & Co (202 Linghi Chetty St, Madras 1 (tel 25756) operate three ships to the Andaman and Nicobar Islands every 15 to 20 days *but there is no regular schedule.*

The disputes which occur in the shipping offices between Indian passengers (who do not require a permit) and the shipping clerks have to be seen to be believed! As a foreigner, your difficulties are compounded by the fact that you need a permit, and that permit states the time (dates) you are allowed to visit the islands. If you've already got your permit and these dates don't correspond with the departure and return of the ship then you've got problems and will have to have your permit altered at the Immigration Office in Madras. Flying out there makes a lot of sense as you can be certain of departure and return dates.

Unfortunately, this isn't the only variable since tickets for the boats are issued only on the basis of the passenger list received at the shipping offices from the authorities at Port Blair. It's necessary to make prior reservations with these people in Port Blair. For cabin class accommodation apply to Assistant Secretary, Chief Commissioner, Andaman and Nicobar Administration, Port Blair. For bunk accommodation apply to the Manager, Shipping Corporation of India, Port Blair. In your application you must state your name, father's name, address, nationality, purpose of visit, duration of stay, the approximate date you want to sail and the class of accommodation required.

If your luck holds out and/or you manage to ride out this ridiculously Kafkaesque miasma, the following table lists the prices (Rs) for the various types of accommodation in the four ships.

Ship 1: *TSS Nancowry* (from Madras)
Ship 2: *MV Harshavardhana* (from Calcutta)
Ship 3: *MV Andamans* (from Vizag)
Ship 4: *MV Akbar* (from Madras)

Ship:	1	2	3	4
Accommodation				
de-luxe cabin	558	558	513	558
A class cabin	500	513	488	500
B class cabin	389	389	389	–
C class cabin	355	355	–	–
air-con bunk	100	100	–	250
ordinary bunk	69	–	69	69

Both the *TSS Nancowry* and the *MV Akbar* depart from Madras. The *MV Harshavardhana* departs from Calcutta and the *MV Andamans* departs from Vizag.

Charges for food on board are Rs 8 per day in bunk class (Indian style) and Rs 28 per day in cabin class accommodation (choice of western or Indian food). The passage from either Calcutta or Madras takes two to three days. The ships stay in Port Blair for four days on average, so if you don't have a lot of time to spare, you could go there just for four days. The *MV Harshavardhana* is the fastest and most modern of the ships.

Read the book *Slow Boats to China*, mentioned in the introductory section on books, for a description of travelling Madras-Port Blair-Calcutta with a short stay in the Andamans.

Inter-Island Ferries
South Andaman Island There is a ferry around South Andaman Island three times daily at 6 am, 12.30 pm and 3 pm from the Fisheries Jetty, Port Blair, which calls at Bamboo Flat, Haddo Harbour, Dandus Point and Junglee Ghat.

Connections to the other islands Two ferries, the *Yerewa* and the *Onge* connect Port Blair with the other islands in the Andaman and Nicobar group on a once-weekly basis. Other small seagoing boats can be chartered from the Harbour Master, Port Blair (tel 528).

Glossary

Indian English is full of interesting little everyday expressions. Where in New York you might get robbed by a mugger, in India it will be a *dacoit* who relieves you of your goods. Politicians may employ strong-arm heavies known in India as *goondas*. There is a plethora of Indian terms for strikes, lock-outs and sit-ins – Indians can have *hartals, bhands* and *gheraos* for example. And then there are all those Indian servants – children get looked after by *ayahs*, your house (and your godown if you have one) is guarded by a *chowkidar* (but they're reputed to be a lazy bunch much given to lying around on *charpois*), and when the toilet needs cleaning there is no way your *bearer* is going to do it, that requires calling in a *sweeper*.

Then there are all the religious terms, the numerous Hindu gods, their attendants, consorts, vehicles and symbols. The multiplicity of religions in India also provides a whole series of terms for temples, shrines, tombs or memorials. It's surprising how many Indian terms have crept into everyday English usage. We can sit out on a *verandah*, wear *pyjamas* (or *dungarees* and *sandals* and they may well be *khaki*), *shampoo* our hair, visit the *jungle*, worry about protecting our *loot* – they're all Indian words.

The glossary that follows is just a sample of words you may come across during your Indian wanderings. See 'food' and 'religion' for lots more.

Acha – OK.

Acharya – revered teacher, originally a spiritual guide or perceptor.

Anikut – weir or dam.

Anna – one sixteenth of a rupee, now extinct but still used in market place conversation, ie eight annas is 50 paise, four annas is 25 paise.

Arrack – spirit drink made from coconut sap or rice wine.

Ashram – spiritual college come retreat.

Avalokitesvara – one of the Buddha's most important disciples.

Ayah – children's nurse or nanny.

Ayurvedic – Indian natural and herbal medicine.

Baba – religious master but also used in a more common manner.

Babu – lower level clerical worker.

Bagh – garden.

Bahadur – brave or chivalrous, honorific title.

Baksheesh – tip, bribe or simply donation to a beggar.

Bandar – port or harbour.

Bandh – general strike.

Banian – T-shirt or under-vest.

Baniya – money lender.

Banyan – Indian fig tree.

Baoli – well, particularly a step well with landings and galleries.

Basti – Jain temple.

Bazaar – market area, a market town is called a bazaar.

Bearer – rather like a butler.

Beedis – (or bidis) small hand-rolled cigarettes – really just a rolled-up tobacco leaf.

Begum – Moslem lady of high rank.

Betel – nut of the betel trees, chewed as a mild intoxicant.

Bhagvadgita – Krishna's lessons to Arjuna, part of the Mahabharata.

Bhang – lassi and charas mixture.

Bhisti – (or bheesti) water carrier.

Bodhisattva – near Buddha, follower of Buddha.

Bo-tree – ficus religiosa, the tree under which the Buddha attained enlightenment.

Brahmin – highest Indian caste.

Bund – embankment or dyke.

Burka – one-piece garment which totally covers Moslem women.

Bustee – slum areas of Calcutta.

Cantonment – administrative and military area of a British Raj-era town.

Caste – what your station in life is.

Chaitya – Buddhist temple.

Chakra – focus of your spiritual power, disc-like weapon of Vishnu.

Chalo, chalo, chalo – 'let's go, let's go, let's go' – what you yell as the bus leaves.

Chance List – the wait list on Indian Airline flights.

Chang – Tibetan rice beer.

Chaoultries – dharamsalas in the south.

Chappals – sandals.

Chappati – unleavened Indian bread.

Charas – ganga.

Charpoi – Indian rope bed.

Chat – general term for small snacks, papris, etc.

Chatri – tomb or mausoleum.

Chauri – fly whisk.

Chela – pupil or follower, as George Harrison was to Ravi Shankar.

Chillum – pipe part of a hookah, commonly used to describe the small pipes for smoking ganga.

Chorten – Tibetan word for stupa.

Chowk – courtyard or market place.

Chowkidah – nightwatchman, often a cook as well.

Cong (I) – Congress Party (India) or Congress Party (Indira) depending on how cynical you are.

Country Liquor – locally-produced liquor.

CPI – Communist Party of India.

CPI (M) – the Communist Party of India (Marxist), it's the bigger, more powerful party and is currently in power in West Bengal (Calcutta).

Crore – 10 million.

Curd – yoghurt.

Cutcherry – office or building for public business.

Dacoit – robber, particularly armed robber.

Dacoity – to suffer at the hands of a dacoit.

Dargah – shrine or place of burial of a Moslem saint.

Darshan – offering or audience with someone, usually a guru.

Darwaza – gateway or door.

Dhal – lentil soup, what most of India lives on.

Dharamsala – religious guest house.

Dharma – Buddhist teachings.

Dhobi – clothes washerman.

Dhopalta – scarf worn by Punjabi women.

Dhoti – like a longhi, but the cloth is then pulled up between your legs.

Diwan – principal officer in a princely state, royal court or council.

Diwan-i-Am – Hall of Public Audience.

Diwan-i-Khas – Hall of Private Audience.

Dooli – covered litter or stretcher, you may still see elderly tourists being carried around some sights in a dooli.

Dravidian – ornate southern Indian architectural style, also southern Indian race.

Durbar – royal court, also used to describe a government.

Durga – same as Kali, terrible manifestation of Parvati.

Dwarpal – door-keeper, sculpture beside the doorways to Hindu or Buddhist shrines.

Fakir – accurately a Moslem who has taken a vow of poverty, but also applied to Hindu ascetics such as sadhus.

Fenni – spirit drink made from cashews, found in Goa.

Firman – a royal order or grant.

Freaks – young westerners wandering India, the '60s live!

Gaddi – throne of a Hindu prince.

Ganesh – god of learning, elephant-headed son of Shiva and Parvati, probably the most popular god in the whole Hindu pantheon.

Ganga – Ganges River.

Ganja – hashish.

Garuda – man-bird vehicle of Vishnu

Ghari – horse carriage.

Ghat – steps or landing on a river, place where corpses are cremated.

Ghazal – Urdu songs, sad love themes.

Ghee – all-purpose cooking oil, clarified butter.

Gherao – lock in, where the workers lock the management in!

Godown – wharehouse.

Gompa – Tibetan-Buddhist monastery.

Gonds – aboriginal Indian race, now mainly found in the jungles in central India.

Goondas – ruffians or toughs, political parties often have gangs of goondas.

Gopis – cowherd girls, Krishna was very fond of them.

Gopuram – soaring pyramidal gateway tower of a Dravidian temple.

Gurdwara – Sikh temple.

Guru – teacher or holy man.

Haji – a Moslem who has made the pilgrimage (haj) to Mecca.

Hanuman – monkey god.

Harijan – literally 'Children of God', but actually it still means simply the lowest casate, the untouchables.

Hartal – strike.

Haveli – traditional mansions with interior courtyards, particularly in Rajasthan and Gujarat.

Hookah – water pipe for smoking tobacco.

Howdah – framework for carrying people on an elephant's back.

Hypothecated – Indian equivalent of leased, you often see a small sign on a taxi or auto-rickshaw that the vehicle is 'hypothecated' to some bank or other.

Idgah – open enclosure to the west of a town where prayers are offered during the Moslem festival of Id.

Imam – Moslem leader.

Imambara – tomb of a Shi'ite Moslem holy man.

IMFL – Indian Made Foreign Liquor – beer or spirits produced in India.

Indra – king of the Vedic gods.

Jaggery – hard, brown sugar-like sweetener made from kitul palm sap.

Janata – people, thus the Janata Party is the People's Party.

Jatakas – tales from the Buddha's various lives.

Jauhar – ritual mass suicide by immolation, traditionally performed by Rajput women at times of military defeat to avoid being dishonoured by their captors.

Ji – honorific title that can be added to the end of almost anything – thus Baba-ji.

Juggernauts – huge, extravagantly decorated temple 'cars', which are dragged through the streets during Hindu festivals.

Jumkahs – ear-rings.

Jyotorlinga – 12 holy Shiva shrines in India are known as the 12 Jyotorlingas.

Kachahri – see Cutcherry.

Kadi – homespun cloth, Mahatma Gandhi spent much energy in encouraging people to spin their own Kadi cloth rather than buy imported English material.

Kali – Parvati's terrible side.

Karmachario – university term.

Kartikiya – god of war, Shiva's son.

Kata – Tibetan prayer shawl, traditionally given to a lama when one is brought into his presence.

Khan – Moslem honorific title.

Kibla – niche in the wall to which Moslems look when praying in order to face Mecca.

Kothi – residence, house or mansion.

Kotwali – police station.

Krishna – Vishnu's eighth incarnation, he's often coloured blue.

Kundalini – coiled serpent, the manifestation of Kali, the place at the base of your spine where your shakti resides.

Lakh – 100,000.

Lama – Tibetan-Buddhist priest or holy man.

Lassi – very refreshing yoghurt and iced water drink.

Lathi – baton, what Indian police hit you with if you get in the way of a lathi charge.

Laxmi (or Lakshmi) – Vishnu's consort, goddess of wealth, very popular in Bombay.

Lingam – phallic symbol, symbol of Shiva.

Lok – people.

Lok Dal – political party, one of the components of the Janata party.

Lok Sabha – lower house in the Indian parliament, comparable to the House of Representatives or House of Commons.

Longhi – loin cloth wrapped around your thighs.

Mahabharata – Vedic epics, one of the two major Hindu epics.

Mahal – house or palace, queen.

Maharaja – Raja, Hindu king or prince.

Mahatma – literally 'great soul'.

Mahayana – large vehicle Buddhism.

Mahout – elephant rider/master.

Maidan – open place or square.

Mali – gardener.

Mandala – Tibetan geometrical and astrological representation of the world.

Mandir – temple.

Mandapam – pillared pavilion in front of a temple.

Mani stone – stone carved with the Tibetan-Buddhist chant 'Om Mani Padme Hum' – 'Hail to the jewel in the lotus'.

Mantra – prayer formula or chant. **Mara** – Buddhist god of death, has three eyes and holds the wheel of life.

Maratha (Mahratta) – war-like central Indian race, who often controlled much of India and gave the Moghuls a lot of trouble.

Masjid – mosque, Jami Masjid is the Friday Mosque or main mosque.

Maund – now largely superseded unit of weight.

Math – monastery.

Mela – a fair.

Memsahib – European married lady, from 'madam-sahib', still more widely used than you'd think.

Mendi – ornate patterns painted on women's hands and feet for important festivals, particularly in Rajasthan.

Mihrab – see Kibla.

Moghul – golden period of Indian history from the emperor Babur to Aurangzeb, the last powerful Moghul ruler.

Monsoon – rainy period from around June to October, when it rains virtually every day.

Moorcha – mob march or protest march.

Mughal – same as Moghul.

Muezzin – one who calls Moslems to prayer from the minaret.

Mullah – Moslem priest.

Munshi – writer, secretary or teacher of languages.

Naga – snake or a person from Nagaland.

Nandi – bull, vehicle of Shiva and usually found at Shiva temples.

Narayan – an incarnation of Vishnu.

Narsimha (or Narsingh) – man-lion incarnation of Vishnu.

Nautch Girls – dancing girls, a nautch is a dance.

Nawab – nobleman or governor.

Naxalites – ultra-leftist political movement, started in northern part of West Bengal where it appeared as a rebellion against landlords by peasants. Characterised by extreme violence, it originated in the village of Naxal and is now fairly subdued in West Bengal, but still exists in Uttar Pradesh.

Nilakantha – form of Shiva with blue throat from swallowing poison that would have destroyed the world.

Nirvana – the ultimate aim of Buddhist existence, a state where one leaves the cycle of existence and does not have to suffer further rebirths.

Nizam – hereditary title of the rulers of Hyderabad.

Nullah – ditch or small stream.

Padyatra – 'foot journey', politicians do it to raise support at the village level.

Pagoda – Buddhist religious monument composed of a solid hemisphere containing relics of the Buddha – also known as a dagoba, stupa or chedi.

Palanquin – box-like enclosure carried on poles on four men's shoulders, occupant sat inside on a seat.

Pali – the original language in which the Buddhist scriptures were recorded, scholars still look to the original Pali texts for the true interpretations.

Pan – betel nut plus the chewing additives.

Pandit – teacher or wiseman, often used in Kashmir where there are many Pandits, sometimes used deprecatingly to mean a bookworm.

Peepul – fig tree, especially a Bo tree.

Peon – lowest grade clerical worker.

Pice – a quarter of an anna.

Pinjrapol – animal hospital maintained by Jains.

Pooja – offering or prayers.

Pranayama – study of breath control.

Prasad – food offering, something you can eat.

Pukkah – proper, very much a Raj era term.

Punkah – cloth fan, swung by pulling a cord.

Puranas – the ancient Hindu scriptures.

Purdah – isolation in which Moslem women are kept.

Raga – somewhat equivalent to a piece, division or movement of western music.

Railhead – station or town at the end of a railway line, termination point.

Raj – rule or sovereignty, but specifically applied to the period of British rule in India.

Raja – king.

Rajput – Hindu warrior caste, royal rulers of Rajasthan.

Ramayana – the story of Rama and Sita and their conflict with Ravana, one of the longest lasting of Indian legends and retold in various forms throughout almost all South-East Asia.

Rani – wife of a princely ruler or a ruler in her own right.

Rath – temple chariot or car used in religious festivals

Raths – rock-cut Dravidian temples at Mahabalipuram.

Rickshaw – two-wheeled vehicle in which one or two passengers are pulled. Only in Calcutta and one or two hill stations do the old man-powered rickshaws still exist. In towns they are now generally bicycle-rickshaws.

Rishis – great sages of old, nowadays applied to any distinguished poet, philosopher or spiritual personality.

Road – railway town which serves as a communication point to a larger town off the line, ie Mt Abu and Abu Road.

Sadhu – wandering holy man, generally Saivaites, mostly laymen who have given everything up to seek religious salvation. They will usually be addressed as 'swamiji' or 'babaji'.

Sahib – 'lord', title applied to any gentlemen and most Europeans.

Saivaite – (or Shaivate) follower of Lord Shiva.

Salwar – blouse worn by Punjabi women.

Samadhi – an ecstatic state, sometimes defined as 'ecstasy, trance, communion with God' or 'ecstatic state of mystic consciousness'. Another definition is the place where a holy man was cremated, usually venerated as a shrine.

Sati – 'honourable woman', what a woman becomes if she throws herself on her husband's funeral pyre, although banned a century or so ago, occasionally satis are still performed.

Satsang – discourse by a swami.

Satyagraha – non-violent protest, involving a fast, popularised by Gandhi. From Sanskrit, literally 'insistence on truth'.

Sepoy – private in the infantry.

Serai – place for accommodation of travellers, specifically a caravanserai where camel caravans once stopped.

Shakti – spiritual energy, life force or strength.

Shikar – hunting expedition, now virtually extinct.

Shikara – gondola-like boat used on Dal Lake in Kashmir.

Shirting – material shirts are made out of.

Sikhara – Hindu temple spire or temple.

Sirdar – leader or commander.

Sitar – Indian stringed instrument, very difficult to tune – which did not prevent it from becoming a '60s craze.

Sof – aniseed seeds, comes with the bill after a meal and you chew a pinch of it as a digestive.

Sonam – karma built up in successive reincarnations.

Sufi – ascetic Moslem mystic.

Suiting – material suits are made out of.

Swami – title given to initiated monks, means 'lord of the self'.

Sweeper – lowest caste servant, who performs the most menial of tasks.

Syce – groom.

Tabla – small drums, almost like bongos.

Tamil – people of south-east India.

Tank – artificial water storage lake.

Tanka – rectangular Tibetan painting on cloth.

Tantric Buddhism – Tibetan Buddhism with strong sexual and occult overtones.

Tatty – woven grass screen which is wetted and hung outside windows in the hot season to provide an effective system of air-cooling.

Tempo – noisy three-wheeler public transport vehicle.

Thali – traditional south Indian 'all-you-can-eat' vegetarian meal – the name derives from the 'thali' plate the food is served on.

Theravada – small vehicle Buddhism.

Thirthayatara – sort of pilgrimage.

Thug – follower of thuggee, religious inspired ritual murderers in the last century.

Tiffin – snack, particularly around lunchtime.

Tirthankars – 24 Jain teachers.

Toddy – mildly alcoholic drink, tapped from the palm tree.

Tonga – two-wheeled horse or pony carriage.

Tope – grove of trees, usually mangoes.

Topi – sun hat much used by the British in the Raj era.

Torana – architrave over temple entrance.

Trimurti – three-faced Shiva image.

Tripitaka – the classical Theravada Buddhist scriptures, which are divided into three categories, hence its name the 'three baskets'. The Mahayanists have other scriptures in addition.

Untouchable – lowest caste for whom the most menial tasks are reserved, the name derives from the fact that higher caste risk defilement if they should touch one.

Upanishads – ancient Vedic scripts, the last part of the Vedas.

Vanaspati – cooking oil, edible oils.

Varuna – supreme Vedic god.

Vedas – ancient spiritual texts, the orthodox Hindu scriptures.

Vihar – monastery.

Vimana – principle part of a Hindu temple.

Wallah – person, can be added on to almost anything, thus dhobi-wallah (clothes washer), taxi-wallah (taxi driver).

Wazir – Prime Minister.

Yagna – religious self mortification, such as a snake-yagna where you sit in a cage full of snakes trying to get yourself in the Guinness Book of Records. Being interred alive is another popular yagna feat.

Yoni – vagina, female fertility symbol.

Zamindar – landowner.

Zenana – area of a high class Moslem household where the women are secluded.

Index

LONELY PLANET NEWSLETTER
We collect an enormous amount of information here at Lonely Planet. Apart from our research we also get a steady stream of letters from people out on the road — some of them are just one line on a postcard, others go on for pages. Plus we always have an ear to the ground for the latest on cheap airfares, new visa regulations, borders opening and closing. A lot of this information goes into our new editions or 'update supplements' in reprints. But we want to make better use of this inform-ation so, we also produce a quarterly newsletter packed full of the latest news from out on the road. It appears in January, April, July and October of each year. If you'd like an airmailed copy of the most recent newsletter just send us A$1.50 (A$1 within Australia) or A$5 (A$4 in Australia) for a year's subscription.

OTHER LONELY PLANET PRODUCTS
We have Lonely Planet T-shirts (A$5, state size and colour preference) and self-adhesive LP stickers (A$1 for two).

THANKS

Writers (apologies if we've mis-spelt your names) to whom thanks must go include:

Adrian Abbotts (UK), Enrico Accorsi (V), Bill Aitken (I), Trevor Akerman (Aus), Masood Akhtar (I), Erik & Elizabeth Alkert (Aus), Pauline Allen (US), Shlomo Amon (US), Ingvar Andersson (Sw), Jane Appleton (Aus), Alison Armstrong (UK), D W & C J Artus (SI), Victor H Ashe (US), Peter E Barcham (UK), C J Barnett (Aus), Steve Barnett, Jenny Bathurst (Aus), Anna Baydell (Aus), Elizabeth Bayley Willis (US), Kym Bayliss (Aus), Susan Beney (Aus), Lari Bennet (C), Paul Berker (UK), John Berridge (C), Moha Bhander (I), Helle Biseth (N), Mark Blazek (Sp), Bob Blumberg (US), N P Boddington, Betty Bohnenblust (I), Alan Bonsteel, Nicholas Brann (UK), David Brewin (UK), David Bridge (Aus), M L Bridge (UK), John Broadbent (UK), David Brown (UK), Steve Brown, Jane Crescent Brundage (US), Linda Buseth (US), Paul Butler (UK), Denise Callichy (SA), Tony & Lena Cansdale (Aus), Justin Carson (UK), William Carter (US), Rakesh Chandra (I), Lyn Charlesworth, Suzanne Chestnut (UK), Katherine Christian (Aus), Julie Christie (!?), C Clark (B), Michael Clayton (UK), Gail & Roger Clements (Aus), Kaye Cummiry (Aus), G Curzon (UK), Wendy & Steven Dahl (US), Gary Daly (Aus), John Daniels, Sam Daniel (US), Penny Dawson (I), John Deane (US), Cetine di Frosini (It), Tine de Giev (Dk), Michael de Haan (US), Paul Descor (Aus), Elizabeth de Stroumillo (UK), Lisa & Nicky Digby (Aus), Mick Donnelly, Natashe Edwards (UK), Kim Ellis (UK), David Erskine (Aus), F J Evans (UK), Richard Everest, Mary Ewer (NZ), Ann Faraday (M), J Fastir (NZ), Margaret Faulkner (C), Mataija Feinberg, Nick Felton (UK), Simon Fick (Aus), Allan Fisher (UK), John Flood (UK), Chris Gammell (UK), Anne Geddie (UK), Keith Gillandes (UK), V Giriraj (I), Don Gittelson (US), Lui Godinho (I), Emily Goldfarb (US), Harry Golding (US), Pete Good (Aus), Dave Goodbar (UK), Helen & Colin Goodwin (Aus), Richard Goransen (C), Loas Gravimko, J Green (UK), Warwick Green (Aus), Helen Guyt (Nl), Don Hammersley (Aus), Julie Hardcastle (Aus), G E Hardie (Aus), Louise Hardy (UK), Janice Harris (C), Anne M Harvie (Aus) Eli Heimann (Isr), B Heywood (UK), P G Hiron (C), Nick Hone (UK), Simon Honywood, J R Hoogenland (Nl), Thomas J Hudak (UK), A R Hudson (UK), Cathryn Hugh (UK), Simon Hunter (UK), Mick Jackson (UK), Jeff Jacobs (US), Rex H James (Aus), Rod James (Aus), Rudy Jansen (Nl), Kathy Jeffery (Aus), Ken Jeffrey (Aus), T G John, Bronwyn Jones (Aus), Lloyd Jones (NZ), Tony Jones (Aus), Margaret & Charles Julian (Aus), Marla & Ron Kantor (US), Sara Kaye (Aus), Murray Kennedy (C), John King (UK), Nick Kirby (UK), Martin Kisler (UK), Sinikha Klemettile (F), Erik Klingzell (Sw), A T (Gladys) Kothavala (I), Mary Krabbe (C), Kathryn Krentz (US), Peter Kutezyckyi (Aus), Claire Kuyes (UK), Rene Lachapelle (C), Margrit Lampe, Louis Landesman (S), Tim Langer (NZ), John Leader (Aus), Marcel Leereveld (Aus), Christine M Levingston (US), Alice Levinson (UK), Liz Lewis (Aus), Colleen Lightbody (C), Bert Lindau (Aus), Stephen Lofage (UK), John Loach, Beate Looser (US), R A Lovell (I), Greg Lowe (Aus), Patrick Macalister (Aus), Ian MacDonald (UK), R MacDonald, Ian MacDonell (C), Graeme Mackay (UK), Will Maclean (Aus), Charlie & John Maier (US), Geoffrey Malone (I), Del Prete Mariano (It), Glenda L Martin (Aus), Kieran & Rosemary Martin (Aus), R Martin (UK), Veronica Matthew (UK), Thomas McCormick (I), Alison J McDougal, Sue & Gez McEvilly (I), Mike & Gerry McMaster, George J McMinn (US), M Meaton (UK), Elan Melamid (US), Frances Meyer (UK), Ulrich Mezger (D), Pamela A Milchrist, Lyn Milnes (NZ), Betsy Moen, Jean Moir (UK), Bill & Joyce Monroe (US), Joanne Morecek (US), Joanne Morey (Aus), Scott Morgan, Jan Morgensen (Dk), David Morris (US), Rene Morse (S), Martin Mueller (D), Berthy Muller (CH), Steve Murray (Nl), Miranda Muschamp (Aus), Werner Mutler (CH), N K Nassau (Aus), John W Nelson, John Nettleship (UK), Mark Newfeld (US), Peter Nicholson (Aus), Charlotte Nielsen (Dk), Naomi Nissen (US), Kristian Nyholm (Dk), David O'Callaghan (US), Maya O'Donnell, Kev O'Neill (Aus), Robert Oostryek (Aus), Geraldine Ormonde (Aus), Donald A Overton (US), Bill Page (L), James Page (UK), Allen Panak (C), S Pandy (I), Bob Parkinson (Aus), Dimitris Partelidis (G), Aap Ki Passand (I), Ray Patch (US), Maddy Paxmor (UK), Mary Peckham (UK), Michael Peluso (Aus), Mark & Desi Pigott (Aus), Eric Pode (UK), Henry Pootjes (Nl), Dale Posgate (C), Andrew Prendergast (UK), C Robert Pryor (US), Norman Quinn (PNG), Graham Ramsey, Alison Randall (UK), Judy Randall (Aus), Scott

Randallesh, Michael Ranger (Aus), Eric Ratner (US), Ronald & Kathy Relemen (US), P A Riolo (Aus), David Roberts (UK), How Robson (UK), Marlene Roeder (US), Mark Roelopsen (Aus), Daniel Ross (US), D J Ryan, Nancy Ryan, Maria Salak (UK), Brenda Samuelson, Peter Saunders (Aus), Elaine & Brian Seargeant (C), Reed Searle (US), Jacqueline Sechuen (Aus), Ellen Semilof (Aus), Jocelyne Sephard (S), Lloyd Sharp (Aus), Colonel John Shipster (UK), Jim Sich (US), Nick Silberstein (Aus), Myrtle Silleman (Dk), Saiyam Sondhi (I), Camille Spielman (UK), Veronika Sptilinger (CH), Fred Stander (SA), Ray Steen (US), Jerry Stein (US), Irmi Steiner (D), Mark C Steinhoff (I), Nick Stephens (US), Peter Stephens (Aus), Terry & Nick Stephens (US), Morris Stewart (UK), Bjarne Stig Hansen, Amos & Ruth Stockfish (Isr), Roger Stoddart (UK), Elizabeth Stuart (UK), Vanessa Stuart (UK), T M Sukumaran (I), Clive Swift (UK), Amon Taurant (UK), Edmunds Teuzon (UK), Chris Tollast, Sver Town, John Tucker (HK), Martin Tuvronningen (I), Linda & Rahamim Udi (US), Jamie Uhrig (I), J Uttamchand (I), Carla van der Sloot (Nl), Martin & Kathy van der Voorn (US), Peter van der Zant (Nl), David C Thomas (UK), Peter van Tilburg (Nl), John Tucker, Daniel P Tyler Jr (US), John C Vanee (Aus), Wolf Wagner (D), William Walford (UK), Chris Walker (Ire), John Walker (Aus), Raymond Ward (UK), Sigrid Wasowicj-Kramer (D), Mark Wass, Shona Watson, Allan Welsh (UK), D Whitehouse (UK), Anthony Whyte, Rick Wicks (US), Margaret Williams (US), Ralph Williams (Aus), Leon Winsky (UK), Roewen Wishart (Aus), David Wratt (NZ), John Wren-Lewis (M), D W Wright (UK), Andrew Wrigley, Steve Wyn-Harris (NZ), Angela Yatri (NZ), Coralie Younger (Aus), Carola Zentner (UK)

Aus – Australia, B – Brunei, C – Canada, CH – Switzerland, D –Germany, Dk –Denmark F – Finland, G – Greece, HK –Hong Kong, I– India, Ire – Ireland, Isr –Israel, It – Italy, L – Luxembourg, M –Malaysia, N – Norway, Nl – Netherlands, NZ – New Zealand, PNG – Papua New Guinea, S – Singapore, SA –South Africa, SI– Solomon Islands, Sp – Spain, Sw –Sweden, UK – UK, US – US, V –Venezuela

UBS

Lonely Planet travel guides

Africa on a Shoestring
Australia – a travel survival kit
Alaska – a travel survival kit
Bali & Lombok – a travel survival kit
Burma – a travel survival kit
Bushwalking in Papua New Guinea
Canada – a travel survival kit
China – a travel survival kit
Hong Kong, Macau & Canton
India – a travel survival kit
Japan – a travel survival kit
Kashmir, Ladakh & and Zanskar
Kathmandu & the Kingdom of Nepal
Korea & Taiwan – a travel survival kit
Malaysia, Singapore & Brunei – a travel
survival kit
Mexico – a travel survival kit
New Zealand – a travel survival kit
North-East Asia on a Shoestring
Pakistan – a travel survival kit
Papua New Guinea – a travel survival kit
The Philippines – a travel survival kit
South America on a Shoestring
South-East Asia on a Shoestring
Sri Lanka – a travel survival kit
Thailand – a travel survival kit
Tramping in New Zealand
Trekking in the Himalayas
Turkey – a travel survival kit
USA West
West Asia on a Shoestring

Lonely Planet phrasebooks

Indonesia Phrasebook
Nepal Phrasebook
Thailand Phrasebook

Lonely Planet travel guides are available around the world. If you can't find them, ask your bookshop to order them from one of the distributors listed below. For countries not listed or if you would like a free copy of our latest booklist write to Lonely Planet in Australia

Australia
Lonely Planet Publications, PO Box 88, South Yarra, Victoria 3141.
Canada
Milestone Publications, Box 2248, Sidney British Columbia, V8L 3S8.
Denmark
Scanvik Books aps, Store Kongensgade 59 A, DK-1264 Copenhagen K.
Hong Kong
The Book Society, GPO Box 7804.
India & Nepal
UBS Distributors, 5 Ansari Rd, New Delhi.
Israel
Geographical Tours Ltd, 8 Tverya St, Tel Aviv 63144.
Japan
Intercontinental Marketing Corp, IPO Box 5056, Tokyo 100-31.
Malaysia
MPH Distributors, 13 Jalan 13/6, Petaling Jaya, Selangor.
Netherlands
Nilsson & Lamm bv, Postbus 195, Pampuslaan 212, 1380 AD Weesp.
New Zealand
Roulston Greene Publishing Associates Ltd, Box 33850, Takapuna, Auckland 9.
Papua New Guinea
Gorden & Gotch (PNG), PO Box 3395, Port Moresby.
Singapore
MPH Distributors, 116-D JTC Factory Building, Lorong 3, Geylang Square, Singapore, 1438.
Sweden
Esselte Kartcentrum AB, Vasagatan 16, S-111 20 Stockholm.
Thailand
Chalermnit, 1-2 Erawan Arcade, Bangkok.
UK
Roger Lascelles, 47 York Rd, Brentford, Middlesex, TW8 0QP.
USA
Lonely Planet Publications, PO Box 2001A, Berkeley, CA 94702.
West Germany
Buchvertrieb Gerda Schettler, Postfach 64, D3415 Hattorf a H.

South-East Asia
on a shoestring

Tony Wheeler